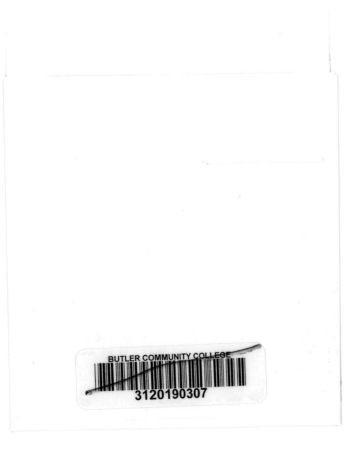

MILESTONE DOCUMENTS OF WORLD RELIGIONS

Exploring Traditions of Faith
Through Primary Sources

MILESTONE DOCUMENTS OF WORLD RELIGIONS

Exploring Traditions of Faith
Through Primary Sources

Second Edition

Volume 3
1604–2002 CE

Editors
David M. Fahey
Aaron J. Gulyas

SCHLAGER GROUP

GREY HOUSE PUBLISHING

Schlager Group, Inc.
325 N. Saint Paul, Suite 3425
Dallas, TX 75201
http://www.schlagergroup.com

Grey House Publishing
4919 Route 22, PO Box 56
Amenia, NY 12501
http://www.greyhouse.com

Milestone Documents, 2016, published by Grey House Publishing, Inc., Amenia, NY.

∞ The paper used in these volumes conforms to the American National Standard for Permanence of Paper for Printed Library Materials, Z39.48 1992 (R2009).

Publisher's Cataloging-In-Publication Data
(Prepared by The Donohue Group, Inc.)

Names: Fahey, David M., editor. | Gulyas, Aaron John, 1975- editor.

Title: Milestone documents of world religions : exploring traditions of faith through primary source documents / David M Fahey, editor in chief ; Aaron Gulyas, editor.

Description: Second edition. | Dallas, Texas : Schlager Group ; Amenia, New York : Grey House Publishing, [2016] | Includes bibliographical references and index. | Contents: Volume 1. 2404 BCE-200 CE — Volume 2. 240-1570 — Volume 3. 1604-2002.

Identifiers: ISBN 978-1-68217-171-4 (set) | ISBN 978-1-68217-173-8 (v.1) | ISBN 978-1-68217-174-5 (v.2) | ISBN 978-1-68217-175-2 (v.3)

Subjects: LCSH: Religions—Sources. | Religions—History—Sources.

Classification: LCC BL85.M55 2016 | DDC 200.9—dc23

Contents

VOLUME 2: 240–1570 CE

VOLUME 3: 1604–2002 CE

MILESTONE DOCUMENTS OF WORLD RELIGIONS

Exploring Traditions of Faith
Through Primary Sources

Guru Nanak with Bhai Bala, Bhai Mardana and Sikh Gurus.

Raag Gond: Document Analysis

"The beggar and the king are all the same to Him. He sustains and fulfills both the ant and the elephant."

Overview

The Sri Guru Granth Sahib is a holy living book that preserves the spirit of the worldview of the ten gurus, or founders, of Sikhism. The book itself is thus considered to be an eternal guru. *Granth* means "holy book," and *sahib* is a term of respect meaning "honorable one." The text is written in Gurmukhi script, mostly in Punjabi (interspersed with other languages, such as Sanskrit, dialects of Hindi, and Farsi) and includes prayers and hymns written by many of the founders of Sikhism as well as by Hindus and Muslims. The compilation of these writings into one book was completed in 1604 by Guru Arjan. The writings were chosen based on both a common ideology of universal religion on the part of their authors and the compiler's intent to be inclusive of local religions by integrating the texts of those religions.

The Sri Guru Granth Sahib consists of thirty-one raga (musical measure) compositions. Raag Gond, treated here, is the seventeenth raga and spans seventeen pages. Unlike other copied scriptures that depend on chapters or verses, the publisher of the Sri Guru Granth Sahib has made its pagination standard, so that pagination is always meant to be the same across all versions. In this excerpt, which deviates from the standard pagination, the text is divided into seventeen parts. Devotional songs in the standard text take up most of the 1,430-page Sikh scripture and are sung according to the season and time of day. The Raag Gond is usually sung in the late afternoon or early evening.

Context

Many of the ideas and works found in this sacred text were formulated during the rise and early rule of the Mughal Empire (1526–1858), an Indian-Islamic power originating in Central Asia that invaded most of India and the regions to the north. The Mughals brought Persian culture as well

as the religion of Islam to the region. Nanak (1469–1538), the founder of Sikhism, was born into a Hindu family in a village near Lahore in present-day Pakistan, but as a spiritual leader he strove to unite the people of his region despite religious differences. He is often quoted as saying, "There is no Hindu; there is no Muslim," and this view is the reason that saints and poets who are well known for being particularly pluralistic in their respective Hindu and Islamic traditions are included in the text of the Sri Guru Granth Sahib. Sikh people, ideas, and text originated in the Punjab region that is divided between Pakistan (70 percent) and northern India (30 percent).

Nanak began his missionary work at age twenty-eight and traveled throughout India, Arabia, and Persia to spread his ideas about what he considered to be true religion: one not unnecessarily contentious, filled with empty or oppressive rituals, or requiring division among people via a caste system—as was the case in Hindu-dominated India at the time. He believed that true religion taught equality of all peoples, men and women, and so he instituted the religious practice of sharing a common meal where people of all religions and castes or stations in life could gather together. This meal, called *langar* (meaning "free kitchen"), continues today in Sikh places of worship. True religion did not, in Nanak's opinion, ask followers to renounce the world but instead to be in perpetual service to it. Although Nanak believed in unification, his message was not evangelistic. Nanak believed that one could get to the core of true religion while remaining in his or her own religious tradition. Nevertheless, those who accepted his teachings called themselves *Sikhs*, a word from Sanskrit that means "disciples." Sikh men eventually began to distinguish themselves by wearing turbans, not trimming their beards, and carrying or wearing five items called the "five Ks": *kesh* (uncut hair), *kanga* (a small comb), *kara* (a band of steel), *kirpan* (a small sword), and *kacha* (special undershorts). In addition, followers of Sikhism eventually began to adopt the names "Singh" (meaning "lion") for men and "Kaur" (meaning "princess") for women.

At the time of the founding of the Sikh religion and throughout the lives of the successive ten gurus, northern India and Pakistan were in perpetual political and cultural transition. During Nanak's life, the region in which he lived changed from Afghan to Mughal rule, and Nanak disapproved of the new social structures that the Mughal Empire brought about, most likely also opposing the new political and militaristic strategies that Babur, the founder of the Mughal Empire in this region, ushered in, such as the use of guns and gunpowder. Nanak comments in the Sri Guru Granth Sahib on the slaughter and the terror as well as the dishonoring of women that he saw accompanying the invasion. Taxes were the primary mode of gaining wealth for the empire, and non-Mughals, especially peasants, felt the brunt of these tax hikes, which spurred many rebellions.

Mughal rule and privilege brought decreasing peace, increasing tension, and probably a feeling of gradual loss of control to Nanak, as someone who was not in power. It was likely in response to his local political environment that the Sikh founder promoted a worldview that was based on ideas of equality and a displacement of secular authority with obedience to a universal God. The Sikh response to persecution thereafter included a militant ideology that was encapsulated in the concept of the soldier-saint, especially following the martyrdom of prominent Sikhs such as the fifth guru, Guru Arjan (1563–1606), the compiler of the Sri Guru Granth Sahib.

Angad Dev (1504–1552), the second Sikh guru, first undertook to preserve the sayings of Nanak as well as his own, and he adopted the Gurmukhi script for this purpose. He chose the Gurmukhi script over the Shahmukhi script, in which the Punjabi language is also written, because Gurmukhi was used by more people in Punjab at that time. This script, which means "from the mouth of the guru," is now associated with Sikhs. The third Sikh guru, Amar Das (1479–1574), extended the desire to create and preserve the Sikh worldview by publishing volumes that included the sayings of all the gurus up to that point, but he also added the sayings of other like-minded poets and peoples. By the time of the fifth guru, Arjan Dev, a substantial collection of material had been produced, to which Arjan added his own and other non-guru works, and he decided to arrange the material as a comprehensive sacred text.

Babur's grandson Akbar (1542–1605), generally considered to be the most tolerant of the Mughal emperors, ruled the kingdom during Arjan's life, yet the growing numbers and power of the Sikh community were accompanied by internal and external dissenters opposed to the Sikh ideology and agenda. Acknowledgement of this volatile situation is likely, in part, to have motivated Arjan to publish the community's compositions in a way that would be understood as authoritative, in the hope of preserving their religious ideology. His composition of the Sri Guru Granth Sahib was completed in 1604. Technically, up until the tenth guru, Guru Gobind Singh, designated the text to be the final and eternal guru and gave it the honorific title of "Holy Book," it was referred to as the Adi Granth, meaning the "First Book."

Time Line	
1270	■ Namdev is born in Maharashtra State in India.
1399(?)	■ Ravi Das is born in Uttar Pradesh State in India.
1441	■ Kabir is born in Uttar Pradesh, India.
1469	■ Guru Nanak is born in what is now Pakistan.
1490s	■ Nanak establishes Sikhism.
1526	■ The Afghan ruler Babur establishes a Mughal empire in India.
1556	■ Akbar, Babur's grandson and the third Mughal emperor, takes the throne.
1574	■ Guru Ram Das becomes the fourth guru of the ten gurus of Sikhism.
1581	■ Guru Arjan becomes the fifth guru of the ten gurus of Sikhism.
1603–1604	■ The Adi Granth is compiled.
1605	■ Akbar dies.
1606	■ Guru Arjan dies in Mughal custody.
1708	■ Guru Gobind Singh, the tenth guru, dies, and the Adi Granth is given the status of the eternal guru, becoming the Sri Guru Granth Sahib.

About the Author

The authors of the Raag Gond section of the Sri Guru Granth Sahib include two of the ten Sikh gurus and three other poet-mystics. The gurus include Guru Ram Das (1534–1581) and Guru Arjan Dev (1563–1606). Guru Ram Das is the first of these authors to appear in the Raag Gond; he became the fourth guru of the Sikh tradition in 1574, at age forty, and was born in the Punjab region. He composed

679 hymns included in the Sri Guru Granth Sahib, and he was the founder of the city of Amritsar (meaning "reservoir of the nectar of immortality), the center of the Sikh religious world and later the site of the religion's most sacred shrine, the Golden Temple (built in 1585–1604).

Guru Arjan Dev, Ram Das's youngest son, became the fifth guru in 1581, at age eighteen. Guru Arjan composed 2,218 of the hymns found in the Sri Guru Granth Sahib, and in 1603–1604 he compiled all the hymns and writings of the saints and poets into a sacred text called the Adi Granth. Guru Arjan Dev was central to the building of the Golden Temple, a place that became renowned as a destination for pilgrimage and daily devotion and prayer. Even though relations between Sikhs and Mughals were not always contentious during Arjan's life under the rule of Akbar, he was tortured and martyred by Akbar's son, Jahangir, who had come to the throne in 1605 and was hostile to the ideologies and activities of Sikhs and the successful religious leadership of Arjan in particular.

Kabir (1441–1518), Namdev (1270–1350), and Ravi Das (whose exact dates of birth and death are debated) are the poets and spiritual guides from other traditions included in the Raag Gond. Kabir was a mystic and saint born in Uttar Pradesh, India, who was one of India's greatest poets. Born to Muslim parents, he became a disciple of a Hindu teacher and leader of the Bhakti movement in India, which emphasizes love and devotion (*bhakti*) to God as the means to spiritual salvation. In the case of Kabir's teacher, that god who was the object of devotion was Rama, an incarnation of the supreme god of Hinduism, Vishnu. Rama is depicted as the ideal human who adheres to dharma (one's duty) despite any difficulty. Kabir wrote 541 hymns in the Sri Guru Granth Sahib.

Namdev was a Hindu religious poet of the thirteenth to fourteenth centuries, born in Maharashtra in India. He was devoted to Vithoba, a form of Vishnu depicted as a dark young boy. He embraced the Bhakti movement, and sixty-one hymns of the Sri Guru Granth Sahib are written by him; his views are understood to be similar to those of Kabir. Ravi Das, born perhaps around 1399 in Uttar Pradesh, was a mystic of the Dalit, or Untouchable, caste. The Sri Guru Granth Sahib contains forty hymns by him. All of these authors were similarly concerned with minimizing the importance of caste in their society, breaking down the barriers between religious communities, and seeking liberation through devotion to a universal, single god.

Explanation and Analysis of the Document

The excerpt here from the Sri Guru Granth Sahib is the Raag Gond, the seventeenth raga. Its sayings identify one god to be supreme above all other gods, and its ideal for humans is to discard empty rituals and authorities and to concentrate the mind on God and on living a holy life filled with respect for others. Hindu mythology and concepts are invoked, commented on, or integrated into the Sikh ideology. Themes of the Raag Gond include equality, social justice, devotion to and intimacy with God, reward and punishment, the soul, and the name of God. The Raag Gond is helpfully organized by author, so that all the sayings of Ram Das are located together, followed by the sayings of Arjan Dev, then Kabir, then Namdev, and, finally, Ravi Das.

◆ Parts 1–3

Ram Das begins the Raag Gond. Raag Gond itself begins with the extended mantra that appears elsewhere in the Sri Guru Granth Sahib: "One Universal Creator God. Truth Is the Name. Creative Being Personified. No Fear. No Hatred. Image of the Undying. Beyond Birth. Self-Existent. By Guru's Grace." Such a mantra directs the reader's/reciter's focus on a monotheistic faith with a god that is eternal, self-sufficient, and worthy of devotion. Ram Das fully describes this god as omniscient, omnipotent, and omnipresent. God is the real truth, and anything perceived as other than God is maya, meaning "not-that." Maya is sometimes translated as "illusion," but it is more particularly an incomplete view of the way things really are, which can lead one away from God (who sees things in all completeness) and can cause distress because of that distortion. Therefore, Ram Das explains, one should meditate and contemplate God and be fully dependent on and trusting of him, because God alone will prove dependable and faithful.

In the first part, Ram Das refers to the Indian/Hindu concepts of attachment and duality. In Hindu spirituality, one who is seeking liberation should practice detachment from the world, including all pleasure, duty, pain, family members and friends, and so on. The concept of detachment is not an ascetic abandonment; instead, one is to refrain from becoming overly dependent or possessive of things and people, even the self. Otherwise, distress would be felt. Dualistic thinking divides a relationship into subject-object, often creating hierarchical divisions instead of allowing subjects to homogeneously relate to one another.

In part 2, Ram Das brings up the idea that chanting the name of the Lord is salvific. This is a major concept in Sikhism and in the Sri Guru Granth Sahib as a whole. The repetition clears the mind of all distraction so that a person can be calm and in control and therefore ready to live a life worthy of God and in service to others. As it is in the Hindu tradition, the mental and emotional health of a person is a spiritual/religious concern in this Sikh text.

Part 3 is centered on the idea that God is the great equalizer. In a society that was based on hierarchies of authority and restricted closeness to God via imperial institutions and caste and gender systems, this was a radical message. Ram Das states that it is only God who has control over the goings-on of the world. Such a message clearly stirs up feelings of intimacy in the devotee, for the section is concluded with poetic lines of desire, need, longing, and the expression of familial ties and friendship between Ram Das and God.

◆ Parts 4–6, 8, and 11

Arjan Dev explains the creator-god in a series of paradoxes using "both/and" language. For instance, God does not either create or destroy, two seemingly opposing acts, but "The Creator forms, and the Creator destroys"; that is, God does both. In part 4, Arjan cannot say that God is this or that because God is everything. Arjan portrays God as the highest and most comprehensive and inclusive being. There is nothing that exists, no perspective that does not include or is not within God. Using animals such as fish, the monkey, the elephant, and birds, Arjan contrasts the eternal God with the temporary, limited entanglements of the world. The five thieves he mentions are the five passions (or desires or demons) that every human struggles with: lust, wrath, greed, attachment, and ego. Arjan attempts to reveal to the reader the suffering that accompanies transitory pursuits and convince the reader that he or she should turn to God.

The name of God, an essential element in the meditation and theology of the Sikhs, is discussed in part 5. The Name, or the Naam, is not only individually salvific but also socially so, correcting social ills and equalizing the beggar and king. The Naam is not just a word but is indeed God, and it is left generic intentionally to encompass all the names that people of other religious communities might call God. God's name is simply Name.

Parts 6 and 8 praise God as Guru, and the Guru as God. Part 7 (not included here) further emphasizes the importance of the name of God by repetitive utterance. The Punjabi word *guru* can mean the spiritual teacher or leader of a community, a founder of Sikhism, God, or the text of the Sri Guru Granth Sahib as well as the ideas or messages or spirit encompassing all these entities. When Arjan says, "I worship and adore my Guru; the Guru is the Lord of the Universe. / My Guru is the Supreme Lord God; the Guru is the Lord God. / My Guru is divine, invisible and mysterious. / I serve at the Guru's feet, which are worshipped by all," he is not indicating that the ten gurus of Sikhism, for instance, are deities or are worthy of worship. Only God is worshipped in Sikhism.

Parts 9 and 10 (not included here) mention the salvation and rewards that come with serving God and deal with the punishment that follows slander. Part 11 further deals with the sin of the slanderer. The Sikhs were a group vulnerable to persecution, marginalization, and division. The condemnation of slander as one of the deepest sins, punishable with being condemned to hell, was strategic. Slander within the group might cause strife and schisms; slander from outside the group toward the gurus, devotees, text, or God might cause distress and self-doubt and cast doubt on the truth of the faith system Sikhs were advancing.

◆ Parts 12–15

Kabir wrote many beautiful poems, and his introspective eloquence is set apart through the philosophic musings in his section of the Raag Gond. Kabir contemplates the concept of the soul in part 12. He is distressed at the seeming pointlessness of human death and contrasts his unknowing living state with the rich reservoirs of the "Akaashic ethers" where God reigns. The term *Akaashic* (usually spelled Akashic) refers to the mystical, nontangible library or compendium of all knowledge of the cosmos and history

of human experience. Kabir believes that a person can truly know anything only after physical death. The soul itself is beyond the usual categories of identity: It is beyond the distinction between human and god. It is beyond ideas about human relationship, spiritual path, vocation, caste. It is eternal and no different from what God is.

In part 13, Kabir presents a series of poeticisms and vignettes that engage the futility of a worldly life in contrast to the holiness of a life given up to God. Most of the world strives after Maya, personified as the bride of the world, a seductress, a captivating prostitute, a monstrous witch, wandering around after the most holy—reminiscent of the rhetoric in the biblical book of Proverbs (7:12–23). The devotee is instructed to stay away from the temptations of the world, which are gendered as female. Female sexuality and the female body are depicted as not only sinful but horrifying and violent as well. In part 14, after Maya sucks the life out of her victim, "she quickly gets up and departs, bare-footed." She has even seduced the Hindu gods Brahma, Shiva, and Vishnu.

While the use of the traditional depiction of Maya as female in Indian mythology is not intended to be taken literally or to be transferred to the female body of a female devotee, feminist theologians have long discussed the connection between sin, or evil, and the female body as participant to the subordination of women within and without the church (temple, mosque, or other place of worship). The equality of women is a prominent feature in Sikh consciousness, as attested by its frequency of mention in almost every text about the Sikh ideology or creed. In addition, negative portrayals of the feminine are often countered by positive depictions of the holiness of women; for instance, at the end of part 14, Kabir announces that a female devotee, the street dancer, is his personal guru. Women appear prominently in Sikh history and thought. Nevertheless, it is important to be aware of how sacred texts portray a particular gender, as privileging or stigmatizing any gender may consequently perpetuate gendered privilege or stigmas in society. Kabir's section ends with some lines at the beginning of part 15 that return to description of the faithful, highlighting the need of the devotee for the holy, as originator, guide, and force.

◆ Parts 15–17

Namdev's sayings, which begin about a third of the way into part 15, are filled with references to events and figures in Hindu mythology. He first discusses the futility of performing religious rituals, worshipping idols, putting faith in scriptural authority such as the Vedas, and making pilgrimages to sacred sites such as Gaya and Benares. For Namdev these places and practices are spiritually insignificant and even distracting to the devotee. The various Hindu gods are made subordinate in this text to the un-imaged, single, universal God that the gurus hoped would unite followers of all religions.

The devotee's emotional and intense relationship with God is described in parts 15 and 16. Namdev compares himself to a lured deer, a fisherman, a goldsmith, a gambler, a man filled with covetous lust, a hungry calf, and a walking stick to the blind. His relationship with God is one of animalistic or basic instinct and addiction, often leading to the extremes of survival and destruction.

Parts 15 and 16 further expound on the God-devotee relationship by mentioning many brief examples from Hindu stories of how people are humbled and how it is God who saves. Dhroo and Naarad, mentioned at the end of part 15, exemplify exceptional devotion and character in the stories in which they feature. Harnaakhash, mentioned in part 16, was a king who had his life taken away because of his uncontrollable ego. The devotees Ajaamal and Ganika are referenced as contrasts to Harnaakhash, because of the way in which they reversed their attachments to the world through acts of kindness and a willingness to take the advice of holy men.

Pootna, or Putana, as she is referred to in many sacred Hindu texts, was also redeemed. Pootna was a demon, sent by Krishna's uncle to murder Krishna. Pootna disguises herself as a beautiful *gopi* (cowherd girl) and persuades Krishna's mother to let her suckle baby Krishna (after she has smeared poison on her breast). In many versions of the story, Krishna ends up killing Pootna by sucking her dry. Namdev, though, reclaims Pootna in the Raag Gond by narrating that she chants the name of Krishna, suggesting that she has a change of heart when she holds the child.

Namdev next makes reference to Dropadi (Draupadi), the wife of the five Pandava brothers in the Hindu sacred epic the Mahabharata. Dropadi did not need to be redeemed from her sinful ways; instead, she often needed to be saved from unjust circumstances, and her faith in Krishna always stirred him to action. Namdev mentions Gautam's wife—her name is Ahalya—who appears in the Ramayana and is turned to stone after she mistakenly makes love with a god who has disguised himself as her husband. In the Ramayana, Ahalya is allowed to return to flesh because of the pity of her husband. Namdev, fitting Ahalya in with this Hall of the Faithful, seems to suggest that Ahalya was acting dutifully and devotedly with her intentions. Kans (also known as Kansa and Kamsa) and Kaysee (also Kesi) are characters who attempt to murder baby Krishna and are killed by God. Kali, by contrast, receives the gift of life from God, in a story that is found in the tenth chapter of the Bhagavata Purana.

For Namdev, these stories from Hindu mythology highlight the virtues of sin, faith, and humility. But at the same time that Namdev uses Hindu figures as moral guides or characters in cautionary tales, he also highlights the failings of the Hindu gods. He mentions Gayatri, for instance, the second wife of the Hindu god Brahma. Namdev's audience would know the story that is alluded to in the one-line reference here: One day, when Brahma's first wife, Saraswati, was away, Brahma asked for a wife to take her place. But when Saraswati came back, she was angry and turned Gayatri into a cow. The subsequent reference, to Shiva, points to the god's cruelty, in a story in which Shiva blesses a wealthy merchant with a son but allows the boy to live for only twelve years.

Part 17 begins with mention of Raam Chand (Lord Rama), the seventh avatar of Vishnu, who manifested on the earth to save the world from the cruelty of a demon king named Ravana, here called Raawan. Rama's wife, Sita, was "lost" when Raawan took advantage of an opportunity to kidnap her and steal her away to his kingdom, resulting in a long and terrible war before Rama finally managed to rescue her. In the Raag Gond, Namdev reads these tales of various Hindu gods as evidence of their imperfections and weakness compared with the one universal creator God, who is portrayed as immaculate and sovereign all the time.

Namdev's use of gender is noteworthy. When, in part 16, Namdev describes his loving need and desire for God, he says, "So is poor Naam Dayv without the Lord's Name. Like the cow's calf, which, when let loose, sucks at her udders and drinks her milk. So has Naam Dayv found the Lord." Here, God is imaged as female. Prostitutes, demon mothers, and good wives are alike saved and praised for their humility. In the same part, Namdev says, "One who worships the Great Goddess Maya will be reincarnated as a woman, and not a man." Here, Namdev might be describing the secondary position of women that was the reality in his society at the time, not necessarily suggesting that being born a woman is a curse or punishment.

◆ Part 17: Final Lines

The remainder of part 17 was written by Ravi Das. In this final section of the Raag Gond, the author focuses on one aspect of God: Liberator, as designated by the Punjabi term *mukanday*. In Sikhism, "Gobinday, Mukanday, Udaaray, Apaaray, Hareeang, Kareeang, Niraamay, Akaamay" is a popular mantra, meaning "Sustainer, Liberator, Enlightener, Infinite, Destroyer, Creator, Nameless, Desireless." These are the eight aspects of God. That Ravi Das, born a member of the lowest class of Hindus, would center on the liberating character of God is significant. He images a God who is concerned about the impoverished and who negates social class and caste altogether. It is not the world or society that has the authority to determine the value of people, but God. The situation of the oppressed, "Untouchable" caste known as Dalits in India has been one of squalor, poverty, degradation, the absence of education, and (from the mainstream perspective) spiritual impoverishment, and that was true in the lifetime of Ravi Das.

According to a classic, normative understanding of karma, any one person's position in life is the result of good or bad deeds in past lives. The suffering experienced by Dalits was therefore often viewed by those of higher castes as merely a reaping of the consequences of past deeds. Far from being able to expect compassion and salvation from God, the Dalit should view his or her situation as reflecting a judgment from God. A Dalit could improve his or her life only in the next life, after rebirth: In the present lifetime, nothing really could or should be done. Such a fatalistic understanding of social and economic status all but negated any chance for liberation or engagement with social justice. But in this writing, Ravi Das repositions himself and his people in relationship to a God whose very nature is to lib-

"Servant Nanak speaks: night and day, chant the Lord's name, O Saints; this is the only true hope for emancipation."

(Section 1)

"There are four castes: Brahmin, Kh'shaatriya, Soodra and Vaishya, and there are four stages of life. One who meditates on the Lord, is the most distinguished and renowned."

(Section 1)

"He fashioned the soul and the breath of life, and infused His Light into the dust; He exalted you and gave you everything to use, and food to eat and enjoy—how can you forsake that God, you fool! Where else will you go?"

(Section 1)

"The beggar and the king are all the same to Him. He sustains and fulfills both the ant and the elephant."

(Section 1)

"By Guru's Grace, the inverted heart-lotus blossoms forth, and the Light shines forth in the darkness."

(Section 1)

"The world loves only the one bride, Maya. / She is the wife of all beings and creatures. / With her necklace around her neck, this bride looks beautiful. / She is poison to the Saint, but the world is delighted with her. / Adorning herself, she sits like a prostitute."

(Section 1)

"I take only the Name of the One Lord. / I have given away all other gods in exchange for Him."

(Section 1)

"The Hindu is sightless; the Muslim has only one eye. / The spiritual teacher is wiser than both of them. / The Hindu worships at the temple, the Muslim at the mosque. / Naam Dayv serves that Lord, who is not limited to either the temple or the mosque."

(Section 1)

erate. He says, "Erasing my social status, I have entered His Court." Ravi Das also asserts the evilness of slander. All the good social and religious deeds that a person might do are negated in light of participation in slander.

Audience

Although the Sri Guru Granth Sahib was compiled, written, and arranged in order to manifest and preserve the foundational ideas of Sikhism as a living memory for its devotees, the cross-faith and cross-cultural subject matter of the text acts as a partial conversation between Sikhs and those of different faiths and cultures who reside in the same world. The text aims to influence its own devotees to higher purity, to persuade nondevotees to take a similar view of holiness, and to negotiate and promote peace among members of society.

Over the centuries, the audience of the Sri Guru Granth Sahib has narrowed. In the beginning, with the first partial writings, the authors tried simply to articulate their vision, and both the text and the audience included members of all faiths. A new religion was not necessarily intended; rather, the authors strove for a perspective that would be a corrective to the realities of the time, one that got at the core of all faiths. Eventually, however, the Sikh faithful acknowledged the text as distinctive from other scriptures and themselves as distinctive followers as well. To preserve their ideology in times of dissention and persecution, they created an increasingly defined community to defend an increasingly defined text that was, in part, a personal message of comfort and encouragement. The text is now almost wholly read, recited, and studied by Sikh followers.

When it was compiled, the Sri Guru Granth Sahib found an audience among Muslims and Hindus from India-Pakistan, the text having integrated both Muslim and Indian beloved authors, incorporated and commented on many of the ideas circulating in their common culture, and borrowed from both faiths. The text was to be taken as a guide on how to be a true Muslim or a true Hindu, and it counted both the Muslim and Hindu god as one. How the text has played to Hindus and Muslims in the past as well as in the present has depended on the extent to which its audience has had a shared or separate culture. Since Muslims had been in India for centuries before Sikhism began, Hindus and Muslims there largely understand each other and understand any texts deriving from the shared elements of their culture better than Hindus and Muslims in other geographic regions. The negative response of the early guru authors to the Mughal invasion was more the result of a foreign culture clash than a religious one.

Impact

These hymns are seen as a result of communication with God, and therefore they are considered to be sacred vessels holding the divine message. The texts that make up the Raag Gond were selected because of the inclusive and pluralistic perspectives of their authors as well as for their focus on *bhakti*, or devotion, toward God. The hymns of the Sri Guru Granth Sahib are not primarily for reading to grasp theology but rather for meditation and for singing at the *gurdwara* (meaning "door to the Guru"), the Sikh place of worship. A hymnbook to evoke the human range of emotions, to console, to transform one's soul, and to bring one closer to God, the Sri Guru Granth Sahib is used actively and continues to promote unity among the Sikh communities in the world.

The writings of the gurus gradually came to be a text expressly belonging to a community that called themselves Sikhs, and the Adi Granth did not take an eternal status all of its own until the tenth guru, Guru Gobind Singh, decided to vest guruship in the text itself rather than in any human successors. During the decades after its compilation, the text had the effect of raising consciousness, of creating unity and comfort, a sense of belonging, among followers who agreed with its ideology. When the Golden Temple was completed in the city of Amritsar in 1604, under the guidance of the fourth guru, Guru Ram Das, it housed the Adi Granth, making the sacred space a throne for a truly sacred text.

When the fourth Mughal emperor treated the Sikhs as a political threat and put Arjan Dev to death in 1606, the sixth guru, Guru Har Gobind (1595–1644), mobilized the Sikhs and constructed the Akal Takht as part of the Golden Temple complex, creating a sacred center for Sikh political and military resistance against the cruelty and injustice they experienced under Mughal rulers. The tenth guru of Sikhism, Guru Gobind Singh (1666–1708), established an army of Sikhs and engaged in battles with rulers attempting to invade and subdue their cities and communities.

During this time, the Sri Guru Granth Sahib served as spiritual armor for actual battles, bolstering ideas of the Sikhs as soldier-saints and defending their existence and their stance on justice. When the Sri Guru Granth Sahib took the position as eternal guru in 1708, it became a solid, unchanging scripture that would be the focal point and unifier of the people, with more authority than any human leader. This also left each member of the community to become his or her own interpreter and example of moral authority, rather than looking for leadership from a guru.

By the mid-eighteenth century, the British had solidified colonial control over India and the Punjab, the Mughal Empire was in decline, and Sikh political power was rising. A confederacy of autonomous Sikh states was formed in the Punjab region in 1801, but this empire lasted only fifty years, eventually dissolving after a series of wars with the British. Over the next century, however, a large portion of freedom fighters involved in the Indian anticolonial movement were Sikhs from the Punjab. During tumultuous times, sacred texts often become political beacons to a future liberation. But in times of peace—which the Sikhs have enjoyed in their progressive state and in the world during the late twentieth and early twenty-first centuries—the Sri Guru Granth Sahib has become more of a devotional text, a songbook for worshipping God and celebrating life.

Further Reading

■ Books

Chilana, Rajwant Singh. *International Bibliography of Sikh Studies*. Dordrecht, Netherlands: Springer, 2005.

Grewal, J. S. *The New Cambridge History of India*. Vol. 2, part 3: *The Sikhs of the Punjab*. Rev. ed. Cambridge, U.K.: Cambridge University Press, 1998.

Harbans Singh, ed. *Encyclopaedia of Sikhism*. 4 vols. Patiala, India: Punjabi University, 1998. Available online. Punjabi University, Patiala Web site. http://www.advancedcentrepunjabi.org/eos/

Kohli, Surinder Singh. *Dictionary of Guru Granth Sahib*. Amritsar, India: Singh Bros., 1996.

—Commentary by LaChelle Shilling

Questions for Further Study

1. Explain, if you can, what it means to regard a book as "living" and, more specifically, to regard the Sri Guru Granth Sahib as a guru.

2. Nanak, the founder of Sikhism, was quoted as saying, "There is no Hindu; there is no Muslim." Compare this statement with the statement by Emanuel Swedenborg in *Invitation to the New Church* that "men and women would no longer be called Evangelicals or Reformed, still less Lutherans or Calvinists, but would simply be Christians." Do you believe that the two leaders shared a common goal? Or do you believe that the context in which each expressed his view gave to his comment an entirely different meaning? Explain.

3. New religions and new expressions of religion often arise in the context of political and social turmoil. Why do you think this is so? What political and social changes gave rise to the Sri Guru Granth Sahib and, more specifically, the Raag Gond?

4. Do you see any contradiction between the ideals of peace and equality in Sikhism and the somewhat militaristic quality of the religion, as reflected, for example, in the carrying of the *kirpan* (sword) and the notion that Sikhs are to consider themselves "soldier-saints"?

5. Some Sikh youth have encountered difficulties in modern public schools because the *kirpan* (sword) and other symbols of Sikhism violate policies against bringing weapons to school. (The *kirpan* can be a large ceremonial sword or, for daily wearing, a smaller weapon, just a few inches long.) Do you believe that this is a reasonable policy? Or do you believe that such a policy violates the rights of Sikh students? Explain your reasoning.

Raag Gond: Document Text

1604 CE

Part 1

One Universal Creator God. Truth Is the Name. Creative Being Personified. No Fear. No Hatred. Image of the Undying. Beyond Birth. Self-Existent. By Guru's Grace:

Raag Gond, Chau-Padas, Fourth Mehl, First House:

If, in his conscious mind, he places his hopes in the Lord, then he shall obtain the fruits of all the many desires of his mind.

The Lord knows everything which happens to the soul. Not even an iota of one's effort goes to waste.

Place your hopes in the Lord, O my mind; the Lord and Master is pervading and permeating all.

O my mind, place your hopes in the Lord of the World, the Master of the Universe.

That hope which is placed in any other than the Lord that hope is fruitless, and totally useless.

That which you can see, Maya, and all attachment to family don't place your hopes in them, or your life will be wasted and lost.

Nothing is in their hands; what can these poor creatures do? By their actions, nothing can be done.

O my mind, place your hopes in the Lord, your Beloved, who shall carry you across, and save your whole family as well.

If you place your hopes in any other, in any friend other than the Lord, then you shall come to know that it is of no use at all.

This hope placed in other friends comes from the love of duality. In an instant, it is gone; it is totally false.

O my mind, place your hopes in the Lord, your True Beloved, who shall approve and reward you for all your efforts.

Hope and desire are all Yours, O my Lord and Master. As You inspire hope, so are the hopes held.

Part 2

Nothing is in the hands of anyone, O my Lord and Master; such is the understanding the True Guru has given me to understand.

You alone know the hope of servant Nanak, O Lord; gazing upon the Blessed Vision of the Lord's Darshan, he is satisfied.

Gond, Fourth Mehl:

Serve such a Lord, and ever meditate on Him, who in an instant erases all sins and mistakes.

If someone forsakes the Lord and places his hopes in another, then all his service to the Lord is rendered fruitless.

O my mind, serve the Lord, the Giver of peace; serving Him, all your hunger shall depart.

O my mind, place your faith in the Lord.

Wherever I go, my Lord and Master is there with me. The Lord saves the honor of His humble servants and slaves.

If you tell your sorrows to another, then he, in return, will tell you of his greater sorrows.

So tell your sorrows to the Lord, your Lord and Master, who shall instantly dispel your pain.

Forsaking such a Lord God, if you tell your sorrows to another, then you shall die of shame.

The relatives, friends and siblings of the world that you see, O my mind, all meet with you for their own purposes.

And that day, when their self-interests are not served, on that day, they shall not come near you.

O my mind, serve your Lord, day and night; He shall help you in good times and bad.

Why place your faith in anyone, O my mind, who cannot come to your rescue at the last instant?

Chant the Lord's Mantra, take the Guru's Teachings, and meditate on Him. In the end, the Lord saves those who love Him in their consciousness.

Servant Nanak speaks: night and day, chant the Lord's Name, O Saints; this is the only true hope for emancipation.

Gond, Fourth Mehl:

Remembering the Lord in meditation, you shall find bliss and peace forever deep within, and your mind will become tranquil and cool.

It is like the harsh sun of Maya, with its burning heat; seeing the moon, the Guru, its heat totally vanishes.

O my mind, night and day, meditate, and chant the Lord's Name.

Here and hereafter, He shall protect you, everywhere; serve such a God forever.

Meditate on the Lord, who contains all treasures, O my mind; as Gurmukh, search for the jewel, the Lord.

Those who meditate on the Lord, find the Lord, my Lord and Master; I wash the feet of those slaves of the Lord.

One who realizes the Word of the Shabad, obtains the sublime essence of the Lord; such a Saint is lofty and sublime, the greatest of the great.

The Lord Himself magnifies the glory of that humble servant. No one can lessen or decrease that glory, not even a bit.

Part 3

He shall give you peace, O my mind; meditate forever, every day on Him, with your palms pressed together.

Please bless servant Nanak with this one gift, O Lord, that Your feet may dwell within my heart forever.

Gond, Fourth Mehl:

All the kings, emperors, nobles, lords and chiefs are false and transitory, engrossed in duality know this well.

The eternal Lord is permanent and unchanging; meditate on Him, O my mind, and you shall be approved.

O my mind, vibrate, and meditate on the Lord's Name, which shall be your defender forever.

One who obtains the Mansion of the Lord's Presence, through the Word of the Guru's Teachings no one else's power is as great as his.

All the wealthy, high class property owners which you see, O my mind, shall vanish, like the fading color of the safflower.

Serve the True, Immaculate Lord forever, O my mind, and you shall be honored in the Court of the Lord.

There are four castes: Brahmin, Kh'shaatriya, Soodra and Vaishya, and there are four stages of life. One who meditates on the Lord, is the most distinguished and renowned.

The poor castor oil plant, growing near the sandalwood tree, becomes fragrant; in the same way, the sinner, associating with the Saints, becomes acceptable and approved.

He, within whose heart the Lord abides, is the highest of all, and the purest of all.

Servant Nanak washes the feet of that humble servant of the Lord; he may be from a low class family, but he is now the Lord's servant.

Gond, Fourth Mehl:

The Lord, the Inner-knower, the Searcher of hearts, is all-pervading. As the Lord causes them to act, so do they act.

So serve forever such a Lord, O my mind, who will protect you from everything.

O my mind, meditate on the Lord, and read about the Lord every day.

Other than the Lord, no one can kill you or save you; so why do you worry, O my mind?

The Creator created the entire universe, and infused His Light into it.

The One Lord speaks, and the One Lord causes all to speak. The Perfect Guru has revealed the One Lord.

The Lord is with you, inside and out; tell me, O mind, how can You hide anything from Him?

Serve the Lord open-heartedly, and then, O my mind, you shall find total peace.

Everything is under His control; He is the greatest of all. O my mind, meditate forever on Him.

O Servant Nanak, that Lord is always with you. Meditate forever on your Lord, and He shall emancipate you.

Gond, Fourth Mehl:

My mind yearns so deeply for the Blessed Vision of the Lord's Darshan, like the thirsty man without water.

My mind is pierced through by the arrow of the Lord's Love.

The Lord God knows my anguish, and the pain deep within my mind.

Whoever tells me the Stories of my Beloved Lord is my Sibling of Destiny, and my friend.

Part 4

Come, and join together, O my companions; let's sing the Glorious Praises of my God, and follow the comforting advice of the True Guru.

Please fulfill the hopes of servant Nanak, O Lord; his body finds peace and tranquility in the Blessed Vision of the Lord's Darshan.

First set of six.

Raag Gond, Fifth Mehl, Chau-Padas, First House:
One Universal Creator God. By the Grace of the True Guru:
He is the Creator of all, He is the Enjoyer of all.
The Creator listens, and the Creator sees.
The Creator is unseen, and the Creator is seen.
The Creator forms, and the Creator destroys.
The Creator touches, and the Creator is detached.
The Creator is the One who speaks, and the Creator is the One who understands.
The Creator comes, and the Creator also goes.
The Creator is absolute and without qualities; the Creator is related, with the most excellent qualities.
By Guru's Grace, Nanak looks upon all the same.
Gond, Fifth Mehl:
You are caught, like the fish and the monkey; you are entangled in the transitory world.
Your foot-steps and your breaths are numbered; only by singing the Glorious Praises of the Lord will you be saved.
O mind, reform yourself, and forsake your aimless wandering.
You have found no place of rest for yourself; so why do you try to teach others?
Like the elephant, driven by sexual desire, you are attached to your family.
People are like birds that come together, and fly apart again; you shall become stable and steady, only when you meditate on the Lord, Har, Har, in the Company of the Holy.
Like the fish, which perishes because of its desire to taste, the fool is ruined by his greed.
You have fallen under the power of the five thieves; escape is only possible in the Sanctuary of the Lord.
Be Merciful to me, O Destroyer of the pains of the meek; all beings and creatures belong to You.
May I obtain the gift of always seeing the Blessed Vision of Your Darshan; meeting with You, Nanak is the slave of Your slaves.
Raag Gond, Fifth Mehl, Chau-Padas, Second House:
One Universal Creator God. By the Grace of the True Guru:
He fashioned the soul and the breath of life, and infused His Light into the dust;
He exalted you and gave you everything to use, and food to eat and enjoy

how can you forsake that God, you fool! Where else will you go?
Commit yourself to the service of the Transcendent Lord.
Through the Guru, one understands the Immaculate, Divine Lord.
He created plays and dramas of all sorts;
He creates and destroys in an instant;
His state and condition cannot be described.
Meditate forever on that God, O my mind.
The unchanging Lord does not come or go.
His Glorious Virtues are infinite; how many of them can I count?

Part 5

His treasure is overflowing with the rubies of the Name.
He gives Support to all hearts.
The Name is the True Primal Being;
millions of sins are washed away in an instant, singing His Praises.
The Lord God is your best friend, your playmate from earliest childhood.
He is the Support of the breath of life; O Nanak, He is love, He is consciousness.
Gond, Fifth Mehl:
I trade in the Naam, the Name of the Lord.
The Naam is the Support of the mind.
My consciousness takes to the Shelter of the Naam.
Chanting the Naam, millions of sins are erased.
The Lord has blessed me with the wealth of the Naam, the Name of the One Lord.
The wish of my mind is to meditate on the Naam, in association with the Guru.
The Naam is the wealth of my soul.
Wherever I go, the Naam is with me.
The Naam is sweet to my mind.
In the water, on the land, and everywhere, I see the Naam.
Through the Naam, one's face becomes radiant in the Court of the Lord.
Through the Naam, all one's generations are saved.
Through the Naam, my affairs are resolved.
My mind is accustomed to the Naam.
Through the Naam, I have become fearless.
Through the Naam, my comings and goings have ceased.

The Perfect Guru has united me with the Lord, the treasure of virtue.

Says Nanak, I dwell in celestial peace.

Gond, Fifth Mehl:

He grants honor to the dishonored, and gives gifts to all the hungry;

he protects those in the terrible womb.

So humbly bow forever to that Lord and Master.

Meditate on such a God in your mind.

He shall be your help and support everywhere, in good times and bad.

The beggar and the king are all the same to Him.

He sustains and fulfills both the ant and the elephant.

He does not consult or seek anyone's advice.

Whatever He does, He does Himself.

No one knows His limit.

He Himself is the Immaculate Lord.

He Himself is formed, and He Himself is formless.

In the heart, in each and every heart, He is the Support of all hearts.

Through the Love of the Naam, the Name of the Lord, the devotees become His Beloveds.

Singing the Praises of the Creator, the Saints are forever in bliss.

Through the Love of the Naam, the Lord's humble servants remain satisfied.

Nanak falls at the feet of those humble servants of the Lord.

Gond, Fifth Mehl:

Associating with them, this mind becomes immaculate and pure.

Associating with them, one meditates in remembrance on the Lord, Har, Har.

Associating with them, all the sins are erased.

Associating with them, the heart is illumined.

Those Saints of the Lord are my friends.

It is their custom to sing only the Naam, the Name of the Lord.

By their mantra, the Lord, Har, Har, dwells in the mind.

By their teachings, doubt and fear are dispelled.

By their kirtan, they become immaculate and sublime.

The world longs for the dust of their feet.

Millions of sinners are saved by associating with them.

They have the Support of the Name of the One Formless Lord.

He knows the secrets of all beings;

He is the treasure of mercy, the divine immaculate Lord.

When the Supreme Lord God becomes merciful,

then one meets the Merciful Holy Guru.

Part 6

Day and night, Nanak meditates on the Naam.

Through the Lord's Name, he is blessed with peace, poise and bliss.

Gond, Fifth Mehl:

Meditate on the image of the Guru within your mind;

let your mind accept the Word of the Guru's Shabad, and His Mantra.

Enshrine the Guru's feet within your heart.

Bow in humility forever before the Guru, the Supreme Lord God.

Let no one wander in doubt in the world.

Without the Guru, no one can cross over.

The Guru shows the Path to those who have wandered off.

He leads them to renounce others, and attaches them to devotional worship of the Lord.

He obliterates the fear of birth and death.

The glorious greatness of the Perfect Guru is endless.

By Guru's Grace, the inverted heart-lotus blossoms forth, and the Light shines forth in the darkness.

Through the Guru, know the One who created you.

By the Guru's Mercy, the foolish mind comes to believe.

The Guru is the Creator; the Guru has the power to do everything.

The Guru is the Transcendent Lord; He is, and always shall be.

Says Nanak, God has inspired me to know this.

Without the Guru, liberation is not obtained, O Siblings of Destiny.

Gond, Fifth Mehl:

Chant Guru, Guru, Guru, O my mind.

I have no other than the Guru.

I lean upon the Support of the Guru, day and night.

No one can decrease His bounty.

Know that the Guru and the Transcendent Lord are One.

Whatever pleases Him is acceptable and approved.
One whose mind is attached to the Guru's feet
his pains, sufferings and doubts run away.
Serving the Guru, honor is obtained.
I am forever a sacrifice to the Guru.
Gazing upon the Blessed Vision of the Guru's Darshan, I am exalted.
The work of the Guru's servant is perfect.
Pain does not afflict the Guru's servant.
The Guru's servant is famous in the ten directions.
The Guru's glory cannot be described.
The Guru remains absorbed in the Supreme Lord God.
Says Nanak, one who is blessed with perfect destiny
his mind is attached to the Guru's feet.
Gond, Fifth Mehl:
I worship and adore my Guru; the Guru is the Lord of the Universe.
My Guru is the Supreme Lord God; the Guru is the Lord God.
My Guru is divine, invisible and mysterious.
I serve at the Guru's feet, which are worshipped by all.
Without the Guru, I have no other place at all.
Night and day, I chant the Name of Guru, Guru.
The Guru is my spiritual wisdom, the Guru is the meditation within my heart.
The Guru is the Lord of the World, the Primal Being, the Lord God.
With my palms pressed together, I remain in the Guru's Sanctuary.
Without the Guru, I have no other at all.
The Guru is the boat to cross over the terrifying world-ocean.
Serving the Guru, one is released from the Messenger of Death.
In the darkness, the Guru's Mantra shines forth.
With the Guru, all are saved.
The Perfect Guru is found, by great good fortune.
Serving the Guru, pain does not afflict anyone.
No one can erase the Word of the Guru's Shabad.
Nanak is the Guru; Nanak is the Lord Himself. . . .

Part 8

Gond, Fifth Mehl:
Bow in humility to the lotus feet of the Guru.

Eliminate sexual desire and anger from this body.
Be the dust of all,
and see the Lord in each and every heart, in all.
In this way, dwell upon the Lord of the World, the Lord of the Universe.
My body and wealth belong to God; my soul belongs to God.
Twenty-four hours a day, sing the Glorious Praises of the Lord.
This is the purpose of human life.
Renounce your egotistical pride, and know that God is with you.
By the Grace of the Holy, let your mind be imbued with the Lord's Love.
Know the One who created you,
and in the world hereafter you shall be honored in the Court of the Lord.
Your mind and body will be immaculate and blissful;
chant the Name of the Lord of the Universe with your tongue.
Grant Your Kind Mercy, O my Lord, Merciful to the meek.
My mind begs for the dust of the feet of the Holy.
Be merciful, and bless me with this gift,
that Nanak may live, chanting God's Name.
Gond, Fifth Mehl:
My incense and lamps are my service to the Lord.
Time and time again, I humbly bow to the Creator.
I have renounced everything, and grasped the Sanctuary of God.
By great good fortune, the Guru has become pleased and satisfied with me.
Twenty-four hours a day, I sing of the Lord of the Universe.
My body and wealth belong to God; my soul belongs to God.
Chanting the Glorious Praises of the Lord, I am in bliss.
The Supreme Lord God is the Perfect Forgiver.
Granting His Mercy, He has linked His humble servants to His service.
He has rid me of the pains of birth and death, and merged me with Himself.
This is the essence of karma, righteous conduct and spiritual wisdom,
to chant the Lord's Name in the Saadh Sangat, the Company of the Holy.

God's Feet are the boat to cross over the world-ocean.

God, the Inner-knower, is the Cause of causes.

Showering His Mercy, He Himself has saved me.

The five hideous demons have run away.

Do not lose your life in the gamble.

The Creator Lord has taken Nanak's side.

Gond, Fifth Mehl:

In His Mercy, He has blessed me with peace and bliss.

The Divine Guru has saved His child.

God is kind and compassionate; He is the Lord of the Universe.

He forgives all beings and creatures.

I seek Your Sanctuary, O God, O Merciful to the meek.

Meditating on the Supreme Lord God, I am forever in ecstasy.

There is no other like the Merciful Lord God.

He is contained deep within each and every heart.

He embellishes His slave, here and hereafter.

It is Your nature, God, to purify sinners.

Meditation on the Lord of the Universe is the medicine to cure millions of illnesses.

My Tantra and Mantra is to meditate, to vibrate upon the Lord God.

Illnesses and pains are dispelled, meditating on God.

The fruits of the mind's desires are fulfilled.

He is the Cause of causes, the All-powerful Merciful Lord.

Contemplating Him is the greatest of all treasures.

God Himself has forgiven Nanak;

forever and ever, he chants the Name of the One Lord.

Gond, Fifth Mehl:

Chant the Name of the Lord, Har, Har, O my friend. . . .

Part 11

Gond, Fifth Mehl:

I am a sacrifice to the Saints.

Associating with the Saints, I sing the Glorious Praises of the Lord.

By the Grace of the Saints, all the sins are taken away.

By great good fortune, one finds the Sanctuary of the Saints.

Meditating on the Lord, no obstacles will block your way.

By Guru's Grace, meditate on God.

When the Supreme Lord God becomes merciful,

he makes me the dust of the feet of the Holy.

Sexual desire and anger leave his body,

and the Lord, the jewel, comes to dwell in his mind.

Fruitful and approved is the life of one

who knows the Supreme Lord God to be close.

One who is committed to loving devotional worship of God, and the Kirtan of His Praises,

awakens from the sleep of countless incarnations.

The Lord's Lotus Feet are the Support of His humble servant.

To chant the Praises of the Lord of the Universe is the true trade.

Please fulfill the hopes of Your humble slave.

Nanak finds peace in the dust of the feet of the humble.

Raag Gond, Ashtapadees, Fifth Mehl, Second House:

One Universal Creator God. By the Grace of the True Guru:

Humbly bow to the Perfect Divine Guru.

Fruitful is His image, and fruitful is service to Him.

He is the Inner-knower, the Searcher of hearts, the Architect of Destiny.

Twenty-four hours a day, he remains imbued with the love of the Naam, the Name of the Lord.

The Guru is the Lord of the Universe, the Guru is the Lord of the World.

He is the Saving Grace of His slaves.

He satisfies the kings, emperors and nobles.

He destroys the egotistical villains.

He puts illness into the mouths of the slanderers.

All the people celebrate His victory.

Supreme bliss fills the minds of the Saints.

The Saints meditate on the Divine Guru, the Lord God.

The faces of His companions become radiant and bright.

The slanderers lose all places of rest.

With each and every breath, the Lord's humble slaves praise Him.

The Supreme Lord God and the Guru are carefree.

All fears are eradicated, in His Sanctuary.
Smashing all the slanderers, the Lord knocks them to the ground.
Let no one slander the Lord's humble servants.
Whoever does so, will be miserable.
Twenty-four hours a day, the Lord's humble servant meditates on Him alone.
The Messenger of Death does not even approach him.
The Lord's humble servant has no vengeance.
The slanderer is egotistical.
The Lord's humble servant wishes well, while the slanderer dwells on evil.
The Sikh of the Guru meditates on the True Guru.
The Lord's humble servants are saved, while the slanderer is cast into hell.
Listen, O my beloved friends and companions: these words shall be true in the Court of the Lord.
As you plant, so shall you harvest.
The proud, egotistical person will surely be uprooted.
O True Guru, You are the Support of the unsupported.
Be merciful, and save Your humble servant.
Says Nanak, I am a sacrifice to the Guru; remembering Him in meditation, my honor has been saved.

Part 12

Raag Gond, The Word Of The Devotees.
Kabeer Jee, First House:
One Universal Creator God. By the Grace of the True Guru:
When you meet a Saint, talk to him and listen.
Meeting with an unsaintly person, just remain silent.
O father, if I speak, what words should I utter?
Speak such words, by which you may remain absorbed in the Name of the Lord.
Speaking with the Saints, one becomes generous.
To speak with a fool is to babble uselessly.
By speaking and only speaking, corruption only increases.
If I do not speak, what can the poor wretch do?
Says Kabeer, the empty pitcher makes noise, but that which is full makes no sound.
GOND:

When a man dies, he is of no use to anyone.
But when an animal dies, it is used in ten ways.
What do I know, about the state of my karma?
What do I know, O Baba?
His bones burn, like a bundle of logs; his hair burns like a bale of hay.
Says Kabeer, the man wakes up, only when the Messenger of Death hits him over the head with his club.
GOND:
The Celestial Lord is in the Akaashic ethers of the skies, the Celestial Lord is in the nether regions of the underworld; in the four directions, the Celestial Lord is pervading.
The Supreme Lord God is forever the source of bliss. When the vessel of the body perishes, the Celestial Lord does not perish.
I have become sad, wondering where the soul comes from, and where it goes.
The body is formed from the union of the five tatvas; but where were the five tatvas created?
You say that the soul is tied to its karma, but who gave karma to the body?
The body is contained in the Lord, and the Lord is contained in the body. He is permeating within all.
Says Kabeer, I shall not renounce the Lord's Name. I shall accept whatever happens.
Raag Gond, The Word Of Kabeer Jee, Second House:
One Universal Creator God. By the Grace of the True Guru:
They tied my arms, bundled me up, and threw me before an elephant.
The elephant driver struck him on the head, and infuriated him.
But the elephant ran away, trumpeting, "I am a sacrifice to this image of the Lord."
O my Lord and Master, You are my strength.
The Qazi shouted at the driver to drive the elephant on.
He yelled out, "O driver, I shall cut you into pieces.
Hit him, and drive him on!"
But the elephant did not move; instead, he began to meditate.
The Lord God abides within his mind.
What sin has this Saint committed, that you have made him into a bundle and thrown him before the elephant?

Lifting up the bundle, the elephant bows down before it.
The Qazi could not understand it; he was blind.
Three times, he tried to do it.

Part 13

Even then, his hardened mind was not satisfied.
Says Kabeer, such is my Lord and Master.
The soul of His humble servant dwells in the fourth state.
GOND:
It is not human, and it is not a god.
It is not called celibate, or a worshipper of Shiva.
It is not a Yogi, and it is not a hermit.
It is not a mother, or anyone's son.
Then what is it, which dwells in this temple of the body?
No one can find its limits.
It is not a house-holder, and it is not a renouncer of the world.
It is not a king, and it is not a beggar.
It has no body, no drop of blood.
It is not a Brahmin, and it is not a Kh'shaatriya.
It is not called a man of austere self-discipline, or a Shaykh.
It does not live, and it is not seen to die.
If someone cries over its death,
that person loses his honor.
By Guru's Grace, I have found the Path.
Birth and death have both been erased.
Says Kabeer, this is formed of the same essence as the Lord.
It is like the ink on the paper which cannot be erased.
GOND:
The threads are broken, and the starch has run out.
Bare reeds glisten at the front door.
The poor brushes are scattered in pieces.
Death has entered this shaven head.
This shaven-headed mendicant has wasted all his wealth.
All this coming and going has irritated him.
He has given up all talk of his weaving equipment.
His mind is attuned to the Lord's Name.
His daughters and sons have nothing to eat,
while the shaven-headed mendicants night and day eat their fill.
One or two are in the house, and one or two more are on the way.

We sleep on the floor, while they sleep in the beds.
They rub their bare heads, and carry prayer-books in their waist-bands.
We get dry grains, while they get loaves of bread.
He will become one of these shaven-headed mendicants.
They are the support of the drowning.
Listen, O blind and unguided Loi:
Kabeer has taken shelter with these shaven-headed mendicants.
GOND:
When her husband dies, the woman does not cry.
Someone else becomes her protector.
When this protector dies,
he falls into the world of hell hereafter, for the sexual pleasures he enjoyed in this world.
The world loves only the one bride, Maya.
She is the wife of all beings and creatures.
With her necklace around her neck, this bride looks beautiful.
She is poison to the Saint, but the world is de-lighted with her.
Adorning herself, she sits like a prostitute.
Cursed by the Saints, she wanders around like a wretch.
She runs around, chasing after the Saints.
She is afraid of being beaten by those blessed with the Guru's Grace.
She is the body, the breath of life, of the faith-less cynics.
She appears to me like a blood-thirsty witch.
I know her secrets well
in His Mercy, the Divine Guru met me.
Says Kabeer, now I have thrown her out.
She clings to the skirt of the world.

Part 14

GOND:
When someone's household has no glory,
the guests who come there depart still hungry.
Deep within, there is no contentment.
Without his bride, the wealth of Maya, he suf-fers in pain.
So praise this bride, which can shake the con-sciousness of even the most dedicated ascetics and sages.
This bride is the daughter of a wretched miser.

Abandoning the Lord's servant, she sleeps with the world.
Standing at the door of the holy man,
she says, "I have come to your sanctuary; now save me!"
This bride is so beautiful.
The bells on her ankles make soft music.
As long as there is the breath of life in the man, she remains attached to him.
But when it is no more, she quickly gets up and departs, bare-footed.
This bride has conquered the three worlds.
The eighteen Puraanas and the sacred shrines of pilgrimage love her as well.
She pierced the hearts of Brahma, Shiva and Vishnu.
She destroyed the great emperors and kings of the world.
This bride has no restraint or limits.
She is in collusion with the five thieving passions.
When the clay pot of these five passions bursts,
then, says Kabeer, by Guru's Mercy, one is released.
GOND:
As the house will not stand when the supporting beams are removed from within it,
just so, without the Naam, the Name of the Lord, how can anyone be carried across?
Without the pitcher, the water is not contained;
just so, without the Holy Saint, the mortal departs in misery.
One who does not remember the Lord let him burn;
his body and mind have remained absorbed in this field of the world.
Without a farmer, the land is not planted;
without a thread, how can the beads be strung?
Without a loop, how can the knot be tied?
Just so, without the Holy Saint, the mortal departs in misery.
Without a mother or father there is no child;
just so, without water, how can the clothes be washed?
Without a horse, how can there be a rider?
Without the Holy Saint, one cannot reach the Court of the Lord.
Just as without music, there is no dancing,
the bride rejected by her husband is dishonored.
Says Kabeer, do this one thing:
become Gurmukh, and you shall never die again.
GOND:
He alone is a pimp, who pounds down his mind.

Pounding down his mind, he escapes from the Messenger of Death.
Pounding and beating his mind, he puts it to the test;
such a pimp attains total liberation.
Who is called a pimp in this world?
In all speech, one must carefully consider.
He alone is a dancer, who dances with his mind.
The Lord is not satisfied with falsehood; He is pleased only with Truth.
So play the beat of the drum in the mind.
The Lord is the Protector of the dancer with such a mind.
She alone is a street-dancer, who cleanses her body-street,
and educates the five passions.
She who embraces devotional worship for the Lord
I accept such a street-dancer as my Guru.
He alone is a thief, who is above envy,
and who uses his sense organs to chant the Lord's Name.
Says Kabeer, these are the qualities of the one
I know as my Blessed Divine Guru, who is the most beautiful and wise.

Part 15

GOND:
Blessed is the Lord of the World. Blessed is the Divine Guru.
Blessed is that grain, by which the heart-lotus of the hungry blossoms forth.
Blessed are those Saints, who know this.
Meeting with them, one meets the Lord, the Sustainer of the World.
This grain comes from the Primal Lord God.
One chants the Naam, the Name of the Lord, only when he tastes this grain.
Meditate on the Naam, and meditate on this grain.
Mixed with water, its taste becomes sublime.
One who abstains from this grain,
loses his honor in the three worlds.
One who discards this grain, is practicing hypocrisy.
She is neither a happy soul-bride, nor a widow.
Those who claim in this world that they live on milk alone,
secretly eat whole loads of food.
Without this grain, time does not pass in peace.

Forsaking this grain, one does not meet the Lord of the World.

Says Kabeer, this I know:

blessed is that grain, which brings faith in the Lord and Master to the mind.

Raag Gond, The Word Of Naam Dayv Jee, First House:

One Universal Creator God. By the Grace of the True Guru:

The ritual sacrifice of horses,

giving one's weight in gold to charities,

and ceremonial cleansing baths

These are not equal to singing the Praises of the Lord's Name.

Meditate on your Lord, you lazy man!

Offering sweet rice at Gaya,

living on the river banks at Benares,

reciting the four Vedas by heart;

Completing all religious rituals,

restraining sexual passion by the spiritual wisdom given by the Guru,

and performing the six rituals;

Expounding on Shiva and Shakti

O man, renounce and abandon all these things.

Meditate, meditate in remembrance on the Lord of the Universe.

Meditate, O Naam Dayv, and cross over the terrifying world-ocean.

GOND:

The deer is lured by the sound of the hunter's bell;

it loses its life, but it cannot stop thinking about it.

In the same way, I look upon my Lord.

I will not abandon my Lord, and turn my thoughts to another.

As the fisherman looks upon the fish,

and the goldsmith looks upon the gold he fashions;

As the man driven by sex looks upon another man's wife,

and the gambler looks upon the throwing of the dice

In the same way, wherever Naam Dayv looks, he sees the Lord.

Naam Dayv meditates continuously on the Feet of the Lord.

GOND:

Carry me across, O Lord, carry me across.

I am ignorant, and I do not know how to swim.

O my Beloved Father, please give me Your arm.

I have been transformed from a mortal being into an angel, in an instant; the True Guru has taught me this.

Born of human flesh, I have conquered the heavens; such is the medicine I was given.

Please place me where You placed Dhroo and Naarad, O my Master.

With the Support of Your Name, so many have been saved; this is Naam Dayv's understanding.

Part 16

GOND:

I am restless and unhappy.

Without her calf, the cow is lonely.

Without water, the fish writhes in pain.

So is poor Naam Dayv without the Lord's Name.

Like the cow's calf, which, when let loose,

sucks at her udders and drinks her milk

So has Naam Dayv found the Lord.

Meeting the Guru, I have seen the Unseen Lord.

As the man driven by sex wants another man's wife,

so does Naam Dayv love the Lord.

As the earth burns in the dazzling sunlight,

so does poor Naam Dayv burn without the Lord's Name.

Raag Gond, The Word Of Naam Dayv Jee, Second House:

One Universal Creator God. By the Grace of the True Guru:

Chanting the Name of the Lord, Har, Har, all doubts are dispelled.

Chanting the Name of the Lord is the highest religion.

Chanting the Name of the Lord, Har, Har, erases social classes and ancestral pedigrees.

The Lord is the walking stick of the blind.

I bow to the Lord, I humbly bow to the Lord.

Chanting the Name of the Lord, Har, Har, you will not be tormented by the Messenger of Death.

The Lord took the life of Harnaakhash,

and gave Ajaamal a place in heaven.

Teaching a parrot to speak the Lord's Name, Ganika the prostitute was saved.

That Lord is the light of my eyes.

Chanting the Name of the Lord, Har, Har, Pootna was saved,

even though she was a deceitful child-killer.

Contemplating the Lord, Dropadi was saved.

Gautam's wife, turned to stone, was saved.

The Lord, who killed Kaysee and Kans,

gave the gift of life to Kali.

Prays Naam Dayv, such is my Lord;
meditating on Him, fear and suffering are dispelled.
GOND:
One who chases after the god Bhairau, evil spirits and the goddess of smallpox,
is riding on a donkey, kicking up the dust.
I take only the Name of the One Lord.
I have given away all other gods in exchange for Him.
That man who chants "Shiva, Shiva,"and meditates on him,
is riding on a bull, shaking a tambourine.
One who worships the Great Goddess Maya
will be reincarnated as a woman, and not a man.
You are called the Primal Goddess.
At the time of liberation, where will you hide then?
Follow the Guru's Teachings, and hold tight to the Lord's Name, O friend.
Thus prays Naam Dayv, and so says the Gita as well.
BILAAVAL GOND:
Today, Naam Dayv saw the Lord, and so I will instruct the ignorant.
O Pandit, O religious scholar, your Gayatri was grazing in the fields.
Taking a stick, the farmer broke its leg, and now it walks with a limp.
O Pandit, I saw your great god Shiva, riding along on a white bull.
In the merchant's house, a banquet was prepared for him he killed the merchant's son.

Part 17

O Pandit, I saw your Raam Chand coming too;
he lost his wife, fighting a war against Raawan.
The Hindu is sightless; the Muslim has only one eye.
The spiritual teacher is wiser than both of them.
The Hindu worships at the temple, the Muslim at the mosque.
Naam Dayv serves that Lord, who is not limited to either the temple or the mosque.
Raag Gond, The Word Of Ravi Daas Jee, Second House:
One Universal Creator God. By the Grace of the True Guru:
Meditate on the Lord Mukanday, the Liberator, O people of the world.

Without Mukanday, the body shall be reduced to ashes.
Mukanday is the Giver of liberation.
Mukanday is my father and mother.
Meditate on Mukanday in life, and meditate on Mukanday in death.
His servant is blissful forever.
The Lord, Mukanday, is my breath of life.
Meditating on Mukanday, one's forehead will bear the Lord's insignia of approval.
The renunciate serves Mukanday.
Mukanday is the wealth of the poor and forlorn.
When the One Liberator does me a favor,
then what can the world do to me?
Erasing my social status, I have entered His Court.
You, Mukanday, are potent throughout the four ages.
Spiritual wisdom has welled up, and I have been enlightened.
In His Mercy, the Lord has made this worm His slave.
Says Ravi Daas, now my thirst is quenched;
I meditate on Mukanday the Liberator, and I serve Him.
GOND:
Someone may bathe at the sixty-eight sacred shrines of pilgrimage,
and worship the twelve Shiva-lingam stones,
and dig wells and pools,
but if he indulges in slander, then all of this is useless.
How can the slanderer of the Holy Saints be saved?
Know for certain, that he shall go to hell.
Someone may bathe at Kuruk-shaytra during a solar eclipse,
and give his decorated wife in offering,
and listen to all the Simritees,
but if he indulges in slander, these are of no account.
Someone may give countless feasts,
and donate land, and build splendid buildings;
he may neglect his own affairs to work for others,
but if he indulges in slander, he shall wander in countless incarnations.
Why do you indulge in slander, O people of the world?
The emptiness of the slanderer is soon exposed.
I have thought, and determined the fate of the slanderer.
Says Ravi Daas, he is a sinner; he shall go to hell.

Ajaamal and Ganika:	figures who reversed their attachments to the world through acts of kindness and a willingness to take the advice of holy men
Akaashic:	also spelled Akashic; referring to the mystical, nontangible library or compendium of all knowledge of the cosmos and history of human experience
Benares:	a sacred site in India
Brahma, Shiva, and Vishnu:	the major Hindu gods
Brahmin:	a member of the priestly caste
Darshan:	usually translated as "viewing" or "meeting"
Dhroo and Naarad:	exemplars of devotion and good character
Dropadi:	a wife in the Hindu sacred epic the Mahabharata who did not need to be redeemed from her sinful ways and maintained her faith in Krishna
Gautam's wife:	a woman who was turned to stone after she mistakenly made love with a god who had disguised himself as her husband
Gaya:	a sacred site in India
Gayatri:	the second wife of the Hindu god Brahma
Gurmukh:	the God-inspired man
Harnaakhash:	a king who had his life taken away because of his uncontrollable ego
Kali:	a figure who receives the gift of life from God, in a story that is found in the Bhagavata Purana
karma:	the effects of a person's actions that determine his destiny in his next incarnation
Kaysee and Kans:	characters who attempt to murder baby Krishna and are killed by God
Kh'shaatriya:	also spelled Kshatriya; a member of the military caste
Loi:	a God-fearing maiden
Maya:	often translated as "illusion" and here personified
Mehl:	literally, "body," or a guru of Sikhism
Mukanday:	that is, "Liberator"
Naam:	that is, "name,"the name of God, or God himself
Nanak:	the founder of Sikhism
Pandit:	a scholar
Pootna:	a demon sent by Krishna's uncle to murder Krishna
Puraanas:	or Puranas, Hindu religious texts
Qazi:	a judge or religious adjudicator who preaches and decides on Islamic religious matters
Raam Chand:	Lord Rama, the seventh avatar of Vishnu
Raawan:	a demon king

Glossary

Saadh Sangat:	the company of Holy people dedicated to the elevation of the person to a higher and better level of understanding of righteousness
Shabad:	a hymn or paragraph in a holy text
Shakti:	the consort of Shiva
Shaykh:	an Islamic religious official; or, a term of respect for elders
Simritees:	traditional ceremonial and legal institutes of the Hindus
Soodra:	the servant or laboring caste
Tantra:	a Hindu or Buddhist religious text, or, doctrine of enlightenment as the realization of the oneness of one's self and the visible world
Vaishya:	the merchant, artisan, and landowner caste
Vedas:	the oldest scriptures of Hinduism

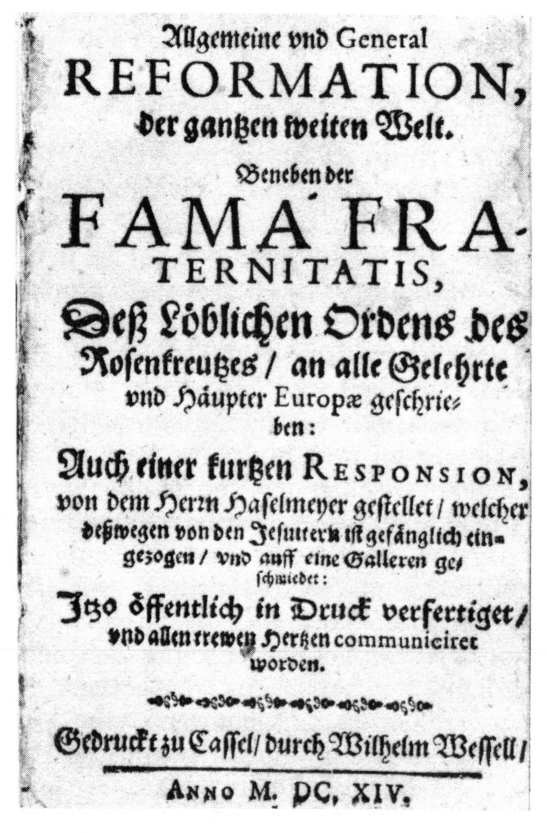

Allgemeine vnd General
REFORMATION,
der gantzen weiten Welt.

Beneben der

FAMA FRA-
TERNITATIS,

Deß Löblichen Ordens des
Rosenkreutzes / an alle Gelehrte
vnd Häupter Europæ geschrie-
ben :

Auch einer kurtzen RESPONSION,
von dem Herrn Haselmeyer gestellet / welcher
deßwegen von den Jesuitern ist gefänglich ein-
gezogen / vnd auff eine Galleren ge-
schmiedet :

Itzo öffentlich in Druck verfertiget /
vnd allen trewen Hertzen communiciret
worden.

Gedruckt zu Cassel / durch Wilhelm Wessell /
ANNO M. DC. XIV.

First page of the *Fama Fraternitatis*, 1614.

FAMA FRATERNITATIS: DOCUMENT ANALYSIS

1610 CE

"There will now be a general reformation, both of divine and human things."

Overview

A masterpiece of Christian utopianism, the *Fama Fraternitatis* (or "Fame of the Fraternity") first appeared as a German manuscript in 1610, almost certainly the work of a young German theologian named Johann Valentin Andreae. The *Fama* seemed to its readers to promise the fruit of a global reformation of science and religion, instigated by an enlightened secret society. This society had allegedly been founded by one "C. R." at the dawn of the fifteenth century.

The manuscript of the *Fama Fraternitatis* was pirated and printed at Kassel, Germany, in 1614, immediately generating a pan-European furor. Dozens of pamphlets and short books were published, arguing for or against the work of the "Brothers R. C." The initialism "R. C." was taken to mean "Rosen Creutz," or "Rosy Cross," while "C. R." was taken to be the name of the brotherhood's alleged founder, "Christian Rosenkreutz." Thus, enthusiasts for the *Fama* came to be called Rosicrucians. To this day, Rosicrucian organizations draw inspiration from the *Fama Fraternitatis*.

The author of the *Fama* believed that an unfortunate side effect of the sixteenth century's Reformation of the Church (which had fractured the Roman Catholic Church, resulting in the formation of various Protestant denominations) was that university learning had been corrupted. Instead of building a future based on shared knowledge and openness to new ideas, sciences, and experiments, education was fostering pretension, bigotry, and persecution. This state of affairs appeared contrary to God's will, for a prophecy of the times held that before the end of the world, a "last light" would deliver the hidden secrets of Nature to human knowledge, and humanity would discover practically unlimited potential.

To generate interest in reform, the *Fama* utilized a mystery story, a satirical play whose script was the document itself. The reader was thus made complicit in its drama.

The *Fama*'s narrative begins in the late fourteenth century and concerns a young German nobleman, referred to as "C. R." or "C. R. C." Having quit his cloister, C. R. is drawn mysteriously to the sages of Damcar in Arabia. They offer him cosmic knowledge in the "Book M," which C. R. translates. When C. R. returns to Germany with the book, the nation's savants reject it, prompting C. R. to form a secret brotherhood dedicated to scientific advance and to healing without charge. Members of the brotherhood assemble in the hidden "House of the Holy Spirit." After a long life, C. R. is interred in a "compendium of the universe," the whereabouts of which is soon forgotten. Hidden, its sealed door declares it will be opened in 120 years.

The *Fama* announces the tomb's discovery as a sign for the world. For readers today, the *Fama*'s appearance not only marks a transitional period in European history—from a concentration on religious controversy to the modern era of scientific experiment and philosophical enlightenment—but also stands as the font of a dream of international reform of science and education. Additionally, the *Fama* is linked to the beginnings of symbolic Freemasonry and modern occult and theosophical societies. The *Fama Fraternitatis* continues to touch the idealistic core of a more hopeful humanity, sickened by bigotry and persecution.

Context

The *Fama Fraternitatis* focuses upon university corruption, something of which Johann Valentin Andreae had personal experience. In 1606 he was temporarily expelled from the Universität Tübingen for objecting to court influence on university governance. Tübingen's chancellor, Matthias Enzlin, was a favorite of the duke of Württemberg's court. Enzlin exploited his connection to the court to prejudice the duke against men he did not approve of—men such as Simon Studion, author of the manuscript *Naometria* ("Temple Measurement," ca. 1604), which joined astronomy to biblical prophecy and apocalyptic numerology and speculation. Whereas learning had once been controlled by the Catholic Church, it was now, in Protestant lands, controlled by princes. The princes ruled over a corruptible system of patronage. The effects of court influence and academic bigotry were observed closely by Andreae in the treatment meted out to his saintly older friend Tobias Hess, an associate of Studion's. Hess, a Tübingen lawyer, mathematician, mechanician, and doctor, dispensed medicine freely to poor people (rejecting the money of the rich) and investigated science through experiment rather than relying on paper authority. He was interrogated and ridiculed by university authorities between 1605 and 1609. Opponents objected to Hess's devotion to the medicine of the Renaissance doctor Paracelsus, a man attacked by many as a heretic, regardless of his great success in curing people.

University interrogators also sought to deny Hess the opportunity to interpret Bible prophecies in the light of recent astronomical events. Indeed, astronomical events provide a key context for understanding the *Fama*'s message and its effect on the times. From indications in the *Fama* and its follow-up manifesto, the *Confessio Fraternitatis* (or "Confession of the Fraternity"), the lost tomb of "C. R." was miraculously discovered by the fraternity in 1604. The discovery signified a new age, possibly even "the last light."

Commentators in Tübingen and across Europe had been excited by observations made by the imperial astronomer and former Tübingen student Johannes Kepler. In September 1604, Kepler observed a massing of planets when Mars joined a conjunction of Saturn and Jupiter on the edge of Scorpio and Sagittarius. Kepler compared it to the appearance of the star of Bethlehem in 7 BCE and wondered whether the world would see a prophet, a new sect, or war. Then, on October 9, as Saturn and Jupiter neared close conjunction in Sagittarius (in the "fiery trigon"), a supernova occurred. This new star was observed for nearly a year in the constellation of Serpens. When the supernova was linked back to the appearance of an earlier new "star" (a comet, in fact) in Cygnus in 1602, commentators prophesied the appearance of a leader and religious movement that would defeat Rome and inaugurate the "last light" before the world's end. The issue was much debated by Kepler and was regarded as highly controversial in Kepler's old university of Tübingen. Hess put the astronomical events in the context of an imminent final defeat of the pope. This wider political context also informs the *Fama*.

Throughout Europe, Protestants felt threatened by a resurgence of Roman Catholic confidence. Since the papacy had given up hope of reconciling Protestants to the Catholic Church, the common expectation was that the papacy would not rest until Protestant lands were completely conquered by Roman Catholic princes. Protestants, on the other hand, sought hope in political alliances and in dreams of supernatural deliverance at the hands of a "Protestant lion," whose leadership would coincide with the "last light" before the world's end. In the fever of the times, it was inevitable that the dreams of the *Fama* would not only be influenced by but also linked to the apocalyptic hopes of Protestants who sought God's help in defeating a power they saw as determined to annihilate God's true witnesses.

The English-language version of the *Fama Fraternitatis*, reproduced here in full, was translated by "Eugenius Philalethes" (the pseudonym used by the Welsh alchemist Thomas Vaughan) as *The Fame and Confession of the Fraternity R: C: Commonly, of the Rosie Cross* (1652). It was the first printed English version, emanating from a London "chemical club" whose members included Vaughan and Thomas Henshaw. Henshaw revered John Hall's translation of Andreae's *Christianae societatis imago* ("A Model of a Christian Society," 1647) and tried to put it into practice in London in 1650. One of the aims of the club, like that of Andreae's Christian Society, was to produce an alchemical encyclopedia, an objective in part achieved in Elias Ashmole's *Theatrum chemicum Britannicum* ("Theatre of British Chemistry," 1652).

About the Author

Johann Valentin Andreae was born at Herrenberg in the duchy of Württemberg. His grandfather Jakob Andreae, the chancellor at Universität Tübingen, contributed to the Lutheran Formula of Concord (1577). The family arms depicted a Saint Andrew's cross with four roses in the quarters—almost certainly the source of the name "Rosenkreutz." Attracted to theater as a means of communicating elusive truth, Andreae believed that salvation involved a mystical transformation of the human being that could be expressed in alchemical symbols. Andreae's family practiced alchemy. His mother, Maria, was apothecary to the court at Tübingen, while he distinguished himself in theology, classics, poetry, Renaissance literature, physics, and chemistry.

Andreae enjoyed what he called "secret friendships"—friendships with people whose religious ideas, for example, might shock or annoy other friends. An ecumenical genius, Andreae did not accept the orthodox idea of heresy. After being ordered to leave the university temporarily in 1606, Andreae visited Frankfurt, Strasbourg, Mainz, Worms, and the Rhineland. He also toured Paris, Geneva, the Alps, Spain, and Italy, earning his keep teaching the sons of noblemen while drafting his play *Turbo*. *Turbo* is dominated by the image of a wanderer, a stranger or alien in the world, saved by Providence, dreams, and angelic care. Andreae returned to Tübingen in 1608, spending time with his close friend, Tobias Hess.

The *Fama* appears to be the product of Andreae's encounter with Hess. In April 1614, Andreae married Bishop Erasmus Grüninger's niece and settled into a Lutheran ministry at Vaihingen, near the southern German city of Stuttgart. That year he published his practical and educational *Collectaneorum mathematicorum* ("Mathematical Collection") at Tübingen. Its contents derived from discussions among members of Andreae's "Mathematical Institute." But the heart of Andreae lies in his works of Christian devotion, classics of a European spiritual movement that would blos-

Time Line	
August 18, 1586	■ Johann Valentin Andreae is born in Herrenberg, near Tübingen, Germany.
1600	■ The natural philosopher Giordano Bruno is burned at the stake in Rome as an "impenitent heretic."
October 9, 1604	■ Johannes Kepler observes the appearance of a supernova in the constellation of Serpens.
1605	■ Andreae writes a work titled *Nuptia chymica* ("Chemical Nuptials"), in which the antihero Christian Rosenkreutz first appears in a fantasy of alchemical regeneration.
1610	■ Andreae travels through France, Italy, and Spain, penning what he referred to as "divers writings" later published by other people; that year, the *Fama Fraternitatis* first appears, as seen by the Paracelsian doctor Adam Haslmayr in the Tyrol (the western part of modern-day Austria).
1613	■ The marriage of Frederick of the Palatinate and Elizabeth, the daughter of James I of England, gives hope to Protestants.
March 1614	■ The *Fama* is published at Kassel, with Trajano Boccalini's *Generale riforma dell' universo* ("The General Reformation of the Whole World") as well as Adam Haslmayr's *Antwort,* or "Answer," to the *Fama* and an account of Haslmayr's imprisonment as a galley slave by Jesuits for promoting the *Fama*.
1615	■ The Latin *Confessio Fraternitatis* ("Confession of the Fraternity") appears in print.
1616	■ Andreae's *Chymische Hochzeit Christiani Rosencreutz* (*The Chemical Wedding of Christian Rosenkreutz*), the first printed edition of his *Nuptia chymica,* is published in Strasbourg.
October 1617	■ Ferdinand of Styria (in modern-day Austria) becomes king of Bohemia and, aided by Jesuits, repeals toleration legislation designed to protect the Bohemian (Protestant) Brethren.
1654	■ Andreae dies in Stuttgart at the age of sixty-seven.

som as Pietism. Intended to bring religion to the mystical heart of the person, Pietism encouraged an inward search for God that could transform the individual's inner life. It was a step beyond mere acceptance of authoritative or dogmatic beliefs; God must be alive in the heart of the believer, not simply an intellectual or philosophical assumption. Andreae's important *Christianopolis* (1619) illustrates his contention that true religion walks with science: Truth must be sought, not imposed.

Andreae put his spiritual and educational ideals into his Societas Christiana, or "Christian Society," a fraternity described in his *Christianae societatis imago* ("Image of the Christian Society," 1620). Under the patronage of a sympathetic prince, members of the society were simply to be "friends of God," dispersed in society but united in faith, whose work would be the amelioration of social, moral, and intellectual life, assisting one another through the storms of political conflict. One of the aims of the society was to produce an encyclopedia. The French scholar Roland Edighofferhas noted, in his *Les Rose-Croix* (1994), its anticipation of the Royal Society and the French Academy. In 1651, Andreae followed his previous year's appointment as abbot and prelate of Bebenhausen with that of superintendent general, equivalent to an archbishopric. He died in Stuttgart in 1654 at the age of sixty-seven.

Explanation and Analysis of the Document

The *Fama Fraternitatis* is an allegorical drama written to inspire debate about how to achieve a reform of knowledge sufficiently dynamic to inaugurate a new era of scientific and spiritual advance.

◆ Paragraph 1
The curtains open on the *Fama Fraternitatis* with an oration based on the idea of human dignity residing in humanity's ability to ascend (or descend) the Great Chain of Being between creaturely life and the realm of the angels. The illuminated intelligence of human beings enables them to grasp the significance of discoveries in geography and science that would be the envy of their ancestors. The author incorporates an idea close to the heart of Paracelsus: The human being is a microcosm of the universe—a little cosmos whose every part is linked to the greater universe. The human's potential is universal and apparently infinite; the human stands on the cusp of something far greater than anything hitherto discovered. A complete system of knowledge awaits humanity if people's minds are willing to penetrate the darkest recesses of nature. Anticipating this opportunity, a fraternity of interest has been secretly at work, in harmony with God and the cosmos.

◆ Paragraphs 2 and 3
Paragraphs 2 and 3 criticize what Andreae views as the stifling effects of closed minds: Instead of seizing the incredible potential of the times, the learned bicker. They scoff at

anyone who lifts his head above the common mud. Rather than working together in an effort to order knowledge based on investigation and experience, they rely on past authority and a religious leadership lacking in spiritual depth and understanding. Indeed, notes Andreae, the great thinkers that they claim to follow would themselves have been the first to abandon old theories for new knowledge. Providentially, the situation had been foreseen by a German whose search for enlightenment necessitated leaving Europe. C. R.'s quitting his monastery allegorizes the Christian—or truly free—spirit suffocating under traditional scholastic and monastic systems.

♦ **Paragraphs 4–7**
Andreae had heard from his friend Christoph Besold, who made a special study of the Middle East, of a sect in Arabia known as the Sabians. They were associated with the university at Damar. "Damcar" was a misprint for "Damar" on Ortelius's world map ("The Theater of the Lands of the Earth," Antwerp, 1570). Located inland from Yemen's coast, Damar was home to a university that permitted the Sabians to pursue their veneration of the stars—a combination of worship and astronomy.

Andreae's polemic concerning the corruption of learning is the *Fama*'s keynote; there was more sense to be found in remote Arabia than in wealthy Tübingen. The theme of cooperative learning is repeated at Fez, where C. R. finds savants sharing their discoveries, unlike their counterparts in Europe. The cartographer Mercator believed *Fez* meant a place "of gold," so knowledge of the art of alchemical transmutation was important to "C. R." Alchemical knowledge involved spiritual and scientific ideals.

♦ **Paragraph 8**
The *Fama Fraternitatis*'s "Elementary Inhabitants" refers to the spirits of the four elements. Paracelsus's book "On Nymphs, Sylphs, Pygmies, and Salamanders" had been published in 1591. Nymphs appeared on the fifth day of Andreae's *Chemical Wedding*, conducting seven symbolic boats to the Olympus tower to witness the nuptial regeneration. Understanding the elements would enable C. R. to gain access to the innermost structure of plants, animals, and minerals and to establish a harmony obscured by perverted learning and pointless contention.

♦ **Paragraphs 9 and 10**
The globe was a staple symbol of harmony in three dimensions. Things that agree are symbolically equidistant to their source or center. C. R.'s *Axiomata* will set knowledge on secure foundations: A second spiritual and scientific reformation is possible, but not inevitable.

Andreae conceives of a "Society" in Europe to help just rulers and to educate those fit to govern. This idea would have long-range effects on European history. Adam Haslmayr responded to it in 1612 in a letter to the Tyrol's archduke, Maximilian, claiming the brotherhood could provide a kind of "superman" to make Maximilian wiser, wealthier, and more successful.

♦ **Paragraph 11**
The *Fama Fraternitatis* has been described as the "gospel according to Paracelsus." While Paracelsus was not a member of the fraternity, his genius, we are cheekily informed, was sparked by the "Book M" (possibly for "Mundus," the world)—a tease to anyone taking the *Fama* literally. In spite of magnificent cures, Paracelsus was dogged by the blind spot that obstructed his contemporaries' vision. Andreae observed the effects of such an obstruction on both himself and his dear friend, Hess, in Tübingen. How this obstruction was to be removed was a principal drive of the *Fama*. It is illustrated in the detail of the nail that must be pulled out to reveal the door to C. R.'s hidden tomb.

♦ **Paragraphs 12–15**
The "magical language" derives from Genesis (2:19) when Adam names every living thing and can thereby summon their essence. When, in the *Fama*, C. R. encounters the wise of Damcar, they know his name. There is a hint that their knowing his hidden being gives them a kind of power over him—hence his attraction to "Damcar."

Some sixteenth-century scholars believed that Hebrew, combined with kabbalah or esoteric interpretation, exhibited the divine language or "word" by which God made the universe. Geometry was also seen as a magical language because Plato believed the universal Architect (God) used five geometrical solids as archetypes to make the cosmos. C. R. integrates all this knowledge in his "habitation" called "Holy Spirit" (compare with 2 Corinthians 5:1–5), restoring not only theoretical science but also the science of healing, a happy by-product of spiritual and rational progress.

♦ **Paragraphs 16–22**
The *Rotae mundi* (wheels of the world) appears to be a mechanical system derived from C. R.'s mathematics. Andreae's "Mathematical Collection" refers to *his* rotary astrolabe and includes a sketch for an astronomical roulette to relate the phases of the moon to the zodiac. In 1643, Andreae sketched a circular cryptographic system called "an alphabet transformed into infinity," an ancestor of the famous Enigma coding machine.

♦ **Paragraphs 23 and 24**
The account of C. R.'s tomb is allegorical. The door that is to be opened to Europe shows that Europe is imprisoned in its own blindness—and pain. The prophecy of 120 years between burial and discovery reflects Tobias Hess's familiarity with Giacopo Brocardo's work *Mystica et prophetica libri Genesis interpretatio* ("The Mystical and Prophetical Interpretation of the Book of Genesis"), published in Bremen in 1585. Brocardo saw Martin Luther's birth in November 1483 as the beginning of the last age, to last 120 years. Luther was the German priest who led the Protestant Reformation.

The early medieval astronomer Abu Ma'shar predicted that a conjunction of Saturn, Jupiter, and Mars in Scorpio would signify the appearance of a prophet to supersede Muhammad. The planets conjoined in 1484. The number

120 derives from Genesis 6:3. The 1607 "Geneva" English Bible notes 120 years as the term given for humankind to repent before the earth's destruction. Andreae spares his readers numerous other esoteric meanings for the figure of 120. Since the *Confessio Fraternitatis* tells us that C. R. was born in 1378 and lived until he was 106 (dying in 1484), then 120 years gives us the signal date of 1604 for the revelation of C. R.'s "compendium of the universe," which would open a door to Europe.

♦ **Paragraphs 25–36**

For those taking the story literally, there is in the text a probably deliberate error. Since Paracelsus was not born until 1493 and the tomb was sealed in 1484, there could hardly be any works of Paracelsus stored within it. The reference to Adam, Moses, and Solomon relates the *Fama*'s itinerary to the "pristine theology." This idea, important to Renaissance religious speculation, refers to a supposed authentic knowledge of God given to Adam, and inspired patriarchs, before the Flood. The "pristine theology" was thought to have persisted through secret verbal transmission.

Note again the appearance of the globe or sphere as an epitome of truth and perfection. The virtues of the sphere were celebrated in the work of the French poet Du Guillaume de Salluste Du Bartas, whose *Devine Weekes and Workes* was published in English in 1608: "See here the Solids: Cubes, Cylinders, Cones, / Pyramids, Prisms, Dodecahedrons: / And there the Sphere, which (World's Type) comprehends / Itself in itself; having neither midst nor ends."

Such a sphere would seem to be the "minute world" hidden in the tomb referred to earlier in the *Fama Fraternitatis*. In 1610, Besold had urged Andreae to study Du Bartas. Du Bartas's poem "The Columns" refers to a gnosis from antiquity brought to Rome from Arabia and thence to Germany: the pristine theology referred to earlier. "The Columns" concerns Seth and Heber, his descendant. Heber's son Phalec witnesses the division of humankind at Babel, when the common language ends. In anticipation of disasters to come, Seth leaves a legacy: two pillars, one of marble to survive flood and one of brick to survive fire. The pillars summarize the main principles of human knowledge. C. R.'s tomb is likewise intended as a compendium of universal knowledge to survive the ravages of time, to be rediscovered when the world needs it most, when the keys to order the harmony of the universe have been lost.

Audience

We cannot be sure of the precise intended audience of the *Fama* or even how far its author was committed to its distribution. Its contents suggest its usefulness to persons desiring reform of university learning. One such was Johann Combach, philosophy professor at Marburg. He published his response to the manuscript in a preface to his *Metaphysicorum liber singularis* ("Peculiar Book of the Metaphysicians") in 1613. Combach shared Andreae's sense that the university system needed reform if it was to properly

educate students subjected to its systems. Combach took the *Fama* very much in the practical sense Andreae had almost certainly intended. Combach's response is only the second known printed response (after Haslmayr's) to the *Fama Fraternitatis*.

Haslmayr's response relied on the fact that he was a devotee of Paracelsus's religious writings, hidden by Paracelsus and not intended to be revealed until after his death. Paracelsus believed in a perpetual "hidden" or spiritual church. This was not to be confused with what he called the "church of stone," the conventional churches related to material power in the world. The spiritual church taught an ancient spiritual doctrine of two "lights": Grace and Nature. The true follower of Christ was one who "sought and found." God's revelation could be seen by the adept within the workings of Nature. Haslmayr took the *Fama* as a work stemming from an esoteric body in touch with Paracelsus's deepest knowledge. While Combach grasped Andreae's polemic about the need for reform of learning, Haslmayr seized upon the *Fama*'s revolutionary potential.

The two responses give an idea of possible intended audiences: one academic and the other made up of people committed to a profound spiritual, experimental revolution in the sciences and in medicine. Furthermore, anyone interested in alchemy, whether within or without the academic system, was interested in what the *Fama Fraternitatis* had to tell them.

Andreae was always ambiguous about how the revolutionary potential of the *Fama* ought to be understood. He knew what it felt like to be a radical outsider to the mainstream. He knew the world was corrupt and that men and women could, with devotion, ameliorate it, but he was highly skeptical about the best wishes of persons who were not utterly regenerated in the spirit of Christ. The completely regenerated Christian, he believed, could not be found in this world.

After the printing of 1614, the greater clamor would come from the sensationalist camps, with the tendency to take the story literally, hoping to bring the fraternity into the open. This is ironic, since the *Fama* itself may in part have been intended to bring forth from obscurity the secret devotees of magic, kabbalah, and alchemy so that they might share any real discoveries they had made and contribute to the greater good of benighted humanity. The *Fama*'s largest audience since the mid-eighteenth century has been constituted of esotericists, theosophists, and spiritual independents rather than persons of mainstream scientific background, who may owe more than they know to the anonymous work of Johann Valentin Andreae.

Impact

The publication of the *Fama Fraternitatis* in 1614 ignited a powder keg. For a start, it appeared together with a satirical chapter from the Venetian liberal Boccalini's *Ragguagli di Parnaso* ("News from Parnassus") titled "The General Reformation of the Whole Wide World." The presence of this

"He hath also made manifest unto us many wonderful, and never-heretofore seen works and creatures of Nature, and, moreover, hath raised men, imbued with great wisdom, who might partly renew and reduce all arts (in this our spotted and imperfect age) to perfection, so that finally man might thereby understand his own nobleness and worth, and why he is called Microcosmus, and how far his knowledge extendeth in Nature."

(Section 1)

"There is now-a-days no want of learned men in Germany, Magicians, Cabalists, Physicians, and Philosophers, were there but more love and kindness among them, or that the most part of them would not keep their secrets close only to themselves."

(Section 1)

"Their agreement was this: First, That none of them should profess any other thing than to cure the sick, and that gratis."

(Section 1)

"Howbeit we know after a time there will now be a general reformation, both of divine and human things, according to our desire, and the expectation of others; for it is fitting, that before the rising of the Sun, there should appear and break forth Aurora, or some clearness, or divine light in the sky."

(Section 1)

comment on the failures of the Catholic Council of Trent (1545–1563) appeared to link imaginary "Rosicrucians" with a covert campaign of global reformation, giving the tract impetus as a tool of Protestant political propaganda.

Politics had moved on since Andreae's writing the *Fama*. For example, the Catholic Henry IV's policy of toleration for French Protestants had ceased following his assassination in 1610 by a Catholic monk. Two years later, in 1612, the tolerant emperor Rudolf II died, replaced by his old brother, Matthias. Matthias's heir, Ferdinand of Styria, threatened the liberties of Bohemian Protestants, who looked to the Protestant Frederick of the Palatinate as the preferred candidate for the Bohemian throne. In

1613, King James I of England gave his daughter Elizabeth in marriage to Frederick to beef up Protestant alliances.

So when the *Fama Fraternitatis* appeared in print in March 1614, it appeared both as an optimistic promise of enlightenment and as a possible cure for political, economic, and religious anxieties. It was embraced by believers in a Protestant redeemer figure and by those seeking alchemical and magical secrets: a potent blend in a fragile political picture.

The scholar Christopher McIntosh has observed the *Fama*'s impact as being comparable to "dropping a pebble into a pool; the ripples go on and on." Initially generating a continental furor of paper debate from 1614 to 1623, the central idea of the hidden fraternity would become a potent ideal of scientific reform on the one hand and the basis for hierarchical, spiritual, and alchemically minded secret societies on the other. Actual neo-Rosicrucian organizations claiming links to the "original fraternity" appeared in the eighteenth century. Rosicrucian influences are peppered throughout Freemasonry, from the Scottish Rite Eighteenth Degree (*Rose Croix*) to the Royal Arch ritual and much so-called fringe Freemasonry.

Ideals discernible within the *Fama* contributed to the European Enlightenment both through the medium of Freemasonry and outside it, among scientific idealists and spiritual pietists. The hypothesis that Accepted Freemasonry itself is the result of an encounter with Rosicrucian sources is historically valid, if unproved absolutely.

The *Fama's* inspiration and the advice of its author also influenced the educational reforms proposed by the seventeenth-century writer on education John Amos Comensky (known as Comenius). Comenius is the father of universal education. Andreae's works served as his inspiration, and Comenius's contribution to global education is acknowledged to this day.

Arguably of greater long-term significance was the impetus given to the development of scientific cooperation for the public good, especially in Great Britain after the 1630s. This development culminated in the establishment of the Royal Society in 1661. While the Royal Society's president, Isaac Newton, was aware the *Fama Fraternitatis* was an "imposture" (a word used by Andreae), he had himself been inspired to join his mind to a scientific movement rendered attractive to men of strong, if unorthodox spiritual drives and religious ideals. Newton shared the Rosicrucian idea

that the original religion was synonymous with the original science. However, while the practical side of that equation has flourished, Andreae would have been disappointed to learn of the slow denigration of spiritual understanding in science's progress toward a materialism only challenged philosophically since the 1920s by physicists responding to the paradoxes of subatomic behavior. The popular idea of a necessary conflict between science and religion is fundamentally challenged by the Rosicrucian phenomenon.

Further Reading

■ Books

Akerman, Susanna. *Rose Cross over the Baltic: The Spread of Rosicrucianism in Northern Europe.* Leiden, Netherlands: Brill, 1998.

Churton, Tobias. *The Invisible History of the Rosicrucians.* Rochester, Vt.: Inner Traditions, 2009.

McIntosh, Christopher. *The Rose Cross and the Age of Reason.* Leiden, Netherlands: Brill, 1992.

Vickers, Brian, ed. *Occult and Scientific Mentalities in the Renaissance.* Cambridge, U.K.: Cambridge University Press, 1984.

Yates, Frances A. *The Rosicrucian Enlightenment.* London, U.K.: RKP, 1983.

—Commentary by Tobias Churton

Questions for Further Study

1. In what sense did the *Fama Fraternitatis* represent a turning point in European thinking about religion, science, and the progress of humanity?

2. What is Rosicrucianism, and why was it an important movement in Europe in the seventeenth century and beyond?

3. What role did conflict between Catholicism and the new Protestant churches play in the emergence of the ideas expressed in the *Fama Fraternitatis*?

4. The entry states that "the publication of the *Fama Fraternitatis* in 1614 ignited a powder keg." Why did it do so? What religious values seemed to come under attack through the document?

5. Compare this document with Martin Luther's *Ninety-five Theses*. Both documents represented a challenge to the accepted order of things. How are the two documents similar, and what different emphases do they have? How did each contribute to religious turmoil in Renaissance Europe?

FAMA FRATERNITATIS: DOCUMENT TEXT

1610 CE

—Johann Valentin Andreae

Seeing the only wise and merciful God in these latter days hath poured out so richly His mercy and goodness to mankind, whereby we do attain more and more to the perfect knowledge of his Son Jesus Christ and of Nature, that justly we may boast of the happy time, wherein there is not only discovered unto us the half part of the world, which was heretofore unknown and hidden, but He hath also made manifest unto us many wonderful, and neverheretofore seen works and creatures of Nature, and, moreover, hath raised men, imbued with great wisdom, who might partly renew and reduce all arts (in this our spotted and imperfect age) to perfection, so that finally man might thereby understand his own nobleness and worth, and why he is called Microcosmus, and how far his knowledge extendeth in Nature.

Although the rude world herewith will be but little pleased, but rather smile and scoff thereat; also the pride and covetousness of the learned is so great, it will not suffer them to agree together; but were they united, they might, out of all those things which in this our age God doth so richly bestow upon us, collect *Librum Naturae*, or, a Perfect Method of All Arts. But such is their opposition that they still keep, and are loth to leave, the old course, esteeming Popery, Aristotle, and Galen, yea, and that which hath but a mere show of learning, more than the clear and manifested Light and Truth. Those, if they were now living, with much joy would leave their erroneous doctrines; but here is too great weakness for such a great work. And although in Theology, Physics, and Mathematics, the truth doth oppose it itself, nevertheless, the old Enemy, by his subtlety and craft, doth show himself in hindering every good purpose by his instruments and contentious wavering people.

To such an intention of a general reformation, the most godly and highly-illuminated Father, our Brother, C. R. C., a German, the chief and original of our Fraternity, hath much and long time laboured, who, by reason of his poverty (although descended of noble parents), in the fifth year of his age was placed in a cloister, where he had learned indifferently the Greek and Latin tongues, and (upon his earnest desire and request), being yet in his growing years, was associated to a Brother, P. A. L., who had determined to go to the Holy Land. Although this Brother died in Ciprus, and so never came to Jerusalem, yet our Brother C. R. C. did not return, but shipped himself over, and went to Damasco, minding from thence to go to Jerusalem. But by reason of the feebleness of his body he remained still there, and by his skill in physic he obtained much favour with the Turks, and in the meantime he became acquainted with the Wise Men of Damcar in Arabia, and beheld what great wonders they wrought, and how Nature was discovered unto them.

Hereby was that high and noble spirit of Brother C. R. C. so stirred up, that Jerusalem was not so much now in his mind as Damasco; also he could not bridle his desires any longer, but made a bargain with the Arabians, that they should carry him for a certain sum of money to Damcar. He was but of the age of sixteen years when he came thither, yet of a strong Dutch constitution. There the Wise Men received him not as a stranger (as he himself witnesseth), but as one whom they had long expected; they called him by his name, and showed him other secrets out of his cloister, whereat he could not but mightily wonder.

He learned there better the Arabian tongue, so that the year following he translated the book M into good Latin, which he afterwards brought with him. This is the place where he did learn his Physick and his Mathematics, whereof the world hath much cause to rejoice, if there were more love, and less envy.

After three years he returned again with good consent, shipped himself over *Sinus Arabicus* [the Red Sea] into Egypt, where he remained not long, but only took better notice there of the plants and creatures. He sailed over the whole Mediterranean Sea for to come unto Fez, where the Arabians had directed him.

And it is a great shame unto us that wise men, so far remote the one from the other, should not only be of one opinion, hating all contentious writings, but also be so willing and ready, under the seal of secrecy to impart their secrets to others. Every year the Arabians and Africans do send one to another, inquiring one of another out of their arts, if happily they had found out some better things, or if experience had weakened their reasons. Yearly there came something to light whereby the Mathematics, Physic, and Magic (for in those are they of Fez most skilful) were amended. There is now-a-days no want of learned men in Germany, Magicians, Cabalists, Physicians, and Philosophers, were there but more love and kindness among them, or that the most part of them would not keep their secrets close only to themselves.

At Fez he did get acquaintance with those which are commonly called the Elementary inhabitants, who revealed unto him many of their secrets, as we Germans likewise might gather together many things, if there were the like unity, and desire of searching out secrets amongst us.

Of these of Fez he often did confess, that their *Magia* [magic] was not altogether pure, and also that their Cabala was defiled with their Religion; but, notwithstanding he knew how to make good use of the same, and found still more better grounds of his faith, altogether agreeable with the harmony of the whole world, and wonderfully impressed with all the periods of time. Thence proceedeth that fair Concord, that as in every several kernel is contained a whole good tree or fruit, so likewise is included in the little body of man, the whole great world, whose religion, policy, health, members, nature, language, words and works, are agreeing, sympathizing, and in equal tune and melody with God, Heaven, and Earth; and that which is disagreeing with them is error, falsehood, and of the devil, who alone is the first, middle, and last cause of strife, blindness, and darkness in the world. Also, might one examine all and several persons upon the earth, he should find that which is good and right, is always agreeing with itself; but all the rest is spotted with a thousand erroneous conceits.

After two years Brother R. C. departed the city of Fez, and sailed with many costly things into Spain, hoping well as he himself had so well and so profitably spent his time in his travel, that the learned in Europe would highly rejoice with him, and begin to rule and order all their studies according to those sure and sound foundations. He therefore conferred with the learned in Spain, showing unto them the errors of our arts, and how they might be corrected, and from whence they should gather the true *Initia* [signs] of the times to come, and wherein they ought to agree with those things that are past; also

how the faults of the Church and the whole *Philosophia Moralis* [moral philosophy] were to be amended. He showed them new growths, new fruits, and beasts, which did concord with old philosophy, and prescribed them new *Axiomata* [axioms], whereby all things might fully be restored. But it was to them a laughing matter; and being a new thing unto them, they feared that their great name would be lessened, if they should now again begin to learn and acknowledge their many years' errors, to which they were accustomed, and wherewith with they had gained them enough. Who so loveth unquietness, let him be reformed (they said). The same song was also sung to him by other Nations, the which moved him the more because it happened to him contrary to his expectation, being then ready bountifully to impart all his arts and secrets to the learned, if they would have but undertaken to write the true and infallible *Axiomata*, out of all faculties, sciences, and arts, and whole nature, as that which he knew would direct them, like a globe or circle, to the only middle point and *centrum* [center], and (as is usual among the Arabians) it should only serve to the wise and learned for a rule, that also there might be a society in Europe, which might have gold, silver, and precious stones, sufficient for to bestow them on kings, for their necessary uses and lawful purposes, with which [society] such as be governors might be brought up for to learn all that which God hath suffered man to know, and thereby to be enabled in all times of need to give their counsel unto those that seek it, like the Heathen Oracles.

Verily we must confess that the world in those days was already big with those great commotions, labouring to be delivered of them, and did bring forth painful, worthy men, who broke with all force through darkness and barbarism, and left us who succeeded to follow them. Assuredly they have been the uppermost point *in Trigono igneo* [in the Fiery Trigon] whose flame now should be more and more bright, and shall undoubtedly give to the world the last light.

Such a one likewise hath Theophrastus been in vocation and callings, although he was none of our Fraternity, yet nevertheless hath he diligently read over the *Book M*, whereby his sharp *ingenium* [intellect] was exalted; but this man was also hindered in his course by the multitude of the learned and wise-seeming men, that he was never able peaceably to confer with others of the knowledge and understanding he had of Nature. And therefore in his writing he rather mocked these busy-bodies, and doth not show them altogether what he was; yet, nevertheless, there is found with him well grounded the afore-named *Harmonia* [harmony], which without doubt he had imparted to the learned, if he had not found them rather worthy of subtle vexation, than to be instructed in greater arts and sciences. He thus with a free and careless life lost his time, and left unto the world their foolish pleasures.

But that we do not forget our loving Father, Brother C. R., he after many painful travels, and his fruitless true instructions, returned again into Germany, the which he heartily loved, by reason of the alterations which were shortly to come, and of the strange and dangerous contentions. There, although he could have bragged with his art, but specially of the transmutations of metals, yet did he esteem more Heaven, and men, the citizens thereof, than all vain glory and pomp.

Nevertheless, he built a fitting and neat habitation, in which he ruminated his voyage and philosophy, and reduced them together in a true memorial. In this house he spent a great time in the mathematics, and made many fine instruments, *ex omnibus hujus artis partibus* [from every part of all the arts], whereof there is but little remaining to us, as hereafter you shall understand.

After five years came again into his mind the wished for Reformation; and in regard [of it] he doubted of the aid and help of others, although he himself was painful, lusty, and unwearisome; howsoever he undertook, with some few adjoined with him, to attempt the same. Wherefore he desired to this end, to have out of his first cloister (to the which he bare a great affection) three of his brethren, Brother G. V., Brother I. A., and Brother I. O., who had some more knowledge of the arts than in that time many others had. He did bind those three unto himself, to be faithful, diligent, and secret; as also to commit carefully to writing all that which he should direct and instruct them in, to the end that those which were to come, and through especial revelation should be received into this Fraternity, might not be deceived of the least syllable and word.

After this manner began the Fraternity of the Rosie Cross—first, by four persons only, and by them was made the magical language and writing, with a large dictionary, which we yet daily use to God's praise and glory, and do find great wisdom therein. They made also the first part of the *Book M*, but in respect that that labour was too heavy, and the unspeakable concourse of the sick hindered them, and also whilst his new building (called *Sancti Spiri-*

tus [Holy Spirit]) was now finished, they concluded to draw and receive yet others more into their Fraternity. To this end was chosen Brother R. C., his deceased father's brother's son; Brother B., a skilful painter; G. G., and P. D., their secretary, all Germans except I. A., so in all they were eight in number, all bachelors and of vowed virginity; by whom was collected a book or volume of all that which man can desire, wish, or hope for.

Although we do now freely confess that the world is much amended within an hundred years, yet we are assured that our *Axiomata* shall immovably remain unto the world's end, and also the world in her highest and last age shall not attain to see anything else; for our *Rota* [wheel] takes her beginning from that day when God spake *Fiat* ["Let there be"] and shall end when he shall speak *Pereat* ["It is over"]; yet God's clock striketh every minute, where ours scarce striketh perfect hours. We also steadfastly believe, that if our Brethren and Fathers had lived in this our present and clear light, they would more roughly have handled the Pope, Mahomet, scribes, artists, and sophisters, and showed themselves more helpful, not simply with sighs and wishing of their end and consummation.

When now these eight Brethren had disposed and ordered all things in such manner, as there was not now need of any great labour, and also that everyone was sufficiently instructed and able perfectly to discourse of secret and manifest philosophy, they would not remain any longer together, but, as in the beginning they had agreed, they separated themselves into several countries, because that not only their *Axiomata* might in secret be more profoundly examined by the learned, but that they themselves, if in some country or other they observed anything, or perceived some error, they might inform one another of it.

Their agreement was this:

First, That none of them should profess any other thing than to cure the sick, and that *gratis*.

Second, None of the posterity should be constrained to wear one certain kind of habit, but therein to follow the custom of the country.

Third, That every year upon the day C., they should meet together in the house *Sancti Spiritus*, or write the cause of his absence.

Fourth, Every Brother should look about for a worthy person, who, after his decease, might succeed him.

Fifth, The word R. C. should be their seal, mark, and character.

Sixth, The Fraternity should remain secret for one hundred years.

These six articles they bound themselves one to another to keep; five of the Brethren departed, only the Brethren B. and D. remained with the Father, Brother R. C., a whole year. When these likewise departed, then remained by him his cousin and Brother I. O. so that he hath all the days of his life with him two of his Brethren. And although that as yet the Church was not cleansed, nevertheless, we know that they did think of her, and what with longing desire they looked for. Every year they assembled together with joy, and made a full resolution of that which they had done. There must certainly have been great pleasure to hear truly and without invention related and rehearsed all the wonders which God had poured out here and there through the world. Everyone may hold it out for certain, that such persons as were sent, and joined together by God, and the Heavens, and chosen out of the wisest of men, as have lived in many ages, did live together above all others in highest unity, greatest secrecy, and most kindness one towards another.

After such a most laudable sort they did spend their lives, but although they were free from all diseases and pain, yet, notwithstanding, they could not live and pass their time appointed of God. The first of this Fraternity which died, and that in England, was I. O., as Brother C. long before had foretold him; he was very expert, and well learned in Cabala, as his book called H. witnesseth. In England he is much spoken of; and chiefly because he cured a young Earl of Norfolk of the leprosie. They had concluded, that, as much as possibly could be, their burial place should be kept secret, as at this day it is not known unto us what is become of some of them, yet everyone's place was supplied with a fit successor. But this we will confess publicly by these presents, to the honour of God, that what secrets soever we have learned out of the Book M, although before our eyes we behold the image and pattern of all the world, yet are there not shown unto us our misfortunes, nor hour of death, the which only is known to God himself, who thereby would have us keep in a continual readiness. But hereof more in our Confession, where we do set down thirty-seven reasons wherefore we now do make known our Fraternity, and proffer such high mysteries freely, without constraint and reward. Also we do promise more gold than both the Indies bring to the King of Spain; for Europe is with child and will bring forth a strong child, who shall stand in need of a great godfather's gift.

After the death of I. O., Brother R. C. rested not, but, as soon as he could, called the rest together, and then, as we suppose, then his grave was made, although hitherto we (who were the latest) did not know when our loving Father R. C. died, and had no more but the bare names of the beginners, and all their successors to us. Yet there came into our memory a secret, which through dark and hidden words, and speeches of the hundred years, Brother A., the successor of D. (who was of the last and second row and succession, and had lived amongst many of us), did impart unto us of the third row and succession; otherwise we must confess, that after the death of the said A. none of us had in any manner known anything of Brother C. R., and of his first fellow-brethren, than that which was extant of them in our philosophical *Bibliotheca* [library], amongst which our *Axiomata* was held for the chiefest, *Rota Mundi* [wheel of the world] for the most artificial, and *Protheus* [power of transformation] the most profitable. Likewise, we do not certainly know if these of the second row have been of the like wisdom as the first, and if they were admitted to all things.

It shall be declared hereafter to the gentle reader, not only what we have heard of the burial of Brother R. C., but also it shall be made manifest publicly, by the foresight, sufferance, and commandment of God, whom we most faithfully obey, that if we shall be answered discreetly and Christian-like, we will not be ashamed to set forth publicly in print our names and surnames, our meetings, or anything else that may be required at our hands.

Now, the true and fundamental relation of the finding out of the high-illuminated man of God, Fra: C. R. C., is this: After that A. in *Gallia Narbonensis* [the province about Narbonne in southwestern France] was deceased, then succeeded in his place our loving Brother N. N. This man after he had repaired unto us to take the solemn oath of fidelity and secrecy, informed us *bona fide* [in good faith], that A. had comforted him in telling him, that this Fraternity should ere long not remain so hidden, but should be to all the whole German nation helpful, needful, and commendable, of the which he was not in anywise in his estate ashamed.

The year following, after he had performed his school right, and was minded now to travel, being for that purpose sufficiently provided with *Fortunatus'* purse, he thought (he being a good architect) to alter something of his building, and to make it more fit. In such renewing, he lighted upon the Memorial Table, which was cast of brass, and containeth all the names of the Brethren, with some few other things. This he would transfer in another more fitting vault, for where or when Brother R. C. died, or in what country he was buried, was by our predecessors concealed and unknown to us. In this table stuck a great nail somewhat strong, so that when it was with force drawn out it took with it an indifferent big stone out of the thin wall or plastering of the hidden door, and so unlooked for uncovered the door, whereat we did with joy and longing throw down the rest of the wall and cleared the door, upon which was written in great letters—

Post CXX Annos Patebo [I will open after 120 Years], with the year of the Lord under it. Therefore we gave God thanks, and let it rest that same night, because first we would overlook our *Rota*—but we refer ourselves again to the Confession, for what we here publish is done for the help of those that are worthy, but to the unworthy, God willing, it will be small profit. For like as our door was after so many years wonderfully discovered, also there shall be opened a door to Europe (when the wall is removed), which already doth begin to appear, and with great desire is expected of many.

In the morning following we opened the door, and there appeared to our sight a vault of seven sides and corners, every side five foot broad, and the height of eight foot. Although the sun never shined in this vault, nevertheless, it was enlightened with another sun, which had learned this from the sun, and was situated in the upper part in the centre of the ceiling. In the midst, instead of a tomb-stone, was a round altar, covered with a plate of brass, and thereon this engraven:

A.C. R.C. Hoc universi compendium unius mihi sepulchrum feci.

[This compendium of the universe I made in my lifetime to be my tomb.]

Round about the first circle or brim stood,

Jesus mihi omnia

[Jesus, everything to me]

In the middle were four figures, inclosed in circles, whose circumscription was,

1. *Nequaquam vacuum.* [A vacuum exists nowhere.]
2. *Legis Jugum.* [The yoke of the law.]
3. *Libertas Evangelii.* [The liberty of the gospel.]
4. *Dei gloria intacta.* [The whole glory of God.]

This is all clear and bright, as also the seventh side and the two heptagons. So we kneeled down together, and gave thanks to the sole wise, sole mighty and sole eternal God, who hath taught us more than all men's wits could have found out, praised be His holy name. This vault we parted in three parts, the upper part or ceiling, the wall or side, the ground or floor. Of the upper part you shall understand no more at this time, but that it was divided according to the seven sides in the triangle, which was in the bright centre; but what therein is contained you (that are desirous of our society) shall, God willing, behold the same with your own eyes. Every side or wall is parted into ten squares, every one with their several figures and sentences, as they are truly shown and set forth *concentratum* [concentrated] here in our book. The bottom again is parted in the triangle, but because therein is described the power and the rule of the Inferior Governors, we leave to manifest the same, for fear of the abuse by the evil and ungodly world. But those that are provided and stored with the Heavenly Antidote, do without fear or hurt, tread on and bruise the head of the old and evil serpent, which this our age is well fitted for. Every side or wall had a door or chest, wherein there lay divers things, especially all our books, which otherwise we had, besides the *Vocabulario* [vocabulary] of Theophrastus Paracelsus of Hohenheim, and these which daily unfalsifieth we do participate. Herein also we found his *Itinerarium* [itinerary] and *Vita* [study of life], whence this relation for the most part is taken. In another chest were looking-glasses of divers virtues, as also in another place were little bells, burning lamps, and chiefly wonderful artificial songs—generally all was done to that end, that if it should happen, after many hundred years the Fraternity should come to nothing, they might by this only vault be restored again.

Now, as we had not yet seen the dead body of our careful and wise Father, we therefore removed the altar aside; there we lifted up a strong plate of brass, and found a fair and worthy body, whole and unconsumed, as the same is here lively counterfeited, with all his ornaments and attires. In his hand he held a parchment, called T., the which next unto the Bible is our greatest treasure, which ought to be delivered to the censure of the world. At the end of this book standeth this following *Elogium* [judicial record]:

Granum pectori Jesu insitum.

C. R. C. ex nobili atque splendida Germaniae R. C. familia oriundus, vir sui seculi divinis revelatiombus, subtilissimis imaginationibus, indefessis laboribus ad coetestia atque humana mysteria; arcanave admissus postquam suam (quam Arabico at Africano itineribus collejerat) plus quam regiam, atque imperatoriam Gazam suo seculo nondum convenientem, posteritati eruendam custodivisset at jam suarum Artium, ut et nominis, fides ac conjunctissimos heredes instituisset, mundum minutum omnibus motibus magno illi respondentem fabricasset hocque tandem preteritarum, praesentium, et futurarum, rerum compendio extracto, centenario major, non morbo (quem ipse nunquam corpore expertus erat, nunquam alios infestare sinebat) ullo pellente sed Spiritis Dei evocante, illuminatam animam (inter Fratrum amplexus et ultima oscula) fidelissimo Creatori Deo reddidisset, Pater delictissimus, Frater suavissimus, praeceptor fidelissimus, amicus integerimus, a suis ad 120 annos hic absconditus est.

[A grain buried in the breast of Jesus.

C. Ros. C., sprung from the noble and renowned German family of R.C.; a man admitted into the mysteries and secrets of heaven and earth through the divine revelations, subtle cogitations and unwearied toil of his life. In his journeies through Arabia and Africa he collected a treasure surpassing that of Kings and Emperors; but finding it not suitable for his times, he kept it guarded for posterity to uncover, and appointed loyal and faithful heirs of his arts and also of his name. He constructed a microcosm corresponding in all motions to the macrocosm and finally drew up this compendium of things past, present and to come. Then, having now passed the century of years, though oppressed by no disease, which he had neither felt in his own body nor allowed to attack others, but summoned by the Spirit of God, amid the last embraces of his brethren he rendered up his illuminated soul to God his Creator. A beloved Father, an affectionate Brother, a faithful Teacher, a loyal Friend, he was hidden here by his disciples for 120 years.]

Underneath they had subscribed themselves,

1. *Fra:* I.A. FR. C.H. *electione Fraternitatis caput* [by the choice of FR. C.H., head of the Fraternity].
2. *Fr:* G.V. M.P.C.
3. *Fra:* R.C. *Iunior haeres S. spiritus* [Junior successor H(oly) Spirit].
4. *Fra:* B.M. P.A. *Pictor et Architectus* [Painter and Architect].
5. *Fr:* G.G. M.P.I. *Cabalista* [Cabalist].

Secundi Circuli.

1. *Fra:* P.A. *Successor,* Fr: I.O. *Mathematicus* [Mathematician].
2. *Fra:* A. *Successor,* Fra. P.D.

3. *Fra:* R. *Successor patris,* C.R.C. *cum Christo Triumphantis* [with Christ Triumphant].

At the end was written,

Ex Deo nascimur, in Jesu morimur, per Spiritum Sanctum revivscimus.

[We are born of God; we die in Jesus; we live again through the Holy Spirit.]

At that time was already dead Brother I. O. and Brother D., but their burial place where is it to be found? We doubt not but our Fra. Senior hath the same, and some especial thing laid in earth, and perhaps likewise hidden. We also hope that this our example will stir up others more diligently to inquire after their names (whom we have therefore published) and to search for the place of their burial; the most part of them, by reason of their practice and physick, are yet known and praised among very old folks; so might perhaps our Gaza be enlarged, or at least be better cleared.

Concerning *Minutum Mundum* [the little universe], we found it kept in another little altar, truly more finer then can be imagined by any understanding man, but we will leave him undescribed, until we shall be truly answered upon this our true-hearted *Fama* [fame]. And so we have covered it again with the plates, and set the altar thereon, shut the door, and made it sure, with all our seals. Moreover, by instruction, and command of our Rota, there are come to sight some books, among which is contained M. (which were made instead of household care by the praiseworthy M. P.). Finally we departed the one from the other, and left the natural heirs in possession of our jewels. And so we do expect the answer and judgment of the learned, or unlearned.

Howbeit we know after a time there will now be a general reformation, both of divine and human things, according to our desire, and the expectation of others; for it is fitting, that before the rising of the Sun, there should appear and break forth *Aurora* [goddess of the morning, or dawn], or some clearness, or divine light in the sky. And so, in the meantime, some few, which shall give their names, may join together, thereby to increase the number and respect of our Fraternity, and make a happy and wished for beginning of our Philosophical Canons, prescribed to us by our Brother R. C., and be partakers with us of our treasures (which never can fail or be wasted), in all humility and love to be eased of this world's labours, and not walk so blindly in the knowledge of the wonderful works of God.

But that also every Christian may know of what Religion and belief we are, we confess to have the knowledge of Jesus Christ (as the same now in these last days, and chiefly in Germany, most clear and pure is professed, and is nowadays cleansed and void of all swerving people, heretics, and false prophets), in certain and noted countries maintained, defended and propagated. Also we use two Sacraments, as they are instituted with all Forms and Ceremonies of the first reformed Church. In *Politia* [politics] we acknowledge the Roman Empire and *Quartam Monarchiam* [the fourth monarchy] for our Christian head; albeit we know what alterations be at hand, and would fain impart the same with all our hearts to other godly learned men, notwithstanding our handwriting which is in our hands, no man (except God alone) can make it common, nor any unworthy person is able to bereave us of it. But we shall help with secret aid this so good a cause, as God shall permit or hinder us. For our God is not blind, as the heathen's *Fortuna* [goddess of luck], but is the Churches' ornament and the honour of the Temple. Our Philosophy also is not a new invention, but as Adam after his fall hath received it, and as Moses and Solomon used it, also it ought not much to be doubted of, or contradicted by other opinions, or meanings; but seeing the truth is peaceable, brief; and always like herself in all things, and especially accorded by with Jesus *in omni parte* [in all parts] and all members, and as He is the true image of the Father, so is His image, so it shall not be said, this is true according to Philosophy, but true according to Theology; and wherein Plato, Aristotle, Pythagoras and others did hit the mark, and wherein Enoch, Abraham, Moses, Solomon did excel, but especially wherewith that wonderful book the Bible agreeth. All that same concurreth together, and makes a sphere or globe whose total parts are equidistant from the centre, as hereof more at large and more plain shall be spoken of in Christianly Conference.

But now concerning, and chiefly in this our age, the ungodly and accursed gold-making, which hath gotten so much the upper hand, whereby under colour of it, many runagates and roguish people do use great villanies and cozen and abuse the credit which is given them; yea, nowadays men of discretion do hold the transmutation of metals to be the highest point and *fastigium* [summit] in philosophy. This is all their intent and desire, and that God would be most esteemed by them, and honoured which could make great store of gold, the which with unpremeditate prayers they hope to attain of the all-knowing God and searcher of all hearts; but we by these presents publicly testify, that the true philosophers are far of another mind, esteeming little the making of gold, which is but a *parergon* [by-product], for besides that they have a thousand better things. We say with our loving Father C. R. C. *Phy. aurium nisi quantum: aurum* [Pish! It is not golden unless it is worth gold], for unto him the whole nature is detected; he doth not rejoice that he can make gold, and that, as saith Christ, the devils are obedient unto him; but is glad that he seeth the Heavens open, and the angels of God ascending and descending, and his name written in the book of life.

Also we do testify that under the name of *Chymia* [chemistry] many books and pictures are set forth in *Contumeliam gloriae Dei* [abusing God's glory], as we will name them in their due season, and will give to the pure-hearted a catalogue, or register of them. And we pray all learned men to take heed of these kind of books; for the Enemy never resteth but soweth his weeds, till a stronger one doth root them out.

So, according to the will and meaning of Fra. C. R. C., we his brethren request again all the learned in Europe who shall read (sent forth in five languages) this our *Fama* and *Confessio* ["The Confession of the Fraternity"], that it would please them with good deliberation to ponder this our offer, and to examine most nearly and sharply their arts, and behold the present time with all diligence, and to declare their mind, either *Communicato consilio* [communicating with others], or *singulatim* [one at a time] by print. And although at this time we make no mention either of names or meetings, yet nevertheless everyone's opinion shall assuredly come to our hands, in what language so ever it be; nor any body shall fail, who so gives but his name, to speak with some of us, either by word of mouth, or else, if there be some let, in writing. And this we say for a truth, that whosoever shall earnestly, and from his heart, bear affection unto us, it shall be beneficial to him in goods, body, and soul; but he that is false-hearted, or only greedy of riches, the same first of all shall not be able in any manner of wise to hurt us, but bring himself to utter ruin and destruction. Also our building, although one hundred thousand people had very near seen and beheld the same, shall for ever remain untouched, undestroyed, and hidden to the wicked world.

Sub umbra alarum tuarum, Jehova.
[Under the shadow of thy wings, Jehova.]

Glossary

Cabalists:	persons associated with kabbalah, or cabala, a mystical movement
Ciprus:	Cyprus, an island in the eastern Mediterranean Sea
Damasco:	Damascus, a city in Syria
Damcar:	a legendary mystical city in ancient Arabia, possibly Damascus
Fez:	a city in Morocco
***Fortunatus'* purse:**	a reference to a legendary story of Fortunatus, who received from a goddess a purse that was replenished whenever he spent money from it; used as a figure of speech for seemingly unlimited wealth
Fra.:	abbreviation for "brother"
Galen:	Aelius Galenus or Claudius Galenus, an ancient Greek physician, surgeon, and philosopher
***gratis*:**	free of charge
heptagons:	polygons with seven sides and seven angles
Mahomet:	an antique spelling of Muhammad, the founder of Islam
Popery:	Catholicism
Rosie Cross:	Rosicrucianism
***Rota*:**	probably a reference to a cylinder built inside a monastery wall and used for exchanging mail and food with cloistered clergy
Theophrastus Paracelsus:	a Renaissance physician, botanist, alchemist, astrologer, and occultist

Portrait of Massachusetts Bay Colony Governor John Winthrop. It was held in the Winthrop family until the 19th century, when it was donated to the American Antiquarian Society.

"A MODEL OF CHRISTIAN CHARITY": DOCUMENT ANALYSIS

"There are two rules whereby we are to walk one towards another: Justice and Mercy."

Overview

As John Winthrop ventured to the Americas in 1630 aboard the *Arbella*, he wrote his guidelines, "A Model of Christian Charity," for the community he and his fellow colonists hoped to establish along New England's shores. Born in 1587/8 into a gentry family in Suffolk, England, Winthrop grew up at Groton Manor as the heir apparent. He attended Cambridge before marrying Mary Forth in 1605. Winthrop's education stretched far beyond lessons from his father and his tutors; he caught the fire of Puritanism. In Winthrop, this manifested as a constant struggle to live in a sinful world without succumbing to temptations. In 1615, after ten years of marriage and five children, Mary Forth Winthrop died from complications of childbirth. By 1618, Winthrop had remarried twice more—first to Thomasine Clopton, who died in childbirth within a year, and finally to Margaret Tyndal. Increasingly frustrated by the disintegrating financial situation and the decadence of the pro-Catholic monarch, Charles I, Winthrop joined the newly reorganized Massachusetts Bay Company. In November 1629 members of the company elected him governor, and he made preparations to depart. On April 8, 1630, he set sail. His wife and numerous children and grandchildren would follow.

In "A Model for Christian Charity," Winthrop outlines his idealized vision of a community, a "holy experiment," based in Christian principles. He also clearly describes his world as he understood it, grounded in the values of order, authority and community. The "Model" explains the responsibilities and privileges of the powerful and those of the "poor and inferior sort." He reminds his audience that in the more perfect society, civil dissention would not occur because all participants would know their places and live accordingly. Those with greater gifts were to honor God and their blessings by ruling well and by providing for and protecting those less fortunate than themselves. Those of lesser means were to express their satisfaction with God's plan through service and acceptance.

Context

The context of John Winthrop's sermon, "A Model of Christian Charity" is rooted in the long history of the English Protestant Reformation. The sixteenth century saw the establishment of the Anglican Church, a national church headed by the English monarch and separate from the Roman Catholic Church. Despite this, some Calvinist Protestants—known pejoratively as "Puritans"—did not believe that the Anglican church was a proper expression of Christianity, believing that in both doctrine and practice it was too close to Roman Catholicism. Persecution of English Puritans varied depending on the religious leadership of particular places—some bishops were more tolerant of these "nonconforming" Christians than others. However, but by the mid-1620s, it was clear that new monarch Charles I (r. 1625-1649) and royal advisors such as William Laud (who would serve as Archbishop of Canterbury from 1633 to his death in 1645) would take a strong position against Puritans and others who refused to accept the primacy of the Anglican church.

Even before this, religious dissenters, who in American history would become known as the Pilgrims, had left England, despairing of the Anglican Church's ability to reform to their liking. These separatists, after first attempting to setting in the Netherlands, established the Plymouth Colony in North America.

Other Calvinists remained in England, believing that the reform of the church would be possible, in time. With the rise of Charles I and William Laud, some began to doubt that this would be possible. In March of 1628, a group of investors established "The New England Company for a Plantation in Massachusetts Bay" and received a land grant from the Council for New England. The company also sought a royal charter which would solidify the groups land claims in North America. While most colonial companies had a board of directors that remained in England while colonists did the hard work of establishing a new life across the ocean. The Massachusetts Bay Company avoided this through a plan known as the Cambridge Agreement. This August 29, 1629 agreement arranged a way for Massachusetts Bay Company shareholders who wished to migrate to North America to purchase shares from those Company members who did not want to leave England. The result of this agreement—and the subsequent share buy-outs—was, as discussed above, that the Massachusetts Bay *Company* and the Massachusetts Bay *Company* were legally indistinguishable. In April, 1630, a group of ships set out from England and arrived at Salem, Massachusetts in June of that year. The ships included the *Arabella*, carrying John Winthrop. It was during this voyage that he wrote and possibly delivered "A Model of Christian Charity."

About the Author

John Winthrop's birth, family, and educational background are discussed above in the "Overview" section. Winthrop, it is important to remember, was trained in the law and had experience as the Lord of Groton Manor in Suffolk, England. Thus, while he was a devoted Puritan, he was also a skilled administrator, being appointed to a position to a post in the Court of Wards and Liveries—part of the royal government's system of revenue collection in 17th century England. Although he was not a part of the establishment of the Massachusetts Bay Company, Winthrop became involved with their efforts to leave England for North America in early 1629. It was in this year that King Charles dissolved Parliament (the legislative body of England) and began nearly a dozen years of rule without legislative input. At the same time, persecutions of Puritans began to increase. Winthrop himself was a victim of this increasing intolerance of Puritans when he was removed from his appointment at the Court of Wards and Liveries. These political events—both for Winthrop personally and for the Company as a whole—were the proximate causes for the decision to head for North America as soon as practical.

At this point, Winthrop became more prominent in the organization. In November, 1629, shareholders elected Winthrop as Governor of the company. The new, emigration minded leaders, including Winthrop, set sail for America in 1630 answerable only to the crown—not a distant board of directors.

Upon arrival at the Massachusetts Bay Colony, Winthrop and his deputies—after some false starts—established what would become the city of Boston. Hundreds of emigrants, including Henry Winthrop—John's son—died during the first year of settlement.

Between the establishment of the colony in 1630 and Winthrop's death in 1649, he was elected to the governorship four times. During his terms of office, he succeeded in negotiating a number of political and religious hurdles as

Time Line	
1588	■ John Winthrop born in Suffolk, England
1629	■ Winthrop elected Governor of the Massachusetts Bay Company
1630	■ Winthrop leads around 700 migrants to establish the Massachusetts Bay colony in North America; Winthrop likely delivered "A Model of Christian Charity" during the voyage.
1630-1634	■ Winthrop's first of four terms as Governor of the Massachusetts Bay Colony
1633-1634	■ Anti-Puritan sentiment in England results in a sharp increase in emigration to the Massachusetts Bay colony.
1649	■ Winthrop dies in Boston

the colony grew rapidly (due, in part, to the persecution of Puritans which drove many out of England to Massachusetts Bay). In general, Winthrop served as a more moderate voice in religious controversies. For example, he had a much closer relationship with dissenter Roger Williams and—possibly—warned him of his impending arrest, giving Williams time to fleet to what would become Rhode Island.

Explanation and Analysis of the Document

Winthrop begins his sermon but explaining that the "condition of mankind" is the result of God's "wise and holy providence," explaining that wealth and status are the result of divine order rather than purely reliant on human beings own actions. He gives a number of reasons for this. These reasons establish a foundation for the entirety of Winthrop's message to his fellow colonists.

The first reason is as a demonstration of God's power and wisdom. As Winthrop will demonstrate, the ways in which God orders His creation—including the ordering of social and economic structures work toward a positive end. In essence, God works through his creation for the benefit of all. Winthrop's second and third reasons for God's ordering of of the human condition build on the first with more specific examples. Winthrop argues that God's Spirit will "restrain" the wicked from exploiting the poor and, at the same time, prevent the "poor and despised" from rising up in revolt. As the well-off care for those less fortunate and the less fortunate exercise "patience, obedience, etc." a society that conforms to God's will work smoothly. In such a society, "every man might have need other others, and from hence they might be all knit more nearly together in the bonds of brotherly affection." Acceptance of God's construction of society leads to harmony.

Winthrop argues that this system is exemplified in the "two rules" of justice and mercy, and hat rich and poor alike can and should act within the bounds of these characteristics. Following this general declaration of justice and mercy being guiding principles of a God-pleasing society, Winthrop addresses several hypothetical questions on the application of these principles, discussing such topics as the amount of money or resources members of the community should contribute for the benefit of the community and the church (in many ways, these were one in the same for the Puritans of Massachusetts Bay), rules for borrowing and lending. In this case, the issue of "mercy" is apparent, as Winthrop asserts that if someone asks to borrow money but does not have the means to repay, those with the means "must give him according to his necessity, rather than lend him" the money. To the question of the forgiveness of debts, Winthrop invokes the New Testament's "Golden Rule" of doing as one would wish to be done by.

Following these somewhat practical considerations, Winthrop moves into a discussion of the nature of mutual love between members of a Christian community. It is in his attempt to "make some application of this discourse" that Winthrop begins to more fully layout the type of society and community that the Massachusetts bay Company would establish when they reached the New World.

First and foremost, Winthrop identifies the group as "a company professing ourselves fellow members of Christ." Thus, from the outset, Winthrop establishes that the people of the Massachusetts Bay Company and Colony are Christians and, by implication, Puritan Christians who had voluntarily set themselves apart from their fellow English subjects. This is not a community that would welcome outsiders or dissenters. His second application declares that the company is establishing a "place of cohabitation and consortship under a due form of government both civil and ecclesiastical." There is no separation between church and state in this society. Additionally, "the care of the public must oversway all private respects": the good of the community takes precedence over individual rights or liberties, because it is a true rule that "particular estates cannot subsist in the ruin of the public."

Winthrop goes on to explain that the fundamental goal of their venture is to "improve [their] lives to do more service to the Lord." The success and prosperity of the "body of Christ" (in the form of the Massachusetts Bay Colony) will enable them to do what they perceived to be God's work and "work out our salvation under the power and purity of his holy ordinances." This is a telling phrase. The Puritans accepted John Calvin's concept of Predestination—the notion that God had determined who was saved from their sins and who was eternally condemned independently of what individual humans did. For Winthrop and his fellow Puritans, the establishment of their Colony was not a way to earn salvation but, rather, a means by which they would demonstrate their devotion to the God who had already saved them. The way to accomplish this goal, Winthrop declares, is to bring consciously and diligently put into action what churches in England "maintain as truth in profession only." In doing so, the Puritans in Massachusetts will continue to receive God's blessings on their efforts. They have been "sanctified," or made holy, and they must maintain that holiness in order to be prosperous.

As Withrop brings his sermon to a close, he declares that the colonists "have entered into covenant with Him" in their efforts and "hath given us leave to draw our own articles" that is, to establish their own form of governance. Their continued obedience to God will lead to continued prosperity. This is not only for the benefit of those in the Massachusetts colony but for those who will come after. For Winthrop intends his colony to be "as a a city of a hill," an example to others. "The eyes of all people," Winthrop explains, "are upon us." Both the Puritans' friends and enemies would see their work, the result of their covenant with God and, with hope, would in them find a worthy example to imitate.

Audience

Initially, Winthrop addressed his message directly to those Puritans who traveled with him to the Massachusetts Bay colony--perhaps even limited to his fellow shipmates on the *Arabella*. Its overall message, including Winthrop's political and theological references would be understandable to those Puritans who came to Massachusetts Bay as well as Puritans who remained behind in England. The sermon speaks to company members of all socio-economic strata. He implores the lowliest among them to be patient and obedient and calls upon the most powerful to be merciful, generous, and just. While his message would have been understood and appreciated by Puritans who remained in England, Winthrop was primarily concerned with setting out the spiritual basis of Massachusetts Bay and connecting that spiritual basis with the social, political, and economic direction of the colony.

While this sermon was directed at his fellow company members who were establishing the Massachusetts Bay Colony, Winthrop was certainly aware that there were other Puritan attempts at colonization in the region, particularly the Plymouth colony that had been established a decade earlier. The title of Winthrop's sermon, "A Model of Christian Charity" clearly indicates that he intended these ideas to spread beyond Massachusetts Bay or Plymouth. As he tells his listeners, "We shall find that the God of Israel is among us, when ten of us shall be able to resist a thousand of our enemies; when He shall make us a praise and glory that men shall say of succeeding plantations, "may the Lord make it like that of New England." Future generations and "succeeding plantations" might not read his words, but Winthrop clearly intended the audience for the *ideas* in his sermon to be much larger than the contingent sailing west in 1630.

"There are two rules whereby we are to walk one towards another: Justice and Mercy."

(Section 1)

"There is a time when a Christian must sell all and give to the poor, as they did in the Apostles' times. There is a time also when Christians (though they give not all yet) must give beyond their ability, as they of Macedonia."

(Section 1)

"So a mother loves her child, because she thoroughly conceives a resemblance of herself in it. Thus it is between the members of Christ; each discerns, by the work of the Spirit, his own Image and resemblance in another, and therefore cannot but love him as he loves himself."

(Section 1)

"For we must consider that we shall be as a city upon a hill. The eyes of all people are upon us. So that if we shall deal falsely with our God in this work we have undertaken, and so cause Him to withdraw His present help from us, we shall be made a story and a by-word through the world. We shall open the mouths of enemies to speak evil of the ways of God, and all professors for God's sake. We shall shame the faces of many of God's worthy servants, and cause their prayers to be turned into curses upon us till we be consumed out of the good land whither we are going."

(Section 1)

Impact

The text of the sermon was not published during Winthrop's lifetime, and the first published copy appeared in the early 19th century. The idealized relationship between difference social and economic strata in the colony was not often reflected in the reality of life in Massachusetts Bay. However, the desire to establish a polity in which God's elect could rule earthly affairs in accordance with his will was a persistent one. Thousands of Puritans would travel from England to New England in the 1630s and 1640s. In England, Puritan political leaders would be one of the combatants in the English Civil Wars, a conflict that resulted in the abolition of the monarchy and the brief establishment of a Puritan republic. "A Model of Christian Charity" serves, in part, as an illustration of the mindset that produced these political, religious, and social events.

There was also imagery and language in the sermon that long outlived John Winthrop and the Massachusetts bay Colony. Winthrop's imagery of the Puritan settlement as a "City on a Hill," a shining beacon and example to other colonies and, indeed, to England would persist in American political culture. In the twentieth and early twenty-first centuries in particular, this phrase would be expanded and shifted to present the United States and its liberal-democratic-capitalist political and economic system, with figures such as American President Ronald Reagan using the phrase to suggest that much broader conception of American exceptionalism.

In 1989, for example, he said of the United States, "I've spoken of the shining city all my political life .... After 200 years, two centuries, she still stands strong and true to the granite ridge, and her glow has held no matter what storm. And she's still a beacon, still a magnet for all who must have freedom, for all the pilgrims from all the lost places who are hurtling through the darkness, toward home." Two and a half centuries later, the scope of the city on the hill had expended greatly.

Further Reading

Bremer, Francis J. *First Founders: American Puritans and Puritanism in an Atlantic World*. Durham, N.H: New Hampshire, 2012. Print.

---. "Remembering--and Forgetting--John Winthrop and the Puritan Founders." *Massachusetts Historical Review* 6 (2004): 38–69. Print.

Dawson, Hugh J. "John Winthrop's Rite of Passage: The Origins of the 'Christian Charitie' Discourse." *Early American Literature* 26.3 (1991): 219–231. Print.

Dunn, Richard S. "John Winthrop Writes His Journal." *The William and Mary Quarterly* 41.2 (1984): 186–212. *JSTOR*. Web.

"John Winthrop: Biography as History: Francis J. Bremer: 9780826429926: Amazon.com: Books." N.p., n.d. Web. 28 Aug. 2016.

Litke, Justin B., ed. "John Winthrop: A Divinely Sanctioned, Practically Cicumscribed Colony." *Twilight of the Republic*. University Press of Kentucky, 2013. 23–52. Web. Empire and Exceptionalism in the American Political Tradition.

Michaelsen, Scott. "John Winthrop's 'Modell' Covenant and the Company Way." *Early American Literature* 27.2 (1992): 85–100. Print.

Parker, Michael. *John Winthrop: Founding the City Upon a Hill*. New York: Routledge, 2013. Print.

Taylor, Alan. *Colonial America: A Very Short Introduction*. 1 edition. Oxford ; New York: Oxford University Press, 2012. Print.

Woodward, Walter W. *Prospero's America: John Winthrop, Jr., Alchemy, and the Creation of New England Culture, 1606-1676*. Chapel Hill: The University of North Carolina Press, 2013. Print.

—Commentary by Aaron J. Gulyas and Martha I. Pallante

Questions for Further Study

1. Both John Winthrop and Brigham Young ("Sermon on Mormon Governance") led religious minorities to a distant place to create a new place in order to build a new society. How did their visions of society differ? How were they similar? How were the contexts of their creation similar or different?

2. How does Winthrop describe the social order of his community? How does it relate to his vision for the colony's future?

3. Would Winthrop recognize or agree with US President Ronald Reagan's use of the "city on a hill" concept? Why or why not?

"A Model of Christian Charity": Document Text

1630 CE

—*John Winthrop*

GOD ALMIGHTY in His most holy and wise providence, hath so disposed of the condition of mankind, as in all times some must be rich, some poor, some high and eminent in power and dignity; others mean and in submission.

The Reason hereof:

1st Reason. First to hold conformity with the rest of His world, being delighted to show forth the glory of his wisdom in the variety and difference of the creatures, and the glory of His power in ordering all these differences for the preservation and good of the whole, and the glory of His greatness, that as it is the glory of princes to have many officers, so this great king will have many stewards, counting himself more honored in dispensing his gifts to man by man, than if he did it by his own immediate hands.

2nd Reason. Secondly, that He might have the more occasion to manifest the work of his Spirit: first upon the wicked in moderating and restraining them, so that the rich and mighty should not eat up the poor, nor the poor and despised rise up against and shake off their yoke. Secondly, in the regenerate, in exercising His graces in them, as in the great ones, their love, mercy, gentleness, temperance etc., and in the poor and inferior sort, their faith, patience, obedience etc.

3rd Reason. Thirdly, that every man might have need of others, and from hence they might be all knit more nearly together in the bonds of brotherly affection. From hence it appears plainly that no man is made more honorable than another or more wealthy etc., out of any particular and singular respect to himself, but for the glory of his Creator and the common good of the creature, man. Therefore God still reserves the property of these gifts to Himself as Ezek. 16:17, He there calls wealth, His gold and His silver, and Prov. 3:9, He claims their service as His due, "Honor the Lord with thy riches," etc.—All men being thus (by divine providence) ranked into two sorts, rich and poor; under the first are comprehended all such as are able to live comfortably by their own means duly improved; and all others are poor according to the former distribution.

There are two rules whereby we are to walk one towards another: Justice and Mercy. These are always distinguished in their act and in their object, yet may they both concur in the same subject in each respect; as sometimes there may be an occasion of showing mercy to a rich man in some sudden danger or distress, and also doing of mere justice to a poor man in regard of some particular contract, etc.

There is likewise a double Law by which we are regulated in our conversation towards another. In both the former respects, the Law of Nature and the Law of Grace (that is, the moral law or the law of the gospel) to omit the rule of justice as not properly belonging to this purpose otherwise than it may fall into consideration in some particular cases. By the first of these laws, man as he was enabled so withal is commanded to love his neighbor as himself. Upon this ground stands all the precepts of the moral law, which concerns our dealings with men. To apply this to the works of mercy, this law requires two things. First, that every man afford his help to another in every want or distress.

Secondly, that he perform this out of the same affection which makes him careful of his own goods, according to the words of our Savior (from Matthew 7:12), whatsoever ye would that men should do to you. This was practiced by Abraham and Lot in entertaining the angels and the old man of Gibea. The law of Grace or of the Gospel hath some difference from the former (the law of nature), as in these respects: First, the law of nature was given to man in the estate of innocence. This of the Gospel in the estate of regeneracy. Secondly, the former propounds one man to another, as the same flesh and image of God. This as a brother in Christ also, and in the communion of the same Spirit, and so teacheth to put a difference between Christians and others. Do good to all, especially to the household of faith. Upon this ground the Israelites were to put a difference between the brethren of such as were strangers, though not of the Canaanites.

Thirdly, the Law of Nature would give no rules for dealing with enemies, for all are to be considered as friends in the state of innocence, but the Gospel commands love to an enemy. Proof: If thine enemy hunger, feed him; "Love your enemies. … Do good to them that hate you" (Matt. 5:44).

This law of the Gospel propounds likewise a difference of seasons and occasions. There is a time when a Christian must sell all and give to the poor, as they did in the Apostles' times. There is a time also when Christians (though they give not all yet) must give beyond their ability, as they of Macedonia (2 Cor. 8). Likewise, community of perils calls for extraordinary liberality, and so doth community in some special service for the church.

Lastly, when there is no other means whereby our Christian brother may be relieved in his distress, we must help him beyond our ability rather than tempt God in putting him upon help by miraculous or extraordinary means. This duty of mercy is exercised in the kinds: giving, lending and forgiving (of a debt).

Question: What rule shall a man observe in giving in respect of the measure?

Answer: If the time and occasion be ordinary he is to give out of his abundance. Let him lay aside as God hath blessed him. If the time and occasion be extraordinary, he must be ruled by them; taking this withal, that then a man cannot likely do too much, especially if he may leave himself and his family under probable means of comfortable subsistence.

Objection: A man must lay up for posterity, the fathers lay up for posterity and children, and he is worse than an infidel that provideth not for his own.

Answer: For the first, it is plain that it being spoken by way of comparison, it must be meant of the ordinary and usual course of fathers, and cannot extend to times and occasions extraordinary. For the other place the Apostle speaks against such as walked inordinately, and it is without question, that he is worse than an infidel who through his own sloth and voluptuousness shall neglect to provide for his family.

Objection: "The wise man's eyes are in his head," saith Solomon, "and foreseeth the plague"; therefore he must forecast and lay up against evil times when he or his may stand in need of all he can gather.

Answer: This very Argument Solomon useth to persuade to liberality (Eccle. 11), "Cast thy bread upon the waters … for thou knowest not what evil may come upon the land." Luke 16:9, "Make you friends of the riches of iniquity.…" You will ask how this shall be? Very well. For first he that gives to the poor, lends to the Lord and He will repay him even in this life an hundredfold to him or his. The righteous is ever merciful and lendeth, and his seed enjoyeth

the blessing; and besides we know what advantage it will be to us in the day of account when many such witnesses shall stand forth for us to witness the improvement of our talent. And I would know of those who plead so much for laying up for time to come, whether they hold that to be Gospel Matthew 6:19, "Lay not up for yourselves treasures upon earth," etc. If they acknowledge it, what extent will they allow it? If only to those primitive times, let them consider the reason whereupon our Savior grounds it. The first is that they are subject to the moth, the rust, the thief. Secondly, they will steal away the heart: "where the treasure is there will your heart be also."

The reasons are of like force at all times. Therefore the exhortation must be general and perpetual, with always in respect of the love and affection to riches and in regard of the things themselves when any special service for the church or particular distress of our brother do call for the use of them; otherwise it is not only lawful but necessary to lay up as Joseph did to have ready upon such occasions, as the Lord (whose stewards we are of them) shall call for them from us. Christ gives us an instance of the first, when he sent his disciples for the donkey, and bids them answer the owner thus, "the Lord hath need of him." So when the Tabernacle was to be built, He sends to His people to call for their silver and gold, etc., and yields no other reason but that it was for His work. When Elisha comes to the widow of Sareptah and finds her preparing to make ready her pittance for herself and family, he bids her first provide for him, he challenges first God's part which she must first give before she must serve her own family. All these teach us that the Lord looks that when He is pleased to call for His right in any thing we have, our own interest we have must stand aside till His turn be served. For the other, we need look no further then to that of 1 John 3:17, "He who hath this world's goods and seeth his brother to need and shuts up his compassion from him, how dwelleth the love of God in him?" Which comes punctually to this conclusion: If thy brother be in want and thou canst help him, thou needst not make doubt of what thou shouldst do; if thou lovest God thou must help him.

Question: What rule must we observe in lending?

Answer: Thou must observe whether thy brother hath present or probable or possible means of repaying thee, if there be none of those, thou must give him according to his necessity, rather then lend him as he requires (requests). If he hath present means of repaying thee, thou art to look at him not as an act of mercy, but by way of commerce, wherein thou art to walk by the rule of justice; but if his means of repaying thee be only probable or possible, then he is an object of thy mercy, thou must lend him, though there be danger of losing it. (Deut. 15:7–8): "If any of thy brethren be poor … thou shalt lend him sufficient." That men might not shift off this duty by the apparent hazard, He tells them that though the year of Jubilee were at hand (when he must remit it, if he were not able to repay it before), yet he must lend him, and that cheerfully. It may not grieve thee to give him, saith He. And because some might object, why so I should soon impoverish myself and my family, he adds, with all thy work, etc., for our Savior said (Matt. 5:42), "From him that would borrow of thee turn not away."

Question: What rule must we observe in forgiving (a debt)?

Answer: Whether thou didst lend by way of commerce or in mercy, if he hath nothing to pay thee, thou must forgive, (except in cause where thou hast a surety or a lawful pledge). Deut. 15:1–2—Every seventh year the creditor was to quit that which he lent to his brother if he were poor, as appears in verse 4. "Save when there shall be no poor with thee." In all these and like cases, Christ gives a general rule (Matt. 7:12), "Whatsoever ye would that men should do to you, do ye the same to them."

Question: What rule must we observe and walk by in cause of community of peril?

Answer: The same as before, but with more enlargement towards others and less respect towards ourselves and our own right. Hence it was that in the primitive Church they sold all, had all things in common, neither did any man say that which he possessed was his own. Likewise in their return out of the captivity, because the work was great for the restoring of the church and the danger of enemies was common to all, Nehemiah directs the Jews to liberality and readiness in remitting their debts to their brethren, and disposing liberally to such as wanted, and stand not upon their own dues which they might have demanded of them. Thus did some of our forefathers in times of persecution in England, and so did many of the faithful of other churches, whereof we keep an honorable remembrance of them; and it is to be observed that both in Scriptures and latter stories of the churches that such as have been most bountiful to the poor saints, especially in those extraordinary times and occasions, God hath left them highly commended to posterity, as Zaccheus, Cornelius, Dorcas, Bishop Hooper, the Cutler of Brussels and divers others. Observe again that the Scripture gives no caution

to restrain any from being over liberal this way; but all men to the liberal and cheerful practice hereof by the sweeter promises; as to instance one for many (Isaiah 58:6–9) "Is not this the fast I have chosen to loose the bonds of wickedness, to take off the heavy burdens, to let the oppressed go free and to break every yoke … to deal thy bread to the hungry and to bring the poor that wander into thy house, when thou seest the naked to cover them … and then shall thy light brake forth as the morning and thy health shall grow speedily, thy righteousness shall go before God, and the glory of the Lord shalt embrace thee; then thou shall call and the Lord shall answer thee," etc. And from Ch. 2:10 [??] "If thou pour out thy soul to the hungry, then shall thy light spring out in darkness, and the Lord shall guide thee continually, and satisfy thy soul in draught, and make fat thy bones, thou shalt be like a watered garden, and they shalt be of thee that shall build the old waste places," etc. On the contrary most heavy curses are laid upon such as are straightened towards the Lord and his people (Judg. 5:23), "Curse ye Meroshe … because they came not to help the Lord." He who shutteth his ears from hearing the cry of the poor, he shall cry and shall not be heard." (Matt. 25) "Go ye cursed into everlasting fire," etc. "I was hungry and ye fed me not." (2 Cor. 9:6) "He that soweth sparingly shall reap sparingly."

Having already set forth the practice of mercy according to the rule of God's law, it will be useful to lay open the grounds of it also, being the other part of the Commandment and that is the affection from which this exercise of mercy must arise, the Apostle tells us that this love is the fulfilling of the law, not that it is enough to love our brother and so no further; but in regard of the excellency of his parts giving any motion to the other as the soul to the body and the power it hath to set all the faculties at work in the outward exercise of this duty; as when we bid one make the clock strike, he doth not lay hand on the hammer, which is the immediate instrument of the sound, but sets on work the first mover or main wheel; knowing that will certainly produce the sound which he intends. So the way to draw men to the works of mercy, is not by force of Argument from the goodness or necessity of the work; for though this cause may enforce, a rational mind to some present act of mercy, as is frequent in experience, yet it cannot work such a habit in a soul, as shall make it prompt upon all occasions to produce the same effect, but by framing these affections of love in the heart which will as naturally bring forth the other, as any cause doth produce the effect.

The definition which the Scripture gives us of love is this: Love is the bond of perfection. First it is a bond or ligament. Secondly, it makes the work perfect. There is no body but consists of parts and that which knits these parts together, gives the body its perfection, because it makes each part so contiguous to others as thereby they do mutually participate with each other, both in strength and infirmity, in pleasure and pain. To instance in the most perfect of all bodies: Christ and his Church make one body. The several parts of this body considered a part before they were united, were as disproportionate and as much disordering as so many contrary qualities or elements, but when Christ comes, and by his spirit and love knits all these parts to himself and each to other, it is become the most perfect and best proportioned body in the world (Eph. 4:15–16). Christ, by whom all the body being knit together by every joint for the furniture thereof, according to the effectual power which is in the measure of every perfection of parts, a glorious body without spot or wrinkle; the ligaments hereof being Christ, or his love, for Christ is love (1 John 4:8). So this definition is right. Love is the bond of perfection.

From hence we may frame these conclusions:

First of all, true Christians are of one body in Christ (1 Cor. 12). Ye are the body of Christ and members of their part. All the parts of this body being thus united are made so contiguous in a special relation as they must needs partake of each other's strength and infirmity; joy and sorrow, weal and woe. If one member suffers, all suffer with it, if one be in honor, all rejoice with it.

Secondly, the ligaments of this body which knit together are love.

Thirdly, no body can be perfect which wants its proper ligament.

Fourthly, All the parts of this body being thus united are made so contiguous in a special relation as they must needs partake of each other's strength and infirmity, joy and sorrow, weal and woe. (1 Cor. 12:26) If one member suffers, all suffer with it; if one be in honor, all rejoice with it.

Fifthly, this sensitivity and sympathy of each other's conditions will necessarily infuse into each part a native desire and endeavor, to strengthen, defend, preserve and comfort the other. To insist a little on this conclusion being the product of all the former, the truth hereof will appear both by precept and pattern. 1 John 3:16, "We ought to lay down our lives for the brethren." Gal. 6:2, "Bear ye one another's burden's and so fulfill the law of Christ."

For patterns we have that first of our Savior who, out of his good will in obedience to his father, becoming a part of this body and being knit with it in the bond of love, found such a native sensitivity of our infirmities and sorrows as he willingly yielded himself to death to ease the infirmities of the rest of his body, and so healed their sorrows. From the like sympathy of parts did the Apostles and many thousands of the Saints lay down their lives for Christ. Again the like we may see in the members of this body among themselves. Rom. 9—Paul could have been contented to have been separated from Christ, that the Jews might not be cut off from the body. It is very observable what he professeth of his affectionate partaking with every member; "Who is weak (saith he) and I am not weak? Who is offended and I burn not?" And again (2 Cor. 7:13), "Therefore we are comforted because ye were comforted." Of Epaphroditus he speaketh (Phil. 2:25–30) that he regarded not his own life to do him service. So Phoebe and others are called the servants of the church. Now it is apparent that they served not for wages, or by constraint, but out of love. The like we shall find in the histories of the church, in all ages; the sweet sympathy of affections which was in the members of this body one towards another; their cheerfulness in serving and suffering together; how liberal they were without repining, harborers without grudging, and helpful without reproaching; and all from hence, because they had fervent love amongst them; which only makes the practice of mercy constant and easy.

The next consideration is how this love comes to be wrought. Adam in his first estate was a perfect model of mankind in all their generations, and in him this love was perfected in regard of the habit. But Adam, himself rent from his Creator, rent all his posterity also one from another; whence it comes that every man is born with this principle in him to love and seek himself only, and thus a man continueth till Christ comes and takes possession of the soul and infuseth another principle, love to God and our brother, and this latter having continual supply from Christ, as the head and root by which he is united, gets predominant in the soul, so by little and little expels the former. 1 John 4:7—Love cometh of God and every one that loveth is born of God, so that this love is the fruit of the new birth, and none can have it but the new creature. Now when this quality is thus formed in the souls of men, it works like the Spirit upon the dry bones. Ezek. 37:7—"Bone came to bone." It gathers together the scattered bones, or perfect old man Adam, and knits them into one body again in Christ, whereby a man is become again a living soul.

The third consideration is concerning the exercise of this love, which is twofold, inward or outward. The outward hath been handled in the former preface of this discourse. From unfolding the other we must take in our way that maxim of philosophy, "simile simili gaudet," or like will to like; for as of things which are turned with disaffection to each other, the ground of it is from a dissimilitude or arising from the contrary or different nature of the things themselves; for the ground of love is an apprehension of some resemblance in the things loved to that which affects it. This is the cause why the Lord loves the creature, so far as it hath any of his Image in it; He loves his elect because they are like Himself, He beholds them in His beloved son.

So a mother loves her child, because she thoroughly conceives a resemblance of herself in it. Thus it is between the members of Christ; each discerns, by the work of the Spirit, his own Image and resemblance in another, and therefore cannot but love him as he loves himself. Now when the soul, which is of a sociable nature, finds anything like to itself, it is like Adam when Eve was brought to him. She must be one with himself. This is flesh of my flesh (saith he) and bone of my bone. So the soul conceives a great delight in it; therefore she desires nearness and familiarity with it. She hath a great propensity to do it good and receives such content in it, as fearing the miscarriage of her beloved, she bestows it in the inmost closet of her heart. She will not endure that it shall want any good which she can give it. If by occasion she be withdrawn from the company of it, she is still looking towards the place where she left her beloved. If she heard it groan, she is with it presently. If she find it sad and disconsolate, she sighs and moans with it. She hath no such joy as to see her beloved merry and thriving. If she see it wronged, she cannot hear it without passion. She sets no bounds to her affections, nor hath any thought of reward. She finds recompense enough in the exercise of her love towards it.

We may see this acted to life in Jonathan and David. Jonathan a valiant man endued with the spirit of love, so soon as he discovered the same spirit in David had presently his heart knit to him by this ligament of love; so that it is said he loved him as his own soul, he takes so great pleasure in him, that he strips himself to adorn his beloved. His father's kingdom was not so precious to him as his beloved David, David shall have it with all his heart.

Himself desires no more but that he may be near to him to rejoice in his good. He chooseth to converse with him in the wilderness even to the hazard of his own life, rather than with the great Courtiers in his father's Palace. When he sees danger towards him, he spares neither rare pains nor peril to direct it. When injury was offered his beloved David, he would not bear it, though from his own father. And when they must part for a season only, they thought their hearts would have broke for sorrow, had not their affections found vent by abundance of tears. Other instances might be brought to show the nature of this affection; as of Ruth and Naomi, and many others; but this truth is cleared enough. If any shall object that it is not possible that love shall be bred or upheld without hope of requital, it is granted; but that is not our cause; for this love is always under reward. It never gives, but it always receives with advantage:

First in regard that among the members of the same body, love and affection are reciprocal in a most equal and sweet kind of commerce.

Secondly, in regard of the pleasure and content that the exercise of love carries with it, as we may see in the natural body. The mouth is at all the pains to receive and mince the food which serves for the nourishment of all the other parts of the body; yet it hath no cause to complain; for first the other parts send back, by several passages, a due proportion of the same nourishment, in a better form for the strengthening and comforting the mouth. Secondly, the labor of the mouth is accompanied with such pleasure and content as far exceeds the pains it takes. So is it in all the labor of love among Christians. The party loving, reaps love again, as was showed before, which the soul covets more than all the wealth in the world.

Thirdly, nothing yields more pleasure and content to the soul then when it finds that which it may love fervently; for to love and live beloved is the soul's paradise both here and in heaven. In the State of wedlock there be many comforts to learn out of the troubles of that condition; but let such as have tried the most, say if there be any sweetness in that condition comparable to the exercise of mutual love.

From the former considerations arise these conclusions:

First, this love among Christians is a real thing, not imaginary.

Secondly, this love is as absolutely necessary to the being of the body of Christ, as the sinews and other ligaments of a natural body are to the being of that body.

Thirdly, this love is a divine, spiritual, nature; free, active, strong, courageous, permanent; undervaluing all things beneath its proper object and of all the graces, this makes us nearer to resemble the virtues of our heavenly father.

Fourthly, it rests in the love and welfare of its beloved. For the full certain knowledge of those truths concerning the nature, use, and excellency of this grace, that which the holy ghost hath left recorded, 1 Cor. 13, may give full satisfaction, which is needful for every true member of this lovely body of the Lord Jesus, to work upon their hearts by prayer, meditation continual exercise at least of the special influence of this grace, till Christ be formed in them and they in him, all in each other, knit together by this bond of love.

It rests now to make some application of this discourse, by the present design, which gave the occasion of writing of it. Herein are four things to be propounded; first the persons, secondly, the work, thirdly the end, fourthly the means.

First, for the persons. We are a company professing ourselves fellow members of Christ, in which respect only, though we were absent from each other many miles, and had our employments as far distant, yet we ought to account ourselves knit together by this bond of love and live in the exercise of it, if we would have comfort of our being in Christ. This was notorious in the practice of the Christians in former times; as is testified of the Waldenses, from the mouth of one of the adversaries Aeneas Sylvius "mutuo ament pene antequam norunt"—they use to love any of their own religion even before they were acquainted with them.

Secondly for the work we have in hand. It is by a mutual consent, through a special overvaluing providence and a more than an ordinary approbation of the churches of Christ, to seek out a place of cohabitation and consortship under a due form of government both civil and ecclesiastical. In such cases as this, the care of the public must oversway all private respects, by which, not only conscience, but mere civil policy, doth bind us. For it is a true rule that particular estates cannot subsist in the ruin of the public.

Thirdly, the end is to improve our lives to do more service to the Lord; the comfort and increase of the body of Christ, whereof we are members, that ourselves and posterity may be the better preserved from the common corruptions of this evil world, to serve the Lord and work out our salvation under the power and purity of his holy ordinances.

Fourthly, for the means whereby this must be effected. They are twofold, a conformity with the work and end we aim at. These we see are extraordinary, therefore we must not content ourselves with usual ordinary means. Whatsoever we did, or ought to have done, when we lived in England, the same must we do, and more also, where we go. That which the most in their churches maintain as truth in profession only, we must bring into familiar and constant practice; as in this duty of love, we must love brotherly without dissimulation, we must love one another with a pure heart fervently. We must bear one another's burdens. We must not look only on our own things, but also on the things of our brethren.

Neither must we think that the Lord will bear with such failings at our hands as he doth from those among whom we have lived; and that for these three reasons:

First, in regard of the more near bond of marriage between Him and us, wherein He hath taken us to be His, after a most strict and peculiar manner, which will make Him the more jealous of our love and obedience. So He tells the people of Israel, you only have I known of all the families of the earth, therefore will I punish you for your transgressions.

Secondly, because the Lord will be sanctified in them that come near Him. We know that there were many that corrupted the service of the Lord; some setting up altars before his own; others offering both strange fire and strange sacrifices also; yet there came no fire from heaven, or other sudden judgment upon them, as did upon Nadab and Abihu, whom yet we may think did not sin presumptuously.

Thirdly, when God gives a special commission He looks to have it strictly observed in every article; When He gave Saul a commission to destroy Amaleck, He indented with him upon certain articles, and because he failed in one of the least, and that upon a fair pretense, it lost him the kingdom, which should have been his reward, if he had observed his commission.

Thus stands the cause between God and us. We are entered into covenant with Him for this work. We have taken out a commission. The Lord hath given us leave to draw our own articles. We have professed to enterprise these and those accounts, upon these and those ends. We have hereupon besought Him of favor and blessing. Now if the Lord shall please to hear us, and bring us in peace to the place we desire, then hath He ratified this covenant and sealed our commission, and will expect a strict performance of the articles contained in it; but if we shall neglect the observation of these articles which are the ends we have propounded, and, dissembling with our God, shall fall to embrace this present world and prosecute our carnal intentions, seeking great things for ourselves and our posterity, the Lord will surely break out in wrath against us, and be revenged of such a people, and make us know the price of the breach of such a covenant.

Now the only way to avoid this shipwreck, and to provide for our posterity, is to follow the counsel of Micah, to do justly, to love mercy, to walk humbly with our God. For this end, we must be knit together, in this work, as one man. We must entertain each other in brotherly affection. We must be willing to abridge ourselves of our superfluities, for the supply of others' necessities. We must uphold a familiar commerce together in all meekness, gentleness, patience and liberality. We must delight in each other; make others' conditions our own; rejoice together, mourn together, labor and suffer together, always having before our eyes our commission and community in the work, as members of the same body. So shall we keep the unity of the spirit in the bond of peace. The Lord will be our God, and delight to dwell among us, as His own people, and will command a blessing upon us in all our ways, so that we shall see much more of His wisdom, power, goodness and truth, than formerly we have been acquainted with. We shall find that the God of Israel is among us, when ten of us shall be able to resist a thousand of our enemies; when He shall make us a praise and glory that men shall say of succeeding plantations, "may the Lord make it like that of New England." For we must consider that we shall be as a city upon a hill. The eyes of all people are upon us. So that if we shall deal falsely with our God in this work we have undertaken, and so cause Him to withdraw His present help from us, we shall be made a story and a byword through the world. We shall open the mouths of enemies to speak evil of the ways of God, and all professors for God's sake. We shall shame the faces of many of God's worthy servants, and cause their prayers to be turned into curses upon us till we be consumed out of the good land whither we are going.

And to shut this discourse with that exhortation of Moses, that faithful servant of the Lord, in his last farewell to Israel, Deut. 30. "Beloved, there is now set before us life and death, good and evil," in that we are commanded this day to love the Lord our God, and to love one another, to walk in his ways and to keep his Commandments and his ordinance and his laws, and the articles of our Covenant with Him, that we may live and be multiplied, and that the Lord our God may bless us in the land whither we go to possess it. But if our hearts shall turn away, so that we will not obey, but shall be seduced, and worship other Gods, our pleasure and profits, and serve them; it is propounded unto us this day, we shall surely perish out of the good land whither we pass over this vast sea to possess it.

- Therefore let us choose life,
- that we and our seed may live,
- by obeying His voice and cleaving to Him,
- for He is our life and our prosperity.

Glossary

"Adam in his first estate"	Refers to the period before Adam and Eve ate of the fruit of the tree of the knowledge of good and evil in Genesis creation story. In his "first estate," Adam was without sin, not in rebellion against God.
Nadab and Abihu	The sons of Aaron, the Hebrew Priest, the brother of Moses. In the book of Leviticus, God killed Nadab and Abihu for violating his ceremonial instructions.
Oversway	To take precedence over.
The Regenerate	Those who are saved by God and granted eternal life.
"We are a company"	Winthrop is referring to the members and leadership of the Massachusetts Bay Company.

WESTMINSTER CONFESSION: DOCUMENT ANALYSIS

1646 CE

"As there is no sin so small but it deserves damnation; so there is no sin so great that it can bring damnation upon those who truly repent."

Overview

The Westminster Confession, written in 1646, is a statement of Christian faith in the tradition of Calvinist, or "Reformed," Protestantism. Its thirty-three chapters were meant to cover all the major issues of Christian theology as they existed in the mid-seventeenth century. The Westminster Confession was created by a group of ministers and theological experts from England and Scotland, mostly Presbyterian in faith, during the English Civil War (1642–1651). The group had originally been summoned by the English parliament to reform the Church of England.

Along with the Westminster Larger and Shorter Catechisms that summarize its doctrines, the Westminster Confession is the most influential statement of faith in the English-speaking Calvinist tradition and remains the theological foundation of most Presbyterian churches as well as strongly influencing churches outside that tradition, including Congregationalist and Baptist bodies.

Context

Reformed theology developed from the Protestant Reformation of the sixteenth century as a mixture whose strongest component was the thought of the French theologian John Calvin (1509–1564). The major issues that distinguished the Reformed tradition from other branches of Protestantism included the Eucharist and infant baptism, which Reformed theologians supported. The issues most identified with a distinctive Reformed tradition, however, were those concerning salvation. As was true of Protestants generally, the Reformed supported the idea of justification by faith alone, not through works. However, Reformed theology was particularly associated with pre-

destination, the theory that God had determined, solely of his own will, who was to be saved (a minority known as the "elect") and who was damned (the rest of humanity, known as the "reprobate.") This was accompanied by the doctrine of "Total Depravity," the belief that human beings, since the fall of Adam, were by their nature utterly corrupt. Only divine grace, which God was completely free to bestow or withhold, could exempt a human from damnation. Jesus Christ had not died to save all, but the elect only—"Limited Atonement." The systematization of these beliefs is often associated with the Synod of Dort, a meeting of Reformed divines from all over Western Europe held at the Dutch city of Dort (or Dordrecht) in 1618 and 1619 that put forward *The Decision of the Synod of Dort on the Five Main Points of Doctrine in Dispute in the Netherlands.* The "Five Points" are Total Depravity; Unconditional Election, not predicated on any quality of saved individuals but solely on God's grace; Irresistible Grace, which cannot be rejected by a human; Limited Atonement; and the Perseverance of the Saints, or the doctrine that grace once given will never be withdrawn. Although the term *Five Points* is not found there, the Westminster Confession follows this model.

The "covenantal" element of Reformed theology was not principally derived from Calvin, although there are elements of Calvin's thought that point to it. Its original sources include the theology of the Swiss minister Heinrich Bullinger (1504–1575). Covenantal theology placed the relationship between God and the saved individual on a contractual basis. By entering into an agreement binding on both sides, God voluntarily limited his absolute power. God's first covenant, the covenant of works made with Adam, was no longer in effect. In the covenant of works, salvation would be granted in return for obedience to the law of God. Adam himself had destroyed the covenant of works by yielding to temptation and violating God's commands. The covenant of grace as originally offered to Abraham replaced the covenant of works. In the covenant of grace, God bound himself to save those who took up their side of the covenant by having faith and striving to follow the moral law, even though they would inevitably fail to live lives of absolute perfection. Covenant theologians sometimes moved far away from Calvin's emphasis on the unknowability and mystery of God's decrees toward a legalistic interpretation of the relationship of God and humanity, although they never viewed the Covenant as abrogating the doctrine of predestination.

Reformed doctrine since the sixteenth century had been put forth in a series of creeds and confessions produced primarily on the European continent. The necessity of establishing a common theological basis for the numerous Reformed churches led to a demand for relatively simple, portable statements of Reformed belief.

Reformed theology had a strong influence on the Church of England when it was formed in the mid-sixteenth century. However, the Church was not a theologically rigid organization. Some leaned toward Arminianism or opposed Calvinism without being very clear what they supported. In the Church of Scotland, however, Reformed theology was combined with a widespread belief in the government of the church by ministers and elders rather than bishops—"Presbyterianism." In 1603 the accession of James VI of Scotland (1566–1625) to the English throne as James I brought the two countries under one royal dynasty, the house of Stuart. James, and far more openly his son Charles I (1600–1649), opposed Presbyterian organization in both kingdoms.

In the years immediately preceding the Westminster Assembly, the principal conflict within the Church of England was between the "Arminians," led by Archbishop of Canterbury William Laud (1573–1645) with the support of King Charles, and "Puritans," most of whom leaned to Calvinist theology. Arminianism is the doctrine associated with the Dutch theologian Jacobus Arminius (1560–1609) that rejects the doctrine of predestination to hold that Christ died for all, not just the elect, and that all are potentially, if not actually, saved. The Arminianism of Laud, sometimes referred to as "English Arminianism," however, was based less on Arminius's doctrinal positions and more on a view of Christianity that emphasized ritual and the "beauty of holiness" over the Calvinist practice of emphasizing doctrine and the sermon.

The conflict between Arminians and Puritans led many Puritans to oppose the institutions of bishops—"Episcopacy"—altogether, in favor of either Presbyterianism or "Congregationalism," built on the supremacy of individual congregations. A similar conflict was raging in Scotland. The outbreak first of the Scottish rebellion (known as the First Bishops' War) in 1639 and then of the English Civil War in 1642 involved political as well as religious issues. However, Arminians in both kingdoms usually supported the king, while many English Puritans along with the Scottish "Covenanters" (so-called for their support of the Scottish National Covenant of 1638) supported the rebellions. By 1642 there was a full-scale civil war in England as well, between the king and the English

parliament The cause of "further Reformation," purging the Church of Catholic and Arminian elements, was popular in Parliament. It voted to reform the Church of England and convoked a meeting at the Henry VII Chapel at Westminster to do so. The gathering was composed of some of England's leading theologians and religious scholars, nearly all Presbyterian or Congregationalist with a small minority of Anglicans.

Shortly afterward, Scottish Covenanters and English Parliamentarians made an alliance, the "Solemn League and Covenant," in 164 3. One goal of the Solemn League and Covenant was to reform the churches in both kingdom, which to the signers meant moving their theology closer to the Reformed tradition. It was followed by the incorporation of Scottish delegates into the Westminster Assembly.

About the Author

The Westminster Assembly of Divines was originally a group of English clergy and lay commissioners assigned to revise the doctrine and practices of the Church of England further away from Catholicism. In addition to drawing up a statement of faith, they were charged with reforming church government and public worship. They initially drew from a diversity of factions in the Church, including Anglicans, but as the proceedings continued, they were dominated by Reformed Presbyterian and Congregational divines. Many members came from the universities, and three ministers of French Reformed churches in London were members. The English members were joined by Scottish lay and clerical delegates following the adoption of the Solemn League and Covenant. The English members were chosen by Parliament and the Scots by the General Assembly of the Church of Scotland. Leaders of the Assembly included the prolocutor, or president, of the Assembly, the philosopher and theologian William Twisse (1578–1646); John Selden (1584–1654), a layman and England's leading Hebrew scholar; and Stephen Marshall (ca. 1594–1655), one of the greatest preachers of the day. The Scottish commissioners included the eminent theologian Samuel Rutherford (ca. 1600–1661), the Presbyterian leader Alexander Henderson (ca. 1583–1646), and the brilliant polemicist George Gillespie (1613–1648). One of the Scottish commissioners, Robert Baille (1602–1662), was only a minor actor in the Assembly, but his gossipy letters are one of our principal historical sources for the making of the Westminster Confession. Despite disagreements over particular points, the Assembly had a broadly Reformed consensus, and there were no openly expressed disagreements over fundamentals. The Assembly did not follow a rigid set of procedures. Much of its work, including the drafting of parts of the Westminster Confession, was entrusted to committees, but some sections were presented to the whole by men who were not members of the relevant or, indeed, of any committee.

Time Line	
July 10, 1509	■ John Calvin is born in Noyon, France.
1529	■ The English Reformation begins.
1536	■ The first edition of Calvin's *Institutes of the Christian Religion*, the foundation of Calvinist theology, is published.
March 24, 1603	■ The English and Scottish thrones are united as James VI of Scotland becomes James I of Great Britain.
November 13, 1618– May 9, 1619	■ The Synod of Dort in the Dutch Republic establishes the classic "Five Points" formulation of Calvinist theology.
1639	■ The Scottish Covenanter rebellion against Charles I (known as the First Bishops' War) breaks out.
1642	■ The English Civil War between Charles I and Parliament erupts.
June 12, 1643	■ Parliament issues an ordinance convoking an assembly of lay commissioners and clergy to reform the Church of England.
July 1, 1643	■ First meeting of the Assembly of Divines is held in the Henry VII Chapel at Westminster.
August 17, 1643	■ The Solemn League and Covenant, an alliance between the Covenanters and Parliament, is approved by the General Assembly of the Church of Scotland.
September 25, 1643	■ The Solemn League and Covenant is approved by the English House of Commons.

October 12, 1643	■ Parliament orders the current work of the Assembly of Divines suspended and substitutes work toward a confession of faith for England, Scotland, and Ireland according to the Solemn League and Covenant.
November 26, 1646	■ The Assembly completes the Westminster Confession.
December 4–7, 1646	■ The Westminster Confession is presented to Parliament.
August 27, 1647	■ The General Assembly of the Church of Scotland at Edinburgh approves the Westminster Confession.
June 20, 1648	■ The English parliament approves the Westminster Confession.
October 1658	■ The Savoy Declaration of English Congregationalists includes a confession of faith that closely follows the Westminster Confession with the exception of those issues of church organization dividing Presbyterians and Congregationalists.
1788	■ The Presbyterian Church in the United States, the first Presbyterian body formed in the newly independent United States, adopts the Westminster Confession with modifications relating to the role of the civil government.

Explanation and Analysis of the Document

The Westminster Confession was meant to be a complete treatment of the major issues of Christian theology. The authors strove for clarity and logic, as befits what was meant to be a definitive doctrinal statement, not a piece of speculative theology.

♦ Chapter I

One of the fundamental principles of the Protestant Reformation was *sola scriptura*—the Bible as the sole source of Christian truth. This principle denied the Catholic belief that the "tradition of the church," independent of the Bible, supplemented it as a source of truth. The Westminster Confession supports this principle by dealing with the Bible first of all, even before God. The first chapter also defines exactly what the Bible is by listing the canonical books of the Old and New Testaments and explicitly excluding the Apocrypha, which Catholics viewed as divinely inspired, but to a lesser degree than the canonical books.

♦ Chapter II

The definition of God was one of the most difficult issues with which the Westminster Assembly grappled. What resulted emphasizes, as the Reformed tradition tends to generally emphasize, God's absoluteness, sovereignty, and utter independence of the created. The doctrine of the Trinity, central to Christian theology, appears almost as an afterthought in this chapter. The Westminster Confession's trinitarianism is in the western Christian mainstream, endorsing the "double procession" of the Holy Spirit from both the Father and the Son, as opposed to the belief of the Eastern Orthodox Churches that the Spirit proceeds from the Father alone.

♦ Chapter III

Predestination is the subject of chapter III. God chose those men and angels who are to be saved and those who are to be damned in eternity, not at a specific moment in time but "before the foundation of the world was laid." This chapter's placement before the chapter on Creation dramatically exemplifies "supralapsarianism," the doctrine that God chose the saved and damned preceding the Fall of Man in the Garden of Eden. (The idea that God chose the saved and damned as a logical consequence of the Fall is called "sublapsarianism.") Its early appearance in the Confession also indicates its overall importance to the writers.

♦ Chapter IV

In chapter IV, Creation is described as a means of expressing God's glory. The first humans were made with the law of God "written on their hearts," meaning that they needed no Bible or other external source for the law. Unlike later humans, the first humans had the power to obey God's law but also the freedom of will to choose not to obey.

♦ Chapter V

Chapter V deals with God's providence, or government of the universe. The concept of providence was central to seventeenth-century Puritan thinking, and the smallest events could be treated as the evidence of God's divine care. The Westminster Confession emphasizes that God's providence can work both within and without what we ordinarily think of cause and effect. Even the Fall of Man was a working out of God's providence, although this in no way transfers the blame from Adam and Eve to God. The idea that God's

omnipotence made him the creator or "author of sin" is one the Westminster writers are very concerned to reject. God's providence is exemplified in exposing both the elect and the regenerate to the temptation of sin, the former to teach them humility and their utter dependence on his grace, the latter to render them still more worthy of damnation. The Confession also points out that the Church is the object of God's particular care.

♦ Chapter VI

After addressing the subject tangentially in the preceding chapters, the Confession here comes to grips with the Fall of the human being and human bondage to sin. The Fall was caused by the temptation of Satan (one of the devil's few appearances in the Confession) but was ultimately ordained to God's glory. In line with Reformed thinking, the Confession emphasizes humanity's utter bondage to sin following the Fall, as we all inherited the "Original Sin" of our first ancestors, completely unable to do that which is good by our own efforts. Everyone, even the elect, remain subject to sin, and each sin, however trivial it seems, is justly punished by eternal death—the Reformed tradition knows nothing of the Catholic distinction between venial sins (which do not alienate the sinner from God completely) and mortal sins (which deprive the sinner of all grace, figuratively "killing" the soul).

♦ Chapter VII

This chapter introduces a key concept of Reformed theology as it developed—the Covenant. There are two Covenants governing the relation between God and humanity. With the original Covenant of Works, humans could be granted salvation by their obedience and conformity with God's will. The Covenant of Works was abrogated by Adam's sin. In its place stands another Covenant, the Covenant of Grace, divided into two dispensations, one between God and the Jews in the pre-Christian era and one between God and the Christian Church. In the Covenant of Grace, God offers salvation to those who have faith in Christ. However, salvation is still utterly dependent on God's grace—only the elect, predestined by God, will receive the grace to have faith.

The Covenant of Grace worked differently in the time of the Old Testament and before Christ's coming to earth—the "time of the law." The elect among the ancient Jews were saved not through explicit faith in the historical figure of Jesus Christ, of whom they knew nothing, but through faith in Jewish ritual practices, all of which prefigured the Messiah, Christ. However, this does not mean that there was a separate covenant operating before Christ; there was one covenant working in two different ways. The coming of Christ ended the earlier operation of the Covenant of Grace. (Chapter X deals with practitioners of religions other than Christianity in the present time, implicitly including the Jews, and states that it is impossible for them to be saved.)

♦ **Chapter VIII**

This chapter deals with the central tenet of Christianity—the redemptive mission of Jesus Christ. The Confession's Christology again is in the Western mainstream, describing Jesus as fully man and fully God in the position established by the Council of Chalcedon in 451. Christ's mission on earth is viewed as a redemptive sacrifice in satisfaction of God's justice, although the Confession avoids the legalism of some interpretations of Christ's redemptive work, such as that of the eleventh-century theologian Anselm's *Cur Deus Homo?* ("Why God Became Man"). Christ's sacrifice applies not to all humankind but only to the elect, "those whom the Father hath given unto him."

♦ **Chapter IX**

The Westminster Assembly here endorsed a fundamental Calvinist tenet, the inability of the fallen human being to will anything spiritually good. This does not mean that human beings are unable by their own efforts to will anything "ethically" good but that these things are irrelevant to salvation. The ability to will the spiritually good, lost by the Fall of Adam and Eve, can be restored only by the grace of God. This is one benefit God gives, but only to his elect. Although their ability to will the spiritually good is restored, even the elect retain the corruption inherent to all humanity and will continue to will evil as well as good. Only in heaven will the saved will only good.

♦ **Chapter X**

A common Reformed belief was in a calling—a time when God made an elect person's status known to him or her. The moment of "calling" was central to the spiritual autobiographies of many Puritans. Calling comes only to the elect, and even for them it comes only at the time of God's choosing---there is nothing the elect person can do to prepare himself or herself for the calling. Even the ability to respond to the calling is a gift of the Holy Spirit. The chapter also speaks of persons who die in infancy (an important issue in early modern societies with a high infant mortality rate), the elect among whom God will save in a way of his choosing. The discussion of infant deaths contains no mention of the sacrament of baptism, in line with the generally secondary role the sacraments play in Reformed theology. (A discussion of the Sacraments does not occur until chapter XXVII.) This chapter also answers the question of whether virtuous persons who are non-Christian can be saved with a firm no.

♦ **Chapter XI**

Chapter XI reaffirms the fundamental Reformation doctrine of justification by faith. There are several important qualifications. Faith is a gift from God to the elect for Christ's sake and not something that can ever be attained by a person's own efforts. Faith is accompanied by other graces, even though these graces are irrelevant to salvation. Once they are saved, the elect can never lose that salvation, but God might still punish them for particular sins.

♦ **Chapter XII**

This chapter describes the glory of the elect in heaven through the metaphor of "adoption," which had a long Christian history. The idea of the elect becoming children of God and his love for them helps soften the stern and arbitrary image of God that is common in Reformed theology.

♦ **Chapter XIII**

Although the Reformed tradition proclaims that works do not matter in salvation, that does not mean that there is no distinction between the saved and unsaved in terms of their behavior. "Sanctification" is the process whereby the elect are changed in this life through the infusion of God's goodness and holiness in them. Although Grace frees the elect from the bondage of sin, in this life they are never entirely freed. The ability to struggle against sinful nature and sometimes to win comes not from one's own strength or virtue but solely from the power of God.

♦ **Chapter XIV**

This chapter discusses the origin and impact of saving faith. The Confession is careful not to limit the ways in which faith comes into the hearts of the saved but emphasizes the most common routes by which it enters and is strengthened—preaching (the "Ministry of the Word") prayer, and sacraments. True faith is followed by obedience to God, though not all the saved are obedient to the same degree. "Strong" and "weak" faith, however, are both saving faith.

♦ **Chapter XV**

Saving faith is also followed by repentance. Since everyone is a vile and filthy sinner, everyone with faith should also be struck by horror at the sins they have committed. The article suggests that while in itself repentance cannot save, it should be felt by every saved person. Confessing one's sins is appropriate, but the article is careful not to follow the Catholic model of treating confession to a priest as a sacrament. Confession should be made to God or to the person or community offended or to the Church at large, but the ministry is not mentioned as playing any role in hearing people's confessions.

♦ **Chapter XVI**

This chapter deals with the complicated topic of good works. The Westminster Assembly, like other Reformed Christians, had to thread a narrow passage between the "Catholic" idea that good works contribute to salvation and the "antinomian" idea that good works are completely irrelevant to the saved. The writers emphasize the importance of good works in glorifying Christ while insisting that the ability to do good works does not come out of our own strength but is instead a gift of God. Once again, they declare that good works are irrelevant to salvation. However, only the saved can do truly good works; even what seem to be the virtuous deeds of the unsaved are not inspired by the right motives or done in the right way and are therefore not truly good works at all.

♦ Chapter XVII

The "Perseverance of the Saints," one of the Five Points of Calvinism, is the belief that God's decree of election will never be undone—that the saved person is saved forever. This doctrine could be a powerful source of spiritual comfort for those who thought themselves children of God. However, saved people could still sin grievously, thereby meriting some kind of chastisement from God delivered in this world.

♦ Chapter XVIII

The assurance of salvation was often a difficult problem for Puritans, who wanted to be assured of their own salvation but also wanted it to be the right kind of assurance, caused by knowledge of God's grace rather than vain hope or overconfidence. In fact, being too certain of one's own salvation could be viewed as evidence that one was not truly saved. The Westminster Confession describes the process by which the elect come to be convinced of their salvation while assuring its readers that doubts and occasional weakening of one's assurance do not mean that one has "lost" it.

Audience

The audience for the Westminster Confession was one of professional theologians, ministers, and the educated laity. Other documents produced by the Assembly, the Larger and Shorter Catechisms, distilled the Confession's teachings in a manner appropriate for ordinary unlearned Christians. The Confession continues to be read by theologians and historians, and books interpreting it are popular among some lay Christians, particularly with the revival of Reformed theology in the twenty-first century.

Impact

Although the Westminster Confession was designed for the reformation of the Church of England, it ultimately had little impact on that body. After the fall of the parliamentary regime and the restoration of the monarchy and the bishops of the Church of England in 1660, the Church moved steadily away from the Calvinism of the Confession. The Westminster Confession's principal impact was on the Church of Scotland, other Scottish Presbyterian churches, and English Dissenting churches, particularly the Presbyterians. Congregationalists and Particular Baptists also accepted many aspects of Reformed theology, if not Presbyterian church order; although the specifically Presbyterian components of the Westminster Confession prevented them from adopting it in toto, statements of faith such as the Congregationalist Savoy Declaration of Faith and Order (1658) and the Particular Baptist Confession of Faith (1689) drew heavily from the Westminster Confession.

From the seventeenth to the nineteenth centuries, the reach of the Westminster Confession grew along with that of the British Empire, as Presbyterian, Congregational, and other Reformed churches in the English-speaking world adopted it in whole or in part as a statement of their faith, including churches in Canada, Australia, and New Zealand. As the former British colonies in North America became independent, the Westminster Confession, like many aspects of the British religious tradition, remained a powerful force in shaping the new nation's religion and has been adopted by many American churches. The Presbyterian Synod of Philadelphia adopted it in 1729, followed by the first official Presbyterian denomination in the newly independent United States, the Presbyterian Church of the United States, in 1788. However, the document has been substantially modified to weaken the power of the state over religious belief in the direction of liberty of conscience. A clause denouncing the pope as Antichrist (not reproduced in this excerpt) is also omitted or repudiated by most modern Presbyterians. For America's largest Presbyterian denomination, the Presbyterian Church (USA), the Westminster Confession has been supplanted by the Confession of 1967, although the Westminster Confession, along with the Westminster Larger and Shorter Catechisms, is included in the Church's Book of Confessions. The Presbyterian Church in America, which broke off from the Presbyterian Church (USA) in part as a response to the theological liberalism it identified in the Confession of 1967, continues to use the Westminster Confession with modifications as its standard, as do many other more conservative Presbyterian bodies.

Further Reading

■ Books

Coffey, John. *Politics, Religion and the British Revolutions: The Mind of Samuel Rutherford*. New York: Cambridge University Press, 1997.

Leith, John H. *Assembly at Westminster: Reformed Theology in the Making*. Richmond, Va.: John Knox Press, 1973.

Letham, Robert. *The Westminster Assembly: Reading Its Theology in Historical Context*. Phillipsburg, N.J.: P & R Publications, 2009.

Rolston, Holmes. *John Calvin versus the Westminster Confession*. Richmond, Va.: John Knox Press, 1972.

■ Web Sites

Center for Reformed Theology and Apologetics Web site. http://www.reformed.org/index.html

—Commentary by William E. Burns

"The authority of the holy Scripture, for which it ought to be believed and obeyed, dependeth not upon the testimony of any man or Church, but wholly upon God (who is truth itself), the Author thereof; and therefore it is to be received, because it is the Word of God."

(Section 1)

"God from all eternity did by the most wise and holy counsel of his own will, freely and unchangeably ordain whatsoever comes to pass; yet so as thereby neither is God the author of sin; nor is violence offered to the will of the creatures, nor is the liberty or contingency of second causes taken away, but rather established."

(Section 1)

"This effectual call is of God's free and special grace alone, not from any thing at all foreseen in man, who is altogether passive therein, until, being quickened and renewed by the Holy Spirit, he is thereby enabled to answer this call, and to embrace the grace offered and conveyed in it."

(Section 1)

"God did, from all eternity, decree to justify the elect; and Christ did, in the fullness of time, die for their sins and rise again for their justification; nevertheless they are not justified until the Holy Spirit doth, in due time, actually apply Christ unto them."

(Section 1)

"As there is no sin so small but it deserves damnation; so there is no sin so great that it can bring damnation upon those who truly repent."

(Section 1)

"They whom God hath accepted in his Beloved, effectually called and sanctified by his Spirit, can neither totally nor finally fall away from the state of grace; but shall certainly persevere therein to the end, and be eternally saved."

(Section 1)

Questions for Further Study

1. Calvinism bears the reputation of being a harsh, dark form of Christianity. How do you think it acquired this reputation?

2. During the seventeenth century, the boundary between politics and religion was often blurred—and, in fact, was often nonexistent. What effects did this merging of politics and religion have, particularly on the British Isles?

3. In what ways did the doctrines of the Reformed churches differ from those of Catholicism? Why were the writers of the Westminster Confession opposed to Catholicism?

4. What similarities, if any, can you find between the doctrines expressed in the Westminster Confession and those expressed in either Martin Luther's *Ninety-five Theses* or John Bunyan's *Pilgrim's Progress?*

5. Why do you think the Church of England distanced itself from the positions of Calvinism?

John Calvin by Holbein.

Westminster Confession: Document Text

1646 CE

—John Calvin

CHAPTER I.

♦ Of the holy Scripture.

I. Although the light of nature, and the works of creation and providence, do so far manifest the goodness, wisdom, and power of God, as to leave men inexcusable; yet are they not sufficient to give that knowledge of God, and of his will, which is necessary unto salvation; therefore it pleased the Lord, at sundry times, and in divers manners, to reveal himself, and to declare that his will unto his Church; and afterwards for the better preserving and propagating of the truth, and for the more sure establishment and comfort of the Church against the corruption of the flesh, and the malice of Satan and of the world, to commit the same wholly unto writing; which maketh the holy Scripture to be most necessary; those former ways of God's revealing his will unto his people being now ceased.

II. Under the name of holy Scripture, or the Word of God written, are now contained all the Books of the Old and New Testament, which are these:

Of the Old Testament:

Genesis
Exodus
Leviticus
Numbers
Deuteronomy
Joshua
Judges
Ruth
I Samuel
II Samuel
I Kings
II Kings
I Chronicles
II Chronicles
Ezra
Nehemiah
Esther
Job
Psalms
Proverbs
Ecclesiastes
The Song of Songs
Isaiah
Jeremiah
Lamentations
Ezekiel
Daniel
Hosea
Joel
Amos
Obadiah
Jonah
Micah
Nahum
Habakkuk
Zephaniah
Haggai
Zechariah
Malachi

Of the New Testament:

The Gospels according to
Matthew
Mark
Luke
John
The Acts of the Apostles
Paul's Epistles to the Romans
Corinthians I
Corinthians II
Galatians
Ephesians
Philippians
Colossians
Thessalonians I
Thessalonians II
Timothy I
Timothy II
Titus
Philemon

The Epistle to the
Hebrews
The Epistle of James
The First and Second
Epistles of Peter
The First, Second, and
Third Epistles of John
The Epistle of Jude
The Revelation

All which are given by inspiration of God, to be the rule of faith and life.

III. The books commonly called Apocrypha, not being of divine inspiration, are no part of the Canon of Scripture; and therefore are of no authority in the Church of God, nor to be any otherwise approved, or made use of, than other human writings.

IV. The authority of the holy Scripture, for which it ought to be believed and obeyed, dependeth not upon the testimony of any man or Church, but wholly upon God (who is truth itself), the Author thereof; and therefore it is to be received, because it is the Word of God.

V. We may be moved and induced by the testimony of the Church to an high and reverent esteem of the holy Scripture; and the heavenliness of the matter, the efficacy of the doctrine, the majesty of the style, the consent of all the parts, the scope of the whole (which is to give all glory to God), the full discovery it makes of the only way of man's salvation, the many other incomparable excellencies, and the entire perfection thereof, are arguments whereby it doth abundantly evidence itself to be the Word of God; yet, notwithstanding, our full persuasion and assurance of the infallible truth and divine authority thereof, is from the inward work of the Holy Spirit, bearing witness by and with the Word in our hearts.

VI. The whole counsel of God, concerning all things necessary for his own glory, man's salvation, faith, and life, is either expressly set down in Scripture, or by good and necessary consequence may be deduced from Scripture: unto which nothing at any time is to be added, whether by new revelations of the Spirit, or traditions of men. Nevertheless we acknowledge the inward illumination of the Spirit of God to be necessary for the saving understanding of such things as are revealed in the Word; and that there are some circumstances concerning the worship of God, and the government of the Church, common to human actions and societies, which are to be ordered by the light of nature and Christian prudence, according to the general rules of the Word, which are always to be observed.

VII. All things in Scripture are not alike plain in themselves, nor alike clear unto all; yet those things which are necessary to be known, believed, and observed, for salvation, are so clearly propounded and opened in some place of Scripture or other, that not only the learned, but the unlearned, in a due use of the ordinary means, may attain unto a sufficient understanding of them.

VIII. The Old Testament in Hebrew (which was the native language of the people of God of old), and the New Testament in Greek (which at the time of the writing of it was most generally known to the nations), being immediately inspired by God, and by his singular care and providence kept pure in all ages, are therefore authentical; so as in all controversies of religion the Church is finally to appeal unto them. But because these original tongues are not known to all the people of God who have right unto, and interest in, the Scriptures, and are commanded, in the fear of God, to read and search them, therefore they are to be translated into the vulgar language of every nation unto which they come, that the Word of God dwelling plentifully in all, they may worship him in an acceptable manner, and, through patience and comfort of the Scriptures, may have hope.

IX. The infallible rule of interpretation of Scripture, is the Scripture itself; and therefore, when there is a question about the true and full sense of any scripture (which is not manifold, but one), it may be searched and known by other places that speak more clearly.

X. The Supreme Judge, by which all controversies of religion are to be determined, and all decrees of councils, opinions of ancient writers, doctrines of men, and private spirits, are to be examined, and in whose sentence we are to rest, can be no other but the Holy Spirit speaking in the Scripture.

CHAPTER II.

♦ Of God, and of the Holy Trinity.

I. There is but one only living and true God, who is infinite in being and perfection, a most pure spirit, invisible, without body, parts, or passions, immutable, immense, eternal, incomprehensible, almighty, most wise, most holy, most free, most absolute, working all things according to the counsel of his own immutable and most righteous will, for his own glory, most loving, gracious, merciful, long-suffering, abundant in goodness and truth, forgiving iniquity, transgression, and sin; the rewarder of them that diligently seek him; and withal most just and terrible in his judgments; hating all sin; and who will by no means clear the guilty.

II. God hath all life, glory, goodness, blessedness, in and of himself; and is alone in and unto himself all-sufficient, not standing in need of any creatures which he hath made, nor deriving any glory from them, but only manifesting his own glory in, by, unto, and upon them; he is the alone foundation of all being, of whom, through whom, and to whom, are all things; and hath most sovereign dominion over them, to do by them, for them, or upon them, whatsoever himself pleaseth. In his sight all things are open and manifest; his knowledge is infinite, infallible, and independent upon the creature; so as nothing is to him contingent or uncertain. He is most holy in all his counsels, in all his works, and in all his commands. To him is due from angels and men, and every other creature, whatsoever worship, service, or obedience he is pleased to require of them.

III. In the unity of the Godhead there be three Persons of one substance, power, and eternity: God the Father, God the Son, and God the Holy Ghost. The Father is of none, neither begotten nor proceeding; the Son is eternally begotten of the Father; the Holy Ghost eternally proceeding from the Father and the Son.

CHAPTER III.

♦ Of God's Eternal Decree.

I. God from all eternity did by the most wise and holy counsel of his own will, freely and unchangeably ordain whatsoever comes to pass; yet so as thereby neither is God the author of sin; nor is violence offered to the will of the creatures, nor is the liberty or contingency of second causes taken away, but rather established.

II. Although God knows whatsoever may or can come to pass, upon all supposed conditions; yet hath he not decreed any thing because he foresaw it as future, as that which would come to pass, upon such conditions.

III. By the decree of God, for the manifestation of his glory, some men and angels are predestinated unto everlasting life, and others foreordained to everlasting death.

IV. These angels and men, thus predestinated and foreordained, are particularly and unchangeably designed; and their number is so certain and definite that it can not be either increased or diminished.

V. Those of mankind that are predestinated unto life, God, before the foundation of the world was laid, according to his eternal and immutable purpose, and the secret counsel and good pleasure of his will, hath chosen in Christ, unto everlasting glory, out of his free grace and love alone, without any foresight of faith or good works, or perseverance in either of them, or any other thing in the creature, as conditions, or causes moving him thereunto; and all to the praise of his glorious grace.

VI. As God hath appointed the elect unto glory, so hath he, by the eternal and most free purpose of his will, foreordained all the means thereunto. Wherefore they who are elected being fallen in Adam are redeemed by Christ, are effectually called unto faith in Christ by his Spirit working in due season; are justified, adopted, sanctified, and kept by his power through faith unto salvation. Neither are any other redeemed by Christ, effectually called, justified, adopted, sanctified, and saved, but the elect only.

VII. The rest of mankind, God was pleased, according to the unsearchable counsel of his own will, whereby he extendeth or withholdeth mercy as he pleaseth, for the glory of his sovereign power over his creatures, to pass by, and to ordain them to dishonor and wrath for their sin, to the praise of his glorious justice.

VIII. The doctrine of this high mystery of predestination is to be handled with special prudence and care, that men attending to the will of God revealed in his Word, and yielding obedience thereunto, may, from the certainty of their effectual vocation, be assured of their eternal election. So shall this doctrine afford matter of praise, reverence, and admiration of God; and of humility, diligence, and abundant consolation to all that sincerely obey the gospel.

CHAPTER IV.

♦ Of Creation.

I. It pleased God the Father, Son, and Holy Ghost, for the manifestation of the glory of his eternal power, wisdom, and goodness, in the beginning, to create or make of nothing the world, and all things therein, whether visible or invisible, in the space of six days, and all very good.

II. After God had made all other creatures, he created man, male and female, with reasonable and immortal souls, endued with knowledge, righteousness, and true holiness after his own image, having the law of God written in their hearts, and power to fulfill it; and yet under a possibility of transgressing, being left to the liberty of their own will, which was subject unto change. Besides this law written in their hearts, they received a command not to eat of the tree of the knowledge of good and evil; which while they kept were happy in their communion with God, and had dominion over the creatures.

CHAPTER V.

♦ Of Providence.

I. God, the great Creator of all things, doth uphold, direct dispose, and govern all creatures, actions, and things, from the greatest even to the least, by his most wise and holy providence, according to his infallible foreknowledge, and the free and immutable counsel of his own will, to the praise of the glory of his wisdom, power, justice, goodness, and mercy.

II. Although in relation to the foreknowledge and decree of God, the first cause, all things come to pass immutably and infallibly, yet, by the same providence, he ordereth them to fall out according to the nature of second causes, either necessarily, freely, or contingently.

III. God, in his ordinary providence, maketh use of means, yet is free to work without, above, and against them, at his pleasure.

IV. The almighty power, unsearchable wisdom, and infinite goodness of God, so far manifest themselves in his providence, that it extendeth itself even to the first Fall, and all other sins of angels and men, and that not by a bare permission, but such as hath joined with it a most wise and powerful bounding, and otherwise ordering and governing of them, in a manifold dispensation, to his own holy ends; yet so, as the sinfulness thereof proceedeth only from the creature, and not from God; who being most holy and righteous, neither is nor can be the author or approver of sin.

V. The most wise, righteous, and gracious God, doth oftentimes leave for a season his own children to manifold temptations and the corruption of their own hearts, to chastise them for their former sins, or to discover unto them the hidden strength of corruption and deceitfulness of their hearts, that they may be humbled; and to raise them to a more close and constant dependence for their support upon himself, and to make them more watchful against all future occasions of sin, and for sundry other just and holy ends.

VI. As for those wicked and ungodly men whom God, as a righteous judge, for former sins, doth blind and harden; from them he not only withholdeth his grace, whereby they might have been enlightened in their understandings, and wrought upon their hearts; but sometimes also withdraweth the gifts which they had; and exposeth them to such objects as their corruption makes occasion of sin; and withal, gives them over to their own lusts, the temptations of the world, and the power of Satan; whereby it comes to pass that they harden themselves, even under those means which God useth for the softening of others.

VII. As the providence of God doth, in general, reach to all creatures, so, after a most special manner, it taketh care of his Church, and disposeth all things to the good thereof.

CHAPTER VI.

♦ Of the Fall of Man, of Sin, and of the Punishment thereof.

I. Our first parents, begin seduced by the subtlety and temptations of Satan, sinned in eating the forbidden fruit. This their sin God was pleased, according to his wise and holy counsel, to permit, having purposed to order it to his own glory.

II. By this sin they fell from their original righteousness and communion with God, and so became dead in sin, and wholly defiled in all the faculties and parts of soul and body.

III. They being the root of mankind, the guilt of this sin was imputed, and the same death in sin and corrupted nature conveyed to all their posterity, descending from them by original generation.

IV. From this original corruption, whereby we are utterly indisposed, disabled, and made opposite to all good, and wholly inclined to all evil, do proceed all actual transgressions.

V. This corruption of nature, during this life, doth remain in those that are regenerated; and although it be through Christ pardoned and mortified, yet both itself, and all the motions thereof, are truly and properly sin.

VI. Every sin, both original and actual, being a transgression of the righteous law of God, and contrary thereunto, doth, in its own nature, bring guilt upon the sinner, whereby he is bound over to the wrath of God, and curse of the law, and so made subject to death, with all miseries spiritual, temporal, and eternal.

CHAPTER VII.

♦ Of God's Covenant with Man.

I. The distance between God and the creature is so great, that although reasonable creatures do owe obedience unto him as their Creator, yet they could never have any fruition of him, as their blessedness and reward, but by some voluntary condescension on God's part, which he hath been pleased to express by way of covenant.

II. The first covenant made with man was a covenant of works, wherein life was promised to Adam, and in him to his posterity, upon condition of perfect and personal obedience.

III. Man by his fall having made himself incapable of life by that covenant, the Lord was pleased to make a second, commonly called the covenant of grace: wherein he freely offered unto sinners life and salvation by Jesus Christ, requiring of them faith in him, that they may be saved, and promising to give unto all those that are ordained unto life, his Holy Spirit, to make them willing and able to believe.

IV. This covenant of grace is frequently set forth in the Scripture by the name of a testament, in reference to the death of Jesus Christ, the testator, and to the everlasting inheritance, with all things belonging to it, therein bequeathed.

V. This covenant was differently administered in the time of the law, and in the time of the gospel: under the law it was administered by promises, prophecies, sacrifices, circumcision, the paschal lamb, and other types and ordinances delivered to the people of the Jews, all fore-signifying Christ to come, which were for that time sufficient and efficacious, through the operation of the Spirit, to instruct and build up the elect in faith in the promised Messiah, by whom they had full remission of sins, and eternal salvation, and is called the Old Testament.

VI. Under the gospel, when Christ the substance was exhibited, the ordinances in which this covenant is dispensed, are the preaching of the Word, and the administration of the sacraments of Baptism and the Lord's Supper; which, though fewer in number, and administered with more simplicity and less outward glory, yet in them it is held forth in more fullness, evidence, and spiritual efficacy, to all nations, both Jews and Gentiles; and is called the New Testament. There are not, therefore, two covenants of grace differing in substance, but one and the same under various dispensations.

CHAPTER VIII.

♦ Of Christ the Mediator.

I. It pleased God, in his eternal purpose, to choose and ordain the Lord Jesus, his only-begotten Son, to be the Mediator between God and men, the prophet, priest, and king; the head and Savior of the Church, the heir or all things, and judge of the world; unto whom he did, from all eternity, give a people to be his seed, and to be by him in time redeemed, called, justified, sanctified, and glorified.

II. The Son of God, the second Person in the Trinity, being very and eternal God, of one substance, and equal with the Father, did, when the fullness of time was come, take upon him man's nature, with all the essential properties and common infirmities thereof; yet without sin: being conceived by he power of the Holy Ghost, in the womb of the Virgin Mary, of her substance. So that two whole, perfect, and distinct natures, the Godhead and the manhood, were inseparably joined together in one person, without conversion, composition, or confusion. Which person is very God and very man, yet one Christ, the only Mediator between God and man.

III. The Lord Jesus in his human nature thus united to the divine, was sanctified and anointed with the Holy Spirit above measure; having in him all the treasures of wisdom and knowledge, in whom it pleased the Father that all fullness should dwell: to the end that being holy, harmless, undefiled, and full of grace and truth, he might be thoroughly furnished to execute the office of a Mediator and Surety. Which office he took not unto himself, but was thereunto called by his Father; who put all power and judgment into his hand, and gave him commandment to execute the same.

IV. This office the Lord Jesus did most willingly undertake, which, that he might discharge, he was made under the law, and did perfectly fulfill it; endured most grievous torments immediately in his soul, and most painful sufferings in his body; was crucified and died; was buried, and remained under the power of death, yet saw no corruption. On the third day he arose from the dead, with the same body in which he suffered; with which also he ascended into heaven, and there sitteth at the right hand of his Father, making intercession; and shall return to judge men and angels, at the end of the world.

V. The Lord Jesus, by his perfect obedience and sacrifice of himself, which he through the eternal Spirit once offered up unto God, hath fully satisfied the justice of his Father; and purchased not only reconciliation, but an everlasting inheritance in the kingdom of heaven, for all those whom the Father hath given unto him.

VI. Although the work of redemption was not actually wrought by Christ till after his incarnation, yet the virtue, efficacy, and benefits thereof were communicated into the elect, in all ages successively from the beginning of the world, in and by those promises, types, and sacrifices wherein he was revealed, and signified to be the seed of the woman, which should bruise the serpent's head, and the Lamb slain from the beginning of the world, being yesterday and today the same and for ever.

VII. Christ, in the work of mediation, acteth according to both natures; by each nature doing that which is proper to itself; yet by reason of the unity of the person, that which is proper to one nature is sometimes, in Scripture, attributed to the person denominated by the other nature.

VIII. To all those for whom Christ hath purchased redemption, he doth certainly and effectually apply and communicate the same; making intercession for them, and revealing unto them, in and by the Word, the mysteries of salvation; effectually persuading them by his Spirit to believe and obey; and governing their hearts by his Word and Spirit; overcoming all their enemies by his almighty power and wisdom, in such manner and ways as are most consonant to his wonderful and unsearchable dispensation.

CHAPTER IX.

♦ Of Free Will.

I. God hath endued the will of man with that natural liberty, that is neither forced, nor by any absolute necessity of nature determined to good or evil.

II. Man, in his state of innocency, had freedom and power to will and to do that which is good and well-pleasing to God; but yet mutably, so that he might fall from it.

III. Man, by his fall into a state of sin, hath wholly lost all ability of will to any spiritual good accompanying salvation; so as a natural man, being altogether averse from that good, and dead in sin, is not able, by his own strength, to convert himself, or to prepare himself thereunto.

IV. When God converts a sinner and translates him into the state of grace, he freeth him from his natural bondage under sin, and, by his grace alone, enables him freely to will and to do that which is spiritually good; yet so as that, by reason of his remaining corruption, he doth not perfectly, nor only, will that which is good, but doth also will that which is evil.

V. The will of man is made perfectly and immutable free to good alone, in the state of glory only.

CHAPTER X.

♦ Of Effectual Calling.

I. All those whom God hath predestinated unto life, and those only, he is pleased, in his appointed and accepted time, effectually to call, by his Word and Spirit, out of that state of sin and death in which they are by nature, to grace and salvation by Jesus Christ: enlightening their minds, spiritually and savingly, to understand the things of God, taking away their heart of stone, and giving unto them an heart of flesh; renewing their wills, and by his almighty power determining them to that which is good; and effectually drawing them to Jesus Christ; yet so as they come most freely, being made willing by his grace.

II. This effectual call is of God's free and special grace alone, not from any thing at all foreseen in man, who is altogether passive therein, until, being quickened and renewed by the Holy Spirit, he is thereby enabled to answer this call, and to embrace the grace offered and conveyed in it.

III. Elect infants, dying in infancy, are regenerated and saved by Christ through the Spirit, who worketh when, and where, and how he pleaseth. So also are all other elect persons who are incapable of being outwardly called by the ministry of the Word.

IV. Others, not elected, although they may be called by the ministry of the Word, and may have some common operations of the Spirit, yet they never truly come to Christ, and therefore can not be saved: much less can men, not professing the Christian religion, be saved in any other way whatsoever, be they never so diligent to frame their lives according to the light of nature, and the law of that religion they do profess; and to assert and maintain that they may is without warrant of the Word of God.

CHAPTER XI.

♦ Of Justification.

I. Those whom God effectually calleth, he also freely justifieth: not by infusing righteousness into them, but by pardoning their sins, and by accounting and accepting their persons as righteous; not for any thing wrought in them, or done by them, but for

Christ's sake alone; not by imputing faith itself, the act of believing, or any other evangelical obedience to them, as their righteousness; but by imputing the obedience and satisfaction of Christ unto them, they receiving and resting on him and his righteousness by faith; which faith they have not of themselves, it is the gift of God.

II. Faith, thus receiving and resting on Christ and his righteousness, is the alone instrument of justification; yet is it not alone in the person justified, but is ever accompanied with all other saving graces, and is no dead faith, but worketh by love.

III. Christ, by his obedience and death, did fully discharge the debt of all those that are thus justified, and did make a proper, real, and full satisfaction of his Father's justice in their behalf. Yet inasmuch as he was given by the Father for them, and his obedience and satisfaction accepted in their stead, and both freely, not for any thing in them, their justification is only of free grace, that both the exact justice and rich grace of God might be glorified in the justification of sinners.

IV. God did, from all eternity, decree to justify the elect; and Christ did, in the fullness of time, die for their sins and rise again for their justification; nevertheless they are not justified until the Holy Spirit doth, in due time, actually apply Christ unto them.

V. God doth continue to forgive the sins of those that are justified; and although they can never fall from the state of justification, yet they may by their sins fall under God's Fatherly displeasure, and not have the light of his countenance restored unto them, until they humble themselves, confess their sins, beg pardon, and renew their faith and repentance.

VI. The justification of believers under the Old Testament was, in all these respect, one and the same with the justification of believers under the New Testament.

CHAPTER XII.

♦ Of Adoption.

All those that are justified, God vouchsafeth, in and for his only Son Jesus Christ, to make partakers of the grace of adoption: by which they are taken into the number, and enjoy the liberties and privileges of the children of God; have his name put upon them; receive the Spirit of adoption; have access to the throne of grace with boldness; are enabled to cry, Abba, Father; are pitied, protected, provided for, and chastened by his as by a father; yet never cast off,

but sealed to the day of redemption, and inherit the promises, as heirs of everlasting salvation.

CHAPTER XIII.

♦ Of Sanctification.

I. They who are effectually called and regenerated, having a new heart and a new spirit created in them, are further sanctified, really and personally, through the virtue of Christ's death and resurrection, by his Word and Spirit dwelling in them; the dominion of the whole body of sin is destroyed, and the several lusts thereof are more and more weakened and mortified, and they more and more quickened and strengthened, in all saving graces, to the practice of true holiness, without which no man shall see the Lord.

II. This sanctification is throughout in the whole man, yet imperfect in this life: there abideth still some remnants of corruption in every part, whence ariseth a continual and irreconcilable war, the flesh lusting against the Spirit, and the Spirit against the flesh.

III. In which war, although the remaining corruption for a time may much prevail, yet, through the continual supply of strength from the sanctifying Spirit of Christ, the regenerate part doth overcome: and so the saints grow in grace, perfecting holiness in the fear of God.

CHAPTER XIV.

♦ Of Saving Faith.

I. The grace of faith, whereby the elect are enabled to believe to the saving of their souls, is the work of the Spirit of Christ in their hearts; and is ordinarily wrought by the ministry of the Word: by which also, and by the administration of the sacraments, and prayer, it is increased and strengthened.

II. By this faith, a Christian believeth to be true whatsoever is revealed in the Word, for the authority of God himself speaking therein; and acteth differently, upon that which each particular passage thereof containeth; yielding obedience to the commands, trembling at the threatenings, and embracing the promises of God for this life, and that which is to come. But the principle acts of saving faith are, accepting, receiving, and resting upon Christ alone for justification, sanctification, and eternal life, by virtue of the covenant of grace.

III. This faith is different in degrees, weak or strong; may be often and many ways assailed and weakened, but gets the victory; growing up in many to the attainment of a full assurance through Christ, who is both the author and finisher of our faith.

CHAPTER XV.

◆ Of Repentance unto Life.

I. Repentance unto life is an evangelical grace, the doctrine whereof is to be preached by every minister of the gospel, as well as that of faith in Christ.

II. By it a sinner, out of the sight and sense, not only of the danger, but also of the filthiness and odiousness of his sins, as contrary to the holy nature and righteous law of God, and upon the apprehension of his mercy in Christ to such as are penitent, so grieves for, and hates his sins, as to turn from them all unto God, purposing and endeavoring to walk with him in all the ways of his commandments.

III. Although repentance be not to be rested in as any satisfaction for sin, or any cause of the pardon thereof, which is the act of God's free grace in Christ; yet is it of such necessity to all sinners, that none may expect pardon without it.

IV. As there is no sin so small but it deserves damnation; so there is no sin so great that it can bring damnation upon those who truly repent.

V. Men ought not to content themselves with a general repentance, but it is every man's duty to endeavor to repent of his particular sins, particularly.

VI. As every man is bound to make private confession of his sins to God, praying for the pardon thereof, upon which, and the forsaking of them, he shall find mercy: so he that scandalizeth his brother, or the Church of Christ, ought to be willing, by a private or public confession and sorrow for his sin, to declare his repentance to those that are offended; who are thereupon to be reconciled to him, and in love to receive him.

CHAPTER XVI.

◆ Of Good Works.

I. Good works are only such as God hath commanded in his holy Word, and not such as, without the warrant thereof, are devised by men out of blind zeal, or upon any pretense of good intention.

II. These good works, done in obedience to God's commandments, are the fruits and evidences of a true and lively faith: and by them believers manifest their thankfulness, strengthen their assurance, edify their brethren, adorn the profession of the gospel, stop the mouths of the adversaries, and glorify God, whose workmanship they are, created in Christ Jesus thereunto, that, having their fruit unto holiness, they may have the end, eternal life.

III. Their ability to do good works is not at all of themselves, but wholly from the Spirit of Christ. And that they may be enabled thereunto, besides the graces they have already received, there is required an actual influence of the same Holy Spirit to work in them to will and to do of his good pleasure; yet are they not hereupon to grow negligent, as if they were not bound to perform any duty unless upon a special motion of the Spirit; but they ought to be diligent in stirring up the grace of God that is in them.

IV. They, who in their obedience, attain to the greatest height which is possible in this life, are so far from being able to supererogate and to do more than God requires, that they fall short of much which in duty they are bound to do.

V. We can not, by our best works, merit pardon of sin, or eternal life, at the hand of God, because of the great disproportion that is between them and the glory to come, and the infinite distance that is between us and God, whom by them we can neither profit, nor satisfy for the debt of our former sins; but when we have done all we can, we have done but our duty, and are unprofitable servants: and because, as they are good, they proceed from his Spirit; and as they are wrought by us, they are defiled and mixed with so much weakness and imperfection that they can not endure the severity of God's judgment.

VI. Yet notwithstanding, the persons of believers being accepted through Christ, their good works also are accepted in him, not as though they were in this life wholly unblamable and unreprovable in God's sight; but that he, looking upon them in his Son, is pleased to accept and reward that which is sincere, although accompanied with many weaknesses and imperfections.

VII. Works done by unregenerate men, although for the matter of them they may be things which God commands, and of good use both to themselves and others; yet, because they proceed not from a heart purified by faith; nor are done in a right manner, according to the Word; nor to a right end, the glory of God; they are therefore sinful and can not please God, or make a man meet to receive grace from God. And yet their neglect of them is more sinful, and displeasing unto God.

CHAPTER XVII.

♦ Of The Perseverance of the Saints.

I. They whom God hath accepted in his Beloved, effectually called and sanctified by his Spirit, can neither totally nor finally fall away from the state of grace; but shall certainly persevere therein to the end, and be eternally saved.

II. This perseverance of the saints depends, not upon their own free-will, but upon the immutability of the decree of election, flowing from the free and unchangeable love of God the Father; upon the efficacy of the merit and intercession of Jesus Christ; the abiding of the Spirit and of the seed of God within them; and the nature of the covenant of grace; from all which ariseth also the certainty and infallibility thereof.

III. Nevertheless they may, through the temptations of Satan and of the world, the prevalancy of corruption remaining in them, and the neglect of the means of their perseverance, fall into grievous sins; ad for a time continue therein: whereby they incur God's displeasure, and grieve his Holy Spirit; come to be deprived of some measure of their graces and comforts; have their hearts hardened, and their consciences wounded; hurt and prevalancy others, and bring temporal judgments upon themselves.

CHAPTER XVIII.

♦ Of the Assurance of Grace and Salvation.

I. Although hypocrites, and other unregenerate men, may vainly deceive themselves with false hopes and carnal presumptions: of being in the favor of God and estate of salvation; which hope of theirs shall perish: yet such as truly believe in the Lord Jesus, and love him in sincerity, endeavoring to walk in all good conscience before him, may in this life be certainly assured that they are in a state of grace, and may rejoice in the hope of the glory of God: which hope shall never make them ashamed.

II. This certainty is not a bare conjectural and probably persuasion, grounded upon a fallible hope; but an infallible assurance of faith, founded upon the divine truth of the promises of salvation, the inward evidence of those graces unto which these promises are made, the testimony of the Spirit of adoption witnessing with our spirits that we are the children of God; which Spirit is the earnest of our inheritance, whereby we are sealed to the day of redemption.

III. This infallible assurance doth not so belong to the essence of faith but that a true believer may wait long and conflict with many difficulties before he be partaker of it: yet, being enabled by the Spirit to know the things which are freely given him of God, he may, without extraordinary revelation, in the right use of ordinary means, attain thereunto. And therefore it is the duty of everyone to give all diligence to make his calling and election sure; that thereby his heart may be enlarged in peace and joy in the Holy Ghost, in love and thankfulness to God, and in strength and cheerfulness in the duties of obedience, the proper fruits of this assurance: so far is it from inclining men to looseness.

IV. True believers may have the assurance of their salvation divers ways shaken, diminished, and intermitted; as, by negligence in preserving of it; by falling into some special sin, which woundeth the conscience, and grieveth the Spirit; by some sudden or vehement temptation; by God's withdrawing the light of his countenance and suffering even such as fear him to walk in darkness and to have no light: yet are they never utterly destitute of that seed of God, and life of faith, that love of Christ and the brethren, that sincerity of heart and conscience of duty, out of which, by the operation of the Spirit, this assurance may in due time be revived, and by the which, in the meantime, they are supported from utter despair.

Abba:	a name infrequently used in the Bible to refer to God the Father
Apocrypha:	any of the various Bible-like books that, for various reasons, are not accepted as scriptural
divers:	diverse, assorted
justification:	in Christian theology, God's act of declaring or making a sinner righteous before God
Lamb:	Christ
paschal lamb:	a lamb the Israelites were to eat with particular rites as a part of the Passover celebration; generally regarded as a prefigurement of Christ
supererogate:	to perform more than a required duty or more than is asked for
Surety:	guarantor; in Christian theology, the concept that Christ functioned as a surety for undeserving sinners by dying for their sins
vouchsafeth:	to grant a right, benefit, or outcome

William Blake: Christian Reading in His Book (Plate 2, 1824–27).

THE PILGRIM'S PROGRESS: DOCUMENT ANALYSIS

"...the man put his fingers in his ears, and ran on crying, Life! life! eternal life!"

Overview

John Bunyan , a self-educated Puritan preacher, wrote his classic book *The Pilgrim's Progress from This World to That Which Is to Come* while he was in jail in 1675 for refusing to conform to the official Church of England. The book, an allegory describing the journey of a Christian from this world to the next, gives a vivid picture of the religious beliefs of Bunyan and other Nonconformists, who rejected the teaching of the state church. In the first part of *Pilgrim's Progress*, written originally to stand alone, Christian, the titular hero, becomes increasingly convinced that he and his community are under a sentence of judgment. Unable to persuade anyone else to flee destruction with him, he sets off alone on a journey to salvation. The second part tells the story of Christian's wife, Christiana, and their children on the same difficult journey.

Pilgrim's Progress, first published in 1678, is a Puritan sermon in the form of a novel, using powerful and charming storytelling to teach the lesson that the world is the venue for the battle of spiritual forces and that victory comes only through denying the world to seek salvation. Bunyan's writings, of which *Pilgrim's Progress* is far and away the best known, allowed him to reach a huge audience despite his incarceration. His account of a religious "everyman" made him a celebrity in his own day and has inspired countless people ever since.

Context

The English Civil War, a series of three armed conflicts (1641–1651), pitted not only Cavaliers (supporters of the king) against Roundheads (supporters of Parliament), or believers in absolutist monarchy by divine right against those who championed some form of constitutional government, it also pitted the official Anglican religious settlement against the religion of the Puritans (Protestants who preferred a more rigorous and Bible-centered faith). Nonconformists, or Dissenters, as Puritans who rejected the Anglican Church were known, formed the backbone of the parliamentary armies led by Oliver Cromwell, which eventually overthrew the monarchy. During the Commonwealth (1649–1660), while first Cromwell and then his son presided over the government, Dissenters were free to practice their religion as they chose.

Shortly after Cromwell's death, England welcomed back Charles II (r. 1660–1685) and, with him, a renewed Anglican settlement. The Restoration government moved quickly and severely against Dissenters, demanding full allegiance to the Church of England, or the Anglican Church. Official Anglicanism had wealth, resources, facilities, and educated clergy. Dissenting churches made do without any of these advantages, and the costs of resistance were high enough that most Dissenters were drawn from the uneducated and poor working classes. Some became involved in political schemes to overthrow Charles or, later, his brother James II (r. 1685–1688). Eventually Dissenters would play a prominent role in ousting the Catholic James for the Protestant Mary and her Dutch Protestant husband William in the Glorious Revolution of 1688. Other Dissenters would leave England for places of refuge such as the New World (as the Pilgrims had done before the English Civil War). But most remained at home and avoided politics as best they could, worshiping according to their beliefs and living with the consequences.

John Bunyan participated personally in all the great happenings of his time. Although he was not yet a committed Puritan, as a teenager he served in the Parliamentary army toward the end of the English Civil War. Later, during the Commonwealth, he experienced his conversion, and used the freedom of that era to become a Dissenting preacher. Like many other Noncomformists, he experienced persecution under the Restoration

THE PILGRIM'S PROGRESS: DOCUMENT ANALYSIS • 1053

government. Bunyan himself spent more than twelve years in jail for preaching without a license. He died just before England's Glorious Revolution allowed some measure of freedom to those who shared his religious beliefs. Yet the ideas about faith he taught in *Pilgrim's Progress*, along with the general English experience on Nonconformity, would contribute toward shaping English views about freedom, government, and the intersection of church and state, not only in Britain but in the United States as well.

About the Author

The English writer and preacher John Bunyan was born in Harrowden in Bedfordshire on November 30, 1628, to an extremely poor family. He received only a minimal education and followed his father into trade as a brazier before he went on to serve in the Parliamentary army during the English Civil War. It was his marriage after the end of military service that changed Bunyan's life. His wife brought as her only dowry two religious texts. Reading those books focused Bunyan's thoughts increasingly on his own spiritual condition and eventually led to what he recognized as a conversion in 1653. A handful of other books, particularly the Bible, the Anglican Book of Common Prayer, and John Foxe's account of the Christian martyrs through history, *Actes and Monuments* (more commonly known as *The Book of Martyrs*), played an important role in Bunyan's self-education. In 1655 he was baptized and received into the Baptist Church.

Bunyan's faith took a public role in religious matters when he began to dispute with local Quakers in 1656; this led to increasing involvement in ministry and finally a call to serve a local Independent congregation as pastor. Under the Commonwealth it was possible for self-proclaimed preachers to lead congregations. With the Restoration of both Charles II and the Anglican Church, however, the government began to move against unlicensed preachers. Bunyan refused to conform to the Church of England and was jailed in 1660. His first period of imprisonment lasted (with occasional interruptions) for twelve years. The confinement was lax, giving him opportunities to write. It was probably during this period that Bunyan began to plan *Pilgrim's Progress*, though he did not begin the writing process until later—certainly he was busy enough turning out his autobiography (*Grace Abounding to the Chief of Sinners*) and other books, pamphlets, sermons, and poetry.

Upon release, Bunyan immediately renewed his career as a pastor, serving a congregation until he was arrested and jailed again in 1675. It was during the following brief stint in prison that he wrote the first part of *Pilgrim's Progress*, although the work was not published for three more years. In 1684 he published the second half of the work. Bunyan's second jail term lasted only six months, and his increasing reputation and popularity protected him from further trouble. He was even offered royal patronage by James II,

Time Line	
November 30, 1628	■ John Bunyan is born in Harrowden in Bedfordshire, England.
1649	■ The English Commonwealth begins.
1651	■ The English Civil War ends.
1655	■ Bunyan experiences a conversion and is baptized and received into the Baptist Church.
1657	■ Bunyan begins his career as a preacher.
1660	■ The end of the Commonwealth brings about the Restoration under Charles II.
1660	■ Bunyan is imprisoned for the first time in Bedford Jail, a confinement that lasts until 1672.
1666	■ Bunyan writes his autobiography, *Grace Abounding to the Chief of Sinners*.
1675	■ Bunyan is imprisoned again in Bedford Jail, where he writes *Pilgrim's Progress*.
1678	■ *Pilgrim's Progress* is published.
1682	■ *The Holy War* is published.
1684	■ The second part of *Pilgrim's Progress* is published.
1685	■ Charles II dies, and James II ascends to the throne.
August 31, 1688	■ Bunyan dies.
1688	■ The Glorious Revolution brings William and Mary to the throne and establishes limited religious freedom for Dissenters.
1692	■ Bunyan's last work, the anti-Catholic *Of Antichrist and His Ruin*, is published.

but Bunyan's religious convictions caused him to refuse the post. He continued writing and preaching until his death on August 31, 1688.

Explanation and Analysis of the Document

The first part of *Pilgrim's Progress* tells the story of Christian's journey from his Native City of Destruction to the Heavenly City. Bunyan presents the trip, meant to represent the life of each Christian, as both ordinary and exciting. The pilgrim on life's journey will encounter fields and towns, friends and neighbors. The pilgrim will also encounter dangerous swamps, monsters, and wild animals. Since the world pilgrims travel through is the meeting place of physical and supernatural life, both the ordinary elements of human experience and encounters with the extraordinary are normal parts of Christian's journey to salvation. The document produced here tells of the beginning of Christian's journey. The style, the imagery, and the constant biblical allusions in the text are typical of the whole work.

♦ As I Walked through the Wilderness of This World

After an introduction in verse, Bunyan sets the stage for his story by describing it as the dream of the author; the author will not reawake until the final line of part 1. As a writer, Bunyan is known for his rich uses of imagery—imagery drawn heavily from the Authorized Version of the Bible. In this opening paragraph, for instance, the description of the future pilgrim is taken from scripture. "Filthy rags" are how the prophet Isaiah describes human attempts to please God; the Psalmist speaks of sins as a "heavy burden… too heavy for me." Similarly, the despairing cry "What shall I do?" is an echo of several biblical passages. The sorrow, as the main character will soon relate, is a sense of impending judgment due for his own sins and the sins of his community. Such sorrow is a natural and appropriate response to encountering God's truth, as the future pilgrim does when he reads his book (the Bible).

♦ In This Plight, Therefore, He Went Home

Bunyan's description of the future pilgrim's dilemma is a reflection of the differing understandings of salvation promoted by the state church (Church of England) and Bunyan's own beliefs. The Church of England did not see society itself under judgment, taught that salvation lay in taking one's appropriate place in society, and emphasized the communal rather than the individual aspects of salvation. Furthermore, the path to salvation offered through the Anglican Church was seen as the default position for any in the community who did not specifically reject it—no one need worry too much about being saved. Independents and other Puritans like Bunyan, however, understood society to be at odds with God. Salvation came only through rejecting society and its religious values and committing one's self entirely to God. Although Bunyan's version of Puritanism had strong communal implications (in part 2 of *Pilgrim's Progress*, Christiana and her children travel together), there was an important individual component to religion. Underlying this stance was the assumption, in contrast to Anglicanism, that every person was lost *unless* he or she converted. The difference between the two positions is typical of a division in Western religiosity classified by sociologists as "church" versus "sect."

The mocking and derision the future pilgrim experienced would have been very familiar to Bunyan's audience. Bunyan himself was in jail when he wrote *Pilgrim's Progress*, and all Nonconformists faced significant penalties—socially, economically, and legally—for rejecting the state church in favor of their own religious beliefs. Adherence to a Dissenting congregation might even mean alienation from family and friends. It was this contempt that Puritans received from the world for their beliefs that strengthened the Puritan notion that the world itself was lost. Certainly the pressure to give up Dissenting beliefs and values taught the Puritans that the battles between good and evil over the destiny of souls were to be fought out in the world.

Bunyan has the first step in the journey to salvation begin with personal anguish. For Puritans, salvation required a strong sense of individual sin and unworthiness. Only those recognizing their sinfulness could turn to God for forgiveness and mercy. It was typical of Puritan values that a decision for conversion only followed many hours of reflection and consideration. While some of their modern-day heirs understand conversion as an instant, once-and-for-all occurrence, for Puritans it was a process involving time and multiple stages.

The phrase (odd to modern ears) "children of my bowels" reflects Bunyan's own familiarity with the Authorized Version of the Bible. The original Greek of the New Testament does indeed use the word correctly translated in the Authorized Version as "bowels" to describe what modern translations render in different places as "heart" or "feeling." Modern Western people usually make the heart the seat of human emotion. The ancients gave that role to the stomach. It is the stomach that receives the rush of acid, for instance, with some strong emotions or that churns with anxiety or hurts during times of stress. The main character is simply adapting a literary expression to describe how dear his children are to him.

♦ Now I Saw… [Him] Reading His Book, and Greatly Distressed in Mind

The importance of reading in the main character's conversion reflects Bunyan's own experience—his conversion was prompted by two books of his wife's. Of course, the book here in the story later proves to be the Bible, the chief source of inspiration for Bunyan, as for all good Puritans. But even these Bible-centered Protestants did not reject the help of other forms of literature. *Pilgrim's Progress* itself was meant to be one of the books that helped Pilgrims on their way.

Evangelist is the first character to be introduced by name. In Bunyan's story, the character of every person met in the pages is revealed by his or her name. Technically speaking, an Evangelist was one of the authors of the four Gospels (Matthew, Mark, Luke, and John), but Bunyan uses the name in the modern sense. Evangelist is someone who can tell the main character about salvation ("the Gospel" or "the Good News"). The future pilgrim has worked out his need for salvation on his own but requires someone to direct him on the path. Evangelist does not take him to salvation or plot the whole journey but merely points him in the right direction.

Notice that up to this point in the story the main character does not have a name. His character has not yet been defined. Only after he makes an important decision can his true nature be revealed by the name he is given. This encounter between Evangelist and the main character emphasizes the individualistic aspect of the Puritan understanding of salvation. To obtain eternal life, the pilgrim must be willing to leave other kinds of life (family life, public life) behind. Underlying Bunyan's beliefs was the conviction that "the world" (society, community, the established order) was opposed to God's will and a hindrance to salvation. One must choose between the world's way and God's way.

At the same time, Puritan religion was communal as well as individualistic. At some point each individual must make a personal decision, but such decisions are not made in isolation. There is no salvation for the main character with Evangelist to point the way. At critical times in the story other individuals appear or reappear to keep the pilgrim on the path. The corporate nature of pilgrim life is emphasized more strongly in the second part of the book, where the pilgrims travel in a group.

The description of the meeting between Evangelist and the main character is a classic depiction of Puritan values. Human sin and its deserved condemnation are self-evident, and many people in the course of life might become aware of them. However, some who recognize their own faults and know they need to be saved might, by society's pressure, decide to ignore their convictions. It is only when the sense of sin is too strong to ignore that the individual is willing to pursue relief. The main character is at this point not saved but a seeker after salvation. And to seek, he must leave his community behind.

♦ **The Neighbors Also Came Out**
The decision to set out on the road to salvation is a momentous one. Only now can the pilgrim be called by his appropriate name, Christian. While the state church would have claimed that all those living in the city of Destruction (which Christian has just fled) were Christians, for the Puritans real Christians were those who were aware of their own sin and who turned to God for salvation.

The experience of opposition was an important part of Puritan self-understanding. Since the world was lost and under judgment, one could expect only opposition from those who lived in it. In the case of Christian, there is gen-

eral contempt and specific opposition from the characters Obstinate and Pliable. Obstinate questions the pilgrim, allowing Christian to describe something of his hope for salvation, words that only bring derision on "the book." Obstinate calls for the pilgrim to give up his silliness and come home, while Pliable proves more open to the message. Ultimately Pliable resolves to travel with the pilgrim, while Obstinate turns back in disgust. It is probably not a good sign for Pliable's future as a pilgrim that he is more attracted to the journey by the joys of heaven than by the conviction of his own sin.

Bunyan's short description of the responses of Christian's neighbors hints at three types of opposition Nonconforming Christians experienced. The first was simple rejection, characterized by mockery—the sort of reaction Bunyan highlights in the story. The second, perhaps implied in the phrase "some cried after him to return," was a more serious effort to persuade Dissenters to abandon their peculiar religious ideas. Mr. Worldly Wiseman, who appears later in the reading, provides one example of this sort as he tries to talk Christian into losing his burden in Morality. The final type of opposition is implied in the attempt "to fetch him back by force." The state church possessed great power from the government to compel conformity. Bunyan himself, of course, wrote *Pilgrim's Progress* while he was in jail for preaching without a license, a license that never would have been issued to him. The amount of legal trouble Dissenters faced varied from place to place and time to time. There were districts and periods where Nonconformists were generally ignored, while on other occasions they might face strict persecution. Even after 1688, though, when the freedom of Protestants to worship was generally allowed, Nonconformists faced severe legal limitations in terms of careers and education. When Bunyan describes the world as actively hostile to Puritan Christians, he is doing no more than recounting a reality he and most Nonconformists experienced.

♦ **Now I Saw in My Dream, That When Obstinate Was Gone Back**
Christian and Pliable travel together while Christian gives more details about the glorious future awaiting believers in heaven. Their conversation demonstrates that the book Christian carries with him is indeed the Bible, a sure source of knowledge about spiritual realities. Although Christian is eager to hurry down the path to the Heavenly City, he finds himself slowed by the burden of sin he still carries on his back like a pack.

The "Slough of Despond" is one of Bunyan's most famous images. Like that of any good allegorical figure, its rich complexity defies simple characterization, but among other things it is a swamp that traps people who are beginning their pilgrimage to the Heavenly City. The Slough itself stains and defiles, and in it the weight of sin is even more burdensome. It is ultimately revealed that the swamp is created from the discouragement that attends an awareness of personal sin. Although it is a trap or hazard on the path to salvation, it is one that cannot be completely mended, because the sorrow and fear created by an awareness of sin is natural (and even necessary) for those seeking to escape judgment.

Even if the Slough cannot ever be entirely drained, it should not be the great obstacle that it is. Here Bunyan is making a typical Puritan complaint against both the Catholic Church and the Anglican Church. Like a monarch ordering his highways to be maintained, God had commanded the road through the Slough to be repaired and provided much teaching to help Christians avoid being caught in the swamp of discouragement and self-doubt, yet these lessons had been mishandled, leaving many stuck in the mire. With appropriate instruction, a believer should be able to find God's firm path through the dangerous slough. This is the fault of the state church, which neglects its essential functions and fails to teach important truths to its adherents, leaving pilgrims to find their own way down the difficult road to salvation.

Despite the hardships, Christian fights his way through the swamp, with the aid of the character Help—yet another reminder of the corporate aspect of Puritan faith. Christian needs others to give him a hand up from the swamp and to point him to the right path. But Pliable, who was so eager to experience the joys of the Heavenly City, is overwhelmed by the challenges of the journey and turns away. Christian continues on his way.

♦ Now I Saw in My Dream That by This Time Pliable Was Got Home

Bunyan's audience would have been very familiar with individuals who had temporarily associated themselves with Dissenting congregations and then returned to the state church. The story of Pliable served as a cautionary tale. Those who went back to their old ways were likely to get just as much grief from their neighbors as if they had remained true, yet they would also miss out on heaven. In fact, since Pliable is around to be derided by his neighbors while Christian has moved on, Pliable may be even be worse off in the present life, just as he will certainly be worse off in the future one.

♦ Now as Christian Was Walking Solitary

Christian continues on his journey and encounters a new figure, a man who has advice for him. The pilgrim has set out on the road to the Heavenly City in order to have the burden lifted from his back. Mr. Worldly Wiseman suggests that there are easier ways to remove the burden, ways that do not involve hardship, danger, or the loss of his family and community standing.

From a Puritan perspective, images of morality and civility promoted by society and the Church of England were traps. As Puritans understood the Bible, human effort ("keeping the law") could not save people from God's judgment. To them, much of what the state church offered was a reliance on human effort, helping people to feel better about themselves so that they no longer noticed their burden of sin but not actually providing salvation. The Puritans saw such teaching as a medicine that masked a patient's

symptoms without curing the deadly disease. In rejecting "morality," the Puritans were not advocating wild, sinful lifestyles—after all, Puritanism today is a byword for ultra-strict conduct. Instead, they were rejecting "moralism," the idea that avoiding certain conspicuous sins was enough to please God. Civility was an even greater trap, elevating politeness and deference to society's ideals of appropriate public behavior as the ultimate standard of human conduct.

Mr. Worldly Wiseman mocks both the teaching of "the book" and Christian's efforts to understand it. The warning not to meddle in things too high for him was typical of the advice that often uneducated Dissenters might frequently receive. Many educated people believed that only the trained experts of the state church were competent to interpret the Bible and God's will and found it offensive that less-educated and less-qualified people would presume to do so. Although it was not necessarily true of the first generation of Puritans, there was an increasing element of class division between Dissenters and the supporters of the established church. This division would grow with time, so that most Nonconforming English groups (Congregationalists, Presbyterians, Baptists, and later Methodists), would be firmly working class in orientation.

For Bunyan, socially acceptable alternatives to fleeing the City of Destruction were foolish tricks. The burden of sin was a real problem pointing to a real solution, and any alleged "cure" that caused a would-be pilgrim to forsake the journey to salvation was a terrible lie. Christian is taken in and leaves the correct road for a dead-end path. Even though the difficult way of salvation is full of misleading tracks, it is always possible to get back on the right road.

♦ So Christian Turned Out of His Way

Bunyan's phrase "so Christian turned out of his way" signals the gravity of Christian's mistake. To leave the path pointed out by Evangelist to seek a shortcut puts the whole pilgrimage at risk. Bunyan and his fellow Dissenters believed that the Church of England ignored biblical directives about the proper way to salvation and pointed the way instead to a path that led only to destruction.

There would be many false trails leading off the true road to the Heavenly City, but Bunyan highlights the path to morality and civility as being particularly dangerous. The way of morality and civility seemed to offer an attractive shortcut to relief from the burden of sin, yet as Christian tries to go in that direction, he finds the burden of sin growing and the path actually harder to follow. Trying to lead a genuinely moral life proves to be more difficult than it seemed initially and does not lead to salvation. Poor Christian despairs of ever reaching the Heavenly City. However, even though his sins are great, it is possible for him to return to the true path Fortunately, the pilgrim is not doomed by his misstep. It is possible for those who have gone astray to return to the right path. Bunyan provides Evangelist as the character who once again can point Christian in the right direction.

One of the ongoing debates within Christianity, going back to the time of Augustine and his opponents, is about the nature of the Christian life. Are pilgrims best represent-ed as super-athletes, who need only an occasional spotter to remain pumped up, or are they more like patients in a hospital, weak and in constant need of medicine? Bunyan presents Christians in the mode of hospital patients. In life, pilgrims make mistakes. They take wrong turns; they fall into swamps; they are led astray and heed bad advice. It is because of human weakness that the journey is dangerous and full of pitfalls. Only by God's help, following the direc-tions given in the Bible and with encouragement and assis-tance from God-given allies along the way, will Christian and other pilgrims arrive at the Heavenly City.

Evangelist's exhortation to Christian is very similar in form to a typical Puritan sermon. The introduction of head-ings (as with the "three things… thou must utterly abhor") is still used in some traditions of preaching even today. Cer-tainly the way in which Evangelist draws on complicated biblical imagery to provide a lesson about life would have been very familiar to anyone who attended a Dissenting congregation.

Audience

Bunyan wrote for the sorts of people who attended or were likely to attend congregations not affiliated with the Church of England. Such Dissenters might lack formal education but often knew the Bible well and were familiar, through sermons, with many of the types of imagery Bun-yan employed in *Pilgrim's Progress*. The book was aimed both at those considering conversion and Christians who needed encouragement to remain faithful.

For many years *Pilgrim's Progress* was appreciated as a classic work of English literature. Most English-language readers encounter it today only in the classroom, but Bun-yan's work still reaches an audience through other authors who have incorporated his values and ideas. Today *Pilgrim's Progress* remains widely read as a religious work, particu-larly by Protestants of almost all denominations. Modern Christians particularly appreciate Bunyan's theological understanding of discouragement as a natural part of faith. The text is also still used by Christian missionaries as a way to introduce Protestant beliefs about conversion and salvation.

Impact

It is often said that, after the Bible, *Pilgrim's Progress* is the most printed, published, and translated book in the world. (It appeared in ninety different editions in the first hun-dred years after its publication and has been translated into more than two hundred languages.) Certainly it was the top best-seller in premodern England and enjoyed a similar popularity in colonial America. For generations Bunyan's allegory was the most popular religious text in the English-speaking world.

Although Bunyan's literary reputation has somewhat diminished in modern times, it was not only his religious views that were influential. Readers who passed over the spiritual message of *Pilgrim's Progress* were often affected by Bunyan's powerful and creative literary style. Bunyan's influence extends even over those who reject his basic val-ues or have never read his work—the popular magazine *Vanity Fair* takes its name from a large community's market in *Pilgrim's Progress*, for Bunyan a place of temptation to avoid. Another of many of Bunyan's phrases to enter popu-lar culture is "Slough of Despond."

As an author, Bunyan still continues to exert influ-ence. C. S. Lewis, the author of the Narnia stories and a popular Christian writer, was inspired by Bunyan to write a modern Christian allegory, which he entitled *The Pilgrim's Regress*. *Pilgrim's Progress* had a discernible impact on such classic literature as Charlotte Brontë's *Jane Eyre*, Louisa May Alcott's *Little Women*, Kurt Von-negut's *Slaughterhouse-Five*, and, of course, William Makepeace Thackeray's *Vanity Fair*, as well as dozens of lesser-known modern works. It was made into an opera by Ralph Vaughan Williams and more recently into a rock opera.

More important to Bunyan would have been the reli-gious legacy of his writing. When Bunyan wrote his classic work, he was expressing the values of a persecuted minority. With time, however, and certainly helped by the wide popu-larity of *Pilgrim's Progress*, Puritan beliefs became more and more mainstream, until today many of their convictions are widely held in the Protestant community worldwide. Bun-yan's understanding of conversion, of Christian mistrust of society, of the role of the individual, and of the author-ity of scripture are shared by the majority of Christians in Britain and the United States today. Perhaps the greatest testimony to how widely accepted *Pilgrim's Progress* is by modern Christians is the inclusion of Christian's hymn "He Who Would Valiant Be" in the Church of England hymnal.

Further Reading

■ Books

Bunyan, John. *Grace Abounding to the Chief of Sinners*. New York: Penguin, 1987.

Furlong, Monica. *Puritan's Progress: A Study of John Bunyan*. Lon-don: Hodder & Stoughton, 1975.

Greaves, Richard L. *Glimpses of Glory: John Bunyan and English Dissent*. Stanford, Calif.: Stanford University Press, 2002.

Hill, Christopher. *A Tinker and a Poor Man: John Bunyan and His Church, 1628–1688*. New York: Knopf, 1988.

Mullett, Michael. *John Bunyan in Context*. Keele, U.K.: Keele Uni-versity Press, 1996.

Vincent Newey, ed. *The Pilgrim's Progress: Critical and Historical Views*. Liverpool, U.K.: University of Liverpool Press, 1980.

Winslow, Ola Elizabeth. *John Bunyan*. New York: Macmillan, 1961.

■ **Journals**

Dutton, Richard A. "'Interesting, but Tough': Reading The Pilgrim's Progress." *Studies in English Literature* 18, no. 3 (Summer 1978): 439–456.

—*Commentary by Raymond Powell*

Essential Quotes

"He answered, 'Sir, I perceive, by the book in my hand, that I am condemned to die, and after that to come to judgment; and I find that I am not willing to do the first, nor able to do the second.'"

(Section 1)

"So I saw in my dream that the man began to run. Now he had not run far from his own door when his wife and children, perceiving it, began to cry after him to return; but the man put his fingers in his ears, and ran on crying, Life! life! eternal life!"

(Section 1)

"So Christian turned out of his way to go to Mr. Legality's house for help: but, behold, when he was got now hard by the hill, it seemed so high, and also that side of it that was next the way-side did hang so much over, that Christian was afraid to venture further, lest the hill should fall on his head; wherefore there he stood still, and wotted not what to do. Also his burden now seemed heavier to him than while he was in his way."

(Section 1)

1. What impact did the English Civil War, which began in 1641 and continued intermittently until 1651, have on the writings of Bunyan?

2. In seventeenth-century England, religion was a topic of widespread discussion and sometimes dispute. In addition to the Church of England (the Anglican Church) and the Catholic Church, there were a variety of religious sects: Quakers, Baptists, Puritans, the Diggers, the Levellers, and others. Additionally, debate raged over such matters as predestination versus free will. How did these debates influence Bunyan's life and the shape of *Pilgrim's Progress?*

3. In seventeenth-century England, disputes arose about proper conduct. Many Puritans (a group that included Bunyan, though nominally he was a Baptist) opposed practices such as sports, festivals, plays, masques (short dramas, usually allegorical, performed by masked actors), mumming (pantomimes), and other supposedly pagan activities that they regarded as sinful. Many of these were rural activities. Why did the Puritans regard these activities as sinful?

4. Just as Christianity split as a result of the Protestant Reformation, Islam split in its early days as a result of a dispute about who should succeed Muhammad as the leader of Islam. The result was the First Fitna, or First Islamic Civil War (656–661). Later in that century, the Second Fitna in the 680s created additional turmoil. In what ways did this split resemble or differ from the split in Christianity?

5. The religious disputes of the seventeenth century, in which Bunyan played a part, continue to influence religious debate in the twenty-first century. What are some of the religious issues that are still debated? How do the roots of these issues extend back to Bunyan's time?

THE PILGRIM'S PROGRESS: DOCUMENT TEXT

1678 CE

—John Bunyan

The First Stage

As I walked through the wilderness of this world, I lighted on a certain place where was a den, and laid me down in that place to sleep; and as I slept, I dreamed a dream. I dreamed, and behold, I saw a man clothed with rags, standing in a certain place, with his face from his own house, a book in his hand, and a great burden upon his back. I looked and saw him open the book, and read therein; and as he read, he wept and trembled; and not being able longer to contain, he brake out with a lamentable cry, saying, "What shall I do?"

In this plight, therefore, he went home, and restrained himself as long as he could, that his wife and children should not perceive his distress; but he could not be silent long, because that his trouble increased. Wherefore at length he brake his mind to his wife and children; and thus he began to talk to them: "O, my dear wife," said he, "and you the children of my bowels, I, your dear friend, am in myself undone by reason of a burden that lieth hard upon me; moreover, I am certainly informed that this our city will be burnt with fire from heaven; in which fearful overthrow, both myself, with thee my wife, and you my sweet babes, shall miserably come to ruin, except (the which yet I see not) some way of escape can be found whereby we may be delivered." At this his relations were sore amazed; not for that they believed that what he had said to them was true, but because they thought that some frenzy distemper had got into his head; therefore, it drawing towards night, and they hoping that sleep might settle his brains, with all haste they got him to bed. But the night was as troublesome to him as the day; wherefore, instead of sleeping, he spent it in sighs and tears. So when the morning was come, they would know how he did. He told them, "Worse and worse:" he also set to talking to them again; but they began to be hardened. They also thought to drive away his distemper by harsh and surly carriage to him; sometimes they would deride, sometimes they would chide, and

sometimes they would quite neglect him. Wherefore he began to retire himself to his chamber to pray for and pity them, and also to condole his own misery; he would also walk solitarily in the fields, sometimes reading, and sometimes praying: and thus for some days he spent his time.

Now I saw, upon a time, when he was walking in the fields, that he was (as he was wont) reading in his book, and greatly distressed in his mind; and as he read, he burst out, as he had done before, crying, "What shall I do to be saved?"

I saw also that he looked this way, and that way, as if he would run; yet he stood still because (as I perceived) he could not tell which way to go. I looked then, and saw a man named Evangelist coming to him, and he asked, "Wherefore dost thou cry?"

He answered, "Sir, I perceive, by the book in my hand, that I am condemned to die, and after that to come to judgment; and I find that I am not willing to do the first, nor able to do the second."

Then said Evangelist, "Why not willing to die, since this life is attended with so many evils?" The man answered, "Because, I fear that this burden that is upon my back will sink me lower than the grave, and I shall fall into Tophet. And Sir, if I be not fit to go to prison, I am not fit to go to judgment, and from thence to execution; and the thoughts of these things make me cry."

Then said Evangelist, "If this be thy condition, why standest thou still?" He answered, "Because I know not whither to go." Then he gave him a parchment roll, and there was written within, "Fly from the wrath to come."

The man therefore read it, and looking upon Evangelist very carefully, said, "Whither must I fly?" Then said Evangelist, (pointing with his finger over a very wide field,) "Do you see yonder wicket-gate?" The man said, "No." Then said the other, "Do you see yonder shining light?" He said, "I think I do." Then said Evangelist, "Keep that light in your eye, and go up directly thereto, so shalt thou see the gate; at which, when thou knockest, it shall be told thee what thou shalt do." So I saw in my dream that the man began to run. Now he had not run far from his own door when his wife and children, perceiving it, began to cry after him to return; but the man put his fingers in his ears, and ran on crying, Life! life! eternal life! So he looked not behind him, but fled towards the middle of the plain.

The neighbors also came out to see him run, and as he ran, some mocked, others threatened, and some cried after him to return; and among those that did so, there were two that were resolved to fetch him back by force. The name of the one was Obstinate and the name of the other Pliable. Now by this time the man was got a good distance from them; but, however, they were resolved to pursue him, which they did, and in a little time they overtook him. Then said the man, "Neighbors, wherefore are you come?" They said, "To persuade you to go back with us." But he said, "That can by no means be: you dwell," said he, "in the city of Destruction, the place also where I was born: I see it to be so; and dying there, sooner or later, you will sink lower than the grave, into a place that burns with fire and brimstone: be content, good neighbors, and go along with me."

Obstinate: What, said Obstinate, and leave our friends and our comforts behind us!

Christian: Yes, said Christian, (for that was his name,) because that all which you forsake is not worthy to be compared with a little of that I am seeking to enjoy, and if you will go along with me, and hold it, you shall fare as I myself; for there, where I go, is enough and to spare. Come away, and prove my words.

Obstinate: What are the things you seek, since you leave all the world to find them?

Christian: I seek an inheritance incorruptible, undefiled, and that fadeth not away, and it is laid up in heaven, and safe there, to be bestowed, at the time appointed, on them that diligently seek it. Read it so, if you will, in my book.

Obstinate: Tush, said Obstinate, away with your book; will you go back with us or no?

Christian: No, not I, said the other, because I have laid my hand to the plough.

Obstinate: Come then, neighbor Pliable, let us turn again, and go home without him: there is a company of these crazy-headed coxcombs, that when they take a fancy by the end, are wiser in their own eyes than seven men that can render a reason.

Pliable: Then said Pliable, Don't revile; if what the good Christian says is true, the things he looks after are better than ours: my heart inclines to go with my neighbor.

Obstinate: What, more fools still! Be ruled by me, and go back; who knows whither such a brain-sick fellow will lead you? Go back, go back, and be wise.

Christian: Nay, but do thou come with thy neighbor Pliable; there are such things to be had which I spoke of, and many more glories besides. If you believe not me, read here in this book, and for the truth of what is expressed therein, behold, all is confirmed by the blood of Him that made it.

Pliable: Well, neighbor Obstinate, said Pliable, I begin to come to a point; I intend to go along with this good man, and to cast in my lot with him: but, my good companion, do you know the way to this desired place?

Christian: I am directed by a man whose name is Evangelist, to speed me to a little gate that is before us, where we shall receive instructions about the way.

Pliable: Come then, good neighbor, let us be going. Then they went both together.

Obstinate: And I will go back to my place, said Obstinate: I will be no companion of such misled, fantastical fellows.

Now I saw in my dream, that when Obstinate was gone back, Christian and Pliable went talking over the plain; and thus they began their discourse.

Christian: Come, neighbor Pliable, how do you do? I am glad you are persuaded to go along with me. Had even Obstinate himself but felt what I have felt of the powers and terrors of what is yet unseen, he would not thus lightly have given us the back.

Pliable: Come, neighbor Christian, since there are none but us two here, tell me now farther, what the things are, and how to be enjoyed, whither we are going.

Christian: I can better conceive of them with my mind, than speak of them with my tongue: but yet, since you are desirous to know, I will read of them in my book.

Pliable: And do you think that the words of your book are certainly true?

Christian: Yes, verily; for it was made by Him that cannot lie.

Pliable: Well said; what things are they?

Christian: There is an endless kingdom to be inhabited, and everlasting life to be given us, that we may inhabit that kingdom for ever.

Pliable: Well said; and what else?

Christian: There are crowns of glory to be given us; and garments that will make us shine like the sun in the firmament of heaven.

Pliable: This is very pleasant; and what else?

Christian: There shall be no more crying, nor sorrow; for he that is owner of the place will wipe all tears from our eyes.

Pliable: And what company shall we have there?

Christian: There we shall be with seraphims and cherubims, creatures that will dazzle your eyes to look on them. There also you shall meet with thousands and ten thousands that have gone before us to that place; none of them are hurtful, but loving and holy; every one walking in the sight of God, and standing in his presence with acceptance for ever. In a word, there we shall see the elders with their golden crowns, there we shall see the holy virgins with their golden harps, there we shall see men, that by the world were cut in pieces, burnt in flames, eaten of beasts, drowned in the seas, for the love they bare to the Lord of the place, all well, and clothed with immortality as with a garment.

Pliable: The hearing of this is enough to ravish one's heart. But are these things to be enjoyed? How shall we get to be sharers thereof?

Christian: The Lord, the governor of the country, hath recorded that in this book, the substance of which is, if we be truly willing to have it, he will bestow it upon us freely.

Pliable: Well, my good companion, glad am I to hear of these things: come on, let us mend our pace.

Christian: I cannot go as fast as I would, by reason of this burden that is on my back.

Now I saw in my dream, that just as they had ended this talk, they drew nigh to a very miry slough that was in the midst of the plain: and they being heedless, did both fall suddenly into the bog. The name of the slough was Despond. Here, therefore, they wallowed for a time, being grievously bedaubed with the dirt; and Christian, because of the burden that was on his back, began to sink in the mire.

Pliable: Then said Pliable, Ah, neighbor Christian, where are you now?

Christian: Truly, said Christian, I do not know.

Pliable: At this Pliable began to be offended, and angrily said to his fellow, Is this the happiness you have told me all this while of? If we have such ill speed at our first setting out, what may we expect between this and our journey's end? May I get out again with my life, you shall possess the brave country alone for me. And with that he gave a desperate struggle or two, and got out of the mire on that side of the slough which was next to his own house: so away he went, and Christian saw him no more.

Wherefore Christian was left to tumble in the Slough of Despond alone; but still he endeavored to struggle to that side of the slough that was farthest from his own house, and next to the wicket-gate; the which he did, but could not get out because of the burden that was upon his back: but I beheld in my dream, that a man came to him, whose name was Help, and asked him what he did there.

Christian: Sir, said Christian, I was bid to go this way by a man called Evangelist, who directed me also to yonder gate, that I might escape the wrath to come. And as I was going thither, I fell in here.

Help: But why did not you look for the steps?

Christian: Fear followed me so hard that I fled the next way, and fell in.

Help: Then, said he, Give me thine hand: so he gave him his hand, and he drew him out, and he set him upon sound ground, and bid him go on his way.

Then I stepped to him that plucked him out, and said, "Sir, wherefore, since over this place is the way from the city of Destruction to yonder gate, is it, that this plat is not mended, that poor travellers might go thither with more security?" And he said unto me, "This miry slough is such a place as cannot be mended: it is the descent whither the scum and filth that attends conviction for sin doth continually run, and therefore it is called the Slough of Despond; for still, as the sinner is awakened about his lost condition, there arise in his soul many fears and doubts, and discouraging apprehensions, which all of them get together, and settle in this place: and this is the reason of the badness of this ground.

"It is not the pleasure of the King that this place should remain so bad. His laborers also have, by the direction of his Majesty's surveyors, been for above this sixteen hundred years employed about this patch of ground, if perhaps it might have been mended: yea, and to my knowledge," said he, "there have been swallowed up at least twenty thousand cart loads, yea, millions of wholesome instructions, that have at all seasons been brought from all places of the King's dominions, (and they that can tell, say, they are the best materials to make good ground of the place,) if so be it might have been mended; but it is the Slough of Despond still, and so will be when they have done what they can.

"True, there are, by the direction of the Lawgiver, certain good and substantial steps, placed even through the very midst of this slough; but at such time as this place doth much spew out its filth, as it doth against change of weather, these steps are hardly seen; or if they be, men, through the dizziness of their heads, step beside, and then they are bemired to purpose, notwithstanding the steps be there: but the ground is good when they are once got in at the gate."

Now I saw in my dream, that by this time Pliable was got home to his house. So his neighbors came to visit him; and some of them called him wise man for coming back, and some called him fool for hazarding himself with Christian: others again did mock at his cowardliness, saying, "Surely, since you began to venture, I would not have been so base as to have given out for a few difficulties:" so Pliable sat sneaking among them. But at last he got more confidence, and then they all turned their tales, and began to deride poor Christian behind his back. And thus much concerning Pliable.

Now as Christian was walking solitary by himself, he espied one afar off come crossing over the field to meet him; and their hap was to meet just as they were crossing the way of each other. The gentleman's name that met him was Mr. Worldly Wiseman: he dwelt in the town of Carnal Policy, a very great town, and also hard by from whence Christian came. This man then, meeting with Christian, and having some inkling of him, (for Christian's setting forth from the city of Destruction was much noised abroad, not only in the town where he dwelt, but also it began to be the town-talk in some other places)—Mr. Worldly Wiseman, therefore, having some guess of him, by beholding his laborious going, by observing his sighs and groans, and the like, began thus to enter into some talk with Christian.

Mr. Worldly Wiseman: How now, good fellow, whither away after this burdened manner?

Christian: A burdened manner indeed, as ever I think poor creature had! And whereas you ask me, Whither away? I tell you, sir, I am going to yonder wicket-gate before me; for there, as I am informed, I shall be put into a way to be rid of my heavy burden.

Mr. Worldly Wiseman: Hast thou a wife and children?

Christian: Yes; but I am so laden with this burden, that I cannot take that pleasure in them as formerly: methinks I am as if I had none.

Mr. Worldly Wiseman: Wilt thou hearken to me, if I give thee counsel?

Christian: If it be good, I will; for I stand in need of good counsel.

Mr. Worldly Wiseman: I would advise thee, then, that thou with all speed get thyself rid of thy burden; for thou wilt never be settled in thy mind till then: nor canst thou enjoy the benefits of the blessings which God hath bestowed upon thee till then.

Christian: That is that which I seek for, even to be rid of this heavy burden: but get it off myself I cannot, nor is there any man in our country that can take it off my shoulders; therefore am I going this way, as I told you, that I may be rid of my burden.

Mr. Worldly Wiseman: Who bid thee go this way to be rid of thy burden?

Christian: A man that appeared to me to be a very great and honorable person: his name, as I remember, is Evangelist.

Mr. Worldly Wiseman: I beshrew him for his counsel! there is not a more dangerous and troublesome way in the world than is that into which he hath directed thee; and that thou shalt find, if thou wilt be ruled by his counsel. Thou hast met with something, as I perceive, already; for I see the dirt of the Slough of Despond is upon thee: but that slough is the beginning of the sorrows that do attend those that go on in that way. Hear me; I am older than thou: thou art like to meet with, in the way which thou goest, wearisomeness, painfulness, hunger, perils, nakedness, sword, lions, dragons, darkness, and, in a word, death, and what not. These things are certainly true, having been confirmed by many testimonies. And should a man so carelessly cast away himself, by giving heed to a stranger?

Christian: Why, sir, this burden on my back is more terrible to me than are all these things which you have mentioned: nay, methinks I care not what I meet with in the way, if so be I can also meet with deliverance from my burden.

Mr. Worldly Wiseman: How camest thou by thy burden at first?

Christian: By reading this book in my hand.

Mr. Worldly Wiseman: I thought so; and it has happened unto thee as to other weak men, who, meddling with things too high for them, do suddenly fall into thy distractions; which distractions do not only unman men, as thine I perceive have done thee, but they run them upon desperate ventures, to obtain they know not what.

Christian: I know what I would obtain; it is ease from my heavy burden.

Mr. Worldly Wiseman: But why wilt thou seek for ease this way, seeing so many dangers attend it? especially since (hadst thou but patience to hear me) I could direct thee to the obtaining of what thou desirest, without the dangers that thou in this way wilt run thyself into. Yea, and the remedy is at hand. Besides, I will add, that instead of those dangers, thou shalt meet with much safety, friendship, and content.

Christian: Sir, I pray open this secret to me.

Mr. Worldly Wiseman: Why, in yonder village (the village is named Morality) there dwells a gentleman whose name is Legality, a very judicious man, and a man of a very good name, that has skill to help men off with such burdens as thine is from their shoulders; yea to my knowledge, he hath done a great deal of good this way; aye, and besides, he hath skill to cure those that are somewhat crazed in their wits with their burdens. To him, as I said, thou mayest go, and be helped presently. His house is not quite a mile from this place; and if he should not be at home himself, he hath a pretty young man to his son, whose name is Civility, that can do it (to speak on) as well as the old gentleman himself: there, I say, thou mayest be eased of thy burden; and if thou art not minded to go back to thy former habitation, (as indeed I would not wish thee,) thou mayest send for thy wife and children to this village, where there are houses now standing empty, one of which thou mayest have at a reasonable rate: provision is there also cheap and good; and that which will make thy life the more happy is, to be sure there thou shalt live by honest neighbors, in credit and good fashion.

Now was Christian somewhat at a stand; but presently he concluded, If this be true which this gentleman hath said, my wisest course is to take his advice: and with that he thus farther spake.

Christian: Sir, which is my way to this honest man's house?

Mr. Worldly Wiseman: Do you see yonder high hill?

Christian: Yes, very well.

Mr. Worldly Wiseman: By that hill you must go, and the first house you come at is his.

So Christian turned out of his way to go to Mr. Legality's house for help: but, behold, when he was got now hard by the hill, it seemed so high, and also that side of it that was next the way-side did hang so much over, that Christian was afraid to venture further, lest the hill should fall on his head; wherefore there he stood still, and wotted not what to do. Also his burden now seemed heavier to him than while he was in his way. There came also flashes of fire, out of the hill, that made Christian afraid that he should be burnt: here therefore he did sweat and quake for fear. And now he began to be sorry that he had taken Mr. Worldly Wiseman's counsel; and with that he saw Evangelist coming to meet him, at the sight also of whom he began to blush for shame. So Evangelist drew nearer and nearer; and coming up to him, he looked upon him, with a severe and dreadful countenance, and thus began to reason with Christian.

Evangelist: What doest thou here, Christian? said he: at which words Christian knew not what to

answer; wherefore at present he stood speechless before him. Then said Evangelist farther, Art not thou the man that I found crying without the walls of the city of Destruction?

Christian: Yes, dear sir, I am the man.

Evangelist: Did not I direct thee the way to the little wicket-gate?

Christian: Yes, dear sir, said Christian.

Evangelist: How is it then thou art so quickly turned aside? For thou art now out of the way.

Christian: I met with a gentleman so soon as I had got over the Slough of Despond, who persuaded me that I might, in the village before me, find a man that could take off my burden.

Evangelist: What was he?

Christian: He looked like a gentleman, and talked much to me, and got me at last to yield: so I came hither; but when I beheld this hill, and how it hangs over the way, I suddenly made a stand, lest it should fall on my head.

Evangelist: What said that gentleman to you?

Christian: Why, he asked me whither I was going; and I told him.

Evangelist: And what said he then?

Christian: He asked me if I had a family; and I told him. But, said I, I am so laden with the burden that is on my back, that I cannot take pleasure in them as formerly.

Evangelist: And what said he then?

Christian: He bid me with speed get rid of my burden; and I told him it was ease that I sought. And, said I, I am therefore going to yonder gate, to receive farther direction how I may get to the place of deliverance. So he said that he would show me a better way, and short, not so attended with difficulties as the way, sir, that you set me in; which way, said he, will direct you to a gentleman's house that hath skill to take off these burdens: so I believed him, and turned out of that way into this, if haply I might be soon eased of my burden. But when I came to this place, and beheld things as they are, I stopped, for fear (as I said) of danger: but I now know not what to do.

Evangelist: Then said Evangelist, Stand still a little, that I show thee the words of God. So he stood trembling. Then said Evangelist, "See that ye refuse not Him that speaketh; for if they escaped not who refused him that spake on earth, much more shall not we escape, if we turn away from Him that speaketh from heaven." He said, moreover, "Now the just shall live by faith; but if any man draw back, my soul shall have no pleasure in him." He also did thus apply them: Thou art the man that art running into this misery; thou hast begun to reject the counsel of the Most High, and to draw back thy foot from the way of peace, even almost to the hazarding of thy perdition.

Then Christian fell down at his feet as dead, crying, Woe is me, for I am undone! At the sight of which Evangelist caught him by the right hand, saying, "All manner of sin and blasphemies shall be forgiven unto men." "Be not faithless, but believing." Then did Christian again a little revive, and stood up trembling, as at first, before Evangelist.

Then Evangelist proceeded, saying, Give more earnest heed to the things that I shall tell thee of. I will now show thee who it was that deluded thee, and who it was also to whom he sent thee. The man that met thee is one Worldly Wiseman, and rightly is he so called; partly because he savoreth only the doctrine of this world, (therefore he always goes to the town of Morality to church;) and partly because he loveth that doctrine best, for it saveth him best from the cross, and because he is of this carnal temper, therefore he seeketh to pervert my ways, though right. Now there are three things in this man's counsel that thou must utterly abhor.

1. His turning thee out of the way.

2. His laboring to render the cross odious to thee.

3. And his setting thy feet in that way that leadeth unto the administration of death.

First, Thou must abhor his turning thee out of the way; yea, and thine own consenting thereto; because this is to reject the counsel of God for the sake of the counsel of a Worldly Wiseman. The Lord says, "Strive to enter in at the straight gate," the gate to which I send thee; "for strait is the gate that leadeth unto life, and few there be that find it." From this little wicket-gate, and from the way thereto, hath this wicked man turned thee, to the bringing of thee almost to destruction: hate, therefore, his turning thee out of the way, and abhor thyself for hearkening to him.

Secondly, Thou must abhor his laboring to render the cross odious unto thee; for thou art to prefer it before the treasures of Egypt. Besides, the King of glory hath told thee, that he that will save his life shall lose it. And he that comes after him, and hates not his father, and mother, and wife, and children, and brethren, and sisters, yea, and his own life also, he cannot be his disciple. I say, therefore, for a man to labor to persuade thee that that shall be thy death, without which, the truth hath said, thou canst not have eternal life, this doctrine thou must abhor.

Thirdly, Thou must hate his setting of thy feet in the way that leadeth to the ministration of death. And

for this thou must consider to whom he sent thee, and also how unable that person was to deliver thee from thy burden.

He to whom thou wast sent for ease, being by name Legality, is the son of the bond-woman which now is, and is in bondage with her children, and is, in a mystery, this Mount Sinai, which thou hast feared will fall on thy head. Now if she with her children are in bondage, how canst thou expect by them to be made free? This Legality, therefore, is not able to set thee free from thy burden. No man was as yet ever rid of his burden by him; no, nor ever is like to be: ye cannot be justified by the works of the law; for by the deeds of the law no man living can be rid of his burden: Therefore Mr. Worldly Wiseman is an alien, and Mr. Legality is a cheat; and for his son Civility, notwithstanding his simpering looks, he is but a hypocrite, and cannot help thee. Believe me, there is nothing in all this noise that thou hast heard of these sottish men, but a design to beguile thee of thy salvation, by turning thee from the way in which I had set thee. After this, Evangelist called aloud to the heavens for confirmation of what he had said; and with that there came words and fire out of the mountain under which poor Christian stood, which made the hair of his flesh stand up. The words were pronounced: "As many as are of the works of the law, are under the curse; for it is written, Cursed is every one that continueth not in all things which are written in the book of the law to do them."

Now Christian looked for nothing but death, and began to cry out lamentably; even cursing the time in which he met with Mr. Worldly Wiseman; still calling himself a thousand fools for hearkening to his counsel. He also was greatly ashamed to think that this gentleman's arguments, flowing only from the flesh, should have the prevalency with him so far as to cause him to forsake the right way. This done, he applied himself again to Evangelist in words and sense as follows.

Christian: Sir, what think you? Is there any hope? May I now go back, and go up to the wicket-gate? Shall I not be abandoned for this, and sent back from thence ashamed? I am sorry I have hearkened to this man's counsel; but may my sin be forgiven?

Evangelist: Then said Evangelist to him, Thy sin is very great, for by it thou hast committed two evils: thou hast forsaken the way that is good, to tread in forbidden paths. Yet will the man at the gate receive thee, for he has good-will for men; only, said he, take heed that thou turn not aside again, lest thou "perish from the way, when his wrath is kindled but a little."

Glossary

beshrew:	to curse, usually mildly
Mount Sinai:	a mountain on the Sinai Peninsula of Egypt, by tradition the place where God gave the Ten Commandments to Moses
seraphims and cherubims:	orders of angels
slough:	any wet, muddy place; typically a stream or a canal in wet marshland or a side canal or inlet
Tophet:	a place in a valley in ancient Jerusalem where human sacrifices were made
wicket-gate:	any small opening or door, usually one that is part of a larger gate or door

Hawai'i State Archives image of King David Kalakaua.

KUMULIPO: DOCUMENT ANALYSIS

"At the time when the earth became hot.... The night gave birth / Born was Kumulipo in the night, a male / Born was Po'ele in the night, a female."

Overview

The Kumulipo, or "Beginning in Deep Darkness," is the 2,102-line Hawaiian chant (consisting of sixteen *wa*, translated here as "chants") describing the creation of everything that lives in the world. The first half of the Kumulipo takes place during the long night in which sea creatures, plants, birds, land animals, and finally humans come into being; in the eighth chant, day breaks as humans increase in number. The rest of the Kumulipo deals with the generations of humans, gods, and goddesses, leading from their origins down to the chief Ka-'i-'i-mamao (or Kalaninui'iamamao, also called Lono-i-ka-makahiki), whose birth the chant honors.

The Kumulipo was published in 1889 by King Kalakaua of Hawaii; in 1897 the King's sister, Queen Lili'uokalani, published her own translation of the text. The short prose note published with the Kalakaua version and revised in the queen's version states that the chant was composed around 1700 and performed twice: once in 1779, when the British explorer Captain James Cook arrived in Hawaii, and once in 1804, when a chief named Ke'eaumoku died. The prose note also explains the genealogical connection between Ka-'i-'i-mamao and Kalakaua. (Ka-'i-'i-mamao was Kalakaua's great-great-great-great-great grandfather.) Since social and political power in Hawaiian society was traditionally linked to bloodlines as well as to martial prowess, a record of divine ancestry was a powerful political symbol.

Context

The Hawaiian archipelago, located between the North American and Asian continents, consists of eight major islands and many smaller ones and is the most isolated island group on earth. An archipelago, or string of islands, is created when a buildup of magma under the seafloor, called a hot spot, causes a series of volcanic eruptions. The magma cools and eventually forms an island, and multiple islands are formed when the tectonic plate to which the islands belong moves, while the hot spot remains in one place. The eight major Hawaiian islands are Oahu (the most densely populated island, where the capital, Honolulu, is located), Hawaii (commonly called "the Big Island"), Maui, Kahoolawe, Lanai, Molokai, Kauai, and Niihau. Hawaii is part of Polynesia, a name given to a number of island groups in the central and southern Pacific Ocean whose languages and cultures are related to one another.

The Kalakaua text of the Kumulipo is based on a manuscript that was owned by Hawaii's King Kalakaua. It had been read and partially translated by a German scholar, Adolf Bastian, who published part of the text and his own translation in an 1881 book on Polynesian sacred chants. Bastian's interest (combined with the fact that the 1880s were tumultuous and uncertain years, to say the least, for the Hawaiian royal family) may have inspired the king to make the full text more widely available. In 1893, four years after the pamphlet was printed, King Kalakaua's sister and successor, Queen Lili'uokalani, was deposed by a coalition of mostly American and European businesspeople. The queen began work on her own translation of the Kalakaua text in 1895, while under house arrest. The publication of a document detailing the genealogical connection of Hawaii's rulers to the land itself was an assertion of the legitimacy of Kalakaua's rule and ultimately of the right of native Hawaiians to political self-determination.

King Kalakaua came to the throne of Hawaii by popular election, not by inheritance. The Kamehameha dynasty, founded by Kamehameha the Great in 1810, had ruled the Kingdom of Hawaii for sixty-two years, but King Kamehameha V died in 1872 without naming a successor. The Hawaiian Constitution called for a popular vote to elect a new king; two members of the *ali'i* ("the chiefly class," or "nobility")—David Kalakaua and William C. Lunalilo—ran for the office. Lunalilo won the 1873 election but died a year later, and Kalakaua was elected king in 1874, though he was challenged by the dowager Queen Emma, the wife of Kamehameha IV.

Kalakaua had supporters and opponents among the electorate. He was more conservative than Lunalilo had been; he wanted more native Hawaiians to hold positions in the Hawaiian government, but he also believed in the rule of the *ali'i* more than in the popular vote of the *maka'ainana* ("common people"). Kalakaua played a major role in the restoration of Hawaiian culture, reviving the practices of hula (which had been banned in 1830), surfing, and Lua, the Hawaiian martial art. Genealogies had always been important to the *ali'i*, so the sacred genealogy in the Kumulipo was significant to Kalakaua both as religious and political support for his rule and as an important part of Hawaiian culture. In addition, Lili'uokalani's translation of the Kumulipo a few years later proved to be an important project: It asserted the longevity and artistic sophistication of Hawaiian culture at a time of disenfranchisement for the Hawaiian people, when political power in the island chain rested primarily in the hands of non-Hawaiian business leaders.

Genealogies were vital to the *ali'i* because an individual's power derived from his or her social rank, and rank was determined by descent. A genealogy was a treasured family possession, and no one outside the family would ordinarily know the entire chant, except for the priest who did the chanting. In fact, the members of the family were not expected to know how to chant their genealogies; that was the responsibility of a few priests attached to the family—part of what might be called a chief's "court." One priest, the *haku mele*, or "master of song," would be called upon to deliver the chant when it was politically necessary for a chief to have his status recognized by other chiefs or, as in the case of the Kumulipo in 1804, as a eulogy. The *haku mele* was also responsible for working a new child of the family into the genealogy, perhaps by composing a new chant, referred to as a *mele inoa*, or "naming song"; this was the origin of the Kumulipo, if we accept that it was composed in honor of Ka-'i-'i-mamao's birth.

According to Hawaiian tradition, a child inherited the combined rank of his or her parents, meaning the union of two high-ranking people would produce a child of even higher rank. Within the *ali'i* class, the closer the relationship between the parents, the higher the rank of the child; for instance, the child of a brother and sister of the "high chief" or *niaupi'o* rank was considered to be an *akua*, a god. A chief did not have to be born a god in order to be part of Hawaiian religious life, however. Chiefs were seen as the link between the commoners, the gods, and the cosmos. The actions and especially the birth of a chief were described in cosmic terms; for example, Hawaiian legends foretold that a king would be born who would unite the islands and that his birth would be marked by the appearance of a comet, which is precisely what occurred upon the birth of Kamehameha I. A chief could also be deified by a special ceremony following his death, becoming an *'aumakua*, or guardian spirit of his family.

Before Kamehameha I unified the islands in 1810, power and territory in Hawaii were very fluid, and warfare was constant. The system by which individuals attempted to acquire and hold on to military, social, and religious power was a complex and often dangerous one. There were several levels of chiefs. Each chiefdom (*aupuni*), which usually included several of the official geographic divisions of one of the larger islands, or one of the smaller islands plus parts of a larger one, was controlled by an *ali'i nui* or "paramount chief," who was elected or appointed by the local aristocracy. Each internal district of an *aupuni* was ruled by a local chief, who in turn had his subordinates. The *aupuni* constantly changed size and shape, since one of the most important responsibilities of an *ali'i nui* was to expand his territory. The chiefdoms frequently made offensive and defensive alliances with one another. A good *ali'i nui* was also expected to maintain peace, security, stability, and prosperity within his *aupuni* through strong military leadership and the maintenance of a harmonic balance between the people and the gods or the forces of nature. Stories exist of Hawaiian rulers who lost their chiefdoms to cruelty and greed, the implication being that the gods had punished them for their military overreaching or impiety. Insurrection and invasion frequently occurred on the death of the *ali'i nui*, while the succession was in question. The island of Hawaii was the site of the most frequent turnovers in power: It was the largest island, which made it hard to control, and neighboring Maui was close enough for its chiefs to launch an invasion easily; Kauai, on the other hand, was divided from Oahu by a rough channel, making it harder to invade and thus relatively stable. Kamehameha I began his great series of conquests with the unification of the island of Hawaii.

The Kalakaua text of the Kumulipo was accompanied by a two-page prose note telling the story of the chant's composition and explaining its connection to King Kalakaua and his queen, Kapi'olani; Queen Lili'uokalani added that the chant was composed in 1700. The chant was performed for Captain Cook because his arrival in the islands on a large sailing ship was seen as fulfilling one of two prophecies: the god Lono's promise to return to Hawaii one day on a floating island (a ship) or a priest's prediction at the time of Ka-'i-'i-mamao's death that Ka-'i-'i-mamao, who was also identified to some extent with Lono, would one day return by sea. Based on the assumption that Captain Cook was, in fact, the reincarnation of Ka-'i-'i-mamao (or Lono), the recitation of the chant served the traditional purpose of announcing the arrival of a chief visiting another chief's territory by establishing his lineage and thus his claim to respect and hospitality. The Kumulipo was chanted by priests known as *kahuna* at religious ceremonies held within a *heiau* (meaning "Hawaiian temple" or "sacred space").

About the Author

In the note accompanying her 1897 translation, Queen Lili'uokalani identifies a chanter named Keaulumoku as the

Time Line	
ca. 1700	■ The Kumulipo is composed.
ca. 1758	■ Kamehameha I (also known as Kamehameha the Great) is born.
1779	■ The English navigator Captain James Cook arrives in Hawaii and participates in a religious ceremony at which the Kumulipo is chanted; he and his men are the first Europeans to visit the islands.
1804	■ The Kumulipo is chanted as Ke'eaumoku (Kamehameha I's uncle, father-in-law, and political supporter) is about to die.
1810	■ Kamehameha I unifies the Hawaiian Islands under his rule and formally creates the Kingdom of Hawaii.
February 12, 1874	■ David Kalakaua is elected king of Hawaii.
1889	■ King Kalakaua publishes the Kumulipo in the form of a pamphlet.
January 20, 1891	■ Kalakaua dies and is succeeded by his sister, Lili'uokalani.
February 1, 1893	■ Hawaii becomes a protectorate of the United States after Queen Lili'uokalani is deposed.
1897	■ Queen Lili'uokalani's translation of the Kumulipo is published in Boston, Massachusetts.
1951	■ Martha Warren Beckwith's translation and annotation of the Kumulipo make the Hawaiian creation chant accessible to a wider audience.
August 21, 1959	■ Hawaii becomes the fiftieth state in the United States.

composer of the Kumulipo. We do know of a famous composer of sacred songs by that name living in the eighteenth century, but as far as scholars have been able to determine he was born around 1716, just sixteen years after the supposed date the Kumulipo was composed. It is possible that there was another, less-well-known Keaulumoku who composed the chant or that over time people forgot the specific dates and simply assumed that the famous chanter had composed the famous chant; scholars have also speculated that "Keaulumoku" was a title passed from one court composer to the next, rather than the given name of an individual. Martha Warren Beckwith, the author of the translation reproduced here, suggested that the Kumulipo, in the form in which it was eventually written down, was in fact a composite—the work of several different writers, possibly compiled over several generations. There is no record of who might have recorded the chant to create the manuscript owned by King Kalakaua.

Explanation and Analysis of the Document

The structure and the meaning of the Kumulipo are open to varying interpretations by different readers or listeners. Three interpretations are particularly well known: The chant may be the straightforward story of the creation of the universe leading to the eventual rise of a particular family line; certain passages may be symbolic of the power struggles between various chiefly families; or the entire chant may be an extended metaphor for the conception, birth, and development of a child. The text is capable of being interpreted in these and other ways because the language used in it is somewhat archaic, including many puns, an abundance of symbolic language, and words that were no longer in use by the time of Kalakaua's reign. Words with double meanings are used throughout, and the chant is rich in allusions to other songs and stories from Hawaiian mythology. This technique is common in Hawaiian poetry, requiring the reader to recognize the symbolism in order to grasp the underlying meaning, or *kaona*, of the text. In the case of the Kumulipo, the best course is probably to follow Beckwith's example and allow for the possibility that the chant has many hidden meanings. (One of Beckwith's advisers on the translation, David Malo Kupihea, suggested that Kalakaua had adapted the original text so that it would have more relevance to the contemporary political situation of the late nineteenth century. Another adviser, Pokini Robinson, thought that the chant should be interpreted as a metaphor for a child's development.) The archaisms and double meanings make the Kumulipo especially difficult to translate. Passages where there is uncertainty about what a word or phrase means are followed by a bracketed question mark. Bracketed words that fill in blanks in the text represent Beckwith's best guess as to the Hawaiian word's meaning. Bracketed words following Hawaiian terms are translations of the Hawaiian.

Of the 2,102 lines of the Kalakaua text, over half consist of paired male and female names; this may mean, as Beckwith suggests, that the Kumulipo as a whole incorporates several different family lines and strings them together with name songs and mythology. The vast majority of these pairs are not reproduced here (including all of Chant 12), but it should be clear from the remaining text that the pairing of opposites is an important structural element of the Kumulipo.

Each of the sixteen sections of the Kumulipo was called a *wa*, which Queen Lili'uokalani translated as "era." In other words, the sixteen divisions of the chant are said to represent the duration of time in which the events described in each chant take place. The first seven chants happen in darkness (*po*), while the rest take place in the light of day (*ao*). One possible interpretation of the division between light and dark is that light represents the emergence of human reasoning, technology, and culture, which follows the creation of animals and plants.

♦ Chant 1

The "time of the rise of the Pleiades" is also the time of the Makahiki, the four lunar months spanning from approximately October to February. This is also the rainy season in Hawaii, during which the dry areas of the islands become green, so it is a particularly appropriate time for a chant about the generation of life to begin.

The first chant emphasizes the roles of the male, the female, and the divine in creating life. The repeated line "Man for the narrow stream, woman for the broad stream" refers to the generation of various forms of life along the shoreline, where the land and the rivers meet the ocean. The pairs of land and sea plants that follow that repeated line are real species, but they are paired on the basis of what their names sound like rather than on any physical relationship. The word "Refrain" in the translation refers to the repetition of three lines: "Darkness slips into light / Earth and water are the food of the plant / The god enters, man cannot enter." This may mean that although the male and female forces of generation are mentioned many times in the chant, only the gods—not humans—are able to make plants and animals grow and flourish. Humans, then, are always at the mercy of nature. Under Kupihea's reading of the Kumulipo as a metaphor for social and political developments, however, the last part of Chant 1—the section in which the water on the roots of the plant allows the top of the plant to grow—represents the role of the commoners in supporting the chiefs.

♦ Chant 2

The male and female forces in this chant are Pouliuli and Powehiwehi. Their names mean "murky" and "obscure," respectively. The *hilu* is a type of brightly colored fish common in the waters around Hawaii. Its name means "elegant," and it was used as a pet name for small children in order to compliment them indirectly, since a direct compliment might tempt bad luck. After listing some of the numerous sea animals that inhabit Hawaiian coastal waters along with the *hilu*, Chant 2 returns to the stream-pair refrain sequence of Chant 1. This time the pairs consist of one sea creature and one land plant. Beckwith suggests that this is meant to reinforce the connection between the actual fish in the ocean and the human *hilu* in a secluded place where children of very high rank were brought up.

♦ Chant 3

The names of the male and female in this chant, Po'ele'ele and Pohaha, mean "time of darkness" and "night breaking into dawn," hinting at the Kumulipo's gradual progression toward daybreak. According to Kupihea's theory, the different parts of the taro plant at the beginning of Chant 3 may symbolize different branches in the chiefly family to which the Kumulipo belonged. After the mention of the taro, the creatures in this chant are all birds or flying insects (except for the stingray, which does appear to swim by flapping its wings); they inhabit the trees and other plants that grew in the second chant. Robinson's theory of the Kumulipo as a metaphor for a child's growth suggests that the series of plants and animals in Chants 2 and 3, which all move about in some way by air or water, are meant to evoke the waving limbs of an infant.

♦ Chant 4

The male name in this chant, Popanopano, is a composite of *po* (night) and *pano* (dark or black). The female name, Polalowehi, combines the words for night, depth, and adornment or decoration. According to Kupihea's theory, the "crawlers" may symbolize the migration of families; according to Robinson's theory, they represent the movements of a child learning to crawl. The creatures in this chant live on the shore, and some, including the turtles, make the transition from sea to land and back. This makes the chant an effective bridge between the creatures living in the sea and in the trees (in Chants 2 and 3) to those living on land (beginning with Chant 5).

♦ Chant 5

The female name here, Polalouli, means "depth of night"; the male name, Pokanokano, which Beckwith translates as "Night-digger" after the first line, has strong sexual connotations. The pig is also associated with male sexuality, because of its role in plowing up the ground and making it ready for crops. The "pig child" in this verse may be the demigod Kamapua'a, who was born to a goddess in the shape of a pig and could shift between pig and human forms at will; he is one of the most popular figures in Hawaiian legend, where he is famous as a fighter and as a lover. The theme of crops and fertility continues with the "children of Lo'iloa" toward the end of the chant; Lo'iloa was the legendary planter of taro, so his children are the different varieties of taro plant. "Oma," in the fourth line from the end of Chant 5, is the word for the leading official at a chief's court; here it refers to the Night-digger, which gives weight to the theory that all the different kinds of people listed in this chant are representatives of different groups and classes coming to pay their respects to the newborn chief whom the Kumulipo honors.

♦ Chant 6

Rats have an ambiguous place in Hawaiian religion. They are believed to be descended from the night gods, and it is said that human spirits can return from the spirit world into rat bodies. However, comparing a person or a thing to a rat or a rat's nest is a bad omen. They "mark the seasons" by migrating to the shore when food becomes scarce in the mountains, and they eat the crops that grew in Chant 5. Kupihea's theory is that their migration symbolizes the development of the *aupuni* structure and the different levels of chiefs, each of which takes a tax on the crops of the level below.

♦ Chant 7

Chant 7 strikes a tone of reverence after the pragmatic description of the habits of rats (and possible playful allusions to the practices of chiefs). It lists some of the ways that a person could violate religious law, or taboo (*kapu* in Hawaiian), including approaching sacred places if one was not a priest or leaving garbage on the paths or in the sacred areas. The brindled dog in the middle of the chant is considered part of the family of the volcano goddess Pele and could not be eaten like other kinds of dogs. (Note that chiefs and other high-ranking men ate dog meat on special occasions.) The "hairless ones" in the same section are the 'Olohe—a name shared by a group of warriors who shaved and oiled their bodies for maximum effectiveness in wrestling and by a supernatural company of dog-headed warriors. The one "without a garment" who is "on the way to Malama" may be the spirit of a dead man making the journey to the afterlife, which in Hawaiian tradition follows a specific geographical path—even though, at this point in the creation myth, humans do not yet exist.

♦ Chant 8

With the birth or arrival of humans in Chant 8, day breaks. Human sexuality reappears with the repetition of "man for the narrow stream, woman for the broad stream." Chants 8 to 11 deal with variations on the ancestry of the first humans, beginning here with the goddess La'ila'i and her two siblings and sexual partners: the god Kane, whose name means "male," and the human Ki'i, whose name means "image." As the firstborn, La'ila'i has power over her brothers. Beckwith suggests that La'ila'i's name, "calmness," evokes the calm before the storm, the storm being human procreation. The expression "the woman sat sideways" refers to a married woman who takes a second man as a husband.

♦ Chant 9

Chant 9 offers further descriptions of the relations between La'ila'i, Ki'i, and Kane, with the references to volcanic activity symbolizing their sexuality and the birth of their children. The line about using sticks to make a fire is also symbolic of sex (the harder stick is held upright and rubbed against the hollowed softer stick in order to generate a spark). It is important to note that Ki'i is always mentioned before Kane as La'ila'i's sexual partner.

♦ Chant 10

This chant continues the story of La'ila'i, Ki'i, and Kane, mentioning more of their children by name and bringing in the conflict between the two males. High-ranking women in traditional Hawaiian society had the freedom to choose their sexual partners after marriage, but virginity before marriage was very important, so that there could be no question that the woman's first child was her husband's. In Chant 10, it appears that La'ila'i is Kane's wife but that Ki'i is the father of her first child. This means that Ki'i's descendants are the senior branch of the family, while Kane's are the junior branch.

♦ Chant 11

Chant 11 gives even more detail to the story: It names about eight hundred pairs of La'ila'i's descendants with Ki'i and Kane, beginning with Ki'i's son Kamaha'ina and Kane's daughter Hali'a. Chant 12 (not reproduced here) consists of eighty-three more pairs of descendants. In the last part of the twelfth chant, Wakea is mentioned with a rooster on his back; he reappears in Chant 13. The rooster, in the context of the Kumulipo, represents a powerful chief who does not belong to the main branch of his family but who makes his own branch the dominant one and whose descendants are ruling chiefs.

♦ Chant 13

The first part of Chant 13 tells the story of Haumea, which is picked up again in Chant 15; the second part turns to the story of Wakea and Papa, his female counterpart. The nine women at the beginning of Chant 13 are all Haumea in different forms. Haumea is a goddess associated with fertility, childbearing, and wild-food plants. She is portrayed variously in Hawaiian mythology as a sister of the gods Kane and Kanaloa and sometimes, as here, as the wife of Kanaloa. She is sometimes identified with La'ila'i (both described as *paha'oha'o*, or "shape-shifters"), sometimes with Papa, and sometimes with her daughter, the volcano goddess Pele.

Papa and Wakea are the legendary couple most commonly referred to as the ancestors of the Hawaiian people (and of many other Polynesian cultures, allowing for some language variations), but they do not seem to play a major role in the Kumulipo. Beckwith speculates that their story was a slightly later addition, added to the Kumulipo when the popularity of these particular figures increased. In some legends, Papa and Wakea are a human couple whose descendants are the chiefs, while Wakea's two brothers are the fathers of the priests and the commoners. The sequence of taboos in Chant 13 is established by Wakea as a cover story so that he can have an affair without making Papa suspicious.

♦ Chant 14

Wakea's affair with Hina is separate from the affair in Chant 13. The significance of the rooster on the ridgepole is that since anyone inferior in rank who allowed his or her shadow to fall on a taboo chief (one whose interactions were governed by sacred laws) could be punished with death, the rooster must be the highest-ranking individual in the area. The rooster also appears elsewhere in Hawaiian poetry as a symbol for a high chief.

♦ Chant 15
The first half of Chant 15 tells us that Haumea (from Chant 13) made herself into a young human woman many times over out of jealousy over her husband's second wife. There are many variations on the story of Haumea in Hawaiian mythology, but they agree that she turned herself into or passed through the trunk of a breadfruit tree so that she and a human husband could escape from a vengeful chief. Chant 15 then launches into a discussion of Maui, one of the most popular demigods in Polynesia, who is sometimes compared to Achilles or Hercules in Greek mythology because of his many superhuman accomplishments. In most stories, he is too clever for his own good, but his actions, such as slowing down the sun to make the days longer and fishing the Hawaiian islands up from the seafloor, are beneficial to humans.

♦ Chant 16
This last section of the Kumulipo is the dedication, a final genealogy leading from Maui to Lono-i-ka-makahiki (Ka-'i-'i-mamao). In other words, it explains the reason for the composition of the entire chant.

Audience

The immediate audience for any genealogical chant was the family to which it belonged, as well as anyone the family wished to impress with the length and possibly the divine nature of its pedigree. In the case of the Kumulipo, the chant was performed and later published for a much larger audience than was usual—namely, the Hawaiian people and anyone else interested in Hawaiian culture—because of the social and political importance of the family in question.

Impact

Genealogical chants are common throughout Polynesia, especially the eastern section of Polynesian islands, which includes Hawaii. Since precontact Hawaii was a nonliterate society, we do not have any records of Hawaiians' reactions to the Kumulipo when it was composed or when it was chanted for Captain Cook. We do know, however, that the Kumulipo is vitally important to the history and the study of Hawaiian religion today. Ten other Hawaiian genealogical creation chants have survived in written form, but after an extended analysis of the Kumulipo and the other chants,

the scholar Dorothy B. Barrère came to the conclusion that the manuscript version of the Kumulipo is the only one that seems to be nearly unaltered by the influence of Christianity and of the various cultures that were introduced to Hawaii in the late eighteenth and nineteenth centuries. Queen Lili'uokalani, in the introduction to her translation, states that one of her reasons for undertaking the project was so that Hawaiian terms and allusions to natural history would be preserved for posterity.

Further Reading

■ Books

Barrère, Dorothy B. *The Kumuhonua Legends: A Study of Late 19th Century Hawaiian Stories of Creation and Origins*. Honolulu: Department of Anthropology, Bernice P. Bishop Museum, 1969.

Beckwith, Martha Warren. *Hawaiian Mythology*. New Haven, Conn.: Yale University Press, 1940.

Beckwith, Martha Warren. *The Kumulipo: A Hawaiian Creation Chant*. Chicago, Ill.: University of Chicago Press, 1951.

Charlot, John. *The Hawaiian Poetry of Religion and Politics: Some Religio-Political Concepts in Post-Contact Literature*. Honolulu: Institute for Polynesian Studies, 1985.

Craig, Robert D. *Handbook of Polynesian Mythology*. Santa Barbara, Calif.: ABC-CLIO, 2004.

Kame'eleihiwa, Lilikala. "Kumulipo." Hawaii: University of Hawaii, 2008.

Lili'uokalani. *The Kumulipo: An Hawaiian Creation Myth*. Kentfield, Calif.: Pueo Press, 1978.

Pukui, Mary Kawena, E. W. Haertig, and Catherine A. Lee. *Nana i ke Kumu: Look to the Source*. 2 vols. Honolulu: Hui Hanai, 1972.

Valeri, Valerio. *Kingship and Sacrifice: Ritual and Society in Ancient Hawaii*, trans. Paula Wissing. Chicago, Ill.: University of Chicago Press, 1985.

■ Journals

Davenport, William. "The 'Hawaiian Cultural Revolution': Some Political and Economic Considerations." *American Anthropologist* 71 (1969): 1–20.

—Commentary by Claudia Arno

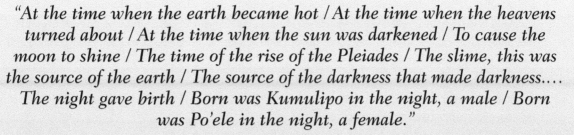

"At the time when the earth became hot / At the time when the heavens turned about / At the time when the sun was darkened / To cause the moon to shine / The time of the rise of the Pleiades / The slime, this was the source of the earth / The source of the darkness that made darkness.... The night gave birth / Born was Kumulipo in the night, a male / Born was Po'ele in the night, a female."

(Section 1)

"The pig child is born / Lodges inland in the bush / Cultivates the water taro patches of Lo'iloa / Tenfold is the increase of the island / Tenfold the increase of the land / The land where the Night-digger dwelt / Long is the line of his ancestry / The ancient line of the pig of chief blood / The pig of highest rank born in the time / The time when the Night-digger lived/ And slept with Po-lalo-uli / The night gave birth."

(Section 1)

"Wakea as Ki'i [image] slept with Hina-ka-we'o-a / Born was the cock, perched on Wakea's back / The cock scratched the back of Wakea / Wakea was jealous, tried to brush it away / Wakea was jealous, vexed and annoyed / Thrust away the cock and it flew to the ridgepole / The cock was on the ridgepole / The cock was lord."

(Section 1)

"Everyone knows about the battle of Maui with the sun / With the loop of Maui's snaring-rope / Winter [?] became the sun's / Summer became Maui's."

(Section 1)

Questions for Further Study

1. It is safe to say that virtually every culture/religion has a creation account, such as the Kumulipo. Each of these accounts is likely to be a reflection of something in the culture's history, social structure, or even geography that defines that culture. In what ways does the creation account of Kumulipo reflect something unique and defining about Hawaiian culture?

2. To what extent is the Kumulipo—or at least publication of a translation of it in the late nineteenth century—a political document as well as a religious one?

3. Historically, the purpose of many religious documents, at least in part, has been to establish the legitimacy of the king or chief by confirming royal descent. This concern, though, seems to have been an obsession in Hawaii; as the entry notes, "A genealogy was a treasured family possession, and no one outside the family would ordinarily know the entire chant, except for the priest who did the chanting." Why do you think the issue of genealogy was a *particular* concern in Hawaii?

4. Why do you think the chant was performed only twice, once in 1779 and once in 1804?

5. Imagine that you are Captain Cook and that you have arrived at the Hawaiian Islands in 1779. What do you think your reaction, as a proper Englishman and sea captain, would be to the Kumulipo?

KUMULIPO: DOCUMENT TEXT

1770 CE

— Kalakaua

Chant 1

At the time when the earth became hot
At the time when the heavens turned about
At the time when the sun was darkened
To cause the moon to shine
The time of the rise of the Pleiades
The slime, this was the source of the earth
The source of the darkness that made darkness
The source of the night that made night
The intense darkness, the deep darkness
Darkness of the sun, darkness of the night
Nothing but night.

The night gave birth
Born was Kumulipo in the night, a male
Born was Po'ele in the night, a female
Born was the coral polyp, born was the coral, came forth
Born was the grub that digs and heaps up the earth, came forth
Born was his [child] an earthworm, came forth
Born was the starfish, his child the small starfish came forth
Born was the sea cucumber, his child the small sea cucumber came forth
Born was the sea urchin, the sea urchin [tribe]
Born was the short-spiked sea urchin, came forth
Born was the smooth sea urchin, his child the long-spiked came forth
Born was the ring-shaped sea urchin, his child the thin-spiked came forth
Born was the barnacle, his child the pearl oyster came forth
Born was the mother-of-pearl, his child the oyster came forth
Born was the mussel, his child the hermit crab came forth
Born was the big limpet, his child the small limpet came forth
Born was the cowry, his child the small cowry came forth

Born was the naka shellfish, the rock oyster his child came forth
Born was the drupa shellfish, his child the bitter white shell fish came forth
Born was the conch shell, his child the small conch shell came forth
Born was the nerita shellfish, the sand-burrowing shellfish his child came forth
Born was the fresh water shellfish, his child the small fresh water shellfish came forth
Born was man for the narrow stream, the woman for the broad stream
Born was the Ekaha moss living in the sea
Guarded by the Ekahakaha fern living on land
Darkness slips into light
Earth and water are the food of the plant
The god enters, man can not enter
Man for the narrow stream, woman for the broad stream
Born was the tough seagrass living in the sea
Guarded by the tough landgrass living on land

Refrain
Man for the narrow stream, woman for the broad stream
Born was the 'Ala'ala moss living in the sea
Guarded by the 'Ala'ala mint living on land

Refrain
Man for the narrow stream, woman for the broad stream
Born was the Manauea moss living in the sea
Guarded by the Manauea taro plant living on land

Refrain
Man for the narrow stream, woman for the broad stream
Born was the Ko'ele seaweed living in the sea
Guarded by the long-jointed sugarcane, the *ko 'ele'ele*, living on land

Refrain
Man for the narrow stream, woman for the broad stream

Born was the Puaki seaweed living in the sea
Guarded by the Akiaki rush living on land

Refrain
Man for the narrow stream, woman for the broad stream
Born was the Kakalamoa living in the sea
Guarded by the moamoa plant living on land

Refrain
Man for the narrow stream, woman for the broad stream
Born was the Kele seaweed living in the sea
Guarded by the Ekele plant living on land

Refrain
Man for the narrow stream, woman for the broad stream
Born was the Kala seaweed living in the sea
Guarded by the 'Akala vine living on land

Refrain
Man for the narrow stream, woman for the broad stream
Born was the Lipu'upu'u living in the sea
Guarded by the Lipu'u living on land

Refrain
Man for the narrow stream, woman for the broad stream
Born was the Long-one living at sea
Guarded by the Long-torch living on land

Refrain
Man for the narrow stream, woman for the broad stream
Born was the Ne seaweed living in the sea
Guarded by the Neneleau [sumach] living on land

Refrain
Man for the narrow stream, woman for the broad stream
Born was the hairy seaweed living in the sea
Guarded by the hairy pandanus vine living on land
Darkness slips into light
Earth and water are the food of the plant
The god enters, man cannot enter
The man with the water gourd, he is a god
Water that causes the withered vine to flourish
Causes the plant top to develop freely
Multiplying in the passing time
The long night slips along
Fruitful, very fruitful
Spreading here, spreading there

Spreading this way, spreading that way
Propping up earth, holding up the sky
The time passes, this night of Kumulipo
Still it is night.

Chant 2

Born is a child to Po-wehiwehi
Cradled in the arms of Po-uliuli[?]
A wrestler, a pusher, [?]
Dweller in the land of Poho-mi-luamea
The sacred scent from the gourd stem proclaims [itself]
The stench breaks forth in the time of infancy
He is doubtful and stands swelling
He crooks himself and straddles
The seven waters just float
Born is the child of the *hilu* fish and swims
The hilu fish rests with spreading tail-fin
A child of renown for Po-uliuli
A little one for Po-wehiwehi
Po-uliuli the male
Po-wehiwehi the female
Born is the I'a [fish], born the Nai'a [porpoise] in the sea there swimming
Born is the Mano [shark], born the Moano [goatfish] in the sea there swimming
Born is the Mau, born the Maumau in the sea there swimming
Born is the Nana, born the Mana fish in the sea there swimming
Born is the Nake, born the Make in the sea there swimming
Born is the Napa, born the Nala in the sea there swimming
Born is the Pala, born the Kala [sturgeon ?] in the sea there swimming
Born is the Paka eel, born is the Papa [crab] in the sea there swimming
Born is the Kalakala, born the Huluhulu [sea slug] in the sea there swimming
Born is the Halahala, born the Palapala in the sea there swimming
Born is the Pe'a [octopus], born is the Lupe [sting ray] in the sea there swimming
Born is the Ao, born is the 'Awa [milkfish] in the sea there swimming
Born is the Aku [bonito], born the Ahi [albacore] in the sea there swimming
Born is the Opelu [mackerel], born the Akule fish in the sea there swimming

Born is the 'Ama'ama [mullet], born the 'Anae [adult mullet] in the sea there swimming
Born is the Ehu, born the Nehu fish in the sea there swimming
Born is the 'Ino, born the 'Ao'ao in the sea there swimming
Born is the 'Ono fish, born the Omo in the sea there swimming
Born is the Pahau, born is the Lauhau in the sea there swimming
Born is the Moi [threadfin], born the Lo'ilo'i in the sea there swimming
Born is the Mao, born is the Maomao in the sea there swimming
Born is the Kaku, born the A'ua'u in the sea there swimming
Born is the Kupou, born the Kupouposu in the sea there swimming
Born is the Weke [mackerel ?], born the Lele in the sea there swimming
Born is the Palani [sturgeon], born the Nuku-moni [cavalla] in the sea there swimming
Born is the Ulua fish, born the Hahalua [devil-fish] in the sea there swimming
Born is the 'Ao'aonui born the Paku'iku'i fish in the sea there swimming
Born is the Ma'i'i'i fish, born the Ala'ihi fish in the sea there swimming
Born is the 'O'o, born the 'Akilolo fish in the sea there swimming
Born is man for the narrow stream, the woman for the broad stream
Born is the Nenue [pickerel] living im the sea
Guarded by the Lauhue [gourd plant] living on land

Refrain
Man for the narrow stream, woman for the broad stream
Born is the Pahaha [young mullet] living in the sea
Guarded by the Puhala [pandanus] living on land

Refrain
Man for the narrow stream, woman for the broad stream
Born is the Pahau living in the sea
Guarded by the Hau tree [hibiscus] living on land

Refrain
Man for the narrow stream, woman for the broad stream
Born is the He'e [squid] living in the sea
Guarded by the Walahe'e [shrub] living on land

Refrain
Man for the narrow stream, woman for the broad stream
Born is the 'O'opu [gobey fish] living in the sea
Guarded by the 'O'opu [fish] living in fresh water

Refrain
Man for the narrow stream, woman for the broad stream
Born is the Kauila eel living in the sea
Guarded by the Kauila tree living on land

Refrain
Man for the narrow stream, woman for the broad stream
Born is the Umaumalei eel living in the sea
Guarded by the 'Ulei tree living on land

Refrain
Man for the narrow stream, woman for the broad stream
Born is the Paku'iku'i fish living in the sea
Guarded by the Kukui tree [candlenut] living on land

Refrain
Man for the narrow stream, woman for the broad stream
Born is the Laumilo eel living in the sea
Guarded by the Milo tree living on land

Refrain
Man for the narrow stream, woman for the broad stream
Born is the Kupoupou fish living in the sea
Guarded by the Kou tree living on land

Refrain
Man for the narrow stream, woman for the broad stream
Born is the Hauliuli [snake mackerel] living in the sea
Guarded by the Uhi yam living on land

Refrain
Man for the narrow stream, woman for the broad stream
Born is the Weke [mackerel] living in the sea
Guarded by the Wauke plant living on land

Refrain
Man for the narrow stream, woman for the broad stream
Born is the 'A'awa. fish living in the sea
Guarded by the 'Awa plant living on land

Refrain

Man for the narrow stream, woman for the broad stream

Born is the Ulae [lizard fish] living in the sea

Guarded by the Mokae rush living on land

Refrain

Man for the narrow stream, woman for the broad stream

Born is the Palaoa [walrus] living in the sea [?]

Guarded by the Aoa [sandalwood] living on land

Refrain

The train of walruses passing by [?]

Milling about in the depths of the sea

The long lines of opule fish

The sea is thick with them

Crabs and hardshelled creatures

[They] go swallowing on the way

Rising and diving under swiftly and silently

Pimoe lurks behind the horizon

On the long waves, the crested waves

Innumerable the coral ridges

Low, heaped-up, jagged

The little ones seek the dark places

Very dark is the ocean and obscure

A sea of coral like the green heights of Paliuli

The land disappears into them

Covered by the darkness of night

Still it is night

Chant 3

A male this, the female that

A male born in the time of black darkness

The female born in the time of groping in the darkness

Overshadowed was the sea, overshadowed the land

Overshadowed the streams, overshadowed the mountains

Overshadowed the dimly brightening night

The rootstalk grew forming nine leaves

Upright it grew with dark leaves

The sprout that shot forth leaves of high chiefs

Born was Po'ele'ele the male

Lived with Pohaha a female

The rootstalk sprouted

The taro stalk grew

Born was the Wood borer, a parent

Out came its child a flying thing, and flew

Born was the Caterpillar, the parent

Out came its child a Moth, and flew

Born was the Ant, the parent

Out came its child a Dragonfly, and flew

Born was the Grub, the parent

Out came its child the Grasshopper, and flew

Born was the Pinworm, the parent

Out came its child a Fly, and flew

Born was the egg [?], the parent

Out came its child a bird, and flew

Born was the Snipe, the parent

Out came its child a Plover, and flew

Born was the A'o bird, the parent

Out came its child an A'u bird, and flew

Born was the Turnstone, the parent

Out came its child a Fly-catcher, and flew

Born was the Mudhen, the parent

Out came its child an Apapane bird, and flew

Born was the Crow, the parent

Out came its child an Alawi bird, and flew

Born was the 'E'ea bird, the parent

Out came its child an Alaaiaha bird, and flew

Born was the Mamo honey-sucker, the parent

Out came its child an 'O'o bird, and flew

Born was the Rail, the parent

Out came its child a brown Albatross, and flew

Born was the Akikiki creeper, the parent

Out came its child an Ukihi bird, and flew

Born was the Curlew, the parent

Out came its child a Stilt, and flew

Born was the Frigate bird, the parent

Out came its child a Tropic bird, and flew

Born was the migrating gray-backed Tern, the parent

Out came its child a red-tailed Tropic-bird, and flew

Born was the Unana bird, the parent

Its offspring the Heron came out and flew

Flew hither in flocks

On the seashore in ranks

Settled down and covered the beach

Covered the land of Kane's-hidden-island

Land birds were born

Sea birds were born

Man born for the narrow stream, woman for the broad stream

Born was the Stingray, living in the sea

Guarded by the Stormy-petrel living on land

Refrain

Man for the narrow stream, woman for the broad stream

Born was the Sea-swallow, living at sea

Guarded by the Hawk living on land

Refrain
Man for the narrow stream, woman for the broad stream
Born was the Duck of the islands, living at sea
Guarded by the Wild-duck living on land

Refrain
Man for the narrow stream, woman for the broad stream
Born was the Hehe, living at sea
Guarded by the Nene [goose] living on land

Refrain
Man for the narrow stream, woman for the broad stream
Born was the Auku'u, living by the sea
Guarded by the Ekupu'u bird living on land

Refrain
Man for the narrow stream, woman for the broad stream
Born was the Noddy [*noio*], living at sea
Guarded by the Owl [*pueo*] living on land

Refrain
This is the flying place of the bird Halulu
Of Kiwa'a, the bird that cries over the canoe house
Birds that fly in a flock shutting out the sun
The earth is covered with the fledgelings of the night breaking into dawn
The time when the dawning light spreads abroad
The young weak 'ape plant rises

A tender plant with spreading leaves
A branching out of the nightborn
Nothing but darkness that
Nothing but darkness this
Darkness alone for Po'ele'ele
A time of dawn indeed for Pohaha
Still it is night

Chant 4

Plant the *'ahi'a* and cause it to propagate
The dusky black *'ape* plant
The sea creeps up to the land
Creeps backward, creeps forward
Producing the family of crawlers
Crawling behind, crawling in front
Advancing the front, settling down at the back
The front of my cherished one [?]

He is dark, splendid,
Popanopano is born as a male [?]
Popanopano, the male
Po-lalo-wehi, the female
Gave birth to those who produce eggs
Produce and multiply in the passing night
Here they are laid
Here they roll about
The children roll about, play in the sand
Child of the night of black darkness is born
The night gives birth
The night gives birth to prolific ones
The night is swollen with plump creatures
The night gives birth to rough-backed turtles
The night produces horn-billed turtles
The night gives birth to dark-red turtles
The night is pregnant with the small lobster
The night gives birth to sluggish-moving geckos
Slippery is the night with sleek-skinned geckos
The night gives birth to clinging creatures
The night proclaims rough ones
The night gives birth to deliberate creatures
The night shrinks from the ineffective
The night gives birth to sharp-nosed creatures
Hollowed is the night for great fat ones
The night gives birth to mud dwellers
The night lingers for track leavers
Born is the male for the narrow stream, the female for the
broad stream
Born is the turtle [*Honu*] living in the sea
Guarded by the *Maile* seedling [*Kubonua*] living on land

Refrain
Man for the narrow stream, woman for the broad stream
Born is the sea-borer [*Wili*] living in the sea
Guarded by the Wiliwili tree living on land

Refrain
Man for the narrow stream, woman for the broad stream
Born is the sea-worm living in the sea
Guarded by the bastard-sandalwood living on land

Refrain
Man for the narrow stream, woman for the broad stream
Born is the Okea living in the sea
Guarded by the Ahakea tree living on land

Refrain

Man for the narrow stream, woman for the broad stream
Born is the sea-urchin [*Wana*] living in the sea
Guarded by the thorny Wanawana plant living on land

Refrain

Man for the narrow stream, woman for the broad stream
Born is the Nene shellfish living in the sea
Guarded by the Manene grass living on land

Refrain

Man for the narrow stream, woman for the broad stream
Born is the Liko living in the sea
Guarded by the Piko tree living on land

Refrain

Man for the narrow stream, woman for the broad stream
Born is the Opeope jellyfish living in the sea
Guarded by the Oheohe [bamboo] living on land

Refrain

Man for the narrow stream, woman for the broad stream
Born is the Nanana [sea spider] living in the sea
Guarded by the Nonanona living on land

Refrain

With a dancing motion they go creeping and crawling
The tail swinging its length
Sullenly, sullenly
They go poking about the dunghill
Filth is their food, they devour it
Eat and rest, eat and belch it up
Eating like common people
Distressful is their eating
They move about and become heated
Act as if exhausted
They stagger as they go
Go in the land of crawlers
The family of crawlers born in the night
Still it is night

Chant 5

The time arrives for Po-kanokano
To increase the progeny of Po-lalo-uli
Dark is the skin of the new generation

Black is the skin of the beloved Po-lalo-uli
Who sleeps as a wife to the Night-digger
The beaked nose that digs the earth is erected
Let it dig at the land, increase it, heap it up
Walling it up at the back
Walling it up in front
The pig child is born
Lodges inland in the bush
Cultivates the water taro patches of Lo'iloa
Tenfold is the increase of the island
Tenfold the increase of the land
The land where the Night-digger dwelt
Long is the line of his ancestry
The ancient line of the pig of chief blood
The pig of highest rank born in the time
The time when the Night-digger lived
And slept with Po-lalo-uli
The night gave birth
Born were the peaked-heads, they were clumsy ones
Born were the flat-heads, they were braggarts
Born were the angular-heads, they were esteemed
Born were the fair-haired, they were strangers
Born were the blonds, their skin was white
Born were those with retreating foreheads, they were bushy haired
Born were the blunt-heads, their heads were round
Born were the dark-heads, they were dark
Born were the common class, they were unsettled
Born were the working class, they were workers
Born were the favorites, they were courted
Born were the slave class, and wild was their nature
Born were the cropped-haired, they were the picked men
Born were the song chanters, they were indolent [?]
Born were the big bellies, big eaters were they
Born were the timid ones, bashful were they
Born were the messengers, they were sent here and there
Born were the slothful, they were lazy
Born were the stingy, they were sour
Born were the puny, they were feeble ones
Born were the thickset, they were stalwart
Born were the broad-chested, broad was their badge in battle
Born were the family men, they were home lovers
Born were the mixed breeds, they had no fixed line of descent

Born were the lousy-headed, they were lice in-
fested
Born were the war leaders, men followed after
them
Born were the high chiefs, they were ruddy
Born were the stragglers, they were dispersed
Scattered here and there
The children of Lo'iloa multiplied
The virgin land sprang into bloom
The gourd of desire was loosened
With desire to extend the family line
To carry on the fruit of Oma's descendants,
The generations from the Night-digger
In that period of the past
Still it is night

Chant 6

Many new fines of chiefs spring up
Cultivation arises, full of taboos
[They go about scratching at the wet lands
It sprouts, the first blades appear, the food is
ready] [?]
Food grown by the water courses
Food grown by the sea
Plentiful and heaped up
The parent rats dwell in holes
The little rats huddle together
Those who mark the seasons
Little tolls from the land
Little tolls from the water courses
Trace of the nibblings of these brown-coated
ones
With whiskers upstanding
They hide here and there
A rat in the upland, a rat by the sea
A rat running beside the wave
Born to the two, child of the Night-falling-away
Born to the two, child of the Night-creeping-
away
The little child creeps as it moves
The little child moves with a spring
Pilfering at the rind
Rind of the 'ohi'a fruit, not a fruit of the upland
A tiny child born as the darkness falls away
A springing child born as the darkness creeps
away
Child of the dark and child in the night now here
Still it is night

Chant 7

Fear falls upon me on the mountain top
Fear of the passing night
Fear of the night approaching
Fear of the pregnant night
Fear of the breach of the law
Dread of the place of offering and the narrow
trail
Dread of the food and the waste part remaining
Dread of the receding night
Awe of the night approaching
Awe of the dog child of the Night-creeping-away
A dog child of the Night-creeping-hither
A dark red dog, a brindled dog
A hairless dog of the hairless ones
A dog as an offering for the oven
Palatable is the sacrifice for supplication
Pitiful in the cold without covering
Pitiful in the heat without a garment
He goes naked on the way to Malama
[Where] the night ends for the children [of
night]
From the growth and the parching [?]
From the cutting off and the quiet [?]
The driving Hula wind his companion
Younger brother of the naked ones, the 'Olohe
Out from the slime come rootlets
Out from the slime comes young growth
Out from the slime come branching leaves
Out from the slime comes outgrowth
Born in the time when men came from afar
Still it is night

Chant 8

Well-formed is the child, well-formed now
Child in the time when men multiplied
Child in the time when men came from afar
Born were men by the hundreds
Born was man for the narrow stream
Born was woman for the broad stream
Born the night of the gods
Men stood together
Men slept together
They two slept together in the time long ago
Wave after wave of men moving in company
Ruddy the forehead of the god
Dark that of man
White-[bearded] the chin
Tranquil was the time when men multiplied

Calm like the time when men came from afar
It was called Calmness [La'ila'i] then
Born was La'ila'i a woman
Born was Ki'i a man
Born was Kane a god
Born was Kanaloa the hot-striking octopus
It was day
The wombs gave birth [?]
Ocean-edge
The-damp-forest, latter of the two
The first chief of the dim past dwelling in cold uplands, their younger
The man of long life and hundreds upon hundreds of chiefs
Scoop out, scoop out,
Hollow out, hollow out, keep hollowing
Hollow out, hollow out, "the woman sat sideways"
La'ila'i, a woman in the time when men came from afar
La'ila'i, a woman in the time when men multiplied
Lived as a woman of the time when men multiplied
Born was Groping-one [Hahapo'ele], a girl
Born was Dim-sighted [Ha-popo], a girl
Born was Beautiful [Maila] called Clothed-in-leaves [Lopalapala]
Naked ['Olohe] was another name
[She] lived in the land of Lua [pit]
[At] that place called "pit of the 'Olohe"
Naked was man born in the day
Naked the woman born in the upland
[She] lived here with man [?]
Born was Creeping-ti-plant [La'i'olo] to man
Born was Expected-day [Kapopo], a female
Born was Midnight [Po'ele-i], born First-light [Po'ele-a]
Opening-wide [Wehi-loa] was their youngest
These were those who gave birth
The little ones, the older ones
Ever increasing in number
Man spread abroad, man was here now
It was Day

Chant 9

Still, trembling stands earth
Hot, rumbling, split is the heaven
This woman ascends to heaven, ascends right up to heaven

Ascends up toward the forest
Tries to touch the earth and the earth splits up
Children of Ki'i sprung from the brain
Came out, flew, flew also to the heavens
Showed the sign, the ruddy tint by which they were known
Showed the fine reddish hair at puberty [?]
Showed on the chin a reddish beard
The offspring of that mysterious woman
The woman of 'Iliponi, of within 'I'ipakalani
"From the female firestick comes the fire that makes men"
That woman dwelt in Nu'umealani
Land where the gods dwelt
"She stripped the dark leaves of the koa tree"
A woman of mysterious body was this
She lived with Ki'i, she lived with Kane
She lived with Kane of the time when men multiplied
Forgotten is the time of this multitude
A multitude the posterity of the time of child-bearing
She returned again upward
Dwelt in the sacred forest of the gods in Nu'umealani
Was pregnant there, the earth broke open
Born was the woman Groping-one [Haha-po'ele]
Born was Dim-sighted [Hapopo], a woman
Last born was Naked-one, 'Olohelohe
Part of the posterity of that woman
It was Day

Chant 10

Come hither, La'ila'i [to] the wall [?]
Kane of Kapokinikini [to] the post; Ki'i be quiet
Born was La'i'olo'olo and lived at Kapapa
Born was Kamaha'ina the first-born, a male
Born was Kamamule, a male
Kamakalua the second child was a girl
Came the child Po'ele-i [Midnight]
Came the child Po'ele-a [First-light]
Wehi-wela-wehi-loa [Opening-to-the heat, opening wide]
La'ila'i returned and lived with Kane
Born was Ha'i, a girl
Born was Hali'a, a girl
Born was Hakea, Fair-haired, a male
There was whispering, lip-smacking and clucking
Smacking, tut-tutting, head-shaking

Sulking, sullenness, silence
Kane kept silence, refused to speak
Sullen, angry, resentful
With the woman for her progeny
Hidden was the man by whom she had children
[The man] to whom her children were born [?]
The chiefess refused him the youngest
Gave the sacred 'ape to Ki'i
She slept with Ki'i
Kane suspected the first-born, became jealous
Suspected Ki'i and La'ila'i of a secret union
They pelted Kane with stones
Hurled a spear; he shouted aloud
"This is fallen to my lot, for the younger [line]"
Kane was angry and jealous because he slept last
with her
His descendants would hence belong to the
younger line
The children of the elder would be lord
First through La'ila'i, first through Ki'i
Child of the two born in the heavens there
Came forth

Chant 11

She was a woman living among chiefs and mar-
ried to her brother
She was a restless woman living among chiefs
She lived above and came bending down over
Ki'i
The earth swarmed with her offspring
Born was Kamaha'ina [First-born], a male
Born was Kamamule, her younger born
Born was Kamamainau, her middle one
Born was Kamakulua her little one, a girl
Kamaha'ina lived as husband to Hali['a]

. . .

Born was Pola'a
Born was rough weather, born the current
Born the booming of the sea, the breaking of
foam
Born the roaring, advancing, and receding of
waves, the
rumbling sound, the earthquake
The sea rages, rises over the beach
Rises silently to the inhabited places
Rises gradually up over the land...

. . .

. . .

Born is Po-elua [Second-night] on the lineage
of Wakea

Born is the stormy night
Born the night of plenty
Born is the cock on the back of Wakea
Ended is [the line of] the first chief of the dim
past dwelling in cold uplands
Dead is the current sweeping in from the navel
of the earth: that was a warrior wave
Many who came vanished, lost in the passing
night

Chant 13

Mulinaha was the husband, 'Ipo'i the wife
Born was Laumiha a woman, lived with Ku-ka-
haku-a-lani ["Ku-the-lord-of-heaven"]
Born was Kaha'ula a woman, lived with Ku-huli-
honua ["Ku-overturning-earth"]
Born was Kahakauakoko a woman, lived with
Ku-lani-'ehu ["Ku-(the)-brown-haired-chief"]
Born was Haumea a woman, lived with the god
Kanaloa
Born was Ku-kaua-kahi a male, lived with
Kuaimehani
Born was Kaua-huli-honua
Born was Hina-mano-ulua'e ["Woman-of-abun-
dance-of food-plants"] a woman
Born was Huhune ["Dainty"] a woman
Born was Haunu'u a woman
Born was Haulani a woman
Born was Hikapuanaiea ["Sickly"] a woman;
Haumea was recognized, this was Haumea
Haumea of mysterious forms, Haumea of eight-
fold forms
Haumea of four-hundred-thousand-fold forms,
Haumea of four-thousand-fold forms
With thousands upon thousands of forms
With Hikapuanaiea the heavenly one became
barren
She lived like a dog, this woman of Nu'umea [?]
Nu'umea the land, Nu'u-papa-kini the division
Haumea spread through her grandchildren
With Ki'o she became barren, ceased bearing
children
This woman bore children through the fontanel
Her children came out from the brain
She was a woman of 'I'ilipo in Nu'umea
She lived with Mulinaha
Born was Laumiha ["Intense-silence"] born
from the brain
Born was the woman Kaha'ula ["Erotic-dreams"]
from the brain

Born was Ka-haka-uakoko ["The-perch-of-the-low-lying rainbow"] from the brain
Haumea was this, that same woman
She lived with the god Kanaloa
The god Kaua-kai ["First-strife"] was born from the brain
Born from the brain were the offspring of that woman
Drivelers were the offspring from the brain
Papa-seeking-earth
Papa-seeking-heaven
Great-Papa-giving-birth-to-islands
Papa lived with Wakea
Born was the woman Ha'alolo
Born was jealousy, anger
Papa was deceived by Wakea
He ordered the sun, the moon
The night to Kane for the younger
The night to Hilo for the first-born
Taboo was the house platform, the place for sitting
Taboo the house where Wakea lived
Taboo was intercourse with the divine parent
Taboo the taro plant, the acrid one
Taboo the poisonous 'akia plant
Taboo the narcotic auhuhu plant
Taboo the medicinal uhaloa
Taboo the bitter part of the taro leaf
Taboo the taro stalk that stood by the woman's taboo house
Haloa was buried [there], a long taro stalk grew
The offspring of Haloa [born] into the day
Came forth

Chant 14

Born was Pau-pani-a[wa]kea
This was Wakea; [born was] Lehu'ula; [born was] Makulu-kulu-the-chief
Their youngest, a man of great bundles
Collected and placed with Makali'i; fixed fast
Fixed are the stars suspended in the sky
[There] swings Ka'awela [Mercury], swings Kupoilaniua
Ha'i swings that way, Ha'i swings this way
Kaha'i swings, swings Kaha'iha'i [in the Milky Way]
Swings Kaua, the star cluster Wahilaninui
Swings the flower of the heavens, Kaulua-i-ha'imoha'i
Puanene swings, the star that reveals a lord

Nu'u swings, Kaha'ilono swings
Wainaku [patron star of Hilo] swings, swings Ikapa'a
Swings Kiki'ula, swings Keho'oea
Pouhanu'u swings, swings Ka-ili-'ula, The-red-skinned
Swings Kapakapaka, [and the morning star) Mananalo [Jupiter or Venus]
Swings Kona, swings Wailea [patron star of Maui]
Swings the Auhaku, swings the Eye-of-Unulau
Swings Hina-of-the-heavens, Hina-lani, swings Keoea
Ka'aka'a swings, swings Polo'ula [star of Oahu]
Kanikania'ula swings, Kauamea swings
Swings Kalalani [of Lanai], swings [the astrologers' star] Kekepue
Swings Ka'alolo [of Ni'ihau], swings the Resting-place-of-the-sun [Kaulana-a-ka-la]
Hua swings, 'Au'a [Betelgeuse] swings
Lena swings, swings Lanikuhana
Swings Ho'oleia, swings Makeaupe'a
Swings Kaniha'alilo, swings 'U'u
Swings Wa [Sirius], swings 'Ololu
Kamaio swings, swings Kaulu[a]lena
Swings Peaked-nose, swings Chicken-nose
Swings Pipa, swings Ho'eu
Swings Malana, swings Kaka'e
Swings Mali'u, swings Kaulua
Lanakamalama swings, Naua swings
Welo swings, swings Ikiiki
Ka'aona swings, swings Hinaia'ele'ele
Puanakau [Rigel] swings, swings Le'ale'a
Swings Hikikauelia [Sirius of navigators], swings Ka'elo
Swings Kapawa, swings Hikikaulonomeha [Sirius of astrologers]
Swings Hoku'ula, swings Poloahilani
Swings Ka'awela, swings Hanakalanai
Uliuli swings, Melemele swings [two lands of old]
Swings the Pleiades, Makali'i, swings the Cluster, na Huihui
Swings Kokoiki [Kamehameha's star], swings Humu [Altair]
Moha'i swings, swings Kaulu[a]okaoka
Kukui swings, swings Konamaukuku
Swings Kamalie, swings Kamalie the first
Swings Kamalie the last
Swings Hina-of-the-yellow-skies, Hina-o-naleilena
Swing the Seven, na Hiku [Big Dipper], swings the first of the Seven

The second of the Seven, the third of the Seven
The fourth of the Seven, the fifth of the Seven
The sixth of the Seven, the last of the Seven
Swings Mahapili, swings the Cluster
Swing the Darts [Kao] of Orion
Sown was the seed of Makali'i, seed of the heavens
Sown was the seed of the gods, the sun is a god
Sown was the seed of Hina, an afterbirth of Lo-no-muku
The food of Hina-ia-ka-malama as Waka
She was found by Wakea in the deep sea
In a sea of coral, a turbulent sea
Hina-ia-ka-malama floated as a bailing gourd
Was hung up in the canoes, hence called Hina-the-bailer [-ke-ka]
Taken ashore, set by the fire
Born were corals, born the eels
Born were the small sea urchins, the large sea urchins
The blackstone was born, the volcanic stone was born
Hence she was called Woman-from-whose-womb-come-various-forms, Hinahalakoa
Hina craved food, Wakea went to fetch it
[He] set up images on the platform
Set them up neatly in a row
Wakea as Ki'i [image] slept with Hina-ka-we'o-a
Born was the cock, perched on Wakea's back
The cock scratched the back of Wakea
Wakea was jealous, tried to brush it away
Wakea was jealous, vexed and annoyed
Thrust away the cock and it flew to the ridgepole
The cock was on the ridgepole
The cock was lord
This was the seed of The-high-one
Begotten in the heavens
The heavens shook
The earth shook
Even to the sacred places.

Chant 15

Haumea, woman of Nu'umea in Kukuiha'a
Of Mehani the impenetrable land of Kuai-healani in Paliuli
The beautiful, the dark [land], darkening the heavens
A solitude for the heavenly one, Kameha-'i-kaua [?]

Kameha-'i-kaua, The-secluded-one-supreme-in-war, god of Kauakahi
At the parting of earth, at the parting of high heaven
Left the land, jealous of her husband's second mate
Came to the land of Lua, to 'Ahu of Lua, lived at Wawau
The goddess became the wife of Makea
Haumea became a woman of Kalihi in Ko'olau
Lived in Kalihi on the edge of the cliff Laumilia
Entered a growing tree, she became a breadfruit tree
A breadfruit body, a trunk and leaves she had
Many forms had this woman Haumea
Great Haumea was mysterious
Mysterious was Haumea in the way she lived
She lived with her grandchildren
She slept with her children
Slept with her child Kauakahi as [?] the wife Kuaimehani
Slept with her grandchild Kaua-huli-honua
As [?] his wife Huli-honua
Slept with her grandchild Haloa
As [?] his wife Hinamano'ulua'e
Slept with her grandchild Waia as [?] his wife Huhune
Slept with her grandchild Hinanalo as [?] his wife Haunu'u
Slept with her grandchild Nanakahili as [?] his wife Haulani
Slept with her grandchild Wailoa as [?] his wife Hikapuaneiea
Ki'o was born, Haumea was recognized
Haumea was seen to be shriveled
Cold and undesirable
The woman was in fact gone sour
Hard to deal with and crabbed
Unsound, a fraud, half blind, a woman generations old
Wrinkled behind, wrinkled before
Bent and grey the breast, worthless was [the one of] Nu'u-mea [?]
She lived licentiously, bore children like a dog
With Ki'o came forth the chiefs
He slept with Kamole, with the woman of the woodland
Born was Ole, Ha'i was the wife
. . .
Waolena was the man, Mahui'e the wife
Akalana was the man, Hina-of-the-fire the wife
Born was Maui the first, born was Maui the middle one

Born was Maui-ki'iki'i, born was Maui of the loincloth
The loincloth with which Akalana girded his loins
Hina-of-the-fire conceived, a fowl was born
The child of Hina was delivered in the shape of an egg
She had not slept with a fowl
But a fowl was born
The child chirped, Hina was puzzled
Not from sleeping with a man did this child come
It was a strange child for Hina-of-the-fire
The two guards [?] were angry, the tall and the short one
The brothers of Hina
The two guards within the cave
Maui fought, those guards fell
Red blood flowed from the brow [?] of Maui
That was Maui's first strife
He fetched the bunch of black kava of Kane and Kanaloa
That was the second strife of Maui
The third strife was the quarrel over the kava strainer
The fourth strife was for the bamboo of Kane and Kanaloa
The fifth strife was over the temple inclosure for images [?]
The sixth strife was over the prayer tower in the heiau [?]
Maui reflected, asked who was his father
Hina denied: "You have no father
The loincloth of Kalana, that was your father"
Hina-of-the-fire longed for fish
He learned to fish, Hina sent him
"Go get [it] of your parent
There is the line, the hook
Manai-a-ka-lani, that is the hook
For drawing together the lands of old ocean"
He seized the great mudhen of Hina
The sister bird
That was the seventh strife of Maui
He hooked the mischievous shape-shifter
The jaw of Pimoe as it snapped open
The lordly fish that shouts over the ocean
Pimoe crouched in the presence of Maui
Love grew for Mahana-ulu-'ehu
Child of Pimoe
Maui drew them [?] ashore and ate all but the tailfin

Kane and Kanaloa were shaken from their foundation
By the ninth strife of Maui
Pimoe "lived through the tailfin"
Mahana-ulu-'ehu "lived through the tail"
Hina-ke-ka was abducted by Pe'ape'a
Pe'ape'a, god of the octopus family
That was Maui's last strife
He scratched out the eyes of the eight-eyed Pe'ape'a
The strife ended with Moemoe
Everyone knows about the battle of Maui with the sun
With the loop of Maui's snaring-rope
Winter [?] became the sun's
Summer became Maui's
He drank the yellow water to the dregs [?]
Of Kane and Kanaloa
He strove with trickery
Around Hawaii, around Maui
Around Kauai, around Oahu
At Kahulu'u was the afterbirth [deposited], at Waikane the navel cord
He died at Hakipu'u in Kualoa
Maui-of-the-loincloth
The lawless shape-shifter of the island
A chief indeed

Chant 16

Maui-son-of-Kalana was the man, Hina-kealo-haila the wife
. . .
Hulu-at-[the]-yellow-sky was the man, Hina-from-the-heavens the wife
'Ai-kanaka was the man, Hina-of-the-moon the wife
Born was Puna-the-first, born was Hema, born was Puna-the-last
Born was Kaha'i the great to Hema, Hina-ulu-'ohi'a was the wife
Hema went after the birthgifts for the wife [?]
Wahieloa was the man, Ho'olaukahili the wife
Laka was the man, Hikawainui the wife
. . .
Palena was the man, Hikawainui the wife
Born was Hanala'a-nui, born was Hanala'a-iki
Hanala'aiki was the man...
. . .
Kahekili [the first] was the man, Hauanuihoni'ala was the wife

Born was Kawauka'ohele and [his sister] Kelea-
nui-noho-ana-'api'api
["Kelea-swimming-like-a-fish"]
She [Kelea] lived as a wife to Kalamakua
Born was La'ie-lohelohe, [she] lived with Pi'ilani,
Pi'ikea was born
Pi'ikea lived with 'Umi, Kumalae-nui-a-'Umi
[was born]
His was the slave-destroying cliff
Kumulae-nui-a-'Umi was the man, Kumu-nui-
puawale the wife

Makua was the man, standing first of *wohi* rank
on the island
Kapo-hele-mai was the wife, a taboo *wohi* chief-
ess, the sacred one
'I, to 'I is the chiefship, the right to offer human
sacrifice
The ruler over the land section of Pakini
With the right to cut down *'ohi'a* wood for im-
ages, the protector of the island of
Hawaii
To Abu, Ahu son of 'I, to Lono
To Lono-i-ka-makahiki

Glossary

Hali'a:	Kane's daughter
Haumea:	a goddess associated with fertility, childbearing, and wild-food plants
He goes naked on the way to Malama:	"He journeys to the afterlife"
hilu:	literally, "elegant," a type of brightly colored fish
Kamaha'ina:	Ki'i's son
Kane:	literally, "male"
Ki'i:	literally, "image"
La'ila'i:	a goddess and sister to Kane and Ki'i
Lo'iloa:	the legendary planter of taro; his children are the different varieties of taro plant.
Lono-i-ka-makahiki:	the chief Ka-'i-'i-mamao (or Kalaninui'iamamao) whose birth the chant honors
Maui:	a popular demigod and hero in Polynesia
Papa and Wakea:	the legendary couple most commonly referred to as the ancestors of the Hawaiian people
Pleiades:	the time of the Makahiki, the four lunar months of the rainy season from approximately October to February
Po'ele'ele:	literally, "time of darkness"
Pohaha:	literally, "night breaking into dawn"
Po-kanokano:	literally, "night-digger"
Po-lalo-uli:	literally, "depth of night"
Po-lalo-wehi:	a combination of words for night, depth, and adornment or decoration
Popanopano:	a composite of *po* (night) and *pano* (dark or black)
Po-uliuli:	literally, "murky"
Po-wehiwehi:	literally, "obscure"

Pagoda of Ichijō-ji Buddhist temple (Japan's National Treasure)**, Kasai, Hyogo prefecture, Japan. This architecture in wayō** (和様, "Japanese")**that is Japanese original design. It was built in 1171.**

"SONG OF MEDITATION": DOCUMENT ANALYSIS

*"Not knowing how near the Truth is, /
People seek it far away, — what a pity!"*

Overview

"Zazen Wasan" ("Song of Meditation") was written in the early eighteenth century CE (ca. 1718) by the Japanese Zen master Hakuin Ekaku, the first Buddhist master in history to put forth the idea of common Zen, the Zen practiced by the ordinary masses, to make the complicated and mysterious Zen thinking and practice understandable in plain, everyday terms. *Zazen* is a term of Zen Buddhism that means seated meditation. The disciples or practitioners of Zen Buddhism are required to sit in a room, with their legs crossed and back straightened, breathing naturally and emptied of all worldly disturbances. In this process, all logic and rational thinking must be abandoned, and the mind must be in a state of focused relaxation. To Hakuin, the mission of Zen is to help people discover their true Buddha nature, to walk on the right path of life, to realize the root of their suffering, and to finally achieve enlightenment. In this song is conveyed the idea that songs are one with the sitting meditation, that the pure land is everywhere on the earth, and that the Buddha nature is none other than one's own nature, which anyone can find within oneself.

The term *zazen* comprises two parts, with *za* meaning "sitting" or "seated," and *zen* meaning "meditation," the latter term being derived from the Sanskrit word for meditation, *dhyana*; hence *zazen* can be translated as "sitting meditation." Huineng, the sixth patriarch of China's Chan Buddhism, expounds *zazen* thus: "To sit means to gain absolute freedom and to be mentally unperturbed in all outward circumstances, be they good or otherwise. To meditate means to realize inwardly the imperturbability of the Essence of Mind." By definition, *zazen* is a meditative state of thought-free, delusion-free, and relaxed yet alertly wakeful attention, from which the sitter can discover his own Buddha nature in a sudden breakthrough of enlightenment. The eulogy and unmediated experience of enlight-

enment by means of sitting meditation is what the "Song of Meditation" expounds for its readers and chanters. This ode is a revolt against traditional Buddhist teaching, which largely concerns itself with ascetic living styles and points to the core of Chan or Zen, which is the identification of self with the Buddha through meditative thinking and intuitive reflection.

Context

Zen Buddhism has exerted a profound impact on the daily lives of the Japanese people, seen in the various aspects of eating, housing, clothing, painting, calligraphy, architecture, gardening, decoration, and so on. Buddhism was first introduced from China into Japan via Korea in the year 522 CE and was securely established by Eisai in 1191. Zen took firm root in Japan during the Kamakura era (1192–1333) and the early Muromachi era (1336–1573), a time of increasing interest in various practices encouraging personal liberation and enlightenment. In Japan there are two main schools of Zen, Rinzai and Soto, similar in teachings yet different slightly in practice. The former depends on the koan as a major way of teaching, while the latter stresses nonreliance on words. The most important restorer and reformer of the Rinzai tradition was Hakuin Ekaku, the greatest master of Rinzai Zen.

Japanese Zen emerged in the context of the country's social and political history: Yoritomo (1148–1199) conquered the entire country and established the samurai government as the first shogun of the Kamakura era. The samurai warriors of this regime could not absorb the complexities of the Tian Tai sect, with its comprehensive systemizations and embracement of all known Buddhist doctrines and practices, but the direct and intuitive Zen practice agreed with their nature. In the fourteenth and fifteenth centuries the alliance between the Rinzai Zen sect and Japan's military government would help to secure the former's social-cultural as well as economic prosperity. At a time when traditional Japanese religions had lost their hold on the people and new ways of spiritual deliverance were in high demand, Hakuin was able to simplify complicated Buddhist teachings and make them accessible to both samurai warriors, who were novices in Buddhist practice, and the common populace. This he accomplished through his innovative and adroit use of the short and paradoxical sayings known as koans. In these troubled times, Buddhist reformers considered it essential to sustain bonds with the government, which dispensed land rights and other means of support for the temples. The so-called Culture of the Five Mountains emerged in this context, representing the high-water mark of Japanese Zen culture, manifested in almost all artistic forms. Many of the Rinzai Zen monasteries were organized into the Gozan, or Five Mountains system, which encompassed hundreds of monasteries. Hakuin is undeniably the most famous reformer of the Rinzai school.

Hakuin lived several centuries later, in the Edo, or Tokugawa, period (1603–1868), considered to be Japan's premodern or late-medieval era. The Tokugawa shogunate was officially established in 1603 by the first Edo shogun, Tokugawa Ieyasu. This was a time of frequent commerce with China, introducing not only goods but also spiritual food like Confucianism, Daoism, and further aspects of Chan (Zen). During the Edo period, in the early 1700s, Hakuin employed koans and also painted many simple but impressive pictures for the illiterate townspeople of Edo, who could not otherwise learn the truth of the Buddha. While most other monks were seeking personal comforts and wealth, Hakuin persevered in simplicity and poverty and guided his followers to do the same. He is often referred to as the father of modern Rinzai Zen, since he reanimated a school that had been deteriorating since the fourteenth century. This proved to be an enduring accomplishment. The Meiji Restoration reestablished Japan's imperial regime in 1868, persecuting Buddhism and establishing Shinto as the state religion. However, Zen was so strongly rooted in the Japanese psyche that it was able to regain its influence and popularity before long. That influence continues to the present day.

About the Author

One of the most influential figures in Japanese Zen Buddhism, the Zen master Hakuin ("White Seclusion") Ekaku, also known as Hakuin Zenji, was born Sugiyama Iwajiro on January 19, 1686, in a small Japanese coastal village at the foot of Mount Fuji on the Tokkaido Road between Tokyo (Edo) and Kyoto. Even as a child, he was oppressed by the fear of hell and had been trying to seek a way of salvation and enlightenment, which he finally discovered in Zen Buddhism. At the age of fifteen, having finally gained the approval of his parents, he joined monastic life by being ordained by Soduko Fueki at the local Zen temple, Shoinji. Soon after, he was sent to the neighboring temple of Daishoji, where he served for four years as a novice and had a chance to read the Lotus Sutra, often considered the best of all Buddhist teachings.

Time Line	
1191	■ Eisai (1141–1215) founds the Rinzai sect of Zen Buddhism.
1603	■ Tokugawa Ieyasu becomes the first shogun of the Edo, or Tokugawa, period, to last until 1868.
January 19, 1686	■ Hakuin is born.
1701	■ Hakuin enters monastic life in being ordained by Soduko Fueki at the local Zen temple, Shoinji.
1704	■ Hakuin is greatly distressed by the murder, centuries earlier, of the Chinese Zen master Yantou Quanhuo and resorts to writing poetry and calligraphy for solace.
1708	■ Hakuin has his first experience of enlightenment at Eiganji Temple.
1717	■ Hakuin becomes the abbot of Shoinji Temple where he was first ordained.
ca. 1718	■ Hakuin writes "Zazen Wasan."
January 18, 1769	■ Ekaku Hakuin Zenji dies in Hara.

At the age of eighteen, reading the story of the brutal murder by bandits of the well-loved ninth-century Chinese Chan master Yantou Quanhuo, with his terminal cries being heard miles away, Hakuin was greatly distressed and resorted to writing poetry and calligraphy for solace. His desperate search for the true path was answered when he read some Zen stories of Ming Dynasty China (1368–1644) collected in *Zekan Sakushin* ("Spurring Students to Break through the Zen Barrier"). From then on, he resolved to practice Zen and resume his Buddhist life for his personal redemption. At the age of twenty-two came his first experience of satori (enlightenment) at Eiganji Temple, after meditating for seven days.

At the age of thirty-one, he returned to Shoinji Temple, where he had been ordained, and became its abbot. It is here that his fame as a Zen master began to soar and he was able to attract numerous monks and lay disciples to study under him. With a teaching style both vigorous and unpredictable, he was bent on driving the students to their utmost efforts and digging out their deepest potential. He set four cardinal principles for his monks to follow: an unshakable faith in the teaching of the Buddha, the constant application of the koan, the perpetual continuity of purpose, and the eventual discovery of nirvana, all through their own efforts. (A koan, from the Chinese *gong'an,* is a story, dialogue, question, or statement whose meaning must be discerned through intuitive, rather than rational, perception. Hakuin is credited with the famous koan "What is the sound of one hand clapping?") Altogether, Hakuin is credited with having trained and cultivated more than ninety enlightened successors.

Hakuin is well known for his penetrating analysis and application of koans, which he made indispensable to the Zen practice. He taught that the struggle to get an answer to a seemingly impossible question by means of meditation would facilitate and quicken one's awakening. In so doing, he was able to revolutionize Japanese Zen. Through his famous koans, he could first arouse doubt in the monks and then urge them to use intuitive insight to crack the mystery. He warned the monks never to rest on the limited enlightenment they had achieved; instead, they should always persevere in finding the truth and exert themselves toward the ultimate enlightenment.

In Hakuin's lifetime, Zen Buddhism had become the court religion and was thus losing some of its purity and essence. Hakuin made a significant contribution to its restoration, rejuvenation, and purification, reclaiming and reinforcing its original genius. His representative works include *Keiso dokuzui* ("Poisonous Stamens and Pistils of Thorns"), *Hogo-roku* ("Record of Talks on the Law"), *Orategama* ("The Embossed Tea Kettle") and *Yasen kanwa* ("A Chat on a Boat in the Evening"). His teachings constituted a new foundation for Rinzai Zen in Japan. On January 18, 1769, Ekaku Hakuin Zenji—*Zenji* being an honorific meaning "Zen Master" or "Zen Teacher"—went to Hara and departed the world there at the age of eighty-three.

Explanation and Analysis of the Document

Hakuin wrote "Zazen Wasan" ("Song of Meditation") in eighteenth-century Japan to make *zazen* understandable in everyday terms to the common people of his era. The song consists of twenty-two couplets in Japanese calligraphy without standard stanza groupings. Some English translators have grouped the lines of this poem into stanzas of different arrangements, and some simply present it without divisions. The version reproduced here has three stanzas. How can one channel one's sitting meditation into the right way? How can one enhance the meditation practice? Such are among the questions dealt with in this song. "Zazen Wasan" has been chanted for generations in countless Buddhist monasteries around the world. Hakuin attaches great importance to meditation in acquiring enlightenment,

proposing that concentrating the spirit in stilled meditation can have a wondrous effect on the reinvigoration of the body. In this famous ode to meditation, the master Hakuin celebrates the power and significance of sitting in meditation for the attainment of enlightenment—the goal of the way of Zen. This practice is regarded as the core of Zen not only by the Japanese Soto and Rinzai schools but also by Zen schools across the world.

◆ Stanza 1

The very first line is not only the essence of the whole poem but also the core of all Buddhist teaching. It means that all sentient beings—all animals, insects, plants, and other living creatures—have the nature or the inherent quality of the Buddha. A person need not go extra miles in seeking the Buddhist truth in the external world and ask for enlightenment from others; all that is needed is to reflect upon oneself, question one's own mind and heart, and locate the true Buddha nature within oneself. If ice may be compared to the Buddha nature, or truth, then water represents the multitudinous human beings living in this world; without water, there can never be ice, since the latter holds or contains the former and the two can never be separated. This water-ice metaphor is traditionally employed in expounding the Buddhist truth. People are burdened by their desires toward the external world ("far away") and the mental constructs forged by those desires, but they cannot be free unless they detect their own Buddha nature.

People do not know that they themselves possess the true Buddha nature, and they start to look for it in books, fervent prayers, or the teaching of Buddhist masters. Too concerned with their own limitations, they do not trust in their perception and insight, which is blurred by their experience of the outside world. What a pity for a man suffering from extreme thirst to cry, "How thirsty I am!" when he is standing up to his waist in water. The metaphor illustrates how, when we find ourselves troubled, we usually seek solutions and help from others when we already possess the cure within ourselves. In this case, Hakuin employs the famous parable of the lost son. The reference is to the Lotus Sutra, an ancient discourse of the Buddha in which a rich man teaches his errant son to recognize his own inheritance instead of blindly living in poverty; it aptly illustrates the Mahayana precept that awakening to one's true nature is more important than seeking it from elders or authorities.

The "six worlds" of line 11 are the realms, or kinds of existence, that sentient beings are subject to: (1) beings in hell, the lowest realm, characterized by aggression; (2) hungry ghosts, the realm of spirits, characterized by craving and hunger; (3) animals, characterized by stupidity; (4) Asura, the realm of demigods, semiblessed beings marked by jealousy and militancy; (5) humans, beings who have enlightenment potentials within, yet are unable to attain it for their own blindness and desires; and (6) the realm of heavenly beings, who also have to inhabit the world of suffering for their overweening pride. All are trapped in this "wheel of life" (as it is called in Tibetan Buddhism). Human beings continuously transmigrate through these worlds and have to go through countless births and deaths before they find enlightenment. They fail simply because they are constantly trapped in worldly desires and mistaken perceptions, "the darkness of ignorance" of line 12, and hence have no hope of redemption and deliverance. Ignorance drives us farther and farther away from Buddhahood on a dead-end road. The rhetorical question "When are we able to get away from birth-and-death?" (line 14) reveals the essence of the Buddhist quest for spiritual enlightenment and freedom.

♦ Stanza 2

Hakuin points out the primary solution to the human dilemma, which is stressed by the Mahayana Buddhist tradition: meditation. Buddhist meditation is a mental process involving concentration, mindfulness, insight, and other faculties for the purpose of gaining enlightenment. The human being cannot use words to define, express, or eulogize it adequately. To some Zen masters, like the Chinese Huineng (d. 713), words cannot be trusted to clarify the truth of the Buddha. The "virtues of perfection," or *paramita,* refer to the commonly recognized six aspects of "completeness": (1) charity, which includes abandoning worldly possessions; (2) following the moral precepts of the Buddha; (3) meekness; (4) strenuousness; (5) contemplation; and (6) spiritual enlightenment. These virtues help believers unshackle themselves from burdens and overcome obstacles on their way to attaining enlightenment or Buddhahood. The invocation of the Buddha's name, commended in line 18, not infrequently refers to the chanting of the prayer "Homage Amida Buddha" of Pure Land Buddhism. Pure Land Buddhism is a devotional branch of Buddhism focused on Amitabha Buddha. People who chant the name "Amitabha Buddha" many times daily will be guided by this Buddha to the Pure Land, or the West, a place of eternity and happiness where the Buddha and all other enlightened beings reside. The six virtues, together with confession and ascetic discipline and other good works, all contribute to the Buddhist concept of merit making, or the accumulation of merits, and will without exception emanate from the practice of meditation.

This stanza clearly delineates the miraculous power of meditation, which can eradicate all one's bad deeds and lead the practitioner away from the wicked paths in the world and into the Pure Land that lies within. Karma (line 22), a concept from Indian Buddhism, here refers to the deeds that bind a person in the endless experience of the six realms mentioned earlier. (Indian Buddhism was the fountainhead of Chinese Chan Buddhism, which in turn gave life to Japanese Zen.) Although good or positive karma will lead to a higher or nobler level of existence, evil or negative karma will lead to living as a beast or ghost. Good or bad, karma is unavoidable in a person's life, and only through the practice of meditation can one escape from the terrible consequences of bad karma and advance in the illuminated directions conferred by the Buddha. By reverencing the Buddha's correct ways toward meditation and enlightenment, praising and implementing this truth, blessings beyond calculation can be attained.

♦ Stanza 3

The final stanza starts by telling us the importance of contemplating one's own nature, what it is that one really wants or lacks, and the significance of the intuitive mind in accessing the Buddha nature through the discarding of external obstacles. As Chinese Zen has stipulated, if one clearly understands one's ultimate nature, and realizes it, one will become the Buddha at that moment. Therefore, one's ultimate nature is the highest wisdom of the Buddha, and only through meditation can a person testify to "the truth of Self-nature," which is none other than the true face of the Buddha and the original inner self. "Self-nature is no-nature" (line 31) illustrates the Buddhist concept of emptiness or nothingness that neither advanced human knowledge nor logical reasoning can ever expect to grasp. The world is nothing and without any significance—a fundamental doctrine in Buddhism. For those who have identified with their true nature, the Buddha's Great Vehicle (Mahayana), the ultimate enlightenment of a person, will be actualized, thus dispersing the differences between cause and effect; that is, once enlightened, a person will see the world as nothing, and the differences between cause and effect will dissolve. Thus, all lesser means of salvation will ultimately culminate in this grand vehicle designed only by the Buddha. When a person realizes that his mind and the universe are one, he has attained nonduality and likewise nontrinity, in other words, oneness or enlightenment.

If one believes in the Buddhist teaching of "not-particular which is in particulars" (line 35), or as a Chinese saying has it, "the form is formlessness, and the formlessness is the form," one will not make distinctions between going or returning, right or wrong, up or down, a girl or a pencil. This is the Buddhist teaching of discarding all subjective distinctions between objects or concepts in the external world. Doing so leads a person to abandon worldly desires and live in peace and harmony, thus relinquishing all causes of suffering and pain. One who can see the world as it is and think about the world without being attached to it or being influenced by it has attained the state of complete freedom. Such a person has refrained from changing or being changed by the world. In Daoist terms, this is a state of *wuwei,* or nonaction, of following the rules of nature and never seeking to analyze or conquer it. In this state anything one does is in accordance with the dharma, the truth of the Buddha, and the way of enlightenment.

Samadhi (line 39) is the highest level of concentrated, complete meditation, in which the conscious subject becomes one with the experienced object. In this state one enters the infinite space, achieving complete freedom. This leads to the "fourfold Wisdom" of line 40. The reference is to the four *prajnas* (or cognitions or cardinal principles) of Buddhahood. Samadhi includes four aspects: (1) the universal mirror *prajna,* the high state of mind that perfectly reflects the world as it is, as through a mirror; (2) the *prajna* of equality (or "equality wisdom," "universal wisdom," "knowledge of equality"), whereby a person can experience the emptiness of the myriad things in the universe, thus perceiving the equality of all; (3) the observing *prajna* or

"all-discerning wisdom," which is the carrying out of the achieved enlightenment in dealing with the realities of the world (in other words, the Buddha in action); and (4) the practical *prajna*, or "perfect wisdom" (or "all-performing wisdom"), which is the wholehearted actualization of Buddhahood with complete enlightenment. Hakuin here celebrates the supremacy of the four wisdoms and their unsurpassed significance to all who practice Zen.

With the achievement of the fourfold Wisdom, a person has obtained genuine insight into the world and is thus beyond any fear of being affected by life or death, pleasure or suffering. What else shall a person want (line 41)? The next line, "As the Truth eternally calm reveals itself to them," envisions the enlightened person coming to the highest state of peace and happiness—nirvana, the purest state of existence, a perfectly peaceful mental state free from all human cravings. To one in this state, the very earth is the Lotus Country; there is no need to seek it elsewhere. One's own body, rather than any external thing or place, is the body of the Buddha. As Bodhidharma, the sixth-century founding father of Chinese Buddhism said: "Once mortals see their nature, all attachments end. Awareness isn't hidden. But you can only find it right now. It's only now. If you really want to find the Way, don't hold on to anything." For those who let go of the self and the attachments, the body is the Buddha's body and the mind the Buddha's mind.

Audience

The original audience of this ode included first of all the Buddhist monks whose goal in life is to achieve nirvana and spiritual awakening. Hakuin cast "Zazen Wasan" in the form of an ode, both lyrical and rhythmical, to make it more pleasing and memorable to chant. Laypeople, burdened by suffering and sometimes confused about the meaning and the necessity of living, also had a strong desire to discover the true way to happiness. Zen Buddhism, like Buddhism in general, holds as its central doctrine a view of the material world as empty or illusory, of all earthly and human activities as fruitless effort, and of life itself as recurring cycles of rebirth. Therefore, "Zazen Wasan," like other similarly memorable Buddhist theories and texts, has ultimately appealed to all people in search of a happier and more carefree way of life.

Impact

In his reform of the Rinzai Zen school and his systematized koan training, Hakuin emphasized once again the importance of *zazen*. His "Zazen Wasan" is a classic text and cornerstone in Zen history worthy of being read, recited, and chanted at any time. It is frequently chanted today in monasteries throughout Japan for its guidance toward the actualization of enlightenment—toward opening the way of the Buddha to all. This ode holds an indispensable place in the history of Japanese religions and culture, influencing the way Zen is approached by Buddhist believers and others

bent on seeking truth and light in life. Through this chant, Hakuin helped to spread the wisdom of the Buddha to all people, especially the poor, uneducated and downtrodden of the Japanese Edo period, who had no other means of accessing the right paths in life.

Further Reading

■ Books

Aitken, Robert. *Taking the Path of Zen.* San Francisco: North Point Press, 1982.

Aitken, Robert. *Encouraging Words: Zen Buddhist Teachings for Western Students.* New York: Pantheon Books, 1994.

Bielefeldt, Carl. *Dogen's Manuals of Zen Meditation.* Berkeley: University of California Press, 1988.

Daoyuan, Shi. *Original Teachings of Ch'an Buddhism*, trans. Chang Chung-yuan. New York: Grove Press, 1982.

Hakuin. *The Zen Master Hakuin: Selected Writings*, trans. Philip Yampolsky. New York: Columbia University Press, 1971.

Hakuin. *The Essential Teachings of Zen Master Hakuin*, trans. Norman Waddell. Boston: Shambhala, 1994.

Hakuin. *Zen Words for the Heart: Hakuin's Commentary on the Heart Sutra*, trans. Norman Waddell. Boston: Shambhala, 1996.

Hakuin. *Wild Ivy: The Spiritual Autobiography of Zen Master Hakuin*, trans. Norman Waddell. Boston: Shambhala, 2001.

Lai, Whalen, and Lewis R. Lancaster, eds. *Early Ch'an in China and Tibet.* Berkeley, Calif.: Asian Humanities Press, 1980.

Nhat Hanh, Thich. *The Heart of the Buddha's Teaching: Transforming Suffering into Peace, Joy, and Liberation.* New York: Broadway Books, 1999.

Schloegl, Irmgard, trans. *The Zen Teachings of Rinzai.* Boulder, Colo.: Shambhala, 1976.

Suzuki, Daisetz T. *The Zen Doctrine of No-Mind.* London: Rider, 1983.

Suzuki, Daisetz T. *An Introduction to Zen.* New York: Grove Press, 2004.

Suzuki, Shunryu. *Branching Streams Flow in the Darkness: Zen Talks on the Sandokai.* Berkeley: University of California Press, 1999.

Suzuki, Shunryu. *Not Always So: Practicing the True Spirit of Zen.* New York: HarperCollins, 2002.

—*Dong Zhao*

"Sentient beings are primarily all Buddhas: / It is like ice and water, / Apart from water no ice can exist; / Outside sentient beings, where do we find the Buddhas?"

(Section 1)

"Not knowing how near the Truth is, / People seek it far away,—what a pity!"

(Section 1)

"Going astray further and further in the darkness, / When are we able to get away from birth-and-death?"

(Section 1)

"And many other good deeds of merit,— / All these issue from the practice of Meditation;

(Section 1)

"Even those who have practised it just for one sitting / Will see all their evil karma wiped clean; / Nowhere will they find the evil paths, / But the Pure Land will be near at hand."

(Section 1)

"Testify … to the truth that Self-nature is no-nature."

(Section 1)

"This very earth is the Lotus Land of Purity, /And this body is the body of the Buddha."

(Section 1)

1. The word *Zen* is one that is tossed around casually in the West, often used to refer loosely to some sort of enlightenment or awareness, as suggested by the famous 1974 book by Robert Pirsig, *Zen and the Art of Motorcycle Maintenance.* Do you think that Hakuin Ekaku would applaud this development or condemn it? Why?

2. On the one hand, Zen Buddhism emphasizes calm, meditation, relaxation, enlightenment, and liberation from rational thought. On the other hand, many observers have suggested that the Japanese people lead extraordinarily hectic lives; the Japanese "salaryman," who works long hours with low prestige in a white-collar profession, has become the subject of frequent commentary. How do you think Japanese society and culture reconcile these two apparently contradictory trends?

3. According to one Japanese baseball coach, "Student baseball must be the baseball of self-discipline, or trying to attain the truth, just as in Zen Buddhism." How do you think Japanese baseball players might apply the principles of Zen Buddhism, and specifically those of the "Zazen Wasan," to the game? What does it even mean to "attain the truth" in a competitive team sport? Do you think that meditation could make a person a better batter or (in basketball) a better free-throw shooter?

4. How can an insect have "the nature or the inherent quality of the Buddha"?

5. In what sense can "Zazen Wasan" be thought of as analogous to modern-English translations of the Bible?

"SONG OF MEDITATION": DOCUMENT TEXT

1718 CE

— Hakuin Ekaku

It is like ice and water,
Apart from water no ice can exist;
Outside sentient beings, where do we find the Buddhas?
Not knowing how near the Truth is,
People seek it far away,—what a pity!
They are like him who, in the midst of water,
Cries in thirst so imploringly;
They are like the son of a rich man
Who wandered away among the poor.
The reason why we transmigrate through the six worlds
Is because we are lost in the darkness of ignorance;
Going astray further and further in the darkness,
When are we able to get away from birth-and-death?

As regards the Meditation practised in the Mahayana,
We have no words to praise it fully:
The virtues of perfection such as charity, morality, etc.,
And the invocation of the Buddha's name, confession, and ascetic discipline,
And many other good deeds of merit,—
All these issue from the practise of Meditation;
Even those who have practised it just for one sitting
Will see all their evil karma wiped clean;

Nowhere will they find the evil paths,
But the Pure Land will be near at hand.
With a reverential heart, let them to this Truth
Listen even for once,
And let them praise it, and gladly embrace it,
And they will surely be blessed most infinitely.

For such as, reflecting within themselves,
Testify to the truth of Self-nature,
To the truth that Self-nature is no-nature,
They have really gone beyond the ken of sophistry.
For them opens the gate of the oneness of cause and effect,
And straight runs the path of non-duality and non-trinity.
Abiding with the not-particular which is in particulars,
Whether going or returning, they remain for ever unmoved;
Taking hold of the not-thought which lies in thoughts,
In every act of theirs they hear the voice of the truth.
How boundless the sky of Samadhi unfettered!
How transparent the perfect moon-light of the fourfold Wisdom!
At that moment what do they lack?
As the Truth eternally calm reveals itself to them,
This very earth is the Lotus Land of Purity,
And this body is the body of the Buddha.

Glossary

Buddha:	a person who has attained full *prajna*, or enlightenment
fourfold Wisdom:	the four *prajnas* (or cognitions or cardinal principles) of Buddhahood
karma:	the effects of a person's actions, which determine his destiny in his next incarnation
Lotus:	in Buddhism, an important symbol of the purification of the mind and body; Lotus Land, or Pure Land, is the celestial realm or pure abode of a Buddha or bodhisattva
Mahayana:	a branch or school of Buddhism whose goal was bodhisattva ("enlightened existence"), the process of becoming a compassionate, heroic person dedicated to saving all beings
Samadhi:	the highest level of concentrated, complete meditation
six worlds:	the realms, or kinds of existence, to which sentient beings are subject

Rev. George Whitefield.

"THE GREAT DUTY OF FAMILY-RELIGION": DOCUMENT ANALYSIS

"If gratitude to God will not, methinks LOVE AND PITY TO YOUR CHILDREN should move you, with your respective families, to serve the Lord."

Overview

"The Great Duty of Family-Religion" was a sermon preached by the British-born clergyman George Whitefield at various times and in various locations in the 1730s before it was published in a collection of his sermons in 1738. The purpose of "The Great Duty of Family-Religion" was simple: to persuade the heads of households to ensure that religion was practiced daily in their homes through prayer and the reading of scripture.

Whitefield's name is largely forgotten today, but as an itinerant preacher in England, the American colonies, and Scotland, Whitefield became a superstar, a cultural hero who attracted audiences often numbering in the tens of thousands. He preached a sermon on Boston Commons to more than 20,000 listeners, likely the largest gathering in American history to that point, and it is estimated that throughout his career he preached 18,000 times, reaching 10 million listeners. Early in life, he seemed destined for a career on the stage, but he gave up acting for the church—and used his skills as a thespian to great effect, holding his audiences spellbound as he wept, screamed, capered, and unleashed the sheer power of his oratory. Great Britain's most famous actor, David Garrick, is reported to have said, "I would give a hundred guineas if I could say 'Oh' like Mr. Whitefield."

Whitefield was one of the most prominent figures in the First Great Awakening, a revival of evangelical religious fervor that peaked in the 1730s through the 1740s and spread from its origins in New Jersey and Pennsylvania into New England, the middle colonies, and eventually the southern colonies. Whitefield, the "Great Itinerant," was one of a legion of missionary preachers who conducted evangelical revivals marked by extemporaneous, high-

ly emotional sermons. Although he was educated under the influence of John and Charles Wesley, the founders of Methodism, and was a proponent of the severe doctrines of John Calvin, his message tended to be softer than theirs. Unlike his contemporary Jonathan Edwards, his sermons were not filled with fire and brimstone. Rather, as in "The Great Duty of Family-Religion," his sermons tried to affect the heart and to lead rather than drive listeners to Christian conversion. He even touched the worldly Benjamin Franklin, who admired Whitefield and published a number of his sermons.

Context

The Protestant religious revival that would later become known as the Great Awakening, and in which George Whitefield would play a major role, began when Protestant clergy became concerned about a decline in peoples' engagement with the church in the 1720s. Many members of the clergy blamed this decline in engagement on including the influx and movement of existing and new colonists, the growing popularity of Enlightenment rationalism and broader trend of American colonists giving more attention to business affairs than religious ones. concerns over spiritual ones.

Beginning in the 1720s, clergy of Presbyterian and Dutch Reformed congregations in New York and New Jersey congregations attracted attention with a more emotive style of preaching that emphasized a deeper and stronger personal connection between individual people and God as well as a higher level of moral behavior as evidence of their strengthened relationship with God. Massachusetts minister Jonathan Edwards, in 1731, gave a talk entitled "God Glorified in the Work of Redemption, by the Greatness of Man's Dependence upon Him, in the Whole of It" that many historians consider the beginning of the

Great Awakening in New England. He drew increasingly large numbers of worshipers to his church in Northampton, Massachusetts during the 1730s. In 1734, Edwards's sermon, "A Divine and Supernatural Light, Immediately Imparted to the Soul by the Spirit of God," established a defining element of the Great Awakening—that salvation imbues the believer with a "spiritual and divine light" that is independent of human imagination or thought. With this notion, Edwards established a break with the older Calvinist theologies prominent in New England that focused on imparting a scholarly understanding of doctrine rather than an emotional connection with the divine. In this split, Edwards and his fellow "new lights" were pitted against the "old lights" of conservative doctrine and practice.

These ideas and the revival triggered by Edwards and other New England preachers would spread throughout the North American colonies through the rest of the 1730s. These revivals were not confined to North America, with similar Protestant religious movements taking place in England and Germany. It was in England that George Whitefield distinguished himself as a preacher and founding figure in the Methodist movement. In 1738, he would travel to North America.

About the Author

George Whitefield was born in 1714 in England, and was educated at Oxford University. During his time at Oxford he became friends with John and Charles Wesley, whose ideas would lead to the founding of the Methodist denomination in 1795. After a conversion experience in the early 1730s, Whitefield continued his education and graduated from Oxford in 1736. Having been ordained as a deacon a year before leaving Oxford, he began preaching soon afterward in his home area of Gloucester as well as in London.

By the late 1730s, Whitefield had reconnected with John Wesley who asked him be a minister in the new colony of Georgia. As he awaited the trip, he began to preach in more and more churches throughout England, sparking a revival akin to those of the Great Awakening in New England. Whitefield had an eye for publicity and began publishing collections of his sermons as well as preaching them throughout the country. It was in an early collection that the "Great Duty" sermon was first published.

Whitefield set out for Georgia in January, 1738 and immediately became convinced of the need for an orphanage—a cause that would be a major part of his life's work. He was only in Goergia for a brief time before returning to England for six months, during which he was ordained as a priest and continued to refine his preaching, including the innovation of moving into from churches to open air, outdoor services to accommodate the growing crowds. As his popularity grew, Church of England officials implored him to preach only has his assigned church. He refused, however, and continued to preach wherever he was invited.

Time Line	
December 27, 1714	■ Whitefield is born in Gloucester, England.
1738	■ Emigrates to Savannah, Georgia to serve as a priest.
1739	■ Whitefield returns to England to raise funds for an orphanage. Construction begins on Bethesda Orphanage in Savannah.
1739-1741	■ Whitefield begins preaching at a series of revival meetings in New England, returning to England afterward.
1763-1765	■ Whitefield undertakes his sixth revival trip to British North America, preaching at revival meetings along the east coast.
September 30, 1770	■ Whitefield dies in Massachusetts Bay Colony.

Whitefield left for his second trip to America in August, 1739. When he arrived in Philadelphia in November, he found that Colonial newspapers had reported on the growth of his revival preaching in England. As a result, Whitefield was already a fairly well-known figure when he arrived in the colonies. He would remain in North America for a little over a year, preaching in every colony, visiting 75 cities and towns and preached over 350 sermons, not including speaking engagements with smaller churches and organizations. While in America, Philadelphia's Benjamin Franklin—despite not sharing Whitefield's religious convictions—served as his publicist and publisher during the tour. During this tour, in 1740, Whitefield established the Bethesda orphanage in Savannah, Georgia.

Throughout this initial and subsequent preaching trips to America, Whitefield came under criticism from fellow clergy members, such as the Bishop who argued that since Whitefield had been assigned to be a minister in Georgia, he should stay in Georgia. Whitefield asserted that his authority to preach came from God, not the Bishop.

Explanation and Analysis of the Document

"The Great Duty of Family-Religion" is a relatively simple sermon. Whitefield takes his text from the story of Joshua

in the Old Testament, using it as a jumping-off point to press his belief that "it is greatly to be feared, that out of those many households that call themselves Christians, there are but few that serve God in their respective families as they ought." He then "begs leave" to explain the duty of a family's "governor" (the male head of household) to ensure that he and those "committed to his charge" serve God, the ways in which a governor and his household ought to do so, and the motives that should "excite" householders to serve God.

Whitefield takes up each of these points in turn. With regard to the first, he argues that every householder is a prophet, a priest, and a king, and that "every house is as it were a little parish, every governor . . . a priest, every family a flock; and if any of them perish through the governor's neglect, their blood will God require at their hands." With regard to the second point, Whitefield maintains that it is the duty of every Christian householder to read aloud the word of God daily, noting: "Besides, servants as well as children, are, for the generality, very ignorant, and mere novices in the laws of God: and how shall they know, unless some one teach them?" Additionally, he calls on householders to lead the family and its servants in daily prayer and to catechize and instruct children and servants.

Whitefield then turns to his third point, the motives that should induce householders to create an atmosphere of family religion. The first is the gratitude they owe to God. The second is love and pity for their children, making family religion "the best testimony they can give of their affection to the darling of their hearts." The third is common honesty and justice; thus, "none can be more liable to such censure, than those who think themselves injured if their servants withdraw themselves from their bodily work, and yet they in return take no care of their inestimable souls." A fourth motivation is self-interest, for family religion is the "best means to promote your own temporal, as well as eternal welfare." Finally, Whitefield refers to the "terrors of the Lord," reminding his listeners that "the time will come, and that perhaps very shortly, when we must all appear before the judgment-seat of Christ" and will not want children and servants as witnesses against us.

Whitefield ends the sermon on a slightly darker, more Calvinist note:

> I beseech you to remember, that you are fallen creatures; that you are by nature lost and estranged from God; and that you can never be restored to your primitive happiness, till by being born again of the Holy Ghost, you arrive at your primitive state of purity, have the image of God restamped upon your souls.

Audience

The year in which this sermon was published—1738—was also the year in which Whitefield made his first trip to the American colonies. Published editions of his sermons, how-ever, had been circulating in America before his arrival. The massive crowds that Whitefield drew—and the large numbers of books sold—lead to the conclusion that, in general, his audience was probably the most diverse of the preachers and evangelists of the Great Awakening. Historians have estimated that as many as half of American colonists of the mid 1700s had—if not heard or read Whitefield's words directly—were at least familiar with him. He was, in many ways, the first celebrity in American culture.

Whitefield wrote this sermon to be broadly applicable to people in a variety of situations in both Britain and Britain's North American colonies. The instructions given here concerning religious instruction of children would have been of use to both working-class people as well as those of a higher socio-economic status. Similarly, the message he gives would be equally useful for both urban and rural families. While he does include a number of Biblical references with little—if any—context, most of them would have been clear to a general Christian audience of the time. He does not get so deeply into questions of theology and doctrine, which suggests that Whitfield knew his messages would be heard or read by Christians of many different denominations.

The most specifically targeted audience of "The Great Duty of Family—Religion" was the heads of households in Britain and the British colonies in America. Several times in the sermon, Whitefield refers to "parents" and "mothers and fathers" indicating that he believe the imparting of religious knowledge and belief was not the responsibility of male or female parents exclusively. Whitefield also specifically addresses the role that the masters of servants played in shaping the religious growth of those under their control. Whitefield often implore slave owners to attend to the religious needs of their slaves so we can reasonably infer that he is also addressing these slave owners in this sermon.

Impact

Broadly, George Whitfield's travels to and through the American colonies—are significant for a number of reasons. Along with being the first "celebrity" in the American colonies, Whitefield's revival tours were a cultural event that united the colonies as nothing before had done. While the Great Awakening was widespread, in its origins it was largely confined to New England and the Mid-Atlantic colonies. Whitefield's preaching was a significant factor in connecting the southern colonies to this broader cultural phenomenon of religious revival. Some scholars, such as Jerome Dean Mahaffey, have argued the Whitefield's influence extended beyond religious revival and was a crucial element in the eventual American Revolution. Whether or not he can be credited with that, it is certain that Whitefield's efforts provided a unifying force that was, at the time, unprecedented in the American colonies.

"The Great Duty of Family—Religion," in particular, illustrates some of the broader and more general

"It is the duty of every governor of a family to take care, that not only he himself, but also that those committed to his charge, 'serve the Lord.'"

(Section 1)

"If gratitude to God will not, methinks LOVE AND PITY TO YOUR CHILDREN should move you, with your respective families, to serve the Lord."

(Section 1)

"However masters may put off their convictions for the present, they will find a time will come, when they shall know they ought to have given them some spiritual as well as temporal wages; and the cry of those that have mowed down their fields, will enter into the ears of the Lord of Sabaoth."

(Section 1)

significance of Whitefield, his ideas, and his preaching. In his emphasis on the role of the parents in the religious education of children, Whitefield is implicitly marginalizing the role of the formal church structure and hierarchy in the spreading of religious knowledge from one generation to another.

Whitefield's assertion that masters must teach and impart religious knowledge and values to their servants as well as their own children is a notion that Whitefield would build upon during his visits to the American colonies. In 1740, Whitefield wrote an open letter to slave owners of the southern colonies (Maryland, Virginia, North Carolina, and South Carolina) in which he condemned brutal methods of discipline towards slaves and asserted that masters should allow their slaves to be taught about and, hopefully, converted to Christianity. While Whitefield did not condemn the institution of slavery (the Bethesda orphanage had, at the time of his death in 1770 50 slaves), he did argue that poor treatment of slaves was a sin.

Although this sermon does not directly address the chattel slavery that was present in Britain's American colonies, the language and arguments Whitefield uses to discuss the obligation of masters to education their servants in religious matters are very similar to later arguments directed at American slave owners. After Whitefield's departure from the colonies, American evangelicals such as the Bryan family of South Carolina, took up the cause of Christianization of slaves in various parts of the south. Historian Allan Gallay has argued that what began as an effort to Christianize slaves evolved into "the utilization of religion as a form of social control" in the slave-owning south.

Further Reading

Cray, Robert E. "Memorialization and Enshrinement: George Whitefield and Popular Religious Culture, 1770-1850." *Journal of the Early Republic* 10.3 (1990): 339–361. JSTOR. Web.

Gallay, Allan. "The Origins of Slaveholders' Paternalism: George Whitefield, the Bryan Family, and the Great Awakening in the South." *The Journal of Southern History* 53.3 (1987): 369–394. JSTOR. Web.

Kidd, Thomas S. *The Great Awakening: A Brief History with Documents.* First Edition edition. Boston: Bedford/St. Martin's, 2007. Print.

Lambert, Frank. "'Pedlar in Divinity': George Whitefield and the Great Awakening, 1737-1745." *The Journal of American History* 77.3 (1990): 812–837. JSTOR. Web.

---. "Subscribing for Profits and Piety: The Friendship of Benjamin Franklin and George Whitefield." *The William and Mary Quarterly* 50.3 (1993): 529–554. *JSTOR*. Web.

---. "The Great Awakening as Artifact: George Whitefield and the Construction of Intercolonial Revival, 1739-1745." *Church History* 60.2 (1991): 223–246. *JSTOR*. Web.

Mahaffey, Jerome Dean. *The Accidental Revolutionary: George Whitefield and the Creation of America.* Waco, Texas: Baylor University Press, 2011.

Smith, John Howard. *The First Great Awakening: Redefining Religion in British America, 1725-1775.* Madison NJ: Fairleigh Dickinson University Press, 2014. Print.

Stout, Harry S. "George Whitefield and Benjamin Franklin: Thoughts on a Peculiar Friendship." *Proceedings of the Massachusetts Historical Society* 103 (1991): 9–23. Print.

---. *The Divine Dramatist: George Whitefield and the Rise of Modern Evangelicalism.* 50465th edition. Grand Rapids, Mich: Eerdmans, 1991. Print.

Tracy, Joseph. *The Great Awakening: A History of the Revival of Religion in the Time of Edwards and Whitefield.* Ed. Mark Riedel. Counted Faithful, 2014. Print.

—*Commentary by Aaron J. Gulyas and Michael J. O'Neal*

Questions for Further Study

1. What specific reasons does Whitefield give for parents being responsible for their children's religious education?

2. George Whitefield and Jonathan Edwards were both prominent figures in the Great Awakening. What similarities and differences do you see in their messages to their audiences?

3. Whitefield addresses the educational and spiritual needs of both children and servants in this sermon. In what ways are his arguments about children and servants similar or different?

"THE GREAT DUTY OF FAMILY-RELIGION": DOCUMENT TEXT

1738 CE

Joshua 24:15 "As for me and my house, we will serve the Lord."

These words contain the holy resolution of pious Joshua, who having in a most moving, affectionate discourse recounted to the Israelites what great things God had done for them, in the verse immediately preceding the text, comes to draw a proper inference from what he had been delivering; and acquaints them, in the most pressing terms, that since God had been so exceeding gracious unto them, they could do not less, than out of gratitude for such uncommon favors and mercies, dedicate both themselves and families to his service. "Now therefore, fear the Lord, and serve him in sincerity and truth, and put away the Gods which your fathers served on the other side of the flood." And by the same engaging motive does the prophet Samuel afterwards enforce their obedience to the commandments of God, 1 Sam. 12:24, "Only fear the Lord, and serve him in truth, with all your heart; for consider how great things he hath done for you." But then, that they might not excuse themselves (as too many might be apt to do) by his giving them a bad example, or think he was laying heavy burdens upon them, whilst he himself touched them not with one of his fingers, he tells them in the text, that whatever regard they might pay to the doctrine he had been preaching, yet he (as all ministers ought to do) was resolved to live up to and practice it himself: "Choose you therefore, whom you will serve, whether the Gods which your fathers served, or the Gods of the Amorites, in whose land ye dwell: but as for me and my house, we will serve the Lord."

A resolution this, worthy of Joshua, and no less becoming, no less necessary for every true son of Joshua, that is entrusted with the care and government of a family in our day: and, if it was ever seasonable for ministers to preach up, or people to put in practice family-religion, it was never more so than in the present age; since it is greatly to be feared, that out of those many households that call themselves Christians, there are but few that serve God in their respective families as they ought.

It is true indeed, visit our churches, and you may perhaps see something of the form of godliness still subsisting amongst us; but even that is scarcely to be met with in private houses. So that were the blessed angels to come, as in the patriarchal age, and observe our spiritual economy at home, would they not be tempted to say as Abraham to Abimilech, "Surely, the fear of God is not in this place?" Gen. 20:11.

How such a general neglect of family-religion first began to overspread the Christian world, is difficult to determine. As for the primitive Christians, I am positive it was not so with them: No, they had not so learned Christ, as falsely to imagine religion was to be confined solely to their assemblies for public worship; but, on the contrary, behaved with such piety and exemplary holiness in their private families, that St. Paul often styles their house a church: "Salute such a one, says he, and the church which is in his house." And, I believe, we must for ever despair of seeing a primitive spirit of piety revived in the world, till we are so happy as to see a revival of primitive family religion; and persons unanimously resolving with good old Joshua, in the words of the text, "As for me and my house, we will serve the Lord."

From which words, I shall beg leave to insist on these three things.

I. First, That it is the duty of every governor of a family to take care, that not only he himself, but also that those committed to his charge, "serve the Lord."

II. Secondly, I shall endeavor to show after what manner a governor and his household ought to serve the Lord. And,

III. Thirdly, I shall offer some motives, in order to excite all governors, with their respective households, to serve the Lord in the manner that shall be recommended.

And First, I am to show that it is the duty of every governor of a family to take care, that not only he himself, but also that those committed to his charge, should serve the Lord.

And this will appear, if we consider that every governor of a family ought to look upon himself as obliged to act in three capacities as a prophet, to instruct: as a priest, to pray for and with; as a king, to govern, direct, and provide for them. It is true indeed, the latter of these, their kingly office, they are not so frequently deficient in, (nay in this they are generally too solicitous) but as for the two former, their priestly and prophetic office, like Gallio, they care for no such things. But however indifferent some governors may be about it, they may be assured, that God will require a due discharge of these offices at their hands. For if, as the apostle argues, "He that does not provide for his own house," in temporal things, has denied the faith, and is worse than an infidel; to what greater degree of apostasy must he have arrived, who takes no thought to provide for the spiritual welfare of his family!

But farther, persons are generally very liberal of their invectives against the clergy, and think they justly blame the conduct of that minister who does not take heed to and watch over the flock, of which the Holy Ghost has made him overseer: but may not every governor of a family, be in a lower degree liable to the same censure, who takes no thought for those souls that are committed to his charge? For every house is as it were a little parish, every governor (as was before observed) a priest, every family a flock; and if any of them perish through the governor's neglect, their blood will God require at their hands.

Was a minister to disregard teaching his people publicly, and from house to house, and to excuse himself by saying, that he had enough to do to work out his own salvation with fear and trembling, without concerning himself with that of others; would you not be apt to think such a minister, to be like the unjust judge, "One that neither feared God, nor regarded man?" And yet, odious as such a character would be, it is no worse than that governor of a family deserves, who thinks himself obliged only to have his own soul, without paying any regard to the souls of his household. For (as was above hinted) every house is as it were a parish, and every master is concerned to secure, as much as in him lies, the spiritual prosperity of every one under his rood, as any minister whatever is obliged to look to the spiritual welfare of every individual person under his charge.

What precedents men who neglect their duty in this particular, can plead for such omission, I cannot tell. Doubtless not the example of holy Job, who was so far from imagining that he had no concern, as governor of a family, with any one's soul but his own, that the scripture acquaints us, "When the days of his children's feasting were gone about, that Job sent and sanctified them, and offered burnt-offerings, according to the number of them all; for Job said, It may be that my sons have sinned and cursed God in their hearts: thus did Job continually." Nor can they plead the practice of good old Joshua, whom, in the

text, we find as much concerned for his household's welfare, as his own. Nor lastly, that of Cornelius, who feared God, not only himself, but with all his house: and were Christians but of the same spirit of Job, Joshua, and the Gentile centurion, they would act as Job, Joshua, and Cornelius did.

But alas! If this be the case, and all governors of families ought not only to serve the Lord themselves, but likewise to see that their respective households do so too; what will then become of those who not only neglect serving God themselves, but also make it their business to ridicule and scoff at any of their house that do? Who are not content with "not entering into the kingdom of heaven themselves; but shoe also that are willing to enter in, they hinder." Surely such men are factors for the devil indeed. Surely their damnation slumbereth not: for although God, is in his good providence, may suffer such stumbling-blocks to be put in his children's way, and suffer their greatest enemies to be those of their own households, for a trial of their sincerity, and improvement of their faith; yet we cannot but pronounce a woe against those masters by whom such offenses come. For if those that only take care of their own souls, can scarcely be saved, where will such monstrous profane and wicked governors appear?

But hoping there are but few of this unhappy stamp, proceed we now to the Second thing proposed: To show after what manner a governor and his household ought to serve the Lord.

1. And the first thing I shall mention, is READING THE WORD OF GOD. This is a duty incumbent on every private person. "Search the scriptures, for in them ye think ye have eternal life," is a precept given by our blessed Lord indifferently to all: but much more so, ought every governor of a family to think it in a peculiar manner spoken to himself, because (as hath been already proved) he ought to look upon himself as a prophet, and therefore agreeably to such a character, bound to instruct those under his charge in the knowledge of the word of God.

This we find was the order God gave to his peculiar people Israel: for thus speaks his representative Moses, Deut. 6:6–7, "These words," that is, the scripture words, "which I command thee this day, shall be in thy heart, and thou shalt teach them diligently unto thy children," that is, as it is generally explained, servants, as well as children, "and shalt talk of them when thou sittest in thy house." From whence we may infer, that the only reason, why so many neglect to read the words of scripture diligently to their children is, because the words of scripture are not in their hearts: for if they were, out of the abundance of the heart their mouth would speak.

Besides, servants as well as children, are, for the generality, very ignorant, and mere novices in the laws of God: and how shall they know, unless some one teach them? And what more proper to teach them by, than the lively oracles of God, "which are able to make them wise unto salvation?" And who more proper to instruct them by these lively oracles, than parents and masters, who (as hath been more than once observed) are as much concerned to feed them with spiritual, as with bodily bread, day by day.

But if these things be so, what a miserable condition are those unhappy governors in, who are so far from feeding those committed to their care with the sincere milk of the word, to the intent they may grow thereby, that they neither search the scriptures themselves, nor are careful to explain them to others? Such families must be in a happy way indeed to do their Master's will, who take such prodigious pains to know it! Would not one imagine that they had turned converts to the Church of Rome, that they thought ignorance to be the mother of devotion; and that those were to be condemned as heretics who read their Bibles? And yet how few families are there amongst us, who do not act after this unseemly manner! But shall I praise them in this? I praise them not; Brethren, this thing ought not so to be.

2. Pass we on now to the second means whereby every governor and his household ought to serve the Lord, FAMILY PRAYER.

This is a duty, though as much neglected, yet as absolutely necessary as the former. Reading is a good preparative for prayer, as prayer is an excellent means to render reading effectual. And the reason why every governor of a family should join both these exercises together, is plain, because a governor of a family cannot perform his priestly office (which we before observed he is in some degree invested with) without performing this duty of family prayer.

We find it therefore remarked, when mention is made of Cain and Abel's offering sacrifices, that they brought them. But to whom did they bring them? Why, in all probability, to their father Adam, who, as priest of the family, was to offer sacrifice in their names. And so ought every spiritual son of the second Adam, who is entrusted with the care of an household, to offer up the spiritual sacrifices of supplications and thanksgivings, acceptable to God through Jesus Christ, in the presence and name of all who wait upon, or eat meat at his table.

Thus we read our blessed Lord behaved, when he tabernacled amongst us: for it is said often, that he prayed with his twelve disciples, which was then his little family. And he himself has promised a particular blessing to joint supplications: "Wheresoever two or three are gathered together in my name, there am I in the midst of them." And again, "If two or three are agreed touching any thing they shall ask, it shall be given them." Add to this, that we are commanded by the Apostle to "pray always, with all manner of supplication," which doubtless includes family prayer. And holy Joshua, when he set up the good resolution in the text, that he and his household would serve the Lord, certainly resolved to pray with his family, which is one of the best testimonies they could give of their serving him.

Besides, there are no families but what have some common blessings, of which they have been all partakers, to give thanks for; some common crosses and afflictions, which they are to pray against; some common sins, which they are all to lament and bewail: but how this can be done, without joining together in one common act of humiliation, supplication, and thanksgiving, is difficult to devise.

From all which considerations put together, it is evident, that family prayer is a great and necessary duty; and consequently, those governors that neglect it, are certainly without excuse. And it is much to be feared, if they live without family prayer, they live without God in the world.

And yet, such an hateful character as this is, it is to be feared, that was God to send out an angel to destroy us, as he did once to destroy the Egyptian first-born, and withal give him a commission, as then, to spare no houses but where they saw the blood of the lintel, sprinkled on the door-post, so now, to let no families escape, but those that called upon him in morning and evening prayer; few would remain unhurt by his avenging sword. Shall I term such families Christians or heathens? Doubtless they deserve not the name of Christians; and heathens will rise up in judgment against such profane families of this generation: for they had always their household gods, whom they worshipped and whose assistance they frequently invoked. And a pretty pass those families surely are arrived at, who must be sent to school to pagans. But will not the Lord be avenged on such profane households as these? Will he not pour out his fury upon those that call not upon his name?

3. But it is time for me to hasten to the third and last means I shall recommend, whereby every governor ought with his household to serve the Lord, CAT-

ECHIZING AND INSTRUCTING their children and servants, and bringing them up in the nurture and admonition of the Lord.

That this, as well as the two former, is a duty incumbent on every governor of an house, appears from that famous encomium or commendation God gives of Abraham: "I know that he will command his children and his household after him, to keep the way of the Lord, to do justice and judgment." And indeed scarce any thing is more frequently pressed upon us in holy writ, than this duty of catechizing. Thus, says God in a passage before cited, "Thou shalt teach these words diligently unto thy children." And parents are commanded in the New Testament, to "bring up their children in the nurture and admonition of the Lord." The holy Psalmist acquaints us, that one great end why God did such great wonders for his people, was, "to the intent that when they grew up, they should show their children, or servants, the same." And in Deut. 6 at the 20th and following verses, God strictly commands his people to instruct their children in the true nature of the ceremonial worship, when they should inquire about it, as he supposed they would do, in time to come. And if servants and children were to be instructed in the nature of Jewish rites, much more ought they now to be initiated and grounded in the doctrines and first principles of the gospel of Christ: not only, because it is a revelation, which has brought life and immortality to a fuller and clearer light, but also, because many seducers are gone abroad into the world, who do their utmost endeavor to destroy not only the superstructure, but likewise to sap the very foundation of our most holy religion.

Would then the present generation have their posterity be true lovers and honorers of God; masters and parents must take Solomon's good advice, and train up and catechize their respective households in the way wherein they should go.

I am aware but of one objection, that can, with any show of reason, be urged against what has been advanced; which is, that such a procedure as this will take up too much time, and hinder families too long from their worldly business. But it is much to be questioned, whether persons that start such an abjection, are not of the same hypocritical spirit as the traitor Judas, who had indignation against devout Mary, for being so profuse of her ointment, in anointing our blessed Lord, and asked why it might not be sold for two hundred pence, and given to the poor. For has God given us so much time to work for ourselves, and shall we not allow some small pittance of it, morn-

ing and evening, to be devoted to his more immediate worship and service? Have not people read, that it is God who gives men power to get wealth, and therefore that the best way to prosper in the world, is to secure his favor? And has not our blessed Lord himself promised, that if we seek first the kingdom of God and his righteousness, all outward necessaries shall be added unto us?

Abraham, no doubt, was a man of as great business as such objectors may be; but yet he would find time to command his household to serve the Lord. Nay, David was a king, and consequently had a great deal of business upon his hands; yet notwithstanding, he professes that he would walk in his house with a perfect heart. And, to instance but one more, holy Joshua was a person certainly engaged very much in temporal affairs; and yet he solemnly declares before all Israel, that as for him and his household, they would serve the Lord. And did persons but redeem their time, as Abraham, David, or Joshua did, they would no longer complain, that family duties kept them too long from the business of the world.

III. But my Third and Last general head, under which I was to offer some motives, in order to excite all governors, with their respective households, to serve the Lord in the manner before recommended, I hope, will serve instead of a thousand arguments, to prove the weakness and folly of any such objection.

1. And the first motive I shall mention is the duty of GRATITUDE, which you that are governors of families owe to God. Your lot, every one must confess, is cast in a fair ground: providence hath given you a goodly heritage, above many of your fellow-creatures, and therefore, bout of a principle of gratitude, you ought to endeavor, as much as in you lies, to make every person of your respective households to call upon him as long as they live: not to mention, that the authority, with which God has invested you as parents and governors of families, is a talent committed to your trust, and which you are bound to improve to your Master's honor. In other things we find governors and parents can exercise lordship over their children and servants readily, and frequently enough can say to one, Go, and he goeth; and to another, Come, and he cometh; to a third, Do this, and he doeth it. And shall this power be so often employed in your own affairs, and never exerted in the things of God? Be astonished, O heavens, at this!

Thus did not faithful Abraham; no, God says, that he knew Abraham would command his servants and children after him. Thus did not Joshua: no, he was resolved not only to walk with God himself, but to improve his authority in making all about him do so too: "As for me and my household, we will serve the Lord." Let us go and do likewise.

2. But Secondly, If gratitude to God will not, methinks LOVE AND PITY TO YOUR CHILDREN should move you, with your respective families, to serve the Lord.

Most people express a great fondness for their children: nay so great, that very often their own lives are wrapped up in those of their offspring. "Can a woman forget her sucking child, that she should not have compassion on the son of her womb?" says God by his Prophet Isaiah. He speaks of it as a monstrous thing, and scarce credible; but the words immediately following, affirm it to be possible, "Yes, they may forget" and experience also assures us they may. Father and mother may both forsake their children: for what greater degree of forgetfulness can they express towards them, than to neglect the improvement of their better part, and not bring them up in the knowledge and fear of God?

It is true indeed, parents seldom forget to provide for their children's bodies, (though, it is to be feared, some men are so far sunk beneath the beasts that perish, as to neglect even that) but then how often do they forget, or rather, when do they remember, to secure the salvation of their immortal souls? But is this their way of expressing their fondness for the fruit of their bodies? Is this the best testimony they can give of their affection to the darling of their hearts? Then was Delilah fond of Samson, when she delivered him up into the hands of the Philistines? Then were those ruffians well affected to Daniel, when they threw him into a den of lions?

3. But Thirdly, If neither gratitude to God, nor love and pity to your children, will prevail on you; yet let a principle of COMMON HONESTY AND JUSTICE move you to set up the holy resolution in the text.

This is a principle which all men would be thought to act upon. But certainly, if any may be truly censured for their injustice, none can be more liable to such censure, than those who think themselves injured if their servants withdraw themselves from their bodily work, and yet they in return take no care of their inestimable souls. For is it just that servants should spend their time and strength in their master's service, and masters not at the same time give them what is just and equal for their service?

It is true, some men may think they have done enough when they give unto their servants food and raiment, and say, "Did not I bargain with thee for so much a year?" But if they give them no other reward than this, what do they less for their very beasts? But are not servants better than they? Doubtless they are: and however masters may put off their convictions for the present, they will find a time will come, when they shall know they ought to have given them some spiritual as well as temporal wages; and the cry of those that have mowed down their fields, will enter into the ears of the Lord of Sabaoth.

4. But Fourthly, If neither gratitude to God, pity to children, nor a principle for common justice to servants, are sufficient to balance all objections; yet let that darling, that prevailing motive of SELF-INTEREST turn the scale, and engage you with your respective households to serve the Lord.

This weighs greatly with you in other matters: be then persuaded to let it have a due and full influence on you in this: and if it has, if you have but faith as a grain of mustard-seed, how can you avoid believing, that promoting family-religion, will be the best means to promote your own temporal, as well as eternal welfare? For "Godliness has the promise of the life that now is, as well as that which is to come."

Besides, you all, doubtless wish for honest servants, and pious children: and to have them prove otherwise, would be as great a grief to you, as it was to Elisha to have a treacherous Gehazi, or David to be troubled with a rebellious Absolom. But how can it be expected they should learn their duty, except those set over them, take care to teach it to them? Is it not as reasonable to expect you should reap where had not sewn, or gather where you had not strawed?

Did Christianity, indeed, give any countenance to children and servants to disregard their parents and masters according to the flesh, or represent their duty to them, as inconsistent with their entire obedience to their father and master who is in heaven, there might then be some pretense to neglect instructing them in the principles of such a religion. But since the precepts of this pure and undefiled religion, are all of them holy, just, and good; and the more they are taught their duty to God, the better they will perform their duties to you; methinks, to neglect the improvement of their souls, out of a dread of spending too much time in religious duties, is acting quite contrary to your own interest as well as duty.

5. Fifthly and Lastly, If neither gratitude to God, love to your children, common justice to your servants, nor even that most prevailing motive self-interest, will excite; yet let a consideration of the terrors of the Lord persuade you to put in practice the pious resolution in the text. Remember, the time will come,

and that perhaps very shortly, when we must all appear before the judgment-seat of Christ; where we must give a solemn and strict account how we have had our conversation, in our respective families in this world. How will you endure to see your children and servants (who ought to be your joy and crown of rejoicing in the day of our Lord Jesus Christ) coming out as so many swift witnesses against you; cursing the father that begot them, the womb that bare them, the paps which they have sucked, and the day they ever entered into your houses? Think you not, the damnation which men must endure for their own sins, will be sufficient, that they need load themselves with the additional guilt of being accessory to the damnation of others also? O consider this, all ye that forget to serve the Lord with your respective households, "lest he pluck you away, and there be none to deliver you!"

But God forbid, brethren, that any such evil should befall you: no, rather will I hope, that you have been in some measure convinced by what has been said of the great importance of FAMILY-RELIGION; and therefore are ready to cry out in the words immediately following the text, "God forbid that we should forsake the Lord;" and again, ver. 21, "Nay, but we will (with our several households) serve the Lord."

And that there may be always such a heart in you, let me exhort all governors of families, in the name of our Lord Jesus Christ, often to reflect on the inesti-mable worth of their own souls, and the infinite ransom, even the precious blood of Jesus Christ, which has been paid down for them. Remember, I beseech you to remember, that you are fallen creatures; that you are by nature lost and estranged from God; and that you can never be restored to your primitive happiness, till by being born again of the Holy Ghost, you arrive at your primitive state of purity, have the image of God restamped upon your souls, and are thereby made meet to be partakers of the inheritance with the saints in light. Do, I say, but seriously and frequently reflect on, and act as persons that believe such important truths, and you will no more neglect your family's spiritual welfare than your own. No, the love of God, which will then be shed abroad in your hearts, will constrain you to do your utmost to preserve them: and the deep sense of God's free grace in Christ Jesus, (which you will then have) in calling you, will excite you to do your utmost to save others, especially those of your own household. And though, after all your pious endeavors, some may continue unreformed; yet you will have this comfortable reflection to make, that you did what you could to make your families religious: and therefore may rest assured of sitting down in the kingdom of heaven, with Abraham, Joshua, and Cornelius, and all the godly householders, who in their several generations shone forth as so many lights in their respective households upon earth. Amen.

Glossary

catechizing:	To teach someone about Christian doctrines by question and answer
"Destroy the Egyptian first-born":	a reference to the Passover story in Exodus, chapter 12
governor of a family:	The head of the household
primitive Christians	The earliest Christians of the first few centuries of church history
servants:	In this context, Whitefield probably meant both free household servants as well as slaves.

SINNERS

In the Hands of an

Angry GOD.

A SERMON

Preached at *Enfield*, *July* 8th 1 7 4 1.

At a Time of great Awakenings ; and attended with remarkable Impreſſions on many of the Hearers.

By *Jonathan Edwards*, A.M.

Paſtor of the Church of CHRIST in *Northampton*.

Amos ix. 2, 3. *Though they dig into Hell, thence ſhall mine Hand take them ; though they climb up to Heaven, thence will I bring them down. And though they hide themſelves in the Top of Carmel, I will ſearch and take them out thence ; and though they be hid from my Sight in the Bottom of the Sea, thence I will command the Serpent, and he ſhall bite them.*

B O S T O N : Printed and Sold by S. KNEELAND and T. GREEN. in Queen-Street over againſt the Priſon. 1 7 4 1.

Edwards, Rev. Jonathan (July 8, 1741), **Sinners in the Hands of an Angry God, A Sermon Preached at Enfield.**

"SINNERS IN THE HANDS OF AN ANGRY GOD": DOCUMENT ANALYSIS

"There is nothing that keeps wicked men, at any one moment, out of hell, but the mere pleasure of God."

Overview

On July 8, 1741, at Enfield, Connecticut, Jonathan Edwards, pastor of the Reformed Church in Northampton, Massachusetts, delivered what is perhaps his most famous sermon, "Sinners in the Hands of an Angry God." The thrust of the sermon is contained in the title: God is an angry, wrathful God, with the power to cast wicked people into hell at any moment. At the same time, God is a merciful God who sent his son, Christ, as a manifestation of his compassion.

Edwards was one of the most prominent figures in the First Great Awakening, a revival of evangelical religious fervor in the 1730s and 1740s. In the American colonies, the awakening paralleled a similar revival in other Protestant countries, including Scotland, England, and Germany. The movement originated with Presbyterians in New Jersey and Pennsylvania and spread outward—first to New England and the middle colonies and then to the southern colonies. In spreading their message, many clergymen conducted revivals marked by highly emotional sermons. The central tenet of the First Great Awakening, one reflected in "Sinners in the Hands of an Angry God," was the primacy of biblical revelation. Among the most prominent proponents of evangelical revival was Edwards, whose fervid sermons, including "Sinners in the Hands of an Angry God," convinced congregants that human nature was depraved and that the terrors of hell awaited those who did not repent.

"Sinners in the Hands of an Angry God" is an important document in the history of religious division in the colonies. Not all clergymen looked on the awakening with approval. They distrusted the emotionalism of preachers like Edwards and believed that these preachers undermined the authority of more established churches, particularly the Anglican Church. Even within such mainline churches as Congregationalism and Presbyterianism, the "New Lights," who approved of the revival, and the "Old Lights," who opposed it, battled for influence. In time, colonial governments were dragged into the dispute as revivalists tried to disestablish mainline churches that received state support.

Context

When Jonathan Edwards delivered "Sinners in the Hands of an Angry God" in the summer of 1741, the Protestant religious revival that would later become known as the Great Awakening had been underway for nearly a decade in the New England colonies. In the early 1730s, Protestant clergy became concerned about a decline in peoples' engagement with the church, which many traced to a number of factors including the increased westward migration of existing and new colonists, the appeal of Enlightenment rationalism and broader trend of American colonists prioritizing commercial concerns over spiritual ones. These were not new concerns, however. In the previous century, New England Puritans had established a "half-way" covenant to enable those who had not fully converted to the Puritan faith to have a stake in the political and economic life of the community.

Beginning in the 1720s, clergy of Presbyterian and Dutch Reformed congregations in the Mid-Atlantic colonies began to attract more parishioners with a more emotive style of preaching that emphasized a deeper and stronger personal connection between individual people and God. Many of these sermons also emphasized the need for Christians to devote themselves to a higher level of moral behavior as evidence of their strengthened relationship with God.

In 1731, Jonathan Edwards brought this new style of preaching to New England, giving a talk in Boston that, upon publishing, was titled "God Glorified in the Work of Redemption, by the Greatness of Man's Dependence upon Him, in the Whole of It." He continued to draw crowds at his home congregation in Northampton, Massachusetts with hundreds of new attendees arriving to hear Edwards's sermons. In 1734, another of Edwards's sermons, "A Divine and Supernatural Light, Immediately Imparted to the Soul by the Spirit of God," established a key part of the Great Awakening—that salvation imbues the believer with a "spiritual and divine light" that is unknowable and unimaginable. This light represents a oneness with God that is independent of human imagination or thought. With this notion, Edwards established a break with the older New England theologies that were much more focused on imparting a scholarly understanding of doctrine rather than an emotional connection with the divine. In this split, Edwards and his fellow "new lights" were pitted against the "old lights" of conservative doctrine and practice.

About the Author

Jonathan Edwards was born in the Connecticut colony on October 5, 1703. Both his father and his maternal grandfather were ministers and, after attending Yale College, he entered the ministry as well while also working as a tutor at Yale. Throughout this time Edwards developed a strong interest in the philosophical and scientific theories of the Enlightenment and Scientific Revolution, reading the works of John Locke and Isaac Newton. Edwards became an assistant minister in Northampton, Massachusetts in 1727.

Four years later, after delivering the Boston address discussed in "Context," above, Edwards oversaw several hundred new members of his church at Northampton. At the same time, he also studied the phenomenon of the massive number of conversions and documented his observations, which often dealt as much with psychological factors as religious ones. Edwards also met with George Whitefield, the revival preacher who swept through the British North American colonies in 1739 and 1741 and worked with him on a preaching tour of New England, including at Edwards's own church in Northampton.

After delivering "Sinners in the Hands of an Angry God" in 1741, Edwards attempted to counter criticisms of the the "New Light" movement and its practices that came from more conservative ministers in the Congregationalist churches of New England. The preaching and teaching of the New Lights was often focused on generating an emotional response. To the consternation of conservative ministers, this emotional response sometimes manifested as fainting, crying out, or other examples of what Edwards called "bodily effects." Edwards argued that these physical manifestations were not the substance of the teaching; that they were instead "incidental" to God's work of salvation. He also wrote extensively on the contribution of the New England revival to what (in his view) was an improvement in the morals of the region.

By the mid-1740s, Edwards's preaching and leadership were becoming less popular in Northampton. In particular, his insistence that Holy Communion be restricted to those who had converted as well has his public denunciation of young people who he felt were engaging in inappropriate behavior led to his eventual dismissal from the pulpit, and he left Northampton in 1751. He remained popular in the wider New England area, however, and preached as a guest minister in several churches and also served as a missionary to local Native American tribes. He continued to preach and write until his death in 1758.

Explanation and Analysis of the Document

"Sinners in the Hands of an Angry God" is a dramatic example of a "fire and brimstone" sermon—one designed to leave the listener shaken, convinced of his or her own sinfulness, and fearful of eternal damnation. According to Edwards, "There is nothing that keeps wicked men, at any one moment, out of hell, but the mere pleasure of God." Not only do people "*deserve* to be cast into hell," they are "*already* under a sentence of condemnation to hell." Throughout the sermon, Edwards repeatedly refers to the "anger" and "wrath" of God, anger that finds expression in the "torments of hell" and the "lake of burning brimstone." Moreover, the devil stands ready to seize souls whenever God allows him to do so, a common belief in frontier communities surrounded by dark forests, Indians, and ever-present dangers. Edwards sums up his argument in this way: "Natural men are held in the hand of God over the pit of hell; they have deserved the fiery pit, and are already sentenced to it." God, he says, "is dreadfully provoked, his anger is as great towards them as to those that are actually suffering the executions of the fierceness of his wrath in hell." One can imagine the terror of his listeners when he thundered, "The devil is waiting for them, hell is gaping for them, the flames gather and flash about them, and would fain lay hold on them, and swallow them up." In one of his most vivid images, Edwards says, "The God that holds you over the pit of hell, much as one holds a spider, or some loathsome insect, over the fire, abhors you, and is dreadfully provoked; his wrath towards you burns like fire."

Calling his listeners to convert, Edwards says, "Thus it will be with you that are in an unconverted state, if you continue in it; the infinite might, and majesty and terribleness of the omnipotent God shall be magnified upon you." Men, though, have an "extraordinary opportunity," for "Christ has flung the door of mercy wide open." Christ cries out to poor sinners, and many of those sinners are flocking to him and "pressing into the kingdom of God." God, he says, "seems now to be hastily gathering in his elect in all parts of the land." Here, Edwards refers to the Calvinist doctrine of "election" or "predestination," which states that God chooses whom to save not on the basis of merit, virtue, or faith but entirely according to his mercy, granted through Christ. Edwards concludes with a call to awakening: "Therefore let everyone that is out of Christ, now awake and fly from the wrath to come."

Audience

Jonathan Edwards initially preached "Sinners in the Hands of an Angry God" to the congregation of his church in Northampton, Massachusetts. It achieved greater attention, however, when it was published following Edwards's delivery of it on July 8, 1741 in Enfield, Connecticut. Edwards had been invited to preach in Enfield but he was not identified as a traveling preacher at that point, rarely journeying to other churches but, rather, relying on his popularity to bring new people into his home congregation. The audience for the preaching of the sermon both in its original form and the version eventually set down in print was composed of New England protestant Christians, mostly Congregationalist but probably including members of other related sects such as Presbyterians. It is important to remember that Edwards's central themes, such as his declaration that those who were unsaved were the subject of God's wrath that there was nothing they could do "to induce God to spare" them was not a new or shocking idea. Those who would have been in the congregation that day or to others from the New England Congregationalist tradition who read the sermon later would certainly recognize Edwards's characterization of God as all powerful and full of wrath at sinful humanity. The total power of God as well as the total depravity of humanity were key aspects of the Calvinist theology upon which New England's Christianity was based. Thus, ideas and imagery that, to a modern audience seem incredibly harsh , were to its original audience a reminder of what they had probably heard from pulpits in New England all their lives.

Impact

While George Whitefield was the preacher of Great Awakening who travelled throughout the North American colonies, it is Jonathan Edwards's "Sinners in the Hands of an Angry God" that remains a standard part not only of books about the history of religion in the United States but also in collections of American literature. As we have seen, the theology presented, and the image of God and His relationship to sinful humans was not far afield from what 18th century Calvinists would have believed. One could argue that some of Edwards's other works, such as those that launched the "new light" movement, were more innovative. However, the extraordinarily vivid language and imagery as well as the emotional, personal appeal that implored "everyone that is out of Christ, now awake and fly from the wrath to come" is what affected those who listened on that summer day in 1741 and has also been a major factor in the sermon's popularity ever since. "Popularity," of course, is a difficult term. "Sinners in the Hands of an Angry God" has been in print in some form ever since it was first published but, at various times in America's history, it has come under criticism and attack from public figures ranging from Mark Twain

to Clarence Darrow. In the Progressive Age of late 19th and early 20th century America, when more liberal theologians began to discount the notion of a literal Hell full of condemned souls, Edwards's sermon was the epitome of a fire and brimstone, fear based sermon. It seemed profoundly old-fashioned, and of a piece with the persecution of religious nonconformists and execution of supposed witches that characterized New England's religious history. In the years following the Second World War, the sermon began to receive some reappraisal, particularly from literary scholars who viewed it as significant and worthy of study less for its theological value than for its use of language. Similarly, as historians began to discuss the changing ways in which Americans (both before and after the War of Independence) viewed themselves and their relationships to God, each other, or the rest of the world, "Sinners in the Hands of an Angry God" served as a vivid example of the New England Puritan/Congregationalist conception of humanity's utter sinfulness and utter dependence on God.

Time Line	
October 5, 1703	■ Jonathan Edwards is born in Connecticut
July 8, 1731	■ Preaches a sermon in Boston published as "God Glorified in the Work of Redemption, by the Greatness of Man's Dependence upon Him, in the Whole of It." This sermon contains many of the themes that he would later develop in "Sinners in the Hands of an Angry God."
1733	■ Protestant revival begins in Northampton, Massachusetts. This revival will grow into the Great Awakening.
1739-1740	■ Edwards meets George Whitefield, another prominent preacher of the Great Awakening.
1741	■ Edwards first preaches his "Sinners in the Hands of an Angry God" sermon in Enfield, Connecticut.
March 22, 1758	■ Edwards dies in New Jersey.

"There is nothing that keeps wicked men, at any one moment, out of hell, but the mere pleasure of God."

(Section 1)

"God has laid himself under no obligation by any promise to keep any natural man out of hell one moment."

(Section 1)

"And now you have an extraordinary opportunity, a day wherein Christ has flung the door of mercy wide open, and stands in the door calling and crying with a loud voice to poor sinners; a day wherein many are flocking to him, and pressing into the kingdom of God."

(Section 1)

Further Reading

"'Is God the Author of Sin?—Jonathan Edwards's Theodicy,' Puritan Reformed Journal 6, no.1 (2014): 98–123. | B. Hoon Woo - Academia.edu." N.p., n.d. Web. 26 Aug. 2016.

Jackson, Brian. "Jonathan Edwards Goes to Hell (House): Fear Appeals in American Evangelism." *Rhetoric Review* 26.1 (2007): 42–59. Print.

Kidd, Thomas S. *The Great Awakening: A Brief History with Documents*. First Edition. Boston: Bedford/St. Martin's, 2007. Print.

Kimnach, Wilson; Maskell, Caleb; Minkema, Kenneth, Jonathan Edwards's Sinners in the Hands of an Angry God, New Haven: Yale University Press, 2010. Print.

Marsden, George M. *Jonathan Edwards: A Life*. Yale University Press, 2003. Print.

Paloff, Benjamin. "Jonathan Edwards in the Old West." *The Antioch Review* 63.4 (2005): 741–741. JSTOR. Web.

Schell, Hannah, and Daniel Ott. *Christian Thought in America: A Brief History*. Augsburg Fortress, Publishers, 2015. JSTOR. Web. 27 Aug. 2016.

Smith, John Howard. *The First Great Awakening: Redefining Religion in British America, 1725-1775*. Madison NJ: Fairleigh Dickinson University Press, 2014. Print.

Tracy, Joseph. *The Great Awakening: A History of the Revival of Religion in the Time of Edwards and Whitefield*. Ed. Mark Riedel. Counted Faithful, 2014. Print.

Yeager, Jonathan M. *Jonathan Edwards and Transatlantic Print Culture*. 1 edition. New York: Oxford University Press, 2016. Print.

—*Commentary by Aaron J. Gulyas and Michael J. O'Neal*

Questions for Further Study

1. Jonathan Edwards and George Whitefield were both prominent figures in the Great Awakening. What similarities and differences do you see in their messages to their audiences?

2. In what ways do you think John Calvin would agree or disagree with Edwards's characterization of God's relationship to humanity, based on your readings of this sermon and Calvin's "Insititutes of the Christian Religion"? Provide specific examples from the texts to support your response.

3. How many different similes or metaphors does Edwards use to describe God's wrath? Which do you think are the most effective? The least?

"Sinners in the Hands of an Angry God": Document Text

1741 CE

—Jonathan Edwards

Their foot shall slide in due time. Deuteronomy 32:35.

In this verse is threatened the vengeance of God on the wicked unbelieving Israelites, that were God's visible people, and lived under means of grace; and that, notwithstanding all God's wonderful works that he had wrought towards that people, yet remained, as is expressed, v. Deuteronomy 32:28, "void of counsel," having no understanding in them; and that, under all the cultivations of heaven, brought forth bitter and poisonous fruit; as in the two verses next preceding the text.

The expression that I have chosen for my text, "Their foot shall slide in due time," seems to imply the following things, relating to the punishment and destruction that these wicked Israelites were exposed to.

1. That they were *always* exposed to destruction, as one that stands or walks in slippery places is always exposed to fall. This is implied in the manner of their destruction's coming upon them, being represented by their foot's sliding. The same is expressed, Psalms 73:18, "Surely thou didst set them in slippery places: thou castedst them down into destruction."

2. It implies that they were always exposed to *sudden* unexpected destruction. As he that walks in slippery places is every moment liable to fall; he can't foresee one moment whether he shall stand or fall the next; and when he does fall, he falls at once, without warning. Which is also expressed in that, Psalms 73:18–19, "Surely thou didst set them in slippery places: thou castedst them down into destruction. How are they brought into desolation as in a moment!"

3. Another thing implied is that they are liable to fall *of themselves*, without being thrown down by the hand of another. As he that stands or walks on slippery ground, needs nothing but his own weight to throw him down.

4. That the reason why they are not fallen already, and don't fall now, is only that God's appointed time is not come. For it is said, that when that due time, or appointed time comes, "their foot shall slide." Then they shall be left to fall as they are inclined by their own weight. God won't hold them up in these slippery places any longer, but will let them go; and then, at that very instant, they shall fall into destruction; as he that stands in such slippery declining ground on the edge of a pit that he can't stand alone, when he is let go he immediately falls and is lost.

The observation from the words that I would now insist upon is this:

[Doctrine.]

There is nothing that keeps wicked men, at any one moment, out of hell, but the mere pleasure of God.

By "the mere pleasure of God," I mean his sovereign pleasure, his arbitrary will, restrained by no obligation, hindered by no manner of difficulty, any more than if nothing else but God's mere will had in the least degree, or in any respect whatsoever, any hand in the preservation of wicked men one moment.

The truth of this observation may appear by the following considerations.

I. There is no want of *power* in God to cast wicked men into hell at any moment. Men's hands can't be strong when God rises up: the strongest have no power to resist him, nor can any deliver out of his hands.

He is not only able to cast wicked men into hell, but he can most *easily* do it. Sometimes an earthly prince meets with a great deal of difficulty to subdue a rebel, that has found means to fortify himself, and has made himself strong by the numbers of his followers. But it is not so with God. There is no fortress that is any defense from the power of God. Though hand join in hand, and vast multitudes of God's enemies combine and associate themselves, they are easily broken in pieces: they are as great heaps of light chaff before the whirlwind; or large quantities of dry stubble before devouring flames. We find it easy to tread on and crush a worm that we see crawling on the earth; so 'tis easy for us to cut or singe a slender thread that anything hangs by; thus easy is it for God when he pleases to cast his enemies down to hell. What are we, that we should think to stand before him, at whose rebuke the earth trembles, and before whom the rocks are thrown down?

II. They *deserve* to be cast into hell; so that divine justice never stands in the way, it makes no objection against God's using his power at any moment to destroy them. Yea, on the contrary, justice calls aloud for an infinite punishment of their sins. Divine justice says of the tree that brings forth such grapes of Sodom, "Cut it down; why cumbreth it the ground" (Luke 13:7). The sword of divine justice is every moment brandished over their heads, and 'tis nothing but the hand of arbitrary mercy, and God's mere will, that holds it back.

III. They are *already* under a sentence of condemnation to hell. They don't only justly deserve to be cast down thither; but the sentence of the law of God, that eternal and immutable rule of righteousness that God has fixed between him and mankind, is gone out against them, and stands against them; so that they are bound over already to hell. John 3:18, "He that believeth not is condemned already." So that every unconverted man properly belongs to hell; that is his place; from thence he is. John 8:23, "Ye are from beneath." And thither he is bound; 'tis the place that justice, and God's Word, and the sentence of his unchangeable law assigns to him.

IV. They are now the objects of that very *same* anger and wrath of God that is expressed in the torments of hell: and the reason why they don't go down to hell at each moment, is not because God, in whose power they are, is not then very angry with them; as angry as he is with many of those miserable creatures that he is now tormenting in hell, and do there feel and bear the fierceness of his wrath. Yea, God is a great deal more angry with great numbers that are now on earth, yea, doubtless with many that are now in this congregation, that it may be are at ease and quiet, than he is with many of those that are now in the flames of hell.

So that it is not because God is unmindful of their wickedness, and don't resent it, that he don't let loose his hand and cut them off. God is not altogether such an one as themselves, though they may imagine him to be so. The wrath of God burns against them, their damnation don't slumber, the pit is prepared, the fire is made ready, the furnace is now hot, ready to receive them, the flames do now rage and glow. The glittering sword is whet, and held over them, and the pit hath opened her mouth under them.

V. The *devil* stands ready to fall upon them and seize them as his own, at what moment God shall permit him. They belong to him; he has their souls in his possession, and under his dominion. The Scripture represents them as his "goods" (Luke 11:21).

The devils watch them; they are ever by them, at their right hand; they stand waiting for them, like greedy hungry lions that see their prey, and expect to have it, but are for the present kept back; if God should withdraw his hand, by which they are restrained, they would in one moment fly upon their poor souls. The old serpent is gaping for them; hell opens its mouth wide to receive them; and if God should permit it, they would be hastily swallowed up and lost.

VI. There are in the souls of wicked men those hellish *principles* reigning, that would presently kindle and flame out into hell fire, if it were not for God's restraints. There is laid in the very nature of carnal men a foundation for the torments of hell: there are those corrupt principles, in reigning power in them, and in full possession of them, that are seeds of hell fire. These principles are active and powerful, and exceeding violent in their nature, and if it were not for the restraining hand of God upon them, they would soon break out, they would flame out after the same manner as the same corruptions, the same enmity does in the hearts of damned souls, and would beget the same torments in 'em as they do in them. The souls of the wicked are in Scripture compared to the troubled sea (Isaiah 57:20). For the present God restrains their wickedness by his mighty power, as he does the raging waves of the troubled sea, saying, "Hitherto shalt thou come, and no further" (Job 38:11); but if God should withdraw that restraining power, it would soon carry all afore it. Sin is the ruin and misery of the soul; it is destructive in its nature; and if God should leave it without restraint, there would need nothing else to make the soul perfectly miserable. The corruption of the heart of man is a thing that is immoderate and boundless in its fury; and while wicked men live here, it is like fire pent up by God's restraints, when as if it were let loose it would set on fire the course of nature; and as the heart is now a sink of sin, so, if sin was not restrained, it would immediately turn the soul into a fiery oven, or a furnace of fire and brimstone.

VII. It is no security to wicked men for one moment, that there are no *visible means of death* at hand. 'Tis no security to a natural man, that he is now in health, and that he don't see which way he should now immediately go out of the world by any accident, and that there is no visible danger in any respect in his circumstances. The manifold and continual experience of the world in all ages shows that this is no evidence that a man is not on the very brink of eternity, and that the next step won't be into another world. The unseen, unthought of ways and means of persons going suddenly out of the world are innumerable and inconceivable. Unconverted men walk over the pit of hell on a rotten covering, and there are innumerable places in this covering so weak that they won't bear their weight, and these places are not seen. The arrows of death fly unseen at noonday; the sharpest sight can't discern them. God has so many different unsearchable ways of taking wicked men out of the world and sending 'em to hell, that there is nothing to make it appear that God had need to be at the expense of a miracle, or go out of the ordinary course of his providence, to destroy any wicked man, at any moment. All the means that there are of sinners going out of the world, are so in God's hands, and so universally absolutely subject to his power and determination, that it don't depend at all less on the mere will of God, whether sinners shall at any moment go to hell, than if means were never made use of, or at all concerned in the case.

VIII. Natural men's *prudence* and *care* to preserve their own *lives*, or the care of others to preserve them, don't secure 'em a moment. This divine providence and universal experience does also bear testimony to. There is this clear evidence that men's own wisdom is no security to them from death: that if it were otherwise we should see some difference between the wise and politic men of the world, and others, with regard to their liableness to early and unexpected death; but how is it in fact? Ecclesiastes 2:16, "How dieth the wise man? as the fool."

IX. All wicked men's *pains* and *contrivance* they use to escape *hell*, while they continue to reject Christ, and so remain wicked men, don't secure 'em from hell one moment. Almost every natural man that hears of hell, flatters himself that he shall escape it; he depends upon himself for his own security; he flatters himself in what he has done, in what he is now doing, or what he intends to do; everyone lays out matters in his own mind how he shall avoid damnation, and flatters himself that he contrives well for himself, and that his schemes won't fail. They hear indeed that there are but few saved, and that the bigger part of men that have died heretofore are gone to hell; but each one imagines that he lays out matters better for his own escape than others have done: he don't intend to come to that place of torment; he says within himself, that he intends to take care that shall be effectual, and to order matters so for himself as not to fail.

But the foolish children of men do miserably delude themselves in their own schemes, and in their confidence in their own strength and wisdom; they trust to nothing but a shadow. The bigger part of those that heretofore have lived under the same means of grace, and are now dead, are undoubtedly gone to hell: and it was not because they were not as wise as those that are now alive; it was not because they did not lay out matters as well for themselves to secure their own escape. If it were so, that we could come to speak with them, and could inquire of them, one by one, whether they expected when alive, and when they used to hear about hell, ever to be the subjects of that misery, we doubtless should hear one and another reply, "No, I never intended to come here; I had laid out matters otherwise in my mind; I thought I should contrive well for myself; I thought my scheme good; I intended to take effectual care; but it came upon me unexpected; I did not look for it at that time, and in that manner; it came as a thief; death outwitted me; God's wrath was too quick for me; O my cursed foolishness! I was flattering myself, and pleasing myself with vain dreams of what I would do hereafter, and when I was saying, 'Peace and safety,' then sudden destruction came upon me" (1 Thessalonians 5:3).

X. God has laid himself under *no obligation* by any promise to keep any natural man out of hell one moment. God certainly has made no promises either of eternal life, or of any deliverance or preservation from eternal death, but what are contained in the covenant of grace, the promises that are given in Christ, in whom all the promises are yea and amen. But surely they have no interest in the promises of the covenant of grace that are not the children of the covenant, and that don't believe in any of the promises of the covenant, and have no interest in the *Mediator* of the covenant.

So that whatever some have imagined and pretended about promises made to natural men's earnest seeking and knocking, 'tis plain and manifest that whatever pains a natural man takes in religion, whatever prayers he makes, till he believes in Christ, God is under no manner of obligation to keep him a *moment* from eternal destruction.

So that thus it is, that natural men are held in the hand of God over the pit of hell; they have deserved the fiery pit, and are already sentenced to it; and God is dreadfully provoked, his anger is as great towards them as to those that are actually suffering the executions of the fierceness of his wrath in hell, and they have done nothing in the least to appease or abate that anger, neither is God in the least bound by any promise to hold 'em up one moment; the devil is waiting for them, hell is gaping for them, the flames gather and flash about them, and would fain lay hold on them, and swallow them up; the fire pent up in their own hearts is struggling to break out; and they have no interest in any mediator, there are no means within reach that can be any security to them. In short, they have no refuge, nothing to take hold of, all that preserves them every moment is the mere arbitrary will, and uncovenanted unobliged forbearance of an incensed God.

[Application.]

The *Use* may be of *Awakening* to unconverted persons in this congregation. This that you have heard is the case of everyone of you that are out of Christ. That world of misery, that lake of burning brimstone is extended abroad under you. *There* is the dreadful pit of the glowing flames of the wrath of God; there is hell's wide gaping mouth open; and you have nothing to stand upon, nor anything to take hold of: there is nothing between you and hell but the air; 'tis only the power and mere pleasure of God that holds you up.

You probably are not sensible of this; you find you are kept out of hell, but don't see the hand of God in it, but look at other things, as the good state of your bodily constitution, your care of your own life, and the means you use for your own preservation. But indeed these things are nothing; if God should withdraw his hand, they would avail no more to keep you from falling, than the thin air to hold up a person that is suspended in it.

Your wickedness makes you as it were heavy as lead, and to tend downwards with great weight and pressure towards hell; and if God should let you go, you would immediately sink and swiftly descend and plunge into the bottomless gulf, and your healthy constitution, and your own care and prudence, and best contrivance, and all your righteousness, would have no more influence to uphold you and keep you out of hell, than a spider's web would have to stop a falling rock. Were it not that so is the sovereign pleasure of God, the earth would not bear you one moment; for you are a burden to it; the creation groans with you; the creature is made subject to the bondage of your corruption, not willingly; the sun don't willingly shine upon you to give you light to serve sin and Satan; the earth don't willingly yield her increase to satisfy your lusts; nor is it willingly a stage for your wickedness to be acted upon; the air don't willingly serve you for breath to maintain the flame of life in your vitals, while you spend your life in the service of God's enemies. God's creatures are good, and were made for men to serve God with, and don't willingly subserve to any other purpose, and groan when

they are abused to purposes so directly contrary to their nature and end. And the world would spew you out, were it not for the sovereign hand of him who hath subjected it in hope. There are the black clouds of God's wrath now hanging directly over your heads, full of the dreadful storm, and big with thunder; and were it not for the restraining hand of God it would immediately burst forth upon you. The sovereign pleasure of God for the present stays his rough wind; otherwise it would come with fury, and your destruction would come like a whirlwind, and you would be like the chaff of the summer threshing floor.

The wrath of God is like great waters that are dammed for the present; they increase more and more, and rise higher and higher, till an outlet is given, and the longer the stream is stopped, the more rapid and mighty is its course, when once it is let loose. 'Tis true, that judgment against your evil works has not been executed hitherto; the floods of God's vengeance have been withheld; but your guilt in the meantime is constantly increasing, and you are every day treasuring up more wrath; the waters are continually rising and waxing more and more mighty; and there is nothing but the mere pleasure of God that holds the waters back that are unwilling to be stopped, and press hard to go forward; if God should only withdraw his hand from the floodgate, it would immediately fly open, and the fiery floods of the fierceness and wrath of God would rush forth with inconceivable fury, and would come upon you with omnipotent power; and if your strength were ten thousand times greater than it is, yea, ten thousand times greater than the strength of the stoutest, sturdiest devil in hell, it would be nothing to withstand or endure it.

The bow of God's wrath is bent, and the arrow made ready on the string, and Justice bends the arrow at your heart, and strains the bow, and it is nothing but the mere pleasure of God, and that of an angry God, without any promise or obligation at all, that keeps the arrow one moment from being made drunk with your blood.

Thus are all you that never passed under a great change of heart, by the mighty power of the Spirit of God upon your souls; all that were never born again, and made new creatures, and raised from being dead in sin, to a state of new, and before altogether unexperienced light and life (however you may have reformed your life in many things, and may have had religious affections, and may keep up a form of religion in your families and closets, and in the house of God, and may be strict in it), you are thus in the hands of an angry God; 'tis nothing but his mere pleasure that keeps you from being this moment swallowed up in everlasting destruction.

However unconvinced you may now be of the truth of what you hear, by and by you will be fully convinced of it. Those that are gone from being in the like circumstances with you, see that it was so with them; for destruction came suddenly upon most of them, when they expected nothing of it, and while they were saying, "Peace and safety": now they see, that those things that they depended on for peace and safety, were nothing but thin air and empty shadows.

The God that holds you over the pit of hell, much as one holds a spider, or some loathsome insect, over the fire, abhors you, and is dreadfully provoked; his wrath towards you burns like fire; he looks upon you as worthy of nothing else, but to be cast into the fire; he is of purer eyes than to bear to have you in his sight; you are ten thousand times so abominable in his eyes as the most hateful venomous serpent is in ours. You have offended him infinitely more than ever a stubborn rebel did his prince: and yet 'tis nothing but his hand that holds you from falling into the fire every moment; 'tis to be ascribed to nothing else, that you did not go to hell the last night; that you was suffered to awake again in this world, after you closed your eyes to sleep: and there is no other reason to be given why you have not dropped into hell since you arose in the morning, but that God's hand has held you up; there is no other reason to be given why you han't gone to hell since you have sat here in the house of God, provoking his pure eyes by your sinful wicked manner of attending his solemn worship: yea, there is nothing else that is to be given as a reason why you don't this very moment drop down into hell.

O sinner! Consider the fearful danger you are in: 'tis a great furnace of wrath, a wide and bottomless pit, full of the fire of wrath, that you are held over in the hand of that God, whose wrath is provoked and incensed as much against you as against many of the damned in hell; you hang by a slender thread, with the flames of divine wrath flashing about it, and ready every moment to singe it, and burn it asunder; and you have no interest in any mediator, and nothing to lay hold of to save yourself, nothing to keep off the flames of wrath, nothing of your own, nothing that you ever have done, nothing that you can do, to induce God to spare you one moment.

And consider here more particularly several things concerning that wrath that you are in such danger of.

First. Whose wrath it is: it is the wrath of the infinite God. If it were only the wrath of man, though it were of the most potent prince, it would be comparatively little to be regarded. The wrath of kings is very much dreaded, especially of absolute monarchs, that have the possessions and lives of their subjects wholly in their power, to be disposed of at their mere will. Proverbs 20:2, "The fear of a king is as the roaring of a lion: whoso provoketh him to anger, sinneth against his own soul." The subject that very much enrages an arbitrary prince, is liable to suffer the most extreme torments, that human art can invent or human power can inflict. But the greatest earthly potentates, in their greatest majesty and strength, and when clothed in their greatest terrors, are but feeble despicable worms of the dust, in comparison of the great and almighty Creator and King of heaven and earth: it is but little that they can do, when most enraged, and when they have exerted the utmost of their fury. All the kings of the earth before God are as grasshoppers, they are nothing and less than nothing: both their love and their hatred is to be despised. The wrath of the great King of kings is as much more terrible than their's, as his majesty is greater. Luke 12:4–5, "And I say unto you my friends, Be not afraid of them that kill the body, and after that have no more that they can do. But I will forewarn you whom ye shall fear: Fear him which after he hath killed hath power to cast into hell; yea, I say unto you, fear him."

Second. 'Tis the *fierceness* of his wrath that you are exposed to. We often read of the *fury* of God; as in Isaiah 59:18, "According to their deeds, accordingly he will repay fury to his adversaries." So Isaiah 66:15, "For, behold, the Lord will come with fire, and with chariots like a whirlwind, to render his anger with fury, and his rebukes with flames of fire." And so in many other places. So we read of God's *fierceness*. Revelation 19:15, there we read of "the winepress of the fierceness and wrath of almighty God." The words are exceeding terrible: if it had only been said, "the wrath of God," the words would have implied that which is infinitely dreadful; but 'tis not only said so, but "the fierceness and wrath of God": the fury of God! the fierceness of Jehovah! Oh how dreadful must that be! Who can utter or conceive what such expressions carry in them! But it is not only said so, but "the fierceness and wrath of *almighty God*." As though there would be a very great manifestation of his almighty power, in what the fierceness of his wrath should inflict, as though omnipotence should be as it were enraged, and exerted, as men are wont to exert their strength in the fierceness of their wrath. Oh! then what will be consequence! What will become of the poor worm that shall suffer it! Whose hands can be strong? and whose heart endure? To what a dreadful, inexpressible, inconceivable depth of misery must the poor creature be sunk, who shall be the subject of this!

Consider this, you that are here present, that yet remain in an unregenerate state. That God will execute the fierceness of his anger, implies that he will inflict wrath without any pity: when God beholds the ineffable extremity of your case, and sees your torment to be so vastly disproportioned to your strength, and sees how your poor soul is crushed and sinks down, as it were into an infinite gloom, he will have no compassion upon you, he will not forbear the executions of his wrath, or in the least lighten his hand; there shall be no moderation or mercy, nor will God then at all stay his rough wind; he will have no regard to your welfare, nor be at all careful lest you should suffer too much, in any other sense than only that you shall not suffer beyond what strict justice requires: nothing shall be withheld, because it's so hard for you to bear. Ezekiel 8:18, "Therefore will I also deal in fury: mine eye shall not spare, neither will I have pity; and though they cry in mine ears with a loud voice, yet I will not hear them." Now God stands ready to pity you; this is a day of mercy; you may cry now with some encouragement of obtaining mercy: but when once the day of mercy is past, your most lamentable and dolorous cries and shrieks will be in vain; you will be wholly lost and thrown away of God as to any regard to your welfare; God will have no other use to put you to but only to suffer misery; you shall be continued in being to no other end; for you will be a vessel of wrath fitted to destruction; and there will be no other use of this vessel but only to be filled full of wrath: God will be so far from pitying you when you cry to him, that 'tis said he will only laugh and mock (Proverbs 1:25–32).

How awful are those words, Isaiah 63:3, which are the words of the great God, "I will tread them in mine anger, and will trample them in my fury, and their blood shall be sprinkled upon my garments, and I will stain all my raiment." 'Tis perhaps impossible to conceive of words that carry in them greater manifestations of these three things, viz. contempt, and hatred, and fierceness of indignation. If you cry to God to pity you, he will be so far from pitying you in your doleful case, or showing you the least regard or favor, that instead of that he'll only tread you under foot: and though he will know that you can't bear the weight of omnipotence treading upon you, yet he won't regard that, but he will crush you under his feet without mercy; he'll crush out your blood, and make it fly, and it shall be sprinkled on his garments, so as to stain all his raiment. He will not only hate you, but he will have you in the utmost contempt; no place shall be thought fit for you, but under his feet, to be trodden down as the mire of the streets.

Third. The misery you are exposed to is that which God will inflict to that end, that he might show what that *wrath* of Jehovah is. God hath had it on his heart to show to angels and men, both how excellent his love is, and also how terrible his wrath is. Sometimes earthly kings have a mind to show how terrible *their* wrath is, by the extreme punishments they would execute on those that provoke 'em. Nebuchadnezzar, that mighty and haughty monarch of the Chaldean empire, was willing to show *his* wrath, when enraged with Shadrach, Meshach, and Abednego; and accordingly gave order that the burning fiery furnace should be het seven times hotter than it was before; doubtless it was raised to the utmost degree of fierceness that human art could raise it: but the great God is also willing to show *his wrath*, and magnify his awful majesty and mighty power in the extreme sufferings of his enemies.

Romans 9:22, "What if God, willing to show *his* wrath, and to make his power known, endured with much longsuffering the vessels of wrath fitted to destruction?" And seeing this is his design, and what he has determined, to show how terrible the unmixed, unrestrained wrath, the fury and fierceness of Jehovah is, he will do it to effect. There will be something accomplished and brought to pass, that will be dreadful with a witness. When the great and angry God hath risen up and executed his awful vengeance on the poor sinner; and the wretch is actually suffering the infinite weight and power of his indignation, then will God call upon the whole universe to behold that awful majesty, and mighty power that is to be seen in it. Isaiah 33:12–14, "And the people shall be as the burning of lime: as thorns cut up shall they be burnt in the fire. Hear, ye that are far off, what I have done; and ye that are near, acknowledge my might. The sinners in Zion are afraid; fearfulness hath surprised the hypocrites. Who among us shall dwell with the devouring fire? who among us shall dwell with everlasting burnings?"

Thus it will be with you that are in an unconverted state, if you continue in it; the infinite might, and majesty and terribleness of the omnipotent God shall be magnified upon you, in the ineffable strength of your torments: you shall be tormented in the presence of the holy angels, and in the presence of the Lamb; and when you shall be in this state of suffering, the glorious inhabitants of heaven shall go forth and look on the awful spectacle, that they may see what the wrath and fierceness of the Almighty is, and when they have seen it, they will fall down and adore that great power and majesty. Isaiah 66:23–24, "And it shall come to pass, that from one new moon to another, and from one Sabbath to another, shall all flesh come to worship before me, saith the Lord. And they shall go forth, and look upon the carcasses of the men that have transgressed against me: for their worm shall not die, neither shall their fire be quenched; and they shall be an abhorring unto all flesh."

Fourth. 'Tis *everlasting* wrath. It would be dreadful to suffer this fierceness and wrath of almighty God one moment; but you must suffer it to all eternity: there will be no end to this exquisite horrible misery. When you look forward, you shall see a long forever, a boundless duration before you, which will swallow up your thoughts, and amaze your soul; and you will absolutely despair of ever having any deliverance, any end, any mitigation, any rest at all; you will know certainly that you must wear out long ages, millions of millions of ages, in wrestling and conflicting with this almighty merciless vengeance; and then when you have so done, when so many ages have actually been spent by you in this manner, you will know that all is but a point to what remains. So that your punishment will indeed be infinite. Oh who can express what the state of a soul in such circumstances is! All that we can possibly say about it, gives but a very feeble faint representation of it; 'tis inexpressible and inconceivable: for "who knows the power of God's anger?" (Psalms 90:11).

How dreadful is the state of those that are daily and hourly in danger of this great wrath, and infinite misery! But this is the dismal case of every soul in this congregation, that has not been born again, however moral and strict, sober and religious they may otherwise be. Oh that you would consider it, whether you be young or old. There is reason to think, that there are many in this congregation now hearing this discourse, that will actually be the subjects of this very misery to all eternity. We know not who they are, or in what seats they sit, or what thoughts they now have: it may be they are now at ease, and hear all these things without much disturbance, and are now flattering themselves that they are not the persons, promising themselves that they shall escape. If we knew that there was one person, and but one, in the whole congregation that was to be the subject of this misery, what an awful thing would it be to think of! If we knew who it was, what an awful sight would it be to see such a person! How might all the rest of the congregation lift up a lamentable and bitter cry over him! But alas! instead of one, how many is it likely will remember this discourse in hell? And it would be a wonder if some that are now present, should not be in hell in a very short time, before this year is out. And it would be no wonder if some person that now sits here in some seat of this meeting house in health, and quiet and secure, should be there before tomorrow morning. Those of you that finally continue in a natural condition, that shall keep out of hell longest, will be there in a little time! your damnation don't slumber; it will come swiftly, and in all probability very suddenly upon many of you. You have reason to wonder, that you are not already in hell. 'Tis doubtless the case of some that heretofore you have seen and known, that never deserved hell more than you, and that heretofore appeared as likely to have been now alive as you: their case is past all hope; they are crying in extreme misery and perfect despair; but here you are in the land of the living, and in the house of God, and have an opportunity to obtain salvation. What would not those poor damned, hopeless souls give for one day's such opportunity as you now enjoy!

And now you have an extraordinary opportunity, a day wherein Christ has flung the door of mercy wide open, and stands in the door calling and crying with a loud voice to poor sinners; a day wherein many are flocking to him, and pressing into the kingdom of God; many are daily coming from the east, west, north and south; many that were very lately in the same miserable condition that you are in, are in now an happy state, with their hearts filled with love to him that has loved them and washed them from their sins in his own blood, and rejoicing in hope of the glory of God. How awful is it to be left behind at such a day! To see so many others feasting, while you are pining and perishing! To see so many rejoicing and singing for joy of heart, while you have cause to mourn for sorrow of heart, and howl for vexation of spirit! How can you rest one moment in such a condition? Are not your souls as precious as the souls of the people at Suffield, where they are flocking from day to day to Christ?

Are there not many here that have lived *long* in the world, that are not to this day born again, and so are aliens from the commonwealth of Israel, and have done nothing ever since they have lived, but treasure up wrath against the day of wrath? Oh sirs, your case in an especial manner is extremely dangerous; your guilt and hardness of heart is extremely great. Don't you see how generally persons of your years are passed over and left, in the present remarkable and wonderful dispensation of God's mercy? You had need to consider yourselves, and wake thoroughly out of sleep; you cannot bear the fierceness and wrath of the infinite God.

And you that are *young men*, and *young women*, will you neglect this precious season that you now enjoy, when so many others of your age are renouncing all youthful vanities, and flocking to Christ? You especially have now an extraordinary opportunity; but if you neglect it, it will soon be with you as it is with those persons that spent away all the precious days of youth in sin, and are now come to such a dreadful pass in blindness and hardness.

And you *children* that are unconverted, don't you know that you are going down to hell, to bear the dreadful wrath of that God that is now angry with you every day, and every night? Will you be content to be the children of the devil, when so many other children in the land are converted, and are become the holy and happy children of the King of kings?

And let everyone that is yet out of Christ, and hanging over the pit of hell, whether they be old men and women, or middle aged, or young people, or little children, now hearken to the loud calls of God's Word and providence. This acceptable year of the Lord, that is a day of such great favor to some, will doubtless be a day of as remarkable vengeance to others. Men's hearts harden, and their guilt increases apace at such a day as this, if they neglect their souls: and never was there so great danger of such persons being given up to hardness of heart, and blindness of mind. God seems now to be hastily gathering in his elect in all parts of the land; and probably the bigger part of adult persons that ever shall be saved, will be brought in now in a little time, and that it will be as it was on that great outpouring of the Spirit upon the Jews in the apostles' days, the election will obtain, and the rest will be blinded. If this should be the case with you, you will eternally curse this day, and will curse the day that ever you was born, to see such a season of the pouring out of God's Spirit; and will wish that you had died and gone to hell before you had seen it. Now undoubtedly it is, as it was in the days of John the Baptist, the ax is in an extraordinary manner laid at the root of the trees, that every tree that brings not forth good fruit, may be hewn down, and cast into the fire.

Therefore let everyone that is out of Christ, now awake and fly from the wrath to come. The wrath of almighty God is now undoubtedly hanging over great part of this congregation: let everyone fly out of Sodom. Haste and escape for your lives, look not behind you, escape to the mountain, lest you be consumed (Genesis 19:17).

Glossary

"an unregenerate state":	A condition of sinfulness. See "natural man" below.
Cumbreth:	To burden or trouble
"Mediator of the covenant":	A reference to Jesus Christ who, in Christian doctrine, "mediated" a new covenant (agreement) between humanity and God, which promises eternal life (the "promises of the covenant" mentioned earlier in the sentence).
Natural man:	One who is not saved by God as opposed to the Spiritual Man.
"No want of *power*":	Sufficient power. In this context, God has sufficient power "to cast wicked men into hell at any moment."

Synagogue of the Baal Shem Tov, founder of Hasidism, in Medzhybizh Ukraine. It gave a new phase to Jewish mysticism, seeking its popularisation through internal correspondence.

"The Holy Epistle": Document Analysis

1752 CE

"I performed an ascent of the soul... and I saw a great accusation until the evil side almost received permission to completely destroy regions and communities...."

Overview

"The Holy Epistle" of Ba'al Shem Tov is one of the signature texts of the founder of Hasidism. Hasidism originated in the late eighteenth century and soon developed into a particularly rich movement of spiritual awakening within Judaism. It has adherents to this day. The founder, whose title literally means "master of the good [holy] name," was also known as the Besht (derived from a shortening of the title Ba'al Shem Tov) or simply as Ba'al Shem. In light of the fact that the vast majority of our knowledge of the movement's first teacher and exemplary saint is at second hand, the modern significance of "The Holy Epistle" to no small degree lies in its authenticity. This lack of firsthand documents stems from the nature of Hasidism at the time of its inception, wherein many of the homilies, discourses, and other manner of teachings were the responsibility of a charismatic teacher's disciples to document and possibly publish. Since the stories surrounding the founder of the movement are especially rich and couched in legend, not to mention stylistically drawn from earlier Jewish hagiographies, Ba'al Shem Tov almost disappears from sight as a genuine person. For a time in the second half of the nineteenth century some historians of the movement doubted that he had even actually existed.

"The Holy Epistle" is the most important of the rare writings that can, with a high degree of certainty, be attributed almost directly to Ba'al Shem Tov. The letter was written by him in 1752, eight years before his death, to his brother-in-law, Rabbi Abraham Gershon of Kitov, a Torah scholar of some renown, who had emigrated from Poland to the Holy Land of ancient Palestine. For unknown reasons the epistle was undelivered, remaining instead in the Besht's immediate circle. It was published about thirty years later, a number of years after its author had passed away. "The Holy Epistle" shows Ba'al Shem in several of his primary roles: among others, as a mystic, as a religious leader involved in contemporary controversies, and as someone who has a warm relationship with his family members. Behind the reported mystical ascents—a prominent feature of the epistle—lies a deep concern for his coreligionists and their problems. Although a number of facets of Hasidism are not present in this rather brief document, it is a powerful witness to the religious inspiration and character of the movement's founder.

Context

Hasidism had its origins in the declining Polish-Lithuanian Commonwealth, where in the eighteenth century approximately four-fifths of the world's Jewish population lived. The decline of the Commonwealth affected the fortunes of the Jews, and many of the coreligionists of the founder of Hasidism experienced great poverty; generally the Podolia region, where the movement arose, was quite depressed economically. Moreover, the tolerance that had allowed the Jewish diaspora to thrive and grow to such an extent in the polity was no longer what it historically had been, and "The Holy Epistle" itself chronicles instances of the persecution of the Jews.

In the eighteenth century there were a number of groups similar to the one centered on Ba'al Shem Tov, often led by kabbalists. However, thanks to Ba'al Shem's particular genius and charismatic nature, his was the group that generated a movement that in a short period of time was to spread throughout the commonwealth beginning from its southeast corner and subsequently through the Jewish communities in Hungary and beyond. From the original simple followers in the small towns, the movement spread quickly to economically more varied regions of the Polish part of the Commonwealth, along the way securing wealthy sponsors that enabled it to flourish. Because its rapid spread and spiritual creativity touched numerous aspects of Jewish life, Hasidism became, above and beyond its religious dimension, the most important cultural development in modern eastern European Jewry before the development of Jewish political movements such as Zionism.

Ba'al Shem Tov was fortunate to attract a talented group of colleague-disciples who were able to develop his original thought and give a viable structure to the movement. The *tzaddikim*, as these teachers and miracle workers were known, established courts and eventually a number of dynasties. The teachings were partly conveyed through appealing stories that assisted in imparting their message to less-sophisticated followers who formed the bulk of the early adherents. These narratives had special appeal to later Jewish thinkers such as the Austrian-born philosopher Martin Buber and the American writer Elie Wiesel, who transmitted them to a wider audience and gave the impression that Hasidism was primarily a folk religion. What attracted these twentieth-century thinkers repelled earlier members of the Haskalah, or Jewish enlightenment, who considered the movement's folksy nature and ecstatic practices signs of ignorance, which were obstacles for Jews in assimilating with the host society. One might add that, tragically, the distinctiveness of the Hasidim made it particularly difficult for them to survive the Holocaust of World War II. The attraction of Hasidism was such that at its height its communities were able to penetrate Haskalah strongholds such as Vilnius. Moreover, the impression of folksiness is only partly correct; in his monumental study *The Religious Thought of Hasidism,* the scholar Norman Lamm details a surprisingly high degree of sophistication present within the movement from its very onset.

Some early observers saw Hasidism as a threat to Orthodox Judaism, but in fact its innovations never challenged the Torah or the *mitzvoth* (commandments). As observant Jews the Hasidim merely stressed that carrying out the *mitzvoth* elevated one only when a spirit of devotion attended the duty. Eventually, the movement took the side of tradition in the face of challenge from the Haskalah in the nineteenth century, in the process becoming one of the rare splinter movements of Judaism that became accepted by Orthodoxy.

The core of classic Hasidic thought was based on its conception of the nature of God. Hasidic thinkers held an unusually broad concept of the Creator and the nature of creation. Some have described this conception as approaching pantheism, but in classic Hasidism it was really a form of panentheism; the difference is that pantheism takes the view that the created world is God, whereas panentheism holds that all exists *within* God. Panentheism remains firmly monotheistic. This conception of God has been present in both Judaism and Christianity at various times. In classical Hasidic thought, everything including the entire cosmos, is a garment of the divine. This perspective had ramifications for the manner in which this thought might be conveyed, implying as it does that creation is a sort of parable; unsurprisingly, parables were one of the favored means of imparting wisdom, starting with the Besht himself.

Thus, for the Hasidim, the absence of God in creation was an illusion, a self-imposed contraction of the divinity. The human ego plays a role in fostering this illusion, while prayer and contemplation aid in reducing the self to assist in restoring unity with the Creator. Hasidism was unusual for its individualistic approach to redemption in Judaism. It encouraged striving for the salvation of one's individual soul in order to bring about the redemption of the world. Although there is no evidence of a direct influence, in this aspect Hasidism was in keeping with the spirit of the eighteenth-century Enlightenment and Christian Pietistic movements, although the latter had little impact on Polish Catholicism or Orthodox Christianity, which were geographically closest to the movement.

Despite this emphasis on the individual, Hasidism held that only within community relations could mystical unity with the divine be achieved. Crucial to Hasidic community was the relationship of the congregation to the *tzaddik*. Hasidism taught that humans must worship and cling to God—that is, attain *devukut*—not only during the practice of religious observances but also in all aspects of life: business, social contacts, and daily affairs. Moreover, Ba'al Shem's insistence that it was important to "serve God in joy" was quite remarkable at the time. From this postulate an ecstatic-prayer-centered regime that critiqued the strenuous asceticism of earlier Jewish mystics evolved within Hasidism. The emphasis placed on joy as essential to the good Jewish life and crucial in the worship of God resulted in the importance of Hasidic song and dance as expressions of piety among the followers and aided in building community cohesion. These practices became prominent among the external elements that identified the movement to outsiders (for instance, as portrayed in the popular modern tale of a Hasidic community in the 1971 film *Fiddler on the Roof*).

Although study of the Torah took second place to prayer and devotion, it was hardly abandoned. The mere accumulation of knowledge was felt to be without spiritual significance; nevertheless, study was praised. The tension between practice and theory stimulated the creativity of the movement and produced the rich body of literature that is an important part of Hasidism's legacy to humanity.

A major reason that the appearance of Hasidism worried Orthodox leaders was its apparent similarity to earlier messianic movements that had stemmed from the Sabbatean movement of the latter seventeenth century, which taught that under the right eschatological conditions, *halakhic* rules—the laws derived from the Hebrew scriptures and Talmud that Jews must follow to abide by Jewish teaching—no longer bound the Jews. Sabbateans also felt that sin might serve as a source of redemption, by provoking the Messiah to come. However, Norman Lamm, among other scholars, has argued that the radical elements in Hasidism were less prominent than they were made out to be in the heat of early polemics over the movement. The influence on Hasidism and Ba'al Shem's reaction to earlier and contemporary messianic movements is evident in "The Holy Epistle."

Ba'al Shem Tov did not put his teachings into writing, and he even opposed the attempts of others to publish them. The first known larger document about him, *Shivhei ha-Besht,* or *In Praise of the Ba'al Shem Tov,* as it was translated into English, was published in Hebrew in 1814, just over half a century after his death. This work contains more than two hundred tales about Ba'al Shem Tov that originally circulated orally; the stories were written down by Rabbi Dov Ber, known as the Maggid of Mezerich, a close associate of the Besht who became the foremost leader within Hasidic circles after the latter's death. It is thus probable that the oral sources of the stories were from among the Besht's closest circle. A number of his other collections were published together with several letters apart from "The Holy Epistle." But despite the fact that the founder of Hasidism lived less than three centuries ago in Europe, surprisingly little is known about him directly: He left no autobiography, no journal or substantial body of correspondence that would allow for a deeper analysis of his character or even for establishing a number of basic biographical facts, including the dates of his birth and marriages, or more than a general trajectory of his educational and career path.

To additionally understand the significance of "The Holy Epistle," it is worth having a closer look at *In Praise of the Ba'al Shem Tov*. The crucial phrase from the title is "in praise of," which signifies the text's primary emphasis. The author of the final version stresses the nature of the work in his introductory remarks: "The reader should realize that I wrote all this not as histories nor as stories. In each tale he should perceive His [Ba'al Shem Tov's] awesome deeds. He should infer the moral of each tale, so that he will be able to attach his heart to the fear of God, the beliefs of the sages and the power of the holy Torah." In other words, the work is clearly more of a hagiography than a historical work. Although the work contains a number of genuine sources pertaining to the Besht's biography, these must be gleaned from among a vast literature that primarily serves another purpose.

Hagiographies are full of edifying tales about holy men or saints. As is typical for this genre, *In Praise of the Ba'al Shem Tov* contains magical transformations of inanimate objects and animals, encounters with a variety of mythical creatures, miraculous healings, the ability to travel through time, and so on. Unsurprisingly, the collection follows a number of generic inspirations. The most evident model is the collection pertaining to the kabbalist Isaac Luria, known as the Holy Ari, that in the seventeenth century came to be known as *In Praise of the Ari*. It has been noted that several details from *In Praise of the Ba'al Shem Tov* are so close to the hero of the earlier work that they can hardly be coincidental.

In contrast to *In Praise of the Ba'al Shem Tov*, which can be said to go out of its way to prove that the Besht was indeed a *ba'al shem*—that is, a miracle worker who could bring about healing and cures—"The Holy Epistle" is a comparatively modest document. Nevertheless, from the contemporary perspective this letter makes it possible to imagine Ba'al Shem Tov as a genuine historical figure embedded in his religious community and time and as someone who expressed a profound concern for his coreligionists, which was a key to his influence.

Time Line

ca. 1700	■ Israel ben Eliezer, known as Ba'al Shem Tov, is born.
1746	■ On Rosh Hashanah of the Hebrew year 5507, Ba'al Shem Tov has the first ascent of the soul to be described in "The Holy Epistle."
1747	■ Rabbi Abraham Gershon of Kitov (Kutów) immigrates to the Holy Land of Israel in ancient Palestine.
1749	■ On Rosh Hashanah of the Hebrew year 5510, the second ascent of the soul to be described by Ba'al Shem Tov occurs.
1752	■ Ba'al Shem Tov writes "The Holy Epistle," intended for Rabbi Gershon, but the letter remains undelivered and circulates only among close associates of the author. These associates create copies of the letter.
1760	■ Ba'al Shem Tov dies.
1781	■ The letter is published as an appendix to Yaakov Yosef of Polonne's *Ben Porat Yosef* with an introduction by the publishers, who refer to it as "Igeret ha-kodesh," or "The Holy Epistle."
1814	■ *In Praise of the Ba'al Shem Tov* is published.
1971	■ Mordecai Bauminger publishes an alternative version of "The Holy Epistle" based on an eighteenth-century manuscript discovered in 1923; scholars claim this version is closer to Ba'al Shem's original than the earlier published version.
1980	■ Yehoshua Mondshine publishes yet another version, based on a manuscript apparently predating the *Ben Porat Yosef* version, but it is the least complete.

About the Author

Israel ben Eliezer was born around 1700 in Okopy in Podolia, now in Ukraine. He began his career as a *ba'al shem* in a nearby town and moved to Miedzybóz, the site of the largest

Jewish community in Podolia, in 1740, where he spent the last twenty years of his life.

The term "founder of Hasidism" that is commonly used regarding Ba'al Shem Tov, even in such reference works as the *Encyclopaedia Judaica*, requires some clarification. Historically speaking, the Besht can more accurately be called the first among equals in a circle of mystics and kabbalists that was formed in the middle of the eighteenth century in Miedzybóz. He gained his reputation as a *ba'al shem*, and it is in this role that the local Jewish community supported him. It is also in this role that non-Jewish sources register him. He was also known as a mystic who had experiences of the "ascent of the soul," two of which are described in "The Holy Epistle." Among his clientele were distinguished rabbis, scholars, wealthy merchants, and prominent estate managers. The Besht was initially not known to a wider public, nor does it seem he strived for one. Rather he was an inspirational figure, certainly quite an original one, who played a central role in the foundation myth of Hasidism established by his enterprising colleague-disciples.

All in all the Besht is known through several published letters, the hagiographical *In Praise of the Ba'al Shem Tov*, and some sermons and homilies published after his death by disciples and associates who claimed that these teachings had been learned from their master. In the traditional tales Ba'al Shem is frequently mentioned in contexts of meeting people and speaking to groups, but he is never depicted teaching in a synagogue. That in reality he was not always taken seriously is evident in anecdotes that tell of the Torah scholar Gershon of Kitov's initial contempt for his "ignorant" brother-in-law—Gershon was the rabbi for whom "The Holy Epistle" was originally intended.

In "The Holy Epistle" there is evidence for one of the keys to the Besht's stature. As Gershon Hundert puts it, "He took on himself, and he did this without holding office and without communal sanction, the task of defending the whole people of Israel." This sense of mission was among his particular contributions to the role of the *ba'al shem*.

Explanation and Analysis of the Document

Since "The Holy Epistle" never reached its addressee and remained in the Besht's immediate circle, where copies of it were made, there is no definitive version of the letter. Three different versions of it exist today. The epistle was first published in 1781 in Koretz as an appendix to *Ben Porat Yosef*, a homiletic work by Yaakov Yosef of Polonne, a disciple of Ba'al Shem Tov. In 1923 a different manuscript version of the letter was discovered that was later published by Mordecai Bauminger in *Sinai* magazine in 1971. The last discovered version, published by Yehoshua Mondshine in 1980 based on a manuscript apparently predating the *Ben Porat Yosef* version, is the least complete. Scholars feel that Bauminger's text is the closest to the version that Ba'al

Shem Tov wrote in 1752, but there is some debate over whether the other versions have material from the lost letter referred to in paragraph 2 that the present letter was supposed to re-create or whether they simply have implants from later Hasidic teaching. The Bauminger version of "The Holy Epistle" is presented here.

♦ **Paragraphs 1 and 2**

After the heading, the first paragraphs of the letter contain a relatively conventional but heartfelt greeting from the Besht to his brother-in-law. The first half of the second paragraph extends the greeting with an account of the meanderings of their earlier correspondence and of how unhappy he was that he had not received a number of letters from Palestine. The plague in the intervening lands that is mentioned as the external deterrent for the carriers of the correspondence is given a deeper moral cause, also serving as an introduction for the main theme of the letter. Moreover, an earlier letter that had been sent to his brother-in-law was evidently lost, and now he intends to briefly recapitulate the "news and the secrets" that it contained.

♦ **Paragraph 3**

The most important part of the Holy Epistle is contained in paragraphs 3 and 4. Each of these paragraphs recounts one of Ba'al Shem Tov's ascents of the soul. An ascent of the soul is a kabbalistic mystical technique. In the related journeys described in these paragraphs, Ba'al Shem Tov's soul in each instance ascended to Paradise. Both ascents take place on Rosh Hashanah, the Jewish New Year, which in Jewish tradition is among the most numinous times of the year, when communication with the divine is deemed more probable. Particularly noteworthy is the deep connection between this mystical experience and the concrete sufferings of Jews in the towns of Zaslaw, Szepetówka, and Dunajów, where there were accusations of ritual murder that led to trials, apostasies, and even executions. Effectively, the Besht attempts a divine intervention on behalf of his coreligionists suffering at the hands of gentiles.

The first vision is described in some detail. The "evil side" is Satan, who accuses Jews and delights in their persecution but nevertheless has access to the heavenly court. The Besht enlists the aid of his celestial "teacher and rabbi," the biblical prophet Ahijah the Shilonite, in this spiritually dangerous encounter. In the palace of the Messiah, Ba'al Shem sees the *Tannaim*, the rabbis whose statements make up the Mishna, a book of the Talmud, as well as the "seven shepherds"—that is, Adam, Seth, Methusaleh, Abraham, Jacob, Moses, and David. He boasts that he was allowed to survive the vision because these righteous enjoyed his "unifications" performed below on the basis of their teaching. He is referring to kabbalistic theurgic acts possessing the mystical effect of unifying the divine.

A particularly telling moment in the vision is Ba'al Shem's confrontation with the Messiah. He asks the stan-

dard question: "When will the master come?" While the question, along with the Messiah's reported response, expresses a deep messianic desire, the tone is far from the antinomian messianism of the Sabbateans, who were willing to provoke the Messiah to come. The importance of this passage has led to a number of emendations in other versions of "The Holy Epistle," which is in accordance with the Hasidic practice of embellishing texts while copying them. All versions, it must be mentioned, are true to the spirit of the version presented here, in that eschatological urgency is absent from them. However, the Messiah's reply is particularly revealing: "Once your Torah will have spread throughout the world." This implies that the Besht will have a central role in the messianic plan of which he himself was conscious.

Regarding the historic events referred to in the paragraph, scholars have noted that the charges of ritual murder against Jews in those towns actually occurred after the date of Rosh Hashanah given in the Epistle, and thus the related vision may contain elements of after-the-fact updating. At any rate, Ba'al Shem's mystical intervention, aided by his celestial teacher and the Messiah, did not succeed in averting the decree. His main success was gaining an explanation for the events via a direct interview with Satan. As Moshe Rosman puts it: "By ascending to Paradise, the Besht was able to ascertain that the suffering was both divine retribution and divine instruction."

♦ Paragraph 4

The Besht describes another ascent that also occurred on Rosh Hashanah, three years later. This heavenly journey is likewise motivated to plead for his fellow Jews. It is noteworthy that this is a departure from the tradition that a soul ascent would be used by a *ba'al shem* primarily to gain divine knowledge. What is also significant in this respect—much like in the earlier ascent—is the direct use of his charismatic presence in celestial courts rather than the use of an objective divine name to carry out his miraculous mission. This new approach is all the more striking in that the literal translation of *Ba'al Shem Tov*, "master of the good [holy] name," connects the founder of Hasidism with the older tradition of use of divine names that he, in fact, supersedes. Both new features, concern for coreligionists and reliance on charisma over holy words, would become characteristic of *tzaddikim*.

Not that this intercession was particularly effective. The Besht describes a great plague that was allegedly a lesser harm than the wholesale destruction that was pending on the Jewish communities of the region, a possible reference to the insecurity of the times evoked by armed uprisings of Ukrainian peasants (Haidamaks), causing Jews to flee. In this paragraph Ba'al Shem continues his mystical intercession with the more traditional kabbalistic technique for preventing death: reciting the *Ketoret* passage with his group, that is, a specific Talmudic passage deemed effective for the purpose. This leads to the celestial rebuke that the action that had been agreed upon in Paradise was thus challenged,

and to the Besht's giving up on this approach, except in response to the worries of his immediate congregation during Hoshanah Rabbah, which is the last day of the Sukkoth holiday, considered to be a time for repentance.

The passage also confirms that Ba'al Shem was the head of a *havurah*, a group of mystics, who assisted him in reciting the *Ketoret* prayer. The fact that the celestial powers insisted that he cease this action for them to carry out their divine plan confirms his importance. However, in the entire spiritual campaign he is less effective as a shaman than as someone who provides a larger perspective to temporal suffering. For his followers, concludes Rosman, "His ability to explain the theodicity of events was proof enough of his communication with God."

♦ Paragraph 5

After having related the "news and secrets," the Besht reaffirms his position as teacher in relation to his brother-in-law. He reminds him of the ethical teachings that he had imparted earlier. A boastful tone is evident when he refers to the "several kinds of sweetness" that it contains. This attitude implies the relationship between the correspondents, indicating who was the instructor and who was the recipient of knowledge. The only teaching directly alluded to in this paragraph concerns the importance of Eretz Yisrael, the "Land of Israel," in Judaism, which is implied in the fact that Ba'al Shem expresses his desire of joining his correspondent there in the future. It is, however, uncertain how seriously he meant this. In a surviving letter that Gershon sent from Palestine and that did not reach the Besht, he makes no mention of the possibility that his brother-in-law will join him. There is a tradition that Ba'al Shem had unsuccessfully attempted such a journey earlier, but it is unsubstantiated.

♦ Paragraphs 6 and 7

Here the Besht presents himself as the head of an extended family, and he explains that the weight of those responsibilities in the face of difficulties closer to home have made the promised support for his brother-in-law in the Holy Land problematic. He is also evidently proud of the progress his grandson has made in the study of the Torah, which he would love to have confirmed by a relative who was renowned in the field. Curiously, considering the circumstances of their actual poverty, Ba'al Shem confirms his teaching against asceticism. Were they to become affluent, he asserts, they could end their enforced asceticism, and they would eat meat if they wished.

♦ Paragraph 8

Toward the end of the missive, in the paragraph preceding the letter's formulaic concluding wishes, Ba'al Shem comes to the probable point of the letter, which was to ask for a recommendation for his disciple, Yaakov Yosef of Polonne (referred to in the letter as Joseph Katz), who at the time of writing intended to settle in the Holy Land and who was to bear the epistle, but who in fact did not.

"I asked the Messiah, 'When will the master come?' And he answered me, 'Once your Torah will have spread throughout the world.'"

(Section 1)

"I performed an ascent of the soul... and I saw a great accusation until the evil side almost received permission to completely destroy regions and communities.... I prayed: 'Let us fall into the hand of God and not fall into the hands of man.' And they gave me permission that instead of this there would be great epidemics and unprecedented plague in all of the regions of Poland and our neighboring areas."

(Section 1)

Audience

As mentioned, the intended addressee of the letter never received it, and the epistle remained in the hands of Ba'al Shem's followers, who passed it on among themselves, occasionally copying it. The copies were partially embellished in the process, so currently historians have difficulty in establishing its exact original content. The bearer of the letter, the Besht's disciple Yaakov Yosef of Polonne, finally published it, and that is the version that had been known to a broader public until the twentieth century, when additional manuscripts were discovered and eventually published. The letter still has a broad audience among contemporary Hasidim, as is witnessed by the Baal Shem Tov Foundation's posting a version on the Internet.

Impact

Hasidism is a movement without a single sacred text. Nonetheless, "The Holy Epistle" does hold a special place among the actual writings of Ba'al Shem Tov. Partly on account of its author's wish not to have his writings published, the letter was not published until well after his death. The fact that the publishers titled the missive "The Holy Epistle" acknowledges the importance attached to it. Nevertheless, equally or more important among texts associated with Ba'al Shem were his words as transcribed by his circle of followers. Thus, when the extremely popular hagiographical *In Praise of Ba'al Shem Tov* was published some three decades after the letter, the position of "The Holy Epistle" became somewhat diminished.

To some extent "The Holy Epistle" gained in meaning when the authenticity of Ba'al Shem's writings became an issue of debate. As of 2010, numerous versions of the letter were available on the Internet, addressing different groups. As the present analysis demonstrates, some kabbalistic practices are evident in it, so one version is addressed to current admirers of the kabbalah. Another version is posted by a Hasidic group, with a comment encouraging Hasidim to return to mystical practices they have largely abandoned over the course of time. Thus the editor of the online version of "The Holy Epistle" provided by the Baal Shem Tov Foundation complains: "Most Chassidim today may be religiously devout, but not much more concerned with mysticism than their non-Chassidic peers." Evidently for the newest generation of Hasidim, "The Holy Epistle" is a potent reminder of a vital part of their tradition apparently neglected at present.

Further Reading

■ Books

Ben-Amos, Dan, and Jerome R. Mintz, eds. *In Praise of the Ba'al Shem Tov: The Earliest Collection of Legends about the Founder of Hasidism.* Northvale, N.J.: Jason Aronson, 1993.

Buber, Martin. *The Legend of the Ba'al-Shem.* Princeton, N.J.: Princeton University Press, 1995.

Dynner, Glenn. *Men of Silk: The Hassidic Conquest of Polish Jewish Society.* Oxford, U.K.: Oxford University Press, 2006.

Etkes, Immanuel. *The Besht: Magician, Mystic, and Leader*, trans. Saadya Sternberg. Waltham, Mass.: Brandeis University Press, 2004.

Hundert, Gershon David. *Jews in Poland-Lithuania in the Eighteenth Century: A Genealogy of Modernity*. Berkeley: University of California Press, 2004.

Lamm, Norman. *The Religious Thought of Hasidism: Text and Commentary*. New York: Michael Scharf Publication Trust of Yeshiva University, 1999.

Rosman, Moshe. *Founder of Hasidism: A Quest for the Historical Ba'al Shem Tov*. Berkeley: University of California Press, 1996.

♦ **Web Site**

The Baal Shem Tov Foundation Web site. http://www.baalshemtov.com/index.php

—Commentary by Christopher Garbowski

Questions for Further Study

1. What is Hasidism, and why was it an important movement in Judaism in the eighteenth century and beyond?

2. Compare this document with the Sefer Yetzirah and the discussion of kabbalah that surrounds it. What, if anything, do the two movements have in common? How do they differ?

3. Respond to the following statement: Hasidism was a form of pantheism and therefore in conflict with Orthodox Judaism in its conception of the nature of God.

4. What is an "ascent of the soul"? What was its link with Jewish mysticism and the kabbalah movement?

5. "The Holy Epistle" is a good example of a key document from the past that exists in different forms such that it is difficult, if not impossible, for scholars to determine precisely what the content of the original letter was. Do you think this diminishes the authenticity or value of the letter? What does this difficulty tell you about the process of transmission of documents in the years after they were written?

"The Holy Epistle": Document Text

1752 CE

—Ba'al Shem Tov

Written [during the week of] the Torah Portion Teruman, 5512, here in the community of Raszkow.

To my honored, beloved brother-in-law, my favorite, my friend in heart and soul, the great sage, the rabbinic paragon, the famous Hasid in Torah and the fear of heaven, his honor, our teacher, Abraham Gershon, may his light shine, and peace to all who belong to him; and to his modest wife, Mrs. Bluma with all of her descendants. May all of them be granted the blessing of life. Amen. Selah.

I received the imprimatur of his holy hand at the Luków fair in 5510, which you sent with the emissary who traveled from Jerusalem, and it was written with great brevity and it said there that you had already written at length to each and every one via a man who traveled to Egypt. However, those letters written at length did not reach me and I was much pained by this that I did not see for form of your holy hand which you wrote in detail. This must have been because of the deterioration of the nations, due to our many sins, for the plague has spread to all the countries and even close to our region, having reached the community of Mohylów, and the areas of Walachia and Kedar. It also stated there that the news and the secrets which I wrote to you via the scribe, the Rabbi, the Preacher of Polonne, did not reach you and I was also greatly pained by this; for you would have assuredly derived great satisfaction if these had reached you. At the present time I have, however, forgotten some of the things in them, but details which I do remember I will write very briefly.

For on Roth Hashana 5507 I performed an adjuration for the ascent of the soul, as you know, and I saw wondrous things in a vision, for the evil side ascended to accuse with great, unparalleled joy and performed his acts—persecutions entailing forced conversion—on several souls so they would meet violent deaths. I was horrified and I literally put my life in jeopardy and asked my teacher and rabbi to go with me because it is very dangerous to go and ascend to the upper worlds. For from the day I attained my position I did not ascend such lofty ascents. I went up step by step until I entered the palace of the Messiah where the Messiah learns Torah with all of the Tannaim and the righteous and also with the seven shepherds. And there I saw exceedingly great joy and I don't know the reason for this joy. I thought this joy was—God forbid—over my departure from this world but they informed me afterward that I was not leaving yet because in the upper spheres they derive pleasure when I perform unifications down below by the means of their holy teachings. The reason for the joy I still do not know. And I asked the Messiah, "When will the master come?" And he answered me, 'Once your Torah will have spread throughout the world,' etc." And I prayed there over why God did thus; wherefore that great wrath that some souls of Israel were given over to the evil side for killing and of them several souls converted and afterward were killed and they gave me permission to ask the evil side himself directly, and I asked the evil side why he did this and how he viewed their converting and then being killed. And he replied to me that his intention was for the sake of heaven. For if they were to remain alive after apostasizing then when there would be some other persecution or libel they would not sanctify the name of heaven; rather everyone would just convert to save themselves. Therefore he acted; those who converted were later killed so that no son of Israel would convert and they would sanctify the name of heaven. Thus it was afterwards, due to our many sins, in the community of Zaslaw there was libel against several souls and two of them converted and later they killed them. The rest sanctified the name of heaven in great holiness and died violent deaths and then there were libels in the communities of Szepetówka and Dunajów and they didn't convert after they saw what happened in Zaslaw, but all of them gave their souls for the sanctification of God's Name and sanctified the name of heaven and withstood the test. And by virtue of this act our Messiah will come and take our vengeance. And God will conciliate his land and his people.

And on Rosh Ha-Shanah 5510 I performed an ascent of the soul, as is known, and I saw a great accusation until the evil side almost received permission to completely destroy regions and communities. I put my life in jeopardy and I prayed: "Let us fall into the hand of God and not fall into the hands of man." And they gave me permission that instead of this there would be great epidemics and unprecedented plague in all of the regions of Poland and our neighboring areas, and so it was that the epidemic spread so much that it could not be measured, and likewise the plague in the other areas. And I arranged with my group to say [*Ketoret*] upon arising to cancel this decree. And they revealed to me in a night vision: "Did not you yourself choose 'Let us fall into God's hand', etc? Why do you want to cancel? Is it not accepted that 'the prosecutor cannot [become the defender]'?" From then on I did not say *Ketoret* and I did not pray about this except by means of several adjurations due to great fear on Hoshannah Rabbah when I went to the synagogue with the entire congregation. And I said *Ketoret* one time so that the plague would not spread to our environs. With the help of God we succeeded.

I would like to go on and meander at length but because of the tears when I recall your departure from me, I cannot speak. But my request of you is to review my words of moral instruction which I said to you several times. They should always be in your consciousness; contemplate them and analyze them. You will certainly find in each and every statement several kinds of sweetness for what I said to you is not a vain thing because God knows that I do not despair of traveling to Eretz Yisrael, if it be God's will, to be together with you, but the times do not allow it.

Also don't be displeased that because of the treacherousness of the times I have not sent you money; there having been in our country plague and famine. Also several dependents from our family rely on me to support and feed them, in addition to the rest of the poor of Israel; and the money has run out. There is nothing left except our bodies. But, if God wills it, "when the Lord enlarges [your territory, as he has promised you]" then, certainly, "[you will say, 'I will eat meat' because you will have the urge to eat meat.]"

And also my grandson, the important young man, the honorable Ephraim, a great prodigy at the highest level of learning; certainly, if the time is propitious, it would be fitting for you to come here yourself and see and be seen with him face to face and to rejoice in our joy as you promised me.

Also my most urgent petition concerning my beloved, the famous rabbi, the Hasid, our teacher Joseph Katz, a servant of the Lord, to bring him close with two hands and with all sorts of favor because his deeds are pleasing before God and all of his deeds are for the sake of heaven. Also please write on his behalf to the wealthy people there with you to keep him well supplied and sustain him so that he "sits with support"; for you will surely derive satisfaction as he will be there together with you.

These are the words of your loving brother-in-law who expects to see you face to face and prays for long life for you, your wife and your progeny; and always seeking your welfare, all the days—including the nights—for good long life. Amen. Selah.

Israel Besht from Miedzybóz

Glossary

Eretz Yisrael:	Hebrew for "Land of Israel"
Ketoret:	incense; figuratively, bonding or connecting
Roth Hashana:	also Rosh Ha-Shanah or Rosh Hashana, the Jewish New Year
Selah:	Hebrew for "stop and listen" or "let those with ears hear"
Tannaim:	Rabbinic sages
Teruman:	also Terumah, Hebrew for "gift" or "offering"—the nineteenth weekly Torah portion in the annual Jewish cycle of Torah reading; it constitutes Exodus 25:1–27:19.

Emanuel Swedenborg.

INVITATION TO THE NEW CHURCH: DOCUMENT ANALYSIS

ca 1760–1772 CE

*"All theologians, when preaching,
know nothing of the falsities of their religion."*

Overview

Emanuel Swedenborg 's *Invitation to the New Church* was not a published work but a draft in Latin that was begun sometime in the 1760s but left unfinished at his death and found among his papers. The concept of the "New Church" was introduced and explored at length in Swedenborg's long book *The True Christian Religion: Containing the Universal Theology of the New Church*, published in Latin in Amsterdam in 1771. The *Invitation* is a summary of some of the salient teachings set out in the work he saw published. The *Invitation* contains some of the author's most important conclusions, namely, that God is one and is recognized in a human form as the Lord Jesus Christ, that the former church must be "consummated" before the new church can be formed, and that reliance on miracles has destroyed the Christian church. The new church will be founded not on miracles but through revelation of the spiritual sense of the Word. Controversially, Swedenborg believed that his body and spirit had been permitted by God to enter the world beyond death so as to know what heaven and hell are and that he was inspired by God to reveal the spiritual sense of the Word, that is, the scriptures. In the "New Church," which accords with the New Jerusalem described by Saint John the Divine in chapters 21 and 22 of the book of Revelation, men and women would no longer be called Evangelicals or Reformed, still less Lutherans or Calvinists, but would simply be Christians.

Context

It was in *The True Christian Religion* that Emanuel Swedenborg introduced the concept of the "New Church," that is, the New Jerusalem foretold at the end of the biblical book of Revelation. Published in Amsterdam in 1771, *The True*

Christian Religion provides a summing-up of the author's theological teachings and contains what he believed to be answers to his critics within the Lutheran Church of Sweden. Swedenborg, who by this time had written numerous books on natural science, anatomy, and theology, was never an ordained clergyman, but he believed that he had received a divine commission to interpret the scriptures and announce a new Christian age. He was accused of propagating new doctrines that his opponents called "Swedenborgianism" but which he himself thought were "genuine Christianity." Like other reformers, he sought to strip away the coats of varnish that encrusted the doctrines of the Christian churches of his day and restore their pristine purity.

In a letter dated August 24, 1771, to Ludwig IX, the landgrave (equivalent to a count) of Hesse-Darmstadt, Swedenborg wrote that he was on the point of leaving Amsterdam for England, where, with the Lord's favor, as he put it, he intended to publish four small works. These planned works were *Invitation to the New Church*, "Concerning the Consummation of the Age," "On the Human Mind," and "Egyptian Hieroglyphics." The latter two works were apparently never undertaken, but drafts of the first two have survived. (The second was published in 1888 as *The Consummation of the Age: The Lord's Second Coming and the New Church*.) *Invitation to the New Church* is addressed to the "whole Christian world." Swedenborg believed that he had witnessed the Second Advent, or Second Coming of the Lord, which he held to be not a physical return by Jesus Christ to this world, as some Christians still believe and expect, but an opening of the inner, or spiritual, meaning of the Word of God. Swedenborg believed that he was serving as an instrument of God in helping to reveal this inner sense by means of the ancient "science of correspondences," whereby words in scripture stand for higher spiritual realities.

In fact, despite the spiritual orientation of *Invitation to the New Church*, Swedenborg wrote as a man of science— not as a narrow specialist in the modern sense but as a man of the Enlightenment curious about all aspects of natural science. While he was not a trained theologian, he was a considerable biblical scholar within the limitations of his age. He was also a patriotic Swede who took great pride in his country's achievements and its status as an important power in northern Europe. He had traveled widely in Catholic European countries, particularly France and Italy, and his Protestant prejudices are sometimes obvious in the text, above all in his dismissal of miracles.

Swedenborg died in March 1772, just half a year after departing for London, which meant that he never saw the publication of his four planned works. By that time, he had made no attempt to attract followers, nor had he sought to establish or encourage the establishment of any separate denomination. It appears that Swedenborg rather envisaged a new spirit that would penetrate the existing Christian churches, perhaps very gradually. He himself, however much his teachings diverged from eighteenth-century Lutheran orthodoxy, remained a member of the Church of Sweden. He received Communion from a Lutheran priest shortly before he died, and his remains were buried in the Swedish church in the East End of London. At the beginning of the twentieth century, they were removed prior to the demolition of that church and, with great ceremony, conveyed to Sweden by warship and interred in the cathedral of Uppsala.

About the Author

Emanuel Swedberg was born in Stockholm on January 29, 1688, the son of Jesper Swedberg, a Lutheran clergyman who later became a bishop. Educated at Uppsala University, the young Swedberg manifested initial interest in science and engineering, drawing up plans for a submarine and a glider aircraft; a model based on his design for the latter is in the Smithsonian Institution in Washington, D.C. In 1716 he was appointed to a position on the Royal Swedish Board of Mines, later becoming assessor, and he held this position until his resignation in 1747. He would later write a treatise on iron and other metals. In 1719 the family was ennobled, taking the name "Swedenborg," and Emanuel took his place in the Riddarhuset, or "House of Nobility" (then equivalent to Great Britain's House of Lords). He was a regular attendee throughout his life, making contributions on financial and economic matters and on foreign affairs until about a year before his death.

Swedenborg's theoretical book on the physical sciences, *The Principia; or, The First Principles of Natural Things*, was published in Latin, the language in which he wrote all his treatises, in 1734. In this he anticipated the nebular hypothesis of the origin of the solar system usually attributed to the German philosopher Immanuel Kant and the French astronomer Pierre-Simon de Laplace. Turning his attention to the human body, Swedenborg studied anatomy

Time Line	
January 29, 1688	■ Emanuel Swedenborg is born in Stockholm, Sweden.
1734	■ Swedenborg launches his career as a scientist with the publication of a theoretical book on the physical sciences, *The Principia; or, The First Principles of Natural Things*.
1740	■ Swedenborg becomes a member of the Royal Swedish Academy of Sciences.
1758	■ Signaling his shift in interest toward the spiritual and metaphysical, Swedenborg publishes *Heaven and Hell*, describing those realms as self-directed states of postmortem consciousness.
ca. 1760–1772	■ Swedenborg writes *Invitation to the New Church*.
1771	■ Swedenborg introduces the concept of the "New Church" with the publication of *The True Christian Religion: Containing the Universal Theology of the New Church*.
March 29, 1772	■ Swedenborg dies in London.
1780s	■ Some readers of Swedenborg's texts in England and the United States form new Protestant Christian denominations with the title "New Church" or "New Jerusalem Church."
1789	■ The first conference of the New Church in held in London.
September 1893	■ Charles Bonney, a Swedenborgian, organizes the first Parliament of the World's Religions in Chicago.

and physiology in an attempt to discover the seat of the soul. He published two books on the human body, *The Economy of the Animal Kingdom* (1740–1741) and *The Animal Kingdom* (1744–1745), and wrote focused manuscripts titled *The Cerebrum* (1738–1740), *The Brain* (1742–1744), *The Generative Organs* (1743), and *The Five Senses* (1744), which were not published until many years after his death. He was made a member of the Royal Swedish Academy of Sciences in 1740.

In the mid-1740s Swedenborg's life took a new direction. After a transitional period characterized by his remarkably frank *Dream Diary*, a private journal written in Swedish and not meant for publication, he abandoned his study of science and embarked on an inward journey. He came to believe that God had called him to interpret the Bible, God's Word, and reveal its inner or spiritual sense with the aid of the ancient science of correspondences, by which the literal sense of the Bible is shown to have a deeper meaning. He also believed that his spiritual eyes had been opened to the world beyond death. In his best-known work, *Heaven and Hell* (1758), he gives a particularly vivid and detailed account of heaven and hell as self-chosen states of postmortem consciousness achievable by men and women of all religions, because God as divine love and divine wisdom condemns no one.

All of Swedenborg's contentions ran counter to the accepted Christianity of the day, Protestant or Catholic. In fact, Swedenborg published detailed exegeses of only the books of Genesis and Exodus, in *Arcana Coelestia* (1749–1756), and the book of Revelation, in *Apocalypse Revealed* (1766) and *Apocalypse Explained* (published posthumously in 1866). His other major theological works include *Divine Love and Wisdom* (1763), *Divine Providence* (1764), *Conjugial Love* (1768), and *The True Christian Religion* (1771). Although he published his religious works anonymously—*Conjugial Love* was the first theological work with his name on the title page—he was rapidly identified as the author of these works. He published in either London or Amsterdam, there not being sufficient religious freedom in Sweden to allow publication in Stockholm. He wrote in Latin, a language that would have had greater currency throughout Europe than his native Swedish, although new books written in Latin were becoming rare by the middle of the eighteenth century. Swedenborg made his last visit to London in the autumn of 1771 and died there on March 29, 1772.

Explanation and Analysis of the Document

Invitation to the New Church was a draft, apparently left uncompleted at Swedenborg's death. As such, it should be treated with caution, and it also makes for somewhat difficult reading. Although Swedenborg does at times use colorful similes—one of the most attractive features of his writing—his thoughts are generally condensed here. One supposes that, had he lived, Swedenborg would have fleshed out the text by developing and illustrating

his arguments further and would have thus produced a more polished and readable volume. Although the whole document has been arranged into fifty-nine consecutive numbered paragraphs (probably done by an amanuensis), in content, it consists of two distinct papers. The first runs from paragraphs 1 to 29 and the second from paragraphs 30 to 59. The numbered paragraphs are preceded by a syllabus, or table of contents, dividing up the text thematically with Roman numerals.

◆ Paragraphs 1–29

The document begins in paragraph 1 with a restatement of the doctrine of the Incarnation, "that in Christ Jesus Man is God, and God Man," but this argument is not developed further here. In paragraph 2 Swedenborg describes the process of the human being's regeneration, or spiritual rebirth, through the instilling of the light and heat of heaven into the higher or spiritual mind. This is how the soul is formed. According to the doctrine of correspondences—which holds that everything in the natural world and every word in the scriptures "corresponds" to a higher spiritual reality—in a spiritual sense, light represents truth, and heat represents love. But there is an even higher state of light and heat (wisdom and love) called the "celestial." Swedenborg illustrates the process of spiritual regeneration in an ecological way by comparing it to the grafting of trees (paragraph 4). He then returns to the theme of the Incarnation (paragraph 5), stating that it was necessary for the regeneration or "saving" of human beings. The following paragraph introduces the attack on miracles, a theme that is developed later. Miracles are said to deprive humans of free will, which is necessary for regeneration. They are like veils or bars that prevent people from receiving spiritual truth.

Paragraphs 7–12 contain an attack on what Swedenborg considered a false orthodoxy in the Lutheran Church of his day, the doctrine of "faith alone." For Swedenborg this was not enough. Humans must repent of their sins, follow the Ten Commandments, and do works of charity for their neighbors with sincerity if they are to live Christian lives. The core of Swedenborg's critique of Lutheranism is contained in paragraph 9, where he states that "a man who has altogether confirmed himself in the faith and doctrine of the present church, makes no account of repentance, of the law of the Decalogue, and of works and charity." Put simply, he rejects the Protestant Reformation notion that salvation can be attained solely through faith.

Paragraph 13 is of particular interest. Swedenborg criticizes Cartesian dualism, which posits the separation of soul and body. The soul is the "inmost" part of the person and is thus the person "from the head to the foot." The soul is to be found in the body, and it is this that gives life. In his books *The Economy of the Animal Kingdom* and *The Animal Kingdom*, Swedenborg had attempted to discover the physical seat of the soul. He did not locate it, but his anatomical studies left him convinced that the soul and body are united. Thus, he is opposed not only to Cartesian dualism but also to modern Western thought that denies there is such a thing as a soul. He had also explored the theme in his short book *Interaction of the Soul and Body*, published in 1769. Swedenborg's religious teachings feature no asceticism, or denial of the flesh and the body's needs. In his work on marriage and the relations of the sexes, *Conjugial Love*, he emphasizes the pleasures of physical love and its spiritual significance.

In paragraph 14 Swedenborg elaborates on his metaphysical scheme, stating once again the three existential degrees of "celestial," "spiritual," and "natural." The soul itself is in the highest, or celestial, degree of existence; the spirit or the mind is in the second, or spiritual, degree; and the body is in the lowest, or natural, degree. The celestial degree is associated with love, while the spiritual degree is associated with wisdom or, more strictly, wisdom derived from love. Love always comes first in the hierarchy, while wisdom is its handmaiden, as Swedenborg makes clear in greater detail in the works *Divine Love and Wisdom* and *Divine Providence*. But it is the body, the "ultimate" or lowest tier, that contains both of these higher degrees. Love and wisdom cannot subsist except in a human person who is able to give effect to them in acts of practical charity and usefulness to others.

In paragraphs 15–20 Swedenborg continues his critique of orthodoxy and what he calls its "falsities." He cites what he seems to characterize as the platitudes of preachers: "They preach that God is one; that the Saviour ought to be adored; that man, therefore, ought to believe in the Word and in preachings; that he ought to exercise charity, and practise repentance, so as to desist from evils." He goes on, though, to suggest that "they remember nothing concerning three Gods, concerning their mystical faith, concerning impotence in spiritual matters, and concerning all the remaining dogmas." That is, the focus is on what they have learned through their theological education and not on the essence of faith. Religious orthodoxy, then, preaches doctrines that effectively overthrow the "very Word" of God and thus true faith itself. Swedenborg then remarks on the nature of evil, arguing that the evil man reverses, or inverts, the inward and the outward, "so that the world is above heaven, that is, heaven below the world."

Swedenborg sums up the whole of the (Lutheran) theology of his day, as he understood it, in paragraphs 21–23, where he describes it as a doctrine of divine omnipotence. God can save whom he wills, can raise the dead from the graves in their original physical bodies, and can destroy the world and create it anew. He shows elsewhere that this picture of a wholly arbitrary God (which may be a caricature of the views of his contemporaries) is false, and he contrasts it with a doctrine of a God who is divine love and wisdom, who wills ill to no one, and who is always true to his own nature. He goes on to explain in paragraph 24 that the Protestant Reformation came about, beginning in 1517, to restore to the Christian world the Word, that is, the Bible, which had been entombed by the Catholic Church. With historic specificity he refers to the rise of the Protestant powers—Sweden, Denmark, Holland, and England. And in an oblique reference to the Thirty Years' War in the Holy Roman Empire (mostly within modern Germany) between Catholic and Protestant factions, he mentions the Swedish King Gustavus II Adolphus, the "Lion of the North," whose armies (financed by the France of Louis XIII and Cardinal Richelieu, Armand-Jean du Plessis) intervened with great effect on the Protestant side in the struggle until the Swedish king was killed while gaining victory at the Battle of Lützen (1632).

The final paragraphs of this section represent a somewhat disjointed summing up of Swedenborg's arguments thus far. He calls for a "healing" of the church through his vision of the New Church. He characterizes the human being as an "organ of life… kept in the middle between heaven and hell, and thus in equilibrium or free will," indicating his rejection of the concept of predestination. He goes on to contend that "the church is the Body of Christ," in that the Lord, through the church, is present in people, just as the soul is present in the body.

♦ **Paragraphs 30–59**
The second part of the document begins with an explanation of the doctrine of the Second Coming of the Lord, starting with the citation of Matthew 25: 31–32. In paragraphs 30–33, Swedenborg cites the Apostles' Creed, the Nicene and Athanasian creeds, and very many passages from scripture, including the Epistles—which he rarely quoted in his works prior to *The True Christian Religion*—in order to demonstrate that the Second Coming has long been foretold. In a remarkable passage (paragraph 34), Swedenborg explains that the old church must be destroyed before the New Church can be established, just as winter must come before spring, night must come before day, and the pain of labor must precede the comfort and joy felt by the new mother. It is said that the Christian churches after the time of the apostles fell into many heresies because people failed to approach the Lord immediately and acknowledge him as the God of heaven. Beginning with paragraph 34, Swedenborg insists that God can be approached by humans because he is manifested as the Lord Jesus Christ, a fully human being. Swedenborg was a Trinitarian (believing in a godhead of three), not a Unitarian (believing in a godhead of only one), but the Trinity for him was not a Trinity of separate persons, or centers of consciousness. Rather, Father, Son and Spirit are the three essentials of the one true God, as he explains at great length in *The True Christian Religion*, but it is through Jesus, the "Divine Human," that God is manifested to humankind. The Lord's truth is apparent in his Word, if it is read aright, that is, in its spiritual or inner sense.

Much of the text of the second part of the document is devoted to an attack on miracles, a theme to which the author returns on several occasions. He mentions (in paragraphs 39 and 46) the Italian tomb of Saint Anthony of Padua, with its plates of gold and silver; the supposed tombs of the wise men in Germany's Cologne Cathedral; and relics in the Loreto, in Prague (now in the Czech Republic).

Swedenborg had visited these cities as a tourist. As a Protestant he would have been unfamiliar with and hostile to the Catholic veneration of saints. Saint Anthony of Padua (who was actually from Lisbon, Portugal, though he died in Padua in 1231) remains a popular Catholic saint and was made a "Doctor of the Church" by Pope Pius XII in 1946. Swedenborg displays his prejudices as a Protestant and as a rational man of the Enlightenment in his attitude toward miracles. They are not done at the present time, he writes, because they seduce people and make them natural, not spiritual. They close the interiors of the mind. In paragraph 55, Swedenborg goes so far as to state not only that miracles seduce and fail to teach but also indeed that "their sole purpose is that they may be invoked as deities." His tone becomes somewhat shrill here. It contrasts strongly with that of his work *A Brief Exposition of the Doctrine of the New Church* (1769), in which he praises the Roman Catholic Church for its insistence on the value of works of charity, as opposed to the Protestant doctrine of faith alone; it also contrasts strongly with that of a famous passage in *Arcana Coelestia*, where he writes that if Protestants and Catholics made love for the Lord and charity to the neighbor the chief aspects of faith, doctrinal differences would be mere shades of opinion concerning the mysteries of faith that true Christians would leave to individual conscience, and the Lord's Kingdom on earth would come.

A characteristic of Swedenborg's thought is that he sees everything as threefold. In everything there is an inmost, a middle, and an outmost aspect. The middle and the outmost are derived from the inmost. For Swedenborg the material world is the effect, mediated through a spiritual efficient cause (*causa efficiens*) from an ultimate cause (*causa causans*)—God himself. Modern scientific thinking starts with the material world and seeks the causes of everything within that world; it sees no need to seek causes outside the material world. This way of thinking was alien to Swedenborg. He was a rational scientist who imbibed the latest scientific discoveries of his age, but fundamental to his thought is his conviction that everything in this world has a spiritual cause. Although he lived on the threshold of the modern world, this aspect of his thinking makes it difficult for the contemporary mind to sympathetically grasp what he has to say. He sometimes seems to belong to a remote age, and, although he was a Protestant often unsympathetic to the Catholic Church, he seems to have more in common with a medieval theologian like Thomas Aquinas than with his Enlightenment contemporaries, let alone with modern-day thinkers. This impression is reinforced by his use of Latin at a time when contemporary scientists, philosophers, and theologians alike were using their vernacular languages. The whole of Swedenborg's thinking is permeated with religion.

In the post-Darwinian age of widespread acceptance of evolution, it is common for scientists and philosophers to see the human race as simply part of the animal kingdom, to emphasize humankind's unity with other creatures, and to deny humanity a special place in the order of creation.

Sensitivity to the destruction of species of fauna and flora, which has proceeded at such an alarming pace in the last century at the hands of humans, and the development of the science of genetics, which explicitly links humans biologically with apes and other primates, have contributed to this attitude of deglorifying humanity. For Swedenborg it is the presence of the Holy Spirit, that spark of God within people, that makes the human race unique. Otherwise, humans would be a species of beast and would have no more life than salt, stones, or stocks (meaning stumps or tree trunks). Humans, he says in paragraph 50, are not born with instinct like the pullet (hen), who at one day old "knows the order of its life better than an infant."

Another great difficulty for the modern reader of this text is Swedenborg's belief that he was granted entry into the spiritual world beyond death. The people of the golden age, he asserts (in paragraph 52), were able to converse with the angels, but they remained in "natural light." Elsewhere, Swedenborg describes this age as the "Most Ancient Church," the expression "church" not having its modern meaning of a religious organization but denoting a spiritual age of humankind. Swedenborg believed that the earliest humans were closer to God because they had no sense of themselves as apart from their surroundings. It was only when self-consciousness emerged, represented mythically by the story of the Fall in Genesis 2 (which is analyzed in great detail in *Arcana Coelestia*), a process that was necessary for humankind's intellectual development, that this unity was broken. Modern readers may be familiar with the theory of Julian Jaynes, presented in *The Origin of Consciousness in the Breakdown of the Bicameral Mind* (1976), that ancient people really did hear "the voice of God," but it is more difficult to accept that a man living in the age of Voltaire and David Hume was able to live in both the natural and spiritual worlds, that he was "granted... to see the wonderful things of heaven, to be together with the angels like one of them, and at the same time to draw forth truths in light, and thus to perceive and teach them; consequently to be led by the Lord" (paragraph 52). Swedenborg believed that he had been granted special gifts by God to gain entrance to the spiritual world. He was no advocate of casual intercourse with spirits and warned others against this—although the pioneers of the Spiritualist movement that arose in the mid-nineteenth century in the United States often claimed inspiration from Swedenborg. The organized New Church, however, tended to keep its distance from Spiritualism and gave it little encouragement.

The essence of *Invitation to the New Church* is not Swedenborg's claim to have been admitted to the spiritual world on a daily basis for many years, but the theological teaching that God is one in essence and person, manifested to humans as the Lord Jesus Christ. The spiritual life that leads to heaven consists of approaching God through his Word, read reverently and rightly with the aid of "correspondences" (paragraph 59), which unite the spiritual and natural worlds and thus join heaven and the Lord with human beings, and doing deeds of love and charity for the neighbor.

"There is no true church unless God is One, and unless He is Jehovah God under a human form—and thus that God is man and man God."

(Section 1)

"Miracles close the internal man, and deprive man of all that free will, through which and in which man is regenerated. Free will really belongs to the internal man; and when this is closed up, the man becomes external and natural; and such a man does not see any spiritual truth."

(Section 1)

"A man who has altogether confirmed himself in the faith and doctrine of the present church, makes no account of repentance, of the law of the Decalogue, and of works and charity."

(Section 1)

"All theologians, when preaching, know nothing of the falsities of their religion."

(Section 1)

"That man cannot discover a single Divine truth, except by approaching the Lord immediately, is due to this, that the Lord alone is the Word, and that He is the Light and the Truth itself; and man does not become spiritual except from the Lord alone, but remains natural; and the natural man, in spiritual things, sees everything in inverted order."

(Section 1)

"That the churches after the times of the Apostles fell away into so many heresies, and that at the present day there are none other than false churches, is because they have not approached the Lord, when yet the Lord is the Word, and the very Light which enlighteneth the whole world."

(Section 1)

Audience

Swedenborg never published *Invitation to the New Church*. Legend has it that when he died in his modest lodgings in Clerkenwell, which was then on the edge of London, this unfinished paper lay on his desk beside his pen. It appears that his anticipated audience included the clergy of the Protestant churches and educated laypeople, who were the most likely to be familiar with Latin. Swedenborg had, however, encouraged and helped to finance the translation of some of his works into English. A clue to his greater intended audience lies in the statement in the syllabus that hereafter men and women were to be called not Evangelical or Reformed and still less Lutherans or Calvinists but rather Christians. It seems that Swedenborg did not envisage the establishment of a new Christian denomination but by the expression "New Church" meant a new spirit that would pervade all of the different Christian churches.

Impact

It cannot be said that this unpublished draft paper had any immediate impact. But Swedenborg's published works were before long translated into English, and by the late 1780s some readers of these texts, first in England and then in the United States, formed new Protestant Christian denominations with the title "New Church" or "New Jerusalem Church." These bodies, including a much later church that broke away from the American New Church and eventually became larger than its parent, still exist, albeit with a total membership that is tiny compared with those of the major Christian denominations. Although these bodies are distinct religious organizations that often have sharp disagreements with one another, they are all founded on a belief that Swedenborg's religious writings contain divinely revealed truths. Yet members of these bodies do not view Swedenborg's concept of the "New Church" as synonymous with their own organizations, either individually or collectively.

One of those who attended the first conference of the New Church in London in 1789 was the poet and artist William Blake, and although he did not stay in the organization, the influence of Swedenborg on his work was profound. In the nineteenth century, Swedenborg's works were read widely, and among those literati who mention him are Ralph Waldo Emerson, Honoré de Balzac, Alfred Lord Tennyson, Robert and Elizabeth Barrett Browning, and Henry James. But the most concrete realization of Swedenborg's concept of a "New Church" came in Chicago in 1893 when Charles Bonney, a lawyer, social reformer, and Swedenborgian, organized the first Parliament of the World's Religions, bringing together representatives of most of the world's religions to celebrate what they had in common—"the love and worship of God, and the love and service of man."

Further Reading

■ Books

Benz, Ernst. *Emanuel Swedenborg: Visionary Savant in the Age of Reason*, trans. Nicholas Goodrick-Clarke. West Chester, Penn.: Swedenborg Foundation, 2002.

Bergquist, Lars. *Swedenborg's Secret: A Biography*. London: Swedenborg Society, 2005.

Jaynes, Julian. *The Origin of Consciousness in the Breakdown of the Bicameral Mind*. Boston: Houghton Mifflin, 1976.

Rose, Jonathan S., et al., eds. *Scribe of Heaven: Swedenborg's Life, Work, and Impact*. West Chester, Penn.: Swedenborg Foundation, 2005.

—Commentary by Richard Lines

1. Like Swedenborg, the English Puritans wanted to "purify" the Christian church—to strip away nonessentials and get to the heart of their Christian faith. Read this document side by side with John Bunyan's *Pilgrim's Progress* and explain what views Bunyan and Swedenborg share—and where they part company.

2. Swedenborg began his career as a prominent scientist, publishing numerous works on natural phenomena and the human body. He then abruptly changed course and, beginning in the mid-1740s, turned his attention to theological matters. Why do you think a scientist would do this?

3. Throughout history, various religions and religious leaders have claimed to supplant or supersede earlier religions; see, for example, Muhammad (the founder of Islam) and the Qur'an, the Baha'i faith as represented by the Bab's Persian Bayan and Baha'u'llah's Kitab-i-aqdas, or Robert Athlyi Rogers and the Holy Piby. What similarities, if any, do you see in the impulses that led these religious leaders to proclaim a new religion that supersedes the old?

4. What was the basis of Swedenborg's opposition to miracles? Do you share Swedenborg's views, or do you believe in miracles?

INVITATION TO THE NEW CHURCH: DOCUMENT TEXT

ca 1760–1772 CE

—*Emanuel Swedenborg*

[Syllabus]

[I.] There is no true church unless God is One, and unless He is Jehovah God under a human form—and thus that God is man and man God.

[II.] The doctrinals contained in True Christian Religion agree with the doctrinals of those of the Roman Catholic Church, and with the doctrinals of those of the Protestants, who acknowledge a personal union in Christ, and approach Christ, and who partake of the two elements in the Eucharist.

[III.] Various causes why now, for the first time, and not before, the above truths of the church [have been revealed]. Among these causes is this, that the New Church is not established before the former church is consummated.

[IV.] The Divine Providence in these matters:

From the heresies which arose after the time of the Apostles.

Why the Romish Church arose.

The causes of the separation from that Church, [as from] an unworthy mother.

Why the Greek Church separated from the Romish.

[V.] Various things concerning miracles; that they have destroyed the church (also from the Lord's words in Matt. 24).

[VI.] That all things tended in this direction, that men who were called saints were to be invoked.

[VII.] That this Church is not instituted and established through miracles, but through the revelation of the spiritual sense, and through the introduction of my spirit, and, at the same time, of my body, into the spiritual world, so that I might know there what heaven and hell are, and that in light I might imbibe immediately from the Lord the truths of faith, where man is led to eternal life.

[VIII.] The Advent of the Lord (from the Word and the creeds).

[IX.] Invitation to the New Church, that men should go and meet the Lord (from Rev. 21–22; and also from Chap. 1, etc.).

[X.] Hereafter they are not to be called the Evangelical, the Reformed, and still less Lutherans and Calvinists, but Christians.

[XI.] Several things concerning miracles.

1. That in Christ Jesus Man is God, and God Man, appears evidently from the Lord's words to His Father:

   All Thine are Mine, and all Mine are Thine (John 17:10).

   From the expression "all Mine are Thine," it is evident that the Man is God; and from the expression, "all Thine are Mine," that God is Man.

2. During man's regeneration, the light of heaven is instilled into natural light, and at the same time the heat of heaven; these two constitute, as it were, the new soul, through which man is formed by the Lord. This light and heat are instilled through the higher mind, which is called the spiritual mind. By virtue of this instilling, or insertion, man becomes a new creature, and becomes more enlightened and more intelligent in matters of the church, and consequently in the reading of the Word. This also is the new understanding and the new will. Afterwards the man is led by the Lord through the above light and through the above heat, and from natural becomes spiritual.

3. There is a still higher or more interior light and heat, which is called celestial. This is inserted and instilled into the former spiritual. The angels of the third heaven who are called celestial, are in this light and heat.

4. This insertion may be explained by a comparison; namely, by the grafting and inoculation of trees; where the grafted slips receive [the sap] interiorly in themselves, according to their form, etc.

5. It is to be clearly shown that without the Lord's Advent, no man could have been regenerated, and hence saved; and that this is meant by "the Lamb taking away the sins of the world." This may be evident from the state of the spiritual world before the Lord's Coming; which was such that not a single truth of faith, nor any good of

charity, could pass from the Lord to man. (This is to be illustrated by the influx of truth and good into evil spirits, into the back part of their heads, etc.)

6. Miracles close the internal man, and deprive man of all that free will, through which and in which man is regenerated. Free will really belongs to the internal man; and when this is closed up, the man becomes external and natural; and such a man does not see any spiritual truth. Miracles also are like veils and bars lest anything might enter. This bar, or this obstruction, however, is gradually broken, and [then] all truths become dispersed.

7. It is said by the church at this day, following Paul, that faith enters through the hearing of the Word; and some add to this, through a certain meditation from the Word. This, however, is to be understood thus, that truths ought to be drawn from the Word, and that man ought to live according to them. In this case, the man approaches the Lord, who is the Word, and the Truth, and receives faith; for each and all truths are from the Word, which is spiritual light. Thus faith is acquired; because faith belongs to truth, and truth belongs to faith; and nothing ought to be believed except the truth.

8. That there are numberless evils interiorly in man; yea, that there are numberless evils in every lust. Every lust of which man becomes conscious, is a mass and a heap of many things. These things the man does not see, but only the one mass. When, therefore, the man by repentance removes this, the Lord, who sees the interior and inmost things of man, removes them. Unless, therefore, a man approaches the Lord, he labors in vain to render himself free from sin. The case herein is as with those things which were written in a Relation concerning turtles [see True Christian Religion 462].

9. That a man who has altogether confirmed himself in the faith and doctrine of the present church, makes no account of repentance, of the law of the Decalogue, and of works and charity. For he can say, "I cannot do goods from myself; they are contained in faith, whence they come forth of their own accord; I can only know them," and so forth. This is the source of the naturalism which prevails at the present time.

10. By the "fulness of time" is signified consummation and desolation; because "time" signifies the state of the church (see Rev. 10:6, and Ezek. 30:3).

The same also is signified by "Time, times, and half a time" (see Rev. 12:14; Dan. 7:25; 12:7). The times in the world are spring, summer, autumn; the fullness of these times is winter. The times as to light are morning, noon, evening; and their fullness is the night, etc., etc. This is meant by the Lord's coming in "the fullness of the time," or of "times"; that is, when there is no longer any truth of faith, and good of charity left. (Concerning "the fullness of the time," see Rom. 11:12, 25; Gal. 4:4; and especially, Eph. 1:9, 10; Gen. 15:16.)

11. That the Lord's love is present with those who are in faith in Him. This may be clearly seen from this circumstance, that place cannot be predicated of love, nor of faith; for both are spiritual. That the Lord Himself is present appears from this consideration, that spiritual love also is not confined to place. It was not in my own case, whenever I was in the spiritual idea. In a word, presence in the spiritual world is according to love. Wherefore, [the Lord] is omnipresent; He does not move about; He is in place, but not through place; He is thus in space and in what is extended, but not through space, and through what is extended.

12. The desolation of the truth of the church may be compared with consummations on the earth; heat, namely, and all the above [times or seasons] are consummated by winter, and then spring [comes]; and light on earth is consummated by the night, when the morning comes. Wherefore, the Lord in Revelation said to those under the altar (Rev. 6:9–11). [See quotation.] A number of passages are to be quoted from Revelation, showing that the church has been laid waste, even to its ultimate.

13. That at the present day nothing is known concerning the union of soul and body, is proved by the hypotheses of the learned concerning the soul; especially by that of Descartes and others, [who maintain] that the soul is a substance separated from the body, in some place or other; when yet the soul is the inmost man; consequently, is the man from the head to the foot. Thence it is, according to the ancients, that the soul is in the whole, and in every part thereof; and that in whatever part the soul does not dwell inmostly, there man has no life. From this union it is, that all things of the soul belong to the body, and all things of the body belong to the soul; as the Lord said concerning His Father, that all His

things are the Father's, and that all things of the Father are His (John 17:10). Thence it is that the Lord is God, even as to the flesh (Rom. 9:5; Col. 2:9); and that [He said], "the Father is in Me," and "I am in the Father" [John 14:10, 11]. Thus they are one.

14. The human mind is of three degrees, which are the celestial, spiritual, and natural. In the first degree is the soul, in the second, is the spirit or the mind, and in the third, is the body. It is the same thing, whether we say that a man's mind is of three degrees, or whether we say that the man himself is. For that of the body which is in principles thus where its first is, is called mind. The remaining parts are derived thence, and are continuations. What is the mind, if it is only to the head, except something that is separated or divorced, in which the mind does not exist through continuation? Let autopsy settle this: The origins of the fibers are the glands of the so-called cortical substance; thence proceed the fibers; and after they are bundled together into nerves, they descend and pass through the whole body, weaving it together and constructing it. The celestial degree, in which is the soul, that is, the inmost man, is a semblance of love; the spiritual degree, in which is the mind, that is, the spirit, which is the mediate man, is a semblance of wisdom from love; and the third degree, in which is the body, which is the ultimate man, is the containant of both; without this third degree, the two higher degrees would not subsist. These things can be further demonstrated from the three heavens, the celestial, spiritual, and natural—where such men are. Wherefore the angels of the higher heavens are invisible to the angels of the lower heavens, if the latter approach the former from their own heavens.

15. Thence it may be seen in light that as a tree exists from its seed, so also the body exists through the soul. Hence also it is that the tree derives its quality from the seed. From this, however, it follows that inasmuch as the soul of Christ was from the Divine essence, His body also must be derived thence.

16. All theologians, when preaching, know nothing of the falsities of their religion. For they preach that God is one; that the Saviour ought to be adored; that man, therefore, ought to believe in the Word and in preachings; that he ought to exercise charity, and practise repentance, so as to desist from evils. While preaching thus, they remember nothing concerning three Gods, concerning their mystical faith, concerning impotence in spiritual matters, and concerning all the remaining dogmas. But let them know, that the falsities which they have imbibed in the schools, are clinging to them interiorly; and other things are merely in the mouth; and that after death they come into the interior things of the spirit; wherefore, these falsities ought by all means to be rooted out. Then also the things that are merely in the mouth, are as the beard on the chin, which afterwards, as is usually the case, is cut off, and he becomes beardless.

17. When orthodoxy enters and explains all those things which priests preach from the Word concerning faith that we ought to believe in God, concerning charity towards the neighbor, conversion, repentance, and the life of piety and spiritual life, they fall as it were into a bucket; then they are overthrown, as when one destroys a dwelling or a house, even so that nothing but ruins remain. The preachers say that these things are not true, unless you believe thus. What does charity, repentance, etc., effect? The very Word then falls, and so forth. It is as if someone undermines a wall, by digging ditches under it. All things are overthrown.

18. Bring an example, where someone preaches devoutly on the above subjects from the Word; and when orthodoxy is brought to bear upon his preaching, you will see that what I saw and declared, is true. (The example will illustrate this....) Thus they affirm, and then deny, if orthodoxy is in the internal man, and the subjects that are preached are in the external man. In this case that which then remains in the external man is regarded as of no account and becomes like froth. It is swept away, like an earthquake, or like a ship broken below by water.

19. An example, also, may be brought from genuine orthodoxy on the subject of faith, charity, and free will. From this example will appear plainly the absurdity of [false orthodoxy].

20. That the spiritual things of heaven flow into the whole man, and that [natural things] flow in through the world, is confirmed in light thus: that spiritual and natural things flow in conjointly, but that the evil man inverts the two. That which is within he places outwardly in his mind; and that which is outmost he places within; so that the world is above heaven, that is, heaven below the world. But the devout and good man

receives both in the order in which they flow in; the spiritual things which flow in through heaven, he places in the mind above, and the natural things which flow in through the world, he places below. This man stands on his feet erect; but the former is, as it were, inverted.

21. The whole of theology at the present day is nothing but the Divine omnipotence. It is said: (1) That God gives faith where and to whom He pleases. (2) That He remits sins. (3) That He regenerates. (4) That He sanctifies. (5) That He imputes and saves. (6) That He will raise the dead bodies from the graves; that He will cause the skeletons to be alive, and will put into them their former souls. (7) That He will destroy the world, with the sun, the stars, the planets, the earths, and will create it anew. (8) Since omnipotence is everything, and since it constitutes the order which is God, and which is from God, in the whole world, it follows that the man of the church can imagine whatever he pleases; that he can raise himself beyond the ethers, that is, above reason; and that, wherever he pleases, he can go counter to reason, and say that "reason is to be held under obedience to our faith. For is not God omnipotent? And who can, and who dares to reason in opposition to His omnipotence?" Such are all things of faith at this day.

22. That man cannot discover a single Divine truth, except by approaching the Lord immediately, is due to this, that the Lord alone is the Word, and that He is the Light and the Truth itself; and man does not become spiritual except from the Lord alone, but remains natural; and the natural man, in spiritual things, sees everything in inverted order; that this is so, is known from Paul. This is the reason why not a single truth has remained in the church, so that now is the consummation, the desolation, the decision, and the fullness [of time]. But still because the Lord is not dead, therefore, according to Daniel, there still remains "a root in the earth"; while, according to Revelation, "man indeed is willing to die, but yet he cannot." That which "remains" is the faculty of being able to understand the truth, and of being able to will good. This is "the root that remains."

23. The students of modern orthodoxy object, that faith, charity, good works, repentance, remission of sins, etc., cannot be given with a man, before he has received the Holy Spirit. But, as has been shown, the Holy Spirit is the Divine which proceeds from the Lord; and the Lord is perpetually present with every man, the evil as well as the good. Without His presence, no one can live; and the Lord constantly acts, urges, and strives to be received; wherefore, the presence of the Holy Spirit is perpetual. For the sake of confirmation, this was proved in the spiritual world, in the case of a certain devil, by the removal from him of the Lord's presence. And the devil lay dead, exactly like a corpse. Thousands from among the spirits and the clergy saw this, and were thunderstruck. From the Lord's perpetual presence, man has the faculty of thinking, understanding, and willing. These faculties are solely from the influx of life from the Lord. Both Melancthon and Luther were present, and they could not open their lips.

24. The only cause why the Reformation was effected, was that the Word which lay buried, might be restored to the world. For many centuries it had been in the world, but at last it was entombed by the Roman Catholics, and not a single truth of the church could then be laid open from it. The Lord thus could not become known, but the Pope was worshipped as God, in the Lord's place. But after the Word had been drawn forth out of its tomb, the Lord could be made known, truth could be derived from it, and conjunction with heaven could be given. For this purpose the Lord raised up simultaneously so many men who contended. He raised up Sweden, Denmark, Holland, England that they might receive; and lest [the Word] should be blotted out in Germany through the Pope, He raised up Gustavus Adolphus, who stood for the Reformation, and rose up against [the Pope].

25. Unless the present little work is added to the preceding work, the church cannot be healed. For it would be a mere palliative cure; a wound in which the corrupt matter remains, and which vitiates the neighboring parts. Orthodoxy is this corrupt matter itself, and the doctrine of the New Church indeed brings a healing, but only exteriorly.

26. The origins of all errors in the church have been this: that they have believed that man lives from himself, or from his own life, and that life has been created in him; when yet man is only an organ of life, and is kept in the middle between heaven and hell, and thus in equilibrium or free will.

27. No one is able to see the desolation of truth in the church, before truths from the Word come into light. What heretic, indeed, knows otherwise than that all that he has are truths? Ev-

eryone can swear to his own. He is in deceptive light arising from confirmations. In such a light is the natural man, when the spiritual man illumines it. Yea the naturalistic atheist can swear that there is no God; and that the existence of God is a mere vain imagination of the common people; wherefore, at heart he scoffs at the doctors of the church.

28. It is known in the church, that the church is the Body of Christ; but how this is has not been known hitherto. Hence it is that the whole heaven is as one man before the Lord; and this man is distinguished into societies, each of which has reference to one member, or organ and viscus in man. In this man or body, the Lord is the soul or life. For the Lord inspires men; and when He is present, He is present through the heavens, as the soul is present through its body. The same is the case with the church on earth; for this is the external man. Wherefore, everyone through death is gathered to his own in that body, etc.

29. The things which are stated in the sequel are not miracles, but they are testimonies that I have been introduced by the Lord into the spiritual world for the sake of the ends which... The causes why no miracles are done at the present time... (Further, from the Lord's words in Matt. 24.) Concerning the miracles of Anthony of Padua, and of most of those who are worshipped as saints; of whose miracles the monasteries are full. Of the miracles of Paris, concerning which there are two volumes in quarto.

30. That the Lord would come in the fullness of time and judge, is meant by His words in Matthew:
When the Son of man shall come in His glory, and all the holy angels with Him, He shall sit on the throne of His glory; and there shall be gathered before Him all nations; and He shall separate them one from another, as the shepherd separateth the sheep from the he-goats (Matt. 25:31–32).
This coming of the Lord is meant by the following words concerning Jesus Christ, in the Apostles' Creed:
He ascended into the heavens, He sitteth at the right hand of God the Father Almighty; from thence He shall come to judge the living and the dead.
And also by these words concerning the Lord Jesus Christ in the Nicene Creed:
He ascended into the heavens, and sitteth on the right hand of the Father; and He shall come

again in glory to judge the living and the dead; of whose kingdom there shall be no end.

31. And also in the Athanasian Creed:
He ascended into the heavens; He sitteth at the right hand of God the Father Almighty; from whence He shall come to judge the living and the dead.... And they shall give account for their own deeds. And they that have done good shall enter into eternal life; and they that have done evil into eternal fire. (Formula Concordiae [Leipsic, 1756], pp. 1, 2, 4.)
Besides, the articles of Schmalkalden teach the same thing as the Apostles', the Nicene, and the Athanasian creeds, namely:
Jesus Christ ascended into the heavens, He sitteth on the right hand of God, He shall come to judge the living and the dead.
Luther in his Lesser Catechism (p. 371) teaches the same thing (Augsburg Confession, pp. 10, 14); and our Catechism [the one used in Sweden] teaches the same (p. 303). From the Augsburg Confession we quote in like manner:
He ascended into the heavens, that He might sit on the right hand of the Father, and reign forever, and rule over all creatures. The same Christ will openly come again to judge the living and the dead, according to the Apostles' Creed (Augsburg Confession, p. 10).

32. That the Lord will not come to judgment, to destroy heaven and earth, appears from many passages in the Word, where His coming is treated of; as for instance where it is said in Luke:
When the Son of man cometh, shall He find faith on the earth? (Luke 18:8).
Besides many more passages which are quoted in True Christian Religion (n. 765); further, that He will not come to destroy the visible heaven and the habitable earth (ibid., n. 768 seq.); but to separate the evil from the good (ibid., n. 772 seq.); and many more passages besides. The same also is declared in the Credal Faith which is inserted in every Book of Psalms in the whole Christian world, where the Apostles' Creed only is set forth. The same is introduced thence into the Psalms. By the "living," in the above places, are meant those who are in charity and faith, and who by the Lord are called "sheep"; but by the "dead" are meant those who are not in charity and faith, and who by the Lord are called "he-goats." (Add here Rev. 11:18; and 20:12.)

33. Title:

THE CONSUMMATION OF THE AGE, AND THE ABOMINATION OF THE DESOLATION THEN.

There is to be adduced what the Lord says,

(1) Concerning the "abomination of the desolation";

(2) What He says [of vastation];

(3) What the Lord says concerning the "affliction";

(4) That "no flesh can be saved";

(5) Concerning the "darkening of the sun and moon";

(6) The things which are declared in Revelation: Behold, I am He that liveth, and was dead; and behold I am He that liveth unto the ages of the ages (Rev. 1:18; also 2:8; and 5:6).

And again, what the Lord said in John:

The night cometh when no man can work (John 9:4).

In that night there shall be two men in one bed (Luke 17:34).

Further, what the Lord said in John (21:18), concerning Peter; also, what Paul said concerning the last times (1 Tim. 4:1–3; 2 Tim. 3:1–7; 4:3, 4). There shall be explained what the Lord says (Matt. 24:27), that this took place on the day of the Last Judgment; also, what He says (Matt. 24:30–31). That this actually has taken place, see True Christian Religion, n. 791.

34. The Lord's Coming is according to order in this respect, that the spring does not come until after the winter; nor the morning, until after the night; that the travailing woman has comfort and joy, only after pain; that states of comfort are after temptations; and that there is genuine life after undergoing death; even as the Lord says, "Unless the grain... die," etc. (John 12:24). The Lord exhibited the type of this order, when He suffered Himself to be crucified and to die, and when afterwards He rose again; this type signifies the state of the church.... The above also is involved in the image which appeared to Nebuchadnezzar, where the Stone at last became a great Rock; it is further involved in the four beasts that came out of the sea; and in what is related there concerning that fearful nation (which is to be explained). It is likewise involved in the four ages known to the ancients, the golden, silver, brazen, and iron ages; further, in the ages through which every man passes, from infancy to old age; then is the end of the life of the body, and then comes the life of the spirit, which is the life of all those who have lived well. The same also is involved in the heaven which has first to pass away (Rev. 21:1, 2). The case with the church is the same.

35. The keys of the kingdom of the heavens were given to Peter, because he represented the Lord as to the Divine Truth; and this is what is meant by "a rock," throughout the whole of the Sacred Scripture. On this account [it is said], "On this rock," that is, on this Divine Truth, "I will build My church," namely, on this that the Lord is "THE SON OF THE LIVING GOD." It shall be shown from the Word, that such is the signification of a "rock." (The "rock" is spoken of in the Word [in the following passages]: Exod. 17:6; 33:21, 22; Num. 20:8–11; Deut. 8:15; 32:4–37; 1 Sam. 2:2; 2 Sam. 22:2, 3, 32, 47; 23:3; Ps. 18:2, 31, 46; 28:1; 31:2, 3; 40:2; 42:9; 62:2, 7; 78:16, 20, 35; 89:26; 92:15; 94:22; 95:1; 105:41; Isa. 2:10; 22:16; 42:11; 51:1; 1 Cor. 10:4.) The "fissures of the rock" mean falsified truths (Rev. 6:15, 16; Isa. 21:19; Jer. 16:16; Song of Sol. 2:14; Isa. 48:21; Jer. 23:29; 49:16; Obad. verse 3; besides in the Evangelists). In this wise also some of the Fathers explained this passage (see Formula Concordiae, p. 345).

36. When the Son alone became Man, and not the whole Trinity, was not then the Divine Essence which is a one and an indivisible trine, separated, that is, disunited or divided?

37. That the whole of the Lord's Prayer, from beginning to end, has respect to this time; that is, to the time when God, the Father will be worshipped in the Human Form. This appears when this prayer is rightly explained.

38. That the churches after the times of the Apostles fell away into so many heresies, and that at the present day there are none other than false churches, is because they have not approached the Lord, when yet the Lord is the Word, and the very Light which enlighteneth the whole world. And yet for them it is as impossible to see one single genuine truth from the Word, except what is encompassed with and steeped in falsities, and coheres with falsities, as it is to sail to the Pleiades, or to dig out the gold which is in the center of the earth. Wherefore, in order that true Christian religion might be manifested, it was absolutely necessary that someone should be introduced into the spiritual world, and derive from the mouth of the Lord genuine truths out of the

Word. The Lord cannot enlighten anyone with His light, unless He is approached immediately, and acknowledged as the God of heaven.

39. That miracles are not done at this day, is on account of the reasons which are stated in True Christian Religion (n. 501); wherefore, the Lord said that they would seduce (Matt. 24:24). Again, what is more common with the Roman Catholics than filling the tombs of the saints, and the walls of monasteries with miracles? How many plates of gold and silver are there not in the tomb of Anthony of Padua? How many are there not where the three wise men are said to be buried? And how many are there not at Prague? And in other places? What else than illusions can be derived thence? The fact that I converse in the spiritual world with angels and spirits, that I have described the states of heaven and hell, and the life after death; and further, the fact that there has been disclosed to me the spiritual sense of the Word—besides many other things—is worth more than all these miracles. Such communication, as far as I know, has not been granted by the Lord to anyone before. These are evidences that this has been granted for the sake of the New Church, which is the crown of all the churches, and which will endure forever. Being in the spiritual world, seeing the wonderful things of heaven, and the miserable things of hell; and being there in the very light of the Lord in which are the angels, surpasses all miracles. Evidences that I am there, may be seen in abundance in my books.

40. The sole cause why the church has immersed itself into so many falsities, that not a single truth has remained in it, and why it is like a ship that has suffered shipwreck, of which the top of the mast only protrudes, is this: that hitherto they have not approached the Lord immediately; and so long as the Lord is not approached immediately, not a single truth can appear in its own light. The reason of this is, that the Lord is the Word, that is, the all of Divine truth in the Word, and that He alone is the Light which enlighteneth all, as He Himself teaches; and further, that every truth of the Word shines from no other source, than from the Lord alone. This light is what is meant by the spiritual; when, therefore, this light is not present, there is nothing spiritual in man's understanding, but what is merely natural; and all things which contain the spiritual, the natural man sees only invertedly; he sees falsity instead of the truth. On reading the Word, therefore, he bends all things towards his own falsities, and thus falsifies truths; and he takes delight in them. For the natural human mind is in such things as belong to the world and to self; it is delighted solely by such things; wherefore, unless in the above things there is spiritual light, the natural man transfers them to those things which belong to the world and to self, and he puts these in the first place. He thus not only shuns spiritual things, and hides them away, but he also scoffs at them. Faith is spiritual from no other source, that is, it cannot be called spiritual, except from the truths which it contains, and thus by virtue of light from the Lord. Unless faith is from this source, it is natural faith which does not conjoin, and which is not saving.

41. That in the spiritual world no one knows another from his name only, but from the idea of his quality. This idea causes that the other becomes present and is known. Thus, and not otherwise, parents are known by their children; children by their parents; and relations, connections by marriage, and friends, by their relations, connections, and friends. In like manner the learned are known from their writings, and from the reputation of their learning; great men and rulers by the fame of their deeds; in like manner kings, emperors, and popes. All are known by these things alone. It was granted to me to converse with such; but with others it is not possible. A spirit himself also is nothing else than his own quality; on this account everyone in that world drops his baptismal name, and the name of his family, and is named according to his quality. Hence it is that "name" in the Word does not signify name, but quality. As the Lord says in Revelation:
Thou hast a few names in Sardis (Rev. 3:4);
and again:
I know thee by name (Exod. 33:7).
Besides, a thousand other places, where "name" is mentioned. From all this, then, it appears, that no one has the Lord present with himself, unless he knows His quality. This quality the truths of the Word make manifest; for, as many truths as there are in the Word, there are just so many mirrors and ideas of the Lord; for He is the Word itself and He is the Truth itself, as He Himself says. Qualities are of two kinds: one kind belongs to the knowledge concerning the Lord Himself, that He is the God of heaven and earth, the Son of God the Father, One with the Father, that all things of the Father are in Him, in a word, that

He is the Human of God the Father. The other kind belongs to the knowledges of those things that proceed from Him; and the things that proceed from Him, are Himself; as, for instance, those things which He teaches concerning charity, freedom, will, repentance, regeneration, the sacraments, and very many other things. These things also make up the idea of the Lord, because they are from Him.

42. It is an arcanum from the spiritual world, that he who does not approach the Lord directly and immediately with the idea concerning Him, presence is not effected, and still less can he become a recipient of any communication. It is as if someone stands at the side, and appears in the dark. In like manner, no one can converse with another, unless he looks directly at him; communication is then granted when each reciprocally looks at the other. Thus, and not otherwise, do ideas enter into another; and if at the same time there is love, conjunction is effected. If anyone, therefore, approaches the Father immediately, He stands as it were at the side; and hence is unable to grant and to impart redemption; that is, He is unable to regenerate, and afterwards to save him.

43. The manifestation of the Lord in Person, and the introduction by the Lord into the spiritual world, both as to sight and as to hearing and speech, surpasses all miracles; for we do not read anywhere in history that such interaction with angels and spirits has been granted from the creation of the world. For I am daily with angels there, even as I am in the world with men; and now for twenty-seven years. Evidences of this interaction are the books which I have published concerning Heaven and Hell, and also the Relations in my last work entitled True Christian Religion; further, what has been stated there concerning Luther, Melancthon, Calvin, and concerning the inhabitants of many kingdoms; besides, the various evidences which are known in the world, and many other evidences besides which are not known. Say, who has ever before known anything concerning heaven and hell? Who has known anything concerning man's state after death? Who has known anything concerning spirits and angels, etc., etc.?

44. In addition to these most manifest evidences, there is the fact that the spiritual sense of the Word has been disclosed by the Lord through me; which has never before been revealed since the Word was written with the sons of Israel; and this sense is the very sanctuary of the Word; the Lord Himself is in this sense with His Divine,

and in the natural sense with His Human. Not a single iota in this sense can be opened except by the Lord alone. This surpasses all the revelations that have hitherto been made since the creation of the world. Through this revelation a communication has been opened between men and the angels of heaven, and the conjunction of the two worlds has been effected; because when man is in the natural sense the angels are in the spiritual sense. See what has been written concerning this sense in the chapter on the Sacred Scripture [in True Christian Religion].

45. The correspondences by which the Word as to each and all of its parts has been written, possess such power and strength, that it may be called the power and strength of the Divine Omnipotence; for through these correspondences the natural acts conjointly with the spiritual, and the spiritual with the natural; thus the all of heaven with the all of the world. Thence it is that the two sacraments are correspondences of spiritual with natural things; thence is their strength and power.

46. What are miracles over against these things? Miracles are not done at this day, because they seduce men, and make them natural. They close the interiors of their minds, wherein faith ought to be rooted; wherefore mere falsities proceed thence (see Matt. 24:24). What did the miracles effect which were done in Egypt with the sons of Israel? What did those miracles effect which were done before them in the desert? What those miracles when they entered into the land of Canaan? What the miracles which were wrought by Elijah and Elisha? What those which the Lord Himself wrought? Was anyone ever made spiritual by their means? What has been the use of miracles among the Roman Catholics? and of those of Anthony at Padua? and of the three wise men at Cologne? And what has been the use of the countless miracles in the monasteries, whose walls are fitted with pictures, plates, and gifts? Has anyone ever been made spiritual thereby? Have they not become natural thereby, so that there is scarcely any truth of the Word among them, but only the external things of worship, which have their origin from men and traditions?

47. That in Christ God is Man, and Man God, is confirmed three times in the Formula Concordiae; and also in the Athanasian Creed, where it treats of the "assumption of the Human into God;" from the Word (Rom. 14:11; Coloss. 2:9; 1 John 5:20, 21), as well as by the declaration of the Lord Himself, that "the Father and Himself are

one;" that "the Father is in Him, and He in the Father;" that "all things of the Father are His;" that "He has Life in Himself;" that "He is the God of heaven and earth"; etc.

48. The soul is the inmost man, and thence according to the ancients it is in the whole and in every part of the body, because the beginning of life resides in the soul; that part of the body in which the soul does not inmostly reside, does not live. Wherefore there is a reciprocal union; and hence the body acts from the soul, but not the soul through the body. Whatever proceeds from God partakes of the human form, because God is Himself the Man; this is especially the case with the soul, which is the first of man.

49. Nothing is more common in the whole heaven and in the whole world, than for one thing to be within another; thus there is an inmost, a middle, and an outmost; and these three intercommunicate, and the power of the middle and outmost are derived from the inmost. That there are three things, one within the other, appears from each and all things in the human body. Around the brain there are three tunics, which are called the dura mater, the pia mater, and the arachnoid; and over these is the skull. Around the whole body there are tunics, one within the other, which taken all together are called the skin. Around each artery and vein there are three tunics; likewise around each muscle and fiber; in like manner around all the rest which are there. In the vegetable kingdom the case is the same. How these parts intercommunicate, and how the inmost enters the middle, and the middle the ultimate, is shown by anatomy, etc. Thence it follows that the same is the case with light; that spiritual light which in its essence is truth, is interiorly in natural light; likewise that spiritual heat which in its essence is love, is in natural heat. By natural heat is meant natural love, because that love becomes warm; and this is clothed with the heat of the blood.

50. All things which people speak concerning the Holy Spirit fall to the ground, as soon as it is believed that man is not life, but only an organ of life; and thus that God is constantly in man, and that He strives, acts, and urges that those things which belong to religion, and consequently those which belong to the church, to heaven and salvation, shall be received. Therefore it is wrong to say that the Holy Spirit is given, or that it is lost. For the Holy Spirit is nothing else than the Divine which proceeds out of the Lord from the Father, and this Divine causes a man's life, and also his understanding and his love; and the presence of this Divine is perpetual. Without the presence of the Lord or the Holy Spirit, man would be nothing but a kind of beast; yea he would not have any more life, than salt, a stone, or a stock. The reason of this is, that man is not born with instinct, like a beast; wherefore a pullet one day old knows the order of its life better than an infant.

51. That it is allowable to confirm the truths of the church by reason or by the understanding, as much as it pleases, and also by various things in nature; and in proportion as truths are so confirmed, they become rooted and shine. It is also allowable to confirm truths by the Word, wherever it pleases, and also to apply for this purpose many things from the Word; and then the Word is not falsified thereby. Those expressions of Scripture through which truths are confirmed, ascend into heaven; they are like the fumes of frankincense; but on the other hand if falsities are confirmed from the Word, they do not ascend into heaven, but are rejected; and they are dispersed on the way with a loud report. This I have heard thousands of times.

52. The manifestation of the Lord, and intromission into the spiritual world, surpass all miracles. This has not been granted to anyone since the creation, as it has been to me. The men of the golden age, indeed, conversed with the angels; but it was not granted to them to be in any other than natural light; but to me it is granted to be in both spiritual and natural light at the same time. By this means it has been granted to me to see the wonderful things of heaven, to be together with the angels like one of them, and at the same time to draw forth truths in light, and thus to perceive and teach them; consequently to be led by the Lord. But as concerns miracles, they would have been nothing else than snares for seducing men; as the Lord says (Matt. 24:24); and as is related of the magician Simon, that:

> He bewitched the nations in Samaria, who believed that these things were done from the great power of God (Acts 8:9 seq.).

What else are the miracles among the Papists, than snares and deceptions? What else do they teach, than that they themselves should be worshipped as deities, and that they should recede from the worship of the Lord? Have wonder-working images any other effect? Have the idols or corpses of saints throughout the papal dominion any other purpose? Those of Anthony of Padua, of the three wise men at Cologne, and of all the rest, whose miracles fill the monasteries? What have these miracles taught concerning Christ? What concerning heaven and life eternal? Not a syllable.

53. That it is impossible for any church, and for any system of religion to exist, unless it is believed that God is one. When, therefore, the Divine Trinity is believed to be divided into three Persons, how can the metaphysical term essence make one out of three? So long as the properties of each person are diverse, yea, so diverse that they are said not to be communicable? And so long as the equal and particular persons subsist by themselves, and one person has no part and no quality in the other person, or of the other person? But when it is believed that the one God is not only the Creator, but also the Redeemer and Operator, then we have one God; and then for the first time the church exists and subsists, and religion lives. And thus union of three cannot be given otherwise, than it is in every man, as soul, body, and proceeding. These three make one man: why not God, who is Himself the Man from firsts to ultimates? These things concerning God Man have been explained in Divine Love and Wisdom, and may be consulted. It is also shown that [the soul] is neither ether, nor air, nor wind; that the soul of every man is the man himself, follows thence. As we have now one God in the church, who is God Man and Man God, this church is called the crown of all the churches.

54. That in Christ man is God is to be shown from three places in the Formula Concordiae (from Paul, Rom. 14:11; Col. 2:9; from John's first Epistle 5:20–21), and from the Lord's words that:
1. God was the Word, and the Word was made flesh.
2. All things of the Father are His.
3. All of the Father come to Him.
4. As the Father hath life in Himself, so has the Son (Life in Himself is God).
5. The Father and He are one.
6. He is in the Father, and the Father in Him.
7. He who seeth Him, seeth the Father.
8. He is the God of heaven and earth.
9. He governs the universe. (From the Creed.)
10. He is called "Jehovah, the Redeemer."
11. He is called "Jehovah, our Righteousness."
12. It is said that "Jehovah would come into the world."
13. In the Apocalypse (Chap. 1) it is said, that He is "the first and the Last."
14. In a word, He is God the Father who is invisible, in the Human which is visible before minds.

Because there is thus One God in the church, the church is the church, etc., etc. From the Athanasian Creed it is said:

As the soul and body is one man: so God and Man in Christ is one Person; then that the Human Nature was taken into God.

55. CONCERNING MIRACLES.
(From the sons of Israel.)
(From the Lord's words concerning Dives and Lazarus.)
(From the Lord's words, Matt. 24:24.)

The Papal miracles (which are to be enumerated). That they only seduce, and do not teach anything; their sole purpose is that they may be invoked as deities; and indeed to this end that gold and silver may be brought to the monasteries; that is, that they may scrape together the treasures of the whole world. The miracles of many of them, as of Anthony at Padua; those by the three wise men at Cologne; those of the wonder-working images, at which treasures are collected, everywhere in the monasteries, where the walls are covered with pictures of the miracles wrought by their saints, and their idols; the books concerning the miracles of Paris and others. What other purpose have they, than that they may be invoked, to the end that gifts may be scraped together? But who among them has thus far taught the way to heaven, and the truths of the church out of the Word?

For this reason it has pleased the Lord to prepare me from my earliest youth to perceive the Word, and He has introduced me into the spiritual world, and has enlightened me with the light of His Word more proximately. From this it is manifest that this surpasses all miracles.

Beelzebub did more miracles than other Gentile gods, as is evident from the Old Testament; and also the magician Simon.

56. That the Lord made the Natural Man in Himself Divine, in order that He might be the First and the Last; and that He might thus enter with men even into their natural man, and might teach and lead it from the Word. For He rose with His whole natural or external man, and did not leave anything of it in the sepulcher; on which account He said that He had bones and flesh, which spirits have not; and [hence it is] that He ate and drank with His disciples of natural food, and in their sight. That He was Divine, He showed by passing through doors, and by becoming invisible, which never could have been done, unless His Natural Man itself also had been made Divine with Him.

57. That all those things which the orthodox at the present day say concerning the sending of the Holy Spirit fall to the ground, as soon as it is known that the Lord is constantly present with every man, and causes the man to live; and that

He resides with man in order that he may go and meet the Lord; and that even if he does not go and meet the Lord, he still has rationality, which would be impossible without the Lord's presence. If the Lord were absent from man, the man would not be a beast, but like some corpse which would be dissipated. This is meant in Genesis by: God breathed into him a living soul (Gen. 2:7).

58. It shall here be shown from the Word, that the Lord is the "Kingdom of God"; thus, that He is heaven and the church.

59. It shall be shown that the greatest power is in correspondences; because in them heaven and the world, or the spiritual and the natural, are together. That for this reason the Word was written by mere correspondences; wherefore, through it there is the conjunction of man with heaven, and thus with the Lord. The Lord also by this means is in firsts and at the same time in ultimates. On this account the sacraments have been instituted through correspondences, and therefore there is the Divine power in them.

Glossary

Advent:	the coming of Christ
Anthony of Padua:	a popular Catholic saint later made a Doctor of the Church by the pope
Apostles' Creed:	a prayer containing the fundamental tenets of the Christian faith, supposedly composed by Christ's twelve apostles
arcanum:	a mystery or deep secret
Athanasian Creed:	a Christian statement of belief that focuses on the Trinity
Augsburg Confession:	the primary profession of faith of the Lutheran Church
Beelzebub:	Satan, the devil
Calvin:	John Calvin, a sixteenth-century French theologian and reformer
Daniel:	an Old Testament prophet
Decalogue:	the Ten Commandments
Descartes:	René Decartes, a prominent seventeenth-century French philosopher, mathematician, and writer
Dives and Lazarus:	a reference to one of Christ's parables in the Gospel of Luke, about a rich man (Dives) who refuses to share his plenty with a poor beggar (Lazarus)
Elijah:	an Old Testament prophet in Israel
Elisha:	Elijah's successor as an Old Testament prophet in Israel
Eucharist:	that is, Holy Communion, the sacrament in which the faithful share in the body and blood of Christ
Gentile:	a non-Jew
Greek Church:	the Eastern branch of Catholicism, comprising numerous "orthodox" churches such as the Greek Orthodox Church
Gustavus Adolphus:	Swedish king Gustavus II Adolphus
Jehovah:	an Old Testament name of God
land of Canaan:	that is, Israel, the biblical homeland of the Jews
Luther:	Martin Luther, the sixteenth-century religious reformer and the impetus behind the Protestant Reformation

Glossary

magician Simon:	Simon Magus, mentioned in the biblical book Acts of the Apostles as a sorcerer and magician
Melancthon:	Philipp Melancthon, a sixteenth-century religious reformer and ally of Martin Luther
Nebuchadnezzar:	a king of the ancient Babylonian Empire
Nicene Creed:	the Catholic profession of faith formulated at the Church's Council of Nicaea in 325
Papists:	followers of the pope; Catholics
Paul:	the author of several New Testament books
Pleiades:	a prominent star cluster
Revelation:	the final book of the New Testament
Romish Church:	the Roman Catholic Church
Schmalkalden:	a town in Germany where, in 1537, Martin Luther and Philipp Melancthon drew up the Smalcald Articles summarizing Lutheran doctrine
three wise men at Cologne:	that is, the three kings who visited Jesus at his birth and whose bodies were supposedly entombed in the cathedral in Cologne, Germany

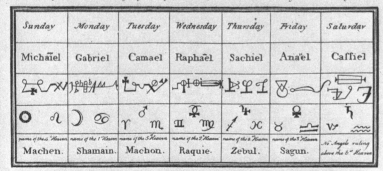

Illustration of Cassiel from
The Magus by Francis Barrett (1801).

THE MAGUS: DOCUMENT ANALYSIS

"The wise ancients knew that in Nature the greatest secrets lay hid, and wonderful active powers were dormant, unless excited by the vigorous faculty of the mind of man..."

Overview

The Magus; or, Celestial Intelligencer, by Francis Barrett , is widely recognized as one of the first influential texts concerning ritualistic magic and the occult in the English-speaking world. Originally printed in 1801, *The Magus* for the first time brought together sections (or complete translations) of many previously rare and difficult-to-find texts in a format that was easily accessible. The works collected in *The Magus* include a previously translated edition of *The Heptameron; or, Magical Elements*, by the medieval Italian physician Peter de Abano; *The Key of Solomon*, a book on magic credited to King Solomon; and, most famously, the *De occulta philosophia libri tres (Three Books on Occult Philosophy)* by the early-sixteenth-century mystic Cornelius Agrippa, along with the *Fourth Book on Occult Philosophy*, which has been attributed to Agrippa. Although it was originally divided into three books, *The Magus* is most commonly printed in one single volume.

The first book of *The Magus* is devoted to the various areas of natural magic, including alchemy (a medieval form of transmutative chemistry), astrology (the belief in and study of the stars' divine influence on human activities), arithmancy (foretelling the future through the use of numbers), and celestial magic (involving spiritual power over planets and other heavenly bodies). The second book deals with magnetism and kabbalistic (utilizing secret or hidden knowledge of the universe, commonly through the exploration of Jewish mysticism) and more ritualistic (ceremonial) magic. Following the more practical areas of the second book, Barrett adds a caution to those wishing to practice magic as described in the book, then includes a personal advertisement to offer individual training in any of the areas covered and described in *The Magus*. The third

book ends with a biographical section of personalities of note in the area of the occult. (There is some uncertainty as to Barrett's authorship of this section.) In this way, Barrett offers *The Magus* as a complete reference work for the entire area of ritualistic magic known and accepted up to that time. It is important to note that, apart from some translating and modernization of the phrasing, the vast majority of *The Magus* is unoriginal in content. However, this fact should not diminish the undeniable influence of the text upon western occult and magic studies. By providing an anthology of works covering different forms of magic and the occult, Barrett made previously esoteric works available to the masses—or at least to those interested—without the need to search for rare texts that, up to this point, had gone out of print; in some cases were never translated; and remained largely unavailable to the general public.

With the onset of the occult revival of the late nineteenth century and a reprint of the work in 1870, *The Magus* once again became a vital reference among followers of more esoteric organizations and beliefs. While the Hermetic Order of the Golden Dawn traces its roots to Rosicrucian sources—the Rosicrucians being an esoteric order (literally, "Fraternity of the Rose Cross") first formed in the early 1600s that espoused the concept of finding enlightenment through occult ritual and magic—it was *The Magus* that was held as a primary source and highly influential to the documents, rituals, and development of the tradition and practices central to the Golden Dawn. The Hermetic Order of the Golden Dawn was a secret organization formed in the late 1800s with the goal of discovering and performing ritualistic magic. Indeed, one of the main points in the development of the Golden Dawn was the practice of some of the rituals and magic listed within *The Magus*. Not surprisingly, some of the rituals and sections in *The Magus* can be found in kabbalistic rituals and more esoteric groups from the late nineteenth century forward. Even with the advent of more opportunities to obtain the original source documents through reprinting and the Internet, the editing and language Barrett applied provided a level of accessibility and understanding that makes *The Magus* a highly inclusive and perhaps the best-known reference to some of the most important works of occult magic and ritual to the modern day.

Context

At the dawn of the nineteenth century, western Europe was still reeling from the effects of years of revolution. Although well within the Romantic era and the Age of Reason, it was a still a time ripe for a work such as *The Magus*: It offered knowledge and opportunities that the earlier Age of Enlightenment had eschewed and that the movement of science and reason would turn away from. In the mid- to late eighteenth century, the role of faith and the divine was losing ground to a more scientific philosophical standpoint. It is important to note the role of religion, and specifically the Christian faith, in the common view of magic at the time: Proponents of reason over tradition and faith did not necessarily treat the concepts of Christianity and the occult as mutually exclusive. Indeed, many aspects of magic required a level of appreciation and belief in the God of the Christian Bible. The role of the devil in magic was one of the great enemy, whose goal was not to promote magic but to prevent humanity from gaining a more complete reconciliation with the soul and, therefore, with God.

The idea of grouping together magic and the church may seem foreign to followers of either magic or established religious paths, but in the eighteenth century and earlier there was slightly more acceptance in certain circles for the concept of melding religion and some forms of magic. Even so, more often than not, the occult had a negative relationship with the church, and, likewise, not all members of the community of magic were fervent believers in Christianity. However, the Age of Reason was nearing its end, and although many texts on magic and the occult were not readily available in the late 1700s, sparks of interest began to appear counter to the popular deism, and more attention began swirling around fringe areas of science and reason (such as alchemy and astrology) that rode the fence between the two camps. It was in this maelstrom of ideas and philosophy that Francis Barrett published *The Magus*.

About the Author

Although few specific and confirmed details exist about Francis Barrett, it is generally agreed that he was born in London, England, sometime between 1770 and 1780. A self-professed alchemist, chemist, and scientist, Barrett was also known as an early pioneer in ballooning, having

Time Line	
1496	■ Peter de Abano prints *The Heptameron*.
1533	■ Cornelius Agrippa publishes *Three Books of Occult Philosophy* in the original Latin.
1651	■ John French translates *Three Books of Occult Philosophy* into English.
1655	■ Robert Turner translates *The Heptameron* into English.
ca. 1770	■ Francis Barrett is born in London, England.
1801	■ Barrett publishes *The Magus*.
1810	■ The French occultist and magician Eliphas Levi is born.
1825	■ Barrett dies.
1870	■ *The Magus* is reprinted by Frederick Hockley.
1888	■ The Hermetic Order of the Golden Dawn is formed.
1974	■ The Mormon historian Dr. Reed Durham releases a medallion worn by Joseph Smith that is later identified as the talisman of Jupiter taken from *The Magus*.

planned and held two events where he attempted to demonstrate balloon flight in front of a crowd of spectators. However, his main interest was in the occult and ritualistic magic. Barrett regularly offered the opportunity for interested students of magic to join him for personalized instruction in natural magic, the kabbalah, and astrology (among other similarly esoteric areas). Specific to ritualistic magic, he provided assistance in reaching the inner soul—a prerequisite for the journey of magic that his pupils would be undertaking. One of the participants from these sessions went on to train the famous French magician Eliphas Levi in the areas of magic. Barrett continued his study and teaching in the areas of natural magic up until his death in 1825.

Explanation and Analysis of the Document

The chosen excerpt from *The Magus* is the "Introduction to the Study of Natural Magic" and the chapter "Of Natural Magic in General: The First Principles of Natural Magic." The introduction lays the foundation for Barrett's concept of ceremonial magic and the importance of God in all aspects of the approach to natural magic. In addition, the role of the stars in the lives of human beings is discussed, seemingly as a way to combat and expose the use of astrology as a tool for soothsaying and determining the impact of the stars and planets on the lives of mortals. To Barrett, humans are created with a microcosm of the universe within themselves. This "inner self" provides a link between the spirit of the human being and the universe and is key to using magic. This inner microcosm gives humans great power; through an acknowledgment of the divine and help from God to focus on the inner self and "tune out" the outer world, people can harness this power (using the rituals and magic discussed) to gain wisdom and knowledge.

The first chapter of *The Magus* deals with a definition of natural magic, that is, magic associated with the forces of nature, the creation of humans in the image of God, the role of magic within the soul, and the role of Satan and sin in the fall of humanity and in keeping human beings from a fuller relationship with God. There are two major concepts being set forth in these excerpts: The first is that people have control over their actions (through free will) and that the greater control one has, the greater is one's ability to connect the inner soul to the outside universe through magic. The second major concept is that God is a vital part of the understanding and use of magic, and this role must be recognized in order for humankind to establish the control needed to perform the spells and rituals discussed.

♦ Introduction to the Study of Natural Magic

From the start of the introduction, Barrett instantly sets a clear signal as to the role of astrology and humanity. Although it was common practice for many to look to the stars and planets as determinates in the actions and experiences of humans, Barrett counters that the heavens do not have the power to go against the gift of free will from God. He argues that the statement that "stars rule men, but a *wise man* rules the stars" is false in two points. First, the actions of humans cannot be determined by celestial bodies if humans have free will; this would place the power of the stars and planets above the God that created them (and humans, whom God imbued with an internal image of himself). Second, the concept that the wise person rules the stars is equally false; instead, Barrett maintains that the wise person has control over his or her *reaction* to events and happenings that might be attributable to the heavens. In this way, free will is demonstrated, and it becomes clear that "a natural wise man is as subject to the slavery of sin as others more ignorant than himself, yet the stars do not incline him to sin." In fact, it is only through the grace of God that the allure of evil can be overcome. Temptation

and sin, therefore, cannot be foisted off as the work of the stars; rather, they are actions of humans themselves. Barrett illustrates his point by quoting Mark 7:21: "Out of the heart of man proceed evil cogitations, murmurs, adulteries, thefts, murders." This development of sin and evil from within man has a direct impact upon the ability to control the inner self; evils of "the heart" negatively affect the soul and spirit, which are vital to the control necessary to gain knowledge through magic. In addition, sin turns man away from God and toward "our spiritual enemy" of the "Infernal Powers."

Having made the point that free will—not the stars and celestial bodies—dictates the actions of the human being, Barrett starts to define more specifically what power the stars, in fact, possess. There are many "great men," Barrett states, who still believe that the stars control not only actions but also more natural occurrences such as illnesses and personal gain or misfortune. Although stars do not control or determine such things, that is not to say that stars do not have other types of power. They, like all things in existence, have a natural connection to each other and possess a power that can be harnessed by humans. While they do not control events, as popular thought at the time suggested, Barrett points out their use as signs of divination to predict naturally occurring events.

Many astrologers of the early nineteenth century (as in the present day) used the stars and planets to determine answers to simple questions, such as the possibility of wealth, power, and the like. In Barrett's opinion, this use of the heavens is well beneath their purpose and is more akin to pandering to the desperate and simple. Furthermore, he suggests that astrologers who use the stars (and therefore God) to answer basic questions of a personal and trivial nature should be regarded as charlatans and frauds. According to Barrett, such people are no more than clowns providing entertainment for money and giving a bad name to those who are more honest and professional in their approach to astrology. Barrett goes into detail about how the deception is developed and presented by the charlatans, comparing their clumsy efforts with the more natural and less humanmade method of magic that Barrett espouses. In this way, he sets up a clear distinction between a common street conjuror and a practitioner of natural magic.

After discussing the common misconception of the causality of the stars over the actions of humans and the role of the stars as agents of divination, Barrett provides more detail to support his claim. Owing to the fact that humanity has been created with an inner microcosm of the universe, which is part of the greater universe as a whole, there is a relationship between the two. What a human does is felt within the universe through the natural connection between the inner and outer universe. Since both are similar in makeup (as Barrett says, "Each mortal creature possesses a Sun and system within himself"), there is a sympathetic harmony between the two made stronger and more perceptive by the similarity. Again, Barrett hastens to point out that this does not mean that although the actions of human beings are perceived by the stars, the action is reciprocal; the stars do not control the evil that humans may do—the ownership of sin is purely the human being's to possess. However, the role of the stars is vital to the work laid out in *The Magus* and must be understood correctly. Barrett takes a jab at both academic approaches to the stars ("the never-ceasing controversies and cavillations of its professors") and to the charlatan astrologers that surrounded his time period ("which we know to be true, without deviation, juggling, fallacy or collusion"). This is an obvious swipe at the main thinkers of the Age of Reason (which Barrett would have been living and suffering through), such as the English mathematician and physicist Sir Isaac Newton, who would give little time to the concept of the occult and mysticism, and also at the common tricksters and parlor-room magicians who gave a bad name to his more "legitimate" approach to magic. He ends this paragraph with a reminder that the role of the true magician is to do right by all who suffer and to do all things for the glory and honor of God. By keeping God uppermost in the mind, proper respect is being paid, and the soul is kept more pure and "right" with the universe, making a stronger connection between the inner universe and the greater outer universe.

The remainder of the introduction is taken up with specific instructions to those who would seek wisdom through magic. Once again, God is vital to the approach and ritual that may be performed, as this positive relationship with God helps center the "student of wisdom" to the correct frame of mind. There follows a prayer to be said prior to beginning, which reiterates the role and power of God in magic and seeking wisdom. There is a call for God to help release the student from the bonds of the mortal flesh and assist him or her in focusing upon the soul and spirit, thereby forming and strengthening the relationship between the soul of the inner universe and the wider universe. What is asked of God for the student is compared to the power and knowledge bestowed upon Solomon, the wise king of Israel, by God in the Old Testament, that with it the magician may be kept with the spirit and soul in focus rather than the earthly temptations and evils of the flesh. Finally, all work done or to be done is given specifically to the glory of God. Following the prayer, Barrett quickly outlines natural magic as a pure magic that has many secrets to be discovered. It is clear that those most successful in uncovering these secrets have not succumbed to temptation or partaken in the sins of the world. The ancient Greek mathematician and philosopher Pythagoras and his followers are held up as the closest to being in tune with the universe and nature through their self-denial of certain foods, emphasis upon silence at times, and general self-denial as a way to separate from the world of the flesh and focus upon the inner world of the soul and spirit. Barrett notes that because Pythagoras and his followers lived centuries before the birth of Jesus, they had no knowledge of Christianity; therefore, while they were capable of attaining great results through their search of the unknown, they were never able to obtain the truer and more pure inspiration bestowed upon the disciples of Jesus Christ. With this final example, Barrett makes

the greatest case for the vital nature of Christianity and magic as co-inhabitants of each individual who wishes to be successful with magic.

♦ Of Natural Magic in General

Barrett begins the first chapter of *The Magus* by defining what natural magic is and what can be gained from its understanding. This form of magic requires an understanding and connection of some degree to all aspects and secrets contained within the created world ("metals, stones, plants and animals"). After creating the world, or macrocosm, God turned to creating humans and the subsequent microcosm. There is an undeniable connection between the two—world and humankind—allowing for a greater understanding of the former. By understanding the specifics of the microcosm, the human being is able to gain a greater understanding of the greater universe and thereby discover the secrets and power hidden within. In order to learn about the macrocosm of the natural world, therefore, it is important to investigate the Creation story in more detail. According to the Creation story in Genesis 1:26, God created humans in his image to rule over all living things. Apart from the Tree of Knowledge, Adam possessed control over all things. The soul of Adam was created by God to be like God, without sin or temptation. However, the enemy of God—the *deceiver*—strove to bring down human beings and pit them against their creator.

Barrett chooses the works of the Belgian chemist and physician Jan Baptist van Helmont (a Catholic) with regard to the philosophy of the fall of the human being and the introduction of fallibility and sin into humanity, as the two men share similar beliefs on the subject. In his *Oraitrike; or, Physick Refined*, van Helmont maintains that the Fall and the subsequent loss of the godlike state that Adam possessed was due first to Adam's choosing to disobey God and partake of the fruit from the Tree of Knowledge but then also (and at great length) to the copulation between and subsequent children of Adam and Eve. The action of reproduction in such a base way creates life separate from the method that would have otherwise involved God directly (which would have resulted in God's creating a more perfect being). Eating the apple created in Adam a desire and lust that had been previously unknown to him and further changed the seed of man to that of a more animalistic and mortal nature.

To Barrett, this transformation in the soul from the desire of sin, as demonstrated in the taking of the apple, to the desire to sin in Adam is a prime example of natural magic and how it works through sympathetic entities toward a change. In this case, by moving Adam and Eve from immortal to animal-like and mortal, the result was severe and permanent. Van Helmont states that this fall from grace caused the "sensitive soul" to leave the body owing to the inability to reside within the mortal, animal body. The Fall also explains the animalistic nature of copulation by men and women as well as the pain of childbirth for the woman. This long section serves to demonstrate an example of natural magic and the role of the soul in this endeavor and also is an answer to Charles Darwin's theory of evolution, as put forward in *On the Origin of Species* (1859). A reprint of *The Magus* was published in 1870, such that Barrett incidentally provided a response to yet another attack upon the beliefs of the mysteries of the occult and magic. In essence, according to van Helmont and Barrett, the human being was created immortal by God and was *transformed* into an animal rather than evolving from an animal.

Barrett concludes the first chapter of *The Magus* with a discussion of Satan and unnatural sex (with supernatural beings). Having both orchestrated and observed the Fall before God, the devil enjoys a short-lived victory of having separated humans from their sensitive soul and therefore from God. Upon realizing that this separation, while permanently altered, will not be permanent in any other way—that is, that eternal life is no longer guaranteed but still attainable—the devil starts to affect and change the mortal world around humans in order to keep them from rejoining with the immortal soul and, instead, to become more base and closer to the sin of the devil. Atheism and heathenism are creations of the devil as temptations and distractors to keep humans from God and a closer union with their own souls. However, discovering that these alone will not suffice, Satan starts to use temptation in the form of lust and eventual cross-breeding of the seed of man with witches or sorceresses in order to create new races of "Faunii, Satyrs, Gnomes, Nymphs, Sylphs, Driades, Hamodriades, Neriads, Mermaids, Syrens, Sphynxes, [and] Monsters." Using some of these creatures to continue mating and entering into marriage with humans, Satan hoped to breed out the human race—at least to a point where reconciliation with God would be all but impossible.

God, seeing these actions taking place, determines to end this abomination by flooding the earth. Barrett defends the existence of these evil species with a last quote from van Helmont, who mentions a discussion with sailors who would periodically find small, dried, human-shaped bodies while traveling among the Canary Islands. Van Helmont considered these to be the bodies of pygmies, which he regarded as the evil offspring from some of the aforementioned breeding engineered by Satan. Barrett includes this continued discussion of the role of sex and sin as a reminder to the initiate of the importance of separating oneself from the mortal and sinful world. Only by focusing on the temptation that Satan worked so hard to create can a magician learn to focus on the inner soul and the necessary link with God.

Audience

While the effect of *The Magus* was impressive for the time in which it was first released, the impact upon the occult revival of the middle to late nineteenth century would not truly be felt until it was reprinted in 1870 by Frederick Hockley. Around this same time, Eliphas Levi, an author and magician who would become highly influential among kabbalists and occult groups in his lifetime and well beyond,

was thought to be learning magic from a former student of Francis Barrett's. There is little doubt of the impact of *The Magus* on Levi as he developed his own philosophy of magic and ritual. Specifically, they shared the belief in the human soul as a miniature copy of the universe that, when linked, is necessary to perform magic. While Barrett had originally written *The Magus* at a time when interest in the unknown was starting to bloom, by the time of the Hockley reprint the hunger for forbidden or secret knowledge was much more pronounced. *The Magus* provided those who wished for it a great wealth of knowledge. Few realized that the majority of the work was unoriginal, and of those who did, fewer cared. These works, which before had been rumored and whispered about for hundreds of years, were now not only available but also translated and edited. Barrett offered an opportunity to possess hundreds of years of writings and philosophy within one book, and with the reprint the opportunity was met with high interest. Since the 1980s, the advances in translation and availability of similarly rare documents have allowed a greater ease of access to previously hard-to-find magic texts (such as those translated by Barrett). However, *The Magus* still enjoys a place of importance among members of occult circles, in part owing to the important nature of the works brought together within one volume. In addition, it is a common text to scholars, based on the historical importance of the work to the rise of interest in the occult from the nineteenth century through to the present.

Impact

The release (and especially the reprinting) of *The Magus* was significant during the rise of interest in the esoteric that took place in the latter decades of the 1800s. While the late nineteenth century saw the emergence of a small number of esoteric movements, the most famous was arguably the Hermetic Order of the Golden Dawn, a group focused on the use of different forms of magic and ritual. One of its more well-known members, Aleister Crowley, was greatly influenced by the works of Levi. Although *The Magus* was available at this time, Levi's more current work—and his ability to speak directly to those interested in the esoteric and occult—made him a larger focus for the magic movement of the late nineteenth and early twentieth centuries. Nevertheless, the concepts and beliefs that fueled Levi's dominance in the field either came directly from or were inspired by Barrett's work and the books that Barrett used in writing and compiling *The Magus*.

There have also been scholarly discussions concerning the possible impact that *The Magus* may have had on Joseph Smith, founder of the Mormon Church. (A medal worn by Joseph Smith was found to have the seal of Jupiter inscribed on it, a talismanic emblem presented in *The Magus*.) Purists at the time and even today may disagree with the value of *The Magus*, citing the blatant plagiarism and unoriginality of the work. However, it cannot be overstated that many of the books included in *The Magus* may

"And as there is in man the power and apprehension of all divination,
and wonderful things, seeing that we have a complete system in ourselves,
therefore are we called the microcosm, or little world; for we carry a heaven in
ourselves from our beginning, for God hath sealed in us the image of himself."

(Section 1)

"By our first declaring the occult qualities and properties that are hid in
the little world, it will serve as a key to the opening of all the treasures
and secrets of the macrocosm, or great world."

(Section 1)

"As the heavens and apprehension of all celestial virtues are scaled by
God in the soul and spirit of man; so when man becomes depraved by
sin and the indulgence of his gross and carnal appetite, he then becomes
the scat of the Infernal Powers, which may be justly deemed a hell; for
then the bodily and fleshly sense obscures the bright purity and thinness
of the spirit, and he becomes the instrument of our spiritual enemy in the
exercise of all infernal lusts and passions."

(Section 1)

"Nevertheless, we do not by these discourses prohibit or deny all influence
to the stars; on the contrary, we affirm there is a natural sympathy and
antipathy amongst all things throughout the whole universe, and this we
shall shew to be displayed through a variety of effects; and likewise that
the stars, as signs, do foreshew great mutations, revolutions, deaths of
great men, governors of provinces, kings, and emperors."

(Section 1)

"The wise ancients knew that in Nature the greatest secrets lay hid, and
wonderful active powers were dormant, unless excited by the vigorous
faculty of the mind of man; but as, in these latter days, men have
themselves almost wholly up to vice and luxury, so their understandings
have become more and more depraved; 'till, being swallowed up in the
gross senses, they become totally unfit for divine contemplations and deep
speculations in Nature."

(Section 1)

not have ever become available to the general public were it not for the efforts of Francis Barrett. The ability to offer such a collection not only fed the rising occult movement of the late nineteenth century but also helped ensure that it would continue well into the twentieth century and beyond.

Further Reading

■ Books

Godwin, Joscelyn. *The Theosophical Enlightenment*. New York: State University of New York Press, 1994.

Lewis, James R. *Satanism Today: An Encyclopedia of Religion, Folklore, and Popular Culture*. Santa Barbara, Calif.: ABC-CLIO, 2001.

Quinn, D. *Early Mormonism and the Magic World View*. Rev. ed. Salt Lake City, Utah: Signature Books, 1998.

Regardie, Israel. *The Golden Dawn*. St. Paul, Minn.: Llewellyn Publications, 1982.

Regardie, Israel, et al., eds. *The Golden Dawn: A Complete Course in Practical Ceremonial Magic*. St. Paul, Minn.: Llewellyn Publications, 1989.

van Helmont, Jan Baptist. *Oriatrike; or, Physick Refined*. London: L. Loyd, 1662.

◆ Web Site

Aho, Barbara. "The Nineteenth Century Occult Revival." Watch unto Prayer Web site. http://watch.pair.com/occult.html

Warnock, Christopher. "Francis Barrett." Renaissance Astrology Web site. http://www.renaissanceastrology.com/barrett.html

—Commentary by Jason Driver

Questions for Further Study

1. Each generation produces individuals, texts, secret societies, and philosophies having to do with magic, mysticism, occultism, and the like. What in your opinion has been the continuing appeal of magic and occult practices for some people throughout the centuries?

2. In what ways did *The Magus* represent a reaction to the Age of Reason of the eighteenth century? How do later books such as Gerald Gardner's *Book of Shadows* represent a reaction against science and rational thought?

3. To what extent does the "natural magic" of *The Magus* resemble the emphasis on the inner self reflected in Hindu and Buddhist documents such as the Noble Eightfold Path or the Vishnu Purana? In what ways does it anticipate the humanist movement as reflected in the Humanist Manifesto?

4. "Magic" and "religion" would seem in many ways to be antithetical (although some people might disagree). In what sense is *The Magus* a "milestone" document in *religious* history?

5. What do you think Barrett's reaction would be to the horoscopes routinely printed in daily newspapers, to modern "magicians" such as David Copperfield, or to people who claim to have psychic powers?

The Magus: Document Text

1801 CE

—*Francis Barrett*

Introduction to the Study of Natural Magic

♦ Of the Influences of the Stars

IT has been a subject of ancient dispute whether or not the stars, as second causes, do so rule and influence man as to ingraft in his nature certain passions, virtues, propensities, &c., and this to take root in him at the very critical moment of his being born into this vale of misery and wretchedness; likewise, if their site and configuration at this time do shew forth his future passions and pursuits; and by their revolutions, transits, and directed aspects, they point out the particular accidents of the body, marriage, sickness, preferments, and such like; the which I have often revolved in my mind for many years past, having been at all times in all places a warm advocate for stellary divination or astrology: therefore in this place it is highly necessary that we examine how far this influence extends to man, seeing that I fully admit that man is endowed with a free-will from God, which the stars can in no wise counteract. And as there is in man the power and apprehension of all divination, and wonderful things, seeing that we have a complete system in ourselves, therefore are we called the microcosm, or little world; for we carry a heaven in ourselves from our beginning, for God hath sealed in us the image of himself; and of all created beings we are the epitome, therefore we must be careful, lest we confound and mix one thing with another. Nevertheless, man, as a pattern of the great world, sympathizes with it according to the stars, which, agreeably to the Holy Scriptures, are set for times and seasons, and not as causes of this or that evil, which may pervade kingdoms or private families, although they do in some measure foreshew them, yet they are in no wise the cause; therefore I conceive in a wide different sense to what is generally understood that "Stars rule men, but a *wise man* rules the stars:" to which I answer, that the stars do not rule men, according to the vulgar and received opinion; as if the stars should stir up men to murders, seditions, broils, lusts, fornications, adulteries, drunkenness, &c., which the common astrologers hold forth as sound and true doctrine; because, they say, Mars and Saturn, being conjunct,

do this and much more, and many other configurations and afflictions of the two great infortunes (*as they are termed*), when the benevolent planets Jupiter, Venus, and Sol, happen to be detrimented or afflicted; therefore, then, they say men influenced by them are most surely excited to the commission of the vices before named; yet a wise man may, by the liberty of his own free-will, make those affections and inclinations void, and this they call "To rule the stars;" but let them know, according to the sense here understood, first, it is not in a wise man to resist evil inclinations, but of the grace of God, and we call none wise but such as are endued with grace; for, as we have said before, all natural wisdom from the hands of man is foolishness in the sight of God; which was not before understood to be a wise man fenced with grace; for why should he rule the stars, who has not any occasion to fear conquered inclinations?—therefore a natural wise man is as subject to the slavery of sin as others more ignorant than himself, yet the stars do not incline him to sin. God created the heavens without spot, and pronounced them good, therefore it is the greatest absurdity to suppose the stars, by a continual inclining of us to this or that misdeed, should be our tempters, which we eventually make them, if we admit they cause inclinations; but know that it is not from without, but within, by sin, that evil inclinations do arise: according to the Scriptures, "Out of the heart of man proceed evil cogitations, murmurs, adulteries, thefts, murders, &c." Because, as the heavens and apprehension of all celestial virtues are scaled by God in the soul and spirit of man; so when man becomes depraved by sin and the indulgence of his gross and carnal appetite, he then becomes the scat of the Infernal Powers, which may be justly deemed a hell; for then the bodily and fleshly sense obscures the bright purity and thinness of the spirit, and he becomes the instrument of our spiritual enemy in the exercise of all infernal lusts and passions.

Therefore it is most necessary for us to know that we are to beware of granting or believing any effects from the influences of the stars more than they have naturally; because there are many whom I have lately conversed with, and great men, too, in this nation, who readily affirm that the *stars* are the causes of any kinds of diseases, inclinations, and fortunes; likewise that they blame the stars for all their misconduct and misfortunes.

Nevertheless, we do not by these discourses prohibit or deny all influence to the stars; on the contrary, we affirm there is a natural sympathy and antipathy amongst all things throughout the whole universe, and this we shall shew to be displayed through a variety of effects; and likewise that the stars, as signs, do foreshew great mutations, revolutions, deaths of great men, governors of provinces, kings, and emperors; likewise the weather, tempests, earthquakes, deluges, &c.; and this according to the law of Providence. The lots of all men do stand in the hands of the Lord, for he is the end and beginning of all things; he can remove crowns and sceptres, and displace the most cautious arrangements and councils of man, who, when he thinks himself most secure, tumbles headlong from the seat of power, and lies grovelling in the dust.

Therefore our astrologers in most of their speculations seek without a light, for they conceive every thing may be known or read in the stars; if an odd silver spoon is but lost, the innocent stars are obliged to give an account of it; if an old maiden loses a favourite puppy, away she goes to an oracle of divination for information of the whelp. Oh! vile credulity, to think that those celestial bodies take cognizance of, and give in their configurations and aspects, continual information of the lowest and vilest transactions of dotards, the most trivial and frivolous questions that are *pretended* to be resolved by an inspection into the figure of the heavens. Well does our legislature justly condemn as juggling impostors all those idle vagabonds who infest various parts of this metropolis, and impose upon the simple and unsuspecting, by answering, for a shilling or half-crown fee, whatever thing or circumstance may be proposed to them, as if they were God's vicegerents on earth, and his deputed privy counsellors.

They do not even scruple ever to persuade poor mortals of the lower class, that they shew images in glasses, as if they actually confederated with evil spirits: a notable instance I will here recite, that happened very lately in this city. Two penurious Frenchmen, taking advantage of the credulity of the common people, who are continually gaping after such toys, had so contrived a telescope or optic glass as that various letters and figures should be reflected in an obscure manner, shewing the images of men and women, &c.; so that when any one came to consult these jugglers, after paying the usual fee, they, according to the urgency of the query, produced answers by those figures or letters; the which affrights the inspector into the glass so much, that he or she supposes they have got some devilish thing or other in hand, by which they remain under the full conviction of having actually beheld the parties they wished to see, though perhaps they may at the same time be residing many hundreds of miles distance therefrom; they, having received this impression from a pre-conceived idea of seeing the image of their friend in this optical machine, go away, and anon report, with an addition of ten hundred lies, that they have been witness of a miracle. I say this kind of deception is only to be acted with the vulgar, who, rather than have their imaginations balked, would swallow the most abominable lies and conceits. For instance, who would suppose that any rational being could be persuaded that a fellow-creature of proper size and stature should be able by any means to thrust his body into a quart bottle?—the which thing was advertised to the public by a merry knave (not thinking there were such fools in existence), to be done by him in a public theatre. Upwards of 600 persons were assembled to behold the transaction, never doubting but the fellow meant to keep his word, when to the great mortification and disgrace of this long-headed audience, the conjuror came forth amidst a general stir and buz of "Ay, now! see! now! see! he is just going to jump in."—"Indeed," says the conjuror, "ladies and gentlemen, I am not; for if you were such fools as to believe such an absurdity, I am not wise enough to do it:"—therefore, making his bow, he disappeared, to the great discomfort of these wiseheads, who straightway withdrew in the best manner they could.

As for the telescope magicians, they were taken into custody by the gentlemen of the police office, in Bow Street; nor would their familiar do them the kindness to attempt their rescue.

But to have done with these things that are unworthy our notice as philosophers, and to proceed to matters of a higher nature: it is to be noted what we have before said, in respect of the influences of the stars, that Ptolemy, in his quadrapartite, in speaking of *generals*, comes pretty near our ideas on the subject of planetary influence, of which we did not at any time doubt, but do not admit (nay, it is not necessary, seeing there is an astrology in Nature), that each action of our life, our afflictions, fortunes, accidents, are deducible to the influential effects of the planets: they proceed from ourselves; but I admit that our thoughts, actions, cogitations, sympathize with the stars upon the principle of general sympathy. Again, there is a much stronger sympathy between persons of like constitution and temperament, for each mortal creature possesses a Sun and system within himself; therefore, according to universal sympathy, we are affected by the general influence or universal spirit of the world, as the vital principle throughout the universe: therefore we are not to look into the configurations of the stars for the cause or incitement of men's bestial inclinations, for brutes have their specifical inclinations from the propagation of their principle by seed, not by the sign of the horoscope; therefore as man is oftentimes capable of the actions and excesses of brutes, they cannot happen to a man naturally from any other source than the seminal being infused in his composition; for seeing likewise that the soul is immortal, and endued with free-will, which acts upon the body, the soul cannot be inclined by any configuration of the stars either to good or evil; but from its own immortal power of willingly being seduced by sin, it prompts to evil; but enlightened by God, it springs to good, on either principle, according to its tendency, the soul feeds while in this frail body; but what further concerns the soul of man in this, and after this, we shall fully investigate the natural magic of the soul, in which we have fully treated every point of enquiry that has been suggested to us by our own imagination, and by scientific experiments have proved its divine virtue originally scaled therein by the Author of its being.

Sufficient it is to return to our subject relative to astrology, especially to know what part of it is necessary for our use, of which we will select that which is pure and to our purpose, for the understanding and effecting of various experiments in the course of our works, leaving the tedious calculation of nativities, the never-ceasing controversies and cavillations of its professors, the dissensions which arise from the various modes of practice; all which we leave to the figure-casting plodder, telling him, by-the-by, that whatever he thinks he can foreshew by inspecting the horoscope of a nativity, by long, tedious, and night-wearied studies and contemplations; I say, whatever he can shew respecting personal or national mutations, changes, accidents, &c. &c., all this we know by a much easier and readier method; and can more comprehensively, clearly, and intelligibly, shew and point out, to the very letter, by our Cabal, which we know to be true, without deviation, juggling, fallacy, or collusion, or any kind of deceit

or imposture whatsoever; which Cabal or spiritual astrology we draw from the Fountain of Knowledge, in all simplicity, humility, and truth; and we boast not of ourselves, but of Him who teaches us through his divine mercy, by the light of whose favour we see into things spiritual and divine: in the possession of which we are secure amidst the severest storms of hatred, malice, pride, envy, hypocrisy, levity, bonds, poverty, imprisonment, or any other outward circumstance; we should still be rich, want nothing, be fed with delicious meats, and enjoy plentifully all good things necessary for our support: all this we do not vainly boast of, as figurative, ideal, or chimerical; but real, solid, and everlasting, in the which we exult and delight, and praise his name forever and ever: Amen.

All which we publicly declare to the world for the honour of our God, being at all times ready to do every kindness we can to our poor neighbour, and, as far as in us lies, to comfort him, sick or afflicted; in doing which we ask no reward: it is sufficient to us that we can do it, and that we may be acceptable to Him who says—"I am the light of the world; to whom with the Father, and Holy Spirit, be ascribed all power, might, majesty, and dominion: Amen."

To the faithful and discreet Student of Wisdom.
Greeting:

TAKE our instructions; in all things ask counsel of God, and he will give it; offer up the following prayer daily for the illumination of thy understanding: depend for all things on God, the first cause; with whom, by whom, and in whom, are all things: see thy first care be to know thyself; and then in humility direct thy prayer as follows.

A Prayer or Oration to God.

ALMIGHTY and most merciful God, we thy servants approach with fear and trembling before thee, and in all humility do most heartily beseech thee to pardon our manifold and blind transgressions, by us committed at any time; and grant, O, most merciful Father, for his sake who died upon the cross, that our minds may be enlightened with the divine radiance of thy holy wisdom; for seeing, O, Lord of might, power, majesty, and dominion, that, by reason of our gross and material bodies, we are scarce apt to receive those spiritual instructions that we so earnestly and heartily desire. Open, O, blessed Spirit, the spiritual eye of our soul, that we may be released from this darkness overspreading us by the delusions of the outward senses, and may perceive and understand those things which are spiritual. We pray thee, oh, Lord, above all to strengthen our souls and bodies against our spiritual enemies, by the blood and righteousness of our blessed Redeemer, thy Son, Jesus Christ; and through him, and in his name, we beseech thee to illuminate the faculties of our souls, so that we may clearly and comprehensively hear with our ears, and understand with our hearts; and remove far from us all hypocrisy, deceitful dealing, profaneness, inconstancy, and levity; so that we may, in word and act, become thy faithful servants, and stand firm and unshaken against all the attacks of our bodily enemies, and likewise be proof against all illusions of evil spirits, with whom we desire no communication or interest; but that we may be instructed in the knowledge of things, natural and celestial: and as it pleased thee to bestow on Solomon all wisdom, both human and divine; in the desire of which knowledge he did so please thy divine majesty, that in a dream, of one night, thou didst inspire him with all wisdom and knowledge, which he did wisely prefer before the riches of this life; so may our desire and prayer be graciously accepted by thee; so that, by a firm dependence on thy word, we may not be led away by the vain and ridiculous pursuits of worldly pleasures and delights, they not being durable, nor of any account to our immortal happiness. Grant us, Lord, power and strength of intellect to carry on this work, for the honour and glory of thy holy name, and to the comfort of our neighbour; and without design of hurt or detriment to any, we may proceed in our labours, through Jesus Christ, our Redeemer: Amen....

♦ **Of Natural Magic in General**

BEFORE we proceed to particulars, it will not be amis to speak of generals; therefore, as an elucidation, we shall briefly show what sciences we comprehend under the title of Natural Magic; and to hasten to the point, we shall regularly proceed from theory to practice; therefore, Natural Magic undoubtedly comprehends a knowledge of all Nature, which we by no means can arrive at but by searching deeply into her treasury, which is inexhaustible; we therefore by long study, labour, and practice, have found out many valuable secrets and experiments, which are either unknown, or are buried in the ignorant knowledge of the present age. The wise ancients knew that in Nature the greatest secrets lay hid, and wonderful active powers were dormant, unless excited by the vigorous faculty of the mind of man; but as, in these latter days, men have themselves almost wholly up to

vice and luxury, so their understandings have become more and more depraved; 'till, being swallowed up in the gross senses, they become totally unfit for divine contemplations and deep speculations in Nature; their intellectual faculty being drowned in obscurity and dulness, by reason of their sloth, intemperance, or sensual appetites. The followers of Pythagoras enjoined silence, and forbade the eating of the flesh of animals; the first, because they were cautious, and aware of the vanity of vain babbling and fruitless cavillations: they studied the power of numbers to the highest extent; they forbade the eating of flesh not so much on the score of transmigration, as to keep the body in a healthful and temperate state, free from gross humours; by these means they qualified themselves for spiritual matters, and attained unto great and excellent mysteries, and continued in the exercise of charitable arts, and the practice of all moral virtues: yet, seeing they were heathens, they attained not unto the high and inspired lights of wisdom and knowledge that were bestowed on the Apostles, and others, after the coming of Christ; but they mortified their lusts, lived temperately, chaste, honest, and virtuous; which government is so contrary to the practice of modern Christians, that they live as if the blessed word had come upon the earth to grant them privilege to sin. However, we will leave Pythagoras and his followers, to hasten to our own work; whereof we will first explain the foundation of Natural Magic, in as clear and intelligible a manner as the same can be done.

The First Principles of Natural Magic

♦ **Natural Magic Defined—Of Man—His Creation—Divine Image—And of the Spiritual and Magical Virtue of the Soul**

NATURAL MAGIC is, as we have said, a comprehensive knowledge of all Nature, by which we search out her secret and occult operations throughout her vast and spacious elaboratory; whereby we come to a knowledge of the component parts, qualities, virtues, and secrets of metals, stones, plants, and animals; but seeing, in the regular order of the creation, man was the work of the sixth day, every thing being prepared for his vicegerency here on earth, and that it pleased the omnipotent God, after he had formed the great world, or macrocosm, and pronounced it good, so he created man the express image of himself; and in man, likewise, an exact model of the great world. We shall describe the wonderful properties of man, in which we may trace in miniature the exact resemblance or copy of the universe; by which means we shall come to the more easy understanding of whatever we may have to declare concerning the knowledge of the inferior nature, such as animals, plants, metals, and stones; for, by our first declaring the occult qualities and properties that are hid in the little world, it will serve as a key to the opening of all the treasures and secrets of the macrocosm, or great world: therefore, we shall hasten to speak of the creation of man, and his divine image; likewise of his fall, in consequence of his disobedience; by which all the train of evils, plagues, diseases, and miseries, were entailed upon his posterity, through the curse of our Creator, but deprecated by the mediation of our blessed Lord, Christ.

The Creation, Disobedience, and Fall of Man

ACCORDING to the word of God, which we take in all things for our guide, in the 1st chapter of Genesis, and the 26th verse, it is said—"God said, let us make man in our image, after our likeness; and let them have dominion over the fish of the sea, and over the fowl of the air, and over the cattle, and over *all the* earth, and over every creeping thing that creepeth upon the earth."—Here is the origin and beginning of our frail human nature; hence every soul was created by the very light itself, and Fountain of Life, after his own express image, likewise immortal, in a beautiful and well-formed body, endued with a most excellent mind, and dominion or unlimited monarchy over all Nature, every thing being subjected to his rule, or command; one creature only being excepted, which was to remain untouched and consecrated, as it were, to the divine mandate: "Of every tree of the garden thou mayest freely eat; But of the tree of the knowledge of good and evil, thou shalt not eat of it; for in the day that thou eatest of it, thou shalt surely die." Gen. ii. ver. 16. Therefore Adam was formed by the finger of God, which is the Holy Spirit; whose figure or outward form was beautiful and proportionate as an angel; in whose voice (before he sinned) every sound was the sweetness of harmony and music: had he remained in the state of innocency in which he was formed, the weakness of mortal man, in his depraved state, would not have been able to bear the virtue and celestial shrillness of his voice. But when the *deceiver* found that man, from the inspiration of God, had began to sing so

shrilly, and to repeat the celestial harmony of the heavenly country, he counterfeited the engines of craft: seeing his wrath against him was in vain, he was much tormented thereby, and began to think how he might entangle him into disobedience of the command of his Creator, whereby he might, as it were, laugh him to scorn, in derision of his new creature, man.

Van Helmont, in his Oriatrike, chap. xcii., speaking of the entrance of death into human nature, &c., finely touches the subject of the creation, and man's disobedience: indeed, his ideas so perfectly coincide with my own, that I have thought fit here to transcribe his philosophy, which so clearly explains the text of Scripture, with so much of the light of truth on his side, that it carries along with it the surest and most positive conviction.

"Man being essentially created after the image of God, after that, he rashly presumed to generate the image of God out of himself; not, indeed, by a certain monster, but by something which was shadowly like himself. With the ravishment of Eve, he, indeed, generated not the image God like unto that which God would have inimitable, as being divine; but in the vital air of the seed he generated dispositions; careful at some time to receive a sensitive, discursive, and motive soul from the Father of Light, yet *mortal*, and *to perish*; yet, nevertheless, he ordinarily inspires, and of his own goodness, the substantial spirit of a mind showing forth his own image: so that man, in this respect, endeavoured to generate his own image; not after the manner of brute beasts, but by the copulation of seeds, which at length should obtain, by request, a soulified light from the Creator; and the which they call a sensitive soul.

"For, from thence hath proceeded another generation, conceived after a beast-like manner, mortal, and uncapable of eternal life, after the manner of beasts; and bringing forth with pains, and subject to diseases, and death; and so much the more sorrowful, and full of misery, by how much that very propagation in our first parents dared to invert the intent of God.

"Therefore the unutterable goodness forewarned them that they should not taste of that tree; and otherwise he foretold, that the same day they should die the death, and should feel all the root of calamities which accompanies death."

Deservedly, therefore, hath the Lord deprived both our parents of the benefit of immortality; namely, death succeeded from a conjugal and brutal copulation; neither remained the spirit of the Lord with man, after that he began to be flesh.

Further; because that defilement of Eve shall thenceforth be continued in the propagation of posterity, even unto the end of the world, from hence the sin of the despised fatherly admonition, and natural deviation from the right way, is now among other sins for an impurity, from an inverted, carnal, and well nigh brutish generation, and is truly called original sin; that is, man being sowed in the pleasure of the concupiscence of the flesh, shall therefore always reap a necessary death in the flesh of sin; but, the knowledge of good and evil, which God placed in the dissuaded apple, did contain in it a seminary virtue of the concupiscence of the flesh, that is, an occult forbidden conjunction, diametrically opposite to the state of innocence, which state was not a state of stupidity; because He was he unto whom, before the corruption of Nature, the essences of all living creatures whatsoever were made known, according to which they were to be named from their property, and at their first sight to be essentially distinguished: *man*, therefore, through eating of the apple, attained a knowledge that he had lost his radical innocency; for, neither before the eating of the apple was he so dull or stupified that he knew not, or did not perceive himself naked; but, with the effect of shame and brutal concupiscence, he then first declared he was naked.

For that the knowledge of good and evil signifies nothing but the concupiscence of the flesh, the Apostle testifies; calling it the law, and desire of sin. For it pleased the Lord of heaven and earth to insert in the apple an incentive to concupiscence; by which he was able safely to abstain, by not eating of the apple, therefore dissuaded therefrom; for otherwise he had never at any time been tempted, or stirred up by his genital members. Therefore the apple being eaten, man, from an occult and natural property ingrafted in the fruit, conceived a lust, and sin became luxurious to him, and from thence was made an animal seed, which, hastening into the previous or foregoing dispositions of a *sensitive soul*, and undergoing the law of other *causes*, reflected itself into the vital spirit of Adam; and, like an ignis-fatuus, presently receiving an archeus or ruling spirit, and animal idea, it presently conceived a power of propagating an animal and mortal seed, ending into life.

Furthermore, the sacred text hath in many places compelled me unto a perfect position, it making Eve an helper like unto Adam; not, indeed, that she should supply the *name*, and *room of a wife*, even as she is called, straightway after sin, for she was a virgin in the intent of the Creator, and afterwards filled with misery: but not, as long as the state of purity presided over innocency, did the will of man overcome her; for the translation of man into Paradise did foreshew another condition of living than that of a beast; and therefore the eating of the apple doth by a most chaste name cover the concupiscence of the *flesh*, while it contains the "knowledge of good and evil" in this name, and calls the ignorance thereof the state of innocence: for, surely, the attainment of that aforesaid knowledge did nourish a most hurtful death, and an irrevocable deprivation of eternal life: for if man had not tasted the apple, he had lived void of concupiscence, and offsprings had appeared out of Eve (a virgin) from the Holy Spirit.

But the apple being eaten, "presently their eyes were opened," and Adam began lustfully to covet copulation with the naked virgin, and defiled her, the which God had appointed for a naked help unto him. But man prevented the intention of God by a strange generation in the flesh of sin; whereupon there followed the corruption of the former nature, or the flesh of sin, accompanied by concupiscence: neither doth the text insinuate any other mark of "*the knowledge of good and evil*," than that they "*knew themselves to be naked*," or, speaking properly, of their virginity being corrupted, polluted with bestial lust, and defiled. Indeed, their whole "knowledge of good and evil" is included in their shame within their privy parts alone; and therefore in the 8th of Leviticus, and many places else in the Holy Scriptures, the privy parts themselves are called by no other etymology than that of shame; for from the copulation of the flesh their eyes were opened, because they then knew that the good being lost, had brought on them a degenerate nature, shamefulness, an intestine and inevitable obligation of death; sent also into their posterity. Alas! too late, indeed they understood, by the unwonted novelty and shamefulness of their concupiscence, why God had so lovingly forbade the eating of the apple. Indeed, the truth being agreeable unto itself, doth attest the filthiness of impure Adamical generation; for the impurity which had received a contagion from any natural issues whatsoever of menstrues or seed, and that by its touching alone is reckoned equal to that which should by degrees creep on a person from a co-touching of dead carcases, and to be expiated by the same ceremonious rite that the text might agreeably denote, that death began by the concupiscence of the flesh lying hid in the fruit forbidden; therefore, also, the one only healing medicine, of so great an impurity contracted by touching, consisted in washing: under the similitude or likeness thereof, faith and hope, which in baptism are poured on us, are strengthened.

For as soon as Adam knew that by fratricide the first born of mortals, whom he had begotten in the concupiscence of the flesh, had killed his brother, guiltless and righteous as he was; and foreseeing the wicked errors of mortals that would come from thence, he likewise perceived his own miseries in himself; certainly knowing that all these calamities had happened unto him from the sin of concupiscence drawn from the apple, which were unavoidably issuing on his posterity, he thought within himself that the most discreet thing he could do, was hereafter wholly to abstain from his wife, whom he had violated; and therefore he mourned, in chastity and sorrow, a full hundred years; hoping that by the merit of that abstinence, and by an opposition to the concupiscence of the flesh, he should not only appease the wrath of the incensed Deity, but that he should again return into the former splendour and majesty of his primitive *innocence* and *purity*. But the repentance of one age being finished, it is most probable the mystery of Christ's incarnation was revealed unto him; neither that man ever could hope to return to the brightness of his ancient purity by his own strength, and much less that himself could reprieve his posterity from death; and that, therefore, marriage was well pleasing, and was after the fall indulged unto him by God because he had determined thus to satisfy his justice at the fulness of times, which should, to the glory of his own *name*, and the confusion of Satan, elevate mankind to a more sublime and eminent state of blessedness.

From that time Adam began to know his wife, *viz.* after he was an hundred years old, and to fill the earth, by multiplying according to the blessing once given him, and the law enjoined him—"Be fruitful and multiply."—Yet so, nevertheless, that although matrimony, by reason of the great want of propagation, and otherwise impossible coursary succession of the primitive divine generation, be admitted as a sacrament of the faithful.

If, therefore, both our first parents, after the eating of the apple, were ashamed, they covered only their privy parts; therefore that shame doth presuppose, and accuse of something committed against justice—against the intent of the Creator—and against their own proper nature: by consequence, therefore, that Adamical generation was not of the primitive constitution of their nature, as neither of the original intent of the Creator; therefore, when God foretels that the earth shall bring forth thistles

and thorns, and that man shall gain his bread by the sweat of his brow, they were not execrations, but admonitions, that those sort of things should be obvious in the earth: and, because that beasts should bring forth in pain—should plow in sweat—should eat their food with labour and fear, that the earth should likewise bring forth very many things besides the intention of the husbandman; therefore, also, that they ought to be nourished like unto brute beasts, who had begun to generate after the manner of brute beasts.

It is likewise told Eve, after her transgression, that she should bring forth in pain. Therefore, what hath the pain of bringing forth common with the eating of the apple, unless the apple had operated about the concupiscence of the flesh, and by consequence stirred up copulation; and the Creator had intended to dissuade it, by dehorting from the eating of the apple. For, why are the genital members of women punished with pains at child-birth, if the eye in seeing the apple, the hands in cropping it, and the mouth in eating of it, have offended? for was it not sufficient to have chastised the life with death, and the health with very many diseases?—Moreover, why is the womb afflicted, as in brutes, with the manner of bringing forth, if the conception granted to beasts were not forbidden to man?

After their fall, therefore, *their eyes were opened, and they were ashamed*: it denotes and signifies that, from the filthiness of concupiscence, they knew that the copulation of the flesh was forbidden in the most pure innocent chastity of nature, and that they were overspread with shame, when, their eyes being opened, their understandings saw that they had committed filthiness most detestable.

But on the serpent and evil spirit alone was the top and summit of the whole curse, even as the privilege of the woman, and the mysterious prerogative of the blessing upon the earth, *viz.* That the woman's seed should bruise the head of the serpent. So that it is not possible that to *bring forth in pain* should be a curse; for truly with the same voice of the Lord is pronounced the blessing of the woman, and victory over the infernal spirit.

Therefore Adam was created in the possession of immortality. God intended not that man should be an *animal* or *sensitive* creature, nor be born, conceived, or live as an animal; for of truth he was created unto a *living soul*, and that after the true image of God; therefore he as far differed from the nature of an animal, as an immortal being from a mortal, and as a God-like creature from a brute.

I am sorry that our school-men, many of them, wish, by their arguments of noise and pride, to draw man into a total animal nature (nothing more), drawing (by their logic) the essence of a man essentially from an animal nature: because, although man afterwards procured death to himself and posterity, and therefore may seem to be made nearer the nature of animal creatures, yet it stood not in his power to be able to pervert the species of the divine image: even so as neither was the evil spirit, of a spirit, made an animal, although he became nearer unto the nature of an animal, by hatred and brutal vices. Therefore man remained in his own species wherein he was created; for as often as man is called an animal, or sensitive living creature, and is in earnest thought to be such, so many times the text is falsified which says, "But the serpent was more crafty than all the living creatures of the earth, which the Lord God had made;" because he speaks of the natural craft and subtilty of that living and creeping animal. Again, if the position be true, man was not directed into the propagation of *seed* or *flesh*, neither did he aspire unto a sensitive soul; and therefore the sensible soul of Adamical generation is not of a brutal species, because it was raised up by a seed which wanted the original ordination and limitation of any species; and so that, as the *sensitive soul* in man arose, besides the intent of the Creator and Nature; so it is of no brutal species, neither can it subsist, unless it be continually tied to the *mind*, from whence it is supported in its life.

Wherefore, while man is of no brutal species, he cannot be an animal in respect to his mind, and much less in respect to his soul, which is of no species.

Therefore know, that neither evil spirit, nor whole nature also, can, by any means or any way whatever, change the essence given unto man from his Creator, and by his foreknowledge determined that he should remain continually such as he was created, although he, in the mean time, hath clothed himself with strange properties, as natural unto him from the vice of his own will; for as it is an absurdity to reckon man glorified among animals, because he is not without sense or feeling, so to be sensitive does not shew the inseparable essence of an animal.

Seeing, therefore, our first parents had both of them now felt the effect throughout their whole bodies of the eating, of the apple, or concupiscence of the flesh in their members in Paradise, it shamed them; because their members, which, before, they could rule at their pleasure, were afterwards moved by a proper incentive to lust.

Therefore, on the same clay, not only mortality entered through concupiscence, but it presently after entered into a conceived generation; for which they were, the same day, also driven out of Paradise: hence followed an adulterous, lascivious, beast-like, devilish generation, and plainly incapable of entering into the kingdom of God, diametrically opposite to God's ordination by which means death, and the threatened punishment, *corruption*, became inseparable to man and his posterity, Therefore, original sin was effectively bred from the concupiscence of the flesh, but occasioned only by the apple being eaten, and the admonition despised: but the stimulative to concupiscence was placed in the dissuaded tree, and that occult lustful property radically inserted and implanted in it. But when Satan (besides his *hope*, and the deflowering of the virgin, nothing hindering of it) saw that man was not taken out of the way, according to the forewarning (for he knew not that the *Son of God* had constituted himself a surety, before the Father, for man) he, indeed, looked at the vile, corrupted, and degenerated nature of man, and saw that a power was withdrawn from him of uniting himself to the God of infinite majesty, and began greatly to rejoice. That joy was of short duration, for, by and by, he likewise knew that marriage was ratified by Heaven—that the divine goodness yet inclined to man—and that Satan's own fallacies and deceits were thus deceived: hence conjecturing that the Son of God was to restore every defect of contagion, and, therefore, perhaps, to be incarnated. He then put himself to work how, or in what manner, he should defile the stock that was to be raised up by matrimony with a mortal soul, so that he might render every conception of God in vain: therefore he stirred up not only his fratricides, and notoriously wicked persons, that there might be evil abounding at all times; but he procured that Atheism might arise, and that, together with Heathenism, it might daily increase, whereby indeed, if he could not hinder the co-knitting of the immortal mind with the sensitive soul, he might, at least, by destroying the law of Nature, bring man unto a level with himself under infernal punishment: but his special care and desire was to expunge totally the immortal mind out of the stock of posterity.

Therefore he (*the Devil*) stirs up, to this day, detestable copulations in Atheistical libertines: but he saw from thence, that nothing but brutish or savage monsters proceeded, to be abhorred by the very parents themselves; and that the copulation with women was far more plausible to men; and that by this method the generation of men should constantly continue; for he endeavoured to prevent the hope of restoring a remnant, that is, to hinder the incarnation of the Son of God; therefore he attempted, by an application of active things, to frame the seed of man according to his own accursed desire; which, when he had found vain and impossible for him to do, he tried again whether an imp or witch might not be fructified by sodomy; and when this did not fully answer his intentions every way, and he saw that of an ass and a horse a mule was bred, which was nearer a-kin to his mother than his father; likewise that of a coney and dormouse being the father, a true coney was bred, being distinct from his mother, only having a tail like the dormouse; he declined these feats, and betook himself to others worthy, indeed, only of the subtile craft of the *Prince of Darkness*.

Therefore Satan instituted a connexion of the seed of man with the seed and in the womb of a junior witch, or sorceress, that he might exclude the dispositions unto an immortal mind from such a new, polished conception: and afterwards came forth an adulterous and lascivious generation of Faunii, Satyrs, Gnomes, Nymphs, Sylphs, Driades, Hamodriades, Neriads, Mermaids, Syrens, Sphynxes, Monsters, &c., using the constellations, and disposing the seed of man for such like monstrous prodigious generations.

And, seeing the Faunii and Nymphs of the woods were preferred before the others in beauty, they afterwards generated their offspring amongst themselves, and at length began wedlocks with men, feigning that, by these copulations, they should obtain an immortal soul for them and their offspring; but this happened through the persuasions and delusions of Satan to admit these monsters to carnal copulation, which the ignorant were easily persuaded to and therefore

these Nymphs are called Succubii: although Satan afterwards committed worse, frequently transchanging himself, by assuming the persons of both Incubii and Succubii, in both sexes; but they conceived not a true young by the males, except the Nymphs alone. The which, indeed, seeing the sons of God (that is, men) had now, without distinction, and in many places, taken to be their wives, God was determined to blot out the whole race begotten by these infernal and detestable marriages, through a deluge of waters, that the intent of the evil spirit might be rendered frustrate.

Of which monsters before mentioned, I will here give a striking example from Helmont: for he says, a merchant of Ægina, a countryman of his, sailing various times unto the Canaries, was asked by Helmont for his serious judgment about certain creatures, which the mariners frequently brought home from the mountains, as often as they went, and called them Tude-squils; for they were dried dead carcasses, almost three-footed, and so small that a boy might easily carry one of them upon the palm of his hand, and they were of an exact human shape; but their whole dead carcass was clear or transparent as any parchment, and their bones flexible like gristles; against the sun, also, their bowels and intestine were plainly to be seen; which thing I, by Spaniards there born, knew to be true. I considered that, to this day, the destroyed race of the Pygmies were there; for the Almighty would render the expectations of the evil spirit, supported by the abominable actions of mankind, void and vain; and he has, therefore, manifoldly saved us from the craft and subtilty of the Devil, unto whom eternal punishments are due, to his extreme and perpetual confusion, unto the everlasting sanctifying of the Divine Name.

Glossary

Ægina: or Aegina, a Greek island

Bow Street: the London street where the city's first professional police force, called the Bow Street Runners, was located

Cabal: a secret society

Canaries: that is, the Canary Islands, off the northwestern coast of Africa

coney: a rabbit

Ptolemy: a second-century Roman astronomer, mathematician, and geographer; "quadripartite" is a reference to his book *Tetrabiblos; or, Quadripartite: Being Four Books of the Influence of the Stars.*

Pythagoras: a Greek philosopher and mathematician of the sixth century BCE

scat: dung

shew: an antique spelling of "show"

Sol: the sun

Succubii: plural form of *succubus,* a female demon believed to have sexual intercourse with sleeping men

Van Helmont: Jean Baptiste van Helmont, a seventeenth-century Flemish chemist and physician; *Oriatrike* is the name of his 1622 book on digestion.

viz.: an abbreviation of the Latin word videlicet, meaning "namely," or "as follows"

DOCTRINE AND COVENANTS

OF

THE CHURCH OF THE

LATTER DAY SAINTS:

CAREFULLY SELECTED

FROM THE REVELATIONS OF GOD,

AND COMPILED BY

JOSEPH SMITH Junior,
OLIVER COWDERY,
SIDNEY RIGDON,
FREDERICK G. WILLIAMS.

[Presiding Elders of said Church.]

PROPRIETORS.

KIRTLAND, OHIO.

PRINTED BY F. G. WILLIAMS & CO.

FOR THE

PROPRIETORS.

1835.

Title page of the original 1835 edition.

Doctrine and Covenants of the Church of Jesus Christ of Latter-day Saints: Document Analysis

1835 CE

"Which commandments were given to Joseph Smith...who was...ordained an apostle of Jesus Christ, to be the first elder of this church."

Overview

Doctrine and Covenants (1835) is the second of three works (along with Book of Mormon and Pearl of Great Price) by Joseph Smith, Jr., the founder of the Church of Jesus Christ of Latter-day Saints (LDS). Doctrine and Covenants is a collection of revelations given to Smith during the 1830s. The content of these revelations ranges from the organization and impetus of the church to specific commandments, such as the proper role and titles of individuals in the LDS church (who are commonly called Mormons), to various theological doctrines.

The book is best known for its explication of rather controversial aspects of the Mormon faith, among them certain theological assertions, including the corporeality of God, the progression of humans toward their own divinity, and the ongoing nature of revelation. The work also covers highly controversial practices, such as the baptism of the dead by proxy and plural marriage, or polygamy. These practices and beliefs set the LDS church apart from the greater Protestant majority in nineteenth-century America and beyond and were the motivating factor behind much of the persecution against Mormons into the twentieth century.

Context

The context of the Mormon faith in general and Doctrine and Covenants specifically reaches back to the series of revivals that swept the United States from around 1790 to 1830. This disparate religious renewal is generally called the Second Great Awakening. Various Protestant denominations attempted to enliven and enlighten the people through religious revivals. This open competition between Christian groups and the creative fervor it produced also engendered new and innovative ideas and practices.

The competition between established and new religious groups was especially vehement in the northern area of New York State. The region was named the "burned-over district" in reference to the numerous revival fires that spread through the area. It was to this "burned-over district" that Joseph Smith, Jr., moved with his family in 1816. Smith's entire family was both excited and confused by the seemingly unlimited religious options open to them. Smith himself was troubled by the various options, with each group claiming to possess the one true way to God. However, one day in 1820, Smith is said to have received an answer to his prayers when he had a vision of a "Father" and "Son" visiting him. The duo informed Smith that all of the present religious groups competing for his devotion were in error and that he must not join any of them. He should rather wait until the true faith was restored to the earth.

This restoration began in the fall of 1823, when the angel Moroni is said to have first visited Smith. According to Smith, Moroni told him of a set of golden tablets that were buried under the hill Cumorah, very close to the Smith family farm. Smith would have to wait four years until he could receive these tablets, and it would take another three years for the tablets, which were written in Reformed Egyptian, to be fully translated. The tablets revealed the ancient story of the lost tribes of Israel, the Lamanites and Nephites, who in 600 BCE came to the land that would later be called America. The two tribes were constantly at war. Jesus was reported to have come to the tribes after his Resurrection, but not even his teachings could deter the groups from their bloody contest. Eventually, the rebellious Lamanites overcame the faithful Nephites, and only the noble warrior Mormon—from whom the work takes its the title—and his son Moroni were left alive. Mormon wrote the epic story of his people on the golden tablets and hid them until God's appointed time.

The publication of these revelations as the Book of Mormon created a great deal of controversy in the United States, especially along the frontier. Many thousands of people flocked to the new Christian movement, yet many others were appalled by the religious innovation and the claim that any work outside of the Bible could be considered true revelation. As opposition to Smith and his new Church of Jesus Christ of Latter-day Saints rose, Smith decided to move the group to Kirtland, Ohio, so that they could receive a fresh start and begin to restore the ancient ways of God on earth. Around this time Smith made it known to his followers that he had been blessed not only with the gift of translation but also with direct revelation from God. In Kirtland, Smith began disclosing additional aspects of the "true" faith. These revelations sometimes dealt with practical matters of church organization, but they also revealed completely new practices and beliefs to Protestant Americans.

The revelations were eventually collected into the work known as Doctrine and Covenants and served to further define the boundaries of the LDS church. They also further distanced Mormons from the Protestant mainstream, so much so that many considered the Mormons to be a sect wholly apart from Christianity itself. However, Smith and his followers insisted that they could do nothing but follow the word of God as it was revealed through Smith and defined themselves over and against the greater culture. This divide between the LDS church and the greater American culture persisted into the twentieth century and, as of the early twenty-first century, had only recently begun to be bridged. The public at large still has very little understanding of actual Mormon practice and belief, and Mormons themselves often exacerbate this ignorance. As such, Doctrine and Covenants is the most concise source for Mormon customs and theology and the clearest window into their sometimes enigmatic world.

About the Author

Joseph Smith, Jr., was the fourth of nine children in a family of modest means. His father and mother, Joseph and Lucy Smith, moved their family from Sharon, Vermont, only a few years after his birth. They subsequently moved several times before finally settling in Palmyra, New York, in 1816. In Palmyra, Smith's mother joined a local Presbyterian congregation, but his father remained unaffiliated with any denomination or sect, choosing instead to test them all for any signs of what he considered to be religious truth. As such, Smith was introduced to numerous theological systems and religious practices but felt no firm obligation to any of them. This openness was further compounded by the family hobby of fortune hunting. Smith took several trips with his family and then with a group of friends to find buried treasure in the hills surrounding their farm in the hope of discovering the hidden secrets of America's mythic past.

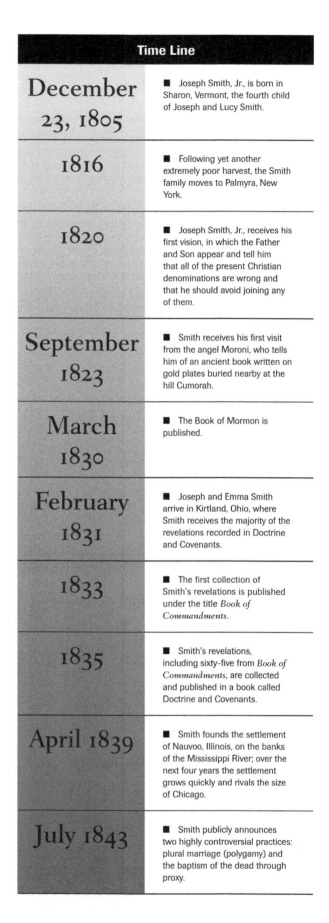

Time Line

December 23, 1805	■ Joseph Smith, Jr., is born in Sharon, Vermont, the fourth child of Joseph and Lucy Smith.
1816	■ Following yet another extremely poor harvest, the Smith family moves to Palmyra, New York.
1820	■ Joseph Smith, Jr., receives his first vision, in which the Father and Son appear and tell him that all of the present Christian denominations are wrong and that he should avoid joining any of them.
September 1823	■ Smith receives his first visit from the angel Moroni, who tells him of an ancient book written on gold plates buried nearby at the hill Cumorah.
March 1830	■ The Book of Mormon is published.
February 1831	■ Joseph and Emma Smith arrive in Kirtland, Ohio, where Smith receives the majority of the revelations recorded in Doctrine and Covenants.
1833	■ The first collection of Smith's revelations is published under the title *Book of Commandments*.
1835	■ Smith's revelations, including sixty-five from *Book of Commandments*, are collected and published in a book called Doctrine and Covenants.
April 1839	■ Smith founds the settlement of Nauvoo, Illinois, on the banks of the Mississippi River; over the next four years the settlement grows quickly and rivals the size of Chicago.
July 1843	■ Smith publicly announces two highly controversial practices: plural marriage (polygamy) and the baptism of the dead through proxy.

1844	■ Smith announces that he will run for the presidency of the United States, a decision that further enflames anti-Mormon sentiment across the United States.
June 27, 1844	■ Smith and his brother Hyrum, who had been arrested for destroying a rival printer in town, are dragged out of an Illinois jail by an angry mob and murdered in cold blood.
February 1846	■ Brigham Young, the new leader of the Church of Jesus Christ of Latter-day Saints, leads the majority of Mormons on a trek to the West, a journey that would eventually lead them to the Great Salt Lake in what is now Utah.
1851	■ The Pearl of Great Price, a collection of Smith's later revelations and translations, is published; the work constitutes the third official work of divinely inspired scripture according to Mormons, along with The Book of Mormon and Doctrine and Covenants.

In the early 1820s, Smith reported that his religious searching had come to an end. He had been chosen by God to be both a prophet and priest of the true religion. This calling involved the miraculous translation of the Book of Mormon and the organization of the Church of Jesus Christ on earth. This new movement was later renamed the Church of Jesus Christ of Latter-day Saints because Smith was convinced that the earth was in its final stage before its destruction and ultimate judgment by God. Under Smith's direction, the LDS church attempted to restore both the early Christian church and numerous practices and concepts of ancient Israel.

Smith chose to move his followers several times after they faced persecution from the local populace. He was once even tarred and feathered while being dragged out of his home. Smith's teachings and actions often fueled the growing anti-Mormon sentiment; he intentionally presented himself and his movement as diametrically opposed to the cultural, political, and religious status quo. Consequently, controversy and even violence followed Smith and his followers to Ohio, Missouri, and Illinois. This violent opposition eventually culminated in the murder of Smith and his brother, Hyrum, by an angry mob in Carthage, Illinois. The brothers were dragged from their jail cell—where they had been arrested for shutting down and then destroying a local printer that had been critical of the Mormons—and subsequently killed in cold blood. Although the tragic

death of their founder and leader devastated the Mormon community, they saw his death in the same way that they had imagined their entire history of persecution: a sign that they were indeed being faithful to the true message of Jesus Christ.

Explanation and Analysis of the Document

The present excerpt from the Doctrine and Covenants contains only 3 of the document's 138 revelations, which are called "sections." The entire work also contains two "official declarations" that, while they are not authoritative revelations themselves, publicly declare 2 revelations received by later presidents of the LDS. The sections reprinted here speak to the church's organization and two of the more controversial aspects of their early doctrine and practice: plural marriage (polygamy) and the baptism of the dead by proxy. Although Smith is recognized as the author of the work—and will be treated as such in the present analysis—Mormons also believe that the revelations in the Doctrine and Covenants come directly from God, and God is sometimes identified as the true speaker within specific sections of the work.

◆ Section 20
Verses 1–7 The opening lines of this section immediately inform the reader of its subject: the official establishment of the LDS church on April 6, 1830. Although there is some debate over the claim, later presidents of the LDS have asserted that the date was chosen by God because it was also the date of Jesus's birth. This section is often called the "Constitution of the Church" within the Mormon community. It refers to the special selection of Joseph Smith, Jr., as God's prophet and the "first elder" of the church. Oliver Cowdery, Smith's longtime friend, an early convert, and scribe, is also identified as an important leader in the movement. Most important, the verses establish Smith as a direct spokesperson for God, an imperfect yet sanctified representative of God on Earth.

Verses 8–16 The section next turns to the divine status of the Book of Mormon. Smith did not write the work, the section immediately points out, but merely translated it. However, the work is divinely inspired and presents all of the necessary practices and beliefs of the people of God, as well as serving as a lens through which previous revelations (that is, the Bible) should be properly understood. This new revelation, which is intimately connected to the previous revelations, shows that God is both consistent and still active in the affairs of humanity. However, Mormons' elevation of the Book of Mormon to the status of divine and authoritative revelation has produced some of their fiercest opposition.

Verses 17–37 The section then affirms many of the common Christian theological doctrines, such as God's nature, humanity's Creation and Fall, and the saving work of God through Jesus Christ. Mormons believe that humankind distorted their proper relationship with God through their incessant pride and constant need to elevate themselves above others and even God. Jesus Christ, through his denial of this temptation and all other temptations and his sacrifice on the Cross justified all of humanity by being what they could not be. This justification culminates in a believer's baptism and ultimately will be concluded when Jesus returns as John prophesied in Revelation. This segment is in harmony with the philosophy of most other Christian groups, yet its appeal to both old and new revelation and godly activity set the stage for further splits between Mormons and the greater Christian world.

Verses 38–67 Attention is then given to the specific organization of the LDS church. Leadership and organizational responsibilities are clearly demarcated in a hierarchical structure. However, these duties are directed to retaining the purity of the organization as much as they address its pragmatic operation. The chief ordinances and sacraments of the church are designated as the responsibility of the apostles, the highest position in the hierarchy. The apostles are responsible for both water baptism and the baptism of fire, the event where the Holy Spirit enters a believer and radically transforms his or her inner being. Although all male members over the age of twelve can administer the bread and wine, apostles are ultimately responsible for the ordinance. In the LDS, the act is seen as symbolic rather than a literal eating and drinking of Christ's body and blood. In most Mormon temples, water actually replaced wine in the sacrament nearly a century ago. This rather basic organizational structure would be refined after the Doctrine and Covenants. Presently, the LDS is led by a president and his two closest advisers. This group is called the "first presidency" and is assisted by a "quorum of twelve" elders who are in charge of the overall operation of the organization. However, the LDS still uses the descriptions in this section to define and select its leaders.

Verses 68–84 This last segment details the requirements of, and expectations for, the general members of the LDS. The specific recitations for the principal rituals of the church—baptism and Communion—are also described. As in the previous segment, the various requirements put on the members explicitly appeal to a strict hierarchical structure within the church, yet they are intended to promote individual and group purity and cohesion. For instance, members are baptized by elders who are "called of God" and have "authority from Jesus Christ to baptize." This simply refers to their station within the church, positions they received because of their demonstrated faith and good works among the community. Mormons have a strict moral code that directs their personal behavior and their attitudes and actions toward others, and this ethical framework is seen as the surest sign of one's true devotion and faith. Since the church is established by God, whoever the church ordains in leadership positions is viewed as having been called by God. In this manner, the hierarchy of the organization is strengthened even as the general members are encouraged to continue to live out their faith in the community.

♦ **Section 127**

Verses 1–4 This section, dated from September 1, 1842, is a letter from Smith to his followers in Nauvoo, Illinois. The first segment relates the persecution Smith had been suffering from his enemies. Subsequently, Smith decided to leave the community and travel to various Mormon settlements for the sake of his safety and that of his followers. Smith then interprets his troubles as a sign of his veracity and special calling from God. After all, Smith argues, God's prophets had always been persecuted. Therefore, the Mormon experience is again linked to an older tradition, and the people are told that God will redeem and save them just as he did Israel. The key, Smith insists, is to remain faithful to God and continue to fulfill God's work.

Verses 5–12 Smith then turns his attention to a rather confusing doctrine he had previously revealed: baptism for the dead. This practice is grounded in several Mormon beliefs. Recognizing that some people do not have the opportunity to hear and therefore act upon God's word while they are living, Mormons believe that those who are dead still have an opportunity to hear and believe in the Gospel of Jesus Christ. Jesus himself first preached to these spirits in the interval between his death and Resurrection. However, all people are required to be baptized by water before they can truly accept God and be joined to the church. Therefore, Mormons are baptized by proxy for those who have died before accepting God's truth. This baptism does not automatically save the deceased, but it does allow them the chance to accept the Gospel while they are spirits awaiting God's final judgment.

Mormons also believe that families are intimately connected, even in the afterlife. Therefore, it is very important that they are baptized on behalf of their entire genealogy. This is the reason that Mormons keep such extensive genealogical records. The present section commands the keeping of these records so that the church will accurately know who has and has not been baptized by proxy and, therefore, given a chance to be saved after they have died.

♦ **Section 132**

Verses 1–14 Section 132 was recorded on July 12, 1843, but its teachings on the eternity of the marriage covenant and plural marriage are said to have been revealed to Smith over a decade earlier. The opening lines suggest that Smith had previously asked God about the authenticity of the patriarchs' marriages to multiple women. God, the speaker in this section, prefaces the response by asserting that he has revealed a new and everlasting covenant and that all who break this covenant will perish. Furthermore, only those covenants, contracts, and bonds that God has ordained and approved will be valid after the Judgment and through eternity. God's approval is revealed through God's prophet: Joseph Smith, Jr. Therefore, Smith, through the power of God, has the ability to discern which contracts, including all marriage bonds, are truly valid.

Verses 15–27 The implications of the previous segment are now revealed. First, only those marriages that Smith has approved are valid in the afterlife. This assertion is proved to be far from inconsequential, because, according to the doctrine of the Church of Jesus Christ of Latter-day Saints, only those who are married can ascend to the highest level in the afterlife. The unmarried are transformed into angels who merely "minister for those who are worthy of... an eternal weight of glory." Unmarried individuals are certainly saved, but they must remain in their lowly current form for all eternity.

However, those who are united in an approved, godly marriage are joined together for all eternity. This familial bond enables them to ascend beyond their mortal capacities and reign with Christ over all creation. Owing to their power and eternal substance, Smith refers to these individuals as gods. Therefore, all true believers, and by default all married Mormons, will be elevated to godhood when they die. This belief was and still is highly contentious for other Christian groups, both for its theological implications and for the immense power it bestows on Smith himself as an arbiter of divine power.

Verses 28–50 The revelation then addresses the subject of plural marriage, specifically that of Abraham. The essential assertion is that God gave Abraham, and numerous additional Jewish leaders, multiple wives and concubines. Therefore, they were correct and even faithful to take these wives or, more correctly, to accept the women as from God. This practice, according to the revelation, has been restored in the new order under Smith's direction and must be accepted by the people. The new order goes so far as to say that whatever Smith approves of, God approves of. Everyone is to obey Smith, God's representative on earth, and never question his orders.

Verses 51–57 This segment of the revelation is addressed specifically to Smith's wife, Emma. At the time of the revelation, Smith had not taken any additional wives other than Emma, whom he had married in 1827. God commands Emma to "receive all those that have been given unto my servant Joseph." God has placed Joseph over "many things." All of this refers, of course, to Smith taking on additional wives. It seems that either God or Smith anticipated a harsh reaction from Emma and informed her of her duties as a follower of God. However, even if Emma would not accept this revelation, Smith was still encouraged to accept what God had given him. After Smith's death, Emma and their son Joseph Smith III, led a dissident group to Missouri and denounced the practice of polygamy.

Verses 58–66 This last segment again validates the leadership and decrees of Smith as coming directly from God and commands everyone to obey him. Finally, the exact nature of plural marriage in the new order is revealed. If any man has one wife and desires another woman who is a virgin, then he is righteous in taking the second woman as a wife as long as Smith approves of the union. As such, both women "belong" to the man because God has given them to him; therefore, the man is not committing adultery. However, if a woman is married to a man and sleeps with another, then she has committed adultery. Also, if a woman is properly wed to a man and does not "administer unto him" because he has taken another wife, then she is at fault, and God will punish her for her sin. President Wilford Woodruff later overturned this practice, which was the source of the greatest antipathy toward the LDS, in 1890. His dissolution of plural marriage paved the way for Utah's admittance as a state six years later. The general perception of polygamy in Mormonism persists even today, yet the practice has been officially banned among members of the church. Although there have been reports of some Mormons still participating in the practice, the majority of them have proved to be unfounded rumors. A splinter group of the LDS church called the Fundamentalist Church of Jesus Christ of Latter-day Saints does actively practice polygamy, but the LDS explicitly rejects the group and their practices.

Audience

Doctrine and Covenants is officially addressed to the entire human population as a witness of God's activity and desires, yet its true audience consisted almost entirely of LDS members. Many converts and even those being evangelized were also introduced to the work, but the Book of Mormon was the movement's primary canon in its first several decades. As noted earlier, the work is now considered one of three authoritative works by the LDS community and is a foundational text in their children's religious education courses.

Impact

Doctrine and Covenants contains the most concise declaration of the LDS's unique theology and practice. Although the Book of Mormon is certainly Smith's best-known and most representative work, its intriguing narrative did not wholly set the movement apart from other burgeoning nineteenth-century religious movements. Stories of America's unique position in world history, tales of the lost tribes of Israel, and millennial expectations were prevalent among the populace. However, the concept of new revelations and especially the content of those revelations set the Mormon movement in stark contrast with its Christian counterparts.

Although plural marriage was officially disallowed in an 1890 revelation, it is still the chief aspect Americans associate with Mormonism. Nearly every other position in the Doctrine and Covenants continues to guide the LDS in the present, and the church continues to grow at a phenomenal rate. Only 10 to 15 percent of Mormons actually live in Utah, and the majority of Mormons live outside the United States. The LDS reports over thirteen million members worldwide, with around five million living in the United States. However, numerous scholars have asserted that these numbers are highly inflated owing to the manner in which Mormons currently count members. Neverthe-

"Which commandments were given to Joseph Smith, Jun., who was called of God, and ordained an apostle of Jesus Christ, to be the first elder of this church."

(Section 1)

"And see that there is no iniquity in the church, neither hardness with each other, neither lying, backbiting, nor evil speaking; And see that the church meet together often, and also see that all the members do their duty."

(Section 1)

"Verily, thus saith the Lord unto you concerning your dead: When any of you are baptized for your dead, let there be a recorder, and let him be eye-witness of your baptisms; let him hear with his ears, that he may testify of a truth, saith the Lord; That in all your recordings it may be recorded in heaven; whatsoever you bind on earth, may be bound in heaven; whatsoever you loose on earth, may be loosed in heaven."

(Section 1)

"Then shall they be gods, because they have no end; therefore shall they be from everlasting to everlasting, because they continue; then shall they be above all, because all things are subject unto them. Then shall they be gods, because they have all power, and the angels are subject unto them."

(Section 1)

"David also received many wives and concubines, and also Solomon and Moses my servants, as also many others of my servants, from the beginning of creation until this time; and in nothing did they sin save in those things which they received not of me."

(Section 1)

less, the LDS is growing rapidly throughout the world, and it seems unlikely this trend will reverse in the near future. The areas of especially high growth rates are in Central and South America, though LDS missions in Southeast Asia have also become very successful in the past few decades.

Further Reading

■ Books

Brodie, Fawn M. *No Man Knows My History: The Life of Joseph Smith*. New York: Random House, 1995.

Bushman, Richard Lyman. *Joseph Smith and the Beginnings of Mormonism*. Chicago: University of Illinois Press, 1984.

Bushman, Richard Lyman. *Joseph Smith: Rough Stone Rolling*. New York: Random House, 2005.

Givens, Terryl L. *By the Hand of Mormon: The American Scripture That Launched a New World Religion*. New York: Oxford University Press, 2002.

Launius, Roger D., and John E. Hallwas, eds. *Kingdom on the Mississippi Revisited: Nauvoo in Mormon History*. Chicago: University of Illinois Press, 1996.

Smith, Joseph. *The Book of Mormon, The Doctrine and Covenants, and The Pearl of Great Price*. Salt Lake City, Utah: Church of Jesus Christ of Latter-day Saints, 1981.

Staker, Mark Lyman. *Hearken, O Ye People: The Historical Setting for Joseph Smith's Ohio Revelations*. Salt Lake City, Utah: Greg Kofford Books, 2009.

■ Web Sites

The Church of Jesus Christ of Latter-day Saints Web site. http://www.lds.org/

—Commentary by Andrew Polk

Questions for Further Study

1. In what ways did Mormonism differ from orthodox Protestantism? What views held by the LDS were regarded as controversial?

2. In what sense was the emergence of Mormonism part of the Second Great Awakening?

3. Mormons consider the Book of Mormon to be divinely revealed, and thus scriptural, in the same sense that the traditional Bible is regarded as the divinely revealed word of God in the Judeo-Christian tradition. Throughout history, numerous religions have considered various texts scriptural. What in your view defines a scriptural text? How can people know that a text is scriptural?

4. In the primary elections leading up to the presidential election of 2008, one of the candidates was Mitt Romney, a businessman, the former governor of Massachusetts, and a Mormon. Some political observers believed that Romney's Mormonism would stand in the way of his nomination, and in fact Romney did not win the nomination. Do you believe that his religion may have been an obstacle? If so, do you believe this was fair?

5. What is the position of the Latter-Day Saints on polygamy? How do you think that the government should respond when a religious practice is contrary to law?

DISTRICT AND COVENANTS OF THE CHURCH OF JESUS CHRIST OF LATTER-DAY SAINTS: DOCUMENT TEXT

1835 CE

—Joseph Smith

Section 20

1. The rise of the Church of Christ in these last days, being one thousand eight hundred and thirty years since the coming of our Lord and Savior Jesus Christ in the flesh, it being regularly organized and established agreeable to the laws of our country, by the will and commandments of God, in the fourth month, and on the sixth day of the month which is called April—

2. Which commandments were given to Joseph Smith, Jun., who was called of God, and ordained an apostle of Jesus Christ, to be the first elder of this church;

3. And to Oliver Cowdery, who was also called of God, an apostle of Jesus Christ, to be the second elder of this church, and ordained under his hand;

4. And this according to the grace of our Lord and Savior Jesus Christ, to whom be all glory, both now and forever. Amen.

5. After it was truly manifested unto this first elder that he had received a remission of his sins, he was entangled again in the vanities of the world;

6. But after repenting, and humbling himself sincerely, through faith, God ministered unto him by an holy angel, whose countenance was as lightning, and whose garments were pure and white above all other whiteness;

7. And gave unto him commandments which inspired him;

8. And gave him power from on high, by the means which were before prepared, to translate the Book of Mormon;

9. Which contains a record of a fallen people, and the fulness of the gospel of Jesus Christ to the Gentiles and to the Jews also;

10. Which was given by inspiration, and is confirmed to others by the ministering of angels, and is declared unto the world by them—

11. Proving to the world that the holy scriptures are true, and that God does inspire men and call them to his holy work in this age and generation, as well as in generations of old;

12. Thereby showing that he is the same God yesterday, today, and forever. Amen.

13. Therefore, having so great witnesses, by them shall the world be judged, even as many as shall hereafter come to a knowledge of this work.

14. And those who receive it in faith, and work righteousness, shall receive a crown of eternal life;

15. But those who harden their hearts in unbelief, and reject it, it shall turn to their own condemnation—

16. For the Lord God has spoken it; and we, the elders of the church, have heard and bear witness to the words of the glorious Majesty on high, to whom be glory forever and ever. Amen.

17. By these things we know that there is a God in heaven, who is infinite and eternal, from everlasting to everlasting the same unchangeable God, the framer of heaven and earth, and all things which are in them;

18. And that he created man, male and female, after his own image and in his own likeness, created he them;

19. And gave unto them commandments that they should love and serve him, the only living and true God, and that he should be the only being whom they should worship.

20. But by the transgression of these holy laws man became sensual and devilish, and became fallen man.

21. Wherefore, the Almighty God gave his Only Begotten Son, as it is written in those scriptures which have been given of him.

22. He suffered temptations but gave no heed unto them.

23. He was crucified, died, and rose again the third day;

24. And ascended into heaven, to sit down on the right hand of the Father, to reign with almighty power according to the will of the Father;

25. That as many as would believe and be baptized in his holy name, and endure in faith to the end, should be saved—

26. Not only those who believed after he came in the meridian of time, in the flesh, but all those from the beginning, even as many as were before he came, who believed in the words of the holy prophets, who spake as they were inspired by the gift of the Holy Ghost, who truly testified of him in all things, should have eternal life,

27. As well as those who should come after, who should believe in the gifts and callings of God by the Holy Ghost, which beareth record of the Father and of the Son;

28. Which Father, Son, and Holy Ghost are one God, infinite and eternal, without end. Amen.

29. And we know that all men must repent and believe in the name of Jesus Christ, and worship the Father in his name, and endure in faith on his name to the end, or they cannot be saved in the kingdom of God.

30. And we know that justification through the grace of our Lord and Savior Jesus Christ is just and true;

31. And we know also, that sanctification through the grace of our Lord and Savior Jesus Christ is just and true, to all those who love and serve God with all their mights, minds, and strength.

32. But there is a possibility that man may fall from grace and depart from the living God;

33. Therefore let the church take heed and pray always, lest they fall into temptation;

34. Yea, and even let those who are sanctified take heed also.

35. And we know that these things are true and according to the revelations of John, neither adding to, nor diminishing from the prophecy of his book, the holy scriptures, or the revelations of God which shall come hereafter by the gift and power of the Holy Ghost, the voice of God, or the ministering of angels.

36. And the Lord God has spoken it; and honor, power and glory be rendered to his holy name, both now and ever. Amen.

37. *And again, by way of commandment to the church concerning the manner of baptism*—All those who humble themselves before God, and desire to be baptized, and come forth with broken hearts and contrite spirits, and witness before the church that they have truly repented of all their sins, and are willing to take upon them the name of Jesus Christ, having a determination to serve him to the end, and truly manifest by their works that they have received of the Spirit of Christ unto the remission of their sins, shall be received by baptism into his church.

38. *The duty of the elders, priests, teachers, deacons, and members of the church of Christ*—An apostle is an elder, and it is his calling to baptize;

39. And to ordain other elders, priests, teachers, and deacons;

40. And to administer bread and wine—the emblems of the flesh and blood of Christ—

41. And to confirm those who are baptized into the church, by the laying on of hands for the baptism of fire and the Holy Ghost, according to the scriptures;

42. And to teach, expound, exhort, baptize, and watch over the church;

43. And to confirm the church by the laying on of the hands, and the giving of the Holy Ghost;

44. And to take the lead of all meetings.

45. The elders are to conduct the meetings as they are led by the Holy Ghost, according to the commandments and revelations of God.

46. The priest's duty is to preach, teach, expound, exhort, and baptize, and administer the sacrament,

47. And visit the house of each member, and exhort them to pray vocally and in secret and attend to all family duties.

48. And he may also ordain other priests, teachers, and deacons.

49. And he is to take the lead of meetings when there is no elder present;

50. But when there is an elder present, he is only to preach, teach, expound, exhort, and baptize,

51. And visit the house of each member, exhorting them to pray vocally and in secret and attend to all family duties.

52. In all these duties the priest is to assist the elder if occasion requires.

53. The teacher's duty is to watch over the church always, and be with and strengthen them;

54. And see that there is no iniquity in the church, neither hardness with each other, neither lying, backbiting, nor evil speaking;

55. And see that the church meet together often, and also see that all the members do their duty.

56. And he is to take the lead of meetings in the absence of the elder or priest—

57. And is to be assisted always, in all his duties in the church, by the deacons, if occasion requires.

58. But neither teachers nor deacons have authority to baptize, administer the sacrament, or lay on hands;

59. They are, however, to warn, expound, exhort, and teach, and invite all to come unto Christ.

60. Every elder, priest, teacher, or deacon is to be ordained according to the gifts and callings of God unto him; and he is to be ordained by the power of the Holy Ghost, which is in the one who ordains him.

61. The several elders composing this church of Christ are to meet in conference once in three months, or from time to time as said conferences shall direct or appoint;

62. And said conferences are to do whatever church business is necessary to be done at the time.

63. The elders are to receive their licenses from other elders, by vote of the church to which they belong, or from the conferences.

64. Each priest, teacher, or deacon, who is ordained by a priest, may take a certificate from him at the time, which certificate, when presented to an elder, shall entitle him to a license, which shall authorize him to perform the duties of his calling, or he may receive it from a conference.

65. No person is to be ordained to any office in this church, where there is a regularly organized branch of the same, without the vote of that church;

66. But the presiding elders, traveling bishops, high councilors, high priests, and elders, may have the privilege of ordaining, where there is no branch of the church that a vote may be called.

67. Every president of the high priesthood (or presiding elder), bishop, high councilor, and high priest, is to be ordained by the direction of a high council or general conference.

68. *The duty of the members after they are received by baptism.*—The elders or priests are to have a sufficient time to expound all things concerning the church of Christ to their understanding, previous to their partaking of the sacrament and being confirmed by the laying on of the hands of the elders, so that all things may be done in order.

69. And the members shall manifest before the church, and also before the elders, by a godly walk and conversation, that they are worthy of it, that there may be works and faith agreeable to the holy scriptures—walking in holiness before the Lord.

70. Every member of the church of Christ having children is to bring them unto the elders before the church, who are to lay their hands upon them in the name of Jesus Christ, and bless them in his name.

71. No one can be received into the church of Christ unless he has arrived unto the years of accountability before God, and is capable of repentance.

72. Baptism is to be administered in the following manner unto all those who repent—

73. The person who is called of God and has authority from Jesus Christ to baptize, shall go down into the water with the person who has presented himself or herself for baptism, and shall say, calling him or her by name: Having been commissioned of Jesus Christ, I baptize you in the name of the Father, and of the Son, and of the Holy Ghost. Amen.

74. Then shall he immerse him or her in the water, and come forth again out of the water.

75. It is expedient that the church meet together often to partake of bread and wine in the remembrance of the Lord Jesus;

76. And the elder or priest shall administer it; and after this manner shall he administer it—he shall kneel with the church and call upon the Father in solemn prayer, saying:

77. O God, the Eternal Father, we ask thee in the name of thy Son, Jesus Christ, to bless and sanctify this bread to the souls of all those who partake of it, that they may eat in remembrance of the body of thy Son, and witness unto thee, O God, the Eternal Father, that they are willing to take upon them the name of thy Son, and always remember him and keep his commandments which he has given them; that they may always have his Spirit to be with them. Amen.

78. The manner of administering the wine—he shall take the cup also, and say:

79. O God, the Eternal Father, we ask thee in the name of thy Son, Jesus Christ, to bless and sanctify this wine to the souls of all those who drink of it, that they may do it in remembrance of the blood of thy Son, which was shed for them; that they may witness unto thee, O God, the Eternal Father, that they do always remember him, that they may have his Spirit to be with them. Amen.

80. Any member of the church of Christ transgressing, or being overtaken in a fault, shall be dealt with as the scriptures direct.

81. It shall be the duty of the several churches, composing the church of Christ, to send one or more

of their teachers to attend the several conferences held by the elders of the church,

82. With a list of the names of the several members uniting themselves with the church since the last conference; or send by the hand of some priest; so that a regular list of all the names of the whole church may be kept in a book by one of the elders, whomsoever the other elders shall appoint from time to time;

83. And also, if any have been expelled from the church, so that their names may be blotted out of the general church record of names.

84. All members removing from the church where they reside, if going to a church where they are not known, may take a letter certifying that they are regular members and in good standing, which certificate may be signed by any elder or priest if the member receiving the letter is personally acquainted with the elder or priest, or it may be signed by the teachers or deacons of the church....

Section 127

1. Forasmuch as the Lord has revealed unto me that my enemies, both in Missouri and this State, were again in the pursuit of me; and inasmuch as they pursue me without a cause, and have not the least shadow or coloring of justice or right on their side in the getting up of their prosecutions against me; and inasmuch as their pretensions are all founded in falsehood of the blackest dye, I have thought it expedient and wisdom in me to leave the place for a short season, for my own safety and the safety of this people. I would say to all those with whom I have business, that I have left my affairs with agents and clerks who will transact all business in a prompt and proper manner, and will see that all my debts are canceled in due time, by turning out property, or otherwise, as the case may require, or as the circumstances may admit of. When I learn that the storm is fully blown over, then I will return to you again.

2. And as for the perils which I am called to pass through, they seem but a small thing to me, as the envy and wrath of man have been my common lot all the days of my life; and for what cause it seems mysterious, unless I was ordained from before the foundation of the world for some good end, or bad, as you may choose to call it. Judge ye for yourselves. God knoweth all these things, whether it be good or bad. But nevertheless, deep water is what I am wont to swim in. It all has become a second nature to me; and I feel, like Paul, to glory in tribulation; for to this day has the God of my fathers delivered me out of them all, and will deliver me from henceforth; for behold, and lo, I shall triumph over all my enemies, for the Lord God hath spoken it.

3. Let all the saints rejoice, therefore, and be exceedingly glad; for Israel's God is their God, and he will mete out a just recompense of reward upon the heads of all their oppressors.

4. And again, verily thus saith the Lord: Let the work of my temple, and all the works which I have appointed unto you, be continued on and not cease; and let your diligence, and your perseverance, and patience, and your works be redoubled, and you shall in nowise lose your reward, saith the Lord of Hosts. And if they persecute you, so persecuted they the prophets and righteous men that were before you. For all this there is a reward in heaven.

5. And again, I give unto you a word in relation to the baptism for your dead.

6. Verily, thus saith the Lord unto you concerning your dead: When any of you are baptized for your dead, let there be a recorder, and let him be eye-witness of your baptisms; let him hear with his ears, that he may testify of a truth, saith the Lord;

7. That in all your recordings it may be recorded in heaven; whatsoever you bind on earth, may be bound in heaven; whatsoever you loose on earth, may be loosed in heaven;

8. For I am about to restore many things to the earth, pertaining to the priesthood, saith the Lord of Hosts.

9. And again, let all the records be had in order, that they may be put in the archives of my holy temple, to be held in remembrance from generation to generation, saith the Lord of Hosts.

10. I will say to all the saints, that I desired, with exceedingly great desire, to have addressed them from the stand on the subject of baptism for the dead, on the following Sabbath. But inasmuch as it is out of my power to do so, I will write the word of the Lord from time to time, on that subject, and send it to you by mail, as well as many other things.

11. I now close my letter for the present, for the want of more time; for the enemy is on the alert, and as the Savior said, the prince of this world cometh, but he hath nothing in me.

12. Behold, my prayer to God is that you all may be saved. And I subscribe myself your servant in the Lord, prophet and seer of the Church of Jesus Christ of Latter-day Saints....

Joseph Smith.

Section 132

1. Verily, thus saith the Lord unto you my servant Joseph, that inasmuch as you have inquired of my hand to know and understand wherein I, the Lord, justified my servants Abraham, Isaac, and Jacob, as also Moses, David and Solomon, my servants, as touching the principle and doctrine of their having many wives and concubines—

2. Behold, and lo, I am the Lord thy God, and will answer thee as touching this matter.

3. Therefore, prepare thy heart to receive and obey the instructions which I am about to give unto you; for all those who have this law revealed unto them must obey the same.

4. For behold, I reveal unto you a new and an everlasting covenant; and if ye abide not that covenant, then are ye damned; for no one can reject this covenant and be permitted to enter into my glory.

5. For all who will have a blessing at my hands shall abide the law which was appointed for that blessing, and the conditions thereof, as were instituted from before the foundation of the world.

6. And as pertaining to the new and everlasting covenant, it was instituted for the fulness of my glory; and he that receiveth a fulness thereof must and shall abide the law, or he shall be damned, saith the Lord God.

7. And verily I say unto you, that the conditions of this law are these: All covenants, contracts, bonds, obligations, oaths, vows, performances, connections, associations, or expectations, that are not made and entered into and sealed by the Holy Spirit of promise, of him who is anointed, both as well for time and for all eternity, and that too most holy, by revelation and commandment through the medium of mine anointed, whom I have appointed on the earth to hold this power (and I have appointed unto my servant Joseph to hold this power in the last days, and there is never but one on the earth at a time on whom this power and the keys of this priesthood are conferred), are of no efficacy, virtue, or force in and after the resurrection from the dead; for all contracts that are not made unto this end have an end when men are dead.

8. Behold, mine house is a house of order, saith the Lord God, and not a house of confusion.

9. Will I accept of an offering, saith the Lord, that is not made in my name?

10. Or will I receive at your hands that which I have not appointed?

11. And will I appoint unto you, saith the Lord, except it be by law, even as I and my Father ordained unto you, before the world was?

12. I am the Lord thy God; and I give unto you this commandment—that no man shall come unto the Father but by me or by my word, which is my law, saith the Lord.

13. And everything that is in the world, whether it be ordained of men, by thrones, or principalities, or powers, or things of name, whatsoever they may be, that are not by me or by my word, saith the Lord, shall be thrown down, and shall not remain after men are dead, neither in nor after the resurrection, saith the Lord your God.

14. For whatsoever things remain are by me; and whatsoever things are not by me shall be shaken and destroyed.

15. Therefore, if a man marry him a wife in the world, and he marry her not by me nor by my word, and he covenant with her so long as he is in the world and she with him, their covenant and marriage are not of force when they are dead, and when they are out of the world; therefore, they are not bound by any law when they are out of the world.

16. Therefore, when they are out of the world they neither marry nor are given in marriage; but are appointed angels in heaven, which angels are ministering servants, to minister for those who are worthy of a far more, and an exceeding, and an eternal weight of glory.

17. For these angels did not abide my law; therefore, they cannot be enlarged, but remain separately and singly, without exaltation, in their saved condition, to all eternity; and from henceforth are not gods, but are angels of God forever and ever.

18. And again, verily I say unto you, if a man marry a wife, and make a covenant with her for time and for all eternity, if that covenant is not by me or by my word, which is my law, and is not sealed by the Holy Spirit of promise, through him whom

I have anointed and appointed unto this power, then it is not valid neither of force when they are out of the world, because they are not joined by me, saith the Lord, neither by my word; when they are out of the world it cannot be received there, because the angels and the gods are appointed there, by whom they cannot pass; they cannot, therefore, inherit my glory; for my house is a house of order, saith the Lord God.

19. And again, verily I say unto you, if a man marry a wife by my word, which is my law, and by the new and everlasting covenant, and it is sealed unto them by the Holy Spirit of promise, by him who is anointed, unto whom I have appointed this power and the keys of this priesthood; and it shall be said unto them—Ye shall come forth in the first resurrection; and if it be after the first resurrection, in the next resurrection; and shall inherit thrones, kingdoms, principalities, and powers, dominions, all heights and depths—then shall it be written in the Lamb's Book of Life, that he shall commit no murder whereby to shed innocent blood, and if ye abide in my covenant, and commit no murder whereby to shed innocent blood, it shall be done unto them in all things whatsoever my servant hath put upon them, in time, and through all eternity; and shall be of full force when they are out of the world; and they shall pass by the angels, and the gods, which are set there, to their exaltation and glory in all things, as hath been sealed upon their heads, which glory shall be a fulness and a continuation of the seeds forever and ever.

20. Then shall they be gods, because they have no end; therefore shall they be from everlasting to everlasting, because they continue; then shall they be above all, because all things are subject unto them. Then shall they be gods, because they have all power, and the angels are subject unto them.

21. Verily, verily, I say unto you, except ye abide my law ye cannot attain to this glory.

22. For strait is the gate, and narrow the way that leadeth unto the exaltation and continuation of the lives, and few there be that find it, because ye receive me not in the world neither do ye know me.

23. But if ye receive me in the world, then shall ye know me, and shall receive your exaltation; that where I am ye shall be also.

24. This is eternal lives—to know the only wise and true God, and Jesus Christ, whom he hath sent. I am he. Receive ye, therefore, my law.

25. Broad is the gate, and wide the way that leadeth to the deaths; and many there are that go in thereat, because they receive me not, neither do they abide in my law.

26. Verily, verily, I say unto you, if a man marry a wife according to my word, and they are sealed by the Holy Spirit of promise, according to mine appointment, and he or she shall commit any sin or transgression of the new and everlasting covenant whatever, and all manner of blasphemies, and if they commit no murder wherein they shed innocent blood, yet they shall come forth in the first resurrection, and enter into their exaltation; but they shall be destroyed in the flesh, and shall be delivered unto the buffetings of Satan unto the day of redemption, saith the Lord God.

27. The blasphemy against the Holy Ghost, which shall not be forgiven in the world nor out of the world, is in that ye commit murder wherein ye shed innocent blood, and assent unto my death, after ye have received my new and everlasting covenant, saith the Lord God; and he that abideth not this law can in nowise enter into my glory, but shall be damned, saith the Lord.

28. I am the Lord thy God, and will give unto thee the law of my Holy Priesthood, as was ordained by me and my Father before the world was.

29. Abraham received all things, whatsoever he received, by revelation and commandment, by my word, saith the Lord, and hath entered into his exaltation and sitteth upon his throne.

30. Abraham received promises concerning his seed, and of the fruit of his loins—from whose loins ye are, namely, my servant Joseph—which were to continue so long as they were in the world; and as touching Abraham and his seed, out of the world they should continue; both in the world and out of the world should they continue as innumerable as the stars; or, if ye were to count the sand upon the seashore ye could not number them.

31. This promise is yours also, because ye are of Abraham, and the promise was made unto Abraham; and by this law is the continuation of the works of my Father, wherein he glorifieth himself.

32. Go ye, therefore, and do the works of Abraham; enter ye into my law and ye shall be saved.

33. But if ye enter not into my law ye cannot receive the promise of my Father, which he made unto Abraham.

34. God commanded Abraham, and Sarah gave Hagar to Abraham to wife. And why did she do it? Because this was the law; and from Hagar sprang many people. This, therefore, was fulfilling, among other things, the promises.

35. Was Abraham, therefore, under condemnation? Verily I say unto you, Nay; for I, the Lord, commanded it.

36. Abraham was commanded to offer his son Isaac; nevertheless, it was written: Thou shalt not kill. Abraham, however, did not refuse, and it was accounted unto him for righteousness.

37. Abraham received concubines, and they bore him children; and it was accounted unto him for righteousness, because they were given unto him, and he abode in my law; as Isaac also and Jacob did none other things than that which they were commanded; and because they did none other things than that which they were commanded, they have entered into their exaltation, according to the promises, and sit upon thrones, and are not angels but are gods.

38. David also received many wives and concubines, and also Solomon and Moses my servants, as also many others of my servants, from the beginning of creation until this time; and in nothing did they sin save in those things which they received not of me.

39. David's wives and concubines were given unto him of me, by the hand of Nathan, my servant, and others of the prophets who had the keys of this power; and in none of these things did he sin against me save in the case of Uriah and his wife; and, therefore he hath fallen from his exaltation, and received his portion; and he shall not inherit them out of the world, for I gave them unto another, saith the Lord.

40. I am the Lord thy God, and I gave unto thee, my servant Joseph, an appointment, and restore all things. Ask what ye will, and it shall be given unto you according to my word.

41. And as ye have asked concerning adultery, verily, verily, I say unto you, if a man receiveth a wife in the new and everlasting covenant, and if she be with another man, and I have not appointed unto her by the holy anointing, she hath committed adultery and shall be destroyed.

42. If she be not in the new and everlasting covenant, and she be with another man, she has committed adultery.

43. And if her husband be with another woman, and he was under a vow, he hath broken his vow and hath committed adultery.

44. And if she hath not committed adultery, but is innocent and hath not broken her vow, and she knoweth it, and I reveal it unto you, my servant Joseph, then shall you have power, by the power of my Holy Priesthood, to take her and give her unto him that hath not committed adultery but hath been faithful; for he shall be made ruler over many.

45. For I have conferred upon you the keys and power of the priesthood, wherein I restore all things, and make known unto you all things in due time.

46. And verily, verily, I say unto you, that whatsoever you seal on earth shall be sealed in heaven; and whatsoever you bind on earth, in my name and by my word, saith the Lord, it shall be eternally bound in the heavens; and whosesoever sins you remit on earth shall be remitted eternally in the heavens; and whosesoever sins you retain on earth shall be retained in heaven.

47. And again, verily I say, whomsoever you bless I will bless, and whomsoever you curse I will curse, saith the Lord; for I, the Lord, am thy God.

48. And again, verily I say unto you, my servant Joseph, that whatsoever you give on earth, and to whomsoever you give any one on earth, by my word and according to my law, it shall be visited with blessings and not cursings, and with my power, saith the Lord, and shall be without condemnation on earth and in heaven.

49. For I am the Lord thy God, and will be with thee even unto the end of the world, and through all eternity; for verily I seal upon you your exaltation, and prepare a throne for you in the kingdom of my Father, with Abraham your father.

50. Behold, I have seen your sacrifices, and will forgive all your sins; I have seen your sacrifices in obedience to that which I have told you. Go, therefore, and I make a way for your escape, as I accepted the offering of Abraham of his son Isaac.

51. Verily, I say unto you: A commandment I give unto mine handmaid, Emma Smith, your wife, whom I have given unto you, that she stay herself and partake not of that which I commanded you to offer unto her; for I did it, saith the Lord, to prove you all, as I did Abraham, and that I might

require an offering at your hand, by covenant and sacrifice.

52. And let mine handmaid, Emma Smith, receive all those that have been given unto my servant Joseph, and who are virtuous and pure before me; and those who are not pure, and have said they were pure, shall be destroyed, saith the Lord God.

53. For I am the Lord thy God, and ye shall obey my voice; and I give unto my servant Joseph that he shall be made ruler over many things; for he hath been faithful over a few things, and from henceforth I will strengthen him.

54. And I command mine handmaid, Emma Smith, to abide and cleave unto my servant Joseph, and to none else. But if she will not abide this commandment she shall be destroyed, saith the Lord; for I am the Lord thy God, and will destroy her if she abide not in my law.

55. But if she will not abide this commandment, then shall my servant Joseph do all things for her, even as he hath said; and I will bless him and multiply him and give unto him an hundredfold in this world, of fathers and mothers, brothers and sisters, houses and lands, wives and children, and crowns of eternal lives in the eternal worlds.

56. And again, verily I say, let mine handmaid forgive my servant Joseph his trespasses; and then shall she be forgiven her trespasses, wherein she has trespassed against me; and I, the Lord thy God, will bless her, and multiply her, and make her heart to rejoice.

57. And again, I say, let not my servant Joseph put his property out of his hands, lest an enemy come and destroy him; for Satan seeketh to destroy; for I am the Lord thy God, and he is my servant; and behold, and lo, I am with him, as I was with Abraham, thy father, even unto his exaltation and glory.

58. Now, as touching the law of the priesthood, there are many things pertaining thereunto.

59. Verily, if a man be called of my Father, as was Aaron, by mine own voice, and by the voice of him that sent me, and I have endowed him with the keys of the power of this priesthood, if he do anything in my name, and according to my law and by my word, he will not commit sin, and I will justify him.

60. Let no one, therefore, set on my servant Joseph; for I will justify him; for he shall do the sacrifice

which I require at his hands for his transgressions, saith the Lord your God.

61. And again, as pertaining to the law of the priesthood—if any man espouse a virgin, and desire to espouse another, and the first give her consent, and if he espouse the second, and they are virgins, and have vowed to no other man, then is he justified; he cannot commit adultery for they are given unto him; for he cannot commit adultery with that that belongeth unto him and to no one else.

62. And if he have ten virgins given unto him by this law, he cannot commit adultery, for they belong to him, and they are given unto him; therefore is he justified.

63. But if one or either of the ten virgins, after she is espoused, shall be with another man, she has committed adultery, and shall be destroyed; for they are given unto him to multiply and replenish the earth, according to my commandment, and to fulfil the promise which was given by my Father before the foundation of the world, and for their exaltation in the eternal worlds, that they may bear the souls of men; for herein is the work of my Father continued, that he may be glorified.

64. And again, verily, verily, I say unto you, if any man have a wife, who holds the keys of this power, and he teaches unto her the law of my priesthood, as pertaining to these things, then shall she believe and administer unto him, or she shall be destroyed, saith the Lord your God; for I will destroy her; for I will magnify my name upon all those who receive and abide in my law.

65. Therefore, it shall be lawful in me, if she receive not this law, for him to receive all things whatsoever I, the Lord his God, will give unto him, because she did not believe and administer unto him according to my word; and she then becomes the transgressor; and he is exempt from the law of Sarah, who administered unto Abraham according to the law when I commanded Abraham to take Hagar to wife.

66. And now, as pertaining to this law, verily, verily, I say unto you, I will reveal more unto you, hereafter; therefore, let this suffice for the present. Behold, I am Alpha and Omega. Amen.

Glossary

Abraham, Isaac, and Jacob, as also Moses, David and Solomon: the line of patriarchs of the biblical Old Testament

Aaron: the brother of Moses and the first high priest of the Israelites

Alpha and Omega: beginning and ending, from the first and last letters of the Greek alphabet

Gentiles: non-Jews, especially Christians

Holy Ghost: in Christianity, the third person of the Trinity; representative of God's spirit in creation

justification through the grace of our Lord…: the Protestant doctrine that salvation is a gift from God through faith and cannot be earned through good works

Nathan: an Old Testament prophet

Paul: an early Christian leader best known for his dramatic conversion to Christianity

Sarah gave Hagar to Abraham to wife: in Genesis, the incident in which Abraham's first wife, Sarah, who was barren, gave her servant Hagar to Abraham as a second wife so that he could have children

Uriah: as recounted in 2 Samuel 11, the husband of Bathsheba, whom King David had killed by putting him in the front line of a battle, so that David could have Uriah's wife

Brigham Young.

SERMON ON MORMON GOVERNANCE: DOCUMENT ANALYSIS

1859 CE

"The world seems to be afraid of the power of God, or rather, as I observed not long since, afraid that we are not in possession of it.

Overview

Once the Church of Jesus Christ of Latter-day Saints (LDS) community became established in Utah, Brigham Young, the church's second president, ordered the publication of the *Journal of Discourses*, which collected the public speeches of Mormon leaders. The vast majority of its contents during his lifetime are by Young, among them his 1859 *Sermon on Mormon Governance*, in which Young characterizes the Mormon political ideal—a theocratic government based on the rule of God.

Context

By 1859, when Brigham Young delivered the Sermon on Mormon Governance, the question of "governance" was one with which the Church of Jesus Christ of Latter Day Saints in the Utah Territory had been dealing for several years. Mormon settlers had been coming to the region of the Great Salt Lake since 1847, leaving the United States for what was, at that point, a remote corner of Mexico. Mormon leaders were aware that, due to the ongoing war between the United States and Mexico, they were still within the US sphere of influence. However, they believed their independence would be maintained by their remoteness from the centers of power in the United States.

In 1848, however, two events brought this region into a closer relationship with the rest of the United States and with the federal government in particular. The first was the conclusion of the Mexican War; under the terms of the treaty of Guadeloupe Hidalgo the entire region was now part of the United States. The second was the discovery of gold in California, which triggered a surge of westward migration, much of it coming through Mormon territory. In 1849, Mormon leaders determined that the best way to maintain their autonomy was to apply for—and be granted—statehood. This way, they could elect Mormon members to positions of authority and preserve their freedom of religion. After facing deadly persecution in previous places like Missouri and Nauvoo, Illinois, strong self-rule was a priority for Mormon leaders, including church President Brigham Young. The fear of persecution was exacerbated by the large number of non-Mormons who were passing through Mormon territory.

The proposed state of Deseret, however, never materialized. Rather, as part of the Compromise of 1850, the Mormon lands were incorporated into the larger Utah Territory. This meant that the President and Congress would be appointing a governor and other officials. To mollify the LDS leadership, however, President Millard Fillmore appointed LDS church President Brigham Young as the new Governor of the Utah Territory.

As the number of Americans in the far west increased, news of the Mormons and their beliefs began to become more prominent in the media. In particular, the practice of plural marriage, or polygamy, raised the hackles of many back east. In fact, the new Republican party equated polygamy with slavery in their first Presidential campaign in 1856. Between 1850 and 1857, an increasing number of important elected and appointed positions within the territory were exclusively under the control of LDS members. Non-Mormon judges appointed to work in the territory left their positions and reported that they territory was approaching a state of theocratic control that was tantamount to rebellion against the authority of the United States. In 1857, US President James Buchanan appointed a new governor to replace Brigham Young and sent 2500 troops to maintain order during the transition.

This led to violence between federal troops and Mormon militia soldiers. The violence extended to those who should have been noncombatants, such as over one hundred westward migrants killed by Mormon militia troops in the Mountain Meadows massacre in September, 1857. The fighting finally subsided in July, 1858. As a result, Brigham Young was forced to step down as governor, but those who had been in rebellion were given amnesty in exchange for acknowledging federal authority.

About the Author

Brigham Young was an early convert to the Mormon Church, which was founded in 1830 by Joseph Smith, Young's relative by marriage. Young quickly advanced within the Mormon hierarchy, becoming president of the Quorum of the Twelve Apostles (the governing body of the church). After Smith's death in 1844, various leaders asserted their claims to become his successor. Rather than settling on a single candidate, the Mormon Church splintered into sects, each with its own leader. Young became the president of the largest faction, then centered in the Mormon city of Nauvoo, Illinois. This faction became the modern-day Church of Jesus Christ of Latter-day Saints (LDS). In 1846 conflict with the local population made the Mormon position in Illinois untenable, so Young ordered the church members to move westward, as many Americans were doing at the time. They established a new LDS center in the Utah Valley around the Great Salt Lake. There Young became the autocratic ruler of a Mormon state whose isolation made it in its early days a virtually independent country.

Young and Joseph Smith both came from poor families and had struggled to find some kind of economic stability prior to the foundation of Mormonism. Although they both had been born in Vermont, their families had moved to the "burnt-over" counties of Upstate New York, so called because the intensity and frequency of fundamentalist religious revivals had left almost no one "unsaved" during the period that was called the Second Great Awakening. Young was typical of many people in this environment. He converted to more than one sect of the Baptist Church and then became a Methodist before encountering the Book of Mormon, the church's sacred scripture, in 1832. Young himself first became accustomed to public speaking as the leader of a series of Bible-reading groups. He was a nervous speaker at first, but he was determined to perfect his skills through practice and rapidly did so. Smith had at one time worked as a treasure hunter, taking fees from landowners in exchange for using his methods of spiritual divination to discover buried treasure on their land. His supposed discovery of the golden tablets on which the Book of Mormon was written, buried on his own land, was an extension of this trade.

Young's work as a Mormon missionary and leader in the 1830s and 1840s accustomed him to addressing very large crowds, both of the converted and of those who had come to hear him with the possibility of becoming Mormons. He regularly spoke before crowds in eastern cities such as Boston or New York and in London. His manner of preaching was very much that of a fundamentalist preacher of that time. He supported his rhetoric with frequent biblical citations and appeals to his own authority and that of the hierarchy and "tradition" he represented. Once he was in control of the LDS Church and was the unquestioned

Time Line	
1830	■ Joseph Smith publishes *The Book of Mormon*, establishing the Mormon Faith
1839	■ After experiencing persecution in Missouri, Brigham Young leads a group of Mormons to Nauvoo, Illinois. Smith follows them later in the year.
1844	■ Joseph Smith and his brother Hyrum are shot and killed while in jail at Nauvoo.
1847	■ The group of Mormons led by Brigham Young settle in the Great Salt Lake valley.
1850	■ Brigham Young is appointed governor of the Utah Territory.
1857	■ Responding to reports that Young is ruling Utah as a theocracy, orders 2500 soldiers to the territory to put down the supposed rebellion. The ensuing conflict will be known as the Mormon War.
1859	■ Young delivers the Sermon on Mormon Governance.

leader of the Mormon community in Utah, he maintained this style, also supporting his political decisions and dictates with an appeal to his own authority as a prophet. He created a carefully crafted public image as a wise and holy authority. As such he made several addresses each week, technically classed as sermons, but given the theocratic nature of his rule, the religious and political functions of his speeches cannot be disentangled. Because Young was a national political figure from at least the late 1830s and increasingly so after Smith's death, his speeches were commonly reproduced and analyzed in national newspapers.

The texts in the *Journal of Discourses* were published first as a monthly magazine starting in January 1853 (continuing through 1886) and then were reprinted as hardbound annual collections the following year. The texts were compiled by stenographers present at the sermons rather than from revised reading scripts. Young did not speak from prepared notes. The historian Stanley Hirshson suggests that this might have been because Young was semiliterate, for the economic circumstances of his early family life allowed him to attend school for less than a year. This was not unusual at the time. Many popular church leaders learned rhetoric and memorized the text of the Bible through a lifetime of hearing sermons, without necessarily knowing how to read. Young's brothers became Methodist ministers despite a complete lack of literacy. This would also tend to explain the high ratio of Young's allusions to and quotations from the Bible as opposed to the Book of Mormon, which he did not hear read repeatedly during his youth. The texts in the *Journal* embody Young's opinions and decisions at the height of his career, when he was the highest authority in the LDS Church and the virtual dictator of Utah. Although Young classed these talks as sermons, his discourses were as often political as religious, for in the Mormon view these two strands were inextricably intertwined.

Explanation and Analysis of the Document

From Henry David Thoreau's retreat at Walden Pond to organized communes such as the Oneida Community, many Americans in the mid-nineteenth century experimented with moving away from mainstream society to find a new way of living in complete independence. The early Mormon movement had much in common with other utopian communes, moving ever farther west to found new settlements. The establishment of the first Mormon community came with the mass conversion of an already-existing Baptist commune in Kirtland, Ohio. But friction with local non-Mormons eventually led to the abandonment of that community and the foundation of new centers at Far West, Missouri (1836), and Nauvoo, Illinois (1839). After the failure of these Mormon centers but the eventual success of the community in Salt Lake City (1847), Young defined the characteristics of the Mormon political ideal. In a sermon delivered on July 31, 1859, he outlines his theoretical understanding of what the government of the Mormon community should be. As with other Utopian movements, Young calls for isolation from the rest of society: "Let us alone, and we will build up the kingdom of God." This statement is most likely conditioned by the history of conflict between Mormon communes and adjacent non-Mormon communities.

The precise form of the government did not matter much to Young, but it had to be theocratic, that is, based on the rule of God. He said: "But few, if any, understand what a theocratic government is. In every sense of the word, it is a republican government, and differs but little in form from our National, State, and Territorial Governments; but its subjects will recognize the will and dictation of the Almighty." A republic or democratic form of government can assume a theocratic character, Young says, when "the power of the Holy Ghost" acts through the voters. Since this power is, in Mormon belief, present only in Mormon "saints," its exercise requires limiting the right to vote to Mormons. In practice Mormons had always voted en bloc following the advice of their prophet, whether Smith or Young. Young thought that the current American government was excellent, but an even better model was "the government of the children of Israel to the time when they elected a king." In his view it was unnecessary to change the executive every four or eight years: "Would it not be better to extend that period during life or good behaviour; and when the people have elected the best man to that office, continue him in it as long as he will serve them?" He is talking about his own rule over the Mormon commune as president and prophet, elected offices that he held for life, though he was ready to apply the same principle to the American presidency should it ever become established as a theocracy. His complaint against the American government was not its form but the fact that the laws "are too often administered in unrighteousness." He meant that laws can be justly administered only by "saints," or Mormons.

In Utah, Young found the isolation that his movement needed, though after Utah came under the authority of the United States in 1848, he and the Mormons found themselves at odds with the federal government until Young resigned as Utah's governor. He retained his position within the LDS Church, however, and thereafter relied on economic measures, such as boycotts, to keep non-Mormons out of Utah. Young tells his audience that non-Mormons inevitably hate and fear Mormons and will act to destroy them. He posits a psychological explanation for this enmity, explaining what he conceives of as the thinking of non-Mormons: "If we had the power to destroy you [Mormons], we would do it; and we are afraid that if you are let alone, you will have the power to destroy us and will do as we would under like circumstances."

Young goes on to emphasize the religious tolerance of Mormonism:

> All denominations and communities would be alike protected in their rights, whether they worshipped the Supreme Author of our existence, or the sun, or the moon, or, as do some of our aborigines [native Americans], a white dog; and none will be permitted to infringe upon their neighbours.... The Hindoos would have the privilege of erecting their temples and of worshipping as they pleased; but they would not be permitted to compel other worshippers to conform to their mode of worship, nor to burn their companions upon the funeral pyre; for that would interfere with individual rights.

Young's rhetoric of religious tolerance served many purposes. It was meant to reassure the federal government that the Mormons would not take steps to exclude non-Mormons from Utah. But Young is also speaking to the most cherished Mormon beliefs when he envisions a situation in which Mormons dominate a state including Hindus and Muslims, in other words, a global state. He still has in mind the same vision of a single theocratic state that impelled Joseph Smith to aim for the presidency of the United States.

It should be emphasized, though, that while Young boasts of Mormon respect for the religions of other communities, in the same speech he constantly emphasizes that his desired theocracy would be run exclusively by "Saints of the Most High ... established upon the earth." So while other religious communities might be tolerated, they would be denied all political rights. Although Young realized by 1859 that he could not directly prohibit the immigration of non-Mormon American citizens into Utah, his actions in regard to religious tolerance were far different from his words. When the Mormons arrived in the Utah basin, they found it inhabited by the Ute Indians. Young imagined that these "Lamanites," as he called them based on the mythology of the Book of Mormon, could be easily converted to Mormonism and integrated into the general community, for the Book of Mormon states that preaching the gospel to Native Americans would make them become "white," since their racial identity is a punishment for past sins. But by 1859 it was clear that the Utes had no interest in conversion and were prepared to resist the Mormon seizure of their land. Accordingly, Young had Mormon militias drive them onto reservations in remote areas of Utah.

Audience

The primary audience of this message is the federal government of the United States. One of the goals of the Sermon on Mormon Governance is to redefine "theocracy" in a manner that would—hopefully—be more palatable to the US government and American citizens. As discussed above, one of the key triggers of the "Utah War" had been reports from non-Mormon political appointees that the degree of political control exercised by the Latter Day Saints church constituted a theocracy and, as such, presented a threat to the dominance of the secular federal government.

One of the complaints President Buchanan's critics levelled at him was that he accepted too readily reports of subversion and theocracy and sent troops to Utah without due diligence and investigation of the reports. Thus, the Sermon on Mormon Governance is, in part, directed at federal authorities in order to persuade them that what the Mormon's consider true theocracy (as opposed to, for example, the theocratic Catholic governments of medieval Europe and their Protestant offshoots). Young asserts that, "In every sense of the word" the theocracy of the Mormons is "a republican government, and differs but little in form from our National, State, and Territorial Governments; but its subjects will recognize the will and dictation of the Almighty." Thus, Young is attempting to persuade non-Mormons—particularly federal officials—that *Mormon* theocracy is compatible with the ideals of the United States. In a way, Young argues that republican ideals are perfected in the government of the Latter Day Saints since such government would be under the control of the righteous, rather than the unrighteous. Young's assertions (discussed above) that government under Mormon control would be tolerant of diverse religions was, likewise, calculated to reassure the public as well as government leaders that a Mormon-dominated government would not be a danger to religious liberty.

Impact

In the years after Brigham Young's removal as governor of the Utah Territory, following the settlement of the Utah War,

members of the Latter Day Saints church retained a great deal of political authority—even if the church itself was not the basis of the government. This was the case despite the increasing numbers of non-Mormons entering the Utah territory on their journeys westward. Some were passing through on their way to California or other areas. Others settled in the territory in search of riches from mineral finds such as silver in the Comstock Lode in the western portion of the Utah Territory that would, eventually, be Nevada.

vIn keeping with the tolerance toward other religious faiths that Brigham Young called for in the Sermon on Mormon Governance, numerous non-Mormon religious communities appeared in Utah during the territorial period. The first known Catholic mass in Utah territory was celebrated in 1859. The Jewish community of the Salt Lake area began formal observances with the celebration of Yom Kippur in 1864. The Presbyterians established their first congregation in the territory in 1870 and a number of Lutheran missionary efforts were in place by the 1880s.

Even given the fact of Mormon control over the territorial government (and local governments as well), Latter Day Saints leaders did increase cooperation with federal officials. This was particularly true following Brigham Young's death in 1877. Territorial militia troops—which were overwhelmingly Mormon—often cooperated with federal troops in the numerous conflicts with Native American tribes. Perhaps the greatest capitulation to federal authority came as a result of federal efforts to end plural marriage, or polygamy. A number of federal laws, such as the Morrill Anti-Bigamy Act of 1862 and the 1882 Edmunds Act established harsh penalties for multiple marriate. The Edmunds-Tucker act of 1887 actually disincorporated the Mormon Church, ending it as a legal entity. When this was upheld by the US Supreme Court in 1890 (*Late Corp. of the Church of Jesus Christ of Latter-Day Saints v. United States*) the Latter Day Saints responded with the 1890 Manifesto which declared:

> There is nothing in my teachings to the Church or in those of my associates, during the time specified, which can be reasonably construed to inculcate or encourage polygamy; and when any Elder of the Church has used language which appeared to convey such teaching, he has been promptly reproved. And I now publicly declare that my advice to the Latter-day Saints is to refrain from contracting any marriage forbidden by the law of the land.

The capitulation led to the approval of Utah's application for statehood. While we may not be able to know for sure the impact of this particular sermon on the Mormon leadership's decision to denounce polygamy but it is likely that they saw their continuing persecution as an obstacle to their creation of a holy society rather than the end of their efforts. For, as Young said

> Let us alone, and we will build up the kingdom of God. We are striving for what all Christendom professes to be, and we will bring it forth. If they persecute us, we will bring it forth the sooner. Could all the Elders of Israel have given "Mormonism" the same impetus that

*"The Constitution and laws of the United States resemble a theocracy more closely than any government; now on the earth." - **Sermon on Mormon Governance***

(Section 1)

*"People are afraid of 'Mormonism,' as they call it. They are afraid of the Gospel of salvation, and say that we have something that others have not—that we have an almighty influence, and that influence is a mystery." - **Sermon on Mormon Governance***

(Section 1)

*"The world seems to be afraid of the power of God, or rather, as I observed not long since, afraid that we are not in possession of it. They need not borrow trouble upon that point; for if we are not what we profess to be, we shall certainly fail, and they will no longer be disturbed about 'Mormonism.'" -**Sermon on Mormon Governance***

(Section 1)

the last quarrel has done? No. The Lord will bring more out of that than all the Elders could have done by any performance of theirs.

Following Young's thinking, the current persecution of polygamists could be used for the broader purpose of the Mormon cause.

Further Reading

Bagley, Will. *Blood of the Prophets: Brigham Young and the Massacre at Mountain Meadows*. First Edition edition. Norman: University of Oklahoma Press, 2002. Print.

Bigler, David L., and Will Bagley. *The Mormon Rebellion: America's First Civil War, 1857–1858*. Reprint edition. Norman: University of Oklahoma Press, 2012. Print.

Bowman, Matthew. *The Mormon People: The Making of an American Faith*. New York: Random House Trade Paperbacks, 2012. Print.

Breslin, Ed. *Brigham Young: A Concise Biography of the Mormon Moses*. y First printing edition. Washington, DC: Regnery History, 2013. Print.

Bushman, Richard Lyman. *Mormonism: A Very Short Introduction*. 1 edition. New York: Oxford University Press, 2008. Print.

Duffy, John Charles, and David J. Howlett. *Mormonism: The Basics*. Reprint edition. Routledge, 2016. Print.

Eliason, Eric A. "Curious Gentiles and Representational Authority in the City of the Saints." *Religion and American Culture: A Journal of Interpretation* 11.2 (2001): 155–190. JSTOR. Web.

Grow, Matthew J. "The Suffering Saints: Thomas L. Kane, Democratic Reform, and the Mormon Question in Antebellum America." *Journal of the Early Republic* 29.4 (2009): 681–710. Print.

Shipps, Jan. *Mormonism: The Story of a New Religious Tradition*. Urbana: University of Illinois Press, 1987. Print.

Turner, John G. *Brigham Young: Pioneer Prophet*. 1st edition. Cambridge, Massachusetts ; London, England: Belknap Press, 2012. Print.

—Commentary by Bradley A. Skeen and Aaron J. Gulyas

1. Both Brigham Young and John Winthrop ("A Model of Christian Charity") led religious minorities to a distant place to create a new place in order to build a new society. How did their visions of society differ? How were they similar? How were the contexts of their creation similar or different?

2. How does Young characterize the notion of "freedom of religion"? Will religions other than the church of the Latter Day Saints have a place in Young's society?

3. How is Brigham Young's definition of "theocracy" similar to or different from other examples of theocracy you have encountered?

4. Discuss some specific examples of the ways in which Young attempts to connect Mormon theocracy to traditional American political, cultural, or social concepts?

SERMON ON MORMON GOVERNANCE: DOCUMENT TEXT

1859 CE

—Brigham Young

Erroneous traditions and the powers of darkness have such sway over mankind, that, when we speak of a theocracy on the earth, the people are frightened. The government of the "Holy Catholic Church," from which all the Protestant churches are offshoots, is professedly theocratic, though it is directly opposed to the theocracy described in the Bible.

But few, if any, understand what a theocratic government is. In every sense of the word, it is a republican government, and differs but little in form from our National, State, and Territorial Governments; but its subjects will recognize the will and dictation of the Almighty. The kingdom of God circumscribes and comprehends the municipal laws for the people in their outward government, to which pertain the Gospel covenants, by which the people can be saved; and those covenants pertain to fellowship and faithfulness.

The Gospel covenants are for those who believe and obey; municipal laws are for both Saint and sinner.

The Constitution and laws of the United States resemble a theocracy more closely than any government; now on the earth, or that ever has been, so far as we know, except the government of the children of Israel to the time when they elected a king.

All governments are more or less under the control of the Almighty, and, in their forms, have sprung from the laws that he has from time to time given to man. Those laws, in passing from generation to generation, have been more or less adulterated, and the result has been the various forms of government now in force among the nations; for, as the Prophet says of Israel, "They have transgressed the laws, changed the ordinances, and broken the everlasting covenant."

Whoever lives to see the kingdom of God fully established upon the earth will see a government that will protect every person in his rights. If that government was now reigning upon this land of Joseph, you would see the Roman Catholic, the Greek Catholic, the Episcopalian, the Presbyterian, the Methodist, the Baptist, the Quaker, the Shaker, the Hindoo, the Mahometan, and every class of worshippers most strictly protected in all their municipal rights and in the privilege of worshipping who, what, and when they pleased, not infringing upon the rights of others. Does any candid person in his sound judgment desire any greater liberty?

The Lord has thus far protected and preserved the human family under their various forms and administrations of government, notwithstanding their wickedness, and is still preserving them; but if the kingdom of God, or a theocratic government, was established on the earth, many practices now prevalent would be abolished.

One community would not be permitted to array itself in opposition to another to coerce them to their standard; one denomination would not be suffered to persecute another because they differed in religious belief and mode of worship. Every one would be fully protected in the enjoyment of all religious and social rights, and no state, no government, no community, no person would have the privilege of infringing on the rights of another one Christian community would not rise up and persecute another.

I will here remark that we are generally looked upon as a dangerous people, and for the reason that there are thousands and millions of people who are afraid that justice will be meted out to them; and they say, to use Scripture language, that "if the Saints are let alone, they will take away our place and nation, and will measure to us what we have measured to them." They conclude thus because they estimate others by themselves, realizing that if they had the power to deprive us of our rights, they would exercise it. "We will judge you Latter-day Saints by ourselves. If we had the power to destroy you, we would do it; and we are afraid that if you are let alone, you will have the power to destroy us and will do as we would under like circumstances." If this people had that power to-day, they would not infringe in the least upon the rights of any person; neither could they, without ceasing to be Saints.

When the Saints of the Most High are established upon the earth, and are prepared to receive the kingdom of God in its fulness, as foretold by the Prophet Daniel, they will have power to protect themselves and all the sons and daughters of Adam in their rights. Then, when a person or community says, "I do not want to believe your religion," they will enjoy liberty to believe as they please, as fully as we shall....

People are afraid of "Mormonism," as they call it. They are afraid of the Gospel of salvation, and say that we have something that others have not—that we have an almighty influence, and that influence is a mystery....

It is recorded in the Bible that in the last days the God of heaven will set up a kingdom. Will that kingdom destroy the human family? No: it will save every person that will and can be saved. The doctrines of the Saviour reveal and place the believers: in possession of principles whereby saviours will come upon Mount Zion to save the house of Esau, which is the Gentile nations, from sin and death,—all except those who have sinned against the Holy Ghost. Men and women will enter into the temples of God, and be, in comparison, pillars there, and officiate year after year for those who have slept thousands of years. The doctrine of the Christian world, which I have already said I was familiar with, sends them to hell irretrievably, which to me is the height of folly. They do not understand what the Lord is doing, nor what he purposes to do.

It is alleged and reiterated that we do not love the institutions of our country. I say, and have so said for many years, that the Constitution and laws of the United States combine the best form of Government in force upon the earth. But does it follow that each officer of the Government administers with justice? No; for it is well known throughout our nation that very many of our public officers are as degraded, debased, corrupt, and regardless of right as men well can be.

I repeat that the Constitution, laws, and institutions of our Government; are as good as can be, with the intelligence now possessed by the people. But they, as also the laws of other nations, are too often administered in unrighteousness; and we do not and cannot love and respect the acts of the administrators of our laws, unless they act justly in their offices.

Jehovah has decreed and plainly foretold the establishment of his kingdom upon this earth; and it will prove to me a shield to the ordinances of his house, in the endowments, and in all the gifts and graces of the Spirit of God with which the Priesthood, so to speak, is clothed. The municipal laws of that kingdom are designed for the protection of all classes of people in their legitimate rights; and were it now in its fulness upon the earth, and the New Jerusalem built upon this continent, which is the land of Zion, the Latter-day Saints would not alone enjoy its blessings, but all denominations and communities would be alike protected in their rights, whether they worshipped the Supreme Author of our existence, or the sun, or the moon, or, as do some of our aborigines, a white dog; and none will be permitted to infringe upon their neighbours, though every knee shall bow and every tongue confess that Jesus is the Christ. The Hindoos would have the privilege of erecting their temples and of worshipping as they pleased; but they would not be permitted to compel other worshippers to conform to their mode of worship, nor to burn their companions upon the funeral pyre; for that would interfere with individual rights.

The kingdom of God will be extended over the earth; and it is written, "I will make thine officers peace, and thine exactors righteousness." Is that day ever coming? It is; and the doctrine we preach leads to that point. Even now the form of the Government of the United States differs but little from that of the kingdom of God.

In our Government a President is elected for four years, and can be reelected but once, thus limiting the time of any one person to but eight years at most. Would it not be better to extend that period during life or good behaviour; and when the people have elected the best man to that office, continue him in it as long as he will serve them?

Would it not be better for the States to elect their Governors upon the same principle; and if they officiate unjustly, hurl them from office? If a good man is thus elected and continues to do his duty, he will keep in advance of the people; and if he does not, he does not magnify his office. Such is the kingdom of God, in comparison.

When the best man is elected President, let him select the best men he can find for his counsellors or cabinet; and let all the officers within the province of the Chief Magistrate to appoint be selected upon the same principle to officiate wisely in different parts of the nation. Our Father in heaven does not visit every place in person to guide and administer the law to the people, and to do this, that, and the other: he never did and never will; but he has officers, whom he sends when and where he pleases, giving to them their credentials and missions, as does our Government to our fellow-men here....

The kingdom that the Almighty will set up in the latter days will have its officers, and those officers will be peace. Every man that officiates in a public capacity will be filled with the Spirit of God, with the light of God, with the power of God, and will understand right from wrong, truth from error, light from darkness, that which tends to life and that which tends to death. They will say, "We offer you life; will you receive it?" "No," some will say. "Then you are at perfect liberty to choose death: the Lord does not, neither will we control you in the least in the exercise of your agency. We place the principles of life before you. Do as you please, and we will protect you in your rights, though you will learn that the system you have chosen to follow brings you to dissolution—to being resolved to native element."

When the government of God is in force upon the earth, there will be many officers and branches to that government, as there now are to that of the United States. There will be such helps, governments, &c., as the people require in their several capacities and circumstances; for the Lord will not administer everywhere in person.

The world seem to be afraid of the power of God, or rather, as I observed not long since, afraid that we are not in possession of it. They need not borrow trouble upon that point; for if we are not what we profess to be, we shall certainly fail, and they will no longer be disturbed about "Mormonism."…

I know that the kingdom of God is in its youth upon this earth, and that the principles of life and salvation are freely proffered to the people all over the world.…

When the kingdom of God is established upon the earth, people will find it to be very different from what they now imagine. Will it be in the least degree tyrannical and oppressive towards any human being? No, it will not; for such is not the kingdom of God.

I believe in a true republican theocracy, and also in a true democratic theocracy, as the term democratic is now used; for they are to me, in their present use, convertible terms.

What do I understand by a theocratic government? One in which all laws are enacted and executed in righteousness, and whose officers possess that power which proceedeth from the Almighty. That is the kind of government I allude to when I speak of a theocratic government, or the kingdom of God upon the earth. It is, in short, the eternal powers of the Gods.

What do the world understand theocracy to be? A poor, rotten government of man, that would say, without the shadow of provocation or just cause, "Cut that man's head off; put that one on the rack; arrest another, and retain him in unlawful and unjust duress while you plunder his property and pollute his wife and daughters; massacre here and there." The Lord Almighty does nothing of that kind, neither does any man who is controlled by his Spirit.

Again, the theocracy I speak of is the power of the Holy Ghost within you—that living and eternal principle that we do not possess in the fulness that we are seeking. When we talk about heavenly things, and see the world grovelling in their sin and misery, and loving iniquity and corruption, the heavens weep over the people, and still they will not infringe upon their rights. God has created them so far perfectly independent as to be able to choose death or life; and he will not infringe upon this right.

And then to see people running after this and that which is calculated to destroy them spiritually and temporally—to bring upon them the first death, and then the second, so that they will be as though they had not been—is enough to make the heavens weep.

When his kingdom is established upon the earth, and Zion built up, the Lord will send his servants as saviours upon Mount Zion. The servants of God who have lived on the earth in ages past will reveal where different persons have lived who have died without the Gospel, give their names, and say, "Now go forth, ye servants of God, and exercise your rights and privileges; go and perform the ordinances of the house of God for those who have passed their probation without the law, and for all who will receive any kind of salvation: bring them up to inherit the celestial, terrestial and telestial kingdoms," and probably many other kingdoms not mentioned in the Scriptures; for every person will receive according to his capacity and according to the deeds done in the body, whether good or bad, much or little.

What will become of the rest? Jesus will reign until he puts all enemies under his feet, and will destroy the death that we are afflicted with, and will also destroy him that hath the power of death; and one eternal life will spread over the earth. Then it will be exalted and become as a sea of glass, as seen by John the Revelator, and become the eternal habitation of those who are so happy as to gain eternal life and live in the presence of our Father and Saviour.

There are millions and millions of kingdoms that the people have no conception of. The Christians of the day have no knowledge of God, of godliness, of eternity, of the worlds that are, that have been, and that are coming forth. There are myriads of people pertaining to this earth who will come up and receive a glory according to their capacity.

A man apostatizes and comes back, and there is a place prepared for him; and so there is for all persons, to suit their several capacities and answer to the lives they have lived in the flesh.

There are many who swear occasionally; others get drunk, &c. Do you not know it? O fools and slow of heart to understand your own existence! But many indulge in such practices, and some will stumble here and there; and we must keep pulling them out of the mire and washing them all the time.

Will they be consigned to eternal damnation for such conduct? No; for those who drink too much will make good servants, if you can get them where whisky will not cloud their brains, or where there is none. Make servants of such characters and set them to work in their different departments, and they can do something: they are not useless. They are the workmanship of God's hands—brothers to Jesus, flesh of his flesh and bone of his bone. The same Father that begat the tabernacle of Jesus on the earth brought forth the world of mankind; and we are all his children, whether we do wickedly or not. We are the offspring of one common Father.

Brother Kimball says that it is a pity there is such a quarrel in the family. In the flesh we are the sons and daughters of Father Adam and Mother Eve: we are all one family; and yet we are contending and quarrelling, and have arrived at such a pass that many do not know whether they belong to one kingdom and family, or not....

With you, my brethren, I have the principles of eternal salvation; and for this cause they quarrel with us. The world say that we have principles that really lay the axe at the roots of the trees of all false creeds; and if we are let alone, their creeds will cease having followers. If they let us alone, and we are wrong and corrupt, as they say we are, we shall come to an end.

Why do they prefer to be corrupt? They do not understand true principles, otherwise they would say, "Praise God! I am thankful that you are here. Do right, prosper, and bring salvation to all the house of Israel, and to the Gentile world so far as you can."

Let us alone, and we will build up the kingdom of God. We are striving for what all Christendom professes to be, and we will bring it forth. If they persecute us, we will bring it forth the sooner. Could all the Elders of Israel have given "Mormonism" the same impetus that the last quarrel has done? No. The Lord will bring more out of that than all the Elders could have done by any performance of theirs.

If the Devil and his servants are permitted to persecute us, why should we complain? Has not the Prophet; said that the servants of the Devil would make lies their refuge, and hide themselves under falsehood? Poor, miserable, lying curses here can write lies and publish them and send them forth in every direction. Traders take our money for goods, and all the time stir up every destructive element in their power to sell our blood, destroy our lives, and pollute our society.

Should the Lord reveal to me that my work on this earth is finished, I am ready to depart this life at any moment he may require. But the time has not yet come, and I expect to live until the Lord is willing that I should die.

I expect to live until I finish my work; and what is that? To promote the welfare of mankind, and save as many of the sons and daughters of Adam as I can prevail upon to be saved. How many I shall prevail upon to be saved is not for me to say.

When I get through my work here, my body will have the privilege to rest; and I understand where my spirit will go, and who will be my associates in the spirit world.

We have more friends behind the vail than on this side, and they will hail us more joyfully than you were ever welcomed by your parents and friends in this world; and you will rejoice more when you meet them than you ever rejoiced to see a friend in this life; and then we shall go on from step to step, from rejoicing to rejoicing, and from one intelligence and power to another, our happiness becoming more and more exquisite and sensible as we proceed in the words and powers of life.

God bless you! Amen.

Glossary

adulterated:	corrupted, mixed with impurities
apostatizes:	abandons beliefs
begat:	to father, or make children
Chief Magistrate:	the president
covenants:	agreements, specifically between God and his people
Gentile:	a Christian (as opposed to a Jew)
house of Esau:	possibly the Edomites, the descendants of the biblical figure Esau, who, according to the biblical book of Obadiah, incur God's wrath for their sins
"if the Saints are let alone ...":	a very loose quotation from the Gospel of John 11:47–49
"I will make thine officers peace ..."	quotation from Isaiah 60:17
Jehovah:	God
John the Revelator:	also called John of Patmos, the author of the biblical Book of Revelation
Mahometan:	Muslim
Mount Zion:	a hill just outside of Jerusalem in Israel, with Zion becoming a figure of speech for all of Israel
New Jerusalem:	literally or figuratively, the city God will prepare for his saints
telestial:	the lowest of the three heavenly kingdoms
theocracy:	rule by God through a state-instituted church
"They have transgressed the laws ...":	from Isaiah 24:5

Shrine of the Báb from North West.

PERSIAN BAYAN: DOCUMENT ANALYSIS

"From eternity unto eternity this Tree of divine Truth hath served and will ever serve as the throne of the revelation and concealment of God among His creatures..."

Overview

The Persian Bayan is a text written by the Bab (Siyyid 'Ali Muhammad Shirazi), a pivotal figure in nineteenth-century Shia Islamic history; the Arabic word *bayan* can be translated as "all things," "divine utterance," or, more generally, "explanation," "eloquence," "expounding," or "revelation." The text is one of numerous mystical, prophetic scriptural works the Bab wrote as the leader of a religious movement called Babism, the forerunner of the religion called Baha'i, which today claims about six to eight million members worldwide. Members of the Baha'i faith converted from Babism, whose members are called Babi Azalis. The Azalis (or Babis) adhere to the original doctrines of the Bab, while members of Baha'i follow the teachings of Baha'u'llah, whose real name was Mirza Husayn-Ali and who saw himself as the divine messianic leader whose imminent arrival the Bab predicted.

Today the Baha'i faith holds the writings of the Bab, including the Persian Bayan, in high regard; the authority of his writings is as important to members of the Baha'i faith as the Bible is to Christians or the Qur'an is to Muslims. Both Babis and Baha'i regard the Bab's writings—particularly the Persian Bayan—as "abrogating," or canceling out, traditionally held Islamic laws. The Bab's writings, in other words, supersede and replace the religious laws and teachings of Islam. Similarly, Baha'is believe that the writings of Baha'u'llah, in turn, supersede many of the teachings and laws of the Bab. They see his writings as an essential phase in the course of human history because they point directly toward the revelation of Baha'u'llah. A comparison may be drawn to the figure of John the Baptist in Christianity; just as John the Baptist prepared a religious minority for the coming of Jesus Christ, the Bab prepared a religious minority for the pronouncements of Baha'u'llah.

The Persian Bayan is considered the "Mother Book" of the Bab; it is his most important and complex text. Baha'is also read the Persian Bayan as having a direct literary and mystical relationship with Baha'u'llah's Kitab-i-iqan ("The Book of Certitude," written in January 1861), in which Baha'u'llah is believed to have negated and fulfilled many of the laws and teachings of the Persian Bayan. Because the Bab left the Persian Bayan in an incomplete state, Baha'is regard the Kitab-i-iqan as its completion.

Many of the Bab's writings have been lost, and more remain archived and unpublished. A claim is often made that no other major religious figure in world history has revealed as much scripture as did the Bab, yet relatively little is available to the general public.

Context

The Bab's writings are intentionally scriptural and take a prophetic and mystical tone rooted in what might be characterized as a very liberal interpretation of the Qur'an. This interpretation arose from a religious and political revolutionary sect called Shaykhism. Shaykhis were Muslims who followed the spiritual teachings of Shaykh Ahmad (1753–1826) and believed that a final Islamic "imam," or teacher, was coming. This final imam's appearance in the world would coincide with the beginning of the final stage of human history. Shaykh Ahmad's teachings were based on the beliefs of Twelver Shias: This Islamic sect believed that Islam was to be led by a series of twelve imams, starting with Ali (the son-in-law of Muhammad, the founder of Islam, and the first imam) and ending with a figure named Muhammad al-Mahdi ("the Mahdi"). While the first eleven imams died, it was believed of the twelfth that he had disappeared but would reappear before the Day of Judgment and make truth and justice triumphant—an event referred to in Islam as "occultation." The Shaykhis believed that if the Mahdi was to provide guidance, someone on earth had to be able to communicate with him; Shaykh Ahmad was regarded as the first person able to do so. This capability gave the sect's leader a kind of divinity in his followers' eyes.

Although the event is largely undocumented, Baha'is believe that the Bab met the successor of Shaykh Amad, Sayyid Kazim (1793–1843), while visiting Karbala (the holy city of Shia Islam in Iraq) in 1839 and 1840. In 1842, shortly before his death, Kazim directed another Shaykhi named Mulla Husayn (1813–1849) to search for the Mahdi, who was believed to be a forerunner to the "final imam." Two years later, in 1844, following a forty-day period of secluded prayer, Mulla Husayn met the Bab in Shiraz (in southwestern Iran), and the Bab declared himself the Mahdi; Husayn became the Bab's first follower.

Although the Bab's writings are understood and accepted as world scripture, it is important to remember that his writings were religiously and politically radical. Many of the Bab's writings were written from prison, contributing to their revolutionary nature and implied audience; the audience of the texts would have been largely limited to the Bab's faithul and other supporters, but the texts themselves are aimed at his theological or political opponents. Many of Baha'u'llah's primary texts were also composed from prison. The Persian Bayan, the Bab's most important text, is believed to have been entirely written while he was imprisoned in Maku in late 1847 or the early months of 1848. The Bab's writings are intentionally heretical to traditional Islam while being theologically playful with Islamic ideas, and his audience viewed his words as negating and replacing Islam itself as a means of preparing humanity for a new religious teaching that would replace all religions. The political systems of the Middle East as well as the Western colonial influences on the region were believed to be ready to be overturned by the new age for which the Bab was preparing his audience.

About the Author

Siyyid 'Ali Muhammad Shirazi is known today primarily as "the Bab," which means "gate" in Arabic. The Bab is revered by Baha'is as a "manifestation of God"; that is, his person and writings share the same significance of the founders of the great world religions—Jesus, Muhammad, and others—but his writings are also rejected in favor of the superiority of Baha'i scriptures. While there have been several "manifestations of God," the one whom the Bab names "Him Whom God shall make manifest" is understood to be a manifestation of God with the authority to supersede all other manifestations.

The Bab was born Siyyid 'Ali Muhammad Shirazi on October 20, 1819, to a middle-class family of prominent merchants in the Persian city of Shiraz; his father died young, and the Bab was taken in by his uncle. The Bab claimed that through both sides of his parents he was a descendant of Muhammad through the lineage of Husayn ibn 'Ali ibn Abi Talib (626–680), an important figure in

Time Line	
October 20, 1819	■ The Bab is born Siyyid 'Ali Muhammad Shirazi.
1839–1840	■ The Bab reportedly attends lectures of Sayyid Kazim while in Karbala.
1842	■ Sayyid Kazim, leader of the Shaykhis, directs Mulla Husayn to search for the Mahdi, believed by Shaykhis to be the companion of Jesus Christ at the apocalypse.
May 22, 1844	■ The Bab confidentially reveals himself to be the Mahdi to Mulla Husayn in Iran.
September 1845	■ The Bab publicly asserts his claim to be the Mahdi.
March 1847	■ The Bab is imprisoned in Maku, where he composes the Persian Bayan.
June-July 1847	■ Early Babis hold the Conference of Badasht, where the nature of the Bab's teachings and the proper context of Babism within the context of Islam is debated; Baha'u'llah is in attendance.
July 9, 1850	■ The Bab is executed in Tabriz. Subh-i-Azal (Mirza Yahya Nuri) is named successor to the Babi movement.
January 1861	■ While in exile in Baghdad, Baha'u'llah writes Kitab-i-iqan, an important theological work in Baha'i faith meant to be a completion of the Persian Bayan.
April 21, 1863	■ Baha'u'llah publicly reveals himself to be "Him Whom God shall make manifest" in Baghdad.
1976	■ The Universal House of Justice of the Baha'i Faith publishes Selections from the Writings of the Bab, including the authoritative translation of the Persian Bayan.

Shia Islam. It is said that at an early age he rejected the merchant trade of his family in favor of the study of religion.

Sometime around 1839 and 1840, the Bab went on a pilgrimage that took him to Iraq and the holy city of Karbala. There he is believed to have met with the Shaykhi leader Sayyid Kazim, who urged his followers to seek out the Mahdi. One of those followers was Mulla Husayn, who traveled to Shiraz, where he met the Bab. A pivotal event took place on May 22, 1844, when Husayn invited the Bab to his home and revealed that he was searching for a successor to Kazim, who had died in December 1843. It was at this meeting that the Bab proclaimed himself to be Kazim's successor, a claim that he made public in September of the following year. Kazim believed him and become his earliest follower. In the years that followed, the Bab proclaimed himself a "hidden" imam, a forefunner to the final and most important teacher, who would be coming to restore Islam.

The Bab, however, became a threat to orthodox Islamic clergy. Accordingly, the governor of Shiraz ordered his arrest in 1845. After a cholera epidemic broke out in the city in 1846, he was released, but as his popularity grew, he was again arrested in January 1847. In an ironic reversal, he was popular among prison authorities and was treated well. During his time in the prison fortress at Maku in Iran, he wrote the Persian Bayan. Meanwhile, in the summer of 1847 early Babis, including Baha'u'llah, held the Conference of Badasht to debate the Bab's teachings and the context of Babism within Islam. Because of his growing popularity, the Bab was put on trial for blasphemy, and during his trial he stated unequivocally that he was the Mahdi. In 1850, Amir Kabir (1807–1852), the premier of Iran, ordered that the Bab be executed. On July 9, 1850, a firing squad proceeded with the execution order, but both the Bab and another follower (who had begged to be executed with him) were unharmed by the firing squad's bullets, and the Bab appeared to have miraculously escaped. When the smoke cleared, the Bab was discovered in hiding in the prison compound. He and his follower were tried again, and the second firing squad killed them both.

Explanation and Analysis of the Document

The Persian Bayan was originally organized into a series of nineteen *vahids*, or "unities," with nineteen *babs*, or "gates," within each unity; the text itself ends with the tenth gate of the ninth unity. The number 19 is considered a holy number by Babis and Baha'is because it is a root of the number of days in the Babi calendar. Spirituality is implied in this organization, for each day of the year is a *bab*, or gate, leading to "Him Whom God shall make manifest."

The Persian Bayan is unavailable in English as a complete text; only selections have been authoritatively translated and published. Even more unfortunate is that in its authoritative published form, released in 1976 as part of a Baha'i edition titled *Selections of the Writings of the Bab*, passages are presented out of order, especially since the opening of the text is essential to understanding the implicit spirituality of the whole. The Arabic term *bayan* means "all things," and the Bab invoked a creation spirituality within his writings, recalling the hymn to Logos, or "the Word," in the Christian Gospel of John. The Bab suggests that his writings are the word of God, and as an apocalyptic text the Persian Bayan suggests that the Bab accompanies Jesus in declaring, "Behold, I am making all things new" (Revelation 21:5). In other words, the text itself of the Persian Bayan reverses the social and religious order of the world in preparation for something entirely new. It is a *bab*, or gate, with many smaller *babs* into a new age for humanity. The reader is invited either to pass through the gates or to passively observe God moving in history. The Persian Bayan, then, sets forth a new religion that is connected to the old and begins the fulfillment of all others, even if the text or the religion itself does not complete this fulfillment.

◆ The Day of Resurrection Is a Day on Which the Sun Riseth

The apocalypse, or final stage, of Islam is not one that comes with great fanfare but is in the ordinariness of the present, and in this case the present is the Bab revealing these words. The Bab here draws a comparison between his revelation and that of Muhammad in the Qur'an—that humanity is now at least partially prepared for the truths about to be given. Yet there is a symbolic reason for a lack of spectacle: "The Day of Resurrection is said to be the greatest of days, yet it is like unto any other day." The Bab's imprisonment, however, is evidence that he is offering a truth for which humanity is not entirely prepared, implying that something else will be coming.

◆ Likewise Consider the Manifestation of the Point of the Bayan

In a clearly heretical statement in the context of Islamic theology, the Bab begins by quoting the Qur'an and then turns to prophesying: "Know thou of a certainty that whenever thou makest mention of Him Whom God shall make manifest, only then art thou making mention of God." The Bab continues: "In like manner shouldst thou hearken unto the verses of the Bayán and acknowledge its truth, only then would the revealed verses of God profit thee." In other words, the text of the Persian Bayan abrogates, or negates, much of what might be considered outdated revelation in the Qur'an, but the Bayan itself is inseparable from a mystical spirituality and messianic expectation of the one who is coming, "Him whom God shall make manifest."

◆ There Is No Doubt That the Almighty Hath Sent Down These Verses unto Him

A text appearing earlier in the Bayan, from the second unity, assures readers of the divine inspiration and source of the Bab's writings. The Bab includes among his revelation all of his previous writings and indicates the voluminous quantity of scripture already given, and he suggests that if he were not imprisoned by his oppressors that the Word of God would be "unhindered."

◆ Since That Day Is a Great Day...

The Bab begins by condemning those who do not wait for "Him Whom God shall make manifest" and then compares the future manifestation with the manifestation of Muhammad, revealing the Qur'an. "Likewise," the Bab continues, "behold this Revelation," that the Persian Bayan has a new authority over the old. Furthermore: "Likewise is the Revelation of Him Whom God shall make manifest," that the coming scripture of the next manifestation of God will abrogate or negate the writings of the Bab.

This passage makes reference to those who followed Muhammad in secret during the initial epoch of Islam, when few people would follow the new faith and even fewer would do so publicly. The Bab's analogy to his own writings is an allusion to his own role as the "hidden" imam, but he is also making the claim that this text will be regarded as an important religious document later. The Bab's point goes further than this, however, suggesting that while the Bayan has authority above the Qur'an, the revelation of the one who is coming will have authority over the Bayan. To this end, the Bayan is a "hidden" text for this preparatory period of the coming new religion.

◆ In the Manifestation of the Apostle of God All Were Eagerly Awaiting Him

All manifestations of God are rejected by many during their lifetimes, the Bab writes, as he gives comfort to his followers, whom he calls "people of the Bayán." Again he draws a comparison between his revelations and those of Muhammad and laments that he is "lonely and forsaken" in prison while those who anticipate the coming of the Messiah live in comfort in their homes. He urges his followers to remain open to divine revelation in the form of the twelfth imam, who will be coming after him.

◆ At the Time of the Manifestation of Him Whom God Shall Make Manifest

The Bab instructs his followers to "be well trained in the teachings of the Bayán," so that they will assist the one who is coming, and he notes that if everyone were knowledgeable of the Bayan, all people would gain admittance to heaven. This teaching is an extension of the Islamic notions of peace and justice, asserting that if a society follows Islamic law, conflicts will cease, and poverty will be eliminated. For the Bab to instruct the text of the Bayan in this way is at once a direct negation of Islamic theology and a bold announcement that he is doing something formally separate from the religion of Islam.

◆ Ye Perform Your Works for God from the Beginning of Your Lives till the End Thereof

The Bab teaches that worship of God is connected to the occultation (emergence from hiding) of the one who is coming, and he suggests that worshiping God without recognizing the manifestations of God does not spiritually move humanity forward. To suggest that the worship of God is inseparable from an expectancy for the one who is coming is another abrogation of Islamic teaching and offers

a different interpretation of some Shia Islamic teachings. For some Shia Muslims the position of spiritually awaiting a final imam is not an unusual idea, but to essentially connect the worship of Allah to this figure would be seen as both undermining Allah and a denial of the status of Muhammad as prophet. Muslims do not worship Muhammad, for he is a prophet; the Bab is speaking of a "manifestation of God" who is coming, and genuine worship of God must coincide with the authority and teaching of this "manifestation."

◆ God Hath, at All Times and under All Conditions, Been Wholly Independent of His Creatures

The transcendence of God is affirmed, and the Bab suggests that a new covenant has been made between the divine and humanity in the revelation of the Bayan and that a new covenant is in the making with the one who is coming. Beyond this, no true holy book is ever revealed without the book's message being one meant for the whole of humanity, not just a specific group of people. This teaching coincides with the Baha'i doctrine that the differences between the world religions are cultural and not theological and that the message behind all of them is essentially the same.

◆ How Veiled Are Ye, O My Creatures

In this passage the Bab condemns those who oppress him, and he affirms the authority of the Bayan. He also continues his condemnation of those who do not recognize his authority; while his authority may appear to be muted by virtue of his location inside a prison, his authority comes from God and will yet be eclipsed by the authority of the one who is coming. In discussing the manifestation who is coming after him, the Bab refers to him as "He Who is the Manifestation of My Self," a peculiar phrase indicating that the Bab sees himself as a "manifestation of God" along with other manifestations, including the one coming next.

◆ How Vast the Number of People Who Are Well Versed in Every Science

In this short passage, the Bab slightly criticizes those who place their faith in science; it is faith in God, he asserts, that will save them. Yet he writes that knowledge of science is not at odds with knowledge of God because the outcome of science is an understanding of God's will. This attitude of harmony between science and religion is an important theme in the Baha'i faith.

◆ No Created Thing Shall Ever Attain Its Paradise...

This passage offers a basic epistemology that was later developed in the Baha'i faith. The gulf between humanity and God is indescribably vast, but within the scope of humanity, the manifestation of God is the highest possible example of humanity, beyond normal understandings of human capacity for knowledge.

The Bab's criticism of education and the sciences is an attack upon those among the elite educated class of his time, who were fascinated with the scientific discoveries of European culture; most technological innovations during this time were coming from Europe and the Americas, not from the Middle East. The point is that religious innovation, which has traditionally arisen in the Middle East, is occuring while few pay attention. In the Baha'i faith, Baha'u'llah would later abrogate these statements of the Bab and encourage scientific and humanities education as essential to the new spiritual age of humanity.

The final paragraph includes a few fairly dense ideas in relatively few words. First, the Bab summarizes his prior points by adding that "true knowledge... is the knowledge of God," adding that this knowledge of God coincides with "the recognition of His Manifestation in each Dispensation." He then offers an analogy about a teenager reaching adulthood and giving thanks for the day of his conception, illustrating the conclusion that every stage in religious history is essential to the next. Therefore, even though the Bayan negates many of the teachings of Islam, the Bab is not suggesting that Islam itself, or the Qur'an and Muhammad, are irrelevant but rather that they are important remnants of an age that has closed. Even "the religion taught by Adam," the first man, long ago, was an essential moment in the new religion whose dawn is now breaking.

♦ Twelve Hundred and Seventy Years Have Elapsed since the Declaration of Muhammad

In this lengthy passage the Bab heretically condemns the pilgrimage practices of Muslims, the hajj, as empty ritual, and urges Muslims to consider their individual faith rather than the faith of the majority. This passage is indicative of the Bab's teaching that the age of Islam has come to an end, demonstrating that its primary rituals have, in his view, lost their spiritual significance and laying the groundwork for the Baha'i teaching that faith practices should be as minimal and simple as possible. The continuation of elaborate rituals that are contingent upon the calendar year prevents individuals from seeing the truth of the Bab's teachings, and these practices are not exclusive to Islam: "Thus in every Dispensation a number of souls enter the fire by reason of their following in the footsteps of others." Not only is the ritual empty, but the ritual has replaced the faith altogether.

♦ Since All Men Have Issued Forth...

Although the point of this passage is repeated elsewhere, the analogy of the sun being reflected by the believers became important in the Baha'i faith, where the faithful mirror the light of the sun, and the manifestations of God reflect the sun more brightly than the rest of humanity and may be mistaken for the sun itself. This is a rejection of the Islamic understanding of *jinn* (mythical spirit creatures) and renders Islamic understandings of human knowledge to be particular to the Islamic faith rather than universal. The sun, on the other hand, is an analogy to which all people of the world may have equal access.

♦ O People of the Bayán!

The Bab again condemns the hajj: "All... people who at this time go on pilgrimage do not do so with true under-

standing that the One Who enjoined this commandment is far greater than the commandment itself." He sees the hajjas an empty ritual that Muslims practice, a ritual that in its practice betrays the greatness of Muhammad, as evidenced by the fact that the Bab is currently imprisoned. This claim of "greatness" with Muhammad is another point of departure with traditional Islam; Islamic theology would not claim such "greatness" for Muhammad, who is understood as having a lower station as a "prophet." The Bab also repeats his analogy of human beings as mirrors reflecting the sun.

♦ Everyone Is Eagerly Awaiting His Appearance

The Bab again draws a comparison between the Qur'an and the Bayan and refers to his own writings—"no less than five hundred thousand verses on different subjects"—which, he predicts, will soon be regarded as scriptural and authoritative. Following the teachings of the Bab leads to peace: "If all men were to observe the ordinances of God no sadness would befall that heavenly Tree."

♦ The Acts of Him Whom God Shall Make Manifest Are Like unto the Sun

The Bab continues his discourse on the analogy of God as the sun, which would be explained further in Baha'i scriptures. The shared "light" of the faithful, who are opening themselves to the light of the one who is coming, renders the individuals as "stars." Their light makes them "starships" whose light is greater than the stars at night, gleaming "forth with light in the night season." He also refers to the manifestation of God as "the Mouthpiece of God."

♦ If at the Time of the Appearance of Him...

In this further discussion of the sun analogy, the Bab suggests that with the one who is coming, the brightness of the sun will be so luminously reflected that regal claims to sovereignty and other assertions of human significance will become meaningless. This text might explain in some ways Baha'u'llah's later writings to the leaders of the world, collected primarily in his Proclamation of Baha'u'llah and elsewhere, declaring his own authority over those very leaders. Like the Bab, Baha'u'llah wrote most of these letters from prison. "I beg forgiveness for making this comparison," the Bab writes, but the "station of one is that of nothingness, while the station of the other... is that of the Reality of things." Those who try to reflect their own light have no comparison to the true light of God.

♦ I Swear by the Most Holy Essence of God

The Persian Bayan's authority, like the authority of other manifestations of God and their texts, will come to an end at the advent of the new manifestation. While many of the Bab's statements regarding his own authority suggest a kind of pretentiousness to an outsider to the religion, a key necessity to understanding the Bab and Babism is the underlying humility of the message that the current teachings are intentionally temporary. In like manner, then, all previous revelations are rendered temporary as well.

The Bab's reference to the "Book of God" is a reference to the Bayan itself, but more deeply the "Book of God" is the spiritual ground out of which all other genuine religious revelations arise. The Persian Bayan is the most recent and most important of revelations emerging from the Book of God, but the one that is following will be much more genuine and powerful.

♦ The Substance of This Chapter Is This

This long passage emphasizes the Islamic affirmation both of the status of Jesus as a prophet and of the Jews as having a shared history of divine revelation. It also denies the Islamic closure of revelation with Muhammad; for Muslims, the Qur'an, revealed by Muhammad, is the final and most absolute revelation of God to humanity. Just as Jesus abrogated the laws of Moses by his teachings, substituting the old law for the new, with the person of Jesus himself fulfilling the law, so also do the Bab and the Bayan itself abrogate and fulfill the Qur'an.

The Bab refers to the date of "the eve of the fifth of Jamádiyu'l-Avval, 1260 A.H.," or May 22, 1844, the day that he revealed himself to be the Mahdi to Mulla Husayn. This date is "the Day of Resurrection of the Qur'an"; so too will the "Resurrection of the Bayan" occur when it is both fulfilled and abrogated by the one who is coming. In other words, the Bab places himself as the most recent revealer of the Word of God within the long history of God and humanity, and just like the former revealers—Moses, Jesus, and Muhammad—the Bab's authority will be at once affirmed and subverted by the next revealer.

♦ In the Name of God, the Most Exalted, the Most Holy

Although this passage appears toward the end of the compiled version of the Bayan in *Selections of the Writings of the Bab*, this text was actually written as the first gate of the first unity of the Persian Bayan. The opening words are a direct reference to the opening of the Qur'an and indirectly are a reference to the biblical book of Genesis and Gospel of John, in their invocation of a creation formula. The opening words of the Persian Bayan, along with the opening words of the Qur'an, constitute nineteen letters, the most perfect number in Babism.

Beyond the numerology, the cryptic meaning of this opening phrase as it appears in Arabic requires some explanation. The phrase, "In the Name of God, the Most Exalted, the Most Holy," is an allusion to the opening words of the Qur'an with some slight changes. This literary connection is relevant given the nature of the theological claims that the Bab offers in the Bayan. A holy book that abrogates the Qur'an begins similarly to the Qur'an itself. In the Bayan's negation of Islam, the Bab acknowledges its roots within Islam and understands himself as branching out onto new religious ground because of Islam, rather than despite Islam.

The Qur'an opens naming Allah, in certain English translations, as "Most Gracious" and "Most Merciful." The Bab names Allah "Most Exalted" and "Most Holy." The Arabic language employed here offers a theologi-

cal and literary allusion to "Twelver" Shia Islam, noting that the Bayan is a text coming from a very specific sect of Islam, a sect that the Bab understands as preparing for fulfillment through schism. The opening phrase thus refers to God but at the same time uses wording that connects the Bayan to scripture of the past while indicating a new beginning.

The rest of this gate is a discourse on the greatness of God, emphasizing the transcendence of God (who is "omnipotent," "Most High," "inaccessible") as being rooted in the Shia Islam of the past, but God is beyond these local understandings. The implication is that the new religious paradigm offered by the Bab is the gateway out of the tribalism of Islam and into something new, even though the Bab and his revelation are just precursors to the new religion. This new, higher understanding of God that the Bab is illuminating for humanity is to be understood as the Primal Unity or Primal Point, the first before all other firsts and the last after all other lasts ("beginning and the end," "manifest and hidden").

♦ The Revelation of the Divine Reality Hath Everlastingly...

Following this passage, the "Point of the Bayan" is here contrasted to "the time of the revelation of the Qur'an" as points along the history of divine revelation, all flowing from each other but equally rooted in the Primal Point of God. This Primal Point is "the Mirror of His Revelation," which will be brought to fuller light by "Him Whom God shall make manifest." The one who is coming "is too high and exalted... for anyone to allude unto Him."

Audience

The Bab seemed to believe, and correctly so, that his writings would carry greater significance long after his own lifetime. As such, much of his intended audience could be considered to be potential converts or imagined followers of a future religion that had not yet been realized. This audience was supposed to hold the Persian Bayan on a par with the Qur'an and yet be prepared to replace it with a new text appearing from the one expected to come later. Specifically, the original audience was a very small group of the Bab's followers and interested Shaykhis and other Shiites, as well as Muslims seeking to discredit and expose the Bab. For the early Babis, the Persian Bayan was immediately recognized as the Bab's most important work of scripture.

Today all of the published writings of the Bab hold an important place among Baha'i scripture as the most recent revelation of God before Baha'u'llah, who announced himself to be "He whom God shall make manifest" in Baghdad on April 21, 1863. The Bab's writings served the purpose for which they were intended, namely, to announce the proper station—the authority and theological significance—of the new manifestation of God. As the Bab predicted that his own writings would be obscured compared with those of the one who is coming, the Baha'is see the Bab's writings as having been superseded by those of Baha'u'llah. That said,

"There is no doubt that the Almighty hath sent down these verses unto Him, even as He sent down unto the Apostle of God. Indeed no less than a hundred thousand verses similar to these have already been disseminated among the people, not to mention His Epistles, His Prayers or His learned and philosophical treatises."

(Section 1)

"From eternity unto eternity this Tree of divine Truth hath served and will ever serve as the throne of the revelation and concealment of God among His creatures, and in every age is made manifest through whomsoever He pleaseth."

(Section 1)

"If at the time of the appearance of Him Whom God will make manifest all the dwellers of the earth were to bear witness unto a thing whereunto He beareth witness differently, His testimony would be like unto the sun, while theirs would be even as a false image produced in a mirror which is not facing the sun. For had it been otherwise their testimony would have proved a faithful reflection of His testimony."

(Section 1)

"The Day of Resurrection is a day on which the sun riseth and setteth like unto any other day. How oft hath the Day of Resurrection dawned, and the people of the land where it occurred did not learn of the event."

(Section 1)

the writings of the Bab were influential on early Baha'is and had at least some influence on Baha'u'llah.

It is difficult to know what relevance any of the writings of the Bab, including the Persian Bayan, have for Azali Babis today, since Azalis are few in number and largely secretive. They follow the teachings of the Bab's successor, Subh-i-Azal (1831–1912), whose writings are believed to supersede those of the Bab.

Impact

Although the religious movements that the Bab directly began were never large, he was a controversial figure during his lifetime and remained influential following his death. His writings' influence continues as an important element of the Baha'is' understanding of revelation, history, and the theological significance of Baha'u'llah, the "manifestation of God" in the Baha'i faith. To this end, perhaps the single most important claim of the Bab is in his description of "He Whom God shall make manifest," the coming *manifestation* of God whom Baha'is believe Baha'u'llah to be.

This claim finds its most significant and fully expounded realization in the Persian Bayan. But beyond this, among the Bab's writings, the Persian Bayan is the most important of Babi sacred literature because of the deep symbolism in the organization of the document itself and because of its revolutionary, if not radical, mystical style. The whole text of the Persian Bayan, read outside its Baha'i interpretations, remains a fascinating example of schismatic movements within Shia Islam in the nineteenth century. The text itself influenced Baha'u'llah, who took it upon himself to complete the Persian Bayan in his landmark text, Kitab-i-iqan, now considered the primary theological text of the Baha'i faith. To this end, the Bab and the Persian Bayan had a deep impact on the beginnings of the Baha'i faith as the only significant religious movement spawned by Islam that survived a century of existence.

For Baha'is today, the writings of the Bab, particularly the Persian Bayan, are held as having supreme authority over previously written world scripture, especially the Qur'an. In other words, Baha'is recognize the authority and importance of other religions' holy texts, such as the Bible, but they hold the Bab's writings to have authority over those. Within Baha'i theology, the Persian Bayan has particularly important significance in that the Bab abrogated much of the Qur'an and by default all other previous divine revelations, so that the next manifestation of God, Baha'u'llah, could begin a revelation completely new for a new era of humanity with as little scriptural baggage as possible remaining from the old eras.

Today the Baha'i faith claims millions of members. Statistics for Babi Azali adherents are difficult to estimate because they are often persecuted and thus secretive: They hold the Shia practice of *taqiyya,* or dissimulation, as an essential component of the religion. In other words, Azalis will deny their religion publicly for their own safety.

Further Reading

■ Books

Baha'i World Centre. "Preface." In *Selections from the Writings of the Bab.* Haifa, Israel: Baha'i World Centre, 1978.

Balyuzi, H. M. *The Bab: The Herald of the Day of Days.* Oxford, U.K.: George Ronald, 1973.

MacEoin, Dennis. *The Sources for Early Babi Doctrine and History.* Leiden, Netherlands: Brill, 1992.

Momen, Moojan, ed. *Selections from the Writings of E. G. Browne on the Babi and Baha'i*

Religions. Oxford, U.K.: George Ronald, 1987.

Saiedi, Nader. *Gate of the Heart.* Waterloo, Canada: Wilfrid Laurier University Press, 2008.

—Commentary by C. D. Rodkey

Questions for Further Study

1. Explain the relationship between the Bab and Babism, on the one hand, and Baha'u'llah and the Baha'i faith on the other. For reference, see the latter's Kitab-i-aqdas. Specifically, how did the Persian Bayan lay the groundwork for Baha'u'llah?

2. Both the Bab and, later, Baha'u'llah wrote many of their documents from prison. Again, referring to the entry on the latter's Kitab-i-aqdas, why were these two men imprisoned? What threat did they represent?

3. Imagine that Muhammad, the founder of Islam (see the entry on the Qur'an), were to engage in a conversation with the Bab. What do you think his reaction to the Bab's beliefs would be? Explain.

4. Babism was a heretical sect of Islam, and, indeed, various religions have had to contend with heresy and offshoots that claimed their version of the faith was truer than the original parent faith. What do you think motivates this tendency toward abrogating the parent faith in favor of a new one, not only in Islam but also in Christianity (see, for example, the entry on Canons and Decrees of the Council of Trent or the Nestorian Book of the Bee) and Buddhism (see, for example, the entry on Buddha's Noble Eightfold Path)?

5. What comparisons might you draw between the Persian Bayan and the New Testament book of Revelation?

PERSIAN BAYAN: DOCUMENT TEXT

1861 CE

—Bab

"THE Day of Resurrection is a day on which the sun riseth"

THE Day of Resurrection is a day on which the sun riseth and setteth like unto any other day. How oft hath the Day of Resurrection dawned, and the people of the land where it occurred did not learn of the event. Had they heard, they would not have believed, and thus they were not told!

When the Apostle of God [Muhammad] appeared, He did not announce unto the unbelievers that the Resurrection had come, for they could not bear the news. That Day is indeed an infinitely mighty Day, for in it the Divine Tree proclaimeth from eternity unto eternity, "Verily, I am God. No God is there but Me." Yet those who are veiled believe that He is one like unto them, and they refuse even to call Him a believer, although such a title in the realm of His heavenly Kingdom is conferred everlastingly upon the most insignificant follower of His previous Dispensation. Thus, had the people in the days of the Apostle of God regarded Him at least as a believer of their time how would they have debarred Him, for seven years while He was in the mountain, from access to His Holy House [Ka'bah]? Likewise in this Dispensation of the Point of the Bayán, if the people had not refused to concede the name believer unto Him, how could they have incarcerated Him on this mountain, without realizing that the quintessence of belief oweth its existence to a word from Him? Their hearts are deprived of the power of true insight, and thus they cannot see, while those endowed with the eyes of the spirit circle like moths round the Light of Truth until they are consumed. It is for this reason that the Day of Resurrection is said to be the greatest of all days, yet it is like unto any other day....

"LIKEWISE consider the manifestation of the Point of the"

LIKEWISE consider the manifestation of the Point of the Bayán. There are people who every night until morning busy themselves with the worship of God, and even at present when the Day-Star of Truth is nearing its zenith in the heaven of its Revelation, they have not yet left their prayer-rugs. If any one of them ever heard the wondrous verses of God recited unto him, he would exclaim: "Why dost thou keep me back from offering my prayers?" O thou who are wrapt in veils! If thou makest mention of God, wherefore sufferest thou thyself to be shut out from Him Who hath kindled the light of worship in thy heart? If He had not previously revealed the injunction: "Verily, make ye mention of God," what would have prompted thee to offer devotion unto God, and whereunto wouldst thou turn in prayer?

Know thou of a certainty that whenever thou makest mention of Him Whom God shall make manifest, only then art thou making mention of God. In like manner shouldst thou hearken unto the verses of the Bayán and acknowledge its truth, only then would the revealed verses of God profit thee. Otherwise what benefit canst thou derive therefrom? For wert thou to prostrate thyself in adoration from the beginning of life till the end and to spend thy days for the sake of God's remembrance, but disbelieve in the Exponent of His Revelation for the age, dost thou imagine that thy deeds would confer any benefit upon thee? On the other hand, if thou believest in Him and dost recognize Him with true understanding, and He saith: "I have accepted thine entire life spent in My adoration," then assuredly hast thou been worshipping Him most ardently. Thy purpose in performing thy deeds is that God may graciously accept them;

and divine acceptance can in no wise be achieved except through the acceptance of Him Who is the Exponent of His Revelation. For instance, if the Apostle of God—may divine blessings rest upon Him—accepted a certain deed, in truth God accepted it; otherwise it hath remained within the selfish desires of the person who wrought it, and did not reach the presence of God. Likewise, any act which is accepted by the Point of the Bayán is accepted by God, inasmuch as the contingent world hath no other access unto the presence of the Ancient of Days. Whatever is sent down cometh through the Exponent of His Revelation, and whatever ascendeth, ascendeth unto the Exponent of His Revelation....

"THERE is no doubt that the Almighty hath sent down"

THERE is no doubt that the Almighty hath sent down these verses unto Him [the Báb], even as He sent down unto the Apostle of God. Indeed no less than a hundred thousand verses similar to these have already been disseminated among the people, not to mention His Epistles, His Prayers or His learned and philosophical treatises. He revealeth no less than a thousand verses within the space of five hours. He reciteth verses at a speed consonant with the capacity of His amanuensis to set them down. Thus, it may well be considered that if from the inception of this Revelation until now He had been left unhindered, how vast then would have been the volume of writings disseminated from His pen.

If ye contend that these verses cannot, of themselves, be regarded as a proof, scan the pages of the Qur'án. If God hath established therein any evidence other than the revealed verses to demonstrate the validity of the prophethood of His Apostle—may the blessings of God rest upon Him—ye may then have your scruples about Him....

Concerning the sufficiency of the Book as a proof, God hath revealed: "Is it not enough for them that We have sent down unto Thee the Book to be recited to them? In this verily is a mercy and a warning to those who believe." When God hath testified that the Book is a sufficient testimony, as is affirmed in the text, how can one dispute this truth by saying that the Book in itself is not a conclusive proof?...

"SINCE that Day is a great Day it would be sorely trying"

SINCE that Day is a great Day it would be sorely trying for thee to identify thyself with the believers. For the believers of that Day are the inmates of Paradise, while the unbelievers are the inmates of the fire. And know thou of a certainty that by Paradise is meant recognition of and submission unto Him Whom God shall make manifest, and by the fire the company of such souls as would fail to submit unto Him or to be resigned to His good-pleasure. On that Day thou wouldst regard thyself as the inmate of Paradise and as a true believer in Him, whereas in reality thou wouldst suffer thyself to be wrapt in veils and thy habitation would be the nethermost fire, though thou thyself wouldst not be cognizant thereof.

Compare His manifestation with that of the Point of the Qur'án. How vast the number of the Letters of the Gospel who eagerly expected Him, yet from the time of His declaration up to five years no one became an inmate of Paradise, except the Commander of the Faithful [Imám 'Alí], and those who secretly believed in Him. All the rest were accounted as inmates of the fire, though they considered themselves as dwellers in Paradise.

Likewise behold this Revelation. The essences of the people have, through divinely-conceived designs, been set in motion and until the present day three hundred and thirteen disciples have been chosen. In the land of Sád [Isfahan], which to outward seeming is a great city, in every corner of whose seminaries are vast numbers of people regarded as divines and doctors, yet when the time came for inmost essences to be drawn forth, only its sifter of wheat donned the robe of discipleship. This is the mystery of what was uttered by the kindred of the Prophet Muḥammad—upon them be the peace of God—concerning this Revelation, saying that the abased shall be exalted and the exalted shall be abased.

Likewise is the Revelation of Him Whom God shall make manifest. Among those to whom it will never occur that they might merit the displeasure of God, and whose pious deeds will be exemplary unto everyone, there will be many who will become the personification of the nethermost fire itself, when they fail to embrace His Cause; while among the lowly servants whom no one would imagine to be of any merit, how great the number who will be honoured with true faith and on whom the Fountainhead of generosity will bestow the robe of authority. For whatever is created in the Faith of God is created through the potency of His Word....

"IN the manifestation of the Apostle of God all were eagerly"

IN the manifestation of the Apostle of God all were eagerly awaiting Him, yet thou hast heard how He was treated at the time of His appearance, in spite of the fact that if ever they beheld Him in their dreams they would take pride in them.

Likewise in the manifestation of the Point of the Bayán, the people stood up at the mention of His Name and fervently implored His advent night and day, and if they dreamt of Him they gloried in their dreams; yet now that He hath revealed Himself, invested with the mightiest testimony, whereby their own religion is vindicated, and despite the incalculable number of people who yearningly anticipate His coming, they are resting comfortably in their homes, after having hearkened to His verses; while He at this moment is confined in the mountain of Mákú, lonely and forsaken.

Take good heed of yourselves, O people of the Bayán, lest ye perform such deeds as to weep sore for His sake night and day, to stand up at the mention of His Name, yet on this Day of fruition—a Day whereon ye should not only arise at His Name, but seek a path unto Him Who personifies that Name—ye shut yourselves out from Him as by as veil....

"AT the time of the manifestation of Him Whom God"

AT the time of the manifestation of Him Whom God shall make manifest everyone should be well trained in the teachings of the Bayán, so that none of the followers may outwardly cling to the Bayán and thus forfeit their allegiance unto Him. If anyone does so, the verdict of "disbeliever in God" shall be passed upon him.

I swear by the holy Essence of God, were all in the Bayán to unite in helping Him Whom God shall make manifest in the days of His Revelation, not a single soul, nay, not a created thing would remain on earth that would not gain admittance into Paradise. Take good heed of yourselves, for the sum total of the religion of God is but to help Him, rather than to observe, in the time of His appearance, such deeds as are prescribed in the Bayán. Should anyone, however, ere He manifesteth Himself, transgress the ordinances, were it to the extent of a grain of barley, he would have trangressed His command.

Seek ye refuge in God from whatsoever might lead you astray from the Source of His Revelation and hold fast unto His Cord, for whoso holdeth fast unto His allegiance, he hath attained and will attain salvation in all the worlds.

"Such is the bounty of God; to whom He will, He giveth it, and God is the Lord of grace abounding...."

"YE perform your works for God from the beginning of"

YE perform your works for God from the beginning of your lives till the end thereof, yet not a single act is for the sake of Him Who is the Manifestation of God, to Whom every good deed reverteth. Had ye acted in such manner, ye would not have suffered so grievously on the Day of Resurrection.

Behold how great is the Cause, and yet how the people are wrapt in veils. I swear by the sanctified Essence of God that every true praise and deed offered unto God is naught but praise and deed offered unto Him Whom God shall make manifest.

Deceive not your own selves that you are being virtuous for the sake of God when you are not. For should ye truly do your works for God, ye would be performing them for Him Whom God shall make manifest and would be magnifying His Name. The dwellers of this mountain who are bereft of true understanding unceasingly utter the words, "No God is there but God"; but what benefit doth it yield them? Ponder awhile that ye may not be shut out as by a veil from Him Who is the Dayspring of Revelation....

"GOD hath, at all times and under all conditions, been"

GOD hath, at all times and under all conditions, been wholly independent of His creatures. He hath cherished and will ever cherish the desire that all men may attain His gardens of Paradise with utmost love, that no one should sadden another, not even for a moment, and that all should dwell within His cradle of protection and security until the Day of Resurrection which marketh the dayspring of the Revelation of Him Whom God will make manifest.

The Lord of the universe hath never raised up a prophet nor hath He sent down a Book unless He hath established His covenant with all men, calling for their acceptance of the next Revelation and of the next Book; inasmuch as the outpourings of His bounty are ceaseless and without limit....

"HOW veiled are ye, O My creatures, who, without"

HOW veiled are ye, O My creatures, who, without any right, have consigned Him unto a mountain [Mákú], not one of whose inhabitants is worthy of mention With Him, which is with Me, there is no one except him who is one of the Letters of the Living of My Book. In His presence, which is My Presence, there is not at night even a lighted lamp! And yet, in places [of worship] which in varying degrees reach out unto Him, unnumbered lamps are shining! All that is on earth hath been created for Him, and all partake with delight of His benefits, and yet they are so veiled from Him as to refuse Him even a lamp!

In this Day therefore I bear witness unto My creatures, for the witness of no one other than Myself hath been or shall ever be worthy of mention in My presence. I affirm that no Paradise is more sublime for My creatures than to stand before My face and to believe in My holy Words, while no fire hath been or will be fiercer for them than to be veiled from the Manifestation of My exalted Self and to disbelieve in My Words.

Ye may contend: "How doth He speak on our behalf?" Have ye not perused the unseemly words ye uttered in the past, as reflected in the text of My Book, and still ye feel not ashamed? Ye have now seen the truth of My Book conclusively established and today every one of you doth profess belief in Me through that Book. The day is not far distant when ye shall readily realize that your glory lieth in your belief in these holy verses. Today, however, when only belief in this Faith truly profiteth you, ye have debarred yourselves therefrom by reason of the things which are disadvantageous unto you and will inflict harm upon you, whereas He Who is the Manifestation of My Self hath been and shall ever remain immune from any harm whatever, and any loss that hath appeared or will appear shall eventually revert unto yourselves....

"HOW vast the number of people who are well versed in"

HOW vast the number of people who are well versed in every science, yet it is their adherence to the holy Word of God which will determine their faith, inasmuch as the fruit of every science is none other than the knowledge of divine precepts and submission unto His good-pleasure....

"NO created thing shall ever attain its paradise unless it"

NO created thing shall ever attain its paradise unless it appeareth in its highest prescribed degree of perfection. For instance, this crystal representeth the paradise of the stone whereof its substance is composed. Likewise there are various stages in the paradise for the crystal itself So long as it was stone it was worthless, but if it attaineth the excellence of ruby—a potentiality which is latent in it—how much a carat will it be worth? Consider likewise every created thing.

Man's highest station, however, is attained through faith in God in every Dispensation and by acceptance of what hath been revealed by Him, and not through learning; inasmuch as in every nation there are learned men who are versed in divers sciences. Nor is it attainable through wealth; for it is similarly evident that among the various classes in every nation there are those possessed of riches. Likewise are other transitory things.

True knowledge, therefore, is the knowledge of God, and this is none other than the recognition of His Manifestation in each Dispensation. Nor is there any wealth save in poverty in all save God and sanctity from aught else but Him—a state that can be realized only when demonstrated towards Him Who is the Dayspring of His Revelation. This doth not mean, however, that one ought not to yield praise unto former Revelations. On no account is this acceptable, inasmuch as it behooveth man, upon reaching the age of nineteen, to render thanksgiving for the day of his conception as an embryo. For had the embryo not existed, how could he have reached his present state? Likewise had the religion taught by Adam not existed, this Faith would not have attained its present stage. Thus consider thou the development of God's Faith until the end that hath no end....

"TWELVE hundred and seventy years have elapsed since"

TWELVE hundred and seventy years have elapsed since the declaration of Muhammad, and each year unnumbered people have circumambulated the House of God [Mecca]. In the concluding year of this period He Who is Himself the Founder of the House went on pilgrimage. Great God! There was a vast concourse of pilgrims from every sect. Yet not one recognized Him, though He recognized every one of them—souls tightly held in the grasp of His former commandment. The only person who recognized Him and performed pilgrimage with Him is the one round whom revolve eight Váhids, in whom God hath gloried before the Concourse on high by virtue of his absolute detachment and for his being wholly devoted to the Will of God. This doth not mean that he was made the object of a special favour, nay, this is a favour which God hath vouchsafed unto all men, yet they have suffered themselves to be veiled from it. The Commentary on the Súrih of Joseph had, in the first year of this Revelation, been widely distributed. Nevertheless, when the people realized that fellow supporters were not forthcoming they hesitated to accept it; while it never occurred to them that the very Qur'án whereunto unnumbered souls bear fealty today, was revealed in the midmost heart of the Arab world, yet to outward seeming for no less than seven years no one acknowledged its truth except the Commander of the Faithful [Imám 'Alí]—may the peace of God rest upon him—who, in response to the conclusive proofs advanced by God's supreme Testimony, recognized the Truth and did not fix his eyes on others. Thus on the Day of Resurrection God will ask everyone of his understanding and not of his following in the footsteps of others. How often a person, having inclined his ears to the holy verses, would bow down in humility and would embrace the Truth, while his leader would not do so. Thus every individual must bear his own responsibility, rather than someone else bearing it for him. At the time of the appearance of Him Whom God will make manifest the most distinguished among the learned and the lowliest of men shall both be judged alike. How often the most insignificant of men have acknowledged the truth, while the most learned have remained wrapt in veils. Thus in every Dispensation a number of souls enter the fire by reason of their following in the footsteps of others....

"SINCE all men have issued forth from the shadow of the"

SINCE all men have issued forth from the shadow of the signs of His Divinity and Lordship, they always tend to take a path, lofty and high. And because they are bereft of a discerning eye to recognize their Beloved, they fall short of their duty to manifest meekness and humility towards Him. Nevertheless, from the beginning of their lives till the end thereof, in conformity with the laws established in the previous religion, they worship God, piously adore Him, bow themselves before His divine Reality and show submissiveness toward His exalted Essence. At the hour of His manifestation, however, they all turn their gaze toward their own selves and are thus shut out from Him, inasmuch as they fancifully regard Him as one like unto themselves. Far from the glory of God is such a comparison. Indeed that august Being resembleth the physical sun, His verses are like its rays, and all believers, should they truly believe in Him, are as mirrors wherein the sun is reflected. Their light is thus a mere reflection....

"O PEOPLE of the Bayán! If ye believe in Him Whom God"

O PEOPLE of the Bayán! If ye believe in Him Whom God shall make manifest, to your own behoof do ye believe. He hath been and ever will remain independent of all men. For instance, were ye to place unnumbered mirrors before the sun, they would all reflect the sun and produce impressions thereof, whereas the sun is in itself wholly independent of the existence of the mirrors and of the suns which they reproduce. Such are the bounds of the contingent beings in their relation to the manifestation of the Eternal Being .

In this day no less than seventy thousand people make pilgrimage every year to the holy House of God in compliance with the bidding of the Apostle of God; while He Himself Who ordained this ordinance took refuge for seven years in the mountains of Mecca. And this notwithstanding that the One Who enjoined this commandment is far greater than the commandment itself. Hence all this people who at this time go on pilgrimage do not do so with true understanding, otherwise in this Day of His Return which is mightier than His former Dispensation, they would have followed His commandment. But now behold what hath happened. People who profess belief in His former religion, who in the daytime and in the night season bow down in worship in His Name, have assigned Him to a dwelling place in a mountain, while each one of them would regard attaining recognition of Him as an honour.…

"EVERYONE is eagerly awaiting His appearance, yet since"

EVERYONE is eagerly awaiting His appearance, yet since their inner eyes are not directed towards Him sorrow must needs befall Him. In the case of the Apostle of God—may the blessings of God rest upon Him—before the revelation of the Qur'án everyone bore witness to His piety and noble virtues. Behold Him then after the revelation of the Qur'án. What outrageous insults were levelled against Him, as indeed the pen is ashamed to recount. Likewise behold the Point of the Bayán. His behaviour prior to the declaration of His mission is clearly evident unto those who knew Him. Now, following His manifestation, although He hath, up to the present, revealed no less than five hundred thousand verses on different subjects, behold what calumnies are uttered, so unseemly that the pen is stricken with shame at the mention of them. But if all men were to observe the ordinances of God no sadness would befall that heavenly Tree.…

"THE acts of Him Whom God shall make manifest are like"

THE acts of Him Whom God shall make manifest are like unto the sun, while the works of men, provided they conform to the good-pleasure of God, resemble the stars or the moon Thus, should the followers of the Bayán observe the precepts of Him Whom God shall make manifest at the time of His appearance, and regard themselves and their own works as stars exposed to the light of the sun, then they will have gathered the fruits of their existence; otherwise the title of "starship" will not apply to them. Rather it will apply to such as truly believe in Him, to those who pale into insignificance in the day-time and gleam forth with light in the night season.

Such indeed is the fruit of this precept, should anyone observe it on the Day of Resurrection. This is the essence of all learning and of all righteous deeds,

should anyone but attain unto it. Had the peoples of the world fixed their gaze upon this principle, no Exponent of divine Revelation would ever have, at the inception of any Dispensation, regarded them as things of naught. However, the fact is that during the night season everyone perceiveth the light which he himself, according to his own capacity, giveth out, oblivious that at the break of day this light shall fade away and be reduced to utter nothingness before the dazzling splendour of the sun.

The light of the people of the world is their knowledge and utterance; while the splendours shed from the glorious acts of Him Whom God shall make manifest are His Words, through whose potency He rolleth up the whole world of existence, sets it under His Own authority by relating it unto Himself, then as the Mouthpiece of God, the Source of His divine light—exalted and glorified be He—proclaimeth: "Verily, verily, I am God, no God is there but Me; in truth all others except Me are My creatures. Say, O My creatures! Me alone, therefore, should ye fear.…"

"IF at the time of the appearance of Him Whom God will"

IF at the time of the appearance of Him Whom God will make manifest all the dwellers of the earth were to bear witness unto a thing whereunto He beareth witness differently, His testimony would be like unto the sun, while theirs would be even as a false image produced in a mirror which is not facing the sun. For had it been otherwise their testimony would have proved a faithful reflection of His testimony.

I swear by the most sacred Essence of God that but one line of the Words uttered by Him is more sublime than the words uttered by all that dwell on earth. Nay, I beg forgiveness for making this comparison. How could the reflections of the sun in the mirror compare with the wondrous rays of the sun in the visible heaven? The station of one is that of nothingness, while the station of the other, by the righteousness of God—hallowed and magnified be His Name—is that of the Reality of things.…

If in the Day of His manifestation a king were to make mention of his own sovereignty, this would be like unto a mirror challenging the sun, saying: "The light is in me." It would be likewise, if a man of learning in His Day were to claim to be an exponent of knowledge, or if he who is possessed of riches were to display his affluence, or if a man wielding power were to assert his own authority, or if one invested with grandeur were to show forth his glory. Nay, such men would become the object of the derision of their peers, and how would they be judged by Him Who is the Sun of Truth!...

"I SWEAR by the most holy Essence of God—exalted and"

I SWEAR by the most holy Essence of God—exalted and glorified be He—that in the Day of the appearance of Him Whom God shall make manifest a thousand perusals of the Bayán cannot equal the perusal of a single verse to be revealed by Him Whom God shall make manifest.

Ponder a while and observe that everything in Islám hath its ultimate and eventual beginning in the Book of God. Consider likewise the Day of the Revelation of Him Whom God shall make manifest, He in Whose grasp lieth the source of proofs, and let not erroneous considerations shut thee out from Him, for He is immeasurably exalted above them, inasmuch as every proof proceedeth from the Book of God which is itself the supreme testimony, as all men are powerless to produce its like. Should myriads of men of learning, versed in logic, in the science of grammar, in law, in jurisprudence and the like, turn away from the Book of God, they would still be pronounced unbelievers. Thus the fruit is within the supreme testimony itself, not in the things derived therefrom. And know thou of a certainty that every letter revealed in the Bayán is solely intended to evoke submission unto Him Whom God shall make manifest, for it is He Who hath revealed the Bayán prior to His Own manifestation....

"THE substance of this chapter is this, that what is intended"

THE substance of this chapter is this, that what is intended by the Day of Resurrection is the Day of the appearance of the Tree of divine Reality, but it is not seen that any one of the followers of Shí'ih Islám hath understood the meaning of the Day of Resurrection; rather have they fancifully imagined a thing which with God hath no reality. In the estimation of God and according to the usage of such as are initiated into divine mysteries, what is meant by the Day of Resurrection is this, that from the time of the appearance of Him Who is the Tree of divine Reality, at whatever period and under whatever name, until the moment of His disappearance, is the Day of Resurrection.

For example, from the inception of the mission of Jesus—may peace be upon Him—till the day of His ascension was the Resurrection of Moses. For during that period the Revelation of God shone forth through the appearance of that divine Reality, Who rewarded by His Word everyone who believed in Moses, and punished by His Word everyone who did not believe; inasmuch as God's Testimony for that Day was that which He had solemnly affirmed in the Gospel. And from the inception of the Revelation of the Apostle of God—may the blessings of God be upon Him—till the day of His ascension was the Resurrection of Jesus—peace be upon Him—wherein the Tree of divine Reality appeared in the person of Muhammad, rewarding by His Word everyone who was a believer in Jesus, and punishing by His Word everyone who was not a believer in Him. And from the moment when the Tree of the Bayán appeared until it disappeareth is the Resurrection of the Apostle of God, as is divinely foretold in the Qur'án; the beginning of which was when two hours and eleven minutes had passed on the eve of the fifth of Jamádiyu'l-Avval, 1260 A.H., which is the year 1270 of the Declaration of the Mission of Muhammad. This was the

beginning of the Day of Resurrection of the Qur'án, and until the disappearance of the Tree of divine Reality is the Resurrection of the Qur'án. The stage of perfection of everything is reached when its resurrection occurreth. The perfection of the religion of Islám was consummated at the beginning of this Revelation; and from the rise of this Revelation until its setting, the fruits of the Tree of Islám, whatever they are, will become apparent. The Resurrection of the Bayán will occur at the time of the appearance of Him Whom God shall make manifest. For today the Bayán is in the stage of seed; at the beginning of the manifestation of Him Whom God shall make manifest its ultimate perfection will become apparent. He is made manifest in order to gather the fruits of the trees He hath planted; even as the Revelation of the Qá'im [He Who ariseth], a descendant of Muhammad—may the blessings of God rest upon Him—is exactly like unto the Revelation of the Apostle of God Himself [Muhammad]. He appeareth not, save for the purpose of gathering the fruits of Islám from the Qur'ánic verses which He [Muhammad] hath sown in the hearts of men. The fruits of Islám cannot be gathered except through allegiance unto Him [the Qá'im] and by believing in Him. At the present time, however, only adverse effects have resulted; for although He hath appeared in the midmost heart of Islám, and all people profess it by reason of their relationship to Him [the Qá'im], yet unjustly have they consigned Him to the Mountain of Mákú, and this notwithstanding that in the Qur'án the advent of the Day of Resurrection hath been promised unto all by God. For on that Day all men will be brought before God and will attain His Presence; which meaneth appearance before Him Who is the Tree of divine Reality and attainment unto His presence; inasmuch as it is not possible to appear before the Most Holy Essence of God, nor is it conceivable to seek reunion with Him. That which is feasible in the matter of appearance before Him and of meeting Him is attainment unto the Primal Tree....

"IN the Name of God, the Most Exalted, the Most Holy"

IN the Name of God, the Most Exalted, the Most Holy. All praise and glory befitteth the sacred and glorious court of the sovereign Lord, Who from everlasting hath dwelt, and unto everlasting will continue to dwell within the mystery of His Own divine Essence, Who from time immemorial hath abided and will forever continue to abide within His transcendent eternity, exalted above the reach and ken of all created beings. The sign of His matchless Revelation as created by Him and imprinted upon the realities of all beings, is none other but their powerlessness to know Him. The light He hath shed upon all things is none but the splendour of His Own Self. He Himself hath at all times been immeasurably exalted above any association with His creatures. He hath fashioned the entire creation in such wise that all beings may, by virtue of their innate powers, bear witness before God on the Day of Resurrection that He hath no peer or equal and is sanctified from any likeness, similitude or comparison. He hath been and will ever be one and incomparable in the transcendent glory of His divine being and He hath ever been indescribably mighty in the sublimity of His sovereign Lordship. No one hath ever been able befittingly to recognize Him nor will any man succeed at any time in comprehending Him as is truly meet and seemly, for any reality to which the term "being" is applicable hath been created by the sovereign Will of the Almighty, Who hath shed upon it the radiance of His

Own Self, shining forth from His most august station. He hath moreover deposited within the realities of all created things the emblem of His recognition, that everyone may know of a certainty that He is the Beginning and the End, the Manifest and the Hidden, the Maker and the Sustainer, the Omnipotent and the All-Knowing, the One Who heareth and perceiveth all things, He Who is invincible in His power and standeth supreme in His Own identity, He Who quickeneth and causeth to die, the All-Powerful, the Inaccessible, the Most Exalted, the Most High. Every revelation of His divine Essence betokens the sublimity of His glory, the loftiness of His sanctity, the inaccessible height of His oneness and the exaltation of His majesty and power. His beginning hath had no beginning other than His Own firstness and His end knoweth no end save His Own lastness....

"THE revelation of the Divine Reality hath everlastingly"

THE revelation of the Divine Reality hath everlastingly been identical with its concealment and its concealment identical with its revelation. That which is intended by "Revelation of God" is the Tree of divine Truth that betokeneth none but Him, and it is this divine Tree that hath raised and will raise up Messengers, and hath revealed and will ever reveal Scriptures. From eternity unto eternity this Tree of divine Truth hath served and will ever serve as the throne of the revelation and concealment of God among His creatures, and in every age is made manifest through whomsoever He pleaseth. At the time of the revelation of the Qur'án He asserted His transcendent power through the advent of Muhammad, and on the occasion of the revelation of the Bayán He demonstrated His sovereign might through the appearance of the Point of the Bayán, and when He Whom God shall make manifest will shine forth, it will be through Him that He will vindicate the truth of His Faith, as He pleaseth, with whatsoever He pleaseth and for whatsoever He pleaseth. He is with all things, yet nothing is with Him. He is not within a thing nor above it nor beside it. Any reference to His being established upon the throne implieth that the Exponent of His Revelation is established upon the seat of transcendent authority... .

He hath everlastingly existed and will everlastingly continue to exist. He hath been and will ever remain inscrutable unto all men, inasmuch as all else besides Him have been and shall ever be created through the potency of His command. He is exalted above every mention or praise and is sanctified beyond every word of commendation or every comparison. No created thing comprehendeth Him, while He in truth comprehendeth all things. Even when it is said "no created thing comprehendeth Him," this refers to the Mirror of His Revelation, that is Him Whom God shall make manifest. Indeed too high and exalted is He for anyone to allude unto Him.

Glossary

A.H.:	an abbreviation of Latin *Anno Hegirae*, or "the year of the Hijri," referring to the flight of Muhammad and his followers to Medina, which marks the beginning of the Islamic calendar
Commentary on the Súrih of Joseph:	the Bab's commentary on the Sura of Joseph in the Qur'an
Declaration of the Mission of Muhammad:	Muhammad's public declaration of his mission as prophet in 611
Imám 'Alí:	the man whom Shia Muslims believe to have been the legitimate successor to Muhammad as the leader of Islam
Ka'bah:	a small, cube-shaped shrine in Mecca, Saudi Arabia
Mákú:	the site of a prison fortress in Iran where the Bab was imprisoned
Mecca:	a city in modern-day Saudi Arabia, Islam's holiest city and the birthplace of Muhammad
Moses:	the Old Testament Hebrew patriarch and lawgiver
Muhammad:	the prophet who founded Islam in the seventh century
Qur'án:	the Islamic sacred scripture
Shí'ih Islám:	or Shia Islam, the minority sect of Islam that claims Ali as the legitimate heir to Muhammad as the leader of the faith
Váhids:	cycles of time; one váhid is nineteen years.

A page from *Yazidi Book of Revelation* manuscript.

KITAB AL-JILWAH: DOCUMENT ANALYSIS

1850 CE

"All treasures and hidden things are known to me; and as I desire, I take them from one and bestow them upon another."

Overview

The Kitab al-jilwah, translated as the "Book of Revelation" or "Book of Divine Effulgence," is one of two alleged sacred books of the Yezidi, the other being the Meshaf resh, or "Black Book." The Yezidi are a religious and ethnic group native to the Kurdish areas of northern Iraq, eastern Turkey, and Transcaucasia (between the southern Black and Caspian seas), with increasing numbers in Europe and the United States. Although its adherents believe themselves to be the oldest group of monotheists, scholars trace Jewish, Christian, Muslim, Gnostic, Zoroastrian, and other influences in their religion. They have often been described as devil worshippers, a misleading claim that has led to violent persecutions.

The Kitab al-jilwah is best described as a celebration of the divine power of the speaker and an exhortation to adhere to the traditional practices of the group and obey its hierarchy. Although it is possible to read the book as dictated by the Creator himself, the speaker is generally considered to be Melek Taus, a name that means "Peacock Angel." Melek Taus is a being created by an almighty God and given authority over the world. Sheikh 'Adi bin Musafir is the putative human author. Sheikh 'Adi is an important Yezidi prophet and one earthly incarnation of Melek Taus; thus, he is also the speaker in the book. However, the historical author was most likely an Arabic-speaking Yezidi scribe writing in the middle of the nineteenth century. The book was written in Arabic and was never meant to be read by the majority of Yezidis, who speak Kurdish dialects. Taken at face value, the Kitab al-jilwah is a secret document of a mystery religion, intended to reinforce the majesty and authority of Yezidi religion and society embodied in the most powerful created being, Melek Taus.

Context

The Kitab al-jilwah appeared in the multicultural context of northern Iraq, probably in the middle of the nineteenth century. It is allegedly a holy book of the Yezidis, a persecuted minority group that has lived on the fringes of more powerful urban peoples of northern Mesopotamia. The precise origins of the Yezidis are unknown, but they are understood to be Kurds, and presently they live in the Kurdish region encompassing parts of Iraq, Turkey, Syria, Azerbaijan, Iran, and Georgia, a region sometimes called Kurdistan. Yezidism is properly a secret tradition. Yezidis are born into their religion, and sharing the tenets of the faith with outsiders or allowing non-Yezidis to observe rituals have traditionally been discouraged. Yezidism is often seen by outsiders as a deviant form of Islam or Christianity, but in reality it is a syncretic religion, a palimpsest of religious traditions layered upon and in dialogue with one another. The tradition is mainly secret and oral. Different aspects of the faith's constitution and heritage are emphasized or deemphasized in the group's changing relationships with other groups. It is therefore difficult to trace the exact appearance of the Kitab al-jilwah.

Though they first appear in historical texts in 1597 CE, the Yezidis as a group are clearly much older. In fact, they believe themselves to follow the oldest monotheistic religion; their earliest traditions are of unwritten local origin. But the Yezidis have complicated relationships with other monotheistic groups arising from their multifaceted shared heritage. Relations with these religious groups have affected the way the Yezidis understand themselves, and this is seen in the Kitab al-jilwah. By the first century CE many groups in the region had converted to Judaism, while in 314 the nearby kingdom of Armenia became the first to accept Christianity as the state religion. Individuals and groups professing less-orthodox creeds related to Judaism and Christianity, including Gnosticism, probably also arrived in the area in the first few centuries before and after Christ.

Yezidis revere Jesus and practice a form of baptism, probably borrowed from Christianity, in the water of the White Spring at their principal shrine at Lalesh, Iraq.

The region of Kurdistan was integrated into the Islamic world within a century of the death of the Muslim prophet Muhammad in 632. Northern Mesopotamia was quickly conquered by 'Umar I, one of the Rashidun, or "rightly guided," caliphs, who reigned between 634 and 644, and the rest of the region eventually followed. However, even long after the Muslim conquest, the Kurdish region remained a stronghold of the Assyrian Church of the East, a Christian denomination often called the Nestorian Church, which parted ways with the Catholic and Orthodox faiths in the fifth century. As minorities in a Muslim region, both of whom experienced great persecutions, Yezidis and Christians have often felt a close kinship.

Nevertheless, Islam, especially in the more mystical strains of Islam known as Sufism, represents one of the most powerful influences on Yezidism. Sufism became particularly important to the Yezidi with the arrival of the great Yezidi reformer and putative author of the Kitab al-jilwah, Sheikh 'Adi bin Musafir, in the early twelfth century. Modern Yezidis often deemphasize these links to Islam, seeing them as corruptions of their traditional faith.

Much of Yezidi practice involves maintaining the inherited social order, the terminology of which is largely borrowed from Islam. Every Yezidi is born within one of three castes: *sheikh*, *pir*, or *murid*. The term *sheikh* can have different meanings, one of which is leader of a Sufi group. The Yezidi *sheikhs* each claim descent from one of Sheikh 'Adi's companions. *Pir* is a shared Kurdish and Persian term usually meaning the same as "sheikh," but in Yezidism it signifies a separate inherited status. *Murid* is another borrowed term, applied to a follower of a *sheikh* in a Sufi brotherhood. Every Yezidi—including every *pir* and *sheikh*—has both a *pir* and a *sheikh* to whom one owes reverence and tithes and from whom one can expect spiritual guidance and, in times of need, financial support. Respecting religious authority is an important theme of the Kitab al-jilwah.

The book first appears historically in the nineteenth century, when the Yezidi faced the threat of extinction and experienced the beginnings of tolerance. The Yezidi have suffered much persecution because of allegations that they worship Shaytan (Satan), arising from the equation, made by the Yezidi themselves, of Melek Taus with Shaytan. The Yezidi believe that Melek Taus always works in accordance with God's will; he is God's agent, not his adversary. In Islam, Shaytan's sin was refusing to bow down to anyone except God—even on God's own orders (Qur'an 18:50). Yezidi devotion to Shaytan may derive from Shaytan's role as a champion of monotheism.

It is this understanding of Shaytan that helped lead to the persecutions of the nineteenth century. One history of the Yezidi, by John S. Guest, is appropriately titled *Survival among the Kurds*. Up until the late nineteenth century the Yezidi were often the targets of purges by local leaders.

Most notoriously, in 1844, Bedr Khan Beg, of Rowanduz, slaughtered an unknown number of Yezidi outside Mosul (in modern-day Iraq) in what came to be called the Soran Massacre. Such killings, often in the name of religion, led the Yezidi to rally around their secret tradition and social hierarchy as a means to survive.

The existence of a holy book among the Yezidi was first alleged by the British historian Sir Paul Rycaut in 1680 in *The History of the Turkish Empire from the Year 1623 to the Year 1677*. In 1730 a book called the Kitab al-jilwah, attributed to Sheikh 'Adi, was first mentioned by Sheikh 'Abd Allah er-Ratabki, a Muslim, in a document that apparently provides a justification for persecuting the Yezidis. However, the scanty descriptions of these books suggest that they were not the Kitab al-jilwah as it exists today. In an 1879 visit to Nicolas Siouffi, a French vice-consul to the Ottoman Empire based in Mosul, Sheikh Nasr, a Yezidi, confirmed the existence of two Yezidi holy books known as the Kitab al-jilwah and the Meshaf resh, appearing to quote from the Kitab al-jilwah as it is now known. However, his words suggest that the books had been in existence and accepted for some time. Thus, the Kitab al-jilwah probably dates to the period around 1850, if not somewhat before, during a time when the Yezidi were struggling to survive and seeking their place as a religious minority in the Ottoman Empire.

Though most of Kurdistan was technically part of the Ottoman Empire in the 1840s, the imperial hold on the region was weak. Kurdistan was a battlefield among local rulers, the most powerful being Bedr Khan Beg, who was famous for his massacres of both Yezidis and Christians. The region was also eyed by the powerful Russian and Persian empires. But in the late 1840s, under the leadership of Tayyar Pasha, the Ottomans were able to regain control of their Kurdish territories through an aggressive policy of suppressing local chieftains. Meanwhile, British and American missionaries had been active in Kurdistan for some time, and the British intervened with the Ottoman authorities on behalf of religious minorities, including the Yezidi. In 1847 Bedr Khan Beg negotiated his surrender and pardon, and the last of the Kurdish chieftains was deposed in 1849. That year, with the secret intervention of the British ambassador, Stratford Canning, the Yezidi normalized their existence in the Ottoman Empire. Yusuf, the chief *qewel*, or religious bard, of the Yezidis, successfully petitioned for their exemption from military service due to strict religious codes of conduct.

The holy books of the Yezidis may have arisen as part of their attempts to legitimize their religion in a predominantly Muslim society. Muslims recognize the special status of "people of the book"—monotheistic religions with a prophet and a revealed scripture (Qur'an 3:64, 29:46). The phrase is usually applied to Jews, Christians, and Sabians (Qur'an 2:62), but many scholars extend the concept to other religions. Codifying scripture would also have helped the Yezidi preserve important tenets of their persecuted faith.

Time Line

314	■ Armenia becomes the first country to adopt Christianity as the state religion.
636–638	■ Mesopotamia is conquered by the Muslim Rashidun ("rightly guided") caliphs.
ca. 1075	■ Sheikh 'Adi bin Musafir is born in Beit Far, in the Bekáa Valley of modern-day Lebanon.
ca. 1100	■ Sheikh 'Adi moves to Lalesh (in present-day Iraq).
January 1162	■ Sheikh 'Adi dies and is buried at Lalesh.
1680	■ Sir Paul Rycaut's history of the Ottoman Empire mentions a book of the law and rituals of the Yezidi.
ca. 1730	■ Sheikh 'Abd Allah er Ratabki, a Muslim, mentions a Kitab al-jilwah supposedly written by Sheikh 'Adi. This is the first clear reference to such a text, but it is probably not the text as it exists today.
1844	■ In the Soran Massacre, an unknown number of Yezidis are killed by Bedr Khan Beg of Rowanduz.
1849	■ Yusuf, the chief qewel (religious bard) of the Yezidis, with the aid of Great Britain's ambassador to the Ottoman Empire, Sir Stratford Canning, successfully petitions for official recognition of the Yezidi religion, and Yezidis are finally granted legal rights in the Ottoman Empire.
ca. 1850	■ The Kitab al-jilwah as it is known today is probably composed.
October 1879	■ Sheikh Nasr, a Yezidi, confirms the existence of two Yezidi holy books known as the Kitab al-jilwah and the Meshaf resh to the French vice-consul Nicolas Siouffi.

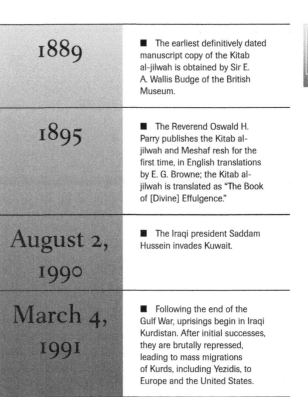

1889	■ The earliest definitively dated manuscript copy of the Kitab al-jilwah is obtained by Sir E. A. Wallis Budge of the British Museum.
1895	■ The Reverend Oswald H. Parry publishes the Kitab al-jilwah and Meshaf resh for the first time, in English translations by E. G. Browne; the Kitab al-jilwah is translated as "The Book of [Divine] Effulgence."
August 2, 1990	■ The Iraqi president Saddam Hussein invades Kuwait.
March 4, 1991	■ Following the end of the Gulf War, uprisings begin in Iraqi Kurdistan. After initial successes, they are brutally repressed, leading to mass migrations of Kurds, including Yezidis, to Europe and the United States.

About the Author

The Kitab al-jilwah is attributed to Sheikh 'Adi bin Musafir. In the prologue of the book, Sheikh 'Adi is referred to as 'Abd Taus, "Servant of the Peacock (Angel)." By some he is also considered to be an earthly manifestation or embodiment of Melek Taus.

The historical Sheikh 'Adi was born about 1075 in Beit Far in the Bekáa Valley of what is now Lebanon. He was descended from the Umayyads, the first Muslim dynasty. Sheikh 'Adi was a Sunni, an orthodox Muslim, but he was also a Sufi, a mystic. He was noted for his piety and his asceticism—it was said by one observer that he was so starved from fasting that, when he bowed in prayer, his brains could be heard knocking about inside his skull "like pebbles in a calabash." He was known for his miraculous powers, and pilgrims visited him from as far away as Morocco. Sheikh 'Adi is believed to have moved to the valley of Lalesh (in modern-day Iraq) as a young man, where he lived a semimonastic life and taught disciples; his title, "sheikh," is an Arabic word given to leaders of Sufi religious communities, and the title is passed down among the Yezidi caste that claims to be descended from his companions. Sheikh 'Adi died in 1162, at more than eighty years of age. What is alleged to be his tomb in Lalesh is the center of Yezidi religious life. All physically able Yezidis are expected to make a pilgrimage to the site at least once a year, during the Autumn Assembly, marking the time when the seven great angels, led by Melek Taus, gather to determine the fate of the world during the coming year. However, the historical Sheikh 'Adi's writings make no mention of Melek Taus or of the special themes mentioned in Yezidi documents. Scholars still debate Sheikh 'Adi's relationship with the Yezidis, but he is generally not believed to be the author of the Kitab al-jilwah as known today.

Some scholars have argued that the Kitab al-jilwah is a fraud. This view was first advanced by Alphonse Mingana in the 1930s, based largely on the fact that most of the sources then available could be traced back to a single manuscript dealer, Jeremiah Shamir. Mingana's argument is that Shamir, a Presbyterian, fabricated the text in order to sell it as "the holy book of the devil worshippers." However, other editions have since come to light. It was also assumed that, since most Yezidis speak Kurdish tongues, any Yezidi holy book would have been in Kurdish, yet the Kitab al-jilwah is in Arabic. Some modern scholars believe that the Kitab al-jilwah was written by a non-Yezidi who was familiar with Yezidi customs and wanted a sacred scripture to present to other non-Yezidis as the bible of the Yezidis, as it were.

Perhaps the most likely author was a Yezidi *qewel*. The *qewels* are a class of religious bards who perpetuate the teachings of Yezidism, communicating the sacred songs and playing musical instruments. The position of *qewel* and the songs are passed down from father to son. The only known Kurdish manuscript of the Kitabl al-Jilwah is a clear forgery, but the *qewels* who would have been most likely to use such a book spoke Arabic; prayers are also often in that language. Although Yezidi culture is mainly an oral tradition, the literate elites are known to have kept texts for their own use alongside the oral works. Indeed, until recently, Yezidis actually discouraged literacy for all but a select few, to the point of its being tabooed. Although the Kitab al-jilwah may not carry the universally binding weight of other holy books such as the Bible, even those scholars who have argued that it is at root a forgery nevertheless believe it contains accurate teachings of the Yezidi religion.

The actual author of the Kitab al-jilwah, then, appears to be an anonymous Arabic speaker, if not a Yezidi, at least one very familiar with Yezidi teachings. It contains teachings meant to be secret, so its history is difficult to trace. The existence of a book known as the Kitab al-jilwah, attributed to Sheikh 'Adi, is noted as early as the eighteenth century, but it is probably not identical to the present version. The manuscripts of the Kitab al-jilwah are written in a form of Arabic used by non-Muslim Arab speakers from the twelfth to the nineteenth centuries. The original manuscript is said to have been housed in Baadra, one of the principal Yezidi towns and the seat of the Mir, the supreme head of the Yezidis. (According to tradition, as Sheikh 'Adi lay dying, his companions quarreled over who would lead the Yezidis. To settle the dispute Sheikh 'Adi prayed, and a man was created out of nothing to lead the people. The family from which the Mir is chosen is descended from this man; the Mir's appointment is for life, and he cannot be removed.) Most of the manuscripts available to scholars, however, have been obtained from various Christians in Mosul.

Explanation and Analysis of the Document

The Kitab al-jilwah consists of a prologue followed by five chapters. After the prologue, the text is arranged like that of the Qur'an, with chapters in order by decreasing length in the original Arabic. However, unlike in the Qur'an (which is much longer, at 114 suras, or chapters), each chapter of the Kitab al-jilwah seems to build on the previous one. Also unlike the Qur'an or the Torah (the first five books of the Hebrew Bible), the Kitab al-jilwah was not edited together from several works or recitations, nor did it build up over time; the book is a unified whole apparently composed by a single author.

♦ Prologue

Isya Joseph's translation of the Kitab al-jilwah (which was included in his academic theses before being published in a journal in 1909 and a book in 1919) begins with a prologue that is not present in some copies of the manuscript. Other translations give a slightly different prologue or none at all. The prologue is written in the third person, while the rest of the book is written in the first person. It is an explanation of the book, and it was likely added to the original text.

This prologue declares that this "revelation"—*jilwah*—existed before creation with Melek Taus, the "Peacock Angel." This is reminiscent of the New Testament Gospel of John's assertion that "in the beginning the Word was with God and was God" (John 1:1). It is also similar to the belief of some Jews that the Torah existed before the creation of the world. The prologue also asserts that Melek Taus sent Sheikh 'Adi—called 'Abd Taus, "Servant of the Peacock (Angel)"—to the Yezidis. Next it stresses the primacy of oral tradition, followed by the authority of the Kitab al-jilwah itself. Finally, Yezidi faith as a secret tradition is stressed—non-Yezidis are forbidden from even seeing this text.

♦ Chapter I

The rest of the Kitab al-jilwah is written in the voice of Melek Taus. In chapter I, Melek Taus describes his eternity, his omnipresence, and his authority over all creatures. The entire universe knows his presence. Outsiders believe that what he does is evil only because they do not understand his actions. For example, the other putative Yezidi holy book, the Meshaf resh, concedes that Melek Taus engineered the fall of Adam. However, it was a necessary part of God's plan. Like many Muslims and even one of the rabbis in the Talmud, the Meshaf resh claims that the forbidden fruit was wheat. Melek Taus knew that Adam needed wheat in order to thrive and reproduce. Thus, what was necessary for the divine plan is seen as evil by those who fail to understand.

Although Melek Taus is omnipotent, different ages have different rulers. Time is cyclical for the Yezidis. According to the Meshaf resh, God first created Melek Taus, and then on each succeeding day for six days, God created another god "from himself and from his light, and their creation was as one lights a lamp from another lamp." Each god, or angel, rules in human form for a set time, establishing laws on earth. Nevertheless, Melek Taus rules over all of these beings. Sheikh 'Adi was the manifestation on earth of Melek Taus, while the other six gods manifested themselves as six sheikhs who are his companions buried at Lalesh and the ancestors of the *sheikh* caste. These are the most important of the many supernatural intermediaries.

Chapter I stresses the favoritism Melek Taus shows to his particular people, the Yezidi. He is there for those who are under the protection of his image, a reference to the *sanjaks*, the seven peacock statues assigned to the areas where Yezidi live; these *sanjaks* are also alluded to in chapter V. Melek Taus aids his people but allows everyone to follow one's own conscience, so that all his opponents will understand why they meet with misfortune. The outsiders—Jews, Christians, and Muslims—have holy books, but even those that were written by genuine prophets and apostles of God have been altered. This is very similar to the common Muslim belief that the holy books of the Christians and Jews, while initially given by God through prophets, have been corrupted over the generations. Melek Taus gives the people "skilled directors" and guidance. Those who obey him are promised "joy, delight, and goodness."

◆ Chapter II

Chapter II continues with the theme of the transcendence of Melek Taus and his special people, the Yezidis. Melek Taus is an agent of God who dispenses both good and evil; there is no evil principle to battle against him. He deals with individuals as they deserve. All dominion over the earth is his to dispense, and those to whom he gives power—the leaders of the Yezidi community—are to be respected.

The Yezidi must remain separate from other peoples, for they "shall not die like the sons of Adam that are without." This is a reference to the belief that the Yezidi are children of Adam but not of Eve. According to this account, Adam and Eve argued between themselves as to which of them contributed more to the life of the child. To resolve the dispute, each put his or her reproductive fluids in jars. When the jars were broken, Eve's jar produced nothing but worms, while Adam's yielded Shehid bin Jer, ancestor of the Yezidi. His descendants are a special people; to them he passed the religious knowledge he miraculously learned during his creation. The seventy-two other nations are the children of Adam and Eve, and it is they who are "the sons of Adam that are without." The Yezidi have strict taboos enforcing endogamy. The Yezidi are forbidden to marry non-Yezidi, and members of the different Yezidi castes must also marry within their own castes.

Melek Taus is the master of life and incarnation, and he at times appears to humans in various forms. If he so chooses, Melek Taus causes a person to reincarnate, either as a human or, in punishment, as an animal such as a dog. Reincarnation, often associated in the Western mind with such religions as Hinduism and Buddhism, may seem to be a strange tenet for a Middle Eastern faith, but it is not

as uncommon as one might expect. Some Sufis, Jews, and Gnostics, as well as the Druze—another minority originally from around Jabal Druze, in Syria, who also follow a secret religion—preach reincarnation.

◆ Chapter III

Chapter III begins with the statement that Melek Taus leads "without a revealed book." Muslim law offers protections to "people of the book"—groups with revealed religious books handed down by prophets. Until the nineteenth century, the Yezidi were without official legal rights under Islamic law because they did not have a prophet or a revealed book recognized by Islam. The writing of the Kitab al-jilwah may have been undertaken in part to establish Yezidism as a legitimate faith in the eyes of outsiders. However, the Kitab al-jilwah itself asserts that such a book is not necessary, reinforcing the priority of oral tradition.

Everything is under the control of Melek Taus, and the universe is his to dispense with as he pleases. His teachings are "applicable to all times and all conditions." This implies that, although chapter I describes the roles of other gods in history, the authority of Melek Taus is eternal; furthermore, time cannot be divided into the period before and the period after revelation, as it is in Christianity and Islam. The text also affirms the concept of retribution after death. Non-Yezidis do not realize that by opposing Melek Taus, they oppose the one who grants all "might, wealth, and riches." At the end of the chapter, Melek Taus claims that all these things are "determined by me from the beginning." This seems to be a claim for predestination of a sort similar to that hinted at in the Qur'an (such as at 7:34).

◆ Chapter IV

Melek Taus has allowed the creation of the four corners of the earth and the four elements—earth, air, fire, and water—from which all things are created, knowing that these things are necessary for existence. (The meaning of "four times" is unknown, but for the Yezidi time is often seen cyclically. Most important, as expressed in the Meshaf resh, different times are accorded to different angels, each of which is also associated with one of the companions of Sheikh 'Adi. The Meshaf resh talks of a cycle of seven angels. This may be a reference to such a cycle, important and well known at the time of composition but now obscure.) Though the other gods have taken part in this creation, Melek Taus maintains his transcendence over them. The similarities between the beliefs of the Yezidi and the Muslims, Christians, and Jews are admitted, but the believer is not to be misled—none of these other faiths is the true faith, and their teachings have been corrupted. Thus, their teachings are to be rejected in favor of the secret teachings of Melek Taus. It is even possible that these religions may be the three unspecified things that "are against" him. Again, the text stresses that Melek Taus has the power to reward after death. He expresses his desire for social cohesion, as this is what will protect the Yezidis against their enemies.

The chapter ends by forbidding the very mention of Melek Taus's name or his attributes. Though they actually may use the name Melek Taus freely, Yezidi are not permitted to say "Shaytan" or any word that sounds like it. The text suggests that this is because of fear of non-Yezidis, who may react negatively toward those who appear to be calling on the aid of the devil. In general, the prohibition seems to be out of reverence, for the same reason devout Jews do not utter the name Yahweh.

♦ Chapter V

The last chapter is an appeal to respect tradition and authority. First, the speaker urges the believer to "honor my symbol and my image, for they remind you of me." This is a reference to the *sanjak*. Between one and three times a year, in a ceremony known as the walking of the peacock, these bronze images of Melek Taus were sent to the seven districts where Yezidi traditionally lived. Because of changing political conditions, this practice has been abandoned in some places. *Qewels* accompany the *sanjaks*, offering an opportunity for all Yezidis, even those in otherwise isolated communities, to hear news of their fellow Yezidis and obtain religious instruction. The Kitab al-jilwah commands the people to obey these representatives. During the walking of the peacock, money is also collected for the Mir. Honoring the image of Melek Taus means both religious and social cohesion.

In closing, the Kitab al-jilwah encourages the Yezidis to learn the teachings of Melek Taus by heart and to not share them with outsiders. The ever-present fear of oppression on the part of the "people of the book" spurs secrecy, and the concern that these outsiders might alter Yezidi teachings contributes to this fear. Just as the concept of the "people of the book" unites these three revealed religions, it alienates them from the Yezidis. The Yezidi are encouraged to learn their own religious precepts by heart—which, in a way, brings the teachings into the individual and makes the beliefs and the believers one.

Audience

The intended audience of the text is naturally a subset of Arabic readers. Presumably, this primarily included the Arabic-speaking *qewels*, the only Arabic speakers in the Yezidi world, who are also responsible for sustaining the oral traditions. The manuscript texts also circulated among Iraqi Christians, who were naturally curious about their neighbors and sympathetic toward other religious minorities. From them the document was obtained by Western and Russian scholars, among whom it has had its greatest impact.

Western scholars like Sir Paul Rycaut were interested in the possible existence of a holy book among the Yezidi at least since the seventeenth century. This interest only grew as American and British missionary societies achieved footholds in Kurdistan in the mid-nineteenth century. Scholars such as the British archaeologist Sir Austen Henry Layard documented their customs and beliefs, and in 1889 Sir E. A. Wallace Budge succeeded in buying copies of the Kitab al-jilwah and the Meshaf resh from a local Christian. In 1895, having bought his own copies of the texts, Reverend Oswald H. Parry published English translations of the Kitab al-jilwah and Meshaf resh by E. G. Browne. This marked the first publication of the books in any language and helped excite interest in and sympathy for the Yezidis and their religion in the West.

Impact

Among scholars in the West, the Kitab al-jilwah and the Meshaf resh have been the focus of Yezidi research, engendering broader knowledge—and sympathy—for this little-known sect. With few exceptions, literacy has been traditionally forbidden to the Yezidi; as such, books about the Yezidi have naturally made little impact among them.

Yet with greater exposure to the outside world, increased education, and movement away from their homeland, the Yezidi are quickly becoming a religious society that turns to books to help the community define itself. On August 2, 1990, President Saddam Hussein of Iraq invaded Kuwait, leading to the Persian Gulf War, in which an allied coalition of thirty-four nations, led by the United States, rushed to aid Kuwait. Iraq surrendered to allied forces on February 28, 1991, but a Kurdish uprising commenced on March 4, 1991. The militants, expecting international aid, were crushed by Hussein's forces, leading to a massive exodus of Kurds, including Yezidis. Still more Yezidis emigrated to Europe and the United States following the 2003 American invasion of Iraq and its subsequent civil unrest. As a result of this instability and in light of encroaching modernization, many Yezidis are increasingly interested in preserving their traditions in writing and turning to documents like the Kitab al-jilwah. Accordingly, literacy and education are rising among the Yezidi, who more and more are turning to further published sources to understand their own religion. The Kitab al-jilwah's impact in the Yezidi world thus has the potential to be greater now than it has ever been before.

Further Reading

■ Books

Edmonds, Cecil J. *A Pilgrimage to Lalish*. London: Royal Asiatic Society of Great Britain and Ireland, 1967.

Guest, John S. *Survival among the Kurds: A History of the Yezidis*. London: Kegan Paul International, 1993.

Joseph, Isya. *Devil Worship: The Sacred Books and Traditions of the Yezidiz*. Boston: Richard G. Badger, 1919.

"I was, am now, and shall have no end.… There is no place in the universe that knows not my presence. I participate in all the affairs which those who are without call evil because their nature is not such as they approve."

(Section 1)

"I lead to the straight path without a revealed book; I direct aright my beloved and my chosen ones by unseen means. All my teachings are easily applicable to all times and all conditions. I punish in another world all who do contrary to my will."

(Section 1)

"All treasures and hidden things are known to me; and as I desire, I take them from one and bestow them upon another. I reveal my wonders to those who seek them, and in due time my miracles to those who receive them from me.… Thus the government of the worlds, the transition of generations, and the changes of their directors are determined by me from the beginning."

(Section 1)

"The books of Jews, Christians, and Moslems, as of those who are without, accept in a sense, i.e., so far as they agree with, and conform to, my statutes. Whatsoever is contrary to these they have altered; do not accept it."

(Section 1)

"O ye that have believed in me, honor my symbol and my image, for they remind you of me. Observe my laws and statutes. Obey my servants and listen to whatever they may dictate to you of the hidden things. Receive that that is dictated, and do not carry it before those who are without, Jews, Christians, Moslems, and others; for they know not the nature of my teaching."

(Section 1)

Meier, Fritz. "The Mystic Path." In *The World of Islam: Faith, People, Culture,* ed. Bernard Lewis. London: Thames and Hudson, 1992.

Spat, Eszter. *The Yezidis.* London: Saqi, 2005.

■ Journals

Mingana, Alphonse. "Devil-Worshippers: Their Beliefs and Their Sacred Books." *Journal of the Royal Asiatic Society of Great Britain and Ireland* 15 (1916): 505–526.

♦ Web Site

Aloian, Zourab. "Shaikh 'Adi, Sufism and the Kurds." Kurdish PEN Center Web site. http://www.pen-kurd.org/englizi/zorab/zorab-SheikhAdi-Sufizm.html

—Commentary by Marc A. Beherec

Questions for Further Study

1. Why do you think that a people such as the Yezidi followed and maintained a secret religion and discouraged contact with outsiders—and even discouraged followers from reading the very text that defines the religion? What cultural and historical factors might account for this practice?

2. In what ways can Yezidism be thought to resemble Nestorianism? (For reference, see the entry on Book of the Bee.) How do the two religions offer a differing interpretation of Christianity?

3. What specific historical circumstances led to the recording of the Kitab al-jilwah?

4. The Yezidi are a good example of a religious sect that historically was persecuted. Why do you think that such sects often meet with hostility and lack of tolerance among majority populations? Do you see any examples of a similar lack of tolerance for a minority religious sect in the modern world?

5. Historically, many religions have been transmitted orally rather than in writing. In this sense, how do the Kitab al-jilwah and the historical circumstances that produced it resemble the Mohawk Thanksgiving Address, which also arose from an oral tradition?

KITAB AL-JILWAH: DOCUMENT TEXT

ca. 1850 CE

Before all creation this revelation was with Melek Taus, who sent 'Abd Taus to this world that he might separate truth known to his particular people. This was done, first of all, by means of oral tradition, and afterward by means of this book, Al-Jilwah, which the outsiders may neither read nor behold.

CHAPTER I

I was, am now, and shall have no end. I exercise dominion over all creatures and over the affairs of all who are under the protection of my image. I am ever present to help all who trust in me and call upon me in time of need. There is no place in the universe that knows not my presence. I participate in all the affairs which those who are without call evil because their nature is not such as they approve. Every age has its own manager, who directs affairs according to my decrees. This office is changeable from generation to generation, that the ruler of this world and his chiefs may discharge the duties of their respective offices every one in his own turn. I allow everyone to follow the dictates of his own nature, but he that opposes me will regret it sorely. No god has a right to interfere in my affairs, and I have made it an imperative rule that everyone shall refrain from worshiping all gods. All the books of those who are without are altered by them; and they have declined from them, although they were written by the prophets and the apostles. That there are interpolations is seen in the fact that each sect endeavors to prove that the others are wrong and to destroy their books. To me truth and falsehood are known. When temptation comes, I give my covenant to him that trusts in me. Moreover, I give counsel to the skilled directors, for I have appointed them for periods that are known to me. I remember necessary affairs and execute them in due time. I teach and guide those who follow my instruction. If anyone obey me and conform to my commandments, he shall have joy, delight, and goodness.

CHAPTER II

I requite the descendants of Adam, and reward them with various rewards that I alone know. Moreover, power and dominion over all that is on earth, both that which is above and that which is beneath, are in my hand. I do not allow friendly association with other people, nor do I deprive them that are my own and that obey me of anything that is good for them. I place my affairs in the hands of those whom I have tried and who are in accord with my desires. I appear in divers manners to those who are faithful and under my command. I give and take away; I enrich and impoverish; I cause both happiness and misery. I do all this in keeping with the characteristics of each epoch. And none has a right to interfere with my management of affairs. Those who oppose me I afflict with disease; but my own shall not die like the sons of Adam that are without. None shall live in this world longer than the time set by me; and if I so desire, I send a person a second or a third time into this world or into some other by the transmigration of souls.

CHAPTER III

I lead to the straight path without a revealed book; I direct aright my beloved and my chosen ones by unseen means. All my teachings are easily applicable to all times and all conditions. I punish in another world all who do contrary to my will. Now the sons of Adam do not know the state of things that is to come. For this reason they fall into many errors. The beasts of the earth, the birds of heaven, and the fish of the sea are all under the control of my hands. All treasures and hidden things are known to me; and as I desire, I take them from one and bestow them upon another. I reveal my wonders to those who seek them, and in due time my miracles to those who receive them from me. But those who are without are my adversaries, hence they oppose me. Nor do they know that such a course is against their own interests, for might, wealth, and riches are in my hand, and I bestow them upon every worthy descendant of Adam. Thus the government of the worlds, the transition of generations, and the changes of their directors are determined by me from the beginning.

CHAPTER IV

I will not give my rights to other gods. I have allowed the creation of four substances, four times, and four corners; because they are necessary things for creatures. The books of Jews, Christians, and Moslems, as of those who are without, accept in a sense, i.e., so far as they agree with, and conform to, my statutes. Whatsoever is contrary to these they have altered; do not accept it. Three things are against me, and I hate three things. But those who keep my secrets shall receive the fulfilment of my promises. Those who suffer for my sake I will surely reward in one of the worlds. It is my desire that all my followers shall unite in a bond of unity, lest those who are without prevail against them. Now, then, all ye who have followed my commandments and my teachings, reject all the teachings and sayings of such as are without. I have not taught these teachings, nor do they proceed from me. Do not mention my name nor my attributes, lest ye regret it; for ye do not know what those who are without may do.

CHAPTER V

O ye that have believed in me, honor my symbol and my image, for they remind you of me. Observe my laws and statutes. Obey my servants and listen to whatever they may dictate to you of the hidden things. Receive that that is dictated, and do not carry it before those who are without, Jews, Christians, Moslems, and others; for they know not the nature of my teaching. Do not give them your books, lest they alter them without your knowledge. Learn by heart the greater part of them, lest they be altered.

Thus endeth the book of Al-Jilwah.

Glossary

'Abd Taus:	the servant of the Peacock Angel, Melek Taus
four corners:	that is, the four corners of the world
four substances:	earth, air, fire, and water
four times:	an obscure reference to the Yezidi belief in the cyclical nature of time
Melek Taus:	the "Peacock Angel," a being created by God and given authority over the world
Moslems:	an antique spelling of Muslims

Allan Kardec and his wife
Amélie Gabrielle Boudet.

THE SPIRITS' BOOK: DOCUMENT ANALYSIS

1857 CE

"...the body often suffers more during life than at the moment of death, when the soul is usually unconscious of what is occurring to the body."

Overview

The Spirits' Book was written by the nineteenth-century Frenchman Hippolyte Léon Denizard Rivail, under the pen name Allan Kardec, and is regarded as one of the five fundamental works of Spiritism. *Le livre des esprits* was first published in 1857 and later underwent several revisions, resulting in more than twenty-five subsequent editions. It has been translated into forty-six languages. Rivail was impelled by the popular religious esotericism that was sweeping North America and Europe during the mid-nineteenth century. After taking a particular interest in Spiritualism, Rivail scrutinized this movement's beliefs and practices in an effort to create a more holistic adaptation of the Spiritualist faith.

In 1855 Rivail began crafting his own version of this paranormal-based movement that he referred to as Spiritism. For Rivail, writing as Kardec, composing *The Spirits' Book* was an attempt to distinguish his new version of Spiritualism from the established tradition. Therein, he describes the use of mediums to conduct séances, wherein, through those mediums, he questions a variety of spirits about their existence and everyday life. Using the answers that these spirits provide, Kardec outlines the major tenets of his Spiritism. *The Spirits' Book* is thus a compilation of extensive interviews with spirits arranged in a question-and-answer format.

Context

The Spirits' Book was written during a period of exploration of esoteric spirit phenomena in both Europe and the United States. The writings of the visionary Swedish scientist Emanuel Swedenborg (1688–1772) inspired the foundation of the Church of the New Jerusalem, whose "Swedenborgian" followers envisioned a new form of Christianity. Swedenborg's visions were said to be conveyed to him through a host of celestial beings, including angels and spirits. The theosophical teachings of the Russian-born Madame Helena Petrovna Blavatsky (1831–1891) also provided major contributions to the popular understanding of spirit encounters. As she traveled through Europe, India, Egypt, and the Americas, Blavatsky acted as a medium in séances and also engaged in "automatic writing"—a method of mediumship in which one unconsciously writes the script as conveyed from a spirit.

Perhaps the single most important impetus to any movement concerning spirit phenomena occurred in the United States in 1848. In the small village of Hydesville, near Rochester, New York—in the part of the state known as the "burned-over district" for being host to so many religious revivals—three young sisters named Kate, Margaret, and Leah Fox purportedly devised a system of communicating with a spirit. This system consisted of correlating the rapping noises made by the spirit with "yes" and "no" answers or letters of the alphabet. According to the official story, Kate and Margaret claimed to have had communication with a particular spirit named Charles B. Rosma, a deceased peddler said to have been buried under the Fox home. As the sisters were the only mediums able to interpret the dialogue between themselves and Rosma, they became central figures in the burgeoning Spiritualist movement.

By the 1850s Kate and Margaret Fox would carry their newly found fame to New York City and other parts of the Northeast, attracting large crowds interested in witnessing a public séance and gathering the interest and support of such influential figures as the editor Horace Greeley and the abolitionist William Lloyd Garrison. News of the Fox sisters' communication with spirits also spread to Europe, which allowed the Parisian Hippolyte Rivail to learn of the Spiritualist movement. Intrigued, he was nevertheless convinced that something was lacking from its belief system. Closely studying the attention that mediumship was receiving, Rivail focused on the concept of reincarnation. For Rivail, the spirit world was the true eternal world, whereas the material world was merely a place where the soul could improve itself on any number of levels. Thus, reincarnation was a journey for the soul to realize its potential, and the spirit world was a place of solace and reflection.

In 1855 Rivail decided to launch a new movement that would challenge some of the tenets of Spiritualism. With his new conjectures about reincarnation, Rivail began composing an alternative text that would offer a different version of the Spiritualist phenomena. This new version of Spiritualism would be referred to as Spiritism, and the alternative text, attributed to Rivail as Allan Kardec, would be titled *The Spirits' Book.*

Kardec's methods of investigation required him to engage in mediumship. He structured the text to appear as an extensive interview between himself and spirits designated as authorities of the spirit world. He used mediums to conduct séances and deliver over seven hundred questions to a variety of spirits, probing into their existence and everyday life within the spirit world. These questions and the spirits' responses constitute the bulk of the *The Spirits' Book.*

In 1888 the credibility of all of the movements associated with spirit phenomena was dealt a potentially devastating blow when the mature Margaret Fox admitted to having manufactured the sessions where she and her sisters communicated with spirits. Despite this admission (later recanted and attributed to Margaret's alcoholism), *The Spirits' Book* served to codify the beliefs in spirit phenomena, allowing Fox's statement to go largely overlooked.

About the Author

Hippolyte Léon Denizard Rivail, also known as Allan Kardec, was born in Lyons, France, on October 3, 1804. Expected to pursue a career in law, owing to his family's substantial history of legal training, he instead took a greater interest in the subjects of philosophy and education. As a young man, Rivail traveled to Yverdun, Switzerland, where he studied pedagogy under Johann Heinrich Pestalozzi. Returning to France, he went on to work as a teacher of general education through his early fifties. Soon Rivail took an interest in a host of esoteric ideas, including alternative healing therapies, parapsychology, physiognomic concepts associated with phrenology, and magnetism, as well as a variety of beliefs and practices emerging from the European occult movement.

After learning of the Hydesville incidents of the late 1840s, Rivail became fascinated by the concept of mediumship and the prospect of reinterpreting the tenets of Spiritualism. He took a particular interest in assessing the extent to which he could engage in dialogue with the "spirit realm." Exploring this interest, Rivail recruited a professional somnambulist named Celina Japhet (or Bequet), who assisted him in participating in séances. During one séance in 1857, Japhet told Rivail that two of his former names were Allan and Kardec. These names Rivail com-

Time Line	
1771	■ Emmanuel Swedenborg publishes *The True Christian Religion*, which prefigures Spiritualism.
OCTOBER 3, 1804	■ Hyppolyte Léon Denizard Rivail is born in Lyons, France.
MARCH 31, 1848	■ The Fox sisters claim to communicate with a spirit in Hydesville, New York.
1857	■ Rivail publishes *The Spirits' Book* under the pen name Allan Kardec.
APRIL 2, 1869	■ Rivail, dead of an aneurysm, is buried in the Cimetière du Père Lachaise and eulogized by the astronomer Camille Flammarion, who claims that "Spiritism is not a religion but a science."
1888	■ Margaret Fox admits that the "tapping" method used in her séances was fraudulent.

bined and adopted as his own pen name for all of his Spiritism writings.

In addition to his seminal 1857 text *The Spirits' Book,* Kardec also composed four other texts including *The Book on Mediums* (1861), *The Gospel according to Spiritism* (1864), *Heaven and Hell* (1865), and *The Genesis according to Spiritism* (1868). These five texts are known among followers of Spiritism as the "Spiritist Codification"—the fundamental canon of the Spiritist belief system.

After achieving considerable fame as the founder of the Spiritism movement, Rivail died of an aneurysm on March 31, 1869. Two days later, on April 2, Rivail was honored at his funeral when the French astronomer Camille Flammarion gave his eulogy, noting that "Spiritism is not a religion but a science." Rivail was buried in the Cimetière du Père Lachaise in Paris.

Explanation and Analysis of the Document

The Spirits' Book consists of four "books," subdivided into chapters. These books contain a total of 1,019 questions posed by Kardec to a number of spirits, including those of the American statesman Benjamin Franklin, Emanuel Swedenborg, the French Catholic theologian François Fénelon, the philosopher and theologian Saint Augustine of Hippo, Saint John the Evangelist, Saint Louis IX of France, Saint Vincent de Paul, the Greek philosophers Socrates and Plato, and "The Spirit of Truth" (the term for God used throughout *The Spirits' Book*). The accompanying excerpt is from book 2, "The Spirit-World; or, The World of Spirits," which contains 537 questions, numbered 76 through 613.

This selection addresses the general nature and experience of a spirit as it exists within the spirit world. Thus the questions involve the definition of a spirit, the postmortem transition from soul into spirit, and several details about the individual spirit's autonomy, consciousness, and relationship to the material world. In the responses, text within quotation marks is understood to be the spirits' words, while additional text (like the note to question 76) is Kardec's. This selection is important for both Spiritism and the wider Spiritualism movement, as it is the first attempt to codify the concept of spirit phenomena.

♦ Chapter I

Questions 76–78 Kardec begins the second book by asking questions to define spirits and their relationship to God. Through this question-and-answer exchange, Kardec concludes that spirits are "intelligent beings" that embody a certain universal ubiquity in contrast to the average mundane concept of the material world. Kardec inquires about the relationship between God and these spirits: Are spirits equal with God or are they created beings? According to Kardec, these spirits' responses suggest that they, like all humankind, are creations of God and are thus inferior to Him. Whereas "God has existed from all eternity," spirits are subsequent creations.

Questions 79–81 Kardec then asks about the nature and creation of spirits. In framing his question, he suggests that there are two general elements within the universe, the "intelligent" and the "material." Kardec is told that spirits are constituted by intelligent elements, whereas the physical body is merely inert matter and made solely of the material element. Through further inquiry, he learns that the creation of spirits is an ongoing process for God and is not confined to a specific time. He acknowledges, however, that any particular details of spirit creation remain a "mystery."

Questions 82 and 83 A paramount question is whether or not spirits are immaterial. In the response, the spirits inform Kardec that human perception cannot understand, much less describe, the nature of spirits, as humans consistently choose to interpret unfamiliar phenomena by contrasting them with the human experience. Instead of "immaterial," spirits propose "incorporeal" as a better description. The spirit is bodiless "quintessentialised matter" and advanced beyond human senses. Kardec also learns that with this incorporeal state comes an endless duration of life. In other words, spirits are immortal.

♦ Chapter III

Questions 149–153 Kardec then asks a series of questions about the soul and death. What happens to one's soul after one dies? The spirits answer that the soul returns

to the spirit realm, where it had resided before life on earth. As this soul once again becomes a spirit, it does retain its autonomy, losing only its corporeal property. The soul retains memories of its former life and experiences a yearning to "go to a better world" in its next incarnation. The spirits add that the very fact that Kardec is communicating with them is proof of their retention of knowledge in the spirit realm. Furthermore, the life of a spirit is "eternal."

Questions 154–157 Kardec then begins to probe into the experience of the soul that is making the transition back into the spirit realm. According to the spirits, the body is merely a transitory state, called the "perispirit," or, more precisely, the perispirit is a "semi-material envelope" that allows the spirit to adhere to the body. Thus life begins in the spirit realm, only to make several lateral journeys into the material world. This separation of soul from body is said to be easy in cases where the individual has lived a life of "intellectual and moral activity, and habitual elevation of thought," but "extremely painful" in other cases, especially suicide, where the spirit is forced to "perceive all the horror of the decomposition" of the body.

After inquiring further about the soul's transitory process, Kardec learns that the soul does not necessarily exit its perispirit instantaneously but rather in a more gradual fashion. Interestingly, Kardec is told that it is also possible for the soul to leave its perispirit prematurely. Furthermore, it is equally possible for the soul to glean a glimpse of the spirit realm just prior to leaving its perispirit, as at this point the soul acquires a degree of independence from its corporeal matter. In this way, Kardec is reminded that the material body will thrive as long as the anatomical capacity is still functioning, regardless of the soul's fleeting transition. The heart may continue to pump even after the soul has departed.

Questions 158–160 Kardec then begins another series of questions relating to reincarnation. Proposing the metaphor of a caterpillar's metamorphosis, Kardec is once again reminded that humankind's earthly conceptualizations cannot be applied literally to the spirit realm. That is, such a metaphor is useful, yet it is also an oversimplification of the reincarnation process.

Probing further, Kardec asks about the experience of encountering the spirit world in relation to a soul's emotional consciousness as well as the possibilities of reuniting with other souls that were part of its perispirit experience. Kardec is told that the emotional consciousness and all other feelings associated with it depend upon the soul's record of malevolence or benevolence. If a soul has engaged in the former, that soul will experience shame, whereas a soul that has engaged in the latter is relieved of all burden and comfortably flourishes among the spirits. In addition, the spirits reveal that a soul can certainly reunite with those whom the soul knew in the material world—some will even "come to meet him on his return to the spirit-world, and help to free him from the bonds of matter."

Questions 161 and 162 Kardec briefly revisits the subject of the separation of the soul to ask about such cases as "violent," "accidental," and rare forms of death—decapitation for example. In such circumstances, though the perispirit's tenure is cut short, the bodily organs otherwise continue to function, and separation of spirit from body is "effected more slowly." Kardec asks if cessation of life takes place simultaneously with the separation of the soul in such instances. The spirits respond by stating that the interval between cessation and separation is brief if there is any at all.

Questions 163–165 Finally, Kardec asks the spirits to address his concerns about "confusion" that he believes may occur among souls passing into the spirit realm. Imagining the transition between the material world and the spirit world to be a confusing one, Kardec seeks a fuller understanding. In response, the spirits concede that many souls may, in fact, experience confusion, depending on their "degree of elevation." Those who have freed themselves from the "thralldom of materiality" make the transition more readily than the "carnally minded." The latter find it more difficult to escape the bonds of matter. However, Kardec is given confirmation that through a knowledge of "Spiritism" a soul may assuage this state of confusion.

Audience

The Spirits' Book was originally written for adherents of Spiritism as a reinterpretation of Spiritualist doctrines. However, followers of a host of syncretic movements have borrowed or adapted aspects of Kardec's book. These movements have included Spiritualism, Theosophy, mediumship, and a host of groups loosely characterized as the New Age movement.

Spiritisim today is a decentralized faith-based movement, whose followers engage in regular meetings to read through Spiritist materials. Among Spiritist societies, the central practice is the interpretation of The Spirits' Book and the rest of Spiritist codification. Thus, The Spirits' Book remains a vital component of sustaining religious belief and practice within Spiritism.

As the Spiritism of Kardec's codification was largely introspective, requiring individuals to assess their own spiritual identities, there were no public Spiritist authorities immediately following his death. A follower of Spiritism had only to read through The Spirits' Book to derive answers to his or her questions, since Kardec had already interviewed particular experts through mediumship. Yet, despite the availability of an authoritative text, a number of individuals have contributed to the proliferation of Spiritism through a variety of different interpretations. Of note were two Brazilian mediums: Zélio Fernandino de Moraes (1891–1975) was instrumental in linking West African religions with Spiritism, and Francisco Cândido "Chico" Xavier (1910–2002) was a charismatic Spiritist who composed hundreds of texts on Spiritism by means of "psychography," or automatic writing.

Impact

As a foundational text of the Spiritism movement, The Spirits' Book helped to establish a broader belief system of spirit phenomena. Within twenty-five years of its publication The Spirits' Book had been translated into several different languages and was found throughout Europe and the Americas, where reincarnation was a relatively novel concept. In particular, the importation of the book and the Spiritist philosophy to Portugal and Portuguese-speaking nations would help to establish long-lasting Spiritist ties with Brazil. This was largely due to the encounters between African religions and the Spiritism of Europe brought about by the Portuguese slave trade of the late fifteenth and early sixteenth centuries. West African religions, such as those of the Yoruba, meshed well with Spiritism because of the shared beliefs in reincarnation and a spirit realm.

Kardec's codifying text is still used today among several different religious traditions associated with Spiritism. By conservative estimates, the adherents of Spiritism range from fifteen to seventeen million worldwide. The majority of these adherents reside in Brazil. The sheer numbers of such a following suggest that the ideas embodied within The Spirits' Book are still relevant.

Further Reading

■ Books

Bragdon, Emma. Kardec's Spirtism: A Home for Healing and Spiritual Evolution. Woodstock, Vt.: Lightening Up Press, 2004.

Kardec, Allan. The Book on Mediums: Guide for Mediums and Invocators, trans. Emma A. Wood. 1874. Reprint. York Beach, Me.: Samuel Weiser, Inc., 1970.

Kardec, Allan. Heaven and Hell; or, Divine Justice according to Spiritism, trans. Darrel W. Kimble with Marcia M. Saiz. Brasilia: International Spiritist Council, 2008.

Lewis, James R. Peculiar Prophets: A Biographical Dictionary of New Religions. Saint Paul, Minn.: Paragon House, 1999.

Monroe, John Warne. Laboratories of Faith: Mesmerisim, Spiritism, and Occultism in Modern France. Ithaca, N.Y.: Cornell University Press, 2008.

Sharp, Lynn L. Secular Spirituality: Reincarnation and Spiritism in Nineteenth-Century France. Lanham, Md.: Lexington Books, 2006.

■ Journals

Hess, David. "The Many Rooms of Spiritism in Brazil." Luso-Brazilian Review 24 (1987): 15–34.

Paulino, Ana. "Spiritism, Santería, Brujería, and Vodooism: A Comparative View of Indigenous Healing Systems." *Journal of Teaching in Social Work* 12 (1996): 105–124.

Warren, Donald. "Spiritism in Brazil." *Journal of Inter-American Studies* 10 (1968): 393–405.

♦ **Web Site**

Explore Spiritism Web site. http://www.explorespiritism.com/index.htm

Allan Kardec Educational Society Web site. http://www.allan-kardec.org/

—Commentary by Salvador Jimenez Murguía

Essential Quotes

82. Is it correct to say that spirits are immaterial? *"How is it possible to define a thing in regard to which no terms of comparison exist, and which your language is incompetent to express? Can one who is born blind define light? 'Immaterial' is not the right word; 'incorporeal' would be nearer the truth, for you must understand that a spirit, being a creation, must be something real."*

(Section 1)

150. Does the soul, after death, preserve its individuality? *"Yes, it never loses its individuality. What would the soul be if it did not preserve it?"*

(Section 1)

—How does the soul preserve the consciousness of its individuality, since it no longer has its material body? *"It still has a fluid peculiar to itself, which it draws from the atmosphere of its planet, and which represents the appearance of its last incarnation—its perispirit."*

(Section 1)

153. —Would it not be more correct to apply the term eternal life to the life of the purified spirits; of those who, having attained to the degree of relative perfection, have no longer to undergo the discipline of suffering? *"The life of that degree might rather be termed eternal happiness; but this is a question of words. You may call things as you please, provided you are agreed among yourselves as to your meaning."*

(Section 1)

154. Is the separation of the soul from the body a painful process? *"No; the body often suffers more during life than at the moment of death, when the soul is usually unconscious of what is occurring to the body. The sensations experienced at the moment of death are often a source of enjoyment for the spirit, who recognizes them as putting an end to the term of his exile.*

(Section 1)

155. —Is this separation effected instantaneously, and by means of an abrupt transition? Is there any distinctly marked line of demarcation between life and death? *"No; the soul disengages itself gradually. It does not escape at once from the body, like a bird whose cage is suddenly opened. The two states touch and run into each other; and the spirit extricates himself, little by little, from his fleshly bonds, which are loosed, but not broken."*

(Section 1)

159. What sensation is experienced by the soul at the moment when it recovers its consciousness in the world of spirits? *"That depends on circumstances. He who has done evil from the love of evil is overwhelmed with shame for his wrong-doing. With the righteous it is very different. His soul seems to be eased of a heavy load, for it does not dread the most searching glance."*

(Section 1)

1. What is the difference between Spiritism and Spiritualism, at least as Kardec understood the terms? Do you think this distinction is significant, or is it a "distinction without a difference"?

2. The entry states that "Rivail [Kardec] took an interest in a host of esoteric ideas, including alternative healing therapies, parapsychology, physiognomic concepts associated with phrenology, and magnetism, as well as a variety of beliefs and practices emerging from the European occult movement." Explain what in your view would cause a person such as Kardec—and he was not alone—to adopt these interests. Dissatisfaction with science and rationality? A religious impulse? A psychological need?

3. Have you ever participated in a séance? Do you believe that it is possible to communicate with the dead through the intervention of a medium? Why or why not?

4. Compare this document with another document that deals with esoteric views. One possibility is Helena Blavatsky's *The Secret Doctrine*. What views do the authors share? How are their views different?

5. Assume for a moment that it is not possible to communicate with spirits and that Kardec's views cannot be defended. What value do you think an interest in Spiritism could have for a person? Do you believe that Spiritism and other esoteric and paranormal activities can aid a person in improving his or her outlook on or understanding of life, death, the soul, consciousness, ethics, morals, or any other abstract concept? Explain.

The Spirits' Book: Document Text

1857 CE

—*Allan Kardec*

Book Second: The Spirit-World, or World of Spirits

♦ CHAPTER I...

Origin and Nature of Spirits 76. *What definition can be given of spirits?*

"Spirits may be defined as the intelligent beings of the creation. They constitute the population of the universe, in contradistinction to the forms of the material world."

NOTE. The word spirit is here employed to designate the individuality of extra-corporeal beings, and not the universal intelligent element.

77. Are spirits beings distinct from the Deity, or are they only emanations from or portions of the Deity, and called, for that reason, "sons" or "children" of God?

"Spirits are the work of God, just as a machine is the work of the mechanician that made it: the machine is the man's work, but it is not the man. You know that when a man has made a fine or useful thing, he calls it his 'child'- his 'creation.' It is thus with us in relation to God. We are His children in this sense, because we are His work."

78. Have spirits had a beginning, or have they existed, like God, from all eternity?

"If spirits had not had a beginning, they would be equal with God; whereas they are His creation, and subject to His will. That God has existed from all eternity is incontestable; but as to when and how He created us, we know nothing. You may say that we have had no beginning in this sense, that, God being eternal, He must have incessantly created. But as to when and how each of us was made, this, I repeat, is known to no one. It is the great mystery."

79. Since there are two general elements in the universe, viz., the intelligent element and the material element, would it be correct to say that spirits are formed from the intelligent element as inert bodies are formed from the material element?

"It is evident that such is the case. Spirits are the individualization of the intelligent principle, as bod-

ies are the individualization of the material principle. It is the epoch and mode of this formation that are unknown to us."

80. Is the creation of spirits always going on, or did it only take place at the beginning of time?

"It is always going on; that is to say, God has never ceased to create."

81. Are spirits formed spontaneously or do they proceed from one another?

"God creates them as He creates all other creatures, by His will. But we must again repeat that their origin is a mystery."

82. Is it correct to say that spirits are immaterial?

"How is it possible to define a thing in regard to which no terms of comparison exist, and which your language is incompetent to express? Can one who is born blind define light?

"'Immaterial' is not the right word; 'incorporeal' would be nearer the truth, for you must understand that a spirit, being a creation, must be something real. Spirit is quintessentialised matter, but matter existing in a state which has no analogue within the circle of your comprehension, and so ethereal that it could not be perceived by your senses."

"We say that spirits are immaterial, because their essence differs from everything that we know under the name of "matter." A nation of blind people would have no terms for expressing light and its effects. One who is born blind imagines that the only modes of perception are hearing, smell, taste, and touch: he does not comprehend the other ideas that would be given him by the sense of sight which he lacks. So, in regard to the essence of superhuman beings, we are really blind. We can only define them by means of comparisons that are necessarily imperfect or by an effort of our imagination."

83. Is there an end to the duration of spirits? We can understand that the principle from which they emanate should be eternal; but what we desire to know is, whether their individuality has a term, and whether, after a given lapse of time, longer or shorter, the ele-

ment from which they are formed is not disseminated, does not return to the mass from which they were produced, as is the case with material bodies? It is difficult to understand that what has had a beginning should not also have an end.

"There are many things that you do not understand, because your intelligence is limited; but that is no reason for rejecting them. The child does not understand all that is understood by its father, nor does an ignorant man understand all that is understood by a learned one. We tell you that the existence of spirits has no end; that is all we can say on the subject at present...."

♦ **CHAPTER III...**

The Soul after Death *149. What becomes of the soul at the moment of death?*

"It becomes again a spirit; that is to say, it returns into the world of spirits, which it had quitted for a short time."

150. Does the soul, after death, preserve its individuality?

"Yes, it never loses its individuality. What would the soul be if it did not preserve it?"

—How does the soul preserve the consciousness of its individuality, since it no longer has its material body?'

"It still has a fluid peculiar to itself, which it draws from the atmosphere of its planet, and which represents the appearance of its last incarnation—its perispirit."

—Does the soul take nothing of this life away with it?

"Nothing but the remembrance of that life and the desire to go to a better world. This remembrance is full of sweetness or of bitterness according to the use it has made of the earthly life it has quitted. The more advanced is the degree of its purification, the more clearly does it perceive the futility of all that it has left behind it upon the earth."

151. What is to be thought of the opinion that the soul after death returns to the universal whole?

"Does not the mass of spirits, considered in its totality, constitute a whole? Does it not constitute a world? When you are in an assembly you form an integral part of that assembly, and yet you still retain your individuality."

152. What proof can we have of the individuality of the soul after death?

"Is not this proof furnished by the communications which you obtain? If you were not blind, you would see; if you were not deaf you would hear; for

you are often spoken to by a voice which reveals to you the existence of a being exterior to yourself."

Those who think that the soul returns after death into the universal whole are in error if they imagine that it loses its individuality, like a drop of water that falls into the ocean; they are right if they mean by the universal whole the totality of incorporeal beings, of which each soul or spirit is an element.

If souls were blended together into a mass, they would possess only the qualities common to the totality of the mass there would be nothing to distinguish them from one another, and they would have no special, intellectual, or moral qualities of their own. But the communications we obtain from spirits give abundant evidence of the possession by each spirit of the consciousness of the me, and of a distinct will, personal to itself; the infinite diversity of characteristics of all kinds presented by them is at once the consequence and the evidence of their distinctive personal individuality. If, after death, there were nothing but what is called the "Great Whole," absorbing all individualities, this whole would be uniform in its characteristics and, in that case, all the communications received from the invisible world would be identical. But as among the denizens of that other world we meet with some who are good and some who are bad, some who are learned and some who are ignorant, some who are happy and some who are unhappy, and as they present us with every shade of character, some being frivolous and other, serious, etc., it is evident that they are different individualities, perfectly distinct from one another. This individuality becomes still more evident when they are able to prove their identity by unmistakable tokens, by personal details relating to their terrestrial life, and susceptible of being verified; and it cannot be a matter of doubt when they manifest themselves to our sight under the form of apparitions. The individuality of the soul has been taught theoretically as an article of faith; Spiritism renders it patent, as an evident, and, so to say, a material fact.

153. In what sense should we understand eternal life?

"It is the life of the spirit that is eternal; that of the body is transitory and fleeting. When the body dies, the soul re-enters the eternal life."

—Would it not be more correct to apply the term eternal life to the life of the purified spirits; of those who, having attained to the degree of relative perfection, have no longer to undergo the discipline of suffering?

"The life of that degree might rather be termed eternal happiness; but this is a question of words. You may call things as you please, provided you are agreed among yourselves as to your meaning."

Separation of Soul and Body *154. Is the separation of the soul from the body a painful process?*

"No; the body often suffers more during life than at the moment of death, when the soul is usually unconscious of what is occurring to the body. The sensations experienced at the moment of death are often a source of enjoyment for the spirit, who recognizes them as putting an end to the term of his exile.

In cases of natural death, where dissolution occurs as a consequence of the exhaustion of the bodily organs through age, man passes out of life without perceiving that he is doing so. It is like the flame of a lamp that goes out for want of aliment.

155. How is the separation of soul and body effected?

"The bonds which retained the soul being broken, it disengages itself from the body."

—Is this separation effected instantaneously, and by means of an abrupt transition? Is there any distinctly marked line of demarcation between life and death?

"No; the soul disengages itself gradually. It does not escape at once from the body, like a bird whose cage is suddenly opened. The two states touch and run into each other; and the spirit extricates himself, little by little, from his fleshly bonds, which are loosed, but not broken."

During life, a spirit is held to the body by his semi-material envelope, *perispirit*. Death is the destruction of the body only. but not of this second envelope, which separates itself from the body when the play of organic life ceases in the latter. Observation shows us that the separation of the *perispirit* from the body is not suddenly completed at the moment of death, but is only effected gradually and more or less slowly in different Individuals. In some cases it is affected so quickly that the *perispirit* is entirely separated from the body within a few hours of the death of the latter but. in other cases, and especially in the case of those whose life has been grossly *material and sensual*, this deliverance is much less rapid, and sometimes takes days, weeks, and even months, for its accomplishment. This delay does not imply the slightest persistence of vitality in the body, nor any possibility of Its return to life, but is simply the result of a certain affinity between the body and the spirit which affinity is always more or less tenacious in proportion to the preponderance of materiality in the affections of the spirit during his earthly life.

It is. in fact, only rational to suppose that the more closely a spirit has identified himself with matter, the greater will be his difficulty in separating himself from his material body; while, on the contrary, intellectual and moral activity, and habitual elevation of thought, effect a commencement of this separation even during the life of the body, and therefore, when death occurs, the separation is almost instantaneous. The study of a great number of individuals after their death has shown that affinity which, in some cases, continues to exist between the soul and the body is sometimes extremely painful for it causes the spirit to perceive all the horror of the decomposition of the latter. This experience is exceptional, and peculiar to certain kinds of life and to certain kinds of death. It sometimes occurs in the case of those who have committed suicide.

156. Can the definitive separation of the soul and body take place before the complete cessation of organic life?

"It sometimes happens that the soul has quitted the body before the last agony comes on, so that the latter is only the closing act of merely organic life. The dying man has no longer any consciousness of himself, and nevertheless there still remains in him a faint breathing of vitality. The body is a machine that is kept in movement by the heart. It continues to live as long as tile heart causes the blood to circulate in the veins, and has no need of the soul to do that."

157. Does the soul sometimes at the moment of death, experience an aspiration or an ecstasy that gives it a fore glimpse of the world into which it is about to return?

"The soul often feels the loosening of the bonds that attach it to the body, and does its utmost to hasten and complete the work of separation. Already partially freed from matter, it beholds the future unrolled before it, and enjoys, in anticipation, the spirit-state upon which it is about to re-enter."

158. Do the transformations of the caterpillar—which, first of all, crawls upon the ground, and then shuts itself up in its chrysalis in seeming death, to be reborn there from into a new and brilliant existence—give us anything like a true idea of the relation between our terrestrial life, the tomb, and our new existence beyond the latter?

"An idea on a very small scale. The image is good; hut, nevertheless, it would not do to accept it literally, as you so often do in regard to such images."

159. What sensation is experienced by the soul at the moment when it recovers its consciousness in the world of spirits?

"That depends on circumstances. He who has done evil from the love of evil is overwhelmed with shame for his wrong-doing. With the righteous it is very different. His soul seems to be eased of a heavy load, for it does not dread the most searching glance."

160. Does the spirit find himself at once in company with those whom he knew upon the earth, and who died before him?

"Yes; and more or less promptly according to the degree of his affection for them and of theirs for him. They often come to meet him on his return to the spirit-world, and help to free him from the bonds of matter. Others whom he formerly knew, but whom he had lost sight of during his sojourn on the earth, also come to meet him. He sees those who are in erraticity, and he goes to visit those who are still incarnated."

161. In cases of violent or accidental death, when the organs have not been weakened by age or by sickness, does the separation of the soul take place simultaneously with the cessation of organic life?

"It does so usually; and, at any rate, the interval between them, in all such cases, is very brief."

162. After decapitation, for instance, does a man retain consciousness for a longer or shorter time?

"He frequently does so for a few minutes, until the organic life of the body is completely extinct; but, on the other hand, the fear of death often causes a man to lose consciousness before the moment of execution."

The question here proposed refers simply to the consciousness which the victim may have of himself as a man, through the intermediary of his bodily organs, and not as a spirit. If he have not lost this consciousness before execution, he may retain it for a few moments afterwards but this persistence of consciousness can only be of very short duration, and must necessarily cease with the cessation of the organic life of the brain. The cessation of the human consciousness, however, by no means implies the complete separation of the perispirit from the body. On the contrary, in all cases in which death has resulted from violence, and not from a gradual extinction of the vital forces, the bonds which unite the body to the perispirit are more tenacious, and the separation is effected more slowly.

Temporarily-Confused State of the Soul after Death *163. Does the soul, on quitting the body, find itself at once in possession of its self-consciousness?*

"Not at once. It is for a time in a state of confusion which obscures all its perceptions."

164. Do all spirits experience, in the same degree and for the same length of time, the confusion which follows the separation of the soul from the body?

"No; this depends entirely on their degree of elevation. He who has already accomplished a certain amount of purification recovers his consciousness almost immediately, because he had already freed himself from the thralldom of materiality during his bodily life; whereas the carnally minded man, he whose conscience is not clear, retains the impression of matter for a much longer time."

165. Does a knowledge of Spiritism exercise any influence on the duration of this state of confusion?

"It exercises a very considerable influence on that duration, because it enables the spirit to understand beforehand the new situation in which it is about to find itself; but the practice of rectitude during the earthly life, and a clear conscience, are the conditions which conduce most powerfully to shorten it."

At the moment of death, everything appears confused. The soul takes some time to recover its self-consciousness, for it Is as though stunned, and in a state similar to that of a man waking out of a deep sleep, and trying to understand his own situation. It gradually regains clearness of thought and the memory of the past in proportion to the weakening of the influence of the material envelope from which it has just freed itself, and the clearing away of the sort of fog that obscured its consciousness.

The duration of the state of confusion that follows death varies greatly in different cases. It may be only of a few hours, and it may be of several months, or even years. Those with whom It lasts the least are they who, during the earthly life, have identified themselves most closely with their future state, because they are soonest able to understand their new situation. This state of confusion assumes special aspects according to character peculiarities, and also according to different modes of death. In all cases of violent or sudden death, by suicide, by capital punishment, accident, apoplexy, etc., the spirit is surprised, astounded, and does not believe himself to be dead. He obstinately persists in asserting the contrary; and, nevertheless, he sees the body he has quitted as something apart from himself he knows that body to be his own, and he cannot make out how it should be separated from him. He goes about among the persons with whom he is united by the ties of affection, speaks to them, and cannot conceive why they do not hear him. This Sort of illusion lasts until the entire separation of the perispirit from the earthly body, for it is only when this is accomplished that the spirit begins to understand his situation, and becomes aware that he no longer forms part of the world of human beings. Death having come upon him by surprise, the spirit is stunned by the suddenness of the change that has taken place in him. For him, death is still synonymous with destruction, annihilation and he thinks, sees, hears, it seems to him that he cannot be dead. And this illusion is still further strengthened by his seeing himself with a body similar in form to the one he has quitted for he does not at first perceive Its ethereal nature, but supposes it to be solid and compact like the other and when his attention has been called to this point, he is astonished at finding that it is not palpable. This phenomenon is analogous to that which occurs in the case of somnambulists, who, when thrown for the first time into the magnetic sleep, cannot believe that they are not awake. Sleep, according to their idea of it, is synonymous with suspension of the perceptive faculties; and as they think freely, and see, they appear to themselves not to be asleep. Some spirits present this peculiarity, even in cases where death has not supervened unexpectedly but it more frequently occurs in the case of those who, although they may have been ill, had no expectation of death. The curious spectacle Is then presented of a spirit attending his own funeral as though it were that of someone else, and speaking of it as of something which in no way concerns him, until the moment when at length he comprehends the true state of the case. In the mental confusion which follows death, there is nothing painful for him who has lived an upright life. He is calm, and his perceptions are those of a peaceful awaking out of sleep. But for him whose conscience is not clean, it is full of anxiety and anguish that become more and more poignant in proportion as he recovers consciousness. In cases of collective death, in which many persons have perished together in the same catastrophe, it has been observed that they do not always see one another immediately afterwards. In the state of confusion which follows death, each spirit goes his own way, or concerns himself only with those in whom he takes an interest.

Glossary

viz.:   an abbreviation of the Latin word *videlicet,* meaning "namely" or "as follows"

Ellen G. White in 1899.

THE GREAT CONTROVERSY: DOCUMENT ANALYSIS

"Christ had come, not to the earth, as they expected, but, as foreshadowed in the type, to the most holy place of the temple of God in heaven."

Overview

The name *Seventh-day Adventist* represents two of the most significant doctrines of the church: the belief that Saturday, the seventh day, is the Sabbath to be observed and the belief in the imminent Second Coming of Christ. These two doctrines are central to the meaning and purpose of Ellen White's chapter "In the Holy of Holies" in her book *The Great Controversy*. Approximately 16 million Adventists today also hold the conviction that White was a prophetess through whom God gave the church special guidance.

Seventh-day Adventists were officially recognized as a church in 1848, and White (1827–1915) went on to spend nearly seventy years of her life in its development. She assisted in the planning, the building, and the operation of Adventist institutions: hospitals, sanitariums, schools, publishing houses, and a worldwide mission work. She wrote thousands of pages of personal advice and institutional counsels on church organization, health reform, and social responsibilities, which are contained in nine volumes called *Testimonies for the Church* (1855–1909).

The Great Controversy is the final book of a five-volume series in which she includes an account of the Millerite Movement of the 1800s. The Second Great Awakening in America arose as pastors from several Christian denominations joined the Millerite group as associates. William Miller, a Baptist preacher, had predicted that Christ would return to the earth on October 22, 1844, but the failure of that prophecy to materialize led to what his followers called "The Great Disappointment." In her essay "In the Holy of Holies," White explains why this prophecy failed, and what Adventists should take away from their study of biblical apocalypticism. White's belief that Christ had actually entered the "heavenly" Sanctuary in 1844 became one of the central doctrines of the church she helped to found.

Context

Ellen G. White wrote The Great Controversy within a religious and cultural environment that we can picture as a series of concentric circles, each providing part of a larger landscape of spiritual and social beliefs and circumstances.

At the broadest level, White's works, including The Great Controversy, were a product of the American religious revival known as the Second Great Awakening. Beginning around the turn of the 19th century and reaching its peak in the 1840s, the Second Great Awakening was characterized by a turning away from the skeptical, rational worldview encouraged by enlightenment thinkers. One of the key beliefs that as common to the preachers and missionaries of the Second Great Awakening was postmillennialism. This was a belief that Jesus Christ's return to Earth would occur after a period called the "millennium," a period of peace, prosperity, and happiness that some believed would be a literal thousand years.

This focus on the end times (or, to use the more theological term, eschatology) moves us inward to the next circle. While many saw the return of Jesus to Earth as a distant event, some believed it was imminent and that the church must convert as many as possible before it was too late for them to receive salvation. One of these was William Miller, a Baptist preacher from northern New York. Miller and his followers (called "Millerites") believed that the second coming (or second advent) would occur sometime between March 1843 and March 1844. during the 1840s, Miller and those who agreed with him published a number of newspapers and pamphlets proclaiming their beliefs. When this did not occur, the Millerites movement began to fracture, with Miller's followers having many, many different explanations for why Christ did not return in 1843-44 and predictions for when, in fact, he might come back. One of the most common predictions was that this would occur October 22, 1844. so many clung to this date that, when it did not occur, it became known as "the Great Disappointment."

The next circle of context is the branch of Protestant Christianity that would become known as Adventism. The Adventists agree with Miller that, based on careful reading of Biblical prophecy, the second advent of Christ was to occur soon. They did not, however, believe that prediction specific dates was appropriate. As most Millerites had, after the Great Disappointment, abandoned the movement, the Adventist movement was quite small and only loosely connected rather than being an organized church body. It is here that we find Ellen G. White. White had been a part of the Millerite tradition since age 12, when her family accepted Miller's teachings. White, along with her husband James White and others would be the establishing figures of the Seventh-day Adventist church in 1863.

About the Author

Ellen Gould White was born Ellen Gould Harmon in Maine in 1827. Her family began following the teachings of William Miller in 1840, when White was twelve years old. beginning in 1844, the year of the Great Disappointment, White claimed to receive visions and would experience thousands between her first at age 17 and her death at age 87. White usually had these in public settings—usually religious meetings and services. These visions formed the basis for her writings, including The Great Controversy. Witnesses described some physical characteristics of her visions that seemed to be fairly consistent over the years: fainting, followed by "superhuman strength," unblinking eyes, and being unaware of what was going on around her while in the midst of a vision. The visions often addressed themes such as the Adventists' pilgrimage toward Heaven.

White married her husband, fellow Millerite James Springer White, in the summer of 1846. Throughout the remainder of the 1840s and 1850s, White and her husband found ways to serve the small but growing Adventist community Ellen continued experiencing and sharing knowledge from her visions, while James published newsletters and books. The vision that inspired White to write The Great Controversy occurred on March 14, 1858 at a funeral in Bowling Green, Ohio. This vision, according to White, consisted of practical education for members of the church as well as a deeper understanding of the conflict between God and Satan.

In 1848, the Adventist church began holding regular meetings in the northeastern United States, usually New York and New England. Ellen White, James White and Joseph Bates were prominent leaders at these meetings, and in 1863, they founded the General Conference Seventh-day Adventist Church at a meeting in Battle Creek, Michigan. Ellen White was a significant figure in the establishment and early decades of the denomination, even though she did not have an official position within the church hierarchy. She continued have visions and to write numerous articles about them as well as other subjects. She also pioneered the denomination's efforts to establish

Time Line	
November 26, 1827	■ Ellen G. Harmon White is born in Maine.
1840	■ White's family becomes involved in the Millerite movement.
1844	■ White experiences her first vision. She would claim to experience over 100 visions between 1844 and 1863.
October 22, 1844	■ William Miller's prediction of the return of Jesus to Earth.
August 30, 1846	■ Marriage to James White.
April, 1848	■ "Sabbath Conferences" take place throughout the northeastern United States, marking the beginnings of the organized Sabbatarian movement in the United States.
1858	■ White writes the first version of "The Great Controversy."
May 21, 1863	■ White, along with James White, Joseph Bates, and J. N. Andrews organize the General Conference of Seventh Day Adventists in Battle Creek, Michigan.
July 16, 1915	■ White dies in California

congregations outside the United States, as well as helping found medical facilities and schools. White was an abolitionist and under her influence the Seventh-day Adventist church took that position as well. White also argued against obeying the federal Fugitive Slave Law, which required people to aid authorities in returning runaway slaves to their masters.

Later in her life, she continued to write not only of her visions but also of broader religious topics as well as theories on health reform. She moved to Australia for nearly a decade in the 1890s and would continue to write for Adventist newspapers and magazines for the rest of her life. she died in 1915.

Explanation and Analysis of the Document

Under William Miller's leadership, the religious awakening of the 1840s focused on Daniel 8:14: "And he said unto me, Unto two thousand and three hundred days; then shall the sanctuary be cleansed." Because the biblical sanctuary no longer existed and it was widely believed among Miller's followers that the word *sanctuary* referred to the earth, Miller took the text as a prediction that Christ would return to cleanse the earth in 2,300 years. He had to explain how a starting point could be determined so that the end of those years could be known.

Daniel 9:25 and 26 seemed to solve the puzzle of the starting and ending dates:

> 25 Know therefore and understand, that from the going forth of the commandment to restore and to build Jerusalem unto the Messiah the Prince shall be seven weeks, and threescore and two weeks: the street shall be built again, and the wall, even in troublous times.

> 26 And after threescore and two weeks shall Messiah be cut off, but not for himself: and the people of the prince that shall come shall destroy the city and the sanctuary; and the end thereof shall be with a flood, and unto the end of the war desolations are determined.

While the symbolic seventy weeks (490 literal years) were allotted to the Jewish people, Miller thought that they were the first 490 of the 2,300 years. If that was not true, he said that his theory of a date for Christ's Second Coming would fail. He believed that the "Messiah" to be "cut off," as noted in verses 25 and 26, applied to Christ and the Crucifixion and that Christ's death would be fulfilled in the last seven-year period of the 490 years. The 490 years would begin when the command goes forth to restore and rebuild Jerusalem following the Babylonian captivity.

Miller took an estimated historical date for the death of Christ and then counted back 490 years to find a decree that allowed the Jews to restore Jerusalem. Following the decree of Cyrus (539 BCE), three other decrees were given by the Persians, but the decree of Artaxerxes in 457 BCE was the only one that could meet the time of Christ without going beyond it. This starting year, Miller reasoned, confirmed that Christ's death actually occurred in 31 CE, leaving the final three and a half years of the 490 to culminate in 34 CE. The remaining 1810 years would terminate in 1844.

When the spring of 1844 passed, Miller looked to find a biblical clue to the exact date for Christ's return, expected that year. He found that the book of Hebrews had made antitypical applications of Christ's death as the sacrificial Lamb and of his ministration as High Priest in heavenly places. Miller met with his associates that summer to study the old Jewish sanctuary. They concluded that the set date for the yearly Day of Atonement in October was the type for the day of Christ's return.

When the Jewish high priest had cleansed the sanctuary and made atonement, he came out to the people, and the camp was cleansed. Miller reasoned, then, that Jesus as High Priest would come out of the "heavenly sanctuary" and return to the earth for its cleansing on October 22. Hiram Edson, a leading pioneer of Adventism, believed that he saw a vision of Christ ministering in the heavenly sanctuary the day following the disappointment. He concluded that instead of Christ's coming out of the "heavenly" sanctuary to the earth on October 22, 1844, he had left the Holy Place and entered the Most Holy Place on that day because he had a work to perform there before returning to the earth. White accepted Edson's vision as light from God and believed that this vision convincingly explained their disappointment.

In the Holy of Holies of heaven, White and her followers believed, resides the original ark of his testament containing the Ten Commandments—the moral standard of God's judgment (Revelation 11:19: "And the temple of God was opened in heaven, and there was seen in his temple the ark of his testament: and there were lightnings, and voices, and thunderings, and an earthquake, and great hail."). Because the fourth commandment to keep holy the Sabbath day must be in the heavenly sanctuary, as in the original "earthly" ark, and before a copy of the commandments was given to Israel, Adventists became Sabbath keepers. As Jesus is in the Most Holy, Adventists believe that the first angel's message (Revelation 14:7: "Saying with a loud voice, Fear God, and give glory to him; for the hour of his judgment is come: and worship him that made heaven, and earth, and the sea, and the fountains of waters") went into effect on October 22, 1844. This judgment is "investigative," or a prejudgment before the Second Coming, because Christ brings the rewards of that judgment with him, when the proverbial "sheep are separated from the goats" and "the wheat from the tares."

The investigative judgment of 1844 has been challenged more than any other doctrine. The cleansing of the sanctuary described in Daniel refers only to the restoration of the ancient sanctuary following the days allotted for 2,300 evening and morning sacrifices that were not offered because the sacred places were defiled by Israel's enemies. Daniel's context draws no antitypical applications to heaven from the Day of Atonement. Certain Adventist leaders, who believe that the theology of the heavenly sanctuary antitypes is biblically supported, accept it as based on Hebrews and not on Daniel. Some have concluded that October 22, 1844, does not belong in the church's theology, but this is not yet the official position of the church.

"Christ had come, not to the earth, as they expected, but, as foreshadowed in the type, to the most holy place of the temple of God in heaven."

(Section 1)

"But the people were not yet ready to meet their Lord. There was still a work of preparation to be accomplished for them. Light was to be given, directing their minds to the temple of God in heaven; and as they should by faith follow their High Priest in His ministration there, new duties would be revealed."

(Section 1)

Audience

Initially, the audience for Ellen White's The Great Controversy was her fellow Adventist believers. Ellen White published the first edition in 1858 and a second edition would follow in 1884. The phrase " Great Controversy" refers to the conflict between Jesus and Satan that raged since the beginning of time both in Heaven and on the Earth. White's book described this battle as she saw it in her vision of 1858. The definitive version would not appear until 1911. Each time a new edition appeared, the text became longer (doubling in word count between the 1858 edition and the 1884 version) with additional discussion of the conflict and the role of the church.

This excerpt comes from the 1888 edition of The Great Controversy. This edition represented an attempt to expand the readership beyond that circle of Seventh-day Adventists and other former Millerites. White added additional material that served to clarify points of Adventist doctrine with those Christians or non-Christians who were not familiar with the history of the Adventist faith. The excerpt presented here is a good example of the ways in which White reached out to those who might have been driven away from the movement after the "Great Disappointment" of 1844 as well as those Christians who were entirely unfamiliar with Adventist beliefs about the return of Jesus.

To make the book and its topics more accessible to these non-Adventist readers, White added additional citations from the Bible to support her arguments and added material on Reformation figures such as Jan Huss and John Calvin, which the Adventist ideas within the context of the broader Protestant tradition.

Impact

Ellen G. White's influence upon Adventism and the Seventh-Day Adventist church particular go beyond her role as one of the founders of the General Conference in 1863. Her writings explaining her visions as well as clarifying Adventist doctrine and practice played a key role in solidifying the Adventist movement and unifying what had been, until the 1860s, a disparate group of believers into an organized force. She was the driving force behind the Adventist church establishing health care facilities, a tradition that continues to this day.

In its latest edition, which was published in 1911, White asserts that the United States will, in the future, merge with such enemies of "true" Christianity as the Roman Catholic church and Protestant churches that had fallen away. One effect of this unholy union would be the enforcement of "Sunday laws" (laws which prohibited certain activities on Sundays, in deference to it being the day of worship for most Christian traditions). White argued that worshiping on Sundays (rather than the Biblically prescribed Sabbath of Saturday) was the "mark of the beast" referred to in the Revelation of St. John. The resulting persecution of Adventists and other Sabbath-keepers would occur, she claimed, shortly before the return of Jesus Christ to Earth. Thus, White was maintaining the tradition of predicting the end of the world but doing so by pointing people to key sequences of events in the future rather than naming a specific date.

The official position of the Seventh-day Adventist church is that Ellen G. White was divinely inspired in her visions and they assert that she possessed the "gift of prophecy" as described in the New Testament. Beyond the realm of the Seventh-day Adventist church, White's visions and the church's support for the role of modern-day prophets as well as the careful study of eschatological passages in the Bible would eventually be echoed elsewhere in American Protestant Christianity. Modern Evangelical attention to the :End Times" such as Hal Lindsey's 1970 book The Late Great Planet Earth owes much to the Millerites and the work of Ellen G. White. Her prediction, in the 1911 edition of *The Great Controversy*, that there was be an evil alliance between the US government, the Roman Catholics, and heretical Protestant churches that would persecute the small remnant of real Christians would become a recurring theme not only in some Bible prophecy studies but also in anti-Catholic conspiracy theory.

◆ **Further Reading**

Aamodt, Terrie Dopp, Gary Land, and Ronald L. Numbers, eds. *Ellen Harmon White: American Prophet*. 1 edition. Oxford ; New York: Oxford University Press, 2014. Print.

Butler, Jonathan M. "Prophecy, Gender, and Culture: Ellen Gould Harmon [White] and the Roots of Seventh-Day Adventism." *Religion and American Culture: A Journal of Interpretation* 1.1 (1991): 3–29. *JSTOR*. Web.

Douglass, Herbert E. *The Heartbeat of Adventism: The Great Controversy Theme in the Writings of Ellen G. White*. Nampa, Idaho: Pacific Press Pub. Association, 2010. Print.

"Ellen G. White®: A Brief Biography." N.p., n.d. Web. 26 Aug. 2016.

Jones, R. Clifford. *James K. Humphrey and the Sabbath-Day Adventists*. University Press of Mississippi, 2006. *JSTOR*. Web. 27 Aug. 2016.

Knight, George R. *Millennial Fever and the End of the World: A Study of Millerite Adventism*. Boise, Idaho: Pacific Press Publishing Association, 1993. Print.

Land, Gary. *Adventism in America: A History*. Revised edition. Berrien Springs, Mich: Andrews University Press, 1998. Print.

Numbers, Ronald L. *Prophetess of Health: A Study of Ellen G. White*. 3 edition. Grand Rapids, Mich: Eerdmans, 2008. Print.

Rowe, David L., and Mark Noll. *God's Strange Work: William Miller and the End of the World*. 1 edition. Grand Rapids, Mich: Eerdmans, 2008. Print.

Schwarz, Richard W. *Light Bearers: A History of the Seventh-Day Adventist Church*. 1 Edition edition. Nampa, Idaho: Pacific Press Publishing Association, 2015. Print.

—Commentary by Sandra Jackson and Aaron J. Gulyas

Questions for Further Study

1. According to White, how did "God's hand" direct "the great advent movement"?

2. In what way, according to White, are the Adventists "like the first disciples"?

3. What does White mean by "the sanctuary above"? Why is it crucial for understanding the Great Disappointment of 1844?

THE GREAT CONTROVERSY: DOCUMENT TEXT

1858 CE

—Ellen G. White

"In the Holy of Holies"

The subject of the sanctuary was the key which unlocked the mystery of the disappointment of 1844. It opened to view a complete system of truth, connected and harmonious, showing that God's hand had directed the great advent movement and revealing present duty as it brought to light the position and work of His people. As the disciples of Jesus after the terrible night of their anguish and disappointment were "glad when they saw the Lord," so did those now rejoice who had looked in faith for His second coming. They had expected Him to appear in glory to give reward to His servants. As their hopes were disappointed, they had lost sight of Jesus, and with Mary at the sepulcher they cried: "They have taken away my Lord, and I know not where they have laid Him." Now in the holy of holies they again beheld Him, their compassionate High Priest, soon to appear as their king and deliverer. Light from the sanctuary illumined the past, the present, and the future. They knew that God had led them by His unerring providence. Though, like the first disciples, they themselves had failed to understand the message which they bore, yet it had been in every respect correct. In proclaiming it they had fulfilled the purpose of God, and their labor had not been in vain in the Lord. Begotten "again unto a lively hope," they rejoiced "with joy unspeakable and full of glory."

Both the prophecy of Daniel 8:14, "Unto two thousand and three hundred days; then shall the sanctuary be cleansed," and the first angel's message, "Fear God, and give glory to Him; for the hour of His judgment is come," pointed to Christ's ministration in the most holy place, to the investigative judgment, and not to the coming of Christ for the redemption of His people and the destruction of the wicked. The mistake had not been in the reckoning of the prophetic periods, but in the *event* to take place at the end of the 2300 days. Through this error the believers had suffered disappointment, yet all that was

foretold by the prophecy, and all that they had any Scripture warrant to expect, had been accomplished. At the very time when they were lamenting the failure of their hopes, the event had taken place which was foretold by the message, and which must be fulfilled before the Lord could appear to give reward to His servants.

Christ had come, not to the earth, as they expected, but, as foreshadowed in the type, to the most holy place of the temple of God in heaven. He is represented by the prophet Daniel as coming at this time to the Ancient of Days: "I saw in the night visions, and behold, one like the Son of man came with the clouds of heaven, and came"—not to the earth, but—"to the Ancient of Days, and they brought Him near before Him." Daniel 7:13.

This coming is foretold also by the prophet Malachi: "The Lord, whom ye seek, shall suddenly come to His temple, even the Messenger of the covenant, whom ye delight in: behold, He shall come, saith the Lord of hosts." Malachi 3:1. The coming of the Lord to His temple was sudden, unexpected, to His people. They were not looking for Him *there*. They expected Him to come to earth, "in flaming fire taking vengeance on them that know not God, and that obey not the gospel." 2 Thessalonians 1:8.

But the people were not yet ready to meet their Lord. There was still a work of preparation to be accomplished for them. Light was to be given, directing their minds to the temple of God in heaven; and as they should by faith follow their High Priest in His ministration there, new duties would be revealed. Another message of warning and instruction was to be given to the church.

Says the prophet: "Who may abide the day of His coming? And who shall stand when He appeareth? For He is like a refiner's fire, and like fullers' soap: and He shall sit as a refiner and purifier of silver: and He shall purify the sons of Levi, and purge them as gold and silver, that they may offer unto the Lord an offering of righteousness." Malachi 3:2, 3. Those who are living upon the earth when the intercession of Christ shall cease in the sanctuary above are to stand in the sight of a holy God without a mediator. Their robes must be spotless; their characters must be purified from sin by the blood of sprinkling. Through the grace of God and their own diligent effort they must be conquerors in the battle with evil. While the investigative judgment is going forward in heaven, while the sins of the penitent believers are being removed from the sanctuary, there is to be a special work of purification, of putting away of sin, among God's people upon earth. This work is more clearly presented in the messages of Revelation 14.

When this work shall have been accomplished, the followers of Christ will be ready for His appearing. "Then shall the offering of Judah and Jerusalem be pleasant unto the Lord, as in the days of old, and as in former years." Malachi 3:4. Then the church which our Lord at His coming is to receive to Himself will be a "glorious church, not having spot or wrinkle, or any such thing." Ephesians 5:27. Then she will look "forth as the morning, fair as the moon, clear as the sun, and terrible as an army with banners." Song of Solomon 6:10.

Besides the coming of the Lord to His temple, Malachi also foretells His second advent, His coming for the execution of the judgment, in these words: "And I will come near to you to judgment; and I will be a swift witness against the sorcerers, and against the adulterers, and against false swearers, and against those that oppress the hireling in his wages, the widow, and the fatherless and that turn aside the stranger from his right, and fear not Me, saith the Lord of hosts." Malachi 3:5. Jude refers to the same scene when he says, "Behold, the Lord cometh with ten thousands of His saints, to execute judgment upon all, and to convince all that are ungodly among them of all their ungodly deeds." Jude 14:15. This coming and the coming of the Lord to His temple are distinct and separate events. ...

The passing of the time in 1844 was followed by a period of great trial to those who still held the advent faith. Their only relief, so far as ascertaining their true position was concerned, was the light which directed their minds to the sanctuary above. Some renounced their faith in their former reckoning of the prophetic periods and ascribed to human or satanic agencies the powerful influence of the Holy Spirit which had attended the advent movement. Another class firmly held that the lord had led them in their past experience; and as they waited and watched and prayed to know the will of God they saw that their great High Priest had entered upon another work of ministration, and, following Him by faith, they were led to see also the closing work of the church. They had a clearer understanding of the first and second angel's messages, and were prepared to receive and give to the world the solemn warning of the third angel of Revelation 14.

Glossary

Advent movement:	A collective name for the 19th century Christians who believed the second coming of Jesus Christ to Earth was imminent.
Disappointment of 1844:	A reference to William Miller's failed prediction that Christ would return on October 22, 1844.
Holy of Holies:	In ancient Israel, the portion of the temple where God was supposed to have dwelt. It could only be entered by certain priests at certain times.
Sepulcher:	A tomb. In this context, the tomb of Jesus Christ.
Solemn warning of the third angel:	The third angel in Revelation, chapter 14, warned that any who worship "the Beast" and take his "mark" will be punished by God.

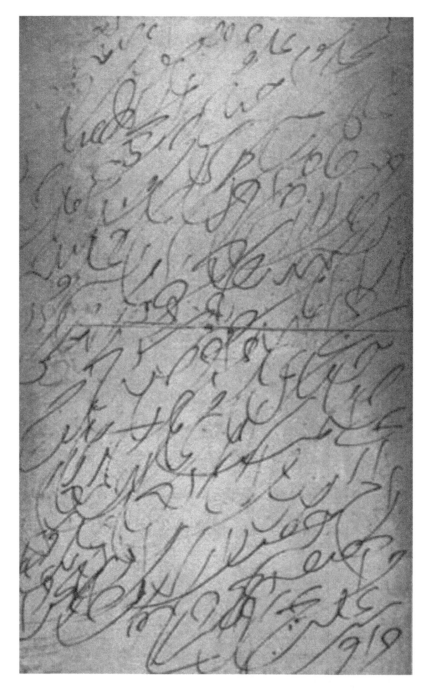

'Revelation writing': The first draft of a page from the Tajallíyát of Bahá'u'lláh.

KITAB-I-AQDAS: DOCUMENT ANALYSIS

"O ye leaders of religion! Who is the man amongst you that can rival Me in vision or insight?"

Overview

The Kitab-i-aqdas, or "Most Holy Book," is regarded as the central document of the Baha'i faith. It was written by Baha'u'llah, or Baha' Allah (born Mirza Hoseyn 'Ali Nuri), whom Baha'is regard as the most recent "manifestation of God" and the founder of the religion that will unify all races and all religions. While the exact dates of the book's composition are unknown, scholars and Baha'is agree that the text was completed around 1873, though some of it may have been written significantly earlier, perhaps as early as 1868. Tradition states that the text was completed while Baha'u'llah lived in the Mansion of Bahji in Acre, Israel, which was also the site of his death in 1892.

Although the text may be characterized as a book of laws, Baha'is regard the Kitab-i-aqdas as not just a book of religious laws and codes but further as a revelatory apology for the new religion and for the authority of Baha'u'llah himself. Baha'is believe that the Kitab-i-aqdas is the foundational document for the new age that Baha'u'llah ushered in; it offers a "blueprint for humanity" for a new era of peace, addressing practical legal topics ranging from inheritances to criminal justice. As a religious text, the Kitab-i-aqdas purposefully abrogates, or negates, religious laws of the Islamic Qur'an and the religious writings of the Bab (originally Mirza 'Ali Mohammad), whose religious movement, Babism, awaited the one "Whom God shall make manifest." This phrase—"He Whom God shall make manifest"—is a recurring theme throughout the writings of the Bab, whose theology claimed that supreme authority would rest with a messenger or manifestation of God to come after him. (A comparison may be drawn to John the Baptist within the Christian tradition; John claimed not to be Christ but to prepare the way for Christ.) Most Babis later became Baha'is by accepting Baha'u'llah as the one who would restore Islam to its roots.

Baha'u'llah began circulating copies of the Kitab-i-aqdas in 1873, and in 1890–1891 he arranged for its publication in India. A few unauthorized English translations emerged in the twentieth century, before Shoghi Effendi Rabbani, who was named the guardian of the Baha'i faith, offered a description and preview of an authoritative translation in his 1944 book *God Passes By*. The Baha'is intended to produce an official translation shortly thereafter, but the complete authoritative translation was not available in English until 1992. This delay in publication emphasizes the Baha'is' belief that humanity should implement the universal laws of the Kitab-i-aqdas gradually rather than immediately. Baha'u'llah's laws, even if they were a starting point for a new era of peace, will take time for humanity to realize and fully implement.

Context

The Baha'i faith began from a small cult of believers called Babis, which was a group within another movement called Shaykhism. Shaykhis were Shia Muslims who followed a teacher named Shaykh Ahmad (1753–1826), who, like many other Shiites, awaited a "hidden imam" who would come to restore and revive Islam. For Ahmad, this hidden imam was coming very soon, and his coming would coincide with the Day of Judgment. Mirza 'Ali Mohammad of Shiraz (1819–1850), who would be later known as "the Bab" (an Arabic word meaning "gate"), would be identified as the Mahdi—not the hidden imam but the teacher who would accompany Jesus at the end of days. The Bab taught that "He Whom God shall make manifest" was coming and that the Bab himself was only preparing humanity for the one who was coming. Baha'u'llah later proclaimed himself to be "He Whom God shall make manifest" and began writing what would be considered by many Babis and the Baha'is as new scripture for the new era of humanity.

Baha'u'llah's writings were considered both politically revolutionary and religiously radical. The earliest followers of Baha'u'llah were exiled, imprisoned, and executed; those who were not were often persecuted and marginalized by the Islamic majority around them. Muslims found the beliefs of the Babis to be incongruent with mainstream Islamic beliefs, and, to be sure, the Bab's writings intentionally negated many central teachings of the Qur'an, the Islamic scripture. In 1848 Babi leaders gathered for the Conference of Badasht, where a central Islamic law was formally abrogated during each day of the conference; the meeting ended when Muslim locals attacked the meeting. Baha'u'llah attended the conference and emerged as a leader in the Babi movement after the death of the Bab in 1850. Even the Bab's appointed leader of the movement, Subh-i-Azal (1831–1912), went into hiding and often publically denied his religious affiliation with the Babi faith.

Baha'u'llah's writings convey the voice of a suppressed and marginalized religion from a part of the world where those of the dominant religion were already considered economically oppressed and exploited by their own governments and the world community. His often bold and pretentious tone should be viewed in this context; the most important event of the world—that is, the revelation of Baha'u'llah—was occurring from a prison while the world was too busy with its own problems to pause to consider the solutions he offered. Most of Baha'u'llah's major works, including the Kitab-i-aqdas, were written in prison and for an audience that either had been imprisoned for religious or political reasons or understood the threat of being imprisoned for their beliefs.

The literature of Baha'u'llah also indicates, perhaps ironically, a keen fascination with the Western world, particularly American ideals of democracy and freedom, that was common among many aristocratic Muslims of the late nineteenth century. Some early Baha'is would later name Baha'u'llah's vision of a world community as the "United States of the World," and Baha'is' support and involvement with the organization of the League of Nations and its successor, the United Nations, were a direct consequence of this influence.

A central Baha'i belief is that the Bab closed the Islamic era, during which the revelation of Muhammad (the founder of Islam) was the most recent and most important word of God for humanity. In turn, the Bab prepared the world, especially the Islamic world, for the revelation of Baha'u'llah. As such, Baha'u'llah is believed by Baha'is to be the fulfillment of the scriptures of all major world religions: He is the Second Coming of Christ for Christians, the Messiah for Jews, the Amitabha Buddha for Buddhists, the twelfth imam for Shia Islam, the Shah Bahram (messiah of prophecy) of Zoroastrianism, and the final incarnation of Vishnu for Hindus. In essence, Baha'u'llah is viewed by his religious faithful as the most recent and most important in a long line of messengers or "manifestations of God" from the Eastern and Western worlds, and he brings together a world divided by religion. The importance of the Kitab-i-aqdas, then, is in its abrogation, its negation or replacement, of all other religious texts and laws. It offers a simple means for the world to begin to get along in a new age of religious peace.

Time Line	
November 12, 1817	■ Baha'u'llah is born Mirza Hoseyn 'Ali Nuri in Tehran, Persia (now Iran).
1845	■ Baha'u'llah converts to Babism.
June–July 1848	■ Early Babis, with Baha'u'llah in attendance, hold the Conference of Badasht to discuss the nature of the Bab's teachings. The conference ends when local villagers attack the Babis.
July 9, 1850	■ The Bab is executed in Tabriz, Persia.
September–December 1852	■ While imprisoned in Tehran, Baha'u'llah concludes that he is the one "Whom God shall make manifest" that the Bab had foretold.
April 21, 1863	■ Baha'u'llah publicly proclaims himself "He Whom God shall make manifest" in the Garden of Ridván, outside of Baghdad.
1873	■ Baha'u'llah completes the Kitab-i-aqdas.
1890–1891	■ Baha'u'llah arranges for the Kitab-i-aqdas to be published in Arabic by a publisher in Bombay.
May 29, 1892	■ Baha'u'llah dies; his will appoints his son 'Abdu'l-Baha as his successor as "Guardian of the Faith."
1900	■ Anton Haddad first translates the Kitab-i-aqdas into English.
1944	■ Shoghi Effendi Rabbani, the new Baha'i guardian of the faith, publishes God Passes By, which contains a description of the Kitab-i-aqdas.

1961	■ A second English translation of the Kitab-i-aqdas appears, prepared by Earl Elder and William Miller.
1973	■ The Baha'is' Universal House of Justice releases *Synopsis and Codification of the Laws and Ordinances of the Kitab-i-Aqdas*, attributed to Baha'u'llah and Shoghi Effendi, to celebrate the one-hundredth anniversary of Baha'u'llah's revelation of the text.
1992	■ The Kitab-i-aqdas is published in an authoritative edition in English.

About the Author

Mirza Hoseyn 'Ali Nuri was born on November 12, 1817, in Tehran, Persia (present-day Iran). He later took the name Baha'u'llah, or Baha' Allah (Arabic for "the glory of God"), and became the primary figure of the Baha'i faith. Baha'u'llah came from an aristocratic family with political connections; his ancestry legendarily connects him directly to both Zoroaster and Jesse of the Jewish tradition, an ancestry that is latent with messianic claims. For example, the Old Testament book of Isaiah says, "And there shall come forth a rod out of the stem of Jesse... and the spirit of the Lord shall rest upon him, the spirit of wisdom and understanding" (11:1–2). Although Baha'u'llah would spend most of his historically important years in prison, his family connections were largely responsible for preventing his execution.

Baha'u'llah converted to Babism at the age of twenty-seven, and as a young man he was immediately viewed by other Babis as a leader within the movement. After the execution of the Bab in 1850, Baha'u'llah gained prominence as an administrator of the small religion while he was in Baghdad, in the Ottoman Empire (now in Iraq). There, on April 21, 1863, Baha'u'llah proclaimed that he was "He Whom God shall make manifest," whom the Babis were awaiting, though he had reached this conclusion nearly a decade earlier. This event split the Babi faith, but the majority of Babis eventually converted to the new religion known today as Baha'i. Baha'u'llah spent most of the rest of his life in exile and in prison. The Islamic government in Persia regarded both the Bab and Baha'u'llah as threats to its authority, so Baha'u'llah was exiled first to Baghdad; then to Constantinople, Turkey (now Istanbul); and finally to Adrianople, Turkey (now Edirne). Later, he was arrested and held at the penal colony in 'Akko (Acre), in present-day Israel. In his final years he was allowed to live at home, although officially he remained a prisoner of the city until he died after a short illness on May 29, 1892. He appointed his eldest son, 'Abdu'l-Baha, to be his spiritual successor.

Explanation and Analysis of the Document

Kitab-i-aqdas is Baha'u'llah's doctrinal vision for the religion he established, outlining the polity and governance of the religion and dictating the practices of the faith. Although the Kitab-i-aqdas is the primary source of religious law for Baha'is, Baha'i law also comprises laws from other texts written by Baha'u'llah, by his son 'Abdu'l-Baha, and by his son's successor, Shoghi Effendi Rabbani and interpreted by the Baha'is' Universal House of Justice. Kitab-i-aqdas is known for its poetic and linguistic originality, but much of its poetry is lost in translation. The text of the Kitab-i-aqdas itself is written in narrative paragraph form and divided into 190 paragraphs in its authoritative translation.

One common device employed by Baha'u'llah throughout the text is the predication of a statement or paragraph with the word "Say," followed by a colon. Baha'u'llah is clearly playing with the language of the Qur'an, as this is a common device in the Qur'an. Theologically, this has several meanings. First, Baha'u'llah is indicating that his writings, as the most recent revelation of God, supercede the authority of the Qur'an. In addition, Baha'u'llah is indicating that he, like Muhammad, is more than a "prophet" of God—as Muhammad is universally claimed to be by Islam—but is instead a "manifestation of God." In other words, manifestations of God are epistemologically—that is, cognitively and spiritually—superior to other humans. Yet Baha'u'llah also uses the "Say" convention to indicate his own heightened authority over that of Muhammad. In the Qur'an, "Say" would predicate a supreme truth being dispensed by the Prophet as derived through a revelation offered by an angelic messenger; in the Kitab-i-aqdas, Baha'u'llah offers supreme truth being revealed by himself alone in his own voice, as he does not require an angel to make supreme statements.

♦ Paragraphs 1–5

These paragraphs address the position of Baha'u'llah and authority of the text. The opening of Kitab-i-aqdas offers a succinct statement of faith for the Baha'i community, which is to accept the authority of the author, Baha'u'llah, and he claims that the laws of Kitab-i-aqdas have supreme authority above all others. Those who follow "Him Who is the Dayspring of His Revelation" are charged with rising above the traditionally accepted ethics of other religions, including Islam. Baha'u'llah implies that Islam has descended into a nihilistic state—preaching morality while tolerating a base immorality—asserting that they "have violated the Covenant of God by breaking His commandments."

Baha'u'llah then directs the world to be his audience. He does not see himself as revealing "a mere code of laws" but rather a spiritual doorway to a higher understanding of morality in general. Laws are the practical means of implementing the divine vision of Baha'u'llah; but the laws are not authoritative simply because they are called "laws."

◆ Paragraph 12

Paragraph 12 is the most important section of a longer discourse on prayer and fasting as the primary religious practices for the new religion. Through this discourse, special instructions and exemptions are given to women while menstruating, to those who are traveling, and in the witness of unnatural events.

In paragraph 12, Baha'u'llah clearly states that restrictions on prayer within Islam and other religions are now abrogated, as restrictions on prayer were previously imposed through misunderstandings on the part of those who interpreted older religions. Individual prayer now takes priority over congregational prayer, with the exception of funeral prayers. These instructions consummate Baha'u'llah's critique of Islamic prayer as being rote and unemotional and of Christian piety as being for show and not offering individual devotion to God alone. This emphasis on personal prayer is maintained in the Baha'i faith today in their temple practices: in Baha'i temples, silence is to be reserved to allow space for prayers, and only the words of sacred texts or music may be offered for gatherings. Individual religious practice is focused primarily upon daily devotions and prayer.

◆ Paragraph 16

This section addresses Naw-Rúz and fasting. Baha'u'llah appropriates the Persian vernal equinox celebration of Naw-Rúz by instituting it as the Baha'i New Year. Naw-Rúz has spiritual significance as a symbol of a new age for humanity, with the equinox symbolic of the manifestation of God. Naw-Rúz is to be a feast for those who practice fasting leading up to the holiday.

◆ Paragraph 30

Paragraph 30 concludes a section on ethics. Through this section, general statements are made forbidding adultery, backbiting, and calumny, and there is a long discussion of proper procedure regarding inheritances. These laws begin with a brief discussion of the necessity of prayer and conclude with a statement affirming the station of Baha'u'llah and the authority of the Kitab-i-aqdas. The discussion of ethics is rooted in the religious practice of Naw-Rúz, not because Naw-Rúz in and of itself makes people more moral but because Naw-Rúz indicates a new beginning of ethical thinking that is a break from the past, rooted in the manifestation of Baha'u'llah.

Paragraph 30 specifically discusses what would be later interpreted as the polity of Baha'i religious institutions, namely, one per city or town. There should not be competing Baha'i communities, as is common with Christian churches and in Shia Muslim culture. This is, Baha'u'llah writes, in the best interests of God. It is for this reason that Baha'is prioritize unity within the faith as a spiritual principle and shun those within the faith who perpetuate dissension.

◆ Paragraph 36

The next section of Kitab-i-aqdas offers exhortations and laws, with instruction given on prayer, declarations of authority, laws of criminal justice, parenting, sexuality, mediation, hunting, and arson. In paragraph 36, Baha'u'llah calls the God of which he speaks "the Lord of all Religions." Referencing the Brahmin (priestly caste) traditions of Hinduism, Baha'u'llah instructs the faithful to "make not your deeds as snares wherewith to entrap the object of your aspiration," critiquing traditional religious ritual as empty devotions wherein the ritual becomes the object rather than God being the "Ultimate Objective." Baha'u'llah further states that all of the good deeds done on earth are meaningless outside of acceptance of his own claim of authority. This lofty claim should be understood within the context of Baha'u'llah's declaration of Naw-Rúz: Doing good deeds is not wrong, but the primary hurdle for peace in the world is acceptance of Baha'u'llah's new religion.

◆ Paragraphs 42 and 43

Paragraph 42 is of particular importance, for Baha'u'llah cryptically bestows upon 'Abdu'l-Baha, and later the House of Justice, the authority to interpret the Kitab-i-aqdas in the future. Today, the Universal House of Justice of the Baha'i faith administers the religion on an international level and is understood to be a reflection of a model for world governance. The Universal House of Justice began operations in 1963 in Haifa, Israel; a small schism occurred within the religion as a result of its establishment. Paragraph 43 describes Baha'u'llah as a mystical means of interpreting religious laws, drawing a comparison to Christian conceptions of Christ as the heart of religious law. From a philosophical perspective, Baha'u'llah appears to be suggesting an Aristotelian ("Middle Way") approach to solving dilemmas, placing himself as the mystical center of right action. The implication here is that while Baha'u'llah's theological and political positions might be considered radical for his time, he represents a common-sense path to morality in the future.

◆ Paragraph 67

The next section famously discusses marriage and sexuality; the discussions of ethics in the previous sections lead Baha'u'llah to pay special attention to marriage. Monogamy is prioritized, and the conditions of marriage are explained: dowries are required, restrictions are placed on travel, and divorce is discouraged. Paragraph 67, in particular, is a well-known passage of Baha'i scripture. Baha'u'llah begins by giving instruction for those with an absent marriage partner, and the later discussion is one of the primary scriptural foundations for the Baha'i understanding of divorce. Although the original text of Baha'u'llah suggests a patriarchal situation in which men typically travel from their wives, within the Baha'i faith, the equality of genders is an important concept. Divorce is discouraged but not absolutely forbidden, requiring a separation, or year of patience, during which the two parties are to attempt to reconcile their differences. If the couple cannot reach a reconciliation, they may divorce. Baha'u'llah also offers instruction for the widowed; they may remarry following a culturally appropriate period of grieving.

♦ Paragraph 77

Baha'u'llah proceeds to offer more laws, including a prohibition of slavery (in paragraph 72). In paragraph 77, Baha'u'llah lifts previous religious instructions to burn books, especially those issued by the Bab in the scripture called the Persian Bayan.

♦ Paragraph 82

In paragraph 82, Baha'u'llah addresses the kings and political rulers of the world. He clearly states that the true authority of the world rests with God alone, and the rulers are subservient to God. Baha'u'llah thus instructs the rulers to accept his authority and submit to the will of God as revealed through him, emphasizing that the world's leaders are made great only through God.

♦ Paragraphs 99–102, 104–105

The next section, one of the most famous of the text, offers exhortations to the world's religious leaders. In paragraph 99, Baha'u'llah asks religious leaders not to compare their holy texts to his, for his book "is the unerring Balance established amongst men." In other words, it is impossible to compare other religious texts to the Kitab-i-aqdas because the quality and purity of religious truth being revealed is on a completely new level (achieving "this most perfect Balance"), above any other previous religious text rendered with authority. In paragraph 100, Baha'u'llah pleads with those who follow other religions to "advance" and says that following the old religions prevents the new revelation of God in the world. This passage not only recalls the Middle Eastern religious trope or archetype of the religious figure updating and fulfilling previous revelation or prophesy but also indicates the closure of an age and the initiation of a new era for humanity. The "Sadratu'l-Muntaha" is a symbol of a tree at the end of a journey; at the end of the horizontal "road" of the previous era of humanity, an entirely new journey begins, moving in a completley new direction, vertically. Baha'u'llah is the conduit for this new, upward movement.

In paragraph 101 Baha'u'llah challenges clerics to compare themselves to him, saying that none could "claim to be My equal in utterance or wisdom." He further claims that the followers of the world's religions will find what they are waiting for in his revelation. Paragraphs 102 and 105 proclaim the Kitab-i-aqdas as the core not only of the new religion but of all religions. Scholars may dispute Baha'u'llah's claims, but those arguments are irrelevant, and those who make such arguments "have perverted the Sublime Word of God." God's grand revelation to the world, not the grandiose "dissertations" of scholars (paragraph 104), is all that matters. Beyond the claims of authority being made in these statements, Baha'is hold as an important spiritual principle the simplicity of the faith that is open to scholarly discussion but does not require scholarly support for legitimacy.

While these claims often seem pretentious, one would expect that if Baha'u'llah believes he is who he claims to be, these kinds of statements would be necessary. The argumentation does, however, accuse the Middle Eastern religions of not taking their own eschatological claims seriously. In other words, Baha'u'llah is condemning the religious faithful of Islam and Christianity, for example, for being too wrapped up in the business and conflicts of their religious institutions to notice that the fulfillment of their own religions is happening right before them. Furthermore, Baha'u'llah's enactment of apocalyptic thinking rejects the violence implicit in Christian and Islamic eschatology.

♦ Paragraphs 115 and 116

Paragraphs 115 and 116 carry some double meaning. Most commonly, Baha'u'llah offers instruction on the proper use of recitation of sacred scripture, which is to be read aloud in worshipful environments and meditated upon in silence or sung, if the "Mashriqu'l-Adhkár" is understood to be a house of worship. 'Abdu'l-Baha taught that this term also refers to the "House of Justice," which Baha'u'llah discusses earlier in the Kitab-i-aqdas. The theological significance is that the administration of the religion and, in essence, the administration of the world are rooted in worship and that sacred speech should be the primary currency within the institution. This is one reason why the Universal House of Justice's resolutions and statements are considered scriptural by Baha'is today.

♦ Paragraphs 120–124

Paragraph 120 abrogates previous understandings of religious ritual. Rituals are empty and meaningless, and ethics are to be prioritized: "Adorn your heads with the garlands of trustworthiness and fidelity, your hearts with the attire of the fear of God, your tongues with absolute truthfulness, your bodies with the vesture of courtesy."

In paragraph 121, Baha'u'llah states, "When the ocean of My presence hath ebbed and the Book of My Revelation is ended, turn your faces toward Him Whom God hath purposed, Who hath branched from this Ancient Root." This line is particularly important for two reasons. First, Baha'is have interpreted 'Abdu'l-Baha to be he "Who hath branched from this Ancient Root," signifying the authority of 'Abdu'l-Baha to succeed Baha'u'llah following his death. Second, just as the Bab understood his own writings and religion to be temporary, so, too, does Baha'u'llah direct that the Baha'i faith will one day come to a close when a new manifestation of God appears. In essence, the Baha'i faith is the only major world religion that predicts the necessity of its own closure and abrogation.

The next section, including paragraphs 122–124, addresses theological anthropology, or the meaning and nature of human existence. Generally speaking, Baha'u'llah takes a dim view of human nature ("consider the pettiness of men's minds"), which is likely influenced by his own belief and claim to be a "manifestation of God," that is, epistemologically and spiritually superior to the rest of humanity. Humans have freedom, but this freedom is only meaningful if it leads "to sedition, whose flames none can quench," in the form of rebellion against the established social and religious order. Humans remain herd animals who "need a shepherd for their protection," and this shepherd is none other than Baha'u'llah, who is the manifestation of God.

Baha'u'llah's teaching on this subject is a significant point of departure from Islam. While Baha'is, for example, elevate the founder of a major religion to be a "manifestation," it is important for Muslims to understand Muhammad as a "prophet," that is, the best possible human being in terms of an open relationship to God but nonetheless only human. From this perspective, Baha'is, then, could be said to have a "higher" view of Muhammad than Muslims. This teaching is considered religiously offensive to most Muslims, as a heretical misappropriation of their religion.

◆ Paragraphs 139 and 144

Later, Baha'u'llah offers exhortations specifically to the Babis. Of particular interest in this section is Baha'u'llah's lifting of the Bab's ban on interreligious marriage (paragraph 139) and his instruction to "consort with all religions with amity and concord, that they may inhale from you the sweet fragrance of God." He thus elevates the status of Babism above that of the major religions of the world, but he specifically instructs Babis to have discourse and dialogue with other faiths. These teachings are among the most distinctive religious practices of the Baha'i faith, in contrast to some other major religions that discourage, if they do not completely ban, interreligious marriage and dialogue.

◆ Paragraph 158, 168, and 173

In the next section, Baha'u'llah offers more laws regarding property and almsgiving, the proper practice of prayer and religious education of children, the frequency of replacing furniture, proper behavior at religious festivals, and more cleanliness codes and instructions on proper dress. He again affirms the authority that the text, being "the Living Book," has above all other "Holy Books." Commentators on Kitab-i-aqdas often mention the mystical tone woven into the passages of this section. In an oft-quoted passage in paragraph 158, Baha'u'llah remarks, "Blessed is the one who discovereth the fragrance of inner meanings from the traces of this Pen through whose movement the breezes of God are wafted over the entire creation, and through whose stillness the very essence of tranquillity appeareth in the realm of being." In paragraph 173 he states, "Ye are the billows of the Most Mighty Ocean, the stars of the firmament of Glory, the standards of triumph waving betwixt earth and heaven. Ye are the manifestations of steadfastness amidst men and the daysprings of Divine Utterance to all that dwell on earth." As is typical in apocalyptic literature, Baha'u'llah here places the reader into an essential and exigent spiritual location within the history of God and humanity. In other words, as the end of the text arrives, the exhortation that is being made throughout the text to various communities (the Babis, Muslims, Christians, and others) now shifts to the future reader, who may or may not have connections to these other audiences. This shift to directly addressing the anonymous reader also serves the function of uniting the various audiences who encounter the text, as a means of spiritually uniting the different peoples of the world.

◆ Paragraphs 174, 181, 182, 185–186

Baha'u'llah concludes the text by addressing his first followers, who would have been Babis. He describes the joy and excitement of being part of the new religion ordained by God through Baha'u'llah. He clarifies that this new religion is serious and not meant to be a means to gain individual power. Social problems not covered in the Kitab-i-aqdas should be prayerfully considered within the context of other revelations, the "ocean" of "Divine knowledge." 'Abdu'l-Baha is again cryptically given authority over the new religion following the death of Baha'u'llah, who refers to his son in paragraph 174 as "Him Who hath branched from this mighty Stock."

The new religion is not simply a new religion but, in fact, a blueprint for humanity in "this new World Order." Baha'u'llah continues, "Mankind's ordered life hath been revolutionized through the agency of this unique, this wondrous System—the like of which mortal eyes have never witnessed." He instructs the faithful to "immerse yourselves in the ocean of My words, that ye may unravel its secrets, and discover all the pearls of wisdom that lie hid in its depths."

Audience

Kitab-i-aqdas is a book of laws written for present and future use, to be culturally translated and appropriated while remaining an authoritative pronouncement from the most recent manifestation of God, Baha'u'llah himself. Its immediate audience, then, would have been the Babi community and the first Baha'is. It is noteworthy, though, that large passages of the text specifically address the Babis and employ theological allusions specific to the Shaykhi sect of Shia Islam. Clearly, Baha'u'llah believed that the Kitab-i-aqdas would become the foundation of a new world order and would likely be read by Muslims and eventually by adherents of all of the world's religions.

Today the Baha'i community is a religion spread very thinly throughout the world, claiming around five million members and with official organizations in 236 countries and territories. Some 2.2 million Baha'is reside in India, while the faith has a considerable oppressed community remaining in Iran. The religion has met with relative success in conversions within Africa and the small nations of Oceania. Baha'i writings have been translated into more than eight hundred languages. Less than 2 percent of Baha'is belong to small schismatic groups that have resulted from disputes over succession of leadership within the mainstream faith.

Impact

Although the Kitab-i-aqdas is regarded as the core text of the Baha'i faith, it was not widely available in an authoritative version until 120 years after its completion. The text is not, at least in terms of its content,

"*The first duty prescribed by God for His servants is the recognition of Him Who is the Dayspring of His Revelation and the Fountain of His laws, Who representeth the Godhead in both the Kingdom of His Cause and the world of creation.*"

(Section 1)

"*Think not that We have revealed unto you a mere code of laws. Nay, rather, We have unsealed the choice Wine with the fingers of might and power. To this beareth witness that which the Pen of Revelation hath revealed. Meditate upon this, O men of insight!*"

(Section 1)

"*O ye leaders of religion! Who is the man amongst you that can rival Me in vision or insight?*"

(Section 1)

"*Adorn your heads with the garlands of trustworthiness and fidelity, your hearts with the attire of the fear of God, your tongues with absolute truthfulness, your bodies with the vesture of courtesy.*"

(Section 1)

"*Blessed is the one who discovereth the fragrance of inner meanings from the traces of this Pen through whose movement the breezes of God are wafted over the entire creation, and through whose stillness the very essence of tranquillity appeareth in the realm of being.*"

(Section 1)

"*The world's equilibrium hath been upset through the vibrating influence of this most great, this new World Order. Mankind's ordered life hath been revolutionized through the agency of this unique, this wondrous System— the like of which mortal eyes have never witnessed.*"

(Section 1)

the most radical or imaginative of Baha'u'llah's writings, but it is taken seriously by Baha'is as the primary and supremely authoritative document regarding religious polity and the administration of what was predicted to become a truly international religion. Baha'u'llah's description of what would later be the Universal House of Justice inevitably became a point of contention that led to a minor schism in the Baha'i religion following the death of Shoghi Effendi (1897–1957), the final guardian of the mainstream Baha'i faith. The primary schism, which resulted in several different small Baha'i sects, arose over the transferal of leadership from Shoghi Effendi as guardian of the faith to the Universal House of Justice. Mason Remey (1874–1974) claimed to be appointed as the next guardian of the faith, a claim disputed by the mainstream faith, though he did have a considerable number of followers for a short time. Supporters of Remey see themselves as having allegiance to the institution of the guardian of the faith rather than to the elected House of Justice, and they took the name "Orthodox Baha'is."

One unique aspect of the Kitab-i-aqdas is its status as a religious text concerning laws and ecclesiastical polity issued as such by the founder of the religion itself. In light of this status, Baha'is have a high regard for the text over other writings of Baha'u'llah, and it contributes to the proofs of the authority of its author as a manifestation of God who established a religion for a new era of humanity.

Further Reading

■ Books

Baha'i World Centre. *A Synopsis and Codification of the Kitab-i-Aqdas: The Most Holy Book of Baha'u'llah*. Haifa, Israel: Baha'i World Centre, 1973.

Bushrui, Suheil. *The Style of the Kitab-i-Aqdas: Aspects of the Sublime*. Bethesda: University of Maryland Press, 1995.

Effendi, Shoghi. "A Description of the Kitab-i-Aqdas." In *Kitab-i-Aqdas*. Haifa, Israel: Baha'i World Centre, 1992.

Elder, Earl. "Preface." In *Al-Kitab al-Aqdas*, trans. Earl Elder and William Miller. London: Royal Asiatic Society, 1961.

Ma'ani, Baharieh Rouhani, and Sovaida Ma'ani Ewing. *Laws of the Kitab-i-Aqdas: Their Evolution in Religious History*. Oxford, U.K.: George Ronald, 2004.

Miller, William. "Introduction." In *Al-Kitab al-Aqdas*, trans. Earl Elder and William Miller. London: Royal Asiatic Society, 1961.

Universal House of Justice. "Introduction." In *Kitab-i-Aqdas*. Haifa, Israel: Baha'i World Centre, 1992.

■ Web Sites

Synopsis and Codification." The Kitab-i-Aqdas: The Most Holy Book Web site. http://www.theaqdas.org/synopsis.php

—Commentary by C. D. Rodkey

Questions for Further Study

1. Numerous religions—Christianity, Judaism, Islam, Zoroastrianism, and the Baha'i, among others—place considerable emphasis on a messiah figure. Why do you believe that the figure of a coming messiah seems to be important in religious belief both now and in the past?

2. Although membership in the Baha'i faith worldwide is relatively small, the religion's membership has grown steadily, and it has become a popular modern religion among some people, even in the United States. Why do you think this is the case? What is the appeal of the religion in the modern world?

3. Outline the relationship between Baha'u'llah and the Kitab-i-aqdas on the one hand and the Bab and the Persian Bayan on the other.

4. Many readers might regard the Kitab-i-aqdas as pretentious, perhaps even arrogant, in expressing the belief that the Baha'i faith abrogates earlier religions such as Christianity and Islam. Do you agree with this assessment of the document? Why or why not?

5. To what extent does the Kitab-i-aqdas resemble other religious texts that establish laws for the followers of the religion? For reference, consider the biblical books of Genesis and Exodus, the Shulchan Arukh and *Mishneh Torah* of Judaism or various Islamic texts such as the Sahih al-Bukhari.

KITAB-I-AQDAS: DOCUMENT TEXT

1860–1873 CE

—Baha'u'llah

IN THE NAME OF HIM WHO IS THE SUPREME RULER OVER ALL THAT HATH BEEN AND ALL THAT IS TO BE.

1. The first duty prescribed by God for His servants is the recognition of Him Who is the Dayspring of His Revelation and the Fountain of His laws, Who representeth the Godhead in both the Kingdom of His Cause and the world of creation. Whoso achieveth this duty hath attained unto all good; and whoso is deprived thereof hath gone astray, though he be the author of every righteous deed. It behoveth every one who reacheth this most sublime station, this summit of transcendent glory, to observe every ordinance of Him Who is the Desire of the world. These twin duties are inseparable. Neither is acceptable without the other. Thus hath it been decreed by Him Who is the Source of Divine inspiration.

2. They whom God hath endued with insight will readily recognize that the precepts laid down by God constitute the highest means for the maintenance of order in the world and the security of its peoples. He that turneth away from them is accounted among the abject and foolish. We, verily, have commanded you to refuse the dictates of your evil passions and corrupt desires, and not to transgress the bounds which the Pen of the Most High hath fixed, for these are the breath of life unto all created things. The seas of Divine wisdom and Divine utterance have risen under the breath of the breeze of the All-Merciful. Hasten to drink your fill, O men of understanding! They that have violated the Covenant of God by breaking His commandments, and have turned back on their heels, these have erred grievously in the sight of God, the All-Possessing, the Most High.

3. O ye peoples of the world! Know assuredly that My commandments are the lamps of My loving providence among My servants, and the keys of My mercy for My creatures. Thus hath it been sent down from the heaven of the Will of your Lord, the Lord of Revelation. Were any man to taste the sweetness of the words which the lips of the All-Merciful have willed to utter, he would, though the treasures of the earth be in his possession, renounce them one and all, that he might vindicate the truth of even one of His commandments, shining above the Dayspring of His bountiful care and loving-kindness.

4. Say: From My laws the sweet-smelling savour of My garment can be smelled, and by their aid the standards of Victory will be planted upon the highest peaks. The Tongue of My power hath, from the heaven of My omnipotent glory, addressed to My creation these words: "Observe My commandments, for the love of My beauty." Happy is the lover that hath inhaled the divine fragrance of his Best-Beloved from these words, laden with the perfume of a grace which no tongue can describe. By My life! He who hath drunk the choice wine of fairness from the hands of My bountiful favour will circle around My commandments that shine above the Dayspring of My creation.

5. Think not that We have revealed unto you a mere code of laws. Nay, rather, We have unsealed the choice Wine with the fingers of might and power. To this beareth witness that which the Pen of Revelation hath revealed. Meditate upon this, O men of insight!…

12. It hath been ordained that obligatory prayer is to be performed by each of you individually. Save in the Prayer for the Dead, the practice of congregational prayer hath been annulled. He, of a truth, is the Ordainer, the All-Wise.…

16. O Pen of the Most High! Say: O people of the world! We have enjoined upon you fasting during a brief period, and at its close have designated for you Naw-Rúz as a feast. Thus hath the Day-Star of Utterance shone forth above the horizon of the Book as decreed by Him Who is the Lord of the beginning and the end. Let the days in excess of the months be placed before the month of fasting. We have ordained that these, amid all nights and days, shall be the manifestations of the letter Há, and thus they have not been

bounded by the limits of the year and its months. It behoveth the people of Bahá, throughout these days, to provide good cheer for themselves, their kindred and, beyond them, the poor and needy, and with joy and exultation to hail and glorify their Lord, to sing His praise and magnify His Name; and when they end—these days of giving that precede the season of restraint—let them enter upon the Fast. Thus hath it been ordained by Him Who is the Lord of all mankind. The traveller, the ailing, those who are with child or giving suck, are not bound by the Fast; they have been exempted by God as a token of His grace. He, verily, is the Almighty, the Most Generous....

30. The Lord hath ordained that in every city a House of Justice be established wherein shall gather counsellors to the number of Bahá, and should it exceed this number it doth not matter. They should consider themselves as entering the Court of the presence of God, the Exalted, the Most High, and as beholding Him Who is the Unseen. It behoveth them to be the trusted ones of the Merciful among men and to regard themselves as the guardians appointed of God for all that dwell on earth. It is incumbent upon them to take counsel together and to have regard for the interests of the servants of God, for His sake, even as they regard their own interests, and to choose that which is meet and seemly. Thus hath the Lord your God commanded you. Beware lest ye put away that which is clearly revealed in His Tablet. Fear God, O ye that perceive....

36. Amongst the people is he who seateth himself amid the sandals by the door whilst coveting in his heart the seat of honour. Say: What manner of man art thou, O vain and heedless one, who wouldst appear as other than thou art? And among the people is he who layeth claim to inner knowledge, and still deeper knowledge concealed within this knowledge. Say: Thou speakest false! By God! What thou dost possess is naught but husks which We have left to thee as bones are left to dogs. By the righteousness of the one true God! Were anyone to wash the feet of all mankind, and were he to worship God in the forests, valleys, and mountains, upon high hills and lofty peaks, to leave no rock or tree, no clod of earth, but was a witness to his worship—yet, should the fragrance of My good pleasure not be inhaled from him, his works would never be acceptable unto God. Thus hath it been decreed by Him Who is the Lord of all. How many a man

hath secluded himself in the climes of India, denied himself the things that God hath decreed as lawful, imposed upon himself austerities and mortifications, and hath not been remembered by God, the Revealer of Verses. Make not your deeds as snares wherewith to entrap the object of your aspiration, and deprive not yourselves of this Ultimate Objective for which have ever yearned all such as have drawn nigh unto God. Say: The very life of all deeds is My good pleasure, and all things depend upon Mine acceptance. Read ye the Tablets that ye may know what hath been purposed in the Books of God, the All-Glorious, the Ever-Bounteous. He who attaineth to My love hath title to a throne of gold, to sit thereon in honour over all the world; he who is deprived thereof, though he sit upon the dust, that dust would seek refuge with God, the Lord of all Religions....

42. Endowments dedicated to charity revert to God, the Revealer of Signs. None hath the right to dispose of them without leave from Him Who is the Dawning-place of Revelation. After Him, this authority shall pass to the Aghsán, and after them to the House of Justice—should it be established in the world by then—that they may use these endowments for the benefit of the Places which have been exalted in this Cause, and for whatsoever hath been enjoined upon them by Him Who is the God of might and power. Otherwise, the endowments shall revert to the people of Bahá who speak not except by His leave and judge not save in accordance with what God hath decreed in this Tablet—lo, they are the champions of victory betwixt heaven and earth—that they may use them in the manner that hath been laid down in the Book by God, the Mighty, the Bountiful....

43. Lament not in your hours of trial, neither rejoice therein; seek ye the Middle Way which is the remembrance of Me in your afflictions and reflection over that which may befall you in future. Thus informeth you He Who is the Omniscient, He Who is aware....

67. It hath been decreed by God that, should any one of His servants intend to travel, he must fix for his wife a time when he will return home. If he return by the promised time, he will have obeyed the bidding of his Lord and shall be numbered by the Pen of His behest among the righteous; otherwise, if there be good reason for delay, he must inform his wife and make the utmost endeavour to return to her. Should neither of these

eventualities occur, it behoveth her to wait for a period of nine months, after which there is no impediment to her taking another husband; but should she wait longer, God, verily, loveth those women and men who show forth patience. Obey ye My commandments, and follow not the ungodly, they who have been reckoned as sinners in God's Holy Tablet. If, during the period of her waiting, word should reach her from her husband, she should choose the course that is praiseworthy. He, of a truth, desireth that His servants and His handmaids should be at peace with one another; take heed lest ye do aught that may provoke intransigence amongst you. Thus hath the decree been fixed and the promise come to pass. If, however, news should reach her of her husband's death or murder, and be confirmed by general report, or by the testimony of two just witnesses, it behoveth her to remain single; then, upon completion of the fixed number of months, she is free to adopt the course of her choosing. Such is the bidding of Him Who is mighty and powerful in His command....

77. God hath relieved you of the ordinance laid down in the Bayán concerning the destruction of books. We have permitted you to read such sciences as are profitable unto you, not such as end in idle disputation; better is this for you, if ye be of them that comprehend....

82. Ye are but vassals, O kings of the earth! He Who is the King of Kings hath appeared, arrayed in His most wondrous glory, and is summoning you unto Himself, the Help in Peril, the Self-Subsisting. Take heed lest pride deter you from recognizing the Source of Revelation, lest the things of this world shut you out as by a veil from Him Who is the Creator of heaven. Arise, and serve Him Who is the Desire of all nations, Who hath created you through a word from Him, and ordained you to be, for all time, the emblems of His sovereignty....

99. Say: O leaders of religion! Weigh not the Book of God with such standards and sciences as are current amongst you, for the Book itself is the unerring Balance established amongst men. In this most perfect Balance whatsoever the peoples and kindreds of the earth possess must be weighed, while the measure of its weight should be tested according to its own standard, did ye but know it....

100. The eye of My loving-kindness weepeth sore over you, inasmuch as ye have failed to recognize the One upon Whom ye have been calling in the daytime and in the night season, at even and at morn. Advance, O people, with snow-white faces and radiant hearts, unto the blest and crimson Spot, wherein the Sadratu'l-Muntahá is calling: "Verily, there is none other God beside Me, the Omnipotent Protector, the Self-Subsisting!"

101. O ye leaders of religion! Who is the man amongst you that can rival Me in vision or insight? Where is he to be found that dareth to claim to be My equal in utterance or wisdom? No, by My Lord, the All-Merciful! All on the earth shall pass away; and this is the face of your Lord, the Almighty, the Well-Beloved.

102. We have decreed, O people, that the highest and last end of all learning be the recognition of Him Who is the Object of all knowledge; and yet, behold how ye have allowed your learning to shut you out, as by a veil, from Him Who is the Dayspring of this Light, through Whom every hidden thing hath been revealed. Could ye but discover the source whence the splendour of this utterance is diffused, ye would cast away the peoples of the world and all that they possess, and would draw nigh unto this most blessed Seat of glory....

104. We have not entered any school, nor read any of your dissertations. Incline your ears to the words of this unlettered One, wherewith He summoneth you unto God, the Ever-Abiding. Better is this for you than all the treasures of the earth, could ye but comprehend it.

105. Whoso interpreteth what hath been sent down from the heaven of Revelation, and altereth its evident meaning, he, verily, is of them that have perverted the Sublime Word of God, and is of the lost ones in the Lucid Book....

115. Blessed is he who, at the hour of dawn, centring his thoughts on God, occupied with His remembrance, and supplicating His forgiveness, directeth his steps to the Mashriqu'l-Adhkár and, entering therein, seateth himself in silence to listen to the verses of God, the Sovereign, the Mighty, the All-Praised. Say: The Mashriqu'l-Adhkár is each and every building which hath been erected in cities and villages for the celebration of My praise. Such is the name by which it hath been designated before the throne of glory, were ye of those who understand.

116. They who recite the verses of the All-Merciful in the most melodious of tones will perceive in them that with which the sovereignty of earth and heaven can never be compared. From them

they will inhale the divine fragrance of My worlds—worlds which today none can discern save those who have been endowed with vision through this sublime, this beauteous Revelation. Say: These verses draw hearts that are pure unto those spiritual worlds that can neither be expressed in words nor intimated by allusion. Blessed be those who hearken....

120. Adorn your heads with the garlands of trustworthiness and fidelity, your hearts with the attire of the fear of God, your tongues with absolute truthfulness, your bodies with the vesture of courtesy. These are in truth seemly adornings unto the temple of man, if ye be of them that reflect. Cling, O ye people of Bahá, to the cord of servitude unto God, the True One, for thereby your stations shall be made manifest, your names written and preserved, your ranks raised and your memory exalted in the Preserved Tablet. Beware lest the dwellers on earth hinder you from this glorious and exalted station. Thus have We exhorted you in most of Our Epistles and now in this, Our Holy Tablet, above which hath beamed the Day-Star of the Laws of the Lord, your God, the Powerful, the All-Wise.

121. When the ocean of My presence hath ebbed and the Book of My Revelation is ended, turn your faces toward Him Whom God hath purposed, Who hath branched from this Ancient Root.

122. Consider the pettiness of men's minds. They ask for that which injureth them, and cast away the thing that profiteth them. They are, indeed, of those that are far astray. We find some men desiring liberty, and priding themselves therein. Such men are in the depths of ignorance.

123. Liberty must, in the end, lead to sedition, whose flames none can quench. Thus warneth you He Who is the Reckoner, the All-Knowing. Know ye that the embodiment of liberty and its symbol is the animal. That which beseemeth man is submission unto such restraints as will protect him from his own ignorance, and guard him against the harm of the mischief-maker. Liberty causeth man to overstep the bounds of propriety, and to infringe on the dignity of his station. It debaseth him to the level of extreme depravity and wickedness.

124. Regard men as a flock of sheep that need a shepherd for their protection. This, verily, is the truth, the certain truth. We approve of liberty in certain circumstances, and refuse to sanction it in others. We, verily, are the All-Knowing....

139. And now consider what hath been revealed in yet another passage, that perchance ye may forsake your own concepts and set your faces towards God, the Lord of being. He hath said: "It is unlawful to enter into marriage save with a believer in the Bayán. Should only one party to a marriage embrace this Cause, his or her possessions will become unlawful to the other, until such time as the latter hath converted. This law, however, will only take effect after the exaltation of the Cause of Him Whom We shall manifest in truth, or of that which hath already been made manifest in justice. Ere this, ye are at liberty to enter into wedlock as ye wish, that haply by this means ye may exalt the Cause of God." Thus hath the Nightingale sung with sweet melody upon the celestial bough, in praise of its Lord, the All-Merciful. Well is it with them that hearken....

144. Consort with all religions with amity and concord, that they may inhale from you the sweet fragrance of God. Beware lest amidst men the flame of foolish ignorance overpower you. All things proceed from God and unto Him they return. He is the source of all things and in Him all things are ended....

158. Blessed is the one who discovereth the fragrance of inner meanings from the traces of this Pen through whose movement the breezes of God are wafted over the entire creation, and through whose stillness the very essence of tranquillity appeareth in the realm of being. Glorified be the All-Merciful, the Revealer of so inestimable a bounty. Say: Because He bore injustice, justice hath appeared on earth, and because He accepted abasement, the majesty of God hath shone forth amidst mankind....

168. We, verily, see amongst you him who taketh hold of the Book of God and citeth from it proofs and arguments wherewith to repudiate his Lord, even as the followers of every other Faith sought reasons in their Holy Books for refuting Him Who is the Help in Peril, the Self-Subsisting. Say: God, the True One, is My witness that neither the Scriptures of the world, nor all the books and writings in existence, shall, in this Day, avail you aught without this, the Living Book, Who proclaimeth in the midmost heart of creation: "Verily, there is none other God but Me, the All-Knowing, the All-Wise...."

173. Happy are ye, O ye the learned ones in Bahá. By the Lord! Ye are the billows of the Most Mighty

Ocean, the stars of the firmament of Glory, the standards of triumph waving betwixt earth and heaven. Ye are the manifestations of steadfastness amidst men and the daysprings of Divine Utterance to all that dwell on earth. Well is it with him that turneth unto you, and woe betide the froward. This day, it behoveth whoso hath quaffed the Mystic Wine of everlasting life from the Hands of the loving-kindness of the Lord his God, the Merciful, to pulsate even as the throbbing artery in the body of mankind, that through him may be quickened the world and every crumbling bone.

174. O people of the world! When the Mystic Dove will have winged its flight from its Sanctuary of Praise and sought its far-off goal, its hidden habitation, refer ye whatsoever ye understand not in the Book to Him Who hath branched from this mighty Stock....

181. The world's equilibrium hath been upset through the vibrating influence of this most great, this new World Order. Mankind's ordered life hath been revolutionized through the agency of this unique, this wondrous System—the like of which mortal eyes have never witnessed.

182. Immerse yourselves in the ocean of My words, that ye may unravel its secrets, and discover all the pearls of wisdom that lie hid in its depths. Take heed that ye do not vacillate in your determination to embrace the truth of this Cause—a Cause through which the potentialities of the might of God have been revealed, and His sovereignty established. With faces beaming with joy, hasten ye unto Him. This is the changeless Faith of God, eternal in the past, eternal in the future. Let him that seeketh, attain it; and as to him that hath refused to seek it—verily, God is Self-Sufficient, above any need of His creatures....

185. This is the Counsel of God; would that thou mightest heed it! This is the Bounty of God; would that thou mightest receive it! This is the Utterance of God; if only thou wouldst apprehend it! This is the Treasure of God; if only thou couldst understand!

186. This is a Book which hath become the Lamp of the Eternal unto the world, and His straight, undeviating Path amidst the peoples of the earth. Say: This is the Dayspring of Divine knowledge, if ye be of them that understand, and the Dawning-place of God's commandments, if ye be of those who comprehend.

Glossary

Aghsánan Arabic word for "branches," used here to designate Baha'u'llah's male descendants

Mashriqu'l-Adhkára house of worship

Naw-Rúzthe Persian vernal equinox celebration and the Baha'i New Year

Sadratu'l-Muntaháa symbol of a tree at the end of a journey or at the end of the horizontal "road" of the previous era of humanity

Mary Baker Eddy.

SCIENCE AND HEALTH WITH KEY TO THE SCRIPTURES: DOCUMENT ANALYSIS

1875 CE

"Disease being a belief...the sensation would not appear if the error of belief was met and destroyed by truth."

Overview

Mary Baker Eddy's *Science and Health with Key to the Scriptures* defines the core principles and healing practices of one of America's most distinctive indigenous religions: Christian Science. Believing that she had rediscovered the spiritual powers utilized by Jesus Christ—the prayers that multiplied loaves and fishes, healed the blind and lame, and raised Lazarus from the dead—Eddy characterized her discovery as "divine Science," which she held to be the "Comforter" promised in the New Testament by John. She argued that the material world is an illusion and that all injuries, illnesses, or disasters suffered by humanity can be "scientifically" healed through an understanding of the principles of "divine Science."

The first edition of *Science and Health* was published in 1875, but Eddy continued to revise and refine the text throughout her life. The final edition, published in 1902 after more than four hundred revisions, remains the official textbook of Christian Science. Eddy decreed that her book, along with the Bible, would serve as the "pastor" of her church; it is read from the pulpits of the original "Mother Church" in Boston, Massachusetts, and at Christian Science branch churches around the world in place of a sermon.

Even before the text achieved its final form, its teachings became hugely popular: Christian Science was one of the fastest-growing sects in the country in the first decades of the twentieth century. The census of 1890 counted 8,724 Christian Scientists; by 1926, that number had leapt to 202,098. Branch churches were established around the world, prominent sanitoriums—rest homes for ailing or elderly Scientists—were constructed, and Christian Science schools, including a college near St. Louis, Missouri, were established.

The extraordinary early momentum of Christian Science was likely driven by the nearly universal nineteenth-century experience of uncured illness and early death. In 1875, when Eddy produced the first edition of her textbook, the practice of medicine was still primitive, ineffective, and often associated with quackery. *Science and Health* offered what followers felt to be a spiritually and emotionally empowering means of taking health care into their own hands. But as the decades passed and medical science made unprecedented advances with the discovery of antibiotics and other treatments, the popularity of Christian Science and its textbook declined sharply. Nonetheless, *Science and Health* remains a powerful and influential expression of the American belief in self-reliance.

Context

From the 1820s to the 1860s, a wave of evangelical, millennialist fervor swept across the country, known in American religious history as the Second Great Awakening, an attempt to restore what was seen as a more primitive, authentic Christianity. (The first awakening had taken place a century earlier, when revivals sprang up in New England in the 1730s, culminating in Jonathan Edwards's famous 1741 sermon, "Sinners in the Hands of an Angry God"). Born in New Hampshire in 1821, the young Mary Baker was exposed to this reformist movement, dubbed a "shopkeeper's millennium" because farmers and other working people made up the majority of participants. Baker is known to have attended a week-long revival meeting in Concord, New Hampshire, in 1834, at the age of twelve and was probably aware of a number of famous religious breakaway sects that came out of the northeast corner of the United States. Such movements would have included the Millerite movement—led by William Miller in a region of western New York State referred to as the "burned-over district" for its thorough exposure to evangelical zeal—which ultimately gave rise to Seventh-Day Adventism. As a youth, she may also have heard of the church launched by Joseph Smith in 1830 in western New York with the publication of the Book of Mormon. Dramatic accounts of faith healings were commonplace during the period and may have been influential in the formation of Eddy's beliefs.

The nineteenth century was also an age of social reform. Abolition, the campaign for women's suffrage, and the temperance movement galvanized American life, and there are references to reform in *Science and Health*. But the most important historical context shaping the book concerns the extraordinary experimentation in dietary and other health regimens, resulting in a welter of treatments. Phrenology (the association of skull conformation with brain function), hydropathy (the "water cure"), and electrotherapy became enormously popular, as did cures based on exposure to cold, light, heat, or magnets. Hypnotists performed demonstrations on crowds eager to experience the unknown powers of the mind. Health fads often sprang from or were combined with religious belief: The Battle Creek Sanitarium, opened in 1866 in Battle Creek, Michigan, by the brothers Kellogg, was inspired by the dietary and health teachings of the Seventh-Day Adventists.

The therapy that directly influenced *Science and Health* was that of Phineas Parkhurst Quimby, a self-taught mesmerist who traveled and lectured during the 1840. Quimby was known for performing mesmeric healings with a partner, Lucius Burkmar, who would diagnose and prescribe treatments for patients while under hypnosis. Eventually, Quimby believed that his partner had cured him of a potentially fatal illness, identifying the curative agent as something akin to the power of suggestion. In 1862, Quimby acquired Eddy (then Mrs. Mary Patterson) as a patient. She had suffered for years from a number of seemingly intractable ailments. Fresh from a failed hydropathic treatment in New Hampshire, Eddy consulted Quimby at his office in Portland, Maine, and their discussions of mental healing would prove profoundly important in Eddy's subsequent thinking and writing. While placing her teachings within the Christian tradition, Eddy felt free to build on that tradition, suggesting that her healing revelations amounted to a rediscovery of the techniques practiced by Jesus. Eventually, as her own teachings grew popular, former students of Quimby and Eddy herself broke away to establish their own sects. Collectively, the breakaway groups, including the Unity School of Christianity and Divine Science, became known as the New Thought movement.

Another influence on *Science and Health* was transcendentalism, a literary and religious movement that emphasized self-reliance and the power of the individual mind to transcend the physical realm. The American transcendentalists—including Ralph Waldo Emerson, Henry David Thoreau, Amos Bronson Alcott, and Margaret Fuller—rejected Enlightenment rationalism in favor of romantic and mystical thought. They were influenced by Vedic philosophy from India counseling an attitude of detachment or serenity, positing an immortal soul capable of sloughing off the physical body for existence on a higher plane. These elements all appear in *Science and Health* in radically simplified and altered ways.

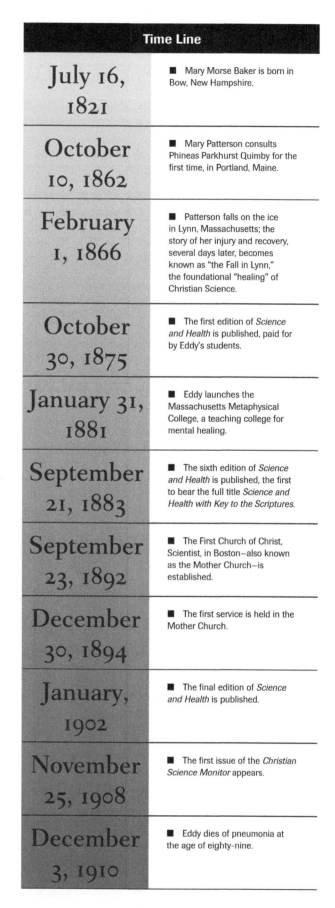

Time Line

July 16, 1821
- Mary Morse Baker is born in Bow, New Hampshire.

October 10, 1862
- Mary Patterson consults Phineas Parkhurst Quimby for the first time, in Portland, Maine.

February 1, 1866
- Patterson falls on the ice in Lynn, Massachusetts; the story of her injury and recovery, several days later, becomes known as "the Fall in Lynn," the foundational "healing" of Christian Science.

October 30, 1875
- The first edition of *Science and Health* is published, paid for by Eddy's students.

January 31, 1881
- Eddy launches the Massachusetts Metaphysical College, a teaching college for mental healing.

September 21, 1883
- The sixth edition of *Science and Health* is published, the first to bear the full title *Science and Health with Key to the Scriptures*.

September 23, 1892
- The First Church of Christ, Scientist, in Boston—also known as the Mother Church—is established.

December 30, 1894
- The first service is held in the Mother Church.

January, 1902
- The final edition of *Science and Health* is published.

November 25, 1908
- The first issue of the *Christian Science Monitor* appears.

December 3, 1910
- Eddy dies of pneumonia at the age of eighty-nine.

About the Author

Born on July 16, 1821, in Bow, New Hampshire, a rural town near the state capital of Concord, Mary Morse Baker was the sixth and youngest child of strict Congregationalist parents. Early on, she showed an enthusiasm for religion and literature, writing poems. As a youth, she reportedly suffered from a variety of maladies, including dyspepsia (indigestion or stomach troubles), ulcers, neuralgia, and spinal problems.

Her early adulthood was unsettled. She married her first husband, George Glover, a builder from South Carolina, at the age of twenty-two. Glover died less than a year after the couple relocated to the South, leaving his pregnant wife to make her way back to New Hampshire. After the birth of her son, George Washington Glover II, Mary Glover taught for a time at a primary school, but after the death of her mother, she spent months traveling from relative to relative, feeling that she and her son were unwelcome in her newly remarried father's home. In 1851 her son was sent to live with former servants of the family and would not see his mother again for twenty-three years. Mary Glover married again in 1853, to a dentist, Daniel Patterson, but her life continued to be plagued by poor health and worries about money. Her husband, serving with the Union forces, was captured by the Confederates in 1862; that same year, Mary Patterson sought treatment at a hydropathic institute for a variety of complaints. When the water cure was unavailing, she traveled to Maine to visit a mesmeric healer, Phineas Parkhurst Quimby. The original mesmerists—including Franz Anton Mesmer, the eighteenth-century German physician for whom the technique was named—used actual magnets to conduct what they took to be healing "energy" through their patients' bodies. Quimby, on the other hand, used the magnetic force of his own hands, often dipping them in "magnetized" water—perhaps weakly acidulated—before rubbing or manipulating the affected limb or body part of his patient.

Rallying, she would spend much of that year and the next in Quimby's care, conferring with him in detail about his methods of mesmerism, spiritualism, and laying-on of hands, which subsequently played a role in formulating her own theories on healing. In an 1862 letter to a Portland newspaper, she called his discoveries "a science capable of demonstration." The following year, in an unpublished manuscript, Quimby coined the term *Christian Science*, and Mrs. Patterson and the doctor continued to confer by letter. She wrote often about Quimby's teachings and healing practice, until his death on January 16, 1866.

On February 1, 1866, two weeks after her mentor's death, Mrs. Patterson fell on the ice in Lynn, Massachusetts, while on her way to a temperance meeting. There has been much subsequent debate over the nature and extent of her injuries. A local newspaper at the time described her injuries as serious, as did a homeopathic physician. After suffering in bed for several days, according to her later account, she experienced an instantaneous healing after reading one of the biblical healings of Jesus. The incident became known among her followers as "the Fall in Lynn," and was considered the breakthrough that resulted in her discovery of Christian Science. Shortly thereafter, deserted by her second husband, Mrs. Patterson began a period of itinerant life, staying in New England rooming houses. In 1872 she began to write a manuscript based on her discussions of healing with Quimby. The first edition of the textbook, called *Science and Health*, was published in 1875, privately printed with donations from a handful of students.

In 1877, after receiving a divorce from Patterson, she married Gilbert Eddy, one of her devoted students. The marriage lasted until his death in 1882. The remaining decades of Mary Baker Eddy's life were spent revising her textbook, teaching the precepts of Christian Science to successive waves of students, and establishing institutions devoted to the religion, including the Mother Church. Mocked by Mark Twain and plagued by lawsuits, sensational attacks in the press, and scandals involving disgruntled students, her later years were tumultuous. Eddy's disgust with the yellow journalism of the day, particularly the coverage in Joseph Pulitzer's *New York World*, inspired her to create a daily newspaper, the *Christian Science Monitor*, in 1908. She died two years later.

Explanation and Analysis of the Document

The final edition of *Science and Health with Key to the Scriptures* runs to seven hundred pages. The bulk of it comprises fourteen chapters: (I) "Prayer," (II) "Atonement and Eucharist," (III) "Marriage," (IV) "Christian Science versus Spiritualism," (V) "Animal Magnetism Unmasked," (VI) "Science, Theology, Medicine," (VII) "Physiology," (VIII) "Footsteps of Truth," (IX) "Creation," (X) "Science of Being," (XI) "Some Objections Answered," (XII) "Christian Science Practice," (XIII) "Teaching Christian Science," and (XIV) "Recapitulation." The "Key to the Scriptures," added to the sixth and subsequent editions of the book, consists of three additional chapters, "Genesis," "The Apocalypse," and a "Glossary," in which Eddy provides definitions of her terms. A final section, "Fruitage," reproduces accounts of healings published in the Christian Science periodicals. Much of the book contains marginal notes written by Eddy, providing a gloss on the text.

Readers of the entire volume will find that while there is no narrative progression, the constant repetition and reiteration of core beliefs seems to serve another function, inducing a sense of immersion in Christian Science rhetoric. For those who practice the religion, this seems to aid in "knowing the Truth," the practice of mentally aligning one's thought with Christian Scientific beliefs.

Science and Health serves as a guide for Christian Scientists in every area of their lives, offering advice on marriage, morality, and health. Most devout Scientists study selections from it every day, as directed by the church's printed Lesson Sermon, published quarterly; the Lesson

Sermon provides actual page and line numbers for daily study. Christian Science "practitioners"—trained and recognized by the church for their ability to pray and facilitate healings—study the textbook assiduously, recommending relevant parts to their patients.

The excerpts from Chapters I, VII, XII, XIV, and XVII presented here are key passages in *Science and Health*, in which Eddy instructs Christian Scientists in the correct method of prayer, warns them away from "drugs and hygiene," and provides definitions of "Mind," "intelligence," "error," and "man." The "scientific statement of being," which occurs in "Recapitulation," is considered the definitive statement of Christian Science. Generations of students have memorized it, and it is read from the podium at every church service and Sunday school service. Eddy's marginal notes, which appear throughout the text of *Science and Health*, have been omitted in these excerpts.

♦ Chapter I: Prayer

Christian Science prayer, Eddy asserts in this passage from the first chapter, is no "mere… pleading" with God, nor is it a rote repetition of formulaic prayers established long ago. While not naming any particular sect, Eddy contrasts her method of prayer with types promoted by established Christian denominations. Directly petitioning God to provide a desired outcome, or praising him relentlessly, she argues, is "lip-service." Rather, prayer is an "understanding" of the true nature of God and the human being, motivated not by a desire for a certain outcome but by an unselfish and constant "watching, and working" to keep hold of that understanding.

She makes strong claims for this form of prayer. Only "spiritual understanding," she argues, can reform sin and heal sickness. Here she lays out the mechanism by which healing and reformation take place: God is defined as perfect "love," "intelligence," and "infinite Mind," and it is the Christian Scientist's responsibility to mirror that "source." She also establishes herself as leader and revelator, in terms repeated throughout the textbook. The second sentence of her first chapter makes the argument that, regardless of what others may offer, "I speak from experience."

The comparison of prayer to solving a mathematics problem is a critical characterization, but readers should realize that Eddy's conception of math and science is uniquely her own. Perfection exists, she argues, and Scientists must comprehend the mathematical "rule" establishing that truth and then "work out the solution." Working through that problem is the way to arrive at "the demonstration of Truth," or healing. Another key concept arrives when Eddy refers to the concept of reflection: God is the perfect origin, and human beings must understand that their nature is to reflect perfection. Such understanding, goes the argument, will enable the Christian Scientist to annihilate sin, sickness, and, ultimately, mortality—as reflected in Eddy's revision of that central Christian prayer, the Lord's Prayer, from "deliver us from evil" to "*delivereth us from sin, disease, and death.*"

At the close of this critical chapter, Eddy offers her gloss on each line of the Lord's Prayer. Her "spiritual interpretation," as the Manual of the Mother Church (the governing document of the Christian Science Church) defines it, is recited at every Sunday service. It notably redefines "Our Father" as "*Our Father-Mother God,*" asserting a matriarchal power in balance with the traditional patriarchal nature of the Almighty. Most important, it rephrases the Christian's fervent hope for the future—"Thy kingdom come"—as an established fact of the present, "*Thy kingdom is come.*" Again, the crucial term *know* arises, as it will throughout *Science and Health*, used in the sense of "understand": "*Enable us to know,—as in heaven, so on earth,—God is omnipotent, supreme.*"

♦ Chapter VII: Physiology

Perhaps the most far-reaching and controversial passage of *Science and Health* in its effects on the lives of the faithful occurs in the chapter "Physiology." The doctrine of "radical reliance" expressed in this section asserts that Christian Scientists can never hope to heal if they serve two masters: One must choose between "Spirit and matter," or between "Truth and error." If Scientists attempt to heal through the practice of "divine Science" while at the same time clinging to a "false belief" in material means—which Eddy identifies as "drugs and hygiene"—then true healing can never occur. There is only one way to achieve healing, she argues: Renounce mortal mind and completely embrace the power of "God's law, the law of Mind." She continues the theme of the mathematical equation that appears in the book's first pages: "An error in the premise must appear in the conclusion."

Eddy again alludes to her personal experience in treating illness, claiming to have "discerned disease in the human mind" months before it appeared physically. She describes the appearance of symptoms as "mental chemicalization," a sign that the patient's outlook is shifting from "a material to a spiritual basis." She interprets such symptoms, however serious, as a positive sign. She asserts that an outbreak of distress may signal a healing on the horizon, despite the fact that the patient himself may be doubtful. Chemicalization, she writes, is one more piece of evidence that all sickness is mental in origin and can thus be treated or healed only by mental means.

She urges the faithful to resist any suggestion that drugs can heal. Such beliefs are actually an attempt by mortal mind to frustrate healing. The type of argument offered here has become the template for the "treatment" offered by Christian Science practitioners, which takes the form of a discussion or argument refuting the power of mortal mind and asserting the primacy of the spiritual. The resistance to "material" means is a standard position taken by church-sanctioned practitioners. By demanding that her followers practice "radical reliance" on the divine Mind and depend solely on Christian Science, eschewing recourse to other means, Eddy ensured that Scientists would come into conflict with a society that increasingly relied on material healing methods and with a medical system that could increasingly prove—through double-blind studies and other scientific methods—the utility of drugs and surgery.

♦ **Chapter XII: Christian Science Practice**

In her illustration of "mental treatment," Eddy identifies fear as a primary causative factor of disease, and she urges students and practitioners to silently repudiate their own fears and those of the patient. Removal of fear, she argues, will result in healing. She counsels healers to convince themselves of a successful outcome in order to produce it. Diseases, she explains, are only to be named "mentally," but not audibly: To say the name of a complaint out loud is to give it power over you. Instantaneous healing, on the other hand, is promised to those capable of driving away the fear of and belief in disease.

Most important, key passages of this chapter take up the treatment of young children and infants. Parents, Eddy writes, must meet a child's needs by correcting their own thought. She cautions against paying attention to the "physical wants or conditions" of children, suggesting that only Mind controls the "stomach, bowels, and food, the temperature of children and of men." If parents hold incorrect or "unwise" views as to their children's health, she suggests, they can cause or prolong illness in their offspring. Parents, she writes, should not bathe their children excessively or give them drugs or pay attention to their digestion. To believe in disease, she writes, is to cause it, both in oneself and in one's children: Only by vanquishing it mentally can Scientists "prevent disease or… cure it."

♦ **Chapter XIV: Recapitulation**

The questions and answers posed in the chapter entitled "Recapitulation" contain the core expression of Christian Science teachings. Often recited and referred to in church services, Sunday school classes, and training sessions for Christian Science practitioners and teachers, these passages are the cornerstone of the religion.

The capitalized seven synonyms for God—"Mind, Spirit, Soul, Principle, Life, Truth, Love"—suggest that these incorporeal, bodiless abstractions stand as the perfect ideal. Eddy suggests that what human beings experience as warring, individual minds; corruptible principles; or lives truncated by mortality is a misperception based on flawed thinking. Given the frailties and flaws of human minds and material bodies, these expressions cannot reflect a perfect God, Eddy reasons; therefore, the material mind and body do not exist. "Matter," she writes, "neither sees, hears, nor feels." She maintains that her position is supported by irrefutable logic: "A priori reasoning shows material existence to be enigmatical." A perfect God implies the existence of a correspondingly perfect creation, a perfect reflection, a perfect Man. As humanity grows to understand this, "Mankind will become perfect in proportion as this fact becomes apparent."

The most concentrated form of Eddy's argument occurs in the "scientific statement of being," which serves a function in Christian Science churches similar to that of the Nicene Creed in conventional Christian churches. In it, matter is defined as "mortal error" or nothing, and the human body and material world are rejected. In their place, Eddy posits an ever-expanding, always perfect God, "infinite Mind and its infinite manifestation." The human being exists only as a spiritual being; all else, including the material body and the material world, is illusion. The ritualistic and repetitive language of the "statement," with its balanced phrases, lends itself to memorization. Its "scientific" quality appears to be associated with Eddy's repeated invocations of logic; later in the chapter, she cites "celestial evidence," comparing humankind's ignorance of its true nature—"divine perfection"—with humanity's inability to perceive "the earth's motions."

"Error"—a term famous in Christian Science discourse—is defined as "a supposition" that matter is real and can cause pain or express intelligence or life. As Eddy muses on the "unreality" of sin and the nature of "Christ," she makes a number of observations that put her teachings at odds with traditional Christian beliefs. She describes "Christ" as the "ideal Truth" or "divine idea" taught and practiced by Jesus, "the human man." To Eddy, Jesus was "not God"—an opinion at odds with the Christian doctrine of the Trinity. Rather, he was the first human man to practice Christian Science healings, which Eddy felt were poorly understood in his day. Jesus's healings were not, she observes, "miracles" but expressions of the true nature of "divine Principle."

Her most stark refutation of the material world comes in answer to the question "What is man?" Eddy's answer leaves no doubt that she holds that the entire physical world is an illusion: "Man is not matter; he is not made up of brain, blood, bones, and other material elements…. . He is not physique." Readers should note her (not entirely consistent) use of the capital letter in insisting that "Man is spiritual and perfect…. Man is idea, the image of Love… incapable of sin, sickness, and death." This idealized "Man" is "the real man." The human being is altogether different: "A mortal sinner is not God's man." Mortal man is seen to be an impostor with satanic origins: "Mortals are the counterfeits of immortals. They are the children of the wicked one, or the one evil, which declares that man begins in dust or as a material embryo." This illusory mortal's fate is to be exposed and annihilated by the truth. "Mortals will disappear," she writes, as "mortality is finally swallowed up in immortality." This is as specific as Eddy allows herself to be on the question of what awaits our material bodies and the visible world.

♦ **Chapter XVII: Glossary**

Eddy's definitions of "God," "Man," and "Matter" are a constant subject of study in Christian Science practice. Here, the description of God verges on the mystical, "the great I AM" (compare Exodus 3:14). "Man" is similarly abstract, the reflection of a perfect ideal. "Matter," on the other hand," is dismissed as a myth, a false expression of "mortal mind" and mortality.

"Who would stand before a blackboard, and pray the principle of mathematics to solve the problem? The rule is already established, and it is our task to work out the solution."

(Section 1)

"Only through radical reliance on Truth can scientific healing power be realized."

(Section 1)

"I have discerned disease in the human mind, and recognized the patient's fear of it, months before the so-called disease made its appearance in the body. Disease being a belief, a latent illusion of mortal mind, the sensation would not appear if the error of belief was met and destroyed by truth."

(Section 1)

"Question.—What is the scientific statement of being? Answer.—There is no life, truth, intelligence, nor substance in matter. All is infinite Mind and its infinite manifestation, for God is All-in-all. Spirit is immortal Truth; matter is mortal error. Spirit is the real and eternal; matter is the unreal and temporal. Spirit is God, and man is His image and likeness. Therefore man is not material; he is spiritual."

(Section 1)

"Question.—What is man? Answer.—Man is not matter; he is not made up of brain, blood, bones, and other material elements. The Scriptures inform us that man is made in the image and likeness of God. Matter is not that likeness. The likeness of Spirit cannot be so unlike Spirit. Man is spiritual and perfect; and because he is spiritual and perfect, he must be so understood in Christian Science. Man is idea, the image, of Love; he is not physique."

(Section 1)

Audience

Eddy began by writing for herself and a handful of students, and her original audience was made up of the close coterie of friends and followers. Gradually, as she refined and edited the book, she expanded her reach to include anyone eager for healing. Thus, her potential audience was huge, and it seems likely that the book reached millions of readers—far more than ever joined the church officially—both in the United States and around the world, especially in English-speaking countries. Eventually translated into seventeen languages, *Science and Health* early on found particular favor in England and Germany, where a number of large branch churches were built. As of 1994, when the church published what it termed a "trade edition" of the textbook—meant to be sold in commercial bookstores as well as its own Christian Science Reading Rooms—the institution claimed that over eight million copies had been sold.

Impact

Eddy forbade her church from keeping a tally of the membership, but scholars have calculated that the number of Christian Science branch churches has declined at 2 percent a year in recent decades, with 823 churches closing since 1987 (while seventy-three have opened in that period). One estimate of church membership suggests that there may be fewer than sixty thousand members worldwide. Nonetheless, despite those losses, the impact of *Science and Health*, along with the church that continues to promote it, has been undeniably profound. Aside from the scores of people attracted to the religion through study of the book, especially during the great flourishing of the faith in the early decades of the twentieth century, the church has had an enormous impact through the lobbying arm that Eddy established, known as the Committee on Publication, renowned for attempting to influence media coverage and public policy.

The church's own members have occupied positions of considerable political and bureaucratic power in the United States. Renowned Hollywood actors—from Elizabeth Taylor and Mickey Rooney to Robert Duvall and Val Kilmer—have at different times espoused Christian Science. Many Scientists—teetotalers and hence good security risks—have been recruited to serve in the FBI and CIA. During the administration of Richard M. Nixon, the president's chief of staff, H. R. Haldeman, and the domestic policy adviser, John Ehrlichman, were lifelong Scientists, as were other key figures in the Nixon campaigns and White House. In 1971 a Christian Scientist, Senator Charles Percy of Illinois, shepherded through Congress a bill reinstating and extending the copyright of *Science and Health*, which had expired; Nixon's powerful aides prevailed upon the president to sign the bill later that year. Challenged by dissident Christian Science groups that wished to print and distribute different editions of Eddy's textbook, the law was declared unconstitutional in 1987, and since then, all editions of *Science and Health* have entered the public domain.

One significant impact of *Science and Health* has been the passage of laws in the United States, on both federal and state levels, designed to exempt Christian Scientists from having their children vaccinated or provided with medical care. Lobbied for by church officials and members, these laws represent the most significant public expression of Eddy's teachings. A recent article in the journal *Pediatrics* documented 170 children's fatalities in the United States between 1975 and 1995 resulting from religiously motivated medical neglect, twenty-eight occurring in Christian Science families. The religious-exemption laws allowing such fatalities potentially endanger minors in all sects eschewing medical care and can be traced directly to Eddy's teachings in *Science and Health*.

Further Reading

■ Books

Bloom, Harold. *The American Religion: The Emergence of the Post-Christian Nation*. New York: Simon & Schuster, 1992.

Braden, Charles S. *Christian Science Today: Power, Policy, Practice*. Dallas, Tex.: Southern Methodist University Press, 1969.

Fraser, Caroline. *God's Perfect Child: Living and Dying in the Christian Science Church*. New York: Metropolitan Books, 2000.

Gardner, Martin. *The Healing Revelations of Mary Baker Eddy: The Rise and Fall of Christian Science*. Buffalo, N.Y.: Prometheus Books, 1993.

Gottschalk, Stephen. *The Emergence of Christian Science in American Religious Life*. Berkeley: University of California Press, 1973.

Meyer, Donald. *The Positive Thinkers: Popular Religious Psychology from Mary Baker Eddy to Norman Vincent Peale and Ronald Reagan*. Rev. ed. Middletown, Conn.: Wesleyan University Press, 1988.

Peel, Robert. *Christian Science: Its Encounter with American Culture*. New York: Holt, Rinehart and Winston, 1950.

Schoepflin, Rennie B. *Christian Science on Trial: Religious Healing in America*. Baltimore, Md.: Johns Hopkins University Press, 2003.

■ Web Sites

"About Science and Health." Spirituality.com Web site. http://www.spirituality.com/science-and-health/index.jhtml

—Commentary by Caroline Fraser

Questions for Further Study

1. The entry notes that "Christian Science was one of the fastest-growing sects in the country in the first decades of the twentieth century." Why do you think this was so? What appeal did Christian Science have? Why do you think the number of Christian Scientists has diminished in more recent decades?

2. Christian Science was one of numerous "breakaway sects" of Christianity that emerged during the nineteenth century in America. What conditions in nineteenth-century America might have given rise to this apparent need for alternative forms of Christianity?

3. To what extent, if any, do you think that Christian Science bears similarities to Eastern religions such as Buddhism and Hinduism? For reference, see, for example, the entries on the Vishnu Purana or the Noble Eightfold Path.

4. In later times, researchers have seemingly established that prayer and other spiritual exercises can, in fact, have a positive impact on a person's health. From a strictly scientific point of view, this would appear to make no sense. But how might such a conclusion be defended?

5. What is your position on the issue of parents denying medical care or immunizations to their children on the basis of religious belief? Do you believe that the state has an interest in forcing such care, or do you believe that the religious rights of parents take precedence? Defend your position.

SCIENCE AND HEALTH WITH KEY TO THE SCRIPTURES: DOCUMENT TEXT

1875 CE

—Mary Baker Eddy

CHAPTER I: Prayer

. . .

THE prayer that reforms the sinner and heals the sick is an absolute faith that all things are possible to God,—a spiritual understanding of Him, an unselfed love. Regardless of what another may say or think on this subject, I speak from experience. Prayer, watching, and working, combined with self-immolation, are God's gracious means for accomplishing whatever has been successfully done for the Christianization and health of mankind.

Thoughts unspoken are not unknown to the divine Mind. Desire is prayer; and no loss can occur from trusting God with our desires, that they may be moulded and exalted before they take form in words and in deeds.

What are the motives for prayer? Do we pray to make ourselves better or to benefit those who hear us, to enlighten the infinite or to be heard of men? Are we benefited by praying? Yes, the desire which goes forth hungering after righteousness is blessed of our Father, and it does not return unto us void.

God is not moved by the breath of praise to do more than He has already done, nor can the infinite do less than bestow all good, since He is unchanging wisdom and Love. We can do more for ourselves by humble fervent petitions, but the All-loving does not grant them simply on the ground of lip-service, for He already knows all.

Prayer cannot change the Science of being, but it tends to bring us into harmony with it. Goodness attains the demonstration of Truth. A request that God will save us is not all that is required. The mere habit of pleading with the divine Mind, as one pleads with a human being, perpetuates the belief in God as humanly circumscribed,—an error which impedes spiritual growth.

God is Love. Can we ask Him to be more? God is intelligence. Can we inform the infinite Mind of anything He does not already comprehend? Do we expect to change perfection? Shall we plead for more at the open fount, which is pouring forth more than we accept? The unspoken desire does bring us nearer the source of all existence and blessedness.

Asking God to *be* God is a vain repetition. God is "the same yesterday, and to-day, and forever;" and He who is immutably right will do right without being reminded of His province. The wisdom of man is not sufficient to warrant him in advising God.

Who would stand before a blackboard, and pray the principle of mathematics to solve the problem? The rule is already established, and it is our task to work out the solution. Shall we ask the divine Principle of all goodness to do His own work? His work is done, and we have only to avail ourselves of God's rule in order to receive His blessing, which enables us to work out our own salvation.

The Divine Being must be reflected by man,—else man is not the image and likeness of the patient, tender, and true, the One "altogether lovely;" but to understand God is the work of eternity, and demands absolute consecration of thought, energy, and desire....

Our Master taught his disciples one brief prayer, which we name after him the Lord's Prayer. Our Master said, "After this manner therefore pray ye," and then he gave that prayer which covers all human needs. There is indeed some doubt among Bible scholars, whether the last line is not an addition to the prayer by a later copyist; but this does not affect the meaning of the prayer itself.

In the phrase, "Deliver us from evil," the original properly reads, "Deliver us from the evil one." This reading strengthens our scientific apprehension of the petition, for Christian Science teaches us that "the evil one," or one evil, is but another name for the first lie and all liars.

Only as we rise above all material sensuousness and sin, can we reach the heaven-born aspiration and spiritual consciousness, which is indicated in the Lord's Prayer and which instantaneously heals the sick.

Here let me give what I understand to be the spiritual sense of the Lord's Prayer:

Our Father which art in heaven, *Our Father-Mother God, all-harmonious,* Hallowed be Thy name. *Adorable One.* Thy kingdom come. *Thy kingdom is come; Thou art ever-present.* Thy will be done in earth, as it is in heaven. *Enable us to know,—as in heaven, so on earth,—God is omnipotent, supreme.* Give us this day our daily bread; *Give us grace for to-day; feed the famished affections;* And forgive us our debts, as we forgive our debtors. *And Love is reflected in love;* And lead us not into temptation, but deliver us from evil; *And God leadeth us not into temptation, but delivereth us from sin, disease, and death.* For Thine is the kingdom, and the power, and the glory, forever. *For God is infinite, all-power, all Life, Truth, Love, over all, and All....*

CHAPTER VII: Physiology

. . .

We cannot serve two masters nor perceive divine Science with the material senses. Drugs and hygiene cannot successfully usurp the place and power of the divine source of all health and perfection. If God made man both good and evil, man must remain thus. What can improve God's work? Again, an error in the premise must appear in the conclusion. To have one God and avail yourself of the power of Spirit, you must love God supremely.

The "flesh lusteth against the Spirit." The flesh and Spirit can no more unite in action than good can coincide with evil. It is not wise to take a halting and half-way position or to expect to work equally with Spirit and matter, Truth and error. There is but one way—namely, God and His idea—which leads to spiritual being. The scientific government of the body must be attained through the divine Mind. It is impossible to gain control over the body in any other way. On this fundamental point, timid conservatism is absolutely inadmissible. Only through radical reliance on Truth can scientific healing power be realized.

Substituting good words for a good life, fair seeming for straightforward character, is a poor shift for the weak and worldly, who think the standard of Christian Science too high for them.

If the scales are evenly adjusted, the removal of a single weight from either scale gives preponderance to the opposite. Whatever influence you cast on the side of matter, you take away from Mind, which would otherwise outweigh all else. Your belief militates against your health, when it ought to be enlisted on the side of health. When sick (according to belief) you rush after drugs, search out the material so-called laws of health, and depend upon them to heal you, though you have already brought yourself into the slough of disease through just this false belief.

Because man-made systems insist that man becomes sick and useless, suffers and dies, all in consonance with the laws of God, are we to believe it? Are we to believe an authority which denies God's spiritual command relating to perfection,—an authority which Jesus proved to be false? He did the will of the Father. He healed sickness in defiance of what is called material law, but in accordance with God's law, the law of Mind.

I have discerned disease in the human mind, and recognized the patient's fear of it, months before the so-called disease made its appearance in the body. Disease being a belief, a latent illusion of mortal mind, the sensation would not appear if the error of belief was met and destroyed by truth.

Here let a word be noticed which will be better understood hereafter,—*chemicalization.* By chemicalization I mean the process which mortal mind and body undergo in the change of belief from a material to a spiritual basis.

Whenever an aggravation of symptoms has occurred through mental chemicalization, I have seen the mental signs, assuring me that danger was over, before the patient felt the change; and I have said to the patient, "You are healed,"—sometimes to his discomfiture, when he was incredulous. But it always came about as I had foretold.

I name these facts to show that disease has a mental, mortal origin,—that faith in rules of health or in drugs begets and fosters disease by attracting the mind to the subject of sickness, by exciting fear of disease, and by dosing the body in order to avoid it. The faith reposed in these things should find stronger supports and a higher home. If we understood the control of Mind over body, we should put no faith in material means.

Science not only reveals the origin of all disease as mental, but it also declares that all disease is cured by divine Mind. There can be no healing except by this Mind, however much we trust a drug or any other means towards which human faith or endeavor is directed. It is mortal mind, not matter, which brings to the sick whatever good they may seem to receive from materiality. But the sick are never really healed except by means of the divine power. Only the action of Truth, Life, and Love can give harmony....

CHAPTER XII: Christian Science Practice

♦ Mental Treatment Illustrated

The Science of mental practice is susceptible of no misuse. Selfishness does not appear in the practice of Truth or Christian Science. If mental practice is abused or is used in any way except to promote right thinking and doing, the power to heal mentally will diminish, until the practitioner's healing ability is wholly lost. Christian scientific practice begins with Christ's keynote of harmony, "Be not afraid!" Said Job: "The thing which I greatly feared is come upon me."

My first discovery in the student's practice was this: If the student silently called the disease by name, when he argued against it, as a general rule the body would respond more quickly,—just as a person replies more readily when his name is spoken; but this was because the student was not perfectly attuned to divine Science, and needed the arguments of truth for reminders. If Spirit or the power of divine Love bear witness to the truth, this is the ultimatum, the scientific way, and the healing is instantaneous.

It is recorded that once Jesus asked the name of a disease,—a disease which moderns would call *dementia*. The demon, or evil, replied that his name was Legion. Thereupon Jesus cast out the evil, and the insane man was changed and straightway became whole. The Scripture seems to import that Jesus caused the evil to be self-seen and so destroyed.

The procuring cause and foundation of all sickness is fear, ignorance, or sin. Disease is always induced by a false sense mentally entertained, not destroyed. Disease is an image of thought externalized. The mental state is called a material state. Whatever is cherished in mortal mind as the physical condition is imaged forth on the body.

Always begin your treatment by allaying the fear of patients. Silently reassure them as to their exemption from disease and danger. Watch the result of this simple rule of Christian Science, and you will find that it alleviates the symptoms of every disease. If you succeed in wholly removing the fear, your patient is healed. The great fact that God lovingly governs all, never punishing aught but sin, is your standpoint, from which to advance and destroy the human fear of sickness. Mentally and silently plead the case scientifically for Truth. You may vary the arguments to meet the peculiar or general symptoms of the case you treat, but be thoroughly persuaded in your own mind concerning the truth which you think or speak, and you will be the victor.

You may call the disease by name when you mentally deny it; but by naming it audibly, you are liable under some circumstances to impress it upon the thought. The power of Christian Science and divine Love is omnipotent. It is indeed adequate to unclasp the hold and to destroy disease, sin, and death.

To prevent disease or to cure it, the power of Truth, of divine Spirit, must break the dream of the material senses. To heal by argument, find the type of the ailment, get its name, and array your mental plea against the physical. Argue at first mentally, not audibly, that the patient has no disease, and conform the argument so as to destroy the evidence of disease. Mentally insist that harmony is the fact, and that sickness is a temporal dream. Realize the presence of health and the fact of harmonious being, until the body corresponds with the normal conditions of health and harmony.

If the case is that of a young child or an infant, it needs to be met mainly through the parent's thought, silently or audibly on the aforesaid basis of Christian Science. The Scientist knows that there can be no hereditary disease, since matter is not intelligent and cannot transmit good or evil intelligence to man, and God, the only Mind, does not produce pain in matter. The act of yielding one's thoughts to the undue contemplation of physical wants or conditions induces those very conditions. A single requirement, beyond what is necessary to meet the simplest needs of the babe is harmful. Mind regulates the condition of the stomach, bowels, and food, the temperature of children and of men, and matter does not. The wise or unwise views of parents and other persons on these subjects produce good or bad effects on the health of children.

The daily ablutions of an infant are no more natural nor necessary than would be the process of taking a fish out of water every day and covering it with dirt in order to make it thrive more vigorously in its own element. "Cleanliness is next to godliness," but washing should be only for the purpose of keeping the body clean, and this can be effected without scrubbing the whole surface daily. Water is not the natural habitat of humanity. I insist on bodily cleanliness within and without. I am not patient with a speck of dirt; but in caring for an infant one need not wash his little body all over each day in order to keep it sweet as the new-blown flower.

Giving drugs to infants, noticing every symptom of flatulency, and constantly directing the mind to such signs,—that mind being laden with illusions about disease, health-laws, and death,—these actions convey mental images to children's budding thoughts, and often stamp them there, making it probable at any time that such ills may be reproduced in the very ailments feared. A child may have worms, if you say so, or any other malady, timorously held in the beliefs concerning his body. Thus are laid the foundations of the belief in disease and death, and thus are children educated into discord....

CHAPTER XIV: Recapitulation

♦ QUESTIONS AND ANSWERS

Question.—What is God?

Answer.—God is incorporeal, divine, supreme, infinite Mind, Spirit, Soul, Principle, Life, Truth, Love.

Question.—Are these terms synonymous?

Answer.—They are. They refer to one absolute God. They are also intended to express the nature, essence, and wholeness of Deity. The attributes of God are justice, mercy, wisdom, goodness, and so on.

Question.—Is there more than one God or Principle?

Answer.—There is not. Principle and its idea is one, and this one is God, omnipotent, omniscient, and omnipresent Being, and His reflection is man and the universe. *Omni* is adopted from the Latin adjective signifying *all.* Hence God combines all-power or potency, all-science or true knowledge, all-presence. The varied manifestations of Christian Science indicate Mind, never matter, and have one Principle.

Question.—What are spirits and souls?

Answer.—To human belief, they are personalities constituted of mind and matter, life and death, truth and error, good and evil; but these contrasting pairs of terms represent contraries, as Christian Science reveals, which neither dwell together nor assimilate. Truth is immortal; error is mortal. Truth is limitless; error is limited. Truth is intelligent; error is non-intelligent. Moreover, Truth is real, and error is unreal. This last statement contains the point you will most reluctantly admit, although first and last it is the most important to understand.

The term *souls* or *spirits* is as improper as the term *gods.* Soul or Spirit signifies Deity and nothing else. There is no finite soul nor spirit. Soul or Spirit means only one Mind, and cannot be rendered in the plural. Heathen mythology and Jewish theology have perpetuated the fallacy that intelligence, soul, and life can be in matter; and idolatry and ritualism are the outcome of all man-made beliefs. The Science of Christianity comes with fan in hand to separate the chaff from the wheat. Science will declare God aright, and Christianity will demonstrate this declaration and its divine Principle, making mankind better physically, morally, and spiritually.

Question.—What are the demands of the Science of Soul

Answer.—The first demand of this Science is, "Thou shalt have no other gods before me." This *me* is Spirit. Therefore the command means this: Thou shalt have no intelligence, no life, no substance, no truth, no love, but that which is spiritual. The second is like unto it, "Thou shalt love thy neighbor as thyself." It should be thoroughly understood that all men have one Mind, one God and Father, one Life, Truth, and Love. Mankind will become perfect in proportion as this fact becomes apparent, war will cease and the true brotherhood of man will be established. Having no other gods, turning to no other but the one perfect Mind to guide him, man is the likeness of God, pure and eternal, having that Mind which was also in Christ.

Science reveals Spirit, Soul, as not in the body, and God as not in man but as reflected by man. The greater cannot be in the lesser. The belief that the greater can be in the lesser is an error that works ill. This is a leading point in the Science of Soul, that Principle is not in its idea. Spirit, Soul, is not confined in man, and is never in matter. We reason imperfectly from effect to cause, when we conclude that matter is the effect of Spirit; but *a priori* reasoning shows material existence to be enigmatical. Spirit gives the true mental idea. We cannot interpret Spirit, Mind, through matter. Matter neither sees, hears, nor feels.

Reasoning from cause to effect in the Science of Mind, we begin with Mind, which must be understood through the idea which expresses it and cannot be learned from its opposite, matter. Thus we arrive at Truth, or intelligence, which evolves its own unerring idea and never can be coordinate with human illusions. If Soul sinned, it would be mortal, for sin is mortality's self, because it kills itself. If Truth is immortal, error must be mortal, because error is unlike Truth. Because Soul is immortal, Soul cannot sin, for sin is not the eternal verity of being.

Question.—What is the scientific statement of being

Answer.—There is no life, truth, intelligence, nor substance in matter. All is infinite Mind and its infinite manifestation, for God is All-in-all. Spirit is immortal Truth; matter is mortal error. Spirit is the real and eternal; matter is the unreal and temporal. Spirit is God, and man is His image and likeness. Therefore man is not material; he is spiritual.

Question.—What is substance?

Answer.—Substance is that which is eternal and incapable of discord and decay. Truth, Life, and Love are substance, as the Scriptures use this word in Hebrews: "The substance of things hoped for, the evidence of things not seen." Spirit, the synonym of Mind, Soul, or God, is the only real substance. The spiritual universe, including individual man, is a compound idea, reflecting the divine substance of Spirit.

Question.—What is Life?

Answer.—Life is divine Principle, Mind, Soul, Spirit. Life is without beginning and without end. Eternity, not time, expresses the thought of Life, and time is no part of eternity. One ceases in proportion as the other is recognized. Time is finite; eternity is forever infinite. Life is neither in nor of matter. What is termed matter is unknown to Spirit, which includes in itself all substance and is Life eternal. Matter is a human concept. Life is divine Mind. Life is not limited. Death and finiteness are unknown to Life. If Life ever had a beginning, it would also have an ending.

Question.—What is intelligence?

Answer.—Intelligence is omniscience, omnipresence, and omnipotence. It is the primal and eternal quality of infinite Mind, of the triune Principle,—Life, Truth, and Love,—named God.

Question.—What is Mind?

Answer.—Mind is God. The exterminator of error is the great truth that God, good, is the *only* Mind, and that the supposititious opposite of infinite Mind—called *devil* or evil—is not Mind, is not Truth, but error, without intelligence or reality. There can be but one Mind, because there is but one God; and if mortals claimed no other Mind and accepted no other, sin would be unknown. We can have but one Mind, if that one is infinite. We bury the sense of infinitude, when we admit that, although God is infinite, evil has a place in this infinity, for evil can have no place, where all space is filled with God.

We lose the high signification of omnipotence, when after admitting that God, or good, is omnipres-

ent and has all-power, we still believe there is another power, named *evil*. This belief that there is more than one mind is as pernicious to divine theology as are ancient mythology and pagan idolatry. With one Father, even God, the whole family of man would be brethren; and with one Mind and that God, or good, the brotherhood of man would consist of Love and Truth, and have unity of Principle and spiritual power which constitute divine Science. The supposed existence of more than one mind was the basic error of idolatry. This error assumed the loss of spiritual power, the loss of the spiritual presence of Life as infinite Truth without an unlikeness, and the loss of Love as ever present and universal.

Divine Science explains the abstract statement that there is one Mind by the following self-evident proposition: If God, or good, is real, then evil, the unlikeness of God, is unreal. And evil can only seem to be real by giving reality to the unreal. The children of God have but one Mind. How can good lapse into evil, when God, the Mind of man, never sins? The standard of perfection was originally God and man. Has God taken down His own standard, and has man fallen?

God is the creator of man, and, the divine Principle of man remaining perfect, the divine idea or reflection, man, remains perfect. Man is the expression of God's being. If there ever was a moment when man did not express the divine perfection, then there was a moment when man did not express God, and consequently a time when Deity was unexpressed—that is, without entity. If man has lost perfection, then he has lost his perfect Principle, the divine Mind. If man ever existed without this perfect Principle or Mind, then man's existence was a myth.

The relations of God and man, divine Principle and idea, are indestructible in Science; and Science knows no lapse from nor return to harmony, but holds the divine order or spiritual law, in which God and all that He creates are perfect and eternal, to have remained unchanged in its eternal history.

The unlikeness of Truth,—named *error*,—the opposite of Science, and the evidence before the five corporeal senses, afford no indication of the grand facts of being; even as these so-called senses receive no intimation of the earth's motions or of the science of astronomy, but yield assent to astronomical propositions on the authority of natural science.

The facts of divine Science should be admitted,—although the evidence as to these facts is not supported by evil, by matter, or by material sense,—because the evidence that God and man coexist is fully sustained by spiritual sense. Man is, and forever has been, God's reflection. God is infinite, therefore ever present, and there is no other power nor presence. Hence the spirituality of the universe is the only fact of creation. "Let God be true, but every [material] man a liar."

Question.—Are doctrines and creeds a benefit to man?

Answer.—The author subscribed to an orthodox creed in early youth, and tried to adhere to it until she caught the first gleam of that which interprets God as above mortal sense. This view rebuked human beliefs, and gave the spiritual import, expressed through Science, of all that proceeds from the divine Mind. Since then her highest creed has been divine Science, which, reduced to human apprehension, she has named Christian Science. This Science teaches man that God is the only Life, and that this Life is Truth and Love; that God is to be understood, adored, and demonstrated; that divine Truth casts out suppositional error and heals the sick.

The way which leads to Christian Science is straight and narrow. God has set His signet upon Science, making it coordinate with all that is real and only with that which is harmonious and eternal. Sickness, sin, and death, being inharmonious, do not originate in God nor belong to His government. His law, rightly understood, destroys them. Jesus furnished proofs of these statements.

Question.—What is error?

Answer.—Error is a supposition that pleasure and pain, that intelligence, substance, life, are existent in matter. Error is neither Mind nor one of Mind's faculties. Error is the contradiction of Truth. Error is a belief without understanding. Error is unreal because untrue. It is that which seemeth to be and is not. If error were true, its truth would be error, and we should have a self-evident absurdity—namely, *erroneous truth.* Thus we should continue to lose the standard of Truth.

Question.—Is there no sin?

Answer.—All reality is in God and His creation, harmonious and eternal. That which He creates is good, and He makes all that is made. Therefore the only reality of sin, sickness, or death is the awful fact that unrealities seem real to human, erring belief, until God strips off their disguise. They are not true, because they are not of God. We learn in Christian Science that all inharmony of mortal mind or body is illusion, possessing neither reality nor identity though seeming to be real and identical.

The Science of Mind disposes of all evil. Truth, God, is not the father of error. Sin, sickness, and death are to be classified as effects of error. Christ came to destroy the belief of sin. The God-principle is omnipresent and omnipotent. God is everywhere, and nothing apart from Him is present or has power. Christ is the ideal Truth, that comes to heal sickness and sin through Christian Science, and attributes all power to God. Jesus is the name of the man who, more than all other men, has presented Christ, the true idea of God, healing the sick and the sinning and destroying the power of death. Jesus is the human man, and Christ is the divine idea; hence the duality of Jesus the Christ.

In an age of ecclesiastical despotism, Jesus introduced the teaching and practice of Christianity, affording the proof of Christianity's truth and love; but to reach his example and to test its unerring Science according to his rule, healing sickness, sin, and death, a better understanding of God as divine Principle, Love, rather than personality or the man Jesus, is required.

Jesus established what he said by demonstration, thus making his acts of higher importance than his words. He proved what he taught. This is the Science of Christianity. Jesus *proved* the Principle, which heals the sick and casts out error, to be divine. Few, however, except his students understood in the least his teachings and their glorious proofs,—namely, that Life, Truth, and Love (the Principle of this unacknowledged Science) destroy all error, evil, disease, and death.

The reception accorded to Truth in the early Christian era is repeated to-day. Whoever introduces the Science of Christianity will be scoffed at and scourged with worse cords than those which cut the flesh. To the ignorant age in which it first appears, Science seems to be a mistake,—hence the misinterpretation and consequent maltreatment which it receives. Christian marvels (and *marvel* is the simple meaning of the Greek word rendered *miracle* in the New Testament) will be misunderstood and misused by many, until the glorious Principle of these marvels is gained.

If sin, sickness, and death are as real as Life, Truth, and Love, then they must all be from the same source; God must be their author. Now Jesus came to destroy sin, sickness, and death; yet the Scriptures aver, "I am not come to destroy, but to fulfil." Is it possible, then, to believe that the evils which Jesus lived to destroy are real or the offspring of the divine will?

Despite the hallowing influence of Truth in the destruction of error, must error still be immortal? Truth spares all that is true. If evil is real, Truth must make it so; but error, not Truth, is the author of the unreal, and the unreal vanishes, while all that is real is eternal. The apostle says that the mission of Christ is to "destroy the works of the devil." Truth destroys falsity and error, for light and darkness cannot dwell together. Light extinguishes the darkness, and the Scripture declares that there is "no night there." To Truth there is no error,—all is Truth. To infinite Spirit there is no matter,—all is Spirit, divine Principle and its idea.

Question.—What is man?

Answer.—Man is not matter; he is not made up of brain, blood, bones, and other material elements. The Scriptures inform us that man is made in the image and likeness of God. Matter is not that likeness. The likeness of Spirit cannot be so unlike Spirit. Man is spiritual and perfect; and because he is spiritual and perfect, he must be so understood in Christian Science. Man is idea, the image, of Love; he is not physique. He is the compound idea of God, including all right ideas; the generic term for all that reflects God's image and likeness; the conscious identity of being as found in Science, in which man is the reflection of God, or Mind, and therefore is eternal; that which has no separate mind from God; that which has not a single quality underived from Deity; that which possesses no life, intelligence, nor creative power of his own, but reflects spiritually all that belongs to his Maker.

And God said: "Let us make man in our image, after our likeness; and let them have dominion over the fish of the sea, and over the fowl of the air, and over the cattle, and over all the earth, and over every creeping thing that creepeth upon the earth."

Man is incapable of sin, sickness, and death. The real man cannot depart from holiness, nor can God, by whom man is evolved, engender the capacity or freedom to sin. A mortal sinner is not God's man. Mortals are the counterfeits of immortals. They are the children of the wicked one, or the one evil, which declares that man begins in dust or as a material embryo. In divine Science, God and the real man are inseparable as divine Principle and idea.

Error, urged to its final limits, is self-destroyed. Error will cease to claim that soul is in body, that life and intelligence are in matter, and that this matter is man. God is the Principle of man, and man is the idea of God. Hence man is not mortal nor material. Mortals will disappear, and immortals, or the children of God, will appear as the only and eternal verities of man. Mortals are not fallen children of God. They never had a perfect state of being, which may subsequently be regained. They were, from the beginning of mortal history, "conceived in sin and brought forth in iniquity." Mortality is finally swallowed up in immortality. Sin, sickness, and death must disappear to give place to the facts which belong to immortal man....

♦ **CHAPTER XVII: Glossary**
. . .

GOD. The great I Am; the all-knowing, all-seeing, all-acting, all-wise, all-loving, and eternal; Principle; Mind; Soul; Spirit; Life; Truth; Love; all substance; intelligence....

MAN. The compound idea of infinite Spirit; the spiritual image and likeness of God; the full representation of Mind.

MATTER. Mythology; mortality; another name for mortal mind; illusion; intelligence, substance, and life in non-intelligence and mortality; life resulting in death, and death in life; sensation in the sensationless; mind originating in matter; the opposite of Truth; the opposite of Spirit; the opposite of God; that of which immortal Mind takes no cognizance; that which mortal mind sees, feels, hears, tastes, and smells only in brief.

Glossary

a priori:	Latin for "prior to"; derived by logic, without observed facts
After this manner therefore pray ye:	from the Gospel of Matthew, chapter 6, verse 9
destroy the works of the devil:	from the first book of John, chapter 3, verse 8
flesh lusteth against the Spirit:	from the book of Galatians, chapter 5, verse 17
Let God be true, but every [material] man a liar:	from Romans, chapter 3, verse 4
Let us make man in our image…:	from Genesis, chapter 1, verse 26
signet:	a seal, as from a ring
substance of things hoped for, the evidence of things not seen:	from Hebrews, chapter 11, verse 1

Portrait photo of German-born U.S. reform rabbi and theologian Dr. Kaufmann Kohler (1843-1926).

PITTSBURGH PLATFORM: DOCUMENT ANALYSIS

"We hold that the modern discoveries of scientific researches in the domains of nature and history are not antagonistic to the doctrines of Judaism, the Bible reflecting the primitive ideas of its own age..."

Overview

In November 1885, concerned about what they saw as a growing disconnect between the strictures of traditional Judaism and the scientific and rational ways of the modern world, nineteen rabbis from the loosely connected Reform movement in Judaism gathered in Pittsburgh, Pennsylvania, to discuss what made the Reform movement both unique and unified. Ultimately, they issued an eight-point platform—the Pittsburgh Platform—that Rabbi Isaac Mayer Wise, one of the participants, called the "Jewish Declaration of Independence" and that Rabbi David Philipson, the secretary of the conference, concluded was "the most succinct expression of the theology of the reform movement that has ever been published to the world."

The Pittsburgh Platform stands as the declaration of the core values of what has come to be known as "classical" Reform Judaism. The platform distinguishes between the ethical, philosophical, and religious elements of traditional Judaism, which the drafters thought essential, and the ceremonial and legalistic behavioral guidelines with which generations of rabbinic thinkers had shrouded those elements. Viewing certain traditions as the discredited relics of a pre-Enlightenment age, the drafters of the platform explicitly rejected all laws regulating diet (the laws of kashruth, or kosher laws), priestly purity (primarily for those claiming descent from Aaron, the brother of Moses), and dress, among other things. In one of its most controversial principles, the Pittsburgh Platform states that Jews are a religious community only and not a people—thus implying that modern Jews should not work for the creation or reestablishment of a Jewish national homeland.

Context

In the late nineteenth century, Reform Jews were facing what they viewed as a dual challenge: on one side, the total estrangement from Judaism of increasing numbers of young American Jews and, on the other side, the drive by those interested in reviving a notion of Jewish traditionalism in America to reject Reform as un-Jewish. In earlier years, some Jewish leaders, including Isaac Mayer Wise, had nurtured the hope that the Reform view of Judaism might become the single Minhag Amerika, or custom of all American Jews. By the mid-1880s, however, it was clear that American Judaism as a whole would never be so united. One remaining question was what beliefs a movement like Reform might defend as fundamental.

To Reform leaders, the challenge from the revivalists was of particular concern. The Reform rabbis viewed their own approach to Judaism as blending the vital aspects of the religion with the realities and rationalities of the modern world. The revivalists, in contrast, insisted that, by abandoning as obsolete various ceremonial and dietary laws, the Reform Jews were effectively abandoning Judaism. Just before he called the Pittsburgh Conference to meet, the influential German American rabbi Kaufmann Kohler had been engaged in a long-running published debate with the equally influential Hungarian American rabbi Alexander Kohut, who ultimately went on to help found the Conservative (more traditional) movement and who clearly viewed Reform as an adulteration of Judaism. As Jonathan D. Sarna recounts in *American Judaism* in describing the debate, Kohut directly and forcefully challenged Kohler's cherished views. "A Reform which seeks to progress without the Mosaic-rabbinical tradition," Kohut declared, "is a deformity—a skeleton without flesh and sinew, without spirit and heart. It is suicide; and suicide is not reform." Kohler vehemently disagreed, and he called the conference together in part to respond. "We cannot afford to stand condemned as *law-breakers*, to be branded as frivolous and as *rebels and traitors* because we transgress these laws on principle," Kohler declared.

In many ways, the stance taken by the Reform movement was dictated by the adherence of Reform leaders to the principles of the eighteenth-century Enlightenment—a belief in human progress and the ability of reason to promote such progress. Enlightenment thinkers tended to believe that the world, which was based on rationality, was continually getting better and that reasoning people could both help improve the world and come to an understanding of how to build a just and ethical society. By rejecting much of the system of Mosaic legislation (the laws as laid out in the Bible) and traditional ceremony, the framers of the Pittsburgh Platform were not attempting to abandon Judaism; instead, they were seeking to retain only those aspects of Judaism that would permit them to help build a just and peaceful society, while nonetheless abandoning meaningless and outdated customs and rules.

Ultimately, the Pittsburgh Platform was enormously influential: It stood as the central statement of the Reform ethos until 1937, when it was replaced by a new statement of principles known as the Columbus Platform. In 1999, the members of the Central Conference of American Rabbis (the professional organization for Reform clergy) returned to Pittsburgh, responding to what they saw as their duty "as rabbis once again to state a set of principles that define Reform Judaism in our own time." In May of that year, they issued a new Statement of Principles, in which (among other things) they declared continued support for the State of Israel, stated that the Bible stands as a record of "God's ongoing revelation," and concluded that Reform Judaism is "committed... to the fulfillment of those [ceremonies and commandments] that address us as individuals and as a community." Seemingly retreating significantly from the Pittsburgh Platform of 1885, which had rejected obsolete and outdated ceremony, the Central Conference of American Rabbis in this new statement observed that some of these "sacred obligations... both ancient and modern, demand renewed attention as the result of the unique context of our own times."

About the Author

Among the nineteen participants in the meetings that led to the promulgation of the Pittsburgh Platform, three—Kohler, Wise, and Rabbi David Philipson—stand out as "authors" of the platform, either because of their roles in assembling and administrating the Pittsburgh Conference or their importance to nineteenth-century Reform Judaism. The conference was initially called by Kohler, who had received both his rabbinical training and his advanced university education in Germany. In 1869, Kohler moved to the United States to become the rabbi of a congregation in Detroit, Michigan. Two years later, he became the rabbi of Chicago's Temple Sinai, and, in

1879, he headed east, becoming the rabbi at Temple Beth-El in New York City (where he succeeded his father-in-law, David Einhorn, who had been the acknowledged leader of the radical Eastern wing of the Reform movement). In all three positions, Kohler encouraged his congregations to abandon what he viewed as outmoded Jewish practices and to adopt such American (or Christian) innovations as Sunday morning services. In 1903, Kohler was elected president of Cincinnati's Hebrew Union College (HUC), which was established to train Reform rabbis in the United States; he served as president until he retired in 1921.

In ascending to the presidency of HUC in 1903, Kohler replaced Wise, who was another towering figure in Reform Judaism. Wise, who had been born in an area that later became Czechoslovakia, was the energetic (if less-well-educated) leader of the more moderate Germanic-oriented wing of Reform Judaism. Wise first came to the United States in 1846 to become the rabbi of the Beth El congregation in Albany, New York, but he left that job in 1850 after a dispute with the temple's lay president literally led to blows in front of the congregation. Wise and his followers founded a new synagogue in Albany, and three years later Wise took up a position as leader of the Bene Yeshurun congregation in Cincinnati. Over subsequent decades, Wise worked tirelessly to promote the concept of a single Minhag Amerika. He served as a leader in the establishment of three key Reform associations: the Union of American Hebrew Congregations (which became the umbrella organization of the Reform movement) in 1873, the HUC in 1875, and the Central Conference of American Rabbis in 1889.

David Philipson, who was born in 1862 in Indiana, served as the secretary of the Pittsburgh Conference. A protégé of Wise's, Philipson was one of the four rabbis to be ordained in the first graduating class of HUC in 1883. He went on to earn a Doctorate of Divinity from Johns Hopkins University in Baltimore, Maryland, and returned to Cincinnati in 1888 to take over for Wise as rabbi of Bene Yeshurun, which was viewed as the Reform movement's largest and most important synagogue. Philipson ultimately retired from that position in 1938. His book *The Reform Movement in Judaism*, published in 1907, is still viewed as an essential work on the history and ideology of Reform Judaism. In that work, Philipson refers to the Pittsburgh Platform as "the utterance most expressive of the teachings of Reform Judaism."

Explanation and Analysis of the Document

The Pittsburgh Platform is remarkable both for its brevity and the direct manner in which it identifies and describes the central principles of contemporary Judaism as viewed by its framers. The text itself is only approximately six hundred words long and is divided into an introductory paragraph and eight "principles," each of which is stated in a few sentences.

Time Line

November 3–6, 1869	■ Twelve Reform rabbis meet in Philadelphia, Pennsylvania, and promulgate a seven-point statement of principles, in part rejecting the belief in bodily resurrection, stressing the importance of praying in the vernacular, and viewing as obsolete any distinction between Jews in general and descendants of the traditional "priestly" classes.
1873	■ Thirty-four Reform Congregations unite in the Union of American Hebrew Congregations, which becomes the umbrella organization for Reform Judaism.
1875	■ Hebrew Union College (HUC) is established in Cincinnati, Ohio, to train Reform rabbis in the United States.
July 11, 1883	■ HUC celebrates the ordination of its first class of graduating rabbis. At the event, which is widely attended by American Jewish leaders of varying beliefs, some more-traditional guests are horrified when the hosts serve non-kosher food.
Summer 1885	■ Rabbi Alexander Kohut (who goes on to help found the Jewish Theological Seminary, which trains Conservative rabbis) and Rabbi Kaufmann Kohler engage in a published debate over the validity of the Reform movement.
November 16–18, 1885	■ At the urging of Rabbi Kaufmann Kohler, nineteen rabbis meet in Pittsburgh and promulgate the Pittsburgh Platform, in which they lay out the core beliefs of Reform Judaism.
1889	■ The Central Conference of American Rabbis is established to serve as the professional organization for all rabbis who consider themselves to be (and are considered to be) part of the organized rabbinate of Reform Judaism.
1937	■ The leaders of the Reform movement promulgate the Columbus Platform, which expands upon many of the principles of the Pittsburgh Platform but substantially restates the Reform movement's view of Zionism and the need for a Jewish homeland.
May 1999	■ The Central Conference of American Rabbis returns to Pittsburgh to issue a new Statement of Principles defining Reform Judaism in the modern era.

Perhaps because of Wise's desire to produce a "Jewish Declaration of Independence," the introductory paragraph (or preamble) to the platform mirrors in form the preamble to the American Declaration of Independence. It lays out the reason for producing the platform: the need, "in view of the wide divergence of opinion and of the conflicting ideas prevailing in Judaism today," for a unified statement of principles. This very general statement clearly references what the framers of the Pittsburgh Platform saw as a dual threat to modern Judaism posed by estranged Jews on the one hand and retraditionalized Jews on the other. The point of the platform was thus (in Kohler's words, as cited in Sarna's *American Judaism*) twofold: to "declare before the world *what Judaism is and what Reform Judaism means and aims at*."

The preamble also seeks to demonstrate a connection between the principles laid out in the Pittsburgh Platform and the principles adopted by the attendees at the Philadelphia Conference in 1869. That earlier meeting in Philadelphia had led to the promulgation of a statement of general principles applicable to American Judaism, including the need to adopt vernacular prayers in addition to Hebrew prayers and the rejection in the modern world of the special place in Judaism previously accorded the "priestly" class. The Philadelphia Conference also led to a number of legal rulings or statements regarding marriage, divorce, and circumcision—critical aspects of normal Jewish life. By linking their work to that done in Philadelphia, the framers presumably hoped to retain a claim to defining the Minhag Amerika.

♦ First Principle: Many Ways to God, with Jewish Primacy

The first principle laid out in the Pittsburgh Platform seems almost paradoxical: It simultaneously recognizes the view that all attempts by people to understand God are in some ways valid but nonetheless holds that Judaism represents the "highest conception" of God. The first principle begins by recognizing "in every religion" an attempt to "grasp the Infinite One." (Alternative versions of the platform recognize instead the more generalized attempt to "grasp the Infinite.") The framers consciously sought to be entirely inclusive: They explicitly recognize a valid belief—the "consciousness of the indwelling of God in man"—in "every mode, source, or book of revelation held sacred in *any* religious system." Even while attempting to be inclusive, however, the framers were clearly influenced by their own fundamental belief in monotheism and the notion that Judaism "presents the highest conception of the God-idea." Put another way, while they ostensibly recognized in all religious expressions the consciousness of the indwelling of God in the human being, they clearly believed that many of those expressions—including, presumably, all those concerning polytheism or animism—were incorrect and that others—including Christianity and Islam—were less correct than the expression found in Judaism.

♦ Second Principle: Understanding of the Bible
The second principle addresses the framers' view of the Bible, which to Jews is called the Tanakh and which is composed of the Torah (the Five Books of Moses: Genesis, Exodus, Leviticus, Numbers, and Deuteronomy), the Nevi'im ("Prophets"), and the Ketuvim ("Writings"). During the late nineteenth century, many Americans of various faiths viewed the Bible (whether Jewish or Christian) as literal truth, or the literal word of God. The second principle of the Pittsburgh Platform stands in direct contrast to that view: To the conference participants, the Bible comprised a "record of the consecration of the Jewish people to its mission as the priest of the one God." In other words, in the eyes of the conference participants, the Bible served as a history rather than as a revelation; it was, they thought, the mission and role of the Jewish people and not the text itself that was critical. That said, however, the Pittsburgh Platform also recognizes the Bible as "the most potent instrument of religious and moral instruction." The platform thus quickly distinguished between moral and religious instruction on the one hand, and the various ceremonies and legalisms described by the Bible on the other.

Having clarified that the Bible was most important as a tool for instructing readers in religion and morals—but not necessarily ceremony and law—the framers then went much further, establishing a firm contrast between any literal reading of the Bible and a reading of the Bible in light of full acceptance of the principles of the Enlightenment. The Bible, the framers declare, "reflect[s] the primitive ideas of its own age," and "sometimes cloth[es] its conception of Divine Providence and Justice dealing with man in miraculous narratives." Despite the Bible's employment of such storytelling tactics, the framers were clearly saying that "modern discoveries of scientific researches in the domain of nature and history" could coexist with the observance and practice of Judaism. To put a point on it: In this second principle, the framers were in part weighing in on the then-raging debate over the relationship between creationism and the theory of evolution as put forth by Charles Darwin in his 1859 book *The Origin of Species*. The authors of the Pittsburgh Platform conclude that the concept of evolution is not "antagonistic to the doctrines of Judaism"—despite the literal text of Genesis, which describes God creating the universe, along with humankind and all of the fauna, in a matter of days.

♦ Third Principle: Recognizing as Binding Only Moral Laws
The third principle presents a more explicit rejection than the second principle of what the Pittsburgh Platform's framers viewed as the "medieval rubbish" and outmoded legalisms explicitly described in or derived (during the preceding two thousand years) from the Tanakh. The framers thus distinguish Judaism "during its national life in Palestine" in literally biblical times from Judaism in the modern world. Given that they rejected the notion of returning to a Jewish homeland in Palestine and that the biblical laws were intended to govern Jewish national practice while living in that ancient homeland, the framers thus accept as binding only Judaism's most enduring moral laws. Along with what they regard as outdated biblical laws, they then explicitly reject all ceremonies "as are not adapted to the views and habits of modern civilization." Interestingly, in stating that they wish to maintain "only such ceremonies as elevate and sanctify our lives," the framers allowed for continued development in Jewish practice in conjunction with continued societal development. The effect of the platform, therefore, was not to freeze Reform Judaism in 1885, but instead to state eternal principles that would find different expression in different periods.

♦ Fourth Principle: Rejecting Outdated Mosaic and Rabbinical Laws
In the fourth principle, the framers focus on exactly what laws and ceremonies they had rejected in the third principle. Among those laws that in their view were "not adapted to the views and habits of modern civilization" were "all such Mosaic and rabbinical laws as regulate diet, priestly purity, and dress." This statement shocked those who embraced traditional Judaism: The framers thus explicitly reject the laws of kashruth, or the laws governing whether certain foods are "kosher" to eat. Among specific foods forbidden to observant Jews under this system are any pork products, shellfish, blood, or any combination of meat and dairy. Those who obey these laws (or, in modern terms, "keep kosher") also focus on how animals are slaughtered, crops are grown, foods are prepared, and dishes are washed. In the eyes of the framers of the Pittsburgh Platform, these rules—even if justified at some point in the past by practical health issues—were now unjustified and were intensely burdensome. While the platform articulates support for maintaining "such ceremonies as elevate and sanctify our lives," the framers conclude that *these* sorts of rules instead "fail to impress the modern Jew with a spirit of priestly holiness."

The fourth principle highlights a subtext to the platform: the desire to bring Judaism fully into conjunction with modern enlightened society. One effect of the laws of kashruth was to keep Jews somehow apart from non-Jews at mealtimes or when eating; by rejecting these laws, which they viewed as nonsensical, the framers of the Pittsburgh Platform were, in effect, abolishing a critical difference between the modern Jewish community in the United States and that community's Christian (and non-Christian) neighbors. Similarly, traditional rules about dress and purity had the effect of keeping Jews apart from modern society. This principle thus, like much of the rest of the platform, sought to permit Jews to fit more seamlessly into the contemporary Western world.

♦ Fifth Principle: No Longer a Nation, but a Religious Community

The fifth principle of the Pittsburgh Platform, which addresses directly the notion of a Jewish identity, is perhaps the most controversial principle of all, because it reflects the rejection by the framers of the theory of Zionism, or the belief that Jews should work to rebuild a Jewish national homeland, perhaps in the area then known as Palestine. In this principle, the framers state that they no longer consider themselves to be the nation of Israel but instead view themselves as belonging to a religious community—and thus, presumably, owing national loyalty only to the United States. (As David Philipson later wrote in *The Reform Movement in Judaism*, to his mind "political Zionism and true Americanism have always seemed mutually exclusive. No man can be a member of two nationalities.") This position was later the first to be rejected by future generations of Reform Jews. While in the final years of the late nineteenth century many prominent Reform rabbis remained staunchly anti-Zionist and Hebrew Union College even fired a pro-Zionist faculty member at the direction of then-president Kohler, most Reform Jews ultimately embraced Zionism in light of the plight of eastern European Jews facing pogroms (mob attacks, either organized or condoned by government officials, on Jewish homes, businesses, and individuals), the promulgation of the British Empire's Balfour Declaration, and (eventually and perhaps most important) the Holocaust. In the Balfour Declaration, which was issued on November 2, 1917, the British government stated that it was in "sympathy with Jewish Zionist aspirations" and accordingly viewed "with favour the establishment in Palestine of a national home for the Jewish people." The Holocaust, of course, was, as the U.S. Holocaust Memorial Museum explains, the "systematic, bureaucratic, state-sponsored persecution and murder of approximately six million Jews by the Nazi regime and its collaborators" in Germany.

Less controversial from a practical standpoint but perhaps more important as a matter of theology, in this principle the framers also effectively reject the concept of the coming of a single Messiah. Instead, they focus on the coming of a Messianic age, or Messianic "kingdom of truth, justice, and peace among all men." They tie this view to a highly optimistic—or perhaps simply naïve—faith in the power of Enlightenment ideas of rationality and concepts of social justice as reflected in "the modern era of universal culture of heart and intellect." This principle effectively places the focus of Reform Judaism not on reestablishing the biblical Temple in Jerusalem, with its attendant ceremonies and sacrifices, but on practicing Judaism in the context of and while contributing to the success and development of the framers' own country.

♦ Sixth Principle: Reason and Monotheism

The sixth principle contains another seemingly paradoxical pairing of ideas: a recognition of Judaism's "progressive" desire to "be in accord with the postulates of reason" but also the firm and unquestioning acceptance of monotheism and faith-based fundamental concepts of moral truth. As the language of the principle makes clear, however, the framers saw no paradox in the simultaneous appeal to reason and the unquestioning acceptance of faith-based monotheism; instead, they clearly believed that any right-thinking rational observers would be forced to accept the validity of Judaism or perhaps its "daughter religions" of Christianity and Islam. Inextricably linked to the framers' belief in the rectitude of monotheism, progressivism, and moral truth is the view that "the spirit of broad humanity" of their age is, in effect, operating together with Jews "in the establishment of the reign of truth and righteousness among men." In other words, as the framers make clear in this principle, they believed that "truth and righteousness among men" is equivalent to the acceptance of monotheism and moral truth; where this leaves polytheistic or animistic religions remains unclear.

♦ Seventh Principle: Basic Doctrine of Judaism

The seventh principle is the framers' attempt to clarify the specific religious beliefs inherent in modern Judaism, separating those beliefs from the practices or broad theistic concepts associated with the Jewish religion. As is often the case with attempts to clarify religious beliefs, however, the principle leaves unanswered a critical question. The soul, the framers declare, is immortal, as they can tell because of the "divine nature of the human spirit, which forever finds bliss in righteousness and misery in wickedness." While this view is shared by representatives of many other religions, including Christianity, the framers' next view is not: "We reject," they explain, "as ideas not rooted in Judaism, the beliefs both in bodily resurrection and in Gehenna and Eden (Hell and Paradise) as abodes for everlasting punishment and reward." In other words, Reform Jews believe that souls are immortal, but they are not punished or rewarded eternally for the actions of ensouled humans on earth; furthermore, as there is no Messiah coming to bring bodily resurrection, souls can never return to an embodied state. As had Jews throughout history, the framers thus left open the difficult religious question of what happens to a soul after death.

♦ Eighth Principle: Judaism as Social Progressivism

The eighth and final principle of the Pittsburgh Platform was added primarily to speak to the Progressive attitudes of many of the conference participants. During the late nineteenth and early twentieth centuries, Progressive reformers had near-absolute faith in the ability of society to craft laws and policies that would alleviate the historical scourges of poverty and ignorance. Traditionally, Jews also embraced the concept of *tikkun olam* , the duty of "repairing the world" to once again make it a paradise. Combining these two concepts, the framers announce that, in conformance with "the spirit of Mosaic legislation," they "deem it our duty to participate in the great task of modern times, to solve, on the basis of justice and righteousness, the problems presented by the contrasts and evils of the present organization of society."

Audience

There were several intended audiences for the Pittsburgh Platform. The platform was primarily intended for American Jews, whom the framers believed and hoped actually subscribed to the platform's rejection of outmoded Jewish ceremonial practice in favor of Jewish ethical and religious principles. More specifically, the platform was aimed both at those American Jews (on the one extreme) who were rejecting the practice of Judaism as being incompatible with modernity and those American Jews (on the other extreme) who were rejecting the practice of *Reform* Judaism as being out of step with the historical understanding of Jewish law and Jewish tradition. To a lesser extent, the platform was also intended for like-minded Enlightenment thinkers of other religions (perhaps particularly American Protestants) who shared the framers' recognition: "in every mode, source, or book of revelation held sacred in any religious system the consciousness of the indwelling of God in man."

Impact

The Pittsburgh Platform was a critical document for what we now consider "classical" Reform Judaism. It had a significant impact in both uniting two wings of Reform Judaism in America (the more radical Eastern wing, which was led by David Einhorn and represented by Kaufmann

---

Essential Quotes

> *"We hold that the modern discoveries of scientific researches in the domains of nature and history are not antagonistic to the doctrines of Judaism, the Bible reflecting the primitive ideas of its own age and at times clothing its conception of divine providence and justice dealing with man in miraculous narratives."*
>
> (Section 1)

> *"We recognize in the Mosaic legislation a system of training the Jewish people for its mission during its national life in Palestine, and to-day we accept as binding only the moral laws and maintain only such ceremonies as elevate and sanctify our lives, but reject all such as are not adapted to the views and habits of modern civilization."*
>
> (Section 1)

> *"We consider ourselves no longer a nation but a religious community, and therefore expect neither a return to Palestine, nor a sacrificial worship under... the sons of Aaron, nor the restoration of any of the laws concerning the Jewish state."*
>
> (Section 1)

Kohler, and the Germanic-oriented wing, which was led by Isaac Mayer Wise and which was strongest in the western United States) and clarifying and promulgating Reform beliefs. While Reform congregations continued to vary (as they do today) in whether they accepted or rejected the laws of kashruth and other ceremonial rules such as those concerning dress, the platform represented two core beliefs: that Judaism was not incompatible with the modern world and Enlightenment principles and that, while ethics and morality might be immutable, outmoded ceremony and tradition should give way in the face of modernity and scientific understanding.

In the decades after the Pittsburgh Platform was promulgated, these core beliefs were in some ways challenged by the more than two million Jewish immigrants—many of them poor and uneducated and most traditionally observant—who journeyed to the United States to join the few hundred thousand who were already living in the country. The platform, or at least the principle stating that Jews were not a people but were simply members of a religious community, also proved extremely controversial even before these waves of immigration, as it contributed to a sharp divide among Reform Jews over the issue of Zionism. The platform continued to exert enormous influence over Reform Judaism until, in 1937, on the eve of World War II, the Central Conference of American Rabbis adopted the Columbus Platform, which expanded upon Reform Jewish notions of religious practice and ethics and which explicitly declared support for the development of a Jewish homeland, which became the modern State of Israel.

Further Reading

■ Books

Heller, James G. *Isaac M. Wise: His Life, Work, and Thought.* New York: Union of American Hebrew Congregations, 1965.

Jacob, Walter, ed. *The Changing World of Reform Judaism: The Pittsburgh Platform in Retrospect.* Pittsburgh, Penn.: Rodef Shalom Congregation, 1985.

Mendes-Flohr, Paul, and Jehuda Reinharz. *The Jew in the Modern World: A Documentary History.* New York: Oxford University Press, 1995.

Philipson, David. *The Reform Movement in Judaism.* Jersey City, N.J.: Ktav Publishing House, 1967.

Raphael, Marc Lee. *Profiles in American Judaism.* San Francisco, Calif.: Harper & Row, 1984.

Sarna, Jonathan D. *American Judaism: A History.* New Haven, Conn.: Yale University Press, 2004.

Telushkin, Joseph. *Jewish Literacy.* New York: William Morrow, 2008.

Temkin, Sefton D. *Isaac Mayer Wise: Shaping American Judaism.* Oxford, U.K.: Oxford University Press, 1992.

♦ Web Site

"The Holocaust." United States Holocaust Memorial Museum "Holocaust Encyclopedia" Web site. http://www.ushmm.org/wlc/en/article.php?ModuleId=10005143

"Platforms Adopted by the CCAR." Central Conference of American Rabbis Web site. http://ccarnet.org/documentsandpositions/platforms/

"A Statement of Principles for Reform Judaism." Central Conference of American Rabbis Web site. http://ccarnet.org/Articles/index.cfm?id=44&pge_id=1606

—Commentary by Samuel Brenner

1. Explain the difference between Reform Judaism and Orthodox Judaism for an audience that might otherwise think that Judaism is a uniform religion.

2. During the late nineteenth century, the findings of modern science were causing many people to question traditional religious beliefs. Compare the way American Jews addressed this issue in the Pittsburgh Platform with the way Quakers did in Essential Truths or Humanists later would in the Humanist Manifesto.

3. Many religions—though by no means all—rely on traditional customs and practices that some observers might regard as outdated, as relics from an age long past. In this regard, Judaism is no exception. In your view, how important do you think these customs and traditions are? Are they relics? Or are the necessary for creating a sense of community and shared heritage among people of a religious faith?

4. Why do you think the more recent Central Conference of American Rabbis backed away from some of the views expressed in the Pittsburgh Platform?

5. What do you think would have been the reaction of Maimonides, the author of the *Mishneh Torah*, to the Pittsburgh Platform? Explain your conclusion.

PITTSBURGH PLATFORM: DOCUMENT TEXT

1885 CE

In view of the wide divergence of opinion and of the conflicting ideas prevailing in Judaism today, we, as representatives of Reform Judaism in America, in continuation of the work begun at Philadelphia in 1869, unite upon the following principles:

First: We recognize in every religion an attempt to grasp the Infinite One, and in every mode, source or book of revelation held sacred in any religions system the consciousness of the indwelling of God in man. We hold that Judaism presents the highest conception of the God-idea as taught in our holy Scriptures and developed and spiritualized by the Jewish teachers in accordance with the moral and philosophical progress of their respective ages. We maintain that Judaism preserved and defended amid continual struggles and trials and under enforced isolation this God-idea as the central religious truth for the human race.

Second: We recognize in the Bible the record of the consecration of the Jewish people to its mission as priest of the One God, and value it as the most potent instrument of religious and moral instruction. We hold that the modern discoveries of scientific researches in the domains of nature and history are not antagonistic to the doctrines of Judaism, the Bible reflecting the primitive ideas of its own age and at times clothing its conception of divine providence and justice dealing with man in miraculous narratives.

Third: We recognize in the Mosaic legislation a system of training the Jewish people for its mission during its national life in Palestine, and to-day we accept as binding only the moral laws and maintain only such ceremonies as elevate and sanctify our lives, but reject all such as are not adapted to the views and habits of modem civilization.

Fourth: We hold that all such Mosaic and Rabbinical laws as regulate diet, priestly purity and dress originated in ages and under the influence of ideas altogether foreign to our present mental and spiritual state. They fail to impress the modern Jew with a spirit of priestly holiness; their observance in our days is apt rather to obstruct than to further modem spiritual elevation.

Fifth: We recognize in the modern era of universal culture of heart and intellect the approach of the realization of Israel's great Messianic hope for the establishment of the kingdom of truth, justice and peace among all men. We consider ourselves no longer a nation but a religious community, and therefore expect neither a return to Palestine, nor a sacrificial worship under the administration of the sons of Aaron, nor the restoration of any of the laws concerning the Jewish state.

Sixth: We recognize in Judaism a progressive religion, ever striving to be in accord with the postulates of reason. We are convinced of the utmost necessity of preserving the historical identity with our great past. Christianity and Islam being daughter-religions of Judaism, we appreciate their mission to aid in the spreading of monotheistic and moral truth. We acknowledge that the spirit of broad humanity of our age is our ally in the fulfillment of our mission, and therefore we extend the hand of fellowship to all who cooperate with us in the establishment of the reign of truth and righteousness among men.

Seventh: We reassert the doctrine of Judaism, that the soul of men is immortal, grounding this belief on the divine nature of the human spirit, which forever finds bliss in righteousness and misery in wickedness. We reject as ideas not rooted in Judaism the belief both in bodily resurrection and in Gehenna and Eden (Hell and Paradise), as abodes for everlasting punishment or reward.

Eighth: In full accordance with the spirit of Mosaic legislation which strives to regulate the relation between rich and poor, we deem it our duty to participate in the great task of modern times, to solve on the basis of justice and righteousness the problems presented by the contrasts and evils of the present organization of society.

Glossary

Messianic: of or relating to the promised arrival of a messiah, that is, a savior or redeemer

Mosaic: pertaining to Moses, the Jewish patriarch and lawgiver in the Hebrew Bible

Rabbinical: pertaining to rabbis, or Jewish teachers who established the foundations of Jewish law and custom during the first centuries of the Common Era

sons of Aaron: those claiming descent from Aaron, the brother of Moses; priests

Blavatsky, c. 1877.

THE SECRET DOCTRINE: DOCUMENT ANALYSIS

"Occult Sciences will have the finger of scorn pointed at them from every street corner..."

Overview

The Secret Doctrine is the magnum opus of Helena Blavatsky. In it, Blavatsky lays out the fundamental basis for Theosophy, a religious philosophy that she believed to be an ageless, universal system for understanding how the earth came to be and humanity's connection to the unseen divine. She drew upon a number of disparate sources to craft her system, including Hindu reincarnation and Darwinian evolution. At its base, Theosophy teaches that everything—the human soul, the earth, the solar system—is proceeding through a set of seven reincarnation periods. The periods can be thought of as one infinitely long breath emanating from the Ultimate Truth. During the outbreath (expansion), everything cycles away from spiritual Oneness, culminating in the fourth period, when we are farthest away and thus visible in material form. After this apex, we begin the journey back, returning to the ultimate goal of all material forms: spiritual Oneness and Truth.

Blavatsky stood at the center of the group of professionals and intellectuals who formed the Theosophical Society in New York City in 1875. *The Secret Doctrine* is the most comprehensive statement of their beliefs, and Blavatsky believed that unseen "Masters" dictated it to her. It is dense and difficult to read in a conventional, logical manner; rather, it is meant to flow over the reader like an ocean, creating an almost meditative state, during which deep truths can penetrate the mind. Although *The Secret Doctrine* is rarely read in its entirety today, the impact of the Theosophy it puts forth is immense. In its own time, it was the most sophisticated synthesis of a number of important religious trends, including the supernatural basis of the occult, the dual nature of human beings that forms the foundation of Spiritualism, and the introduction of Asian religions such as Hinduism into the West. Additionally, Theosophy addressed the question of how science and religion could coexist in the wake of Charles Darwin's contentious theory of evolution. It was also a key antecedent of Indian independence and gave rise to many New Age religious movements that gained popularity in the 1960s.

Context

The members of Blavatsky's Theosophical Society, all of whom were upper-middle-class professionals from New York City, were searching for answers: How did our world come to be? Where do we go after we die? Are there unseen forces that control human action? The answers that Theosophists formulated to these age-old questions cannot be understood apart from their particular historical period and place.

The occult has a long history in the West, having developed alongside Christianity and provided another way to view the world and our place in it. Occult groups often had secret societies, brotherhoods, and complicated initiations, and adherents to occultism believed in mystical beings that populated the earth. Medieval European societies, like the Rosicrucians and Freemasons, were imported to and flourished in the United States. A mid-nineteenth-century U.S. movement called Spiritualism was influenced by these earlier groups but was also more widely popular. Spiritualists believed that spirits of the dead returned and spoke with the living, generally through a medium at a séance. This concept permeated American culture after the 1848 "Hydesville Rappings," when two young girls allegedly communicated through a series of knocks—much like the newly invented Morse code—with a man they called Mr. Splithoof (the Devil). The case caused a sensation, and séances were soon being held across the northeastern United States—even Mary Todd Lincoln, the wife of President Abraham Lincoln, held one in the White House in order to contact her deceased son. Spiritualism remained popular through the American Civil War (1861–1865) but began to lose credibility in the late 1860s, when a number of mediums were exposed as frauds.

The Theosophical Society arose directly out of the context of Spiritualism. It was fostered through collaboration between Blavatsky and Henry Steel Olcott, a New York lawyer descended of Puritans. A believer in Spiritualism and the occult, Olcott was contracted by newspapers in 1874 to write a series of articles about séances in Vermont. It was there that he met Blavatsky, a recent immigrant to the United States who had already distinguished herself as a medium of extraordinary ability. She was charismatic and exotic—telling of travels and spiritual encounters all over the world, particularly in Egypt and Tibet. Blavatsky told Olcott that the messages she received were not just from spirits but of a more unusual sort: She said she spoke with Masters (or Adepts), people so spiritually evolved that they were invisible.

In 1875 these Masters also began to speak to Olcott, through Blavatsky. In letters addressed to Olcott as "Brother Neophyte," the Masters are said to have commanded him to get Blavatsky an apartment in New York City and to learn from her. Olcott did so, and together they began to hold a series of philosophical gatherings in her new apartment that brought together Spiritualists and occultists from across New York City. As Spiritualism waned in popularity, Blavatsky and her circle sought new ways to explain mysterious happenings. Thus, they formed the Theosophical Society in order to tap into ancient sources of wisdom. Although Theosophists' ultimate goal was to become one with the Ultimate Truth, they did not engage in ritual, prayer, or other facets of religion, strictly speaking. Rather, they gave speeches to one another, held forums for discussion, and made intellectual links with occultists in Europe. They believed that Spiritualism and other occult phenomena could be investigated, discussed, and understood.

Besides the occult, Theosophy arose out of a series of societal shifts that, to many upper-middle-class white Americans, seemed profoundly disruptive: the Industrial Revolution, the influx of millions of new immigrants to the United States, the Civil War, and the rise of Darwinian science. Large numbers of immigrants were poor Catholics and Jews who settled in overcrowded city tenements; many wealthy Protestants felt that they lacked moral fiber, which resulted in the spread of disease and vice. Immorality and chaos seemed to have infiltrated the United States during the Civil War: Americans killed each other on an unprecedented scale, and many observers felt that the Apocalypse might be at hand. Just as destabilizing were new intellectual trends coming out of Europe: German biblical criticism and Darwinian evolution. Biblical critics maintained that the Bible was not the literal word of God, as most Christians at that time believed, but should be read allegorically and as a product of its own historical time. Darwin's *On the Origin of Species* (1859) offered a new explanation for how humans came to be: They were not created by God but were evolved from monkeys. For many Christians, it seemed dangerous to say that nature's law was "survival of the fittest." What, then, was there to stop men from killing those weaker than they or committing more atrocities like those perpetrated during the Civil War? Pressure mounted to harmonize these new sciences—biblical criticism and evolution—with religion. At the same time, Victorian-era Protestants embraced new trends, such as the expansion of American missions to foreign lands. To many Americans, it seemed as if Christian progress and civilization could save the world. Missionaries' writings were popular readings and introduced American audiences to the Eastern religions of Hinduism and Buddhism. For Americans who were unhappy in Christian denominations and dabbled in the occult, these exotic faiths seem to have offered new possibilities.

Theosophists were on the cutting edge of these trends in Victorian society. Blavatsky developed the most coherent (and complicated) system of beliefs related to the occult, casting aside Spiritualism when it was no longer credible and proposing her own system as a substitute. Within Theosophy, Blavatsky and her group were able to bring together contemporary ideas about evolutionary science and the new interest in Eastern religions, as is evident in the excerpt reprinted here. Theosophy focused on the individual soul's journey, proposing that we each have the power to improve our own spiritual circumstances. Consequently, it appealed to a U.S. culture based on individualism, free will, and progress. By harnessing these various strands, Theosophy succeeded in neutralizing the fear and discomfort that new ideas caused, while also appealing to the sense of exotic mystery that occultists craved. It is within this context that one can understand how a tome as dense as *The Secret Doctrine* has had such long-lasting impact.

About the Author

Helena Petrovna Blavatsky was a colorful character who flouted traditional gender norms in an era when most women stayed home. She was known for being charismatic and magnetic; her contemporaries described her as a powerful force, able to communicate with spirits. Born in Russia in 1831, Blavatsky was of royal blood. Her grandmother had been a princess, and both she and Blavatsky's mother were noted authors in their own right. As a child, Helena was imaginative but tempestuous. At age sixteen, she married a man in his forties but ran away shortly after and, by age twenty, was in London, where she later claimed to have first met an invisible Master. For the next two decades or so, Blavatsky disappeared: These "lost years" are the source of much debate. Theosophists (and Blavatsky herself) claim that she wandered the earth, learning from Masters in places like Tibet. Such stories are unsubstantiated historically, although in 1871 and 1872, she certainly was in Egypt, where she started a Société Spirite (Spiritualist Society).

Blavatsky arrived in New York City in July 1873 and immediately became involved in Spiritualist circles. She began the Theosophical Society in 1875 and wrote *Isis Revealed* two years later. The book caused some controversy because of rumors of plagiarism. Although sections of it were directly attributable to others, Blavatsky explained that this was a miscommunication that stemmed from her low level of fluency in English as well as from the complex

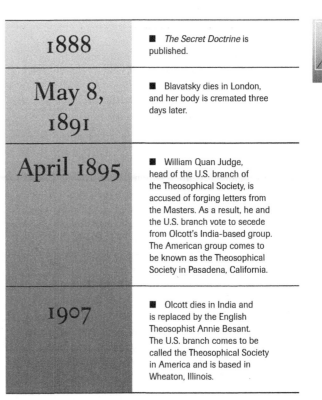

Time Line	
1831	■ Blavatsky is born in Yekaterinoslav, Russia (now Dnipropetrovsk, Ukraine).
1832	■ Henry Steel Olcott is born in Orange, New Jersey.
1848	■ The "Hydesville Rappings" take place in upstate New York, beginning the Spiritualism craze.
ca. 1851	■ Blavatsky leaves Russia and claims to meet her first spiritual Master in London, England.
July 1873	■ Blavatsky immigrates to New York City.
1874	■ Olcott travels to Vermont to write about Spiritualism.
October 1874	■ Olcott and Blavatsky meet in Vermont.
March 9, 1875	■ Olcott receives the first "Brother Neophyte" letter from an Egyptian Master, marking the beginning of Olcott and Blavatsky's break with Spiritualism.
November 17, 1875	■ The first regular meeting of the Theosophical Society takes place at Blavatsky's New York City apartment.
1877	■ Blavatsky publishes her first English-language book, *Isis Revealed*. Accusations of plagiarism follow.
1878	■ Olcott and Blavatsky set out for India.
1879	■ Olcott and Blavatsky establish the Theosophical Society World Headquarters in Adyar, India.
1885	■ Blavatsky leaves India and settles in London with her followers in 1887.

1888	■ *The Secret Doctrine* is published.
May 8, 1891	■ Blavatsky dies in London, and her body is cremated three days later.
April 1895	■ William Quan Judge, head of the U.S. branch of the Theosophical Society, is accused of forging letters from the Masters. As a result, he and the U.S. branch vote to secede from Olcott's India-based group. The American group comes to be known as the Theosophical Society in Pasadena, California.
1907	■ Olcott dies in India and is replaced by the English Theosophist Annie Besant. The U.S. branch comes to be called the Theosophical Society in America and is based in Wheaton, Illinois.

nature of the dictations from the invisible Masters. Nevertheless, accusations of plagiarism and fraud followed Blavatsky throughout her career.

In 1878, Blavatsky convinced Olcott that the future of the society lay in India, where they could be closest to the most important Masters. Shortly after their arrival there, an English theosophist in India, A. P. Sinnett, began to receive letters from "KH," a Master named Koot Hoomi. The letters apparently appeared on napkins or fell from the ceiling or were hand-delivered by Blavatsky herself. When controversy erupted within the Theosophical Society about whether she was actually producing them, Blavatsky left India and went to live with followers in London. She published *The Secret Doctrine* in 1888 and died three years later. Her body was cremated, a practice that Theosophists imported from India and introduced into the West. Blavatsky's ashes were divided into three portions: Olcott carried one part back to India and buried it at the Theosophist headquarters in Adyar; another portion was taken to New York and is now housed at the Theosophical Society in Pasadena, California; and a third was transported to India and scattered in the Ganges.

Explanation and Analysis of the Document

The Secret Doctrine, subtitled *The Synthesis of Science, Religion, and Philosophy*, was originally published as two volumes that totaled more than fifteen hundred pages. The excerpt here comes from the first volume, *Cosmogenesis*, in which Blavatsky lays out the creation of the universe. The second volume, *Anthropogenesis*, deals with the evolution of humanity through seven "root races." For Theosophists, *The Secret Doctrine* was the first modern description of an ancient and universal truth out of which religion, science, and philosophy have grown. In the section that follows, Blavatsky introduces the reader to the fundamental principles upon which Theosophy is based.

◆ Proem

The stanzas from the *Book of Dzyan* are the mysterious, ancient religious text upon which Blavatsky said *The Secret Doctrine* was based. Although she identified *Dzyan* as the oldest book in the world, archeologists have pointed out that no such book is known to have existed. In the Proem, or preface, to *The Secret Doctrine*, Blavatsky says that she is translating a section of the *Book of Dzyan* that describes a chain of evolution of which our visible earth is one part. This chain links everything into infinity: the earth to the planets, the planets to the solar system, the solar system to the universe until, writes Blavatsky, "the mind reels and is exhausted in the effort." Blavatsky claims that there are seven stanzas of the *Book of Dzyan* that lay out the seven great stages of creation. The number 7 is a key symbol in Theosophy, and most aspects of Blavatsky's system occur in 7s.

◆ Three Fundamental Propositions

Immediately after the "Proem," Blavatsky lays out the three fundamental propositions of Theosophy. The first is that there is an omnipresent and eternal principle that guides all action. Theosophists reject any anthropomorphic conception of a deity—either animal or human—but believe in this universal principle (also called the "One," "Absolute Reality," or "Be-ness"), which is beyond human comprehension. She describes how "Matter" (Substance) and "Spirit" (Ideation) are joined within the Absolute Reality. When our souls move from this consciousness, we lose the link between Matter and Spirit, becoming Matter only. From there, we must struggle to reach a perfect reality once more. Note how Blavatsky uses scientific terms such as "electrifying every atom into life." Because Theosophy was seen as a perfect union of science and religion, Blavatsky used much of the scientific language of the day.

The second proposition, according to Blavatsky, concerns a universal law of periodicity, of ebb and flow. Here, again, the author appeals to science, although the concept of ebb and flow is also drawn from Hinduism. What it means is that all actions have an opposite, and the two depend on each other: "Day and Night and Life and Death" are just two examples. At the same time, all aspects of existence—from the smallest soul to whole universes—are engaged in a constant process of evolution and reincarnation: manifesting, going through cyclical stages of development, and then disappearing, only to be reborn again in other forms.

The last proposition lays out where our souls come from: They are "sparks" from the "Over-Soul," which is the Absolute Reality mentioned earlier. It is key to note the importance of the individual. Blavatsky writes that the "pivotal doctrine" is that the human being must struggle "through personal effort and merit." Unlike traditional Christianity, Judaism, and Islam, all of which have elaborate systems of community (the People of God, the Chosen People, and the Ummah, respectively), Theosophy as it is explained in *The Secret Doctrine* is starkly individualist. It focuses on the soul's own journey through cycles of reincarnation. Blavatsky goes on to mention both the Bible and the Hindu Puranas, writing that the seven stages of creation in the *Book of Dzyan* are, in fact, the same as what is described in these two texts. Her purpose is to underline that *Dzyan* is the most ancient source of knowledge, from which all others are derived. In this sense, Theosophists believe that all current religious traditions are fundamentally linked.

◆ Seven Stages of the Creation of the Universe: Stanzas I–VII

In this section, Blavatsky lays out how the universe was created in seven stages, according to the seven stanzas in *Dzyan*. She holds that the human (or Western) mind cannot comprehend the first two stages, so she tells the reader that it is best to stop trying. Apparently, an individual either has the intuition to understand the idea of an Absolute nothingness (Pralaya) or does not.

Stanza III describes the first separation from Absolute Oneness—in other words, the first creation of "Monads," which means any type of substance that materializes separately from the One. Stanza IV identifies the first Monads created out of the One as the seven "Dhyan Chohans." These seven intelligent Beings adjust and control evolution. Thus, Theosophists expound upon evolution, differing from traditional Christianity (where each animal is created in toto from the beginning) and from traditional science (where the mechanism for change is contained with evolution itself). Theosophists believe that evolution is occurring but that there are intelligent Beings directing it.

Stanza V describes how the earth came into material form. Theosophy states that each planet (and, indeed, each soul on the planet) is cycling through an evolution of seven stages, where the first and last are closest to the Absolute Reality. The fourth stage (or, as Blavatsky refers to it, the "fourth great period") is the farthest away from the One and is therefore when we are at our most material. After this period (which might take millions of years), the earth will begin the cycle back to its spirit state.

Blavatsky then gives a sense of the elitist nature of Theosophy. It was never meant to be a philosophy for the masses; only a select few were ever expected to begin to understand it. Blavatsky identifies herself as one of the profane material creatures, albeit more able to understand than most. She also calls herself "the writer, or rather the humble recorder" and, at the end of the section, refers to "a Master and his chelas (or disciples)." Blavatsky believed that invisible Masters dictated the text of *The Secret Doctrine* to her. Theosophists explain that there are seven Masters (also called "Adepts") who keep a library of the world's knowledge, helped by disciples called chelas. The Masters are men who have "perfected their physical, mental, psychic, and spiritual" states and have reached higher states of consciousness. They are thus far from the material and invisible to most men and women.

♦ Theosophy and Science

The question of how popular science accorded with the world of the spirit is essential to *The Secret Doctrine* and surfaces many times. Although Blavatsky draws on modern science in *The Secret Doctrine*, she criticizes scientists in this section, beginning with the first point under the subhead "Summing Up." She feels that scientists are fundamentally flawed, since they do not believe in the "soul of things." Preempting the criticism with which she is sure she will be met, Blavatsky maintains that it is useless to try to convince scientists of the ancient cosmogony, which, she writes, is based on facts passed down over thousands of generations. The author again points to the hubris of the human being: Just because we cannot see it does not mean that it is not there.

A few paragraphs later, Blavatsky issues an invective against materialist scientists, who are seen to be so authoritative that people believe whatever they say. She casts doubt upon their competency to judge her work by penning an addendum (not included here) showing how scientists often make mistakes. She also criticizes them for assuming "that Truth is the exclusive property of the Western world." She says that scientists follow Aristotle's Western perspective, whereas Theosophists follow Hermes' universal wisdom. This is a reference to an early Gnostic text (ca. 50–300 CE) attributed to Hermes Trismegistus, a Greco-Egyptian god. Blavatsky and her circle inherited this idea of "Hermetic" texts from earlier European occultists, such as the Rosicrucians. She writes that Theosophists recognize that "heathens"—Hindus and Hermeticists—offer the key to Truth.

Blavatsky readily admits that Theosophy adopted aspects of evolutionary science. In fact, this a restatement of themes discussed earlier—namely, how evolution functions by its own mechanism but is directed by beings according to karmic laws. The author refers to the "survival of the fittest" specifically, the aspect of Darwinian theory that was the focus of much debate. Many Christians worried that this concept would undermine charity and protection of the weak and encourage militarism. Blavatsky does not share this concern, since she believes that the One directs evolution.

♦ Divinity and Ritual

In the sixth point under "Summing Up," Blavatsky elaborates on her notion of the divine. She ridicules the concept of anthropomorphic deities and dismisses the idea that God and angels have personalities and offer protection or punishment. Rather, she explains, there is a great hierarchy of beings, each of which is connected to the One and is simply applying immutable karmic and cosmic laws. These beings are not men but have been or will be men in a past or coming cycle. At the end of this section, Blavatsky describes how even material humans (as a follower of Theosophy)

can succeed in arriving at full knowledge of the infinite harmony and, in doing so, be protected within it.

Theosophy was profoundly anticlerical and did away with old conceptions of ritual administered by a priest or pastor. The Americans who gathered in Blavatsky's New York apartment were sure that ultimate Truth lay outside of their Protestant denominations. Here, that anticlericalism is reflected when Blavatsky counsels Theosophists to create an altar in their hearts, where it will be invisible and unmentioned, and to privilege their own souls as the sole mediators with the "Universal Spirit." This idea draws on Protestantism, which also privileges an individual's connection to God but goes beyond it, describing all forms of external worship practice as unnecessary.

♦ West Meets East

In the last quarter of the excerpt, Blavatsky gives weight to occultist truths by explaining that they have been passed down "from time immemorial." She mentions Hermes again and ends with Paracelsus, a well-known fifteenth-century alchemist and occultist. The quote that ends this paragraph is usually attributed to Seneca, a first-century Roman philosopher and dramatist. These allusions link Theosophists to a long line of earlier and contemporaneous Western occultists. The main purpose of this paragraph is to underscore the constant cycles (evolutions) in which all matter travels. There is, therefore, no such thing as death; matter exists but is manifested materially or not at any given point during its cycle.

Blavatsky then writes that, in fact, Western and Eastern philosophies are in agreement regarding the root of all things. At the end of this long paragraph, she begins to tell the reader how human essence (also called Ego or soul) evolves into matter: it cycles through vegetable and animal stages first. In this sense, Theosophy draws loosely on the idea of the evolution of species but believes that each Ego simultaneously contains the elements of all past and future incarnations.

In a reference to the Christian Bible ("render unto Caesar what is Caesar's"), Blavatsky demonstrates that the material world has a role to play in her theology of spirit, understanding that Theosophists must also participate in secular activities in their everyday lives. Like the Gospel writers, however, she warns them not to forget the preeminence of the spirit. Although the biblical quote relates primarily to taxation, here Blavatsky refers to the role of science. There is a place for science, she writes, but Theosophy rejects scientists' attempts to equate consciousness with physiological processes. She is being sarcastic when she refers to science's "high priests."

In the final paragraph of the excerpt, Blavatsky acknowledges that in our current incarnation (the "Fifth Race" of seven that will appear), we humans are likely too far away from the ultimate Truth—too close to the material—to truly understand the Theosophical message. When the Sixth Race looks back on this time, Blavatsky predicts, it will be obvious to them that *The Secret Doctrine* is true, but until that time Theosophists are destined to be ridiculed.

"There is one absolute Reality which antecedes all manifested, conditioned, being. This Infinite and Eternal Cause... is the rootless root of 'all that was, is, or ever shall be.'"

(Section 1)

"The Eternity of the Universe in toto as a boundless plane; periodically 'the playground of numberless Universes incessantly manifesting and disappearing,' called 'the manifesting stars,' and the 'sparks of Eternity.'... [There is] absolute universality of that law of periodicity, of flux and reflux, ebb and flow, which physical science has observed and recorded in all departments of nature."

(Section 1)

"The pivotal doctrine of the Esoteric philosophy admits no privileges or special gifts in man, save those won by his own Ego through personal effort and merit throughout a long series of metempsychoses and reincarnations."

(Section 1)

"Meanwhile the generations of our Fifth Race will continue to be led away by prejudice and preconceptions. Occult Sciences will have the finger of scorn pointed at them from every street corner, and everyone will seek to ridicule and crush them in the name, and for the greater glory, of Materialism and its so-called Science."

(Section 1)

Audience

Although Blavatsky addresses her book to the "general reader," the actual readership of *The Secret Doctrine* has been comparatively small, composed mainly of dedicated Theosophists and occultists. The book was written in English, and Blavatsky's intended audience was Western. This is why she continually compares Western to Eastern sources and refers to Western precedents such as the works of Hermes and Paracelsus, which were familiar to Victorian occultists. Much of *The Secret Doctrine*'s influence is indirect and best realized through the publication of many Theosophist, Spiritualist, and New Age books that are rooted in its teachings. Today, *The Secret Doctrine* is available online, and Theosophist societies hold lectures and book studies to help first-time readers better comprehend its meaning.

Impact

The Secret Doctrine and the Theosophical Society have had a tremendous impact on certain populations, particularly in North America, England, Germany, India, and Sri Lanka. Theosophists still exist today, but Blavatsky's ideas have permeated more widely as well, particularly in encouraging the second flowering of Spiritualism in the 1920s and 1930s and the development of New Age in the 1960s. A number of new religious groups claim to have received direct communication from the Masters: the German Anthroposophical movement, the English Liberal Catholic Church, and the American "I am" movement.

More broadly, scholars have traced the impact of Theosophy in abstract art, in interfaith dialogue, and in the Indian independence movement. Theosophists were among the first Westerners to live in India and tell Hindus and Buddhists that their beliefs were not only valid but also the basis of all knowledge. This concept provided inspiration to a number of key Indian intellectuals who called for independence from colonial Britain in the first several decades of the twentieth century. The Theosophist Bhagwan Das was an important public advocate for freedom from British rule, and Annie Besant, the president of the Theosophical Society in India, was a tireless promoter of Indian self-rule. As well, Jawaharlal Nehru, the first prime minister of India, was tutored as a teen by a Theosophist and later wrote about the deep intellectual debt he owed the movement.

Further Reading

■ Books

Campbell, Bruce F. *Ancient Wisdom Revived: A History of the Theosophical Movement*. Berkeley: University of California Press, 1980.

Godwin, Joscelyn. *The Theosophical Enlightenment*. Albany: State University of New York Press, 1994.

Johnson, K. Paul. *The Masters Revealed: Madame Blavatsky and the Myth of the Great White Lodge*. Albany: State University of New York Press, 1994.

Prothero, Stephen R. *The White Buddhist: The Asian Odyssey of Henry Steel Olcott*. Bloomington: Indiana University Press, 1996.

◆ Web Site

Blavatsky Net—Theosophy Web site. http://www.blavatsky.net/blavatsky/secret_doctrine/secret_doctrine.htm

—Commentary by Hillary Kaell

Questions for Further Study

1. Why do you think that *The Secret Doctrine* and Theosophy in general had such appeal for upper-class professional people? Why was it not a grassroots movement among working-class people or the masses?

2. Blavatsky's name, along with Theosophy, is often associated with New Age, occultist, and spiritualist movements—and, indeed, the late 1800s in America was a time when spiritualism, séances, and the like became immensely popular. For this reason, she and the movement might be regarded by some as "flakey" or eccentric. Is this a fair representation of her, her work, and the movement? Explain.

3. To the extent that it synthesizes science and religion, what similarities, if any, does *The Secret Doctrine* have with *On the Nature of Things* by the Roman writer Lucretius? How do the two philosophies differ?

4. Through the Western world since at least the time that Blavatsky wrote, a significant number of people have become, as the entry puts it, "unhappy in Christian denominations" and have turned to mysticism, occultism, and Eastern religions such as Hinduism. Why do you think this is so? What do these belief systems offer that Christianity and other traditional Western religions fail to offer? Or do you think that these alternative systems fulfill some people's need for things exotic and foreign?

5. Consider a meeting between Helena Blavatsky and Emma Goldman, author of "The Philosophy of Atheism," in which they discuss theology. To what extent, if any, do you think Goldman would agree with this statement from *The Secret Doctrine:* " The pivotal doctrine of the Esoteric philosophy admits no privileges or special gifts in man, save those won by his own Ego through personal effort and merit"?

THE SECRET DOCTRINE: DOCUMENT TEXT

1875 CE

—*Helena Blavatsky*

♦ Proem

. . .

Before the reader proceeds to the consideration of the Stanzas from the Book of Dzyan which form the basis of the present work, it is absolutely necessary that he should be made acquainted with the few fundamental conceptions which underlie and pervade the entire system of thought to which his attention is invited. These basic ideas are few in number, and on their clear apprehension depends the understanding of all that follows.

The Secret Doctrine establishes three fundamental propositions:—

(a) An Omnipresent, Eternal, Boundless, and Immutable PRINCIPLE on which all speculation is impossible, since it transcends the power of human conception and could only be dwarfed by any human expression or similitude. It is beyond the range and reach of thought—in the words of Mandukya, "unthinkable and unspeakable."

To render these ideas clearer to the general reader, let him set out with the postulate that there is one absolute Reality which antecedes all manifested, conditioned, being. This Infinite and Eternal Cause—dimly formulated in the "Unconscious" and "Unknowable" of current European philosophy—is the rootless root of "all that was, is, or ever shall be." It is of course devoid of all attributes and is essentially without any relation to manifested, finite Being. It is "Be-ness" rather than Being (in Sanskrit, Sat), and is beyond all thought or speculation.

This "Be-ness" is symbolised in the Secret Doctrine under two aspects. On the one hand, absolute abstract Space, representing bare subjectivity, the one thing which no human mind can either exclude from any conception, or conceive of by itself. On the other, absolute Abstract Motion representing Unconditioned Consciousness. Even our Western thinkers have shown that Consciousness is inconceivable to us apart from change, and motion best symbolises change, its essential characteristic. This latter aspect of the one Reality, is also symbolised by the term

"The Great Breath," a symbol sufficiently graphic to need no further elucidation. Thus, then, the first fundamental axiom of the Secret Doctrine is this metaphysical ONE ABSOLUTE—BE-NESS—symbolised by finite intelligence as the theological Trinity....

Parabrahm (the One Reality, the Absolute) is the field of Absolute Consciousness, i.e., that Essence which is out of all relation to conditioned existence, and of which conscious existence is a conditioned symbol. But once that we pass in thought from this (to us) Absolute Negation, duality supervenes in the contrast of Spirit (or consciousness) and Matter, Subject and Object.

Spirit (or Consciousness) and Matter are, however, to be regarded, not as independent realities, but as the two facets or aspects of the Absolute (Parabrahm), which constitute the basis of conditioned Being whether subjective or objective.

Considering this metaphysical triad as the Root from which proceeds all manifestation, the great Breath assumes the character of precosmic Ideation. It is the fons et origo of force and of all individual consciousness, and supplies the guiding intelligence in the vast scheme of cosmic Evolution. On the other hand, precosmic root-substance (Mulaprakriti) is that aspect of the Absolute which underlies all the objective planes of Nature.

Just as pre-Cosmic Ideation is the root of all individual consciousness, so pre-Cosmic Substance is the substratum of matter in the various grades of its differentiation.

Hence it will be apparent that the contrast of these two aspects of the Absolute is essential to the existence of the "Manifested Universe." Apart from Cosmic Substance, Cosmic Ideation could not manifest as individual consciousness, since it is only through a vehicle of matter that consciousness wells up as "I am I," a physical basis being necessary to focus a ray of the Universal Mind at a certain stage of complexity. Again, apart from Cosmic Ideation, Cosmic Substance would remain an empty abstraction, and no emergence of consciousness could ensue.

The "Manifested Universe," therefore, is pervaded by duality, which is, as it were, the very essence of its EX-istence as "manifestation."

But just as the opposite poles of subject and object, spirit and matter, are but aspects of the One Unity in which they are synthesized, so, in the manifested Universe, there is "that" which links spirit to matter, subject to object.

This something, at present unknown to Western speculation, is called by the occultists Fohat. It is the "bridge" by which the "Ideas" existing in the "Divine Thought" are impressed on Cosmic substance as the "laws of Nature." Fohat is thus the dynamic energy of Cosmic Ideation; or, regarded from the other side, it is the intelligent medium, the guiding power of all manifestation, the "Thought Divine" transmitted and made manifest through the Dhyan Chohans, the Architects of the visible World. Thus from Spirit, or Cosmic Ideation, comes our consciousness; from Cosmic Substance the several vehicles in which that consciousness is individualised and attains to self—or reflective—consciousness; while Fohat, in its various manifestations, is the mysterious link between Mind and Matter, the animating principle electrifying every atom into life....

Further, the Secret Doctrine affirms:—

(b) The Eternity of the Universe in toto as a boundless plane; periodically "the playground of numberless Universes incessantly manifesting and disappearing," called "the manifesting stars," and the "sparks of Eternity." "The Eternity of the Pilgrim" is like a wink of the Eye of Self-Existence (Book of Dzyan). "The appearance and disappearance of Worlds is like a regular tidal ebb of flux and reflux."

This second assertion of the Secret Doctrine is the absolute universality of that law of periodicity, of flux and reflux, ebb and flow, which physical science has observed and recorded in all departments of nature. An alternation such as that of Day and Night, Life and Death, Sleeping and Waking, is a fact so common, so perfectly universal and without exception, that it is easy to comprehend that in it we see one of the absolutely fundamental laws of the universe.

Moreover, the Secret Doctrine teaches:—

(c) The fundamental identity of all Souls with the Universal Over-Soul, the latter being itself an aspect of the Unknown Root; and the obligatory pilgrimage for every Soul—a spark of the former—through the Cycle of Incarnation (or "Necessity") in accordance with Cyclic and Karmic law, during the whole term. In other words, no purely spiritual Buddhi (divine Soul) can have an independent (conscious) existence before the spark which issued from the pure Essence of the Universal Sixth principle,—or the OVER-SOUL,—has (a) passed through every elemental form of the phenomenal world of that Manvantara, and (b) acquired individuality, first by natural impulse, and then by self-induced and self-devised efforts (checked by its Karma), thus ascending through all the degrees of intelligence, from the lowest to the highest Manas, from mineral and plant, up to the holiest archangel (Dhyani-Buddha). The pivotal doctrine of the Esoteric philosophy admits no privileges or special gifts in man, save those won by his own Ego through personal effort and merit throughout a long series of metempsychoses and reincarnations....

Such are the basic conceptions on which the Secret Doctrine rests.

It would not be in place here to enter upon any defence or proof of their inherent reasonableness; nor can I pause to show how they are, in fact, contained—though too often under a misleading guise—in every system of thought or philosophy worthy of the name.

Once that the reader has gained a clear comprehension of them and realised the light which they throw on every problem of life, they will need no further justification in his eyes, because their truth will be to him as evident as the sun in heaven. I pass on, therefore, to the subject matter of the Stanzas as given in this volume, adding a skeleton outline of them, in the hope of thereby rendering the task of the student more easy, by placing before him in a few words the general conception therein explained.

. . . The history of cosmic evolution, as traced in the Stanzas, is, so to say, the abstract algebraical formula of that Evolution. Hence the student must not expect to find there an account of all the stages and transformations which intervene between the first beginnings of "Universal" evolution and our present state. To give such an account would be as impossible as it would be incomprehensible to men who cannot even grasp the nature of the plane of existence next to that to which, for the moment, their consciousness is limited.

The Stanzas, therefore, give an abstract formula which can be applied, mutatis mutandis, to all evolution: to that of our tiny earth, to that of the chain of planets of which that earth forms one, to the solar Universe to which that chain belongs, and so on, in an ascending scale, till the mind reels and is exhausted in the effort.

The seven Stanzas given in this volume represent the seven terms of this abstract formula. They refer to, and describe the seven great stages of the evolutionary process, which are spoken of in the Puranas as the "Seven Creations," and in the Bible as the "Days" of Creation.

The First Stanza describes the state of the ONE ALL during Pralaya, before the first flutter of re-awakening manifestation.

A moment's thought shows that such a state can only be symbolised; to describe it is impossible. Nor can it be symbolised except in negatives; for, since it is the state of Absoluteness per se, it can possess none of those specific attributes which serve us to describe objects in positive terms. Hence that state can only be suggested by the negatives of all those most abstract attributes which men feel rather than conceive, as the remotest limits attainable by their power of conception.

The stage described in Stanza II is, to a western mind, so nearly identical with that mentioned in the first Stanza, that to express the idea of its difference would require a treatise in itself. Hence it must be left to the intuition and the higher faculties of the reader to grasp, as far as he can, the meaning of the allegorical phrases used. Indeed it must be remembered that all these Stanzas appeal to the inner faculties rather than to the ordinary comprehension of the physical brain.

Stanza III describes the Re-awakening of the Universe to life after Pralaya. It depicts the emergence of the "Monads" from their state of absorption within the ONE; the earliest and highest stage in the formation of "Worlds," the term Monad being one which may apply equally to the vastest Solar System or the tiniest atom.

Stanza IV shows the differentiation of the "Germ" of the Universe into the septenary hierarchy of conscious Divine Powers, who are the active manifestations of the One Supreme Energy. They are the framers, shapers, and ultimately the creators of all the manifested Universe, in the only sense in which the name "Creator" is intelligible; they inform and guide it; they are the intelligent Beings who adjust and control evolution, embodying in themselves those manifestations of the ONE LAW, which we know as "The Laws of Nature."

Generically, they are known as the Dhyan Chohans, though each of the various groups has its own designation in the Secret Doctrine.

This stage of evolution is spoken of in Hindu mythology as the "Creation" of the Gods.

In Stanza V the process of world-formation is described:—First, diffused Cosmic Matter, then the fiery "whirlwind," the first stage in the formation of a nebula. That nebula condenses, and after passing through various transformations, forms a Solar Universe, a planetary chain, or a single planet, as the case may be.

The subsequent stages in the formation of a "World" are indicated in Stanza VI, which brings the evolution of such a world down to its fourth great period, corresponding to the period in which we are now living.

Stanza VII continues the history, tracing the descent of life down to the appearance of Man; and thus closes the first Book of the Secret Doctrine.

The development of "Man" from his first appearance on this earth in this Round to the state in which we now find him will form the subject of Book II.

The Stanzas which form the thesis of every section are given throughout in their modern translated version, as it would be worse than useless to make the subject still more difficult by introducing the archaic phraseology of the original, with its puzzling style and words. Extracts are given from the Chinese Thibetan and Sanskrit translations of the original Senzar Commentaries and Glosses on the Book of Dzyan—these being now rendered for the first time into a European language. It is almost unnecessary to state that only portions of the seven Stanzas are here given. Were they published complete they would remain incomprehensible to all save the few higher occultists. Nor is there any need to assure the reader that, no more than most of the profane, does the writer, or rather the humble recorder, understand those forbidden passages. To facilitate the reading, and to avoid the too frequent reference to foot-notes, it was thought best to blend together texts and glosses, using the Sanskrit and Tibetan proper names whenever those cannot be avoided, in preference to giving the originals. The more so as the said terms are all accepted synonyms, the former only being used between a Master and his chelas (or disciples)....

♦ **Summing Up**

. . .

Let us recapitulate and show, by the vastness of the subjects expounded, how difficult, if not impossible, it is to do them full justice.

(1) The Secret Doctrine is the accumulated Wisdom of the Ages, and its cosmogony alone is the most stupendous and elaborate system: e.g., even in the exotericism of the Puranas. But such is the mysterious power of Occult symbolism, that the facts which have actually occupied countless gen-

erations of initiated seers and prophets to marshal, to set down and explain, in the bewildering series of evolutionary progress, are all recorded on a few pages of geometrical signs and glyphs. The flashing gaze of those seers has penetrated into the very kernel of matter, and recorded the soul of things there, where an ordinary profane, however learned, would have perceived but the external work of form. But modern science believes not in the "soul of things," and hence will reject the whole system of ancient cosmogony. It is useless to say that the system in question is no fancy of one or several isolated individuals. That it is the uninterrupted record covering thousands of generations of Seers whose respective experiences were made to test and to verify the traditions passed orally by one early race to another, of the teachings of higher and exalted beings, who watched over the childhood of Humanity. That for long ages, the "Wise Men" of the Fifth Race, of the stock saved and rescued from the last cataclysm and shifting of continents, had passed their lives in learning, not teaching. How did they do so? It is answered: by checking, testing, and verifying in every department of nature the traditions of old by the independent visions of great adepts; i.e., men who have developed and perfected their physical, mental, psychic, and spiritual organisations to the utmost possible degree. No vision of one adept was accepted till it was checked and confirmed by the visions—so obtained as to stand as independent evidence—of other adepts, and by centuries of experiences.

(2) The fundamental Law in that system, the central point from which all emerged, around and toward which all gravitates, and upon which is hung the philosophy of the rest, is the One homogeneous divine Substance-Principle, the one radical cause.... It is called "Substance-Principle," for it becomes "substance" on the plane of the manifested Universe, an illusion, while it remains a "principle" in the beginningless and endless abstract, visible and invisible Space. It is the omnipresent Reality: impersonal, because it contains all and everything. Its impersonality is the fundamental conception of the System. It is latent in every atom in the Universe, and is the Universe itself. (See in chapters on Symbolism, "Primordial Substance, and Divine Thought.")

(3) The Universe is the periodical manifestation of this unknown Absolute Essence. To call it "essence," however, is to sin against the very spirit of the philosophy. For though the noun may be derived in this case from the verb esse, "to be," yet It cannot

be identified with a being of any kind, that can be conceived by human intellect. It is best described as neither Spirit nor matter, but both. "Parabrahmam and Mulaprakriti" are One, in reality, yet two in the Universal conception of the manifested, even in the conception of the One Logos, its first manifestation, to which, as the able lecturer in the "Notes on the Bhagavadgita" shows, It appears from the objective standpoint of the One Logos as Mulaprakriti and not as Parabrahmam; as its veil and not the one reality hidden behind, which is unconditioned and absolute.

(4) The Universe is called, with everything in it, Maya, because all is temporary therein, from the ephemeral life of a fire-fly to that of the Sun. Compared to the eternal immutability of the One, and the changelessness of that Principle, the Universe, with its evanescent ever-changing forms, must be necessarily, in the mind of a philosopher, no better than a will-o'-the-wisp. Yet, the Universe is real enough to the conscious beings in it, which are as unreal as it is itself.

(5) Everything in the Universe, throughout all its kingdoms, is conscious: i.e., endowed with a consciousness of its own kind and on its own plane of perception. We men must remember that because we do not perceive any signs—which we can recognise—of consciousness, say, in stones, we have no right to say that no consciousness exists there. There is no such thing as either "dead" or "blind" matter, as there is no "Blind" or "Unconscious" Law. These find no place among the conceptions of Occult philosophy. The latter never stops at surface appearances, and for it the noumenal essences have more reality than their objective counterparts; it resembles therein the mediaeval Nominalists, for whom it was the Universals that were the realities and the particulars which existed only in name and human fancy.

(6) The Universe is worked and guided from within outwards. As above so it is below, as in heaven so on earth; and man—the microcosm and miniature copy of the macrocosm—is the living witness to this Universal Law, and to the mode of its action. We see that every external motion, act, gesture, whether voluntary or mechanical, organic or mental, is produced and preceded by internal feeling or emotion, will or volition, and thought or mind. As no outward motion or change, when normal, in man's external body can take place unless provoked by an inward impulse, given through one of the three functions named, so with the external or manifested Universe. The whole Kosmos is guided, controlled, and animated by almost endless series of Hierarchies of

sentient Beings, each having a mission to perform, and who—whether we give to them one name or another, and call them Dhyan-Chohans or Angels— are "messengers" in the sense only that they are the agents of Karmic and Cosmic Laws. They vary infinitely in their respective degrees of consciousness and intelligence; and to call them all pure Spirits without any of the earthly alloy "which time is wont to prey upon" is only to indulge in poetical fancy. For each of these Beings either was, or prepares to become, a man, if not in the present, then in a past or a coming cycle (Manvantara). They are perfected, when not incipient, men; and differ morally from the terrestrial human beings on their higher (less material) spheres, only in that they are devoid of the feeling of personality and of the human emotional nature—two purely earthly characteristics. The former, or the "perfected," have become free from those feelings, because (a) they have no longer fleshly bodies—an ever-numbing weight on the Soul; and (b) the pure spiritual element being left untrammelled and more free, they are less influenced by maya than man can ever be, unless he is an adept who keeps his two personalities—the spiritual and the physical—entirely separated. The incipient monads, having never had terrestrial bodies yet, can have no sense of personality or ego-ism. That which is meant by "personality," being a limitation and a relation, or, as defined by Coleridge, "individuality existing in itself but with a nature as a ground," the term cannot of course be applied to non-human entities; but, as a fact insisted upon by generations of Seers, none of these Beings, high or low, have either individuality or personality as separate Entities, i.e., they have no individuality in the sense in which a man says, "I am myself and no one else;" in other words, they are conscious of no such distinct separateness as men and things have on earth. Individuality is the characteristic of their respective hierarchies, not of their units; and these characteristics vary only with the degree of the plane to which those hierarchies belong: the nearer to the region of Homogeneity and the One Divine, the purer and the less accentuated that individuality in the Hierarchy. They are finite, in all respects, with the exception of their higher principles—the immortal sparks reflecting the universal divine flame—individualized and separated only on the spheres of Illusion by a differentiation as illusive as the rest. They are "Living Ones," because they are the streams projected on the Kosmic screen of illusion from the absolute life; beings in whom life cannot become extinct, before

the fire of ignorance is extinct in those who sense these "Lives." Having sprung into being under the quickening influence of the uncreated beam, the reflection of the great Central Sun that radiates on the shores of the river of Life, it is the inner principle in them which belongs to the waters of immortality, while its differentiated clothing is as perishable as man's body. Therefore Young was right in saying that "Angels are men of a superior kind" and no more. They are neither "ministering" nor "protecting" angels; nor are they "Harbingers of the Most High" still less the "Messengers of wrath" of any God such as man's fancy has created. To appeal to their protection is as foolish as to believe that their sympathy may be secured by any kind of propitiation; for they are, as much as man himself is, the slaves and creatures of immutable Karmic and Kosmic law. The reason for it is evident. Having no elements of personality in their essence they can have no personal qualities, such as attributed by men, in their exoteric religions, to their anthropomorphic God—a jealous and exclusive God who rejoices and feels wrathful, is pleased with sacrifice, and is more despotic in his vanity than any finite foolish man. Man, as shown in Book II, being a compound of the essences of all those celestial Hierarchies may succeed in making himself, as such, superior, in one sense, to any hierarchy or class, or even combination of them. "Man can neither propitiate nor command the Devas," it is said. But, by paralyzing his lower personality, and arriving thereby at the full knowledge of the non-separateness of his higher Self from the One absolute Self, man can, even during his terrestrial life, become as "One of Us." Thus it is, by eating of the fruit of knowledge which dispels ignorance, that man becomes like one of the Elohim or the Dhyanis; and once on their plane the Spirit of Solidarity and perfect Harmony, which reigns in every Hierarchy, must extend over him and protect him in every particular.

The chief difficulty which prevents men of science from believing in divine as well as in nature Spirits is their materialism. The main impediment before the Spiritualist which hinders him from believing in the same, while preserving a blind belief in the "Spirits" of the Departed, is the general ignorance of all, except some Occultists and Kabalists, about the true essence and nature of matter. It is on the acceptance or rejection of the theory of the Unity of all in Nature, in its ultimate Essence, that mainly rests the belief or unbelief in the existence around us of other conscious beings besides the Spirits of the Dead. It is on the right comprehension of the primeval Evolution of Spirit-Matter and its real essence that the student has to depend for the further elucidation in his mind of the Occult Cosmogony, and for the only sure clue which can guide his subsequent studies.

In sober truth, as just shown, every "Spirit" so-called is either a disembodied or a future man. As from the highest Archangel (Dhyan Chohan) down to the last conscious "Builder" (the inferior class of Spiritual Entities), all such are men, having lived aeons ago, in other Manvantaras, on this or other Spheres; so the inferior, semi-intelligent and non-intelligent Elementals—are all future men. That fact alone—that a Spirit is endowed with intelligence—is a proof to the Occultist that that Being must have been a man, and acquired his knowledge and intelligence throughout the human cycle. There is but one indivisible and absolute Omniscience and Intelligence in the Universe, and this thrills throughout every atom and infinitesimal point of the whole finite Kosmos which hath no bounds, and which people call Space, considered independently of anything contained in it. But the first differentiation of its reflection in the manifested World is purely Spiritual, and the Beings generated in it are not endowed with a consciousness that has any relation to the one we conceive of. They can have no human consciousness or Intelligence before they have acquired such, personally and individually. This may be a mystery, yet it is a fact, in Esoteric philosophy, and a very apparent one too.

The whole order of nature evinces a progressive march towards a higher life. There is design in the action of the seemingly blindest forces. The whole process of evolution with its endless adaptations is a proof of this. The immutable laws that weed out the weak and feeble species, to make room for the strong, and which ensure the "survival of the fittest," though so cruel in their immediate action—all are working toward the grand end. The very fact that adaptations do occur, that the fittest do survive in the struggle for existence, shows that what is called "unconscious Nature" is in reality an aggregate of forces manipulated by semi-intelligent beings (Elementals) guided by High Planetary Spirits, (Dhyan Chohans), whose collective aggregate forms the manifested verbum of the unmanifested logos, and constitutes at one and the same time the mind of the Universe and its immutable law.

Three distinct representations of the Universe in its three distinct aspects are impressed upon our thought by the esoteric philosophy: the pre-existing (evolved from) the ever-existing; and the phenomenal—the world of illusion, the reflection, and shadow thereof. During the great mystery and drama of life known as the Manvantara, real Kosmos is like the object placed behind the white screen upon which are thrown the Chinese shadows, called forth by the magic lantern. The actual figures and things remain invisible, while the wires of evolution are pulled by the unseen hands; and men and things are thus but the reflections, on the white field, of the realities behind the snares of Mahamaya, or the great Illusion. This was taught in every philosophy, in every religion, ante as well as post diluvian, in India and Chaldea, by the Chinese as by the Grecian Sages. In the former countries these three Universes were allegorized, in exoteric teachings, by the three trinities emanating from the Central eternal germ and forming with it a Supreme Unity: the initial, the manifested, and the Creative Triad, or the three in One. The last is but the symbol, in its concrete expression, of the first ideal two. Hence Esoteric philosophy passes over the necessarianism of this purely metaphysical conception, and calls the first one, only, the Ever Existing....

The writer hopes that, superficially handled as may be the comments on the Seven Stanzas, enough has been given in this cosmogonic portion of the work to show Archaic teachings to be more scientific (in the modern sense of the word) on their very face, than any other ancient Scriptures left to be regarded and judged on their exoteric aspect. Since, however, as confessed before, this work withholds far more than it gives out, the student is invited to use his own intuitions. Our chief care is to elucidate that which has already been given out, and, to our regret, very incorrectly at times; to supplement the knowledge hinted at—whenever and wherever possible—by additional matter; and to bulwark our doctrines against the too strong attacks of modern Sectarianism, and more especially against those of our latter-day Materialism, very often miscalled Science, whereas, in reality, the words "Scientists" and "Sciolists" ought alone to bear the responsibility for the many illogical theories offered to the world. In its great ignorance, the public, while blindly accepting everything that emanates from "authorities," and feeling it to be its duty to regard every dictum coming from a man of Science as a proven fact—the public, we say, is taught to scoff at anything brought forward from "heathen" sources. Therefore, as materialistic Scientists can be fought solely with their own weapons—those of controversy and argument—an

Addendum is added to every Book contrasting our respective views and showing how even great authorities may often err. We believe that this can be done effectually by showing the weak points of our opponents, and by proving their too frequent sophisms—made to pass for scientific dicta—to be incorrect. We hold to Hermes and his "Wisdom"—in its universal character; they — to Aristotle as against intuition and the experience of the ages, fancying that Truth is the exclusive property of the Western world. Hence the disagreement. As Hermes says, "Knowledge differs much from sense; for sense is of things that surmount it, but Knowledge (gyi) is the end of sense"—i.e., of the illusion of our physical brain and its intellect; thus emphasizing the contrast between the laboriously acquired knowledge of the senses and mind (manas), and the intuitive omniscience of the Spiritual divine Soul—Buddhi.

Whatever may be the destiny of these actual writings in a remote future, we hope to have proven so far the following facts:

(1) The Secret Doctrine teaches no Atheism, except in the Hindu sense of the word nastika, or the rejection of idols, including every anthropomorphic god. In this sense every Occultist is a Nastika.

(2) It admits a Logos or a collective "Creator" of the Universe; a Demi-urgos—in the sense implied when one speaks of an "Architect" as the "Creator" of an edifice, whereas that Architect has never touched one stone of it, but, while furnishing the plan, left all the manual labour to the masons; in our case the plan was furnished by the Ideation of the Universe, and the constructive labour was left to the Hosts of intelligent Powers and Forces. But that Demiurgos is no personal deity,—i.e., an imperfect extra-cosmic god,—but only the aggregate of the Dhyan-Chohans and the other forces.

As to the latter—

(3) They are dual in their character; being composed of (a) the irrational brute energy, inherent in matter, and (b) the intelligent soul or cosmic consciousness which directs and guides that energy, and which is the Dhyan-Chohanic thought reflecting the Ideation of the Universal mind. This results in a perpetual series of physical manifestations and moral effects on Earth, during manvantaric periods, the whole being subservient to Karma. As that process is not always perfect; and since, however many proofs it may exhibit of a guiding intelligence behind the veil, it still shows gaps and flaws, and even results very often in evident failures—therefore, neither the collective Host (Demiurgos), nor any of the working powers individually, are proper subjects for divine honours or worship. All are entitled to the grateful reverence of Humanity, however, and man ought to be ever striving to help the divine evolution of Ideas, by becoming to the best of his ability a co-worker with nature in the cyclic task. The ever unknowable and incognizable Karana alone, the Causeless Cause of all causes, should have its shrine and altar on the holy and ever untrodden ground of our heart—invisible, intangible, unmentioned, save through "the still small voice" of our spiritual consciousness. Those who worship before it, ought to do so in the silence and the sanctified solitude of their Souls; making their spirit the sole mediator between them and the Universal Spirit, their good actions the only priests, and their sinful intentions the only visible and objective sacrificial victims to the Presence.

(4) Matter is Eternal. It is the Upadhi (the physical basis) for the One infinite Universal Mind to build thereon its ideations. Therefore, the Esotericists maintain that there is no inorganic or dead matter in nature, the distinction between the two made by Science being as unfounded as it is arbitrary and devoid of reason. Whatever Science may think, however—and exact Science is a fickle dame, as we all know by experience—Occultism knows and teaches differently, from time immemorial—from Manu and Hermes down to Paracelsus and his successors.... "Everything is the product of one universal creative effort.... There is nothing dead in Nature. Everything is organic and living, and therefore the whole world appears to be a living organism."

(5) The Universe was evolved out of its ideal plan, upheld through Eternity in the unconsciousness of that which the Vedantins call Parabrahm. This is practically identical with the conclusions of the highest Western Philosophy—"the innate, eternal, and self-existing Ideas" of Plato, now reflected by Von Hartmann. The "unknowable" of Herbert Spencer bears only a faint resemblance to that transcendental Reality believed in by Occultists, often appearing merely a personification of a "force behind phenomena"—an infinite and eternal Energy from which all things proceed, while the author of the "Philosophy of the Unconscious" has come (in this respect only) as near to a solution of the great Mystery as mortal man can.... All the Christian Kabalists understood well the Eastern root idea: The active Power, the "Perpetual motion of the great Breath" only awakens Kosmos at the dawn of every new Period, setting it into motion by means of the two contrary Forces, and

thus causing it to become objective on the plane of Illusion. In other words, that dual motion transfers Kosmos from the plane of the Eternal Ideal into that of finite manifestation, or from the Noumenal to the phenomenal plane. Everything that is, was, and will be, eternally is, even the countless forms, which are finite and perishable only in their objective, not in their ideal Form. They existed as Ideas, in the Eternity, and, when they pass away, will exist as reflections. Neither the form of man, nor that of any animal, plant or stone has ever been created, and it is only on this plane of ours that it commenced "becoming," i.e., objectivising into its present materiality, or expanding from within outwards, from the most sublimated and supersensuous essence into its grossest appearance. Therefore our human forms have existed in the Eternity as astral or ethereal prototypes; according to which models, the Spiritual Beings (or Gods) whose duty it was to bring them into objective being and terrestrial Life, evolved the protoplasmic forms of the future Egos from their own essence. After which, when this human Upadhi, or basic mould was ready, the natural terrestrial Forces began to work on those supersensuous moulds which contained, besides their own, the elements of all the past vegetable and future animal forms of this globe in them. Therefore, man's outward shell passed through every vegetable and animal body before it assumed the human shape. As this will be fully described in Book II, with the Commentaries thereupon, there is no need to say more of it here....

Thus it may be shown that all the fundamental truths of nature were universal in antiquity, and that the basic ideas upon spirit, matter, and the universe, or upon God, Substance, and man, were identical. Taking the two most ancient religious philosophies on the globe, Hinduism and Hermetism, from the scriptures of India and Egypt, the identity of the two is easily recognisable.

Neither the Occultists generally, nor the Theosophists, reject, as erroneously believed by some, the views and theories of the modern scientists, only because these views are opposed to Theosophy. The first rule of our Society is to render unto Caesar what is Caesar's. The Theosophists, therefore, are the first to recognize the intrinsic value of science. But when its high priests resolve consciousness into a secretion from the grey matter of the brain, and everything else in nature into a mode of motion, we protest against the doctrine as being unphilosophical, self-contradictory, and simply absurd, from a scientific point of view, as much and even more than from the occult aspect of the esoteric knowledge.

It is barely possible that the minds of the present generations are not quite ripe for the reception of Occult truths. Such will be the retrospect furnished to the advanced thinkers of the Sixth Root Race of the history of the acceptance of Esoteric Philosophy—fully and unconditionally. Meanwhile the generations of our Fifth Race will continue to be led away by prejudice and preconceptions. Occult Sciences will have the finger of scorn pointed at them from every street corner, and everyone will seek to ridicule and crush them in the name, and for the greater glory, of Materialism and its so-called Science.

Book of Dzyan:	a mysterious, ancient text that archeologists believe never existed
cosmogony:	the study of the origin, evolution, and structure of the universe
fons et origo:	Latin for "source and origin"
Hermes:	Hermes Trismegistus, a Greco-Egyptian god and putative author of a Gnostic text
Kabalists:	followers of Kabbalah, or Jewish mysticism
Karmic law:	the Hindu law of moral causation
Manas:	"mind"
Mandukya:	the name of one of the Hindu Upanishads
Manvantara:	an astronomical measure of a time period, an "age of a Manu," or progenitor of humankind
mutatis mutandis:	Latin for "by changing those things that need to be changed" or, more simply, "the necessary changes having been made"
"Notes on the Bhagavadgita":	a book published by the Theosophical Society; the "able lecturer" was the author T. Subba Row
Paracelsus:	a fifteenth-century alchemist and occultist
Pralaya:	"dissolution"
Puranas:	the scriptural texts that contain the mythologies of Hinduism
Sciolists:	amateurs, dabblers
Senzar Commentaries and Glosses:	mythical commentaries written in Atlantis in the Senzar language
Vedantins:	those who follow the Vedanta, one of the systems of Indian philosophy; essentially, Hindus
Von Hartmann:	Karl Robert Eduard von Hartmann, a nineteenth-century German philosopher
Young:	British poet Edward Young; the quotation is from his 1742 poem "The Complaint; or, Night Thoughts on Life, Death, and Immortality"

Oblong Friends Meeting House (Pawling, Dutchess County, USA).

"ESSENTIAL TRUTHS": DOCUMENT ANALYSIS

"The Friends believe war to be incompatible with Christianity, and seek to promote peaceful methods for the settlement of all the differences between nations and between men."

Overview

"Essential Truths", written by Rufus M. Jones, is a statement of belief of the Religious Society of Friends from the early twentieth century. It is an excerpt from a larger document known as the Uniform Discipline, which was completed in 1900 by Jones and another American Friend, James E. Wood (1839–1925). A discipline is a document that outlines the organizational structure, standards, and beliefs of the Religious Society of Friends and acts a guide for the gathered community of faith. The earliest discipline was written in 1668 by George Fox and served as the basis for later disciplines in England and America. The Uniform Discipline was adopted by a group of Quakers (the informal name for Friends) in 1902, the Five Years Meeting of the Friends in America. The "Essential Truths" section was one of three documents included in the Five Years Meeting's Authorized Declaration of Faith in 1922. The other two documents are George Fox's Letter to the Governor of Barbados, from 1671, and the Declaration of Faith (or Richmond Declaration) put forward at a conference held in Richmond, Indiana, in 1887, written by the English Quaker Joseph Bevan Braithwaite, with the help of two American Quakers, James E. Rhoads and James Carey Thomas.

The Religious Society of Friends was founded in the late 1640s in England by George Fox (1624–1691). Today most Quakers affirm that they are Christians like the Protestant denominations established during and after the Reformation era, including Lutherans, Baptists, Methodists, and the Reformed. Some Quakers do not affirm a strictly Christian identity, however, and have embraced a more universalist perspective about the role of Jesus in history. "Essential Truths" does not represent the beliefs of all Quakers. It applies chiefly to the yearly meetings that

hold membership in the Five Years Meeting, known since 1960 as Friends United Meeting (FUM). (*Yearly meeting* is the Quaker term for both the annual sessions at which the business of a region is done and the name of that geographic region that contains the individual congregations or monthly meetings.) The Quakers of these yearly meetings were most influenced by the evangelical Protestantism of the nineteenth century. They are known as Orthodox Friends or Gurneyite Friends, after the influential English Quaker minister Joseph John Gurney (1788–1847). By the late nineteenth century there were, in fact, three distinct branches of Quakerism in America—Hicksite, Orthodox, and Conservative—all divided over Quaker beliefs and practices. Historically, "Essential Truths" represents an attempt by the Orthodox Quakers to carve out their own religious identity vis-à;-vis the other branches of Quakerism and other Protestant denominations. It followed earlier efforts at Orthodox self-definition, most notably that of the Richmond Conference in 1887 and the Declaration of Faith that came out of that conference.

The member yearly meetings of FUM do not believe that the "Essential Truths" or the other statements in the Authorized Declaration of Faith are authoritative in the same manner as creeds in the Protestant and Catholic churches. The session of the Five Years Meeting in 1912 concluded that the Richmond Declaration and other statements of faith were "not to be regarded as constituting a creed." When the Five Years Meeting finally adopted the three statements into the Authorized Declaration of Faith in 1922, it again emphasized that the statements were not creeds. Further, a study done by the General Board of FUM in 1974 affirmed the decisions of the 1922 meeting of the Five Years Meeting, and it too pointed out the limitations of doctrinal statements.

The Five Years Meeting had recognized the Authorized Declaration of Faith as a statement of belief for over twenty years when a committee drafted a revision of the

Uniform Discipline in 1945. The member yearly meetings could not agree on the doctrinal statements in the revised version, however, and the yearly meetings were left to use those statements as they saw fit. Despite the lack of unity with respect to the Uniform Discipline and the Authorized Declaration of Faith since that time, the "Essential Truths" remains an important statement of Quaker belief within FUM. Of the three documents that comprise the Authorized Declaration of Faith, Essential Truths has been the least controversial, characterized as it is by simplicity and brevity. FUM member yearly meetings still use it as a guide for understanding what they believe about God, Jesus Christ, the Holy Spirit, ministry, the Fall, the Resurrection, the Bible, and other matters of their faith.

Context

The context necessary for understanding "Essential Truths" extends back to the early nineteenth century in America, when the Religious Society of Friends was united by distinct beliefs and practices that separated it from its Protestant and Catholic neighbors. Quakers were quietists, which means that they sought to live a life of meditation and reflection. They focused on the workings of the Holy Spirit on the soul, not on liturgical forms of worship. Friends believed that scripted preaching, sacraments, and other external forms of the expression of grace were distractions in their quest for unity with and obedience to God, and they maintained silence in their worship where they listened for the Holy Spirit. When preaching did occur, it was to be under the direct inspiration of the Holy Spirit, as planning and preparation in the form of writing out the sermon in advance or memorizing it were frowned upon. Such spontaneous preaching could be offered by anyone sitting in the silent worship—man, woman, or child—in obedience to the prompting of the Holy Spirit.

The hallmark belief of the historical Quakers was George Fox's doctrine of the Light, the divine light of Christ within each soul that, if followed, could lead to salvation. This has come to be referred to as the Inward Light or, more commonly, Inner Light. Fox and other early Friends affirmed the Atonement, that is, the belief that Christ died for one's sins, but they subordinated it to their focus on following the Light through the trials and tribulations of life. Unlike the Protestant notion of justification by grace, which privileged the moment of salvation, Quakers rarely spoke of a decisive moment of conversion and instead focused on the process of obeying the Light. Moreover, Quakers did not speak of going to a "church" but gathered together with fellow believers to worship in silence at the "meeting for worship," which did not need a special building and might be held anywhere.

The concept of the Inner Light became controversial in the early nineteenth century as Quakers came into contact with evangelical preachers of the Second Great

Awakening who used revivals to win converts to their faith. Evangelicalism is difficult to define, but the primary characteristic shared by most evangelicals is the emotional conversion experience through which the believer could claim a personal relationship with God. Many evangelicals of the day united justification (the moment of salvation) and sanctification (the process of becoming more holy) into the conversion experience, which meant that a new believer could claim a life of complete holiness and freedom from sin. This was incongruous with the Quaker ideal of gradually working out one's salvation by obeying the Inner Light.

The Great Separation of 1827–1828 at the sessions of Philadelphia Yearly Meeting divided Quakers sympathetic to the beliefs of the evangelicals from those who maintained the centrality of the Inner Light at the expense of traditional "orthodox" Christian doctrines. The latter group, called Hicksites after their leader Elias Hicks (1748–1830), a Long Island farmer, tended to spiritualize Jesus and did not believe in a moment of justification through the death and resurrection of Christ on the cross. Hicks argued that Jesus was the Son of God in the same sense that all people were. Jesus was an example to follow because he had perfectly obeyed his Inner Light. Hicks also claimed that the revelation of scripture was subordinate to the power of the Holy Spirit. In so doing, he did away with many of the doctrines central to traditional Christianity, most notably the atonement and original sin. This prompted the Orthodox group to denounce Hicks and his followers and to emphasize the divinity of Christ, the atonement, and the authority of the Bible over the authority of the Holy Spirit.

The Second Separation, between the Gurneyite Orthodox and the Wilburite Conservatives, happened at New England Yearly Meeting sessions in 1845–1846. The Orthodox Friends were led by Joseph John Gurney, a British biblical scholar, church historian, linguist, and preacher who traveled extensively as a missionary in Europe and America. Although he was a proponent of the Inner Light and the traditional Quaker form of silent worship, Gurney believed (with the evangelicals) that the Bible was the divinely inspired Word of God and that salvation depended on faith in the atoning death of Jesus Christ. His opponent, John Wilbur (1774–1856), was a Rhode Island farmer and land surveyor who traveled in the ministry among Friends in New England and New York yearly meetings during the years 1821–1827 and 1833–1837. Wilbur disagreed with Gurney's belief in the higher authority of the Bible over the Holy Spirit and therefore opposed the Gurneyite focus on Bible study. The Wilburites chose to separate themselves from the "world" that they believed had corrupted Gurney and his followers. Many Orthodox meetings in America were soon divided into Gurneyite and Wilburite factions.

The Orthodox Gurneyite Quakers found themselves divided yet again in the decades after the Civil War. During that period, some Orthodox meetings began implementing a system of planned "programmed" worship in imitation of their evangelical peers, even going so far as to hire pastors who brought prepared messages every Sunday, in direct opposition to George Fox's many injunctions against "the hireling ministry." Friends in Iowa, Indiana, and Kansas resisted these changes and established their own yearly meetings. These so-called Conservative Friends held to the older "unprogrammed" mode of Quaker worship shared by the Hicksites and by the Wilburites, from whom they became largely indistinguishable over time. The contrast between the pastoral and silent modes of Quaker worship is the most visible difference between the Orthodox and the Conservative and Hicksite Friends today, and it reflects the theological divide between those nineteenth-century Quakers who were more receptive to evangelical theology and those who held to Fox's notion of the Light as a gradual quietist means to salvation.

The late nineteenth century introduced new challenges to the Orthodox heirs of Gurney, including a crisis over the place of the ordinances of water baptism and physical communion shared by most evangelical Christians. The Orthodox grew increasingly concerned about the diversity of belief and practice in their yearly meetings. Many were sympathetic with the Conservatives, while others, known as "Waterites," were clearly in the evangelical camp; the latter supported the toleration of water baptism in their worship services. Some Orthodox Quakers, including David B. Updegraff (1830–1894) of Ohio Yearly Meeting, also believed in the evangelical "holiness" notion that once one was saved one could live a sanctified life free of all propensity or desire to sin. As early as 1870, one of the Orthodox yearly meetings, Western Yearly Meeting (of western Indiana), proposed a general council of all the yearly meetings to try to resolve this growing disunity. In 1887 the representatives from the Orthodox yearly meetings finally convened in Richmond, Indiana, to deal with the three major issues that had proved most divisive: the nature of sanctification through the Holy Spirit, the professional ministry, and the ordinances of baptism and Communion. The major players included those committed to evangelical theological principles of the wider Christian world such as Updegraff, conservatives like Joseph Bevan Braithwaite who valued the historic Quaker writings, and a middle party that sought to steer the Orthodox between the extremes of evangelical and Conservative Quakerism.

The Richmond Declaration's statements about God, the Holy Spirit, the Fall, the Bible, and conversion show the influence of evangelical Christianity. The Declaration devotes no attention to Fox's doctrine of the Light except to disavow it by claiming that there is no spiritual light inherent in human beings. On the other hand, it does not explicitly endorse an extreme evangelical "holiness" view on sanctification, as it affirms both justification and sanctification without claiming that one can live a life free from temptation. Nevertheless, its critics have argued that the language of the Declaration on sanctification strays too far from the historical Quaker focus on a life of quiet obedience to God. On the question of a professional min-

istry, the Declaration is rather vague, claiming that worship "stands neither in forms nor in the formal disuse of forms: it may be without words as well as with them, but it must be in spirit and in truth (John 4:24)." Finally, against the Waterites and those who tolerated the ordinances, the Declaration affirms the spiritual meaning of baptism and Communion as means of fellowship with Christ and the Holy Spirit.

The Richmond Conference did not resolve all the issues within Orthodox Quakerism, but it did manage to address pressing concerns for the Orthodox Quakers. The Richmond Declaration provided a statement of belief for the yearly meetings, although not all yearly meetings took identical actions toward it. Western (Indiana), Iowa, Kansas, and North Carolina yearly meetings adopted the Richmond Declaration into their books of discipline, while London, Ohio, and New England only noted it in their meeting minutes. New York, Baltimore, and Dublin yearly meetings approved the declaration but did not formally adopt it. Nonetheless, the Richmond Declaration set the Orthodox Quakers on the path to further self-definition, a path that led to the drafting of the Uniform Discipline a decade later. Indeed, William Nicholson (1826–1899), the clerk of Kansas Yearly Meeting, proposed forming a triennial conference of yearly meetings. His proposal led to quinquennial meetings, with the next meeting in 1892—hence the name Five Years Meeting adopted in 1902. It was at the meeting in 1897 that the delegates decided to draft the Uniform Discipline, which was completed in 1900 and from which "Essential Truths" is taken.

About the Author

Rufus M. Jones was a scholar, peace activist, and mystic who emerged as a leading voice among Orthodox Quakers in the decade following the Richmond Conference in 1887. He was particularly influential for his role in the rise of modernist Quakerism, the attempt to reconcile Quaker beliefs with the conclusions of both modern science and historical criticism of the Bible (the application of scientific methods of study to the Bible not as a sacred text but as a historical document). Modernist Quakers hold the position that scientific and historical findings do not endanger their beliefs because, as many Friends contend, God progressively reveals new truths about the world and the Christian faith to humanity.

Jones was born in South China, Maine, in 1863 to a devout Gurneyite Quaker family and went to Quaker schools, including Providence Friends School in Rhode Island and Haverford College in Pennsylvania. While at Haverford, Jones encountered the founder of the Quakers, George Fox, through his reading of Ralph Waldo Emerson's *Essays*. He was especially impressed by Fox's focus on direct spiritual experience of the divine, and he regarded Fox as a mystic, that is, someone who seeks direct contact with the divine through religious experience.

Time Line

1640s	■ George Fox founds the Society of Friends in England.
1668	■ Fox writes the first Quaker Discipline.
1671	■ Fox writes the Letter to the Governor of Barbados, an important statement of Quaker belief.
1691	■ Fox dies.
1827–1828	■ The "Great Separation" at the Philadelphia Yearly Meeting takes place between the followers of Elias Hicks and Friends sympathetic to evangelical theology.
1845–1846	■ The "Second Separation" at the New England Yearly Meeting takes place between the followers of John Wilbur and those of the British Friend Joseph John Gurney.
1860s	■ Division occurs between Orthodox and Conservative Friends over "programmed" versus "unprogrammed" worship.
1870	■ Western Yearly Meeting proposes a council to deal with divisions among Gurneyite Friends.
1887	■ Delegates from Orthodox yearly meetings meet in Richmond, Indiana, and produce the Declaration of Faith (Richmond Declaration); various yearly meetings take different actions regarding the declaration.
1893	■ Rufus Jones becomes editor of *Friends Review*, which later becomes *American Friend*, published out of Philadelphia.
1897	■ Delegates of Orthodox quinquennial meeting decide to draft the Uniform Discipline.
1900	■ The Uniform Discipline, containing "Essential Truths," is completed by Rufus Jones and James E. Wood.
1902	■ The Five Years Meeting of Friends in America is formed on the basis of the Uniform Discipline; most Orthodox yearly meetings accept "Essential Truths" as a statement of belief.
1917	■ Walter C. Woodward is appointed to the post of executive secretary of the Five Years Meeting.
1922	■ Delegates of Five Years Meeting produce the Authorized Declaration of Faith, which includes "Essential Truths," the Richmond Declaration, and George Fox's Letter to the Governor of Barbados.
1925–1930	■ Orthodox Friends sympathetic to fundamentalism leave the Five Years Meeting, including Friends in Oregon, Indiana, and California.
1945	■ The Five Years Meeting drafts a revision of the Uniform Discipline, but there is no agreement on the doctrinal statements among member yearly meetings.
1960	■ The Five Years Meeting of the Friends in America changes its name to Friends United Meeting (FUM) and establishes triennial meetings to replace the previous practice of meeting every five years.
1987	■ FUM triennial meeting chooses not to reaffirm the Richmond Declaration, instead issuing a compromise statement known as the Two o'Clock Minute.
2007	■ FUM General Board meets in Kenya, to reaffirm the Richmond Declaration but not require the adoption of the declaration for continued membership in FUM.
2010	■ FUM is the largest body of Friends in the world.

Jones's work for the Orthodox Friends in America cannot be overstated, nor can his impact on American Quakerism. In the early 1890s he became deeply involved in the Religious Society of Friends, and in 1893 he became editor of the *Friends Review*, the most influential journal of Gurneyite Quakerism. One year later he was instrumental in the merger of the *Friends Review* with the *Christian Worker*, a Quaker publication based in Chicago. The result was a new journal published in Philadelphia called *American Friend*. Through *American Friend*, Jones became more popular and influential among Quakers of all persuasions and began moving toward a modernist theological position, especially after an extended trip to Europe in 1897. During this trip, Jones became close to a group of modernist Quakers in England who accepted the theory of evolution as well as historical critical study of the Bible. Among others, these Friends included John Wilhelm Rowntree and William Braithwaite.

Jones's work with James Woods on the Uniform Discipline, especially the "Essential Truths" section, is but one of many examples of his enduring influence on Orthodox Quakerism by his death in 1948. He lectured widely across the United States, Europe, and parts of Asia, and he was highly respected by Quakers around the world. He produced fifty-four books between 1889 and 1948 in addition to countless book chapters and introductions, journal and magazine articles, and book reviews. He trained volunteers at Haverford College for relief work in France during World War I, an effort that led to the formation of the American Friends Service Committee. Jones also helped establish the Friends World Committee for Consultation in 1937, an organization that grew out of a global All Friends Conference in London in the midst of World War I. In 1945, Jones managed to reunite New England Yearly Meeting, the setting of the original Gurneyite-Wilburite split; the Gurneyite yearly meeting, the Wilburite yearly meeting, and five independent Quaker monthly meetings came together to form one yearly meeting. Jones's influence was such that many Friends around the world regarded him as the preeminent spokesperson of Quakerism to non-Quakers. He died in 1948.

Explanation and Analysis of the Document

"Essential Truths" is rather short, being only thirteen paragraphs long and less than a thousand words in length. As such, it lends itself to detailed analysis. It portrays the Quaker faith as spiritualist, that is, unattached to the external ceremonies or ordinances of the Protestants and Catholics. Jones opposed the evangelicalism of some of the Orthodox yearly meetings, and "Essential Truths" reflects this point of view throughout the text. The evangelical tone of the Richmond Declaration is noticeably absent. In fact, Jones was opposed to the Declaration, calling it a "poor thin mediocre expression" of the Quaker faith, as quoted in Elizabeth Vining's biography. He used his influence at the formation of the Five Years Meeting in 1902 to prevent its inclusion in the Uniform Discipline.

◆ Paragraph 1

Jones begins by focusing on the nature of the soul's relationship to God, claiming that the "vital principle of the Christian faith" is a personal relationship between the soul and God. This statement affirms the evangelical claim that the Christian faith is personal, yet it also includes Jones's vision of Quaker spirituality. Jones's use of the term *higher life* alongside *salvation* suggests that the Christian faith is about more than salvation, the final destination of the believer. It is also about the spiritual journey of the soul to God.

◆ Paragraph 2

Jones makes the traditional claim that salvation is "deliverance from sin," through a "personal" faith in Christ and also notes that Christ's "love and sacrifice" draw the believer to God. It is noteworthy that the word *sacrifice* follows *love* and that there is no mention of the nature of this sacrifice. It is left to the reader to decide if Jones means the atonement (Christ's death and Resurrection) or some other kind of sacrifice, for he does not use the traditional evangelical code words such as *blood*, *cross*, or *propitiation*. Instead, Jones's focus is on how Jesus Christ "draws us to Him," which again suggests that the Christian life is a journey of the believer to God.

◆ Paragraph 3

Jones introduces the role of the Holy Spirit in salvation. There is no mention of the Inner Light, as the historic Quaker doctrine was too controversial for the Orthodox yearly meetings that preferred the Richmond Declaration. Although Jones would soon offer his thoughts on the Inner Light in his *Social Law and the Spiritual World* from 1904, "Essential Truths" is entirely silent on the matter. Instead, Jones writes a statement acceptable to the traditional position that there is no innate divine light or spark that allows a soul to move toward God on its own. The Holy Spirit must awaken a conviction for sin and act as the first mover, as it were, in the conversion experience. In addition, Jones denies the traditional Catholic notion of the priest as a go-between, or intercessor, between the believer and God. He also denies the notions of ordinances and ceremonies.

◆ Paragraph 4

Jones comments here on the "whole spiritual life" of cooperation with God in contrast to the religious life of outward ceremonies and material aids. For Jones in "Essential Truths," these external forms are of no avail with respect to the spiritual life of the believer. Thus he reasserts the conclusions of the preceding paragraph: True Quaker Christianity looks inward to the soul, not outward to ceremonies used by Protestants and Catholics.

♦ **Paragraph 5**

This is the section on the Quaker understanding of baptism and Communion. Unlike most Christians, who retained an actual water baptism for infants or adults, the Quakers affirmed a spiritual, inward baptism of the Holy Spirit. Jones does not stray from that historic Quaker position, noting that the spiritual baptism of the Holy Spirit empowers the believer's soul and bestows the believer with "gifts for service." He then addresses Holy Communion, which Protestants and Catholics usually celebrate with bread and wine or similar symbols of Christ's Last Supper. Jones again turns to the historic Quaker position that Christ is "Spiritual bread" that nourishes the soul of the believer. Using the Platonic language of "participation," that is, the idea that a physical, temporal being can somehow share or "participate" in an eternal spiritual being, he emphasizes that the goal of the Christian life for the believer is to unite with Christ. Moreover, those who unite with Christ are also united in a "living union with each other as members of one body."

♦ **Paragraph 6**

Jones notes that Christian worship and fellowship are the fruits of the Quaker spiritualist belief in a personal relationship with God. For Jones, as well as for many other modernist Orthodox Quakers, a common fear was that too much emphasis on a personal, spiritualist faith would lead to isolated quietist spiritualism outside the gathering of the faithful. Thus Jones asserts that true spiritual religion is necessarily social, since it springs out of the relationship between believers and Christ.

♦ **Paragraph 7**

Jones addresses the authority of holy scripture, and here "Essential Truths" departs from the Richmond Declaration. While Christians are "bound to accept" its doctrines and are to regulate their lives by its moral teachings, Jones does not privilege any one interpretation of the Bible over another, noting instead that scripture is to be "interpreted and unfolded" by the leadings of the Holy Spirit in the soul of the believer.

♦ **Paragraph 8**

This is the first paragraph in which the Jones uses the word *Friends* to identify his audience. He confirms the importance of the traditional "apostolic" beliefs of Christianity: God understood as Father; the "Deity and humanity of the Son," both God and man; "the gift of the Holy Spirit"; the atonement; and the Resurrection. Jones also affirms the "High priesthood of Christ" and the "individual priesthood of believers," references to the traditional Protestant claim, against the Catholic Church, that believers do not require a priestly mediator between themselves and God for forgiveness of their sins and, ultimately, their salvation.

♦ **Paragraph 9**

Jones turns to the missionary impulse of Christianity in this paragraph. He notes that because Christ died for the sins of humanity, it is the just calling of Quakers that they work together with God "in extending His kingdom" by going wherever they may be needed, whether at home or in foreign mission fields. They are to proclaim the truth of their beliefs through the leading of the Holy Spirit. This is the only place in "Essential Truths" where Jones uses traditional Atonement language, including the words *blood* and *cleansing*. He also affirms that the condition of humanity is sinful and "prone to temptation," which contradicts the "holiness" claims of evangelical Friends like David B. Updegraff.

♦ **Paragraph 10**

Jones addresses the issue of authority in this paragraph. He notes that surrender to the Holy Spirit and obedience to "Him" are what believers should strive for, but not at the expense of the judgments of the community as a whole. He argues that "the sanctified conclusions of the Church are above the judgment of a single individual." This is Jones's first use of the word *Church* in the document, and it is used in the traditional sense of the gathered community of faith, wherever it may be.

♦ **Paragraph 11**

The Quaker spiritualist focus dominates this paragraph, as Jones affirms the historic Quaker conviction that there is no scriptural evidence for "sacerdotalism," that is, a system of worship that requires priests (the Latin *sacerdos* means "priest") to act as mediators between God and humans by engaging in religious ceremonies. For Jones, it is impossible to promote the spiritual life "through the ceremonial application of material things," since the presence of Jesus Christ in the believer's heart is sufficient for true religion. Jones writes that Christ's teaching, his life, his death, and his Resurrection "virtually destroy every ceremonial system and point the soul to the only satisfying source of spiritual life and power."

♦ **Paragraph 12**

Jones here refers to the historic Quaker commitment to nonviolence, a commitment shared by certain other radical Christian groups from the sixteenth and seventeenth centuries, most notably the Anabaptists (the Mennonites, Amish, and Hutterite Brethren). Historically, the Anabaptists were those Christians during the Reformation era who rejected infant baptism; they believed that one must have faith in Christ before being baptized. From their reading of the New Testament, most Anabaptists also believed that that they should not bear arms and wage war and thus followed the example of Christ and his apostles. Jones again uses the word *Church* to describe the community of faith that is to work for justice, the alleviation of suffering, and the spiritual and moral improvement of humanity in general. For Quakers, war is "incompatible with Christianity."

♦ **Paragraph 13**

Jones takes up the matter of oaths in this paragraph. Historically, the Quakers had always been opposed to swear-

"The vital principle of the Christian faith is the truth that man's salvation and higher life are personal matters between the individual soul and God."

(Section 1)

"The whole spiritual life grows out of the soul's relation to God and its co-operation with Him, not from any outward or traditional observances."

(Section 1)

"The Holy Scriptures were given by inspiration of God and are the divinely authorized record of the doctrines which Christians are bound to accept, and of the moral principles which are to regulate their lives and actions. In them, as interpreted and unfolded by the Holy Spirit, is an ever fresh and unfailing source of spiritual truth for the proper guidance of life and practice."

(Section 1)

"The Friends find no scriptural evidence or authority for any form or degree of sacerdotalism in the Christian Church, or for the establishment of any ordinance or ceremonial rite for perpetual observance."

(Section 1)

"The Friends believe war to be incompatible with Christianity, and seek to promote peaceful methods for the settlement of all the differences between nations and between men."

(Section 1)

ing oaths. In this they were again like the Anabaptist groups. For the Quakers, telling the truth has always been a fundamental aspect of faith, and they believe that the taking of an oath (for example, an oath of loyalty or an oath to tell the truth) suggests that a person might otherwise not be truthful. Jones thus emphasizes the historic Quaker commitment to telling the truth by claiming that it is an essential part of faith that one's words match one's beliefs.

Audience

The original audience for the Uniform Discipline, from which "Essential Truths" is taken, was the Five Years Meeting of Friends in America, officially formed in 1902. The first yearly meeting to accept the Uniform Discipline was New England Yearly Meeting in 1900. The Orthodox yearly meetings in Baltimore, California, Indiana, Iowa, New York, North Carolina, Oregon, Western (Indiana), and

Wilmington (Ohio) accepted it soon afterward, but Ohio Yearly Meeting did not. As the Five Years Meeting grew, so did the audience for the Uniform Discipline. For example, Canadian Yearly Meeting joined the Five Years Meeting in 1907, as did Nebraska Yearly Meeting in 1908.

Nevertheless, several yearly meetings were divided or left the Five Years Meeting because of further controversies over Orthodox Quaker identity. The decision of the Five Years Meeting to appoint the modernist Walter C. Woodward to the post of executive secretary in 1917 rankled those yearly meetings more sympathetic to fundamentalism. The inclusion of the Richmond Declaration in the Authorized Declaration of Faith in 1922 also proved controversial. Many meetings were divided between modernists like Rufus Jones and fundamentalist-friendly Quakers who wanted the Authorized Declaration to have the creedal authority to push the "unsound" modernists out of the Five Years Meeting. Oregon Yearly Meeting left in 1925, and many Friends sympathetic to fundamentalism in Indiana, Western, and California yearly meetings had left the Five Years Meeting by 1930.

The audience for the Uniform Discipline and "Essential Truths" has remained fluid to this day, as FUM has experienced both divisions and reunifications ever since. Moreover, the Orthodox failure to reach a consensus on the doctrinal statements in the 1945 revision of the Uniform Discipline has led to more diversity among the yearly meetings. The only fail-safe way to determine which FUM yearly meetings use the Essential Truths section is to read their individual disciplines.

Impact

"Essential Truths" is an important statement of faith for FUM and a testament to the influence of modernist thought within Orthodox Quakerism at the turn of the twentieth century. The moderate language used by Rufus Jones contrasts with the evangelical tone that characterizes the Richmond Declaration of Faith. Nevertheless, "Essential Truths" has clearly been overshadowed by the Richmond Declaration, which has become far more controversial within FUM and the Religious Society of Friends generally. For example, an evangelical splinter group from FUM formed in the mid-twentieth century, Evangelical Friends Alliance (now International), adapted its constitution from the Richmond Declaration of Faith. Moreover, in 1987, the FUM Triennial Meeting could not agree about the status of the Richmond Declaration and therefore did not reaffirm it, opting instead for a statement known among Friends as the Two o'Clock Minute. Twenty years later, however, the FUM General Board, meeting in Kenya, reaffirmed the Richmond Declaration as a statement of faith while not requiring adoption of it for membership, a development that has troubled some FUM Friends and prompted scholars to reflect on the future direction of FUM.

Ongoing Quaker debates about the status of the Richmond Declaration stand in full relief to the relative silence with respect to "Essential Truths." This silence speaks to the unifying character of "Essential Truths," which manages to assert Quaker distinctiveness with respect to its historical spiritualism and pacifism while also affirming "orthodox" Christian beliefs about God, Christ, the Holy Spirit, justification and sanctification, the Bible, and the church. With the Uniform Discipline and its "Essential Truths," the Orthodox Quakers were able to establish the Five Years Meeting in America in 1902. This group eventually became FUM, now headquartered in Richmond, Indiana. As of 2010 FUM is the largest organization of Quakers in the world, with eleven yearly meetings in North America in addition to yearly meetings in the Caribbean and East Africa. Kenya is particularly significant, with fifteen yearly meetings as of 2010 and the majority of FUM members.

Further Reading

■ Books

Abbott, Margery Post, et al., eds. *Historical Dictionary of the Friends (Quakers)*. Lanham, Md.: Scarecrow Press, 2003.

Fox, George. *The Works of George Fox*. 8 vols. Philadelphia: Marcus T. C. Gould, 1831.

Hamm, Thomas D. *The Transformation of American Quakerism: Orthodox Friends, 1800–1907*. Bloomington: Indiana University Press, 1988.

Jones, Rufus M. *Social Law in the Spiritual World: Studies in Human and Divine Inter-Relationship*. New York: Swarthmore Press, 1923.

Mekeel, Arthur J. *Quakerism and a Creed*. Philadelphia: Friends Book Store, 1936.

Minear, Mark. *Richmond 1887: A Quaker Drama Unfolds*. Richmond, Ind.: Friends United Press, 1987.

Minutes and Proceedings of the Five Years Meeting of the American Yearly Meetings Held in Indianapolis, Indiana, 1902. Philadelphia: J. C. Winston, 1903.

Proceedings, Including the Declaration of Christian Doctrine: Of the General Conference of Friends, Held in Richmond, Ind., U.S.A., 1887. Richmond, Ind.: Nicholson, 1887.

Vining, Elizabeth Gray. *Friend of Life: The Biography of Rufus M. Jones*. Philadelphia: Lippincott, 1958.

■ **Journals**

Hamm, Thomas D. "Friends United Meeting and Its Identity: An Interpretative History." *Quaker Life* (January–February 2009): 10–15. Available online at http://www.fum.org/QL/issues/0901/FUM_Identity_Hamm.htm

■ **Web Site**

"Friends United Meeting: About FUM—Declaration of Faith." Friends United Meeting Web site. http://www.fum.org/about/declarationfaith.htm#Worship

—Commentary by Adam Darlage

Questions for Further Study

1. The authors of "Essential Truths" emphasized that they were not composing a "creed." What did they mean by that, and how did the resistance to writing a creed reflect something about the fundamental nature and beliefs of the Society of Friends?

2. Members of the Society of Friends are called Quakers because of the belief that they shook and quaked from religious ecstasy during observances—although the origin of the term is disputed. Do you think that "Quaker" is offensive, a religious stereotype?

3. Through the nineteenth century, the Society of Friends went through a series of disputes leading to the emergence of different branches or sects. Why do you think this was the case? Is there anything fundamental to Quaker belief that would lead to this kind of dissension? Explain.

4. Evangelicals tend to hold to a literal interpretation of the Bible. Yet modern Quakerism, thought of as an evangelical form of Christianity, takes the position that its beliefs are not challenged by modern science or historical study of the Bible, which both call into question literal interpretations of scripture. On what basis do modern Quakers hold this position?

5. What is your position on the issue of the U.S. government's granting pacifist status to certain religious groups such as the Amish and the Society of Friends? Do you support this practice, or do you think that all American citizens, whatever religious group they belong to, should be available for military service in a time of crisis? Defend your position.

"ESSENTIAL TRUTHS": DOCUMENT TEXT

1900 CE

—Rufus M. Jones

The vital principle of the Christian faith is the truth that man's salvation and higher life are personal matters between the individual soul and God.

Salvation is deliverance from sin and the possession of spiritual life. This comes through a personal faith in Jesus Christ as the Savior, who, through his love and sacrifice draws us to Him.

Conviction for sin is awakened by the operation of the Holy Spirit causing the soul to feel its need of reconciliation with God. When Christ is seen as the only hope of Salvation, and a man yields to Him, he is brought into newness of life, and realizes that his sonship to God has become an actual reality. This transformation is wrought without the necessary agency of any human priest, or ordinance, or ceremony whatsoever. A changed nature and life bear witness to this new relation to Him.

The whole spiritual life grows out of the soul's relation to God and its co-operation with Him, not from any outward or traditional observances.

Christ Himself baptizes the surrendered soul with the Holy Spirit, enduing it with power, bestowing gifts for service. This is an efficient baptism, a direct incoming of divine power for the transformation and control of the whole man. Christ Himself is the Spiritual bread which nourishes the soul, and He thus enters into and becomes a part of the being of those who partake of Him. This participation with Christ and apprehension of Him become the goal of life for the Christian. Those who thus enter into oneness with Him become also joined in living union with each other as members of one body.

Both worship and Christian fellowship spring out of this immediate relation of believing souls with their Lord.

The Holy Scriptures were given by inspiration of God and are the divinely authorized record of the doctrines which Christians are bound to accept, and of the moral principles which are to regulate their lives and actions. In them, as interpreted and unfolded by the Holy Spirit, is an ever fresh and unfailing source of spiritual truth for the proper guidance of life and practice.

The doctrines of the apostolic days are held by the Friends as essentials of Christianity. The Fatherhood of God, the Deity and humanity of the Son; the gift of the Holy Spirit; the atonement through Jesus Christ by which men are reconciled to God; the Resurrection; the High priesthood of Christ, and the individual priesthood of believers, are most precious truths, to be held, not as traditional dogmas, but as vital, life-giving realities.

The sinful condition of man and his proneness to yield to temptation, the world's absolute need of a Saviour, and the cleansing from sin in forgiveness and sanctification through the blood of Jesus Christ, are unceasing incentives to all who believe to become laborers together with God in extending His kingdom. By this high calling the Friends are pledged to the proclamation of the truth wherever the Spirit leads, both in home and in foreign fields.

The indwelling Spirit guides and controls the surrendered life, and the Christian's constant and supreme business is obedience to Him. But while the importance of individual guidance and obedience is thus emphasized, this fact gives no ground for license; the sanctified conclusions of the Church are above the judgment of a single individual.

The Friends find no scriptural evidence or authority for any form or degree of sacerdotalism in the Christian Church, or for the establishment of any ordinance or ceremonial rite for perpetual observance. The teachings of Jesus Christ concerning the spiritual nature of religion, the impossibility of promoting the spiritual life by the ceremonial application of material things, the fact that faith in Jesus Christ Himself is all-sufficient, the purpose of His life, death, resurrection and ascension, and His presence in the believer's heart, virtually destroy every ceremonial system and point the soul to the only satisfying source of spiritual life and power.

With faith in the wisdom of Almighty God, the Father, the Son and the Holy Spirit, and believing that it is His purpose to make His Church on earth a power for righteousness and truth, the Friends labor for the alleviation of human suffering; for the intellectual, moral and spiritual elevation of mankind; and for purified and exalted citizenship. The Friends believe war to be incompatible with Christianity, and seek to promote peaceful methods for the settlement of all the differences between nations and between men.

It is an essential part of the faith that a man should be in truth what he professes in word, and the underlying principle of life and action for individuals, and also for society, is transformation through the power of God and implicit obedience to His revealed will.

Glossary

apostolic days:	New Testament times, when Christ's apostles preached and spread Christianity
sacerdotalism:	a system of worship that requires priests to act as mediators between God and humans by engaging in religious ceremonies

Rudolf Steiner, 1905.

THEOSOPHY: DOCUMENT ANALYSIS

"In each life the human spirit appears as a repetition of itself with the fruits of its former experiences in previous lives."

Overview

Rudolph Steiner wrote *Theosophy: An Introduction to the Spiritual Processes in Human Life and in the Cosmos* (1904) as part of his lifelong project to reconcile the sensory and supersensory realms in the study of the nature of human beings. These two dimensions are clearly evident from the very subtitle of the book, in which spiritual processes are perceived to be part of human life. The book identifies three spheres of existence—body, soul, and spirit, which are interdependent and structure human life. At the heart of the book lies Steiner's reworking of the concepts of reincarnation of the spirit and karma, which the author elaborates differently from Oriental philosophies and identifies as a doctrine that could give purpose to human existence.

According to his autobiography, Steiner was aware from a very early age of the existence of the visible as well as an invisible world—the latter world with which he felt more at ease. He admits candidly to his difficulty in learning factual and measurable data about natural objects and phenomena. Accordingly, he states his preference for the spiritual realm, which, to him, always bore the genuine character of reality. Steiner thus set out to modify the prevailing materialist and positivist beliefs, rooted in sensory experience and empirical evidence, that marked philosophical thought at the turn of the twentieth century in favor of the spiritual science that he called Anthroposophy; he worked to create a connection between the physical and the spiritual worlds. The very term *Anthroposophy* identifies knowledge of the human condition that encompasses both its spirituality and its physicality (with *anthropo* referencing the human being and *sophia* meaning "wisdom"). Steiner's mode of thought entails the belief that to understand the world, knowledge of the physical must be complemented with the spiritual dimensions, as both are equally part of the human condition. A type of knowledge that rests merely on sensory impressions cannot lead to the satisfaction of the innate spiritual quest of the human soul.

Steiner intended *Theosophy* as an introduction to the knowledge of the spiritual world and the fate of the human being. The book grew out of his intense activity as a lecturer in the German and other European theosophical circles in which he was engaged at the turn of the century. Its genesis is also to be found in Steiner's reworking of the articles in *Lucifer* and *Lucifer-Gnosis*, two successive theosophical reviews that he founded and edited in Berlin. With *Theosophy*, Steiner gave his spiritual philosophy book-length treatment, dedicating it to the spirit of Giordano Bruno, the sixteenth-century Italian philosopher who was burned at the stake as a heretic by the Catholic Inquisition for his claim that the universal soul continuously reincarnates in different forms.

Context

The cultural seeds for the composition of *Theosophy* and the establishment of the discipline as a "spiritual science" date back to Steiner's scientific studies at Vienna's Technical University in the late 1870s. There Steiner studied mathematics, biology, physics, and chemistry as principal subjects, coming to understand the importance of scrupulous research. Significantly, Steiner's doctorate, which he would obtain in Germany in 1891 at Rostock University, would be on the relationship between truth and science in the thinking of the German philosopher Johann Gottlieb Fichte and would be published in 1892 as *Truth and Science*. Fichte's influence on Steiner would be lasting, and the German idealist is quoted at the beginning of *Theosophy*. At the same time, Steiner developed a keen interest in the classics, the arts, and the humanities. As a result of his double focus on science and classics, Rudolf was fascinated by the German poet and intellectual Johann Wolfgang von Goethe's scientific writings, whose spiritual view on the world he came to share. At only twenty-two years of age,

Steiner was appointed to edit Goethe's scientific writings for the Deutsche National Literatur, a scholarly series of German literary classics, and this task acquainted him with Goethe's notion of the "sensory-supersensory" form, which would be an important influence on *Theosophy*. This form represents an interposition between natural vision and spiritual perception, between a sensory and a spiritual apprehension. At this point, Steiner became clearly interested in overcoming the boundaries of single disciplines and to depart from received notions of what formed orthodox and acceptable fields of enquiry. Goethe showed Steiner that thinking could be an organ of perception just as a material organ like an ear or an eye. While these organs perceive material events, thinking recognizes ideas.

Goethe's "sensory-supersensory form" and Fichte's idealist philosophy were two unlikely models for a young researcher to observe, given the prevailing intellectual milieu at the turn of the century. This milieu was characterized by the fast dissemination of the French philosopher Auguste Comte's positivist beliefs. Comte's philosophy aimed at demonstrating how humankind had finally succeeded in throwing off all religious superstitions and was moving toward an understanding of the world in purely material terms without any recourse to spiritual realms. To Comte's optimistic teleology of human existence, based on belief in linear progress, philosophers like the Germans Arthur Schopenhauer and Friedrich Nietzsche, whom Steiner would meet in 1896, opposed a nihilistic vision of humankind, whose evolution they found ultimately meaningless. Such a pessimistic vision would receive impetus from the tragic historical events that took place during Steiner's life and which, culminating with World War I, brought to an end the Russian, German, Ottoman, and Austro-Hungarian empires. Theosophy rejects the positivist understanding of the world in mere material terms and its tenet that the visible and earthly world encompasses the entire reality that humans can experience. At the same time, Steiner could not share Nietzsche's skepticism and agnosticism because his awareness of the spiritual led him to believe that human life has a purpose.

Theosophy originated in Steiner's conviction that, in addition to his numerous lectures on the issue, he had to find a more inclusive mode of communication for his anthroposophical work. After the foundation of the German section of the Theosophical Society in 1901, the following year Steiner launched the monthly journal *Lucifer* with the help of Marie von Sivers, one of Steiner's closest collaborators and his second wife. The title refers to the doctrine found in the ancient mysteries that Christ is the true Lucifer, in its literal meaning as "bearer of light." (The mysteries were secret religious groups that flourished during the Hellenistic period and sought to initiate individuals into cults of deities, stressing private worship and a personal relationship with the god rather than a public expression of faith.) As the number of subscribers increased quickly, the journal absorbed the Viennese publication *Gnosis* and was renamed *Lucifer-Gnosis*. Steiner wrote most of the articles for the journal, and its reputation grew steadily.

Steiner did not initially conceive his lectures to be later published in volumes. His first cycles of lectures were given to the small audiences who attended the Theosophical Society and the Theosophical Library in Berlin. But Steiner's oratorical skills were rapidly appreciated by the most diverse audiences, as the author is estimated to have given over six thousand lectures throughout his career. In contrast to the simple language of the lectures, the written books, including *Theosophy*, may baffle the reader in several passages. Steiner reflects in the preface to the first edition of the book that the reader will have to figure out each and every page as well as many individual sentences. The author goes on to explain that this is intentional, so as to make the reader experience and live the truths that the book has to communicate. This reflection points to the tension and difficulty of describing phenomena belonging to an immaterial world with a means—language—usually employed to represent the physical world. Form and content, therefore, are closely interrelated, as the style in which the material is narrated leads the reader to pursue an active path of knowledge. Reading thus becomes a form of spiritual exercise.

Steiner found an initial forum for his ideas in European theosophical circles, but he also immediately marked the difference between his thought and the prevailing ideas in those circles formed by the Russian medium and Theosophical Society founder Helena Blavatsky and the Theosophist and political activist Annie Besant. While these thinkers looked at Oriental philosophies to substantiate Theosophy, Steiner identified the incarnation of Christ or, in his preferred designation, "the Mystery of Golgotha" (referring to the site where Jesus was crucified), as the central event in the history of humanity for his spiritual science. Although he was critical of religious dogmas, Steiner regarded as unique the appearance on earth of the Son of God as Jesus of Nazareth. Blavatsky and Besant did not accept this centrality and this uniqueness, as their goal was to reach a synthesis of all different religions, which they held to all contain equally valid truths. After a years-long process of separation, in 1911 a section of the Theosophical Society encouraged by Besant founded the Order of the Star in the East, a branch that believed that Christ had reincarnated in a Hindu boy, Jiddu Krishnamurti, in a new earthly existence. By 1913 it had become apparent to Steiner that the two branches could not remain together, and he decided to found an independent Anthroposophical Society.

About the Author

Rudolf Steiner was born on February 25, 1861, in Kraljevic, in the eastern Slavic provinces of the Austrian Empire. At the time of Steiner's birth, the vast empire ruled by the Hapsburg monarchy was beginning to dissolve under the pressures for independence among its different populations. After its humiliating defeat against Prussia in the Austro-Prussian War of 1866, the Austrian Empire found that the only way to survive was to strengthen its links with

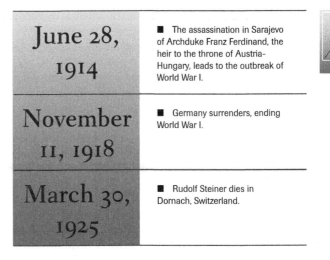

Time Line

February 25, 1861	■ Rudolf Steiner is born in Kraljevic, Hungary (now part of Croatia).
1882	■ Steiner is commissioned to edit Johann Wolfgang von Goethe's scientific writings for the prestigious Deutsche National Literatur series.
1891	■ Steiner earns a doctorate of philosophy from Rostock University.
1900	■ Steiner begins to lecture at the Theosophical Library in Berlin, in the house of the count and countess Brockdorff.
January 17, 1902	■ Steiner joins the Theosophical Society.
1904	■ Steiner's *Theosophy: An Introduction to the Spiritual Processes in Human Life and in the Cosmos* is published.
1905	■ Steiner begins to lecture exclusively on theosophical matters.
1909	■ Disagreements emerge in the Theosophical Society, as Jiddu Krishnamurti is proclaimed the reincarnation of Christ against Steiner's complaints.
January 1911	■ The rift between Steiner and the Theosophical Society deepens as the Order of the Star in the East, a new branch of the society believing Krishnamurti to be the reincarnation of Christ, is founded.
February 2–3, 1913	■ The foundational meeting of the Anthroposophical Society takes place, making Steiner's break with the Theosophical Society official.
September 20, 1913	■ In Dornach, Switzerland, Steiner lays the foundation stone of the Goetheanum, which will take six years to complete.
June 28, 1914	■ The assassination in Sarajevo of Archduke Franz Ferdinand, the heir to the throne of Austria-Hungary, leads to the outbreak of World War I.
November 11, 1918	■ Germany surrenders, ending World War I.
March 30, 1925	■ Rudolf Steiner dies in Dornach, Switzerland.

its eastern Slavic provinces. While consenting to greater independence for the Hungarian provinces in internal matters, the central government disregarded appeals for the preservation of the linguistic and cultural heritage of these regions. It tried to force a unified Germanic identity, against which Hungarian patriots vehemently reacted. Steiner was to experience firsthand the cultural clashes that took place in Austria-Hungary, as both of his parents were German speakers from Lower Austria but worked in the eastern provinces for much of his childhood and adolescence. His father, Johann, was an employee of the Austrian Southern Railway. Rudolf was the eldest of the three children born to Johann and his wife, Franziska. Because of their father's job, the family often moved during Rudolf's early life, at a time when he had already begun to experience visions of a higher, spiritual world.

For a few years the family lived in the Lower Austrian town of Pottschach, near the Hungarian border, where Steiner received private instruction at his home, owing to disagreements between his father and the village teacher. However, in 1869, the family moved to the Hungarian village of Neudörfl, where patriots were trying to revive the traditional Magyar language and culture in opposition to what they considered the imperialist policies of the Austrian government. Meanwhile, because Steiner's father wanted him to become a railway civil engineer, his formal studies were mainly scientific and technical. From a very early age, however, he also developed a keen interest in philosophy and psychology. Because his family lived at a subsistence level, Steiner had to use his pocket money to buy secondhand philosophy books. He began reading the German philosopher Immanuel Kant's *Critique of Pure Reason* (1781) at age fourteen and became convinced that he could find the bridge between the material and spiritual worlds only by acquiring and mastering the philosophical method advocated by Kant, which postulates that knowledge is independent of experience. During his childhood and adolescence, Steiner also discovered that he had supersensory abilities. At the age of seven, he saw the form of one of his aunts asking for help; unknown to his family, the aunt had died in a distant town. His childhood visions initially contributed to a deep feeling of loneliness, as he understood that he could not communicate the visions to his friends. With adolescence and maturity, these supersensory perceptions developed in the author the persuasion that he should translate them into conceptual structures so that they could be communicated to others in words.

Steiner's experiences of ethnic tensions can account for his decision, once his studies at Vienna's Technical University were complete in 1883, not to live in Austria again. Indeed, the cultural conflicts and crumbling of the existing social and political order left a deep mark on Steiner, as reflected in the cosmopolitanism of Anthroposophy and its rejection of preconceived ideas. He would remark directly in *The Threefold Commonwealth* (1919) on the failure of Austria-Hungary to find a balance between its peoples that could have had historical significance. Through the 1880s, 1890s, and early twentieth century, Steiner lectured extensively throughout western Europe, with the German cities of Berlin, Munich, and Stuttgart proving particularly important in the development of anthroposophical circles. When World War I broke out, he settled in Dornach, Switzerland, where he supervised the building of the Goetheanum, "a school for spiritual science" that he himself had designed and which would be used to spread Anthroposophy.

The carnage that Steiner witnessed during World War I certainly stimulated his reflection on life after death, which became a major theme in his postwar works. After the conflict, Steiner continued lecturing to disseminate anthroposophical ideas through initiatives with an ever-widening scope, embracing pedagogy, medicine, and agriculture. The folly of the war had persuaded Steiner that cultural renewal was essential, and to such a process he devoted the last years of his life, continuing to lecture tirelessly and focusing, in particular, on education. His ideas in this area gave rise to the first Waldorf School in 1919. Despite disagreements within the Anthroposophical Society, the burning of the Goetheanum in 1922 (with arson suspected), and his weakening health, Steiner embarked on a major reformation of the society he had founded, a project he worked on until his death on March 30, 1925.

Explanation and Analysis of the Document

The present excerpt from *Theosophy: An Introduction to the Spiritual Processes in Human Life and in the Cosmos* includes parts of chapter 1, "The Constitution of the Human Being," and chapter 2, "Re-embodiment of the Spirit and Destiny." The term *Theosophy* is a compound of the Greek words *theos* (God) and *sophia* (wisdom), standing for "divine wisdom." Steiner argues that because of the prevailing materialist conceptions of existence at the turn of the century, people are blind to their spiritual dimension and consider only the physical world of sensory perceptions. In the text, Steiner describes the threefold nature of human beings as body, soul, and spirit, which allows them to go beyond sensory impressions and discover the deeper

and truer layers of experience. Steiner also recognizes the eternal nature of the spirit, thus introducing a Christian path to reincarnation that diverges from Eastern models. In the thirty-third chapter of his autobiography, Steiner states that his goal in writing *Theosophy* was to stimulate understanding in his readers through descriptions drawn from supersensory realms but using language taken from the world of sense perception and intellect.

♦ Chapter 1: "The Constitution of the Human Being"
In the first chapter Steiner argues that human beings have three means by which they experience the outside world. The body allows them to enter into sensory and physical contact with the external features of the objects that they perceive, like flowers and their colors. The soul allows the human to link perceived objects to one's own being and express the feelings that they provoke. For example, looking at flowers, one will have certain reactions of pleasure, making them one's own. Through the spirit, the human being discovers the inherent and eternal qualities of the surrounding world. In experiencing something repeatedly, the spirit allows humans to detect timeless characteristics and thus the laws and true being of what surrounds them.

The whole being of a person is revealed only when these three aspects are taken into account, because through each aspect, one is connected to the rest of the world in a different way. Through sensory perceptions, one is able to observe objects from without and gain an understanding of bodily existence. But the feelings that such objects stimulate represent the region of the soul; they cannot be understood through the senses and are not directly accessible to others. Through the soul, one creates one's own private world and establishes a bridge between the body and the spirit. The spirit connects with the surrounding world on a higher plane, revealing what is significant in it not merely for one's subjectivity but more universally for the world itself. Citing the observation of "the starry heavens" as an example, Steiner writes that while the delight experienced by virtue of the soul belongs to the human being, the eternal laws of the stars apprehended through the spirit belong to the stars themselves.

♦ Chapter 2: "Re-embodiment of the Spirit and Destiny"
The second chapter starts by considering the intermediary position of the soul, between body and spirit. The body sends to the soul impressions that are temporary and which require the activation of a sensory organ by the presence of an object. But the soul passes to the spirit the emotional reactions to sensory perceptions and thus preserves the present for remembrance, conferring timelessness upon it. What the soul retains after the initial impression becomes the conception that one has of the object. One does not need to see a red rose constantly to have an idea of it, because the soul reworks the outer world into its inner world and stores its remembrance. Steiner defines the soul as "the faithful preserver of the past" and argues that it is thanks to the soul that past external impressions are remembered. The spirit,

in turn, filters these remembrances of the past, extracting what can effectively enrich human abilities and human life. Steiner takes as an example the process of acquiring reading and writing skills in childhood. One obviously cannot remember all the experiences one has had while learning but will remember "their fruits… in the form of abilities."

Steiner then broadens his argument to consider the spirit and soul beyond the period "between birth and death." In this section, the author introduces his own vision of reincarnation and karma. According to Steiner, physical matter and forces cannot account for the human form in its entirety, because the human form is passed on by propagation. While physical materials and forces constitute the body during life, it is the forces of propagation that enable the inheritance of the form by another body. Steiner calls this second body "the bearer of the same life-body" and defines it as "a repetition of its forefathers." The spirit of a person, too, appears to be the result of this process of propagation. The differences of human beings in their spiritual dimension cannot arise only from the differences in their environment and upbringing, because people who are reared in the same environment or receive the same upbringing develop in different ways. Steiner therefore concludes that humans' spirits enter their path of life with different attitudes. These differences in nature are what make each human being unique, a fact that becomes apparent when one looks at the different life stories that exist because of these differences. "In regard to spiritual things," Steiner concludes, "each man is a species by himself."

Just as the physical outlook of a person can be understood with reference to physical heredity, so can the spiritual dimension be understood with reference to what Steiner calls spiritual heredity. Yet this is not a mechanical or deterministic process, and it would be wrong to assume that the spiritual heritage of a given person comes from his family members. On the contrary, Steiner explains that a human being's spiritual dimension is the result of one's development of the predispositions with which one enters life. Such work begins before birth, and, in spiritual terms, each man or woman is "the repetition of one through whose biography [his or hers] can be explained." The process of reincarnation ("re-embodiment") of the spiritual human being does not concern external physical facts but occurs in the supersensory realm, where none of the human faculties can be applied except for thought. With this conceptual development, Steiner rescues his argument from irrationality, pointing out that thinking can shed light on higher spiritual facts. Still, one should not approach spiritual matters with the eyes, seeking material evidence as a natural scientist would. This is the attitude that Steiner finds predominant in his era and that he calls a "materialistic spell" preventing the human being from considering the relationships between different phenomena in a true light. The reembodiment of the spirit shows the importance of the soul beyond physical death.

Because the soul acts as a mediator between the body and the spirit, the latter is able to recognize when a particular experience has occurred and decide what attitude to adopt. This produces learning; so the spirit confers eternity to the results of transitory experience. These resulting attitudes and conceptions remain as the heritage of the spirit, which brings them within itself in its next reembodiment. Again, Steiner rejects a purely automatic model of transmission that would exclude human agency by arguing that the spirit acquires this heritage "by work." He also adds that a human's "deeds" are extremely important for this spiritual heritage, as the effects of yesterday's actions are present in today's being and will be relevant for a person's fate. To exemplify his theory, Steiner draws a parallel between sleep and death. Just as a person waking up in the morning brings along into the new day all of one's previous experiences in life, so does the human spirit begin earthly life with the eternal fruits of previous lives. The spirit holds throughout eternity the conceptions that the soul has elaborated from the sensations provoked by bodily organs. Therefore, the physical world that the spirit enters is not completely foreign ground, as the spirit encounters again the same situations that it has already encountered in previous lives.

The last part of the document introduces the concept of fate created by a person through actions—karma. The human spirit decides its fate through its actions, because the results of its actions remain in its heritage and link its present life with its former one. The destiny of the present life is inscribed in the spirit's previous incarnations and past actions. Steiner emphasizes the influence of past actions in human fate and calls this destiny "self-created" because it is dependent on the conceptions that the soul has elaborated from sensory experiences. In conclusion, the text summarizes the threefold nature of the human being, stressing that the spirit is eternal and subject to the laws of reincarnation, while the body is subject to the laws of heredity. The soul links spirit and body during earthly life.

Audience

Steiner's mature conviction that he should find a way to communicate his supersensory experiences to large audiences accounts for the large number of written volumes and lectures on Anthroposophy, including *Theosophy*. The majority of Steiner's books were actually transcriptions of his lectures, which his followers helped collect and publish in order to disseminate Anthroposophy. Steiner had acquired a reputation as an editor, reviewer, and lecturer of philosophy, literature, and pedagogy in Berlin circles by the 1890s. At the turn of the century, he decided to devote his intellectual strengths to Theosophy and subsequently, after the 1913 break with the Theosophical Society, to Anthroposophy. His primary audience was therefore represented by those attending meetings and lectures of the Theosophical Society. Steiner's ambition was to increase the number of people interested in the subject and to produce a true change of direction in the minds of his contemporaries. He thought that the turn of the century represented the peak in the separation of human thinking and willing from the spirit. Theosophy was designed to contribute to that "turn

"Man has three sides to his nature.... By body is here meant that by which the things in the environment of a man reveal themselves to him.... By the word soul is signified that by which he links the things to his own being.... By spirit is meant that which becomes manifest in him when, as Goethe expressed it, he looks at things as 'a so-to-speak divine being.'"

(Section 1)

"The soul is placed between the present and eternity, in that it holds the middle place between body and spirit. But it is also the intermediary between the present and eternity. It preserves the present for the remembrance. It thereby rescues it from impermanence, and brings it nearer to the eternity of the spiritual."

(Section 1)

"The spirit of man therefore carries each moment of its life a twofold possession within itself, firstly, the eternal laws of the good and the true; secondly, the remembrance of the experiences of the past.... To understand a human spirit we must therefore know two different things about him, first, how much of the eternal has revealed itself to him; second, how much treasure from the past is stored up within him."

(Section 1)

"The human form can never be explained by what lies between birth and death.... Physical materials and forces build up the body during life; the forces of propagation enable another body, inheriting its form, to proceed from it; that is to say, one which is able to be the bearer of the same life-body. Each life-body is a repetition of its forefathers."

(Section 1)

"In each life the human spirit appears as a repetition of itself with the fruits of its former experiences in previous lives. This life is consequently the repetition of another, and brings with it what the spirit-self has, by *work, acquired for itself in the previous life. When the spirit-self absorbs something that can develop into fruit, it penetrates itself with the life-spirit."*

(Section 1)

"A physical body, receiving its form through the laws of heredity, comes upon the scene. This body becomes the bearer of a spirit which repeats a previous life in a new form. Between the two stands the soul, which… receives the impressions of the outer world and carries them to the spirit, in order that the spirit may extract from them the fruits that are for eternity."

(Section 1)

"Life in the present is not independent of the previous lives. For the incarnating spirit brings its destiny with it from its previous incarnations, and this destiny decides the kind of life…. The life of the soul is therefore the result of the self-created destiny of the human spirit…. One calls this fate created by the man himself his karma. The spirit is under the law of re-embodiment or reincarnation."

(Section 1)

or reversal of direction in human evolution" that seemed so necessary to the author. Anthroposophy is today a world-wide movement, and *Theosophy* remains an important point of reference for Steiner's followers. They are mostly concentrated in Germany, Britain, and the United States.

Impact

Theosophy, as well as the author's other writings and lectures, helped revise the religious philosophy that had been identified with the Theosophical Society, established by Helena Blavatsky and Henry Steel Olcott, an American military officer and journalist, in New York in 1875. The Theosophical Society emphasized the importance of mysticism by stressing that God must be experienced directly to be known. In addition, it refused to identify one supreme religion but claimed that all faiths shared universal values and that their teachings represented quests for truth. Steiner became the head of the German branch of the society

in 1902 but, less than a decade after the publication of *Theosophy*, broke away from it in 1913, founding his own Anthroposophical Society.

One of the main reasons for the theosophical controversy was Steiner's interest in finding a Western spiritual path to knowledge that would not discount Christianity to privilege Oriental and Eastern philosophies. Steiner also did not accept what he perceived as the uncritical adoption of occult traditions as a tenet of Theosophy as formulated by Blavatsky and Annie Besant. Steiner, whose training as a scientist taught him to value rigorous standards of research, constantly argued for the application of such standards to all types of observations. Significantly, his biographer, A. P. Shepherd, describes him as a "scientist of the invisible" because, throughout his oeuvre, the philosopher suggests means for a scientific investigation of the spiritual world that would not transcend a rigorous methodology of observation. Steiner's oeuvre has not only contributed to the fields of religion and mysticism but has also had far-reaching effects on education, agriculture, and medicine.

Further Reading

■ Books

Childs, Gilbert. *Rudolf Steiner: His Life and Work*. Hudson, N.Y.: Anthroposophic Press, 1996.

Easton, Stewart C. *Rudolf Steiner: Herald of a New Epoch*. Spring Valley, N.Y.: Anthroposophic Press, 1980.

Hemleben, Johannes. *Rudolf Steiner: An Illustrated Biography*. London: Sophia Books, 2000.

Lachman, Gary. *Rudolf Steiner: An Introduction to His Life and Work*. New York: Jeremy P. Tarcher/Penguin, 2007.

Shepherd, A. P. *Scientist of the Invisible: Spiritual Science, the Life and Work of Rudolf Steiner*. Rochester, Vt.: Inner Traditions International, 1983.

Steiner, Rudolf. *Autobiography: Chapters in the Course of My Life, 1861–1907*, trans. Rita Stebbing. Great Barrington, Mass.: SteinerBooks, 2006.

Wilkinson, Roy. *Rudolf Steiner: An Introduction to His Spiritual World-View, Anthroposophy*. Forest Row, U.K.: Temple Lodge Publishing, 2001.

Wilson, Colin. *Rudolf Steiner: The Man and His Vision*. London: Aeon Books, 2005.

♦ Web Site

Lachman, Gary. "Rudolf Steiner." Fortean Times Web site. http://www.forteantimes.com/features/profiles/109/rudolf_steiner.html

Rudolf Steiner Archive Web site. http://www.rsarchive.org/index1.php

—Commentary by Luca Prono

Questions for Further Study

1. How does Steiner's understanding of reincarnation and karma differ from that found in various documents from Eastern religions? For reference, see, for example, the entries on the Noble Eightfold Path, the *Bodhicaryavatara,* or the Bhagavad Gita.

2. What was the fundamental dispute between Steiner's views and those of the positivists? Why do you think these sets of views came into conflict during this period of history?

3. Helena Blavatsky (see *The Secret Doctrine*) and Steiner both wrote about Theosophy. Although their works contain many similarities, there is one fundamental difference—one that led to Steiner's split from the Theosophical movement. What is that difference? How do the two writers defend their differing positions?

4. In discussing *Theosophy,* the entry states that "through the spirit, the human being discovers the inherent and eternal qualities of the surrounding world. In experiencing something repeatedly, the spirit allows humans to detect timeless characteristics and thus the laws and true being of what surrounds them." Now, a century later, scientists have largely unlocked the genetic makeup of humans and have identified certain emotions and tendencies (love, violence, risk taking, alcoholism) with chemical processes in the brain—or at least claim to have done so. Do you believe that these scientific discoveries have effectively negated Steiner's views? Or do you believe that there still exists a nonmaterial spiritual dimension to life?

THEOSOPHY: DOCUMENT TEXT

1904 CE

—*Rudolf Steiner*

Chapter 1: The Constitution of the Human Being

♦ Introduction

. . .

Man continually links himself in this threefold way with the things of the world. One should not for the time being read anything into this fact, but merely take it as it presents itself. It makes it evident that man has three sides to his nature. This and nothing else will for the present be indicated here by the three words body, soul, and spirit. He who connects any preconceived meanings, or even hypotheses, with these three words will necessarily misunderstand the following explanations. By body is here meant that by which the things in the environment of a man reveal themselves to him, as in the example just cited, the flowers of the meadow. By the word soul is signified that by which he links the things to his own being, through which he experiences pleasure and displeasure, desire and aversion, joy and sorrow. By spirit is meant that which becomes manifest in him when, as Goethe expressed it, he looks at things as "a so-to-speak divine being." In this sense the human being consists of body, soul, and spirit.

Through his body man is able to place himself for the time being in connection with the things; through his soul he retains in himself the impressions which they make on him; through his spirit there reveals itself to him what the things retain in themselves. Only when one observes man in these three aspects can one hope to gain light on his whole being. For these three aspects show him to be related in a threefold way to the rest of the world.

Through his body he is related to the objects which present themselves to his senses from without. The materials from the outer world compose this body of his; and the forces of the outer world work also in it. And just as he observes the things of the outer world with his senses, he can also observe his own bodily existence. But it is impossible to observe the soul existence in the same way. All occurrences connected with my body can be perceived with my bodily senses. My likes and dislikes, my joy and pain, neither I nor anyone else can perceive with bodily senses. The region of the soul is one which is inaccessible to bodily perception. The bodily existence of a man is manifest to all eyes; the soul existence he carries within himself as HIS world. Through the spirit, however, the outer world is revealed to him in a higher way. The mysteries of the outer world, indeed, unveil themselves in his inner being; but he steps in spirit out of himself and lets the things speak about themselves, about that which has significance not for him but for them. Man looks up at the starry heavens; the delight his soul experiences belongs to him; the eternal laws of the stars which he comprehends in thought, in spirit, belong not to him but to the stars themselves.

Thus man is citizen of three worlds. Through his body he belongs to the world which he perceives through his body; through his soul he constructs for himself his own world; through his spirit a world reveals itself to him which is exalted above both the others.

It is evident that because of the essential differences of these three worlds, one can obtain a clear understanding of them and of man's share in them only by means of three different modes of observation....

Chapter 2: Re-embodiment of the Spirit and Destiny

♦ Reincarnation and Karma

In the midst between body and spirit lives the soul. The impressions which come to it through the body are transitory. They are present only as long as the body opens its organs to the things of the outer world. My eye perceives the color of the rose only so long as the rose is opposite to it and my eye is itself open. The presence of the things of the outer world as well as of the bodily organs is necessary in order that an impression, a sensation, or a perception can take place. But what I have recognized in my spirit as truth concerning the rose does not pass with the present moment. And, as regards its truth, it is not in the least dependent on me. It would be true even although I had never stood in front of the rose. What I know through the spirit is timeless or eternal. The soul is placed between the present and eternity, in that it holds the middle place between body and spirit. But it is also the intermediary between the present and eternity. It preserves the present for the remembrance. It thereby rescues it from impermanence, and brings it nearer to the eternity of the spiritual. It stamps eternity on the temporal and impermanent by not merely yielding itself up to the transitory incitements, but by determining things from out its own initiative, and embodying its own nature in them by means of the actions it performs. By remembrance the soul preserves the yesterday, by action it prepares the to-morrow.

My soul would have to perceive the red of the rose always afresh if it could not store it up in remembrance. What remains after an external impression, what can be retained by the soul, is the conception. Through the power of forming conceptions the soul makes the corporal outer world so far into its own inner world that it can then retain the latter in the memory for remembrance and, independent of the gained impressions, lead with it thereafter a life of its own. The soul-life thus becomes the enduring result of the transitory impressions of the external world.

But an action also receives permanence when once it is stamped on the outer world. If I cut a branch from a tree something has taken place by means of my soul which completely changes the course of events in the outer world. Something quite different would have happened to the branch of the tree if I had not interfered by my action. I have called forth into life a series of effects which, without my existence, would not have been present. What I have done to-day endures for to-morrow; it becomes permanent through the deed, as my impressions of yesterday have become permanent for my soul through memory.

Let us first consider memory. How does it originate? Evidently in quite a different way from sensation or perception, because these are made possible by the corporality. Without the eye I cannot have the sensation "blue." But in no way do I have the remembrance of "blue" through the eye. If the eye is to give me this sensation now, a blue thing must come before it. The corporality would always allow impressions to sink back into nothingness if it alone existed. I remember; that is, I experience something which is itself no longer present. I unite a past experience with my present life. This is the case with every remembrance. Let us say, for instance, that I meet a man and recognize him again because I met him yesterday. He would be a complete stranger to me were I not able to unite the picture perception with my impression of him to-day. The picture of to-day is given me by the perception, that is to say, by my corporality. But who conjures that of yesterday into my soul? It is the same being in me that was present during my experience yesterday, and that is also present in that of to-day. In the previous explanations it has been called soul. Were it not for this faithful preserver of the past each external impression would be always new to a man.

As preserver of the past the soul continually gathers treasures for the spirit. That I can distinguish right from wrong follows because I, as a human being, am a thinking being, able to grasp the truth in my spirit. Truth is eternal; and it could always reveal itself to me again in things, even if I were always to lose sight of the past and each impression were to be a new one to me. But the spirit within me is not restricted to the impressions of the present alone; the soul extends its horizon over the past. And the more it is able to bring to the spirit out of the past, the richer does it make the spirit. In this way the soul transmits to the spirit what it has received from the body. The spirit of man therefore carries each moment of its life a twofold possession within itself, firstly, the eternal laws of the good and the true; secondly, the remembrance of the experiences of the past. What he does, he accomplishes under the influence of these two factors. If we wish to understand a human spirit we must therefore know two different things about him, first, how much of the eternal has revealed itself to him; second, how much treasure from the past is stored up within him.

The treasure by no means remains in the spirit in an unchanged shape. The conceptions which man extracts from his experiences fade gradually from the memory. Not so, however, their fruits. One does not remember all the experiences one had during childhood when acquiring the arts of reading and writing. But one could not read or write if one had not had the experiences, and if their fruits had not been preserved in the form of abilities. And that is the transmutation which the spirit effects on the treasures of memory. It consigns the pictures of the separate experiences to their fate, and only extracts from them the force necessary for enhancing and increasing its abilities. Thus not one experience passes by unused; the soul preserves each one as memory, and from each the spirit draws forth all that can enrich its abilities and the whole content of its life. The human spirit grows through assimilated experiences. And, although one cannot find the past experiences in the spirit preserved as if in a storeroom, one nevertheless finds their effects in the abilities which the man has acquired.

Thus far spirit and soul have been considered only within the period lying between life and death. One cannot rest there. Anyone wishing to do that would be like the man who observes the human body also within the same limits only. Much can certainly be discovered within these limits. But the human form can never be explained by what lies between birth and death. It cannot build itself up unaided out of mere physical matter and forces. It takes rise in a form like its own, which has been passed on to it by propagation. Physical materials and forces build up the body during life; the forces of propagation enable another body, inheriting its form, to proceed from it; that is to say, one which is able to be the bearer of the same life-body. Each life-body is a repetition of its forefathers. Only because it is such does it appear, not in any chance form, but in that passed on to it. The forces which have given me human form lay in my forefathers. But the spirit also of a man appears in a definite form. And the forms of the spirit are the most varied imaginable in different persons. No two men have the same spiritual form. One ought to make investigations in this region in just as quiet and matter-of-fact a manner as in the physical world. It cannot be said that the differences in human beings in spiritual respects arise only from the differences in their environment, their upbringing, etc. No, this is by no means the case, for two people under similar influences as regards environments, upbringing, etc., develop in quite different ways. One is therefore forced to admit that they have entered on their path of life with quite different predispositions. Here one is brought face to face with an important fact which, when its full bearing is recognized, sheds light on the nature of man.

Human beings differ from their animal fellow-creatures on the earth as regards their physical form. But among each other human beings are, within certain limits, the same in regard to their physical form. There is only one human species. However great may be the differences between rac-

es, peoples, tribes, and personalities as regards the physical body, the resemblance between man and man is greater than between man and any brute species. All that expresses itself as human species passes on from forefather to descendants. And the human form is bound to this heredity. As the lion can inherit its physical form from lion forefathers only, so the human being inherits his physical body from human forefathers only.

Just as the physical similarity of men is quite evident to the eye, the difference of their spiritual forms reveals itself to the unprejudiced spiritual gaze. There is one very evident fact which shows this clearly. It consists in the existence of the biography of a human being. Were a human being merely a member of a species, no biography could exist. A lion, a dove, lay claim to interest in so far as they belong to the lion, the dove genus. One has understood the separate being in all its essentials when one has described the genus. It matters little whether one has to do with father, son, or grandson. What is of interest in them, father, son, and grandson have in common. But what a human being signifies begins, not where he is a mere member of a genus, but only where he is a separate being. I have not in the least understood the nature of Mr. Smith of Crowcorner if I have described his son or his father. I must know his own biography. Anyone who reflects accurately on the essence of biography becomes aware that in regard to spiritual things each man is a species by himself.

Those people, to be sure, who regard a biography merely as a collection of external incidents in the life of a person, may claim that they can write the biography of a dog in the same way as that of a man. But anyone who depicts in a biography the real individuality of a man, grasps the fact that he has in the biography of one human being something that corresponds to the description of a whole genus in the animal kingdom.

Now if genus or species in the physical sense becomes intelligible only when one understands it as the result of heredity, the spiritual being can be intelligible only through a similar spiritual heredity. I have received my physical human form from my forefathers. Whence have I that which comes to expression in my biography? As physical man, I repeat the shape of my forefathers. What do I repeat as spiritual man? Anyone claiming that what is comprised in my biography requires no further explanation has to be regarded as having no other course open to him than to claim equally that he has seen, somewhere, an earth mound on which the lumps of matter have aggregated quite by themselves into a living man.

As physical man I spring from other physical men, for I have the same shape as the whole human species. The qualities of the species, accordingly, could be bequeathed to me within the genus. As spiritual man I have my own shape as I have my own biography. I therefore can have obtained this shape from no one but myself. Since I entered the world not with un-defined but with defined predispositions; and since the course of my life as it comes to expression in my biography is determined by these predispositions, my work on myself cannot have begun with my birth. I must, as spiritual man, have existed before my birth. In my forefathers I have certainly not been existent, for they as spiritual human beings are different from me. My biography is not explainable through theirs. On the contrary, I must, as spiritual being, be the repetition of one through whose biography mine can be explained. The physical form which Schiller bore he inherited from his forefathers. But just as little as Schiller's physical form can have grown out of the earth, so little can his spiritual being have done so. It must be the repetition of another spiritual being through whose biography his will be explainable as his physical human form is explainable through human propagation. In the same way, therefore, that the physical human form is ever again and again a repetition, a reincarnation of the distinctively human species, the spiritual human being must be a reincarnation of the same spiritual human being. For as spiritual human being, each one is in fact his own species.

It might be said in objection to what has been stated here that it is pure spinning of thoughts, and such external proof might be demanded as one is accustomed to in ordinary natural science. The reply to this is that the re-embodiment of the spiritual human being is, naturally, a process which does not belong to the region of external physical facts, but is one that takes place entirely in the spiritual region. And to this region no other of our ordinary powers of intelligence has entrance, save that of thinking. He who is unwilling to trust to the power of thinking cannot, in fact, enlighten himself regarding higher spiritual facts. For him whose spiritual eye is opened the above train of thoughts acts with exactly the same force as does an event that takes place before his physical eyes. He who ascribes to a so-called "proof," constructed according to the methods of natural science, greater power to convince than the above observations concerning the significance of biography, may be in the ordinary sense

of the word a great scientist, but from the paths of true spiritual investigation he is very far distant.

One of the gravest prejudices consists in trying to explain the spiritual qualities of a man by inheritance from father, mother, or other ancestors. He who contracts the prejudice, for example, that Goethe inherited what constitutes his essential being from father or mother will at first be hardly approachable with arguments, for there lies within him a deep antipathy to unprejudiced observation. A materialistic spell prevents him from seeing the relations of phenomena in the true light....

How does the interaction between body and soul proceed? During life the spirit is bound up with the soul in the way shown above. The soul receives from it the power of living in the Good and the True, and of thereby bringing in its own life, in its tendencies, impulses, and passions, the spirit itself to expression. The spirit-self brings to the I, from the world of the spirit, the eternal laws of the True and the Good. These link themselves through the consciousness-soul with the experiences of the soul's own life. These experiences themselves pass away, but their fruits remain. The spirit-self receives an abiding impression by having been linked with them. When the human spirit approaches an experience similar to one with which it has already been linked, it sees in it something familiar, and is able to take up a different attitude toward it than if it were facing it for the first time. This is the basis of all learning. And the fruits of learning are acquired capacities. The fruits of the transitory life are in this way graven on the eternal spirit.... In each life the human spirit appears as a repetition of itself with the fruits of its former experiences in previous lives. This life is consequently the repetition of another, and brings with it what the spirit-self has, by work, acquired for itself in the previous life. When the spirit-self absorbs something that can develop into fruit, it penetrates itself with the life-spirit. Just as the life-body reproduces the form, from genus to genus, so does the life-spirit reproduce the soul from personal existence to personal existence.

Thus the experiences of the soul become enduring not only within the boundaries of birth and death, but out beyond death. But the soul does not stamp its experiences only on the spirit which flashes up in it, it stamps them, as has been shown, on the outer world, also, through the deed. What a man did yesterday is to-day still present in its effects. A picture of the connection between cause and effect is given in the simile of sleep and death. Sleep has often been called the younger brother of death. I get up in the morning. Night has interrupted my consecutive activity. Now, under ordinary circumstances, it is not possible for me to begin my activity again just as I like. I must connect it with my doings of yesterday if there is to be order and coherence in my life. My actions of yesterday are the conditions predetermining those I have to do to-day. I have created my fate of to-day by what I did yesterday. I have separated myself for a while from my activity; but this activity belongs to me and draws me again to itself after I have withdrawn myself from it for a while. My past remains bound up with me; it lives on in my present, and will follow me into my future. If the effects of my deeds of yesterday were not to be my fate to-day, I should have had, not to awake this morning, but to be newly created out of nothing. It would be absurd if under ordinary circumstances I were not to occupy a house that I have had built for me.

The human spirit is just as little newly created when it begins its earthly life as is a man newly created every morning. Let us try to make clear to ourselves what happens when an entrance into this life takes place. A physical body, receiving its form through the laws of heredity, comes upon the scene. This body becomes the bearer of a spirit which repeats a previous life in a new form. Between the two stands the soul, which leads a self-contained life of its own. Its inclinations and disinclinations, its wishes and desires minister to it; it takes thought into its service. As sentient-soul it receives the impressions of the outer world and carries them to the spirit, in order that the spirit may extract from them the fruits that are for eternity. It plays, as it were, the part of intermediary; and its task is fully accomplished when it is able to do this. The body forms impressions for the sentient-soul which transforms them into sensations, retains them in the memory as conceptions, and hands them over to the spirit to hold throughout eternity. The soul is really that through which man belongs to his earthly life. Through his body he belongs to the physical human species. Through it he is a member of this species. With his spirit he lives in a higher world. The soul binds the two worlds for a time together.

But the physical world on which the human spirit enters is no strange field of action to it. On it the traces of its actions are imprinted. Something in this field of action belongs to the spirit. It bears the impress of its being. It is related to it. As the soul formerly transmitted the impressions from the outer world to the spirit in order that they might become enduring in it, so now the soul, as the spirit's organ, converts the capacities bestowed by the spirit into deeds which are also enduring through their effects. Thus the soul has actually flowed into these actions. In the effects of his actions man's soul lives on in a second independent life. And it is inevitable that the human spirit should meet again the effect of these actions. For only the one part of my deed is in the outer world; the other is in myself....

By means of his actions, therefore, the human spirit has really carved his fate. In a new life he finds himself linked to what he did in a former one.... The human spirit can only live in the surroundings which by its acts it has created for itself. There can be no more appropriate comparison than that of sleep with death. That I find in the morning a state of affairs which I on the previous day created, is brought about by the immediate progress of the events themselves. That I, when I reincarnate myself, find surroundings which correspond with the results of my deeds in a previous life, is brought about by the relationship of my reincarnated spirit with the things in the world around. From this it stands out clearly how the soul forms a member of the constitution of man. The physical body is subject to the laws of heredity. The human spirit, on the contrary, has to incarnate over and over again, and its law consists in its bringing over the fruits of the former lives into the following ones. The soul lives in the present. But this life in the present is not independent of the previous lives. For the incarnating spirit brings its destiny with it from its previous incarnations, and this destiny decides the kind of life. Whatever impressions the soul will be able to have, with what wishes it will be able to be gratified, what sorrows and joys spring forth for it, depend on the nature of the actions in the past incarnations of the spirit. The life of the soul is therefore the result of the self-created destiny of the human spirit. The course of man's life between birth and death is therefore determined in a three-fold way. And he is by these means dependent in a threefold way on factors which lie on the other side of birth and death. The body is subject to the laws of heredity; the soul is subject to the self-created fate. One calls this fate created by the man himself his karma. The spirit is under the law of re-embodiment or reincarnation. One can accordingly express the relationship between spirit, soul, and body in the following way as well. The spirit is eternal; birth and death have dominion over the corporality according to the laws of the physical world; the soul-life, which is subject to destiny, links them together during an earthly life.

Photographer Unknown (Bain News Service): en:Emma Goldman on a Street Car (1917) **This candid photograph was probably taken during one of the many strikes or antiwar demonstrations in which the anarchist and feminist was active during World War I. Two years later, at the height of the Red Scare, Goldman was deported to the Soviet Union, to return in 1934, disenchanted with the Soviet experiment and with the violent political repression in Stalin's Russia. No doubt the photographer saw the irony in the patriotic Uncle Sam poster visible here behind the feisty ideologue's head.**

"THE PHILOSOPHY OF ATHEISM": DOCUMENT ANALYSIS

1916 CE

"Atheism in its negation of gods is at the same time the strongest affirmation of man, and through man, the eternal yea to life, purpose, and beauty."

Overview

Emma Goldman's essay "The Philosophy of Atheism" was published in *Mother Earth* in 1916, but an earlier version was delivered as a lecture for the Congress of Religious Philosophies on July 29, 1915, as part of the Panama-Pacific International Exposition in San Francisco. This locates the essay in the context of Goldman's extensive lecture tours and of one of the most important radical journals in U.S. history. The journal was edited by Goldman and Alexander Berkman from its founding in 1906 until it ceased publication in August 1917 under pressure from the U.S. government for its opposition to American entry into World War I.

Both the lecture tours and the journal were products of Goldman's commitment to popular education, a critical component of her anarchist theory. The originality of her theory lay in its synthesis of the two main streams of anarchism prevalent at the time she wrote: the individualism of the Russian philosopher Pyotr Kropotkin (1842–1921) and the German philosopher Johann Kaspar Schmidt (1806–1856), who wrote under the name Max Stirner, and the collective revolutionary action of the Russian philosopher Mikhail Bakunin (1814–1876). Goldman saw religion, like the state, as antithetical to liberty. Like Bakunin and the German political philosopher Karl Marx (1818–1883), she also saw it as an indicator of the level of maturity of human thought, and, like Kropotkin and Marx, she approached it in an evolutionary context in which its importance would diminish as human thought evolved.

Context

In thinking about Goldman's essay, it is worth bearing in mind that philosophical writing is a conversation, not simply the statement of an independent conclusion. Goldman was engaged in a lively conversation with the events around her and also with the work of other philosophers. Like many radical thinkers in the nineteenth century, she reasoned in accord with the inversion of orthodox Christian theology proposed by the German philosopher Ludwig Feuerbach (1804–1872). This inversion includes the assumptions that God is a human construct and that not only have people made God in their image (an idea that can be traced back as far as the pre-Socratic philosophers) but they also make gods to compensate for shortcomings and explain what is found inexplicable.

"God," as John Lennon would later write, "is a concept by which we measure our pain." This is essentially the argument that Marx made in his critique of Georg Wilhelm Friedrich Hegel's *Philosophy of Right* (1821). Goldman's essay is rooted in the reaction to the Hegelian system identified with Marx and Feuerbach but also present in Bakunin, whose *God and the State* (1882) was a direct influence on Goldman. Like Marx, Goldman roots the concept of God in the true needs of real human beings while also defining religion as the process by which that concept is constructed. The concept of God is a product of religion, and religion is a response to human need: Thus, God is the product of a social process. The more needy humankind is, the more likely it is that religion will be put into play as a way to produce a god (or gods) that satisfies particular human needs. Religion, then, is a sign of human need, and the amelioration of human need reduces the necessity of religion.

This connection of religion with need partly explains the connection between atheism and radical politics. Goldman stands in a line of political radicals who were convinced that addressing the real needs of human beings would reduce the dependence of human beings on religion. The word *dependence* is critical. When Marx describes religion as the opiate of the people (an image close to those Bakunin used at about the same time), he classifies it as a painkiller—not a bad thing for a people in pain but a distraction if the cause of the pain is not addressed. Nineteenth-century radical political thought based on Feuerbach's criticism of Hegel saw a danger of dependence in religion that could be exploited by the powerful to keep the mass of the people powerless. The German philosopher Friedrich Nietzsche (1844–1900) took this up in his dismissal of Christianity as weak, as a religion of slaves.

Marx, Bakunin, and Kropotkin saw religion as a means of political oppression as well as a sign of neediness because it encourages dependence. But they also viewed it as a means of oppression because it can serve as a distraction. Nineteenth- and early-twentieth-century political radicals were particularly critical of Christianity because it promised a reward in another life that made this life important only as something to be endured. An attack on religion was understood as a way to turn the attention of suffering people to the cause of their suffering in this life.

European theorists, in particular, had reason to see both church and state as centers of power, and they often took up the "protestant" principle of resistance to global power as a way to make a space in which to exercise power locally. The tension between local and global permeated debates over organization and strategy that shaped radical movements in Europe and the United States, the movements within which Goldman's thought developed.

The International Workingmen's Association, the First International, was formed in 1864 as a response to the need for an organization of workers to confront the organized powers that oppressed them. It split in 1872 because there were irreconcilable differences over whether the power of the state could be harnessed by the oppressed against their oppressors. The split separated anarchists (including Bakunin) from Communists (including Marx) and both from syndicalists, who embraced communal organization but rejected the power of the state as inherently oppressive. Goldman was particularly attuned to the split, critical of Marx for his embrace of the power of the state while sympathetic to both anarchists and syndicalists.

In the United States, the radical thought of the late nineteenth and early twentieth centuries is inextricably connected with the labor movement—which made questions of organization decidedly practical for workers struggling for a living wage and decent working conditions. The practical questions led to coalitions that had an impact on the political philosophy of the time. In Chicago, for example, radical theorists who saw reforms such as the eight-hour workday as cosmetic nevertheless lent their support to labor actions organized around "eight hours for work, eight hours for rest, and eight hours for what you will." One such action targeted the McCormick Reaper plant and culminated in the Haymarket tragedy of May 4, 1886. An explosion near the end of a peaceful demonstration led to gunfire in which eight police officers and a number of civilians were killed. As a result, local anarchist and Socialist leaders were arrested (whether or not they had been present at the time of the explosion). Eight anarchists were tried and convicted; one committed suicide in prison, and four were executed on November 11, 1887. Goldman points to that date as the moment that inspired her anarchism and galvanized

her political activities for the remainder of her life, as it did for many radical thinkers in the United States and abroad.

The period between the Haymarket tragedy and World War I was one of the most active in the history of labor organizing in the United States, encompassing the organization of both the American Federation of Labor in 1886 and the Industrial Workers of the World in 1905. It was also a period of growth for progressive and radical political movements. Goldman played a significant role in both, often speaking on behalf of workers and tirelessly devoting herself to educating popular audiences on the philosophy of anarchism. It is within the context of that work that Goldman developed her philosophy of atheism, as presented in her lecture in San Francisco on July 29, 1915, which led to her publication of "The Philosophy of Atheism" in *Mother Earth* in February 1916.

About the Author

Emma Goldman was born on June 27, 1869, in Kovno (now Kaunas), Lithuania, which was then part of the Russian Empire. Kovno was part of the area Empress Catherine II had set aside in 1791 for Jewish settlement after the Russian annexation of Poland. Goldman's father, Abraham, was an Orthodox Jew, and although her mother, Taube, belonged to a more liberal tradition, Emma grew up in a conservative Jewish family in a context of persistent anti-Semitism. Her autobiography recounts a childhood that was often difficult under a father who was stern, distant, and sometimes abusive. By her account, her Jewish background—particularly in the anti-Semitic context of czarist Russia—was important to her anarchism. First, it gave her reason to be suspicious of electoral politics (when her father lost an election because, as he explained, he was Jewish and the winner gave more vodka). Second, it gave her firsthand experience of the brutality of militarism. Emma's formal schooling in Königsberg ended when she moved with her family to Saint Petersburg in 1881. But her education continued, as it did throughout her life. She was introduced to radical literature by her sister Helena, and she grew familiar with Russian revolutionary movements during the four years she spent in Saint Petersburg. In December 1885, she immigrated to the United States, settling first in Rochester, where her older sister Lena had already moved. Pressured into an unhappy marriage in 1887, she divorced and moved to New Haven, Connecticut, ten months later. She returned briefly to Rochester for health reasons, remarried and divorced a second time, and then moved to New York City.

She begins her autobiography with her arrival in New York at the age of twenty, on August 15, 1889. On her arrival, she settled on the Lower East Side, where she met Johann Most and Alexander Berkman. Most, editor of *Die Freiheit* ("Freedom"), became Goldman's mentor. Most began publication of *Die Freiheit* in London, where he continued to publish it until he was expelled from the Social Democratic Party as a result of differences with Marx over the role of the state. Most went to New York at the invitation of the

Time Line

June 27, 1869	■ Goldman is born in Kovno (now Kaunas), Lithuania.
May 4, 1886	■ The Haymarket tragedy takes place in Chicago.
December 1886	■ The American Federation of Labor, one of the earliest U.S. labor-union federations, is founded.
March 3, 1903	■ The Anarchist Exclusion Act is passed by the U.S. Congress.
1905	■ The labor organization Industrial Workers of the World is founded.
March 1906	■ The first issue of *Mother Earth* is published.
1911	■ Goldman's *Anarchism and Other Essays* is published.
July 29, 1915	■ Goldman lectures on "The Philosophy of Atheism" in San Francisco.
February 1916	■ "The Philosophy of Atheism" is published in *Mother Earth*.
April 6, 1917	■ The United States enters World War I.
July 9, 1917	■ Goldman is sentenced to two years in prison for conspiracy to avoid the draft.
August 1917	■ *Mother Earth* ceases publication.
October 16, 1918	■ Immigration Act of 1918 is signed into law.
December 21, 1919	■ Goldman is deported to Russia.
1921	■ Goldman leaves Russia.
1923	■ Goldman's *My Disillusionment in Russia* is published.
1931	■ *Living My Life* (Goldman's autobiography) is published.
May 14, 1940	■ Goldman dies in Toronto.

Social Revolutionary Club and resumed publication there. It was Most who first encouraged Goldman to begin speaking in public. She went on her first tour in 1890, speaking in Yiddish. She later said that her experience on the tour cured her of her "childlike faith" in the "infallibility" of her teacher and taught her the importance of thinking independently. Although the tour was not entirely successful, it made her aware that she could sway people with words—and that led to her becoming one of the most influential spokespersons for anarchism in the United States in the twentieth century. Her association with Berkman, which developed from a love affair into a lifelong friendship, led indirectly to her imprisonment at Blackwell's Island Penitentiary for incitement to riot. Her year there gave her time to read and also provided an opportunity for formal training as a nurse. That training and her work with fellow prisoners improved her English so that she was ready to move beyond the Yiddish-speaking audience by the time she resumed her lectures after her release. Her medical training in prison prompted her to travel to Vienna for further study. There she heard Sigmund Freud lecture and continued to develop connections with radical thinkers in Europe.

Goldman spoke and wrote on a variety of issues, all determined by her fierce defense of individuals threatened by institutional power, all connected by her commitment to anarchism: the rights of workers, the rights of women (including outspoken advocacy of birth control), the right to refuse conscription into the military. She was a consistent critic of militarism, and it was her opposition to U.S. entry into World War I that led to her arrest and imprisonment in 1917; under the Immigration Act of 1918, which expanded the provisions of the 1903 Anarchist Exclusion Act, she was deported to Russia in 1919. She never wavered in her support for the Russian Revolution, but she grew disillusioned with the Bolsheviks for what she saw as their statism, or support for extensive state controls, and she wrote a critical account after she left Russia. She lived the last years of her life in exile in Germany, Britain, and France and continued to write and speak on issues including the Spanish Civil War. She died in Toronto in 1940 and was buried near the Haymarket martyrs in Waldheim cemetery, just outside Chicago.

Explanation and Analysis of the Document

Goldman's philosophy of atheism draws on Bakunin, and her essay is partly intended to make his ideas accessible to a mass audience. But it is more than popularization. Goldman's contribution lies not only in her ability to popularize but also in her ability to synthesize two apparently antithetical strands of anarchist thought—individualist and collectivist—and in the resulting movement toward an ethic that can underwrite politically consistent action beyond the constraints of electoral politics. While the essay is by no means a comprehensive theory of ethics, it is a significant contribution to understanding the consistency of Goldman's actions across a remarkable range of issues. It is a contribution to theology because of the clarity with which it delineates the relationship between concepts of god and human consciousness—a relationship that Goldman did not discover or invent but that she articulates in a singularly accessible way.

♦ Paragraphs 1 and 2

Goldman begins with an assertion familiar to readers of Marx and Bakunin, an assertion that shows the indirect influence of Hegel on her thinking: An exposition of the philosophy of atheism is necessarily a "genetic" one, that is, it has to attend to the historical transformation of the belief in a deity. Goldman says that the concept of "god" "has become more indefinite and obscure in the course of time and progress." As science advances (particularly in terms of correlating "human and social events"), the "God idea" grows more impersonal and less distinct. It is worth bearing in mind that discussions of theology—as the thirteenth-century philosopher Thomas Aquinas noted in his famous five "proofs" of the existence of God, in his *Summa theologiae*—are about language or concepts of god, not about God. As Goldman maintains, "God" does not represent what it represented in the beginning. The concept expresses "a sort of spiritualistic stimulus to satisfy the fads and fancies of every shade of human weakness." Because the God idea adapts to human development, it is an indicator of where human beings are in that development. Although Goldman does not pursue this idea, it is a rationale for the study of religion, and it has been taken as such by a number of twentieth-century theologians, including liberation theologians, who consider salvation as providing freedom

from social injustice and who employ Marxist social theory in considering reflection on action.

♦ Paragraphs 3–5

Goldman asserts that the conception of gods originated in fear and curiosity. The concept is used to explain something that appears inexplicable. This, of course, is not the only theory of god or gods, but it is a consistent one that has guided a good deal of work in the history of religions and the sociology of religion. Goldman quotes Bakunin: "The history of religions… is nothing… but the development of the collective intelligence and conscience of mankind." The long quotation Goldman cites concludes with the assertion that "the idea of God implies the abdication of human reason and justice; it is the most decisive negation of human liberty, and necessarily ends in the enslavement of mankind, both in theory and practice." The reason for looking at the history of religions is to get a reading of human social development.

With this reason comes a warning. Both the reason and the warning are important keys to Goldman's use of Bakunin. The state of religion, like the state of the state or the state of the economy or the state of sexual relations, can tell us something about the state of human development. But it can also be an abdication of autonomy and a tool in the service of oppression. Following Bakunin, Goldman maintains that theism becomes superfluous as human beings become autonomous. She also maintains, however, that human freedom depends on "outgrowing" dependence on God. This is consistent with Bakunin's connection of God and the state in his revolutionary theory, and it puts Goldman's apparently militant atheism in context. The God idea is equivalent to the idea of the state. While it is possible to argue that both will wither away as human beings mature, it is also possible to argue that, because both the state and the god concept foster dependence, both must be actively opposed and neither can be trusted as a tool in the service of liberation.

♦ Paragraphs 6–8

When Goldman refers to theism as "the theory of speculation" and atheism as "the science of demonstration," she places atheism at the heart of her social theory. This does not so much rule out religion as redefine it by redirecting its attention. "It is the earth," she writes, "not heaven, which man must rescue if he is truly to be saved." This bears a striking resemblance to some variations on the "Social Gospel" being articulated at about the same time Goldman was writing, and it also resonates with later articulations of liberation theology. It is telling that all of these approaches were written "on the fly" by practitioners rather than theorists and that all had intimate connections with workers involved in practical struggles that could not be easily contained within politics narrowly defined. Goldman locates herself in a twentieth-century tradition deeply committed to action and deeply suspicious of theory. Her thought resonates with pragmatism, particularly as it developed (again, at about the same time she was writing and speaking) in the work of the American philosopher John Dewey. When Goldman writes that the "theists" realize that "the masses are growing daily more atheistic," that "more and more the masses are becoming engrossed in the problems of their immediate existence," she turns a liability into a strength. The everyday struggle for survival turns "the masses" away from the god concept.

Presenting this turn as "natural" seems, uncharacteristically, to ignore the strategies of those with whom Goldman most often found herself at odds, represented in this essay by the immensely popular athlete-turned-evangelist Billy Sunday (1862–1935). More properly, within the context of this essay and Goldman's work as a whole, immersion in the everyday appears to be an opportunity to turn the masses away from the God idea, and that turning is one way to describe Goldman's work. Enlightenment is not a "natural" process that unfolds apart from conscious activity; it is a process of popular education. Goldman's clearest indictment of the church comes when she says that the theists are concerned with bringing the masses back to the God idea because atheism threatens "the largest, the most corrupt and pernicious, the most powerful and lucrative industry in the world, not excepting the industry of manufacturing guns and munitions," which she identifies as "the industry of befogging the human mind and stifling the human heart." She does not quite identify that industry with the church, but she certainly identifies the theists as its apologists. This identification of an "industry" intent on "befogging the human mind" anticipates the culture industry of critical theory and is an important indicator of the consistency of Goldman's thought. She chose her targets on the basis of their role in a *system* that worked to befog the human mind. Like Marx and the critical theorists who were influenced by him, she sets her sights on social processes by which "false consciousness" and alienation are manufactured—not the symptoms, but the process and the causes.

◆ Paragraphs 9–11

Given the context, Goldman's description of the tolerance of denominations as a sign of their weakness rather than their understanding is a frontal attack. The Congress of Religious Philosophy was one of many interfaith and interdenominational gatherings organized at the time. Goldman dismisses the very platform on which she stands when she says that "it is characteristic of theistic 'tolerance' that no one really cares what the people believe in, just so they believe or pretend to believe." Religious belief is a means of control. Referring to political and business leaders, she writes, "They know that capital invested in Billy Sunday, the Y.M.C.A., Christian Science, and various other religious institutions will return enormous profits from the subdued, tamed, and dull masses." The state of religion is an indicator of the state of human development, but it is also a tool by which to arrest that development. "Consciously or unconsciously," she writes, "most theists see in gods and devils, heaven and hell; reward and punishment, a whip to lash the people into obedience, meekness and contentment."

◆ Paragraphs 12–15

Goldman's response is a variation on the assertion that has spawned a long line of theodicies, or defenses of God's goodness and omnipotence despite the existence of evil in the world. She points to "the agony of the human race" as a demonstration of how bankrupt the theistic idea is. No god arises to end injustice, so humankind must do so.

Turning from the bankruptcy of theism, Goldman outlines her positive vision of atheism as a philosophy of human development concerned with consciousness. "The philosophy of Atheism," she writes, "expresses the expansion and growth of the human mind." Theism is static, atheism dynamic. Goldman's comment that "things do not act in a particular way because there is a law, but we state the 'law' because they act in that way" is an important key to her embrace of atheism. "The philosophy of Atheism," she writes, "represents a concept of life without any metaphysical Beyond or Divine Regulator. It is the concept of an actual, real world with its liberating, expanding and beautifying possibilities, as against an unreal world, which, with its spirits, oracles, and mean contentment has kept humanity in helpless degradation." This is a variation, common to Goldman, Bakunin, and Kropotkin, on Marxian materialism. The turn is not from the "ideal" to the "material" but from an illusory "other" world to this one. Goldman states her philosophy of atheism as a variation on the theme of engagement in this world, an argument against the kind of escapism that she believes can underwrite and reinforce enslavement.

◆ Paragraphs 16–18

"Gods in their individual function," Goldman says, "are not half as pernicious as the principle of theism which represents the belief in a supernatural, or even omnipotent, power to rule the earth and man upon it. It is the absolutism of theism, its pernicious influence upon humanity, its paralyzing effect upon thought and action, which Atheism is fighting with all its power." Goldman's atheism is one facet of her opposition to absolutism in all forms, the same opposition that underwrites her suspicion of the state and centralized power. Once again taking up language that echoes Hebrew prophecy, Goldman writes that humankind "has been punished long and heavily for having created its gods; nothing but pain and persecution have been man's lot since gods began. There is but one way out of this blunder: Man must break his fetters which have chained him to the gates of heaven and hell, so that he can begin to fashion out of his reawakened and illumined consciousness a new world upon earth." The argument concerns the turn human beings take in our relation to the world in which we live—and the way the things we make and the way we make them *turn* us. Goldman objects to every system that turns human beings from the world. "Beauty as a gift from heaven," she says, "has proved useless. It will, however, become the essence and impetus of life when man learns to see in the earth the only heaven fit for man."

♦ **Paragraphs 19–22**

Turning to an often-repeated argument in defense of religion, Goldman asks, "Do not all theists insist that there can be no morality, no justice, honesty or fidelity without the belief in a Divine Power?" Her answer echoes Kropotkin and offers another direction for ethical theory. "Based upon fear and hope," she says, "such morality has always been a vile product, imbued partly with self-righteousness, partly with hypocrisy." These closing paragraphs hint at an ethical theory that values autonomy: "Thoughtful people are beginning to realize that moral precepts, imposed upon humanity through religious terror, have become stereotyped and have therefore lost all vitality." What she is looking for in her espousal of atheism are *vital* moral precepts. She repeats the phrase familiar from prophetic literature: "Man must get back to himself before he can learn his relation to his fellows." The phrase is a reflection of Goldman's original appropriation of Max Stirner, of her insistence on holding together the individual and the communal, that is, in her understanding, always an affirmation and embrace of the human: "Atheism in its negation of gods is at the same time the strongest affirmation of man, and through man, the eternal yea to life, purpose, and beauty."

Audience

The original audience for "The Philosophy of Atheism" was a gathering occasioned by the Congress of Religious Philosophies that was part of the 1915 Panama-Pacific International Exposition in San Francisco. At that time, Goldman shared the stage with representatives of a variety of denominations and religious traditions, and she spoke to a popular audience disposed to support interfaith and ecumenical activities. When the present version of the essay was published a year later in *Mother Earth,* the audience expanded to include a readership interested in progressive and radical ideas, attentive not only to politics but also to literature and the arts.

Goldman's essay found a receptive audience among activists rethinking anarchism and feminism in the late 1960s, and it continues to be of interest to activists across a broad range of social justice movements, especially those who are interested in nonviolence and alternatives to electoral politics. Goldman's atheism continues to be of particular interest to those who see organized religion as a barrier to social progress and wish to avoid approaching atheism as a belief system that functions as one denomination among others. This makes the essay of interest, too, to readers who do not so much wish to dismiss faith as to practice it outside established institutions.

Impact

Goldman reached a large audience during her lifetime and achieved a degree of notoriety reflected in her designation as "the most dangerous woman in America." She was best known for her antimilitarism and her unfailing support for the rights of workers. Her views on religion, including this piece on atheism, generated controversy but also prompted serious attention from audiences interested in theology (including students at Union Theological Seminary in New York). Her work enjoyed a revival in the 1970s and has continued to influence writing on feminist and anarchist theory as well as antimilitarism.

The revival of interest in Goldman's work in the late 1960s and the 1970s had a particular impact on anarchist thinking of the time, which in turn had an impact on the antiglobalization movement—both on the street, where demonstrators cite her as an influence, and in the theoretical writing that has developed from the movement. Her influence spans the political spectrum, ranging from theorists of the left to libertarians on the right. At a time when more and more people see such distinctions as meaningless or irrelevant, the difficulty of locating her on a political spectrum gives her added appeal. A line attributed to Goldman, "If I can't dance, I don't want to be part of your revolution" (though probably a paraphrase of ideas she stated a bit more prosaically in her autobiography), continues to be a popular slogan among cultural anarchists disaffected not only with the powers that be but also with a political Left that has sometimes appeared humorless and puritanical.

Further Reading

■ Books

Falk, Candace. *Love, Anarchy, and Emma Goldman.* Rev. ed. New Brunswick, N.J.: Rutgers University Press, 1990.

Goldman, Emma. *Anarchism and Other Essays.* New York: Mother Earth Publishing Association, 1910.

Goldman, Emma. *Living My Life.* 2 vols. New York: Alfred A. Knopf, 1931.

Morton, Marian J. *Emma Goldman and the American Left: "Nowhere at Home."* New York: Twayne Publishers, 1992.

Shulman, Alix. *To the Barricades: The Anarchist Life of Emma Goldman.* New York: Thomas Y. Crowell, 1971.

Zinn, Howard. "Emma." In *Playbook,* ed. Maxine Klein et al. Boston: South End Press, 1986.

■ Web Sites

Emma Goldman Papers. Berkeley Digital Library Sunsite. http://sunsite.berkeley.edu/Goldman/

—Commentary by Steven Schroeder

"In proportion as man learns to realize himself and mold his own destiny theism becomes superfluous. How far man will be able to find his relation to his fellows will depend entirely upon how much he can outgrow his dependence upon God."

(Section 1)

"It is the earth, not heaven, which man must rescue if he is truly to be saved."

(Section 1)

"Consciously or unconsciously, most theists see in gods and devils, heaven and hell; reward and punishment, a whip to lash the people into obedience, meekness and contentment."

(Section 1)

"Mankind has been punished long and heavily for having created its gods; nothing but pain and persecution have been man's lot since gods began. There is but one way out of this blunder: Man must break his fetters which have chained him to the gates of heaven and hell, so that he can begin to fashion out of his reawakened and illumined consciousness a new world upon earth."

(Section 1)

"Man must get back to himself before he can learn his relation to his fellows. Prometheus chained to the Rock of Ages is doomed to remain the prey of the vultures of darkness. Unbind Prometheus, and you dispel the night and its horrors."

(Section 1)

"Atheism in its negation of gods is at the same time the strongest affirmation of man, and through man, the eternal yea to life, purpose, and beauty."

(Section 1)

1. Why, in your opinion, are scientists more likely to consider themselves atheists than are nonscientists?

2. Compare how atheists examine the "problem of evil" with the way this problem is examined in a religious tradition you may be familiar with.

3. Goldman refers to organized religion as "the most powerful and lucrative industry in the world." Explain what she means by this statement and express agreement or disagreement. Does it trouble you that many religious institutions own considerable economic assets?

4. What was the connection between atheism and radical politics at the time? Do you think that if Goldman had lived in a different time period, she might not have become an atheist?

5. Goldman described herself not only as an atheist but also as an anarchist. What connection do you see between atheism and anarchism? What historical events at the time forged a connection between these two "-isms," at least in Goldman's mind?

"THE PHILOSOPHY OF ATHEISM: DOCUMENT TEXT

1916 CE

—*Emma Goldman*

To give an adequate exposition of the Philosophy of Atheism, it would be necessary to go into the historical changes of the belief in a Deity, from its earliest beginning to the present day. But that is not within the scope of the present paper. However, it is not out of place to mention, in passing, that the concept of God, Supernatural Power, Spirit, Deity, or in whatever other term the essence of Theism may have found expression, has become more indefinite and obscure in the course of time and progress. In other words, the God idea is growing more impersonal and nebulous in proportion as the human mind is learning to understand natural phenomena and in the degree that science progressively correlates human and social events.

God, today, no longer represents the same forces as in the beginning of His existence; neither does He direct human destiny with the same Iron hand as of yore. Rather does the God idea express a sort of spiritualistic stimulus to satisfy the fads and fancies of every shade of human weakness. In the course of human development the God idea has been forced to adapt itself to every phase of human affairs, which is perfectly consistent with the origin of the idea itself.

The conception of gods originated in fear and curiosity. Primitive man, unable to understand the phenomena of nature and harassed by them, saw in every terrifying manifestation some sinister force expressly directed against him; and as ignorance and fear are the parents of all superstition, the troubled fancy of primitive man wove the God idea.

Very aptly, the world-renowned atheist and anarchist, Michael Bakunin, says in his great work *God and the State*: "All religions, with their gods, their demi-gods, and their prophets, their messiahs and their saints, were created by the prejudiced fancy of men who had not attained the full development and full possession of their faculties. Consequently, the religious heaven is nothing but the mirage in which man, exalted by ignorance and faith, discovered his own image, but enlarged and reversed—that is divinised. The history of religions, of the birth, grandeur, and the decline of the gods who had succeeded one

another in human belief, is nothing, therefore, but the development of the collective intelligence and conscience of mankind. As fast as they discovered, in the course of their historically progressive advance, either in themselves or in external nature, a quality, or even any great defect whatever, they attributed it to their gods, after having exaggerated and enlarged it beyond measure, after the manner of children, by an act of their religious fancy.... With all due respect, then, to the metaphysicians and religious idealists, philosophers, politicians or poets: the idea of God implies the abdication of human reason and justice; it is the most decisive negation of human liberty, and necessarily ends in the enslavement of mankind, both in theory and practice."

Thus the God idea, revived, readjusted, and enlarged or narrowed, according to the necessity of the time, has dominated humanity and will continue to do so until man will raise his head to the sunlit day, unafraid and with an awakened will to himself. In proportion as man learns to realize himself and mold his own destiny theism becomes superfluous. How far man will be able to find his relation to his fellows will depend entirely upon how much he can outgrow his dependence upon God.

Already there are indications that theism, which is the theory of speculation, is being replaced by Atheism, the science of demonstration; the one hangs in the metaphysical clouds of the Beyond, while the other has its roots firmly in the soil. It is the earth, not heaven, which man must rescue if he is truly to be saved.

The decline of theism is a most interesting spectacle, especially as manifested in the anxiety of the theists, whatever their particular brand. They realize, much to their distress, that the masses are growing daily more atheistic, more anti-religious; that they are quite willing to leave the Great Beyond and its heavenly domain to the angels and sparrows; because more and more the masses are becoming engrossed in the problems of their immediate existence.

How to bring the masses back to the God idea, the spirit, the First Cause, etc.—that is the most pressing question to all theists. Metaphysical as all these questions seem to be, they yet have a very marked physical background. Inasmuch as religion, "Divine Truth," rewards and punishments are the trade-marks of the largest, the most corrupt and pernicious, the most powerful and lucrative industry in the world, not excepting the industry of manufacturing guns and munitions. It is the industry of befogging the human mind and stifling the human heart. Necessity knows no law; hence the majority of theists are compelled to take up every subject, even if it has no bearing upon a deity or revelation or the Great Beyond. Perhaps they sense the fact that humanity is growing weary of the hundred and one brands of God.

How to raise this dead level of theistic belief is really a matter of life and death for all denominations. Therefore their tolerance; but it is a tolerance not of understanding; but of weakness. Perhaps that explains the efforts fostered in all religious publications to combine variegated religious philosophies and conflicting theistic theories into one denominational trust. More and more, the various concepts "of the only true God, the only pure spirit, the only true religion" are tolerantly glossed over in the frantic effort to establish a common ground to rescue the modern mass from the "pernicious" influence of atheistic ideas.

It is characteristic of theistic "tolerance" that no one really cares what the people believe in, just so they believe or pretend to believe. To accomplish this end, the crudest and vulgarest methods are being used. Religious endeavor meetings and revivals with Billy Sunday as their champion—methods which must outrage every refined sense, and which in their effect upon the ignorant and curious often tend to create a mild state of insanity not infrequently coupled with eroto-mania. All these frantic efforts find approval and support from the earthly powers; from the Russian despot to the American President; from Rockefeller and Wanamaker down to the pettiest business man. They know that capital invested in Billy Sunday, the Y.M.C.A., Christian Science, and various other religious institutions will return enormous profits from the subdued, tamed, and dull masses.

Consciously or unconsciously, most theists see in gods and devils, heaven and hell; reward and punishment, a whip to lash the people into obedience, meekness and contentment. The truth is that theism would have lost its footing long before this but for the combined support of Mammon and power.

How thoroughly bankrupt it really is, is being demonstrated in the trenches and battlefields of Europe today.

Have not all theists painted their Deity as the god of love and goodness? Yet after thousands of years of such preachments the gods remain deaf to the agony of the human race. Confucius cares not for the poverty, squalor and misery of people of China. Buddha remains undisturbed in his philosophical indifference to the famine and starvation of outraged Hindoos; Jahve continues deaf to the bitter cry of Israel; while Jesus refuses to rise from the dead against his Christians who are butchering each other.

The burden of all song and praise "unto the Highest" has been that God stands for justice and mercy. Yet injustice among men is ever on the increase; the outrages committed against the masses in this country alone would seem enough to overflow the very heavens. But where are the gods to make an end to all these horrors, these wrongs, this inhumanity to man? No, not the gods, but MAN must rise in his mighty wrath. He, deceived by all the deities, betrayed by their emissaries, he, himself, must undertake to usher in justice upon the earth.

The philosophy of Atheism expresses the expansion and growth of the human mind. The philosophy of theism, if we can call it philosophy, is static and fixed. Even the mere attempt to pierce these mysteries represents, from the theistic point of view, nonbelief in the all-embracing omnipotence, and even a denial of the wisdom of the divine powers outside of man. Fortunately, however, the human mind never was, and never can be, bound by fixities. Hence it is forging ahead in its restless march towards knowledge and life. The human mind is realizing "that the universe is not the result of a creative fiat by some divine intelligence, out of nothing, producing a masterpiece chaotic in perfect operation," but that it is the product of chaotic forces operating through aeons of time, of clashes and cataclysms, of repulsion and attraction crystalizing through the principle of selection into what the theists call, "the universe guided into order and beauty." As Joseph McCabe well points out in his *Existence of God*: "a law of nature is not a formula drawn up by a legislator, but a mere summary of the observed facts—a 'bundle of facts.' Things do not act in a particular way because there is a law, but we state the 'law' because they act in that way."

The philosophy of Atheism represents a concept of life without any metaphysical Beyond or Divine

Regulator. It is the concept of an actual, real world with its liberating, expanding and beautifying possibilities, as against an unreal world, which, with its spirits, oracles, and mean contentment has kept humanity in helpless degradation.

It may seem a wild paradox, and yet it is pathetically true, that this real, visible world and our life should have been so long under the influence of metaphysical speculation, rather than of physical demonstrable forces. Under the lash of the theistic idea, this earth has served no other purpose than as a temporary station to test man's capacity for immolation to the will of God. But the moment man attempted to ascertain the nature of that will, he was told that it was utterly futile for "finite human intelligence" to get beyond the all-powerful infinite will. Under the terrific weight of this omnipotence, man has been bowed into the dust—a will-less creature, broken and sweating in the dark. The triumph of the philosophy of Atheism is to free man from the nightmare of gods; it means the dissolution of the phantoms of the beyond. Again and again the light of reason has dispelled the theistic nightmare, but poverty, misery and fear have recreated the phantoms—though whether old or new, whatever their external form, they differed little in their essence. Atheism, on the other hand, in its philosophic aspect refuses allegiance not merely to a definite concept of God, but it refuses all servitude to the God idea, and opposes the theistic principle as such. Gods in their individual function are not half as pernicious as the principle of theism which represents the belief in a supernatural, or even omnipotent, power to rule the earth and man upon it. It is the absolutism of theism, its pernicious influence upon humanity, its paralyzing effect upon thought and action, which Atheism is fighting with all its power.

The philosophy of Atheism has its root in the earth, in this life; its aim is the emancipation of the human race from all God-heads, be they Judaic, Christian, Mohammedan, Buddhistic, Brahministic, or what not. Mankind has been punished long and heavily for having created its gods; nothing but pain and persecution have been man's lot since gods began. There is but one way out of this blunder: Man must break his fetters which have chained him to the gates of heaven and hell, so that he can begin to fashion out of his reawakened and illumined consciousness a new world upon earth.

Only after the triumph of the Atheistic philosophy in the minds and hearts of man will freedom and beauty be realized. Beauty as a gift from heaven has proved useless. It will, however, become the essence and impetus of life when man learns to see in the earth the only heaven fit for man. Atheism is already helping to free man from his dependence upon punishment and reward as the heavenly bargain-counter for the poor in spirit.

Do not all theists insist that there can be no morality, no justice, honesty or fidelity without the belief in a Divine Power? Based upon fear and hope, such morality has always been a vile product, imbued partly with self-righteousness, partly with hypocrisy. As to truth, justice, and fidelity, who have been their brave exponents and daring proclaimers? Nearly always the godless ones: the Atheists; they lived, fought, and died for them. They knew that justice, truth, and fidelity are not conditioned in heaven, but that they are related to and interwoven with the tremendous changes going on in the social and material life of the human race; not fixed and eternal, but fluctuating, even as life itself. To what heights the philosophy of Atheism may yet attain, no one can prophesy. But this much can already be predicted: only by its regenerating fire will human relations be purged from the horrors of the past

Thoughtful people are beginning to realize that moral precepts, imposed upon humanity through religious terror, have become stereotyped and have therefore lost all vitality. A glance at life today, at its disintegrating character, its conflicting interests with their hatreds, crimes, and greed, suffices to prove the sterility of theistic morality.

Man must get back to himself before he can learn his relation to his fellows. Prometheus chained to the Rock of Ages is doomed to remain the prey of the vultures of darkness. Unbind Prometheus, and you dispel the night and its horrors.

Atheism in its negation of gods is at the same time the strongest affirmation of man, and through man, the eternal yea to life, purpose, and beauty.

Glossary

Billy Sunday: a former professional baseball player who became a prominent evangelist

Christian Science: a religion founded in 1866 by Mary Baker Eddy

Jahve: a variant of Yahweh, used in the Hebrew Bible to refer to God

Mammon: a biblical term that signifies wealth combined with greed

metaphysical: of or relating to an order of existence beyond the visible, observable universe

Mohammedan: an antique term used to refer to a follower of Islam, now regarded as objectionable

Rockefeller: industrialist John D. Rockefeller

theistic: pertaining to a belief system that accepts a transcendent and personal God who created, preserves, and governs the world

Wanamaker: John Wanamaker, a merchant and religious leader considered by many to be the father of modern advertising

Y.M.C.A.: Young Men's Christian Association

Selassie I in the 1930s.

HOLY PIBY: DOCUMENT ANALYSIS

1924 CE

"I heard a great voice uttered from the end of the world saying, behold the map of the new Negroes..."

Overview

The Holy Piby, an early document in the Rastafari tradition that is sometimes referred to as "the black man's Bible," was compiled by Robert Athlyi Rogers from 1913 to 1917 and first published in 1924 in Newark, New Jersey. According to to Rastafarians and members of certain Afrocentric churches, Rogers recovered the original message of the Bible out of the belief that the Bible had undergone significant tampering to the extent that it had acquired socially constructed deficiencies. The intended practical purpose of the Holy Piby is to provide instructions in the form of laws that guide and direct the transformation of global Pan-African society toward liberation from political, economic, and cultural domination to a state of autonomy. The Holy Piby also played a key role in the development of a black theology, one that posits a black Jesus and calls attention to blacks in the Old Testament. This theology laid the groundwork for black liberation theology in the following decades.

The word *Rastafarianism* is often used to refer to the religious movement that the Holy Piby helped launch. Followers of the movement, however, reject this term. They contend that they do not want to be associated with an "-ism," arguing that the world has been the scene of too many "-isms" such as Communism and capitalism. Accordingly, the term *Rastafari* is preferred, and its adherents are called either Rastafarians or, preferably, Rastas.

Context

Rogers composed the Holy Piby at a time of sweeping racial change in the United States. A decade earlier, for example, W. E. B. Du Bois had published *The Souls of Black Folk,*

a 1903 collection of essays that constituted an indictment of racism and segregation in the United States but that, more important, called on the black community to seize its own destiny and assert its independence. Then, in 1905, black leaders, including Du Bois and the journalist William Monroe Trotter, launched the Niagara Movement to combat segregation, disenfranchisement, and lynchings. The movement gained prominence in 1908 after a race riot erupted in Springfield, Illinois, when a white woman claimed that a black man had tried to rape her—a charge she later recanted. These and other events led to the formation of the National Association for the Advancement of Colored People in 1909.

At roughly the same time, Marcus Garvey, a black nationalist born in Jamaica, was gaining prominence as the founder of the Universal Negro Improvement Association (UNIA). Garvey founded the UNIA in 1914, and by the early 1920s it boasted nearly a million members and was the largest secular black organization in the United States. Garvey's central message was one of black pride and self-help—the belief that only black enterprise could improve the condition of blacks. The UNIA transformed black political thought as well as African Americans' and West Indians' expectations of what was politically possible in the contemporary world, and Garvey preached a message of race pride, Pan-African unity, and self-determination. Transformation for people of African descent, he regularly asserted to his followers, could be achieved only through their own initiatives and not through the good graces of other races. To empower his race, Garvey organized the UNIA; formed various economic cooperatives and initiatives; hosted international conventions; and started a newspaper, the *Negro World,* with a readership that spanned the globe. Such endeavors gave Garvey a huge following, particularly in the United States, where hundreds of thousands of African Americans and West Indians championed his agenda. It should be noted that Garvey would later be highly critical of the Rastafari movement, but his message gained traction with Rastas, and his ideology strongly influenced the movement.

Then, in 1919, the African Blood Brotherhood, a black liberation and self-defense organization with ties to the Communist Party, was formed. The Brotherhood, like the UNIA, had a West Indian connection in the person of Cyril V. Briggs, an immigrant who composed *The Summary of the Program and Aims of the African Blood Brotherhood*, published in 1920. In this document, he listed the eight goals of the Brotherhood, a secret, all-black society he founded to unite people of African descent from around the world and counter what he saw as the menacing forces of capitalism and white racism. This concern became especially acute in the period following World War I, when many black servicemen returned home to meet with hostility and when numerous American cities were the scenes of race riots.

It was in this context of emerging black nationalism and Pan-Africanism that Rogers compiled the Holy Piby. The early twentieth century was an era marked by the florescence of postbiblical Afrocentric literature in response to increased black suspicion of traditional biblical interpretation. Post-Judeo-Christian Pan-African movements in the Western Hemisphere, specifically in the United States and the Caribbean, faced the challenge of finding meaning in an ancient faith and its scriptures that would give a clear sense of mission in light of widespread human suffering in the global African diaspora. Western Christians of African origin, almost all of them victims of Euro-American slavery, had collectively experienced a disconnect from their own African culture. Cultural ties are important in the context of religious discourse. The Holy Piby was written to reconnect Christians of African descent with their African roots. Although new readers of the Holy Piby encounter a multitude of references from both the Hebrew Bible and the Christian New Testament, they also find much that is distinctive.

In accord with the Christian belief that the Bible has a divine origin, members and affiliates of the church that Rogers founded, the Afro-Athlican Constructive Church, accepted the Holy Piby as authored by the Holy Spirit independently from the Hebrew and Christian bibles. Throughout, the document refers repeatedly to "Ethiopia," which traditionally stands for Africans in general. The Holy Piby arose out of a response to the African American cultural disconnect from Africa and its oral traditions, rituals, and oracles. Rastafari was one of several Pan-African religious movements to emerge in the Western Hemisphere during the early twentieth century. Although Rastafari does not hold a single text as the official and final authority, the Holy Piby ranks as a text of divine inspiration that directly addresses the needs of the people of the African diaspora. Ultimately, the Holy Piby tries to restore the original word of God, out of the widespread belief that most approved versions of the Bible underwent significant tampering at the hands of white Christians, resulting in severe distortion that leads people astray and causes dissent.

Time Line

1909	■ The National Association for the Advancement of Colored People is formed.
1913	■ Robert Athlyi Rogers begins to compile and write the Holy Piby, a process that continues until 1917.
1914	■ Marcus Garvey forms the Universal Negro Improvement Association.
1917	■ Rogers begins his missionary journey in Newark, New Jersey.
1919	■ Rogers is designated as Shepherd of the Afro-Athlican Constructive Church.
1924	■ The Holy Piby is published.
1925	■ Charles F. Goodridge and Grace Jenkins Garrison found a branch of the Afro-Athlican Constructive Church called the Hamatic Church in Jamaica.
November 2, 1930	■ Ras Tafari Makonnen, known as Haile Selassie, becomes emperor of Ethiopia.
August 24, 1931	■ Rogers commits suicide.

About the Author

Very little is known about the life of Robert Athlyi Rogers, and, indeed, copies of the Holy Piby were rare until recently, in large part because the work was banned in Jamaica and other Caribbean islands in the 1920s. He was originally from Anguilla, a small island located in the British Lesser Antilles. After spending several years compiling and producing the text entitled the Holy Piby, Athlyi undertook a missionary journey to Newark, New Jersey, and then proceeded to Springfield, Massachusetts. Within a relatively brief period, he acquired the support and resources to proselytize actively and spread the new message to South America and the isles of the Caribbean. On August 24, 1931, Rogers died a self-inflicted death.

Explanation and Analysis of the Document

The Holy Piby consists of four books. The second of these books is titled *The Second Book of Athlyi Called Aggregation*. The selection consists of excerpts from chapters 3 through 6 of this second book.

♦ Chapter 3: God's Holy Law to the Children of Ethiopia

The heart of the Holy Law of the Children of Ethiopia is explicitly stated in the form of twelve Holy Commandments. The division of the law into twelve commandments is likely intended to distinguish the Piby from the established Ten Commandments of the Old Testament, which are themselves diversely stated in the biblical books of Exodus (20:2–17) and Deuteronomy (5:6–21). Additionally, the numbering connects the Holy Piby with the tradition of the established significance of twelve, as in the Twelve Tribes of Israel and the Twelve Disciples of Christ.

The first commandment, to love one another, has obvious common ground with the universal golden rule of using the desired way of being treated as the measuring stick for treating others. In addition, this initial commandment corresponds with Deuteronomy 6:5, Leviticus 19:18, and the New Testament of Christianity in its insistence that loving one's fellow humanity serves as the gateway or prerequisite to loving God. It is unclear whether the implication of the initial command, "Love ye one another," is to include universal love for all humankind or strictly fellow Ethiopians. If the latter, then a problem arises, since the word "Ethiopians" cannot refer literally to the people of Ethiopia. Athlyi was not an Ethiopian by nationality. An inclusive interpretation of "Ethiopia" might range from the Pan-African population to all oppressed persons of the world. Oppression, in turn, may include not only the economically deprived but also the oppressor, who experiences oppression within himself.

The second commandment, "Be thou industrious, thrifty and fruitful," parallels Genesis 1:28, "Be fruitful and multiply." The common Rastafarian expression "Jah [Jehovah] provides" describes the essence of the second commandment, based on an understanding of the global environment as containing the essential resources for the human population. Human creatures, as rational beings, have the responsibility to cultivate and maintain adequate access to life's necessities for all. Because Pan-African societies rank among the lowest in the global social-political hierarchy, concentrated efforts must prioritize the neediest. The command to be "industrious" includes charity in the short run, but the ultimate goal includes working toward the restructuring and transformation of society for a more equitable outcome.

The third commandment calls for solidarity. It is a testament to a traditional cultural attribute and a warning to shun individualism and social isolation. Empowerment comes through cooperation rather than competition. In his 1968 sermon titled The Drum Major Instinct, the American civil rights leader Martin Luther King, Jr., echoed this theme when he acknowledged that the human creature has an innate instinct to "surpass others and achieve distinction." King argued that the unchecked instinct can be

counterproductive for humanity unless it is rechanneled to advocate for justice. The phrase "demand respect of the nations" remains an ongoing objective for the African diaspora, with the understanding that internal conflict poses a threat to collective efforts toward redemption.

Revisiting Deuteronomy 6:5 in the fourth commandment, Rogers uses the expressive combination of heart, soul, and strength in reference to the motive and intensity behind one's labor. Although the Drum Major sermon was delivered some fifty years after the compilation of the Holy Piby, the essence of King's message contains a significant parallel. Both Rogers and King present a paradox: that the natural human urge for greatness cannot succeed through fighting for supremacy but only through service to humanity and standing firm for justice.

In the fifth commandment, external cleanliness and a pleasant countenance are said to signify the embodiment of the sacred. The prescribed Rastafari diet and its variations have been described as *ital*, a Rastafarian culture colloquial term that resembles the Islamic halal or Jewish kosher practices. The theological understanding implies that the physical body functions as the property of God, such that care for the body signifies reverence to God. The anointing of the generation of Ethiopia means that persons regarded as part of Ethiopia have been set apart from the remaining population. This command makes no reference to the superior or inferior status of any select group.

Virtues and the cultivation of character are emphasized in the sixth commandment; the "Children of Ethiopia" must avoid the temptation of taking moral shortcuts toward upward social mobility. Prosperity is a goal, but flawed character can nullify the words and deeds of individuals and institutions that could otherwise improve society.

The seventh commandment corresponds to the traditional "Thou shall not steal" but takes a radically different approach. There is an implied understanding that taking the possessions of another without consent constitutes a transgression against humanity and God. However, the Holy Piby implies a broader context by acknowledging that everything belongs to God and that God holds humanity as stewards. Thus, defending property and safeguarding fundamental individual and group rights become divine mandates. Such rights were directly violated during the slavery era and continued to be violated in the postslavery African diaspora through colonialism, America's Jim Crow laws, and all the institutions that compel people of African descent to endure positions of servitude. Allowing the violation of human rights is itself sinful, because it tolerates conditions that impede the worship of God.

The eighth commandment warns against hypocrisy and passing judgment on others. While moral judgment may seem unavoidable, the rational person must seek to view the transgressor in a favorable light. Likewise, gossip and malicious speech (which murders the victim's character) should not be accepted as true. The commandment emphasizes instead such favorable attitudes as understanding, tolerance, and forgiveness.

The ninth commandment corresponds to the biblical "Thou shall not kill." The Piby, however, not only assumes the wrongfulness of shedding blood but also specifically addresses the ancient problem of fratricide. This command forbids violent acts against individuals and groups that ought to be allies. In a polarized society, intragroup murders only empower enemies and competitors.

The tenth commandment calls for social, political, and economic independence. Contrary to pure separatist nationalism, the command endorses self-reliance as the antidote to the collective problem of Pan-African political impotence. Blacks are cautioned against relying on outside institutions, whose "denial" may signal fickleness or inconstancy. In addition, the living have an obligation to sacrifice and labor so that future generations (the "offsprings of the womb") can inherit a life with more favorable conditions within an optimally just society.

The eleventh commandment addresses the form and manner of worship, calling on the "children of Ethiopia" to "establish ye upon the Law a Holy temple for the Lord according to thy name" and to become "concretized" in the law. This word is one the author favors and seems to refer to the notion of becoming firm in one's faith.

Finally, the twelfth commandment recapitulates parts of the first and couples this statement with an injunction to worship and sacrifice and observe the Sabbath. As the Lord rested on the seventh day, his followers are enjoined to do likewise, in language echoing the biblical fourth commandment (Deuteronomy 5:12).

The "Shepherd's Prayer" that concludes chapter 3 corresponds with the Lord's Prayer of Matthew and Luke of the Christian New Testament Gospels. By addressing the "God of Ethiopia," that is, our God, the prayer becomes a collective prayer on behalf of the entire African diaspora rather than a merely personal prayer.

◆ Chapter 4: The Law Preached

The life and preaching of Robert Athlyi Rogers are here presented in a manner that recalls the Gospel of Mark. The preaching and baptism of "Shepherd Athlyi" is similar to that of John the Baptist. Just as the biblical John appeared from the wilderness, Rogers emerged from obscurity. John performed water baptisms, proclaimed a message of repentance, and announced the coming of one much greater. His words and deeds unified rival groups such that people from both Jerusalem and Judea came forth. Rogers's message of concretion entails sending forth people to play an active role in eradicating human suffering. The implication of this message is to acknowledge the necessity of advancing humanity by focusing directly on those who have been generationally regarded as the least. The lifespan of the philosophy that has derived from the laws can be attributed to basing the laws on religion rather than on purely secular law. Purely secular laws at their best contain logical validity and soundness; however, such laws must appeal to the emotional faculties because emotions make common shared experiences possible.

◆ Chapter 5: Athlicanity Preached

The excerpt from chapter 5 (with the coined term "Athlicanity" paralleling "Christianity" in the title) stresses the role that race relations play in terms of mission. If the Holy Piby is to be compared with the Judeo-Christian Bible, the historical context needs to be examined. When the documents that constitute the Bible were compiled from the first millennium BCE to about 100 CE, there was no racial taxonomy for humankind. Ethnic groups, tribes, families, and nationalities existed, but they were not categorized in the scientific (and sometimes pseudoscientific) manner characteristic of the West during the twentieth century.

Race categories in Western society can become distorting lenses when viewing the world of sacred texts; in particular, race becomes a challenging concept in connection with texts written in a preracial or nonracial setting. In the Holy Piby, however, racial solidarity has an explicit thematic purpose. Rogers warns against "a race of people who forsake their own" but does not specify a particular race. A sympathetic critique of Rogers's doctrine of racial solidarity would see humanitarianism (emerging from self-evaluation), group solidarity, and reaching out to other groups as long-term goals. Undoubtedly, some Rastafarians do embrace xenophobia as a means of survival and a requisite to redemption. Rastafari, after all, lacks a central authority or unifying creed. However, along with the Bible, especially the book of Revelation, the Holy Piby has been revered as sacred.

◆ Chapter 6: Solemnity Feast

The excerpt from the sixth chapter highlights one of the most prominent features of the Holy Piby, the significance of the sacraments. Although the text does not explicitly cite a Trinitarian doctrine like that of Christianity, the Athlican faith acknowledges that its sacrament of baptism exists under the authority of "one God, his Holy Law and the Holy Ghost."

When properly observed, the monthly Solemnity Feast is a three-day observance that culminates with a cessation from secular labor and a feast on the third day. The Solemnity Feast parallels the Jewish Passover meal and the Christian Holy Communion in its consumption of bread and water as an act of ongoing remembrance. The proper ritual includes devoutly kneeling at the altar and then rising to renew one's commitment to lead a new life and leave all previous iniquities at the altar.

The "remission of their iniquities" granted by Athlican baptism can best be understood in the context of the African diaspora. A common belief shared by both the Athlican and the greater Rastafari communities is that subjection through political oppression and economic exploitation in the United States and the Caribbean is a consequence of past transgressions by non-Africans. Thus, the text draws a parallel between the exile of the Israelites in Babylon and the displacement of Africans in the Western Hemisphere. Hope lies in redemption and an eventual return to Ethiopia.

Baptism also symbolizes unity of spirit, which contrasts with the Protestant emphasis on personal salvation. It is through the sacrament that the individual transcends his or her self and is commissioned to play an active role in saving humanity from suffering and in rebuilding Ethiopia. "Ethiopia," again, signifies more than a particular African political nation. It refers to a decolonized, free, and independent Africa. A large sector of modern-day Rastafarians equate Ethiopia with heaven, despite the human suffering of the earthly Ethiopia. The faith of the movement in the face of suffering defies the fatalistic view of never-ending trials and envisions the end of African deprivation. Therefore, baptism functions as the outward expression of turning against a nonproductive life to unite with a community of believers who are committed to becoming advocates for Ethiopia's redemption and restoration.

The Holy Piby substitutes water for the Judeo-Christian consumption of wine (or grape juice in some denominations). This practice is compatible with the dietary practice of abstaining from wine or grape products in the Nazirite vow in Numbers 6:1–21. Partaking of water instead of wine enables the sacrament to include those under the Nazirite vow, which requires abstinence from consuming wine and grapes.

Audience

The Holy Piby addresses primarily persons of African origin in North and Central America who have a Judeo-Christian religious orientation. The original audience was the Afro-Athlican Constructive Church, including the Hamatic Church in Jamaica. However, Rastafari philosophical discourse is in part derived from the Holy Piby, which revises (in the sense of "re-sees") traditional biblical truths in terms that reflect the African experience and the African diaspora. The Holy Piby underpins the Rastafari belief in a monotheistic God and in Christ as the redeemer; at the same time, it appeals to those who believe that the message of the Bible has been corrupted by Western society, that the people of Ethiopia are God's chosen people (the children of Israel), and that Ethiopia is the promised land.

Impact

Although the Holy Piby is regarded as a foundational document for Rastafari, strictly speaking it is not a Rastafari document, for that movement did not take shape until the 1930s. Nevertheless, the Holy Piby holds pride of place with Rastafarians for its articulation of a black, Pan-African vision of Christianity.

According to Rastafari tradition, five key events occurred within a brief period to inaugurate the Rastafari movement. First was the publication of the Holy Piby in 1924, providing a literary framework for establishing Rastafari doctrines. Second, Charles F. Goodridge and Grace Jenkins Garrison carried the Holy Piby to Jamaica beginning in 1925 and founded the Hamatic Church. They faced immediate opposition from both mainline and fundamentalist Christian authorities, which led toward their retreating to the remote Saint Thomas Parish, which is regarded as the birthplace of the Rastafari movement. Third, during the late 1920s Marcus Garvey prophesied that a great king would come from Africa. Garvey made several references linking the coronation of an African king with the redemption and deliverance of persons of African origin living in the West. Fourth, Ras Tafari Makonnen, also known as Haile Selassie (which means "strength of the Trinity") was crowned emperor of Ethiopia in 1930; notice that the word *Rastafari* is derived from "Ras Tafari." Fifth, Leonard P. Howell, often referred to as the "first Rastafarian," began preaching in Jamaica that Haile Selassie was a living Messiah and the Second Advent (or Second Coming of Christ). Followers of Howell's teachings became known as Rastafarians.

Rastafari is characterized as less a religion and more a movement, an ideology, and a way of life. Most Rastafarians do not claim to adhere to any Christian sect or denomination, and they encourage others to find inspiration and faith internally rather than through an institutionalized church. The Rastafari movement advocates the use of cannabis for spiritual purposes and rejects Western social institutions, referring to the West as "Babylon," an allusion to the figurative Babylon of the New Testament Book of Revelation, where the ancient city becomes a symbol of corruption. At the same time it holds that Africa is the "Zion," or promised land, referred to in the Bible, and it calls for a variety of Afrocentric social and political aspirations. In the contemporary world, awareness of the Rastafari movement has spread in large part through interest in reggae music, such as that of Jamaican singer-songwriter Bob Marley (1945–1981). Roughly 5–10 percent of Jamaicans identify themselves as Rastafari.

Further Reading

■ Books

Forsythe, Dennis. *Rastafari: For the Healing of the Nation*. New York: One Drop Books, 1983.

Garvey, Amy Jacques. *The Philosophy and Opinions of Marcus Garvey; or, Africa for the Africans*. Dover, Mass.: Majority Press, 1986.

Hill, Robert A. *Dread History: Leonard P. Howell and Millenarian Visions in the Early Rastafarian Religion*. Chicago: Frontline Distribution International, 2001.

King, Martin Luther, Jr. "Drum Major Instinct." In *A Knock at Midnight: Inspiration from the Great Sermons of Reverend Martin Luther King Jr.*, ed. Peter Holloran and Clayborne Carson. New York: Warner Books, 2000.

Murrell, Nathaniel S., and Lewin Williams. "The Black Biblical Hermeneutics of Rastafari." In *Chanting Down Babylon: The Rastafari Reader*, ed. Nathaniel S. Murrell et al. Philadelphia: Temple University Press, 1998.

Page, Hugh R., Jr., ed. *The Africana Bible: Reading Israel's Scriptures from Africa and the African Diaspora*. Minneapolis, Minn.: Fortress Press, 2010.

Smith, Theophus H. *Conjuring Culture: Biblical Formations of Black America*. New York: Oxford University Press, 1994.

West, Cornel. "Philosophy and the Afro-American Experience." In *A Companion to African-American Philosophy*, ed. Tommy L. Lott and John P. Pittman. Malden, Mass.: Blackwell Publishing, 2003.

Wimbush, Vincent L., ed. *African Americans and the Bible: Sacred Texts and Social Textures*. New York: Continuum International Press, 2000.

■ **Journals**

Davidson, Steed V. "Leave Babylon: The Trope of Babylon in Rastafarian Discourse." *Black Theology* 6, no. 1 (2008): 46–60.

—*Commentary by Michael D. Royster*

Essential Quotes

"Let the people be baptized with water by submersion for the remission of their iniquities in the name of one God, his Holy Law and the Holy Ghost."

(Section 1)

"Let the people assemble once a month on their knees before the altar at Solemnity feast, then shall the parson and ordained cleffs administer to them bread and water, saying 'eat in remembrance of your pledge to God, yielding yourselves into actual work for the welfare of your generation through the up building of Ethiopia and for the rescue of suffering humanity.'"

(Section 1)

"We believe in one God, maker of all things, Father of Ethiopia and then in His Holy Law as it is written in the book Piby, the sincerity of Angel Douglas and the power of the Holy Ghost. We believe in one Shepherd Athlyi as an anointed apostle of the Lord our God, then in the Afro Athlican Constructive Church unto the most Holy House of Athlyi."

(Section 1)

"I heard a great voice uttered from the end of the world saying, behold the map of the new Negroes, by this shall ye know the apostle of the twentieth century whom the Almighty God hath commanded to save Ethiopia and her posterities."

(Section 1)

---

1. What does the entry mean when it states that, in the view of Rogers, the Bible contains "socially constructed deficiencies"? What are these deficiencies, and how were they supposed to have been socially constructed?

2. In what sense is the Holy Piby the "black man's Bible"?

3. In the eyes of many people who know little about it, Rastafari would probably not even be thought of as a religion but rather some kind of drug-using voodoo cult. Disabuse them of that notion, based on your reading of the Holy Piby.

4. Underlying the Holy Piby is a strong social and economic message. What is the essence of Rogers's view of religion as an engine for social and economic change?

5. Rastafari bears many similarities with Christianity, yet Rastas themselves would probably not claim adherence to any particular Christian faith. How might a Rasta explain the apparent contradiction?

Holy Piby: Document Text

1924 CE

—Robert Athlyi Rogers

Chapter 3: God's Holy Law to the Children of Ethiopia

Great and manifold are the blessings bestowed upon us the oppressed children of Ethiopia, by His Divine Majesty, Lord God Almighty, King of all mercies, when by his most holy command His divine highness, Christ, Prince of the Heavenly Kingdom, descended and anointed us that we may be prepared to receive these noble men, servants of God and redeemers of Ethiopia's posterities. His honor, Marcus Garvey and colleague, his holiness the shepherd Athlyi, supreme minister of God's Holy Law to the children of Ethiopia, may we show gratitude to our God by being submissive to his teachings through these his humble servants, and submitting ourselves in obedience to his Holy Law that we a suffering people may reap the fruit thereof.

When as it was the intention of others to keep us forever in darkness, by our faithfulness to the Law we shall in time prove to the nations that God has not forsaken Ethiopia.

♦ The Holy Commandments

I

Love ye one another, O children of Ethiopia, for by no other way can ye love the Lord your God.

II

Be thou industrious, thrifty and fruitful, O offsprings of Ethiopia, for by no other way can ye show gratitude to the Lord your God, for the many blessings he has bestowed upon earth free to all mankind.

III

Be ye concretized and ever united, for by the power of unity ye shall demand respect of the nations.

IV

Work ye willingly with all thy heart with all thy soul and with all thy strength to relieve suffering and oppressed humanity, for by no other way can ye render integral service to the Lord your God.

V

Be thou clean and pleasant, O generation of Ethiopia, for thou art anointed, moreover the angels of the Lord dwelleth with thee.

VI

Be thou punctual, honest and truthful that ye gain flavor in the sight of the Lord your God, and that your pathway be prosperous.

VII

Let no people take away that which the Lord thy God giveth thee, for the Lord shall inquire of it and if ye shall say some one hath taken it, ye shall in no wise escape punishment, for he that dieth in retreat of his enemy the Lord shall not hold him guiltless, but a people who dieth in pursuit of their enemy for the protection of that which the Lord God giveth them, shall receive a reward in the kingdom of their Father.

VIII

Thou shalt first bind up the wound of thy brother and correct the mistakes in thine own household before ye can see the sore on the body of your friend, or the error in the household of thy neighbour.

IX

O generation of Ethiopia, shed not the blood of thine own for the welfare of others for such is the pathway to destruction and contempt.

X

Be ye not contented in the vineyard or household of others, for ye know not the day or the hour when denial shall appear, prepare ye rather for yourselves a foundation, for by no other way can man manifest love for the offsprings of the womb.

XI

Athlyi, Athlyi, thou shepherd of the holy law and of the children of Ethiopia, establish ye upon the Law a Holy temple for the Lord according to thy name and there shall all the children of Ethiopia worship the Lord their God, and there shall the apostles of the shepherd administer the law and receive pledges thereto and concretize within the Law. Verily he that is concretized within the Law shall be a follower and a defender thereof, more-over the generations born of him that is concretized within the law are also of the law.

XII

O generation of Ethiopia, thou shalt have no other God but the Creator of Heaven and Earth and the things thereof. Sing ye praises and shout Hosanna to the Lord your God, while for a foundation ye sacrifice on earth for His Divine Majesty the Lord our Lord in six days created. the heaven and earth and rested the seventh; ye also shall hallow the seventh day, for it is blessed by the Lord, therefore on this day thou shall do no manner of work or any within thy gates.

♦ The Shepherd's Prayer by Athlyi

O God of Ethiopia, thy divine majesty; thy spirit come in our hearts to dwell in the path of righteousness, lead us, help us to forgive that we may be forgiven, teach us love and loyalty on earth as in Heaven, endow us with wisdom and understanding to do thy will, thy blessing to us that the hungry be fed, the naked clothed, the sick nourished, the aged protected and the infants cared for. Deliver us from the hands of our enemies that we prove fruitful, then in the last day when life is o'er, our bodies in the clay, or in the depths of the sea, or in the belly of a beast, O give our souls a place in thy kingdom forever and forever. Amen.

Chapter 4: The Law Preached

Now in the year of 1917 A.D., Shepherd Athlyi first went about the City of Newark, New Jersey, U.S.A., telling of the Law and preaching concretation saying, I come not only to baptize but to concretize for the rescue of suffering humanity, for verily I say unto you, first seek ye righteousness toward men and all things will be added unto you, even the kingdom of God.

There came to him many to be concretized and he concretized them with water, men and women. And the names of his stars were: Rev. J.H. Harris, Sister R.J. Hamilton, Brother J. Reid, Rev. and Mrs. J. Barber, Brother C.C. Harris, Sister Leila Best, Sister Thurston, Brother H. Pope, Rev. and Mrs. Flanagan, Brother Charles McLaurin, Sister Letica Johnson, Brother and Sister Adam Costly, Brother and Sister W.D. Sullivan, Sister Sarah Johnson, Brother G.W. Roberts, Rev. J.J. Derricks, Rev. A.J. Green, Rev. W. Barclift, Sister Bertha Johnson, Her holiness, the

Shepherdess Miriam, Her Holiness the Shepherd-miss Muriel, Brother F.L. Redd. These are those who followed the shepherd from place to place.

And it came to pass that his holiness, the shepherd, traveled to Springfield, Massachusetts, U.S.A., there he concretized with water, and the names of his stars who followed him around were: Sister Sylvie Randall, Brother and Sister Eugene Kitchen, Brother and Sister Joseph Rutherford, Rev. R.G. Gaines, Brother J. When, Sister Ellen Frazier, Sister Minnieolo Walker, Sister M.A. Bryant, Irene Chambers, E. Dempsey. From there he traveled all around South America and the West Indies, preaching of the law and concretation by water for the sake of suffering humanity.

Moreover, in the year of 1919 Athlyi, after he was anointed shepherd, paraded the streets of Newark with a host of Negroes, protected by riding officers of the city and accompanied by a Salvation Army carrying banners, proclaiming a universal holiday for Negroes and foretelling of their industrial and national independence.

Chapter 5: Athlicanity Preached

For as much as the doctrine preached by Athlyi gained favor in the hearts of the people, and that it was efficient for the Salvation of Ethiopia's generations: On the thirteenth day of the seventh month, in the nineteen hundred and eighteen year, the followers of Athlyi assembled at the Israel Memorial A.M.E. Church, West Kinney Street, Newark, New Jersey, U.S.A. They declared themselves Athlyians by name and in faith.

And they consolidated themselves within the faith. They sang songs of praises and offered thanksgiving to the Lord God of Ethiopia.

And it came to pass that a committee was appointed from among them to confirm the Shepherd, and the names of those appointed and consolidated were Sister Rachel Hamilton, Rev. James Barber, Sister Gilby Rose, Bro. C.E. Harris and Bro. James Reed.

The committee decorated the Shepherd in four colors and committed in his right hand a staff so as to confirm the authority conferred upon him by the heavenly officials.

Now when the Shepherd was adorned and anointed by prayer, the Athlyians shouted with great joy and cried "Lead on, Shepherd of the Athlyians."

And it came to pass after the performance, the Shepherd stood up, and he was in four colors which were blue, black, red and green, and he explained the meaning of the colors and of the staff.

Saying Ethiopia's generations shall respect the heaven while for a foundation they sacrifice on earth; moreover a king sits on the throne of his organized government, but a Shepherd must seek his sheep and prepare a pasture for them that they be fed.

Then the Shepherd commanded his followers to stand, and he taught them saying, great is His Divine Majesty, the Lord God of all mankind, Father of Ethiopia; Who is greater than the Lord God? Even from the beginning of the world hath he prepared for his children unto the end.

The sun, the moon, the stars, the wind, the rain, the land and the sea hath he given free to mankind; who is so philanthropic, so magnificent, who can give such a gift? There is none so great as the Lord our God.

Let all the generations of Ethiopia hear the voice of Athlyi, for in his hands the law is given unto them.

Let not be devil persuade you that you turn your back against the Lord God of Ethiopia.

Woe be unto you should the heavenly father because of your ingratitudes turn against thee, revengely the hands of thy enemies and shall come upon thee with horror.

Let the Athlyians walk in the path of righteousness and all impediments shall be their foot stool and the spirit of the Lord shall dwell with them for ever and ever.

Blessed are the industrious hearts for they are those who use the blessing and the power of God for the good of mankind. Great shall be their reward in the kingdom of heaven.

Blessed are those who seek the Lord and by actual work prove to the nations that they have found him; for the power of God shall be as two kings feeling in darkness for an electric switch and he that found it immediately there was light throughout his palace and all the people rejoiced because of its splendor, but in the palace of him that found it not, there was no light, therefore his people wandered and became the servants of others.

Blessed are a people who seek their own, beautify and maintain it, for in their barns there shall be plenty; great shall they be among men. The Lord shall glory in them and their daughters shall be the wives of mighty men.

Woe be unto a people, a race who seek not their own foundation; their wives shall be servants for the wives of other men, and their daughters shall be wives of poor men and of vagabonds, and there shall be tears because of privation, then in the end hell everlasting for there shall be no reward in the kingdom of heaven for slothful nor the unconcerned.

Woe be unto a race of people who forsake their own and adhere to the doctrine of another. They shall be slaves to the people thereof

Verily I say unto you, O children of Ethiopia, boast not of the progress of other races, believing that thou are a part of the project for at any time thou shall be cast over the bridge of death both body and soul.

Forget not the assembling of thy selves and unitedly working for the up building of Ethiopia and her generations.

Then shall the nations of the earth respect thee and thy commodities shall be for their gold and their commodities for thy gold, but there shall be none to fool thee neither shall ye be their slaves.

For thy emblem shall rank among their emblems; thy ships among their ships, and thy men-of-war among their men-of-war; great shall be thy name among the nations.

The Lord God, Father of Ethiopia, shall glory in thee, with thee shall all the angels rejoice, great is thy reward in the kingdom of heaven.

Thy daughters shall work with clean hands and in soft clothing, thy sons shall enjoy the fruits of their colleges.

Chapter 6: Solemnity Feast

The following meeting after the Shepherd was confirmed, there came to him men and women to be concretized, and he concretized them with water.

And the Shepherd taught the form Solemnity feast, which the Christians call sacrament, and he taught the form of baptism also concretation and the period of concord according to the Athlican faith.

Let the people be baptized with water by submersion for the remission of their iniquities in the name of one God, his Holy Law and the Holy Ghost.

Let the people be concretized also with water that they be binded into one united band from one generation to another and let them pledge their lives loyally to the cause of actual work for the up building of Ethiopia and for the rescue of suffering humanity, suffer them to wash their hands against the slothful and fruitless life of the past. Then shall the parson give to them a hand of fellowship, bringing them forward into a new and ever productive life.

Let the people assemble once a month on their knees before the altar at Solemnity feast, then shall the parson and ordained cleffs administer to them bread and water, saying "eat in remembrance of your pledge to God, yielding yourselves into actual work for the welfare of your generation through the up building of Ethiopia and for the rescue of suffering humanity."

Drink in remembrance of your baptism when thy sins hath been washed away, bid far the devil and his iniquities; arise and go in the name of one God, His Law and the Holy Ghost.

For as much as angel Douglas binded the heaven and earth for the rescue of Ethiopia and her posterities, suffer the children of Ethiopia to assemble for three days celebration, beginning from the setting of the sun on the twenty-ninth day of the seventh month unto the setting of the sun of the first day of the eighth month of the year, which shall be known throughout the world as the period of concord in accordance with the celestial and terrestrial concord led by the mighty angel Douglas.

Hear, oh generations of Ethiopia, for I, Athlyi, speak not as a mere man but with authority from the kingdom of God.

Verily, I say unto you, the first days of the concord thou shall not eat the flesh of any animals, nor large fishes, neither shall ye drink of their blood or of their milk, thy victuals shall be of fowl and tiny fishes, devote thyself in communing with the Lord God of Ethiopia.

Be aware of improper conduct, for the angels of heaven are participating in the concord.

On the third day, which is the last day of concord, let there be a great feast and joviality among the people.

Let the atmosphere be teemed with balloons of colors carried in the hands of the people; let also the possessions of all Ethiopia's generations be adorned with the colors.

During the concord the house of Athlyi shall order the release of the people from all Athlican factories, or other enterprises so that they can commune with the Lord their God.

In time of concord let the Athlican ships fly the colors of the Great Negro Civilization where so ever they are; pray that the captains thereof are of the Athlican faith so as to celebrate concord in its fullness.

Hear ye, O generations of Ethiopia, for I, Athlyi, speak unto you, for as the Lord God of Ethiopia liveth, this is a serious affair which must not be forsaken.

The Holy finger print of the Almighty God signed the issue in the name of His Majesty, His Law, and for the sake of suffering humanity.

And it came to pass that one of the newcomers into the Athlican Faith who sat in the midst of the audience spoke, saying, "May I ask his Holiness, what is the principal belief of the Athlyians?"

Straight-way the Shepherd answered saying, the fundamental belief of the Athlican faith is justice to all, but hear ye, also, the Athlyian's creed:

♦ The Athlyian's Creed

We believe in one God, maker of all things, Father of Ethiopia and then in His Holy Law as it is written in the book Piby, the sincerity of Angel Douglas and the power of the Holy Ghost. We believe in one Shepherd Athlyi as an anointed apostle of the Lord our God, then in the Afro Athlican Constructive Church unto the most Holy House of Athlyi. We believe in the Freedom of Ethiopia and the maintenance of an efficient government recorded upon the catalog of nations in honor of her posterities and the glory of her God, the establishment of true love and the administration of Justice to all men, the celebration of concord, the virtue of the Solemnity feast and in the form of baptism and concretation as taught by our Shepherd Athlyi.

We believe in the utilization of the power and blessings of God for the good of mankind, the creation of industries, the maintenance of colleges and the unity of force, then in the end when earth toil is over we shall be rewarded a place of rest in the kingdom of Heaven, thereto sing with the saints of Ethiopia, singing Hallelujah, hosanna to the Lord our God forever and ever Amen.

Then the Athlyians shouted "Hosanna to the Lord God, surely the Lord has sent us not only a Shepherd but a savior."

Straight-way the Shepherd Athlyi spake, saying "Upon those words the Afro Athlican Constructive Church stands firm over which the hosts of hell nor the armies of the earth shall not prevail."

And the Shepherd being full with the Holy Spirit recited from his heart saying: "Father, thou God of all, closer to thee even though afar we stray; thou hast called us back, now all in one we come, children in Africa: Closer, oh God, to thee; closer to thee."

And he began to tell his followers about the wonderful works of God; how he hath sent apostles of the twentieth century, to save Ethiopia and her generations from the oppressive feet of the nations that they prove themselves fruitful for the good of their children and the glory of their God.

"Know ye that I am not the only one sent by the Lord our God to rescue the children of Ethiopia, for before me there were two others sent forth to prepare the minds of the people for the great things that shall come to pass.

"I saw an angel resembling a mighty Negro, and upon his head were horns of a great structure and on his breast was a map of life.

"I heard a great voice uttered from the end of the world saying, behold the map of the new Negroes, by this shall ye know the apostle of the twentieth century whom the Almighty God hath commanded to save Ethiopia and her posterities.

"At the sound of the mighty voice the structure descended from the head of the angel and stood upon the ground and the map surrounded it, then was the writing plain to be understood."

And the Shepherd showed the people a copy of the map, and said "Behold the map as I have seen it, straight-way at midnight I reproduce the mystery."

Then the Athlyians shouted for joy and the Shepherd spake with a loud voice saying "Thou sun that shines upon the waters of the utmost world, that gives light to the earth, stand thou still over mountains of Africa and give light to her righteous armies."

Where are those? There is none to compare with the Athlyians in united spirits and a determination; a people, lovers of freedom and of justice, fearless of death.

Glossary

A.M.E. Church: any African Methodist Episcopal church

angel Douglas: conceived here as a messenger from God

Ethiopia: a generic term for Africa

Marcus Garvey: a black nationalist born in Jamaica and founder of the Universal Negro Improvement Association 1914

Albert Einstein, Portrait taken in 1935 in Princeton.

HUMANIST MANIFESTO: DOCUMENT ANALYSIS

"Humanism asserts that the nature of the universe depicted by modern science makes unacceptable any supernatural or cosmic guarantees of human values."

Overview

The Humanist Manifesto, written in 1933 and published in the May–June 1933 issue of the *New Humanist* magazine, is a twelve-hundred-word document that lays out the tenets of religious humanism. Its primary author was Raymond B. Bragg, a Unitarian minister and at the time the secretary of the Western Unitarian Conference, who was joined by thirty-three other signatories. The 1933 document is generally referred to as Humanist Manifesto I, to distinguish it from later manifestos published in 1973 and 2003.

The aim of the Humanist Manifesto was to outline a new religious movement that rejected the dogmas and creeds of traditional deity-based religions. In particular, the document presents fifteen "affirmations" stating that the universe is "self-existing and not created," that "the nature of the universe depicted by modern science makes unacceptable any supernatural or cosmic guarantees of human values," and that "the humanist finds his religious emotions expressed in a heightened sense of personal life and in a cooperative effort to promote social well-being," among other tenets. Put simply, humanism is a belief system that rejects appeals to supernatural authority and focuses instead on the concerns and values of the human community and on the social and ethical development of the individual.

Context

Humanism is a term that can have different meanings to different people and, because it refers to a philosophical and ethical belief system, any discussion of humanism is necessarily complicated. The term is used, for example, to refer to a Renaissance movement that emphasized "the humanities," that is, secular knowledge, particularly the knowledge obtainable from study of the Greek and Roman classics. One of the key figures in this movement was Desiderius Erasmus, a Dutch humanist who did his most important work in the early decades of the sixteenth century. Erasmus was a Catholic priest who published new, groundbreaking Latin and Greek translations of the Bible and contributed to the burgeoning quest for secular knowledge during the Renaissance.

In the modern world, references are made to such subdivisions as cultural humanism, environmental humanism, philosophical humanism, literary humanism, and numerous others; additionally, there are people who classify themselves as Christian humanists, Jewish humanists, Islamic humanists, and even Buddhist humanists. However, two broad types of humanism are widely recognized: secular humanism and religious humanism, although the distinctions between the two sets of views is not always sharp or clear. Secular humanism, as the name implies, is an entirely secular philosophy. It emphasizes justice, ethics, and human reason. It rejects any and all appeals to the supernatural or religious dogma. It takes the position that humans can lead upright, happy, and functional lives without any appeal to God or traditional religious tenets. As a practical matter, secular humanists tend to regard traditional religions as regressive, oppressive, backward, superstitious, and closed-minded. Secular humanism has sometimes been referred to as scientific humanism, for the belief system is based in large part on humans' growing understanding of the processes of the natural order. Many secular humanists, in fact, have been scientists; among them were Albert Einstein, Linus Pauling, E. O. Wilson, and Carl Sagan. In contemporary life, the term *secular humanism* is often used as an insult by some people who adhere to traditional religions. They believe that secular humanists have a disproportionate effect on politics, culture, art, and entertainment and that the goal of secular humanists is specifically to undermine the traditional religious beliefs of the majority of the population. Religious fundamentalists, in particular, cast a wary eye on those they regard as secular humanists.

The other broad type of humanism is referred to as religious humanism, and it is this type of humanism that is espoused in the Humanist Manifesto—whose authors, it should be noted, included numerous ministers and professors of theology. Although religious humanists occupy common ground with secular humanists, there are important differences. Religious humanists, for example, are more likely to believe in religious experiences that imply the presence of a deity; secular humanists reject the validity of these experiences. While religious humanists tend not to believe in traditional conceptions of God, they do recognize the existence of the divine, of ideals and beliefs that transcend physical reality; secular humanists regard the so-called divine as a metaphor that refers to purely material truths. Finally, many forms of religious humanism explicitly express a belief in God; secular humanists, in contrast, regard belief in God as irrational.

The history of humanism is long and complex. Although humanist views date back to the ancient Greeks and Romans as well as to Renaissance thinkers, modern humanism can trace its roots back to the Enlightenment philosophy of the eighteenth century, which elevated science and human reason and rejected at least some of the dogmatism of traditional religion. The principal religious philosophy of Enlightenment thinkers was deism. Deists believed in God, but they rejected the notion that God involved himself in human affairs and that knowledge about creation was obtainable only through religious revelation, arguing instead for the primacy of human reason and observation. In the nineteenth century, Auguste Comte published *A General View of Positivism* (1844), which outlined the positivist philosophy—essentially a sociological view of the human condition based on science rather than theology and that Comte called the "religion of humanity." Also during the nineteenth century, writers such as Henri de Saint-Simon and Karl Marx outlined influential historical and philosophical views that rejected theological interpretations of the human experience.

As a more organized movement, humanism took shape through the formation of the Humanistic Religious Association in 1853 in London. The purpose of the organization was to promote knowledge of science, philosophy, and the arts. The organization's constitution stated: "In forming ourselves into a progressive religious body, we have adopted the name 'Humanistic Religious Association' to convey the idea that Religion is a principle inherent in man and is a means of developing his being towards greater perfection." The constitution went on: "We have emancipated ourselves from the ancient compulsory dogmas, myths and ceremonies borrowed of old from Asia [that is, the Middle East, the birthplace of Christianity, Judaism, and Islam] and still pervading the ruling churches of our age." A next step was the founding of the Free Religious Association in 1867. The goals of the association, founded in part by William J. Potter and David Atwood Wasson, were to emancipate religion from dogmatic traditions and to affirm the validity of individual reason and conscience.

Yet another step in the organization of a humanist movement was the formation of the Society for Ethical Culture by Felix Adler in 1876. Adler, a German Jew and rationalist, regarded Ethical Culture as a new form of religion. It would eliminate the unscientific dogmas of former ages, but it was to retain the ethical messages of those religions. In Adler's view, traditional religious dogma was incompatible with the findings of modern science, although Adler wanted to retain the good works and moral views of traditional religion. One signer of the 1933 manifesto was V. T. Thayer, the educational director of the network of Ethical Culture Schools.

In the United States, religious humanism gained a foothold after a Unitarian minister, John H. Dietrich, came across the term *humanism* in a magazine and adopted it to describe his own religious views; some historians regard Dietrich as the "father" of religious humanism—particularly after the publication of his book *The Religion of Humanity* in 1919. A decade later, in 1929, Charles Francis Potter (who also signed the Humanist Manifesto) established the First Humanist Society of New York. His advisory board included luminaries such as the evolutionary biologist Julian Huxley, the educator John Dewey, the novelist Thomas Mann, and the physicist Albert Einstein. Potter and his wife, Clara Cook Potter, published *Humanism: A New Religion* in 1930, and throughout the 1930s the two advocated women's rights, birth control, an end to the death penalty, and divorce law reform. Meanwhile, in 1927, a group of professors and seminarians at the University of Chicago formed the Humanist Fellowship, which published *The New Humanist*.

The publication of the Humanist Manifesto was not the result of an organized movement, nor did it emerge from a conference or symposium. In 1933 Raymond B. Bragg, a Unitarian minister, was the associate editor of *The New Humanist*. He was also the secretary of the Western Unitarian Conference (the organization that oversaw the Unitarian Church in the central third of the nation), and, as he traveled about, people suggested to him that the journal should publish some kind of statement outlining the religious humanist position. Interestingly, thought was given to having Charles Francis Potter write such a statement, but the idea was rejected because, in the eyes of some, Potter was not regarded as entirely reliable. The task of preparing a first draft was turned over to Roy Wood Sellars, a professor of philosophy at the University of Michigan. The draft was passed around among like-minded people, rewritten, and edited until it appeared in the May–June issue of *The New Humanist*. Its signatories included clerics, college professors, journalists, and others. Perhaps the most famous signer of the manifesto was John Dewey, whose name survives as that of one of the United States' most famous progressive educators.

About the Author

The person regarded as the principal author and motive force behind the Humanist Manifesto is Raymond Bennett

Time Line	
1844	■ Auguste Comte publishes *A General View of Positivism*.
1853	■ The Humanistic Religious Association is formed in London.
1867	■ The Free Religious Association is formed, in part by William J. Potter and David Atwood Wasson.
October 10, 1902	■ Raymond Bennett Bragg, principal author of the Humanist Manifesto, is born in Worcester, Massachusetts.
1919	■ John H. Dietrich, a Unitarian minister, publishes *The Religion of Humanity*.
1927	■ Professors and seminarians at the University of Chicago organize the Humanist Fellowship and begin publication of *The New Humanist* magazine the next year.
1929	■ Charles Francis Potter forms the First Humanist Society of New York; he and his wife, Clara Cook Potter, publish *Humanism: A New Religion* the following year.
1933	■ A group of thirty-four men compose and sign the Humanist Manifesto I; it is published in the May–June edition of *The New Humanist*.
1973	■ The Humanist Manifesto II is published in the September–October issue of *The Humanist*.
2003	■ *Humanism and Its Aspirations*, also called the Humanist Manifesto III, is published by the American Humanist Association.

of All Souls in Evanston, Illinois. After he was appointed secretary of the Western Unitarian Conference, he traveled up to fifty thousand miles a year to help keep Unitarian churches open during the Great Depression. As if that were not enough to occupy him, Bragg was the associate editor of *The New Humanist* from 1932 to 1935 and editor in 1935–1936.

Throughout the 1930s Bragg traveled across Europe, witnessing the rise of Adolf Hitler and the Nazi Party. In 1935 he accepted a job as associate pastor of the First Unitarian Society under John Dietrich in Minneapolis. Three years later he succeeded Dietrich as the church's senior minister. In this position he became an outspoken critic of Fascism. During World War II he served on the board of directors of the American Unitarian Association and chaired the Committee on Foreign Churches. After the war he served in various administrative positions for the Unitarian Church, but in 1952 he returned to pastoral work when he accepted a position at the All Souls Unitarian Church in Kansas City, Missouri, where he was one of the founders of the Kansas City Civil Liberties Union. He retired from the ministry in 1973 and died on February 15, 1979.

Roy Wood Sellars was the author of the first draft of the Humanist Manifesto. Sellars was born in 1880 in Ontario, Canada. He enjoyed a distinguished academic career as a professor of philosophy at the University of Michigan until he retired in 1950. He was the author of numerous influential books that dealt with humanist themes, including *Critical Realism* (1916), *The Next Step in Religion* (1918), *Evolutionary Naturalism* (1922), and *Religion Coming of Age* (1928). He died on September 5, 1973.

Explanation and Analysis of the Document

The Humanist Manifesto begins with a brief statement from Raymond B. Bragg. He notes that the manifesto was produced by many people, as intended to represent not a creed but a developing point of view. Although many religious humanists believe in God, they reject the dogmas and creeds of traditional religions, and humanists in the early 1930s sedulously avoided any sense that they were forming a new creed. Bragg concludes the opening statement by pointing out that humanism represents an attempt to form a new philosophy that takes into account the realities of the modern world. Indeed, scientific and technological advances dating back to at least the nineteenth century caused many people to question traditional religious beliefs and seek a new path.

The manifesto itself begins with a recognition that there have been "radical changes in religious beliefs" in the modern world. Humanists reject the notion that traditional religious beliefs have to be revised. Because of scientific advances and economic change—the United States and the world were mired in a deep economic depression in 1933—old beliefs are being turned on their heads, and religion has to find new ways for people to come to terms with new conditions. The opening paragraph then announces that the

Bragg. Bragg was born on October 10, 1902, in Worcester, Massachusetts. He attended Bates College in Maine from 1921 to 1924 and then transferred to Brown University, where he studied until 1925. His interest in theology grew, so he attended the Meadville Theological School, graduating in 1928. It was here that his humanist views developed. From 1927 to 1930 he served as the pastor of the Church purpose of the manifesto is to make "certain affirmations" demanded by the facts of contemporary life.

The manifesto's second paragraph notes that the doctrines and methods of traditional religion "are powerless to solve the problem of human living in the Twentieth Century." The paragraph goes on to affirm the legitimacy of "the highest values of life." In the past, these values have been achieved through theology, its goals and ideals, and the "cult," which the document refers to as "technique." Any change in these values results in change in the "outward forms of religion" that have been witnessed over time. Religion itself, though, remains a constant as people take part in the "abiding" quest for values.

The third paragraph again alludes to science and the way it has changed people's understanding of the world. It also refers to "brotherhood," suggesting that one of humanism's chief goals is the creation of a community of people without the divisions of the past. The passage acknowledges that people owe a debt to traditional religions, but religion has to adapt to the needs of the present age. It is important to note that humanists are not atheists—at least not necessarily. Religious humanists believe in God and believe that religion in some form can aid people in their quest for a peaceful, ethical life.

The manifesto then turns to its fifteen affirmations. The first rejects the literalism of the biblical book of Genesis by saying that the universe is "self-existing and not created." The findings of geology, as well as the work of Charles Darwin on evolution in the nineteenth century, had undermined traditional, literal interpretations of the Bible and the biblical account of creation. The second affirmation picks up the evolutionary theme by saying that humans are "part of nature" and have "emerged as a result of a continuous process." In other words, humanists reject the traditional view that humans hold some special status in the created world.

The third affirmation refers to this as the "organic" view of life and rejects the concept of a dualism of mind and body—referring to the notion that the soul is distinct from a person's physical body and that the body is just a vehicle for the soul. In the eyes of humanists, the traditional dualist view relieves humans of the need to forge a better order on earth, for earthly existence is merely a way station on the road to an afterlife.

The fourth affirmation calls attention to "man's religious culture and civilization" and characterizes them as a product of a "gradual development" resulting from human "interaction" with the "natural environment" and "social heritage." By saying that a person "born into a particular culture is largely molded by that culture," humanists reject the notion that one set of religious beliefs is superior to any other; all religious beliefs are the product of culture.

In the early decades of the twentieth century, scientists such as Albert Einstein were changing people's understanding of the very nature of matter and the universe. Thus, the fifth affirmation of the manifesto asserts that modern science has demonstrated that human values cannot be guaranteed by "supernatural or cosmic" forces. Further, the findings of science suggest that the only way to understand reality is through the "scientific spirit and method."

In the sixth affirmation, the manifesto explicitly rejects various religious philosophies. One is theism, the belief in a personal and transcendent God who created the world and preserves and governs it. Additionally, the manifesto rejects deism, a belief system associated with the eighteenth-century Enlightenment and that acknowledged God as the creator of the universe. Also mentioned is "modernism." It is difficult to specify what the authors mean here, though the word has been used to refer to any unspecified set of religious views that represent a break with the past.

The seventh affirmation broadly defines religion as any form of human endeavor, including labor, art, science, philosophy, love, friendship, and recreation. All these activities are expressions of intelligence. Thus humanists reject any distinction between the sacred and the secular. The eighth affirmation explicitly refers to "Religious Humanism" and states that the end of life is the "realization of the human personality" in the here and now. The end is achieved through "social passion," or a recognition of the brotherhood of people referred to earlier in the document.

The ninth affirmation turns to issues of "worship and prayer." Humanists see traditional forms of worship and prayer as ineffectual, for these forms assume the theistic view: If humans pray to a transcendent God, he will answer those prayers because he is actively involved in human affairs. Humanists define "worship" as a "heightened sense of personal life" and, perhaps more important, "a cooperative effort to promote social well-being." These aspirations can produce the same kind of religious emotion that traditional worship and prayer do. The tenth affirmation rejects the view that these "uniquely religious" emotions can be achieved by belief in a transcendent supernatural being—God.

With the tenth affirmation, the manifesto turns to the role of people in social affairs. Education can foster "reasonable and manly attitudes." (The masculine language was made gender neutral in the later manifestos.) Rather than encouraging "sentimental and unreal hopes," humanism, according to the eleventh affirmation, follows the path of "social and mental hygiene." Here, hygiene refers not to cleanliness but to any practice that promotes health, including mental health and the "health" of the society.

The twelfth affirmation asserts that a purpose of religion is "joy in living" and that one way to promote that joy is through creative endeavors. In the same vein, the thirteenth affirmation states that associations and institutions can add to human fulfillment. Again, religious institutions must be reformed to substitute intelligence for "ritualistic forms, ecclesiastical methods, and communal activities." Many early religious humanists were Unitarians, a denomination that places little or no emphasis on ritual and ecclesiastical methods.

The most controversial affirmation of the manifesto was the fourteenth, which attacks "acquisitive and profit-motivated society." The statement calls for "a socialized and cooperative economic order" and the "equitable distribu-

"Religions the world over are under the necessity of coming to terms with new conditions created by a vastly increased knowledge and experience."

(Section 1)

"Today man's larger understanding of the universe, his scientific achievements, and deeper appreciation of brotherhood, have created a situation which requires a new statement of the means and purposes of religion."

(Section 1)

"Humanism asserts that the nature of the universe depicted by modern science makes unacceptable any supernatural or cosmic guarantees of human values."

(Section 1)

"The humanists are firmly convinced that existing acquisitive and profit-motivated society has shown itself to be inadequate and that a radical change in methods, controls, and motives must be instituted. A socialized and cooperative economic order must be established to the end that the equitable distribution of the means of life be possible."

(Section 1)

"Man is at last becoming aware that he alone is responsible for the realization of the world of his dreams, that he has within himself the power for its achievement. He must set intelligence and will to the task."

(Section 1)

tion of the means of life." This seemed to many to be a call for Socialism, perhaps even Communism. For this reason, some people who were invited to sign the manifesto refused to do so.

The final affirmation calls for an affirmation of life and its possibilities and, consistent with the fourteenth affirmation, conditions for a "satisfactory life for all, not merely for the few." The final paragraph is a summing up. The values of the "religious forms and ideas of our fathers" are no longer equal to the task of creating meaning in life. However, those traditional religions did promote a "quest for the good

life," and humanists still regard that quest as central. The manifesto concludes by stating that man alone has the power to achieve his dreams, but he must turn his intelligence and will to the task.

Audience

The Humanist Manifesto was published in the May–June 1933 edition of magazine *The New Humanist*, which was subtitled "a Bulletin of the Humanist Fellowship." The magazine had been founded in 1927 and published its first issue in 1928. In the inaugural issue, the president of the Humanist Fellowship, H. C. Creel, wrote:

> The membership of the Fellowship is not, at present, limited to persons of any single type of interest or any single walk of life. It is hoped that, as it grows, this will continue to be the case. Humanism, to be worthy of its ideals, neither can be a neo-ecclesiasticism nor a neo-scholasticism. We are interested, primarily, in building a society in which every human being shall have the greatest possible opportunity for the best possible life. Insofar as we are Humanists, every secondary interest must be judged by this prime criterion.

In the second issue, Creel wrote that the purpose of the publication was to bring "the Humanists of this country (and of the world, if possible) into relations of mutual awareness and cooperation." Thus, the audience for the Humanist Manifesto included not only people interested in humanism per se but also people interested in religious dialogue, particularly dialogue about the role, function, and meaning of religion in the modern world. Additionally, the magazine functioned as a resource for clerics, especially Unitarian clerics, who found in it ideas for the content of services.

Impact

One of the longer-term effects of the 1933 Humanist Manifesto was the need for a second manifesto, which was published in 1973. Humanists believed that major cultural and socioeconomic changes were affecting the ability of people to assign meaning to their lives and that the original document was too naive and optimistic. It was noted that the 1930s and 1940s saw the rise of Nazism, with its unspeakable brutality. In the years following World War II, other regimes used warfare, espionage, and military power to enforce their wills. Racism and sexism continued to plague societies. The belief emerged that the principles of humanism had to adapt to these realities. Further, humanists came to believe that the supporters of the 1933 document still held to some form of traditional theism and that prayer provided a path to salvation. By 1973 humanists had come to regard these as outmoded beliefs.

Another problem raised by the 1933 document was that it was frequently misunderstood and misused. Some observers saw the document as the articulation of a creed—even though the document's originators specifically indicated that they were not advancing a creed. Still others regarded the document as in some measure responsible for a decline in morality. In effect, humanism became a scapegoat for many of the ills plaguing modern society. In particular, many religious conservatives, including such figures as Jerry Falwell, Pat Robertson, Jim Bakker, and Jimmy Swaggart, saw the Humanist Manifesto

as a statement intended to substitute ethical opportunism for religious belief. These and other critics were particularly agitated by what they saw as the creeping influence of humanism in the schools.

Even at the time, the Humanist Manifesto was controversial, at least in some ways. A particular point of controversy—and one that prompted some people to refuse to sign the document—was the fourteenth point, which states in part: "The humanists are firmly convinced that existing acquisitive and profit-motivated society has shown itself to be inadequate and that a radical change in methods, controls, and motives must be instituted. A socialized and cooperative economic order must be established to the end that the equitable distribution of the means of life be possible." During the 1930s, many people in the West were watching the rise of Communism with fear; indeed, the threat of Communism in post–World War I Germany contributed to the rise to power of Adolf Hitler and the Nazis. In the United States, anti-Communist hysteria had been a feature of American life since the Russian Revolution of 1917. During the "Red Scare" of 1919–1920, thousands of foreign-born radicals and anarchists were arrested. Many Americans attributed the labor unrest of the 1920s to Communist influences. But during the Great Depression of the 1930s, many Americans became sympathetic to Communist ideology because of the unemployment and poverty presumably created by the excesses of capitalism. In this climate, the House Un-American Activities Committee would be formed in 1938, and after World War II its chief mandate was to root out Communists. Thus, statements about "acquisitive and profit-motivated society" and "equitable distribution of the means of life" were perceived by some as an attack on the foundations of American capitalism and self-sufficiency.

Humanism and Its Aspirations, often referred to as Humanist Manifesto III, was promulgated in 2003. It is briefer and simpler than the two earlier documents, but the fundamental views remain the same. The manifesto was signed by a large number of people, including twenty-one Nobel Prize winners.

Further Reading

■ Books

Davies, Tony. *Humanism: The New Critical Idiom.* London: Routledge, 1997.

Fowler, Jeaneane D. *Humanism: Beliefs and Practices.* Brighton, U.K.: Sussex Academic Press, 1999.

Herrick, Jim. *Humanism: An Introduction.* Amherst, N.Y.: Prometheus Books, 2005.

Lamont, Corliss. *The Philosophy of Humanism*, 8th ed. Amherst, N.Y.: Humanist Press, 1997.

Norman, Richard. *On Humanism*. London: Routledge, 2004.

♦ **Web Site**

Wilson, Edwin H. *The Genesis of a Humanist Manifesto*. 1995. http://www.infidels.org/library/modern/edwin_wilson/manifesto/

—*Commentary by Michael J. O'Neal*

Questions for Further Study

1. Respond to the following statement: Humanism is not really a religion, for it is a form of atheism that rejects appeals to a deity and focuses instead on the human community.

2. What is the distinction between secular humanism and religious humanism? Why are so-called secular humanists so often the target of attack by people who adhere to traditional religious beliefs, particularly fundamentalist Christian beliefs?

3. What social, historical, and economic circumstances may have played a part in the decision to formulate the Humanist Manifesto?

4. Can you see any commonalities in the views of the authors of the Humanist Manifesto and those of the Pittsburgh Platform, which articulated the views of Reform Jews?

5. Some people who participated in the discussions surrounding the Humanist Manifesto ultimately refused to sign it. Why?

6. Do you agree that the "doctrines and methods" of traditional religion have "lost their significance and... are powerless to solve the problem of human living in the Twentieth Century"?

Humanist Manifesto: Document Text

1933 CE

—Raymond B. Bragg

The time has come for widespread recognition of the radical changes in religious beliefs throughout the modern world. The time is past for mere revision of traditional attitudes. Science and economic change have disrupted the old beliefs. Religions the world over are under the necessity of coming to terms with new conditions created by a vastly increased knowledge and experience. In every field of human activity, the vital movement is now in the direction of a candid and explicit humanism. In order that religious humanism may be better understood we, the undersigned, desire to make certain affirmations which we believe the facts of our contemporary life demonstrate.

There is great danger of a final, and we believe fatal, identification of the word religion with doctrines and methods which have lost their significance and which are powerless to solve the problem of human living in the Twentieth Century. Religions have always been means for realizing the highest values of life. Their end has been accomplished through the interpretation of the total environing situation (theology or world view), the sense of values resulting therefrom (goal or ideal), and the technique (cult), established for realizing the satisfactory life. A change in any of these factors results in alteration of the outward forms of religion. This fact explains the changefulness of religions through the centuries. But through all changes religion itself remains constant in its quest for abiding values, an inseparable feature of human life.

Today man's larger understanding of the universe, his scientific achievements, and deeper appreciation of brotherhood, have created a situation which requires a new statement of the means and purposes of religion. Such a vital, fearless, and frank religion capable of furnishing adequate social goals and personal satisfactions may appear to many people as a complete break with the past. While this age does owe a vast debt to the traditional religions, it is none the less obvious that any religion that can hope to be a synthesizing and dynamic force for today must be shaped for the needs of this age. To establish such a religion is a major necessity of the present. It is a responsibility which rests upon this generation. We therefore affirm the following:

FIRST: Religious humanists regard the universe as self-existing and not created.

SECOND: Humanism believes that man is a part of nature and that he has emerged as a result of a continuous process.

THIRD: Holding an organic view of life, humanists find that the traditional dualism of mind and body must be rejected.

FOURTH: Humanism recognizes that man's religious culture and civilization, as clearly depicted by anthropology and history, are the product of a gradual development due to his interaction with his natural environment and with his social heritage. The individual born into a particular culture is largely molded by that culture.

FIFTH: Humanism asserts that the nature of the universe depicted by modern science makes unacceptable any supernatural or cosmic guarantees of human values. Obviously humanism does not deny the possibility of realities as yet undiscovered, but it does insist that the way to determine the existence and value of any and all realities is by means of intelligent inquiry and by the assessment of their relations to human needs. Religion must formulate its hopes and plans in the light of the scientific spirit and method.

SIXTH: We are convinced that the time has passed for theism, deism, modernism, and the several varieties of "new thought".

SEVENTH: Religion consists of those actions, purposes, and experiences which are humanly significant. Nothing human is alien to the religious. It includes labor, art, science, philosophy, love, friendship, recreation—all that is in its degree expressive of intelligently satisfying human living. The distinction between the sacred and the secular can no longer be maintained.

EIGHTH: Religious Humanism considers the complete realization of human personality to be the end of man's life and seeks its development and fulfillment in the here and now. This is the explanation of the humanist's social passion.

NINTH: In the place of the old attitudes involved in worship and prayer the humanist finds his religious emotions expressed in a heightened sense of personal life and in a cooperative effort to promote social well-being.

TENTH: It follows that there will be no uniquely religious emotions and attitudes of the kind hitherto associated with belief in the supernatural.

ELEVENTH: Man will learn to face the crises of life in terms of his knowledge of their naturalness and probability. Reasonable and manly attitudes will be fostered by education and supported by custom. We assume that humanism will take the path of social and mental hygiene and discourage sentimental and unreal hopes and wishful thinking.

TWELFTH: Believing that religion must work increasingly for joy in living, religious humanists aim to foster the creative in man and to encourage achievements that add to the satisfactions of life.

THIRTEENTH: Religious humanism maintains that all associations and institutions exist for the fulfillment of human life. The intelligent evaluation, transformation, control, and direction of such associations and institutions with a view to the enhancement of human life is the purpose and program of humanism. Certainly religious institutions, their ritualistic forms, ecclesiastical methods, and communal activities must be reconstituted as rapidly as experience allows, in order to function effectively in the modern world.

FOURTEENTH: The humanists are firmly convinced that existing acquisitive and profit-motivated society has shown itself to be inadequate and that a radical change in methods, controls, and motives must be instituted. A socialized and cooperative economic order must be established to the end that the equitable distribution of the means of life be possible. The goal of humanism is a free and universal society in which people voluntarily and intelligently cooperate for the common good. Humanists demand a shared life in a shared world.

FIFTEENTH AND LAST: We assert that humanism will: (a) affirm life rather than deny it; (b) seek to elicit the possibilities of life, not flee from them; and (c) endeavor to establish the conditions of a satisfactory life for all, not merely for the few. By this positive morale and intention humanism will be guided, and from this perspective and alignment the techniques and efforts of humanism will flow.

So stand the theses of religious humanism. Though we consider the religious forms and ideas of our fathers no longer adequate, the quest for the good life is still the central task for mankind. Man is at last becoming aware that he alone is responsible for the realization of the world of his dreams, that he has within himself the power for its achievement. He must set intelligence and will to the task.

(Signed)

J.A.C. Fagginger Auer—Parkman Professor of Church History and Theology, Harvard University; Professor of Church History, Tufts College. *E. Burdette Backus*—Unitarian Minister. *Harry Elmer Barnes*—General Editorial Department, ScrippsHoward Newspapers. *L.M. Birkhead*—The Liberal Center, Kansas City, Missouri. *Raymond B. Bragg*—Secretary, Western Unitarian Conference. *Edwin Arthur Burtt*—Professor of Philosophy, Sage School of Philosophy, Cornell University. *Ernest Caldecott*—Minister, First Unitarian Church, Los Angeles, California. *A.J. Carlson*—Professor of Physiology, University of Chicago. *John Dewey*—Columbia University. *Albert C. Dieffenbach*—Formerly Editor of *The Christian Register*. *John H. Dietrich*—Minister, First Unitarian Society, Minneapolis. *Bernard Fantus*—Professor of Therapeutics, College of Medicine, University of Illinois. *William Floyd*—Editor of *The Arbitrator*, New York City. *F.H. Hankins*—Professor of Economics and Sociology, Smith College. *A. Eustace Haydon*—Professor of History of Religions, University of Chicago. *Llewellyn Jones*—Literary critic and author. *Robert Morss Lovett*—Editor, *The New Republic*; Professor of English, University of Chicago. *Harold P. Marley*—Minister, The Fellowship of Liberal Religion, Ann Arbor, Michigan. *R. Lester Mondale*—Minister, Unitarian Church, Evanston, Illinois. *Charles Francis Potter*—Leader and Founder, the First Humanist Society of New York, Inc. *John Herman Randall, Jr.*—Department of Philosophy, Columbia University. *Curtis W. Reese*—Dean, Abraham Lincoln Center, Chicago. *Oliver L. Reiser*—Associate Professor of Philosophy, University of Pittsburgh. *Roy Wood Sellars*—Professor of Philosophy, University of Michigan. *Clinton Lee Scott*—Minister, Universalist Church, Peoria, Illinois. *Maynard Shipley*—President, The Science League of America. *W. Frank Swift*—Director, Boston Ethical Society. *V.T. Thayer*—Educational Director, Ethical Culture Schools. *Eldred C. Vanderlaan*—Leader of the Free Fellowship, Berkeley, California. *Joseph Walker*—Attorney, Boston, Massachusetts. *Jacob J. Weinstein*—Rabbi; Advisor to Jewish Students, Columbia University. *Frank S.C. Wicks*—All Souls Unitarian Church, Indianapolis. *David Rhys Williams*—Minister, Unitarian Church, Rochester, New York. *Edwin H. Wilson*—Managing Editor, *The New Humanist*, Chicago, Illinois; Minister, Third Unitarian Church, Chicago, Illinois.

Glossary

deism:	a belief system associated with the eighteenth-century Enlightenment and that acknowledged God as the creator of the universe
theism:	the belief in a personal and transcendent God who created the world and preserves and governs it

From 1925 until 1954 Meher Baba communicated by pointing to letters on an alphabet board.

DISCOURSES: DOCUMENT ANALYSIS

"...the one redeeming feature about human nature is that even in the midst of disruptive forces there invariably exists some form of love."

Overview

The *Discourses* are a compilation of the teachings of the Indian mystic and spiritual master Meher Baba, given to his inner circle of disciples in the 1930s and 1940s. Although this series of messages was offered over an extended period (usually cited as being between 1938 and 1943), the *Discourses* present a coherent set of guidelines for the spiritual advancement of humanity. This book is generally considered by followers of Meher Baba to be his second most important work after *God Speaks* (1955), which offers his most complete description of the process and meaning of life.

Meher Baba's followers do not consider the *Discourses* to be a sacred text, and Meher Baba himself was opposed to the formation of a religion based on his work. Instead, the *Discourses* are designed to further an aspirant's progress on the path of spiritual evolution while ensuring engagement in the affairs of the world. The book does make it clear that a guide on the path, a "Master," is required in order to overcome life's myriad challenges, and it offers both practical and metaphysical insights to the reader. The text also reinforces Meher Baba's conviction that while all religions may lead one to ultimate happiness and peace or salvation, one can achieve this goal only through utter faith, devotion, and surrender to God.

Originally printed at the request of the Italian-born princess Norina Matchabelli, an early Western disciple, as articles in the New York–based *Meher Baba Journal*, the monthly pieces were edited by Chakradhar D. Deshmukh, approved by Meher Baba, and bound into volumes at the end of each year. The *Journal* ceased printing after four years, and a subsequent fifth volume of other messages by Meher Baba was later printed in India. In 1955, with earlier editions of the writings out of print, Meher Baba authorized Charles B. Purdom (an English author and also Meher Baba's first biographer) to put together a condensed

volume to be published in the West. In 1967 he next authorized a three-volume set (the sixth edition) to be released with some corrections and minor modifications. A seventh edition was published in the United States in 1987.

Context

As an assemblage of writings, the *Discourses* have no singular inspiration but rest firmly on the religious ideals of Meher Baba's upbringing and his extensive study with well-respected living teachers of various religious traditions, notably Sufi, Muslim, and Hindu. The Zoroastrianism in which he was immersed as a child provided a strong framework for the development of his commitment to truth as a guiding principle of faith and the importance placed on doing beneficent works in the world to help ensure an ordered reality—one in which good prevails over evil and chaos is kept at bay.

Meher Baba's first teacher, Hazrat Babajan, was an ethnic Baloch Muslim saint who, though she was born a princess, inspired knowledge in Meher Baba through her own story of the limitedness of wealth and status. Meher Baba met her in 1913; he received a kiss on the forehead from her under a neem tree in January 1914 at the age of nineteen and is said to have gone immediately into a state of divine bliss that lasted about nine months. During this time he is said to have first experienced himself as one with all of creation, though others initially questioned his sanity. Meher Baba's belief in the equality of all life and the disregard for caste within Hindu India as well as his willing personal care and provision of treatment for the physically and mentally ill have strong roots in the years spent with Hazrat Babajan.

Other teachers too, specifically the remaining four of the five "Perfect Masters" named by Meher Baba as providing the ground for his spiritual explorations and impetus for their furtherance, give additional context for his *Discourses*. These Perfect Masters were Upasni Maharaj (1870–1941),

Sai Baba of Shirdi (ca. 1830–1918), Hazrat Tajuddin Baba (1861–1925), and Narayan Maharaj (1885–1945). The purpose of the Masters of any time, Meher Baba believed, is to help humanity understand its true nature by facilitating an awakening to truth and in this way helping uplift humankind toward the goal of eternal happiness. From these Masters he claimed to have received the lessons and qualities that made him who he was as a spiritual teacher.

Of the five Perfect Masters, the life and teachings of Sai Baba of Shirdi are perhaps the best documented and most well known. Cutting across religious boundaries with a key message of the oneness of God, he is honored as a saint by both Muslims and Hindus to this day. Sai Baba was committed to all seekers and paths, although he preferred that one simply live by example in accordance with universal spiritual principles. His life inspired many, and Meher Baba found motivation for several of the teachings provided in his *Discourses* in the combination of practical and spiritual wisdom espoused by Sai Baba. For example, when Meher Baba states in volume 1, chapter 2, of the *Discourses* that "forms, ceremonies and rituals, traditions and conventions are in most cases fetters to the release of infinite life," he is invoking Sai Baba's call to humanity's greater spiritual creativity as unbound from religious and cultural dogma.

Upasni Maharaj (born Kashinath Govindrao Upasni), is the only one of the Five Perfect Masters who left writings, and it is from these that his teachings have been disseminated beyond the oral tradition. His central message was "Be as it may," by which he meant to convey that one should adopt an attitude of acceptance toward whatever life presents. Upasni, who was a personal disciple of Sai Baba of Shirdi, taught a position of acceptance because he believed, as did Sai Baba, that God is in everything. Thus, to do other than willingly embrace life's challenges would be to deny God. Meher Baba and Upasni Maharaj met for the first time in 1914 when Upasni was still in Shirdi with Sai Baba, but the two spent more time together when Upasni relocated to Sakori in 1917. Overall, they were in contact for seven years, and because of the length of their contact, Upasni is considered by many to be Meher Baba's main teacher. The *Discourses* echo Upasni's main point, with their stress on cultivation of spiritual maturity based on one's everyday responses to the world—responses that are themselves, according to Meher Baba, expressions of divinity.

Tajuddin Baba of Nagpur and Narayan Maharaj of Kedgaon, the final two Perfect Masters, both lost their parents as children and came to a spiritual life quite young. Tajuddin, a Muslim by birth, was known both for the love he showed his devotees and for his ability to perform miracles. Committed to an insane asylum for sixteen years, he was finally released after having turned the asylum into a place of pilgrimage for many seeking his blessings, healings, and gifts. Narayan Maharaj, a Hindu by birth, was also said to have performed miracles for devotees. He invited disciples to find devotion in their hearts and to treat everyone as God. Meher Baba's *Discourses* reflect these Masters' commitment to the heart of humanity through an emphasis on divine love as expressed among even the most poor and destitute.

The *Discourses* came at a time of global significance, with World War II (which began on September 1, 1939, and lasted until 1945) largely framing their transmission. This backdrop provided Meher Baba with a unique opportunity to discuss the facts of war relative to his message of the oneness of life. Dispelling the spiritual ignorance of interconnectedness, he believed, would prove wars of all varieties (military and economic chief among them) unnecessary and unreasonable because their root cause—selfishness—would be eliminated. Such a message resonated with many in the West because it addressed widespread problems such as crime and unemployment. Especially in the United States, where the Great Depression had cut the average family income by 40 percent and left a quarter of those in the workforce jobless, many were questioning the fabric of American society and the principles of capitalism, democracy, and individualism that had heretofore made the country the land of opportunity.

In India, the independence movement was growing at the time the *Discourses* were initially given, and Mohandas K. Gandhi's activation of the principle of ahimsa (nonviolence) and civil disobedience in response to British rule inspired millions in the struggle that led to a free India in 1947. Gandhi's important role in this period of Indian history and the alignment of spiritual values and moral action in his life cannot be ignored as an influence on Meher Baba's thought, although devotees reported that Meher Baba told Gandhi to abandon politics when the two met in 1931 during a voyage to England. Nevertheless, Gandhi's commitment to truth as God, refusal of the Hindu caste system, and stance of peaceful resistance naturally aligned with Meher Baba's ideas and provided the basis for respect to emerge between the two men. Gandhi's position regarding British rule—which led to his imprisonment in August 1942—also fortified Meher Baba's stand in the *Discourses* on the subject of engagement in the problems of the world as a matter of spiritual discipline.

Finally, the *Discourses* follow an important period of Meher Baba's engagement with the West, and their writing and dissemination was supported by the popularity he gained during the early 1930s in the course of several trips abroad, notably to the United States and Europe. His book *Message to America* (1932) sowed the seeds for Meher Baba's American disciples to emerge and the *Discourses* to be printed from original talks given to a group of his closest disciples, called *mandali* (a Sanskrit word meaning "circle"), in India beginning in November 1938. From these small initial lectures (dictated on an alphabet board) to monthly articles printed in the United States to later bound volumes distributed around the world, the *Discourses* have continued to be of value to those seeking guidance on matters of the soul's development and what it is to live a spiritual life within the constraints of everyday existence.

Time Line	
February 25, 1894	■ Merwan Sheriar Irani, later known as Meher Baba, is born.
1913	■ Meher Baba meets Hazrat Babajan (née Gulrukh, meaning "Face of a Rose"), a Muslim spiritual master and world renunciate.
January 14, 1914	■ Meher Baba receives his first experience of divine bliss by the grace of Hazrat Babajan.
1921	■ Meher Baba receives another spiritual awakening, from Upasni Maharaj of Sakori, India; from this point, his spiritual work and public life commence, and he is given the name Meher Baba by his disciples.
April 1923	■ Meher Baba establishes Meherabad as an ashram with a free school and hospital as well as shelters for the poor and destitute. Facilities are open to all without regard for caste or religion.
July 10, 1925	■ Meher Baba begins forty-four years of silence, communicating only with an alphabet board until 1954 and then relying solely on hand gestures to convey his messages.
1931	■ Meher Baba first travels to England, visiting with Mahatma Gandhi several times during a three-week voyage on the SS *Rajputana*.
May 20, 1932	■ Meher Baba, on a tour of the United States, issues his *Message to America*.
November 1938	■ Meher Baba begins dictating *Discourses* on his alphabet board for publication. They are collected over the span of five years.
September 1, 1939	■ World War II begins.
August 9, 1942	■ Gandhi is imprisoned after his call for an independent India.
February 10, 1954	■ Meher Baba declares himself the Avatar of the Age.
November 1962	■ Meher Baba calls followers from around the world to India for a series of meetings over four days, called the East-West Gathering. Thousands attend.
January 31, 1969	■ Meher Baba dies in Meherabad.

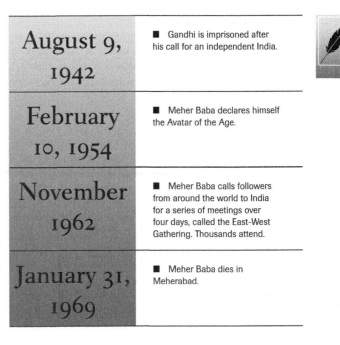

About the Author

A noted mystic and spiritual master, Merwan Sheriar Irani, called Meher Baba ("Compassionate Father") by his circle of followers, was born in Pune (formerly Poona), India, to Persian parents of the Zoroastrian religion on February 25, 1894. The name Irani in his family's adopted homeland of India tells of his ancestry in Iran (formerly Persia). He was a charismatic youth—handsome, well versed in several languages, said to be knowledgeable about the world for his age, and both a poet and musician. Although his father was a man of faith, Meher Baba did not follow any particular spiritual calling until his meeting with Hazrat Babajan in 1913. He was attending Deccan College in Pune at the time, and from that meeting his interest in spiritual matters took precedence in his life.

When Meher Baba was twenty-seven, he received a spiritual awakening from his teacher Upasni Maharaj; his inclinations for God thereafter took on public proportions, and his work with the *mandali* ensued. His dedication to spiritual values and a devout following of men and women eventually led to the creation of Meherabad (near Ahmednagar in the state of Maharashtra). An ashram built on a former British military site, Meherabad opened in April 1923 and by 1925 was a robust community complete with a post office and a free school as well as medical care and other community services offered to visitors, including the poor and infirm, without regard for caste or religion. Later, Meher Baba's work with *masts* ("God-intoxicated persons") dominated his time. He spent more than ten years traveling throughout South Asia with his disciples to find them. His efforts, he said, served to guide the inner fire of those he deemed to be spiritually advanced and not suffering from madness.

Meher Baba is perhaps most known for his almost life-long silence. For forty-four years, beginning in 1925, he communicated without vocalization, using first his own handwritten messages, then an alphabet board, and later in his life a unique system of hand gestures to put across his intended meaning. Meher Baba traveled the world spreading his love of God, traversing India countless times and visiting Europe, Australia, and the United States on thirteen voyages over a span of twenty years. On his first trip to England, in 1931, he met several times with Mahatma Gandhi during a three-week voyage on the SS *Rajputana*. In America, he was particularly interested in working "to break down all religious barriers and destroy America's materialism and amalgamate all creeds into a common element of love." This is the central tenet of his *Message to America*, published on May 20, 1932. In 1954, Meher Baba publicly declared himself to be Avatar of the Age, naming himself as a direct descendant of God in human form (akin to Jesus, Muhammad, and Krishna in other faiths), manifested in order to facilitate the awakening of humanity. In 1962, Meher Baba called thousands of worldwide followers to India for a four-day series of meetings called the East-West Gathering. At the end of the decade, bedridden, his body suffering intense muscle spasms of unknown origin, he died in Pimplegaon, India, on January 31, 1969, and was buried at Meherabad. The day of his death is remembered by followers as Amartithi (Deathless Day), and every year on July 10, in honor of his vow of silence, devotees themselves speak no words. Meher Baba is reported to have gestured, "Remember that I am God" as he took his last breaths.

Explanation and Analysis of the Document

The text provided here contains three early chapters from the *Discourses* that provide the ground for understanding Meher Baba's overall objectives and that set the stage for his universal message to be heard, by opening the reader to potentials for self-reflection. The use of gendered language in the text (for example, "man" instead of "human being" or "person") is generally recognized as more a sign of the times in which the pieces were written than a reflection on the inclusiveness of Meher Baba's own thought or teachings.

◆ The Seven Realities

The first chapter is concise and makes it clear that Meher Baba's teachings are available to all who seek spiritual guidance, irrespective of religious, ethnic, or national background and without regard for ceremony and ritual. In it, he lays out the seven key principles that are the basis for his work. An understanding of these "Seven Realities" is considered essential to full engagement with the *Discourses*.

The first Reality is Real Existence. With this, Meher Baba conveys his belief in the oneness of all creation, stating that God is found in every person. Real Love is both infinite and finite. God's presence ignites a longing within the individual to regain awareness of connection to the

source, to the oneness of God, which is Truth. While in pursuit of Real Love, everything that stands in the way of knowing and experiencing it is surrendered—through Real Sacrifice. Only a release, through Real Renunciation, of selfish thoughts and desires, including those had while conducting one's daily duties, can prepare one for the experience of oneness with God. Real Knowledge is an awareness of God in all people—whether they are considered good or bad—carried into all interactions and situations, so that one helps all people equally and harms none. In seeking to align with the qualities of God, one must exert a discipline of the senses, Real Control, in order to resist temptations and retain a good character. An acceptance of the will of God in one's life means release of selfish tendencies or agendas, through Real Surrender, so that perfect calm and equanimity prevail.

◆ The New Humanity

In the opening paragraphs of this chapter, Meher Baba argues for the spiritual rebirth of humanity, stating that creative forces, though silent, are operating according to the divine plan and that human transformation toward increasingly advanced spiritual states is assured. The conflicts and destruction wrought by war and competition in our everyday lives challenge us to look at the root cause of our suffering, which is self-interest. Once we understand this on all levels, material, intellectual, emotional, and cultural, we recognize the unity of life and, with it, the naturalness of being cooperative with one another. Until "self-interest gives way to self-giving love," he says, "humanity cannot avoid conflict and insufficiency."

A "New Humanity" can emerge "from the travail of the present struggle and suffering," Meher Baba tells us, in which science, as much as spirituality, can be a vehicle for the finite (individual) to know the infinite (God) and for lasting progress to be made toward the coming expressions of a human existence steeped in spiritual awareness. He writes, "Just as true art expresses spirituality, science, when properly handled, can be the expression and fulfillment of the spirit." This is possible, however, only when we can put science and religion to work hand in hand alongside time-tested spiritual values that guide the application of science and its objectives. For example, abiding religious dictates about the sanctity of all life within the scientific sphere would create a moral position prohibitive of vivisection and perhaps other forms of animal experimentation as well.

Similarly, spiritual experience, often considered to be at odds with the rational intellect, is not at all to be dismissed. Rather, it is to be embraced as a pathway to deeper understanding. For example, opening science to include insight and revelation obtained through what might be called spiritual means, such as dreams and visions, would pave the way for the emergence and validation of alternative epistemologies that help broaden humanity's awareness of Reality. The point for Meher Baba was the importance of bringing together seemingly disparate ways of being in and understanding the world, reconciling them through temperance, surrender, patience, and love.

Meher Baba goes on to say that when the intellect is transcended, the experience may be deemed mystical, meaning that a depth of spiritual experience so profound has been reached as to go beyond limitations of the body and mind. While connection to the infinite through these experiences can be articulated with the aid of the intellect, one must experience such states firsthand in order to fully know and comprehend them. Thus, one cannot be taught the nature of the mystical through books but rather can discover them only through dedicated practice on a spiritual path or be led to them by a qualified guide.

Finally, with all of this, the world and one's actions within it cannot be forgotten. An appropriate response to the demands and difficulties of life must be maintained, for to do otherwise would be to create a false sense of security built on illusions, foremost of which is a disconnected sense of self; that is, an ignorance of the oneness of creation, leading to separateness and suffering. If spiritual experience is unconnected to everyday life, he asserts, it is merely "a neurotic reaction."

"The spiritual experience that is to enliven and energize the New Humanity cannot be a reaction to the stern and uncompromising demands made by the realities of life," he continues. In the next paragraphs, Meher Baba outlines the forms and methods of our attachments in the world, stating that a creative life of the spirit, one that knows no limitations, is the destiny of the New Humanity. Categories of identity such as gender, class, religion, and so on, in addition to the obstacles of adherence to tradition and convention, only serve to burden individual existence and keep us far from the experience of universal life. When we are encumbered by limitedness, our worldview is equally small.

"What results from identification with narrow groups or limited ideals is not a real merging of the separative self, but only a semblance of it," he states. "A real merging of the limited self in the ocean of universal life involves complete surrender of separative existence in all its forms." Thus, Meher Baba advocates dropping ties to even acculturated identities that polarize individuals (for example, forms of dress, recreation, language, and other distinctions) in order to fully realize our inherent oneness with the divine. Although such unity may be difficult to accomplish or even imagine, given the narrow-mindedness of humankind in its present state, Meher Baba assures us that hope is possible for a joyful life because the force of love continues to exist despite oppositional categories of distinction.

In the final paragraphs of this chapter, Meher Baba makes an effort to affirm the potentials of humanity that could be realized if limitedness is released. He states that expanded, spontaneous forms of contagious love "in measureless abundance" could be awakened. This can be facilitated with the aid of the Masters, and our species as a whole can experience new kinds of love that are free from corruption, more deeply connected with one another and all life, and evocative of peace, happiness, and harmony in all spheres of our world. Acknowledging the fact of war, he points out that even in the ideologies that lead to war, love exists, but it is a misguided, limited, and tainted love: "Even

wars require cooperative functioning, but the scope of this cooperative functioning is artificially restricted by identification with a limited group or ideal. Wars often are carried on by a form of love, though it is a love that has not been understood properly. In order that love should come into its own, it must be untrammeled and unlimited."

By adopting a position open to spontaneous love and actively cultivating it from within, humanity can be released from the forces of corruption, greed, and coercion. When these forces no longer hold sway, asserts Meher Baba, the people of the world will become genuinely free.

◆ The Search for God

The first four paragraphs of this chapter discuss various gradations of belief in God. Regarding the infinite, Meher Baba tells us that many people are convinced of God's existence merely because of their upbringing; others maintain belief by faith, and still others cultivate belief through philosophical speculation. Such belief, however, is not the same as having personal knowledge of God, and those seeking a rich inner life will benefit first from a direct experience of that which they seek. Meher Baba illustrates his point by telling a story in the style of the Hindu Puranas (religious texts written in the form of stories) of an unknown sage who, upon seeing a dead body pass in the street and hearing a friend comment on the immortality of the soul, asks how the friend can know that the soul does not perish without having seen a soul firsthand. Because the sage insists on personal knowledge, he remains skeptical of the veracity of the friend's claim.

Although the story is intended to illustrate that firsthand experience is preferable to blind acceptance or mere inference, Meher Baba goes on to make a second point: The wisdom to remain open to possibilities for the existence of things not yet directly perceived is also important. He continues with a story of the same sage, who also happens to be a prince. The prince is traveling on a road blocked by a pedestrian who, when asked to move for the prince, refuses and asks how he can know the prince is truly who he says he is. With this, the prince realizes, by analogy, that he can know that God may exist even without any direct perception of God.

"God either exists or does not exist," says the discourse, but the search for God is not usually undertaken lightly. Meher Baba tells us that it is typically the case that difficulty, despair, and disillusionment create the opening for a quest—or at least the questioning—to begin. For example, as we use the world to search for pleasure and happiness (with accompanying habits of thought and behavior), we can have experiences of unmet expectations that lead to frustration and, in some cases, cause psychic upset or shock. Desperation in these circumstances can serve the powers of destruction, or, in the thoughtful person, can alternatively lead to spiritual insight.

In the final paragraphs of this chapter, Meher Baba concludes that the spiritual seeker at this juncture either experiences as rational the argument for belief in God or determines that life is meaningless. With the former perspective,

"Economic adjustment is impossible unless people realize that there can be no planned and cooperative action in economic matters until self-interest gives way to self-giving love. Otherwise, with the best of equipment and efficiency in the material spheres, humanity cannot avoid conflict and insufficiency."

(Section 1)

"Science is a help or hindrance to spirituality according to the use to which it is put. Just as true art expresses spirituality, science, when properly handled, can be the expression and fulfillment of the spirit."

(Section 1)

"There is nothing irrational in true mysticism when it is, as it should be, a vision of Reality. It is a form of perception that is absolutely unclouded, and it is so practical that it can be lived every moment of life and expressed in everyday duties."

(Section 1)

"The forces of lust, hate, and greed produce incalculable suffering and chaos. However, the one redeeming feature about human nature is that even in the midst of disruptive forces there invariably exists some form of love."

(Section 1)

"God either exists or does not exist. If He exists, the search for Him is amply justified. And if He does not exist, there is nothing to lose by seeking Him."

(Section 1)

"The spiritual journey does not consist in arriving at a new destination where a person gains what he did not have or becomes what he was not. It consists in the dissipation of his ignorance concerning himself and life, and the gradual growth of that understanding which begins with spiritual awakening. The finding of God is a coming to one's own Self."

(Section 1)

reengagement with the daily grind of life takes on new significance because a pathway to the transpersonal is sought out from within the mundane, and life becomes "a real experiment with perceived spiritual values." In this way, life gradually takes on a spiritual dimension that gives life meaning, and fulfillment is at hand. The discoveries along the way, however, are not an unveiling of something new; instead, the seeker discovers that they are the revelation of something ancient, of what has always been true—"The finding of God is a coming to one's own Self."

Audience

The original audience for the *Discourses* was Meher Baba's own small group of disciples, to whom they were spoken directly. These men and women came from various walks of life and different castes and creeds. They included, among others, Meher Baba's sister (younger by twenty-four years), Manija; his closest disciple, Mehera Jehangir Irani; Bhau Kalchuri, an author who later became Meher Baba's chief biographer; and Eruch Byramshaw Jessawala, the primary interpreter of Meher Baba's alphabet board and sign language.

Once *Discourses* was published, its first audience was American. Meher Baba's 1932 *Message to America* and his tours all over the United States had integrated East and West for many, offering an appealing call to the universality of divine love and an honoring of the truth expressed through both science and spirituality. When Meher Baba spoke to this audience of the need to eradicate self-interest so that this larger truth might be experienced and peace realized, many listened, and American disciples embraced his ideas throughout the country. Initially, the *Discourses* helped serve these individuals' need for ready teachings by Meher Baba, and later, when the *Discourses* were printed in India, the volumes brought even greater numbers of spiritual seekers together across caste, creed, and other boundaries of difference.

Those who read and find value in the *Discourses* today come from all backgrounds, nations, and faiths. In accordance with his wishes, Meher Baba's followers do not proselytize, and there is no centralized authority on his work. Thus, Meher Baba's worldwide following, though it is substantive, is impossible to quantify.

Impact

With the first publication of the *Discourses*, those previously introduced to Meher Baba but without other connection to him had access to a regular flow of his teachings. His popularity in the West had been growing since 1932, when such Hollywood celebrities as Mary Pickford, Boris Karloff, Tallulah Bankhead, and Charles Laughton, among others, gathered at a welcoming reception to hear his message. Millions in India and thousands in the United States and Europe are said to have become followers during the peak of his popularity, and today many in the West know Meher Baba for the quote "Don't worry—be happy"

through the Grammy Award–winning 1988 Bobby McFerrin song inspired by it.

The contemporary rock-and-roll legend Pete Townshend of the Who became a fan after initiating a spiritual quest in 1968. The Who's rock opera *Tommy* of 1969 was inspired in part by Meher Baba's silence, and the album was dedicated to him. Other Townshend works—from both his time with the Who (for instance the song "Baba O'Riley" in 1971) and as an independent artist—reflected his connection to Meher Baba. Townshend has said that his recording of Jim Reeves's song "There's a Heartache Following Me," on his first solo album, was a tribute to Meher Baba because it was Baba's favorite song.

With a universal message of selfless service, love, and spiritual guidance applicable more than seventy years after its first publication, the *Discourses* remain relevant to many today, and myriad centers devoted to Meher Baba and his teachings have been created around the world. Two of the more prominent are Avatar Meher Baba Trust in Ahmednagar, India, and Sufism Reoriented in California. Both were established by Meher Baba with specific instructions as to their purpose, and both act as spiritual centers for pilgrims and followers. Through these and other organizations both local and international dedicated to Meher Baba's simple message, his life and work continue to inspire.

Further Reading

■ Books

Adriel, Jean. *Avatar: The Life Story of Avatar Meher Baba*. Berkeley, Calif.: John F. Kennedy University Press, 1971.

Donkin, William. *The Wayfarers: Meher Baba with the God-Intoxicated*. Myrtle Beach, S.C.: Sheriar Foundation, 2001.

Haynes, Charles. *Meher Baba: The Awakener*. Myrtle Beach, S.C.: Avatar Foundation, 1989.

Kalchuri, Bhau. *Lord MeherPrabhu: The Biography of the Avatar of the Age, Meher Baba*. Asheville, N.C.: Manifestation, 1986.

Meher Baba. *God Speaks: The Theme of Creation and Its Purpose*. 2nd ed. New York: Dodd, Mead, 1973.

Purdom, Charles B. *The God-Man: The Life, Journeys, and Work of Meher Baba with an Interpretation of His Silence and Spiritual Teaching*. London: Allen and Unwin, 1964.

◆ Web Site
"Meher Baba's Message to America." Excerpt from *Message to America*. Avatar Meher Baba Lovers of Tampa Bay Web site. http://www.meherbabatampabay.org/america-message.php

—Commentary by Chandra Alexandre

Questions for Further Study

1. The entry states that in Baba's view, the purpose of "Masters" is to "help humanity understand its true nature by facilitating an awakening to truth and in this way help uplift humankind toward the goal of eternal happiness." What does Baba mean by "happiness"? What is your position on "happiness" as a goal? Do you think that the quest for happiness might be essentially a selfish one, or do you think that the achievement of happiness marks the attainment of a higher state of awareness and consciousness?

2. Baba's views are laced with such words and concepts as *happiness, acceptance, peace, oneness of life, interconnectedness, truth, awakening, understanding, surrender,* and *Real Existence.* These are positive values, but how, according to Baba, does one achieve such abstract and vaguely defined states of mind? What place would *competition* or *struggle* have in Baba's worldview?

3. What impact might economic and historical events in the 1930s and 1940s have had on Baba and the *Discourses?*

4. How do you think a Nobel Prize–winning chemist or physicist would respond to Baba's statement that "science, when properly handled, can be the expression and fulfillment of the spirit"?

DISCOURSES: DOCUMENT TEXT

1938–1943 CE

—Meher Baba

The Seven Realities

♦ Existence, Love, Sacrifice, Renunciation, Knowledge, Control, and Surrender

I give no importance to creed, dogma, caste, or the performance of religious ceremonies and rites but to the *understanding* of the following seven Realities:

1. The only Real Existence is that of the one and only God, who is the Self in every finite self.
2. The only Real Love is the love for this Infinity (God), which arouses an intense longing to see, know, and become one with its Truth (God).
3. The only Real Sacrifice is that in which, in pursuance of this love, all things-body, mind, position, welfare, and even life itself-are sacrificed.
4. The only Real Renunciation is that which abandons, even in the midst of worldly duties, all selfish thoughts and desires.
5. The only Real Knowledge is the knowledge that God is the inner dweller in good people and in so-called bad, in saint and in so-called sinner. This knowledge requires you to help all equally as circumstances demand without expectation of reward; when compelled to take part in a dispute, to act without the slightest trace of enmity or hatred, to try to make others happy with brotherly or sisterly feeling for each one; and to harm no one in thought, word, or deed—not even those who harm you.
6. The only Real Control is the discipline of the senses to abstain from indulgence in low desires, which alone ensures absolute purity of character.
7. The only Real Surrender is that in which poise is undisturbed by any adverse circumstance; and the individual, amidst every kind of hardship, is resigned with perfect calm to the will of God.

The New Humanity

As in all great critical periods of human history, humanity is now going through the agonizing travail of spiritual rebirth. Great forces of destruction are afoot and seem to be dominant at the moment, but constructive and creative forces that will redeem humanity are also being released through several channels. Although the working of these forces of light is chiefly silent, they are eventually bound to bring about those transformations that will make the further spiritual advance of humanity safe and steady. It is all a part of the divine plan, which is to give to the hungry and weary world a fresh dispensation of the eternal and only Truth.

At present the urgent problem facing humanity is to devise ways and means of eliminating competition, conflict, and rivalry in all the subtle and gross forms that they assume in the various spheres of life. Military wars are, of course, the most obvious sources of chaos and destruction. However, wars in themselves do not constitute the central problem for humanity but are rather the external symptoms of something graver at their root. Wars and the suffering they bring cannot be completely avoided by mere propaganda against war; if they are to disappear from human history, it will be necessary to tackle their root cause. Even when military wars are not being waged, individuals or groups of individuals are constantly engaged in economic or some other subtle form of warfare. Military wars, with all the cruelty they involve, arise only when these underlying causes are aggravated.

The cause of the chaos that precipitates itself in wars is that most persons are in the grip of egoism and selfish considerations, and they express their egoism and self-interest individually as well as collectively. This is the life of illusory values in which man is caught. To face the truth is to realize that life is one, in and through its manifold manifestations. To have this understanding is to forget the limiting self in the realization of the unity of life.

With the dawn of true understanding, the problem of wars would immediately disappear. Wars have to be so clearly seen as both unnecessary and unreasonable that the immediate problem would not be how to stop wars but to wage them spiritually against the attitude of mind responsible for such a cruel and painful state of things. In the light of the truth of the unity of all life, cooperative and harmonious action becomes natural and inevitable. Hence, the chief task before those who are deeply concerned with the rebuilding of humanity is to do their utmost to dispel the spiritual ignorance that envelops humanity.

Wars do not arise merely to secure material adjustment. They are often the product of uncritical identification with narrow interests, which through association come to be included in that part of the world regarded as "mine." Material adjustment is only part of the wider problem of establishing spiritual adjustment. Spiritual adjustment requires the elimination of self, not only from the material aspects of life, but also from those spheres that affect the intellectual, emotional, and cultural life of man.

To understand the problem of humanity as merely a problem of bread is to reduce humanity to the level of animality. But even when man sets himself the limited task of securing purely material adjustment, he can only succeed in this attempt if he has spiritual understanding. Economic adjustment is impossible unless people realize that there can be no planned and cooperative action in economic matters until self-interest gives way to self-giving love. Otherwise, with the best of equipment and efficiency in the material spheres, humanity cannot avoid conflict and insufficiency.

The *New Humanity* that emerges from the travail of the present struggle and suffering will not ignore science or its practical attainments. It is a mistake to look upon science as antispiritual. Science is a help or hindrance to spirituality according to the use to which it is put. Just as true art expresses spirituality, science, when properly handled, can be the expression and fulfillment of the spirit. Scientific truths concerning the physical body and its life in the gross world can become mediums for the soul to know itself; but to serve this purpose they must be properly fitted into larger spiritual understanding. This includes a steady perception of true and lasting values. In the absence of such spiritual understanding, scientific truths and attainments are liable to be used for mutual destruction and for a life that will tend to strengthen the chains that bind the spirit. All-sided progress of humanity can be assured only if science and religion proceed hand in hand.

The coming civilization of the New Humanity shall be ensouled not by dry intellectual doc-trines but by living spiritual experience. Spiritual experience has a hold on the deeper truths that are inaccessible to mere intellect; it cannot be born of unaided intellect. Spiritual truth can often be stated and expressed through the intellect, and the intellect surely is of some help for the communication of spiritual experience. But by itself, the intellect is insufficient to enable man to have spiritual experience or to communicate it to others. If two persons have had headaches, they can cooperatively examine their experience of headaches and make it explicit to themselves through the work of the intellect. If a person has never experienced a headache, no amount of intellectual explanation will suffice for making him understand what a headache is. Intellectual explanation can never be a substitute for spiritual experience; it can at best prepare the ground for it.

Spiritual experience involves more than can be grasped by mere intellect. This is often emphasized by calling it a mystical experience. Mysticism is often regarded as something anti-intellectual, obscure and confused, or impractical and unconnected with experience. In fact, true mysticism is none of these. There is nothing irrational in true mysticism when it is, as it should be, a vision of Reality. It is a form of perception that is absolutely unclouded, and it is so practical that it can be lived every moment of life and expressed in everyday duties. Its connection with experience is so deep that, in one sense, it is the final understanding of all experience.

When spiritual experience is described as mystical, one should not assume that it is something supernatural or entirely beyond the grasp of human consciousness. All that is meant is that it is not accessible to the limited human intellect until the intellect transcends its limits and is illumined by direct realization of the Infinite. Jesus Christ pointed out the way to spiritual experience when He said, "Leave all and follow me." This means that man must leave limitations and establish himself in the infinite life of God. A real spiritual experience involves not only realization of the nature of the soul while traversing the higher planes of consciousness but also a right attitude toward worldly duties. If it loses its connection with the different phases of life, what we have is a neurotic reaction that is far from being a spiritual experience.

The spiritual experience that is to enliven and energize the New Humanity cannot be a reaction to the stern and uncompromising demands made by the realities of life. Those without the capacity for adjustment to the flow of life have a tendency to recoil from the realities of life and to seek shelter and protection in a self-created fortress of illusions. Such a reaction is an attempt to perpetuate one's separate existence by protecting it from the demands made by life. It can only give a pseudo solution to the problems of life by providing a false sense of security and self-completeness. It is not even an advance toward the real and lasting solution; on the contrary, it is a sidetrack from the true spiritual path. Man will be dislodged again and again from his illusory shelters by fresh and irresistible waves of life, and will invite upon himself fresh forms of suffering by seeking to protect his separative existence through escape.

Just as a person may seek to hold on to his separative experience through escape, he may also seek to hold on to it through uncritical identification with forms, ceremonies and rituals, or with traditions and conventions. Forms, ceremonies and rituals, traditions and conventions, are in most cases fetters to the release of infinite life. If they were pliant mediums for the expression of unlimited life, they would be an asset rather than a handicap for securing the fulfillment of divine life on earth. But they mostly have a tendency to gather prestige and claims in their own right, independently of the life they might express. When this happens, any attachment to them must eventually lead to a drastic curtailment and restriction of life.

The New Humanity will be freed from a life of limitations, allowing unhampered scope for the creative life of the spirit; and it will break the attachment to external forms and learn to subordinate them to the claims of the spirit. The limited life of illusions and false values will then be replaced by unlimited life in the Truth; and the limitations, through which the separative self lives, will wither away at the touch of true understanding.

Just as a person may seek to hold on to his separative existence through escape or identification with external forms, he may seek to hold on to it through identification with some narrow class, creed, sect, or religion, or with the divisions based upon sex. Here the individual may seem to have lost his separative existence through identification with a larger whole. But, in fact, he is often *expressing* his separative existence through such an identification, which enables him to delight in his feeling of being separate from others who belong to another class, nationality, creed, sect, religion, or sex.

Separative existence derives its being and strength from identifying itself with one of the opposites and contrasting itself with the others. An individual may seek to protect his separate existence through iden-

tification with one ideology rather than another or with his conception of good as contrasted with his idea of evil. What results from identification with narrow groups or limited ideals is not a real merging of the separative self but only a semblance of it. A real merging of the limited self in the ocean of universal life involves complete surrender of separative existence in all its forms.

The large mass of humanity is caught up in the clutches of separative and assertive tendencies. For one who is overpowered by the spectacle of these fetters of humanity, there is bound to be nothing but unrelieved despair about its future. One must look deeper into the realities of the day if one is to get a correct perspective on the present distress of humanity. The real possibilities of the New Humanity are hidden to those who look only at the surface of the world situation, but they exist and only need the spark of spiritual understanding to come into full play and effect. The forces of lust, hate, and greed produce incalculable suffering and chaos. However, the one redeeming feature about human nature is that even in the midst of disruptive forces there invariably exists some form of love.

Even wars require cooperative functioning, but the scope of this cooperative functioning is artificially restricted by identification with a limited group or ideal. Wars often are carried on by a form of love, though it is a love that has not been understood properly. In order that love should come into its own, it must be untrammeled and unlimited. Love does exist in all phases of human life; but it is latent or is limited and poisoned by personal ambition, racial pride, narrow loyalties and rivalries, and attachment to sex, nationality, sect, caste, or religion. If there is to be a resurrection of humanity, the heart of man will have to be unlocked so that a new love is born into it—a love that knows no corruption and is entirely free from individual or collective greed.

The New Humanity will come into existence through a release of love in measureless abundance, and this release of love can come through the spiritual awakening brought about by the Perfect Masters. Love cannot be born of mere determination; through the exercise of will one can at best be dutiful. Through struggle and effort, one may succeed in assuring that one's external action is in conformity with one's concept of what is right; but such action is spiritually barren because it lacks the inward beauty of spontaneous love.

Love has to spring spontaneously from within; it is in no way amenable to any form of inner or outer force. Love and coercion can never go together; but while love cannot be forced upon anyone, it can be awakened through love itself. Love is essentially self-communicative; those who do not have it catch it from those who have it. Those who receive love from others cannot be its recipients without giving a response that, in itself, is the nature of love. True love is unconquerable and irresistible. It goes on gathering power and spreading itself until eventually it transforms everyone it touches. Humanity will attain a new mode of being and life through the free and unhampered interplay of pure love from heart to heart.

When it is recognized that there are no claims greater than the claims of the universal Divine Life-which, without exception, includes everyone and everything—love will not only establish peace, harmony, and happiness in social, national, and international spheres but it will shine in its own purity and beauty. Divine love is unassailable to the onslaughts of duality and is an expression of divinity itself. It is through divine love that the New Humanity will tune in to the divine plan. Divine love will not only introduce imperishable sweetness and infinite bliss into personal life but it will also make possible an era of New Humanity. Through divine love the New Humanity will learn the art of cooperative and harmonious life. It will free itself from the tyranny of dead forms and release the creative life of spiritual wisdom; it will shed all illusions and get established in the Truth; it will enjoy peace and abiding happiness; it will be initiated in the life of Eternity.

The Search for God

Most persons do not even suspect the real existence of God, and naturally they are not very keen about God. There are others who, through the influence of tradition, belong to some faith or another and acquire the belief in the existence of God from their surroundings. Their faith is just strong enough to keep them bound to certain rituals, ceremonies, or beliefs; and it rarely possesses that vitality which is necessary to bring about a radical change in one's entire attitude toward life. There are still others who are philosophically minded and have an inclination to believe in the existence of God, either because of their own speculations or because of the assertions of others. For them, God is at best an hypothesis or an intellectual idea. Such lukewarm belief in itself can never be sufficient incentive for launching upon

a serious search for God. Such persons do not know of God from personal knowledge, and for them God is not an object of intense desire or endeavor.

A true aspirant is not content with knowledge of spiritual realities based on hearsay, nor is he satisfied with pure inferential knowledge. For him the spiritual realities are not the object of idle thinking, and the acceptance or rejection of these realities is fraught with momentous implications for his inner life. Hence he naturally insists upon direct knowledge about them. This may be illustrated from an occurrence in the life of a great sage. One day he was discussing spiritual topics with a friend who was quite advanced upon the path. While they were engaged in this discussion their attention was diverted to a dead body that was being carried past them. "This is the end of the body but not of the soul," the friend remarked. "Have you *seen* the soul?" asked the sage. "No," the friend answered. And the sage remained skeptical about the soul, for he insisted upon *personal* knowledge.

Although the aspirant cannot be content with secondhand knowledge or mere guesses, he does not close his mind to the possibility that there could be spiritual realities that have not come within his experience. In other words, he is conscious of the limitations of his own individual experience and refrains from making it the measure of all possibilities. He has an open mind toward all things that are beyond the scope of his experience. While he does not accept them on hearsay, he also does not rush to deny them. The limitation of experience often tends to restrict the scope of imagination; and thus a person comes to believe that there are no realities other than those which may have come within the ken of his past experience. But usually some incidents or happenings in his own life will cause him to break out of his dogmatic enclosure and become really open-minded.

This stage of transition may also be illustrated by a story from the life of the same sage, who happened to be a prince. Some days after the incident mentioned above, as he was riding on horseback, he came upon a pedestrian advancing toward him. Since the way of the horse was blocked by the presence of the pedestrian, the sage arrogantly ordered the man out of the way. The pedestrian refused, so the sage dismounted and the following conversation was held: "Who are you?" asked the pedestrian. "I am the prince," answered the sage. "But I do not *know* you to be the prince," said the pedestrian and continued, "I shall accept you as a prince only when I know you to be a prince and not otherwise." This encounter awakened the sage to the fact that God *may* exist even though he did not know Him from personal experience, just as he was actually a prince although the pedestrian did not know it from his own personal experience. Now that his mind was open to the possible existence of God, he set himself to the task of deciding that question in earnest.

God either exists or does not exist. If He exists, the search for Him is amply justified. And if He does not exist, there is nothing to lose by seeking Him. However, man does not usually turn to a real search for God as a matter of voluntary and joyous enterprise. He has to be driven to this search by disillusionment with those worldly things that allure him and from which he cannot deflect his mind. The ordinary person is completely engrossed in his activities in the gross world. He lives through its manifold experiences of joys and sorrows without even suspecting the existence of the deeper Reality. He tries as best he can to have pleasures of the senses and to avoid different kinds of suffering.

"Eat, drink, and be merry" is the ordinary individual's philosophy. But in spite of his unceasing search for pleasure, he cannot altogether avoid suffering; and even when he succeeds in having pleasures of the senses, he is often satiated by them. While he thus goes through the daily round of varied experiences, there often arises some occasion when he begins to ask himself, "What is the point of all this?" Such a thought may arise from some untoward happening for which the person is not mentally prepared. It may be the frustration of some confident expectation, or it may be an important change in his situation demanding radical readjustment and the giving up of established ways of thought and conduct. Usually such an occasion arises from the frustration of some deep craving. If a deep craving happens to meet an impasse so that there is not the slightest chance of it ever being fulfilled, the psyche receives such a shock that it can no longer accept the type of life that may have been accepted hitherto without question.

Under such circumstances a person may be driven to utter desperation. And if the tremendous power generated by this disturbance of the psyche remains uncontrolled and undirected, it may even lead to serious mental derangement or attempts to commit suicide. Such a catastrophe overcomes those in whom desperateness is allied with thoughtlessness, for they allow impulse to have free and full sway. The unharnessed power of desperateness can only work destruction. The desperateness of a thoughtful person under similar circumstances is altogether differ-

ent in results because the energy it releases is intelligently harnessed and directed toward a purpose. In the moment of such *divine* desperateness, a person makes the important decision to discover and realize the aim of life. There thus comes into existence a true search for lasting values. Henceforth the burning query that refuses to be silenced is, "What does it all lead to?"

When the mental energy of an individual is thus centered upon discovering the goal of life, he uses the power of desperateness creatively. He can no longer be content with the fleeting things of this life, and he is thoroughly skeptical about the ordinary values he had so far accepted without doubt. His only desire is to find the Truth at any cost, and he does not rest satisfied with anything short of the Truth.

Divine desperateness is the beginning of spiritual awakening because it gives rise to the aspiration for God-realization. In the moment of divine desperateness, when everything seems to give way, the person decides to take any risk to ascertain what of significance to his life lies *behind* the veil.

All the usual solaces have failed him, but at the same time his inner voice refuses to reconcile itself completely with the position that life is devoid of all meaning. If he does not posit some hidden reality he has not hitherto known, then there is nothing at all worth living for. For him there are only two alternatives: either there is a hidden spiritual Reality, which prophets have described as God, or everything is meaningless. The second alternative is utterly unacceptable to the whole of man's personality, so he must try the first alternative. Thus the individual turns to God when he is at bay in worldly affairs.

Now since there is no direct access to this hidden reality that he posits, he inspects his usual experiences for possible avenues leading to a significant *beyond*. Thus he goes back to his usual experiences with the purpose of gathering some light on the path. This involves looking at everything from a new angle and entails a reinterpretation of each experience. He now not only has experience but tries to fathom its spiritual significance. He is not merely concerned with what it is but with what it *means* in the march toward this hidden goal of existence.

All this careful reevaluation of experience results in his gaining an insight that could not come to him before he began his new search. Reevaluation of an experience amounts to a new bit of wisdom, and each addition to spiritual wisdom necessarily brings about a modification of one's general attitude toward life. So the purely intellectual search for God—or the hidden spiritual Reality—has its reverberations in the practical life of a person. His life now becomes a real experiment with perceived spiritual values.

The more he carries on this intelligent and purposive experimentation with his own life, the deeper becomes his comprehension of the true meaning of life. Until finally he discovers that as he is undergoing a complete transformation of his being, he is arriving at a true perception of the real significance of life as it is. With a clear and tranquil vision of the real nature and worth of life he realizes that God, whom he has been so desperately seeking, is no stranger nor hidden and foreign entity. He is Reality itself and not a hypothesis. He is Reality seen with undimmed vision—that very Reality of which he is a part and in which he has had his entire being and with which he is in fact identical.

Thus, though he begins by seeking something utterly new, he really arrives at a new understanding of something ancient. The spiritual journey does not consist in arriving at a new destination where a person gains what he did not have or becomes what he was not. It consists in the dissipation of his ignorance concerning himself and life, and the gradual growth of that understanding which begins with spiritual awakening. The finding of God is a coming to one's own Self.

Gardner with his Irish nursemaid, Com, during the 1880s.

BOOK OF SHADOWS: DOCUMENT ANALYSIS

"...let there ever be joy in your heart. Greet people with joy, be glad to see them."

Overview

The Wiccan *Book of Shadows* is often attributed to the British author Gerald Brosseau Gardner. Gardner declared that in 1939 he was initiated into a coven of witches in Highcliffe, England, who claimed to be followers of an ancient faith that had preserved pre-Christian pagan religion. This "Old Religion" taught a magical worldview and worshipped the gods of ancient times. It was called Wica (pronounced "witcha") and had survived over millennia, despite being driven underground during the witch hunts of early-modern Europe. Gardner sought to publicize his newfound faith and soon began to gather interest from the press; he found that people were keen to learn more about this "craft of the wise." Gardner began to train people and gave them a short book that contained the practical rites, spells, and ceremonies of the witches. This book was to be copied by hand, in candlelight, and never let out of one's possession. It was called the *Book of Shadows*.

Gardner said that the *Book of Shadows* he was given by his initiators contained only the outline of the rites of the religion, and he sought to flesh it out with more material. He started to work on editing and adding to the book, and he was joined by Doreen Valiente in 1953. She made some of the most significant changes, particularly in rewriting the words spoken by the priestess when representing the Goddess in rituals, which became known as "The Charge of the Goddess," a core sacred text for modern paganism.

Today Gardner's Wica has grown into many different denominations of modern pagan witchcraft, from international networks of initiatory Wiccans to covens of self-styled teen witches. It is now widely known as Wicca (pronounced "wicka") and falls under the umbrella term of contemporary pagan religion. The *Book of Shadows* is still passed from witch to witch and copied by hand. The corpus of Wiccan literature that is the *Book of Shadows* has continued to change over the years, as the *Book of Shadows* has been

described as a "cookbook" rather than an unchangeable sacred text, and many variants can be found. The version reproduced here represents the *Book of Shadows* used when Gardner first publicized Wicca.

Context

Gardner is not the sole author of the *Book of Shadows*, but he is the person who brought it to the attention of the world. In publicizing Wicca and working for its growth, he is one of the founding fathers of contemporary pagan religion in the West, particularly modern pagan witchcraft. Having first written about Wicca as a means to preserve a small group he thought was about to die out—the coven at Highcliffe—he has become known as the founder of one of the world's fastest-growing religions, the only religion Britain has given to the world.

Gardner's research and writings about witchcraft were supported by such figures as Margaret Murray, a well-known Egyptologist who was the president of the Folklore Society in London when she wrote the foreword to Gardner's *Witchcraft Today* in 1954. Murray's own books, particularly *The Witch Cult in Western Europe* (1921) and *The God of the Witches* (1931), had already helped to create and contribute greatly to the hypothesis that witches are not evil sorcerers but are, in fact, the persecuted keepers of the ancient wisdom of a long-hidden European paganism.

These books were published at a time when many people wanted to believe in an Old Religion, as Britain became increasingly secular and esoteric and Eastern-oriented religious models such as Spiritualism, Theosophy, Buddhism, and Anthroposophy were being experimented with as alternatives to traditional Christianity. Wicca had some philosophical elements in common with these spiritualities, such as a belief in reincarnation and karma—the view that the effects of a person's actions in the present life determine his or her destiny in a subsequent incarnation. It also harked back to the magical and folk traditions of Europe and to the practices and philosophies of the magical societies that had dominated the esoteric milieu of the turn of the nineteenth and twentieth centuries, societies such as the Hermetic Order of the Golden Dawn and the Society of the Inner Light. The *Book of Shadows* itself is a survivor of the tradition of the *grimoire*, or a textbook of magic that is passed down among the magical community and copied from one mage (practitioner of witchcraft) to another.

Gardner's Old Religion emerged from this creative cauldron as a repository of ancient wisdom, pagan religion, folk practices, and magical knowledge. In common with the other magical societies, it was concerned with the place of women in magical orders and in wider society. However, unlike the more formal societies, it wove the witch and the goddess into a mythos of the passionate resistance of the common people against oppressive patriarchal forces. This resistance was led by women who were magicians and healers. This was a very appealing mix at this time, when the place of women in society and, indeed, society itself was rapidly changing in the context of civil rights agitation, the end of colonialism, the loss of faith in more traditional, orthodox religions, world war, the proliferation of more sophisticated and destructive weapons, and the spread of Soviet-style Communist ideology—changes that gave rise to modern forms of anxiety. The time was ripe for Wicca to emerge, and thus the *Book of Shadows* came out of the shadows and into the public eye.

About the Author

Gerald Gardner was born on June 13, 1884, in Liverpool, to a rich family. After traveling widely throughout his youth, he settled in the Far East and worked as a tea and rubber plantation manager and government opium inspector. He was always fascinated by magic, and he joined many esoteric societies—from the Freemasons (whom he joined in 1910), to whose meetings he traveled through the jungle carrying his uniform in a box, to the Dyak tribe headhunters of Borneo, who allowed him to attend their rites at a time when few colonial white men would have been invited. Despite having had little formal education, he became an amateur anthropologist and a successful author, and he published a book on Malaysian ritual daggers that remains the definitive work today.

He retired to England in 1936 and continued to mix in a diverse magical milieu. He joined the Folklore Society and the Society for Psychical Research. He was friendly with Ross Nicholls, who founded the Order of Bards, Ovates, and Druids, and was even appointed the head of the magical order the Ordo Templi Orientis by the notorious magician Aleister Crowley. However, his most important and enduring influence came after he moved to the borough of Christchurch, near the New Forest in the south of England. There he discovered the Crotona Fellowship, a thriving community of people who were exploring alternative lifestyle practices such as vegetarianism, naturism, and

Time Line	
June 13, 1884	■ Gerald Gardner is born in Liverpool.
1910	■ Gardner becomes a Freemason.
1912	■ Gardner starts to study the magic of Malaysia and Borneo and is allowed to join in native rites with the headhunting Dyak tribe.
January 4, 1922	■ Doreen (Dominy) Valiente is born in South London.
January 1936	■ Gardner retires to England and moves to Christchurch, where he joins the Crotona Fellowship and meets his first English witches.
September 1939	■ Gardner is brought into a coven at the Mill House, Highcliffe, and is given the *Book of Shadows*.
1939	■ Gardner publishes *A Goddess Arrives*, a novel about reincarnation and goddess worship.
1949	■ Gardner publishes *High Magic's Aid*, a novel about witchcraft, magic, and resistance.
1951	■ The Witchcraft Act is repealed and replaced by the Fraudulent Mediums Act, making witchcraft legal in Great Britain.
1953	■ Gardner invites Doreen Valiente to rewrite parts of the *Book of Shadows*.
1954	■ Gardner publishes *Witchcraft Today*.
1959	■ Gardner publishes *The Meaning of Witchcraft*.
February 12, 1964	■ Gardner dies while on a sea voyage and is buried in Tunisia.
September 1, 1999	■ Doreen Valiente dies.

biodynamics and were actively interested in reincarnation, herbs, divination, fairies, magic, and witchcraft. Within the Crotona Fellowship he met a group of people who were members of a coven of witches. He was welcomed into their coven at the Mill House, in the village of Highcliffe, in September 1939. "Then I knew that which I had thought burnt out hundreds of years ago still survived," he later said. Gardner dedicated the rest of his life to publicizing witchcraft, including living as the resident witch in the Museum of Witchcraft and Magic on the Isle of Man.

He was keen to publish books about his new faith. With the blessing of his coven, he started with two novels, *A Goddess Arrives* (1939) and *High Magic's Aid* (1949). In 1951 the centuries-old Witchcraft Act was repealed as part of the modernization of British law; witchcraft was no longer illegal, and Gardner was free to publish the first factual books about living as a modern witch. These were *Witchcraft Today* (1954) and *The Meaning of Witchcraft* (1959), in which Gardner used his anthropological skills to describe Wicca from the hitherto unique position of someone who had been brought into a coven and had attended the witches' rites. Gardner died while on a voyage at sea on February 12, 1964, and was buried in Tunisia.

Doreen Valiente was born Doreen Dominy on January 4, 1922, in South London. To squelch her growing interest in magic and sorcery, her parents sent her to a convent school, but she left at age fifteen and refused to return. In 1941 she married a sailor who went missing in action during World War II. In 1944 she married Casimiro Valiente, who never shared her interest in magic and occultism. In 1952 the couple moved to southern England, where she struck up a correspondence with Gerald Gardner, who in 1953 invited her to join his Bricket Wood coven, where she rose to the position of high priestess. Valiente was concerned that much of the material in the *Book of Shadows* came not from ancient sources but from the writings of Aleister Crowley. With Gardner's permission, she rewrote much of the book, deleting sections that came from Crowley's works. By 1957, she and Gardner were in conflict—Valiente believed that Gardner was too interested in publicity—and she broke away to form her own coven. Later, in 1964, she joined a coven, the Clan of Tubal Cain, run by Robert Cochrane, a charismatic leader of traditional witchcraft who combined shamanism and Wicca. She left that coven because she disapproved of Cochrane's use of hallucinogenic drugs. She published her first book, *Where Witchcraft Lives*, in 1962, and in the years that followed she wrote numerous others: *An ABC of Witchcraft* (1972), *Natural Magic* (1975), and *Witchcraft for Tomorrow* (1978). She died on September 1, 1999.

Explanation and Analysis of the Document

The Wiccan phrase "book of shadows" can be ambiguous. Some traditional Wiccans keep two "books of shadows," one containing core Wiccan practices and rituals and that is shared with initiates and the second a book for a

coven that differs from coven to coven. This second "book of shadows" may contain all manner of material, including herbal lore, astrological predictions, and the like. Sometimes covens trade these books. Additionally, some Wiccans keep a personal book in the form of a journal that is also often referred to as a "book of shadows." Meanwhile, Gardner's *Book of Shadows* has evolved continually over the years. Certain core elements remain, however, and the following excerpts, which represent some of the ideology and practices of Wicca, are from one of the earliest forms of the book.

♦ To Help the Sick

"To Help the Sick" is an excerpt from the *Book of Shadows* that gives instructions on how to live as a witch and how to engage in the psychology of healing others, a preoccupation of Gardner's witches. Gardner's emphasis on the power and importance of the Goddess in Wicca is repeated throughout the *Book of Shadows*, along with the reminder that she is a goddess of love and joy. Although some Wiccans pay tribute to a specific goddess, "Goddess" here represents an all-encompassing feminine principle. Wiccans are instructed here to always remember the powerful joyous emotions of their rites, and their love for those they have met through Wicca, and to use this as a form of positive thinking that will improve their own health. A "mind over matter" approach can be used to nullify pain.

The methods described here are psychological rather than magical, although they would be used in conjunction with practical magic. Along with positive thinking, techniques to help a patient include distraction from pain, using sedatives, and practicing hypnosis. The reputation of the witch as someone wielding magical power is also drawn upon in this psychological healing methodology; the text recommends that patients should be encouraged to believe that the witch has the power to heal them magically—thus making use of the placebo effect, whereby patients can sometimes cure themselves if they believe strongly enough that a harmless but nonactive substance is a potent cure. The text notes that these techniques require subtlety and conviction, as well as knowledge of when and how to administer medicines in conjunction with the psychological technique. Hence Wicca has come to be known as "white witchcraft," the art of using magic and persuasion to perform helpful acts.

Gardner continues with instructions on the use of hypnosis. He describes where and how to look at patients and how to talk to them. He also instructs the healer to infuse the medicines with the feelings of ecstasy that are felt in the witches' rites. Gardner discusses how it is easier to heal people who can be trusted with the fact that the healer is a witch. Otherwise, one must attempt the healing without revealing too much of one's Wiccan identity and by working with the unconscious rather than the conscious mind of the person being healed.

Gardner emphasizes the need for secrecy and discretion, reminding the reader of the persecutions of the witch hunts. Although no evidence exists that the people persecuted in the witch hunts actually practiced magic—rather, they seem to have been victims of neighborhood feuds and hysteria—the foundation myth of Wicca was built on this premise. Further, not all victims of the witch hunts were burned at the stake, nor is there any proof that they were Goddess worshippers, but this section further underlines the strong mythos that Gardner built up in his writings, which pervaded literature on the revival of paganism until the 1970s.

The final paragraph of this section refers to the prayer "The Amalthean Horn," an adaption of a poem published by Aleister Crowley in 1907. In classical mythology, Amalthea, whose name means "tender goddess," was a foster mother of the Greek god Zeus. She is typically depicted with a "horn," that is, a cornucopia overflowing with grains and fruits.

♦ The Warning

"The Warning" further illustrates the early Gardnerian belief that witches were the persecuted priesthood of the Old Religion. It urges witches to hide their ritual tools and tells them how to avoid capture or confession, and it emphasizes the secrecy in which the Book of Shadows should be held and its personal nature. The fact that the book is not published but rather is meant to be copied by hand reflects Wicca's foundation in the *grimoire* tradition of magical texts, which were individually copied by hand before the invention of photocopying and electronic data transfer. Reference is made to a pentacle, which is a five-pointed star surrounded by a circle. The pentacle has long been a prominent religious symbol not only among Wiccans but, historically, among Christians, Jews, the ancient Greeks, the ancient Egyptians, and others. While the symbolic significance of the pentacle can vary from tradition to tradition, generally it has connotations of evoking some kind of life force, energy, or spirit. In this particular passage, Gardner is referring to a round disc engraved with a five-pointed star and symbols of the God and the Goddess and initiation. This has various ritual uses, including symbolizing earth and "grounding" magic. Since this passage is about avoiding capture as a witch, Gardner advises that the pentacle should be made of wax, that is, easily disposable and easily remade. This may have a precedence in the Elizabethan magic of John Dee, which uses several complex wax pentacles, including the Sigillum Dei Aemeth, also known as "the seal of God's truth."

♦ The Eightfold Way

This is a specific training document—that is, it comprises the notes of a teaching session within the oral tradition of Wicca. Most Wiccans use dance, chanting, spells, and visualization, accompanied by incense and wine, as aids in the practice of making magic. The *Book of Shadows* does not contain many specific examples of chants and spells, however, for these would be memorized from practice.

Many of the items or actions briefly referred to in "The Eightfold Way" are self-explanatory, but a few bear comment. For instance, the second "way" is given as "trance,

projection of the Astral." *Astral,* a word that has been used in numerous philosophical traditions, can be understood as the "astral body" or the intermediate realm between the physical body and the mind. Astral projection or astral journey is an out-of-body experience. Among Wiccans, "projection of the Astral" is essentially a form of meditation.

Cautious drug use is mentioned as a valid method of consciousness expansion, along with use of wine and incense. In Gardner's time, all Wiccans were initiated adults who viewed themselves as pioneers of a new consciousness; they were indeed forebears of the New Age movement. Other ways of raising consciousness and achieving trance states include dancing or control of breath and blood flow, which could include carrying out such techniques as binding of the wrists, holding a yoga position, or undergoing light scourging of the back (all done carefully to avoid harm). The "Great Rite" refers to ritual sex. Sometimes the sex is literal, undertaken in private by the high priest and priestess, but generally it is symbolic and consists of the high priestess plunging a ritual knife, which is a male symbol, into a chalice filled with wine, a female symbol, which is held by the high priest as he kneels before her. The rite symbolizes a union between the Mother Goddess and the male principle and is essentially a fertility rite.

The short notes in this section thus indicate the variety of techniques that can be used to concentrate the mind and aid creative visualization, trance induction, and alternative states of consciousness. These techniques are used within the consecrated circle, so the practitioner is immersed completely in the magical mind-set of Wicca before starting to direct his or her consciousness toward the outcome.

♦ The Working Tools

This section tells new witches how to start their craft with little equipment, although an athame (the black-handled dagger that the *Book of Shadows* elsewhere calls the weapon of the true witch) is essential. The importance of preparing and consecrating tools for use in "magical operations" is emphasized, along with the the importance of keying up mental energy for such undertakings and the importance of using natural or handmade materials. The text explains that because there is a transmission of charisma within the witch's tools, a ritual weapon gains or loses value according to how it has been made and consecrated.

♦ A Revision of the Casting Procedure

Wiccan rites are always conducted within the circle, a sacred space that is consecrated anew each time, even in a permanently dedicated temple. Considerable preparation by the participants may include ritual bathing and wearing a special robe. This version of the words spoken to effect the circle-casting procedure, revised from the text available only to priestesses, retains the earlier titles "magus" and "high priestess," although "magus" (that is, "magician" or "sorcerer") is not normally used. The consecrations are drawn from *The Key of Solomon the King*, a medieval *gri-*

moire on magic attributed to the biblical King Solomon. Only when the consecration is done may the rite proceed. The procedure begins by invoking two figures: Aradia, who was the daughter of Lucifer and the goddess Diana, sent to earth to teach oppressed Italian peasants how to use witchcraft against the upper classes; and Cerunnos, known as "the Horned One," a Celtic god of fertility as well as of life, animals, and the underworld. It calls for use of an aspergillum, which is a perforated container or a brush used to sprinkle holy water.

Following the casting of the circle, the four elements are summoned, and then "The Witches' Rune" is chanted while the witches dance to raise energy. At this point the circle is fully opened, and the gods are invoked into those who will represent them as living embodiments of the divine. "The Charge of the Goddess," which is often spoken at full moon Esbat rites and at initiations, may then be undertaken. While the poetic version of the charge is presented here, the prose version is one of the most loved and used pieces of Wiccan ritual text, encapsulating the longing for union with the Goddess, the Wiccan understanding of the Goddess, and some of the philosophy behind Wiccan spirituality. The charge makes reference to a number of ancient goddesses, including Aphrodite, the Greek goddess of love and sexuality; Diana, the Roman goddess of the hunt; and Cerridwen (the goddess of dark prophetic powers and also the keeper of the Cauldron of the Underworld, where inspiration and knowledge are brewed). Artemis was the Greek goddess of the wilderness, the hunt and wild animals, and fertility; Brigid was the Celtic goddess of poetry, healing, and craft; and Melusine was a feminine spirit of freshwater in sacred springs and rivers in European folklore. Gardner says that by invoking these and other goddesses, "thine inmost divine self shall be enfolded in the raptures of the infinite."

◆ Cakes and Wine

The "Cakes and Wine" act concludes the serious part of the rite, before participants relax and feast. Here, the high priestess, embodying the Goddess, is seated on the altar, while the magus, or high priest, kneels; together they consecrate the food and drink and partake. During this simple act, the high priestess releases the energy of the Goddess, and the force is believed to "charge" the food and wine. The consecration itself is a symbolic sex act in which the woman is enthroned and holding the "positive" sexual symbol of the athame (knife), while the man kneels before her holding the "negative" sexual symbol of the grail (a chalice or cup). This interplay of male and female energy and empowerment is described by Wiccans as "polarity magic." Polarity magic is the theme of Dion Fortune's influential novels *The Sea Priestess* (1938) and *Moon Magic* (1956), both of which have been drawn upon in later versions of the *Book of Shadows*.

◆ The Sabbat Rituals

The Sabbats are seasonal festivals that celebrate the "wheel of the year." They incorporate ideas and customs drawn from folklore with ritual drama used in a religious context. This dramatized enactment of the turning of the seasons is believed to bring the celebrants closer to the cycle of nature and allow them to contemplate the mysteries of birth, life, death, and rebirth as the wheel turns.

These celebrations fulfill the universal desire for marking and celebrating the passage of time with ceremony, a desire that is seen in all religions, and are modern interpretations of ancient pagan rites. The festivals printed in this section of Gardner's *Book of Shadows* celebrate the main solstices and equinoxes, fulcrum points in the solar calendar, but Wiccans also celebrate the "cross-quarter days," fire festivals that fall between the solstices and equinoxes and mark the high point of each astronomical season. Their names hark back to pre-Christian Celtic festivals: Imbolc celebrates the first light after the darkness, on February 2; Beltane celebrates the beginning of summer, on May 1; Lammas, or Lughnasadh, celebrates the time of the corn harvest, on August 1; and Samhain acknowledges the darkness of winter's beginning and is a time for remembering the dead, on October 31.

The Sabbat festivals form the backbone of the modern pagan ritual year, and they are celebrated in many ways: from a simple walk in the countryside to complex, richly decorated rites with hundreds of participants. The Sabbats are also seen as a time of celebration and partying, with invited guests and shared feasts. This contrasts with the Esbats, or full moon rites, where a coven meets with just its members to train in the art of magic and to work healing rites. The solstices are both times of great celebration. The turning of the year wheel at the equinoxes is believed to be a potent time for spellcraft and working for change, as it is seen as a time when the tides of the universe are in flux and thus a great time for magic.

The solar festivals discussed here track the annual journey of the sun (relative to the earth) and reflect that journey in the human life cycle. The spring equinox is a celebration of new life and light, as the wheel of life has turned toward summer, and the *Book of Shadows* calls for observing this date with fire, dancing, and games. The summer solstice celebrates the peak of the sun's power, with the sun's intensified rays symbolized by a spear wielded by the high priest. The arrival of the sun in its zenith at midsummer happens on the cusp of the astrological sign of Cancer, referred to here as "the sign of the waters of life." The passage on the autumn equinox expresses the idea of the solar force departing from the land but journeying on to the realms of darkness, to continue transformed. The fruits of the autumn are on the altar, including corn, which symbolizes the secret seeds of life that germinate in the winter and burgeon into new life in due course. For the winter solstice the altar is decorated with evergreens, which defy the frosts of winter, and candles symbolize the light of hope in the darkest time of the year. The witches move in a circle holding candles, lighting them one at a time, so the light grows as the dance goes on. Eventually a fire is kindled, while a chant to the Great Mother is sung, as she brings forth the new light and hope. All jump the flaming cauldron in festive spirit as the birth of light of a new sun is celebrated.

♦ The Witches' Chant or Rune

The poem-song called "The Witches' Rune" was written by Doreen Valiente and incorporated by Gardner into the *Book of Shadows*. A "rune" is a character from ancient Germanic alphabets, of significance to Wiccans because runes were thought to have magical powers; indeed, the word *rune* comes from the word *runa*, meaning "secret" or "mystery." The witches dance rhythmically round the circle chanting this rune, or rhyme, to "raise the cone of power" in the final stage of casting the circle. Sometimes the rune is used as a spell: The members of the coven visualize their goal, and at the right moment their energy is sent to a sick person in a form of distant healing. The rhythmic rhyme used here is a good example of spell writing, where the words occupy the conscious mind, as the chant occupies the body, and the witch can then concentrate entirely on the goal of the spell.

♦ Consecrating Tools

As noted earlier, Wiccans believe that it is essential to prepare, purify, and consecrate every tool before it can be used. The text here notes that it is preferable to consecrate a new item with one that is already consecrated. This transfer of magical energy is reinforced by activating the tool through the elements—for instance, burying it in the earth for a time, leaving it in a river, or "charging" it up by the light of a full moon—and then dedicating it to the gods. The tool's personal nature is reinforced by the owner's sleeping with it or holding it each night for at least six months, until it becomes truly the person's own. The tools that are used to cast the circle, the sword and athame, are given a slightly different consecration from that of the other tools, since they are being consecrated as weapons of protection rather than for magical operation. While Wiccans may not make all their own tools anymore, many compromise by cutting and whittling their own wands, etching their own pentacles, and personalizing their athames, then ritually consecrating them. This is one way contemporary practitioners are finding to walk between the worlds of late capitalist consumerism and the authenticity they seek in living as a witch.

Audience

The *Book of Shadows* was originally meant to be copied by hand by each new witch and possibly was never meant to be published. It is still seen as a cookbook of spells, ceremonies, and advice for modern practitioners of magic, even though many versions are now available in print and on the Internet. Its contemporary audience includes scholars of religion, history, myth, and culture, but its main consumers remain those people who are interested in learning about Goddess religion and the practical application of magic in theory and practice.

Impact

As Wicca grew and became more formalized, the *Book of Shadows* became known as "oath-bound material" that should be passed only from witch to witch and never shown to anyone who had not taken oaths of allegiance to Wicca. Needless to say, this increased its value to those who sought to find out the secrets of Gardner's Wicca. In 1964, the commercially minded witch Charles Cardell (using the pseudonym Rex Nemorensis) published parts of the 1953 *Book of Shadows* (which he had obtained underhandedly) as a thin booklet titled "Witch." Aidan Kelley republished the book in 1991, with extensive analysis of its text, in *Crafting the Art of Magic*. Kelley's study established that some *Book of Shadows* material was drawn from previously published matter, and he concluded that the *Book of Shadows* and the religion of Wicca were fundamentally creations of Gardner's, rather than being the preserved remnants of an ancient pagan religion. Meanwhile, the myth of an unbroken line of an Old Religion had been proved impossible by historians.

Since the 1990s, however, scholars such as Ronald Hutton, Sorita D'Este, David Rankine, and Philip Heselton have demonstrated the importance of the *Book of Shadows* for the way it represents a published synthesis of the Western esoteric traditions, in a simple form, that has been adopted by the adherents of a successful modern religion that draws on ancient roots. It offers a template for magical religiosity that is easily followed and adapted. It contains some of the favorite liturgy of Wicca and reflects the early mythos of Wicca. Although it is not seen as doctrine or creed or even a "holy book," the *Book of Shadows* as a text has fueled much discussion and literature about modern pagan witchcraft and has been widely replicated in many forms.

Further Reading

■ Books

Clifton, Chas, and Graham Harvey. *The Paganism Reader*. New York: Routledge, 2004.

Crowley, Vivianne. *Wicca: The Old Religion in the New Age*. London: Aquarian Press, 1989.

D'Este, Sorita, and David Rankine. *Wicca Magickal Beginnings: A Study of the Possible Origins of the Rituals and Practices Found in This Modern Tradition of Pagan Witchcraft and Magick*. London: Avalonia, 2008.

Farrar, Janet, and Stewart Farrar. *The Witches' Way: Principles, Rituals, and Beliefs of Modern Witchcraft*. London: Robert Hale, 1984.

Farrar, Janet, and Stewart Farrar. *The Witches' Goddess: The Feminine Principle of Divinity*. Blaine, Wash.: Phoenix, 1987.

"Ever remember the promise of the goddess, 'For ecstasy is mine and joy on earth' so let there ever be joy in your heart. Greet people with joy, be glad to see them. If times be hard, think, 'It might have been worse. I at least have known the joys of the Sabbath, and I will know them again.'"

(Section 1)

"Never boast, never threaten, never say you wish ill to anyone."

(Section 1)

"I am the Gracious Goddess who gives the gift of Joy unto the heart of Man. Upon Earth I give the knowledge of the Spirit Eternal, and beyond death I give peace and freedom, and reunion with those who have gone before. Nor do I demand aught in sacrifice, for behold, I am the Mother of all things, and my love is poured out upon earth."

(Section 1)

"And thou who thinkest to seek me, know that thy seeking and yearning shall avail thee not unless thou know the mystery, that if that which thou seekest thou findest not within thee, thou wilt never find it without thee, for behold; I have been with thee from the beginning, and I am that which is attained at the end of desire."

(Section 1)

"Oh Queen most secret, bless this food unto our bodies, bestowing health, wealth, strength, joy and peace, and that fulfillment of love that is perpetual happiness."

(Section 1)

Harvey, Graham. *Contemporary Paganism: Listening People, Speaking Earth*. London: Hurst, 1997.

Harvey, Graham, and Charlotte Hardman, eds. *Paganism Today*. San Francisco: Thorsons, 1996.

Heselton, Philip. *Wiccan Roots: Gerald Gardner and the Modern Witchcraft Revival*. Milverton, U.K.: Cappall Bann, 2000.

Heselton Philip. *Gerald Gardner and the Cauldron of Inspiration: An Investigation into the Sources of Gardnerian Witchcraft*. Milverton, U.K.: Cappall Bann, 2003.

Hutton, Ronald. *The Stations of the Sun*. Oxford, U.K.: Oxford University Press, 1996.

Hutton, Ronald. *The Triumph of the Moon: A History of Modern Pagan Witchcraft*. Oxford, U.K.: Oxford 1999.

Partridge, Christopher. *The Re-Enchantment of the West.* Vol. 1: *Alternative Spiritualities, Sacralization, Popular Culture, and Occulture.* London: Continuum, 2004.

Starhawk. *The Spiral Dance: A Rebirth of the Ancient Religion of the Great Goddess.* San Francisco: Harper, 1999.

Valiente, Doreen. *The Rebirth of Witchcraft.* London: Robert Hale, 1989.

Valiente, Doreen. *The Charge of the Goddess.* Brighton, U.K.: Hexagon Hoopix, 2000.

♦ **Web Site**

Gerald Gardner Archive Web site. http://www.geraldgardner.com/archive/index.php

The Wica Web site. http://www.thewica.co.uk/

—Commentary by Melissa Harrington

Questions for Further Study

1. Historically, the word *pagan* has had negative connotations, associated with heathenism, ignorance, and even decadence. How do you think Gardner and his followers would respond to this view?

2. The origin of the word *pagan* is the Latin word *paganus,* meaning "country dweller" (as opposed to someone living in a city). How do you think the word came to be applied to polytheistic religions such as Wicca? Do you think that there is any logic to the application of the word to such religions?

3. Compare this document with *The Voyage of Bran,* another document that while in many respects Christian still incorporates pagan beliefs. What do the two documents taken together tell you about pagan beliefs and practices in the British Isles?

4. Compare the biography of Gerald Gardner with that of Allan Kardec, the author of *The Spirits' Book.* Do you see any similarities? What influence might these similarities have had on the respective authors' interests?

5. Wicca seems in many respects to be a "feminine" religion. Wiccans worship the "Goddess," and rites are often conducted by "high priestesses." While Wicca certainly includes men, discussion often centers on witches (female) rather than warlocks (male). Historically, the witches who have been persecuted have tended to be women more so than men. Why do you think Wicca in particular and witchcraft in general are associated so much with women?

BOOK OF SHADOWS: DOCUMENT TEXT

1953-1957 CE

—Gerald Brosseau Gardner

To Help the Sick

(1953)

[1] Ever remember the promise of the goddess, "For ecstasy is mine and joy on earth" so let there ever be joy in your heart. Greet people with joy, be glad to see them. If times be hard, think, "It might have been worse. I at least have known the joys of the Sabbath, and I will know them again." Think of the grandeur, beauty, and Poetry of the rites, of the loved ones you meet through them. If you dwell on this inner joy, your health will be better. You must try to banish all fear, for it will really touch you. It may hurt your body, but your soul is beyond it all.

[2] And ever remember, that if you help others it makes you forget your own woes. And if another be in pain, do what you may to distract his attention from it. Do not say "You have no pain," but if you may, administer the drugs which sooth as well as those that cure. But ever strive to make them believe they are getting better. Install into them happy thoughts. If you can only get this into his inner mind so that it be always believed.

[3] To this end it is not wrong to let people think that we of the cult have more power than we have. For the truth is that if they believe we have more power than we really possess, we do really possess these powers, insomuch we can do good to them.

[4] You must try to find out about people. If you tell a slightly sick man, "You are looking better. You will soon be well," he will feel better, but if he is really ill, or in pain, his Knowledge that he is in pain will cause him to doubt your words in future. But if you give him one of the drugs and then say, "The pain is growing less. Soon it will be gone," because the pain goes, the next time you say, "The pain is going," he will believe you and the pain will really get less. But you must ever say so with conviction, and this conviction must come from your believing it yourself, because you yourself know that if you can fix his mind so that he believes you, it is true.

[5] 'Tis often better to look exactly between their eyes, looking as if your eyes pierced their heads, opening your eyes as wide as you may and never blink. This continued gazing oft causes the patient to grow sleepy. If they show signs of this, say "You are growing sleepy. You will sleep, you are tired. Sleep. Your eyes grow tired. Sleep." If they close their eyes, say "Your eyes close, you are tired, you cannot open your eyes." If they cannot, say "Your arms are tired, you cannot raise them." If they cannot, say "I am master of your mind. You must ever believe what I tell you. When I look like this into your eyes you will sleep and be subject to my will," then tell them they will sleep and wake up refreshed, feeling better. Continue this with soothing and healing drugs, and try to infuse into them the feeling of ecstasy that you feel at the Sabbath. They cannot feel it in full, but you can command them to feel what is in your own mind, and try to concentrate on this ecstasy. If you may safely tell that you are of the Cult, your task may be easier. And it were well to command them to know it only with their sleeping mind, and forget it, or to be at least unable to tell anyone about it when awake. A good way is to command them that, if they are ever questioned about Witchcraft or Witches, to immediately fall asleep.

[6] Ever remember if tempted to admit or boast of belonging to the cult you be endangering your brothers, for though now the fires of persecution may have died down, who knows when they may be revived? Many priests have knowledge of our secrets, and they well know that, though much religious bigotry has calmed down, many people would wish to join our cult. And if the truth were known of its joys, the Churches would lose power, so if we take many recruits, we may loose the fires of persecution against us again. So ever keep the secrets.

[7] Think joy, think love, try to help others and bring joy into their lives. Children are naturally easier to influence than grown people. Ever strive to work through people's existing beliefs. For instance, more than half of the world believe in amulets. An ordinary stone is not an amulet but if it hath a natural hole

in it, it must be something unusual, so if the patient hath this belief give him one. But first carry it next your skin for a few days, forcing your will into it, to cure pain, to feel safe, or against their particular fear, and this amulet may keep imposing your will when you are absent. The masters of talismans knew this full well when they say they must be made in a circle, to avoid distraction, by someone whose mind is on the subject of the work.

[8] But keep your own mind happy. Remember the Words of the Goddess: "I give unimaginable joys on Earth, certainty, not faith, while in life, and upon death, peace unutterable, rest, and ecstasy, and the promise that you will return again." In the old days many of us went to the flames laughing and singing, and so we may again. We may have joy in life and beauty, and peace and Death and the promise of return.

[9] The Bible speaks sooth, "A merry heart doeth good like a medicine but a broken spirit breaketh the bones." But you may not have a merry heart. Perchance you were born under an evil star. I think that the effects of the stars are overestimated, but you cannot make a merry heart to order, you say. But you can, in the Cult; there be secret processes by which your will and imagination may be influenced. This process also affects the body, and brings it to joy. Your body is happy, so your mind is happy . You are well because you are happy, and you are happy because you are well.

[10] Prayer may be used with good result if the patient believes it can and will work. Many believe it can, but do not believe their God or saint will help. Prayers to the Goddess help, especially the Amalthean Horn Prayer, as it causes stimulation to the body as well as to the mind.

The Warning

(1953)

Keep this book in your own hand of write. Let brothers and Sisters copy what they will, but never let this book out of your hands, and never keep the writings of another, for if it be found in their hand of write, they may well be taken and tortured. Each should guard his own writings and destroy them whenever danger threatens. Learn as much as you may by heart, and when the danger is past, rewrite your book. For this reason, if any die, destroy their book if they have not been able to, for, if it be found and, 'tis clear proof against them. "Ye may not be a Witch alone"; so all their friends be in danger of the torture. So destroy everything not necessary. If your book be found on

you, 'tis clear proof against you. You may be tortured. Keep all thought of the cult from your mind. Say you had bad dreams, that a Devil caused you to write this without your knowledge. Think to yourself, "I Know Nothing. I Remember nothing. I have forgotten all." Drive this into your mind. If the torture be too great to bear, say, "I will confess. I cannot bear this torment. What do you want me to say? Tell me and I will say it." If they try to make you talk of the broth, do not, but if they try to make you speak of impossibilities, such as flying through the air, consorting with the Devil, sacrificing children, or eating men's flesh, say, "I had an evil dream. I was not myself. I was crazed." Not all Magistrates are bad. If there be an excuse, they may show you mercy. If you have confessed aught, deny it afterwards. Say you babbled under the torture; you knew not what you did or said. If you be condemned, fear not. The Brotherhood is powerful. They may help you to escape if you are steadfast. If you betray aught, there is no hope for you, in this life, or in that which is to come. But, 'tis sure, that if steadfast you go to the pyre, drugs will reach you. You will feel naught, and you go but to Death and what lies beyond, the ecstasy of the Goddess. The same with the working Tools. Let them be as ordinary things that anyone may have in their homes. The Pentacles shall be of wax that they may be melted or broken at once. Have no sword unless your rank allows you one. Have no names or signs on anything. Write them on in ink before consecrating them and wash it off at once when finished. Never boast, never threaten, never say you wish ill to anyone. If any speak of the craft, say, "Speak not to me of such, it frightens me, 'tis evil luck to speak of it."

The Eightfold Way

(1953)

Eightfold Path or Ways to the Centre.

1. Meditation or Concentration. This in practice means forming a mental image of what is desired, and forcing yourself to see that it is fulfilled, with the fierce belief and knowledge that it can and will be fulfilled, and that you will go on willing till you force it to be fulfilled. Called for short, "Intent"
2. Trance, projection of the Astral.
3. Rites, Chants, Spells, Runes, Charms, etc.
4. Incense, Drugs, Wine, etc., whatever is used to release the Spirit. (Note. One must be very careful

about this. Incense is usually harmless, but you must be careful. If it has bad aftereffects, reduce the amount used, or the duration of the time it is inhaled. Drugs are very dangerous if taken to excess, but it must be remembered that there are drugs that are absolutely harmless, though people talk of them with bated breath, but Hemp is especially dangerous, because it unlocks the inner eye swiftly and easily, so one is tempted to use it more and more. If it is used at all, it must be with the strictest precautions, to see that the person who uses it has no control over the supply. This should be doled out by some responsible person, and the supply strictly limited.)

5. The Dance, and kindred practices.
6. Blood control (the Cords), Breath Control, and kindred practices.
7. The Scourge.
8. The Great Rite.

These are all the ways. You may combine many of them into the one experiment, the more the better.

The Five Essentials:

1. The most important is "Intention": you must know that you can and will succeed; it is essential in every operation.
2. Preparation. (You must be properly prepared according to the rules of the Art; otherwise you will never succeed.)
3. The Circle must be properly formed and purified.
4. You all must be properly purified, several times if necessary, and this purification should be repeated several times during the rite.
5. You must have properly consecrated tools.

These five essentials and Eight Paths or Ways cannot all be combined in one rite. Meditation and dancing do not combine well, but forming the mental image and the dance may be well combined with Chants. Spells, etc., combined with scourging and No. 6, followed by No. 8, form a splendid combination. Meditation, following scourging, combined with Nos. 3 and 4 and 5, are also very Good. For short cuts concentration, Nos. 5, 6, 7, and 8 are excellent.

The Working Tools

(1953)

There are no magical supply shops, so unless you are lucky enough to be given or sold tools, a poor witch must extemporize. But when made you should be able to borrow or obtain an Athame. So having made your circle, erect an altar. Any small table or chest will do. There must be fire on it (a candle will suffice) and your book. For good results incense is best if you can get it, but coals in a chafing dish burning sweet-smelling herbs will do. A cup if you would have cakes and wine, and a platter with the signs drawn into the same in ink, showing a pentacle. A scourge is easily made (note, the scourge has eight tails and five knots in each tail). Get a white-hilted knife and a wand (a sword is not necessary). Cut the marks with Athame. Purify everything, then consecrate your tools in proper form and ever be properly prepared. But ever remember, magical operations are useless unless the mind can be brought to the proper attitude, keyed to the utmost pitch. Affirmations must be made clearly, and the mind should be inflamed with desire. With this frenzy of will, you may do as much with simple tools as with the most complete set. But good and especially ancient tools have their own aura. They do help to bring about that reverential spirit, the desire to learn and develop your powers. For this reason witches ever try to obtain tools from sorcerers, who, being skilled men, make good tools and consecrate them well, giving them mighty power. But a great witch's tools also gain much power; and you should ever strive to make any tools you manufacture of the finest materials you can obtain, to the end that they may absorb your power the more easily. And of course if you may inherit or obtain another witch's tools, power will flow from them. It is an old belief that the best substances for making tools are those that have once had life in them, as opposed to artificial substances. Thus wood or ivory is better for a wand than metal, which is more appropriate for knives or swords. Virgin parchment is better than manufactured paper for talismans, etc. And things which have been made by hand are good, because there is life in them.

A Revision of the Casting Procedure

(1957)
ALL ARE PURIFIED

[1] Magus consecrates salt and water.
[2] High Priestess kneels at Altar, takes up Sword, says, "I conjure thee, O Sword of Steel, to serve me as a defence in all Magical Operations. Guard me at all times against mine enemies, both visible and invisible. Grant that I may obtain what I desire in

all things wherein I may use Thee, Wherefore do I bless Thee and invoke Thee in the names of Aradia and Cernunnos." Gives Sword to Magus.

[3] Magus kneeling hands her vessel of consecrated Water and Aspergillum. He Casts the Circle, three circles, on the lines marked out, starting at the East and returning to the East. High Priestess follows, Asperging Circle (sprinkling it to purify it) and all present and finally herself. Then she goes round again censing it. (Everyone in the circle must be sprinkled and censed.) She returns vessel, etc., to Magus, who places them on altar, or convenient place, and hands her Sword [handwritten].

[4] She walks slowly round Circle, saying, "I conjure Thee, O Circle of Space, that thou be a Boundary and a Protection and a meeting place between the world of Men and that of the Dread Lords of the OUTER SPACES, that Thou be cleansed, Purified, and strengthened to be a Guardian and a Protection that shall preserve and contain THAT POWER which we so earnestly desire to raise within thy bounds this night, wherefore do I bless thee and entreat thee to aid me in the endeavor, in the names of Aradia and Cernunnos." Hands sword to Magus [handwritten].

[5] Magus then summons the Mighty Ones as usual. (*The Verse Charge*)

[6] High Priestess stands in front of Altar (which may be pushed back for this). High Priestess assumes Goddess position (arms crossed). Magus kneeling in front of her, draws pentacle on her body with Phallus-headed Wand, Invokes (Drawing down the Moon), "I Invoke and beseech Thee, O mighty MOTHER of all life and fertility. 'By seed and root, by stem and bud, by leaf and flower and fruit, by Life and Love, do I invoke Thee' to descend into the body of thy servant and High Priestess (name)." (The Moon having been drawn down, i.e., link established, Magus and all male officers give fivefold kiss; all others bow.)

[7] High Priestess in Goddess position says, arms crossed,

"Mother, Darksome and Divine, Mine the Scourge and Mine the Kiss, The Five-point Star of Love and Bliss; Here I charge ye in this Sign. (Opens out Arms to pentacle position)

Bow before my Spirit bright (All bow) Aphrodite, Arianrhod, Lover of the Horned God, Queen of Witchery and Night.

Diana, Brigid, Melusine, Am I named of old by men, Artemis and Cerridwen, Hell's dark mistress, Heaven's Queen.

Ye who ask of me a boon, Meet ye in some hidden shade, Lead my dance in greenwood glade By the light of the full moon.

Dance about mine altar stone, Work my holy magistry, Ye who are fain of sorcery, I bring ye secrets yet unknown.

No more shall ye know slavery who tread my round the Sabbat night. Come ye all naked to the rite In sign that ye are truly free.

Keep ye my mysteries in mirth, Heart joined to heart and lip to lip. Five are the points of fellowship That bring ye ecstasy on Earth.

No other law but love I know; By naught but love may I be known, And all that liveth is my own: From me they come, to me they go.

THE CHARGE, to be read while the initiate stands, properly prepared before the Circle.

[Magus]: Listen to the words of the Great mother, who was of old also called among men, Artemis, Astarte, Dione, Melusine, Aphrodite, Cerridwen, Diana, Arianrhod, Bride, and by many other names.

[High Priestess]: "At mine Altars the youth of Lacedaemon in Sparta made due sacrifice. Whenever ye have need of anything, once in the month, and better it be when the moon is full. Then ye shall assemble in some secret place and adore the spirit of Me who am Queen of all Witcheries. There ye shall assemble, ye who are fain to learn all sorcery, yet who have not won its deepest secrets. To these will I teach things that are yet unknown. And ye shall be free from slavery, and as a sign that ye be really free, ye shall be naked in your rites, and ye shall dance, sing, feast, make music, and love, all in my praise. For mine is the ecstasy of the Spirit, and mine is also joy on earth. For my Law is Love unto all beings. Keep pure your highest ideals. Strive ever towards it. Let naught stop you or turn you aside. For mine is the secret which opens upon the door of youth; and mine is the cup of the Wine of Life: and the Cauldron of Cerridwen, which is the Holy Grail of Immortality. I am the Gracious Goddess who gives the gift of Joy unto the heart of Man. Upon Earth I give the knowledge of the Spirit Eternal, and beyond death I give peace and freedom, and reunion with those who have gone before. Nor do I demand aught in sacrifice, for behold, I am the Mother of all things, and my love is poured out upon earth."

[Magus]: Hear ye the words of the Star Goddess, She in the dust of whose feet are the hosts of Heaven, whose body encircleth the universe.

[High Priestess]: "I who am the beauty of the green earth; and the White Moon amongst the Stars; and the mystery of the Waters; and the desire of the heart of man. I call unto thy soul: arise and come unto me. For I am the Soul of nature who giveth life to the Universe; 'From me all things proceed; and unto me, all things must return.' Beloved of the Gods and men, thine inmost divine self shall be enfolded in the raptures of the infinite. Let my worship be within the heart that rejoiceth, for behold: all acts of love and pleasure are my rituals; and therefore let there be Beauty and Strength, Power and Compassion, Honour and Humility, Mirth and reverence within you. And thou who thinkest to seek me, know that thy seeking and yearning shall avail thee not unless thou know the mystery, that if that which thou seekest thou findest not within thee, thou wilt never find it without thee, for behold; I have been with thee from the beginning, and I am that which is attained at the end of desire."

Cakes and Wine

(1957)

High Priestess seated on Altar, God position.

Magus, kneeling, kisses her feet, then knees, bows with head below her knees, extends arms along her thighs, and adores.

Magus fills cup and offers it to High Priestess, who, holding Athame between palms, places point in cup.

Magus says: "As the Athame is the male, so the cup is the female, and conjoined they bring blessedness."

High Priestess lays Athame aside, and takes Cup and drinks, gives Cup to server, who puts a little in each glass.

Magus presents Pentacle with cakes to High Priestess, saying, "Oh Queen most secret, bless this food unto our bodies, bestowing health, wealth, strength, joy and peace, and that fulfillment of love that is perpetual happiness".

High Priestess blesses them with Athame, takes Cake and eats, while the Magus gives her the Cup again and kisses knees and adores.

All sit as Witches, and invite High Priestess to join them.

The Sabbat Rituals

♦ **Spring Equinox**
(1957)

The symbol of the wheel should be placed on the altar upright, decked with flowers, flanked with burning candles. The Cauldron, containing spirits, is in the east. Magus in west, High Priestess in east with Phallic wand or pinecone-tipped wand, or broomstick, or riding pole, broom upwards. High Priestess lights Cauldron, saying,

"We kindle fire this day! In the presence of the Holy Ones:Without malice, without jealousy, without envy. Without fear of aught beneath the sun. But the High Gods.

Thee we invoke: O light of life: Be thou a bright flame before us: Be thou a guiding star above us: Be thou a smooth path beneath us;

Kindle thou in our hearts within, A flame of love for our neighbor, To our foes, to our friends, to our kindred all: To all men on this broad Earth.

O merciful son of Cerridwen, From the lowest thing that liveth To the name that is highest of all."

High Priestess draw pentacle upon Magus with wand, kiss, gives it to him. He does likewise. They lead the dance round the circle, all couples leaping burning fire. The last couple as the fire goes out should be well-purified three times, and each should give Fivefold Kiss to all of opposite sex.

Cakes and wine.

If the people will, the Cauldron dance can be done again, many times, or other games can be played.

♦ **Summer Solstice**
Form circle. Invoke, Purify. Cauldron is placed before altar filled with water, wreathed with summer flowers. The people, men and women alternately, stand round circle. High Priestess stands in north, before Cauldron, holding raised wand, which should be Phallic or tipped with a pinecone (anciently the thyrsus) or a riding pole or a broomstick, invokes the sun.

"Great One of Heaven, Power of the Sun, we invoke thee in thine ancient names, Michael, Balin, Arthur, Lugh, Herne. Come again, as of old, into this thy land. Lift up thy shining spear of light to protect us. Put to flight the powers of darkness, give us fair woodlands and green fields, blossoming orchards and ripening corn. Bring us to stand upon thy hill of vision, and show us the path to the lovely realms of the gods."

High Priestess draws invoking pentacle on Magus with wand.

Magus comes forward sunwise and takes wand with kiss, plunges wand into Cauldron and holds it upright, saying, "The spear to the Cauldron, the lance to the Grail, spirit to flesh, man to woman, sun to earth." He salutes High Priestess over Cauldron, then rejoins people, still bearing wand.

High Priestess takes aspergillum, stands by Cauldron, says, "Dance ye about the Cauldron of Cerridwen the Goddess, and be ye blessed with the touch of this consecrated water, even as the sun, the lord of light, arriveth in his strength in the sign of the waters of life."

The people dance sunwise about the altar and Cauldron, led by Magus bearing wand. High Priestess sprinkles them lightly as they pass her.

Ritual of cakes and wine.

Any other dances, rites, or games as the Priestess and people wish.

♦ Autumn Equinox

The altar should be decorated with symbols of autumn, pine cones, oak sprigs, acorns, or ears of corn, and should have fire or burning incense on it as usual. After usual purification, the people stand round, men and women alternately. Magus at west of altar in God position.

High Priestess stands at east of altar, facing him, and reads the incantation.

"Farewell, O Sun, ever returning light. The hidden god, who ever yet remains. He departs to the land of youth, through the gates of death, to dwell enthroned, the judge of gods and man. The horned leader of the hosts of air. Yet, even as stand unseen about the circle the forms of the Mighty Lords of the Outer Spaces,. So dwelleth he, 'the lord within ourselves'. So dwelleth he within the secret seed, the seed of new reaped grain, the seed of flesh, hidden in the earth, the marvellous seed of the stars.

'In him is life, and life is the light of men [John 1:4],' that which was never born and never dies. Therefore the Wicca weep not, but rejoice."

The High Priestess goes to the Magus with a kiss. He lays aside Athame and scourge, and kisses her. The High Priestess hands him her wand, which should be Phallic, or a branch tipped with a pinecone, Or a riding pole, or a broomstick (anciently the thyrsus). They lead the dance, she with a systrum or rattle, he with wand, the people falling in behind them, dancing three times round the altar. Then the candle game is played.

Cakes and wine.

Great Rite if possible.

Dances and games.

♦ Winter Solstice

Form circle in usual manner, invoking the Mighty Ones.

The Cauldron of Cerridwen is placed in the circle at the south wreathed with holly, ivy, and mistletoe, with fire lighted within it. There should be no other light except for the candles on the altar and about the circle.

After all are purified, the Moon should be drawn down.

Then the High Priestess stands behind the Cauldron in pentacle position, symbolizing the rebirth of the sun. The people, man and woman alternately, stand round the circle. The Magus stands facing the High Priestess with a bundle of torches, or candles, and the book of words of the incantation. One of the officers stands beside him with a lighted candle, so that he may have light to read by.

The people begin to slowly move round the circle sunwise. As each passes him the Magus lights his candle or torch from the fire in the Cauldron, which may be simply a candle, till all have lighted candles or torches. Then the people dance round slowly as he reads the incantation. (A real fire must now be kindled in the Cauldron.)

Queen of the Moon, Queen of the Sun. Queen of the Heavens, Queen of the Stars.

Queen of the Waters, Queen of the Earth. Who ordained to us the child of promise:

It is the Great Mother who gives birth to him, He is the Lord of Life who is born again, Darkness and tears are set behind, And the star of guidance comes up early.

Golden sun of hill and mountain illumine the land, illumine the world, illumine the seas, illumine the rivers, Grief be laid, and joy be raised.

Blessed be the Great Mother, Without beginning, without ending, To everlasting, to eternity, I. O. Evohe, Blessed be."

The dance commences slowly, in rhythm with the chant, all taking up the call "I. O. Blessed be." The Priestess joins dance and leads them with a quicker rhythm. The cauldron with burning fire is pushed so that the dancers leap or step over it, in couples. Whichever couple is passing it as it goes out, should be well-purified, three times each, and may pay any amusing forfeit as the High Priestess may ordain. Sometimes the cauldron is relighted several times for this purpose.

The Witches' Chant or Rune

(1957)

Darksome night and Shining Moon, East, then South, then West, then North, Harken to the Witches Rune: Here come I to call thee forth.

Earth and Water, Air and Fire, Wand and Pentacle and Sword, Work ye unto my desire, Harken ye unto my word.

Cords and Censer, Scourge and knife, Powers of the Witches Blade, Waken all ye into life, Come ye as the Charm is made:

Queen of Heaven, Queen of Hell, Horned Hunter of the Night, Lend your power unto the Spell, Work my will by Magic Rite.

If chant is used to reinforce a work already begun, end with this:

By all the power of land and sea, by all the might of moon and sun,

What is my will—So mote it be, What I do say—It shall be done."

Consecrating Tools

(1957)

(Note: if possible lay any new weapon touching an already consecrated one, Sword to sword, Athame to Athame, etc.)

[1] Prepare Circle and purify. All tools must be consecrated by a man and a woman, both as naked as drawn swords; they must be purified, clean, and properly prepared.

[2] Place tool on pentacle on altar. Magus sprinkles it with salt and water. Witch passes it through smoke of incense, replaces it on pentacle. Touching with already consecrated weapon, they say the First Conjuration.

[2a] For sword or athame, say "I conjure thee, O Sword (or Athame) of Steel, that thou servest me for a strength and a defence in all magical operations, against all mine enemies, visible and invisible, in the names of Aradia and Cernunnos. I conjure thee anew by the Holy Names Aradia and Cernunnos, that thou

servest me for a protection in all adversities, so aid me."

[2b] For any other tool, say, "Aradia and Cernunnos, deign to bless and to consecrate this [tool], that it may obtain necessary virtue through thee for all acts of love and Beauty."

[3] Again they sprinkle and cense, and say the Second Conjuration:

[3a] For sword or athame, say, "I conjure thee, O Sword [Athame] of Steel, by the Great Gods and the Gentle Goddesses, by the virtue of the Heavens, of the Stars, of the Spirits who preside over them, that thou mayest receive such virtues that I may obtain the end that I desire in all things wherein I shall use thee, by the power of Aradia and Cernunnos."

[3b] For any other tool, say, "Aradia and Cernunnos, bless this instrument prepared in thine honour." (For the scourge or cords, add, "That it may only serve for a good use and end, and to thy Glory.")

[4] All instruments when consecrated should be presented to their User by giving the [point-down triangle] sign salute (if they are working in the 1st degree, or the sign of the higher degree if they are working that.)

[5] Then the one who is not the owner should give the Fivefold Kiss to the owner. For the final kiss, the tool should be placed between the breasts, and the two workers should embrace for as long as they feel like, it being held in place by their bodies. The new owner should use it immediately, i.e., cast (trace) Circle with Sword or Athame, wave wand to 4 quarters, cut something with white-handled knife, etc. Cords and scourge should be used at once.

The tool should be kept in as close connection as possible to the naked body for at least a month, i.e., kept under pillow, etc. When not in use, all tools and weapons should be put away in a secret place; and it is good that this should be near your sleeping place, and that you handle them each night before retiring. Do not allow anyone to touch or handle any of your tools until they are thoroughly impregnated with your aura; say, six months or as near as possible. But a couple working together may own the same tools, which will be impregnated with the aura of both.

Glossary

Amalthean Horn Prayer:	an adaption of a poem published by Aleister Crowley in 1907; in classical mythology, Amalthea, a foster mother of the Greek god Zeus, was depicted with a "horn," that is, a cornucopia overflowing with grains and fruits.
amulet:	a piece of jewelry thought to provide magical protection against evil or disease
Aphrodite:	the Greek goddess of love and sexuality
Aradia:	the daughter of Lucifer and the goddess Diana, sent to earth to teach oppressed Italian peasants how to use witchcraft against the upper classes
Arianrhod:	a Celtic goddess famed for her beauty
Artemis:	the Greek goddess of the wilderness, the hunt and wild animals, and fertility
aspergillum:	an implement (such as a brush, branch, or perforated ball) used to sprinkle holy water
Asperging Circle:	the circle in which people are "asperged," or sprinkled with holy water
Astarte:	an ancient goddess of love and fertility
Athame:	a black-handled dagger
Bride:	that is, Bridget, the patron saint of Ireland
Brigid:	the Celtic goddess of poetry, healing, and craft
Cernunnos:	"the Horned One," a Celtic god of fertility as well as of life, animals, and the underworld
Cerridwen:	the goddess of dark prophetic powers and the keeper of the Cauldron of the Underworld, where inspiration and knowledge are brewed
Cords:	girdles or belts, typically nine feet long and used to measure the circumference of a magic circle
Diana:	the Roman goddess of the hunt
Dione:	a minor Greek goddess
Lacedaemon:	usually used synonymously with Sparta, a city-state of ancient Greece
Magus:	magician, sorcerer
Melusine: a	feminine spirit of freshwater in sacred springs and rivers in European folklore
A merry heart doeth good like a medicine but a broken spirit breaketh the bones:	quotation from the biblical book of Proverbs, chapter 17, verse 22
pentacle:	a five-pointed star surrounded by a circle
Sabbat:	a seasonal festival that celebrates the "wheel of the year"
sooth:	truth
talisman:	an amulet or other object thought to have magical powers

VATICAN II: DOCUMENT ANALYSIS

"The rites should be distinguished by a noble simplicity; they should be short, clear, and unencumbered by useless repetitions..."

Overview

The Second Vatican Council was summoned by Pope John XXIII on January 25, 1959, as an ecumenical council charged with renewal of the Roman Catholic Church. The preceding post-Reformation Councils of Trent (1543–1565) and First Vatican Council (1869–1870) had sought to define the Church dogmatically in relation, respectively, to Protestantism and the liberal ideas unleashed by the French Revolution, which had come to inform the practices of secular governments in western Europe and North America. In contrast, Vatican II sought to redefine the Church's identity and its relationship with the world. Preparatory commissions were appointed in 1959, and then, from October 11, 1962, to December 8, 1965, the bishops of the Church gathered at Vatican City in Rome for four separate sessions, to debate draft documents prepared by the papal bureaucracy and—in certain cases—issues hitherto unaddressed. Every conciliar document was reviewed and amended by commissions of bishops elected from within the council, to take account of criticisms and concerns raised during debate, and was ultimately approved by (generally overwhelming) majority vote.

The final documents promulgated by Vatican II addressed all aspects of the Church's internal and external life, including its forms of worship; the respective roles of bishops, members of religious orders, priests, and laypeople; its relationships with other Christians, non-Christians, and the secular world; and such singular topics as the nature of religious freedom. The range of subject matter addressed was unprecedented, and the very tone of the council arguably marked the most dramatic shift in the Church's self-understanding since the Counter-Reformation.

Context

When John XXIII (formerly Angelo Roncalli) gave notice of the Second Vatican Council only a few months after his election to office (on October 28, 1958), few anticipated the momentous changes that would follow. But the new pope radiated a personal approachability far removed from his predecessor (Pius XII), and his incorporation of a plea to non-Catholic Christians to join with Rome in seeking organic Christian unity signaled a noteworthy departure from the Roman Catholic Church's earlier emphasis on ecumenical reunion not through dialogue between churches but solely as a process of conversion by non-Catholics to a belief in the authenticity of Rome's claims to primacy.

The seemingly revolutionary character of the council should not be overstated. A century earlier, the Church had considered itself in the forefront of resistance to a liberal revolution, marked not only by the political ascendancy of the bourgeoisie in much of western Europe but also by an emphasis on personal liberty in religious matters and on scientific approaches to biblical scholarship. The classic response was Pope Pius IX's Syllabus of Errors (1864), which condemned many—if not most—aspects of classical liberalism. By the early twentieth century, however, such defensiveness was giving way to a flowering of Catholic interest in modern biblical scholarship, liturgical renewal, and ministries undertaken and directed primarily by laypeople rather than clergy. Although the pace of change varied from nation to nation, after 1933 the threat posed by German National Socialism also forced the Church to abandon its earlier resolve to stand aloof from secular politics.

During World War II and in the years immediately following, further dramatic changes in the character of Western Catholicism took place. The Church's willingness to negotiate concordats (agreements securing it privileged status from the state) with totalitarian regimes in Germany, Italy, and Spain during the 1920s and 1930s had compromised it in the eyes of many liberals who came to prominence in Europe's postwar governments. As lay Catholics came to play an increasing role in the emerging Christian Democrat parties in France, Germany, and Italy, moreover, they increasingly voiced a language of religious pluralism that sat uncomfortably with the ethos prevailing in the corridors of the Vatican.

The new world of the 1950s brought other changes that did not sit comfortably with the earlier Catholic ethos. Suburbanization—particularly in countries with a long tradition of Catholic immigration—produced a new type of college-educated Catholic, increasingly resistant to notions of subordination to clerical authority and desirous of carving out a separate sphere of lay activity. Such Catholics were encouraged by a postwar generation of parish priests, many of whom were proponents of participatory liturgical worship and wanted the Church to a play more active role in the struggles against poverty, racism, and injustice.

As the pace of decolonization increased during the 1950s, moreover, the Church witnessed the emergence of new Catholic indigenous leadership in Africa and Asia. Without in any way calling into question the ultimate authority of the papacy, third-world bishops sought a degree of discretion in implementing the mission of the Church that took account of the unique gifts and problems of their particular region. Increasingly aware of the diversity of Catholicism, many bishops—not all of them from the third world—would use their time at the council to articulate a vision of episcopal collegiality (that is, the pope and the bishops acting together) that had not been seen in Western Catholicism for over a century. The final documents promulgated were the product of the bishops assembled in council expressing approval (or disapproval) of what had been presented to them, a far more participatory process than had been the case at the First Vatican Council.

About the Author

While the documents of Vatican II were begun under the authority of one pope (John XXIII, who died in 1963) and promulgated under the authority of another (Paul VI), neither was an "author" of the conciliar documents to the extent that they were authors of such encyclicals as Pacem in Terris (On Establishing Universal Peace in Truth, Justice, Charity and Liberty, 1963) or Humanae Vitae (On the Regulation of Birth, 1968)—although Paul VI played a more active role in commenting on drafts of council documents and occasionally demanding modifications than did John XXIII. The council, acting in its corporate capacity, was the ultimate author, and thus every participating bishop could claim a share in the final

Time Line

October 28, 1958
- Angelo Roncalli is elected pope as John XXIII.

June 5, 1959
- The preparatory commissions for the council (staffed by Vatican personnel) are appointed.

October 11, 1962
- The first session of the council begins.

November 20, 1962
- A vote by the bishops against the schema on revelation, which held divine revelation to be independent of the Bible and Catholic tradition, demonstrates their resolve to affirm the role of scripture and the value of biblical criticism.

April 11, 1963
- John XXIII issues the encyclical *Pacem in Terris* (Peace on Earth), endorsing the concept of inherent human rights and the action of the Holy Spirit in improving the social conditions of working people.

June 3, 1963
- John XXIII dies.

June 21, 1963
- Giovanni Montini is elected pope as Paul VI.

September 29, 1963
- The second session of the council begins.

December 4, 1963
- The Constitution on the Sacred Liturgy (*Sacrosanctum Concilium*) is approved.

January 4–6, 1964
- Paul VI meets with Ecumenical Patriarch Athenagoras I of Constantinople, a significant ecumenical gesture between the Catholic and Eastern Orthodox churches.

September 14, 1964	■ The third session of the council begins.
November 16–21, 1964	■ During what is to be known as "Black Week," Paul VI decides to delay the vote on the Declaration on Religious Freedom and insist on amendments to the Decree on Ecumenism to meet conservative concerns.
November 20, 1964	■ The Decree on Ecumenism (*Unitatis Redintegratio*) is approved.
September 14, 1965	■ The fourth session of the council begins.
October 28, 1965	■ The Declaration on Religious Freedom (*Dignitatis Humanae*) is approved.
December 7, 1965	■ The Pastoral Constitution on the Church in the Modern World (*Gaudium et Spes*) is approved.
December 8, 1965	■ The Vatican Council is formally closed by Paul VI.

theologian Karl Rahner, an influential voice in pushing the council in radical directions.

Explanation and Analysis of the Document

By the time Pope Paul VI closed the Second Vatican Council in 1965, the bishops had endorsed a total of sixteen documents: four constitutions, nine decrees, and three declarations. While they are not of equal weight, all reveal a common willingness to address certain key themes, foremost among which was an interest in rediscovering the forms of early Christian worship and practice prevailing before the traditions of the High Middle Ages became the universal standard for post-Reformation Western Catholicism. Many bishops also embraced the notion of *aggiornamento*—a phrase of John XXIII's describing the Church's ability to appropriate certain aspects of contemporary culture—intended not to alter the Church's doctrine but to render it more comprehensible to human society of the twentieth century. Since the volume of Vatican II material makes it impossible to address every aspect, this discussion examines how four specific conciliar documents reflect these concerns.

◆ Sacrosanctum Concilium (Constitution on the Sacred Liturgy)

The liturgical forms employed by the Roman Catholic Church in 1959 were, with a few exceptions, those codified at the Council of Trent (1545–1563). Based upon a Latin liturgy—except in parts of Eastern Europe and the Middle East—Roman Catholic worship emphasized a form of religious practice in which laypeople had acquired the status of observers of a rite centered on the priestly celebrant. Pressure for the rediscovery of premedieval liturgies and greater congregational participation arose in France in the eighteenth century, spread to parts of Germany in the nineteenth century, and was encouraged by Pope Pius XII during the 1940s and 1950s.

The Vatican II debate over the document promulgated in 1963 as the Sacrosanctum Concilium (Constitution on the Sacred Liturgy, approved on December 4, 1963) also set the tone for later sessions of the council. Pressure from within the papal bureaucracy had led to the elimination of many changes proposed by the preparatory commission on the liturgy and the insistence that the process of liturgical reform be vested in the hands of the Holy See. At the opening session of the council, however, the bishops demanded restoration of the original text, and a preliminary draft was approved by 2,162 votes to 46 in November 1962. The final draft passed almost unanimously only a month later.

III. The Reform of the Sacred Liturgy Given later complaints about radical liturgical experimentation, it is illuminating that the governing instruments of the third section of chapter 1 of the Sacrosanctum Concilium, "The Reform of the Sacred Liturgy," emphasized a hierarchical approach to reform extending from the pope in Rome to the

documents. That said, the members of the commissions elected by the council to prepare amended drafts played a major role in shaping the form of the documents that finally emerged.

A disproportionate influence may also be said to have been exerted by several cardinals who took the lead in moving proceedings forward. Within the papal bureaucracy the most notable figure was Augustin Bea, a German Jesuit, former rector of the Pontifical Bible Institute and head of the Secretariat for the Promotion of Christian Unity. Outside the Vatican establishment, the key figures were Leon-Josef Suenens (the archbishop of Malines-Brussels) and Franz Konig (the archbishop of Vienna), who played central roles on the Central Preparatory Commission. Suenens was a leading figure in drafting the Pastoral Constitution on the Church in the Modern World, while Konig served on the Doctrinal Commission and was the sponsor of the German diocesan bishop (22). Furthermore, the principle of change for change's sake was emphatically rejected in favor of a deliberate process grounded in theological and historical inquiry and incorporating the experience of liturgical experimentation (23). Arguably the most radical innovation was the call for a renewed engagement with scripture as the basis for liturgical action, something neglected in the post-Reformation period (24).

A central aspect of the renewed liturgy was that it was to be corporate in nature and required to display a "public and social nature," which emphasized that the priest alone did not "make" the sacrament but rather that it was a communal event celebrated in conjunction with the body of the faithful (26–27). Lay participation (hitherto confined largely to altar boys assisting the priest and professional choirs) was expanded to include a variety of functions, including such offices as lector and prayer leader that had existed in the early Church, though critics would later argue that such participants sometimes failed to "perform their functions in a correct and orderly manner" (28–29). Even those laypeople without an assigned role were urged actively to demonstrate the corporate nature of the Eucharistic celebration through "acclamations, responses, psalmody, antiphons and songs" as well as "reverent silence." No longer was the Catholic layman to be in any sense a spectator (30–32).

The new Eucharistic rite was to be both simplified and comprehensible (33–34). It also revived something familiar to most Protestants, namely, the liturgy of the Word. Readings from the scriptures—particularly the Old Testament—had been greatly curtailed in Catholic liturgy, and Sacrosanctum Concilium sought to restore a liturgical calendar that exposed worshippers to a greater variety of Bible texts. Furthermore, priests were instructed to introduce more scriptural material into their preaching, providing their congregations with a greater appreciation of how the promises of the Old Testament prefigured the coming of the Messiah authenticated in the New Testament. Bible services—something few would have considered Catholic in the early twentieth century—were also recommended, particularly for communities where priests were in short supply (35).

The most revolutionary aspect of liturgical renewal, however, concerned the language of worship, hitherto Latin except in the Greek Catholic churches of Eastern Europe and the Middle East. Pressure for an entirely vernacular liturgy (that is, worship conducted in the native tongue of the participants) came in the first instance from the Greek Catholic archbishop Maximos IV Saigh of Antioch, although the initial focus of translation was applied to Bible readings, prayers, and chants rather than the central aspects of the liturgy (36).

Equally striking was a growing readiness to substitute cultural adaptation in liturgical practice for the "rigid uniformity" of the past, provided that "substantial unity of the Roman rite" was maintained (37–38). During the late 1960s, the papacy permitted the incorporation of certain local ritual elements, including the Thai gesture of peace and the Chinese celebration of rites in honor of the dead, and introduced Japanese and Ugandan martyrs into the calendar of saints. Even more noteworthy was the granting of permission to both bishops and episcopal conferences to authorize liturgical experimentation and make the final determination of liturgical norms (39–40).

♦ **Unitatis Redintegratio (Decree on Ecumenism)**
For much of the twentieth century the Roman Catholic Church stood apart from the ecumenical movement, insisting that Christian reunion could come only from the submission of non-Catholics to the authority of the See of Rome. When John XXIII first summoned the council, however, he laid particular stress on reconciliation with the "separated brethren," and he suited actions to words by establishing the Secretariat for Promoting Christian Unity in 1960, which urged the bishops to acknowledge the elements of divine grace that persisted among both the Eastern Orthodox churches and the heirs of the Protestant Reformation. Four years later, his successor, Paul VI, would hold a hitherto unprecedented meeting with the Ecumenical patriarch Athenagoras I of Constantinople.

Despite the Secretariat for Promoting Christian Unity's interest in Protestantism, the earliest version of the Unitatis Redintegratio (Decree on Ecumenism, approved November 20, 1964) dealt only with the Orthodox churches and still called on them to submit to Rome. Such wording was rejected during the 1962 session of the council, the bishops agreeing that the emphasis on Rome's authority and jurisdiction must be lessened and its pastoral role emphasized. They also argued that the text must be expanded to address not merely the Orthodox churches but also the Protestant ones. On November 20, 1964, after intervention by the pope, the Decree on Ecumenism was approved by 2,054 votes to 64.

Chapter I: Catholic Principles on Ecumenism The final version of the Decree on Ecumenism offered a hitherto unprecedented admission that "men who believe in Christ and have been truly baptized are in communion with the Catholic Church even though this communion is imperfect." No longer were non-Catholics viewed as outside the bonds of Christian community, nor was the ecumenical movement treated as meritless. Furthermore, the decree conceded that "significant elements and endowments" existed within both Orthodoxy and Protestantism and offered the basis for the pursuit of unity, thus acknowledging the corporate identity of the non-Catholic churches for the first time (3–4).

Chapter II: The Practice of Ecumenism For the first time, Catholics were encouraged to participate in the work of the ecumenical movement, albeit within defined limits. Prayers for unity both among Catholics and in common with other ecumenically minded Christians were welcomed as affirming the goal of the ecumenical movement, but on common (shared) worship the bishops were more cautious, emphasizing the Catholic position that unity generally preceded common worship and requiring episcopal permission for any such activity (8). Far more important for them was the development of a better understanding of other Christian traditions, not only their doctrine but also their history, spirituality, and cultural background, for only through mutual understanding would the cause of Christian unity be advanced (9).

♦ Gaudium et Spes (Pastoral Constitution on the Church in the Modern World)

Of all the conciliar documents, the Gaudium et Spes (Pastoral Constitution on the Church in the Modern World, approved on December 7, 1965) represents the council's most sustained effort to explore and renew the relationship between the Catholic Church and the twentieth-century state. It is all the more noteworthy, then, that such a topic did not figure among the documents introduced by the preparatory commissions in 1962, an absence that provoked a sharp response from many bishops, most notably Dom Helder Camara of Rio de Janeiro and Cardinals Leo Suenens and Giovanni Montini (the future Pope Paul VI).

A coordinating commission headed by Suenens, which included fourteen lay participants, subsequently produced a document that maintained that Christians should seek to make the Church present to the world through service and witness. Acknowledging that the Church need not reject rational solutions to social problems, the commission nevertheless warned of the importance of understanding that the Church should not be *of* the world but *in and for* the world. First presented at the 1964 session, the constitution was ultimately approved in December 1965 by 2,111 votes to 251.

Gaudium et Spes sought to demonstrate how the Christian message should be presented in secular environments and in non-European cultural contexts. "The Church is not the petrification of what once was," wrote Joseph Ratzinger (the future Pope Benedict XVI), "but its living presence in every age. The Church's dimension is therefore the present and the future no less than the past." For the bishops, however, the social order was never an end in itself. Accepting that the Church no longer exercised formal political power, they nevertheless rejected the notion that it should be confined to a purely "religious" domain, while acknowledging the present need for a degree of autonomy for the secular sphere.

Preface Gaudium et Spes exemplified the depth of Vatican II's commitment to the renewal of the social order. Humanity, particularly in the wake of the horrors of World Wars I and II, had entered a period of doubt about the inevitability of progress and the "ultimate destiny of reality and of humanity." The pastoral constitution affirmed the Church's willingness to foster the "brotherhood of all men," in a spirit of reconciliation rather than judgment (3).

Part I: Chapter IV—The Role of the Church in the Modern World Part I of Gaudium et Spes sought to articulate a theology of the Church in the world, noting that a commitment to unity was the essence of the Church and that this was a unity realized not by "external dominion exercised by merely human means" but rather by "faith and charity put into vital practice." The Church, the constitution argued, offered the prospect of a human unity that transcended cultural, political, and economic distinctions, but it was also capable of discerning the positive aspects of human institutions and willing to assist those institutions in developing their capacities where they did not conflict with the Church's own mission. (42)

Part II: Chapter III—Economic and Social Life In the economic arena, Gaudium et Spes criticized concentrations of power, whether among nations or individuals. Objecting to both inadequate and excessive economic regulation, the constitution encouraged individuals to contribute to their nation's economic life to the full extent of their ability (65). The document's greatest concern was over economic inequality, which it viewed as destructive of human dignity. Discrimination in matters of wages or working conditions was condemned, and the need for migrant workers to be incorporated into the communities in which they resided was emphasized. This recurring emphasis on the preservation of human dignity would be a feature of this and other conciliar documents (66).

The Constitution on the Church in the Modern World adopted a more radical tone in an article devoted solely to the rights of workers, contending that the autonomy of management should not be used as an excuse to limit worker participation in business decisions. Thus, the ability to belong to a trade union and to take part in its activities without fear of reprisal was deemed a "basic right," and the bishops went so far as to define the right to strike as "a necessary, though ultimate, aid for defense of the workers' own rights," albeit only after negotiations had broken down (68).

While the bishops were generally careful to refrain from offering detailed economic prescriptions, they did not shrink from reminding even investors of their social obligations in establishing a proper balance between consumption and investment. Perhaps with the concerns of the representatives from newly independent and soon-to-be-independent countries in Africa in mind, they urged that particular care be devoted to the needs of "underdeveloped countries or regions" (70).

Having adopted (what seemed to some) a radical note, the bishops concluded their reflections on economic responsibility with an affirmation of private property as essential to individual and family autonomy, while recognizing that the nature of such property varied over time. Public property was accepted as compatible with a just society, but only when acquired by due process of law, for the common good, and with fair compensation for any individual or group who suffered loss (71).

Part II: Chapter IV—The Life of the Political Community Departing from the nineteenth-century Church's hostility to democracy, Gaudium et Spes also sought to promote the development of civil rights that enhanced human dignity and the greater involvement of ordinary citizens in the process of government, a theme that echoed John XXIII's 1963 encyclical "Pacem in Terris." The constitution accepted the need for greater state intervention in the

modern world but warned against "dictatorial systems or totalitarian methods" and insisted upon the importance of tolerating a diversity of political viewpoints and the necessity of proper training in citizenship (75).

The Church's willingness to concede the principle of pluralism was one of the most remarkable aspects of the fourth chapter. What individuals do as Christians is not necessarily identical to what they do as members of the Church, the constitution conceded. The Church and the political community were to be regarded as autonomous, with the Church identified with no political party and respecting the "political freedom and responsibility" of all citizens (76).

Part II: Chapter V—The Fostering of Peace and the Promotion of a Community of Nations The bishops also broke new ground in the debate over world peace, by moving from a simple indictment of war to an emphasis on how more effectively to strive for peace. Unlikely support for the promotion of international cooperation between citizens and governments came from the otherwise conservative Cardinal Alfredo Ottaviani, who recommended a worldwide federation of states and binding authority for a body like the United Nations. International organizations received praise in the constitution, particularly for their endeavors in the developing world and their role in helping Christians and non-Christians work positively together (84). The constitution also affirmed the role of economic cooperation and the benefits to the developing world of experts motivated more by genuine altruism than national considerations (85).

The constitution nevertheless warned against the dangers of governments pursuing solutions to such contemporary issues as the population explosion, which ran counter to the principle of human dignity. Acknowledging the occasional necessity of such imposed changes as land reform and improvement of the social order, it repudiated interventions that contravened the inalienable rights of individuals and families (forcible sterilization being a topic of considerable contemporary debate) (87–88).

♦ Dignitatis Humanae (Declaration on Religious Freedom)

The Vatican II document titled Dignitatis Humanae (Declaration on Religious Freedom, approved on October 28, 1965) represented one of the most dramatic departures by the Roman Catholic Church from its earlier position that "error has no rights." Although it was initially incorporated into the Decree on Ecumenism, the declaration received independent status following the 1963 and 1964 sessions of the council. So vigorous were those debates that Pope Paul VI postponed the vote on the declaration until the 1965 session, when it was approved by a margin of 1,954 to 249. The occasion of the debates of November 1964 came to be known to progressives as "Black Week" and was feared for a time to mark a retreat by the pope from the principles previously asserted by the council.

Conservative bishops argued that governments of nations in which Catholicism was a minority faith were obliged to respect the religious freedom of Catholics and the mission of the Church but that no Catholic state was obliged to accord such a status to non-Catholics within its jurisdiction. The new understanding of religious freedom that emerged from the council was that no state should compel persons of faith to act against their conscience or prevent them from acting in accord with it. The declaration reiterated the importance of personal human dignity and the fact that this extended to freedom of religious profession (2).

The freedom from coercion required by individuals applied equally to families and to religious communities, the declaration added, and should be recognized as a civil right. By the same token, while religious communities should enjoy freedom from state coercion, the former should not abuse that privilege by evangelizing individuals in ways that undermined the latter's personal religious freedom. Governments had a duty to protect and foster religious freedom, the bishops agreed, and the sole justification for the state to limit religious freedom was a clear threat to the public order (4).

Audience

The audience for Vatican II varied to some extent from document to document. Some concerned the activities of particular functional groups within the Church (bishops, priests and members of religious orders, and Eastern Rite Catholics); some were primarily addressed to groups outside the Catholic Church (non-Catholic Christians and non-Christians). The four foundational constitutions (those on the Sacred Liturgy, Revelation [Die Verbum], the Church [Luman Gentium], and the Church in the Modern World) were addressed both to Catholics and non-Catholics in that they sought to demonstrate how the Church should act and how it defined itself in serving as the link between God and Man. Perhaps the document with the most immediate impact on ordinary Catholics was the Constitution on the Sacred Liturgy, which, at a stroke, altered worship practices throughout the Catholic world.

One of the problems in defining the audience for Vatican II is that while lay activists frequently placed an expansive interpretation on the conciliar documents, arguing that they must be read in accordance with the "spirit of Vatican II," many clerical leaders—including the late Pope John Paul II—rejected the notion that the council did away with the traditional understanding of hierarchical authority within the Catholic Church. In the former interpretation, Vatican II was a blueprint for transformation of the Church from the grassroots upward; under the latter view, it represented guidelines for the evolutionary transformation of the Church—in its own eyes and in the eyes of others—consistent with past tradition and in conformity with episcopal and papal authority.

"The rites should be distinguished by a noble simplicity; they should be short, clear, and unencumbered by useless repetitions; they should be within the people's powers of comprehension, and normally should not require much explanation."

(Section 1)

"The brethren divided from us also use many liturgical actions of the Christian religion. These most certainly can truly engender a life of grace in ways that vary according to the condition of each Church or Community. These liturgical actions must be regarded as capable of giving access to the community of salvation."

(Section 1)

"With great respect, therefore, this Council regards all the true, good and just elements inherent in the very wide variety of institutions which the human race has established for itself and constantly continues to establish. The council affirms, moreover, that the Church is willing to assist and promote all these institutions to the extent that such a service depends on her and can be associated with her mission."

(Section 1)

"Therefore the right to religious freedom has its foundation not in the subjective disposition of the person, but in his very nature. In consequence, the right to this immunity continues to exist even in those who do not live up to their obligation of seeking the truth and adhering to it, and the exercise of this right is not to be impeded, provided that just public order be observed."

(Section 1)

Impact

Scholars remain divided over the extent to which the Second Vatican Council reflected continuity with existing tradition and practice and how much it departed from it, yet any account of the visible aspects of changes effected by the council cannot fail to note that the Church did not act in the same fashion after 1965 as previously. Exceeded in length only by the ecumenical councils of Constance (1414–1418) and Trent, Vatican II involved far more preparatory planning than any earlier council and witnessed an attendance of 2,400 bishops at any one time, with participants from every continent and almost every nation.

For the Roman Catholic Church, Vatican II marked a final acknowledgment that the era of establishment (the privileged status accorded by the state to a particular church) was over. Its deliberations also reflected a growing desire to reconcile with what were termed the "separated churches" (the products of the Protestant Reformation) and to at least modify the harsh rhetoric the Church had employed against secular modernity since at least the 1870s. It was no longer enough simply to identify and condemn the failings of secular society; rather, Catholics were obliged to become involved in the process of devising solutions. Such an approach had implications not only for laypeople but also for priests and even bishops.

When Pope Paul VI closed the Second Vatican Council in 1965, the future course for the Catholic Church seemed propitious. Lay Catholics were encouraged to study the conciliar documents and work with clergy and bishops to ensure Vatican II's effectual implementation at the provincial, diocesan, and parish levels. Catholic life promised to be invigorated by the active participation of the laity, Catholic relations with fellow Christians would henceforth be governed by a sense of mutual respect, and the Catholic Church's commitment to the upbuilding of the secular world was firmly delineated. The ensuing turmoil of the late 1960s, however, demonstrated that the council had raised excessively high expectations on the part of some, and at the same it elicited alarm from many who still looked to the Church as a bulwark against modernity. Within a few short years, activist laypeople and clergy would find themselves opposed to the episcopal hierarchy whose interventions at the council had given rise to the documents on which the more radical elements claimed to base their interpretation of the new Catholicism. The refusal of successive popes to abandon opposition to artificial birth control and concern about the extent of liturgical diversity provoked a reaction among the hierarchy that culminated in the election of Pope John Paul II in 197

8. While dubbed by some a conservative reaction, however, it did not represent a repudiation of Vatican II in its entirety but rather was an attempt to restore the balance between change and tradition.

Further Reading

■ Books

Alberigo, Giuseppe. *A Brief History of Vatican II*. Maryknoll, N.Y.: Orbis Books, 2006.

Hastings, Adrian, ed. *Modern Catholicism: Vatican II and After*. New York: Oxford University Press, 1991.

Lamb, Matthew, and Matthew Levering, eds. *Vatican II: Renewal within Tradition*. New York: Oxford University Press, 2008.

O'Malley, John W. *What Happened at Vatican II*. Cambridge, Mass.: Harvard University Press, 2008.

Ratzinger, Joseph. "The Dignity of the Human Person." In *Commentary on the Documents of Vatican II*, Vol. 5: *Pastoral Constitution on the Church in the Modern World*, ed. Herbert Vorgrimler. New York: Herder and Herder, 1969.

Rynne, Xavier. *Vatican Council II*. New York: Farrar, Straus and Giroux, 1968.

Vorgrimler, Herbert, ed. *Commentary on the Documents of Vatican II*. 5 vols. New York: Herder and Herder, 1967–1969.

■ Web Sites

Vatican II: Voice of the Church Web site. http://www.vatican-2voice.org/default.htm

Documents of the II Vatican Council. The Vatican Web site. http://www.vatican.va/archive/hist_councils/ii_vatican_council/

—Commentary by Jeremy Bonner

Questions for Further Study

1. In your view, did the Second Vatican Council change Catholicism, or did the council reflect and institutionalize changes in Catholicism that had already taken place? Or both? Explain your position.

2. The Second Vatican Council could be regarded as an end point in a host of geopolitical, economic, and historical changes throughout the world in the preceding decades. Explain in detail how this is the case.

3. Still in the twenty-first century, some conservative Catholics grumble about Vatican II, arguing that it liberalized the church beyond recognition. They prefer masses conducted in Latin, use of traditional hymns (accompanied by an organ rather than guitars), and adherence to traditional practices that Vatican II either eliminated or deemphasized. Why do you think some Catholics feel this way?

4. Make the argument that Vatican II was part and parcel of the revolutionary, anticapitalist, countercultural decade of the 1960s.

5. One commentator remarked pithily, "If the post-Vatican II theology did anything, it drew attention to the person in the pew instead of the priest in the pulpit." Explain this statement in light of the Vatican II documents.

Picture of Pope Paul VI.

VATICAN II: DOCUMENT TEXT

III. The Reform of the Sacred Liturgy

A) General norms. . .

22. 1. Regulation of the sacred liturgy depends solely on the authority of the Church, that is, on the Apostolic See and, as laws may determine, on the bishop.
    2. In virtue of power conceded by the law, the regulation of the liturgy within certain defined limits belongs also to various kinds of competent territorial bodies of bishops legitimately established.
    3. Therefore no other person, even if he be a priest, may add, remove, or change anything in the liturgy on his own authority.

23. That sound tradition may be retained, and yet the way remains open to legitimate progress, a careful investigation is always to be made into each part of the liturgy which is to be revised. This investigation should be theological, historical, and pastoral. Also the general laws governing the structure and meaning of the liturgy must be studied in conjunction with the experience derived from recent liturgical reforms and from the indults conceded to various places. Finally, there must be no innovations unless the good of the Church genuinely and certainly requires them; and care must be taken that any new forms adopted should in some way grow organically from forms already existing.

    As far as possible, notable differences between the rites used in adjacent regions must be carefully avoided.

24. Sacred Scripture is of the greatest importance in the celebration of the liturgy. For it is from scripture that lessons are read and explained in the homily, and psalms are sung; the prayers, collects, and liturgical songs are scriptural in their inspiration and their force, and it is from the Scriptures that actions and signs derive their meaning. Thus to achieve the restoration, progress, and adaptation of the sacred liturgy, it is essential to promote that warm and living love for Scripture to which the venerable tradition of both Eastern and Western rites gives testimony.

25. The liturgical books are to be revised as soon as possible; experts are to be employed on the task, and bishops are to be consulted, from various parts of the world.

B) Norms drawn from the hierarchic and communal nature of the Liturgy

26. Liturgical services are not private functions, but are celebrations of the Church, which is the "sacrament of unity," namely, the holy people united and ordered under their bishops.

    Therefore liturgical services pertain to the whole body of the Church; they manifest it and have effects upon it; but they concern the individual members of the Church in different ways, according to their differing rank, office, and actual participation.

27. It is to be stressed that whenever rites, according to their specific nature, make provision for communal celebration involving the presence and active participation of the faithful, this way of celebrating them is to be preferred, so far as possible, to a celebration that is individual and quasi-private.

    This applies with especial force to the celebration of Mass and the administration of the sacraments, even though every Mass has of itself a public and social nature.

28. In liturgical celebrations each person, minister or layman, who has an office to perform, should do all of, but only, those parts which pertain to his office by the nature of the rite and the principles of liturgy.

29. Servers, lectors commentators, and members of the choir also exercise a genuine liturgical function. They ought, therefore, to discharge their office with the sincere piety and decorum demanded by so exalted a ministry and rightly expected of them by God's people.

    Consequently they must all be deeply imbued with the spirit of the liturgy, each in his own measure, and they must be trained to perform their functions in a correct and orderly manner.

30. To promote active participation, the people should be encouraged to take part by means of

acclamations, responses, psalmody, antiphons, and songs, as well as by actions, gestures, and bodily attitudes. And at the proper times all should observe a reverent silence.

31. The revision of the liturgical books must carefully attend to the provision of rubrics also for the people's parts.

32. The liturgy makes distinctions between persons according to their liturgical function and sacred Orders, and there are liturgical laws providing for due honors to be given to civil authorities. Apart from these instances, no special honors are to be paid in the liturgy to any private persons or classes of persons, whether in the ceremonies or by external display.

C) Norms based upon the didactic and pastoral nature of the Liturgy

33. Although the sacred liturgy is above all things the worship of the divine Majesty, it likewise contains much instruction for the faithful. For in the liturgy God speaks to His people and Christ is still proclaiming His gospel. And the people reply to God both by song and prayer.

Moreover, the prayers addressed to God by the priest who presides over the assembly in the person of Christ are said in the name of the entire holy people and of all present. And the visible signs used by the liturgy to signify invisible divine things have been chosen by Christ or the Church. Thus not only when things are read "which were written for our instruction" (Rom. 15:4), but also when the Church prays or sings or acts, the faith of those taking part is nourished and their minds are raised to God, so that they may offer Him their rational service and more abundantly receive His grace.

Wherefore, in the revision of the liturgy, the following general norms should be observed:

34. The rites should be distinguished by a noble simplicity; they should be short, clear, and unencumbered by useless repetitions; they should be within the people's powers of comprehension, and normally should not require much explanation.

35. That the intimate connection between words and rites may be apparent in the liturgy:

1) In sacred celebrations there is to be more reading from holy Scripture, and it is to be more varied and suitable.

2) Because the sermon is part of the liturgical service, the best place for it is to be indicated even in the rubrics, as far as the nature of the rite will allow; the ministry of preaching is to be fulfilled with exactitude and fidelity. The sermon, moreover, should draw its content mainly from scriptural and liturgical sources, and its character should be that of a proclamation of God's wonderful works in the history of salvation, the mystery of Christ, ever made present and active within us, especially in the celebration of the liturgy.

3) Instruction which is more explicitly liturgical should also be given in a variety of ways; if necessary, short directives to be spoken by the priest or proper minister should be provided within the rites themselves. But they should occur only at the more suitable moments, and be in prescribed or similar words.

4) Bible services should be encouraged, especially on the vigils of the more solemn feasts, on some weekdays in Advent and Lent, and on Sundays and feast days. They are particularly to be commended in places where no priest is available; when this is so, a deacon or some other person authorized by the bishop should preside over the celebration.

36. 1. Particular law remaining in force, the use of the Latin language is to be preserved in the Latin rites.

2. But since the use of the mother tongue, whether in the Mass, the administration of the sacraments, or other parts of the liturgy, frequently may be of great advantage to the people, the limits of its employment may be extended. This will apply in the first place to the readings and directives, and to some of the prayers and chants, according to the regulations on this matter to be laid down separately in subsequent chapters.

3. These norms being observed, it is for the competent territorial ecclesiastical authority mentioned in Art. 22:2, to decide whether, and to what extent, the vernacular language is to be used; their decrees are to be approved, that is, confirmed, by the Apostolic See. And, whenever it seems to be called for, this authority is to consult with bishops of neighboring regions which have the same language.

4. Translations from the Latin text into the mother tongue intended for use in the liturgy must be approved by the competent territorial ecclesiastical authority mentioned above.

D) Norms for adapting the Liturgy to the culture and traditions of peoples

37. Even in the liturgy, the Church has no wish to impose a rigid uniformity in matters which do not implicate the faith or the good of the whole community; rather does she respect and foster the genius and talents of the various races and peoples. Anything in these peoples' way of life which is not indissolubly bound up with superstition and error she studies with sympathy and, if possible, preserves intact. Sometimes in fact she admits such things into the liturgy itself, so long as they harmonize with its true and authentic spirit.

38. Provisions shall also be made, when revising the liturgical books, for legitimate variations and adaptations to different groups, regions, and peoples, especially in mission lands, provided that the substantial unity of the Roman rite is preserved, and this should be borne in mind when drawing up the rites and devising rubrics.

39. Within the limits set by the typical editions of the liturgical books, it shall be for the competent territorial ecclesiastical authority mentioned in Art. 22:2, to specify adaptations, especially in the case of the administration of the sacraments, the sacramentals, processions, liturgical language, sacred music, and the arts, but according to the fundamental norms laid down in this Constitution.

40. In some places and circumstances, however, an even more radical adaptation of the liturgy is needed, and this entails greater difficulties. Wherefore:

    1) The competent territorial ecclesiastical authority mentioned in Art. 22, 2, must, in this matter, carefully and prudently consider which elements from the traditions and culture of individual peoples might appropriately be admitted into divine worship. Adaptations which are judged to be useful or necessary should then be submitted to the Apostolic See, by whose consent they may be introduced.

    2) To ensure that adaptations may be made with all the circumspection which they demand, the Apostolic See will grant power to this same territorial ecclesiastical authority to permit and to direct, as the case requires, the necessary preliminary experiments over a de-

termined period of time among certain groups suited for the purpose.

    3) Because liturgical laws often involve special difficulties with respect to adaptation, particularly in mission lands, men who are experts in these matters must be employed to formulate them.

Unitatis Redintegratio (Decree on Ecumenism)

♦ **Chapter I: Catholic Principles on Ecumenism**

3. Even in the beginnings of this one and only Church of God there arose certain rifts, which the Apostle strongly condemned. But in subsequent centuries much more serious dissensions made their appearance and quite large communities came to be separated from full communion with the Catholic Church—for which, often enough, men of both sides were to blame. The children who are born into these Communities and who grow up believing in Christ cannot be accused of the sin involved in the separation, and the Catholic Church embraces them as brothers, with respect and affection. For men who believe in Christ and have been truly baptized are in communion with the Catholic Church even though this communion is imperfect. The differences that exist in varying degrees between them and the Catholic Church—whether in doctrine and sometimes in discipline, or concerning the structure of the Church—do indeed create many obstacles, sometimes serious ones, to full ecclesiastical communion. The ecumenical movement is striving to overcome these obstacles. But even in spite of them it remains true that all who have been justified by faith in Baptism are members of Christ's body, and have a right to be called Christian, and so are correctly accepted as brothers by the children of the Catholic Church.

Moreover, some and even very many of the significant elements and endowments which together go to build up and give life to the Church itself, can exist outside the visible boundaries of the Catholic Church: the written word of God; the life of grace; faith, hope and charity, with the other interior gifts of the Holy Spirit, and visible elements too. All of these, which come from Christ and lead back to Christ, belong by right to the one Church of Christ.

The brethren divided from us also use many liturgical actions of the Christian religion. These most certainly can truly engender a life of grace in ways that vary according to the condition of each Church or Community. These liturgical actions must be regarded as capable of giving access to the community of salvation....

4. Today, in many parts of the world, under the inspiring grace of the Holy Spirit, many efforts are being made in prayer, word and action to attain that fullness of unity which Jesus Christ desires. The Sacred Council exhorts all the Catholic faithful to recognize the signs of the times and to take an active and intelligent part in the work of ecumenism....

♦ Chapter II: The Practice of Ecumenism

. . .

8. This change of heart and holiness of life, along with public and private prayer for the unity of Christians, should be regarded as the soul of the whole ecumenical movement, and merits the name, "spiritual ecumenism."

It is a recognized custom for Catholics to have frequent recourse to that prayer for the unity of the Church which the Saviour Himself on the eve of His death so fervently appealed to His Father: "That they may all be one."

In certain special circumstances, such as the prescribed prayers "for unity," and during ecumenical gatherings, it is allowable, indeed desirable that Catholics should join in prayer with their separated brethren. Such prayers in common are certainly an effective means of obtaining the grace of unity, and they are a true expression of the ties which still bind Catholics to their separated brethren. "For where two or three are gathered together in my name, there am I in the midst of them."

Yet worship in common (communicatio in sacris) is not to be considered as a means to be used indiscriminately for the restoration of Christian unity. There are two main principles governing the practice of such common worship: first, the bearing witness to the unity of the Church, and second, the sharing in the means of grace. Witness to the unity of the Church very generally forbids common worship to Christians, but the grace to be had from it sometimes commends this practice. The course to be adopted, with due regard to all the circumstances of time, place, and persons, is to be decided by local episcopal authority, unless otherwise provided for by the Bishops' Conference according to its statutes, or by the Holy See.

9. We must get to know the outlook of our separated brethren. To achieve this purpose, study is of necessity required, and this must be pursued with a sense of realism and good will. Catholics, who already have a proper grounding, need to acquire a more adequate understanding of the respective doctrines of our separated brethren, their history, their spiritual and liturgical life, their religious psychology and general background. Most valuable for this purpose are meetings of the two sides—especially for discussion of theological problems—where each can treat with the other on an equal footing—provided that those who take part in them are truly competent and have the approval of the bishops. From such dialogue will emerge still more clearly what the situation of the Catholic Church really is. In this way too the outlook of our separated brethren will be better understood, and our own belief more aptly explained.

Gaudium et Spes (Pastoral Constitution on the Church in the Modern World)

♦ Preface

. . .

3. Though mankind is stricken with wonder at its own discoveries and its power, it often raises anxious questions about the current trend of the world, about the place and role of man in the universe, about the meaning of its individual and collective strivings, and about the ultimate destiny of reality and of humanity. Hence, giving witness and voice to the faith of the whole people of God gathered together by Christ, this Council can provide no more eloquent proof of its solidarity with, as well as its respect and love for the entire human family with which it is bound up, than by engaging with it in conversation about these various problems. The council brings to mankind light kindled from the Gospel, and puts at its disposal those saving resources which the Church herself, under the guidance of the Holy Spirit, receives from her Founder. For the human person deserves to be preserved; human society deserves to be renewed. Hence the focal point of our total presentation will be man himself, whole and entire,

body and soul, heart and conscience, mind and will.

Therefore, this sacred synod, proclaiming the noble destiny of man and championing the God-like seed which has been sown in him, offers to mankind the honest assistance of the Church in fostering that brotherhood of all men which corresponds to this destiny of theirs. Inspired by no earthly ambition, the Church seeks but a solitary goal: to carry forward the work of Christ under the lead of the befriending Spirit. And Christ entered this world to give witness to the truth, to rescue and not to sit in judgment, to serve and not to be served....

♦ **Part I**

. . .

Chapter IV: The Role of the Church in the Modern World . . .

42.... The Church recognizes that worthy elements are found in today's social movements, especially an evolution toward unity, a process of wholesome socialization and of association in civic and economic realms. The promotion of unity belongs to the innermost nature of the Church, for she is, "thanks to her relationship with Christ, a sacramental sign and an instrument of intimate union with God, and of the unity of the whole human race." Thus she shows the world that an authentic union, social and external, results from a union of minds and hearts, namely from that faith and charity by which her own unity is unbreakably rooted in the Holy Spirit. For the force which the Church can inject into the modern society of man consists in that faith and charity put into vital practice, not in any external dominion exercised by merely human means.

Moreover, since in virtue of her mission and nature she is bound to no particular form of human culture, nor to any political, economic or social system, the Church by her very universality can be a very close bond between diverse human communities and nations, provided these trust her and truly acknowledge her right to true freedom in fulfilling her mission. For this reason, the Church admonishes her own sons, but also humanity as a whole, to overcome all strife between nations and race in this family spirit of God's children, and in the same way, to give internal strength to human associations which are just.

With great respect, therefore, this Council regards all the true, good and just elements inherent in the very wide variety of institutions which the human race has established for itself and constantly continues to establish. The council affirms, moreover, that the Church is willing to assist and promote all these institutions to the extent that such a service depends on her and can be associated with her mission. She has no fiercer desire than that in pursuit of the welfare of all she may be able to develop herself freely under any kind of government which grants recognition to the basic rights of person and family, to the demands of the common good and to the free exercise of her own mission....

♦ **Part II**

. . .

Chapter III: Economic and Social Life

. . .

65. Economic development must remain under man's determination and must not be left to the judgment of a few men or groups possessing too much economic power or of the political community alone or of certain more powerful nations. It is necessary, on the contrary, that at every level the largest possible number of people and, when it is a question of international relations, all nations have an active share in directing that development. There is need as well of the coordination and fitting and harmonious combination of the spontaneous efforts of individuals and of free groups with the undertakings of public authorities.

Growth is not to be left solely to a kind of mechanical course of the economic activity of individuals, nor to the authority of government. For this reason, doctrines which obstruct the necessary reforms under the guise of a false liberty, and those which subordinate the basic rights of individual persons and groups to the collective organization of production must be shown to be erroneous.

Citizens, on the other hand, should remember that it is their right and duty, which is also to be recognized by the civil authority, to contribute to the true progress of their own community according to their ability. Especially in underdeveloped areas, where all resources must urgently be employed, those who hold back their unproductive resources or who deprive their community of the material or spiritual aid that it needs—saving the personal right of migration—gravely endanger the common good.

66. To satisfy the demands of justice and equity, strenuous efforts must be made, without disregarding the rights of persons or the natural qualities of each country, to remove as quickly as possible the immense economic inequalities, which now exist and in many cases are growing and which are connected with individual and social discrimination. Likewise, in many areas, in view of the special difficulties of agriculture relative to the raising and selling of produce, country people must be helped both to increase and to market what they produce, and to introduce the necessary development and renewal and also obtain a fair income. Otherwise, as too often happens, they will remain in the condition of lower-class citizens. Let farmers themselves, especially young ones, apply themselves to perfecting their professional skill, for without it, there can be no agricultural advance.

Justice and equity likewise require that the mobility, which is necessary in a developing economy, be regulated in such a way as to keep the life of individuals and their families from becoming insecure and precarious. When workers come from another country or district and contribute to the economic advancement of a nation or region by their labor, all discrimination as regards wages and working conditions must be carefully avoided. All the people, moreover, above all the public authorities, must treat them not as mere tools of production but as persons, and must help them to bring their families to live with them and to provide themselves with a decent dwelling; they must also see to it that these workers are incorporated into the social life of the country or region that receives them. Employment opportunities, however, should be created in their own areas as far as possible.

In economic affairs which today are subject to change, as in the new forms of industrial society in which automation, for example, is advancing, care must be taken that sufficient and suitable work and the possibility of the appropriate technical and professional formation are furnished. The livelihood and the human dignity especially of those who are in very difficult conditions because of illness or old age must be guaranteed....

68. In economic enterprises it is persons who are joined together, that is, free and independent human beings created to the image of God. Therefore, with attention to the functions of each—owners or employers, management or labor—and without doing harm to the necessary unity of management, the active sharing of all in the administration and profits of these enterprises in ways to be properly determined is to be promoted. Since more often, however, decisions concerning economic and social conditions, on which the future lot of the workers and of their children depends, are made not within the business itself but by institutions on a higher level, the workers themselves should have a share also in determining these conditions—in person or through freely elected delegates.

Among the basic rights of the human person is to be numbered the right of freely founding unions for working people. These should be able truly to represent them and to contribute to the organizing of economic life in the right way. Included is the right of freely taking part in the activity of these unions without risk of reprisal. Through this orderly participation joined to progressive economic and social formation, all will grow day by day in the awareness of their own function and responsibility, and thus they will be brought to feel that they are comrades in the whole task of economic development and in the attainment of the universal common good according to their capacities and aptitudes.

When, however, socio-economic disputes arise, efforts must be made to come to a peaceful settlement. Although recourse must always be had first to a sincere dialogue between the parties, a strike, nevertheless, can remain even in present-day circumstances a necessary, though ultimate, aid for the defense of the workers' own rights and the fulfillment of their just desires. As soon as possible, however, ways should be sought to resume negotiation and the discussion of reconciliation....

70. Investments, for their part, must be directed toward procuring employment and sufficient income for the people both now and in the future. Whoever makes decisions concerning these investments and the planning of the economy—whether they be individuals or groups of public authorities—are bound to keep these objectives in mind and to recognize their serious obligation

of watching, on the one hand, that provision be made for the necessities required for a decent life both of individuals and of the whole community and, on the other, of looking out for the future and of establishing a right balance between the needs of present-day consumption, both individual and collective, and the demands of investing for the generation to come. They should also always bear in mind the urgent needs of underdeveloped countries or regions. In monetary matters they should beware of hurting the welfare of their own country or of other countries. Care should also be taken lest the economically weak countries unjustly suffer any loss from a change in the value of money.

71. Since property and other forms of private ownership of external goods contribute to the expression of the personality, and since, moreover, they furnish one an occasion to exercise his function in society and in the economy, it is very important that the access of both individuals and communities to some ownership of external goods be fostered.

Private property or some ownership of external goods confers on everyone a sphere wholly necessary for the autonomy of the person and the family, and it should be regarded as an extension of human freedom. Lastly, since it adds incentives for carrying on one's function and charge, it constitutes one of the conditions for civil liberties.

The forms of such ownership or property are varied today and are becoming increasingly diversified. They all remain, however, a cause of security not to be underestimated, in spite of social funds, rights, and services provided by society. This is true not only of material property but also of immaterial things such as professional capacities.

The right of private ownership, however, is not opposed to the right inherent in various forms of public property. Goods can be transferred to the public domain only by the competent authority, according to the demands and within the limits of the common good, and with fair compensation. Furthermore, it is the right of public authority to prevent anyone from abusing his private property to the detriment of the common good.

By its very nature private property has a social quality which is based on the law of the common destination of earthly goods. If this social quality is overlooked, property often becomes an occasion of passionate desires for wealth and serious disturbances, so that a pretext is given to the attackers for calling the right itself into question....

Chapter IV: The Life of the Political Community . . .

75. It is in full conformity with human nature that there should be juridico-political structures providing all citizens in an ever better fashion and without any discrimination the practical possibility of freely and actively taking part in the establishment of the juridical foundations of the political community and in the direction of public affairs, in fixing the terms of reference of the various public bodies and in the election of political leaders. All citizens, therefore, should be mindful of the right and also the duty to use their free vote to further the common good. The Church praises and esteems the work of those who for the good of men devote themselves to the service of the state and take on the burdens of this office.

If the citizens' responsible cooperation is to produce the good results which may be expected in the normal course of political life, there must be a statute of positive law providing for a suitable division of the functions and bodies of authority and an efficient and independent system for the protection of rights. The rights of all persons, families and groups, and their practical application, must be recognized, respected and furthered, together with the duties binding on all citizen. Among the latter, it will be well to recall the duty of rendering the political community such material and personal service as are required by the common good. Rulers must be careful not to hamper the development of family, social or cultural groups, nor that of intermediate bodies or organizations, and not to deprive them of opportunities for legitimate and constructive activity; they should willingly seek rather to promote the orderly pursuit of such activity. Citizens, for their part, either individually or collectively, must be careful not to attribute excessive power to public authority, not to make exaggerated and untimely demands upon it in their own interests, lessening in this way the responsible role of persons, families and social groups.

The complex circumstances of our day make it necessary for public authority to intervene more often in social, economic and cultural matters in order to bring about favorable conditions which will give more effective help to citizens and groups in their free pursuit of man's total well-being. The relations, however, between socialization and the autonomy and development of the person can be understood in different ways according to various regions and the evolution of peoples. But when the exercise of rights is restricted temporarily for the common good, freedom should be restored immediately upon change of circumstances. Moreover, it is inhuman for public authority to fall back on dictatorial systems or totalitarian methods which violate the rights of the person or social groups.

Citizens must cultivate a generous and loyal spirit of patriotism, but without being narrow-minded. This means that they will always direct their attention to the good of the whole human family, united by the different ties which bind together races, people and nations.

All Christians must be aware of their own specific vocation within the political community. It is for them to give an example by their sense of responsibility and their service of the common good. In this way they are to demonstrate concretely how authority can be compatible with freedom, personal initiative with the solidarity of the whole social organism, and the advantages of unity with fruitful diversity. They must recognize the legitimacy of different opinions with regard to temporal solutions, and respect citizens, who, even as a group, defend their points of view by honest methods. Political parties, for their part, must promote those things which in their judgement are required for the common good; it is never allowable to give their interests priority over the common good.

Great care must be taken about civic and political formation, which is of the utmost necessity today for the population as a whole, and especially for youth, so that all citizens can play their part in the life of the political community. Those who are suited or can become suited should prepare themselves for the difficult, but at the same time, the very noble art of politics, and should seek to practice this art without regard for their own interests or for material advantages. With integrity and wisdom, they must take action against any form of injustice and tyranny, against arbitrary domination by an individual or a political party and any intolerance. They should dedicate themselves to the service of all with sincerity and fairness, indeed, with the charity and fortitude demanded by political life.

76. It is very important, especially where a pluralistic society prevails, that there be a correct notion of the relationship between the political community and the Church, and a clear distinction between the tasks which Christians undertake, individually or as a group, on their own responsibility as citizens guided by the dictates of a Christian conscience, and the activities which, in union with their pastors, they carry out in the name of the Church.

The Church, by reason of her role and competence, is not identified in any way with the political community nor bound to any political system. She is at once a sign and a safeguard of the transcendent character of the human person.

The Church and the political community in their own fields are autonomous and independent from each other. Yet both, under different titles, are devoted to the personal and social vocation of the same men. The more that both foster sounder cooperation between themselves with due consideration for the circumstances of time and place, the more effective will their service be exercised for the good of all. For man's horizons are not limited only to the temporal order; while living in the context of human history, he preserves intact his eternal vocation. The Church, for her part, founded on the love of the Redeemer, contributes toward the reign of justice and charity within the borders of a nation and between nations. By preaching the truths of the Gospel, and bringing to bear on all fields of human endeavor the light of her doctrine and of a Christian witness, she respects and fosters the political freedom and responsibility of citizens....

Chapter V: The Fostering of Peace and the Promotion of a Community of Nations ...

84. In view of the increasingly close ties of mutual dependence today between all the inhabitants and peoples of the earth, the apt pursuit and efficacious attainment of the universal common good now require of the community of nations that it organize itself in a manner suited to its present responsibilities, especially toward the many parts of the world which are still suffering from unbearable want.

To reach this goal, organizations of the international community, for their part, must make provision for men's different needs, both in the fields of social life—such as food supplies, health, education, labor and also in certain special circumstances which can crop up here and there, e.g., the need to promote the general improvement of developing countries, or to alleviate the distressing conditions in which refugees dispersed throughout the world find themselves, or also to assist migrants and their families.

Already existing international and regional organizations are certainly well-deserving of the human race. These are the first efforts at laying the foundations on an international level for a community of all men to work for the solution to the serious problems of our times, to encourage progress everywhere, and to obviate wars of whatever kind. In all of these activities the Church takes joy in the spirit of true brotherhood flourishing between Christians and non-Christians as it strives to make ever more strenuous efforts to relieve abundant misery.

85. The present solidarity of mankind also calls for a revival of greater international cooperation in the economic field. Although nearly all peoples have become autonomous, they are far from being free of every form of undue dependence, and far from escaping all danger of serious internal difficulties.

The development of a nation depends on human and financial aids. The citizens of each country must be prepared by education and professional training to discharge the various tasks of economic and social life. But this in turn requires the aid of foreign specialists who, when they give aid, will not act as overlords, but as helpers and fellow-workers. Developing nations will not be able to procure material assistance unless radical changes are made in the established procedures of modern world commerce. Other aid should be provided as well by advanced nations in the form of gifts, loans or financial investments. Such help should be accorded with generosity and without greed on the one side, and received with complete honesty on the other side.

If an authentic economic order is to be established on a world-wide basis, an end will have to be put to profiteering, to national ambitions, to the appetite for political supremacy, to militaristic calculations, and to machinations for the sake of spreading and imposing ideologies....

87. International cooperation is needed today especially for those peoples who, besides facing so many other difficulties, likewise undergo pressures due to a rapid increase in population. There is an urgent need to explore, with the full and intense cooperation of all, and especially of the wealthier nations, ways whereby the human necessities of food and a suitable education can be furnished and shared with the entire human community. But some peoples could greatly improve upon the conditions of their life if they would change over from antiquated methods of farming to the new technical methods, applying them with needed prudence according to their own circumstances. Their life would likewise be improved by the establishment of a better social order and by a fairer system for the distribution of land ownership.

Governments undoubtedly have rights and duties, within the limits of their proper competency, regarding the population problem in their respective countries, for instance, in the line of social and family life legislation, or regarding the migration of country-dwellers to the cities, or with respect to information concerning the condition and needs of the country. Since men today are giving thought to this problem and are so greatly disturbed over it, it is desirable in addition that Catholic specialists, especially in the universities, skillfully pursue and develop studies and projects on all these matters.

But there are many today who maintain that the increase in world population, or at least the population increase in some countries, must be radically curbed by every means possible and by any kind of intervention on the part of public authority. In view of this contention, the council urges everyone to guard against solutions, whether publicly or privately supported, or at times even imposed, which are contrary to the moral law. For in keeping with man's inalienable right to marry and generate children, a decision concerning the number of children they will have depends on the right judgment of the parents and it cannot in any way be left to the judgment of public authority. But since the judgment of the parents presupposes a rightly formed conscience, it is of the utmost importance that the way be open for everyone to develop a correct and genuinely human responsibility which respects the divine law and takes into consideration the circumstances of the situation and the time. But sometimes this requires an improvement in educational and social conditions, and, above all, formation in religion or at least a complete moral training. Men should discreetly be informed, furthermore, of scientific advances in exploring methods whereby spouses can be helped in regulating the number of their children and whose

safeness has been well proven and whose harmony with the moral order has been ascertained.

88. Christians should cooperate willingly and wholeheartedly in establishing an international order that includes a genuine respect for all freedoms and amicable brotherhood between all. This is all the more pressing since the greater part of the world is still suffering from so much poverty that it is as if Christ Himself were crying out in these poor to beg the charity of the disciples. Do not let men, then, be scandalized because some countries with a majority of citizens who are counted as Christians have an abundance of wealth, whereas others are deprived of the necessities of life and are tormented with hunger, disease, and every kind of misery. The spirit of poverty and charity are the glory and witness of the Church of Christ.

Those Christians are to be praised and supported, therefore, who volunteer their services to help other men and nations. Indeed, it is the duty of the whole People of God, following the word and example of the bishops, to alleviate as far as they are able the sufferings of the modern age. They should do this too, as was the ancient custom in the Church, out of the substance of their goods, and not only out of what is superfluous.

The procedure of collecting and distributing aids, without being inflexible and completely uniform, should nevertheless be carried on in an orderly fashion in dioceses, nations, and throughout the entire world. Wherever it seems convenient, this activity of Catholics should be carried on in unison with other Christian brothers. For the spirit of charity does not forbid, but on the contrary commands that charitable activity be carried out in a careful and orderly manner. Therefore, it is essential for those who intend to dedicate themselves to the services of the developing nations to be properly trained in appropriate institutes.

Dignitatis Humanae (Declaration on Religious Freedom)

. . .

2. This Vatican Council declares that the human person has a right to religious freedom. This freedom means that all men are to be immune from coercion on the part of individuals or of social groups and of any human power, in such wise that no one is to be forced to act in a manner contrary to his own beliefs, whether privately or publicly, whether alone or in association with others, within due limits.

The Council further declares that the right to religious freedom has its foundation in the very dignity of the human person as this dignity is known through the revealed word of God and by reason itself. This right of the human person to religious freedom is to be recognized in the constitutional law whereby society is governed and thus it is to become a civil right.

It is in accordance with their dignity as persons—that is, beings endowed with reason and free will and therefore privileged to bear personal responsibility—that all men should be at once impelled by nature and also bound by a moral obligation to seek the truth, especially religious truth. They are also bound to adhere to the truth, once it is known, and to order their whole lives in accord with the demands of truth. However, men cannot discharge these obligations in a manner in keeping with their own nature unless they enjoy immunity from external coercion as well as psychological freedom. Therefore the right to religious freedom has its foundation not in the subjective disposition of the person, but in his very nature. In consequence, the right to this immunity continues to exist even in those who do not live up to their obligation of seeking the truth and adhering to it, and the exercise of this right is not to be impeded, provided that just public order be observed....

4. The freedom or immunity from coercion in matters religious, which is the endowment of persons as individuals, is also to be recognized as their right when they act in community. Religious communities are a requirement of the social nature both of man and of religion itself.

Provided the just demands of public order are observed, religious communities rightfully claim freedom in order that they may govern themselves according to their own norms, honor the Supreme Being in public worship, assist their members in the practice of the religious life, strengthen them by instruction, and promote institutions in which they may join together for the purpose of ordering their own lives in accordance with their religious principles.

Religious communities also have the right not to be hindered, either by legal measures or by administrative action on the part of government, in the selection, training, appointment, and transferral of their own ministers, in communicating with religious authorities and communities abroad, in erecting buildings for religious purposes, and in the acquisition and use of suitable funds or properties.

Religious communities also have the right not to be hindered in their public teaching and witness to their faith, whether by the spoken or by the written word. However, in spreading religious faith and in introducing religious practices

everyone ought at all times to refrain from any manner of action which might seem to carry a hint of coercion or of a kind of persuasion that would be dishonorable or unworthy, especially when dealing with poor or uneducated people. Such a manner of action would have to be considered an abuse of one's right and a violation of the right of others.

In addition, it comes within the meaning of religious freedom that religious communities should not be prohibited from freely undertaking to show the special value of their doctrine in what concerns the organization of society and the inspiration of the whole of human activity. Finally, the social nature of man and the very nature of religion afford the foundation of the right of men freely to hold meetings and to establish educational, cultural, charitable and social organizations, under the impulse of their own religious sense.

Glossary

Advent:	the period encompassing the four Sundays preceding the birth of Christ (that is, Christmas)
Apostolic See:	also Holy See, the central government of the Catholic Church, based in the Vatican
For where two or three are gathered together in my name…:	quotation from the New Testament Gospel of Matthew, chapter 18, verse 20
homily:	a sermon, usually one based on a reading from scripture
indult:	a permission or privilege granted by a church authority for an exception from a particular church law
Lent:	the forty days preceding the resurrection of Christ (that is, Easter), a time of penitence for Christians
liturgy:	in Catholicism, the mass, especially the sacrament of the Holy Eucharist (or Holy Communion)
Redeemer:	Christ

ISLAMIC GOVERNMENT: GOVERNANCE OF THE JURIST: DOCUMENT ANALYSIS

Overview

Ayatollah Ruhollah Musawi Khomeini's Islamic Government: Governance of the Jurist (in Persian, Hokumat-e Islami: Velay-at-e faqih, which is sometimes translated as "Islamic Government: Guardianship of the Juirst") is an argument for the estab-lishement of Islamic law in the ayatollah's native Iran and elsewhere. The essence of Khomeini's belief is that because the laws of God govern society, all government leaders should be knowledgeable in Islamic law. And since Islamic jurists, call *faqih*, have studied Islamic law, many ruler should also be a *faqih* and thus able to counter anti-Islamic influences emanating from non-Muslim sources, a role that Khomeini calls "guardianship."

The book had its origins in a series of speeches given by Khomeini in Januray and February 1970 to students in An Najaf, Iraq. An Najaf remains an important center of Islamic scholarship and the spiritual center of Shia Islam, the second-largest branch of the religion, behind Sunni Islam. The city is the location of a shrine to Imam ⊠Ali, the first Shia leader and a son-in-law of the prophet Muhammad, the founder of Islam. It was also where the ayatollah (a title meaning "signs of God," given to high-ranking Shia clerics) spent thirteen years as a teacher at the Shaykh Murtaza Ansari madrassa, a religious school. Later that year, the speeches, which had been recorded and transcribed by a student, were collected and published in Beirut, Lebanon.

In the 1970s the book had to be smuggled into Iran under different titles, including *Authority of the Jurist* and *A Letter from Imam Musavi Kashef al-Qita*, the latter using a fake name to deceive government censors. At that time, Iran was under the control of a secular regime headed by a shah (or king), Mohammad Reza Pahlavi, who enforced his rule through his notorious and feared secret police, the SAVAK, short for Sazeman-e Ettela⊠at va Aminiyat-e Kesh-var, or National Intelligence and Security Organization. In the face of growing revolutionary activity, the shah institut-ed repressive measures against militant Muslims, including Khomeini. In 1964 Khomeini was exiled from Iran in an effort to lessen his domestic influence. In 1977 Khomei-ni's son died uner mysterious circumstances; many Iranian believed that his death was the work of SAVAK. Despite the shah's efforts to retain power, his regine was overthrown in the 1979 Islamic Revolution.

Islamic Government: Governance of the Jurist became an important text in the establishment of the Islamic Republic of Iran, when Khomeini was proclaimed the nation's supreme leader. Khomeini was a revered figure in Iran, acquiring the title imam, which means "guide" or "one who walks in front"; the title had previously been reserved for Shia Islam's original twelve infallible leaders, the right-ful successors to the prophet Muhammad. During the revo-lution, Khomeini's name and face became familiar to West-erners primarily for his support of the seizure of fifty-three Americans who were held hostage at the American embassy in Tehram, Iran, from November 4, 1979, to January 20, 1981.

Context

The context for Khomeini's militancy and for *Islamic Gov-ernment* extends back at least to World War II, when Iran's oil and strategic geographical position were vital to Allied interests in the fight against Nazi Germany. In 1941 the Allies installed Mohammad Reza Pahlavi as shah, cor-rectly believing that he would support the Allies against Germany, unlike his father, who had declared neutral-ity in the war. After the war, Mohammad Mosaddeq was democratically elected as Iran's prime minister, but the U.S. government believed that Mosaddeq's sympathies were increasingly leaning toward the Communist Soviet Union. Accordingly, the U.S. Central Intelligence Agency, in concert with its British counterpart, engineered a 1953 coup d'état that deposed Mosaddeq. The United States and Great Britain supported the shah because of his secu-larism and pro-West stance, seen as crucial at a time when the West feared the expansion of Iran's northern neighbor, the Soviet Union. These events set the stage for ongoing clashes between Iran's secular government and Muslims, who believed that the monarchal government was cor-rupt, extravagant, repressive, godless, and a puppet of the United States.

Khomeini rose to prominence in the 1960s during the so-called White Revolution—an effort on the part of Shah Pahlavi to promote Western values, break up the landhold-ings of religious institutions, give women the right to vote, increase literacy in state-run schools, and allow non-Muslims to hold political office, among other measures. Khomeini strongly denounced the shah and his pro-Western plans in a statement released on January 22, 1963. Then, on June 3 of that year, he delivered a speech further denouncing the shah. Two days later he was arrested, sparking three days of mass protests called the Movement of 15 Khordad, the date on the Persian calendar corresponding to June 5 on the Western calendar. Khomeini was held under house arrest until April 1964. After his release, he continued his antigovernment agitation, singling out the government's cooperation with Israel and its "capitulations" giving diplomatic immunity to Western military personnel in Iran. He was arrested again in November 1964 and went into exile, eventually settling in An Najaf, Iraq.

During these years Khomeini and others developed the ideology that would lead to the Islamic Revolution in Iran. Jalal Al-e-Ahmad, a political activist and writer, coined the term *gharbzadegi*, translated variously as "westoxification," "weststruckness," or "occidentosis"; the present document refers to those afflicted with this condition as "xenomaniacs." *Gharbzadegi* refers to Muslims who have become intoxicated or seduced by Western cultural models, which Al-e-Ahmad believed constituted a plague that had to be done away with; he used the word as the title of his most influential book, published in 1952. Ali Shariati, a sociologist regarded as the intellectual father of the Islamic Revolution, taught that Islam was uniquely able to liberate the Third World from repressive colonialism and capitalism. Khomeini began to formulate the views that would become the basis of *Islamic Government*, particularly what he called *vilāyat-i faqīh*, meaning "guardianship of the jurist." This is the belief that Muslims require the guardianship of Islamic jurists, whose knowledge of sharia, or Islamic law, can protect Muslims from plundering by foreign, non-Muslim influences. As his views spread through Iran, often in the form of speeches and sermons recorded on smuggled cassette tapes, revolutionary fervor began to grow. In response, the shah's regime became more oppressive. The fuse was lit for the 1979 Islamic Revolution, which drove the shah into exile, established the Islamic Republic of Iran, and created the post of supreme leader based on principles outlined in *Islamic Government*.

Explanation and Analysis of the Document

The present excerpt from *Islamic Government* is the book's introduction. The introduction does not lay down a thorough plan for an Islamist government. Rather, it expounds a number of ideas that form the historical justification for such a government. The core of Khomeini's argument is that the Qur'an and sharia law provide humans with all the guidance they need; accordingly, a secular government is not necessary. The favorable alternative is a government under the leadership of Muslim jurists, or clerics who are knowledgeable about Islamic law.

Time Line	
1902 ca. September 24	■ Ruhollah Musawi (Khomeini) is born in Khomein, Iran.
1941 September 16	■ Mohammad Reza Pahlavi replaces his father as shah of Iran.
1951 April 28	■ Mohammad Mosaddeq is elected Iranian prime minister, thenceforth competing with the shah for power.
1953 August 19	■ An American-sponsored coup d'état removes Mosaddeq from office; Shah Pahlavi returns from temporary exile to resume full power three days later.
1957	■ The Sazeman-e Ettela'at va Amniyat-e Keshvar (SAVAK), Iran's feared secret police, is formed.
1963 January 9	■ The Iranian shah announces the White Revolution, a series of reforms perceived by Muslim clerics as pro-Western.
January 22	■ Ayatollah Khomeini denounces the White Revolution.
June 5	■ Khomeini is placed under house arrest for ten months for opposition to the shah, sparking the Movement of 15 Khordad.
1964 November	■ Khomeini is again arrested and is driven into exile.
1970 January 21	■ In the city of An Najaf, Iraq, Khomeini gives the first of a series of lectures that would form the basis of Islamic Government; the final lecture is given on February 8.
1978	■ The Iranian government under Shah Pahlavi begins to break down in the face of widespread protests.

1979 January 16	■ Shah Pahlavi leaves Iran and goes into exile.
February 1	■ Khomeini returns to Iran and denounces the provisional government. February 11 ■ The Islamic Revolution in Iran is completed when the nation's Supreme Military Council declares itself neutral in the political disputes, allowing Muslim revolutionaries to overrun the provisional government.
November 4	■ Iranian revolutionaries take fifty-three Americans hostage in Tehran.
December 3	■ Khomeini takes the oath as Iran's supreme leader.
1981 January 20	■ The American hostages in Tehran are released.
1989 June 3	■ Khomeini dies of a heart attack.

◆ Paragraphs 1–3

The opening paragraphs of the introduction set the tone for Khomeini's exposition. He argues that the principles of governance of the jurist are "self-evident" but that they have been neglected because of historical circumstances. He refers to "anti-Islamic propaganda" from Jews and other groups; although he does not refer by name to the United States, it is likely that the United States and its allies, particularly Great Britain, are the groups he had in mind. He states that the goal of these outside influences has been "imperialist penetration of the Muslim countries," a process that began at least three hundred years before but which could be traced back to the Crusades, the two-hundred-year-long series of wars between Christian Europe and Muslim Arabs for the control of Palestine in the twelfth and thirteenth centuries. He argues that it was not the purpose of these groups to eliminate Islam and replace it with Christianity, for "the imperialists really have no religious belief." He goes on to say that the imperialists instead planted agents in the government, publishing, and education to "distort the principles of Islam," as the religion was considered an obstacle to political power and materialism.

◆ Paragraphs 4–7

Khomeini next draws a distinction between true Islam and Islam as it has been depicted by its adversaries. He states that "Islam is the religion of militant individuals who are committed to truth and justice" and that it is only by fulfilling the ordinances of Islam that Muslims can live full lives. He also emphasizes the revolutionary aspect of Islam in opposing imperialism. He then proceeds to develop a core argument. Countering the belief that Islam "is not a comprehensive religion" and "has nothing to say about human life in general and the ordering of society," he argues that, on the contrary, Islam is about much more than ritual observances. He refers to the Qur'an, Islam's sacred scripture. Muslims believe that the Qur'an, from an Arabic word meaning "the recitation," is the literal word of Allah, revealed to the prophet Muhammad by the archangel Jibra'il (Gabriel) beginning in 610 until his death. Reference is also made to the hadiths, or compilations of the Prophet's sayings during his lifetime; some twenty-six hundred hadiths, out of six hundred thousand that were gathered, are regarded as authentic, and they provide guidance in matters ranging from law to personal behavior. Khomeini notes that large portions of both the Qur'an and the hadiths deal with "social, economic, legal, and political questions—in short, the gestation of society." His point is that the sacred writings of Islam provide people with all the guidance they need, not just in private matters but in public, social matters as well.

◆ Paragraphs 8–11

After urging young people to be of service to Islam, Khomeini sketches in the historical background of his views. He notes that in Muhammad's time, the West was in a state of "darkness and obscurity," while nations such as Iran were under tyrannical rule. In this context the Prophet emerged and, from God, "sent laws that astound people with their magnitude." He continues by saying that God "instituted laws and practices for all human affairs and laid injunctions for man extending from even before the embryo is formed until after he is placed in the tomb." This key point reinforces Khomeini's view that Islam is sufficient for governing all human affairs. He concludes by saying that "there is not a single topic in human life for which Islam has not provided instructions and established a norm." He dismisses the views of ākhūnds—a word that literally means "Muslim clerics" but that has become a derogatory term for misguided and hypocritical clerics—and argues that they have been in part responsible for the view that Islam concerns itself only with rituals. He even concedes that some of the 'ulamā, or Islamic scholars, have been guilty.

◆ Paragraphs 12–19

Khomeini turns next to some specific matters of law. He begins by noting that the nation's constitution, as implemented under the monarchy, is essentially a Western document, borrowing heavily from the constitutions of Britain, Belgium, and France; the few Islamic ordinances contained in the constitution were inserted as a way of deceiving Muslims into believing that the constitution reflected Islamic law. He continues by insisting that while the Iranian constitution thus embodies a monarchal form of government, Islam "proclaims monarchy and hereditary succession wrong and invalid." He reviews historical circumstances, recalling how Muhammad enjoined the rulers of the Byzantine Empire and Iran to abandon monarchy, as had been done in Islamic countries such as Egypt. Arguing that God is the only true monarch, he calls monarchy a "sinister, evil system of government." Its influence was what caused Imam Husayn ibn ʿAlī, Muhammad's grandson, to refuse to pledge his allegiance to Yazīd I, head of the Umayyad Caliphate, in the seventh century. Husayn became the "Doyen of the Martyrs" when he was killed during the Battle of Karbala in 680, a major historical event in the development of the Shia movement.

Khomeini addresses the fact that Islam has no specific laws against such behaviors as usury, the consumption of alcohol, and sexual vice. For Khomeini, the fact that Islamic countries have not had to enact laws forbidding these practices is a sign of the religion's "perfection." He goes on to say that this legal system was "worked out by the imperialist government of Britain" to render Islam impotent. Khomeini then outlines some of the inadequacies of the Western legal system imposed on Iran, suggesting that it has been a source of delayed justice owing to endless litigation. Legal matters are not resolved swiftly, and people have to waste their time trying to enforce their rights. In earlier times, sharia (spelled *sharīʿah* in the document) law could quickly settle matters. Western law, in contrast, is a source of "frustration and perplexity" as well as corruption and bribery.

♦ **Paragraphs 20–23**

Khomeini takes up the issue of whether Islamic law is "too harsh," a view he says is widely prevalent in the West because of the work of "agents of imperialism." He notes that in the West a person can be executed for the possession of ten grams of heroin and asks whether this is not a harsh punishment, one that is disproportionate to the crime. He acknowledges that a person living under Islamic rule can receive eighty lashes for the consumption of alcohol, but he is indignant at the notion that this punishment is "too harsh" in light of Western laws governing drug possession. This leads to a discussion of alcohol. Khomeini argues that "many forms of corruption that have appeared in society derive from alcohol," including road accidents, murders, and suicides, and that alcohol addiction can lead to heroin addiction. Yet in the West alcohol can be bought and sold freely. He defends the practice of whipping fornicators and stoning adulterers by saying that "these penal provisions of Islam are intended to keep great nations from being destroyed by corruption." He concludes by asking, "Why should it be regarded as harsh if Islam stipulates that an offender must be publicly flogged in order to protect the younger generation from corruption?"

♦ **Paragraphs 24–31**

Khomeini next returns to a discussion of history. He begins by observing that Western powers can wage war in Vietnam but that wars waged by Islam to stamp out corruption are considered questionable. He asserts that everything he has discussed so far represents "plans drawn up several centuries ago that are now being implemented and bearing fruit." He objects to the establishment of schools that turn people into "Christians or unbelievers." He says that the Western plan has been to keep Muslims "backward" and to exploit the resources of Muslim lands. In preaching Islam, clerics have to practice *taqiyyah*, or circumspection in the face of danger, a practice sanctioned in the Qur'an. He defends the wearing of military apparel, pointing out that the early leaders of Islam, including the "Commander of the Faithful," ʿAlī ibn Abī Ṭālib, who was the Prophet's cousin and son-in-law and the first of the Twelve Imams, proudly wore military attire. All of the anti-Islamic developments he discusses are considered the result of a "wave of propaganda."

♦ **Paragraphs 32–35**

Khomeini turns from the external factors that have corrupted and diminished Islam to internal factors, in particular, "the dazzling effect that the material progress of the imperialist countries has had on some members of our society." He argues that morality and happiness derive not from technical and scientific progress, such as going to the moon (accomplished by the Americans in the summer of 1969) but from "the faith, the conviction, and the morality of Islam," which "serve humanity instead of endangering it." Meanwhile, some Muslims have been seduced by the Western idea that Islam has no "specific form of government or governmental institutions." Khomeini sees this as part of the propaganda campaign designed to prevent the creation of an Islamic society.

Examining government from a historical perspective, Khomeini says that the Prophet established a system for determining his successors. The purpose of those successors, though, was not simply to expound law, for the law had already been expounded in the Qur'an and other documents. Rather, the successors' purpose was to execute the laws, for laws are of no avail unless they are carried out. Islamic law, then, was part of the prophetic mission of God, carried out by Muhammad. It was this argument that led to the creation of the position of supreme leader after the Islamic Revolution in Iran.

♦ **Paragraphs 36–41**

In the final paragraphs, Khomeini addresses his audience directly. He urges Muslims to fulfill the prophetic mission: *"Know that it is your duty to establish an Islamic government."* He tells them to present Islam in its true form and to make clear to others that Islam is not a religion of forms and observances but a vital part of the political structure of Islamic nations. He says that Muslims must engage not only in prayer and study but also in political agitation. Otherwise, the imperialists will maintain control of Islamic countries through industrialization and the exploitation of oil, not caring about Islam if it restricts itself to *azān*, or the call to prayer. He concludes by warning that the imperialists want to "prevent you from intervening in the affairs of society and struggling against treacherous governments and their anti-national and anti-Islamic politics."

About the Author

Ruhollah Musawi was born in Khomein, Iran, the source of "Khomeini," a later addition to his name. Regarding the date of his birth, some contend that he was born in 1900, but many others cite his birth date as September 24 or 25, 1902. The early decades of his life were spent in study, teaching, and writing. He was particularly interested in philosophy, ethics, and Islamic law, and he also wrote a considerable amount of poetry. He rose to political power in 1963, when he gained the title ayatollah and led Muslim clerics in their opposition to Shah Pahlavi's White Revolution, for which he was placed under house arrest from June 5, 1963, until April the following year. After his release he continued to oppose the shah, and he was forced into exile in November 1964, first in Turkey and then in An Najaf, Iraq, where he delivered the speeches that would form *Islamic Government*. In 1978 he was forced out of Iraq by the future dictator Saddam Hussein, and he spent the last few months of his exile just outside Paris, France.

Throughout the 1970s, while he was living in Iraq, Khomeini consolidated his position as Iran's immensely popular spiritual leader. When he believed that he had the backing of Iran's important clerics and of the Iranian people, he ordered the revolution against the shah to begin. In the face of widespread protest in 1978, the government broke down. The shah fled Iran on January 16, 1979, and Khomeini returned in triumph on February 1, to denounce the provisional government and call for a referendum on replacing the monarchy with an Islamic republic. The referendum was held on March 30 and 31, 1979, and passed with an overwhelming majority of the vote. In the months that followed, Khomeini and his supporters accomplished the prompt passage of a constitution that would place the spiritual and governmental leadership of the country under a supreme religious leader. Khomeini himself took the oath of office as supreme leader on December 3, 1979. Despite his popularity, numerous political organizations throughout the country opposed the type of theocracy Khomeini envisioned. The supreme leader banned these organizations and proceeded to rule Iran with an iron fist.

Throughout the 1980s Khomeini was the face of Islam, particularly radical Islam, to the West. He supported the seizure of hostages at the American embassy in Iran, setting off a 444-day crisis that dominated headlines in the United States; ironically, the precipitating invasion of the embassy by students was intended merely to be symbolic. Khomeini led the nation through the Iran-Iraq War of the 1980s, and he was back in the headlines in 1989 when he issued a fatwa, or theocratic ruling, that called for the

assassination of the British author Salman Rushdie, whose novel *The Satanic Verses* was perceived to be offensive to Islam. Khomeini died on June 3, 1989, of a heart attack suffered while recovering from surgery.

Audience

The original audience for the ideas of *Islamic Government: Governance of the Jurist* consisted of students at An Najaf, Iraq. Khomeini's series of speeches was recorded and transcribed to form the basis of the book, which was published in Lebanon. In time it was smuggled into Iran under various titles and was circulated among the ayatollah's core supporters. It is uncertain whether and to what extent Khomeini intended the book to have wider circulation. Some observers have maintained that he deliberately restricted circulation of the book because he did not want to alienate Iranian moderates, who likely would have opposed the establishment of a theocracy and would therefore have impeded progress toward the revolution. It was only after Khomeini's supporters had consolidated their own positions of power that the book was given wider circulation. After the success of the revolution, the book was disseminated to the wider public, and many of the views expressed therein became part of the new constitution passed by the Islamic Republic of Iran.

Impact

Islamic Government: Governance of the Jurist was Khomeini's most influential text. It established the principles of guardianship by jurists, meaning that governance in Islamic countries (and ideally all countries) is to be placed under the authority of Islamic clerics and Islamic sharia law. To the extent that Iran became an Islamic republic, Khomeini succeeded in his principal objectives. Iran, which was an ally of the United States and the West during the cold war (the state of tension and hostility between the West and the Communist Soviet bloc), became in the late twentieth century a firm adversary.

The question of whether "governance of the jurist" has been successful in Iran remains an open one. Many conservative Muslims in that nation would argue that it has, for, they would say, Iran was purged of Western influences and came under the control of Islamist leaders committed to enforcing Islamic law. Nominally democratic, Iran has an elected president, a 290-member elected Majlis (the parliament), and an elected eighty-six-member Assembly of Experts, who appoint the supreme leader. Real power in Iran, however, is held by unelected officials, in particular, the supreme leader—Khomeini's successor since 1989 has been Ayatollah Ali Khamenei—and the twelve-member Guardian Council. Although members of the latter group have to be approved by the parliament, they are appointed or screened by the supreme leader, they have veto power over any measures passed by parliament that they deem

"Islam is the religion of militant individuals who are committed to truth and justice. It is the religion of those who desire freedom and independence. It is the school of those who struggle against imperialism."

(Section 1)

"God, Exalted and Almighty ... instituted laws and practices for all human affairs and laid injunctions for man extending from even before the embryo is formed until after he is placed in the tomb. In just the same way that there are laws setting forth the duties of worship for man, so too there are laws, practices, and norms for the affairs of society and government."

(Section 1)

"Their plan is to keep us backward, to keep us in our present miserable state so they can exploit our riches, our underground wealth, our lands, and our human resources. They want us to remain afflicted and wretched, and our poor to be trapped in their misery. Instead of surrendering to the injunctions of Islam ... they and their agents wish to ... enjoy lives of abominable luxury.

(Section 1)

"The necessity for the implementation of divine law, the need for an executive power, and the importance of that power in fulfilling the goals of the prophetic mission and establishing a just order that would result in the happiness of mankind—all of this made the appointment of a successor synonymous with the completion of the prophetic mission."

(Section 1)

"If you pay no attention to the policies of the imperialists, and consider Islam to be simply the few topics you are always studying and never go beyond them, then the imperialists will leave you alone. Pray as much as you like; it is your oil they are after—why should they worry about your prayers? They are after our minerals, and want to turn our country into a market for their goods."

(Section 1)

to be inconsistent with Islamic law, and they control the military and the media. The council can also bar candidates from standing for election to parliament or the presidency. Effectively, then, the government in Iran is answerable to clerics.

Thus, in the short term, Khomeini achieved the objectives he articulated in *Islamic Government: Governance of the Jurist*—though many observers would argue that he did so at a terrible price, for he silenced criticism, and thousands were put to death for opposition to his theocratic rule. In the longer term, though, there has been growing resistance to Iran's theocratic government. As of 2010, Iran is a young country, with large numbers of voters under the age of thirty. Many are coming to resent the influence of the Basij, or morality police, and would like to live in an Iran that is more liberal and less repressive. Reformers in Iran want the nation to continue to be an Islamic republic but would also like the government to respect the democratic institutions enshrined in the nation's constitution. They believe that the legacy left by Ayatollah Khomeini is inconsistent with the democratic freedoms written into the constitution that he and his backers produced.

Further Reading

■ Books

Arjomand, Said Amir. *Turban for the Crown: The Islamic Revolution in Iran*. New York: Oxford University Press, 1988.

Bakhash, Shaul. *The Reign of the Ayatollahs: Iran and the Islamic Revolution*. New York: Basic Books, 1984.

Brumberg, Daniel. *Reinventing Khomeini: The Struggle for Reform in Iran*. Chicago: University of Chicago Press, 2001.

Coughlin, Con. *Khomeini's Ghost: The Iranian Revolution and the Rise of Militant Islam*. New York: Ecco, 2009.

Dabashi, Hamid. *Theology of Discontent: The Ideological Foundations of the Islamic Revolution in Iran*. New York: New York University Press, 1993.

Hoveyda, Fereydoun. *The Shah and the Ayatollah: Iranian Mythology and Islamic Revolution*. Westport, Conn.: Greenwood, 2003.

Keddie, Nikki. *Roots of Revolution: An Interpretive History of Modern Iran*. New Haven, Conn.: Yale University Press, 1981.

Wright, Robin. *In the Name of God: The Khomeini Decade*. New York: Simon and Schuster, 1989.

■ Web Sites

Fukuyama, Francis. "Authoritarian Iran, Islam and the Rule of Law." Livemint.com Web site. http://www.livemint.com/2009/07/28204901/Authoritarian-Iran-Islam-and.html.

—Commentary by Michael J. O'Neal

Questions for Further Study

1. Explain what Khomeini means by the concept of "guardianship."

2. What historical circumstances enabled Khomeini to rise to a position of power and influence in Iran?

3. Compare this selection with Al-Māwardī's "On Qāḍis," particularly as the latter pertains to Islamic jurisprudence. What do you think Al-Māwardī's reaction to Khomeini's text might have been?

4. What does Khomeini regard as the weakness of the Western legal system? Why did he believe that concepts of Western law are inapplicable in Islamic countries?

5. Ayatollah Khomeini became a figure who was feared, perhaps even hated, among many people in the West. At the very least, he was looked on with suspicion. Why do you think this was so?

ISLAMIC GOVERNMENT: GOVERNANCE OF THE JURIST: DOCUMENT TEXT

1970 CE

—Ayatollah Khomeini

Introduction

The subject of the governance of the jurist *(vilāyat-i faqīh)* provides us with the opportunity to discuss certain related matters and questions. The governance of the *faqīh* is a subject that in itself elicits immediate assent and has little need of demonstration, for anyone who has some general awareness of the beliefs and ordinances of Islam will unhesitatingly give his assent to the principle of the governance of the *faqīh* as soon as he encounters it; he will recognize it as necessary and self-evident. If little attention is paid to this principle today, so that it has come to require demonstration, it is because of the social circumstances prevailing among the Muslims in general and the teaching institution in particular. These circumstances, in turn, have certain historical roots to which I will now briefly refer.

From the very beginning, the historical movement of Islam has had to contend with the Jews, for it was they who first established anti-Islamic propaganda and engaged in various stratagems, and as you can see, this activity continues down to the present. Later they were joined by other groups, who were in certain respects, more satanic than they. These new groups began their imperialist penetration of the Muslim countries about three hundred years ago, and they regarded it as necessary to work for the extirpation of Islam in order to attain their ultimate goals. It was not their aim to alienate the people from Islam in order to promote Christianity among them, for the imperialists really have no religious belief, Christian or Islamic. Rather, throughout this long historical period, and going back to the Crusades, they felt that the major obstacle in the path of their materialistic ambitions and the chief threat to their political power was nothing but Islam and its ordinances, and the belief of the people in Islam. They therefore plotted and campaigned against Islam by various means.

The preachers they planted in the religious teaching institution, the agents they employed in the universities, government educational institutions, and publishing houses, and the orientalists who work in the service of the imperialistic states—all these people have pooled their energies in an effort to distort the principles of Islam. As a result, many persons, particularly the educated, have formed misguided and incorrect notions of Islam.

Islam is the religion of militant individuals who are committed to truth and justice. It is the religion of those who desire freedom and independence. It is the school of those who struggle against imperialism. But the servants of imperialism have presented Islam in a totally different light. They have created in men's minds a false notion of Islam. The defective version of Islam, which they have presented in the religious teaching institution, is intended to deprive Islam of its vital, revolutionary aspect and to prevent Muslims from arousing themselves in order to gain their freedom, fulfill the ordinances of Islam, and create a government that will assure their happiness and allow them to live lives worthy of human beings.

For example, the servants of imperialism declared that Islam is not a comprehensive religion providing for every aspect of human life and has no laws or ordinances pertaining to society. It has no particular form of government. Islam concerns itself only with rules of ritual purity after menstruation and parturition. It may have a few ethical principles, but it certainly has nothing to say about human life in general and the ordering of society.

This kind of evil propaganda has unfortunately had an effect. Quite apart from the masses, the educated class—university students and also many students at the religious teaching institutions—have failed to understand Islam correctly and have erroneous notions. Just as people may, in general, be unacquainted with a stranger, so too they are unacquainted with Islam. Islam lives among the people of this world as if it were a stranger. If somebody were to present Islam as it truly is, he would find it difficult to make people believe him. In fact, the agents of imperialism in the religious teaching institutions would raise a hue and cry against him.

In order to demonstrate to some extent, the difference between Islam and what is presented as Islam, I would like to draw your attention to the difference between the Holy Qur'an and the books of *hadīth*, on the one hand, and the practical treatises of jurisprudence, on the other. The Holy Qur'an and the books of *hadīth*, which represent the sources for the commands and ordinances of Islam, are completely different from the treatises written by the *mujtahīds* of the present age both in breadth of scope and in the effects they are capable of exerting on the life of society. The ratio of Qur'anic verses concerned with the affairs of society to those concerned with ritual worship is greater than a hundred to one. Of the approximately fifty sections of the corpus of *hadīth* containing all the ordinances of Islam, not more than three or four sections relate to matters of ritual worship and the duties of man toward his Creator and Sustainer. A few more are concerned with questions of ethics, and all the rest are concerned with social, economic, legal, and political questions—in short, the gestation of society.

You who represent the younger generation and who, God willing, will be of service to Islam in the future must strive diligently all your lives to pursue the aims I will now set forth and to impart the laws and ordinances of Islam. In whatever way you deem most beneficial, in writing or in speech, instruct the people about the problems Islam has had to contend with since its inception and about the enemies and afflictions that now threaten it. Do not allow the true nature of Islam to remain hidden, or people will imagine that Islam is like Christianity (nominal, not true Christianity), a collection of injunctions pertaining to man's relation to God, and the mosques will be equated with the church.

At a time when the West was a realm of darkness and obscurity—with its inhabitants living in a state of barbarism, and America still peopled by half-savaged redskins—and the two vast empires of Iran and Byzantium were under the rule of tyranny, class privilege, and discrimination, and the powerful dominated all without any trace of law or popular government, God, Exalted and Almighty, by means of the Most Noble Messenger(s), sent laws that astound people with their magnitude. He instituted laws and practices for all human affairs and laid injunctions for man extending from even before the embryo is formed until after he is placed in the tomb. In just the same way that

there are laws setting forth the duties of worship for man, so too there are laws, practices, and norms for the affairs of society and government. Islamic law is a progressive, evolving, and comprehensive system. All the voluminous books that have been compiled from the earliest times on different areas of law, such as judicial procedure, social transactions, penal law, retribution, international relations, regulations pertaining to peace and war, private and public law— taken together, these contain a mere sample of the laws and injunctions of Islam. There is not a single topic in human life for which Islam has not provided instructions and established a norm.

In order to make the Muslims, especially the intellectuals, and the younger generation, deviate from the path of Islam, foreign agents have constantly insinuated that Islam has nothing to offer, that Islam consists of a few ordinances concerning menstruation and parturition, and that this is the proper field of study for the *ākhūnds*.

There is something of truth here, for it is fitting that those *ākhūnds* who have no intention of expounding the theories, injunctions and worldview of Islam and who spend most of their time on precisely such matters, forgetting all the other topics of Islamic law, be attacked and accused in this manner. They too are at fault; foreigners are not the only ones to be blamed. For several centuries, as might be expected, the foreigners laid certain plans to realize their political and economic ambitions, and the neglect that has overtaken the religious teaching institution has made it possible for them to succeed. There have been individuals among us, the *'ulamā*, who have unwittingly contributed to the fulfillment of those aims, with the result that you now see.

It is sometimes insinuated that the injunctions of Islam are defective, and said that the laws of judicial procedure, for example, are not all that they should be. In keeping with this insinuation and propaganda, agents of Britain were instructed by their masters to take advantage of the idea of constitutionalism in order to deceive the people and conceal the true nature of their political crimes (the pertinent proofs and documents are now available). At the beginning of the constitutional movement, when people wanted to write laws and draw up a constitution, a copy of the Belgian legal code was borrowed from the Belgian embassy and a handful of individuals (whose names I do not wish to mention here) used it as the basis for the constitution they then wrote, supplementing its deficiencies with borrowings from the French and British legal codes. True, they added some of the ordinances of Islam in order to deceive the people, but the basis of the laws that were now thrust upon the people was alien and borrowed.

What connections do all the various articles of the Constitution as well as the body of Supplementary Law concerning the monarchy, the succession, and so forth, have with Islam? They are all opposed to Islam; they violate the system of government and the laws of Islam.

Islam proclaims monarchy and hereditary succession wrong and invalid. When Islam first appeared in Iran, the Byzantine Empire, Egypt, and the Yemen, the entire institution of monarchy was abolished. In the blessed letters that the Most Noble Messenger wrote to the Byzantine Emperor Heraclius and the Shāhanshāh of Iran, he called upon them to abandon the monarchical and imperial form of government, to cease compelling the servants of God to worship them with absolute obedience, and to permit men to worship God, Who has no partner and is the True Monarch. Monarchy and hereditary succession represent the same sinister, evil system of government that prompted the Doyen of the Martyrs to rise up in revolt and seek martyrdom in an effort to prevent its establishment. He revolted in repudiation of the hereditary succession of Yazīd, to refuse it his recognition.

Islam, then, does not recognize monarchy and hereditary succession; they have no place in Islam. If that is what is meant by the so-called deficiency of Islam, then Islam is indeed deficient. Islam has laid down no laws for the practice of usury, for banking on the basis of usury, for the consumption of alcohol, or for the cultivation of sexual vice, having radically prohibited all of these. The ruling cliques, therefore, who are the puppets of imperialism and wish to promote these vices in the Islamic world, will naturally regard Islam as defective. They must import the appropriate laws from Britain, France, Belgium, and most recently, America. The fact that Islam makes no provision for the orderly pursuit of these illicit activities, far from being a deficiency, is a sign of perfection and a source of pride.

The conspiracy worked out by the imperialist government of Britain at the beginning of the constitutional movement had two purposes. The first, which was already known at that time, was to eliminate the influence of Tsarist Russia in Iran, and the second was to take the laws of Islam out of force and operation by introducing Western laws.

The imposition of foreign laws on our Islamic society has been the source of numerous problems and difficulties. Knowledgeable people working in our judicial system have many complaints concerning the existing laws and their mode of operation. If a person becomes caught up in the judicial system of Iran or that of analogous countries, he may have to spend a whole lifetime trying to prove his case. In my youth I once encountered a learned lawyer who said, "I can spend my whole life following a litigation back and forth through the judicial machinery, and then bequeath it to my son for him to do the same thing!" That is the situation that now prevails, except, of course, when one of the parties has influence, in which case the matter is examined and settled swiftly, albeit unjustly.

Our present judicial laws have brought our people nothing but trouble, causing them to neglect their daily tasks and providing the occasion for all kinds of misuse. Very few people are able to obtain their legitimate rights. In the adjudication of cases, it is necessary not only that everyone should obtain his rights, but also that correct procedure be followed. People's time must be considered, as well as the way of life and profession of both parties, so that matters are resolved as swiftly and simply as possible.

A case that a *shari'ah* judge in earlier times settled in one or two days cannot be settled now in twenty years. The needy, young, and old alike, must spend the entire day at the Ministry of Justice, from morning to evening, wasting their time in corridors or standing in front of some official's desk, and in the end they will still not know what has transpired. Anyone who is more cunning, and more willing and able to give bribes, has his case settled expeditiously, but at the cost of justice. Otherwise, they must wait in frustration and perplexity until their entire lives are gone.

The agents of imperialism sometimes write in their books and their newspapers that the legal provisions of Islam are too harsh. One person was even so impudent as to write that the laws of Islam are harsh because they have originated with the Arabs, so that the "harshness" of the Arabs is reflected in the harshness of Islamic law!

I am amazed at the way these people think. They kill people for possessing ten grams of heroin and say, "That is the law" (I have been informed that ten people were put to death some time ago, and another person more recently, for possession of ten grams of heroin). Inhuman laws like this are concocted in the name of a campaign against corruption, and they are not to be regarded as harsh. (I am not saying it is permissible to sell heroin, but this is not the appropriate punishment. The sale of heroin must indeed be prohibited but the punishment must be in proportion to the crime.) When Islam, however, stipulates that the drinker of alcohol should receive eighty lashes, they consider it "too harsh." They can *execute* someone for possessing ten grams of heroin and the question of harshness does not even arise!

Many forms of corruption that have appeared in society derive from alcohol. The collisions that take place on our roads, and the murders and suicides are very often caused by the consumption of alcohol. Indeed, even the use of heroin is said to derive from addiction to alcohol. But still, some say, it is quite unobjectionable for someone to drink alcohol (after all, they do it in the West); so let alcohol be bought and sold freely.

But when Islam wishes to prevent the consumption of alcohol—one of the major evils—stipulating that the drinker should receive eighty lashes, or sexual vice, decreeing that the fornicator be given one hundred lashes (and the married man or woman be stoned), then they start wailing and lamenting: "What a harsh law that is, reflecting the harshness of the Arabs!" They are not aware that these penal provisions of Islam are intended to keep great nations from being destroyed by corruption. Sexual vice has now reached such proportions that it is destroying entire generations, corrupting our youth, and causing them to neglect all forms of work. They are all rushing to enjoy the various forms of vice that have become so freely available and so enthusiastically promoted. Why should it be regarded as harsh if Islam stipulates that an offender must be publicly flogged in order to protect the younger generation from corruption?

At the same time, we see the masters of this ruling class of ours enacting slaughters in Vietnam over fifteen years, devoting enormous budgets to this business of bloodshed, and no one has the right to object! But if Islam commands its followers to engage in warfare or defense in order to make men submit to laws that are beneficial for them, and kill a few corrupt people or instigators of corruption, then they ask: "What's the purpose for that war?"

All of the foregoing represent plans drawn up several centuries ago that are now being implemented and bearing fruit.

First, they opened a school in a certain place and we overlooked the matter and said nothing. Our colleagues also were negligent in the matter and failed to prevent it from being established so that now, as you can observe, these schools have multiplied, and their missionaries have gone out into the provinces and villages, turning our children into Christians or unbelievers.

Their plan is to keep us backward, to keep us in our present miserable state so they can exploit our riches, our underground wealth, our lands, and our human resources. They want us to remain afflicted and wretched, and our poor to be trapped in their misery. Instead of surrendering to the injunctions of Islam, which provide a solution for the problem of poverty, they and their agents wish to go on living in huge places and enjoy lives of abominable luxury.

These plans of theirs are so broad in scope that they have even touched the institutions of religious learning. If someone wishes to speak about an Islamic government and the establishment of Islamic government, he must observe the principle of *taqiyyah* and count upon the opposition of those who have sold themselves to imperialism. When this book was first printed, the agents of the embassy undertook certain desperate measures to prevent its dissemination, which succeeded only in disgracing themselves more than before.

Matters have now come to the point where some people consider the apparel of a soldier incompatible with true manliness and justice, even though the leaders of our religion were all soldiers, commanders, and warriors. They put on military dress and went into battle in the wars that are described for us in our history; they killed and they were killed. The Commander of the Faithful himself would place a helmet on his blessed head, don his coat of chain mail, and gird on a sword. Imām Hasan and the Doyen of the Martyrs acted likewise. The later Imāms did not have the opportunity to go into battle, even though Imām Bāqir was also a warrior by nature. But now the wearing of military apparel is thought to detract from a man's quality of justice, and it is said that one should not wear military dress. If we want to form an Islamic government, then we must do it in our cloaks and turbans; otherwise, we commit an offense against decency and justice!

This is all the result of the wave of propaganda that has now reached the religious institution and imposed on us the duty of proving that Islam also possesses rules of government.

That is our situation then—created for us by the foreigners through their propaganda and their agents.

They have removed from operation all the judicial processes and political laws of Islam and replaced them with European importations, thus diminishing the scope of Islam and ousting it from Islamic society. For the sake of exploitation they have installed their agents in power.

So far, we have sketched the subversive and corrupting plan of imperialism. We must now take into consideration as well certain internal factors notably the dazzling effect that the material progress of the imperialist countries has had on some members of our society. As the imperialist countries attained a high degree of wealth and affluence—the result both of scientific and technical progress and of their plunder of the nations of Asia and Africa—these individuals lost all their self-confidence and imagined that the only way to achieve technical progress was to abandon their own laws and beliefs. When the moon landings took place, for instance, they concluded that Muslims should jettison their laws! But what is the connection between going to the moon and the laws of Islam? Do they not see that countries having opposing laws and social systems compete with each other in technical and scientific progress and the conquest of space? Let them go all the way to Mars or beyond the Milky Way; they will still be deprived of true happiness, moral virtues and spiritual advancement and be unable to solve their own social problems. For the solution of social problems and the relief of human misery require foundations in faith and moral; merely acquiring material power and wealth, conquering nature and space, have no effect in this regard. They must be supplemented by, and balanced with, the faith, the conviction, and the morality of Islam in order truly to serve humanity instead of endangering it. This conviction, this morality, and these laws that are needed, we already possess. So, as soon as someone goes somewhere or invents something, we should not hurry to abandon our religion and its laws, which regulate the life of man and provide for his well being in this world and hereafter.

The same applies to the propaganda of the imperialists. Unfortunately some members of our society have been influenced by their hostile propaganda, although they should not have been. The imperialists have propagated among us the view that Islam does not have a specific form of government or governmental institutions. They say further that even if Islam does have certain laws, it has no method for enforcing them, so that its function is purely legisla-

tive. This kind of propaganda forms part of the overall plan of the imperialists to prevent the Muslims from becoming involved in political activity and establishing an Islamic government. It is in total contradiction with our fundamental beliefs.

We believe in government and believe that the Prophet was bound to appoint a successor, as he indeed did. Was a successor designated purely for the sake of expounding law? The expounding of law did not require a successor to the Prophet. He himself, after all, had expounded the laws; it would have been enough for the laws to be written down in a book and put into people's hands to guide them in their actions. It was logically necessary for a successor to be appointed for the sake of exercising government. Law requires a person to execute it. The same holds true in all countries of the world, for the establishment of a law is of little benefit in itself and cannot secure the happiness of man. After a law is established, it is necessary also to create an executive power. If a system of law or government lacks an executive power, it is clearly deficient. Thus Islam, just as it established laws, also brought into being an executive power.

There was still a further question: who was to hold the executive power? If the Prophet had not appointed a successor to assume the executive power, he would have failed to complete his mission, as the Qur'an testifies. The necessity for the implementation of divine law, the need for an executive power, and the importance of that power in fulfilling the goals of the prophetic mission and establishing a just order that would result in the happiness of mankind—all of this made the appointment of a successor synonymous with the completion of the prophetic mission. In the time of the Prophet, laws were not merely expounded and promulgated; they were also implemented. The Messenger of God was an executor of the law. For example, he implemented the penal provisions of Islam: he cut off the hand of the thief and administered lashings and stonings. The successor to the Prophet must do the same; his task is not legislation, but the implementation of the divine laws that the Prophet has promulgated. It is for this reason that the formation of a government and the establishment of executive organs are necessary. Belief in the necessity for these is part of the general belief in the Imamate, as are, too, exertion and struggle for the sake of establishing them.

Pay close attention. Whereas hostility toward you has led them to misrepresent Islam, it is necessary for you to present Islam and the doctrine of the Imamate correctly. You must tell people: "We believe in the Imamate; we believe that the Prophet appointed a successor to assume responsibility for the affairs of the Muslims, and that he did so in conformity with the divine will. Therefore, we must also believe in the necessity for the establishment of government, and we must strive to establish organs for the execution of law and the administration of affairs." Write and publish books concerning the laws of Islam and their beneficial effects on society. Improve your style and method of preaching and related activity. *Know that it is your duty to establish an Islamic government.* Have confidence in yourselves and know that you are capable of fulfilling this task. The imperialists began laying their plans three or four centuries ago; they started out with nothing, but see where they are now! We too will begin with nothing, and we will pay no attention to the uproar created by a few "xenomaniacs" and devoted servants of imperialism.

Present Islam to the people in its true form, so that our youth do not picture the *ākhūnds* as sitting in some corner in Najaf or Qum, studying the questions of menstruation and parturition instead of concerning themselves with politics, and draw the conclusion that religion must be separate from politics. This slogan of the separation of religion from politics and the demand that Islamic scholars should not intervene in social and political affairs have been formulated and propagated by the imperialists; it is only the irreligious who repeat them. Were religion and politics separate in the time of the Prophet? Did there exist, on one side, a group of clerics, and opposite it, a group of politicians and leaders? Were religion and politics separate in the time of the caliphs—even if they were not legitimate—or in the time of the Commander of the Faithful? Did two separate authorities exist? These slogans and claims have been advanced by the imperialists and their political agents in order to prevent religion from ordering the affairs of this world and shaping Muslim society, and at the same time to create a rift between the scholars of Islam, on the one hand, and the masses and those struggling for freedom and independence, on the other. They will thus been able to gain dominance over our peo-

ple and plunder our resources, for such has always been their ultimate goal.

If we Muslims do nothing but engage in the canonical prayer, petition God, and invoke His name, the imperialists and the oppressive governments allied with them will leave us alone. If we were to say "Let us concentrate on calling the *azān* and saying our prayers. Let them come and rob us of everything we own—God will take care of them! There is no power or recourse except in Him, and God willing, we will be rewarded in the hereafter!"—if this were our logic, they would not disturb us.

Once during the occupation of Iraq, a certain British officer asked, "Is the *azān* I hear being called now on the minaret harmful to British policy?" When he was told that it was harmless, he said: "Then let him call for prayers as much as he wants!"

If you pay no attention to the policies of the imperialists, and consider Islam to be simply the few topics you are always studying and never go beyond them, then the imperialists will leave you alone. Pray as much as you like; it is your oil they are after—why should they worry about your prayers? They are after our minerals, and want to turn our country into a market for their goods. That is the reason the puppet governments they have installed prevent us from industrializing, and instead, establish only assembly plants and industry that is dependent on the outside world.

They do not want us to be true human beings, for they are afraid of true human beings. Even if only one true human being appears, they fear him, because others will follow him and he will have an impact that can destroy the whole foundation of tyranny, imperialism, and government by puppets. So, whenever some true human being has appeared they have either killed or imprisoned and exiled him, and tried to defame him by saying: "This is a political *ākhūnd!*" Now the Prophet was also a political person. This evil propaganda is undertaken by the political agents of imperialism only to make you shun politics, to prevent you from intervening in the affairs of society and struggling against treacherous governments and their anti-national and anti-Islamic politics. They want to work their will as they please, with no one to bar their way.

Glossary

a school in a certain place: elsewhere in the document source, it is acknowledged that no particular school among the various foreign-run schools in Iran can be identified.

… as the Qur'an testifies: at 4:67

Commander of the Faithful: leader of the Muslims

desperate measures: attempts by the Iranian embassy in Baghdad to prevent the dissemination of earlier versions of this document

Imāam Hasan and …
Imāam Bāqir: respectively, the second and fifth imams

Most Noble Messenger: the Prophet Muhammad

mujtahids: an Islamic legal authority whose opinions on a law's specific provisions are based on deductions from Muslim principles and ordinances

These new groups: European countries, beginning with the Portuguese in the mid-1500s, that colonized Muslim countries

"xenomaniacs":   English rendition of a Persian term designating persons excessively partial to the culture of foreign, especially Western, nations

Sango tribe members, 1906.

YORUBA PRAISE POEM TO SANGO: DOCUMENT ANALYSIS

ca. 1970 CE

"The day fire produces great puffs of smoke, / The same day it produces flames, / Grant whatever I ask of you."

Overview

The Yoruba people of West Africa worship and pay homage to approximately two hundred deities. While some are recognized by relatively small communities, their worship even confined to single villages, some are universally acknowledged by all Yoruba, both within Africa and among their descendants in the Americas. Among these most powerful gods is Sango, god of thunder and lightning. Associated with royal power and justice and feared for his volatile temper and incredible destructive power, Sango is worshipped regularly to ensure his protection and goodwill. As with other Yoruba deities, the chief expression of devotion is praise poetry, a form of laudatory prayer. Devotees sing poems to offer praise, request aid, and remind worshippers that acknowledging Sango is essential to their well-being. The praise poem considered here contains all of the aforementioned elements, and though it was recorded in the late twentieth century, it is typical of the kind of oral scriptures that have been an essential part of Yoruba spiritual life for centuries.

Context

The ancestors of the Yoruba people can be traced to the confluence of the Benue and Niger rivers between 2000 and 1000 BCE. Groups of these ancestral peoples migrated westward from the eighth to the eleventh centuries CE to what is now southwestern Nigeria and southeastern Benin, thereby establishing the origins of Yorubaland. These migrants organized themselves into highly urbanized city-states. The two most important city-states were Ile-Ife, where Yoruba folklore says their people originated, and Oyo, the city-state that eventually created the most powerful Yoruba empire. Although the Yoruba share common ancestry, mythology, culture, and artistic tradition,

their identities and languages were principally shaped by local loyalties to city-states. To this day some dialects of Yoruba are barely mutually intelligible, and regional identities remain strong. The precise year for the emergence of Yoruba praise poetry (*oríkì*) cannot be known, but the practice likely dates from the formative eighth to eleventh centuries, when Yoruba culture and religion took shape. Individual examples of praise poetry have come and gone over the course of Yoruba history, being shaped and molded by the generations and by each individual reciter. The particular praise poem to Sango considered here was recorded around 1970, yet aspects of it may be centuries old. Oral scriptures cannot always be dated precisely.

Likewise, the exact year that Yoruba religion began cannot be dated precisely, but it is certainly just about as old as the Yoruba themselves. The Yoruba people pay homage to approximately two hundred deities, *òrìsàs*, which range in significance from the primordial gods said to have had a hand in the ordering of the universe to those who protect local villages. While most of the major gods are believed to have existed from the beginning of the universe, some others are said to have once been human—heroes who performed memorable deeds and were deified. This was particularly common among kings, who were considered divine representatives. Sango, god of thunder and lightning and one of the greatest gods, is known differently by different worshippers. In some oral traditions he is called Irunmole and is known as a primordial deity. Yet other traditions refer to him as Oba Alaafin and say he was once mortal and ruled as the *aláàfin*, or divine monarch, of the Oyo Empire.

In some regions, especially in the Americas, the tales of Sango as the deified Oba Alaafin have became more powerful than those that describe him as a primordial deity. Sango is therefore a complex deity whose definition and conception vary in different locations. For some worshippers, he remains a primordial figure who existed at the very origins of the universe; for others he is a historical figure, a king of Oyo who was so powerful that he became a god upon his departure from earth. Over time, the mythic Sango and the historical Sango have overlapped—so much so that the legends surrounding them, even when they are contradictory, are accepted by worshippers as describing the same being. Whether he is believed to be a primordial entity or a deified emperor, both traditions agree on a common "essence" of Sango. He is known for his devotion to justice, his use of lightning and thunder to carry out his will and express his displeasure, his military prowess, and his fiery temper. In this fashion, the behavior of Sango described in Yoruba mythology and by his believers is akin to thunder and lightning: It is powerful, swift, and generally unpredictable.

According to the praise poetry that recounts the lives of the deities, the mythical Sango was a contemporary of Ogun, Orunmila, Obatala, Ese, Osun, and the other primordial deities and was present at the creation of the world. He is the embodiment of atmospheric power, as exemplified in thunder and lightning. He has a restless and unpredictable nature, tending to be irrational and impatient with a predilection for violence. He is honored on the day Jakuta, one of the four Yoruba days of the week. Jakuta was an ancient solar deity who also controlled lightning and had a strong hatred for immorality, and he is now identified with Sango, regarded either as his predecessor or as the same deity. The conception of the primordial Sango, as described in oral traditions, appears to be the more ancient. However, the historical Sango is the conception that was first written down, in the nineteenth century. The power of texts and the written word began to elevate traditions of the historical Sango in significance. Most worshippers would agree that the differences in the traditions do not matter; they simply describe different sides of Sango over time.

The historical Sango has his beginnings in the Oyo Empire. A Yoruba city-state that expanded into a substantial empire by the late seventeenth century, Oyo was, at its peak between approximately 1700 and 1750, arguably the largest and strongest of all Yoruba kingdoms. It bordered several other Yoruba kingdoms to the east, roughly following the Osun River north to the Niger, and encompassed the empire of Dahomey (modern-day Benin) in the west all the way south to the coast of the Atlantic Ocean. According to tradition, the city was founded by Oduduwa, son of Olorun (also called Olodumare), god of the sky. It is generally agreed that the historical Sango was a descendant of Oduduwa and that he was the fourth emperor of Oyo. He was known to be aggressive and impulsive and is credited with being a great warrior and skilled military leader who consolidated the Oyo Empire. Accounts of his rule describe his personality alternatively as impartial and just or as exacting and tyrannical. He was reputed to have an intense hatred for liars, a love for honor, a volatile temperament, and a gift for working magical charms. According to myth, he had the ability to shoot fire from his mouth, and he possessed the power to control lightning.

Various stories of the historical Sango's death and subsequent deification exist, but there are three common versions. One states that while experimenting with a newly acquired charm that gave him the power to call lightning

Time Line	
ca. 2000– 1000 BCE	■ The ancestors of the Yoruba emerge near the confluence of the Benue and Niger rivers.
ca. 700– 1100 CE	■ Peoples from the Benue-Niger region migrate westward and settle in what is now southwestern Nigeria and southeastern Benin, thereby establishing Yorubaland. Yoruba religion, Sango worship, and the practice of praise poetry have their roots in this formative period.
ca. 1600– 1700	■ The Oyo Empire expands significantly and introduces Sango worship to other parts of West Africa, including Dahomey (now much of Benin), Borgu (northern Benin and western Nigeria), and Nupe (central and northern Nigeria).
ca. 1700– 1750	■ The fourth emperor of Oyo reigns, at the height of Oyo's political power and territorial expansion.
1780–1850	■ Yoruba enslavement is at its peak, and Yoruba-based religions travel with enslaved populations to the Americas.
1789	■ The last emperor of Oyo to wield substantial power, Abiodun, dies.
1820s	■ The Oyo Empire collapses, owing largely to civil war and a weakened administration.
ca. 1970	■ The scholar Akinwumi Isola records a praise poem to Sango, as recited by a priest of Sango in the city of Oyo.

down from the sky, he inadvertently caused it to strike his palace, killing his own people. Horrified and ashamed, he then hung himself. Another account says that, troubled by quarrelling among his wives and complaints from his subjects, he left his palace and climbed a chain into the sky. There he remained, choosing to rule his kingdom with lightning from that day forward. The most well-known rendition, however, tells that two members of Sango's court, Timi and Gbonnka, had become very powerful. Because he felt threatened by them, Sango schemed to set the two against each other in battle. He hoped they might kill each other, but Gbonnka emerged victorious. Sango then had him thrown into a fire—some versions claim Gbonnka asked to have this done, to demonstrate his power—and when he came forth unharmed and challenged Sango's rule, Sango abdicated and then hung himself. Afterward, his priests went to the site of his supposed death but did not find him there. They spread the word among his former subjects that he had become a god, and firestones fell from the sky upon his detractors.

Naturally, after he became deified, worship of Sango remained at its strongest in his kingdom of Oyo, and he is still the deity most identified with kingship in Oyo. While the celebration of Sango is a religious activity, it was also strongly associated with royal power. This fact contributed to the power of Oyo during its expansion. Yorubaland had, and still has, a very high occurrence of lightning, and so a royal court that claimed strong ties with the deity who controlled such a powerful, ever-present force was one to be reckoned with. The Sango cult therefore effectively sanctioned the authority of the emperor, and any emperor was expected to participate in Sango festivals and to worship at Sango's shrine in Oyo. The highest members of the emperor's court were also traditionally heavily involved in the cult of Sango. Sango worship became an integral part of ruling the populace; the emperor regularly sent priests of Sango to provinces under Oyo's control to maintain his jurisdiction, and the religion was imposed on conquered peoples during the empire's expansion. It was primarily in this way that Sango's religion was spread in West Africa, and it is for this reason that his worship in Africa is most concentrated in the areas where Oyo's influence was greatest. Nonetheless, the worship of Sango can be also be found in many regions of West Africa that were only marginally under the political rule of Oyo, such as Sabe and Ketu (in modern-day Benin). In still other cases, Sango worship can be found among people who were affected by Oyo culturally though never under Oyo's political control, such as Fon- and Ewe-speaking peoples of contemporary Benin and Togo.

Approximately one million Yoruba were taken from West Africa and brought to the Americas as slaves from the late seventeenth to the mid-nineteenth centuries. Early in that period, captives were taken by the Yoruba during Oyo's wars of expansion. Yet when civil war broke out in the mid-nineteenth century and the empire's administration and leadership consequently degenerated, the Oyo Empire collapsed, and the Yoruba became a particularly vulnerable target of the transatlantic slave trade. The neighbors of the Yoruba began to raid them, and hundreds of thousands were captured and subsequently transported across the Atlantic. The majority of these slaves were transported to Brazil and the islands of the Caribbean Sea, especially Cuba. In these places a number of Yoruba-based religions formed, such as Candomblé, Santería, Lucumi, Batuque, and Winti, with many containing elements of Sango worship.

Sango worship is therefore an international phenomenon that can be found in Nigeria, Benin, and Togo in West Africa and throughout the Americas, especially in Brazil and the Caribbean islands of Cuba, Haiti, Trinidad, and Puerto Rico. Sango worship has, in turn, been brought by emigrants from these nations to their new homes, spreading to virtually all nations of the Americas, particularly the United States and Canada. In traveling from Africa, however, Sango could not remain unchanged. He retained certain features—his power to manipulate thunder and lightning, his double-headed ax, his violent temper, and his association with royalty. However, he gathered new traits as he went, borrowing from the identities of distinctly non-Yoruba deities. For instance, in many Yoruba-based religions of the Americas, Sango has been combined with the Catholic saint Barbara, the patron saint of protection from thunderstorms and fire. Scholars generally agree that in such cases, the origin of this religious blending is likely to be found in the past criminalization of African religions. To continue practicing their own worship, slaves called their gods by Christian names, feigning devotion to Christianity in public in order to preserve their own religion in private. Over time, the two divinities came to be seen as the same deity by two different names. Elsewhere, in Haiti, the god is affectionately called "Papa Sango," and in Trinidad, he holds such an important place that Afro-Trinidadian religion has frequently been referred to simply as "Sango."

It is clear, therefore, that regardless of how far Oyo's political dominance extended, worship of Sango now reaches well beyond, stretching from West Africa to Brazil to Canada. As a powerful primordial deity with dominion over the fearsome natural phenomenon of lightning and thunder, he is respected and feared. The implication is that among certain peoples, there is no choice but to pay homage to Sango. To do otherwise is to invite his wrath.

About the Author

This praise poem was orally recited by a priest (*mogbà*) of Sango in the city of Oyo around 1970 and recorded in writing by the scholar Akinwumi Isola. Priests pay homage to Sango on a daily basis, and this habitual worship includes the chanting of a praise poem. Knowing the ritual has been performed, worshippers are able to proceed confidently with their day, trusting they then have Sango's goodwill and protection. Priests are the guardians of Sango's sacred objects—such as his double-headed ax and sixteen cowries for divination—maintainers of Sango's shrine, and the officials of all weekly and annual ceremonies pertaining to him. They also compose and recite praise poems dedicated to Sango, such as this one. During periodic rituals, praise poems are sung, and the shrine is cleaned to assure Sango of his worshippers' continued devotion. Routine practices such as this are performed by priests on behalf of the entire community.

Explanation and Analysis of the Document

This praise poem declares the speaker's readiness and willingness to serve Sango and also seeks his assistance in all endeavors. It is intended to appease him and also to encourage him to offer his service to his worshippers. The first thirteen lines of the poem indicate that paying homage to Sango, respecting and recognizing his power, is essential to one's well-being, and failing to do so brings serious repercussions. Descriptive praise names are used, such as Oosase (hailing a deity's power and authority) and Awo (which refers to a deity's mystery); the poem's references to Sango as the "son of Oosase" likely refers to Sango as a descendant of Olorun/Olodumare, the Yoruba creator god. The poem acknowledges Sango not only as a god but also as a military leader and emperor: "We greet the king as well as the captain." He is called the "ever-successful-architect," a reference to him as a designer of men's destinies and perhaps also to his historical role as the *aláàfin* who consolidated the Oyo kingdom, or the "architect" of the great empire.

After the opening lines saluting Sango, the poem shifts into a request for his aid in accomplishing goals and resolving problems. He is reputed to have assisted humans with a wide variety of issues, helping women to bear their children, ending droughts by opening the clouds, and making it possible for leaders to conquer their enemies. The poem calls on all his mighty and mysterious powers, referring first to his magical abilities. Most notable among them is his ability to manipulate fire, an energy that transcends boundaries and has tremendous destructive and creative powers. There is an implication that while the speaker understands that humans may act independently, with Sango's help they are capable of doing greater things than they might do alone. Regarding the reference to Igede, a drum made from a hollow log, in many African societies, drums are said to "speak." The placement, timing, and force of the drummers' hits upon the log can produce a variety of tones that mimic human speech. In this manner, the Igede drum, too, can be commanded to praise Sango. In addition to a broad request for his assistance, the poem seems also to ask that Sango address only the issues that the speaker brings to him, making reference to a proverb—"Oro 'kills' only the trees that are marked for him"—that suggests that one should contribute only to issues about which one is knowledgeable. This part of the praise poem thus reveals that worshippers of Sango sometimes implore him for protection in a broad and generalized way while at other times requesting his assistance in a very precise manner.

The final lines of the poem echo the belief that those who praise Sango and express gratitude for his assistance enjoy his blessings. It refers to animals that, though they live in constant danger, wake up each day without fear, just as devotees may do when they wake up each day greeting Sango. The poem also discusses the benefits that respect and gratitude bring, using the analogy of the relationship between buyers and sellers at the market. Being gracious to the seller, the provider of one's needs at the market, results in generosity on the part of the seller. In the same way, paying homage to Sango reaps similar benefits. The end of the poem reiterates the positive effects of acknowledging Sango by referring to constants found in the world: "The red-billed firefinch always gets up hale and hearty. / One does not find an invalid bird in a nest. / The Lord of outdoors is always found outdoors. / The ajilete leaf is always found outdoors." The implication is that when devotees praise Sango as they ought, all will be as it should.

Audience

As with prayers in almost every religion, prayers to the Yoruba gods are a central and most basic religious activity. The intended audience for this prayer is Sango himself, as it serves as an expression of the worshipper's devotion and a petition for the god's aid. The essential purpose of all Yoruba praise poetry is the acquisition of one or more of the following three virtues: good fortune, fertility, and longevity. The belief is that these desires, known as *ire*, ultimately belong to Olorun, or Olodumare, the parent deity of the gods. Access to Olorun is provided by the deity one worships, because humans may not approach him directly. Therefore, *ire* is supplied to humans by the gods, including Sango, who are prepared to dispense it when the appropriate prayers are said and proper sacrifices are offered by devotees.

Impact

Yoruba praise poetry, like most forms of prayer, serves both to reinforce belief and to remind devotees that the attainment of worldly desires and good fortune are at the very least improbable, if not impossible, without the aid of their deities. This understanding permeates all levels of Yoruba society and, transcending international boundaries, can be found among people of Yoruba ancestry.

Praise poetry and prayer are also unifying activities that reinforce the identities of religious communities and the connections shared by members. Sango is manifest among the many cultural descendants of the Yoruba throughout the world, from Brazilian Candomblé to Cuban Santería to Nigerian *òrìsà* worship. All such groups respect Sango and address him regularly. They recognize his power, seek his protection, and ask that he assist them in their endeavors. They do so because they genuinely believe that their success, worldly or otherwise, is contingent on Sango's willingness to provide access to it, and that willingness is contingent on their devotion.

> *"Good morning, Sango. /Good morning, the Almighty. / The-ever-successful-architect, I pay homage to you. /Acting without first paying homage brings evil repercussions. / He who pays due homage is safe, / May I be safe."*
>
> (Section 1)

> *"The day fire produces great puffs of smoke, / The same day it produces flames, / Grant whatever I ask of you. / Do whatever I ask of you, Sango Almighty."*
>
> (Section 1)

> *"The black snake in the disused ant-hill, though in constant danger of death, wakes up well. / Money purchases merchandise and merchandise fetches money. / When one wishes the seller well, she gives one an eni. / No horse thanks one for its decorations, / I thank you Sango for my well-being."*
>
> (Section 1)

Further Reading

■ Books

Atanda, J. A. *The New Oyo Empire: Indirect Rule and Change in Western Nigeria, 1894–1934.* London: Longman, 1973.

Awolalu, J. Omosade. *Yoruba Beliefs and Sacrificial Rites.* Brooklyn, N.Y.: Athelia Henrietta Press, 2001.

Beier, Ulli, ed. *Yoruba Myths.* Cambridge, U.K.: Cambridge University Press, 1980.

Houk, James T. *Spirits, Blood, and Drums: The Orisha Religion in Trinidad.* Philadelphia: Temple University Press, 1995.

Isola, Akinwumi. "Religious Politics and the Myth of Sango." In *African Traditional Religions in Contemporary Society*, ed. Jacob K. Olupona. New York: Paragon, 1991.

Tishken, Joel E., Toyin Falola, and Akíntúndé Akínyemí, eds. *Sàngó in Africa and the African Diaspora.* Bloomington: Indiana University Press, 2009.

■ Journals

Isola, Akinwumi. "Yoruba Beliefs about Sango as a Deity." *Orita: Ibadan Journal of Religious Studies* 11, no. 2 (1977): 100–120.

—Allison Sellers and Joel E. Tishken

1. Compare this document with Emma Goldman's essay "The Philosophy of Atheism." What would Goldman have to say about the inclination of the Yoruba to worship a god such as Sango, the god of thunder and lightning?

2. Early cultures often exhibited a tendency to conflate gods with mortal heroes. In what sense did the Yoruba do so? How does their conception of heroes-as-gods compare with, for example, the notion that the hero of the *Epic of Gilgamesh* was in part divine?

3. The entry states that "the Sango cult therefore effectively sanctioned the authority of the emperor." In what ways have other religions served to "sanction the authority" of an emperor? See, for example, either the discussion in the Shinto entry Yengishiki or the discussion of the Egyptian "Great Hymn to the Aten."

4. What historical events helped to make Yoruba religion an international one?

5. Religion often serves not just a spiritual function but a social function as well. In what ways might Yoruba religion in general and the Yoruba Praise Poem in particular have contributed to the social cohesion of the Yoruba people?

YORUBA PRAISE POEM TO SANGO: DOCUMENT TEXT

1970 CE

I trust you are hearing me, Sango.
When we wake up, we salute the Lord,
The Almighty,
Good morning, son of Oosase,
When we wake, we greet Awo,
We greet the king as well as the captain.
He who wakes up and greets one not is one's enemy.
Good morning, Sango.
Good morning, the Almighty.
The-ever-successful-architect, I pay homage to you.
Acting without first paying homage brings evil repercussions.
He who pays due homage is safe,
May I be safe.
By its peculiar power, fire consumes wood.
Put the magic power of utterance-fulfillment on my tongue, Sango.
By its peculiar power, the sun shines forth.
Put the magic power of utterance-fulfillment on my tongue, son of Oosase.
The day fire produces great puffs of smoke,
The same day it produces flames,
Grant whatever I ask of you.
Do whatever I ask of you, Sango Almighty.

I pray you, whatever command we give Igede,
The same Igede obeys.
Oro "kills" only the trees that are marked for him.
Fire gets acquainted with wood within a day.
Accept all I tell you, Sango.
Good morning, son of Oosase.
The *emo* rat wakes up well on its track,
Good morning, Sango.
The *afe-imojo* wakes up well in its hole,
Good morning, son of Oosase.
The black snake in the disused ant-hill, though in constant danger of death, wakes up well.
Money purchases merchandise and merchandise fetches money.
When one wishes the seller well, she gives one an *eni*.
No horse thanks one for its decorations,
I thank you Sango for my well-being.
The red-billed firefinch always gets up hale and hearty.
One does not find an invalid bird in a nest.
The Lord of outdoors is always found outdoors.
The *ajilete* leaf is always found outdoors.
May I always wake up well, Sango.

Glossary

afe-imojo: spotted grass mouse (*Lemnicomys striatus*)

ajilete leaf: leaf from a local shrub named after the Yoruba town Ajilete

Awo: mystery, here referring to the divine mystery and might of Sango

emo rat: the Tullberg's mouse (*Praomys tullbergi*)

eni: a bonus

Igede: a type of drum made from a hollowed log and used in religious ceremonies

Oosase: praise name literally meaning "the deity that has authority and power"

Oro "kills" only the trees that are marked for him: Yoruba proverb meaning that one should contribute only to those issues in which one is knowledgeable because to do otherwise might create problems

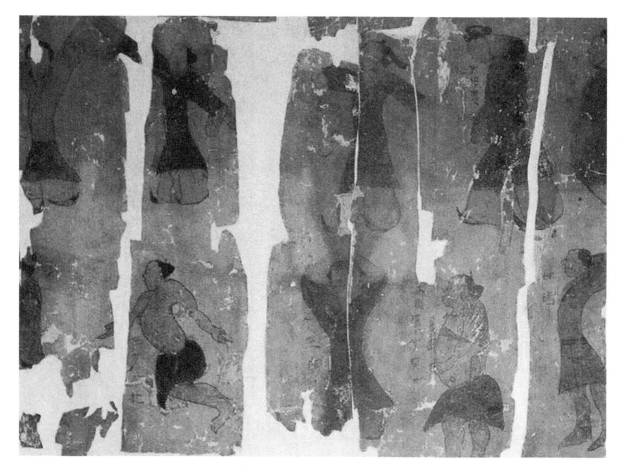

The physical exercise chart; a painting on silk depicting the practice of Qigong Taiji; unearthed in 1973 in HunanProvince, China, from the 2nd-century BC Western Han burial site of Mawangdui Han tombs site, Tomb Number 3.

ZHUAN FALUN: DOCUMENT ANALYSIS

1994 CE

"The whole process of cultivation is a process of constantly getting rid of human attachments."

Overview

Zhuan falun is the central text of Falun Dafa (also known as Falun Gong), a Chinese spiritual movement founded by Li Hongzhi in 1992. Falun Dafa, meaning "the great way of the dharma wheel," was originally a form of *qigong*, "the discipline of the vital breath," and emerged in the context of the *qigong* boom of the 1980s and 1990s. In this mass movement, hundreds of millions of Chinese practiced a wide variety of *qigong* cultivation techniques to improve their physical, mental, and spiritual well-being. The *qigong* boom has been likened to a new religious movement by some Western scholars.

Zhuan falun is a transcription of a series of nine lectures given by Li Hongzhi in the southern Chinese city of Guangzhou in December 1994. Such lectures, often delivered before paying customers in large venues like sports stadiums, were one of the main tools employed by *qigong* masters to spread their teachings and recruit new followers. *Zhuan falun* was published in Chinese that same month and has served as the bible of the movement ever since. It has subsequently been translated into at least thirty-eight languages and is available free on the Internet.

Li's teachings were shaped by criticisms directed at other schools of *qigong* in the 1990s, criticisms that focused on magical claims made by some *qigong* masters to possess extraordinary powers to cure diseases and perform other miracles. The teachings found in *Zhuan falun* emphasize instead "higher-level" cultivation, involving personal moral practice and a deeper understanding of the principles of the universe, even while providing exercise—and curing illnesses—as did other schools of *qigong*. As a result, while some *qigong* books read like how-to exercise manuals, Li's *Zhuan falun* more closely approximates a sacred religious text, indeed making numerous direct and indirect references to Buddhism, Daoism, and other traditional Chinese religions.

Context

The essential context for understanding *Zhuan falun* and Li Hongzhi is *qigong*. *Qigong* was popularized in the People's Republic of China in the 1950s as part of a nationalistic reaction to the perceived Westernization of Chinese medical practices. The creation of modern *qigong* entailed refurbishing traditional practices involving techniques such as directed breathing, meditation, visualization, and certain physical exercises, many of which had previously been taught as parts of spiritual or religious disciplines. *Qigong* became a part of official "traditional Chinese medicine"— a scientized version of traditional Chinese healing practices—and was practiced in clinics that were part of the Socialist Chinese medical establishment.

The Great Proletarian Cultural Revolution was launched in 1966 with the goal of eliminating all vestiges of traditional Chinese culture, seen at the time as "feudal," so as to build a new, Socialist culture. Given its roots in traditional religious and spiritual practices, *qigong* was condemned as "feudal superstition." Although official *qigong* clinics were closed down, a somewhat different form of *qigong* reappeared in public parks in Beijing in the early 1970s, taught by charismatic masters who had few links to China's medical establishment and whose teachings were often grounded in traditional spiritual discourses and practices. Their chief appeal was their self-proclaimed healing abilities, while their immediate impact was relatively minor. In the late 1970s, however, reputable Chinese scientists claimed to have proved the material existence of *qi* in laboratory experiments, which gave *qi* and *qigong* a new scientific legitimacy and ultimately facilitated the *qigong* boom.

Mao Zedong served as China's supreme leader until his death in 1976—the last year of the Cultural Revolution—and was a consistent advocate of revolutionary change, even at the expense of economic development. Deng Xiaoping, who succeeded Mao, abandoned class revolution in favor of markets, money, and greater freedom for most Chinese, thereby contributing to the creation of modern-day

China. The *qigong* boom was a major cultural moment in post-Mao China, extending from the late 1970s through the beginning of the campaign against Falun Gong in 1999. The most important actors were hugely charismatic *qigong* masters such as Yan Xin and Zhang Hongbao, who built powerful and profitable nationwide organizations on the strength of their claims to emit their miraculous personal *qi*. There were hundreds of such masters and hundreds of millions of followers, whose enthusiasm was fueled by the rise of journalists who chronicled and publicized the movement in *qigong* newspapers and magazines. Crucially, Chinese authorities—even leaders of the Chinese military-industrial complex—supported the movement, seeing in *qigong* a new Chinese science constructed on the basis of ancient Chinese civilization, which many *qigong* masters cited as the source of their power. The application of ancient Chinese spiritual principles to the challenges of contemporary Chinese life lent religious overtones to the *qigong* movement, although it was not identified as such. In his *Zhuan falun*, Li Hongzhi developed the spiritual elements of *qigong* further than did most other masters, even if his teachings share much with other schools of *qigong*.

About the Author

According to official Chinese records, Li Hongzhi was born on July 7, 1952, in Jilin Province. (Li himself claims to have been born on May 13, 1951—the day on which many Chinese celebrate the birthday of the historical Buddha, Siddhartha Gautama—and blames the confusion on the chaos of the Cultural Revolution.) According to an early Falun Gong biography, Li was exceptional from a very young age and was educated—in secrecy, for political reasons—in the spiritual arts by Buddhist and Daoist teachers, in preparation for his eventual vocation as spiritual leader. By contrast, available school and employment records suggest that Li had an ordinary childhood, although his education was disrupted by the Cultural Revolution, which began when he was a teenager, as schools were closed so that youths could "make revolution." He held a series of menial jobs—trumpet player, hotel attendant, security guard—before becoming interested in *qigong*.

It is not known at what point Li began to practice *qigong*, but in 1991 he quit his job so as to devote himself to cultivation. Like other *qigong* masters, Li taught a series of physical exercises, described in *China Falun Gong*, although the reading and rereading of *Zhuan falun* eventually came to be more important to Falun Dafa practice than the exercises. He first presented his Falun Dafa teachings in public in Changchun, Jilin, in May 1992, and his success grew rapidly, particularly after his appearance at the Oriental Health Expo held in Beijing—the center of the *qigong* world—in December 1992, where Li and Falun Dafa were warmly welcomed. Falun Dafa was accepted into the Chinese Qigong Research Society, the umbrella organization that governed *qigong*, and Li went on to give some fifty-four

Time Line	
March 1949	■ Modern *qigong* is invented by the Socialist Chinese medical establishment.
July 7, 1952	■ Li Hongzhi is born in Gongzhuling, Jilin Province.
1966	■ The Great Proletarian Cultural Revolution begins, and *qigong* is banned as a "feudal superstition."
1970	■ Charismatic *qigong* masters begin teaching healing *qigong* practices in public parks in Beijing, without the express approval of Chinese authorities.
March 1978	■ Well-known Chinese scientists announce the discovery of the material existence of *qi* in a scientific laboratory in Shanghai.
1991	■ Li quits his job to concentrate on *qigong* practice.
May 13, 1992	■ Li first presents his Falun Dafa teachings in public in Changchun, Jilin; he will give fifty-four lectures in many major venues in China through January 1995, establishing Falun Dafa as a major *qigong* organization.
December 1992	■ Li presents his teachings in Beijing, the center of China's *qigong* world, at the Oriental Health Expo.
1993	■ Li publishes his first book, *China Falun Gong*.
December 1994	■ Li publishes *Zhuan falun*.
January 1995	■ Li announces that his ministry in China is completed and leaves on a speaking tour in Europe before settling in the United States.

1996–1999	■ Conflicts increase between Falun Gong and Chinese authorities as part of a general decline of enthusiasm for *qigong*.
April 25, 1999	■ Falun Gong organizes a major demonstration outside the gates of Communist Party headquarters in Beijing.
July 20, 1999	■ The Chinese campaign outlawing Falun Gong begins.
December 29, 2000	■ Li Hongzhi comes out of hiding and begins once again to address followers at experience-sharing conferences.

lectures between May 1992 and January 1995 to audiences totaling some sixty thousand. He published his first book, *China Falun Gong*, in April 1993. On the strength of these successes, Li built a nationwide organization eventually consisting of more than twenty-eight thousand base-level practice centers, nineteen hundred training stations, and thirty-nine main coordinating stations. Li published *Zhuan falun* in late December 1994. By early 1995, Falun Gong was one of the largest *qigong* groups in China.

Li left China in early 1995 and eventually became a permanent resident of the United States. He continued to give lectures to Falun Gong practitioners in the Chinese diaspora throughout the world and, until the spring of 1999, returned frequently to China to continue his work there. Li presumably played a role in devising the Falun Gong response to increasing official criticism of *qigong* and Falun Gong over the course of the decade, a response that consisted of persistent but nonviolent protests of perceived media slights. There were about three hundred such small-scale demonstrations between 1996 and 1999, culminating in a much larger demonstration on April 25, 1999, in Beijing, which provoked a strong counterreaction by the Chinese government and altered the course of the Falun Gong movement and the *qigong* boom.

China issued an international arrest warrant for Li Hongzhi in late July 1999, shortly after outlawing Falun Gong. Although Interpol refused to honor the warrant, Li Hongzhi nonetheless went into hiding in the United States and was not seen in public for more than a year. Since reemerging in late 2000, his only appearances have been at the "experience-sharing conferences" held by Falun Gong practitioners, chiefly in North America. For security reasons, his appearances are not announced beforehand, and he is whisked away by bodyguards at the end of his speeches. Li communicates with practitioners through Falun Dafa Web

sites, which also carry transcripts of his speeches at experience-sharing conferences. Since 1999, many of his communications have focused on the bitter conflict between Falun Gong and Chinese authorities, and the movement has grown increasingly anti-Communist.

Explanation and Analysis of the Document

The present excerpt from *Zhuan falun* is part of the first chapter of Li's book. Li speaks as a *qigong* master to *qigong* enthusiasts, and his central argument is that he has the personal knowledge, experience, and power to teach "high-level" cultivation. In making this claim, Li broadened the definition of *qigong* cultivation to include individual moral and physical transformation and a theory of cyclical world destruction and renewal—guided by the creative force of *qigong*. Li's Falun Gong thus came to resemble a religion in many ways.

♦ "Truly Guiding People Up to High Levels"

The central message of *Zhuan falun* is contained in this initial passage: While other schools of *qigong* focus solely on improving the health of practitioners, Li Hongzhi's Falun Dafa enables dedicated followers to "cultivate" at a high level. For the practitioner, high-level cultivation of the self is a process of shedding attachments to wealth, fame, and human sentimentality. Li's discussion of attachments underscores Falun Dafa's important debts to Buddhism, references to which are found throughout *Zhuan falun*. At the same time, Li presents himself as the only person in the world teaching cultivation at high levels, and he suggests that even if health is not the ultimate goal of cultivation, he will personally heal dedicated practitioners so that they can focus on genuine cultivation rather than on health issues. This reveals the considerable power Li claims to possess, both to cure illness and to intervene in the basic law of karmic retribution, according to which illness and other forms of suffering are the result of bad behavior in previous or present lives. Later, the reader learns that genuine cultivation cannot take place without the guidance of a true master, which Li is. Elsewhere in this passage, Li hints at his theory of the multiple "levels" that make up reality. He argues that humankind originally existed at a high level but has declined over time as humans have developed "attachments" to earthly things. From this perspective, the goal of cultivation is to return to one's original self, found at the original level. This idea is often associated with Daoism and suggests the syncretic nature of Falun Gong beliefs and practices.

♦ "Different Levels Have Different Laws"

In this passage, Li introduces a new concept, *gong*, which means "cultivation level as determined by moral practice." Most of this section, however, is devoted to a discussion of the history of Buddhism, the goal of which is to suggest that some teachings are better than others and that cultivation practice is not possible without correct teachings. Li's negative example is that of Zen (in Chinese, Chan) Buddhism, which famously rejects scriptural teachings in favor of sudden individual enlightenment—occasionally with the aid of a well-placed blow to the body of the practitioner. The original justification for the rejection of scripture was the statement by the historical Buddha (Shakyamuni, meaning "Sage of the Shakyas"—the preferred Chinese name for Siddhartha Gautama) that "no law is absolute." Li interprets this statement to mean that no law is great enough to encompass all levels; as the Buddha deepened his enlightenment over time and advanced to new levels, he understood the limitations of the laws that had guided him to that point. Here, Li is comparing himself implicitly to the Buddha while arguing against what he sees as the relativism of Zen. In Li's eyes, his teachings are the greatest currently available, and cultivation without proper teachings is futile.

♦ "One Standard Alone Determines If Someone Is Good or Bad: Whether He Is Able to Be True, Good, and Forbearing [Endure]"

This section is meant to convey the heart of Li's own law, contained within the slogan "Truth, Goodness, and Forbearance." In Li's view, these three virtues are what practitioners must strive to embody in the cultivation of their individual character. "Truth," or the idea of becoming a "true person," is a central ideal of Daoism. "Goodness," or compassion, represents a central ideal of the Buddhist Mahayana tradition. "Forbearance" may well refer to Li's teaching that enduring suffering enables us to reduce our karma and build virtue. At the same time, Li wants the reader to understand that "Truth, Goodness, and Forbearance" are also the constituent elements of the material universe. Such a view is largely in accord with many Chinese teachings that insist on the unity of spirit and matter.

♦ "Qigong Is Part of Prehistoric Culture"

Li Hongzhi argues at many places in Zhuan falun that the modern scientific worldview, if useful, is also limited. He claims to have achieved a broader, deeper, understanding of reality and history through cultivation, and his statements in this passage are part of those claims. More specifically, he argues against Charles Darwin and his linear, progressive view of the evolution of humankind, insisting that, in fact, the world has been created and destroyed at least eighty-one times. (Chinese authorities later criticized Li for such "apocalyptic" views, but these statements were not viewed as particularly controversial prior to the campaign against Falun Gong, and they did not originate with Li.) At the beginning of each new kalpa—an unimaginably long period of time—only the elect, who understand and practice genuine cultivation, survive and push civilization toward development, until human feelings of attachment to earthly things begin the next cycle toward destruction. From this point of view, qigong has always served as the creative spark of cultural development throughout the history of humankind.

♦ "Qigong Is about Cultivation"

In this passage, Li Hongzhi continues his discussion of the relationship between qigong and science. He claims that qi and qigong have a material existence, as "with the use of scientific instruments people have now detected on the bodies of qigong masters things like infrasonic waves, ultrasonic waves, electromagnetic waves, infrared, ultraviolet, gamma rays, neutrons, atoms, and trace metal elements." In other words, some functions of qi and qigong can be described and measured using scientific language. At the same time, Li notes that cultivation can "bring out a person's supernatural abilities." And while such claims are often dismissed by skeptics as being founded in superstition, Li argues that many current technological developments would surely have been seen as "superstition" by our less-advanced ancestors. Cultivation is on the cutting edge of the development of human potential, and supernatural abilities are one expression of that development.

♦ "Why Doing Cultivation Exercises Doesn't Increase Gong"

In this passage, Li returns to the fundamental issue of character, linking it to the theme of the unity of matter and spirit. Once again condemning the facile equation of qigong with health, he repeats his arguments that cultivation requires the abandonment of attachments and willingness to suffer loss. He further argues that the "virtue" one cultivates is a white matter found within the human body, while karma—in many ways the opposite of virtue—is a black matter. There is a constant exchange of white and black matter as people go about their daily lives. Striving, self-directed behavior increases karma and black matter; selfless cultivation and forbearance in the face of suffering increase virtue and white matter. The presence of a master is necessary to transform the white matter into gong, which might be understood as the positive energy resulting from virtuous behavior. Genuine, transformative cultivation requires the special powers of the master, as suggested by the oft-repeated phrase "Cultivation is up to you, gong is up to the master." The master can discern instantly the cultivation level of a practitioner by looking at his gong pillar, which exists at a different level from that of human life but which is nonetheless visible to the master.

♦ "Falun Dafa's Special Features"

In this final section, Li attempts to summarize the character and benefits of his teachings, which are being made available for the first time to human civilization as the turning of the kalpa approaches. He repeats his argument that cultivation of gong is more important than exercises that seek to improve health, but he notes nonetheless that Falun Dafa offers exercises as well. This is because the body remains important for Falun Dafa practitioners as they develop their supernatural capacities and continue to cultivate within the human world. In the language of cultivation, this is referred to as dual cultivation of mind and body. Under Li's guidance, Falun Gong practitioners transform the material nature of their bodies as they cultivate their virtue, which

"The whole process of cultivation is a process of constantly getting rid of human attachments. Out in the ordinary world, people fight each other, they deceive each other, and they harm other people just to benefit themselves a little. The thoughts behind that all have to go. And this is especially true for us folks learning the practice today—you have all the more reason to get rid of those thoughts."

(Section 1)

"Those things other people are spreading are all just about healing and fitness, and if you want to cultivate up to high levels, you won't get anywhere, because you don't have a higher Law to guide you. It's just like going to school: if you used elementary school books in college you'd still just be an elementary school student."

(Section 1)

"So just what is Buddha Law? The universe's most fundamental nature, to be True, Good, and Forbearing [Endure], that's the highest expression of Buddha Law, that's the essence of Buddha Law. Buddha Law is expressed in different forms at different levels, and at different levels it acts as a guide in different ways, with its manifestations getting more diverse as the level gets lower."

(Section 1)

"Cultivation can bring out a person's supernatural abilities. Six types of abilities are recognized in the world today, but... I'd say there's around 10,000 true abilities. Just suppose that while sitting in place, and without moving his hands or feet, somebody could do what other people can't do even with their hands and feet, and he could see the true laws governing every dimension of the universe, and the reality of the universe."

(Section 1)

"Let's talk about how virtue is evolved into gong. There's a saying in the cultivation world, 'Cultivation is up to you, gong is up to the master.'... When it comes to who's actually doing it, it's the master. There's no way

you could do that. You've just got an ordinary human body, and you think you can evolve a higher being's body that's made of high-energy matter? Not a chance."

(Section 1)

"After our Falun Dafa students cultivate a while the way they look changes a lot. Their skin becomes delicate and fair, it glows with health, and older people begin to have fewer wrinkles—some will hardly have any. This is all common. There's nothing far-fetched about it. A lot of the veteran students here in the audience know this."

(Section 1)

explains their youthful appearance and vitality. Finally, Li explains that he installs in the stomach of each practitioner a revolving law wheel. Turning clockwise, it absorbs energy from the universe to benefit the practitioner. Turning counterclockwise, it diffuses the practitioner's energy outward, thus benefiting those around him.

Audience

Zhuan falun was originally presented orally as a series of lectures to people who wished to hear Li Hongzhi's message, and the book similarly targets *qigong* enthusiasts. Consequently, Li makes little effort to explain himself or his arguments to those unfamiliar with the *qigong* world. He assumes a certain level of knowledge and commitment on the part of his readers, and he dismisses out of hand those who might not agree with him, whether they be practitioners of "lesser" forms of *qigong* or *qigong* skeptics. Li's audience in China has presumably declined radically since the government crackdown, although there are signs that an underground movement remains. Outside of China, the movement is small but vocal. In North America, most practitioners are ethnic Chinese, while in Europe, Falun Gong appeals more to Europeans.

Impact

Li Hongzhi's teachings, as conveyed in *Zhuan falun*, earned him immense popularity in China's *qigong* world in the 1990s, as Falun Dafa became one of the most widely cul-

tivated forms of *qigong* during that period. Li criticized *qigong* as it was then practiced in China as being overly concerned with healing and magic tricks, and he sought to connect *qigong* with a much more ambitious project of "high-level cultivation." From the moment of its publication in 1994, *Zhuan falun* became the central sacred text of the movement, and the reading and rereading of this text by practitioners came to be the most important part of Falun Dafa cultivation. Such devotion to a text set Falun Gong off from other schools of *qigong* and perhaps encouraged heightened intensity and commitment on the part of practitioners.

The religious overtones of *Zhuan falun* and Li's pretentions to godlike knowledge and powers likely played some role in the eventual conflict between Falun Gong and Chinese authorities. At the same time, Falun Dafa had enjoyed considerable support from some Chinese leaders up until the beginning of the conflict in April 1999, and virtually all of the vitriolic criticism directed at Li Hongzhi and Falun Dafa was a product of the subsequent campaign against the movement. *Zhuan falun* was largely unknown outside the context of the *qigong* movement until the Chinese government decided to ban Falun Gong, such that nonpractitioners first encountered the text in a highly politicized environment in which the Chinese government sought to demonize Li and his teachings. Although the politics of the anti–Falun Gong campaign have dominated discussion of *Zhuan falun* since 1999, it is important to remember that the text was originally composed as a recruitment device, aimed at building a following for Li's teachings. These teachings took *qigong* in a new, more "religious" direction but did not at the outset seek conflict with Chinese authorities.

Li Hongzhi left China in 1995 and subsequently took up residence in the United States in an apparent effort to decrease tensions with Chinese authorities who worried that Falun Gong was growing too quickly. According to some sources, there may have been as many as sixty million practitioners at the height of the movement in the mid- to late 1990s. Rather than cede control of the Falun Dafa organization in China to subordinates in his absence, Li instead insisted all the more on the central importance of *Zhuan falun* to Falun Gong practice, arguing that repeated study of the text would establish a lasting one-to-one relationship between practitioner and master regardless of Li's absence from China.

Despite Li's departure, tensions between Falun Dafa and Chinese authorities multiplied, culminating in the large, peaceful demonstration of Falun Gong practitioners outside the gates of Communist Party headquarters in Beijing on April 25, 1999. The demonstrators demanded the right to practice in peace, which they felt had been threatened by increasing media criticism and police intervention. The demonstration shocked President Jiang Zemin, and within a few weeks, Chinese authorities declared Falun Dafa illegal and launched a campaign of brutal suppression that continued through the first decade of the twenty-first century. The conflict between Falun Gong and the Chinese authorities constituted a major problem in relations between China and the United States between 1999 and 2001, and human rights organizations continue to criticize China for its treatment of Falun Dafa practitioners. Most such media attention has focused on political and human rights issues rather than on the religious teachings at the core of Falun Gong.

Further Reading

■ Books

Ownby, David. *Falun Gong and the Future of China*. New York: Oxford University Press, 2008.

Palmer, David A. *Qigong Fever: Body, Science, and Utopia in China*. New York: Columbia University Press, 2007.

Tong, James W. *Revenge of the Forbidden City: The Suppression of the Falungong in China, 1999–2005*. New York: Oxford University Press, 2009.

■ Web Sites

Falun Dafa Clearwisdom.net Web site. http://www.clearwisdom.net

Falun Dafa Web site. http://www.falundafa.org/eng/home.html

—Commentary by David Ownby

Questions for Further Study

1. What similarities, if any, do you see between *Zhuan falun* and the *qigong* movement and religious revivalism practiced by nondenominational preachers in the United States, who often claim healing powers and preach before mass audiences?

2. How does the relationship between *qigong* and Chinese Communism reflect the relationship between religion and politics historically? For comparison, see the entry on the Canons and Decrees of the Council of Trent.

3. In your opinion, is *qigong*, as reflected in *Zhuan falun*, a genuine religion? What characteristics of a religion does it have, as you understand the term *religion*? How does it differ from traditional religions? In what ways, if any, can *Zhuan falun* be regarded as a "sacred text"?

4. To many westerners, Li Hongzhi's views would seem characteristically eastern, with similarities to Buddhism and perhaps such religions as Hinduism and Japanese Shinto. Is this a stereotype? Or is there something fundamentally "eastern" or "Asian" about *qigong*? Explain.

5. Why do you think the type of religion Li Hongzhi promoted became so immensely popular in China? What do you think was its fundamental appeal?

ZHUAN FALUN: DOCUMENT TEXT

1994 CE

—Li Hongzhi

Truly Guiding People Up to High Levels

For the whole time I've been transmitting our teachings and exercises, I've made a point of being responsible to society and to our students. The results have been good, and the impact on the whole society has been pretty good, too. A few years back there were a lot of masters of the qigong arts spreading their qigong practices, but the things they taught were all just at the level of healing and fitness. Of course, I'm not saying that other people's practices aren't good. I'm just saying they haven't passed on any higher things. I know the state of qigong all across the country, and I can say that right now, whether we're talking about inside China or abroad, I'm the only one who's really transmitting a practice that takes you to higher levels....

Transmitting a practice that takes you to high levels—now think about it, what's that mean? Isn't it about saving people? It's saving people—you are truly cultivating yourself, and not just getting healthy or fit. It's true cultivation, so the demands on the student's character are higher. Now us folks sitting here, we've come here to learn the Great Law, so you need to have the mindset of a true practitioner while you sit here, and you need to let go of your attachments. If you're coming here to learn the exercises, or the Great Law, with the goal of getting all kinds of things, then you won't learn anything. I'll tell you a truth: the whole process of cultivation is a process of constantly getting rid of human attachments. Out in the ordinary world, people fight each other, they deceive each other, and they harm other people just to benefit themselves a little. The thoughts behind that all have to go. And this is especially true for us folks learning the practice today—you have all the more reason to get rid of those thoughts.

I'm not going to talk about doing healing here. We don't do healing. But if you want to do true cultivation, and you've come here with an ailing body, then you can't cultivate yet. So I have to purify your body. I only purify the body for people who've truly come here to learn the practice, who truly come to learn the Law. There's one thing we stress: if you can't set aside those thoughts of yours, if you can't set aside that health problem, then there's nothing we can do and we can't help you. And why is that? Because there's a truth in this universe: the things that happen to ordinary people, as Buddhists put it, all have underlying causes, and for ordinary people things like birth, aging, sickness, and death are just a fact of life. People only have health problems and suffering because they did bad things in the past and made *karma*. When they go through hard times they are paying off a karmic debt, so nobody can just go and change that at will. If it's changed, that's like letting somebody who's in debt get off without paying it back, and you can't just go and do that on a whim. That's the same as doing something bad....

So why is it okay to do that for cultivators, then? Because nobody is more precious than a cultivator. He wants to cultivate, and that's the most precious thought. In Buddhism they talk about Buddha-nature, and that when a person's Buddha-nature comes out the Enlightened Beings can help him. And what do they mean by that? If you ask me, since I'm transmitting a practice on a higher level, it involves truths from high levels, and the issues it touches on are huge. In this universe, human life, as we see it, isn't generated in the ordinary world. A person's true life is generated in the space of the universe. The reason being, there are many types of matter in this universe that produce life, and these types of matter can generate life through motion and interaction. What this means is that a person's earliest life originates in the universe. The space of the universe is inherently good, and its nature is to be True, Good, and Forbearing [Endure], and when a person is born he has the same nature as the universe. But as more beings are created, community-like social relationships form. Some of the beings might grow selfish and gradually lower their levels, so they can't stay at that level and have to drop. But then at the next level they become not so good again, and again they can't stay there, so they keep dropping down and down, until at some point they finally drop to this level of human beings.

The whole human society is at one level. When they drop down this far, these beings were supposed to be destroyed if they are looked at only in terms of abilities, or only from the standpoint of the Great Enlightened Beings. But Great Enlightened Beings take compassion as their starting point, so they gave them another chance and made this special environment and this special dimension. The beings in this dimension are different from the beings in all other dimensions in the universe. The beings in this dimension can't see the beings in other dimensions, and they can't see how the universe really is, so it's just like these people have dropped into a realm of delusion. If they want to get healed, get rid of adversity, or eliminate their karma, then they've got to cultivate and return to their original, true selves. That's how all the different cultivation ways see it. A person should return to his original, true self—that's actually the true purpose of being human. So, once somebody wants to cultivate, they'd say his Buddha-nature has come out. That thought is the most precious, because he wants to return to his original, true self, he wants to break out of this level of ordinary people....

Some people think, "I'll cultivate if I can just get my health back." But cultivation doesn't have any conditions attached—if you want to cultivate, then you just cultivate. Some people's bodies are sick, though, and some people have messed-up messages in their bodies, some haven't ever cultivated, and then there are others who've cultivated for decades but are still milling around in the realm of *qi* energy, and haven't gotten anywhere cultivating.

So what should we do about that? We need to purify their bodies and make it possible for them to cultivate up to high levels. When you're cultivating at the lowest level there's a process, which is, we totally purify your body. We take all the bad things in your mind, that karma field around your body, and all those factors that make your body unhealthy, and we clean the whole thing out. If we didn't, then how could you, and that dirty body of yours that's all dark, and that filthy mind of yours, how could you cultivate up to high levels? And we don't work on qi here. You don't need to work on those low-level things. We'll push you past that and help your body reach an illness-free state. And at the same time, we'll give you a complete, ready-made set of things that are needed

at the low level to build a foundation. That way, we'll start right off at a high level....

Different Levels Have Different Laws

. . .

During these ten classes I'll expound higher truths and leave nothing out, and then you'll be able to cultivate. If I didn't do that you'd have no way to cultivate. Those things other people are spreading are all just about healing and fitness, and if you want to cultivate up to high levels, you won't get anywhere, because you don't have a higher Law to guide you. It's just like going to school: if you used elementary school books in college you'd still just be an elementary school student. Some people think they've learned a lot of practice methods, and they ramble on about such-and-such methods, and they've got a big old pile of completion certificates, but guess what, their gong still hasn't gone up. They think those things are the heart of qigong and that that's all there is to it. Hardly. That's just qigong's outer shell, that's its lowest things. Qigong is about more than that, it's cultivation, which is wide-ranging and profound. And besides, at different levels there are different Laws. So it's not like the qi-based approaches we know about today, where learning more of them doesn't do anything for you. Let's say you've studied Britain's elementary school books, you've studied America's elementary school books, you've studied Japan's elementary school books, and you've studied China's elementary school books—well, you're still just an elementary school student. The more low-level qigong lessons you take in, and the more that gets crammed in your head, it turns out, the worse that is for you, and you'll wreck your body.

Now, there's a point I want to make: when you cultivate, you have to have both practice methods and teachings passed on to you. Maybe the monks in some monasteries, like the Zen Buddhist ones, probably, they might have a different opinion. The minute they hear the words "pass on teachings," they don't want to listen. And why is that? Zen Buddhism believes that the Law isn't something you can teach, that as soon as you explain the Law it's not Law anymore, and that there's no Law that can be taught, you just have to figure it out intuitively. That's why Zen can't teach any Law today. The Zen Buddhist Bodhidharma spread this idea, and it was based on one thing Buddha Shakyamuni said. Shakyamuni said, "no Law is absolute." So he founded the Zen sect based on that statement from Shakyamuni. We'd say the sect is going down a dead end. How so? Back at the beginning, when Bodhidharma went down it, he thought it was pretty spacious, while for Patriarch II it wasn't that spacious; for Patriarch III it was so-so, but by the time of Patriarch IV it was already really narrow; basically there wasn't much to go down for Patriarch V, and by the time of Patriarch VI, Huineng, they'd hit the end of it, and they couldn't go any further. Today if you go to Zen to learn the Law, don't ask them anything, because if you ask them something they'll whack you right on the head, and they call it a "stick wake up." The idea is, you shouldn't ask, and that you've got to awaken on your own. You'd say, "I came here to learn because I don't know anything. What am I supposed to 'awaken' to? You just hit me with a stick!" That's the end that they've reached, and they have nothing left to teach. Even Bodhidharma said that Zen could only be passed down for six generations, and that after that it wouldn't work. Hundreds of years have gone by, but today there are still people who cling for dear life to Zen's doctrines and just won't let go. So then what's the real meaning of Shakyamuni's "no Law is absolute"? Shakyamuni was at the Tathagata level. People later on, and even a lot of monks, weren't able to awaken to things at Shakyamuni's level, nor to the state of mind at his level of awareness, to the true meaning of the Law he taught, or the true meaning of his words. That's why people who came after him interpreted it just about however you could imagine, and they interpreted it into a big mess. And they took "no Law is absolute" to mean you shouldn't teach it, and that once it's taught it's not Law. But that's actually not what it means. After Shakyamuni became Unlocked, or Enlightened, under the Bodhi tree, he didn't reach the Tathagata level right away. For all of the 49 years he was preaching the Law he was constantly improving himself. Every time he improved one level he'd look back and see that the Law he had just taught wasn't correct. After he improved more, he'd realize that the Law he had preached wasn't correct again. And when he improved even more, he realized that the Law he'd just taught wasn't correct yet again. For all 49 years he was constantly raising his level like that, and every time he went up one level he'd realize that the Law he taught before had a low understanding. He also realized that the Law at each level is that level's manifestation of the Law, and that every level has a Law, but that not one of them is the absolute Truth of the universe, although the Laws at higher levels are closer to the nature of the universe than the Laws at lower levels. That's why he said, "no Law is absolute.…"

One Standard Alone Determines If Someone is Good or Bad: Whether He Is Able to Be True, Good, and Forbearing [Endure]

There have always been people in Buddhism examining what Buddha Law is. And some people think that the Law taught in Buddhism is the whole Buddha Law. But it's actually not. The Law that Shakyamuni taught was for those ordinary people 2,500 years ago with a really low degree of civilization, they were people who'd just emerged from a primitive society and whose minds were kind of simple. He talked about, "the Age of the Law's End." *That's today.* Modern people can't cultivate with that Law anymore. In the Age of the Law's End it's hard for monks in monasteries to save even themselves, let alone save others. The Law Shakyamuni preached back then was specific to that situation, and also, he didn't teach people everything he knew at his level about Buddha Law. And if you want to keep it from ever changing, that's just not possible.

Society has been developing and the human mind has gotten more and more complicated, so it's hard now for a person to cultivate that way. Buddhism's Law doesn't cover the entire Buddha Law—it's just a tiny little part of Buddha Law. There are a lot of Buddhist Great Law practices that have been passed down among common folks, or passed down over the generations in a lineage-type way. Different levels have different Laws, and different dimensions have different Laws, and all of this is the Buddha Law's manifestation in different dimensions and at different levels.…

So just what is Buddha Law? The universe's most fundamental nature, to be True, Good, and Forbearing [Endure], that's the highest expression of Buddha Law, that's the essence of Buddha Law. Buddha Law is expressed in different forms at different levels, and at different levels it acts as a guide in different ways, with its manifestations getting more diverse as the level gets lower. Air particles, stone, wood, soil, steel, the human body—all matter has this nature, to be True, Good, Forbearing [Endure]. In ancient times they believed that the Five Elements form all the myriad things of the universe. And they, too, have this nature—to be True, Good, and Forbearing [Endure]. A cultivator can only know the specific manifestation of Buddha Law at the level he has cultivated to, and that's his cultivation Fruition, his level. If you spell it out in detail, the Law is huge. But when you reach its highest point, then it's simple, because the Law stacks up in a pyramid-like shape. Up at an extremely high level you can summarize it in just three words: Truth, Goodness, and Forbearance [True, Good, Endure]. But as it manifests at each different level it gets extremely complicated....

This nature, to be True, Good, and Forbearing [Endure], is the standard that determines what is good and bad in the universe. What's good? What's bad? You use this nature to tell. The same goes for the idea of "virtue" that people used to talk about. Of course, now society's moral level has changed, and even the moral standard has been perverted. Nowadays, if somebody models himself after that good Samaritan, Lei Feng, people will probably say he's crazy. But in the 1950s or 60s, tell me, who would have said he's crazy? Mankind's moral standard is on a big downslide, the world is going to the dogs, people are just controlled by greed, they harm others just to benefit themselves a little, and people just compete and fight—they go at it by hook or by crook.... But it doesn't matter how mankind's moral standard changes, the nature of the universe *doesn't* change, and *it* is the only standard for determining who's good and who's bad. So to be a cultivator you have to take the nature of the universe as your guide for improving yourself. You can't go by ordinary people's standards. If you want to return to your original, true self, if you want to raise your level by cultivating, you have to live by this standard. For anybody here, only if you can follow the universe's nature, to be True, Good, and Forbearing [Endure], only then you can call yourself a good person. And a person who goes against this nature, now that's somebody who's truly bad. Maybe when you're at work or out and about, someone will say that you're bad. But maybe you aren't really bad. Or maybe someone says that you're good. But, turns out, maybe you aren't really good. And for a cultivator, if you assimilate to this nature you're someone who has attained the Dao. The truth is really just that simple.

Daoists cultivate Truth, Goodness and Forbearance [True, Good, Endure] with an emphasis on being True. That's why Daoists strive to, "cultivate truth and nourish inborn nature, say true words, do true things, be a truthful person, return to your original, true self, and ultimately cultivate into a True Person." But they also have Forbearance [Endure], and they also have Goodness [Good], it's just that the emphasis is on cultivating the True part. Bud-

dhists emphasize the Goodness [Good] of Truth, Goodness, and Forbearance [True, Good, Endure], in their cultivation. Cultivation of Goodness [Good] can develop a heart of great compassion, and once this heart of great compassion comes out you can see that all sentient beings are suffering, so you'll be filled with one wish: to save all sentient beings. But they also have Truth [True], and they also have Endure [Endurance], it's just that the emphasis is on cultivating Good. Our Falun Dafa discipline, the Law Wheel Great Way, goes by the highest standard of the universe, to be True, Good, and Forbearing [Endure], and we cultivate these all together. So what we cultivate is huge.

Qigong is Part of Prehistoric Culture

What is qigong? A lot of qigong masters are trying to address this question, but what I have to say is completely different.... Some qigong masters say that qigong has a 2,000-year history in our country. And others say qigong has a 3,000-year history. Some say it has a 5,000-year history, which would be about the same as the history of our Chinese civilization. And there are people who say that if you go by historic artifacts it has a 7,000-year history, which goes way beyond the history of our Chinese civilization. But all the same, the date doesn't go much beyond the history of this civilization. Now, according to Darwin's theory of evolution, man first evolved from aquatic plants into aquatic animals, then he climbed onto land, and later up into trees, then he came back down and turned into an ape, and then finally he evolved into modern man, who has culture and thought, which puts human civilization at only about 10,000 years old, if you figure that way. Go back a little further and there wouldn't have even been quipu record-keeping, and they would have worn leaves and eaten raw meat. Go even further back, and maybe they wouldn't even know how to make fire, and they would have been those totally savage, primitive people.

But something just doesn't add up. There are a lot of places around the world where traces of ancient cultures have been left, and they're really a lot older than our civilization. These ancient remains are excellent in terms of their craftsmanship, and if you look at the artistry they're superb. It's almost like modern folks are imitating the arts of ancient people, and they have great aesthetic value. But they're from more than 100,000 years ago, hundreds of thousands of years ago, millions of years ago, or even more than

100 million years ago. Then think about it, isn't this making a joke of "history" as we know it? But this really isn't just another amusing idea, since mankind is perfecting itself and rediscovering itself on an ongoing basis, and that's just how a society develops, so chances are what it knows at the beginning isn't totally correct.

A good number of you have probably heard of the term prehistoric culture, which is also called prehistoric civilization. Let's talk about prehistoric civilization. On the earth there is Asia, Europe, South America, North America, Oceania, Africa, and Antarctica, which geologists group together as continental plates. It's been tens of millions of years since the continental plates formed, or you could say, a number of land masses rose from the ocean floor, and a lot of land masses sank to the bottom of the sea, and it's been tens of millions of years since they stabilized as they are now. But at the bottom of a lot of oceans people have found tall and large ancient structures, the structures have elegant designs, and they aren't cultural remains from today's human race. So they must have been built before they sank to the sea bottom. Then who was it tens of millions of years ago that started those civilizations? Back then, our human race wouldn't have even been monkeys, right—how could we have created such intelligent things? Today archaeologists have discovered that there was an organism called a trilobite, and that creature was active from 600 million years ago up until 260 million years ago. It hasn't been around for 260 million years. Yet there's an American scientist who discovered a trilobite fossil, and what was on it but a human footprint, the footprint of somebody wearing shoes, and the print was unmistakable. Isn't that like playing a joke on historians? If you go by Darwin's theory of evolution, tell me, could there be human beings 260 million years ago?...

There are a lot of brave scientists in other countries who have publicly acknowledged that these things come from prehistoric cultures, and that they're from a civilization that came before this human civilization of ours, meaning, before this civilization of ours there were other periods of civilization, and not just one. You can tell by looking at archeological objects that they weren't all from one period of civilization. So they think that after the many times civilization suffered a devastating blow, only a small number of people survived, they lived primitively, then gradually multiplied into a new human race, and began a new civilization. Then it would head for destruction again, and again they would multiply into a new human race. So that's how it's gone through all of these different cyclical changes, time after time. Physicists say that the motion of matter has patterns. Our entire universe's changes also have patterns.

The movement of our planet earth, when it's in this vast universe, and when it's in this turning Milky Way, there's just no way it could have always had smooth sailing, and chances are it's run into other planets, or had other problems, and these would have brought about huge catastrophes. If we look at it from the perspective of abilities, that's just how it was arranged. One time I traced it back carefully and found out that there have been 81 times when mankind lay in total ruin, and only a few people survived, only a little of the prehistoric civilization was left, and then they entered the next period and lived primitively. When the people multiplied enough, civilization would finally appear again. So it's gone through 81 of these cycles, and I didn't trace it back to the end. The Chinese people talk about timely moments [opportunities of time] granted by Heaven, geographical advantages, and unity among the people. Different changes in celestial phenomena, or different times granted by Heaven, these can bring about different situations in the ordinary world. In physics they say that the motion of matter follows patterns. Well, the same goes for the motion of the universe.

The main reason I just talked about prehistoric culture was to make this point: qigong is not something that today's human race came up with, it was handed down from ages ago, and it's part of prehistoric culture. And we can find some passages about this in scriptures. Back in his day, Shakyamuni said that he completed his cultivation and became Enlightened many, many hundreds of millions of *kalpa* ago. So then how many years are in a kalpa? One kalpa is many, many hundreds of millions of years. You really can't even imagine a number that huge. So if what he said is true, then doesn't it match up with mankind's history and the changes the whole earth has been through? And another thing Shakyamuni said was that before him there were six Buddhas of the primeval age, that he had masters, and so on, and that all of them had cultivated and become Enlightened many, many hundreds of millions of kalpa ago. So if these things are really true, then could some of those authentic, real practices and some of the legitimately passed down ones that are spread in the world today, could they include those types of cultivation ways? If you ask me, I'd say of course, sure. But you don't see them much. Nowadays those fake qigong, phony qigong, and those people who are possessed go and recklessly concoct some stuff to con people, and they outnumber the true qigongs by umpteen times. It's hard to make out which is real and which is fake. And it's hard to tell if something is real qigong. It's not that easy to find....

Qigong Is about Cultivation

Qigong has been around for ages, so just what exactly is it for? I'm going to tell you, what we have here is a Buddhist cultivation Great Law, so of course it's for cultivating Buddhahood. And Daoists, of course, cultivate the Dao to attain the Dao....

So let's think about it. Cultivation can bring out a person's supernatural abilities. Six types of abilities are recognized in the world today, but there are more than just those. I'd say there's around 10,000 true abilities. Just suppose that while sitting in place, and without moving his hands or feet, somebody could do what other people can't do even with their hands and feet, and he could see the true laws governing every dimension of the universe, and the reality of the universe—he could see things that ordinary people can't. Isn't that somebody who's attained the Dao by cultivating? Isn't he a Great Enlightened Being? Could you say he's the same as an ordinary person? Isn't he somebody who's become Enlightened by cultivating? Isn't it only right to call him "an Enlightened Being"? When you put it into the language of ancient India, that's a "Buddha." And *that* is what it's really about— *that* is what qigong is for.

The moment qigong comes up there's always somebody who says, "Why would you want to practice qigong if you don't have health problems?" He's implying that qigong is just for healing, and that's a really, really shallow understanding of it. But you can't blame him, because a lot of qigong masters are just healing people and helping them stay fit, that stuff, they just talk about healing and fitness, and nobody is teaching higher things. I'm not trying to say their practices aren't good. It's actually their mission to teach things at the level of healing and fitness, and popularize qigong. But there are a lot of folks who want to cultivate to high levels. They think about this, and they have the heart for it, but they don't know how to cultivate themselves, and this has brought them a lot of hardship, and they've run into a lot of problems. Now of course, really transmitting a practice at high levels is going to involve higher things. So we've made a point of being responsible to society, and to all people, and the overall results

of transmitting this practice have been good. Some of the things *are* high-level, and maybe it sounds like we're talking about superstitions [blind beliefs], but we'll try our best to use modern science when we explain them.

When we mention certain things some people blurt right out, "superstition [blind belief]." Why do they do that? Their criteria for something being "superstition [blind belief]" or "quackery" is that it's whatever science hasn't grasped, or whatever they haven't experienced first-hand, or whatever they think can't possibly exist. That's their way of thinking. So is that way of thinking correct? Can you just dismiss something as superstition [blind belief] or quackery just because science hasn't grasped it yet, or just because science isn't far enough along to explain it yet? Aren't these people themselves full of superstition [blind belief]? And aren't they caught up in quackery? If everybody thought that way, could science develop? Could it move forward? Society wouldn't be able to make progress. The things that our scientific and technological community has invented are all things that people didn't have at one time. If those things were all thought of as superstition [blind belief], then there'd be no point in talking about progress, right? Qigong isn't quackery. But there are always a lot of people who think it is, since they don't understand it. But with the use of scientific instruments people have now detected on the bodies of qigong masters things like infrasonic waves, ultrasonic waves, electromagnetic waves, infrared, ultraviolet, gamma rays, neutrons, atoms, and trace metal elements. Aren't those all concrete things? They're matter. Aren't all things made of matter? Aren't other space-times made of matter? Could you call *them* superstitions [blind beliefs]? Qigong is for cultivating Buddhahood, so of course there are going to be a lot of profound things involved. And we're going to explain all of them.

So if that's what qigong is for, why do people call it qigong? It's not really called qigong. What's it called? It's called cultivation—it is *cultivation*. Of course, it has other specific names, but as a whole it's called cultivation. So why do people call it qigong, then? You know, qigong has been popular for over 20 years. It started as early as the middle of the Cultural Revolution, and at the end of the Cultural Revolution it began to peak. Now think about it. Back then the ultra-leftist, Maoist thought was going strong. Let's not get into what names qigong had in prehistoric cultures. But as this civilization of ours was developing, it went through a feudal period, so it had names that sounded pretty medieval. And the ones related to religions often had names that sounded pretty religious, like, "Dafa of Cultivating Dao," "Vajra Meditation," "Way of Arhat," "Dafa of Cultivating Buddha," "Nine-Fold Immortality Elixir Method." They were names like those. If you used those names during the Cultural Revolution, wouldn't you have been publicly denounced? That wish that qigong masters had to popularize qigong was good, and they did it to heal the masses and keep them fit, it was to improve people's physical conditions—that was great, wasn't it?—but it still wouldn't have gone over well, so they didn't dare use those names. So to popularize qigong, a lot of qigong masters plucked two words from *The Book of Elixir* and the *Daoist Canon* and then called it "qi gong." Some people even dig into the term qigong and research it, but there's nothing there to study. It just used to be called cultivation. Qigong is just a new term that came along in order to suit modern people's thinking. That's all.

Why Doing Cultivation Exercises Doesn't Increase Gong

Why doesn't doing cultivation exercises increase your gong? Here's what a lot of people think: "I haven't been given any of the real things in my practice. But I know my gong would just shoot right up if a teacher showed me his signature move or let me in on some top-notch tricks." That's how 95% of people think these days. I'd say that's pretty silly. And why do I say that? Because qigong isn't some ordinary technique, it's entirely a higher thing, and so you have to use higher truths to size it up. I can tell you that the fundamental reason people's gong doesn't go up is that between the two words "cultivation" and "exercises," people only pay attention to the "exercises" part but not to "cultivation." Looking outward won't get you anywhere…. But in true cultivation you have to cultivate your mind, and it's called cultivating your character. To illustrate it, when you and another person are having a problem with each other, you try to take those emotions and desires of yours, all those passions of yours, take them a little less seriously. Otherwise, you're over there fighting tooth and nail to benefit yourself, and you want to increase your gong? Forget it! Aren't you just like an ordinary person, then? You think you could increase your gong? That's why you have to focus on character cultivation. That's what it takes for your gong to grow, and that's what it takes for your level to rise.

So what is character? Character includes virtue (which is a type of matter), it includes forbearance [enduring], it includes awakening to things, it includes giving up things—giving up all the desires and all the attachments that are found in an ordinary person—and you also have to endure hardship, to name just a few things. So it includes a lot of different things. You need to improve every aspect of your character, and only when you do that will you really improve. That's one of the key factors in improving your potency.

Some people think, "This 'character' you're talking about, it's just a philosophical thing. It's a matter of a person's level of awareness. It's different from the gong we want to cultivate." What do you mean "different"?! In intellectual circles there's always been the question of whether matter is primary or mind is primary. They've been talking about this and debating it for a long time. I'm going to tell you, in reality, matter and mind are one and the same. The scientists in the field of human-body science are now thinking that the thoughts the human brain produces are matter. So they exist materially. But aren't they also in people's minds? Aren't they one and the same? It's just like what I've said about the universe—it has its material side, and at the same time, it has its nature side. The universe's nature, to be True, Good, and Forbearing [Endure], isn't something ordinary people can sense, and that's because ordinary people are all on this one level's plane. When you go beyond the level of ordinary people then you can experience this nature. How do you experience it? In this universe all things, and this includes even all the matter that permeates the whole universe, they're all living entities, they all have thinking, and they're all forms that the Law of the universe exists in at different levels. If they don't let you rise to a higher level, maybe you want to go higher, but you just can't go up, they just won't let you come up. And why don't they? Because your character hasn't improved. Every level has different standards, and if you want to raise your level, you have to put a stop to your bad thoughts and dump out your filth, and you have to assimilate to that level's standard. That's the only way you can go up.

When your character improves, your body really changes. When your character improves, the matter in your body definitely changes. And what are the changes? You'll throw out those bad things that you stubbornly go after. Let me illustrate it. Take a bottle that's filled with filth, cap it tightly, and throw it into water, and it'll sink right down to the bottom. Then dump out that filth inside it, and the more you dump out, the more it'll float up. And when it's dumped all the way out it'll float all the way up. What we're doing when we cultivate is getting rid of every kind of bad thing that's in the body, and that's the only way to rise to higher levels....

Let's talk a little about this virtue thing.... Virtue is a type of white matter, and it's actually not some spiritual thing, or just something philosophical, like some people used to think. It's definitely material. And that's why at one time older people said "Build up virtue!" and "Don't lose virtue!" They hit it right on the head! That virtue is all around the human body, and it forms a field. Daoists used to say that the master looks for a disciple, not that the disciple looks for a master. And what does that mean? They just had to look at the proportion of virtue on the disciple to see if it was large. And if it was large, it'd be easy for him to cultivate. If it wasn't large, it'd be hard for him to cultivate, and he'd have a really tough time raising his gong up high.

At the same time there's a black type of matter. Here we call it karma, while in Buddhism it's called bad karma. There's white matter and black matter, and these two kinds of matter coexist. So how are these two types of matter related? The matter called virtue is something we get through suffering, going through hard times, or by doing good things for people. While the black matter, on the other hand, people get that by doing terrible things or things that aren't good, like taking advantage of other people. Nowadays, it doesn't stop at people just being controlled by greed, some people will even stop at no evil and do anything for money. They murder innocent people, hire people to kill, engage in homosexuality, do drugs, you name it—there's all kinds of stuff. When people do bad things they lose virtue. How do they lose it? When a person insults somebody, he thinks he's come out on top and let off steam. But there's a law in this universe, called "a person doesn't gain anything if he doesn't lose"—to gain, you have to lose, and if you don't lose you'll be made to lose. Who enforces this? It's the nature of the universe that does. So only wanting to gain just won't do it. So how's it work?

When a person insults somebody, or when he takes advantage of someone, he flings his virtue over to him. He's being wronged, he's losing out, and he's suffering, so he's compensated for it. So when that person insults him over here, right when those words come out a piece of virtue flies out of that person's own dimensional field and it lands right on him....

Let's talk about how virtue is evolved into gong. There's a saying in the cultivation world, "Cultivation is up to you, gong is up to the master...." if you just have that wish you're all set. When it comes to who's actually doing it, it's the master. There's no way you could do that. You've just got an ordinary human body, and you think you can evolve a higher being's body that's made of high-energy matter? Not a chance....

So then what does your master give you? He gives you the gong that increases gong. Virtue is outside the human body, and a person's true gong is developed from virtue, so the height of a person's level, and how much potency a person has, these both come from virtue. He evolves your virtue into gong, which grows upward like a spiral (the gong that really determines a person's level grows outside the body), it grows in a spiral shape until at some point it forms a gong pillar after reaching the top of your head. Want to know how high somebody's gong is? It just takes one glance at how high his gong pillar is, and that's his level, or what they call "Fruition" in Buddhism....

Also, to tell how high a person's character is, there is a measuring stick you can look at. The measuring stick and the gong pillar don't exist in the same dimension, but they do co-exist. When you've improved your character by cultivating, like for example, maybe you're around ordinary people and somebody insults you, but you don't say anything back and you're totally calm inside, or maybe somebody punches you, and again you don't say a thing and you just shrug it off, and you get through it. Then that shows that your character is high. You're a practitioner, so what should you get? Don't you get gong? When your character improves, your gong rises. However high your character is, that's how high your gong is....

Falun Dafa's Special Features

Our Falun Dafa is one of the Buddhist system's 84,000 disciplines. It's never been passed on to the general public before during this period of civilization, but it did once save people on a large scale in a prehistoric age. Today I'm spreading it again widely during this final period of the kalpa's end, so it's just extremely precious. I've talked about the way virtue is transformed directly into gong. And gong, it turns out, doesn't come from doing exercises—it comes from cultivation. A lot of people are really looking to build up their gong, but they only think exercises are important and they don't take cultivation seriously.

But the fact is, gong all comes from cultivating your character. Then why do we teach you exercises here? Let me first say a little about why monks don't do exercises. They mainly meditate, chant scripture, and cultivate their character, and then their gong increases—they increase that gong which decides your level. Shakyamuni talked about renouncing everything in the world, and that includes your innate body, so they don't need to do any movements. Daoists don't talk about saving all sentient beings. The people they teach don't have all kinds of mentalities, or all kinds of levels, and they don't deal with just whoever, with some people being really selfish and others less so. They choose their disciples. They might find three disciples, but only one of them is taught the essence, so that disciple is sure to have a lot of virtue, be good, and not run into problems. So they focus on teaching manual techniques, and that's to cultivate longevity. They work on things like supernatural powers and technique-type things, and that means they have to do some movements.

Falun Dafa is a practice that cultivates both your character and destiny [nature and longevity], so it has to have some movements to do. For one thing, the movements are for reinforcing abilities. And what's "reinforcing" about? It's about using your mighty potency to fortify your abilities, and it makes them stronger and stronger. And secondly, your body needs to evolve a lot of living things. When they reach a high level of cultivation, Daoists talk about "the Cultivated Infant coming to birth," just as Buddhists talk about "the Indestructible Adamantine Body," and lots and lots of technical things need to be evolved, too. All of these things need to be evolved through manual techniques, and they're what the movements are for. Looking at it this way, a complete system of both character and destiny [nature and longevity] cultivation needs to have cultivation, and it needs to have exercises. So I think you now know how gong comes about: the gong that really decides your level doesn't in fact come from exercises. It comes from cultivation. It has to do with you cultivating yourself, and how when you improve your character in the midst of ordinary people, and when you assimilate to the universe's nature, then the universe's nature doesn't hold you back, and you're able to rise higher. That's when your virtue starts evolving into gong, and as your character improves, it goes right up with it. That's how it works.

This practice of ours really counts as a practice of character and destiny [nature and longevity] cultivation. The gong we develop is stored up in every cell in

our bodies, and it goes all the way down to the microscopic particles of the original matter that exists in an extremely microcosmic state, and they all store up that high-energy-matter gong. As your potency grows higher and higher, its density becomes greater and greater, and its power becomes greater and greater, too. This type of high-energy matter has intelligence, and because it's stored in every cell in your body, right down to the origin of your being, over time it takes on the same form as the cells in your body, and it has the same arrangement as the molecules, and the same form as all the nuclei. But its nature changes, and now your body isn't the same flesh and blood that your cells used to make up....

After our Falun Dafa students cultivate a while the way they look changes a lot. Their skin becomes delicate and fair, it glows with health, and older people begin to have fewer wrinkles—some will hardly have any. This is all common. There's nothing far-fetched about it. A lot of the veteran students here in the audience know this. Also, older women are likely to get their period back, because a practice that cultivates both your nature and longevity needs to have the qi of essence and blood to cultivate longevity. They'll get their period, but it won't be heavy. They'll have just a little bit at this stage, only the amount that's needed. That's another thing that's common. If that didn't happen, how would you cultivate longevity when you don't have it? The same goes for men—the old and the young alike will all feel energized from head to toe. So I can say to our true cultivators: you will feel these changes....

Our Falun Dafa has another major feature that's extremely special and that sets it apart from all other practices.... What our practice does is cultivate a Law Wheel at the lower abdomen, and I personally place it in students during my classes. While I'm teaching Falun Dafa we place a Law Wheel in you one by one. Some people feel it, some don't, but most people feel it, and that has to do with people each having different physical conditions.... The Law Wheel is a miniature universe, it has all the functions of a universe, and it can operate and rotate automatically. It will turn forever at your lower abdomen, once it's placed in you it won't stop, and it'll turn like that year in and year out. When it's turning clockwise it automatically absorbs energy from the universe, and it can evolve energy by itself, and supply the energy that's needed to evolve every part of your body. In the same way, when it turns counterclockwise it sends out energy, and drives used material out of you, which then dissipates around your body. When it sends out energy, it shoots it out very far and brings in new energy again. And the energy it shoots out benefits everyone who's near your body. Buddhists believe in saving oneself and saving others, saving all sentient beings, so you don't just need to cultivate yourself, but you also have to save other beings. Other people benefit along with you, and you can adjust other people's bodies and heal other people without even meaning to, and other things. But of course you won't lose the energy. When the Law Wheel turns clockwise it draws it back in by itself, because it turns constantly and never stops.

Glossary

Bodhi tree:	a fig tree in India under which the Buddha achieved enlightenment
Bodhidharma:	a fifth- to sixth-century Buddhist monk thought to be the first transmitter of Zen Buddhism
The Book of Elixir:	an ancient Chinese text
Cultural Revolution:	the "Great Proletarian Cultural Revolution," launched by Mao Zedong in 1966 to eliminate vestiges of traditional Chinese culture and turn China into a modern Socialist state
Daoists:	or Taoists, practitioners of Daoism, a religious/philosophical system developed by Lao-tzu and Chuang-tzu in the sixth century BCE
Darwin:	Charles Darwin, a nineteenth-century British naturalist whose name has become synonymous with the theory of evolution
Great Law:	that is, the Great Law of Buddhism
karma:	the notion that the effects of a person's actions determine his destiny in his next incarnation
Lei Feng:	a young soldier in the Chinese army; after his death in 1962, the Communist Party used his image and story as a propaganda tool to inspire youths to serve the party.
Maoist:	pertaining to Mao Zedong, the leader of Chinese Communism until his death in 1976
Patriarch:	any leader of Zen Buddhism
qi:	the active life principle in a person's body
Shakyamuni:	Siddhartha Gautama, the historical Buddha
Tathagata:	the name the historical Buddha, Siddhartha Gautama, used in referring to himself
Zen Buddhism:	a school of Mahayana Buddhism that believes that enlightenment can come through meditation and intuition rather than faith

Soviet authorities break up a demonstration of Jewish refuseniks in front of the
Ministry of Internal Affairs for the right to make aliyah, January 10, 1973.

"The grandeur of God is rarely compromised by the hunger to see or by the need to capture God in human language. And yet, God's nearness and compassion are sensually asserted."

Overview

The Sacred Cluster (1995) is a mission statement for Conservative Judaism written by Ismar Schorsch, the Rabbi Herman Abramovitz Professor of Jewish History and sixth chancellor of New York City's Jewish Theological Seminary, with the latter post recognized as the highest academic and rabbinic position within the Conservative movement. The text identifies seven distinct issues as constituting the core of the movement's identity. Schorsch emphasizes that they reflect not so much an abstract theological system, but rather the ideals and practices of a living community. Thus, they include issues of a theological nature but also, and perhaps primarily, issues bearing on social life. The seven issues are the importance of the relationship of the American Conservative Jews with the State of Israel; the place of the Hebrew language in Jewish life; the relationship of the individual Jew to Jews in general; the role of the sacred book of the Torah—the five books of Moses (also called the Pentateuch), the first part of the Hebrew Bible—in reshaping Jewish life; the way the Torah should be studied; the authority of religious law, halakha, in everyday life; and, finally, the idea the Conservative movement forms about God.

The need for a clear, public Conservative mission statement became more and more pressing during the last three decades of the twentieth century, because of particular internal and external challenges and changes to the movement from the end of the 1960s onward. Aiming to recoup its status as the most attractive option for religious Jewry in North America while at the same time to also support particular trends within the movement, many Conservative leaders felt the need to offer an articulate and up-to-date programmatic agenda, one that would succeed in pairing modernism with respect for tradition. While the text contains the ideas and values of one particular leader of the movement, it can certainly be viewed as representative of the more conservative mainstream of the Conservative movement as well. It seeks to represent every element that differentiates the movement from the Orthodox and Reform, or Reconstructionist, Jewish worlds. While it was written at the end of the twentieth century, it reiterates almost all the major points of a much earlier program written by the rabbi and scholar Louis Finkelstein in 1927, "The Things That Unite Us."

In fact, The Sacred Cluster, subtitled The Core Values of Conservative Judaism, was not the first attempt at a description of what Conservative Judaism was and was not at the end of the twentieth century. It was preceded by Emet Ve-Emunah: Statement of Principles of Conservative Judaism, a mission statement, titled with the Hebrew words for "Truth and Faith," that was drafted in 1988 by a very large board of Conservative leaders. This statement, precisely on account of being inclusive, was deemed excessively general and noncommittal regarding some very controversial issues, and more specificity was called for. The Sacred Cluster avoids the pitfalls of excessive inclusiveness and generalization, indicating, at least in the short run, the success of the more conservative constituency within the movement. However, the early twenty-first century witnessed violent debates within the Jewish Theological Seminary around the issue of the role of homosexuals within the leadership, with Schorsch being one of the most prominent leaders to take a conservative stance against the ordination of gays. But when Schorsch ended his chancellorship in 2006, the more liberal position of the other, by-and-large younger leadership was ultimately accepted, essentially marking the end of the conservative stream of Conservative Judaism.

Context

The writing of The Sacred Cluster was spurred by the social, ideological, and political changes that affected the Conservative Jewish movement from the 1950s onward in the United States. The most important of these social changes were the growth of intermarriage among members of the movement, the rift caused by the violent disagreement over women's roles among the leadership of the movement, the somewhat similar issue of openly homosexual members' eligibility for rabbinic positions, the decline of the movement's appeal to Jewish youth, and the related phenomenon of the shrinking number of synagogues belonging to the movement. These changes were accompanied by the unexpected revival of Orthodox Jewry beginning in the 1970s in North America. A very important ideological change within the Conservative movement was the leadership's growing acceptance of political Zionism, the basic objective of which had been to achieve statehood in Palestine for Jews. Earlier leaders of the Jewish Theological Seminary—such as Solomon Schechter (president from 1902 to 1915) and Louis Finkelstein (chancellor from 1940 to 1972)—endorsed religious and cultural Zionism but opposed political Zionism, even during the years of World War II, when the bulk of the movement's membership was already attuned to that mode of Zionism. This gap between the membership and leadership of the Jewish Theological Seminary diminished with time, and later chancellors, especially Schorsch, began to fully support political Zionism.

Support for political Zionism was not restricted to the Conservative American Jews; from the end of the 1960s, the American government's stance on the Near East also took a dramatic change. In 1966, Mossad, the Israeli secret service, obtained from Iraq a Soviet-produced MiG-21 fighting plane, which was then unfamiliar to Western powers and as such the object of much curiosity in the United States. Since at the time U.S. diplomacy was not particularly supportive of Israel, the Israelis' offering of the captured MiG-21 to the United States came as a surprise. The following year, in June 1967, the Israeli army achieved a stunning victory over the armies of Egypt, Syria, Jordan, and Iraq in the Six-Day War, leading American foreign policy to tilt toward support for Israel. By the early 1970s, the United States had become a vocal supporter of Israel and as such of political Zionism.

The success of women's rights groups in the larger American social context led to feminist concerns within the Conservative movement during the second half of the twentieth century. Already in the 1950s some steps were taken to actively defend women's rights, such as the 1954 decision by Saul Lieberman, a highly distinguished professor of the Jewish Theological Seminary and one of the most important Talmudic scholars of the modern era, aimed at coercing recalcitrant husbands to give their wives divorces. According to tradition, only the husband, never the wife, could give a *get*, the divorce document, thus making divorce the prerogative of men. In 1972 a small group of female intellectuals called Ezrat Nashim (or "Women's Section," referring to the section reserved for and restricted to women in Orthodox synagogues) published an influential petition called "Jewish Women Call for Change," which asked for complete equality with men within the movement,

Time Line	
November 3, 1935	■ Ismar Schorsch is born in Hannover, Germany.
1950	■ The Committee on Jewish Law and Standards rules it permissible to drive to the synagogue on the Sabbath (Saturday), the holy day in Judaism when traditionally no "work" is allowed.
1954	■ The important Talmudic scholar Saul Lieberman empowers a new joint rabbinic court of the Rabbinic Assembly of the Conservative movement and Jewish Theological Seminary to force recalcitrant husbands to allow their wives a *get*, the divorce document.
1962	■ Schorsch is ordained as a rabbi.
1966	■ The American-Israeli relationship becomes warmer following Mossad's unexpected offering of a Soviet MiG-21 jet fighter to the U.S. government.
June 1967	■ After the Israeli victory over Egypt, Syria, Jordan, and Iraq in the Six-Day War, American foreign policy and most Conservative Jews become supportive of political Zionism.
1972	■ Ezrat Nashim make public their petition "Jewish Women Call for Change," demanding a greater role for women from the Rabbinical Assembly.
1974	■ The Committee on Jewish Law and Standards makes the decision to count women in the minyan.
1983	■ Following the death of Lieberman, the decision is taken that women can be ordained as rabbis. Several rabbis disagree with the decision and leave the movement.
1986	■ Schorsch becomes the sixth chancellor of the Jewish Theological Seminary.

1987	■ Schorsch admits women into the Conservative cantorial schools.
1988	■ *Emet Ve-Emunah: Statement of Principles of Conservative Judaism,* written by twenty-five rabbis, is published.
1995	■ Schorsch publishes *The Sacred Cluster: The Core Values of Conservative Judaism.*
2006	■ Schorsch's chancellorship at the seminary ends.
2007	■ Schorsch publishes *Canon without Closure,* a diverse collection of Torah commentaries written during his chancellorship.

including the rights for women to initiate divorce, to be counted as witnesses, and to fully participate in religious observances, such as being counted into a minyan, the quorum of ten necessary for public prayer. Even though the group was not allowed to directly address the Rabbinical Assembly, the official legislative body of the Conservative movement, their petition was published by the *New York Times* and was well received. The groups' demands were gradually met—for example, women could be counted in a minyan beginning in 1974—and in 1983, following the death of Lieberman, who was adamantly opposed to women's ordination, women were finally admitted to rabbinical and cantorial schools at the New York City seminary. The decision, however, was not met with the full approval of the leadership, and three rabbis, including the Holocaust survivor and author David Weiss Halivni, left the movement on account of it.

About the Author

Ismar Schorsch was born in 1935 in Hannover, Germany, into an upper-middle-class rabbinic family, his father being a well-known and respected rabbi. Schorsch's immediate family left Germany in the last years of the 1930s, when emigration was still an option for Jewish families, and settled in the United States. From early on, Schorsch had a keen interest in history and rabbinic studies, and he became a devoted student, excelling especially in the humanities. He received his undergraduate diploma from Pennsylvania's Ursinus College in 1957, was ordained in 1962, and completed his doctorate in Jewish history at Columbia University in 1969.

Schorsch's interests turned to unaffiliated and persecuted Jews, and his conviction that faith and scholarship

could bring solutions to human problems encouraged him to create in 1991 the academic Project Judaica in Moscow, a joint effort between the Jewish Theological Seminary and the Russian State University for the Humanities. The objective of the program was to help create a new Jewish intelligentsia, to reestablish the academic study of Judaism, and to reinvigorate Jewish life in Russia in general. As an acknowledgment of his work, Schorsch received an honorary degree from the Russian State University for the Humanities in 1998.

While thus engaged in Russia, he also wrote *The Sacred Cluster* in 1995, a mission statement for the movement that met with acclaim. At the same time, he became interested in and committed to contributing to the educational system of Jews in America. He helped establish at the seminary the Solomon Schechter High School of New York in 1992 and the William Davidson Graduate School of Jewish Education in 1996.

Schorsch's interest in the political fate of the State of Israel and his prestige within the Conservative Jewish movement earned him an invitation by President Bill Clinton to be part of the official presidential delegation to witness the signing of the peace treaty between Jordan and Israel in October 1994. His position on the Israeli-Palestinian conflict can be construed as clearly Zionist; for example, he considered the territorial gains accrued during the successful Israeli wars with the neighboring Arab nations as legitimate extensions of the existence of the State of Israel. However, he was not against the idea of mutual compromises and negotiations with the Arab world, and he held out hope for a peaceful solution to the conflict. During and after the end of his chancellorship he continued to publish, including *Polarities in Balance* (2004), a two-volume collection of articles and essays that he wrote while chancellor, and *Canon without Closure* (2007), a collection of Torah commentaries also written during his chancellorship.

Explanation and Analysis of the Document

The present text is the full text of *The Sacred Cluster*. It concentrates on seven very specific issues that constitute in Schorsch's estimation the heart of the Conservative movement. These issues are of an intellectual as well as religious/cultural nature, drawing heavily on tradition while also transforming it. Overall, this writing is intended to offer an ideal description of what the Conservative movement should strive to be.

♦ "The Centrality of Modern Israel"
The first core value that Schorsch describes is that of Zionism. He claims that all Conservative Jews feel a special connectedness to the State of Israel, but they are also affected by anti-Semitism, which then affects their ability to fully identify with their home country—to feel a "sense of at-homeness" in the diaspora, as he puts it. He hints at the possibility that anti-Semitism in America might still be at least a theoretical problem, which likewise prevents

American Jews from fully identifying with their diasporic home. This testifies to profound changes that took place in the Conservative movement in the second half of the twentieth century, especially following the Six-Day War in 1967. After the Israeli victory, there was a much deeper identification with political Zionism and, consequently, a strong willingness to support the State of Israel in both financial and political ways. While the earlier leadership of the Conservative movement was dedicated to the idea of being American—in fact, the Jewish Theological Seminary was founded to help Jewish immigrants assimilate and become American while maintaining their Jewish identity and tradition—with time, perceptions about Americanization and Zionism changed.

While the religious and cultural facets of Zionism were always on the horizon of the movement, they did not take a political hue, as the approaches of previous Conservative leaders, such as Finkelstein or Mordecai Kaplan, the founder of Reconstructionism, show. Those leaders believed in the necessity of a strong Jewish cultural presence within the land of Israel without it assuming a political character such as a state; they thought that Jews should live in the land of Israel or participate and build a culturally and religiously Jewish entity, which would yet never become a state. (It should be noted that by 2010, the Zionism of both the leadership and the constituency of the Conservative movement was more inclusive of leftist views than it had been even a decade earlier.) The intellectual gesture of identifying politics as the most important issue for the Conservative movement is emblematic of the movement's engagement with matters beyond those traditionally deemed religious.

Schorsch asserts that the Conservative movement's Zionism does not question the legitimacy of the diaspora, especially since, according to him, the positive interdependence of Jewish identity and Judaism exists only outside the State of Israel. This is held to be so partly because in the modern State of Israel, the educational system's secular character deprives most people of a meaningful encounter with Judaism, so that consequently Israeli identity is not enriched or informed by Judaism. Although he does not specify as much here, he hints at the fact that the other reason for the Israeli failure to be more welcoming to Conservative Judaism is the hegemony of the Orthodox establishment. During his chancellorship, Schorsch more than once articulated his view on this point, advocating for religious equality for all Jews in Israel regardless of denomination.

♦ "Hebrew: The Irreplaceable Language of Jewish Expression"

The second core value cited by Schorsch is the centrality of the Hebrew language. He holds that it is intrinsically bound up with and is part of Judaism, since all the sacred texts of Judaism are revealed—at least partially—in the medium of classical, or Mishnaic-Talmudic, Hebrew. He insists that Hebrew literacy should remain a main objective of the Conservative movement. He employs the inspiring example of the German rabbi Zacharias Frankel, the intellectual and spiritual father of Conservative Judaism, who broke with Reform Judaism in 1854 over the latter's decision to discard the Hebrew liturgy. Schorsch supplies evidence of his movement's efforts to maintain and spread Hebrew literacy during the latter part of the twentieth century: The official language of the Jewish Theological Seminary's Teachers Institute is Hebrew. The Ramah summer camps, found in locations across North America and in Israel, insist on the usage of Hebrew on a daily basis. The liturgy's language is overwhelmingly Hebrew. And the Solomon Schechter day schools—a pride of the elementary educational system of the Conservative movement—are particularly invested in excellence in Hebrew. This list needs to be offered with a caveat: The Teachers Institute's original academic program has changed with time, in that, contrary to the aims of the founding dean Mordecai Kaplan, the institution today offers a broad liberal arts education that does not necessarily aim at training Jewish intelligentsia or Jewish communal leaders. Consequently, the official language of the school, now known as the Albert A. List College of Jewish Studies, is no longer Hebrew.

Schorsch's conviction about the centrality of this issue is well illustrated by his bold statement that the spread of Hebrew literacy would serve the objectives of Zionism better than anything else. The fact that he views the World Zionist Organization's objectives and the spread of the Hebrew language as interrelated is an example of how political Zionism and cultural Zionism go hand in hand in his thinking.

♦ "Devotion to the Ideal of Klal Yisrael"

Schorsch's interpretation of *klal yisrael*—the collectivity of all Jews—is in line with Solomon Schechter's interpretation of the term. The original idea of *klal yisrael* appears in the late antique text Pirke Avot, which is one of the most well-known parts of the Mishnah and which serves as the best "reference book" to the worldview and culture of fourth- and fifth-century rabbis. Schechter coined the term "Catholic Israel" to convey that the Jewish people are the ultimate source of authority regarding which religious laws should be regarded as eternally binding and which as temporary. Though this definition voices an old principle within religious law, given Schechter's views and position within the Conservative movement—especially his leniency concerning the mutability of religious law—his definition was clearly meant to oppose Orthodox Judaism's stance on how religious law should be observed. In Schechter's mind, Orthodox Judaism disregarded social change, whereas Conservative Judaism succeeded in striking the right balance between being faithful to tradition and applying it to the world in its current circumstances. While in Schechter's formulation the term *klal yisrael* is intricately linked both to the Conservative movement's stance on religious law and its belief in the importance of unity between Jews, as it is understood by Schorsch, it evokes the national character and unity among Jews in general.

◆ "The Defining Role of Torah in the Reshaping of Judaism"

Schorsch next discusses the role of the Torah in the reshaping of modern Judaism, and in these paragraphs he continues to fundamentally distinguish the theological beliefs of his movement from those of Orthodoxy. The traditionally cherished triad of Torah–synagogue–learning (whereby the practices of reading the Torah, attending synagogue, and learning Jewish traditions reinforce one another) continues, according to Schorsch, to occupy a central position in the Conservative practice. He admits, however, that the way Torah study is actualized in his movement is less than ideal. He sees the root of the problem in the practice of the triennial system of reading the Torah, which divides the reading of the entire text into weekly portions in such a way that it takes three years to finish it. Since the liturgical year, which governs the dates of the festivals, is based on the tradition of finishing the reading of the Torah in just one year, the difference between the two systems results in discrepancies between the weekly and yearly celebrations of sacred moments. This renders the festival of Simchas (or Simkhat) Torah, that of the finishing of the reading of the Torah, in particular somewhat contradictory.

Schorsch also deplores the widespread practice of reading only a small part of the actual weekly Torah portion, and he advocates a change in the liturgy to enable people to fully access the sacred texts. Schorsch spells out his views on the nature of the authorship of the Torah, which, according to him, while not divine, is still sacred. The distinction is crucial for him, and it serves as a watershed between the Conservative movement and Orthodoxy. His denial of divine authorship is not absolute, as he allows for divine participation in the creation of the Torah, but he ascribes the bulk of it to human effort. The sanctity, as he explains, of this mainly human product stems from the ancient and continuous esteem in which Jews throughout history have held it, as well as from its having generated so many other sacred texts within Judaism. It is interesting to see how well the previously mentioned idea of the power of the collectivity of the Jewish people harmonizes with this idea of sacred but not divine authorship of the Torah. Highlighting at every juncture the crucial points on which his movement differs from Orthodox Judaism, Schorsch concludes his outline of the place of the Torah in the modern Conservative movement by claiming sacred and foundational status for it.

◆ "The Study of Torah"

Following the discussion concerning the role of the Torah in reshaping modern Judaism, Schorsch sets out to define the value of Torah study, the fifth of his core values. The distinction between the two is clear: Whereas the issue of the role of the Torah in reshaping modern Judaism touches upon its liturgical usage, the study of the Torah is an interpretive activity based on the text of the Torah.

In Schorsch's analysis, Conservative Jewry gives a primary place to the study of the Torah and the Talmud, the late antique and early medieval commentary on the Mishnah, with the movement's major contribution being its promotion of modern critical scholarship. By applying all available scholarship and academic methods to the sacred texts and by reading contextually and thus broadening the range of questions one can ask concerning the texts, one can enrich one's religious experience, since the texts will yield new, as-yet unknown meanings. Like the idea of the nondivine Torah, this idea is also in well-known contrast to Orthodox views—although there is more variety concerning the use of critical methods in Orthodoxy than there used to be, and this seems to be a continuing development. Aware, on one hand, of this tension between the positions of contemporary denominations and, on the other, of the staggering erudition and intense labor that went into creating and shaping the traditional texts, Schorsch emphasizes that the Conservative approach in no way denies or questions the merit of the premodern approach to Torah study. On the contrary, it sees an intellectual and spiritual continuum between the endeavors of premodern Jewish commentators and the work of latter-day Conservative interpreters.

◆ "The Governance of Jewish Life by Halakha"

The sixth core value is the place halakha, or halacha (religious law), should occupy in the life of a Jew. Yet again, this issue is one that clearly distinguishes the different stances of Orthodox and Conservative Judaism on issues of religious law. Schorsch identifies three areas where he sees the beneficial impact of halakha: in the focusing and harnessing of human energy, in the shaping of human community, and in the shaping and creating of times and places where the presence of the divine can be discernible for humans. Schorsch identifies the holy day of Sabbath as unifying all of these three areas.

While Schorsch's position on the importance of halakha is clear, he also acknowledges the challenges created by the presence of these laws, in particular, the constant tension between the demands of very ancient laws and the demands of a larger contemporary world in which Jews and non-Jews live side by side with equal rights. Since he sees halakha as the optimal means for balancing these contradictory demands, he opts for a Jewish life in which constant negotiation between the two takes place. Because both sets of demands are regarded as legitimate, both must be subject to consideration and compromise. Such a position is obviously at odds with the stance of the Orthodox world and in line with the Conservative movement's traditional position. There is a long and consistent Conservative path leading to Schorsch's take on the subject; in 1950, for example, the Committee on Jewish Law and Standards decided that it is halakhically acceptable to ride to the synagogue on Sabbath. This decision was clearly influenced by the acceptance of the reality of urban and suburban life, where synagogues might be far from homes.

◆ "Belief in God"

The last core value on Schorsch's list is what he identifies as the central aspect of the religious enterprise: God. Schorsch pronounces the Jewish experience of revelation

"For Conservative Jews, as for their ancestors, Israel is not only the birthplace of the Jewish people, but also its final destiny."

(Section 1)

"[Hebrew] was never merely a vehicle of communication, but part of the fabric and texture of Judaism. Words vibrate with religious meaning, moral values, and literary associations. Torah and Hebrew are inseparable and Jewish education was always predicated on mastering Hebrew. Hebrew literacy is the key to Judaism."

(Section 1)

"For Conservative Jews, the Torah is no less sacred, if less central, than it was for their pre-modern ancestors. I use the word "sacred" advisedly. The Torah is the foundation text of Judaism, the apex of an inverted pyramid of infinite commentary, not because it is divine, but because it is sacred, that is, adopted by the Jewish people as its spiritual font."

(Section 1)

"Collectively, the injunctions of Jewish law articulate Judaism's deep-seated sense of covenant, a partnership with the divine to finish the task of creation."

(Section 1)

"For Judaism, then, God is a felt presence rather than a visible form, a voice rather than a vision. Revelation tends to be an auditory and not a visual experience. The grandeur of God is rarely compromised by the hunger to see or by the need to capture God in human language. And yet, God's nearness and compassion are sensually asserted."

(Section 1)

"Jewish tradition continues unbroken in Conservative Judaism, where yearning for God wells up primarily not from reason or revelation but from the blood-soaked, value-laden, and textually rooted historical experience of the Jewish people."

(Section 1)

as restricted in nature in the sense that, while revelation of God's presence definitely occurs and is documented in its sacred texts, it is always described as partial, invisible, and auditory. God, according to Schorsch, is portrayed as both nearby and remote. He believes that these characteristics are best expressed in the *berakhah* ("blessing") of the *pesukei de-zimra*, the psalms that are chanted during the morning service, by the constant usage of verbs instead of nouns in the text that is supposed to describe God. To balance this portrayal of a God that might be called remote, Schorsch also asserts that God is compassionate to all beings, Jews and non-Jews alike.

Schorsch finishes his essay on a very optimistic note when he expresses his belief that the Ramah summer camps embody and exemplify the simultaneous existence of all seven core values. It is noteworthy that while Schorsch does not consider the Torah to be divinely authored, he definitely thinks that it documents divine revelation and expresses the essence of God. By pronouncing God to be the central figure of Conservative Judaism while at the same time refusing to believe in the divine authorship of the Torah, he strikes a subtle theological balance.

Audience

The target audience of *The Sacred Cluster* was first and foremost American Jews who were susceptible to being interested in Conservative Judaism either because they were on the left side of Orthodoxy or on the more conservative and halakhically minded side of Reform Judaism. However, the statement was not intended only for those who were outside the fold; it was written just as well for the Conservative constituency, a constituency that felt in need of guidance on account of the challenge brought by a suddenly resurfacing, vigorous Orthodoxy and which also felt the transformative experiences of the mid- to late-twentieth century. That era proved to be a trying period on account of both the oppression, persecution, and genocide of the Holocaust and the attractive assimilative power of contemporary Western values. *The Sacred Cluster* was not the first Conservative attempt at a mission statement offering guidance in the last decades of the century, and its precursor, *Emet Ve-Emunah* deserves to be remembered as well.

Impact

The Sacred Cluster was well received as a Conservative mission statement for its optimism, the prestige of its author, and the clarity of its message. However, *The Sacred Cluster* does not mention some extremely important issues, which resulted in a prolonged, controversial, and very emotional debate within the movement that began while Schorsch was still chancellor and did not end until after he stepped down. Schorsch's silence has spoken volumes regarding his position on these issues—and

the fact that his successor took a diametrically opposing stance on them indicates that Schorsch's influence was not perceived as positive.

During the last two decades of the twentieth century, the issue of gay ordination and the related twin issues of same-sex marriage and homosexual intercourse received particular interest and attention among both the leadership and the rank and file of the Conservative movement. Opinions about these issues differed greatly. During the 2006 vote, Rabbis Joel Roth and Leonard Levy, prominent members of the Rabbinical Assembly, maintained that homosexual intercourse could not be sanctioned by halakha (that is, according to Jewish religious law). The ultimate ruling by the Committee on Jewish Law and Standards allowed for both same-sex marriage and gay ordination, but it stopped short at ruling homosexual intercourse as sanctioned. Ismar Schorsch's view on this issue was well known and considered conservative, certainly among students of the Jewish Theological Seminary. He believed that ordaining homosexuals would only alienate the more conservative and older members, who then, he feared, would join the ranks of the modern Orthodox. He also argued that the numbers of more liberal Jews who would be attracted to the Conservative movement by a more tolerant stance on homosexuality would be negligible, because the supporters of such a liberal ruling demonstrated loyalties that lay more with the Reform movement in any case.

It is interesting to note that the dean of the Ziegler School of Rabbinic Studies of the American Jewish University—the West Coast equivalent of the Jewish Theological Seminary, located in Los Angeles—Rabbi Bradley Shavit Artson, held a completely different view on the subject. Artson was not only a supporter of the rights of gay people within Judaism but also was, in fact, the person who wrote a *tsuvah* ("responsum," a type of religious legislation that interprets biblical law) about it in 1992, proposing a radical shift in perspective, according to which both homosexual partnership and sexual practice would be halakhically acceptable, and thus the ordination of homosexuals would be a nonissue. While Artson's *tsuvah* was rejected in 1992, a later one adopted in 2006 included most of the same propositions. The 2006 vote bore the trademark of a generational leadership change, in that Rabbi Arnold Eisen, the newly elected chancellor of the Jewish Theological Seminary, was well known for his liberal views. The very fact of his appointment to head the seminary was a clear sign of a much broader change within the movement.

Further Reading

■ Books

Eisen, Arnold M. *Rethinking Modern Judaism: Ritual, Commandment, Community.* Chicago: University of Chicago Press, 1998.

Feinstein, Edward, ed. *Jews and Judaism in the 21st Century: Human Responsibility, the Presence of God and the Future of the Covenant*. Woodstock, Vt.: Jewish Lights, 2007.

Fishman, Sylvia Barack. *A Breath of Life: Feminism in the American Jewish Community*. Boston: Brandeis University Press, 1993.

Medding, Peter Y., ed. *Studies in Contemporary Jewry*, Vol. 5: *Israel: State and Society, 1948–1988*. New York: Oxford University Press, 1989.

Medding, Peter Y., ed. *Studies in Contemporary Jewry*, Vol. 8: *A New Jewry? America since the Second World War*. New York: Oxford University Press, 1992.

■ Journals

Eisen, Arnold M., ed. *The Problem of Judaism in America: In Commemoration of the 350th Anniversary of Jewish Settlement in North America*. Special issue, *Conservative Judaism Journal* 56 (2004).

Schorsch, Ismar. "Schechter's Seminary: Polarities in Balance." *Conservative Judaism* 55, no. 2 (Winter 2003): 3–23.

—*Commentary by Agnes Veto*

Questions for Further Study

1. *The Sacred Cluster* bears obvious comparison with the Pittsburgh Platform, the statement issued by Reform Jews in 1885. What opposing views do the two documents express with regard to Judaism?

2. Describe the complex relationship between American Judaism and Zionism. Why do you think Zionism has been appealing to Conservative Jews in particular?

3. *The Sacred Cluster* could be regarded, at least in part, as a document originating in geopolitical circumstances. What were those circumstances, and how did they have an impact on Schorsch's thinking?

4. A question that has often been discussed is whether Judaism is just a religion or an ethnic identity, a cultural identity, or a nationality—or some combination of them. How do you think Schorsch would answer that question?

5. The Hebrew language and Judaism have historically been closely intertwined. For centuries, Latin and Christianity were similarly intertwined, yet Christianity has essentially abandoned Latin (with the notable exception of certain documents issued by the pope as leader of the Catholic Church). How are the two situations different? Why do many Jews want to retain Hebrew (when Jews are scattered around the world and speak many languages) while Christianity gave up on Latin and few Christians miss it? For reference, see the entry on Vatican II.

THE SACRED CLUSTER: DOCUMENT TEXT

1995 CE

—Ismar Schorsch

If dogmas or doctrines are the propositional language of a theological system, core values are the felt commitments of lived religion, the refraction of what people practice and profess. To identify them calls for keen observation as well as theoretical analysis. Conservative Judaism is best understood as a sacred cluster of core values. No single propositional statement comes close to identifying its center of gravity. Nor does Conservative Judaism occupy the center of the contemporary religious spectrum because it is an arbitrary and facile composite of what may be found on the left or the right. On the contrary, its location flows from an organic and coherent world view best captured in terms of core values of relatively equal worth.

There are seven such core values, to my mind, that imprint Conservative Judaism with a principled receptivity to modernity balanced by a deep reverence for tradition. Whereas other movements in modern Judaism rest on a single tenet, such as the autonomy of the individual or the inclusiveness of God's revelation at Sinai (*Torah mi-Sinai*), Conservative Judaism manifests a kaleidoscopic cluster of discrete and unprioritized core values. Conceptually they fall into two sets—three national and three religious—which are grounded and joined to each other by the overarching presence of God, who represents the seventh and ultimate core value. The dual nature of Judaism as polity and piety, a world religion that never transcended its national origins, is unified by God. In sum, a total of seven core values corresponding to the most basic number in Judaism's construction of reality.

The Centrality of Modern Israel

The centrality of modern Israel heads our list of core values. For Conservative Jews, as for their ancestors, Israel is not only the birthplace of the Jewish people, but also its final destiny. Sacred texts, historical experience, and liturgical memory have conspired to make it for them, in the words of Ezekiel, "the most

desirable of all lands (20:6)." Its welfare is never out of mind. Conservative Jews are the backbone of Federation leadership in North America and the major source of its annual campaign. They visit Israel, send their children over a summer or for a year, and support financially every one of its worthy institutions. (1) Israeli accomplishments on the battlefield and in the laboratory, in literature and politics, fill them with pride. Their life is a dialectic between homeland and exile. No matter how prosperous or assimilated, they betray an existential angst about anti-Semitism that denies them a complete sense of at-homeness anywhere in the diaspora.

And their behavior reflects the dominant thrust of Conservative Judaism not to denationalize Judaism. Even in the era of emancipation, Zion remained the goal, as it was for the Torah, an arena in which to translate monotheism into social justice. A world governed by realpolitik needed a polity of a different order. The liturgy of the Conservative synagogue preserved the full text of the daily amida (the silent devotion) with its frequent pleas for the restoration of Zion. Heinrich Graetz, who taught at the Movement's rabbinical seminary in Breslau and authored the most nationalistic history of the Jews ever written, inspired Moses Hess to pen one of the earliest Zionist tracts in 1862 and would not write of the biblical period until he had personally visited Palestine in early 1872. During the last two decades, well over one hundred Conservative rabbis have made aliyah, often at the cost of professional satisfaction, attesting not only to movement ideology, but personal courage.

This is not to say that Conservative Judaism divests the diaspora of all spiritual value or demands of all Jews to settle in Israel. Ironically, the state of Judaism is far healthier outside the Jewish state, where Judaism is indispensable for a resilient Jewish identity. Most Israelis have sadly been severed from any meaningful contact with Judaism by the absence of religious alternatives and by the erosion of sacred Jewish content in the secular school system where 75% of Israel's Jewish children are educated. And yet, the miracle and mystery of Israel's restoration after two millennia out of the ashes of the Holocaust continues to overwhelm Conservative Jews with radical amazement and deep joy.

Hebrew: The Irreplaceable Language of Jewish Expression

Hebrew as the irreplaceable language of Jewish expression is the second core value of Conservative Judaism. Its existence is coterminous with that of the Jewish people and the many layers of the language mirror the cultures in which Jews perpetuated Judaism. It was never merely a vehicle of communication, but part of the fabric and texture of Judaism. Words vibrate with religious meaning, moral values, and literary associations. Torah and Hebrew are inseparable and Jewish education was always predicated on mastering Hebrew. Hebrew literacy is the key to Judaism, to joining the unending dialectic between sacred texts, between Jews of different ages, between God and Israel. To know Judaism only in translation is, to quote Bialik, akin to kissing the bride through the veil.

These are some of the sentiments which prompted Zacharias Frankel, the founder of Conservative Judaism in central Europe, to break with Reform over the issue of Hebrew at the Frankfurt Rabbinical Conference in 1845. Despite the leniency of Jewish law, he was not prepared to endorse a resolution which would acknowledge that synagogue services could theoretically dispense with Hebrew. Given the rapid shrinkage of Judaism with the advent of emancipation, the fostering of Hebrew for Frankel became a symbol of historical continuity and national unity. Much of his scholarly oeuvre was intentionally written in Hebrew. And the language has remained at the heart of the Conservative agenda ever since.

Hebrew became the language of instruction of JTS's Teachers Institute not too long after its opening in 1909, as well as the language of daily conversation in the Ramah summer camps which it launched in the late 1940s. The Conservative synagogue never expunged Hebrew from the liturgy, and its supplementary Hebrew school, despite the constraints of a very pared-down curriculum, never gave up the struggle to teach a modicum of Hebrew literacy to the young. If anything, the Solomon Schechter day schools of the movement, an achievement of the past two decades, excel in the teaching of Hebrew language.

The revival of Hebrew in the last century-and-a-half, that is *Hebrew Reborn* as Sholom Spiegel put it in the title of his celebratory book of 1930, is as singular a feat as the creation of the Jewish state. Hebrew has been wholly transformed from an unwieldy classical medium of liturgy and learning into a modern Western language fit for the sciences and sensibilities of secular society. Diaspora Jews can little afford to remain deaf to the sounds of Hebrew as they can ignore the fate of the Jewish state.

In a Jewish world of sundry and proliferating divisions, Hebrew must emerge as the common and unifying language of the Jewish people, and nothing would advance that vision more effectively than to redefine Zionism today solely in terms of the ability to speak Hebrew. To restructure the World Zionist Organization by earmarking all of its budget to the intensive teaching of Hebrew to diaspora Jews would create many more Zionists (that is, Jews who appreciate the centrality of Israel) than all the atavistic politics of the current Zionist establishment. The natural bonds of language and culture bind more firmly than those of abstruse ideological constructs.

I offer as example the young Mordecai Kaplan, then dean of the Teachers Institute, struggling to perfect his command of Hebrew to the point where he could preside over its faculty meetings and public events in Hebrew. In the 1920s he made the following poignant entry in his diary:

"Here is another failure I have to register against myself. Due to the lack of energy necessary to train myself to speak and write Hebrew with ease, I am afraid to venture on those occasions to give an address in Hebrew."

Of such failures, the fabric of Jewish unity is sewn!

Devotion to the Ideal of Klal Yisrael

The third core value is an undiminished devotion to the ideal of klal yisrael, the unfractured totality of Jewish existence and the ultimate significance of every single Jew. In the consciousness of Conservative Jews, there yet resonates the affirmation of haverim kol yisrael (all Israel is still joined in fellowship)—despite all the dispersion, dichotomies and politicization that history has visited upon us, Jews remain united in a tenacious pilgrimage of universal import. It is that residue of Jewish solidarity that makes Conservative Jews the least sectarian or parochial members of the community, that renders them the ideal donor of Federation campaigns and brings them to support unstintingly every worthy cause in Jewish life. Often communal needs will prompt them to compromise the needs of the Movement.

Such admirable commitment to the welfare of the whole does not spring from any special measure of ethnicity, as is so often ascribed to Conservative Jews. Rather, I would argue that it is nurtured by the acute historical sense cultivated by their leadership. In opposition to exclusively rational, moral or halahkic criteria for change, Conservative Judaism embraced a historical romanticism that rooted tradition in the normative power of a heroic past. To be sure, history infused an awareness of the richness and diversity of the Jewish experience. But it also presumed to identify a normative Judaism and invest it with the sanctity of antiquity. It is that mixture of critical breadth and romantic reverence that imbued men like Frankel, Graetz, Schechter, Kaplan, and Louis Finkelstein with the love of klal yisrael. And, fortunately, they all commanded the literary gifts to disseminate and popularize their views.

The Defining Role of Torah in the Reshaping of Judaism

The fourth core value is the defining role of Torah in the reshaping of Judaism after the loss of political sovereignty in 63 B.C.E. and the Second Temple in 70 C.E. to the Romans. In their stead, the rabbis fashioned the Torah into a portable homeland, the synagogue into a national theater for religious drama, and study into a form of worship. Conservative Judaism never repudiated any of these remarkable transformations. Chanting the Torah each Shabbat is still the centerpiece of the Conservative service, even if all too often it is lamentably done according to the triennial cycle and then without liturgical aplomb. Though historically defensible, the cycle makes a sham of Simhat Torah, even as it suggests the decline of Torah in our lives.

More substantively, the cycle misses a precious chance to reinvigorate Shabbat. As the rhythm of the Jewish week is to be set by Shabbat, so should the content of individual home study be informed by the weekly Torah portion. Conservative Jews increasingly evince a hunger for access to holy texts. To restore the reading of the entire parasha each Shabbat, to train a cadre of congregants, both young and old, to become proficient Torah readers, and to help congregants in studying the parasha prior to Shabbat would

create a *kahal kadosh*, a holy community, joined by a sacred calendar and text. Jews would then come to the synagogue on Shabbat morning prepared and primed to listen to the Torah reading, to recapture a touch of the numinous of the Sinai experience which, at best, it is designed to reenact.

For Conservative Jews, the Torah is no less sacred, if less central, than it was for their pre-modern ancestors. I use the word "sacred" advisedly. The Torah is the foundation text of Judaism, the apex of an inverted pyramid of infinite commentary, not because it is divine, but because it is sacred, that is, adopted by the Jewish people as its spiritual font. The term skirts the divisive and futile question of origins, the fetid swamp of heresy. The sense of individual obligation, of being commanded, does not derive from divine authorship, but communal consent. The Written Torah, no less than the Oral Torah, reverberates with the divine-human encounter, with "a minimum of revelation and a maximum of interpretation." It is no longer possible to separate the tinder from the spark. What history can attest is that the community of Israel has always huddled in the warmth of the flame.

The Study of Torah

Accordingly, the study of Torah, in both the narrow and extended sense, is the fifth core value of Conservative Judaism. As a canon without closure, the Hebrew Bible became the unfailing stimulus for midrash, the medium of an I-Thou relationship with the text and with God. Each generation and every community appropriated the Torah afresh through their own interpretive activity, creating a vast exegetical dialogue in which differences of opinion were valid and preserved. The undogmatic preeminence of Torah spawned a textually-based culture that prized individual creativity and legitimate conflict.

What Conservative Judaism brings to this ancient and unfinished dialectic are the tools and perspectives of modern scholarship blended with traditional learning and empathy. The full meaning of sacred texts will always elude those who restrict the range of acceptable questions, fear to read contextually, and who engage in willful ignorance. It is precisely the sacredness of these texts that requires of serious students to employ every piece of scholarly equipment to unpack their contents. Their power is crippled by inflicting upon them readings that no longer carry any intellectual cogency. Modern Jews deserve the right to study Torah in consonance with their mental world and not solely through the eyes of their ancestors. Judaism does not seek to limit our thinking, only our actions.

This is not to say that earlier generations got it all wrong. Nothing could be further from the truth. To witness their deep engagement with Torah and Talmud is to tap into inexhaustible wellsprings of mental acuity and spiritual power. It is to discover the multiple and ingenious ways—critical, midrashic, kabbalistic, and philosophical—in which they explicated these texts. Like them, Conservative scholars take their place in an unbroken chain of exegetes, but with their own arsenal of questions, resources, and methodologies. No matter how differently done, the study of Torah remains at the heart of the Conservative spiritual enterprise.

Moreover, it is pursued with the conviction that critical scholarship will yield new religious meaning for the inner life of contemporary Jews. It is not the tools of the trade that make philology or history or anthropology or feminist studies threatening, but the spirit in which they are applied. Rigorous yet engaged and empathetic research often rises above the pedestrian to bristle with relevance. Witness the tribute paid by Moshe Greenberg, professor of biblical studies at the Hebrew University and a graduate of the Seminary, to Yehezkel Kaufmann, who a generation earlier pioneered a Jewish approach to the critical study of the Hebrew Bible.

Yehezkel Kaufmann embodied a passionate commitment to grand ideas, combining the philosopher's power of analysis and generalization with the attention to detail of the philological exegete. His lifework is a demonstration that the study of ancient texts does not necessitate losing contact with the vital currents of the spirit and the intellect.

The Governance of Jewish Life by Halakha

The sixth core value is the governance of Jewish life by halakha, which expresses the fundamental thrust of Judaism to concretize ethics and theology into daily practice. The native language of Judaism has always been the medium of deeds. Conservative Jews are rabbinic and not biblical Jews. They avow the sanctity of the Oral Torah erected by Rabbinic Judaism alongside the Written Torah as complementary and vital to deepen, enrich, and transform it. Even if in their individual lives they may often fall short on observance, they generally do not ask of their rabbinic leadership to dismantle wholesale the entire halakhic system in order to translate personal behavior into public policy. Imbued with devotion to klal yisrael and a pervasive respect for tradition, they are more inclined to sacrifice personal autonomy for a reasonable degree of consensus and uniformity in communal life.

Collectively, the injunctions of Jewish law articulate Judaism's deep-seated sense of covenant, a partnership with the divine to finish the task of creation. Individually, the mitzvot accomplish different ends. Some serve to harness and focus human energy by forging a regimen made up of boundaries, standards, and rituals. To indulge in everything we are able to do, does not necessarily enhance human happiness or well-being. Some mitzvot provide the definitions and norms for the formation of community, while others still generate respites of holiness in which the feeling of God's nearness pervades and overwhelms.

The institution of Shabbat, perhaps the greatest legacy of the Jewish religious imagination, realizes all three. The weekly rest it imposes both humbles and elevates. By desisting from all productive work for an entire day, Jews acknowledge God's sovereignty over the world and the status of human beings as mere tenants and stewards. But the repose also conveys an echo of Eden, for Shabbat is the one fragment left over from the lost perfection of creation. Shabbat seeds the tortuous course of human history with moments of eternity, linking beginning to end while softening the massive suffering in between. Stopping the clock and diminishing the self allow others to reenter our lives. We are transposed to another dimension of reality.

Shabbat is an exquisite work of religious art created out of whole cloth by the meticulous performance of countless mitzvot. We join with family, friends, and community in a symphony of ritual—clothing, candles, table-setting, prayer, food, song, and study—to turn Shabbat into the Jewish equivalent of a country home. To gain renewal, we give up a measure of dominion. The hallowed tranquility that ensues helps us reach beyond ourselves. Like the halakha as a whole, Shabbat at its best invests the ordinary with eternity and life with ultimate meaning. Submission to God sets us free.

Never has this heroic effort to generate pockets of holiness in our personal lives been more important than today. Emancipation has thrust Jews irreversibly into the mainstream of contemporary civilization, with incalculable benefit to both. We are determined to live in two worlds and have won the right to be different, individually and collectively, without impairing our integration. The question is whether our Judaism will survive intact? Our sensibilities as Jews have been transformed and the discrepancies between the two worlds beg for accommodation.

The challenge, however, has not induced Conservative Judaism to assert blithely that the halakha is immutable. Its historical sense is simply too keen. The halakhic system, historically considered, evinces a constant pattern of responsiveness, change, and variety. Conservative Judaism did not read that record as carte blanche for a radical revision or even rejection of the system, but rather as warrant for valid adjustment where absolutely necessary. The result is a body of Conservative law sensitive to human need, halakhic integrity, and the worldwide character of the Jewish community. Due deliberation generally avoided the adoption of positions which turned out to be ill-advised and unacceptable.

Nevertheless, what is critical for the present crisis is the reaffirmation of halakha as a bulwark against syncretism, the overwhelming of Judaism by American society, not by coercion but seduction. Judaism is not a quilt of random patches onto which anything might be sewn. Its extraordinary individuality is marked by integrity and coherence. The supreme function of halakha (and Hebrew, for that matter) is to replace external barriers with internal ones, to create the private space in which Jews can cultivate their separate identities while participating in the open society that engulfs them.

Belief in God

I come, at last, to the seventh and most basic core value of Conservative Judaism: its belief in God. It is this value which plants the religious nationalism and national religion that are inseparable from Judaism in the universal soil of monotheism. Remove God, the object of Israel's millennial quest, and the rest will soon unravel. But this is precisely what Conservative Judaism refused to do, even after the Holocaust. Abraham Joshua Heschel, who came to the United States in March, 1940, to emerge after the war as the most significant Jewish theologian of the modern period, placed God squarely at the center of his rich exposition of the totality of the Jewish religious experience.

To speak of God is akin to speaking about the undetected matter of the universe. Beyond the reach of our instruments, it constitutes at least 90 per cent of the mass in the universe. Its existence is inferred solely from its effects: the gravitational force, otherwise unaccounted for, that it exerts on specific galactic shapes and rotational patterns and that it contributes in general to holding the universe together.

Similarly, Heschel was wont to stress the partial and restricted nature of biblical revelation.

"With amazing consistency the Bible records that the theophanies witnessed by Moses occurred in a cloud. Again and again we hear that the Lord "called to Moses out of the midst of the cloud" (Exodus 24:16)....

We must neither willfully ignore nor abuse by allegorization these important terms. Whatever specific fact it may denote, it unequivocally conveys to the mind the fundamental truth that God was concealed even when He revealed, that even while His voice became manifest, His essence remained hidden."

For Judaism, then, God is a felt presence rather than a visible form, a voice rather than a vision. Revelation tends to be an auditory and not a visual experience. The grandeur of God is rarely compromised by the hunger to see or by the need to capture God in human language. And yet, God's nearness and compassion are sensually asserted. The austerity of the one and the intimacy of the other are the difference between what we know and what we feel. God is both remote and nearby, transcendent and immanent. To do justice to our head and heart, that is, to the whole person, Judaism has never vitiated the polarity that lies in the midst of its monotheistic faith.

I know of no finer example of this theological view than the berakhah which introduces the psalms (*pesukei de-zimra*) of the morning service. Its function is to praise God before we make our petitions. But, in essence, it is really a meditation on the nature of the deity we are about to address. Before we pray, we take a moment to orient ourselves. My quite literal translation of the text encompasses the first few lines, which are all I wish to comment on.

Praised be the one who spoke and the world sprang into being. Praised be that one. Praised be the maker of the beginning. Praised be the one who spoke and acted. Praised be the one who ordered and executed. Praised be the one who has compassion for all the earth. Praised be the one who has compassion for all of nature's creatures. Praised be the one who rewards those who fear God. Praised be the one who lives forever and endures till eternity. Praised be the one who redeems and rescues. Praised be God's name.

What I find striking and altogether typical of Judaism in this ancient paean is the crescendo of appellations for God through a preference for circuitous verb forms. Despite a fervent desire to encounter and behold God, there is a palpable reluctance to depict or render God concrete, to traduce the mystery. The author takes refuge in verbs rather than nouns.

The very first appellation alludes to the strategy: "Praised be the one who spoke and the world sprang into being"—an awkward name for God that quickly brings to mind the majestic and imageless description of creation in the opening chapter of Genesis. Not a word is wasted there on what God looks like, on what God's sex might be, on what God did before creation. The Torah simply implies that there is but a single God who is absolutely transcendent and chose at some point to call forth the cosmos. And that creation is effected with effortless elegance through ten verbal commands. No consultations, no warfare, no labor!

It is wholly in the spirit of that supreme expression of biblical monotheism that our rabbinic author works. The act of creation becomes the name by which God is known. Theology compels us to turn verbs into nouns. We know God not through appearance, but effect. Only the experience of divine action falls within our ken. Our author even forms an adverb "bereshit" (in the beginning) into a noun and God rises before us as "the maker of the beginning."

But an unchanging, soaring, bodiless deity is also beyond human suffering. To counter that conclusion, the prayer immediately moves from creation to love. The God of Israel remains engaged, a soul mate as much as a prime mover. God's compassion extends to our planet and all its creatures as well as to the chosen people, "those who fear God." God is not an ineffable "It" but a caring "Thou," or, as Buber once said of his own faith in God: "If believing in God means being able to speak of Him in the third person, then I probably do not believe in God; or at least, I do not know if it is permissible for me to say that I believe in God. For I know, when I speak of him in the third person, whenever it happens, and it has to happen again and again, there is no other way, then my tongue cleaves to the roof of my mouth so quickly that one cannot even call it speech."

As this lilting paean makes so clear, for the rabbinic mind God was conceived in polarities, lofty yet loving, imageless yet intimate, hidden yet revealed. Conservative Judaism is very much part of that ancient Jewish quest for a comprehensive understanding of God.

More broadly still, Jewish tradition continues unbroken in Conservative Judaism, where yearning for God wells up primarily not from reason or revelation but from the blood-soaked, value-laden, and textually rooted historical experience of the Jewish people. It is surely in order to ask in closing whether this unique constellation of core values has ever coalesced into a vivifying ideal. I would submit that in its Ramah summer camps the Seminary created an extension of itself: a controlled environment for the formation of a model religious community. Over the past half-century Ramah has compiled an extraordinary record of touching and transforming young Jews to become the most effective educational setting ever generated by the movement. All the core values of Conservative Judaism are present in spades, defining and pervading the culture.

Let me single them out. The centrality of Israel finds expression in the large contingent of Israeli staff members brought over each summer, who often return to Israel themselves enamored of Conservative Judaism in the wake of experiencing Ramah. Their presence also reinforces the use of Hebrew as the camp's official language, while the value of klal yisrael promotes the priority of community and the inclusive spirit of camp programming.

On the religious side of the ledger, the Torah constitutes the lifeblood of camp life. The parasha is a basic text of study during the week and read in full every Shabbat, giving dozens of youngsters the chance to master the skill. A myriad of daily classes and Shabbat study groups symbolize the devotion to learning (in the Conservative manner), and halakha governs every aspect of life, from daily services to human relationships to relating to the environment. Each week culminates in the magnificent choreography of Shabbat that puts Judaism to music by imbuing everyone with a sense of belonging and intimacy, of uplift and holiness. And finally, the engaged figure of a Seminary scholar-in-residence teaches and personifies the core values that animate the whole noble experiment.

Ramah is not the conscious articulation of an ideological blueprint but rather the natural impulse of a vibrant, authentically Jewish religious culture, proof positive that Conservative Judaism bespeaks an organic, distinctive, and transformational reality. What Solomon Schechter once said of Rabbinic Judaism, when he ventured to crystallize its theological underpinnings, holds true no less for its modern counterpart:

A great English writer has remarked that "the true health of a man is to have a soul without being aware of it." In a similar way, the old Rabbis seem to have thought that the true health of a religion is to have a theology without being aware of it; and thus they hardly ever made—nor could they make—any attempt towards working their theology into a formal system, or giving us a full exposition of it.

Today, Conservative Judaism pulsates with many pockets of intense religious energy. Its congregational life, national conventions, USY pilgrimages and Schechter day schools increasingly manifest models of religious community shaped by its core values. More than ever, the lay leadership of these ventures consists of serious Jews for whom Conservative Judaism is hardly "a halfway house" (Sklare). The long-standing gap between Seminary and synagogue has also been largely transformed into a common calling to perpetuate rabbinic Judaism in an open society. What Conservative Judaism offers the growing number of Jews hungry for the holy is a sacred cluster where standards are coupled with compassion, scholarship with spirit, piety with intellectual honesty, and parochial passion with universalism—a prescription for salvation in this world and the one to come.

Glossary

aliyah:	"going up" or "ascent," the immigration of Jews to Israel
atavistic:	referring to the tendency to revert to ancestral type; a throwback
diaspora:	the scattering of Jews (or any religious, racial, or ethnic group) throughout the world
halahka:	religious law
kabbalistic:	pertaining to kabbalah, or Jewish mysticism
midrashic:	pertaining to the Midrash, an ancient commentary on Hebrew scriptures
mitzvoth:	plural of *mitzvah*, or the 613 commandments given in the Torah and the seven rabbinic commandments instituted later
Oral Torah:	the legal and interpretative traditions that were transmitted orally to Moses by God from Mount Sinai and were not written in the Torah
parasha:	a section of a book in the Hebrew Bible
Ramah summer camps:	camps in North America and in Israel that insist on the daily usage of Hebrew
Shabbat:	sundown Friday to sundown Saturday, the Jewish day of rest
Simhat Torah:	a Jewish holy day to celebrate the completion of the annual cycle of readings of the Torah
Solomon Schechter day schools:	private elementary schools (and some high schools) conducted by the United Synagogue of Conservative Judaism's Commission on Jewish Education
Talmud:	the late antique and early medieval commentary on the Mishnah, the first written compilation of Oral Law
theophanies:	appearances of God to people in visible but not material form
Torah:	the first five books of the Hebrew Bible: Genesis, Exodus, Leviticus, Numbers, and Deuteronomy
USY:	United Synagogue Youth
Written Torah:	the first five books of the Hebrew Bible, as opposed to the Oral Torah
Zion:	the biblical land of Israel

A medieval missionary tells that he has found the point where heaven and Earth meet.

CALLING HUMANITY: DOCUMENT ANALYSIS

2002 CE

"Presently, there is a call coming from different constellations...; for humans to express their rightful cosmic heritage."

Overview

José Trigueirinho's *Calling Humanity* (in Portuguese, *Um chamado especial*; literally, "A Special Calling") is a selected collection of previous works by the Brazilian writer, translated for the first time into English (as well as Spanish and French). The core of Trigueirinho's belief, outlined in these selections, is that humanity is just one of the many living societies in the universe, since there are countless life forms at all dimensions and levels. Trigueirinho maintains that if people let their consciousness dominate their inner and outer selves, then humans could actually interact interdimensionally with all these life forms, regardless of their place in the cosmos.

Calling Humanity, issued in 2002, along with Trigueirinho's numerous other published works and recorded lectures, belongs to that form of spirituality called mysticism or esotericism. Defining *mysticism* is notoriously difficult, for the term embraces a vast range of belief systems, some of them practiced within traditional religions. In general, though, mysticism centers on the belief that people can pursue communion or identity with some sort of ultimate divinity, spiritual truth, or God less through traditional religious dogma and more through insight, intuition, instinct, or some other form of direct awareness. As a form of religion, mysticism advocates practices that are designed to promote those kinds of experiences, leading to heightened awareness of a higher reality.

Context

The type of mystical experiences Trigueirinho describes in *Calling Humanity* have deep historical roots, beginning with the intellectual and spiritual models of second- and third-century Gnosticism (a heresy that said that people could transcend the corrupt physical world through esoter-

ic spiritual knowledge); the teachings of Joachim of Flora (ca. 1135–1202), an Italian monastic and Christian visionary; and the philosophy of the thirteenth- and fourteenth-century Brethren of the Free Spirit, a lay Christian movement in northern Europe that maintained that God is both transcendent and immanent.

The mystical tradition persisted into more modern times. In 1875, Alice Ann Bailey (1880–1949), a British-born American teacher and writer, and the Ukrainian-born American esotericist Helena P. Blavatsky (1831–1891) cofounded the modern Theosophical movement, holding that through independent spiritual search, humans could reach and realize the oneness of all life, which they saw as a fact of nature, and form a universal brotherhood. Then, in 1923, Bailey founded the Arcane School, whose followers were initiated into occult and paranormal practices. Less than a decade later, in 1932, she established the World Good Will Association, which advocated for the return of the "World Instructor," Christ. According to the association, Christ would establish a universal religion and, with the help of each human being—who, in his or her turn, had to undergo a transformation—would also establish a new society, one more mature and more knowledgeable than the present one and consequently in perfect harmony with its members and the universe. Blavatsky, meanwhile, envisioned the mythical kingdom of Shamballa (also spelled *Shambala* or *Shambhala*; Sanskrit for "peaceful place"), thought by many to be located in Inner Asia. This was conceived as a special place that only a few could reach. Bailey, though, saw it as a hidden place populated by a select, mystic society toiling for the good of all humankind. As such, Shamballa possessed a spiritual dimension (etheric plane) inhabited by earth, and the Sanat Kumara, lord of earth and humanity, was recognized as the highest avatar, that is, one of the true expressions of the will of God.

Numerous other mystics and followers of esoteric views could be cited, including the Croatian-born Austrian architect and philosopher Rudolf Steiner (1861–1925), who founded the Anthroposophical Society in 1912.

Anthroposophists hold that all humans can access the spiritual world by cultivating a form of thinking that is independent of the senses and that tries to achieve the same precision and clarity that the natural sciences do in studying the physical world.

The late twentieth century revisited some of these views as people attempted to find the spiritual essence of the cosmos by returning to nature and Mother Earth. New mystic sensibilities suitable for this new era thus arose under the heading of New Age philosophy, one devoid of sacred texts, dogmas, and spiritual leaders. The message of New Age philosophy is based on a mystique that embraces all religions as well as the cosmos and science. Humans can thus live in harmony with nature, the universe, and the supernatural.

Some historians regard New Age philosophy as a byproduct of the 1930s and the Great Depression, a time when social inequities called for resolute spiritual answers. But it was not until the end of World War II, in 1945, that individuals began to feel a profound transformation in their spiritual lives. The New Age is a spiritual climate or sensibility rather than a structured spiritual movement. Thus, it should be considered as an attitude, a desire to unite in harmony the personal, inner sphere with the outer sphere, the cosmos. Humans have to reach a profound experience with the divine in everything, on earth and in the universe, which is seen as a living, spiritual body governed by qualitative relationships and where cosmic energy permeates everything and everyone.

As a way of reaching this mystic experience, humans must undergo transcendental meditations or, better yet, rely on spiritual leaders as a way of being illuminated and becoming one with the universe. Humans in their transpersonal experiences submerge themselves in the universal conscience; hence, they come into contact with beings distant in time and space, below, on, and outside this earth. Nature, the universe, and the spiritual world can thus communicate with humans and instruct them.

One strand of this line of thinking has to do with belief in extraterrestrial beings. Some people believe not only in their existence but also in their manifestation through paranormal phenomena or reincarnations. Others focus instead on the spiritual nature of the extraterrestrials; whereas some adherents interact frequently with extraterrestrials, only a few chosen humans—namely, those who have undergone a complete inner cleansing or transformation—can act as intermediaries or messengers.

It is precisely against this background that we have to place Trigueirinho's universal spiritual message, which is a natural continuation of these earlier movements and an adaptation of older forms of mystic and theological schools. Like the Rosicrucians—a secret society of mystics formed in seventeenth-century Germany—Trigueirinho suggests that only a select few have access to esoteric truths and can read minds, prophesize, speak different languages, and have contact with (spiritual) beings from higher hierarchies. Trigueirinho proposes a new kind of spirituality, one

that could provide all humankind, through proper training and guidance, with insight into nature, the world below the terrestrial surface, the universe, and the spiritual world. Further, his vision of spirituality allows humans to become one with supernatural/extraterrestrial beings, thus enjoying everlasting peace and harmony.

Through a process known as "transmutation" (an exchange of souls), the inner self of each person is able to leave the physical body so that another inner self can occupy it. In his capacity of spiritual leader, Trigueirinho came into contact with an incarnate member of the spiritual hierarchy, Sarumah, who encouraged him to help humanity. Trigueirinho explains in *Calling Humanity* that he was taken to the Erks Valley in Argentina, where he remained until he received a new inner self. ERKS is an acronym for Encontro de Remanescentes Kósmicos Siderais (Gathering of Sidereal Cosmic Remnants), where the "remnants" are the extraterrestrial beings on earth who work to further cosmic fulfillment and wisdom. Trigueirinho's time at Erks is said to have been a turning point beginning a new phase in his life. In more than ninety books and countless lectures, Trigueirinho has shared his experiences. He gathers the core of his beliefs in *Calling Humanity*.

About the Author

José Hipólito Trigueirinho Netto, also spelled Neto, was born in São Paulo, Brazil, in 1931. He began his career as a scriptwriter/filmmaker with the Companhia Cinematográfica Vera Cruz, a studio based in the greater São Paulo area. From 1953 to 1958 he studied at the Centro Sperimentale di Cinematografia in Rome and produced his first and only documentary, *Bahia de Todos os Santos* ("Bahia of All the Saints," the name of a famous Brazilian city), in 1961. He also worked as a hotel manager, in the radio industry, and as a restaurant owner, but he abandoned these careers to become a spiritual leader, dedicating his life to inspirational writing.

Trigueirinho began his career as a spiritual writer in 1987 with the publication of *Nossa vida nos sonhos* ("Our Lives in Our Dreams") and *A energia dos raios em nossa vida* ("The Energy of Rays in Our Lives"). The former is a guide to understanding the powerful creative energy found in the inner world. In the latter work, Trigueirinho exposes the seven qualities of energy that inhabit the manifested forms found in the universe, thus molding human behavior and suggesting new ways of collaborating with them.

Also in 1987, Trigueirinho founded the Comunidade Espiritual Figueira (Figueira Spiritual Community), a nondenominational spiritual monastery in the rural area of Carmo da Cachoeira, Minas Gerais, in Brazil. Its members practice celibacy, are vegetarian, and grow their own food. The center has a school and research center, publishes books on food and health, and maintains contact between nature and the cosmos.

Time Line

1875	■ Alice Ann Bailey and Helena P. Blavatsky cofound the Modern Theosophical Movement.
1912	■ Rudolf Steiner founds the Anthroposophical Society.
1923	■ Bailey founds the Arcane School.
September 24, 1931	■ José Hipólito Trigueirinho Netto is born in São Paulo, Brazil.
1987	■ Trigueirinho founds the nondenominational spiritual monastery Comunidade Espiritual Figueira (Figueira Spiritual Community) in Brazil and publishes his first two books: *Nossa vida nos sonhos* ("Our Lives in Our Dreams") and *A energia dos raios em nossa vida* ("The Energy of Rays in Our Lives").
1988	■ In Erks Valley, Córdoba, Argentina, Trigueirinho comes into contact with an incarnate member of the spiritual hierarchy.
2002	■ Trigueirinho publishes *Calling Humanity*, a collection of his earlier works.

Explanation and Analysis of the Document

The following excerpts from *Calling Humanity* represent the core of Trigueirinho's thought. As an anthology of some of the author's works on spirituality, *Calling Humanity* contains the most fundamental concepts that form his movement. The essence of Trigueirinho's message is to provide humanity with all the necessary tools to reach oneness with one another, the earth, and the universe. The excerpts reproduced are all from part 1 of the book, by far the most important component, since it sets the scene for Trigueirinho's overall message.

♦ A Message from an Earlier Civilization

According to Trigueirinho, there are three kinds of worlds: the extraterrestrial (cosmos), the intraterrestrial (hollow earth), and the surface area (society of the surface, where human beings live). Yet, because of human nature, these three civilizations have never truly related to one another; hence, the main desire is to see cooperation among these three worlds.

Like most philosophers and religious leaders before him, Trigueirinho underscores the fact that, at a given time in history, civilizations have come and gone, reaching heights unimaginable for their time, only to fall later or at least become dormant, powerless, and destitute societies. In this respect, civilizations can be compared to evolving and revolving cycles, from creation to destruction.

Trigueirinho exalts human-made machines and inventions such as nuclear energy that are capable of marvels. Unfortunately, however, because of their not-so-peaceful innate nature, humans have taken a long time to reach such high levels of technological sophistication. Trigueirinho states that human beings had to be programmed in order to curb acts of violence against their own species, nature, and the universe. Moreover, the advancement in technology was not accompanied by a higher, sophisticated, and more tolerant behavior and attitude among humans; this lack of consciousness dictated extreme measures.

Trigueirinho goes on to explain that wise governors with full decision-making powers were allowed to take charge by the Governing Council. Hence, a new race was programmed—a race of people willing to collaborate fully with the evolution plan. In order to do so, birthrates were checked, and the elderly and the sickly were removed. At this time, the society of the surface was using motors fueled exclusively by atomic energy. Even though the radioactive residue was recycled, in time, a glitch arose. After hundreds of years, the "spectro-magnetic lines" of all this recycled energy refused to obey the "rigid laws" of science. Despite a few successes, radioactivity reached the atmosphere, destroying the ozone layer. Consequently, humans did not progress as a race, since Technotronics (supertechnology) had taken them over and ruled the world.

In order to avoid a massive exodus of people from the cities, the governors ordered that—with the equator as a starting point—new cities should be built in four perfect rings around the surface of the earth. People were evacuated in stages, but many preferred to stay in the cities despite the high level of radiation, which eventually caused diseases and physical deformations. Others ventured into the unknown wilderness, facing unfamiliar illnesses and dangerous animals. Still others could not adapt to the food they ate and survived by ingesting pills that facilitated the intake of food and water to which their bodies were reacting.

Among the very few ways of escaping annihilation, humans had to seek refuge in the inner part of the hollow earth. There, they were surrounded by the marine sources moved by *ono-zone*, also known as the "One Cosmic Energy of Life," driven by universal, omniscient harmony. Meanwhile, natural disasters began occurring outside, affecting the outer portion of the earth: cataclysms split the planet's external layer into millions of pieces. Still, humans survived; in order to prevent imperfect humans from being born, four couples were selected to reproduce in laboratories. As a result, "three perfect children" were born and later raised "in the jungles." Since they had no knowledge of and no contact with their ancestors, they "began a new society" based on their own experience.

Trigueirinho goes on to describe this new society, focusing first on communication. Since their ancestors had given up the use of languages, substituting "brain-to-brain transmission" (thanks to "extra-cerebral receivers" implanted by machines), members of the new society had great difficulties in starting to speak again, and some were never capable of doing so. In order to record what had happened and transmit it to the future generations, they began to write down their history using a script. They explained that while the world on the surface was fading away because of natural disasters, their civilization was prospering inside, below the surface of the earth. Mother Earth had given these new humans a second chance; this time, they could start all over again at a point in time just before the world was contaminated by atomic energy.

Four hundred years went by, and the new society of humans living below the surface of the earth had finally arrived at the point that their ancestors had reached at the time of the atomic disaster. In hindsight, relates Trigueirinho, the new humans decided not to explore atomic energy. They also studied the magnetic force but decided against harnessing it, since it was causing alterations in objects and beings. Eventually they opted for energy derived from stellar *ono-zone* photons that reached the inner parts of earth through "inter-magnetic channels" or crevices. Hence, they were able to reach even deeper into the earth and build new cities. Society prospered beyond imagination.

Some members of the new society decided to find their ancestral roots: They wandered through the lands above (the surface of the earth) and found themselves in Victoria Land (southern Antarctica), the sea of New Zealand, Australia, Melanesia, Japan, and China. Most of those who ventured to these lands never returned, for they were fascinated by the flora and the fauna that they encountered. After a geophysical study of the surface of the earth, it was declared that the surface had recovered from the disasters that occurred thousands of years before. Many humans wanted to follow the example of their fellow citizens and go to the surface. However, in an effort to prevent them from repeating the mistakes of their ancestors, the governors put a halt to their quests. Those who did leave went on to become the forefathers of the Asian peoples of China, Japan, the east coast of Mexico, and the southern region of Argentina.

As mentioned earlier, the few human survivors of the disasters that had hit the earth thousands of years before—some white, some black—had undergone many changes, regressing to a low level of intelligence. Some of them were white, and others were black. In time, though, all humans apparently repeated the same mistakes of their forefathers and made new mistakes that were even worse, as in the case of the atomic bomb, which could also cause the destruction of the intraterrestrials. Something had to be done to prevent this from happening. The intraterrestrials thus warned the representatives of some of the "most significant countries" of this immediate danger. As a way of rewarding these leaders for their cooperation, the intraterrestrials were willing to disclose the "secret for the utilization of magnetic energy."

♦ **The Greatest of the Mirrors of Light**

Trigueirinho's narrative continues with a description of highly evolved beings who see to it that the world goes in the right direction. They belong to Aurora (dawn), Erks, and Miz Tli Tlan, three supraphysical planetary centers on earth, almost unknown to most humans, which bear the same name as their terrestrial counterparts located in South America. These beings receive their energy from the "mother-source." Material bodies are made of circuits, set in motion by a force. Energy is distributed from top to bottom, from the highest to the lowest. A higher source triggers points of energy called mirrors, or rather, nuclei of a well-designed network of exchange of energy. What determines whether a given planet, civilization, people, or a person is a mirror is the aura of consciousness.

Even though all beings are connected with their respective network of mirrors, only some are actually involved in this exchange. Hence, there are designated souls, called "mirror beings," that are assigned the task of receiving and reflecting energy in its simple form. Beings with feminine polarity are in charge of these mirrors and see that everything runs smoothly; they are assisted in this task by other beings, and some incarnated souls are being trained as helpers. Moreover, mirrors have a vital role in transmitting planetary energy.

Energy is distributed among planes of existence, and, in their turn, the mirrors can radiate its essence. Since energy decreases as it descends, obviously there will be planes of existence with different degrees of energy, commensurate with their internal evolution.

Intraterrestrials are in charge of these mirrors, though in the future humans will be assigned to them. Mirrors transmit information, are in charge of the formation of the new race, and assist in the descent of beings onto earth, hence completing the law of science. Yet, as explained by other occult followers such as the Theosophists, this does not contradict the role of the devic hierarchy—a ranking of nature spirits who communicate on different levels. Trigueirinho emphasizes the fact that currently on earth the *devas* (Sanskrit for the "shining ones"; "invisible beings" who make up the devic hierarchy) are in charge of flora, fauna, the waters, and the mineral world, whereas the monads—entities that "work to perfect human beings and their spiritual formation"—and the spiritual hierarchies look after human evolution.

Some beings have special missions—like the archangels of the monotheistic tradition, the only difference being that these beings have a more direct contact with humans. In order to come into contact, though, they have to mitigate their energy charge, lest they would harm humans. Trigueirinho gives here the example of an evolved being known as Nicolas. This being was the soul of a person who returned to earth as a man to serve as the representative of the extraterrestrial hierarchies to humans in Aurora, one of the greater mirrors in South America.

These beings communicate with humans through transmission of energy in space aided by beings from different planes, as in the case of the mirrors, where some beings are actually trained. In order for humans to benefit from this transmission of energies, they have to activate the "right side of Consciousness," or rather, they have to allow the energies of their mind to flow freely, thus meeting with those of their creator. The same would apply to the mental side of earth; hence, it would have an impact on the atmospheric occurrences controlled by the *devas*. In order for humans to have a role in all of this, they must first fully understand the function and capability of the mirrors. The example given is healing: Mental waves emanate from the body and enter the space where they are charged with pure energy. They then return to the emitter, causing the right side of the physical body to vibrate; from there, they enter the body of the sick person.

Cosmic and human energies have the capability of transforming everything, yet humans have ignored this fact. Below the earth there are hidden lost civilizations with vast amounts of knowledge. In the past, mirrors were known in the spiritual centers of ancient civilizations; hence, they prospered.

The three intraterrestrial mirrors—Miz Tli Tlan, in the Amazonian jungles of Peru, with branches in adjacent Brazil; Erks, in Córdoba, Argentina; and Aurora, in Salto, Uruguay—work as a triad, each with a specific task. Although they have existed since the beginning of time, people had no knowledge of them until the end of the period of Shamballa (ca. 1920s), at which point they became known to everyone because the time had come to assist humanity in an unprecedented way.

Following along the tradition of the modern Theosophical movement, Trigueirinho places Shamballa in Central Asia (Tibet), conferring upon it a special, mystical power and designating it as the Great Asian Mirror; Miz Tli Tlan, though, is the birthplace of the new race. Just as in the past, when the human races left present-day South America and spread to Europe and Asia, Trigueirinho tells readers that today we are witnessing a change that started on August 8, 1988 (8/8/88). On that date, the earth entered a new era (new solar cycle), the Phase of Purification or Transition.

A total awakening of the right side of consciousness, notes Trigueirinho, will trigger complete harmony: The inner self will finally be in tune with the cosmos; hence, humans will become complete. Nevertheless, they will continue to search for their creator. This is the reason the hierarchies have come to earth—to see that humans claim their legacy. The mirrors on earth have the special task of reconnecting humans with themselves as well as with the extraterrestrial.

With the help of the monads, humans can reach cosmic perfection of the soul if they let the mirrors guide them (through the feminine rays of creation). The aforementioned Sanat Kumara is identified as Arnuna Khur, a high consciousness representing the Almighty. Humans have to develop as cosmic souls—and take inner pleasure in their spiritual growth—in order to integrate themselves with the universe. Humanity is predestined to reach this perfection, but human beings must first gain self-knowledge (knowledge of the inner self) in order to become one with the cosmos. Once this is complete, humans can then reunite with their inner selves, which they must revere as divine. Without doing so, humans cannot meet the Supreme Being.

Erks and Aurora are part of a larger unit of intraterrestrial and extraterrestrial beings who, in order to take human form, transmute (inhabit the body of a dead person). In Miz Tli Tlan, some hierarchies collaborate with Arnuna Khur on many levels but always according to the Council of Central Celestial Government, a committee where creation is planned and set into motion.

♦ Presences That Make Themselves Known

Mirna Jad is a planetary center that, though it is directly linked to Miz Tli Tlan, holds the energy of all three supraphysical planetary mirrors, sending energy to humans. Here Trigueirinho talks about contacts between humans and intraterrestrials. Although they are always in contact with one another, only a few humans—such as teachers and disciples in spiritual monasteries—had knowledge and were in charge of contacts. Yet today, according to the author, the frequency of contacts has intensified. We just need to seek them and they shall remain permanent.

Again, Trigueirinho emphasizes the fact that God's will is our will if the latter is guided by and represents Universal Law, something that humans can do effect if they are filled with the law. Healing energy is a quality that we, as humans, have been receiving from intraterrestrials, now more than ever. At Mirna Jad are many members of the hierarchy who transmit the will of the Almighty through vibrations of praise.

♦ The Transfer of Planetary Energies

To complete earth's evolution and restore balance to the planet, ancient energy centers on earth are now operating full force. This has a tremendous impact on humans, since there will no longer be barriers separating us from one another. Just as Shamballa came and went, serving its purpose, so is Mirna Jad now at its peak, emanating the energy that it receives it from the Mother-center. There are pockets of energy between the earth and the intraterrestrial space where humans are restored and prepared. Spacecrafts are currently being used for this purpose. Here Trigueirinho inserts a personal experience: While he was aware of being physically in a place, he saw an oval-shaped craft. After asking his inner self if what he was seeing was true, he received confirmation of it by finding himself in a chamber looking at the vessel. Trigueirinho thus realized that his inner conscience was witnessing this: He had, in fact, witnessed the intermediate level between the earth and the intraterrestrial world.

Trigueirinho's message is that we must let our human consciousness reach the cosmic sphere. We can attain this only through inner work and by letting the self be guided by the higher sources of life. Our human mind has to be transformed: For example, in Mirna Jad, also known as the Realm of Eternal Light, mental energy partakes with the *ono-zone* activities; it is lighter and communicates with the higher planes, where there is no concept of time or space.

"Highly evolved beings have been able to enter the realm of energies and are working toward the progress of the worlds. This is the case of those who inhabit Aurora, Erks and Miz Tli Tlan and who cooperate with the evolution of humanity of the surface. Their work is carried out on the subjective levels of life as well as directly on the material planes."

(Section 1)

"There are beings who have achieved the same level of evolution as the ones we call 'archangels,' yet they descend to the more material planes. When doing this, they must divest themselves of certain energy charges, for their vibration is so intense that the terrestrial human would not be able to withstand their presence without having been prepared."

(Section 1)

"If given the right direction, both cosmic and human energies are able to generate transformations through a powerful action that so far has been ignored by humans from the surface of the Earth. Human beings have an incalculable treasury of knowledge currently hidden in the depths of their own world."

(Section 1)

"Presently, there is a call coming from different constellations…; for humans to express their rightful cosmic heritage. Human beings are cosmic in their essence. Their reality is transcendent. They are divine beings, capable of living within themselves and of rising above their own world. Despite the appeal of their earthly surroundings and the lure of this world, human beings do still continue to seek their source of creation."

(Section 1)

"This entire process begins when human beings discover the thread of light that connects them with their spirit and when they become devoted to their inner Self. There can be no divinization of external existence if there is no divinization (or progress) of the inner Self. Although veiled, divinity exists in the spiritual core of humans."

(Section 1)

Essential Quotes

> *"There is a process of elevation of consciousness to go from human to cosmic evolution that develops through different levels which are transcended during the unfolding of the consciousness. This process is carried out through inner work and surrender of the self to the higher Sources of Life."*
>
> (Section 1)

Given that the new genetic code is still not completely functioning in humans, the latter can remain in Mirna Jad only for a short while. Later, when the genetic mutation is complete, they can remain as Children of the Sun.

Audience

Trigueirinho has an audience estimated at two million people. They follow him in order to make sure that, through his guidance, they can amend their ways, purify their inner selves, and reach moral perfection. This is done through transmutation: The inner self has to leave the body so that a different inner self can replace it. The possibility of being rescued is thus an incentive to change one's lifestyle and personality.

Impact

Trigueirinho's message is intended to help humanity become aware of its inner and outer nature, thus attuning humans to the rhythm of the earth/cosmos. He also calls for a (re)discovery of the spiritual hierarchies within humanity as well as below, above, and beyond the earth/cosmos. It is no surprise, then, that this message of rediscovery and inner/outer search appeals to many, particularly those who are dissatisfied with the rituals of an established religion or philosophy of life. Although Trigueirinho's message does not run counter to any of these established practices, it thus completes their mission and purpose.

Further Reading

Buehler, Marilyn L. "Life before Birth: Esoteric Thought on the Soul's Experience Prior to Birth and Formation of the Physical Body." Davis: University of California at Davis Medical Center, 2007.

Dawson, Andrew. *New Era—New Religions: Religious Transformation in Contemporary Brazil*. Burlington, Vt.: Ashgate, 2007.

Faivre, Antoine. *Theosophy, Imagination, Tradition: Studies in Western Esotericism*. Albany: State University of New York Press, 2000.

Parrish-Harra, Carol E. *Messengers of Hope: The Walk-In Phenomenon*. 1983. Tahlequah, Okla.: Sparrow Hawk Press, 2001.

—Commentary by Joseph Abraham Levi

1. What similarities do Trigueirinho's views have with those of the seventeenth-century Rosicrucians, as reflected in *Fama Fraternitatis*?

2. Respond to the following statement: Trigueirinho is a fraud, a con artist who turned away from his conventional jobs to support himself by writing books, articles, and speeches for the gullible; at best, he is a writer of science fiction.

3. In what way could Trigueirinho's message be said to complete the mission and purpose of conventional, traditional religions?

4. In what sense might Trigueirinho's message resemble some of the precepts of Eastern religions such as Hinduism and Buddhism? For reference, consult such documents as the Buddha's Noble Eightfold Path or the Vishnu Purana.

CALLING HUMANITY: DOCUMENT TEXT

2002 CE

—José Trigueirinho

Milestone Documents

A Message from an Earlier Civilization

"To your world:

"It would be good to underscore the fact that there are three types of worlds and even though integration of their civilizations has always been desired, their inhabitants have never truly related to one another. These worlds are: the extraterrestrial world of the cosmos, the intraterrestrial world of the hollow Earth and the world of its surface. The world where you are on the surface of the Earth is moving rapidly toward the destruction that our ancestors also could not avoid, and that once turned planet Earth into a hideous gigantic tomb full of corpses, ruin and desolation.

"All this happened at a very remote time, way beyond your conjecture. At that time humans witnessed the events that were taking place but could do nothing. Each civilization reaches a maximum point of development and then immediately or gradually disappears. It is consumed like the stars. Universal life is an eternal mathematical game, composed of cycles that contain certain annihilating aspects.

"Our technological development had reached impressive levels of perfection. Even at astonishing distances we were able to break down matter into units of energy and also reconstruct it. The effects of the radioactive residue were kept under control.

"This practice brought about the use of disintegrator plants (or stations), where machinery could transform a physical form into energy and project that energy to any city on the Earth, where another machine would transform that energy back into the same form. It later became commonplace for individuals to have their own machines.

"There were practically no secrets for us.

"Thanks to our scientific knowledge we could do almost anything we wanted to, including to extend life indefinitely. This was made possible by using the process of hibernation, which our social system allowed. Hibernation consisted of having our vital functions suspended for years and later simply taking a pill to return to active life.

"The governing class had managed to correct the problem of the agglomeration of living creatures. It was able to control the excessive growth that had occurred in the population and its resulting contamination. Evidently, lengthy periods of time were needed for everything to be adjusted because our peaceful nature did not allow us to adopt any aggressive measures against those who transgressed the norm.

"In the assistance centers the newly born received programming pills that produced the effect of curbing any violent action against a fellow being.

"Nevertheless, serious problems began to arise due to the lack of growth in consciousness regarding continual technological progress. On a memorable date the governing council finally thought up a solution for these problems. In order to avoid death, from then on we had to have governors with total decision-making power. They then programmed a new race that cooperated with the plan of evolution. Prepared to look beyond both the bad and the good, they legislated with extraordinary wisdom. The population growth was limited and under this regime, conception was controlled and prevented. Furthermore, the decrepit, the senile and those considered to be socially unrecoverable were eliminated.

"But we had been making a mistake. An aberration in the structure upon which we had consolidated the society of the surface went by unnoticed: the motors of our powerful technology were being fueled exclusively by atomic energy. We knew about other forms to produce clean energy but we were satisfied with the degree of security obtained from controlling the splitting of the atom. Evidently, in the beginning we had to deal with the radioactive residue, which we placed in special capsules and then buried. Later we were able to transform that residue and finally we reached what we called the point of a no-loss consumer chain. It could be compared to an engine of today, powered by gasoline, that could continually collect and reutilize all of the gases generated by its combustion. We had reached the point where we thought we had achieved everything when one of our mathematicians warned us that after a certain time (which you would measure in terms of hundreds of years) the spectro-magnetic lines of the recycled energy were unexpectedly no longer responding to the rigid laws they had followed up until then.

"In other words, they rebelled. For, what else could this anarchy of the spectro-magnetic lines of atomic recycling mean? When we found this out, it was too late. Our science had completed its cycle and all of us remembered the wise words of the last philosopher: 'However, death still exists.'

"The radioactive content of the atmosphere began to increase tremendously, producing black holes in the ozone layers that surrounded the Earth. The super-complex machinery that supported the structure of our civilizations rapidly became useless. You must realize that we had constructed real cybernetic monsters, capable of restoring, on their own, the parts of the machinery that had become damaged for whatever reason. Some, therefore, lasted for a longer time and we managed to obtain a regulator for the rate of increase of radioactivity. But this was of little help. We had not bothered to obtain immunity to the radioactivity, which we depended upon totally, just as today you would not go in search of immunity to the water of your rivers, thinking that tomorrow they could be converted into a factor of death.

"We suddenly knew that we were alone and defenseless.

"We had not progressed as a race; on the contrary, we remained at an elementary stage. Without being aware of it, we had simply contributed to the emergence, the splendor and the twilight of super-technology. Technotronics had controlled us.

"We had to flee from the cities. Fortunately, we knew which direction to take and we attempted to carry out the exodus strictly within the directives set by the governors. These same governors had once been obliged to adopt extreme measures to avoid a demographic explosion and had ordered the new cities to be built in four perfect rings around the surface of the planet, going through the area that today is called the equator. One of the things that I must warn you about is that the topography of the planet was different then. At that time the continental platform was a wide strip that covered the space between the tropics, to the south and to the north. In the area where today the poles are located there were upwelling marine currents, which is to say, natural lines of communication placed in the form of a geometric network under the seas. Through them waters came up from the interior of the planet to the surface and then returned.

"Nowadays that network is completely fragmented. The waters come out of the intraterrestrial world and return to it through only four openings. These, according to your cartography, are located in the triangles of Tokyo-Shanghai-Vladivostok, in the sea of Japan; of Sydney-Melbourne-New Zealand, in the Tasmanian Sea; of Malvinas-Río Gallegos-Viedma, in the Argentine Sea; and of Bermuda-San Juan, Puerto Rico-Bahamas, in the North Atlantic Ocean.

"The evacuation of our population was carried out in stages. First those who lived in the inner rings were transferred to the outer ones so as not to wait until the last minute and then be obliged to cross a deadly belt composed of the areas where the laws had been most changed. Meanwhile, desperate efforts were still being made to find a solution. Yet, we did not know what to do, as we had to base ourselves exclusively on our own knowledge, without the support of the artificial brains. The technological brains had even gone so far as to console us when our psychic system suffered from the impact of the upheaval of the situation.

"We had become accustomed to using recyclable matter as a source of energy and we finally came face to face with a reality we had not expected. We did not have the means to use the more primitive forms of energy controlled by the natural laws of matter. We had inadvertently held back the development of consciousness to a technological level of progress and had allowed matter to overrule it.

"What would be the use of trying to return to those sources if we no longer had the devices that could run on those types of fuel? You would understand us if you could imagine yourself being told today to go back to using steam ships. You could produce steam—but where are the ships?

"This is when the crisis broke out. That perfect, super-developed society was nothing more than a parasite on a gigantic technological animal. The only parasite on the only animal. If it died, what would be left?

"Decadence set in rapidly. The capacity to give orders had long depended on complete records of information that foresaw the need and the consequences of the order being given. It had become very difficult for us to think for ourselves!

"Many chose to remain in the cities, defying the rising level of radiation. They soon became distortions of what they had been. They suffered bone deformations, went blind because of eye cataracts, and finally died through lack of motor coordination.

"Those who fled wandered through the jungles which we had never bothered about. They faced unfamiliar animals that were unknown to us because the populated belts were protected by strips of total barrenness. They drank water from the streams and many died because they had lost the genetic coding that allowed them to assimilate water in its pure state.

"Others collapsed while they were eating. They had lost almost all their capacity to adapt to the terrestrial environment. Some gathered together in coordinated cells, attempting to survive what awaited them.

"Special pills gave many the balance that the body needed and only by taking these pills could they be assured that food and water would not turn into their enemies.

"The journey was very strenuous. Super-specialization had caused Us to become invalids. However, we continued to stay alive, in spite of the warning of the last philosopher: 'Death still exists.'

"One of our alternatives for survival was to reach the marine sources moved by ono-zone and get to the inner part of the hollow Earth, where we hoped we would not be ravaged by radioactive contamination. Yet, how could we get there?

"How will somebody who lives in Philadelphia and always uses the telephone to communicate with somebody in New York feel when, one day, he or she discovers that no telephones work?

"We wandered through the jungles.... Old age caught up with us. We discovered that our existence as senile parasites was miserable. Meanwhile, radiation had reached intolerable levels and the survivors hurried toward the seaboard, searching for the coastlines of the ocean. Enormous cataclysms fragmented the external layer of the Earth into millions of pieces, as if a massive explosion had overtaken our devastated world. Nevertheless, in the midst of this conflagration, our race continued to retain its archetypes.

"By not permitting debilitated couples to procreate, we managed to select four who could serve as reproducers in laboratories, and even in the most inhospitable conditions we managed to have three perfect children generated from them. Raised in the jungles, not knowing the benefits that their ancestors had enjoyed, the little ones began a new society.

"Like us, they spoke very little. We had long given up the spoken language and had chosen brain-to-brain transmission, thanks to the good performance of extra-cerebral receivers provided by the great technological monster that supported us. After that, it was very difficult to start speaking again and some never managed to do so.

"One of the coordinator groups took on the task of telling the story of what had happened to the terrestrials in symbols that were used for communication at that time. This was done in order to pass history down to the new humans who were already starting to have children. A new biological chain began with a shift in the genetic code.

"This is the story of the race of those who live in the depths of the Earth, the race of those who, in order to rise out of the ashes of a civilization, had to bear much more than you have had to undergo. It is told here and could serve as a basis for today's humans, if they wish to take advantage of these experiences.

"While the world on the surface was falling apart through innumerable cataclysms, our civilization began to regenerate, gradually yet surely. The new Earth, inside the planet, bestowed its resources on us in the same way that the previous one had done. However, there was a fundamental difference: it allowed us to start again from a point of no contamination. It was our 'second chance' of which philosophers spoke in the past. It was only then that we realized how important these philosophers were. They knew more than any supermachine and yet we had actually mocked them!

"About four hundred centuries had to go by before we felt we were strong again. We knew that once again we had reached the exact point where the road forked, where those who molded the race had once erred and had begun to proclaim the death of the race. We made good use of this second chance, faithfully following the principles contained in the decalogue that we had inherited from the 'first ones' and which tradition had kept alive. These mandates included things that addressed the experience of past times lived on the surface of the Earth which, for millennia, we had been unable to understand. Gradually, with the advance of a new science, precepts such as, 'Atomic energy is the cause of death and must not be employed' began to make sense to us. The rediscovery we made of the atom unveiled the meaning of this first article, which warned us not to go on with that study.

"This time we chose to look into magnetic force, but we discovered that magnetic fields of a certain intensity cause physical changes in objects and in beings. So we abandoned that system as well and tried others, until we selected the energy obtained from picking up ono-zone photons coming from the stars. These photons reached us from the outside through inter-magnetic channels or holes. Thanks to the knowledge and control of this energy, we were able to penetrate even deeper areas of the planet that we had always considered to be dark. We were thus able to build new cities and finally to suspend the restrictions set on birth control. Our race continued to grow.

"There were always those among us who, stimulated by the philosophers, set out to find the original land, that is to say, the birthplace of our species. They headed for the marine currents, passing through the frozen lands unknown to our ancestors. These lands were the outcome of the ecological disaster caused by our predecessors. They reached the continental soil after having crossed extensive marine areas. According to your cartography, they went through the land of Victoria, going on by sea to New Zealand, and from there to Australia, across Melanesia, after which they arrived in Japan and the coasts of China between Canton and Tientsin.

"Of those who left, few returned. They were mesmerized by the luminosity of the days, by the blue sky, by the sea breezes, by the abundance of the vegetation that offered them fruits without needing to plant, and by the quantity of wild animals available for hunting, a sport that was discovered accidentally and which fascinated them.

"Our governors decided to study the geophysical year of the outside surface with the intention of verifying the conditions there for life to progress. The results were wonderful. It was observed that, for thousands of years there had been no signs of the radioactive eruption that had scathed our ancestors. Nature had slowly but relentlessly eliminated all vestiges of contamination.

"Thousands then decided to leave the inner part of the Earth. As had happened previously in our history, the governors once again had to make an important decision. They forbade us to leave the world inside the Earth. This was done in order to stop us from going back to that point of degeneration that we had reached at the time when we had been humans of the surface. The governors set a time limit for the return of those who had already left. After that they would no longer be re-admitted because they would have even acquired a different physical structure. The unity of the intraterrestrial race was preserved. Those who did not return formed the foundations of the yellow race based in China, Japan, the east coast

of Mexico and the southernmost part of Argentina. Prior to that, the population in China was either white or black. The yellow race that we know today has intraterrestrial origins.

"Escape from the intraterrestrial world occurred through the natural conduits under the seas that interconnect the world of the surface with that of the interior of the Earth. But this was being kept under control.

"The geophysical year on the outside had revealed some interesting facts, besides that of the lack of radiation in the environment. We learned that the human race had not disappeared completely from the surface of the Earth but, because of the extensive mutations it had undergone over time, its humans had a slightly different form than ours, as well as radical changes in their physical appearance. We did not find any representatives of the original race there, but we did come across black and white people in a near-animal state, with a very low level of intelligence.

"We were also able to verify that our permanent source of water for the inner rings had remained intact. We are referring to what you call Lake Baikal, in Siberia. Around it we found some colonies of animals bearing almost the same characteristics that tradition assigns to the animals that lived together with our ancestors on the surface.

"Now that a gradual evolution has granted human beings from the surface of the Earth moderate intelligence, they rush headlong into the same trap that caused the destruction of the primordial race. The first step in that direction was the building of the atomic bomb, an artifact with unlimited potential for harm that will serve to create governments of terror, throwing the world into total disaster. This disaster may reach us also, because it is impossible to know how far a confrontation using nuclear weapons can reach.

"We are not about to let this happen. This is why we are warning the world of the surface, through its most significant countries, of this danger. We want them to form an international committee against the use of nuclear energy. In exchange, we are willing to reveal the secret for the utilization of magnetic energy."

The Greatest of the Mirrors of Light

Highly evolved beings have been able to enter the realm of energies and are working toward the progress of the worlds. This is the case of those who inhabit Aurora, Erks and Miz Tli Tlan and who cooperate with the evolution of humanity of the surface. Their work is carried out on the subjective levels of life as well as directly on the material planes. However, most human beings know very little about these activities.

In this context, "energy" refers to that which comes from the mother-source, while "force" is the name given to the action that occurs within the material body, the body formed of circuits. The one energy subdivides as it externalizes. All of its parts emanate from the same source, reflect on each plane or dimension and permeate those planes from the highest to the lowest. Thus the one energy is manifested in descending gradations.

The "mirrors" are focal points of energy that are activated by a higher source. Currently beings of feminine polarity carry out the work of these mirrors. These beings are also aware of the movements of the forces so that, by keeping them under control, the laws may be accurately carried out. Those who work with the mirrors (and at this time there are some incarnated souls being trained for this) are in charge of seeing that no circumstance and no person should obstruct the fulfillment of the laws. They do this for the benefit of other beings and of the universe.

When passing through different planes, energy infuses a certain quality in each of them and radiates its essence by means of the mirrors. As energy descends, the power of its expression gradually decreases. Therefore, each plane of existence corresponds to a specific gradation of this power and receives it according to its own evolution.

The energy wave that activates the mirrors extends itself. In this way it adapts itself to, and also brings about consequent adaptations in, the beings according to their evolutionary state, thus forming a vast field. This energy field has a broad spectrum but it also serves each individual, for each one receives it according to his or her Hierarchy, task, evolution and corresponding part of the Plan of Evolution.

All energies respond to the mirror systems. Some systems are short-range, while others act more universally. The systems receive energies and transmit them to all that is within their range of action. In this way, through these systems the energies reach the terrestrial plane with the maximum possible potential and they are absorbed according to the level of evolution of the beings who receive them. The energies create a circuitry and communicate through it.

Intraterrestrial civilizations are responsible for the work with the mirrors. In time, this will also be the task of civilizations of the surface as they begin to take on this work. The mirrors are active in the transmission of information, and in the formation of the new race, as well as in the transition of those who wish to come down to this physical plane and fulfill the Law of Service. This does not preclude the work of the Devic Hierarchy in the construction of forms, a work known and disseminated by occultists of all times. The various Hierarchies communicate on different levels, which makes cooperative activities possible. During this phase of the Earth, however, the devas are more dedicated to the mineral, plant and animal kingdoms, and specifically to water in all forms. The work of stimulating and supporting the evolution of the civilizations of the human kingdom is delegated mainly to the monads and the spiritual Hierarchies.

When energy is emitted in its original state of purity for the purpose of reaching a specific plane of existence, the mirrors absorb the power that is expended, eliminated or discharged during its trajectory. The circulating energy is continually worked on and restored to its original state. In this way, because of this perpetual renewal, the energy is able to reach the level of destination fully charged.

As we can see, the work of the mirrors is extremely important for the transmutation of the planetary energies. When the wave of pure energy reaches the terrestrial plane, it immediately transforms the charge emitted by this plane, a charge which is negative due to the charge emitted by this plane, a charge which is negative due to the atomic residue present there. The activity of the mirrors becomes unified with this transformed positive polarization in transmitting the renewed charge to the future race of the surface.

Everything is generated and emitted by the energies. The mirrors give matter-body the vibratory element that corresponds to its attunement. When combined with the body itself, this vibratory element produces the wave needed by the being. The vibrations of the energies govern all aspects of nature, from the beginning of the first cell of an embryo to the completion of its development. Not for an instant do these vibrations cease being produced. They reach the matter-body through the mirror-wave. The more advanced the being, the greater is the level of his or her vibration, assimilation and information.

There are beings who have achieved the same level of evolution as the ones we call "archangels," yet they descend to the more material planes. When doing this, they must divest themselves of certain energy charges, for their vibration is so intense that the terrestrial human would not be able to withstand their presence without having been prepared. This vibration, comparable in potency to that of a ray, has a very brilliant luminosity that some clairvoyants can see. This luminosity is produced by the friction between that high energy and the atoms of matter, which also evolve as the energies pass through them. Nicolás, for example, is one of those evolved beings. Once he lived on this planet and now he has returned to carry out a specific mission of bringing the voice of the extraterrestrial Hierarchies to the humans of the surface. Nicolás is capable of taking on human form at will. Currently he is in Aurora, which is one of the greater mirrors of South America.

The energy waves emitted by evolved beings such as Nicolás are permeated with vibrations of the fluidic worlds and their radiation can be transmitted to the other worlds. However, those who are on very high planes can only partially descend to the terrestrial planes because the imprint of their reflection on the material world is too strong. The transmission of energy that emanates from them, that is, their communication with the terrestrial levels, is carried out in space with the help of individuals from different planes, including the physical, who are ready for the task. It is through this task, which is one aspect of the broad work performed by the mirrors, that some individuals are prepared for service.

The creator-energies intervene in everything that takes place in such a circuit of transmission, as well as in the circuits where they polarize the energies of those individuals preparing for service and of their worlds. But in order for a creative vibratory circuit such as this to become possible, it is necessary for the mental atoms of the right side consciousness of individuals to become activated. This circuit emerges out of the combination of the creator-energies and energies emitted by the mind.

The merging of the creator-energies with those emanated by the mental world of the planet also has an impact on the atmospheric phenomena controlled by the devas. To bring about these phenomena requires an integration of all those mental waves.

It is not possible for human beings to cooperate with this work without having an understanding of the vibratory waves of the mirrors. One must have the necessary knowledge in order to channel them. For example, in the case of healing, the mental waves begin vibrating, marking out a circuit that is dislodged from the mental body. They enter the space or the atmosphere that surrounds them and there they receive the necessary positive charge of original pure energy. Becoming polarized, they then return to the emitter, causing the sensory centers of the right side of the physical body to vibrate. From there, fully charged, they enter the physical body of the infirm person.

If given the right direction, both cosmic and human energies are able to generate transformations through a powerful action that so far has been ignored by humans from the surface of the Earth. Human beings have an incalculable treasury of knowledge currently hidden in the depths of their own world. The lack of understanding that is characteristic of the superficial levels of human consciousness has caused that treasure to remain buried together with long vanished civilizations. The mirrors were known in the spiritual centers of those ancient civilizations. If love is present in those who accept responsibilities in silence, the mirrors will impart information far beyond what one could foresee.

There are three great mirrors active in what we here refer to as the southern cone, which actually includes the whole of South America. The first of these mirrors is Miz Tli Tlan, located in the Amazonian jungles of Peru. Miz Tli Tlan, which is now awakening, branches out into the jungles of Brazil and is the greatest mirror of light created on the planet by ono-zone energy. The second mirror is Aurora, in the area of Salto, Uruguay. Like Erks and Miz Tli Tlan, Aurora is an intraterrestrial center, however it is a channel for healing through cosmic energy. The third, Erks, is located in the province of Cordoba, in Argentina. Each of these intraterrestrial centers has a specific task, while at the same time, it is part of a triad.

These mirrors have been known since the creation of planet Earth in order for the races to be able to inhabit it when the planetary Law of Procreation would go into effect. These mirrors remained undisclosed until the end of the period of Shamballa, which has now entered a dormant state. In spite of the fact that their existence was known by all the ancient hermetic schools, only today are they being revealed to the general public because it is only in these times that their activity of helping humanity of the surface has begun to be intensified. This is the hour of need and for this reason the reality of their presence on the planet can be announced more openly.

The mirrors were known in the most ancient civilizations. Some of the work done with them has been documented. For example, the French narrative, *à; l'ombre des monastè res thibé tains* (In the Shadow of the Tibetan Monasteries), states: "The mirror becomes alluring; in a yellow and gold cloud of scintillating fire, beings pass by, shadows are traced and strange scenes and visions from beyond appear. It seems as if the mirror oscillates under the magic power that impregnates it. It is the sign of the secret societies of Asia, which unifies millions and millions of the yellow race."

This narrative about Tibet also states that "the ancient one now throws handfuls of aromatic herbs into a great incense burner and uncovers a magic mirror on the altar." This is the Great Asian Mirror, in the world of Shamballa of those times.

Today, however, Miz Tli Tlan has awakened to be the originator of the new race. As happened in the past, when the races left the region that is presently the continent of South America to go to what are now the European and Asian continents, another transfer is taking place. The greater mirror known as Shamballa is beginning a period of dormancy and Miz Tli Tlan is now becoming the significant mirror for the new times.

Since the date of 8/8/88 (August 8, 1988) many have awakened in response to the call to become renewed. The spiritual growth of this world is to take place according to the vast cosmic plan to which this greatest of the mirrors of light is linked. Something harmonious and perfect in human beings will happen when the awakening of their right side consciousness becomes total rather than merely partial. They will feel the call of the three major intraterrestrial centers: Miz Tli Tlan, Aurora, and Erks. They will become aware of this stimulation on their individual being and on their inner life. Their aim will be to reach a new and complete state of consciousness based on the dynamic perfection of the being, a state that will be more consonant with what humans are intended to manifest.

Presently, there is a call coming from different constellations, directed by the Hierarchies that are present on this planet, for humans to express their rightful cosmic heritage. Human beings are cosmic in their essence. Their reality is transcendent. They are divine beings, capable of living within themselves and of rising above their own world. Despite the appeal of their earthly surroundings and the lure of this world, human beings do still continue to seek their source of creation.

This is where the light of the mirrors comes in to help human beings to become integrated with their world as well as with the extraterrestrial dimension, guiding them to go beyond the conditions of the current race of the surface. With the light of the mirrors there will be a more harmonious relationship between what is material and what is nonmaterial, for humans will go on seeking inner perfection and spiritual liberation, all the way to the cosmic world. The cosmic world calls for the return of human beings to its bosom.

But the reality within each one must be based on direct knowledge of divine life. Therefore, growth of spirit is to be the primary concern of the new humans because they must vibrate in harmony with divine life even while interacting with the planet and its material levels. Reality touches individual mental beings through the divinity that they perceive, or try to perceive. They will thus become attuned with the monad or the Logos and will grow in divinity. All this is an inward movement.

The monads work to perfect human beings and their spiritual formation. The Planetary Logos draws them toward a complete change, integrating them with the evolutionary law of the cosmic plane. Cosmic life can be found through integration with the mirrors. Currently the Mirror of the Semi-God, Amuna Khur is awakening. Amuna Khur is there in Miz Tli Tlan, as He was in Shamballa. However, whether in Aurora, Erks or Miz Tli Tlan, the power and the perfection of this divine spirit are always present. The entire process is spiritual and this is why we are expressing it in these terms. The process consists above all in seeking the patterns of the higher worlds and not merely the patterns of Earth. The doors are open. Is this not clear?

Individual work must still be carried out, although human behavior in general is to be guided by the Hierarchies of the Cosmos through the education that will come with the new law that will govern planet Earth. New genes are already free of terrestrial karma. The soul is cosmic and matter is terrestrial; mind and life are powers of the being and these powers can either be developed or left undeveloped.

In Miz Tli Tlan a process of development controlled by the universal mind and carried out by Amuna Khur will make it possible for humans to express the inner sense of the soul. Mind and life alone cannot bring about this process. The new human beings can help the growth of their inner self by projecting a mental attunement upon it, acquired through the stimulating rays of the mirrors, or rather, of the greater mirror that controls the *feminine* light of creation, and determines the influence of the energies on human beings.

Human beings are predestined to grow in this way. Aided in their self-development, they will harmoniously bring forces under control. A sense of religiousness of the embodied spirit is the expression of the new child of light and of the cosmic universe. The embodiment of the supra-conscious mind is an emerging tendency. This does not take place through what is already known within the boundaries of current thought, but through evolutionary essence, through self-knowledge.

When this phase is completed the present structure of the inner self will have changed and the feminine aspect will be the source of the new creator-action. The task now is to enter into the new rhythm within one's own self. This is the condition that the Supreme Being is presenting to humanity today. Philosophy lives within. Once they perceive this, humans begin to create from their own cosmic level. Their lives and their more subtle bodies are then instruments that will become integrated with the new world, a world that will be born at the end of these times.

This entire process begins when human beings discover the thread of light that connects them with their spirit and when they become *devoted* to their inner Self. There can be no divinization of external existence if there is no divinization (or progress) of the inner Self. Although veiled, divinity exists in the spiritual core of humans. When they perceive that the aim of nature is to exist in cosmic fullness, this also becomes their only goal.

Without surrender, the total transformation of the current basic structures will not occur. The new Law of Mutation is the light of the mirrors. The call is there, and the decision made by human beings is the work of the Will that claims them as its children. The Will is present, in varying nuances, in each and every individual.

The spiritual growth to which we refer goes beyond prayer, or rather beyond the known limitations of prayer. The vessels of the Space Gardeners are already crossing the skies and they symbolize this consciousness that is being formed. The vessels seek to awaken human beings to self-knowledge. Individuals must feel a total delight in being, for without this they continue to be minimized; they have existence but lack the full Light of the Self. This delight is not external, but intrinsic, self-engendering and independent of whatever may be manifested outside of the human being.

We have been given to know of the existence of the three great mirrors, so let us look at each one. Aurora is a mirror where extraterrestrial civilizations converge and unite with its intraterrestrial civilization. This is carried out in order to fulfill the Divine Plan for the transition of planet Earth. Aurora provides the base from which to carry out the projects in this transition that are unknown to human beings of the race of the surface.

Erks is a mirror that is integrated with Aurora and is composed of an intraterrestrial civilization and of extraterrestrial beings who also come from other galaxies to contribute to the great mission of changing the race of the surface. When necessary, their task includes taking on physical bodies. In order to do this they perform a transmutation, which means that they bring back to life and use a body that has gone through clinical death. They can also use the bodies of those who have already completed their spiritual-evolutionary stage on Earth and who are leaving for more subtle dimensions, in full knowledge that their sheathes will be used as instruments by more evolved entities to fulfill part of the great plan.

The Law of Procreation, which normally governs the process of terrestrial incarnation, is not followed by these beings from Erks because of the short period of time in which the Law of Mutation is to be applied on planet Earth, and for other reasons as well. In these cases, when a sheath is ready, the being who inhabited it is transmuted to a higher plane. At the same time, one of the higher beings gives up its present state in order to descend to this physical plane, with the intent of assisting the race of the surface to fulfill its evolutionary cycle.

In Miz Tli Tlan, the greatest of the mirrors, certain Hierarchies work with Amuna Khur, directing the missions of Aurora, Erks and other planetary centers and regulating the development of the plan for the transition of planet Earth and of the race of its surface....

Presences That Make Themselves Known

When one's aura is attuned and in harmony with the Commands, contacts with intra or extra-terrestrial supraphysical reality take place no matter where one may be. This is because these contacts come from one's inner world and emerge into consciousness, like daylight filtering through slats in the blinds.

Certain areas on the physical plane of the Earth, however, have a specific role and their magnetic field can be organized in such a way that these contacts may more easily take place. These areas are important for the preparation of groups for the planetary rescue, and for the work to support the transition....

Contact between humans from the surface of the Earth and intraterrestrial civilizations has been cultivated since Antiquity. This contact has been the privilege of a few because dense forces of involution wandering the Earth did not allow it to happen on a wider scale. Those who dedicated themselves to inner life in the old monasteries knew a great deal about the existence of these civilizations. However, since they practiced a vow of silence, their experiences were only revealed to their teachers.

What we understand to be God's ways are also humanity's ways when they are followed in fulfillment of Universal Law. We can recognize these ways when we are imbued with that Law.

Intraterrestrial civilizations have always sent healing energy and vibrations of equilibrium to the surface of the Earth and now our link with them is being revitalized. Our Being can contact its cosmic essence in the inner sanctuary of Mirna Jad.

Many Hierarchies are present in the heart of Mirna Jad. Certain patterns of vibration that emanate from the Great Central Council of Miz Tli Tlan imprint the designs of the Most High on the ethers as they become incorporated on each plane of the civilization of Mirna Jad.

A subtle system of short range mirrors interconnects several sublevels of the civilization of Mirna Jad. The activities of those mirrors is accompanied by a vibration of praise.

Intraterrestrial brothers are more and more frequently drawing near our material bodies. As has been announced, once again the Great Brotherhood will be in the midst of humanity of the surface. The pathway goes on being prepared whenever we open ourselves to these contacts. It is as though an eternal and blessed Presence were being glimpsed, if only for brief moments. Part of our group work is to nurture these contacts so that awareness of this reality may endure, nevermore to vanish.

The Transfer of Planetary Energies

Ancient energy centers of the Earth are being deactivated and their energies are being transferred to other regions of the planet. This, and other changes in the planetary body, are attempting to bring about the all-round balance that has to be attained during a given phase of the Earth's evolution. Therefore, we must let go of nationalism and not be confined to the boundaries or to previous phases of spiritual teaching. We must transcend both external reality and traditions.

One intraterrestrial realm can withdraw from activity, as in the case of Shamballa, while another can enter into activity, as in the case of Miz Tli Tlan. The departing one continues to exist and remains on its own level, but its light is no longer being manifested. Therefore it does not participate directly in the interaction process of the various spheres of consciousness of the planet. On the other hand, the one that enters into activity becomes lighted up. This light then radiates out to all those spheres and interacts with them.

The realm of Mirna Jad is also awakening today, spreading its light throughout the planet and sending out to every corner the essence of life emanating from the Mother-center, Miz Tli Tlan. It is active on the inner planes, where there is no sense of space, but taken from an external point of view, it is situated in South America. Mirna Jad can project itself directly on the surface plane in four different areas of this continent.

Inter-dimensional entrances exist throughout the physical level, regardless of physical and material conditions. At the time of the rescue several intraterrestrial centers will receive a portion of humankind from the surface of the Earth through these centers. Like Mirna Jad, they interact with the centers that fulfill a broader task on the planetary energy circuit.

Intermediate areas between the surface and the intraterrestrial worlds are being prepared to receive human beings who are to be rescued and who will have their subtle bodies worked on before they can enter the intraterrestrial civilizations. In these areas, which are like pockets of energy, they may go into a state of dormancy, assisted by those beings of the surface who were rescued previously and have been prepared for this task, as well as by their intraterrestrial fellow beings. Part of this work is already being carried out today, some of which takes place in space vessels. Nevertheless, during the massive rescue operation, many subtle bodies, scarred by their experiences on the outer planes, will need an intermediate field of vibration for their transfer to occur harmoniously.

Even knowing all this, one should always take into account that the Hierarchies in charge of the tasks are continually revising the plans for the planetary evacuation. In regard to these inter-dimensional entrances, one day I noticed a type of very large chamber, on a dimension close to the physical plane, in the basement of the place where we used to meet. Several beings were working in this apparently oval-shaped space. Because it was something that appeared to be so concrete, I asked my Inner Self for confirmation on the veracity of that impression. The perception continued to be present and after a while it seemed as if I myself were inside the chamber although my dense physical body remained on the surface.

The day before, while we were trying to pick up the correct wording of a new mantra, I had the feeling that we were in a special part of that area. A subtle "door" opened up in the floor, leading to the inner world. Some hours later we perceived something similar while we worked with the same mantra. Once again we felt as if we were in that place but this time we had already established a link with it.

I knew at the time that something from another dimension was being experienced inwardly and it was being received by my conscious self through these impressions. But in the contact with that chamber it was different. The reality that was being revealed was physical even though it was more subtle than the physical sphere of the surface. I was in contact with an intermediate place between the world of the surface and the intraterrestrial strata where great civilizations live their cycles of evolution.

There is a process of elevation of consciousness to go from human to cosmic evolution that develops through different levels which are transcended during the unfolding of the consciousness. This process is carried out through inner work and surrender of the self to the higher Sources of Life.

The mental state of humanity of the surface is very different from the intraterrestrial one. In Mirna Jad and in other planetary centers mental energy is perfectly integrated with the transformative activity of ono-zone. Since these centers have a crystalline connection with the higher planes, this mental energy has become a working instrument for them. The goal sought and the task to be fulfilled are recognized as soon as the impulses sent to them emanate from the Main Council. This is similar to what happens in a healthy organism in which life energy reaches all the cells with the intensity and quality that are appropriate for their functioning.

Since the Realm of Mirna Jad is governed by laws that are higher than the ones we know, there is no struggle for life nor is there a sense of time such as we know it. The succession of events is perceived in a different way on each plane and consciousnesses move from one plane to another, according to the need of the whole Realm. When these consciousnesses contact inhabitants of the terrestrial sphere to take instruction or healing to them the auras and the bodies of the intraterrestrial beings must undergo continual rebalancing.

Even when human bodies from the surface are within the intraterrestrial aura, they continue to be governed by the Law of Disintegration of Matter. Until the new genetic code is fully implanted in them, they can only remain in Mirna Jad for certain periods of time. The healing work carried out there makes it possible for molecules to respond to the new genetic code that is being incorporated by those who, on the surface, are embodying their real identity as *Children of the Sun*.

The Realm of Mirna Jad, Realm of Eternal Light, extends its radiance to humans of the surface who are pure of heart and who can receive into themselves the rays of a new dawn.

Glossary

Aurora:	according to the author, the location of one of the supraphysical planetary mirrors in the area of Salto, Uruguay
cybernetic:	pertaining to the study of communication, feedback, and control mechanisms in living systems and machines
decalogue:	an allusion to the Ten Commandments
Devic Hierarchy:	the ranks of spiritual beings or intelligences called *devas*
Erks:	according to the author, the location of one of the supraphysical planetary mirrors in the province of Cordoba, Argentina
hermetic:	pertaining to alchemy or occult practices
karma:	the effects of a person's actions that determine one's destiny in one's next incarnation
Logos:	the divine word of God; traditionally used to refer to God's son, Christ
Mirna Jad:	a planetary center that holds the energy of the three supraphysical planetary mirrors, sending energy to humans
Miz Tli Tlan:	according to the author, the location of one of the supraphysical planetary mirrors in the Amazonian jungles of Peru
monad:	the Supreme Being; a single metaphysical entity
ono-zone:	the "One Cosmic Energy of Life"
ozone layers:	the layers of gas, composed of molecules consisting of three oxygen atoms, that protect the earth from ultraviolet radiation
photons:	discrete quantities of electromagnetic energy; subatomic particles
Shamballa:	a mystical place in Central Asia
Technotronics:	super-technology

List of Documents by Religious Tradition

Ancient Religions: Mesopotamia, Egypt, Greece, Rome

Pyramid Texts (ca. 2404–2193 BCE)
"Instructions of Ptahhotep" (ca. 2200 BCE)
"Hymn to the Nile" (ca. 1990–1950 BCE)
Hymn of the Righteous Sufferer (ca. 1770–600 BCE)
Egyptian Book of the Dead (ca. 1569–1315 BCE)
Enuma Elish (ca. 1500 BCE)
"Great Hymn to the Aten" (ca. 1348 BCE)
Epic of Gilgamesh (ca. 1300 BCE)
Orphic Tablets and Hymns (ca. 400 BCE–300 CE)
Cleanthes: "Hymn to Zeus" (ca. 280–276 BCE)
Pseudo-Sibylline Oracles (ca. 150 BCE–700 CE)
Lucretius: *On the Nature of Things* (ca. 59–55 BCE)

Atheism

Emma Goldman: "The Philosophy of Atheism" (1916)

Baha'i

Bab: Persian Bayan (1848)
Baha'u'llah: Kitab-i-aqdas (1873)

Buddhism

Noble Eightfold Path (ca. 528 BCE)
Lotus Sutra (ca. 100 BCE–200 CE)
Heart Sutra (ca. 250–400)
Shantideva: *Bodhicaryavatara* (ca. 700–763)
Tibetan Book of the Dead (ca. 750)
Hakuin Ekaku: "Song of Meditation" (ca. 1718)

Bon

gZi-brjid (ca. 1400)

Christianity

Bible: Exodus (ca.1446 BCE)
Bible: Genesis (ca. 1400–400 BCE)
Book of Enoch (ca. 300–100 BCE)
Gospel of Thomas (ca. 50–180)
Bible: Revelation (ca. 94–96)
Ptolemy: "Letter to Flora" (ca. 150)
Nicene Creed (325)
Dionysius the Areopagite: *The Celestial Hierarchy* (ca. 500)
Book of the Cave of Treasures (ca. 500–600)
Book of the Bee (ca. 1200–1300)
Francis of Assisi: "Canticle of the Creatures" (1224–1225)
Thomas Aquinas: *Summa theologiae* (1266–1273)
Martin Luther: *Ninety-five Theses* (1517)
Canons and Decrees of the Council of Trent (1564)
The Life of St. Teresa of Jesus (1565)
Fama Fraternitatis (ca. 1610)
Westminster Confession (1646)
John Bunyan: *Pilgrim's Progress* (1678)
Emanuel Swedenborg: *Invitation to the New Church* (ca. 1760–1772)
Doctrine and Covenants of the Church of Jesus Christ of Latter-day Saints (1835)
Mary Baker Eddy: *Science and Health with Key to the Scriptures* (1875)
Rufus M. Jones: "Essential Truths" (1900)
Rudolf Steiner: *Theosophy* (1904)
Vatican II (1962–1965)

Confucianism

Confucius: Analects (ca. 479–249 BCE)
Han Feizi (ca. 230 BCE)
Book of Rites (ca. 200–100 BCE)

Daoism

Dao De Jing (ca. 300–200 BCE)

Esotericism and Mysticism

Dionysius the Areopagite: *The Celestial Hierarchy* (ca. 500)
Fama Fraternitatis (ca. 1610)
Allan Kardec: *The Spirits' Book* (1857)
Helena Blavatsky: *The Secret Doctrine* (1888)
Rudolf Steiner: *Theosophy* (1904)
Meher Baba: *Discourses* (1938–1943)
Jose Trigueirinho: *Calling Humanity* (2002)

Falun Gong

Li Hongzhi: *Zhuan falun* (1994)

Gnosticism and Hermetica

Ptolemy: "Letter to Flora" (ca. 150)
Emerald Tablet (ca. 500–700)
Paracelsus: *Concerning the Nature of Things* (1537)

Hinduism

Rig Veda (ca. 1700–1200 BCE)
Upanishads (ca. 500 BCE–200 CE)
Bhagavad Gita (ca. 200 BCE–200 CE)
Laws of Manu (ca. 200 BCE–200 CE)
Tirumular: "Atbudha Dance" (ca. 400–700)
Vishnu Purana (ca. 1045)

Humanism

Humanist Manifesto (1933)

Indigenous Religions

Yoruba Praise Poem to Sango (ca. 1970)
Popol Vuh (ca. 250–925)
gZi-brjid (ca. 1400)
Mohawk Thanksgiving Address (ca. 1451)
Rig Veda Americanus (ca. 1540–1585)
Kumulipo (ca. 1700)
Nihongi (720)
Yengishiki (927)
Kitab al-jilwah (ca. 1850)
Li Hongzhi: *Zhuan falun* (1994)

Islam

Qur'an (ca. 610–632)
Sahih al-Bukhari (870)
Usul al-kafi (921–940)
Ibn al-'Arabi: *The Meccan Illuminations* (1203–1224)
Ayatollah Khomeini: Islamic Government: Governance of the Jurist (1970)

Jainism

Jain Sutras (ca. 500–200 BCE)

Judaism

Bible: Exodus (1446 BCE)
Bible: Genesis (ca. 1400–400 BCE)
Pirke Avot (ca. 200)
Sefer Yetzirah (ca. 200)
Mishneh Torah (1170–1180)
Shulchan Arukh (ca. 1570)
Ba'al Shem Tov: "The Holy Epistle" (1752)
Pittsburgh Platform (1885)
Ismar Schorsch: *The Sacred Cluster* (1995)

Legends and Myths

Epic of Gilgamesh (ca. 1300 BCE)
Popol Vuh (ca. 250–925)
The Voyage of Bran (ca. 700–800)
Nihongi (720)
Snorra Edda (ca. 1220)

Magic and Witchcraft

Henricus Institoris and Jacobas Sprenger: *Malleus maleficarum* (1486)
The Key of Solomon the King (ca. 1525)
Francis Barrett: *The Magus* (1801)
Gerald Gardner: *Book of Shadows* (ca. 1953)

Manichaeanism

Mani: Evangelium (ca. 240–270)

Rastafari

Robert Athlyi Rogers: Holy Piby (1924)

Shinto

Nihongi (720)
Yengishiki (927)

Sikhism

Raag Gond (1604)

Yazidism

Kitab al-jilwah (ca. 1850)

INDEX

A

Abbasid Caliphate, 707
An ABC of Witchcraft (Valiente), 1383
Abraham, 82, 107, 109–110, 115, 117, 119, 121, 123, 125, 244, 439, 506, 522, 527, 596, 623
Acaranga Sutra, 201–205, 208. *See also* Jain Sutras
Actes and Monuments (Foxe), 1054
Adam and Eve, 122, 153, 191, 293, 389, 649, 793, 796, 1038–1039, 1160, 1225
Adams, John, 324
Adi Granth, 986
Aesir, 791, 793–796
Afro-Athlican Constructive Church, 1346, 1349
Age of Reason, 1158, 1160
Agrippa, Heinrich Cornelius, 614, 616, 1157
Agum-Kakrime, 89
Aitareya Upanishad, 217
Akbar (1542-1605), 222, 986–987
Akhenaten, 42, 138, 139–144
Akkadian Empire, 14
Alaric, King, 569, 571
al-Bukhari, Muhammad ibn Abu Abdullah ibn Ismail, 691–697
    Sahib al-Bukhari, 691–705
Aldred, Cyril, 140
Alexander the Great, 94, 222, 289, 388, 612
Alhambra Decree, 971, 972
'Ali ibn Abi Talib, Hysayn, 708, 709, 715, 1204
al-Kulayni, 707–712
    Usul al-kafi, 707–719
Allan Kardec, 1231–1234
al-Mahdi, Muhammad, 1203
Amar Das, Guru, 986
Amaterasu, 663, 664, 721
The Analects, 231–242
Anathema, 551
Andreae, Jakob, 1008
Andreae, Johann Valentin, 1007–1013
Angad Dev, Guru (1504–1552), 986
Anglican Church, 1023, 1053–1055, 1057, 1113
The Animal Kingdom (Swedenborg), 1139
Anquetil-Duperron, Abraham-Hyacinthe, 224
Anthroposophy, 1319, 1322–1323, 1325, 1381
Anti-Judaism, 449
Apocalypse Explained (Swedenborg), 1139
Apocalypse Revealed (Swedenborg), 1139
Aquinas, Thomas, 581, 585, 815–821
    Summa theologiae, 815–831
Aquinas, Thomas, 1141, 1336

Arab Empire, 90
Arcana Coelestia, (Swedenborg), 1139, 1141
Arianism, 548, 550, 551
Aristotelianism, 324
Arjan Dev, Guru, 985, 986–987
Arminianism, 1036
Arminians, 1036
Arminius, Jacobus, 1036
Arsheya Upanishad, 217
Aruru, 151
Ashoka, 189, 372
Assyrian Empire, 14, 50, 94, 166, 243
"Atbudha Dance," 556
Aten, 140, 141–144
Athanasius, 548–552
    Nicene Creed, 547–554
Augustine, Saint, 82, 122, 293, 454, 456, 458–459, 485, 524, 569, 570, 574–577, 585
Augustine of Hippo. *See* Augustine, Saint
Authority of the Jurist, 1417
Azalis, 1203–1210
Aztec Empire, 924, 929
Aztecs, 923–930

B

Ba'al Shem Tov, 1126, 1127–1132
    "The Holy Epistle," 1127–1135
Bab, 1203–1210
    Babism, 1203–1208, 1251–1253, 1256
    Persian Bayan, 1203–1210
Babism, 1203–1208, 1203–1210, 1251–1253, 1256
Bablyoniaca (Berossus), 94
Babylonian Captivity, 94, 596, 976
Baha' Allah, 1251–1258
    Kitab-i-aqdas, 1203–1210, 1251–1258
Baha'i, 1203–1210, 1251–1258
Baha'u'llah, 1203–1210. *See also* Baha' Allah
Baille, Robert, 1036
Bakunin, Mikhail, 1333–1337
Barrère, Dorothy B., 1074
Barrett, Francis, 1157–1163
    The Magus, 1157–1173
Bashkala Upanishad, 217
Battle of Kalinga. *See* Kalinga War
Ber, Rabbi Dov, 1129
Bergson, Henri, 428
Besant, Annie, 1297, 1320, 1325
Besold, Christoph, 1010